Brill's
New Pauly

SUPPLEMENTS 11

GREEK AND ROMAN
MILITARY HISTORY

Brill's New Pauly
SUPPLEMENTS

EDITORS

Manfred Landfester
Jörg Rüpke
Helmuth Schneider

Brill's
Greek and Roman Military History
New Pauly

Edited by
Leonhard Burckhardt and Michael A. Speidel

English edition by
Michael Graves

Translated by
Duncan Alexander Smart

LEIDEN – BOSTON
2025

BRILL

Original German language edition: Leonhard Burckhardt & Michael A. Speidel (eds.): Militärgeschichte der griechisch-römischen Antike: Lexikon (= Der Neue Pauly Supplemente 12), published by J.B. Metzler'sche Verlagsbuchhandlung und Carl Ernst Poeschel Verlag GmbH Stuttgart, Germany. Copyright © 2022.

Cover design: TopicA (Antoinette Hanekuyk)
Front: Delphi, temple area.

The Library of Congress Cataloging-in-Publication Data is available online at https://catalog.loc.gov

Typeface for the Latin, Greek, and Cyrillic scripts: "Brill". See and download: brill.com/brill-typeface.

ISBN 978-90-04-33934-7

Copyright 2025 by Koninklijke Brill BV, Plantijnstraat 2, 2321 JC Leiden, The Netherlands.
Koninklijke Brill BV incorporates the imprints Brill, Brill Nijhoff, Brill Schöningh, Brill Fink, Brill mentis, Brill Wageningen Academic, Vandenhoeck & Ruprecht, Böhlau and V&R unipress.

All rights reserved. No part of this publication may be reproduced, translated, stored in a retrieval system, or transmitted in any form or by any means, electronic, mechanical, photocopying, recording or otherwise, without prior written permission from the publisher.
Requests for re-use and/or translations must be addressed to Koninklijke Brill BV via brill.com or copyright.com.
For more information: info@brill.com.

This book is printed on acid-free paper and produced in a sustainable manner.

PRINTED BY DRUKKERIJ WILCO B.V. - AMERSFOORT, THE NETHERLANDS

Contents

List of Contributors	VII
List of Contributions	IX
Introduction	XI
Notes to the User	XV
Ancient Greek Transcription Table	XV
List of Abbreviations	XVII
List of Illustrations	LXV
Contributions A–Z	1
Index	
A. Index of Persons	517
B. Geographical Index	530
C. Subject Index	546

Contributors

Sheila L. **Ager** (Waterloo, Canada): Diplomacy
Nathan **Arrington** (Princeton): Descriptions of war
Lukas de **Blois** (Nijmegen): Wars of note, G. Aurelian's Palmyrene War
Henning **Börm** (Rostock): Civil war
Leonhard **Burckhardt** (Basle): Battles of note, F. Marathon; Generals of note, B. Alexander; F. Epaminondas; K. Marius; O. Scipio Africanus; Mercenaries; State and army; Wars of note, A. Campaign of Alexander; J. Persian Wars
François **Cadiou** (Bordeaux): Battles of note, H. Pharsalus; Generals of note, C. Caesar; N. Pompey; Wars of note, D. Gallic Wars
Charalampos I. **Chrysafis** (Augsburg): Specialists; Symbols
Pierre **Cosme** (Rouen): Army; Cavalry; Civil war; Infantry; Militia
Jean-Christophe **Couvenhes** (Paris): Camp; Consequences of war; Supply; War
Hélène **Cuvigny** (Paris): Language
Dan **Dana** (Lyon): Recruitment
Alexander **Demandt** (Berlin): Enemies
Eckhard **Deschler-Erb** (Cologne): Armament; Artillery; Equipment
Martin **Dreher** (Magdeburg): Administration
Werner **Eck** (Cologne): Descriptions of war; Empire; Honours; Sources; Wars of note, B. Bar Kochba Revolt; E. Jewish War
Immacolata **Eramo** (Bari): Consequences of war
Patrice **Faure** (Lyon): Elite troops; Guards; Oath; Officers; Victory titles
Thomas **Fischer** (Mainburg): Camp; Slavery
Michael A. **Flower** (Princeton): Religion
Klaus **Geus** (Berlin): Maps
Martin **Guggisberg** (Basel): Acropolis
Matthäus **Heil** (Berlin): Generals of note, D. Corbulo
Henry **Heitmann-Gordon** (Munich): Terror
Olivier **Hekster** (Nijmegen): State and army
Peter **Herz** (Regensburg): Production system; Rear; Supply
Alfred Michael **Hirt** (Liverpool): Battles of note, E. Magnesia ad Sipylum; Chariot; Dogs; Elephants
Paul **Holder** (Manchester): Auxiliaries
Tonio **Hölscher** (Heidelberg): Representations of war
Benjamin **Isaac** (Tel Aviv): Colonies; Garrison
Tanja **Itgenshorst** (Fribourg): Parades; Triumph
Anna Maria **Kaiser** (Krems): Civilians; Law of war
Georgy **Kantor** (Oxford): Alliances
Arthur **Keaveney** † (Kent): Veterans
Anne **Kolb** (Zürich): Infrastructure; Vehicles
David **Konstan** (New York): Emotions
Yann **Le Bohec** (Paris): Rank; Valour

Detlef **Liebs** (Freiburg im Breisgau): Law of war
Josef **Löffl** (Lemgo): Military service; War
Christian **Mann** (Mannheim): Heroism; Motivation
Christian **Marek** (Zürich): Wars of note, F. Mithridatic Wars
Florian **Matei-Popescu** (Bucharest): Bandits; Education; Esprit de corps; Hunting; Motivation; Policing; Training
Jan B. **Meister** (Bern): Generals of note, E. Demetrius Poliorketes
Peter Franz **Mittag** (Cologne): Costs of war
Andrew **Monson** (New York): Empire
Joëlle **Napoli** (Boulogne-sur-Mer): Siege warfare
Bernhard **Palme** (Vienna): Army; Rank; Sources
Michael **Peachin** (New York): Society and army
Ioan **Piso** (Cluj-Napoca): Wars of note, C. Trajan's Dacian Wars
David M. **Pritchard** (Brisbane): Pay
Kurt A. **Raaflaub** (Providence): Law of war; Phalanx
Philip **Rance** (Berlin): Battles of note, B. Adrianople; G. Milvian Bridge; Generals of note, H. Julian; Generals of note, J. Constantine; Wars of note, I. Julian's Persian War
Boris **Rankov** (London): Reconnaissance; Transmission of orders
Michel **Reddé** (Paris): Borders; Fortification
Patrick **Sänger** (Münster): Music; Veterans
John **Scheid** (Paris): Death; Religion
Sandra **Scheuble-Reiter** (Saarbrücken): Administration; Army; Camels; Cavalry; Officers; Rank; Reconnaissance
Stefanie **Schmidt** (Berlin): Costs of war
Sebastian **Schmidt-Hofner** (Tübingen): Borders; Generals of note, M. Philip of Macedon; Wars of note, H. Peloponnesian War
Winfried **Schmitz** (Bonn): Sources
Helmuth **Schneider** (Kassel): Innovation
Wolfgang **Schuller** (Constance): Garrison
Raimund **Schulz** (Bielefeld): Battles of note, I. Salamis; Fleet
Nicholas **Sekunda** (Gdańsk): Armament; Customs of war; Equipment; Society and army
Michael A. **Speidel** (Istanbul/Zürich): Battles of note, A. Actium; C. Cannae; Generals of note, L. Marcus Aurelius; Legion; Pay; Specialists
Konrad **Stauner** (Hagen): Administration
Oliver **Stoll** (Passau): Prisoners; Standard
Joachim **Szidat** (Riedholz): Sources
Michel **Tarpin** (Grenoble): Booty
Lukas **Thommen** (Basle): Sparta
Kai Michael **Töpfer** (Heidelberg): Symbols
Giusto **Traina** (Paris): Battles of note, D. Carrhae; Honour; Scorched earth
Lawrence A. **Tritle** (Los Angeles): Military service

Jürgen von **Ungern-Sternberg** (Basle): Peace
Gregory F. **Viggiano** (Fairfield, CT): Army; Discipline; Mutiny
Uwe **Walter** (Bielefeld): Descriptions of war; Generals of note, I. Cimon; State and army; Timeframe of war
Peter **Weiß** (Kiel): Military diploma
Gabriele **Wesch-Klein** (Heidelberg): Avoidance of military service; Conscription; Discipline; Marriage; Medical corps; Mutiny
Everett L. **Wheeler** (Durham, NC): Battle; Eve-of-battle speech; General; March; Military literature; Strategy
Johannes **Wienand** (Braunschweig): Victory
Jeroen W.P. **Wijnendaele** (Ghent): Generals of note, A. Aëtius; Generals of note, P. Stilicho
Jessica **Wißmann** (Osnabrück): Cowardice; Valour
Catherine **Wolff** (Lyon): Hostages
Reinhard **Wolters** (Vienna): Battles of note, J. Teutoburg Forest; Representations of war; Sources
Bernhard **Zimmermann** (Freiburg im Breisgau): Descriptions of war
Klaus **Zimmermann** (Münster): Generals of note, G. Hannibal; Wars of note, K. Punic Wars

Contributions

Acropolis
Administration
Alliances
Armament
Army
Artillery
Auxiliaries
Avoidance of military service

Bandits
Battle
Battles of note
Booty
Borders

Camels
Camp
Cavalry
Chariot
Civil war
Civilians
Colonies
Conscription
Consequences of war
Costs of war
Cowardice
Customs of war

Death
Descriptions of war
Diplomacy
Discipline
Dogs

Education
Elephants
Elite troops
Emotions
Empire
Enemies
Equipment
Esprit de corps
Eve-of-battle speech

Fleet
Fortification

Garrison
General
Generals of note
Guards

Heroism
Honour
Honours

Hostages
Hunting

Infantry
Infrastructure
Innovation

Language
Law of war
Legion

Maps
March
Marriage
Medical corps
Mercenaries
Military diploma
Military law
Military literature
Military service
Militia
Motivation
Music
Mutiny

Oath
Officers

Parades
Pay
Peace
Phalanx
Policing
Prisoners
Production system

Rank
Rear
Reconnaissance
Recruitment
Religion
Representations of war

Scorched earth
Siege warfare
Slavery
Society and army
Sources
Sparta
Specialists
Standard
State and army
Strategy
Supply
Symbols

Terror
Timeframe of war
Training
Transmission of orders
Triumph

Valour
Vehicles

Veterans
Victory
Victory titles

War
Wars of note

Introduction

Within the field of European Antiquity, military history is one of the oldest subjects of historiographic investigation. Drawing on the narratives of the great epics and the accounts of the classical historians, research in this area has largely been concerned with war, strategy, armies and their weaponry and organization, military alliances, naval forces, heroism, prominent generals and the campaigns they and their armies conducted and the battles they fought. In this form, military history has long been one of the cornerstones of ancient history. From this perspective, Greco-Roman Antiquity appears as a warlike era, during which weapons clashed, battlecries resounded, armies marched near or far and warships collided – and all of this created the conditions for shaping European civilization through Greco-Roman culture.

After World War II, however, and particularly in the German-speaking world, military history lost much of its importance. It was now felt unseemly, in academic circles here, to study ancient armies in terms of their actual function – the threat or infliction of bloody violence. As a result, the history and historical significance of battles and wars, as well as their effects on wider aspects of history, faded into the background as subjects of academic study. However, in countries whose relationship with their own armed forces remained essentially unchanged, military history did continue to be studied, albeit to a lesser degree than before. Meticulous study of the military organizations of the Greek *poleis*, Hellenistic monarchies, Roman Republic and Roman Empire remained part of academic activity.

Yet, it would be inaccurate to claim that the military history of Antiquity before the second half of the 20th century had its roots entirely in enthusiasm for wars, battles, victories and great generals. This suspicion, arising after World War II and especially (though not exclusively) in the German-speaking world, overlooked the fact that even in the second half of the 19th century, there were scholars, particularly of Roman history and archaeology (and above all Alfred von Domaszewski), who devoted themselves to structural, societal, economic and religious issues connected with the armies of the ancient world, and who sought to make use of all available sources, including inscriptions, coins, archaeology and papyri (the last of which at that period were still only available in relatively small numbers).

With the end of World War II, research in the historical sciences shifted in emphasis. Interest now focused on social history and issues of economics, cultural anthropology, religious history, psychology and settlement topography. Historical investigations of war and the military were also affected by this. Against the backdrop of a vastly enlarged horizon, modern military history with its many new avenues and approaches has attracted great and renewed interest over recent decades, and has expanded in scope, so much so that it now counts as one of the most dynamic fields of research in classical studies. A cornucopia of issues and perspectives has yielded discoveries that, going beyond traditional research, have merged the military history of the ancient world into current trends of historiography.

Particularly advantageous for this new interest in studying ancient military history is the comparatively good state of the sources. This is especially true of the material remains, namely, physical structures of a military character or at least with military connotations, images, objects related in some way to war and the military, coins and new types of written monuments, such as inscriptions and papyri, which yield abundant information on many different manifestations and aspects of military life with more immediacy and detail than historiographic sources.

By now, the intensity of ancient military history, its dimensions, the quality of its issues and the discoveries made have reached such a point that, particularly in the German-speaking world, a comprehensive survey seems not only possible and reasonable, but also necessary. This reference work offers such a survey. The purpose of the volume is to render ancient military history accessible not only to the specialist reader, but also to an interested readership from related fields. The lemmata selected are intended to offer thematic overviews and quick access to the most important sources and the relevant research literature on Greco-Roman military history.

From the above, it will be evident that military history is not understood here as merely the history of war. Rather, the broadest possible definition is adopted, to include all societal, political, economic, technical, cultural, psychological and religious phenomena that were related to war and the military in the Greek and Roman worlds. Interwovennesses and overlaps between various spheres of life and the military will be discussed, light will be shed on the importance and participation of social groups, and attention will be paid to the influence of societal models and traditions on the army and warfare. In addition, aspects of the representation of war and the military will be considered, and relevant methodological issues investigated. Nevertheless, accompanying these structural approaches, important individuals, events, campaigns and wars of the period will also be presented by way of example.

The necessary selection of subject areas follows the fundamental principle described above. The spectrum ranges, accordingly, from basic issues of warfare and the attitude of society towards the military in general, to individual battles. Still, the editors do not labour under the illusion that completeness is achievable. We do hope, however, that our selection is appropriate, encompassing the horizon of issues as they now stand and representing the status quo in ancient military history, so as to provide a sound introduction.

The survey is confined to 'classical', that is, Greco-Roman Antiquity for pragmatic rather than substantial reasons. The prescribed length of the volume would not permit the ancient Mediterranean and neighbouring cultures as a whole to be included in a way that would be desirable. Nonetheless, the adversaries of the Greeks and Romans (e.g. Persians, Carthaginians, Germanic tribes) are regularly taken into account where it makes sense to do so. The chronological span runs from the Homeric-Archaic period (8th/7th centuries BC) through to Late Antiquity (4th/5th centuries AD).

Given the breadth of subject matter and the dynamics of recent developments in ancient military history, it is no surprise that contributors represent a broad range of opinions and, on occasion, divergent approaches to military history and its constituent areas. The editors have deliberately avoided harmonizing these differences to bring about what would be an artificial *unité de doctrine*. Rather, the encyclopedia represents the diversity that exists in opinions, interpretations and theoretical approaches. The high degree of specialization that has affected ancient military history as much as other fields, along with the complexity of the subject matter, also frequently necessitates subdividing an entry and assigning it to multiple authors. A number of articles are therefore divided into two or even three sections. It has proved useful to split texts into Greek and Roman sections, and Late Antiquity is also occasionally treated separately.

The volume also contains articles of different lengths. The weightiest topics relevant to Greek and Roman military history cover approximately eight printed pages (e.g. *Military service*, *Religion* and *Sources*). Most lemmata, however, are dealt with in articles of medium length, at about four pages (e.g. *Booty*, *Mutiny* and *Civilians*), permitting an adequate if brief discussion of the key aspects of the subject in question. Specific topics of narrative and biographical history are presented in articles of about one page in length (e.g. *Hunting*, *Chariot*, individual generals such as *Demetrius Poliorketes*, wars like Julian's *Persian campaign*, battles like *Pharsalus*).

In the case of these last three, namely, *Generals of note*, *Wars of note* and *Battles of note* (where articles are located and ordered under these respective main index headings), considerations of space have imposed a need for rigorous selection. Readers will therefore note the absence from the lists of many important events and personages. Here in particular, it has been impossible to avoid considerable problems of delimitation. For instance, there is an article on *Cimon*, but not Pericles, *Epameinondas*, but not Agesilaus, *Marius*, but not Sulla. *Marcus Aurelius* has an entry, but Trajan appears only in the context of the *Dacian Wars*. The biographical and narrative articles are selected simply as representative of a period, a type of warfare, a historical trend or an important watershed in military history. The many omissions do not reflect disdain for the subject matter or person omitted, but occur only because of the focus of the volume and the need for restraint. Like the other volumes in this series, this supplement is closely aligned to *Brill's New Pauly*. In general, but especially for the historical figures and topics not discussed here, it is advisable to look back at the foundational work, and to consult the multi-volume encyclopedia for its treatment of the subject in question. In order to make clear that the specific generals, wars and battles in this volume do not merely represent themselves, they are presented – as mentioned above – in collective lemmata, with the general treatment of the subject consigned to three separate articles. Thus, the individual generals are brought together in the lemma *Generals of note*, following on from the lemma discussing the overall concept of a *General*. The same applies to *War* and *Wars of note*, and to *Battle* and *Battles of note*.

In general, the editors were careful to define the lemmata in such a way as to facilitate an overview of a particular phenomenon or subject area of military history, rather than focusing on specific details. This means, for example, that an officer rank such as centurion does not appear in an article of that title, but is discussed in the articles *Officers* and *Rank*. Weapons are examined in the articles *Armament* and *Equipment*, battleships under the lemma *Fleet*.

Of course, such an approach only makes sense if the volume is easy to navigate. This is achieved through comprehensive indices of persons, places and subjects, permitting rapid and precise orientation to the articles themselves, and easing access to subjects under discussion that do not have their own headword. In addition, cross-references within the texts and references below them highlight parallel or related subjects contained in the volume, and a lemma list gives an overview of all articles. Further assistance for readers – not least for deciphering bibliographies and the quotations from ancient sources contained in the articles – is provided in various lists of abbreviations and a transcription table for Ancient Greek.

Some articles of this volume contain illustrations. As is the usual practice in the supplement series of *Brill's New Pauly*, we have sought to ensure that images are not purely illustrative, but that they (together with their explanatory captions) enrich the encyclopedia by taking up and expanding on specific aspects of the subjects under discussion. These illustrations, therefore, offer a further layer in the exploration of ancient military history alongside the texts of the articles.

An undertaking like this volume is always a major collaborative effort. Many participants have contributed to it. As editors in this sense, we wish first of all to thank the authors whose articles have provided the substance of the book. The quality of this work depends on the quality of their texts.

René Zimmermann has checked the articles with the utmost conscientiousness and competence, and carefully verified the many references. For this, we are greatly indebted to him.

Immacolata Eramo and Guido Helmig have undertaken thorough reworkings of individual articles and adapted them to the standards of the volume. Our grateful thanks to them.

Helmuth Schneider has offered expert advice on the selection of lemmata, for which we are extremely thankful.

Many articles were originally written in English, French or Italian, and have been translated into flawless German. The translators deserve our profound gratitude for their careful work.

Brigitte Egger, Susanne Mall, Thomas Stichler and Oliver Schütze of Metzler Verlag have applied much expertise, patience and willing flexibility to bringing the work into a presentable form in conformity with DNP. We thank them profusely.

LEONHARD BURCKHARDT (BASLE)
MICHAEL A. SPEIDEL (ISTANBUL/ZÜRICH)

Notes to the User

This volume on Greek and Roman military history forms part of the second set (volumes 7–13) of Brill's New Pauly Supplement series which complements and expands the content of the fifteen-volume *Brill's New Pauly: Encyclopaedia of the Ancient World* and the five-volume *Brill's New Pauly: Classical Tradition*. Each of the supplement volumes can be used as a self-contained reference work and in conjunction with the encyclopaedia volumes.

Articles are in alphabetical order. The cross-references ☞ at the end of each article point to other articles on related themes.

Spellings of geographical and personal names and their transcriptions from ancient and other modern languages have only been standardized to a limited extent. In general, the conventions of particular specialist disciplines are observed and English terms in current use respected. Transcriptions from the Ancient Greek follow the conventions of Brill's New Pauly (cf. the table below).

In article texts, a number in square brackets (e.g. [12]) refers to the corresponding number of the bibliographical references at the end of the article; these numbers may be supplemented by specific page numbers (e.g. [15. 227–234]). Arrows (→) in front of terms represent cross-references to other articles in the volume. The indices offer further thematic search options.

General and bibliographic abbreviations and abbreviations for ancient authors and works are explained in the List of Abbreviations. Abbreviations for books of the Bible (Old and New Testaments) follow the conventions of *Brill's New Pauly*. References in the alphabetical section (e.g. Desertion *see* Avoidance of military service) and the indices will assist in the finding of terms and names, particularly those that are mentioned in the volume but that have no entry of their own. Other persons, places and subject terms are listed here with references to their occurrence in the volume. Entries marked with an asterisk (*) in the indexes – with homonym numbers if applicable (e.g. [7]*) – if they have an entry in *Brill's New Pauly*, to facilitate identification and further research.

Further details on the illustrations are given in the List of Illustrations.

Ancient Greek Transcription Table

α	a	Alpha	ν	n	Nu	
αι	ai		ξ	x	Xi	
αυ	au		ο	o	Omicron	
β	b	Beta	οι	oi		
γ	g	Gamma (but γγ, γκ, γχ: ng, nk, nch)	ου	ou		
δ	d	Delta	π	p	Pi	
ε	e	Epsilon	ρ	r	Rho	
ει	ei		σ, ς	s	Sigma	
ευ	eu		τ	t	Tau	
ζ	z	Zeta	υ	y	Ypsilon	
η	ē	Eta	φ	ph	Phi	
ηυ	ēu		χ	ch	Chi	
θ	th	Theta	ψ	ps	Psi	
ι	i	Iota	ω	ō	Omega	
κ	k	Kappa	ʽ	h	Rough breathing	
λ	l	Lambda	ᾳ	ai	Iota subscript (η, ēi; ῳ, ōi)	
μ	m	Mu				

Greek diacritics are omitted, except where the Greek word itself is under discussion, in which cases all diacritical marks are represented by an acute (´) accent and long vowels by a macron (¯).

Abbreviations

A. General

AD	Anno Domini	l., ll.	line(s)
art.	article	Ms., Mss.	manuscript(s)
b.	born	N.F.	Neue Folge
BC	Before Christ	n.p.	no page
ca.	circa	n.s./N.S.	new series/Neue Serie
cap.	capitulum (= chapter)	no.	number
cf.	confer (= compare)	p., pp.	page(s)
Cod., Codd.	Codex, Codices	pl.	plate
col.	column	r	recto
comm.	commentary; commentator	s. v., s. vv.	sub voce, sub vocibus (= under the heading(s))
d.	died		
diss.	dissertation	s.a.	sine anno (year of publication unknown)
e.g.	exempli gratia (= for example)		
ed.	edition; editor; edited by	s.l.	sine loco (place of publication unknown)
esp.	especially		
et al.	et alii, et aliae (and others)	sc.	scilicet (= namely)
etc.	et cetera	suppl.	supplement
fig.	figure (illustration)	tab.	table
fn.	footnote	trans.	translation; translator; translated by
fol.	folium		
i.e.	id est (= that is)	v	verso
intro.	introduction; introduced by	vol., vols.	volume, volumes

B. Lexica, journals, standard works

A&A	Antike und Abendland
A&R	Atene e Roma
AA	Archäologischer Anzeiger
AAA	Annals of Archaeology and Anthropology
AAAlg	S. Gsell, Atlas archéologique de l'Algérie. Édition spéciale des cartes au 200000$_e$ du Service Géographique de l'Armeé, 1911 (repr. 1973)
AAHG	Anzeiger für die Altertumswissenschaften, edited by the Österreichischen Humanistischen Gesellschaft
AArch	Acta archeologica
AASO	The Annual of the American Schools of Oriental Research
AATun 050	E. Babelon et al. (eds.), Atlas archéologique de la Tunisie (1:50000), 1893
AATun 100	R. Cagnat / A. Merlin (eds.), Atlas archéologique de la Tunisie (1:100000), 1914
AAWG	Abhandlungen der Akademie der Wissenschaften in Göttingen. Philologisch-historische Klasse
AAWM	Abhandlungen der Akademie der Wissenschaften und Literatur in Mainz. Geistes- und sozialwissenschaftliche Klasse
AAWW	Anzeiger der Österreichischen Akademie der Wissenschaften in Wien. Philosophisch-historische Klasse
ABAW	Abhandlungen der Bayerischen Akademie der Wissenschaften. Philosophisch-historische Klasse
Abel	F.-M. Abel, Géographie de la Palestine, 2 vols., 1933–1938
ABG	Archiv für Begriffsgeschichte. Bausteine zu einem historischen Wörterbuch der Philosophie
ABr	P. Arndt / F. Bruckmann (eds.), Griechische und römische Porträts, 1891–1912; E. Lippold (ed.), Textband, 1958
ABSA	Annual of the British School at Athens
AC	L'Antiquité Classique
AchHist	H. Sancisi-Weerdenburg et al. (eds.), Achaemenid History, 8 vols., 1987–1996

Acta	Acta conventus neo-latini Lovaniensis, 1973
AD	Archaiologikon Deltion
ADAIK	Abhandlungen des Deutschen Archäologischen Instituts Kairo
Adam	J. P. Adam, La construction romaine. Matériaux et techniques, 1984
ADAW	Abhandlungen der Deutschen Akademie der Wissenschaften zu Berlin. Klasse für Sprachen, Literatur und Kunst
ADB	Allgemeine Deutsche Biographie
AdI	Annali dell'Instituto di Corrispondenza Archeologica
AE	L'Année épigraphique
AEA	Archivo Espanol de Arqueología
AEM	Archäologisch-epigraphische Mitteilungen aus Österreich
AfO	Archiv für Orientforschung
AGD	Antike Gemmen in Deutschen Sammlungen, 4 vols., 1968–1975
AGM	Archiv für Geschichte der Medizin
Agora	The Athenian Agora. Results of the Excavations by the American School of Classical Studies of Athens, 1953 ff.
AGPh	Archiv für Geschichte der Philosophie
AGR	Akten der Gesellschaft für griechische und hellenistische Rechtsgeschichte
AHAW	Abhandlungen der Heidelberger Akademie der Wissenschaften. Philosophisch-historische Klasse
AHES	Archive for History of Exact Sciences
AIHS	Archives internationales d'histoire des sciences
AION	Annali del Seminario di Studi del Mondo Classico, Sezione di Archeologia e Storia antica
AJ	The Archaeological Journal of the Royal Archaeological Institute of Great Britain and Ireland
AJA	American Journal of Archaeology
AKL	G. Meissner (ed.), Allgemeines Künsterlexikon. Die bildenden Künstler aller Zeiten und Völker, ²1991 ff.
AJAH	American Journal of Ancient History
AJBA	Australian Journal of Biblical Archaeology
AJN	American Journal of Numismatics
AJPh	American Journal of Philology
AK	Antike Kunst
AKG	Archiv für Kulturgeschichte
AKM	Abhandlungen für die Kunde des Morgenlandes
Albrecht	M. von Albrecht, Geschichte der römischen Literatur, ²1994
Alessio	G. Alessio, Lexicon etymologicum. Supplemento ai Dizionari etimologici latini e romanzi, 1976
Alexander	M. C. Alexander, Trials in the Late Roman Republic, 149 BC to 50 BC (Phoenix Suppl.-vol. 26), 1990
Alföldi	A. Alföldi, Die monarchische Repräsentation im römischen Kaiserreiche, 1970 (repr. ³1980)
Alföldy, FH	G. Alföldy, Fasti Hispanienses. Senatorische Reichsbeamte und Offiziere in den spanischen Provinzen des römischen Reiches von Augustus bis Diokletian, 1969
Alföldy, Konsulat	G. Alföldy, Konsulat und Senatorenstand unter den Antoninen. Prosopographische Untersuchungen zur senatorischen Führungsschicht (Antiquitas 1,27), 1977
Alföldy, RG	G. Alföldy, Die römische Gesellschaft. Ausgewählte Beiträge, 1986
Alföldy, RH	G. Alföldy, Römische Heeresgeschichte, 1987
Alföldy, RS	G. Alföldy, Römische Sozialgeschichte, ³1984
ALLG	Archiv für lateinische Lexikographie und Grammatik
Altaner/Stuiber	B. Altaner / B. Stuiber, Patrologie. Leben, Schriften und Lehre der Kirchenväter, ⁹1980
AMI	Archäologische Mitteilungen aus Iran
Amyx, Addenda	C. W. Neeft, Addenda et Corrigenda to D. A. Amyx, Corinthian Vase-Painting, 1991
Amyx, CVP	D. A. Amyx, Corinthian Vase-Painting of the Archaic Period, 3 vols., 1988

Anadolu	Anadolu (Anatolia)
AncSoc	Ancient Society
Anderson	J. G. Anderson, A Journey of Exploration in Pontus (Studia pontica 1), 1903
Anderson/Cumont/Grégoire	J. G. Anderson / F. Cumont / H. Grégoire, Recueil des inscriptions grecques et latines du Pont et de l'Arménie (Studia pontica 3), 1910
André, botan.	J. André, Lexique des termes de botanique en latin, 1956
André, oiseaux	J. André, Les noms d'oiseaux en latin, 1967
André, plantes	J. André, Les noms de plantes dans la Rome antique, 1985
Andrews	K. Andrews, The Castles of Morea, 1953
ANET	J. B. Pritchard, Ancient Near Eastern Texts Relating to the Old Testament, ^{3}1969 (repr. 1992)
AnnSAAt	Annuario della Scuola Archeologica di Atene
ANRW	H. Temporini / W. Haase (Hrsg.), Aufstieg und Niedergang der römischen Welt, 1972 ff.
ANSMusN	Museum Notes. American Numismatic Society
AntAfr	Antiquités africaines
AntChr	Antike und Christentum
AntPl	Antike Plastik
AO	Der Alte Orient
AOAT	Alter Orient und Altes Testament
APF	Archiv für Papyrusforschung und verwandte Gebiete
APh	L'Année philologique
Arangio-Ruiz	V. Arangio-Ruiz, Storia del diritto romano, ^{6}1953
Arcadia	Arcadia. Zeitschrift für vergleichende Literaturwissenschaft
ArchCl	Archeologia Classica
ArchE	Archaiologike ephemeris
ArcheologijaSof	Archeologija. Organ na Archeologiceskija institut i muzej pri Bălgarskata akademija na naukite
ArchHom	Archaeologia Homerica, 1967 ff.
ArtAntMod	Arte antica e moderna
ARW	Archiv für Religionswissenschaft
AS	Anatolian Studies
ASAA	Annuario della Scuola Archeologica di Atene e delle Missioni italiane in Oriente
ASARI	F. Bagherzadel (ed.), Annual Symposium on Archeological Research in Iran
ASL	Archiv für das Studium der neueren Sprachen und Literaturen
ASNP	Annali della Scuola Normale Superiore di Pisa, Classe di Lettere e Filosofia
ASpr	Die Alten Sprachen
ASR	B. Andreae (ed.), Die antiken Sarkophagreliefs, 1952 ff.
ATL	B. D. Meritt et al., Athenian Tribute Lists, 4 vols., 1939-1953
AU	Der altsprachliche Unterricht
Aulock	H. von Aulock, Münzen und Städte Pisidiens (MDAI(Ist) Beiheft 8), 2 vols., 1977-1979
Austin	C. Austin (ed.), Comicorum graecorum fragmenta in papyris reperta, 1973
BA	Bolletino d'Arte del Ministero della Publica Istruzione
BAB	Bulletin de l'Académie Royale de Belgique. Classe des Lettres
BABesch	Bulletin antieke beschaving. Annual Papers on Classical Archaeology
Badian, Clientelae	E. Badian, Foreign Clientelae, 1958
Badian, Imperialism	E. Badian, Roman Imperialism in the Late Republic, 1967
BaF	Baghdader Forschungen
Bagnall	R. S. Bagnall et al., Consuls of the Later Roman Empire (Philological Monographs of the American Philological Association 36), 1987
BalkE	Balkansko ezikoznanie
BalkSt	Balkan Studies
BaM	Baghdader Mitteilungen

Bardenhewer, GAL	O. Bardenhewer, Geschichte der altkirchlichen Literatur, vols. 1–2, ²1913–1914; vols. 3–5, 1912–1932 (repr. vols. 1–5, 1962)
Bardenhewer, Patr.	O. Bardenhewer, Patrologie, ³1910
Bardon	H. Bardon, La littérature latine inconnue, 2 vols., 1952–1956
Baron	W. Baron (ed.), Beiträge zur Methode der Wissenschaftsgeschichte, 1967
BASO	Bulletin of the American Schools of Oriental Research
BASP	Bulletin of the American Society of Papyrologists
Bauer/Aland	W. Bauer / K. Aland (eds.), Griechisch-deutsches Wörterbuch zu den Schriften des Neuen Testamentes und der frühchristlichen Literatur, ⁶1988
Baumann, LRRP	R. A. Bauman, Lawyers in Roman Republican Politics. A Study of the Roman Jurists in Their Political Setting, 316–82 BC (Münchener Beiträge zur Papyrusforschung und antiken Rechtsgeschichte), 1983
Baumann, LRTP	R. A. Bauman, Lawyers in Roman Transitional Politics. A Study of the Roman Jurists in Their Political Setting in the Late Republic and Triumvirate (Münchener Beiträge zur Papyrusforschung und antiken Rechtsgeschichte), 1985
BB	Bezzenbergers Beiträge zur Kunde der indogermanischen Sprachen
BCAR	Bullettino della Commissione Archeologica Comunale di Roma
BCH	Bulletin de Correspondance Hellénique
BE	Bulletin épigraphique
Beazley, ABV	J. D. Beazley, Attic Black-Figure Vase-Painters, 1956
Beazley, Addenda2	T. H. Carpenter (ed.), Beazley Addenda, ²1989
Beazley, ARV2	J. D. Beazley, Attic Red-Figure Vase-Painters, ²1963
Beazley, EVP	J. D. Beazley, Etruscan Vase Painting, 1947
Beazley, Paralipomena	J. D. Beazley, Paralipomena. Additions to Attic Black-Figure Vase-Painters and to Attic Red-Figure Vase-Painters, ²1971
Bechtel, Dial.	F. Bechtel, Die griechischen Dialekte, 3 vols., 1921–1924 (repr. 1963)
Bechtel, HPN	F. Bechtel, Die historischen Personennamen des Griechischen bis zur Kaiserzeit, 1917
Belke	K. Belke, Galatien und Lykaonien (Denkschriften der Österreichischen Akademie der Wissenschaften. Philosophisch- Historische Klasse 172; TIB 4), 1984
Belke/Mersich	K. Belke / N. Mersich, Phrygien und Pisidien (Denk- schriften der Österreichischen Akademie der Wissenschaften. Philosophisch- Historische Klasse 211; TIB 7), 1990
Bell	R. E. Bell, Place-Names in Classical Mythology, Greece, 1989
Beloch, Bevölkerung	K. J. Beloch, Die Bevölkerung der griechisch-römischen Welt, 1886
Beloch, GG	K. J. Beloch, Griechische Geschichte, 4 vols., ²1912–1927 (repr. 1967)
Beloch, RG	K. J. Beloch, Römische Geschichte bis zum Beginn der Punischen Kriege, 1926
Bengtson	H. Bengtson, Die Strategie in der hellenistischen Zeit. Ein Beitrag zum antiken Staatsrecht (Münchener Beiträge zur Papyrusforschung und antiken Rechtsgeschichte 26, 32, 36), 3 vols., 1937–1952 (corrected repr. 1964–1967)
Berendes	J. Berendes (ed.), Des Pedanios Dioskurides Arznei- mittellehre übers. und mit Erl. versehen, 1902 (repr. 1970)
Berger	E. H. Berger, Geschichte der wissenschaftlichen Erdkunde der Griechen, ²1903
Berve	H. Berve, Das Alexanderreich auf prosopographischer Grundlage, 1926
Beyen	H. G. Beyen, Die pompejanische Wanddekoration vom zweiten bis zum vierten Stil, 2 vols., 1938–1960
BFC	Bolletino di filologia classica
BGU	Ägyptische Urkunden aus den Kaiserlichen (from vol. 6 Staatlichen) Museen zu Berlin: Griechische Urkunden, 20 vols., 1895–2014
BHM	Bulletin of the History of Medicine
BIAO	Bulletin de l'Institut français d'Archéologie Orientale
BiblH&R	Bibliothèque d'Humanisme et Renaissance
BiblLing	Bibliographie linguistique / Linguistic Bibliography

BIBR	Bulletin de l'Institut Belge de Rome
Bickerman	E. Bickermann, Chronologie (Einleitung in die Altertumswissenschaft 3,5), 1933
BICS	Bulletin of the Institute of Classical Studies of the University of London
BIES	The Bulletin of the Israel Exploration Society
BiogJahr	Biographisches Jahrbuch für Altertumskunde
Birley	A. R. Birley, The Fasti of Roman Britain, 1981
BJ	Bonner Jahrbücher des Rheinischen Landesmuseums in Bonn und des Vereins von Altertumsfreunden im Rheinlande
BKT	Berliner Klassikertexte, 8 vols., 1904–1939
BKV	Bibliothek der Kirchenväter (Kemptener Ausg.), 63 vols., ^{2}1911–1931
Blänsdorf	J. Blänsdorf (ed.), Theater und Gesellschaft im Imperium Romanum, 1990
Blass	F. Blass, Die attische Beredsamkeit, 3 vols., ^{3}1887–1898 (repr. 1979)
Blass/Debrunner/Rehkopf	F. Blass / A. Debrunner / F. Rehkopf, Grammatik des neutestamentlichen Griechisch, ^{15}1979
Blümner, PrAlt.	H. Blümner, Die römischen Privataltertümer (HdbA 4/2,2), ^{3}1911
Blümner, Techn.	H. Blümner, Technologie und Terminologie der Gewerbe und Künste bei Griechen und Römern, vol. 1, ^{2}1912; vols. 2–4, 1875–1887 (repr. 1969)
BMC, Gr	A Catalogue of the Greek Coins in the British Museum, 29 vols., 1873–1965
BMCByz	W. Wroth (ed.), Catalogue of the Imperial Byzantine Coins in the British Museum, 2 vols., 1908 (repr. 1966)
BMClR	Bryn Mawr Classical Review
BMCRE	H. Mattingly (ed.), Coins of the Roman Empire in the British Museum, 6 vols., 1962–1976
BMCRR	H. A. Grueber (ed.), Coins of the Roman Republic in the British Museum, 3 vols., 1970
BN	Beiträge zur Namensforschung
BNP	Brill's New Pauly. Encyclopaedia of the Ancient World, ed. H. Cancik et al., 2002–2011
Bolgar, Culture 1	R. Bolgar, Classical Influences on European Culture A.D. 500–1500, 1971
Bolgar, Culture 2	R. Bolgar, Classical Influences on European Culture A.D. 1500–1700, 1974
Bolgar, Thought	R. Bolgar, Classical Influences on Western Thought AD 1650–1870, 1977
Bon	A. Bon, La Morée franque, 2 vols., 1969
Bonner	S. F. Bonner, Education in Ancient Rome, 1977
Bopearachchi	O. Bopearachchi, Monnaies gréco-bactriennes et indo-grecques. Catalogue raisonné, 1991
Borinski	K. Borinski, Die Antike in Poetik und Kunsttheorie vom Ausgang des klassischen Altertums bis auf Goethe und Wilhelm von Humboldt, 2 vols., 1914–1924 (repr. 1965)
Borza	E. N. Borza, In the Shadow of Olympus. The Emergence of Macedon, 1990
Bouché-Leclerq	A. Bouché-Leclerq, Histoire de la divination dans l'antiquité, 3 vols., 1879–1882 (repr. 1978 in 4 vols.)
BPhC	Bibliotheca Philologica Classica
BrBr	H. Brunn / F. Bruckmann, Denkmäler griechischer und römischer Skulpturen, 1888–1947
BRGK	Bericht der Römisch-Germanischen Kommission des Deutschen Archäologischen Instituts
Briant	P. Briant, Histoire de l'empire perse de Cyrus à Alexandre, 1996
Briggs/Calder	W. W. Briggs / W. M. Calder III, Classical Scholarship. A Biographical Encyclopedia, 1990
Bruchmann	C. F. H. Bruchmann, Epitheta deorum quae apud poetas graecos leguntur, 1893
Brugmann/Delbrück	K. Brugmann / B. Delbrück, Grundriß der vergleichenden Grammatik der indogermanischen Sprachen, vols. 1–2, ^{2}1897–1916; vols. 3–5, 1893–1900
Brugmann/Thumb	K. Brugmann / A. Thumb (eds.), Griechische Grammatik, ^{4}1913

Brunhölzl	F. Brunhölzl, Geschichte der lateinischen Literatur des Mittelalters, 2 vols., 1975–1992
Brunt	P. A. Brunt, Italian Manpower 222 B. C.–A. D. 14, 1971
Bruun	C. Bruun, The Water Supply of Ancient Rome. A Study of Imperial Administration (Commentationes Humanarum Litterarum 93), 1991
Bryer/Winfield	A. Bryer / D. Winfield, The Byzantine Monuments and Topography of Pontus (Dumbarton Oaks Studies 20), 2 vols., 1985
BSABR	Bulletin de Liaison de la Société des Amis de la Bibliothèque Salomon Reinach
BSL	Bulletin de la Société de Linguistique de Paris
BSO(A)S	Bulletin of the School of Oriental (from vol. 10 ff.: and African) Studies
BTCGI	G. Nenci (ed.), Bibliografia topografica della colonizzazione greca in Italia e nelle isole tirreniche, 1980 ff.
Buck	A. Buck (ed.), Die Rezeption der Antike, 1981
Burkert	W. Burkert, Griechische Religion der archaischen und klassischen Epoche, 1977
Busolt/Swoboda	G. Busolt / H. Swoboda, Griechische Staatskunde (HdbA 4/1,1), 2 vols., ^{3}1920–1926 (repr. 1972–1979)
BWG	Berichte zur Wissenschaftsgeschichte
BWPr	Winckelmanns-Programm der Archäologischen Gesellschaft zu Berlin
Byzantion	Byzantion. Revue internationale des études byzantines
ByzF	Byzantinische Forschungen. Internationale Zeitschrift für Byzantinistik
ByzZ	Byzantinische Zeitschrift
C. Jud. Syr. Eg.	E. van't Dack (ed.), The Judean-Syrian-Egyptian Conflict of 103–101 B.C. A Multilingual Dossier Concerning a 'War of Sceptres' (Collectanea hellenistica 1), 1989
C. Ord. Ptol.	M.-T. Lenger (ed.), Corpus des ordonnances des Ptolémées, ^{2}1980
Caballos (Senadores)	A. Caballos, Los senadores hispanoromanos y la romanización de Hispania (Siglos I al III p.C.), vol. 1: Prosopografía (Monografías del Departamento de Historia Antigua de la Universidad de Sevilla 5), 1990
CAF	T. Kock (ed.), Comicorum Atticorum Fragmenta, 3 vols., 1880–1888
CAG	Commentaria in Aristotelem Graeca, 18 vols., 1885–1909
CAH	The Cambridge Ancient History, 12 text vols. and 5 table vols., 1924–1939, (vol. 1 as 2. ed.); vols. 1–2, ^{3}1970–1975; vols. 3,1 and 3,3 ff., ^{2}1982 ff.; vol. 3,2, ^{1}1991
Carney	T. F. Carney, Bureaucracy in Traditional Society. Romano-Byzantine Bureaucracies Viewed from within, 1971
Cartledge/Millett/Todd	P. Cartledge / P. Millett / S. Todd (eds.), Nomos, Essays in Athenian Law, Politics and Society, 1990
Cary	M. Cary, The Geographical Background of Greek and Roman History, 1949
Casson, Ships	L. Casson, Ships and Seamanship in the Ancient World, 1971
Casson, Trade	L. Casson, Ancient Trade and Society, 1984
CAT	Catalogus Tragicorum et Tragoediarum (in TrGF vol. 1)
CatLitPap	H. J. M. Milne (ed.), Catalogue of the Literary Papyri in the British Museum, 1927
CCAG	F. Cumont et al. (eds.), Catalogus Codicum Astrologorum Graecorum, 12 vols. in 20 parts, 1898–1940
CCG	Corpus Christianorum. Series Graeca, 1977 ff.
CCL	Corpus Christianorum. Series Latina, 1954 ff.
CE	Cronache Ercolanesi
CEG	P. A. Hansen (ed.), Carmina epigraphica Graeca (Texte und Kommentare 12; 15), 1983 ff.
CeM	Classica et Mediaevalia
CGF	G. Kaibel (ed.), Comicorum Graecorum Fragmenta, 21958
CGL	G. Götz (ed.), Corpus glossariorum Latinorum, 7 vols., 1888–1923 (repr. 1965)
Chantraine	P. Chantraine, Dictionnaire étymologique de la langue grecque, 4 vols., 1968–1980

CHCL-G	E. J. Kenney (ed.), The Cambridge History of Classical Literature. Greek Literature, 1985 ff.
CHCL-L	E. J. Kenney (ed.), The Cambridge History of Classical Literature. Latin Literature, 1982 ff.
Chiron	Chiron. Mitteilungen der Kommission für alte Geschichte und Epigraphik des Deutschen Archäologischen Instituts
ChLA	A. Bruckner / R. Marichal (eds.), Chartae Latinae Antiquiores, 1954 ff.
Christ	K. Christ, Geschichte der römischen Kaiserzeit von Augustus bis zu Konstantin, 1988
Christ, RGG	K. Christ, Römische Geschichte und deutsche Geschichtswissenschaft, 1982
Christ, RGW	K. Christ, Römische Geschichte und Wissenschaftsgeschichte, 3 vols., 1982–1983
Christ/Momigliano	K. Christ / A. Momigliano, Die Antike im 19. Jahrhundert in Italien und Deutschland, 1988
Chron. min.	Chronica minora saec. IV. V. VI.VII., 3 vols., 1892–1898
CIA	A. Kirchhoff et al. (eds.), Corpus Inscriptionum Atticarum, 1873 (Suppl. 1877–1891)
CIC	Corpus Iuris Canonici, 2 vols., 1879–1881 (repr. 1959)
CID	Corpus des inscriptions de Delphes, 3 vols., 1977–1992
CIE	C. Pauli (ed.), Corpus Inscriptionum Etruscarum, vol. 1–2, 1893–1921; vol. 3,1 ff., 1982 ff.
CIG	Corpus Inscriptionum Graecarum, 4 vols., 1828–1877
CIIP	W. Ameling et al. (eds.), Corpus Inscriptionum Iudaeae / Palaestinae, 2010 ff.
CIL	Corpus Inscriptionum Latinarum, 1863 ff.
CIL III Add.	M. Sasel-Kos, Inscriptiones latinae in Graecia repertae. Additamenta ad CIL III (Epigrafia e antichità 5), 1979
CIRB	Corpus Inscriptionum regni Bosporani, 1965
CIS	Corpus Inscriptionum Semiticarum, 5 parts, 1881–1951
CJ	Classical Journal
CL	Cultura Neolatina
Clairmont	C. W. Clairmont, Attic Classical Tombstones, 7 vols., 1993
Clauss	M. Clauss, Der magister officiorum in der Spätantike (4.–6. Jahrhundert). Das Amt und sein Einfluß auf die kaiserliche Politik (Vestigia 32), 1981
CLE	F. Bücheler / E. Lommatzsch (eds.), Carmina Latina Epigraphica (Anthologia latina 2), 3 vols., 1895–1926
CM	Clio Medica. Acta Academiae historiae medicinae
CMA	Cahiers de l'Institut du Moyen Age grec et latin
CMB	W. M. Calder III / D. J. Kramer, An Introductory Bibliography to the History of Classical Scholarship, Chiefly in the XIXth and XXth Centuries, 1992
CMG	Corpus Medicorum Graecorum, 1908 ff.
CMIK	J. Chadwick, Corpus of Mycenaean Inscriptions from Knossos (Incunabula Graeca 88), 1986 ff.
CML	Corpus Medicorum Latinorum, 1915 ff.
CMS	F. Matz et al. (eds.), Corpus der minoischen und mykenischen Siegel, 1964 ff.
CodMan	Codices manuscripti. Zeitschrift für Handschriftenkunde
Coing	H. Coing, Europäisches Privatrecht, 2 vols., 1985–1989
CollAlex	I. U. Powell (ed.), Collectanea Alexandrina, 1925
CollRau	J. von Ungern-Sternberg (ed.), Colloquia Raurica, 1988 ff.
Conway/Johnson/Whatmough	R. S. Conway/S. E. Johnson/J. Whatmough, The Prae-Italic Dialects of Italy, 3 vols., 1933 (repr. 1968)
Conze	A. Conze, Die attischen Grabreliefs, 4 vols., 1893–1922
C.Pap.Lat.	R. Cavenaile, Corpus Papyrorum Latinarum, 1958
Courtney	E. Courtney, The Fragmentary Latin Poets, 1993
CPF	F. Adorno (ed.), Corpus dei Papiri Filosofici greci e latini, 1989 ff.

CPG	M. Geerard (vols. 1–5) / F. Glorie (vol. 5), Clavis patrum graecorum, 5 vols., 1974–1987
CPh	Classical Philology
CPL	E. Dekkers / A. Gaar, Clavis patrum latinorum (CCL), ^{3}1995
CPR	C. Wessely et al. (eds.), Corpus Papyrorum Raineri, 1895 ff.
CQ	Classical Quarterly
CR	Classical Review
CRAI	Comptes rendus des séances de l'Académie des inscriptions et belles-lettres
CRF	O. Ribbeck (ed.), Comicorum Romanorum Fragmenta, 1871 (repr. 1962)
CSCO	Corpus Scriptorum Christianorum Orientalium, bisher 663 vols., 1903 ff.
CSCT	Columbia Studies in the Classical Tradition
CSE	Corpus Speculorum Etruscorum, 1990 ff.
CSEL	Corpus Scriptorum ecclesiasticorum Latinorum, 1866 ff.
CSIR	Corpus Signorum Imperii Romani, 1963 ff.
Cumont, Pont	F. Cumont / E. Cumont, Voyage d'exploration archéologique dans le Pont et la Petite Arménie (Studia pontica 2), 1906
Cumont, Religions	F. Cumont, Les religions orientales dans le paganism romain, ^{3}1929 (repr. 1981)
Curtius	E. R. Curtius, Europäische Literatur und lateinisches Mittelalter, ^{11}1993
CVA	Corpus Vasorum Antiquorum, 1923 ff.
CW	The Classical World
D'Arms	J. H. d'Arms, Commerce and Social Standing in Ancient Rome, 1981
D'Arms/Kopff	J. H. d'Arms / E. C. Kopff (eds.), The Seaborne Commerce of Ancient Rome. Studies in Archaeology and History (Memoirs of the American Academy in Rome 36), 1980
Dacia	Dacia. Revue d'archéologie et d'histoire ancienne
Davies	J. K. Davies, Athenian Propertied Families 600–300 B.C., 1971
DB	F. Vigouroux (ed.), Dictionnaire de la Bible, 1881 ff.
DCPP	E. Lipiński et al. (eds.), Dictionnaire de la civilization phénicienne et punique, 1992
Degrassi, FCap.	A. Degrassi, Fasti Capitolini (Corpus scriptorium Latinorum Paravianum), 1954
Degrassi, FCIR (= FC)	A. Degrassi, I Fasti consolari dell'Impero Romano, 1952
Deichgräber	K. Deichgräber, Die griechische Empirikerschule, 1930
Delmaire	R. Delmaire, Les responsables des finances impériales au Bas-Empire romain (IVe-VIe s.). Études prosopographiques (Collection Latomus 203), 1989
Demandt	A. Demandt, Der Fall Roms. Die Auflösung des römischen Reiches im Urteil der Nachwelt, 1984
Demougin	S. Demougin, Prosopographie des Chevaliers romains Julio-Claudiens (43 av. J.-C.–70 ap. J.-C.) (Collection de l'École Française de Rome 153), 1992
Deubner	L. Deubner, Attische Feste, 1932
Develin	R. Develin, Athenian Officials 684–321 B. C., 1989
Devijver	H. Devijver, Prosopographia militiarum equestrium quae fuerunt ab Augusto ad Gallienum (Symbolae Facultatis Litterarum et Philosophiae Lovaniensis Ser. A 3), 3 vols., 1976–1980 (2 Suppl.-vols., 1987–1993)
DHA	Dialogues d'histoire ancienne
DHGE	A. Baudrillart / R. Aubert (eds.), Dictionnaire d'histoire et de géographie ecclésiastiques, 1912 ff.
DID	Didascaliae Tragicae/Ludorum Tragicorum (in TrGF vol. 1)
Diels, DG	H. Diels, Doxographi Graeci, 1879
Diels/Kranz	H. Diels / W. Kranz (eds.), Fragmente der Vorsokratiker, 3 vols., ^{6}1951–1952 (repr. vol. 1, 1992; vol. 2, 1985; vol. 3, 1993)
Dierauer	U. Dierauer, Tier und Mensch im Denken der Antike, 1977
Dietz	K. Dietz, Senatus contra principem. Untersuchungen zur senatorischen Opposition gegen Kaiser Maximinus Thrax (Vestigia 29), 1980
Dihle	A. Dihle, Die griechische und lateinische Literatur der Kaiserzeit. Von Augustus bis Justinian, 1989

DiskAB	Diskussionen zur archäologischen Bauforschung, 1974 ff.
Dixon	S. Dixon, The Roman Family, 1992
DJD	Discoveries in the Judaean Desert, 1955 ff.
DLZ	Deutsche Literaturzeitung für Kritik der internationalen Wissenschaft
DMA	J. R. Strayer et al. (eds.), Dictionary of the Middle Ages, 13 vols., 1982–1989
DMic	F. Aura Jorro, Diccionario Micénico, 1985
Dörrie/Baltes	H. Dörrie / M. Baltes (eds.), Der Platonismus in der Antike, 1987 ff.
Domaszewski	A. von Domaszewski, Aufsätze zur römischen Heeresgeschichte, 1972
Domaszewski/Dobson	A. von Domaszewski / B. Dobson, Die Rangordnung des römischen Heeres, ²1967
Domergue	C. Domergue, Les mines de la péninsule ibérique dans l'Antiquité romaine, 1990
Drumann/Groebe	W. Drumann / P. Groebe (eds.), Geschichte Roms in seinem Übergange von der republikanischen zur monarchischen Verfassung, 6 vols., ²1899–1929 (repr. 1964)
DS	C. Daremberg / E. Saglio (eds.), Dictionnaire des antiquités grecques et romaines d'après les textes et les monuments, 6 vols., 1877–1919 (repr. 1969)
Dulckeit/Schwarz/Waldstein	G. Dulckeit / F. Schwarz / W. Waldstein, Römische Rechtsgeschichte. Ein Studienbuch (Juristische Kurz-Lehrbücher), ⁹1995
Dumézil	G. Dumézil, La religion romaine archaïque, suivi d'un appendice sur la religion des Etrusques, ²1974
Duncan-Jones, Economy	R. Duncan-Jones, The Economy of the Roman Empire. Quantitative Studies, 1974
Duncan-Jones, Structure	R. Duncan-Jones, Structure and Scale in the Roman Economy, 1990
DVjS	Deutsche Vierteljahrsschrift für Literaturwissenschaft und Geistesgeschichte
EA	Epigraphica Anatolica. Zeitschrift für Epigraphik und historische Geographie Anatoliens
EAA	R. Bianchi Bandinelli (ed.), Enciclopedia dell'arte antica classica e orientale, 1958 ff.
EB	G. Camps, Encyclopédie Berbère, 1984 ff.
Ebert	F. Ebert, Fachausdrücke des griechischen Bauhandwerks, vol. 1: Der Tempel, 1910
EC	Essays in Criticism
Eck (Statthalter)	W. Eck, Die Statthalter der germanischen Provinzen vom 1.–3. Jahrhundert (Epigraphische Studien 14), 1985
Eckstein	F. A. Eckstein, Nomenclator philologorum, 1871
EDCS	Epigraphische Datenbank Clauss/Slaby (http://www.manfredclauss.de/)
Edelstein, AM	L. Edelstein, Ancient Medicine, 1967
Edelstein, Asclepius	E. J. Edelstein / L. Edelstein, Asclepius. A Collection and Interpretation of the Testimonies, 1945
Eder, Demokratie	W. Eder (ed.), Die athenische Demokratie im 4. Jahrhundert v.Chr. Vollendung oder Verfall einer Verfassungsform? Akten eines Symposiums, 3.–7. August 1992, 1995
Eder, Staat	W. Eder (ed.), Staat und Staatlichkeit in der frühen römischen Republik. Akten eines Symposiums, 12.–15. Juli 1988, 1990
EDM	K. Ranke / W. Brednich (eds.), Enzyklopädie des Märchens. Handwörterbuch zur historischen und vergleichenden Erzählforschung, 1977 ff.
EDRL	A. Berger, Encyclopedic Dictionary of Roman Law (TAPhA N. S. 43,2), 1953 (repr. 1968)
EEpigr	Ephemeris Epigraphica
EI	Encyclopaedia of Islam, ²1960 ff.
Eissfeldt	O. Eissfeldt (ed.), Handbuch zum Alten Testament, ³1964 ff.
Emerita	Emerita. Revista de linguistica y filologia clasica
EncIr	E. Yarshater (ed.), Encyclopaedia Iranica, 1985
Entretiens	Entretiens sur l'antiquité classique (Fondation Hardt)

EOMIA	C. H. Turner (ed.), Ecclesiae Occidentalis Monumenta Iuris Antiquissima, 1899–1939 (Suppl. 1930 ff.)
EOS	Atti del Colloquio Internaziona- le AIEGL su Epigrafia e Ordine Senatorio, Roma, 14–20 maggio 1981, 2 vols., 1982
EpGF	M. Davies, Epicorum graecorum fragmenta, 1988
EpGr	G. Kaibel (ed.), Epigrammata Graeca ex lapidibus conlecta, 1878
Epicurea	H. Usener (ed.), Epicurea, 1887 (repr. 1963)
EPRO	Études préliminaires aux religions orientales dans l'Empire Romain, 1961 ff.
Eranos	Eranos. Acta Philologica Suecana
Eranos-Jb	Eranos-Jahrbuch
Erasmus	Erasmus. Speculum Scientiarum. Internationales Literaturblatt der Geisteswissenschaften
Eretz-Israel	Eretz-Israel. Archaeological, Historical and Geographical Studies
Ernout/Meillet	A. Ernout / A. Meillet, Dictionnaire étymologique de la langue latine, ^{4}1959
Errington	R. M. Errington, Geschichte Makedoniens. Von den Anfängen bis zum Untergang des Königreiches, 1986
ESAR	T. Frank (ed.), An Economic Survey of Ancient Rome, 6 vols., 1933–1940
Espérandieu, Inscr.	E. Espérandieu (ed.), Inscriptions latines de Gaule, 2 vols., 1929–1936
Espérandieu, Rec.	E. Espérandieu, Recueil général des bas-reliefs, statues et bustes de la Gaule romaine, 16 vols., 1907–1981
ET	H. Rix (ed.), Etruskische Texte (ScriptOralia 23,24, Reihe A 6,7), 2 vols., 1991
ETAM	Ergänzungsbände zu den Tituli Asiae minoris, 1966 ff.
Euph.	Euphorion
EV	F. Della Corte et al. (eds.), Enciclopedia Virgiliana, 5 vols. in 6 parts, 1984–1991
Evans	D. E. Evans, Gaulish Personal Names. A Study of Some Continental Celtic Formations, 1967
F&F	Forschungen und Fortschritte
Farnell, Cults	L. R. Farnell, The Cults of theGreek States, 5 vols., 1896–1909
Farnell, GHC	L. R. Farnell, Greek Hero Cults and Ideas of Immortality, 1921
FCG	A. Meineke (ed.), Fragmenta Comicorum Graecorum, 5 vols., 1839–1857 (repr. 1970)
FCS	Fifteenth-Century Studies
FdD	Fouilles de Delphes, 1902 ff.
FGE	D. L. Page, Further Greek Epigrams, 1981
FGrH	F. Jacoby, Die Fragmente der griechischen Historiker, 3 parts in 14 vols., 1923–1958 (part 1: ^{2}1957)
FHG	C. Müller (ed.), Fragmenta Historicorum Graecorum, 5 vols., 1841–1870
Fick/Bechtel	A. Fick / F. Bechtel, Die griechischen Personennamen, ^{2}1894
FiE	Forschungen in Ephesos, 1906 ff.
Filologia	La Filologia Greca e Latina nel secolo XX, 1989
Finley, Ancient Economy	M. I. Finley, The Ancient Economy, ^{2}1984
Finley, Ancient Slavery	M. I. Finley, Ancient Slavery and Modern Ideology, 1980
Finley, Economy	M. I. Finley et al. (eds.), Economy and Society in Ancient Greece, 1981
Finley, Property	M. I. Finley (ed.), Studies in Roman Property, 1976
FIRA	S. Riccobono / J. Baviera (eds.), Fontes iuris Romani anteiustiniani, 3 vols., ^{2}1968
FIRBruns	K. G. Bruns et al. (eds.), Fontes iuris Romani antiqui, ^{7}1909 (repr. 1969)
Fittschen/Zanker	K. Fittschen / P. Zanker, Katalog der römischen Porträts in den capitolinischen Museen und den anderen kommunalen Museen der Stadt Rom, 1983 ff.
Flach	D. Flach, Römische Agrargeschichte (HdbA 3/9), 1990
Flashar	H. Flashar, Inszenierung der Antike. Das griechische Drama auf der Bühne der Neuzeit, 1991
Flashar, Medizin	H. Flashar (ed.), Antike Medizin, 1971

FMS	Frühmittelalterliche Studien, Jahrbuch des Instituts für Frühmittelalter-Forschung der Universität Münster
FO2	L. Vidman, Fasti Ostienses, 1982
Fossey	J. M. Fossey, Topography and Population of Ancient Boiotia, vol. 1, 1988
FOst	L. Vidman, Fasti Ostienses, 1982
Fowler	W. W. Fowler, The Roman Festivals of the Period of the Republic. An Introduction to the Study of the Religion of the Romans, 1899
FPD	I. Piso, Fasti Provinciae Daciae, vol. 1: Die senatorischen Amtsträger (Antiquitas 1,43), 1993
FPL2	W. Morel / C. Büchner (eds.), Fragmenta Poetarum Latinorum epicorum et lyricorum, ^{2}1982
FPL3	W. Morel et al. (eds.), Fragmenta Poetarum Latinorum epicorum et lyricorum, ^{3}1995
FPR	A. Bährens (ed.), Fragmenta poetarum Romanorum, 1886
Frazer	J. G. Frazer, The Golden Bough. A Study in Magic and Religion, 8 parts in 12 vols.; vols. 1–3, 5–9, ^{3}1911–1914; vols. 4, 10–12, 1911–1915
Freis	H. Freis (ed.), Historische Inschriften zur römischen Kaiserzeit. Von Augustus bis Konstantin, ^{2}1994
Frenzel	E. Frenzel, Stoffe der Weltliteratur, ^{8}1992
FRH	H. Beck / U. Walter (eds.), Die frühen römischen Historiker, 2 vols., 2001-2004
Friedländer	L. Friedländer / G. Wissowa (eds.), Darstellungen aus der Sittengeschichte Roms, 4 vols., ^{10}1921–1923
Frier, Landlords	B. W. Frier, Landlords and Tenants in Imperial Rome, 1980
Frier, PontMax	B. W. Frier, Libri annales pontificum maximorum. The Origins of the Annalistic Tradition (Papers and Monographs of the American Academy in Rome 27), 1979
Frisk	H. Frisk, Griechisches etymologisches Wörterbuch (Indogermanische Bibliothek: Reihe 2), 3 vols., 1960–1972
FRLANT	Forschungen zur Religion und Literatur des Alten und Neuen Testaments
Fuchs/Floren	W. Fuchs / J. Floren, Die Griechische Plastik, vol. 1: Die geometrische und archaische Plastik, 1987
Furtwängler	A. Furtwängler, Die antiken Gemmen. Geschichte der Steinschneidekunst im klassischen Altertum, 3 vols., 1900
Furtwängler/Reichhold	A. Furtwängler/K. Reichhold, Griechische Vasenmalerei, 3 vols., 1904–1932
Fushöller	D. Fushöller, Tunesien und Ostalgerien in der Römerzeit, 1979
G&R	Greece and Rome
GA	A. S. F. Gow / D. L. Page, The Greek Anthology, vol. 1: Hellenistic Epigrams, 1965; vol. 2: The Garland of Philip, 1968
Gardner	P. Gardner, A History of Ancient Coinage, 700–300 B. C., 1918
Gardthausen	V. Gardthausen, Augustus und seine Zeit, 2 parts in 6 vols., 1891–1904
Garnsey	P. Garnsey, Famine and Food Supply in the Graeco-Roman World. Responses to Risk and Crisis, 1988
Garnsey/Hopkins/Whittaker	P. Garnsey / K. Hopkins / C. R. Whittaker (eds.), Trade in the Ancient Economy, 1983
Garnsey/Saller	P. Garnsey / R. Saller, The Roman Empire, Economy, Society and Culture, 1987
GCS	Die griechischen christlichen Schriftsteller der ersten Jahrhunderte, 1897 ff.
Gehrke	H.-J. Gehrke, Jenseits von Athen und Sparta. Das Dritte Griechenland und seine Staatenwelt, 1986
Gentili/Prato	B. Gentili / C. Prato (eds.), Poetarvm elegiacorvm tetestimona et fragmenta, vol. 1, ^{2}1988; vol. 2, 1985
Georges	K. E. Georges, Ausführliches lateinisch-deutsches Handwörterbuch, 2 vols., ^{8}1912–1918 (repr. 1992)
Gérard-Rousseau	M. Gérard-Rousseau, Les mentions religieuses dans les tablettes mycéniennes, 1968

Germania	Germania. Anzeiger der Römisch-Germanischen Kommission des Deutschen Archäologischen Instituts
Gernet	L. Gernet, Droit et société dans la Grèce ancienne (Institut de droit romain, Publication 13), 1955 (repr. 1964)
Geus	K. Geus, Prosopographie der literarisch bezeugten Karthager (Studia Phoenicia 13; Orientalia Lovaniensia analecta 59), 1994
GG	Grammatici Graeci, vols. 1,1– 4,2, 1867–1910
GGA	Göttingische Gelehrte Anzeigen
GGM	C. Müller (ed.), Geographi Graeci Minores, 2 vols., Tabulae, 1855–1861
GGPh1	Grundriß der Geschichte der Philosophie (founded by F. Überweg); K. Prächter (ed.), vol. 1: Die Philosophie des Altertums, ^{12}1926 (repr. 1953)
GGPh2	Grundriß der Geschichte der Philosophie (founded by F. Überweg); H. Flashar (ed.), vol. 3: Die Philosophie der Antike, 1983; vol. 4: Die hellenistische Philosophie, 1994
GHW 1	H. Bengtson et al., Großer Historischer Weltatlas des Bayrischen Schulbuchverlages, vol. 1: Vorgeschichte und Altertum, ^{6}1978
GHW 2	J. Engel et al., Großer Historischer Weltatlas des Bayrischen Schulbuchverlages, vol. 2: Mittelalter, ^{2}1979
GIBM	C. T. Newton et al. (eds.), The Collection of Ancient Greek Inscriptions in the British Museum, 4 vols., 1874–1916
Gillispie	C. C. Gillispie (ed.), Dictionary of Scientific Biography, 14 vols. and index, 1970–1980 (repr. 1981; 2 Suppl.-vols., 1978–1990)
GL	H. Keil (ed.), Grammatici Latini, 7 vols., 1855–1880
GLM	A. Riese (ed.), Geographi Latini Minores, 1878
Glotta	Glotta. Zeitschrift für griechische und lateinische Sprache
GMth	F. Zaminer (ed.), Geschichte der Musiktheorie, 1984 ff.
Gnomon	Gnomon. Kritische Zeitschrift für die gesamte klassische Altertumswissenschaft
Göbl	R. Göbl, Antike Numismatik, 2 vols., 1978
Goleniščev	I. N. Goleniščev-Kutuzov, Il Rinascimento italiano e le letterature slave dei secoli XV e XVI, 1973
Gordon	A. E. Gordon, Album of Dated Latin Inscriptions, 4 vols., 1958–1965
Goulet	R. Goulet (ed.), Dictionnaire des philosophes antiques, 1989 ff.
Graf	F. Graf, Nordionische Kulte. Religionsgeschichtliche und epigraphische Untersuchungen zu den Kulten von Chios, Erythrai, Klazomenai und Phokaia, 1985
GRBS	Greek, Roman and Byzantine Studies
Grenier	A. Grenier, Manuel d'archéologie gallo-romaine, 4 vols., 1931–1960 (repr. vols. 1–2, 1985)
GRF	H. Funaioli (ed.), Grammaticae Romanae Fragmenta, 1907
GRF(add)	A. Mazzarino, Grammaticae Romanae Fragmenta aetatis Caesareae (accedunt volumini Funaioliano addenda), 1955
GRLMA	Grundriß der romanischen Literaturen des Mittelalters
Gruen, Last Gen.	E. S. Gruen, The Last Generation of the Roman Republic, 1974
Gruen, Rome	E. S. Gruen, The Hellenistic World and the Coming of Rome, 1984 (repr. 1986)
Gruppe	O. Gruppe, Geschichte der klassischen Mythologie und Religionsgeschichte während des Mittelalters im Abendland und während der Neuzeit, 1921
Gundel	W. Gundel / H.-G. Gundel, Astrologumena. Die astrologische Literatur in der Antike und ihre Geschichte, 1966
Guthrie	W. K. C. Guthrie, A History of Greek Philosophy, 6 vols., 1962–1981
GVI	W. Peek (ed.), Griechische Versinschriften, vol. 1, 1955
Gymnasium	Gymnasium. Zeitschrift für Kultur der Antike und humanistische Bildung
HABES	Heidelberger althistorische Beiträge und epigraphische Studien, 1986 ff.
Habicht	C. Habicht, Athen. Die Geschichte der Stadt in hellenistischer Zeit, 1995
Haehling	R. von Haehling, Die Religionszugehörigkeit der hohen Amtsträger des Römischen Reiches seit Constantins I. Alleinherrschaft bis zum Ende der

	Theodosianischen Dynastie (324–450 bzw. 455 n.Chr.) (Antiquitas 3,23), 1978
Hakkert	A. M. Hakkert (ed.), Lexicon of Greek and Roman Cities and Place-Names in Antiquity c. 1500 B.C.–c. A.D. 500, 1992 ff.
Halfmann	H. Halfmann, Die Senatoren aus dem östlichen Teil des Imperium Romanum bis zum Ende des 2. Jahrhunderts n.Chr. (Hypomnemata 58), 1979
Hamburger	K. Hamburger, Von Sophokles zu Sartre. Griechische Dramenfiguren antik und modern, 1962
Hannestad	N. Hannestad, Roman Art and Imperial Policy, 1986
Hansen, Democracy	M. H. Hansen, The Athenian Democracy in the Age of Demosthenes. Structure, Principles and Ideology, 1991 (repr. 1993)
Harris	W. V. Harris, War and Imperialism in Republican Rome 327–70 B.C., 1979
Hasebroek	J. Hasebroek, Griechische Wirtschafts- und Gesellschaftsgeschichte bis zur Perserzeit, 1931
HbdOr	B. Spuler (ed.), Handbuch der Orientalistik, 1952 ff.
HbdrA	J. Marquardt / T. Mommsen, Handbuch der römischen Alterthümer, vol. 1–3, ^{3}1887–1888; vol. 4–7, ^{2}1881–1986
HBr	P. Herrmann / R. Herbig (eds.), Denkmäler der Malerei des Altertums, 2 vols., 1904–1950
HDA	H. Bächtold-Stäubli et al. (eds.), Handwörterbuch des deutschen Aberglaubens, 10 vols., 1927–1942 (repr. 1987)
HdArch	W. Otto / U. Hausmann (eds.), Handbuch der Archäologie. Im Rahmen des HdbA, 7 vols., 1969–1990
HdbA	I. von Müller et al. (eds.), Handbuch der Altertumswissenschaft, ^{5}1977 ff.
Heckel	W. Heckel, Marshals of Alexander's Empire, 1978
Heinemann	K. Heinemann, Die tragischen Gestalten der Griechen in der Weltliteratur, 1920
Helbig	W. Helbig, Führer durch die öffentlichen Sammlungen klassischer Altertümer in Rom, 4 vols., ^{4}1963–1972
Hephaistos	Hephaistos. Kritische Zeitschrift zu Theorie und Praxis der Archäologie, Kunstwissenschaft und angrenzender Gebiete
Hermes	Hermes. Zeitschrift für klassische Philologie
Herrscherbild	Das römische Herrscherbild, 1939 ff.
Herzog, Staatsverfassung	E. von Herzog, Geschichte und System der römischen Staatsverfassung, 2 vols., 1884–1891 (repr. 1965)
Hesperia	Hesperia. Journal of the American School of Classical Studies at Athens
Heubeck	A. Heubeck, Schrift (Archaeologia Homerica Kapitel X vol. 3), 1979
Heumann/Seckel	H. G. Heumann / E. Seckel (eds.), Handlexikon zu den Quellen des römischen Rechts, ^{11}1971
HGIÜ	K. Brodersen (ed.), Historische griechische Inschriften in Übersetzung, 3 vols., 1992–1999
Highet	G. Highet, The Classical Tradition. Greek and Roman Influences on Western Literature, ^{4}1968 (repr. 1985)
Hild/Hellenkemper	F. Hild / H. Hellenkemper, Kilikien und Isaurien (Denkschriften der Österreichischen Akademie der Wissenschaften. Philosophisch-Historische Klasse 215; TIB 5), 2 vols., 1990
Hild/Restle	F. Hild / M. Restle, Kappadokien (Kappadokia, Charsianon, Sebasteia und Lykandos) (Denkschriften der Österreichischen Akademie der Wissenschaften. Philosophisch-Historische Klasse 149; TIB 2), 1981
Hirschfeld	O. Hirschfeld, Die kaiserlichen Verwaltungsbeamten bis auf Diocletian, ^{2}1905
Historia	Historia. Zeitschrift für Alte Geschichte
HJb	Historisches Jahrbuch
HLav	Humanistica Lavanensia
HLL	R. Herzog / P. L. Schmidt (eds.), Handbuch der lateinischen Literatur der Antike, 1989 ff.

HM	A History of Macedonia, vol. 1: N. G. L. Hammond, Historical Geography and Prehistory, 1972; vol. 2: N. G. L. Hammond/G. T. Griffith, 550–336 BC, 1979; vol. 3: N. G. L. Hammond/F. W. Walbank, 336–167 BC, 1988
HmT	H. H. Eggebrecht, Handwörterbuch der musikalischen Terminologie, 1972 ff.
HN	B. V. Head, Historia numorum. A Manual of Greek Numismatics, ^{2}1911
Hodge	T. A. Hodge, Roman Aqueducts and Water Supply, 1992
Hölbl	G. Hölbl, Geschichte des Ptolemäerreiches. Politik, Ideologie und religiöse Kultur von Alexander dem Großen bis zur römischen Eroberung, 1994
Hölkeskamp	K.-J. Hölkeskamp, Die Entstehung der Nobilität. Studien zur sozialen und politischen Geschichte der Römischen Republik im 4. Jh. v.Chr., 1987
Hoffmann	D. Hoffmann, Das spätrömische Bewegungsheer und die Notitia dignitatum (Epigraphische Studien 7), 2 vols., 1969–1970 (Diss. Universität Basel, 1958)
Hofmann/Szantyr	J. B. Hofmann / A. Szantyr, Lateinische Syntax und Stilistik, ^{2}1972
Holder	A. Holder, Alt-celtischer Sprachschatz, 3 vols., 1896–1913 (repr. 1961–1962)
Honsell	H. Honsell, Römisches Recht (Springer-Lehrbuch), ^{3}1994
Honsell/Mayer-Maly/Selb	H. Honsell / T. Mayer-Maly / W. Selb, Römisches Recht, ^{4}1987
Hopfner	T. Hopfner, Griechisch-ägyptischer Offenbarungszauber, 2 vols. in 3 parts, 1921–1924 (repr. 1974–1990)
Hopkins, Conquerors	K. Hopkins, Conquerors and Slaves. Sociological Studies in Roman History, vol. 1, 1978
Hopkins, Death	K. Hopkins, Death and Renewal. Sociological Studies in Roman History, vol. 2, 1983
HR	History of Religions
HRR	H. Peter (ed.), Historicorum Romanorum Reliquiae, vol. 1, ^{2}1914; vol. 2, 1906 (repr. 1967)
HrwG	H. Cancik et al. (from vol. 2: K.-H. Kohl) (ed.), Handbuch religionswissenschaftlicher Grundbegriffe, 1988 ff.
HS	Historische Sprachforschung
HSM	Histoire des sciences médicales
HSPh	Harvard Studies in Classical Philology
Hülser	K. Hülser, Die Fragmente zur Dialektik der Stoiker. Neue Sammlung der Texte mit deutscher Übersetzung und Kommentaren, 4 vols., 1987–1988
Humphrey	J. H. Humphrey, Roman Circuses. Arenas for Chariot Racing, 1986
Hunger, Literatur	H. Hunger, Die hochsprachlich profane Literatur der Byzantiner (HdbA 12,5), 2 vols., 1978
Hunger, Mythologie	H. Hunger (ed.), Lexikon der griechischen und römischen Mythologie, ^{6}1969
Huss	W. Huss, Geschichte der Karthager (HdbA 3,8), 1985
HWdPh	J. Ritter / K. Gründer (eds.), Historisches Wörterbuch der Philosophie, 13 vols., 1971 ff.
HWdR	G. Ueding (eds.), Historisches Wörterbuch der Rhetorik, 12 vols., 1992 ff.
HZ	Historische Zeitschrift
IA	Iranica Antiqua
IAquileia	J. B. Brusin, Inscriptiones Aquileiae, 3 vols., 1991–1993
IconRel	T. P. V. Baaren (ed.), Iconography of Religions, 1970 ff.
ICret	M. Guarducci (ed.), Inscriptiones Creticae, 4 vols., 1935–1950
ICUR	A. Ferrua / G. B. de Rossi, Inscriptiones christianae urbis Romae
IDélos	Inscriptions de Délos, 1926 ff.
IDidyma	A. Rehm (ed.), Didyma, vol. 2: Die Inschriften, 1958
IDR	I. I. Russu (ed.), Inscripţiile Daciei Romane = Inscriptiones Daciae Romanae, 1975 ff.
IDRE	C. C. Petulescu (ed.), Inscriptions de la Dacie romaine. Inscriptions externes concernant l'histoire de la Dacie (Ier– IIIe siècles), 1996 ff.
IEG	M. L. West (ed.), Iambi et elegi Graeci ante Alexandrum cantati, 2 vols., ^{2}1989–1992
IEJ	Israel Exploration Journal

IEph	Die Inschriften von Ephesos, parts 1–7 (= Inschriften griechischer Städte aus Kleinasien 11–17,4), 1979–1984
IER	Illustrierte Enzyklopädie der Renaissance
IEry	H. Engelmann (ed.), Die Inschriften von Erythrai und Klazomenai, 2 vols., 1972–1973
IF	Indogermanische Forschungen
IFay	É. Bernand, Recueil des inscriptions grecques du Fayoum, 3 vols., 1975–1981
IG	Inscriptiones Graecae, 1873 ff.
IGA	H. Roehl (ed.), Inscriptiones Graecae antiquissimae praeter Atticas in Attica repertas, 1882 (repr. 1977)
IGBulg	G. Mihailov (ed.), Inscriptiones Graecae in Bulgaria Repertae, 5 vols., 1956–1996
IGLS	Inscriptions grecques et latines de la Syrie, 1929 ff.
IGR	R. Cagnat et al. (eds.), Inscriptiones Graecae ad res Romanas pertinentes, 4 vols., 1906–1927
IGUR	L. Moretti, Inscriptiones Graecae urbis Romae, 4 vols., 1968–1990
IHG	J.-M. Bertrand (ed.), Inscriptions Historiques Grecques, 1992
IJCT	International Journal of the Classical Tradition
IJsewijn	J. IJsewijn, Companion to Neo Latin Studies, ²1990 ff.
IK	Die Inschriften griechischer Städte aus Kleinasien, 1972 ff.
ILAlg	S. Gsell, Inscriptions Latines de l'Algérie, vol. 1, 1922 (repr. 1965; vol. 2 (ed. H. G. Pflaum), 1957)
ILBulg	B. Gerov (ed.), Inscriptiones Latinae in Bulgaria repertae, 1989
ILCV	E. Diehl (ed.), Inscriptiones Latinae Christianae Veteres orientis, 3 vols., 1925–1931 (repr. 1961); J. Moreau / H. I. Marrou (eds.), Suppl., 1967
ILLRP	A. Degrassi (ed.), Inscriptiones Latinae liberae rei publicae, 2 vols., 1957–1963 (repr. 1972)
ILS	H. Dessau (ed.), Inscriptiones Latinae Selectae, 3 vols., 1892–1916 (repr. ⁴1974)
ILTun	A. Merlin (ed.), Inscriptions latines de la Tunisie, 1944
IMagn.	O. Kern (ed.), Die Inschriften von Magnesia am Mäander, 1900 (repr. 1967)
IMU	Italia medioevale e umanistica
Index	Index. Quaderni camerti di studi romanistici
InscrIt	A. Degrassi (ed.), Inscriptiones Italiae, 1931 ff.
IOlympia	W. Dittenberger / K. Purgold, Inschriften von Olympia, 1896 (repr. 1966)
IOSPE	V. Latyschew (ed.), Inscriptiones antiquae orae septentrionalis ponti Euxini Graecae et Latinae, 3 vols., 1885–1901 (repr. 1965), vol. 1 ²1916
IPArk	G. Thür / H. Taeuber, Prozeßrechtliche Inschriften der griechischen Poleis. Arkadien, 1994
IPerg	M. Fraenkel (ed.), Die Inschriften von Pergamon (Altertümer von Pergamon, vol. 8,1 und 8,2), 1890 und 1895
IPNB	M. Mayrhofer / R. Schmitt (eds.), Iranisches Personennamenbuch, 1979 ff.
IPQ	International Philosophical Quaterly
IPriene	F. Hiller von Gärtringen, Inschriften von Priene, 1906
Irmscher	J. Irmscher (ed.), Renaissance und Humanismus in Mittel- und Osteuropa, 1962
ISmyrna	G. Petzl, Die Inschriften von Smyrna (Die Inschriften griechischer Städte in Kleinasien 24.1), vol. 1–2,2, 1982–1990
Isager/Skydsgaa	S. Isager / J. E. Skydsgaard, Ancient Greek Agriculture. An Introduction, 1992
ISE	L. Moretti (ed.), Iscrizioni storiche ellenistiche, 2 vols., 1967–1976
IScM	Inscriptiones Scythiae Minoris Graecae et Latinae, 1980 ff.
IstForsch	Istanbuler Forschungen des Deutschen Archäologischen Instituts
IThrakAig	L. D. Loukopoulou et al. (eds.), Epigraphes tēs Thrakēs tou Aigaiou. Metaxy tōn potamōn Nestou kai Hevrou (nomoi Xanthēs, Rhodopēs kai Hevrou), 2005

IThSy	A. Bernand, De Thèbes à Syène, 1989
Iura	IVRA, Rivista internazionale di diritto romano e antico
Jaffé	P. Jaffé, Regesta pontificum Romanorum ab condita ecclesia ad annum 1198, 2 vols., ²1985–1988
JBAA	The Journal of the British Archaeological Association
JbAC	Jahrbuch für Antike und Christentum
JCS	Journal of Cuneiform Studies
JDAI	Jahrbuch des Deutschen Archäologischen Instituts
JEA	The Journal of Egyptian Archaeology
Jenkyns, DaD	R. Jenkyns, Dignity and Decadence. Classicism and the Victorians, 1992
Jenkyns, Legacy	R. Jenkyns, The Legacy of Rome. A New Appraisal, 1992
JHAS	Journal for the History of Arabic Science
JHB	Journal of the History of Biology
JHM	Journal of the History of Medicine and Allied Sciences
JHPh	Journal of the History of Philosophy
JHS	Journal of Hellenic Studies
JLW	Jahrbuch für Liturgiewissenschaft
JMRS	Journal of Medieval and Renaissance Studies
JNES	Journal of Near Eastern Studies
JNG	Jahrbuch für Numismatik und Geldgeschichte
JÖAI	Jahreshefte des Österreichischen Archäologischen Instituts
Jones, Cities	A. H. M. Jones, The Cities of the Eastern Roman Provinces, ²1971
Jones, Economy	A. H. M. Jones, The Roman Economy. Studies in Ancient Economic and Administrative History, 1974
Jones, LRE	A. H. M. Jones, The Later Roman Empire 284–602. A Social, Economic and Administrative Survey, 1964
Jones, RGL	A. H. M. Jones, Studies in Roman Government and Law, 1968
Jost	M. Jost, Sanctuaires et cultes d'Arcadie, 1985
JPh	Journal of Philosophy
JRGZ	Jahrbuch des Römisch-Germanischen Zentralmuseums
JRS	Journal of Roman Studies
JSJ	Journal for the Study of Judaism
Justi	F. Justi, Iranisches Namenbuch, 1895
JWG	Jahrbuch für Wirtschaftsgeschichte
JWI	Journal of the Warburg and Courtauld Institutes
Kadmos	Kadmos. Zeitschrift für vor- und frühgriechische Epigraphik
KAI	H. Donner / W. Röllig, Kanaanaeische und aramaeische Inschriften, 3 vols., ³1971–1976
Kajanto, Cognomina	I. Kajanto, The Latin Cognomina, 1965
Kajanto, Supernomina	I. Kajanto, Supernomina. A Study in Latin Epigraphy (Commentationes humanarum litterarum 40,1), 1966
Kamptz	H. von Kamptz, Homerische Personennamen. Sprachwissenschaftliche und historische Klassifikation, 1982 = H. von Kamptz, Sprachwissenschaftliche und historische Klassifikation der homerischen Personennamen, 1958 (Diss. Universität Jena)
Karlowa	O. Karlowa, Römische Rechtsgeschichte, 2 vols., 1885–1901
Kaser, AJ	M. Kaser, Das altrömische Jus. Studien zur Rechtsvorstellung und Rechtsgeschichte der Römer, 1949
Kaser, RPR	M. Kaser, Das römische Privatrecht (Rechtsgeschichte des Altertums part 3, vol. 3; HbdA 10/3,3), 2 vols., ²1971–1975
Kaser, RZ	M. Kaser, Das römische Zivilprozessrecht (Rechtsgeschichte des Altertums part 3, vol. 4; HbdA 10/3,4), 1966
Kearns	E. Kearns, The Heroes of Attica, 1989 (BICS Suppl. 57)
Keller	O. Keller, Die antike Tierwelt, 2 vols., 1909–1920 (repr. 1963)
Kelnhofer	F. Kelnhofer, Die topographische Bezugsgrundlage der Tabula Imperii Byzantini (Denkschriften der Österreichischen Akademie der Wissenschaften. Philosophisch-Historische Klasse 125, Beiheft; TIB 1, Beiheft), 1976

Kienast	D. Kienast, Römische Kaisertabelle. Grundzüge einer römischen Kaiserchronologie, ^{1}1990 (^{2}1996)
Kindler	W. Jens (ed.), Kindlers Neues Literatur Lexikon, 20 vols., 1988–1992
Kinkel	G. Kinkel (ed.), Epicorum Graecorum Fragmenta, 1877
Kirsten/Kraiker	E. Kirsten / W. Kraiker, Griechenlandkunde. Ein Führer zu klassischen Stätten, ^{5}1967
Kleberg	T. Kleberg, Hôtels, restaurants et cabarets dans l'antiquité Romaine. Études historiques et philologiques, 1957
Klio	Klio. Beiträge zur Alten Geschichte
KlP	K. Ziegler (ed.), Der Kleine Pauly. Lexikon der Antike, 5 vols., 1964–1975 (repr. 1979)
Knobloch	J. Knobloch et al. (ed.), Sprachwissenschaftliches Wörterbuch (Indogermanische Bibliothek 2), 1986 ff. (1st fasc. 1961)
Koch/Sichtermann	G. Koch / H. Sichtermann, Römische Sarkophage, 1982
Koder	J. Koder, Der Lebensraum der Byzantiner. Historisch-geographischer Abriß ihres mittelalterlichen Staates im östlichen Mittelmeerraum, 1984
Koder/Hild	J. Koder / F. Hild, Hellas und Thessalia (Denkschriften der Österreichischen Akademie der Wissenschaften. Philosophisch-Historische Klasse 125; TIB 1), 1976
Kolb, Bauverwaltung	A. Kolb, Die kaiserliche Bauverwaltung in der Stadt Rom, 1993
Kraft	K. Kraft, Gesammelte Aufsätze zur antiken Geschichte und Militärgeschichte, 1973
Kromayer/Veith	J. Kromayer / G. Veith, Heerwesen und Kriegführung der Griechen und Römer, 1928 (repr. 1963)
Krumbacher	K. Krumbacher, Geschichte der byzantinischen Litteratur von Justinian bis zum Ende des oströmischen Reiches (527–1453) (HdbA 9,1), ^{2}1897 (repr. 1970)
KSd	J. Friedrich (ed.), Klein asiatische Sprachdenkmäler (Kleine Texte für Vorlesungen und Übungen 163), 1932
KUB	Keilschrifturkunden von Boghazköi
Kühner/Blass	R. Kühner / F. Blass, Ausführliche Grammatik der griechischen Sprache, part 1: Elementar- und Formenlehre, 2 vols., ^{3}1890–1892
Kühner/Gerth	R. Kühner / B. Gerth, Ausführliche Grammatik der griechischen Sprache, part 2: Satzlehre, 2 vols., ^{3}1898–1904; W. M. Calder III, Index locorum, 1965
Kühner/Holzweißig	R. Kühner / F. Holzweissig, Ausführliche Grammatik der lateinischen Sprache, part 1: Elementar-, Formen- und Wortlehre, ^{2}1912
Kühner/Stegmann	R. Kühner / C. Stegmann, Ausführliche Grammatik der lateinischen Sprache, part 2: Satzlehre, 2 vols., ^{4}1962 (durchgesehen von A. Thierfelder); G. S. Schwarz / R. L. Wertis, Index locorum, 1980
Kullmann/Althoff	W. Kullmann / J. Althoff (eds.), Vermittlung und Tradierung von Wissen in der griechischen Kultur, 1993
Kunkel	W. Kunkel, Herkunft und soziale Stellung der römischen Juristen, ^{2}1967
KWdH	H. H. Schmitt (ed.), Kleines Wörterbuch des Hellenismus, ^{2}1993
Lacey	W. K. Lacey, The Family in Classical Greece, 1968
LÄ	W. Helck et al. (eds.), Lexikon der Ägyptologie, 7 vols., 1975–1992 (1st fasc. 1972)
LAK	H. Brunner et al. (eds.), Lexikon Alte Kulturen, 3 vols., 1990–1993
Lanciani	R. Lanciani, Forma urbis Romae, 1893–1901
Lange	C. C. L. Lange, Römische Altertümer, vols. 1–2, ^{2}1876–1879; vol. 3, 1876
Langosch	K. Langosch, Mittellatein und Europa, 1990
Latomus	Latomus. Revue d'études latines
Latte	K. Latte, Römische Religions- geschichte (HdbA 5,4), 1960 (repr. 1992)
Lauffer, BL	S. Lauffer, Die Bergwerkssklaven von Laureion, ^{2}1979
Lauffer, Griechenland	S. Lauffer (ed.), Griechenland. Lexikon der historischen Stätten von den Anfängen bis zur Gegenwart, 1989
Lausberg	H. Lausberg, Handbuch der literarischen Rhetorik. Eine Grundlegung der Literaturwissenschaft, ^{3}1990
LAW	C. Andresen et al. (eds.), Lexikon der Alten Welt, 1965 (repr. 1990)

LCI	E. Kirschbaum (ed.), Lexikon der christlichen Ikonographie, 8 vols., 1968–1976
LdA	J. Irmscher (ed.), Lexikon der Antike, ^{10}1990
Le Bohec	Y. le Bohec, L'armée romaine sous le Haut-Empire, ^{4}2018
Leitner	H. Leitner, Zoologische Terminologie beim Älteren Plinius, 1972 (Diss. Universität Wien)
Leo	F. Leo, Geschichte der römischen Literatur, vol. 1: Die archaische Literatur, 1913 (repr. 1958)
Lesky	A. Lesky, Geschichte der griechischen Literatur, ^{3}1971 (repr. 1993)
Leumann	M. Leumann, Lateinische Laut- und Formenlehre (HdbA 2/2,1), 1977
Leunissen (Konsuln)	P. M. M. Leunissen, Konsuln und Konsulare in der Zeit von Commodus bis zu Alexander Severus (180–235 n.Chr.) (Dutch Monographs in Ancient History and Archaeology 6), 1989
Lewis/Short	C. T. Lewis / C. Short, A Latin Dictionary, ^{2}1980
LFE	B. Snell (ed.), Lexikon des frühgriechischen Epos, 1979 ff. (1st fasc. 1955)
LfgrE	B. Snell (ed.), Lexikon des frühgriechischen Epos, 4 vols., 1955–2010
LGPN	P. M. Fraser et al. (eds.), A Lexicon of Greek Personal Names, 1987 ff.
Liebenam	W. Liebenam, Städteverwaltung im römischen Kaiserreich, 1900
Lietzmann	H. Lietzmann, Geschichte der Alten Kirche, $^{4/5}$1975
LIMC	J. Boardman et al. (eds.), Lexicon Iconographicum Mythologiae Classicae, 1981 ff.
Lippold	G. Lippold, Die griechische Plastik (HdArch 3), 1950
Lipsius	J. H. Lipsius, Das attische Recht und Rechtsverfahren Mit Benutzung des Attischen Processes, 3 vols., 1905–1915 (repr. 1984)
Lloyd-Jones	H. Lloyd-Jones, Blood for the Ghosts. Classical Influences in the Nineteenth and Twentieth Centuries, 1982
LMA	R.-H. Bautier / R. Auty (eds.), Lexikon des Mittelalters, 7 vols., 1980–1993 (1st fasc. 1977) (repr. vol. 3, 1995)
Lobel/Page	E. Lobel / D. Page (eds.), Poetarum lesbiorum fragmenta, 1955 (repr. 1968)
Loewy	E. Loewy (ed.), Inschriften griechischer Bildhauer, 1885 (repr. 1965)
LPh	T. Schneider, Lexikon der Pharaonen. Die altägyptischen Könige von der Frühzeit bis zur Römerherrschaft, 1994
LRKA	Friedrich Lübkers Reallexikon des Klassischen Altertums, ^{8}1914
LSAG	L. H. Jeffery, The Local Scripts of Archaic Greece. A Study of the Origin of the Greek Alphabet and its Development from the Eighth to the Fifth Centuries B. C., ^{2}1990
LSAM	F. Sokolowski, Lois sacrées de l'Asie mineure, 1955
LSCG	F. Sokolowski, Lois sacrées des cités grecques, 1969
LSCG, Suppl	F. Sokolowski, Lois sacrées des cités grecques. Supplément, 1962
LSJ	H. G. Liddell / R. Scott / H. S. Jones et al. (eds.), A Greek-English Lexicon, ^{9}1940 (Suppl. 1968; repr. 1992)
LThK2	J. Höfer / K. Rahner (eds.), Lexikon für Theologie und Kirche, 14 vols., ^{2}1957–1986
LThK3	W. Kasper et al. (eds.), Lexikon für Theologie und Kirche, ^{3}1993 ff.
LTUR	E. M. Steinby (ed.), Lexicon Topographicum Urbis Romae, 1993 ff.
LUA	Lunds Universitets Arsskrift/ Acta Universitatis Lundensis
Lugli, Fontes	G. Lugli (ed.), Fontes ad topographiam veteris urbis Romae pertinentes, 6 of 8 vols. partly published, 1952–1962 Lugli, Monumenti G. Lugli, I Monumenti antichi di Roma e suburbio, 3 vols., 1930–1938 (Suppl. 1940)
Lustrum	Lustrum. Internationale Forschungsberichte aus dem Bereich des klassischen Altertums
M&H	Mediaevalia et Humanistica. Studies in Medieval and Renaissance Society
MacDonald	G. Macdonald, Catalogue of Greek Coins in the Hunterian Collection. University of Glasgow, 3 vols., 1899–1905
MacDowell	D. M. Macdowell, The Law in Classical Athens (Aspects of Greek and Roman Life), 1978
MAev.	Medium Aevum

Magie	D. Magie, Roman Rule in Asia Minor to the End of the Third Century after Christ, 1950 (repr. 1975)
MAII	Mosaici Antichi in Italia, 1967 ff.
MAMA	W. Calder / M. Balance (eds.), Monumenta Asiae minoris Antiqua, 1927 ff.
Manitius	M. Manitius, Geschichte der lateinischen Literatur des Mittelalters (HdbA 9,2), 3 vols., 1911–1931 (repr. 1973–1976)
MarbWPr	Marburger-Winckelmann-Programm
Marganne	M. H. Marganne, Inventaire analytique des papyrus grecs de médicine, 1981
Marrou	H.-I. Marrou, Geschichte der Erziehung im klassischen Altertum (Übersetzung der Histoire de l'éducation dans l'antiquité), ²1977
Martinelli	M. Martinelli (ed.), La ceramica degli Etruschi, 1987
Martino, SCR	F. de Martino, Storia della costituzione romana, 5 vols., ²1972–1975; Indici ²1990
Martino, WG	F. de Martino, Wirtschaftsgeschichte des alten Rom, ²1991
Masson	O. Masson, Les inscriptions chypriotes syllabiques. Recueil critique et commenté (Études chypriotes 1), ²1983
Matz/Duhn	F. Matz/F. von Duhn (eds.), Antike Bildwerke in Rom mit Ausschluß der größeren Sammlungen, 3 vols., 1881–1882
MAVORS	M. P. Speidel (ed.), Roman Army Researches 1984 ff.
MBAH	Münsterische Beiträge zur antiken Handelsgeschichte
M. Chr.	L. Mitteis / U. Wilcken, Grundzüge und Chrestomathie der Papyruskunde, vol. 2: Juristischer Teil, 2. Hälfte: Chrestomathie, 1912
MDAI(A)	Mitteilungen des Deutschen Archäologischen Instituts, Athenische Abteilung
MDAI(Dam)	Damaszener Mitteilungen des Deutschen Archäologischen Instituts
MDAI(Ist)	Istanbuler Mitteilungen des Deutschen Archäologischen Instituts
MDAI(K)	Mitteilungen des Deutschen Archäologischen Instituts. Abteilung Kairo
MDAI(R)	Mitteilungen des Deutschen Archäologischen Instituts. Römische Abteilung
MDOG	Mitteilungen der Deutschen Orient-Gesellschaft zu Berlin
MededRom	Mededelingen van het Nederlands Historisch Instituut te Rome
Mediaevistik	Mediaevistik. Internationale Zeitschrift für interdisziplinäre Mittelalterforschung
MEFRA	Mélanges d'Archéologie et d'Histoire de l'École Française de Rome. Antiquité
Meiggs	R. Meiggs, Trees and Timber in the Ancient Mediterranean World, 1982
Merkelbach/West	R. Merkelbach / M. L. West (eds.), Fragmenta Hesiodea, 1967
Mette	H. J. Mette, Urkunden dramatischer Aufführungen in Griechenland, 1977
MG	Monuments Grecs
MGG1	F. Blume (ed.), Die Musik in Geschichte und Gegenwart. Allgemeine Enzyklopädie der Musik, 17 vols., 1949–1986 (repr. 1989)
MGG2	L. Finscher (ed.), Die Musik in Geschichte und Gegenwart, 20 vols., ²1994 ff.
MGH	Monumenta Germaniae Historica inde ab anno Christi quingentesimo usque ad annum millesimum et quingentesimum, 1826 ff.
MGH AA	Monumenta Germaniae Historica. Auctores Antiquissimi
MGH DD	Monumenta Germaniae Historica. Diplomata
MGH Epp	Monumenta Germaniae Historica. Epistulae
MGH PL	Monumenta Germaniae Historica. Poetae Latini medii aevi
MGH SS	Monumenta Germaniae Historica. Scriptores
MGrecs	Monuments Grecs publié par l'Association pour l'Encouragement des Études grecques en France, 2 vols., 1872–1997
MH	Museum Helveticum
MiB	Musikgeschichte in Bildern
Millar, Emperor	F. G. B. Millar, The Emperor in the Roman World, 1977
Millar, Near East	F. G. B. Millar, The Roman Near East, 1993

Miller	K. Miller, Itineraria Romana. Römische Reisewege an der Hand der Tabula Peutingeriana, 1916 (repr. 1988)
Millett	P. Millett, Lending and Borrowing in Ancient Athens, 1991
MIO	Mitteilungen des Instituts für Orientforschung
MIR	Moneta Imperii Romani. Österreichische Akademie der Wissenschaften. Veröffentlichungen der Numismatischen Kommission
Mitchell	S. Mitchell, Anatolia. Land, Men, and Gods in Asia Minor, 2 vols., 1993
Mitteis	L. Mitteis, Reichsrecht und Volksrecht in den östlichen Provinzen des römischen Kaiserreichs. Mit Beiträgen zur Kenntnis des griechischen Rechts und der spätrömischen Rechtsentwicklung, 1891 (repr. 1984)
Mitteis/Wilcken	L. Mitteis / U. Wilcken, Grundzüge und Chrestomathie der Papyruskunde, 1912 (repr. 1978)
ML	R. Meiggs / D. Lewis (eds.), A Selection of Greek Historical Inscriptions to the End of the Fifth Century B. C., ^{2}1988
MLatJb	Mittellateinisches Jahrbuch. Internationale Zeitschrift für Mediävistik
Mnemosyne	Mnemosyne. Bibliotheca Classica Batava
MNVP	Mitteilungen und Nachrichten des Deutschen Palästinavereins
MNW	H. Meier et al. (eds.), Kulturwissenschaftliche Bibliographie zum Nachleben der Antike, 2 vols., 1931–1938
Mollard-Besques	S. Mollard-Besques, Museé National du Louvre. Catalogue raisonné des figurines et reliefs en terre-cuite grecs, étrusques et romains, 4 vols., 1954–1986
Momigliano	A. Momigliano, Contributi alla storia degli studi classici, 1955 ff.
Mommsen, Schriften	T. Mommsen, Gesammelte Schriften, 8 vols., 1904–1913 (repr. 1965)
Mommsen, Staatsrecht	T. Mommsen, Römisches Staatsrecht, 3 vols., vol. 1, ^{3}1887; vol. 2–3, 1887–1888
Mommsen, Strafrecht	T. Mommsen, Römisches Strafrecht, 1899 (repr. 1955)
Mon. Ant. ined.	Monumenti Antichi inediti
Moos	P. von Moos, Geschichte als Topik, 1988
Moraux	P. Moraux, Der Aristotelismus bei den Griechen von Andronikos bis Alexander von Aphrodisias (Peripatoi 5 & 6), 2 vols., 1973–1984
Moreau	J. Moreau, Dictionnaire de géographie historique de la Gaule et de la France, 1972 (Suppl. 1983)
MP	Modern Philology
MPalerne	Mémoires du Centre Jean Palerne
MRR	T. R. S. Broughton, The Magistrates of the Roman Republic, 2 vols., 1951–1952 (Suppl. 1986)
MSG	C. Jan (ed.), Musici scriptores Graeci, 1895 (Suppl. 1899; repr. 1962)
Müller	D. Müller, Topographischer Bildkommentar zu den Historien Herodots. Griechenland im Umfang des heutigen griechischen Staatsgebiets, 1987
Müller-Wiener	W. Müller-Wiener, Bildlexikon zur Topographie Istanbuls, 1977
Münzer[1]	F. Münzer, Römische Adelsparteien und Adelsfamilien, 1920
Münzer[2]	F. Münzer, Römische Adelsparteien und Adelsfamilien, ^{2}1963
Murray/Price	O. Murray / S. Price (eds.), The Greek City. From Homer to Alexander, 1990
Muséon	Le Muséon. Revue d'Études Orientales
Musurillo	H. Musurillo, The Acts of the Christian Martyrs, 1972
MVAG	Mitteilungen der Vorderasiatischen (Ägyptischen) Gesellschaft
MVPhW	Mitteilungen des Vereins klassischer Philologen in Wien
MythGr	Mythographi Graeci, 3 vols., 1894–1902 (vol. 1, ^{2}1926)
Nash	E. Nash, Bildlexikon zur Topographie des antiken Rom, 1961–1962
NC	Numismatic Chronicle
NClio	La Nouvelle Clio
NDB	Neue Deutsche Biographie, 1953 ff. (repr. vols. 1–6, 1971)
NEAEHL	E. Stern (ed.), The New Encyclopedia of Archaeological Excavations in the Holy Land, 4 vols., 1993
Neoph.	Neophilologus
Newald	R. Newald, Nachleben des antiken Geistes im Abendland bis zum Beginn des Humanismus, 1960

NGrove	The New Grove Dictionary of Music and Musicians, ^{6}1980
NGroveInst	The New Grove Dictionary of Musical Instruments, 1984
NHCod	Nag Hammadi Codex
NHL	Neues Handbuch der Literaturwissenschaft, vol. 1: W. Röllig (ed.), Altorientalische Literaturen, 1978; vol. 2: E. Voigt (ed.), Griechische Literatur, 1981; vol. 3: M. Fuhrmann (ed.), Römische Literatur, 1974; vol. 4: L. J. Engels / H. Hofmann (eds.), Spätantike, 1997; vol. 5: W. Heinrichs (ed.), Orientalisches Mittelalter, 1990
NHS	Nag Hammadi Studies
Nicolet	C. Nicolet, L' Ordre équestre à l'époque républicaine 312–43 av. J.-C., 2 vols., 1966–1974
Nilsson, Feste	M. P. Nilsson, Griechische Feste von religiöser Bedeutung mit Ausschluss der attischen, 1906
Nilsson, GGR	M. P. Nilsson, Geschichte der griechischen Religion (HdbA 5,2), vol. 1, ^{3}1967; vol. 2, ^{4}1988 (repr. vol. 1, 1992)
Nilsson, MMR	M. P. Nilsson, The Minoan-Mycenaean Religion and Its Survival in Greek Religion, ^{2}1950
Nissen	H. Nissen, Italische Landeskunde, 2 vols., 1883–1902
Nock	A. D. Nock, Essays on Religion and the Ancient World, 1972
Noethlichs	K. L. Noethlichs, Beamtentum und Dienstvergehen. Zur Staatsverwaltung in der Spätantike, 1981
Norden, Kunstprosa	E. Norden, Die antike Kunstprosa vom 6. Jh. v. Chr. bis in die Zeit der Renaissance, ^{6}1961
Norden, Literatur	E. Norden, Die römische Literatur, ^{6}1961
OA	J. G. Baiter / H. Sauppe (eds.), Oratores Attici, 3 parts, 1839–1843
NSA	Notizie degli scavi di antichità
NTM	Schriftenreihe für Geschichte der Naturwissenschaften, Technik und Medizin
Nutton	V. Nutton, From Democedes to Harvey. Studies in the History of Medicine (Collected Studies Series 277), 1988
NZ	Numismatische Zeitschrift
O. BuNjem	R. Marichal (ed.), Les Ostraca de Bu Njem (Libya Anti qua, Suppl. 7), 1992
O. Claud.	J. Bingen et al. (eds.), Mons Claudianus. Ostraca graeca et Latina, 4 vols., 1992–2009
O. Did.	H. Cuvigny et al. (eds.), Didymoi. Une garnison romaine dans le désert Oriental d'Égypte, vol. 2: Les textes (Praesidia du désert de Bérénice 4), 2012
O. Douch	Les ostraca grecs de Douch, vol. 1: H. Cuvigny / G. Wagner (eds.) (Institut Français d'Archéologie Orientale, Documents de Fouilles 24/1), 1986; vol. 2: H. Cuvigny / G. Wagner (eds.) (Documents de Fouilles 24/2), 1988; vol. 3: H. Cuvigny / G. Wagner (eds.) (Documents de Fouilles 24/3); vol. 4: G. Wagner (ed.) (Documents de Fouilles 24/4), 1999; vol. 5: G. Wagner (ed.) (Documents de Fouilles 24/5)
O. Krok.	H. Cuvigny (ed.), Ostraca de Krokodilô, vol. 1: La correspondance militaire et sa circulation (O. Krok. 1–151). Praesidia du désert de Bérénice II (Fouilles de l'IFAO 51), 2005
O. Trim.	Amheida I. Ostraka from Trimithis, vol. 1: R. S. Bagnall/G. R. Ruffini (eds.), Texts from the 2004–2007 Seasons, 2012; vol. 2: R. Ast / R. S. Bagnall (eds.), Greek Texts from the 2008–2013 Seasons, 2012
O&R	R. Osborne / P. J. Rhodes (eds.), Greek Historical Inscriptions, 478-404 BC, 2017
OBO	Orbis Biblicus et Orientalis
OCD	N. G. Hammond / H. H. Scullard (eds.), The Oxford Classical Dictionary, ^{2}1970 (^{3}1996)
ODB	A. P. Kazhdan et al. (eds.), The Oxford Dictionary of Byzantium, 1991 ff.
OF	O. Kern (ed.), Orphicorum Fragmenta, 31972
OGIS	W. Dittenberger (ed.), Orientis Graeci Inscriptiones Selectae, 2 vols., 1903–1905 (repr. 1960)

OLD	P. G. W. Glare (ed.), Oxford Latin Dictionary, 1982 (1st fasc. 1968)
OlF	Olympische Forschungen, 1941 ff.
Oliver	J. H. Oliver, Greek Constitutions of Early Roman Emperors from Inscriptions and Papyri, 1989
Olivieri	D. Olivieri, Dizionario di toponomastica lombarda. Nomi di comuni, frazioni, casali, monti, corsi d'acqua, ecc. della regione lombarda, studiati in rapporto alla loro origine, ²1961
Olshausen/Biller/Wagner	E. Olshausen / J. Biller / J. Wagner, Historisch-geographische Aspekte der Geschichte des Pontischen und Armenischen Reiches. Untersuchungen zur historischen Geographie von Pontos unter den Mithradatiden (TAVO 29), vol. 1, 1984
OLZ	Orientalistische Literaturzeitung
OpAth	Opuscula Atheniensia, 1953 ff.
OpRom	Opuscula Romana
ORF	E. Malcovati, Oratorum Romanorum Fragmenta (Corpus scriptorum Latinorum Paravianum 56–58), 3 vols., 1930
Orientalia	Orientalia, Neue Folge
Osborne	R. Osborne, Classical Landscape with Figures. The Ancient Greek City and Its Countryside, 1987
Overbeck	J. Overbeck, Die antiken Schriftquellen zur Geschichte der bildenden Künste bei den Griechen, 1868 (repr. 1959)
P.	Papyri editions usually after E. G. Turner, Greek Papyri. An Introduction, 1968, 159–178 or the "Checklist of Editions" (https://papyri.info/docs/checklist)
P. Aberd.	E. G. Turner, Catalogue of Greek and Latin Papyri and Ostraca in the Possession of the University of Aberdeen, 1939
P. Abinn.	H. I. Bell et al. (eds.), The Abinnaeus Archive. Papers of a Roman Officer in the Reign of Constantius II, 1962
P. Anastasi 1	A. H. Gardiner (ed.), The Papyrus Anastasi I., 1911
P. Benaki	E. Papapolychoniou (ed.), Greek Papyri in the Benaki Museum, from the Collections of the Historical Archive, 2000
P. Bodmer	V. Martin et al. (eds.), Papyrus Bodmer, 1954 ff.
P. Cair. Isid.	A. E. R. Boak / H. C. Youtie (eds.), The Archive of Aurelius Isidorus in the Egyptian Museum, Cairo, and the University of Michigan, 1960
P. Cair. Masp.	J. Maspero, Papyrus grecs d'époque byzantine (Catalogue général des antiquités égyptiennes du Musée du Caire), 1911-1916
P. Cair. Zen.	C. C. Edgar (ed.), Zenon Papyri (Catalogue général des antiquités égyptiennes du Musée du Caire), 5 vols., 1925-1940
P. Col.	W. L. Westermann et al. (eds.), Columbia Papyri, 11 vols., 1929–1998
P. Diog.	P. Schubert (ed.), Les archives de Marcus Lucretius Diogenes et textes apparentés (Pap. Texte Abh. 39), 1990
P. Diosk.	J. M. S. Cowey et al. (eds.), Das Archiv des Phrurarchen Dioskurides (Papyrologica Coloniensia 30), 2003
P. Dryton	K. Vandorpe (ed.), The Bilingual Family Archive of Dryton, His Wife Apollonia and Their Daughter Senmouthis (Collectanea hellenistica 4), 2002
P. Dura	C. B. Welles / J. F. Gilliam (eds.), The Excavations at Dura-Europos conducted by Yale University and the French Academy of Inscriptions and Letters, Final Report 5, part 1: The Parchments and Papyri, 1959
P. Flor.	Papiri greco-egizii, Papiri Fiorentini (Supplementi Filologico-Storici ai Monumenti Antichi), vol. 1: G. Vitelli (ed.), Documenti pubblici e privati dell'età romana e bizantina, 1906; vol. 2: D. Comparetti (ed.), Papiri letterari ed epistolari, 1908–1910; vol. 3: G. Vitelli (ed.), Documenti e testi letterari dell'età romana e bizantina, 1915
P. Gen.	J. Nicole et al. (eds.), Les Papyrus de Genève, 6 vols., 1896–2010
P. Gen. Lat.	J. Nicole / C. Morel (eds.), Archives militaires du 1er siècle (Texte inédit du Papyrus Latin de Genève No. 1), 1900

P. Giss. Apoll.	M. Kortus (ed.), Briefe des Apollonios-Archives aus der Sammlung Papyri Gissenses (Berichte und Arbeiten aus der Universitätsbibliothek und dem Universitätsarchiv Giessen 49), 1999
P. Grenf.	B. P. Grenfell (ed.), An Alexandrian Erotic Fragment and other Greek Papyri chiefly Ptolemaic, vol. 1, 1896; B. P. Grenfell (ed.), New Classical Fragments and Other Greek and Latin Papyri, vol. 2, 1897
P. Heid.	E. Siegmann (ed.), Literarische griechische Texte der Heidelberger Papyrussammlung, 1956
P. Herc.	M. Gigante (ed.), Catalogo dei Papiri Ercolanesi, 1979
P. Hib.	B. P. Grenfell et al. (eds.), The Hibeh Papyri, 2. vols., 1906-1955 (Egypt Exploration Society, Graeco-Roman Memoirs 7; 32)
P. IFAO	J. Schwartz / G. Wagner (eds.), Papyrus grecs de l'Institut Français d'Archéologie Orientale, 3. vols., 1971-1975
P. Lond.	F. G. Kenyon et al. (eds.), Greek Papyri in the British Museum, 7 vols., 1893–1974
P. Masada	H. M. Cotton / J. Geiger (eds.), Masada. The Yigael Yadin Excavations 1963–1965. Final Reports, vol. 2: The Latin and Greek Documents, 1989
P. Mich.	C. C. Edgar et al. (eds.), Papyri in the University of Michigan Collection, 1931 ff.
P. Münch.	Die Papyri der Bayerischen Staatsbibliothek München, vol. 1: A. Heisenberg / L. Wenger (eds.), Byzantinische Papyri der Bayerischen Staatsbibliothek München, 1986; vol. 2: A. Carlini (ed.), Papiri letterari greci, 1986; vol. 3: D. Hagedorn et al. (eds.), Griechische Urkundenpapyri der Bayerischen Staatsbibliothek München, 1986
P. Ness.	Excavations at Nessana, vol. 1: H. D. Colt (ed.), [Introductory volume], 1962; vol. 2: L. Casson / E. L. Hettich (eds.), Literary Papyri, 1950; vol. 3: C. J. Kraemer, Jr. (ed.), Non-Literary Papyri, 1958
P. Oxy.	B. P. Grenfell et al. (eds.), The Oxyrhynchus Papyri, 1898 ff.
P. Panop. Beatty	T. C. Skeat (ed.), Papyri from Panopolis in the Chester Beatty Library Dublin, 1933 ff.
P. Paramone	J. M. S. Cowey / B. Kramer (eds.), Editionen und Aufsätze von Mitgliedern des heidelberger Instituts für Papyrologie zwischen 1982 und 2004 (Archiv Beihefte 16), 2004
P. Petr.	J. P. Mahaffy (vol. 1–3) / J. G. Smyly (vol. 3) (ed.), The Flinders Petrie Papyri, 3 vols., 1891–1905
P. Petra	J. Frösén et al. (eds.), The Petra Papyri, 2002 ff.
P. Princ.	A. C. Johnson et al. (eds.), Papyri in the Princeton University Collections, 3 vols., 1931–1942
P. Ross. Georg.	G. Zereteli et. al. (eds.), Papyri russischer und georgischer Sammlungen, 5. vols., 1925-1935
P. Ryl.	A. S. Hunt et al. (eds.), Catalogue of the Greek and Latin Papyri in the John Rylands Library, Manchester, 4 vols., 1911–1952
P. Sakaon	G. M. Parássoglou, The Archive of Aurelius Sakaon: Papers of an Egyptian Farmer in the Last Century of Theadelphia (Papyrologische Texte und Abhandlungen vol. 23), 1978
P. Stras.	F. Preisigke et al. (eds.), Griechische Papyrus der Kaiserlichen Universitäts- und Landesbibliothek zu Strassburg, 10 vols., 1912-2014
P. Turner	P. J. Parsons et al. (eds.), Papyri Greek and Egyptian Edited by Various Hands in Honour of Eric Gardner Turner on the Occasion of his Seventieth Birthday (Egypt Exploration Society, Graeco-Roman Memoirs 68), 1981
P. Yale	J. F. Oates et al. (eds.), Yale Papyri in the Beinecke Rare Book and Manuscript Library, 3 vols., 1967-2001
PA	J. Kirchner, Prosopographia Attica, 2 vols., 1901–1903 (repr. 1966)
Pack	R. A. Pack (ed.), The Greek and Latin Literary Texts from Greco-Roman Egypt, ²1965
Panofsky	E. Panofsky, Renaissance und Renaissancen in Western Art, 1960
Pape/Benseler	W. Pape / G. E. Benseler, Wörterbuch der griechischen Eigennamen, 2 vols., 1863–1870

PAPhS	Proceedings of the American Philosophical Society
Parke	H. W. Parke, Festivals of the Athenians, 1977
Parke/Wormell	H. W. Parke / D. E. W. Wormell, The Delphic Oracle, 1956
PBSR	Papers of the British School at Rome
PCA	Proceedings of the Classical Association. London
PCG	R. Kassel / C. Austin (eds.), Poetae comici graeci, 1983 ff.
PCPhS	Proceedings of the Cambridge Philological Society
PdP	La Parola del Passato
PE	R. Stillwell et al. (eds.), The Princeton Encyclopedia of Classical Sites, 1976
Peacock	D. P. S. Peacock, Pottery in the Roman World. An Ethnoarchaeological Approach, 1982
PEG I	A. Bernabé (ed.), Poetae epici graeci. Testimonia et Fragmenta, part 1, 1987
Pfeiffer, KPI	R. Pfeiffer, Geschichte der Klassischen Philologie. Von den Anfängen bis zum Ende des Hellenismus, ²1978
Pfeiffer, KPII	R. Pfeiffer, Die Klassische Philologie von Petrarca bis Mommsen, 1982
Pfiffig	A. J. Pfiffig, Religio Etrusca, 1975
Pflaum	H.-G. Pflaum, Les carrières procuratoriennes équestres sous le Haut-Empire Romain, 3 vols. and plates, 1960–1961 (Suppl. 1982)
Pfuhl	E. Pfuhl, Malerei und Zeichnung der Griechen, 1923
Pfuhl/Möbius	E. Pfuhl / H. Möbius, Die ostgriechischen Grabreliefs, 2 vols., 1977–1979
PG	J. P. Migne (ed.), Patrologiae cursus completus, series Graeca, 161 vols., 1857–1866 (Conspectus auctorum 1882; Indices, 2 vols., 1912–1932)
PGM	K. Preisendanz / A. Henrichs (eds.), Papyri Graecae Magicae. Die griechischen Zauberpapyri, 2 vols., ²1973– 1974 (repr. von 1928–1931)
Philippson/Kirsten	A. Philippson / A. Lehmann et al. (eds.), Die griechischen Landschaften. Eine Landeskunde, 4 vols., 1950–1959
Philologus	Philologus. Zeitschrift für klassische Philologie
PhQ	Philological Quarterly
PhU	Philologische Untersuchungen
PhW	Berliner Philologische Wochenschrift
Picard	C. Picard, Manuel d'archéologie grecque. La sculpture, 1935 ff.
Pickard-Cambridge/Gould/Lewis	A. W. Pickard-Cambridge / J. Gould / D. M. Lewis, The Dramatic Festivals of Athens, ²1988
Pickard-Cambridge/Webster	A. W. Pickard-Cambridge / T. B. L. Webster, Dithyramb, Tragedy and Comedy, ²1962
Pigler, 1	A. Pigler, Barockthemen. Eine Auswahl von Verzeichnissen zur Ikonographie des 17. und 18. Jahrhunderts, 2 vols., ²1974; ill. vol., 1974
PIR	Prosopographia imperii Romani saeculi, 8 vols., ²1933–2009
PISO, FPD	I. Piso, Fasti Provinciae Daciae, 2 vols., 1993–2014
PL	J. P. Migne (ed.), Patrologiae cursus completus, series Latina, 221 vols., 1844–1865 (partial repr.; 5 Suppl.-vols., 1958–1974; Index 1965)
PLM	A. Baehrens (ed.), Poetae Latini Minores, 5 vols., 1879–1883
PLRE	A. H. M. Jones et al. (eds.), The Prosopography of the Later Roman Empire, 3 vols., 1971–1992
PME	H. Devijver, Prosopographia militiarum equestrium quae fuerunt ab Augusto ad Gallienum (Symbolae Facultatis Litterarum et Philosophiae Lovaniensis Ser. A 3), 3 vols., 1976–1980; 2 Suppl.-vols., 1987–1993
PMG	D. L. Page, Poetae melici graeci, 1962
PMGF	M. Davies (ed.), Poetarum melicorum graecorum fragmenta, 1991
PMGTr	H. D. Betz (ed.), The Greek Magical Papyri in Translation, Including the Demotic Spells, ²1992
Poccetti	P. Poccetti, Nuovi documenti italici a complemento del manuale di E. Vetter (Orientamenti linguistici 8), 1979
Pökel	W. Pökel, Philologisches Schriftstellerlexikon, 1882 (repr. ²1974)
Poetica	Poetica. Zeitschrift für Sprach- und Literaturwissenschaft
Pokorny	J. Pokorny, Indogermanisches etymologisches Wörterbuch, 2 vols., ²1989

Poulsen	F. Poulsen, Catalogue of Ancient Sculpture in the Ny Carlsberg Glyptotek, 1951
PP	W. Peremans (ed.), Prosopographia Ptolemaica (Studia hellenistica), 9 vols., 1950–1981 (repr. vol. 1–3, 1977)
PPM	Pompei, Pitture e Mosaici, 1990 ff.
Praktika	Praktika tes en Athenais Archaiologikes Hetaireias
Préaux	C. Préaux, L'économie royale des Lagides, 1939 (repr. 1980)
Preller/Robert	L. Preller / C. Robert, Griechische Mythologie, ^{5}1964 ff.
Pritchett	K. Pritchett, Studies in Ancient Greek Topography (University of California Publications. Classical Studies) 8 vols., 1969–1992
PropKg	K. Bittel et al. (eds.), Propyläen Kunstgeschichte, 22 vols., 1966–1980 (repr. 1985)
Prosdocimi	A. L. Prosdocimi / M.Cristofani, Lingue e dialetti dell'Italia antica, 1978; A.Marinetti, Aggiornamenti ed Indici, 1984
PrZ	Prähistorische Zeitschrift
PSI	G. Vitelli et al. (eds.), Papiri greci e latini (Pubblicazione della Società Italiana per la ricerca dei papiri Greci e latini in Egitto), 1912 ff.
QSt	Quellen und Studien zur Geschichte und Kultur des Altertums und des Mittelalters
Quasten	J. Quasten, Patrology, 3 vols., 1950–1960
R&O	P. J. Rhodes / R. Osborne (eds.), Greek Historical Inscriptions, 404-323 BC, 2007
RA	Revue Archéologique
Rabe	H. Rabe (ed.), Rhetores Graeci, vols. 6, 10, 14–16, 1892–1931
RAC	T. Klauser / E. Dassmann (eds.), Reallexikon für Antike und Christentum. Sachwörterbuch zur Auseinandersetzung des Christentums mit der antiken Welt, 1950 ff. (1st fasc. 1941)
RACr	Rivista di Archeologia Cristiana
Radermacher	L. Radermacher (ed.), Artium Scriptores. Reste der voraristotelischen Rhetorik, 1951
Radke	G. Radke, Die Götter Altitaliens, ^{2}1979
Raepsaet-Charlier	M.-T. Raepsaet-Charlier, Prosopographie des femmes de l'ordre sénatorial (I.–II. siècles) (Fonds René Draguet 4), 2 vols., 1987
RÄRG	H. Bonnet, Reallexikon der ägyptischen Religionsgeschichte, ^{2}1971
RAL	Rendiconti della Classe di Scienze morali, storiche e filologiche dell'Academia dei Lincei
Ramsay	W. M. Ramsay, The Cities and Bishoprics of Phrygia, 2 vols., 1895–1897
RAssyr	Revue d'assyriologie et d'archéologie orientale
Rawson, Culture	E. Rawson, Roman Culture and Society. Collected Papers, 1991
Rawson, Family	B. Rawson (ed.), The Family in Ancient Rome. New Perspectives, 1986
RB	P. Wirth (ed.), Reallexikon der Byzantinistik, 6 parts, 1968–1976
RBA	Revue Belge d'archéologie et d'histoire de l'art
RBi	Revue biblique
RBK	K. Wessel / M. Restle (eds.), Reallexikon zur byzantinischen Kunst, 1966 ff. (1st fasc. 1963)
RBN	Revue Belge de numismatique
RBPh	Revue Belge de philologie et d'histoire
RDAC	Report of the Department of Antiquities, Cyprus
RDK	O. Schmitt (ed.), Reallexikon zur deutschen Kunstgeschichte, 10 vols., 1937–2014
RE	G. Wissowa et al. (eds.), Paulys Real-Encyclopädie der classischen Altertumswissenschaft, Neue Bearbeitung, 1893–1980; C. Frateantonio et al., Gesamtregister 1. Alphabetischer Teil, 1997
REA	Revue des études anciennes
REByz	Revue des études byzantines
REG	Revue des études grecques
Rehm	W. Rehm, Griechentum und Goethezeit, ^{3}1952, ^{4}1968
Reinach, RP	S. Reinach, Répertoire de peintures greques et romaines, 1922
Reinach, RR	S. Reinach, Répertoire de reliefs grecs et romains, 3 vols., 1909–1912

Reinach, RSt	S. Reinach, Répertoire de la statuaire greque et romaine, 6 vols., 1897–1930 (repr. 1965–1969)
REL	Revue des études latines Rer. nat. scr. Gr. min. O. Keller (ed.), Rerum naturalium scriptores Graeci minores, 1877
Reynolds	L. D. Reynolds (ed.), Texts and Transmission. A Survey of the Latin Classics, 1983
Reynolds/Wilson	L. D. Reynolds / N. G. Wilson, Scribes and Scholars. A Guide to the Transmission of Greek and Latin Literature, ³1991
RFIC	Rivista di filologia e di istruzione classica
RG	W. H. Waddington / E. Babelon, Recueil général des monnaies grecques d'Asie mineure (Subsidia epigraphica 5), 2 vols., 1908–1925 (repr. 1976)
RGA	H. Beck et al. (eds.), Reallexikon der germanischen Altertumskunde, 21973 ff. (1st fasc. 1968; Suppl.-vols. 1986 ff.)
RGG	K. Galling (ed.), Die Religion in Geschichte und Gegenwart. Handwörterbuch für Theologie und Religionswissenschaft, 7 vols., ³1957–1965 (repr. 1986)
RGRW	Religion in the Graeco-Roman World
RGVV	Religionsgeschichtliche Versuche und Vorarbeiten
RGZM	B. Pferdehirt, Römische Militärdiplome und Entlassungsurkunden in der Sammlung des Römisch-Germanischen Zentralmuseums, 2 vols. (Kataloge vor- und frühgeschichtlicher Altertümer 37), 2004
RH	Revue historique
RHA	Revue hittite et asianique
RhM	Rheinisches Museum für Philologie
Rhodes	P. J. Rhodes, A Commentary on the Aristotelian Athenaion Politeia, ²1993
RHPhR	Revue d'histoire et de philosophie religieuses
RHR	Revue de l'histoire des religions
RHS	Revue historique des Sciences et leurs applications
RIA	Rivista dell'Istituto nazionale d'archeologia e storia dell'arte
RIB	R. G. Collingwood / R. P. Wright (eds.), The Roman Inscriptions of Britain, 1965 ff.
RIC	H. Mattingly / E. A. Sydenham, The Roman Imperial Coinage, 10 vols., 1923–1994
Richardson	L. Richardson (Jr.), A New Topographical Dictionary of Ancient Rome, 1992
Richter, Furniture	G. M. A. Richter, The Furniture of the Greeks, Etruscans and Romans, 1969
Richter, Korai	G. M. A. Richter, Korai. Archaic Greek Maidens, 1968
Richter, Kouroi	G. M. A. Richter, Kouroi. Archaic Greek Youths, 31970
Richter, Portraits	G. M. A. Richter, The Portraits of the Greeks, 3 vols. and suppl., 1965–1972
RIDA	Revue internationale des droits de l'antiquité
RIG	P.-M. Duval (ed.), Recueil des inscriptions gauloises, 1985 ff.
RIL	Rendiconti dell'Istituto Lombardo, classe di lettere, scienze morali e storiche
RIU	L. Barkóczi et al. (eds.), Die römischen Inschriften Ungarns, 1972 ff.
Rivet	A. L. F. Rivet, Gallia Narbonensis with a Chapter on Alpes Maritimae. Southern France in Roman Times, 1988
Rivet/Smith	A. L. F. Rivet / C. Smith, The Place-Names of Roman Britain, 1979
Rix, HGG	H. Rix, Historische Grammatik des Griechischen, ²1992
RLA	E. Ebeling et al. (eds.), Reallexikon der Assyriologie und vorderasiatischen Archäologie, 1928 ff.
RLV	M. Ebert (ed.), Reallexikon der Vorgeschichte, 15 vols., 1924–1932
RMD	M. M. Roxan / P. Holder (eds.), Roman Military Diplomas (Occasional Publications of the Institute of Archaeology of the University of London), 1978 ff.
RMR	R. O. Fink (ed.), Roman Military Records on Papyrus, 1971
RN	Revue numismatique
Robert, OMS	L. Robert, Opera minora selecta, 7 vols., 1969–1990
Robert, Villes	L. Robert, Villes d'Asie Mineure. Études de géographie ancienne, ²1962

Robertson	A. S. Robertson, Roman Imperial Coins in the Hunter Coin Cabinet, University of Glasgow, 5 vols., 1962–1982
Rohde	E. Rohde, Psyche. Seelenkult und Unsterblichkeitsglaube der Griechen, ²1898 (repr. 1991)
Roscher	W. H. Roscher, Ausführliches Lexikon der griechischen und römischen Mythologie, 6 vols., ³1884–1937 (4 Suppl.-vols., 1893–1921; repr. 1992–1993)
Rostovtzeff, Hellenistic World	M. I. Rostovtzeff, The Social and Economic History of the Hellenistic World, ²1953
Rostovtzeff, Roman Empire	M. I. Rostovtzeff, The Social and Economic History of the Roman Empire, ²1957
Rotondi	G. Rotondi, Leges publicae populi Romani. Elenco cronologico con una introduzione sull'attività legislative dei comizi romani, 1912 (repr. 1990)
RPAA	Rendiconti della Pontificia Accademia di Archeologia
RPC	A. Burnett et al. (eds.), Roman Provincial Coinage, 1992 ff.
RPh	Revue de philologie
RQ	Renaissance Quarterly
RQA	Römische Quartalsschrift für christliche Altertumskunde und für Kirchengeschichte
RRC	M. Crawford, Roman Republican Coinage, 1974 (repr. 1991)
RSC	Rivista di Studi Classici
Rubin	B. Rubin, Das Zeitalter Iustinians, 1960
Ruggiero	E. de Ruggiero, Dizionario epigrafico di antichità roma- na, 1895 ff. (repr. vols. 1–3, 1961–1962)
Saeculum	Saeculum. Jahrbuch für Universalgeschichte
Saller	R. Saller, Personal Patronage under the Early Empire, 1982
Salomies	O. Salomies, Die römischen Vornamen. Studien zur römischen Namengebung (Commentationes humanarum litterarum 82), 1987
Salomies, Nomenclature	O. Salomies, Adoptive and Polyonymous Nomenclature in the Roman Empire, 1992
Samuel	A. E. Samuel, Greek and Roman Chronology. Calendars and Years in Classical Antiquity (HdbA 1/7), 1972
Sandys	J. E. Sandys, A History of Classical Scholarship, 3 vols., ²1906–1921 (repr. 1964)
SAWW	Sitzungsberichte der Österreichischen Akademie der Wissenschaften in Wien
SB	Sammelbuch griechischer Urkunden aus Ägypten (Inschriften und Papyri), vols. 1–2: F. Preisigke (ed.), 1913–1922; vols. 3–5: F. Bilabel (ed.), 1926–1934
SBAW	Sitzungsberichte der Bayerischen Akademie der Wissenschaften
SCCGF	J. Demiańczuk (ed.), Supplementum comicum comoediae Graecae fragmenta, 1912
Schachter	A. Schachter, The Cults of Boiotia, 4 vols., 1981–1994
Schäfer	A. Schäfer, Demosthenes und seine Zeit, 3 vols., ²1885–1887 (repr. 1967)
Schanz/Hosius	M. Schanz / C. Hosius et al., Geschichte der römischen Literatur bis zum Gesetzgebungswerk des Kaisers Justinian (HdbA 8), vol. 1, ⁴1927 (repr. 1979); vol. 2, ⁴1935, (repr. 1980); vol. 3, ³1922 (repr. 1969); vol. 4,1, ²1914 (repr. 1970); vol. 4,2, 1920 (repr. 1971)
Scheid, Collège	J. Scheid, Le collège des frères arvales. Étude prosopographique du recrutement (69–304) (Saggi di storia antica 1), 1990
Scheid, Recrutement (Frères)	J. Scheid, Les frères arvales. Recrutement et origine sociale sous les empereurs julio-claudiens (Bibliothèque de l'École des Hautes Études, Section des Sciences Religieuses 77), 1975
Schlesier	R. Schlesier, Kulte, Mythen und Gelehrte. Anthropologie der Antike seit 1800, 1994
Schmid/Stählin I	W. Schmid / O. Stählin, Geschichte der griechischen Literatur, part 1: Die klassische Periode der griechischen Literatur (HdbA 7/1), 5 vols., 1929–1948 (repr. 1961–1980)
Schmid/Stählin II	W. Christ / W. Schmid / O. Stählin, Geschichte der griechischen Litteratur bis auf die Zeit Justinians, part 2: Die nachklassische Periode

	der griechischen Litteratur (HdbA 7/2), 2 vols., ⁶1920–1924 (repr. 1961–1981)
Schmidt	K. H. Schmidt, Die Komposition in gallischen Personennamen, in: Zeitschrift für celtische Philologie 26, 1957, 33–301, 1954 (Diss. Universität Bonn)
Schönfeld	M. Schönfeld, Wörterbuch der altgermanischen Personen- und Völkernamen (Germanische Bibliothek 1/4/2), 1911 (repr. ²1965)
ScholiaIl	H. Erbse (ed.), Scholia Graeca in Homeri Iliadem (Scholia vetera), 7 vols., 1969–1988
SChr	Sources Chrétiennes, 300 vols., 1942 ff.
Schrötter	F. von Schrötter (ed.), Wörterbuch der Münzkunde, ²1970
Schürer	E. Schürer / G. Vermès, The History of the Jewish People in the Age of Jesus Christ (175 B. C.–A. D. 135), 3 vols., 1973–1987
Schulten, Landeskunde	A. Schulten, Iberische Landeskunde. Geographie des antiken Spanien, 2 vols., 1955–1957 (Übersetzung der spanischen Ausgabe von 1952)
Schulz	F. Schulz, Geschichte der römischen Rechtswissenschaft, 1961 (repr. 1975)
Schulze	W. Schulze, Zur Geschichte lateinischer Eigennamen, 1904
Schwyzer, Dial.	E. Schwyzer (ed.), Dialectorum Graecarum exempla epigraphica potiora, ³1923
Schwyzer, Gramm.	E. Schwyzer, Griechische Grammatik, vol. 1: Allgemeiner Teil. Lautlehre, Wortbildung, Flexion (HdbA 2/1,1), 1939
Schwyzer/Debrunner	E. Schwyzer / A. Debrunner, Griechische Grammatik, vol. 2: Syntax und syntaktische Stilistik (HdbA 2/1,2), 1950; D. J. Georgacas, Index to both volumes, 1953; F. Radt / S. Radt, Index locorum, 1971
Scullard	H. H. Scullard, Festivals and Ceremonies of the Roman Republic, 1981
SDAW	Sitzungsberichte der Deutschen Akademie der Wissenschaften zu Berlin
SDHI	Studia et documenta historiae et iuris
SE	Studi Etruschi
Seeck	O. Seeck, Regesten der Kaiser und Päpste für die Jahre 311 bis 476 n.Chr. Vorarbeiten zu einer Prosopographie der christlichen Kaiserzeit, 1919 (repr. 1964)
SEG	Supplementum epigraphicum Graecum, 1923 ff.
Sel. Pap.	A. S. Hunt / C. C. Edgar (eds.), Select Papyri (The Loeb Classical Library), 3 vols., 1932–1942
Seltman	C. Seltman, Greek Coins. A History of Metallic Currency and Coinage down to the Fall of the Hellenistic Kingdoms, ²1965
Sezgin	F. Sezgin, Geschichte des arabischen Schrifttums, vol. 3: Medizin, Pharmazie, Zoologie, Tierheilkunde bis ca. 430 H., 1970
SGAW	Sitzungsberichte der Göttinger Akademie der Wissenschaften
SGDI	H. Collitz et al. (eds.), Sammlung der griechischen Dialekt-Inschriften, 4 vols., 1884–1915
SGLG	K. Alpers et al. (eds.), Sammlung griechischer und lateinischer Grammatiker, 7 vols., 1974–1988
SH	H. Lloyd-Jones / P. Parsons (edes.), Supplementum Hellenisticum, 1983
SHAW	Sitzungsberichte der Heidelberger Akademie der Wissenschaften
Sherk	R. K. Sherk, Roman Documents from the Greek East. Senatus Consulta and Epistulae to the Age of Augustus, 1969
SicA	Sicilia archeologica
SIFC	Studi italiani di filologia classica
SiH	Studies in the Humanities
Simon, GG	E. Simon, Die Götter der Griechen, ⁴1992
Simon, GR	E. Simon, Die Götter der Römer, 1990
SLG	D. Page (ed.), Supplementum lyricis graecis, 1974
SM	Schweizer Münzblätter
SMEA	Studi Micenei ed Egeo-Anatolici
Smith	W. D. Smith, The Hippocratic Tradition (Cornell Publications in the History of Science), 1979
SMSR	Studi e materiali di storia delle religioni

SMV	Studi mediolatini e volgari
SNG	Sylloge Nummorum Graecorum
SNR	Schweizerische Numismatische Rundschau Solin/Salomies
	H. Solin / O. Salomies, Repertorium nominum gentilium et cognominum Latinorum (Alpha–Omega: Reihe A 80), ²1994
Sommer	F. Sommer, Handbuch der lateinischen Laut- und Formenlehre. Eine Einführung in das sprachwissenschaftliche Studium des Lateins (Indogermanische Bibliothek Abt. 1, Reihe 1, vol. 3, Tl. 1), ²/³1914
Sommer/Pfister	F. Sommer / R. Pfister, Handbuch der lateinischen Laut-und Formenlehre, vol. 1, ⁴1977
Soustal, Nikopolis	P. Soustal, Nikopolis und Kephallenia (Denkschriften der Österreichischen Akademie der Wissenschaften. Philosophisch-Historische Klasse 150; TIB 3), 1981
Soustal, Thrakien	P. Soustal, Thrakien. Thrake, Rodope und Haimimontos (Denkschriften der Österreichischen Akademie der Wissenschaften. Philosophisch-Historische Klasse 221; TIB 6), 1991
Sovoronos	J. N. Sovoronos, Das Athener Nationalmuseum, 3 vols., 1908–1937
Spec.	Speculum
Spengel	L. Spengel (ed.), Rhetores Graeci, 3 vols., 1853–1956 (repr. 1966)
SPrAW	Sitzungsberichte der Preußischen Akademie der Wissenschaften
SSAC	Studi storici per l'antichità classica
SSR	G. Giannantoni (ed.), Socratis et Socraticorum Reliquiae, 4 vols., 1990
Staden	H. von Staden, Herophilus. The Art of Medicine in Early Alexandria, 1989
Stein, Präfekten	A. Stein, Die Präfekten von Ägypten in der römischen Kaiserzeit (Dissertationes Bernenses Series 1,1), 1950
Stein, Spätröm.	R. E. Stein, Geschichte des spätrömischen Reiches, vol. 1, 1928 (French 1959; vol. 2 only in French, 1949)
Stewart	A. Stewart, Greek Sculpture. An exploration, 2 vols., 1990
StM	Studi Medievali
Strong/Brown	D. Strong / D. Brown (eds.), Roman Crafts, 1976
StV	Die Staatsverträge des Altertums, vol. 2: H. Bengtson / R. Werner (eds.), Die Verträge der griechisch-römischen Welt von 700 bis 338, ²1975; vol. 3: H. H. Schmitt (ed.), Die Verträge der griechisch-römischen Welt 338 bis 200 v. Chr., 1969; vol. 4: R. M. Errington (ed.), Die Verträge der griechisch-römischen Welt von ca. 200 v. Chr. bis zum Beginn der Kaiserzeit, 2020
SVF	J. von Arnim (ed.), Stoicorum veterum fragmenta, 3 vols., 1903–1905 (Index 1924; repr. 1964)
Syll.2	W. Dittenberger, Sylloge inscriptionum Graecarum, 3 vols., ²1898–1909
Syll.3	F. Hiller von Gaertringen et al. (eds.), Sylloge inscriptionum Graecarum, 4 vols., ³1915–1924 (repr. 1960)
Syme, AA	R. Syme, The Augustan Aristocracy, 1986
Syme, RP	E. Badian (vols. 1–2), A. R. Birley (vols. 3–7) (ed.) R. Syme, Roman Papers, 7 vols., 1979–1991
Syme, RR	R. Syme, The Roman Revolution 1939
Syme, Tacitus	R. Syme, Tacitus, 2 vols., 1958
Symposion	Symposion, Akten der Gesellschaft für Griechische und Hellenistische Rechtsgeschichte
Syria	Syria. Revue d'art oriental et d'archéologie
TAM	Tituli Asiae minoris, 1901 ff.
TAPhA	Transactions and Proceedings of the American Philological Association
Taubenschlag	R. Taubenschlag, The Law of Greco-Roman Egypt in the Light of the Papyri, 332 B. C.–640 A. D., ²1955
TAVO	H. Brunner / W. Röllig (eds.), Tübinger Atlas des Vorderen Orients, Beihefte, Tl. B: Geschichte, 1969 ff.
TeherF	Teheraner Forschungen
TGF	A. Nauck (ed.), Tragicorum Graecorum Fragmenta, ²1889 (2. repr. 1983)
ThGL	H. Stephanus et al. (eds.), Thesaurus graecae linguae, 1831 ff. (repr. 1954)

ThlL	Thesaurus linguae Latinae, 1900 ff.
ThlL, Onom.	Thesaurus linguae Latinae, Supplementum onomasticon. Nomina propria Latina, vol. 2: C–Cyzistra, 1907–1913; vol. 3: D–Donusa), 1918–1923
ThLZ	Theologische Literaturzeitung. Monatsschrift für das gesamte Gebiet der Theologie und Religionswissenschaft
Thomasson	B. E. Thomasson, Laterculi Praesidum, 3 vols. in 5 parts, 1972–1990
Thomasson, Fasti Africani	B. E. Thomasson, Fasti Africani. Senatorische und ritterliche Amtsträger in den römischen Provinzen Nordafrikas von Augustus bis Diokletian, 1996
Thumb/Kieckers	A. Thumb / E. Kieckers, Handbuch der griechischen Dialekte (Indogermanische Bibliothek Abt. 1, Reihe 1, Tl. 1), ^{2}1932
Thumb/Scherer	A. Thumb / A. Scherer, Handbuch der griechischen Dialekte (Indogermanische Bibliothek Abt. 1, Reihe 1, Tl. 2), ^{2}1959
ThWAT	G. J. Botterweck / H.-J. Fabry (eds.), Theologisches Wörterbuch zum Alten Testament, 1973 ff.
ThWB	G. Kittel / G. Friedrich (eds.), Theologisches Wörterbuch zum Neuen Testament, 11 vols., 1933–1979 (repr. 1990)
TIB	H. Hunger (ed.), Tabula Imperii Byzantini, 12 vols., 1976–2014
Timm	S. Timm, Das christlich-koptische Ägypten in arabischer Zeit. Eine Sammlung christlicher Stätten in Ägypten in arabischer Zeit, unter Ausschluß von Alexandria, Kairo, des Apa-Mena-Klosters (Der Abu Mina), des Sketis (Wadi n-Natrun) und der Sinai-Region (TAVO 41), 6 parts, 1984–1992
TIR	Tabula Imperii Romani, 1934 ff.
TIR/IP	Y. Tsafrir et al., Tabula Imperii Romani. Iudaea Palaestina. Eretz Israel in the Hellenistic, Roman and Byzantine Periods, 1994
Tod	M. N. Tod (ed.), A Selection of Greek Historical Inscriptions to the End of the Fifth Century BC, 2 vols., ^{2}1951–1950 (repr. vol. 1, 1985)
Tovar	A. Tovar, Iberische Landeskunde, part 2: Die Völker und Städte des antiken Hispanien, vol. 1: Baetica, 1974; vol. 2: Lusitanien, 1976; vol. 3: Tarraconensis, 1989
Toynbee, Hannibal	A. J. Toynbee, Hannibal's Legacy. The Hannibalic War's Effects on Roman Life, 2 vols., 1965
Toynbee, Tierwelt	J. M. C. Toynbee, Tierwelt der Antike, 1983
TPhS	Transactions of the Philological Society Oxford
Traill, Attica	J. S. Traill, The Political Organization of Attica, 1975
Traill, PAA	J. S. Traill, Persons of Ancient Athens, 1994 ff.
Travlos, Athen	J. Travlos, Bildlexikon zur Topographie des antiken Athen, 1971
Travlos, Attika	J. Travlos, Bildlexikon zur Topographie des antiken Attika, 1988
TRE	G. Krause / G. Müller (eds.), Theologische Realenzyklopädie, 1977 ff. (1. Lfg. 1976)
Treggiari	S. Treggiari, Roman Marriage. Iusti Coniuges from the Time of Cicero to the Time of Ulpian, 1991
Treitinger	O. Treitinger, Die Oströmische Kaiser- und Reichsidee nach ihrer Gestaltung im hoefischen Zeremoniell, 1938 (repr. 1969)
Trendall, Lucania	A. D. Trendall, The Red-Figured Vases of Lucania, Campania and Sicily, 1967
Trendall, Paestum	A. D. Trendall, The Red-Figured Vases of Paestum, 1987
Trendall/Cambitoglou	A. D. Trendall / A. Cambitoglou, The Red-Figured Vases of Apulia, 2 vols., 1978–1982
TRF	O. Ribbeck (ed.), Tragicorum Romanorum Fragmenta, ^{2}1871 (repr. 1962)
TRG	Tijdschrift voor rechtsgeschiedenis
TrGF	B. Snell et al. (eds.), Tragicorum graecorum fragmenta, vol. 1, ^{2}1986; vols. 2–4, 1977–1985
Trombley	F. R. Trombley, Hellenic Religion and Christianization c. 370–529 (Religions in the Graeco-Roman World 115), 2 vols., 1993–1994
TU	Texte und Untersuchungen zur Geschichte der altchristlichen Literatur

TUAT	O. Kaiser (ed.), Texte aus der Umwelt des Alten Testaments, 1985 ff. (1st fasc. 1982)
TZ	Trierer Zeitschrift für Geschichte und Kunst des Trierer Landes und seiner Nachbargebiete. Trier, Rheinisches Landesmuseum
TürkAD	Türk arkeoloji dergisi
Ullmann	M. Ullmann, Die Medizin im Islam, 1970
UPZ	U. Wilcken (ed.), Urkunden der Ptolemäerzeit (Ältere Funde), 2 vols., 1927–1957
van den Hout	M. P. J. van den Hout (ed.), M. Cornelii Frontonis Epistulae. Schedis tam ed. quam ined. Edmundi Hauleri usus iterum editum, 1988
VDI	Vestnik Drevnej Istorii
Ventris/Chadwick	M. Ventris / J. Chadwick, Documents in Mycenean Greek, ^{2}1973
Vetter	E. Vetter, Handbuch der italischen Dialekte, 1953
VIR	Vocabularium iurisprudentiae Romanae, 5 vols., 1903–1939
VisRel	Visible Religion
Vittinghoff	F. Vittinghoff (ed.), Europäische Wirtschafts- und Sozialgeschichte in der römischen Kaiserzeit, 1990
VL	W. Stammler et al. (eds.), Die deutsche Literatur des Mittelalters. Verfasserlexikon, ^{2}1978 ff.
Vogel-Weidemann	U. Vogel-Weidemann, Die Statthalter von Africa und Asia in den Jahren 14–68 n.Chr. Eine Untersuchung zum Ver- hältnis von Princeps und Senat (Antiquitas 1,31), 1982
VT	Vetus Testamentum. Quarterly Published by the International Organization of Old Testament Scholars
Wacher	R. Wacher (ed.), The Roman World, 2 vols., 1987
Wachter	R. Wachter, Altlateinische Inschriften, 1987
Walde/Hofmann	A. Walde / J. B. Hofmann, Lateinisches etymologisches Wörterbuch, 3 vols., ^{3}1938–1956
Walde/Pokorny	A. Walde / J. Pokorny (eds.), Vergleichendes Wörterbuch der indogermanischen Sprachen, 3 vols., 1927–1932 (repr. 1973)
Walz	C. Walz (ed.), Rhetores Graeci, 9 vols., 1832–1836 (repr. 1968)
WbMyth	H. W. Haussig (ed.), Wörterbuch der Mythologie, section 1: Die alten Kulturvölker, 1965 ff.
Weber	W. Weber, Biographisches Lexikon zur Geschichtswissenschaft in Deutschland, Österreich und der Schweiz, ^{2}1987
Wehrli, Erbe	F. Wehrli (ed.), Das Erbe der Antike, 1963
Wehrli, Schule	F. Wehrli (ed.), Die Schule des Aristoteles, 10 vols., 1967–1969 (2 Suppl.-vols., 1974–1978)
Welles	C. B. Welles, Royal Correspondence in the Hellenistic Period. A Study in Greek Epigraphy, 1934
Wellmann	M. Wellmann (ed.), Pedanii Dioscuridis de materia medica, vol. 1, 1907; vol. 2, 1906; vol. 3, 1914 (repr. 1958)
Wenger	L. Wenger, Die Quellen des römischen Rechts (Denkschriften der Österreichischen Akademie der Wissenschaften. Philosophisch-Historische Klasse 2), 1953
Wernicke	I. Wernicke, Die Kelten in Italien. Die Einwanderung und die frühen Handelsbeziehungen zu den Etruskern (Palingenesia 33), 1991 (Diss. Universität Berlin, 1989)
Whatmough	J. Whatmough, The Dialects of Ancient Gaul. Prolegomena and Records of the Dialects, 5 vols., 1949–1951, (repr. in 1 vol., 1970)
White, Farming	K. D. White, Roman Farming, 1970
White, Technology	K. D. White, Greek and Roman Technology, 1983 (repr. 1986)
Whitehead	D. Whitehead, The Demes of Attica, 1986
Whittaker	C. R. Whittaker (ed.), Pastoral Economies in Classical Antiquity, 1988
Wide	S. Wide, Lakonische Kulte, 1893
Wieacker, PGN	F. Wieacker, Privatrechtsgeschichte der Neuzeit, ^{2}1967
Wieacker, RRG	F. Wieacker, Römische Rechtsgeschichte, vol. 1, 1988

Wilamowitz	U. von Wilamowitz-Moellendorff, Der Glaube der Hellenen, 2 vols., ²1955 (repr. 1994)
Will	E. Will, Histoire politique du monde hellénistique (323–30 av. J. C.), 2 vols., ²1979–1982
Winter	R. Kekulé (ed.), Die antiken Terrakotten, vol. 3, part 1–2: Die Typen der figürlichen Terrakotten, ed. F. Winter, 1903
WJA	Würzburger Jahrbücher für die Altertumswissenschaft
WMT	L. I. Conrad et al., The Western Medical Tradition. 800 BC to AD 1800, 1995
WO	Die Welt des Orients. Wissenschaftliche Beiträge zur Kunde des Morgenlandes
Wolff	H. J. Wolff, Das Recht der griechischen Papyri Ägyptens in der Zeit der Ptolemaeer und des Prinzipats (Rechtsgeschichte des Altertums Tl. 5; HbdA 10/5), 1978
WS	Wiener Studien. Zeitschrift für klassische Philologie und Patristik
WUNT	Wissenschaftliche Untersuchungen zum Neuen Testament
WVDOG	Wissenschaftliche Veröffentlichungen der Deutschen Orient-Gesellschaft
WZKM	Wiener Zeitschrift für die Kunde des Morgenlandes
YClS	Yale Classical Studies
ZA	Zeitschrift für Assyriologie und Vorderasiatische Archäologie
ZÄS	Zeitschrift für ägyptische Sprache und Altertumskunde
ZATW	Zeitschrift für die Alttestamentliche Wissenschaft
Zazoff, AG	P. Zazoff, Die antiken Gemmen, 1983
Zazoff, GuG	P. Zazoff / H. Zazoff, Gemmensammler und Gemmenforscher. Von einer noblen Passion zur Wissenschaft, 1983
ZDMG	Zeitschrift der Deutschen Morgenländischen Gesellschaft
ZDP	Zeitschrift für deutsche Philologie
Zeller	E. Zeller, Die Philosophie der Griechen in ihrer geschichtlichen Entwicklung, 4 vols., 1844–1852 (repr. 1963)
Zeller/Mondolfo	E. Zeller / R. Mondolfo, La filosofia dei Greci nel suo sviluppo storico, vol. 3, 1961
ZfN	Zeitschrift für Numismatik
Zgusta	L. Zgusta, Kleinasiatische Ortsnamen, 1984
Zimmer	G. Zimmer, Römische Berufsdarstellungen, 1982
ZKG	Zeitschrift für Kirchengeschichte
ZNTW	Zeitschrift für die Neutestamentliche Wissenschaft und die Kunde der älteren Kirche
ZPalV	Zeitschrift des Deutschen Palästina-Vereins
ZPE	Zeitschrift für Papyrologie und Epigraphik
ZRG	Zeitschrift der Savigny-Stiftung für Rechtsgeschichte. Romanistische Abteilung
ZRGG	Zeitschrift für Religions- und Geistesgeschichte
ZVRW	Zeitschrift für vergleichende Rechtswissenschaft
ZVS	Zeitschrift für vergleichende Sprachforschung

C. Ancient authors and works

Abd	Abdias
Acc.	Accius
Ach.Tat.	Achilles Tatius
Act. Arv.	Acta fratrum Arvalium
Ael.	Aelianus
NA	De natura animalium
VH	Varia historia
Aen. Tact.	Aeneas Tacticus
Aesch.	Aeschylus
Ag.	Agamemnon
Cho.	Choephori

Eum.	Eumenides
Pers.	Persae
PV	Prometheus
Sept.	Septem adversus Thebas
Supp.	Supplices
Aeschin.	Aeschines
In Ctes.	In Ctesiphontem
In Tim.	In Timarchum
Leg.	De falsa legatione
Aesop.	Aesopus
Aet.	Aetius
Aeth.	Aetheriae peregrinatio
Alc.	Alcaeus
Alc. Avit.	Alcimus Ecdicius Avitus
Alci.	Alciphron
Alcm.	Alcman
Alex. Aphr.	Alexander of Aphrodisias
Alex. Polyh.	Alexander Polyhistor
Ambr.	Ambrosius
Epist.	Epistulae
Exc. Sat.	De excessu Fratris (Satyri)
Obit. Theod.	De obitu Theodosii
Obit. Valent.	De obitu Valentiniani (iunioris)
Off.	De officiis ministrorum
Paenit.	De paenitentia
Amm. Marc.	Ammianus Marcellinus
Anac.	Anacreon
Anaxag.	Anaxagoras
Anaximand.	Anaximander
Anaximen.	Anaximenes
And.	Andocides
Anecd. Bekk.	Anecdota Graeca ed. I. Bekker
Anecd. Par.	Anecdota Graeca ed. J.A. Kramer
Anon. De rebus bell.	Anonymus de rebus bellicis
Anth. Gr.	Anthologia Graeca
Anth. Lat.	Anthologia Latina
Anth. Pal.	Anthologia Palatina
Anth. Plan.	Anthologia Planudea
Antiph.	Antiphon
Antisth.	Antisthenes
Anton. Lib.	Antoninus Liberalis
(Met.)	(Metamorphoseon Synagoge)
Apoll. Rhod.	Apollonius Rhodius
Apollod.	Apollodorus, Library
Apollod. epit.	Apollodorus, Epitome
App.	Appianus
B Civ.	Bella civilia
Celt.	Celtica
Hann.	Hannibalica
Hisp.	Iberica
Ill.	Illyrica
It.	Italica
Lib.	Libyca
Mac.	Macedonica
Mith.	Mithridatius
Num.	Numidica
Pun.	Punica
Reg.	Regia

Sam.	Samnitica
Sic.	Sicula
Syr.	Syriaca
App. Verg.	Appendix Vergiliana
Apul.	Apuleius
Apol.	Apologia
Flor.	Florida
Met.	Metamorphoses
Arat.	Aratus
Archil.	Archilochus
Archim.	Archimedes
Archyt.	Archytas
Arist. Quint.	Aristides Quintilianus
Aristaen.	Aristaenetus
Aristid.	Aelius Aristides
Aristob.	Aristoboulus
Aristoph.	Aristophanes
Ach.	Acharnenses
Av.	Aves
Eccl.	Ecclesiazusae
Equ.	Equites
Lys.	Lysistrata
Nub.	Nubes
Pax	Pax
Plut.	Plutus
Ran.	Ranae
Thesm.	Thesmophoriazusae
Vesp.	Vespae
Aristot.	Aristotle
An.	De anima
An. post.	Analytica posteriora
An. pr.	Analytica priora
Ath. pol.	Athenaion Politeia
Aud.	De audibilibus
Cael.	De caelo
Cat.	Categoriae
Col.	De coloribus
Div.	De divinatione
Eth. Eud.	Ethica Eudemia
Eth. Nic.	Ethica Nicomachea
Gen. an.	De generatione animalium
Gen. corr.	De generatione et corruptione
Hist. an.	Historia animalium
Mag. mor.	Magna moralia
Metaph.	Metaphysica
Mete.	Meteorologica
Mir.	Mirabilia
Mot. an.	De motu animalium
Mund.	De mundo
Oec.	Oeconomica
Part. an.	De partibus animalium
Ph.	Physica
Phgn.	Physiognomica
Poet.	Poetica
Pol.	Politica
Pr.	Problemata
Rh.	Rhetorica
Rh. Al.	Rhetorica ad Alexandrum

	Sens.	De sensu
	Somn.	De somno et vigilia
	Soph. el.	Sophistici elenchi
	Spir.	De spiritu
	Top.	Topica
Aristox. Harm.		Aristoxenus, Harmonica
Arnob.		Arnobius, Adversus nationes
Arr.		Arrianus
	Anab.	Anabasis
	Cyn.	Cynegeticus
	Ind.	Indica
	Peripl. p. eux.	Periplus ponti Euxini
	Succ.	Historia successorum Alexandri
	Tact.	Tactica
Artem.		Artemidorus
Ascl.		Asclepius
Ascon.		Asconius
Ath.		Athenaeus
Athan.		Athanasius
	ad Const.	Apologia ad Constantium
	c. Ar.	Apologia contra Arianos
	Fuga	Apologia de fuga sua
	Hist. Ar.	Historia Arianorum ad monachos
Athenag. leg.		Athenagoras, Legatio sive supplicatio pro Christianis
Aug.		Augustinus
	Civ.	De civitate dei
	Conf.	Confessiones
	Doctr. christ.	De doctrina christiana
	Epist.	Epistulae
	Retract.	Retractationes
	Serm.	Sermones
	Soliloq.	Soliloquia
	Trin.	De trinitate
Aur. Vict. Caes.		Aurelius Victor, Caesares (Liber de Caesaribus)
Auson.		Ausonius
	Mos.	Mosella
	Urb.	Ordo nobilium urbium
Avell.		Collectio Avellana
Avien.		Avienus
Babr.		Babrius
Bacchyl.		Bacchylides
Bas.		Basilicorum libri LX
Basil.		Basilius
Batr.		Batrachomyomachia
Bell. Afr.		Bellum Africum
Bell. Alex.		Bellum Alexandrinum
Bell. Hisp.		Bellum Hispaniense
Bion Epit. Ad.		Bion, Epitaph to Adonis
Bocc. Gen.		Boccaccio, De genealogia deorum gentilium
Boeth.		Boethius
Caes.		Caesar
	B Civ.	De bello civili
	B Gall.	De bello Gallico
Calp. Ecl.		Calpurnius Siculus, Eclogae
Cass. Dio		Cassius Dio
Cassian.		Iohannes Cassianus

Cassiod.	Cassiodorus
Inst.	Institutiones
Var.	Variae
Cato	Cato
Agr.	De agri cultura
Orig.	Origines (HRR)
Catull.	Catullus, Carmina
Cels. artes	Cornelius Celsus, Artes
Celsus, Dig.	Iuventius Celsus, Digesta
Censorinus, DN	Censorinus, De die natali
Chalcid.	Chalcidius
Charisius, Gramm.	Charisius, Ars grammatica
Chron. min.	Chronica minora
Chron. pasch.	Chronicon paschale
Cic.	Cicero
Acad. 1	Academicorum posteriorum liber 1
Acad. 2	Lucullus sive Academicorum priorum liber 2
Ad Brut.	Epistulae ad Brutum
Ad Q. Fr.	Epistulae ad Quintum fratrem
Arat.	Aratea
Arch.	Pro Archia poeta
Att.	Epistulae ad Atticum
Balb.	Pro L. Balbo
Brut.	Brutus
Caecin.	Pro A. Caecina
Cael.	Pro M. Caelio
Cat.	In Catilinam
Cato	Cato maior de senectute
Clu.	Pro A. Cluentio
De or.	De oratore
Deiot.	Pro rege Deiotaro
Div.	De divinatione
Div. Caec.	Divinatio in Q. Caecilium
Dom.	De domo sua
Fam.	Epistulae ad familiares
Fat.	De fato
Fin.	De finibus bonorum et malorum
Flac.	Pro L. Valerio Flacco
Font.	Pro M. Fonteio
Har. resp.	De haruspicum responso
Inv.	De inventione
Lael.	Laelius de amicitia
Leg.	De legibus
Leg. agr.	De lege agraria
Leg. Man.	Pro lege Manilia (de imperio Cn. Pompei)
Lig.	Pro Q. Ligario
Marcell.	Pro M. Marcello
Mil.	Pro T. Annio Milone
Mur.	Pro L. Murena
Nat. D.	De natura deorum
Off.	De officiis
Opt. gen.	De optimo genere oratorum
Orat.	Orator
P. Red. Quir.	Oratio post reditum ad Quirites
P. Red. Sen.	Oratio post reditum in senatu
Parad.	Paradoxa
Part. or.	Partitiones oratoriae
Phil.	In M. Antonium orationes Philippicae
Philo.	Libri philosophici

Pis.	In L. Pisonem
Planc.	Pro Cn. Plancio
Prov. cons.	De provinciis consularibus
Q. Rosc.	Pro Q. Roscio comoedo
Quinct.	Pro P. Quinctio
Rab. perd.	Pro C. Rabirio perduellionis reo
Rab. Post.	Pro C. Rabirio Postumo
Rep.	De re publica
Rosc. Am.	Pro Sex. Roscio Amerino
Scaur.	Pro M. Aemilio Scauro
Sest.	Pro P. Sestio
Sull.	Pro P. Sulla
Tim.	Timaeus
Top.	Topica
Tull.	Pro M. Tullio
Tusc.	Tusculanae disputationes
Vatin.	In P. Vatinium testem interrogatio
Verr. 1, 2	In Verrem actio prima, secunda

Claud. Claudius Claudianus
  Carm. Carmina
  Rapt. Pros. De raptu Proserpinae

Clem. Al. Clemens Alexandrinus
  Prot. Protrepticus
  Strom. Stromata

Cod. Iust. Corpus Iuris Civilis, Codex Iustinianus
Cod. Theod. Codex Theodosianus
Colum. Columella
Comm. Commodianus
Const. Constitutio Sirmondiana
Coripp. Joh. Corippus, Johannis
Curt. Curtius Rufus, Historiae Alexandri Magni
Cypr. Cyprianus

Dares Dares Phrygius
Dem. Eloc. Demetrius, De elocutione
Dem. Or. Demosthenes, Orationes
Demad. Demades
Democr. Democritus
Dict. Dictys Cretensis
Dig. Corpus Iuris Civilis, Digesta
Din. Dinarchus
Diod. Sic. Diodorus Siculus
Diog. Laert. Diogenes Laertius
Diom. Diomedes, Ars grammatica
Dion. Chrys. Dion Chrysostomus

Dion. Hal. Dionysius Halicarnasseus
  Ant. Rom. Antiquitates Romanae
  Comp. De compositione verborum
  Rhet. Ars rhetorica

Dion. Thrax Dionysius Thrax
Dionys. Per. Dionysius Periegeta
DK Diels/Kranz (preceded by fragment number)
Donat. Donatus grammaticus

Drac. Dracontius
  Romul. Romulea
  Satisf. Satisfactio

Ed. Diocl. Edictum Diocletiani
EM Etymologicum magnum

Emp.	Empedocles
Enn.	Ennius
Ann.	Annales
Sat.	Saturae
Scaen.	Fragmenta scaenica
Ennod.	Ennodius
Ephor.	Ephorus of Cyme (FGrH 70)
Epict.	Epictetus
Eratosth.	Eratosthenes
Et. Gen.	Etymologicum genuinum
Et. Gud.	Etymologicum Gudianum
Euc.	Euclides, Elementa
Euhem. (Mess.)	Euhemerus Messenius
Eunap. VS	Eunapius, Vitae sophistarum
Eur.	Euripides
Alc.	Alcestis
Andr.	Andromache
Bacch.	Bacchae
Beller.	Bellerophon
Cyc.	Cyclops
El.	Electra
Hec.	Hecuba
Hel.	Helena
Heracl.	Heraclidae
Herc.	Hercules
Hipp.	Hippolytus
Hyps.	Hypsipyle
IA	Iphigenia Aulidensis
Ion	Ion
IT	Iphigenia Taurica
Med.	Medea
Or.	Orestes
Phoen.	Phoenissae
Rhes.	Rhesus
Supp.	Supplices
Tro.	Troades
Euseb.	Eusebios
Dem. evang.	Demonstratio Evangelica
Hist. eccl.	Historia Ecclesiastica
On.	Onomasticon
Praep. evang.	Praeparatio Evangelica
Vita Const.	De vita Constantini
Eust.	Eustathius
Eutr.	Eutropius
Ev. Ver.	Evangelium Veritatis
Fast.	Fasti
Fest.	Festus
Firm. Mat.	Firmicus Maternus, Matheseos libri VIII
Err.	De errore profanarum religionum
Flor. Epit.	Florus, Epitoma de Tito Livio
Florent.	Florentinus
Frontin.	Frontinus
Aq.	De aquae ductu urbis Romae
Str.	Strategemata
Fulg.	Fulgentius Afer
Aet.	De aetatibus mundi
Myth.	Mythologiae
Fulg. Rusp.	Fulgentius Ruspensis

Gai. Inst.	Gaius, Institutiones
Gal.	Galenus
Gell. NA	Gellius, Noctes Atticae
Geogr. Rav	Geographus Ravennas
Gorg.	Gorgias
Gp.	Geoponica
Greg. M.	Gregorius Magnus
Dial.	Dialogi (de miraculis patrum Italicorum)
Epist.	Epistulae
Past.	Regula pastoralis
Greg. Naz.	Gregorius Nazianzenus
Epist.	Epistulae
Or.	Orationes
Greg. Nyss.	Gregorius Nyssenus
Greg. Tur.	Gregorius of Tours
Hist.	Decem libri historiarum
Mart.	De virtutibus Martini
Vit. patr.	De vita patrum
H. Hom.	Hymni Homerici
Harpocr.	Harpocrates
Hdn.	Herodianus
Hdt.	Herodotus
Hecat.	Hecataeus
Hell. Oxy.	Hellennica Oxyrhynchia
Hen	Henoch
Heph.	Hephaestio grammaticus (Alexandrinus)
Heracl.	Heraclitus
Heraclid. Pont.	Heraclides Ponticus
Herc. O.	Hercules Oetaeus
Herm.	Hermas
Mand.	Mandata
Sim.	Similitudines
Vis.	Visiones
Herm. Trism.	Hermes Trismegistus
Hermog.	Hermogenes
Hes.	Hesiodus
Cat.	Catalogus feminarum
Op.	Opera et dies
Sc.	Scutum
Theog.	Theogonia
Hil.	Hilarius
Hippoc.	Hippocrates
Hom.	Homerus
Il.	Ilias
Od.	Odyssea
Hor.	Horatius
Ars P.	Ars poetica
Carm.	Carmina
Carm. saec.	Carmen saeculare
Epist.	Epistulae
Epod.	Epodi
Sat.	Satirae (sermones)
Hsch.	Hesychius
Hyg.	Hyginus
Astr.	Astronomica
Fab.	Fabulae
Hyp.	Hypereides

Iambl.	Iamblichus
Myst.	De mysteriis
Protr.	Protrepticus in philosophiam
VP	De vita Pythagorica
Iav.	Iavolenus Priscus
Inst. Iust.	Corpus Juris Civilis, Institutiones
Ioh. Chrys.	Iohannes Chrysostomus
Epist.	Epistulae
Hom. ...	Homiliae in ...
Ioh. Mal.	Iohannes Malalas, Chronographia
Iord. Get.	Iordanes, De origine actibusque Getarum
Iren.	Irenaeus
Isid.	Isidorus
Nat.	De natura rerum
Orig.	Origines
Isoc. Or.	Isocrates, Orationes
It.	Itinerarium
Ant.	Antonini
Aug.	Augusti
Burd.	Burdigalense vel Hierosolymitanum
Plac.	Placentini
Iul. Vict. Rhet.	C. Iulius Victor, Ars rhetorica
Iuvenc.	Iuvencus, Evangelia
Jer.	Jerome
Chron.	Chronicon
Comm. in Ez.	Commentaria in Ezechielem (PL 25)
Ep.	Epistulae
On.	Onomasticon
Vir. ill.	De viris illustribus
Jos.	Josephus
Ant. Iud.	Antiquitates Iudaicae
Ap.	Contra Apionem
BI	Bellum Iudaicum
Vit.	De sua vita
Julian.	Julianus
Ep.	Epistulae
In Gal.	In Galilaeos
Mis.	Misopogon
Or.	Orationes
Symp.	Symposium
Just. Epit.	Justinus, Epitoma historiarum Philippicarum
Justin.	Justinus Martyr
Apol.	Apologia
Dial.	Dialogus cum Tryphone
Juv.	Juvenalis, Saturae
Lactant.	Lactantius
De mort. pers.	De mortibus persecutorum
Div. inst.	Divinae institutiones
Ira	De ira dei
Opif.	De opificio dei
Lex Irnit.	Lex Irnitana
Lex Malac.	Lex municipii Malacitani
Lex Rubr.	Lex Rubria de Gallia cisalpina
Lex Salpens.	Lex municipii Salpensani
Lex Urson.	Lex coloniae Iuliae Genetivae Ursonensis
Lex Visig.	Leges Visigothorum
Lex XII tab.	Lex duodecim tabularum

Lib.	Libanius
Ep.	Epistulae
Or.	Orationes
Liv.	Livius, Ab urbe condita
Luc.	Lucanus, Bellum civile
Lucian.	Lucianus
Dial. D.	Dialogi deorum
Dial. mar.	Dialogi marini
Imag.	Imagines
Salt.	De saltatione
Syr. D.	De Syria dea
Lucil.	Lucilius, Saturae
Lucr.	Lucretius, De rerum natura
Lycoph.	Lycophron
Lycurg.	Lycurgus
Leocr.	Oratio contra Leocratem
Lydus	Lydus
Mag.	De magistratibus
Mens.	De mensibus
Lys.	Lysias
M. Aur.	Marcus Aurelius Antoninus Augustus
Macrob.	Macrobius
In Somn.	Commentarii in Ciceronis somnium Scipionis
Sat.	Saturnalia
Manil.	Manilius, Astronomica
Mar. Vict.	Marius Victorinus
Mart.	Martialis
Mart. Cap.	Martianus Capella
Max. Tyr.	Maximus Tyrius
Mela	Pomponius Mela
Melanipp.	Melanippides
Men.	Menander
Dys.	Dyskolos
Epit.	Epitrepontes
Fr.	Fragmentum
Pk.	Perikeiromene
Sam.	Samia
Mimn.	Mimnermus
Min. Fel.	Minucius Felix, Octavius
Mod.	Herennius Modestinus
Mosch.	Moschus
Naev.	Naevius
Nemes.	Nemesianus
Nep.	Cornelius Nepos
Att.	Atticus
Epam.	Epaminondas
Hann.	Hannibal
Milt.	Miltiades
Timoth.	Timotheus
Nic.	Nicander
Alex.	Alexipharmaca
Ther.	Theriaca
Nicom.	Nicomachus
Non.	Nonius Marcellus
Nonnus Dion.	Nonnus, Dionysiaca
Not. Dign. Occ.	Notitia dignitatum occidentis
Not. Dign. Or.	Notitia dignitatum orientis

Not. Episc.	Notitia dignitatum et episcoporum
Nov.	Corpus Iuris Civilis, Leges Novellae
Obseq.	Julius Obsequens, Prodigia
Onas.	Onasander
Opp.	Oppianus
Cyn.	Cynegetica
Hal.	Halieutica
Or. Sib.	Oracula Sibyllina
Orib.	Oribasius
Orig.	Origenes
Oros.	Orosius
Orph.	[Orpheus]
A.	Argonautica
Fr.	Fragmentum
H.	Hymni
Ov.	Ovidius
Am.	Amores
Ars am.	Ars amatoria
Epist.	Epistulae
Fast.	Fasti
Ib.	Ibis
Medic.	Medicamina faciei femineae
Met.	Metamorphoses
Pont.	Epistulae ex Ponto
Rem. am.	Remedia amoris
Tr.	Tristia
P. Oxy.	Oxyrhynchus Papyri
Pall.	Palladius
Agric.	Opus agriculturae
Laus.	Historia Lausiaca
Pan. Lat.	Panegyrici Latini
Papin.	Aemilius Papinianus
Par.	Dante, Paradiso
Paroemiogr.	Paroemiographi Graeci
Pass. mart.	Passiones martyrum
Paul Fest.	Paulus Diaconus, Epitoma Festi
Paul Nol.	Paulinus Nolanus
Paulus, Sent.	Julius Paulus, Sententiae
Paus.	Pausanias
Pelag.	Pelagius
Peripl.	Periplus
m.eux.	maris Euxini
m.m.	maris magni
m.r.	maris rubri
Pers.	Persius, Saturae
Petron. Sat.	Petronius, Satyrica
Phaedr.	Phaedrus, Fabulae
Phil.	Philo
Philarg.Verg. ecl.	Philargyrius grammaticus, Explanatio in eclogas Vergilii
Philod.	Philodemus
Philostr.	Philostratus
Imag.	Imagines
VA	Vita Apollonii
VS	Vitae sophistarum
Phlp.	Philoponus
Phot.	Photius
Phryn.	Phrynichus
Pind.	Pindar

Fr.	Fragments
Isthm.	Isthmian Odes
Nem.	Nemean Odes
Ol.	Olympian Odes
Pae.	Paeanes
Pyth.	Pythian Odes
Pl.	Plato
Alc. 1	Alcibiades 1
Alc. 2	Alcibiades 2
Ap.	Apologia
Ax.	Axiochus
Chrm.	Charmides
Clit.	Clitopho
Crat.	Cratylus
Crit.	Crito
Criti.	Critias
Def.	Definitiones
Demod.	Demodocus
Ep.	Epistulae
Epin.	Epinomis
Erast.	Erastae
Eryx.	Eryxias
Euthd.	Euthydemus
Euthphr.	Euthyphro
Grg.	Gorgias
Hipparch.	Hipparchus
Hp. mai.	Hippias maior
Hp. mi.	Hippias minor
Ion	Ion
La.	Laches
Leg.	Leges
Ly.	Lysis
Men.	Menon
Menex.	Menexenus
Min.	Minos
Phd.	Phaedo
Phdr.	Phaedrus
Phlb.	Philebus
Plt.	Politicus
Prm.	Parmenides
Prt.	Protagoras
Resp.	Res publica
Sis.	Sisyphus
Soph.	Sophista
Symp.	Symposium
Thg.	Theages
Tht.	Theaetetus
Ti.	Timaeus
Plaut.	Plautus
Amph.	Amphitruo
Asin.	Asinaria
Aul.	Aulularia
Bacch.	Bacchides
Capt.	Captivi
Cas.	Casina
Cist.	Cistellaria
Curc.	Curculio
Epid.	Epidicus
Men.	Menaechmi
Merc.	Mercator

Mil.	Miles gloriosus
Mostell.	Mostellaria
Poen.	Poenulus
Pseud.	Pseudolus
Rud.	Rudens
Stich.	Stichus
Trin.	Trinummus
Truc.	Truculentus
Vid.	Vidularia
Plin.	Plinius minor
Ep.	Epistulae
Pan.	Panegyricus
Plin. HN	Plinius maior, Naturalis historia
Plot.	Plotinus
Plut.	Plutarchus, Vitae parallelae
Ages.	Agesilaus
Alex.	Alexander
Amat.	Amatorius
Ant.	Antonius
Arist.	Aristides
Brut.	Brutus
De def. or.	De defectu oraculorum
De E	De E apud Delphos
De fluv.	De fluviis
De Is. et Os.	De Iside et Osiride
De Pyth. or.	De Pythiae oraculis
De sera	De sera numinis vindicta
Mor.	Moralia
Pel.	Pelopidas
Pyrrh.	Pyrrhus
Quaest. Graec.	Quaestiones Graecae
Quaest. Rom.	Quaestiones Romanae
Symp.	Quaestiones convivales
Them.	Themistocles
Thes.	Theseus
Pol.	Polybius
Pol. Silv.	Polemius Silvius
Poll.	Pollux
Polyaenus, Strat.	Polyaenus, Strategemata
Polyc.	Polycarpus, Letter
Pomp. Trog.	Pompeius Trogus
Pompon.	Sextus Pomponius
Porph.	Porphyrius
Porph. Hor. comm.	Porphyrio, Commentum in Horatii carmina
Posidon.	Posidonius
Priap.	Priapea
Prisc.	Priscianus
Prob.	Pseudo-Probian writings
Procl. Chr.	Proclus, Chrestomathia
Procop.	Procopius
Aed.	De aedificiis
Arc.	Historia arcana
Goth.	Bellum Gothicum
Pers.	Bellum Persicum
Vand.	Bellum Vandalicum
Prop.	Propertius, Elegiae
Prosp.	Prosper Tiro
Prudent.	Prudentius
Ps.-Acro	Ps.-Acro in Horatium

Ps.-Aristot.	Pseudo-Aristotle
Lin. insec.	De lineis insecabilibus
Mech.	Mechanica
(Ps.-)Aur. Vict.	(Pseudo-)Aurelius Victor
Epit. Caes.	Epitome de Caesaribus
Ps.-Long. Subl.	Pseudo-Longinus, De sublimi
Ps.-Sall. In Tull.	Pseudo-Sallustius
In Tull.	In M.Tullium Ciceronem invectiva
Rep.	Epistulae ad Caesarem senem de re publica
Ptol.	Ptolemy
Alm.	Almagest
Geog.	Geographia
Harm.	Harmonica
Tetr.	Tetrabiblos
Purg.	Dante, Purgatorio
Quint.	Quintilianus
Decl.	Declamationes minores
Inst.	Institutio oratoria
Quint. Smyrn.	Quintus Smyrnaeus
R. Gest. div. Aug.	Res gestae divi Augusti
Rhet. Her.	Rhetorica ad C. Herennium
Rufin.	Tyrannius Rufinus
Rut. Namat.	Rutilius Claudius Namatianus, De reditu suo
RVF	Petrarca, Rerum vulgarium fragmenta (Canzoniere)
Sall.	Sallustius
Catil.	De coniuratione Catilinae
Hist.	Historiae
Iug.	De bello Iugurthino
Salv. Gub.	Salvianus, De gubernatione dei
Scyl.	Scylax, Periplus
Scymn.	Scymnus, Periegesis
Sedul.	Sedulius
Sen.	Seneca maior
Controv.	Controversiae
Suas.	Suasoriae
Sen.	Seneca minor
Ag.	Agamemno
Apocol.	Divi Claudii apocolocyntosis
Ben.	De beneficiis
Clem.	De clementia
Dial.	Dialogi
Ep.	Epistulae morales ad Lucilium
Herc. f.	Hercules furens
Med.	Medea
Oed.	Oedipus
Phaedr.	Phaedra
Phoen.	Phoenissae
Q Nat.	Naturales quaestiones
Thy.	Thyestes
Tranq.	De tranquillitate animi
Tro.	Troades
Vit. beat.	De vita beata
Serv.	Servius
Aen.	Commentarius in Vergilii Aeneida
Ecl.	Commentarius in Vergilii eclogas
Georg.	Commentarius in Vergilii georgica

Serv. auct.	Servius auctus Danielis
Sext. Emp.	Sextus Empiricus
Adv. math.	Adversus mathematicos
P. H.	Pyrrhoniae Hypotyposes
SHA	Scriptores Historiae Augustae
Ael.	Aelius
Alb.	Clodius Albinus
Alex. Sev.	Alexander Severus
Aur.	M. Aurelius
Aurel.	Aurelianus
Avid. Cass.	Avidius Cassius
Car.	Carus et Carinus et Numerianus
Carac.	Antoninus Caracalla
Clod.	Claudius
Comm.	Commodus
Diad.	Diadumenus Antoninus
Did. Iul.	Didius Iulianus
Gall.	Gallieni duo
Gord.	Gordiani tres
Hadr.	Hadrianus
Heliogab.	Heliogabalus
Max. Balb.	Maximus et Balbus
Opil.	Opilius Macrinus
Pert.	Helvius Pertinax
Pesc. Nig.	Pescennius Niger
Pius	Antoninus Pius
Quadr. tyr.	Quadraginta tyranni
Sev.	Severus
Tac.	Tacitus
Tyr. Trig.	Triginta Tyranni
Valer.	Valeriani duo
Sid. Apoll.	Apollinaris Sidonius
Carm.	Carmina
Epist.	Epistulae
Sil. Pun.	Silius Italicus, Punica
Simon.	Simonides
Simpl.	Simplicius
Socr.	Socrates, Historia ecclesiastica
Sol.	Solon
Solin.	Solinus
Soph.	Sophocles
Aj.	Ajax
Ant.	Antigone
El.	Electra
Ichn.	Ichneutae
OC	Oedipus Coloneus
OT	Oedipus Tyrannus
Phil.	Philoctetes
Trach.	Trachiniae
Sor. Gyn.	Soranus, Gynaecia
Sozom. Hist. eccl.	Sozomenus, Historia ecclesiastica
Stat.	Statius
Achil.	Achilleis
Silv.	Silvae
Theb.	Thebais
Steph. Byz.	Stephanus Byzantius
Stesich.	Stesichorus
Stob.	Stobaeus
Str.	Strabo

Suda	Suda = Suidas
Suet.	Suetonius
Aug.	Divus Augustus
Caes.	Caesar
Calig.	Caligula
Claud.	Divus Claudius
Dom.	Domitianus
Gram.	De grammaticis
Iul.	Divus Iulius
Tib.	Divus Tiberius
Tit.	Divus Titus
Vesp.	Divus Vespasianus
Vit.	Vitellius
Sulp. Sev.	Sulpicius Severus
Symmachus	Symmachus
Ep.	Epistulae
Or.	Orationes
Relat.	Relationes
Sync.	Syncellus
Synes. epist.	Synesius, Epistulae
Tab. Peut.	Tabula Peutingeriana
Tac.	Tacitus
Agr.	Agricola
Ann.	Annales
Dial.	Dialogus de oratoribus
Germ.	Germania
Hist.	Historiae
Ter.	Terentius
Ad.	Adelphoe
An.	Andria
Eun.	Eunuchus
Haut.	H(e)autontimorumenos
Hec.	Hecyra
Phorm.	Phormio
Ter. Maur.	Terentianus Maurus
Tert.	Tertullianus
Ad nat.	Ad nationes
Apol.	Apologeticum
Them. Or.	Themistius, Orationes
Theoc.	Theocritus
Theod.	Theodoretus
Epist.	Epistulae
Gr. aff. Cur.	Graecarum affectionum curatio
Hist. eccl.	Historia ecclesiastica
Theophr.	Theophrastus
Caus. pl.	De causis plantarum
Char.	Characteres
Hist. pl.	Historia plantarum
Theopomp.	Theopompus
Thgn.	Theognis
Thuc.	Thucydides
Tib.	Tibullus, Elegiae
Tyrt.	Tyrtaeus
Tzetz.	Tzetzes
Anteh.	Antehomerica
Chil.	Chiliades
Posth.	Posthomerica

Ulp.	Ulpianus (Ulpiani regulae)
Val. Fl.	Valerius Flaccus, Argonautica
Val. Max.	Valerius Maximus, Facta et dicta memorabilia
Varro	Varro
Ling.	De lingua Latina
Rust.	Res rusticae
Sat. Men.	Saturae Menippeae
Vat.	Fragmenta Vaticana
Vat. Palat.	Vaticanus Palatinus
Veg. Mil.	Vegetius, Epitoma rei militaris
Vell. Pat.	Velleius Paterculus, Historiae Romanae
Ven. Fort.	Venantius Fortunatus
Verg.	Vergilius
Aen.	Aeneis
Catal.	Catalepton
Ecl.	Eclogae
G.	Georgica
Vir. ill.	De viris illustribus
Vitr. De arch.	Vitruvius, De architectura
Vulg.	Vulgate
Xen.	Xenophon
Ages.	Agesilaus
An.	Anabasis
Ap.	Apologia
Ath. pol.	Athenaion politeia
Cyn.	Cynegeticus
Cyr.	Cyropaedia
Eq.	De equitandi ratione
Eq. mag.	De equitum magistro
Hell.	Hellenica
Hier.	Hiero
Hipp.	Hipparchicus
Lac.	Respublica Lacedaemoniorum
Mem.	Memorabilia
Oec.	Oeconomicus
Symp.	Symposium
Vect.	De vectigalibus
Xenoph.	Xenophanes
Zen.	Zeno
Zenob.	Zenobius
Zenod.	Zenodotus
Zon.	Zonaras
Zos.	Zosimus

Illustrations

It has not been possible in all cases to identify the rights holders of protected images. The publishers will of course meet all legitimate claims even after publication.

ACROPOLIS

Fig. 1: The Acropolis of Eretria with defensive wall and north tower. Photo: École Suisse d'Archéologie en Grece, A. Görtz and V. Festeau, 2015.

ARMAMENT

Fig. 1: Mainz-type *gladius*, in its sheath, with corresponding belt (mid-1st cent. AD, from a ditch at the legionary camp of Vindonissa, modern Windisch, Switzerland). Kantonsarchäologie Aargau, CH-5200 Brugg.

Fig. 2: Iron helmet of the Weisenau type (mid-1st century AD, from the legionary camp at Vindonissa, modern Windisch, Switzerland). Kantonsarchäologie Aargau, CH-5200 Brugg. Photo: Béla A. Polyvás.

ARMY

Fig. 1: Frieze from the Monument of the Nereids at Xanthus, Lycia (relief, c. 400 BC; British Museum, London). akg-images / WHA / World History Archive.

ARTILLERY

Fig. 1: Tombstone of Gaius Vedennius Moderatus (Rome, 1st century AD; from: H.-J. Schalles, 'Die frühkaiserzeitliche Torsionsarmbrust aus Xanten-Wardt – Fundgeschichte, Beschreibung und Datierung', in: H.-J. Schalles (ed.), *Die frühkaiserzeitliche Manuballista aus Xanten-Wardt* (Xantener Berichte 18), 2010, 5.

Fig. 2: Detail from the spiral relief on the Trajan Column (image 25, scene 69; Rome, AD 112/13; plaster cast, 1861). Museo della Civilta Romana, Rome. akg-images.

AUXILIARIES

Table 1: Strength and organization of units. Paul Holder.

Table 2: Units in the reign of Hadrian (after: P. Holder, 'Auxiliary Development in the Reign of Hadrian', in: J. J. Wilkes (ed.), *Documenting the Roman Army. Essays in Honour of Margaret Roxan* (Bulletin of the Institute of Classical Studies Suppl. 81), 2003, 101–145, updated 2021).

BATTLES OF NOTE

Fig. 1: Battle formation at the Battle of Magnesia after Liv. 37,39f. (diagram). Alfred Michael Hirt.

Fig. 2: Tombstone of the centurion Marcus Caelius of Bononia (now Bologna; Lorraine limestone, 1.37m tall). Rheinisches Landesmuseum, Bonn. akg / Bildarchiv Steffens.

ELEPHANTS

Fig. 1: War elephant (interior of a ceramic bowl, 3rd cent. BC). Museo Nazionale Etrusco di Villa Giulia, Rome, Inv.-Nr. 23949. akg-images.

EQUIPMENT

Fig. 1: Legionary of the 1st century AD (drawing by Graham Sumner). © Graham Sumner.

Fig. 2: Soldiers of Late Antiquity (drawings by Graham Sumner). © Graham Sumner.

FLEET

Fig. 1: Lenormant Relief (marble, 4th century BC; excavated on the Athenian Acropolis by the archaeologist François Lenormant in 1852). Acropolis Museum, Athens. akg-images / Pictures From History.

Fig. 2: Part of a ram bow (bronze, 3rd century BC). Photo: Sb2s3, 2016 (https://commons.wikimedia.org/wiki/File:Carthaginian_naval_ram_(2).jpg). CC BY-SA 4.0 international license.

Fig. 3: Denarius of mint master Q. Nasidius (44/43 BC; RRC 483/2; 3.81g; diameter: 20.23mm). British Museum R 9115. akg-images / Erich Lessing.

GENERALS OF NOTE

Fig. 1: Alexander Mosaic (2nd century BC). Museo Archeologico Nazionale, Napels. Photo: © Zev Radovan / Bridgeman Images.

Fig. 2: Gold *stater* of Demetrius Poliorketes (probably from Euboea, after c. 290 BC; 8.56g; diameter: 18mm). LeuNumismatik AG, Web Auction 2 (3.12.2017), Nr. 151. Private collection.

Fig. 3: Relief on a monument honouring Marcus Aurelius (marble, c. AD 176–180). Musei Capitolini, Palazzo dei Conservatori, Rome. Eric Vandeville / akg-images.

Fig. 4: Bust of Scipio Africanus (bronze, 1st century AD). Museo Archeologico Nazionale, Napels. © Iberfoto / Bridgeman Images.

HUNTING

Fig. 1: Hunt scene from the mosaic at the Villa Romana del Casale, Piazza Armerina, Sicily (detail; first half of 4th century AD). akg-images / Erich Lessing.

INFRASTRUCTURE

Fig. 1: Detail from the spiral relief on the Trajan Column (Rome, AD 112/13; plaster cast taken 1934–1940). Muzeul Național de Istorie a României, Bucharest. akg-images / Erich Lessing.

Fig. 2a: Detail from the spiral relief on the Trajan Column (Rome, AD 112/13; plaster cast taken 1934–1940). Muzeul Național de Istorie a României, Bucharest. akg-images / Erich Lessing.

Fig. 2b: Trajan Bridge on the Danube. Photo: Anne Kolb.

LANGUAGE

Fig. 1: O. Claud. II 331 (mid-2nd century AD). © A. Bülow-Jacobsen.

LEGION

Fig. 1: Formation of the manipular legion (diagram). Michael A. Speidel.

Fig. 2: The ten cohorts of a legion (diagram). Michael A. Speidel.

Map 1: Distribution of the legions c. AD 200; based on: BNP 7, 2005, pp. 361-362. © J. B. Metzler/ Springer-Verlag GmbH.

MILITARY DIPLOMA

Figs. 1–4: Diploma of Titus from September 8, AD 79 for the auxiliaries of the province of Noricum (two-part document on metal tablets). © Andreas Pangerl, www.romancoins.info.

MUSIC

Fig. 1: Detail from the upper frieze on the Chigi Vase (Olpe, overall height: 26cm; c. 675–625 BC). Museo Nazionale Etrusco di Villa Giulia, Rome, Inv.-Nr. 22679. akg-images / André Held.

Fig. 2: Detail from the spiral relief on the Trajan Column (Rome, AD 112/13; marble). Trajan Forum, Rome. akg-images.

OFFICERS

Fig. 1: The so-called 'Praetorian relief' (marble, 163 × 134 × 28 cm; found in Rome). Musée du Louvre, Paris. bpk | RMN – Grand Palais | Hervé Lewandowski.

PAY

Table 1: Annual basic pay in the Roman army in *denarii* (from: M. A. Speidel, *Heer und Herrschaft im Römischen Reich der Hohen Kaiserzeit*, 2009, 427).

RECRUITMENT

Fig. 1: Imperial rescript of Gordianus III, dated December 13, BC 240 (transcript on bronze). © Andreas Pangerl, www.romancoins.info.

Fig. 2: Latin papyrus from the reign of Hadrian (ChLA X 422). © Staatliche Museen zu Berlin – Egyptian Museum and Papyrus Collection, Scan: Berliner Papyrusdatenbank (Berlin Papyrus Database), P 11596 R.

RELIGION

Fig. 1: Frieze from a red-figured *stamnos* (c. 450–400 BC, attributed to the Cleophon Painter); from: A. Furtwängler / K. Reichhold (eds.), *Griechische Vasenmalerei. Auswahl hervorragender Vasenbilder*, Serie I (pl. 1– 60), 1904, pl. 35.

Fig. 2: Silver *tetradrachma* of Agathocles, tyrant of Syracuse (310/08–306/05 BC; 17.18 g; diameter: ca. 24.4 mm). Classical Numismatic Group, Triton XI (8. – 9.1.2021), Nr. 68. Private collection.

Fig. 3: Louis Noguet, reconstruction of the main façade of the Temple of Mars Ultor (watercolour, ink, gold highlights, 1868/69). École nationale supérieure des Beaux-Arts, Paris. bpk / RMN – Grand Palais / Image Beaux-Arts de Paris.

REPRESENTATIONS OF WAR

Fig. 1: Greek victory monument: Nike, Goddess of Victory, atop a pillar (Olympia, Sanctuary of Zeus, 425 BC; reconstruction). Bildarchiv Institut für Klassische Archäologie, Universität Heidelberg.

Fig. 2: Roman war scene: relief on the Column of Marcus Aurelius in Rome (Field of Mars, Rome, AD 180–192); from: Giovanni Becatti, *Colonna di Marco Aurelio*, 1957, fig. 14).

Fig. 3: Quintuple *shekel* (c. 327 BC; 40.08 g; diameter: c. 34 mm). New York Sale XXVII (4.2.2012), Nr. 304. Private collection.

Fig. 4: *Denarius* of mint master Q. Minucius Thermus (Rome, 103 BC; RRC 319/1; 4.02 g; diameter: 19 mm). Classical Numismatic Group, Electronic Auction 492, 26.5.2021, Nr. 324. Private collection.

Fig. 5: *Denarius* of mint master M. Sergius Silus (Rome, 116/115 BC; RRC 286/1; 3.92 g; diameter c. 20 mm). American Numismatic Society 1941.131.92. Private collection.

Fig. 6: *Sestertius* of Hadrian (Rome, c. AD 130–133; RIC 915; 26.66 g; diameter: c. 33 mm). Numismatica Ars Classica 10.5.2021, Nr. 1326. Private collection.

Fig. 7: Bronze medaillon from the reign of Constantine II (Rome, AD 337/340; RIC 347; 31.68 g; diameter: 38.7 mm). Kunsthistorisches Museum Wien, Coin Collection, Inv.-Nr. RÖ 32338. © KHM-Museumsverband.

SIEGE WARFARE

Fig. 1: Reconstruction of a stone catapult based on the manual by Hero of Alexandria (drawing, from: E. W. Marsden, *Greek and Roman Artillery, vol. 2, Technical Treatises*, 1971, 56, fig. 20).

Fig. 2: Reconstruction of a *helepolis*, a *chelone* and a battering ram (etching; after: *Les dix livres d'Architecture de Vitruve*, trans. C. Perrault, 2nd edition 1684, 345).

SOURCES

Fig. 1: List of soldiers of the *legio III Cyrenaica* and *legio XXII Deiotariana* (P. Vindob. L 2, edited as ChLA XLIII 1242; SB XXII 15638; origin: Aegyptus, AD 98–120). © Österreichische Nationalbibliothek, Papyrus Collection.

SPECIALISTS

Fig. 1: Gravestone of the *structor* M. Iulius Maximus, soldier of the *legio XI* at Vindonissa (AD 70–101). Photo: Schweizerisches Nationalmuseum, A-3326.

STANDARD

Fig. 1: Detail from the relief band of the Trajan Column (Scenes IV–V; Rome, AD 112/13; plaster cast, 1861). Museo della Civilta Romana, Rome. akgimages.

Fig. 2a/b: Funerary stele of Gnaeus Musius from Veleia, *aquilifer* of the *legio XIIII Gemina* (relief; found in Mainz). Cast from the Museo della Civilta Romana, Rome. bpk | Scala. Original in Landesmuseum Mainz.

SUPPLY

Fig. 1: Demaenetus Decree from Eleusis (211/10 BC; IG II21304, ll. 32 ff.). Epigraphic Museum, Athens. Photo: Jean-Christophe Couvenhes.

Fig. 2: Detail from the relief band of the Trajan Column (Rome, AD 112/13; plaster cast, 1861). Museo della Civilta Romana, Rome. akg-images.

Fig. 3: *Horreum* at the Roman fort of Vercovicium on Hadrian's Wall (built AD 122; Housesteads Roman Fort near Hexham, Northumberland, England). akg-images / Richard Booth.

VEHICLES

Fig. 1: Gravestone from Viminacium (near Kostolac, Serbia, CIL III 1650). Photo: Anne Kolb, 2018.

WARS OF NOTE

Map 1: Alexander's campaigns (336–323 BC); from: BNP 1, 2002, pp. 471-472). © J. B. Metzler/Springer-Verlag GmbH.

Map 2: Caesar's proconsulship in Gaul (58–50 BC); from: BNP Suppl. 3, 2007, p. 165). © J. B. Metzler/Springer-Verlag GmbH.

Map 3: The Peloponnesian War (431–404 BC); from: BNP 10, 2007, pp. 705-706). © J. B. Metzler/Springer-Verlag GmbH.

Map 4: The First Punic War (264–241 BC); from: BNP 12, 2008, pp. 207-208). © J. B. Metzler/Springer-Verlag GmbH.

Map 5: The Second Punic War (218–201 BC); from: BNP 12, 2008, pp. 209-210). © J. B. Metzler/Springer-Verlag GmbH.

Acropolis

First mention of the term 'acropolis' comes in Hom. Od. 8,494 and 8,504, in reference to the delivery of the Wooden Horse into the walled city of Troy. Hom. Il. 6,88 mentions the Temple of Athena that was located *en polei akrei* ('at the highest point of the city') (the same term is also found in Hom. Il. 6,257; 6,297; 6,317; 7,345; 20,52; 22,172; 22,383). 'Acropolis' here probably refers to the city as a whole, thought of as occupying a hilltop and segregated from the surrounding country by fortifications, its political and religious centre at its highest point [15]. The passage in the *Odyssey* is striking, displaying as it already does the primary idea of the settlement's use as a fortification, encircled by a defensive wall. With the sole exception of the 'fortresses' of the Mycenaean period, the first fortified settlements on the Greek mainland appeared only in the Archaic period. Not so on the islands of the Aegean, where fortified hillside settlements have been identified dating back as far as the 8th century BC, with walls blocking access to the town only partially (Zagora [3]; [7], Vroulia [10]; [7]) or entirely (Heraclea Minoa [7]), or partially (Emporio(n) [2]; [7]) encircling it. At Emporio on Chios, a wall separates an 'upper town', with prestigious residences and a sanctuary on the hilltop, from the unfortified 'lower town'. The walled part of the settlement was the centre of political and religious power and offered inhabitants a place of refuge when danger arose. As they grew in size and social stratification increased from the Archaic period onwards, entire settlements came to need extensive protection. Walls were now planned in response to topographical and strategic demands, sometimes even enclosing heights that were inhabited only sparsely or not at all, as for instance on Samos (Ampelus) [9]. The acropolis now increasingly became the exclusive venue of the cult (Pind. Ol. 7,49; Aesch. Sept. 240). The classic example here is the Acropolis of Athens, which was probably still inhabited in the 8th century, but which from the early Archaic period onwards became exclusively a cultic precinct [14]. Even so, the plateau at the summit of the Acropolis, ringed by a Mycenaean Cyclopean wall, continued to serve as a defensive installation in times of crisis, the last such occasion being during the Persian Wars, when those Athenians who had stayed behind sought safety there in vain (Hdt. 8,51–53). Little is known of how the Mycenaean wall was developed as a fortification during historical times. The Pelargikon mentioned in the sources as a fortified wall ascribed to the 'Pelasgians' may be partly identifiable with the Mycenaean encircling wall, but much remains unclear in regard to its extent, location and fortification [16]. The Athenian Acropolis did, however, certainly benefit from a well, which was accessible via steps cut into the rock.

Military use of acropoleis is better understood for smaller settlements than in the case of Athens. At Rhamnus, for example, the acropolis forms part of a fortress that was probably built during the Peloponnesian War (431–404 BC) [7]. Like the settlement as a whole, the acropolis is fortified with a separate circular wall defended with turrets.

As siegecraft and the architecture of fortifications were steadily perfected during the late Classical and Hellenistic periods, the military control of acropoleis became increasingly important [1]; [5]. Cross walls (*diateichisma*) and circular walls now often cut them off from the rest of the settlement and defended them separately (e.g. Aegosthena [13]; [7], Dystus [8]; [7], Eretria (cf. fig. 1) [4]; [7], Lisus [7], Nea Halos [7], Stratos [1]), or else they were enclosed within the settlement's encircling wall, even where they were inhabited only thinly or not at all (e.g. Acrocorinth [1], Ephesus [1], Priene [7]; [1]). Simple interior structures and hollow turrets invite the supposition that troops were at least temporarily garrisoned on some acropoleis (Eretria [4], Priene [18]). There is also epigraphic evidence for the stationing of troops on acropoleis. A text from Eretria, for example, mentions an officer of the occupying Macedonian force who was stationed *en tei akrai tei Eretrieon* ('in the citadel of the Eretrians') [11.296 note 179]. An inscription from Priene refers to a garrison commander who 'remained in the fortress on the hill' for the entire period when he was stationed there [17.463].

Besides serving the defence of the settlement itself, fortifications on hilltops also enabled control of the settlement and territory, as shown for instance by the bastion on the exposed north-eastern corner of the Acropolis of Eretria (cf. fig. 1), in that it faces not only the surrounding countryside, but also the town. Acropoleis (called citadels), integrated into town walls and often protected by more walls on the side facing the town, also became a firm fixture of urban planning in new towns of the Hellenistic east (e.g. Dura-Europus [7], Ai Khanum [7]).

☞ **Fortification; Garrison; Infrastructure; Siege warfare**

BIBLIOGRAPHY

[1] J.-P. ADAM, L'architecture militaire grecque, 1981 [2] J. BOARDMAN, Excavations in Chios 1952–1955. Greek Emporio, 1967 [3] A. CAMBITOLOGOU et al. (eds.), Zagora, vol. 2: Excavation of a Geometric Town on the Island of Andros, 1988 [4] S. FACHARD, Les fortifications de l'acropole. Sondage dans le secteur de la Tour nord, in: AK 50, 2007, 129–134 [5] Y. GARLAND, Recherches sur la poliorcétique grecque (Bibliothèque des écoles françaises d'Athènes et de Rome 223), 1974 [6] A. VON GERKAN, Griechische Städteanlagen, 1924 [7] M.-C. HELLMANN, L'architecture grecque, vol. 3: Habitat, urbanisme et fortification. Les manuels d'art et d'archéologie antiques,

Fig. 1: The Acropolis of Eretria with defensive wall and north tower. The fortification of the acropolis with a wall and defensive towers built of polygonal stones took place after the town's destruction by the Persians, in the second quarter of the 5th century BC or at its end circa 400 BC, at which time the circular wall on the plain was also newly built. The course of the Archaic stone wall in the vicinity of the acropolis is unknown.

2010 (esp. 294–359)   [8] E.L. HICKS, An Inscription from Priene, in: JHS 4, 1883, 237–242   [9] H. KIENAST, Die Stadtmauer von Samos (Samos 15), 1978   [10] K.F. KINCH, Vroulia, 1914   [11] D. KNOEPFLER, Décrets érétriens de proxénie et de citoyenneté (Eretria 11), 2001   [12] A. MCNICOLL, Hellenistic Fortifications from the Aegean to the Euphrates, 1997   [13] M.B. SAKELLARIOU / N. PHARAKLAS, Megaris, Aigosthena, Ereneia, 1972   [14] A. SCHOLL, ΑΝΑΘΜΑΤΑ ΤΩΝ ΑΡΧΩΝ. Die Akropolisvotive aus dem 8. bis frühen 6. Jahrhundert v.Chr. und die Staatswerdung Athens, in: JDAI 121, 2006, 1–173   [15] M. STOEVESANDT, Sechster Gesang (Z), in: A. BIERL / J. LATACZ (eds.), Homer Ilias, Gesamtkommentar IV 2, 2008   [16] I.N. TRAVLOS, Bildlexikon zur Topographie Athens, 1971   [17] T. WIEGAND, Dystos, in: MDAI(A) 24, 1899, 458–467   [18] F.E. WINTER, Greek Fortifications, 1971.

MARTIN GUGGISBERG

Administration

A. Greek
B. Hellenistic period
C. Roman

A. GREEK

A.1. The army
A.2. The navy

Our only detailed knowledge of the military administration of a Greek *polis* pertains to Athens, and more to the 4th century BC than to the 5th. There is little to add from other, typically smaller *poleis*. It must be assumed, however, that these had much simpler administrative systems.

A.1. THE ARMY

Every Greek *polis* had a military company that was essentially composed of private citizens who provided their own equipment. Registration of Athenian citizens who were of legal age took place in the individual demes and was certified by the Council of Five Hundred (*boule*; Aristot. Ath. pol. 42,1). From at least the 4th century BC onwards, men over the age of 18 had to complete a two-year military training as *ephebes*. The people elected the director (*kosmetes*) and trainers, and the fathers of the *ephebes* elected the superintendents (*sophronistes*), each of whom was responsible for one division (*phyle*). The equivalent system in Sparta had a longer period of training and military education (*agoge*), which was supervised by a *paidonomos* (Xen. Lac. pol. 2–4).

In Aristotle's time, the *boule* was responsible for organising the cavalry, which at Athens was first established in the mid-5th century from among the wealthier citizens of the *polis* (Aristot. Ath. pol. 49). The *boule* inspected the horses and would withhold the allotted feed subsidy from the animals' keeper if they were poorly maintained. The *boule* also inspected the mounted vanguard (*prodromoi*) and the light foot soldiers (*hamhippoi*). Ten men known as *katalogeis* who were elected by the people kept the register of the 'normal' cavalry. They presented this register to the commanders, who in turn submitted it to the *boule*. Anyone registered who swore that he was physically or financially incapable of cavalry service was deleted from the list.

All military commanders were elected for one-year terms by the popular assembly of the Athenian democracy. During the 4th century (Aristot. Ath. pol. 61), the most important positions were the ten *strategoi*, who could be dismissed by the popular assembly only with confirmation from the citizens' court (*dikasterion*), ten taxiarchs, who appointed their own company captains (*lochagoi*), two hipparchs, who acted as supreme cavalry commanders, ten phylarchs, who served as lower-ranking commanders, and lastly a hipparch for the cavalry stationed on the island of Lemnos.

In Sparta, the 'kings' (*basileis*) were also supreme commanders of the army. As the frequency of warfare increased, prominent Spartiates who held no formal office were also given military commands [5.148f.].

Both Athens and Sparta enlisted their active military company by age group. At Athens, a hoplite catalogue (*katalogos*) was specially prepared on each occasion for this purpose (Thuc. 7,16 et al.), once the popular assembly had stipulated how many age groups were to be enlisted (Aristot. Ath. pol. 53,7). The ephors made this decision in Sparta.

Campaigns were financed through a resolution of the *polis*. At Athens, a specific tax (*eisphora*) could be imposed for this purpose on a case-by-case basis. In the field, supreme commanders were responsible for the war chest. Like all Athenian officials, *strategoi* had to give an account of their financial activities. By the Late Classical period, a treasurer (*tamias*) elected by the people was in charge of the (by now permanent) war chest. At Sparta, kings on military campaigns were accompanied by judges (*hellanodikai*) and treasurers (*tamiai*) (Xen. Lac. pol. 13,11). Spartan kings could impose capital punishment for infractions, whereas the Athenian *strategoi* had only lesser penalties at their disposal (Aristot. Ath. pol. 61,2). However, a Spartan who proved to be a 'fleer' (*tresantes*) in battle could be stripped of his full citizenship only by a civil court (Plut. Ages. 30).

A.2. THE NAVY

Most Greek *poleis* had only a few warships. Only the leading cities, notably Athens, could raise significant navies.

Building, equipping and maintaining navies, as well as supplying crews for them, were very costly commitments. The largest naval fleets therefore tended to be assembled by fighting alliances (symmachies). The Athenians appointed a committee of ten *hellenotamiai* (Thuc. 1,96,2), accompanied by a further ten assessors and one or two scribes, to manage the allies' contributions (*phoroi*) in the Delian League. The league's treasury was transferred from Delos to Athens in 454. From then on, the Athenians offered one sixtieth of all tribute payments to Athena. These offerings were recorded annually on large stone tablets, some of which are preserved (tribute lists). The Second Athenian League had no communal treasury. If the *syntaxeis* (contributions) were not collected directly by the *strategoi* on the expedition, they may have been administered by Athenian members of the league's council (*synhedrion*) [1.65ff.].

The organization of warships within the Archaic Athenian *polis* was traditionally thought to have been the responsibility of a group known as the *naukrariai* (cf. e.g. Aristot. Ath. pol. 8,3). However, objections have been raised to the etymological interpretation that would suggest this understanding of the word (*naukraros*, 'chief of ships'; e.g. [3.19ff.]). The ships that undoubtedly undertook coastal watch duties in early Athens were probably the private responsibility of wealthy aristocrats.

When, from 483/82 BC onwards, Athens began using the revenues from the Attic silver mines to build a fleet of 200 triremes, the financing and equipping of ships and crews were again entrusted to wealthy private individuals. The trierarchy, which at first involved each individual trierarch being responsible for one ship, was one of the most important privately funded public service projects of the *polis*. In 410 BC, the burden for each ship came to be shared by two trierarchs. In about 358 BC, a law of Periander expanded the system of 'taxation groups' (*symmoriai*) to the trierarchy. Finally, in 340 BC, Demosthenes stipulated that this public service should be required, not from the existing 1,200 *symmoria* members, but only from the 300 richest. Special curators (*epimeletai*) headed the *symmoriai* (Dem. Or. 47,21). One of the ten *strategoi* was put in charge of the trierarchy system around 330 BC (Aristot. Ath. pol. 61,1).

Overall responsibility for the supervision of the triremes, their equipment and boathouses lay with the *boule* (Aristot. Ath. pol. 46). This council elected ten boatmasters (*trieropoioi*) from its own ranks as supervisors, and the people then elected the boatbuilders. A committee of ten *epimeletai* was put in charge of the wharves in the 4th century. That committee's annual registers, which were recorded on stone, inform us of a great many Athenian ships by name along with the condition of their equipment (IG II² 1604ff.).

☞ **State and army**

BIBLIOGRAPHY

[1] M. DREHER, Hegemon und Symmachoi. Untersuchungen zum Zweiten Athenischen Seebund, 1995 [2] M. DREHER, Sparta als Seemacht, in: E. BALTRUSCH et al. (eds.), Seemacht, Seeherrschaft und die Antike, 2016, 189–203 [3] V. GABRIELSEN, Financing the Athenian Fleet. Public Taxation and Social Relations, 1994 [4] M.H. HANSEN, Die athenische Demokratie im Zeitalter des Demosthenes. Struktur, Prinzipien und Selbstverständnis, trans. W. Schuller, 1995 [5] L. THOMMEN, Sparta. Verfassungs- und Sozialgeschichte einer griechischen Polis, 2003.

MARTIN DREHER

B. Hellenistic period

B.1. Writing and archives
B.2. Antigonids
B.3. Ptolemies
B.4. Seleucids

Administration of the army and troops was carried out by assorted military officials, including overseers (*epistatai*), secretaries (*grammateis*) and adjutants (*hyperetai*), organized at different levels and with diverse responsibilities. It is uncertain whether any precisely regulated hierarchy of offices existed. Hierarchies among the various functions can be discerned to a certain extent from court titles suggesting rank, combinations of offices, officials' career paths and authorizations to issue directives. Rarely, however, is a clear sequence of ranks attested, at least in the higher administrative echelons, and it is likely that no such sequence existed. The administration of the army was also subject to increasing bureaucratization. While various administrative functions were initially performed by officers, such tasks were gradually transferred to bureaucrats, whose numbers increased markedly. It was also commonplace for responsibility to be shared among several functionaries of equal rank, which indicates an increase in administrative regulation.

B.1. Writing and archives

Writing seems to have played little part in Ptolemaic army administration, with the exception of administrative procedures connected with the disbursal of soldier's pay and other benefits (see e.g. C. Ord. Ptol. 19f.), and the allocation and – in the broadest sense – management of land allotments (*kleroi*). Despite the abundance of papyrological evidence, only four official military archives have been preserved: the archive of the commander of the guard (*phrourarchos*) Dioscurides (P. Diosc.), the archive of thecontribution manager (*pros te syntaxei*) Pancrates (SB XIV 12159–12166), the archive of the 'general' Herianoupis [8] and the correspondence of the commander (*strategos*) Platon in the Pathyris Archives [12.95–97]. However, the first of these contains mostly complaints made to the *phrourarchos*, the archive of Pancrates is too fragmentary for its contents to be determined, and the archive of Herianoupis deals only with civilian matters. Only the 'Correspondence of Plato' is concerned with military issues, as seen in the context of a revolt in the Thebaid in 88 BC. The archive of the cavalry commander (*hipparches*) Dryton (P. Dryton) is a family archive, and that of the leaders (*hegemones*) Pates and Pachrates from the time of the Judaeo-Syro-Egyptian conflict of 103–101 BC (C. Jud. Syr. Eg.) contains private correspondence.

No comparable documentary sources are available for the two other Hellenistic kingdoms. In the case of the Antigonid army, however, several ordinances do survive in inscriptions in various cities, possibly representing a single royal edict (*diagramma*) of Philip V (238–179 BC) concerning military service in the Macedonian army. These offer detailed insights into administrative structures and procedures [7.151–164]. Complementing these inscriptions are the law regulating the office of gymnasiarch at Beroea (SEG 43, 381) and the ephebarchic law of Amphipolis (REG 100, 1987, pp. 434f., BE 1987, 704, [13]).

B.2. Antigonids

Under the Antigonids, reference is made to the *epi tou grammateiou* (Pol. 4,87,8), probably the chief secretary to the armed forces. Together with the *epi tas diagraphas* ('keeper of the regsiters'), he kept the army register. At the level of *strategia* ('military command'), there was found a secretary (*grammateus*), a chief adjutant (*archyperetes*) and an administrator (*cheiristes*). Among the responsibilities of the *grammateus* was the collection of fines. Adjutants (*hyperetai*) at the *speira* ('cohort') and *chiliarchia* ('group of a thousand soldiers') levels were in charge of the confiscation of spoils and the collection of fines. They may also have been responsible for the distribution of pay on behalf of the treasurer (*dioiketes*), as in the other Hellenistic armies. Horses were inspected by cavalry commanders (*hipparchoi*), who submitted their findings to the *epistatai*, urban overseers appointed by the king, and to their secretaries (*grammateis*). It may be that the *grammateis* also had the task of distributing to the mobilized army weapons and grain rations that were stored in the cities, while the *epistatai* may also have dealt with enlisting and mobilizing recruits.

In garrisons, several colleagues assisted the commander of the guard (*phrourarchos*), in particular a financial administrator (*oikonomos*) and administrators (*cheiristai*). The latter were responsible for the storage of the king's portion of the spoils [4.217–220]; [6.454–456]; [7.48f., 77–79]; [11.99–107].

B.3. Ptolemies

Assorted overseers (*epistatai*), secretaries (*grammateis*) and the adjutants (*hyperetai*) assigned to them worked in the Ptolemaic army administration. They bore responsibility for specific units, the names of which were suffixed to their titles in the genitive case, thus appearing at a variety of hierarchical levels. Their competencies ranged from organizational units like the hipparchy to territories incorporating several nomes and even all Upper or Lower Egypt. Although officials' titles display a striking variety, their individual responsibilities are seldom clearly identifiable. Alongside those mentioned above, other, lesser official positions emerged over time, their competencies purely financial (*oikonomoi*, 'financial administrators', *logeoutai*, 'tax callectors', and *sitologoi*, 'officials in charge of grain') [9]. 'Horse inspectors' (*hipposkopoi*) are attested in charge of cavalry mounts.

Administrative institutions concerned with the management of land allotments (*kleroi*) are particularly well documented. Besides the relevant overseers (*epistatai*) and secretaries (*grammateis*), responsibility for the *klerouchoi* ('those who possessed land allotments') and their land lay with the high-ranking contribution manager (*pros te syntaxei*). Answerable to him, the 'acquisition manager' (*tageis pros te proslepsei*) was in charge of recruitment to and registration in the *klerouchia* ('allotment of land'). Subordinate by still one more level, the 'distribution manager' (*pros tois katalochismois*) probably kept the registers [10.206–233].

Responsibility for paying wages to mercenaries lay chiefly with the secretaries (*grammateis*), who worked on these matters together with various officials of the nomes' financial administration, such as the financial administrator (*oikonomos*) and the Royal Scribe [1].

B.4. SELEUCIDS
In the absence of documentary sources, almost nothing is known about administrative organization in the Seleucid army. The administrative headquarters of the army (*logisterion to strategikon*), which included the royal stud and the elephants, was located at Apamea (Str. 16,2,10). The chief secretary of the armed forces (*archigrammateus tes dynameos / ton dynameon*), whose rank at court was 'among the first friends', appears to have been an officer with responsibility for financial affairs, especially pay (Pol. 5,54,12; SEG 19, 904; cf. [2.86f.]). We also know of chief adjutants (*archyperetai*) in the Seleucid army (OGIS II 754; cf. [3.92]), so presumably there were adjutants (*hyperetai*). The scribes of the *tagmata* ('companies of soldiers') were responsible for keeping troop lists (ISmyrna 573,45f.).

☞ Rank; Supply

BIBLIOGRAPHY
[1] C. ARMONI, Zum amtlichen Procedere bei der Auszahlung von Soldatenlöhnen im hellenistischen Ägypten, in: R. EBERHARDT et al. (eds.), '... vor dem Papyrus sind alle gleich!' Papyrologische Beiträge zu Ehren von Bärbel Kramer, 2009, 12–21 [2] B. BAR-KOKHVA, The Seleucid Army. Organization and Tactics in the Great Campaigns, 1976 [3] E. BIKERMAN, Institutions des Séleucides, 1938 [4] R.M. ERRINGTON, Geschichte Makedoniens. Von den Anfängen bis zum Untergang des Königreiches, 1986 [5] C. FISCHER-BOVET, Army and Society in Ptolemaic Egypt, 2014 [6] M.B. HATZOPOULOS, Macedonian Institutions under the Kings, vol. 1: A Historical and Epigraphic Study, 1996 [7] M.B. HATZOPOULOS, L'organisation de l'armée macédonienne sous les Antigonides. Problèmes anciens et documents nouveaux, 2001 [8] B. MUHS, Two Demotic Letters from the Archive of Herianoupis, from the Curzon Collection Now in the British Museum, in: H. KNUF (ed.), Honi soit qui mal y pense. Studien zum pharaonischen, griechisch-römischen und spätantiken Ägypten zu Ehren von Heinz-Josef Thissen, 2010, 397–404 [9] W. PEREMANS / E. VAN'T DACK, Prosopographia Ptolemaica, vol. 2: L'armée de terre et la police, 1952 [10] S. SCHEUBLE-REITER, Die Katökenreiter im ptolemäischen Ägypten, 2012 [11] N.V. SEKUNDA, The Antigonid Army, 2013 [12] K. VANDORPE / S. WAEBENS, Reconstructing Pathyris' Archives. A Multicultural Community in Hellenistic Egypt, 2009.

ADDITIONS TO THE ENGLISH VERSION
[13] K. D. Lazaridou, Ἐφηβαρχικὸς νόμος ἀπὸ τὴν Ἀμφίπολη, ArchE 154, 2015, 1–45.

SANDRA SCHEUBLE-REITER

C. ROMAN

C.1. Roman Republic (c. 5th cent.–30 BC)
C.2. Principate (30/27 BC–c. AD 284)
C.3. Dominate (c. 284–c. early 7th cent. AD)

The role of Roman military administration encompassed several activities, namely, acquiring, organizing and distributing soldiers, equipment, and provisions, disbursing pay to the infantry, cavalry and fleets, and planning and executing deployments of soldiers and materials. Measures necessary for these purposes were undertaken at a variety of levels: in the central administration of the Empire, at high commands in the provinces and within individual units. The ultimate purpose of the documentation kept by the army was to preserve the *disciplina militaris*, that is, the orderly performance of military service.

C.1. ROMAN REPUBLIC
(C. 5TH CENT.–30 BC)
Reconstruction of military administration during the Republican period, when Rome had no standing army, relies almost entirely on literary sources (especially Pol., Liv.). Administratively, military operations were prepared and carried out on at least two levels: at a superordinate level by the Senate, and at the level of individual armies by their commanders. The Senate debated questions of declaring (Pol. 6,13,6; Liv. 10,25,11f.; 24,11,1) and conducting war (*administratio belli*, Liv. 26,1,1). It established what strategy to pursue and what was required in terms of soldiers, equipment and

funding (Cic. Pis. 5). Moreover, the Senate enlisted legions, transferred command (*imperium*) of those legions to consuls, praetors and promagistrates (*propraetores, proconsules*), and assigned the promagistrates to the province in which they were to exercise their command (Liv. 23,32,2; 24,10, 1–5). The consuls and praetors, by contrast, were assigned campaigns and provinces by lot (Liv. 21,63,1; 32,28). If the consuls' year of office expired, the Senate either extended their command (*prorogatio*) or dispatched a successor (Pol. 6,15,6). It could also strip a consul of command. Decisions of the Senate (*senatus consulta*) had to be confirmed by the popular assembly (Pol. 6,16,2).

The popular assembly elected the consuls, whereas the military tribunes were either selected by the consuls or were elected by the people. The consuls together with the military tribunes recruited Roman citizens aged between 17 and 46, with the age range determined by need, and released them from service at the end of the campaign (Liv. 24,11,4f.; 32,3,6f.; Pol. 6,19f.). Lists (*tabulae*) of men fit for duty were kept for such recruitment processes. The censors regularly updated the lists, which showed when a particular man had last performed military service, and whether a valid exemption applied to any non-participation in a campaign (*vacatio iusta militiae*, Liv. 24,18,7). The consuls reported to the Senate on the strength and location of forces (Liv. 24,11,1). Rome's allies would also request lists of men fit to bear arms and lists of troop contingents (Pol. 2,23,9; 6,21,4).

At the individual army level, the commander had unlimited authority to wage and end war (Pol. 6,14,2). He could also negotiate peace terms, although these had to be confirmed by the popular assembly (Pol. 6,15,9). While on campaign, he relied on cooperation with the Senate, since it approved the army's → supply of grain, clothing and→ pay, some of which might be provided by Rome's allies (Pol. 6,15,4; Liv. 26,2,4). However, commanders' freedom to make their own decisions likely grew in proportion to the distance that separated the theatre of war from Rome and Italy. Beginning in the Second Punic War (218–201 BC), each year might see the conscription of over twenty legions, who were deployed alongside allied forces within and beyond Italy. During this period, it became critical for army supplies to be organized efficiently, and various strategies were devised to achieve this. In part, needed supplies were obtained by means of levies on the provinces (Liv. 30,3,2f.), by payment (Liv. 25,15,4), as voluntary contributions from allies (Liv. 23,21,5) or by requisition (Liv. 23,32,9). Alongside these sources of revenue, the Senate and senior officers in the field also worked with private entrepreneurs to provide troops with (additional) goods (App. Civ. 3,26) [4]. To aid them in the fulfilment of logistical and administrative tasks, commanders had officers, public servants (*apparitores, scribae* [6.39f.]; [11.64f.]) and their own → slaves and freedmen working with them (Liv. 42,27,8; App. Civ. 5,78).

Every consular (and probably praetorian, proconsular and propraetorian) company of men had a quaestor appointed by the popular assembly, who ranked immediately below the commander. As administrator of the treasury and stores, the quaestor distributed pay, provisions, clothing and (probably substitute) weapons to soldiers according to their rank. The standard prices of these items were deducted from pay, while allies received them free of charge (Pol. 6,39,12–15). The quaestor also sold booty and shared out the proceeds among the soldiers (Liv. 35,1,12). Given that a regular consular army of two legions could comprise as many as ten thousand men (Pol. 6,20,8), along with perhaps an equal complement of allies, it required considerable effort to document all soldiers by name, rank, unit and financial obligations for consumables used. The quaestor therefore had the support of scribes (*scribae*) and other public servants [6]; [11]; [12]. On relinquishing their command, commanders were required to account for their actions before the popular assembly (Pol. 6,15,10) and the quaestors of the public treasury (*aerarium*; Cic. Fam. 5,20,2).

In Polybius' time (2nd cent. BC), each legion regularly had six tribunes as the highest-ranking officers alongside the commander (Pol. 6,19,7–20,1). Two of them would take turns for two months at a time as 'serving tribunes' in the → camp and the field (Pol. 6,34,2f.). Their duties were mainly administrative. They carried out the enlisting of soldiers (Pol. 6,20), took the soldiers' oaths of service (Pol. 6,21,1–3; Liv. 22,38,1–5), assigned duties to the soldiers (Pol. 6,33,3), monitored construction work and routine tasks (Pol. 6,34,1–3), conveyed orders from the consul to the cavalry and centurions (Pol. 6,34,6), and generally advised the commander (Liv. 25,23,15; 34,35,1). In the field, they commanded individual military units (Liv. 6,2,7f.; 8,25,13; 22,21,4; 38,13,4) and occasionally entire legions (Liv. 41,5,8). They distributed booty to the soldiers (Pol. 10,16,1), functioned as judges (Pol. 6,39,6) and supervised guard duty. A written procedure was established to enforce performance of guard duty that imposed harsh penalties for dereliction (Pol. 6,34,7–37,6). Polybius' detailed descriptions suggest the existence of a military manual that described how the various official tasks were to be carried out.

C.2. Principate (30/27 BC–c. AD 284)

C.2.1. Military diploma: an administrative procedure privileging soldiers
C.2.2. Internal company administrative personnel
C.2.3. Content and function of administrative documentation

Under Augustus (27 BC–AD 14), what had been a citizens' militia became a standing professional army that swore an oath (*sacramentum*) of loyalty to the emperor as supreme commander [15]; [27.799f.]. This made it necessary to establish the military administration as a permanent institution. Of the 60 or so legions in existence at the end of the Civil War (30 BC), 28 were ultimately preserved, most of them dating back to the Caesarean legions. As they were adopted into the standing army, so too in all likelihood was the administrative experience gleaned from the long years of intense and successful campaigning in the field. This experience allowed for the efficient documentation of operational and logistical demands on personnel and materials. Certainly, this is the impression given by Suetonius, who reports that although Augustus' army reforms of 13 BC introduced many innovations, he also drew on what was tried and tested [19]. He enacted measures to safeguard → discipline among the troops and set out rules of conduct for commanders (Suet. Aug. 24). He also stipulated the number of years of expected service and the level of veterans' benefits, tiered according to rank and military branch (Cass. Dio 54,25,5f.; 55,23,1). These provisions imply that soldiers' personal information (name, age, distinguishing features, date of first service, unit, military career, place of service; cf. Rom. Mil. Rec. 87; 64) was systematically recorded and archived for purposes of recruitment and making monetary payments. At least a selective compilation of details on the strength and deployment of troops (Cass. Dio 55,23f.) was contained in Augustus' *breviarium totius imperii*, a statistical survey of the state (Suet. Aug. 101,4; cf. 28,1). All emperors probably received similar surveys [20]; [25.75]. In AD 6, Augustus established a special fund for financing veterans' benefits, the *aerarium militare* (Suet. Aug. 49,2).

C.2.1. Military diploma: an administrative procedure privileging soldiers

Later emperors also introduced innovations. Claudius (AD 41–54), for instance, regulated the service and careers of equestrian officers (*equestris militiae*, Suet. Claud. 25,1). → Military diplomas, bronze tablets about the size of a postcard, began to be issued in his reign. These had the effect of confirming in the name of the emperor that a soldier or → veteran of the auxiliary forces (*alae, cohortes*), praetorian fleets (*classes praetoriae*) or imperial mounted guards (*equites singulares Augusti*) held Roman citizenship (*civitas*) and was entitled to marry (*conubium*). They also granted the right of *conubium* to members of the praetorian guard (*cohortes praetoriae*) and urban guard (*cohortes urbanae*). These privileges created a considerable and continuous need for administration and documentation, particularly on behalf of the auxiliary forces [18]. The offices of company commanders created lists containing the names of soldiers who were to receive a given privilege, together with the names of any wives and children. All the auxiliary units in a province would submit these lists to the governor as supreme commander of the provincial army, and he then forwarded them to Rome. The imperial administration there created the text for bestowing the privileges (*constitutio*), and presented it to the emperor for approval. The *constitutio* was then engraved on bronze and published by means of public display. At the same time, individual diplomas stating the conferral of the privileges were created for the registered soldiers, and these were sent to the province, where the governor or company commander presented them to the soldiers.

C.2.2. Internal company administrative personnel

Of the later emperors who introduced administrative regulations for the army, special mention is warranted for Hadrian (AD 117–138), who even made detailed alterations to procedures while inspecting troops in the provinces (Cass. Dio 69,9,1–4; cf. HA Hadr. 10,3–11,1 [25.71]). Such interventions by the emperor illustrate the evolutionary nature of army administration, which can also be seen in army documentation [25.64] and the gradual expansion of the adminsitrative staff. Inscriptions from the legionary camp of Lambaesis in Numidia, dating from the late 2nd and 3rd centuries AD, show that the legion's internal administrative staff and allocations to assorted offices and archives (*scholae, tabularia*) reached their highest levels of complexity during this High Imperial period (AE 1898, 108f.; CIL VIII 2560; 2553–2555). The titles given to administrators (*cornicularius*, 'adjutant', *actuarius*, 'record keeper', *exactus*, 'supervisor', *librarius*, 'secretary' [23]) imply a clearly defined organization with specialized roles for creating, managing and archiving [26.230–236] documents, and this is confirmed by the variety of hands discernible in papyri that preserve army records (e.g. P. Masada 722). The military challenges of the 3rd century spawned new roles, some associated with legionary *vexillationes* (temporary military detachments), for example *canalicularius* ('adjutant') and *codiciarius* ('book keeper') [5. no. 314], which then vanished again in the course of the Diocletianic reforms. These illustrate the great importance that was attached to military documentation, even in what were at first merely temporary units. Thus, the use of writing for administrative purposes was not a local phenomenon confined only to the regular quarters of permanent army units. Rather, it was an essential instrument in managing the deployment and supply of military forces, regardless of the size, composition and lifespan of the unit.

Abundant written documents pertaining to military administration are preserved from many provinces (especially Aegyptus, Africa, Britannia, Syria), centuries and administrative levels (e.g. O. BuNjem, O. Did. [27], O. Krok., Rom. Mil. Rec., Tab. Vindol.). Written on wooden tablets, clay sherds (*ostraka*) or papyri, some of these documents were produced by governors' offices and others were created by legions, but most originated from auxiliary units. Within an individual company, documents were created and managed in a range of administrative contexts, as attested by inscriptions detailing specific soldiers' careers. For example, the cavalryman C. Iulius Dexter served successively as *curator* ('manager'), *armorum custos* ('keeper of arms') and *signifer* ('standard bearer'), and was thus responsible for administrative tasks in his unit's provisioning system, armoury and treasury (CIL VIII 2094). Promotion to *centurio* ('centurion') was generally also conditional upon having held a number of administrative posts (CIL VIII 217 [16]).

C.2.3. CONTENT AND FUNCTION OF
ADMINISTRATIVE DOCUMENTATION

Documentation for military units conveyed orders in structured form and answered implicit questions (*who, by/with/for whom, how much/many, what, when, where?*) at a context-specific level of detail regarding the deployment and supply of forces. It thus enabled the transparent rendering of accounts (*reddere rationem*, Veg. Mil. 2,20,7), which ultimately stabilized, documented and verified the *disciplina militaris* in all its dimensions, including personnel-related, logistical, and operational (cf. the *renuntia* from Vindolanda on the execution of orders: Tab. Vindol. III 574–579).

Administrative documents are characterized by a general consistency of form (layout, structure) and content (terminology, phraseology, abbreviations, symbols) that remains stable throughout this period for all types of military units. Several factors explain this. First, the subject matter of documents (the mustering, deployment and supply of soldiers) remained basically the same throughout the centuries for all bodies of men everywhere in the Empire. Second, consistency was maintained through the presence of internal training mechanisms for administrative posts within companies [26.239f.]. Lastly, the principle of advancing one's career by redeploying within and between military units (in different provinces) and by serving in civilian imperial administration had a standardizing effect on documentation.

With a strength of around 400,000 men in the High Imperial period, the Roman army was relatively small in relation to the size of the Empire. Its broad range of duties – for example, protecting Roman territories from attack, conducting offensive operations, serving with civilian officials, and maintaining peace and good order in the provinces – made it necessary to take soldiers out of their home units and dispatch them in all directions on a continuous basis, as Hadrian's address to the *legio III Augusta* at Lambaesis illustrates (CIL VIII 2532 [22]). Administrative documentation was an indispensable foundation and precondition for such a complex deployment of forces, exhibiting as it did the army's current conditions at any given time with regard to personnel and materials (cf. Tab. Vindol. II 154).

C.3. DOMINATE
(C. 284–C. EARLY 7TH CENT. AD)

C.3.1. Comprehensive army reforms
C.3.2. Continuities in army administration

There are more literary (esp. Amm. Marc., Veg. Mil., Not. Dign., Procop., Ps.-Maur. Strat.) and papyrological sources for the administration of the later Roman army than for the earlier period [14], but fewer epigraphic testimonies. Legal texts in particular afford insights into what emperors expected (Dig., Cod. Theod. 7, Cod. Iust. passim; cf. Ps.-Maur. Strat. 1,6; 12B, pr.; 12B,10) in terms of the administrative work of senior commanders (*magistri militum* (*praesentales*)), military governors (*comites, duces*) and company commanders (*tribuni, praefecti, praepositi*). The largely fragmentary papyrological record, meanwhile, comes mostly from the sphere of supplies, but its uneven chronological distribution limits its usefulness.

C.3.1. COMPREHENSIVE ARMY REFORMS

Many reorganizations of the military beginning around the middle of the 3rd century led to profound organizational changes in the army. Traditional units (*legiones*, 'legions', *alae*, 'wings', *cohortes*, 'cohorts'), some of which were now reduced in size, were joined by new ones (*auxiliares*, 'auxiliaries', *cunei*, 'divisions', *equites*, 'cavalry' and others [3]). Administrative staffs (*officia*) at various levels, the compositions of which sometimes varied from place to place and period to period, began exhibiting new and sometimes increasingly abstract official titles (e.g. *primiscri-*

nius, primicerius, ducenarius, domesticus, numerarius, scriniarius; P. Abinn., Not. Dign. passim; SEG 9, 356; 9, 414; Cod. Theod. 8,1,16; Cod. Iust. 1,27,2,19–34; P. Ness. III *passim*). This implies yet further administrative specialization. The basic division of the army into higher-ranking field armies (*comitatenses*) that could be deployed from place to place, and lower-ranking units stationed in frontier regions (*limitanei, riparienses*), as well as the transfer of responsibility for army supplies (Cod. Theod. 7,4) and recruitment [17]; [7] to the civilian administration, gave rise to what became a more complex military administration in comparison with the High Imperial period. This increasingly complex administration probably generated a heavier flow of documentation, reporting and monitoring within and between the various administrative levels of the military hierarchy, and also between the military and civilian administrations (P. Panop. Beatty 1,72–76; Nov. 130). Illustrating the close interweaving of civilian and military administration in army supplies is the fact that some officials working within units were now civilians (Lyd. Mag. 3,31;35) [24]. The *de facto* division of the Empire in the late 4th century also spawned divergent developments in army administration in the two halves. For example, in the East, the civilian *quaestor sacri palatii* ('Quaestor of the Sacred Palace'), as a high-ranking legal advisor to the Emperor, was responsible for keeping the register of officers below the rank of *dux* ('commander') (*minus laterculum*, Cod. Theod. 1,8,2), whereas this was probably the task of the *magister militum praesentalis* ('Master of Soldiers in the (Imperial) Presence') in the West from the time of Stilicho onwards [2.282].

C.3.2. CONTINUITIES IN ARMY ADMINISTRATION

Administrative activity and the form and content of surviving documentation, most of which is from the Eastern Empire, displays continuities from the early and High Imperial periods, although Greek was coming into increasingly frequent use in military adminsitration alongside the official language of command, Latin (Ps.-Maur. Strat. 1,8; 3,5; 12B,24). The imperial administration held complete registers of the armed forces (cf. Not. Dign. passim), and it made decisions regarding promotions and transfers (P. Abinn. 1; 2; Cod. Theod. 7,1,18). Senior commanders had documentation on the strength, deployment and → supply of their forces (Amm. Marc. 18,5,1), and they issued written instructions to company commanders (Ps.-Maur. Strat. 3,11; 7A,4; 7B,16f.; P. Abinn. 2). Those company commanders in turn submitted reports to their superiors (Cod. Theod. 7,17,1), and they kept and archived lists of their units' personnel (muster rolls). Regular transcripts of these lists (*matrices*) were sent to the civilian authorities via the military governor, so that provisions could be allocated according to rank (*adaeratio*; P. Panop. Beatty 1,72–76; Cod. Theod. 11,5,1; CPR XXIV 15; SEG 32, 1554 [9]). → Veterans received discharge papers (*emeritae missionis epistulae*) bestowing privileges that were graded by company membership, rank and term of service. This too required that information regarding personnal be documented (ChLA XLIII 1248; Cod. Theod. 7,20). However, the orderly performance of military service (*disciplina militaris*) was the subject of frequent imperial reforms provoked by abuses (corruption [10]) in the army and administration (Cod. Theod. 7,20,12; Zos. 4,31,1) [13].

In terms of the technicalities of documentation, the 'rendering of accounts' structure of soldier lists essentially continued from the preceding era (e.g. ChLA XI 499; XI 504; XLIII 1244; X 429; X 430; P. Ness. III 37: list of soldiers sent away for duty with indication of their destinations; cf. Rom. Mil. Rec. 1; 2; Tab. Vindol. II 154; cf. also the level of detail on sick leave in the latter document with details on grounds for discharge in ChLA XLIII 1248,3). The sources also still exhibit scribal conventions familiar from the early and High Imperial periods. These include abbreviations and symbols for titles (e.g. *tesse(rarios)*, O. Douch 12 et al.; *centurio/hekatontarchos*, O. Trim. I 322; P. Lond. V 1722; 1729; P. Oxy. LIX 4000; cf. Ps.-Maur. Strat. 12,1,1; *dec(urio)*, *eq(ues)*, ChLA XLIII 1248,3), technical military terms (e.g. *sti(pendiorum)*, *k(astr.)*, ChLA XLIII 1248,3), units of measurement (e.g. *artabe, litra*, P. Abinn., P. Ness. III *passim*), indications of amount (*gi(netai/nontai)*, e.g. O. Douch *passim*) and terminology for lists (*gnosis/logos* in the sense of *ratio*, P. Abinn. 69,V 1; O. Douch I 15; P. Benaki 3; P. Ness. III 37; *matricula*, ChLA XLIII 1248,3). Literate staff thus remained a necessity at all levels of administration, and in the East such staff were probably available (cf. the Taurinos Archive, documenting the advancement of members of an army family in military administration over three generations in the 5th/6th centuries; CPR XXIV 10, Introduction; but cf. Ps.-Maur. Strat. 1,4: senior commanders and their adjutants were expected to be literate). As in the High Imperial period, these staff members also undertook private scribal duties (P. Lond. V 1722,51; 54–60; 1729,46–52; P. Ness. III 19,6f.; P. Münch. I 14,104–110). Overall, however, the overly elaborate rhetoric of late Imperial administrative language, along with the improprieties of civilian and military officials that are a constant theme in the sources, probably undermined the effectiveness and efficiency of adminsitrative procedures [8].

☞ **State and army; Supply**

Bibliography

Sources
[1] Maurikios, Das Strategikon des Maurikios, edited by G.T. Dennis and E. Gamillscheg, 1981.

Secondary literature
[2] A. Demandt, Die Spätantike. Römische Geschichte von Diocletian bis Justinian, 284–565 n.Chr., 2007 [3] H. Elton, Military Forces, in: P. Sabin et al. (eds.), The Cambridge History of Greek and Roman Warfare, vol. 2, 2007, 270–309 [4] P. Erdkamp, Manpower and Food Supply in the First and Second Punic Wars, in: D. Hoyos (ed.), Companion to the Punic Wars, 2011, 58–76 [5] V. Hoffiller / B. Saria, Antike Inschriften aus Jugoslawien, vol. 1, 1938 [6] A.H.M. Jones, The Roman Civil Service (Clerical and Sub-Clerical Grades), in: JRS 39, 1949, 38–55 [7] Y. Le Bohec, Das römische Heer in der Späten Kaiserzeit, 2010 [8] R. MacMullen, Roman Bureaucratese, in: Traditio 18, 1962, 364–378 [9] F. Mitthof, Annona militaris. Die Heeresversorgung im spätantiken Ägypten. Ein Beitrag zur Verwaltungs- und Heeresgeschichte des Römischen Reiches im 3. bis 6. Jh. n.Chr., 2 vols., 2001 [10] F. Mitthof / K. Stauner, Zwei Kassen in der römischen Armee und die Rolle der signiferi. Ein neues Papyruszeugnis: P. Hamb. inv. 445, in: Tyche 31, 2016, 205–225 [11] J. Muñiz Coello, Empleados y subalternos de la administración romana I: Los scribae, 1982 [12] J. Muñiz Coello, Empleados y subalternos de la administración romana II: Los praecones, in: Habis 14, 1983, 117–145 [13] F. Onur, The Anastasian Military Decree from Perge in Pamphylia. Revised 2nd Edition, in: Gephyra 14, 2017, 133–212 [14] B. Palme, Die römische Armee von Diokletian bis Valentinian I. Die papyrologische Evidenz, in: Y. Le Bohec / C. Wolff (eds.), L'armée romaine de Dioclétien à Valentinien Ier, 2004, 101–115 [15] S. Phang, Roman Military Service. Ideologies of Discipline in the Late Republic and Early Principate, 2008 [16] B. Rankov, Military Forces, in: P. Sabin et al. (eds.), The Cambridge History of Greek and Roman Warfare, vol. 2, 2007, 30–75 [17] G. Ravegnani, Soldati di Bisanzio in età Giustinianea, 1988 [18] N. Scheuerbrandt, Kaiserliche Konstitutionen und ihre beglaubigten Abschriften. Diplomatik und Aktengang der Militärdiplome, 2009 [19] M.A. Speidel, Augustus' militärische Neuordnung und ihr Beitrag zum Erfolg des Imperium Romanum. Zu Heer und Reichskonzept, in: M.A. Speidel, Heer und Herrschaft im römischen Reich der Hohen Kaiserzeit, 2009, 19–51 [20] M.A. Speidel, Geld und Macht. Die Neuordnung des staatlichen Finanzwesens unter Augustus, in: M.A. Speidel, Heer und Herrschaft im römischen Reich der Hohen Kaiserzeit, 2009, 53–84 [21] M.A. Speidel, Heer und Herrschaft im Römischen Reich der Hohen Kaiserzeit, 2009 [22] M.P. Speidel, Emperor Hadrian's Speeches to the African Army. A New Text, 2006 [23] K. Stauner, Das offizielle Schriftwesen des römischen Heeres von Augustus bis Gallienus (27 v.Chr.–268 n.Chr.). Eine Untersuchung zu Struktur, Funktion und Bedeutung der offiziellen militärischen Verwaltungsdokumentation und zu deren Schreibern, 2004 [24] K. Stauner, Der cornicularius in den Büros der ducalen und ducalen Kommandeure in der Notitia dignitatum, in: Tyche 25, 2010, 131–171 [25] K. Stauner, Rationes ad milites pertinentes. Organisation und Funktion der Binnenadministration militärischer Einheiten in der Frühen und Hohen Kaiserzeit, in: A. Eich (ed.), Die Verwaltung der kaiserzeitlichen römischen Armee. Studien für Hartmut Wolff, 2010, 37–85 [26] K. Stauner, Finanzliteralität im Imperium Romanum am Beispiel der argentarii und signiferi. Dokumentationsexperten im zivilen und militärischen Finanzwesen (späte Republik – Prinzipatszeit), in: Tyche 29, 2014, 193–253 [27] K. Stauner, New Documents from the Roman Military Administration in Egypt's Eastern Desert. The Ostraca from the Praesidium of Didymoi, in: B. Takmer et al. (eds.), Vir Doctus Anatolicus. Studies in Memory of Sencer Şahin Anısına Yazılar, 2016, 796–815

Konrad Stauner

Alliances

Alliances always had a role to play in the world of the Graeco-Roman city states. In times of war, the pooling of resources offered obvious benefits, notably when the Greeks allied against the Persians, and also when Greek city states formed the Peloponnesian League or the Athenian-dominated Delian League. Some of these alliances obtained a more durable character and served as the basis for federal states or empires. Alliances enabled the expanding Roman Republic to harness the resources of dependent states and thereby contain the costs of establishing and maintaining its empire. In Late Antiquity, Rome used its alliances to incorporate 'barbarian' tribes into the administrative and defensive structures of the Roman Empire.

A. Early Greece
B. Greece: Late Archaic period
C. Greece: Classical period
D. Hellenistic period
E. Early Rome and Italy
F. Roman Republic, 3rd cent.–1st cent. bc
G. Imperial period

A. Early Greece
Classical literature begins with the story of a military alliance against Troy as recounted in Homer's *Iliad* (in which the 'Catalogue of Ships' contains a list of allies from 178 places) and in other works of the Epic Cycle [39.64–69]. The second great cycle, the Theban Cycle, deals with the alliance of the Seven Against Thebes. Examples from mythographic sources include the alliance of Dioynsus with the Thracian king Lycurgus (Diod. Sic. 3,65,4) and that of Minos with the Carians (other instances: [26.1–34]). Although this reveals the importance of military alliances in the earliest phase of Greek culture, it is not necessary to trace later treaties of alliance back to the Mycenaean or Homeric periods (the notion of a correlation between the oath 'to have the same friends and enemies' and Hittite antecedents is not convincing [17.298]). At a more

historical period around 700 BC, the war on the island of Euboea between Chalcis and Eretria over the Lelantine Plain is said to have been fought out between two alliances in which most of Greece took sides (Thuc. 1,15; Hdt. 1,18; 5,99; Pol. 13,3,4; Str. 10,1,12; Plut. Mor. 760f.), although many details in later sources probably originated in the conflation of unrelated conflicts from the Archaic period that were combined to present the Lelantine War as a confrontation akin to the Trojan War [39.137–145].

From about 600 BC onwards, sporadic and fragmentary reports of alliances among individual Greek cities and between Greek cities and non-Greek dynastic states become more reliable, though admittedly much of the record may be coloured by later diplomatic practice ([22.346–349, nos. 5–25; 27f.]; survey: [39.70–138]). One phenomenon important for understanding the early history of the alliance as an institution is that some of the terminology used (e.g., *xenia*, 'hospitality', *philia*, 'friendship') resembles the vocabulary used for personal relationships among the elites. By the Classical period at the latest, a terminological distinction was achieved between a full military alliance (*symmachia*) and a purely defensive one (*epimachia*; Thuc. 1,44,1; cf. Thuc. 5,48 contrasting the various alliances of Argos; on the uneven terminology [17.328]). As throughout subsequent Greek history, the defining formal feature of alliance accords in this period was the swearing of → oaths (details: [1.92–188]).

Among the earliest epigraphic witnesses, dating from the late 6th century BC, are the treaty between Sybaris and the otherwise unknown 'Serdaioi' of Southern Italy (ML 10), and the treaty between Elis and Heraea (ML 17). Both are extremely terse and limited to essentials. The accord between Elis and Heraea, which was to be in force for 100 years, stipulated that the allies 'should support each other in all things, especially in war', and set a penalty payable to the Olympian Zeus as the sanction for any breach of the treaty. The late Classical tradition emphasized the obligations assumed by members of the Delphic Amphictyony if any member violated the terms of their military alliance: 'that they would neither lay waste to any city of the Amphictyonic states, nor shut them off from running water either in war or in peace; but that if anyone should violate this oath, they would advance against such a one and lay waste to its cities' (Aeschin. Leg. 2,115). In emphasizing this, the oath associates this alliance with the concerted action of the member states during the First Sacred War (traditionally dated to 594–585 BC). Although certain details of the obligations attached to the Amphictyony may have been extrapolated from later practice, there is probably a historical basis to the tradition [39.34–47].

B. GREECE: LATE ARCHAIC PERIOD

The Late Archaic and Classical periods saw the emergence of alliances among multiple partners, both on a regional and a theoretically pan-Hellenic basis. Such alliances became a hallmark of the Greek military and diplomatic sphere. Some regional alliances merged into federal states (typology of federal states: [8]; historiographical survey: [14]; historical survey up to the 5th cent. BC: [1.3–91]). It may be that the distinction between a multilateral alliance and a federal state was not always clear at first. Aristotle emphasized in a famous passage that the *polis* was 'not the same as a military alliance (*symmachia*): a military alliance is useful by virtue of its quantity, even if there is no difference in quality (for mutual assistance is the desired goal)' (Aristot. Pol. 2,1261A24–26). Yet, the view that *poleis* in a federal state had a right to autonomy and independent political action simmered never far below the surface (cf. [4.11] on the difference between the federal Boeotia and the Peloponnesian League, which 'had precious little, if any, influence on the communities involved in terms of their actual qualities as states'; cf. [30] on 'precursors to federal states'; [25.21–57]; [13.223–240]). Another distinction that can be made is between unequal alliances led by a recognized *hegemon* ('leader'), such as the Peloponnesian League, the Delian League of the 5th century and the Athenian League of the 4th century, and partnerships of equals, such as the League of Corinth of 395 BC [22.356f., no. 136] or the 369 BC alliance between Athens and Sparta [22.370f., no. 192].

The early history of what became federal states is obscure, as is the early history of military alliances in the strict sense. For example, it is not presently clear what the pressure Thebes exerted on Plataeae to join 'the Boeotians' (Hdt. 6,108,5) in 519 BC really entailed. At the time of Xerxes' invasion, however, the sources report the *boiotarchai* as a college at the head of the Boeotian League (later known as League Generals; cf. Hdt. 9,15; on unpublished epigraphic evidence cf. [6.138]). Likewise unclear in detail is the genesis of the Spartan system of military alliances on and beyond the Peloponnese in the 6th century (at least from the time of Sparta's victory over Tegea). In the Classical period, these alliances entailed the obligation 'to follow where the Lacedaemonians lead, on land and sea, and to have the same friend and the same enemy as the Lacedaemonians' (O&R 128, ll. 4–9: epigraphic treaty with the Aetolian Erxadieis, c. 450–400 BC; cf. Xen. Hell. 2,2,20; 4,6,2; 5,3,26). But controversy still surrounds the date when these unequal services were rendered, as well as the questions of when a core group of allies formally organized into what we now call the Peloponnesian League and when it became necessary for them to assent to offensive campaigns (as opposed to defensive support rendered to an ally).

Instances are attested of decisions in favor of war or peace being presented to the allies after being ratified by the Spartan popular assembly (the best-known being in Thucydides' account of the origins of the Peloponnesian War, Thuc. 1,87,3f.; 1,118–125). It has been suggested that this 'bicameral' procedure originated in the campaign of Cleomenes against Athens in approximately 506 BC and his subsequent attempt to reinstall Hippias (Hdt. 5,74–76; 5,91–93). Sparta's previous right to call upon its allies unilaterally [17.101–151, 333–341] was then curtailed. After this, whatever obligations Sparta had to consult its allies and adhere to majority decisions would have rested entirely on ad hoc arrangements [23]. Perhaps the most convincing approach here is to date the emergence of offensive elements in the Spartan alliance, along with the bicameral procedure, to the time after Xerxes' invasion [11.54–73]. By 371 BC, it was possible to criticize Sparta for taking allies to war without their agreement (Xen. Hell. 6,3,7f.).

C. GREECE: CLASSICAL PERIOD

We are on more secure ground with the 'Hellenic League' formed in 481 against the Persians, again under the leadership of Sparta (Hdt. 7,132; 7,145–169: alliance negotiations; ML 27: dedication by 31 member cities after the Battle of Plataeae; [10]; [1]). The allies took on an obligation of mutual military support, probably not against the Persians alone (Sparta invoked the alliance during the Third Messenian War of the 460s BC). Command resided with Sparta on land and water, although Herodotus' account ascribes an active role even on campaigns to the war council, on which each member *polis* had a voice. In 478/77 BC, this anti-Persian alliance was superseded by the Delian League under Athenian command [32.14–21]; [1.52–64]; [17.298–307]. Allies now swore 'to have the same friends and the same enemies' (Aristot. Ath. Pol. 23,5). Some members contributed naval forces, while others made tribute payments (*phoros*) to the joint war chest, as Athens dictated. At first, the allies were led 'on the basis of equality' (*apo tou isou*, Thuc. 3,10f.), although what exactly this phraseology implied remains uncertain. In 454/53, the joint treasury of the League was transferred from Delos to Athens, and there were probably no more general meetings of all members. By the time of the Peloponnesian War (431–404 BC), only Chios and Lesbos still had independent fleets. The tribute payments set for the other allies were rising sharply, and additional obligations were being imposed on them, particularly the requirement to use Athenian coinage, weights and measures (O&R 152–155; there is much debate over the chronology).

Treaties between Athens and the more independent *poleis* tended to focus more on mutual military support. The 420 BC defensive alliance (*epimachia*) with Argos, Mantinea and Elis (O&R 165), for instance, transferred command of all allied forces to whichever *polis* had invoked the treaty, and obliged that *polis* to provide food and pay for troops at the agreed rates after thirty days. The Second Athenian League founded in 378/77 conspicuously avoided the more imperialistic practices of the Delian League, instead prescribing a more active military role for the confederates, whose freedoms were guaranteed in matters of occupation, the appointment of governors and the exaction of tribute. The *synhedrion* ('assembly') of the League had an important role, subsequently regulating the joint financial contributions (*syntaxeis*) (R&O 22: Athenian decree establishing the League and its membership list) [11.192–240].

By contrast, the Peloponnesian League imposed no tribute obligation on its members (cf. O&R 151 on smaller financial contributions from outside cities). It offered the possibility of converting military obligations to monetary payments (Xen. Hell. 5,2,20f.: in 382 BC, the rate was 3 Aeginetan *oboloi* per foot soldier and 12 per cavalryman; Xen. Hell. 6,2,16). A reform of the allies' military obligations in 376 subdivided the League into ten geographical regions. It also declared that one hoplite (a heavily armed soldier) was equivalent to two lightly armed foot soldiers, and that one cavalryman was equivalent to four hoplites (Diod. Sic. 15,31). Some allies provided ships rather than infantry (Thuc. 2,9). The principle of seeking out allies with different military strengths was generally established (e.g. Thuc. 1,68,4 on Corcyra; Diod. Sic. 15,78,4–79,2 on Epaminondas' plans for a Theban naval alliance). Alliances with powers outside Greece, particularly the Persians during the Peloponnesian War (Thuc. 8,18; 8,36; 8,58), often centred on financial aid, but also sometimes included commitments to mutual military support. Revenue could also be obtained by conducting military campaigns for allies outside the world of the *poleis*, that is, by providing what were essentially mercenary services. This was done by the Spartans Brasidas in Macedonia and Agesilaus II in Egypt.

D. HELLENISTIC PERIOD

Three key developments took place in the alliances of the Hellenistic period: the creation of pan-Hellenic alliances under the command of the Macedonians and Diadochi in the wake of the Battle of Chaeronea (338 BC) [38]; the emergence of federal states as a new and important factor [5]; [25] and the evolution of royal treaty diplomacy in the Diadoch states. A considerable number of detailed epigraphic testimonies concerning bilateral agreements between individual *poleis* also survives, especially from Crete (survey:

[12.87–100]; cf. [22.372–393, nos. 345–371, 376f., 399, 402, 428, 437–441, 443, 447–449, 462f., 482, 487, 493, 495–499, 505, 508–510, 514, 519, 548–550, 567–587, 610–612]). King Philip II of Macedon founded the League of Corinth in 338/27 BC with the intention of leading it as *hegemon* ('leader') and enforcing a general peace. Allies undertook to participate in whatever punitive actions were ordered by the joint *synhedrion* ('assembly') and the *hegemon* (R&O 76: oath of the confederates and membership; other evidence: StV III 403). The new League of Corinth found itself engaged almost immediately in a joint campaign against Persia, and contingents from the league also took part in the campaign of Alexander the Great. This alliance was revived by Demetrius Poliorketes in 302 BC (StV III 446), and Antigonus III Doson and Philip V imitated it in their Hellenic League (224–197; on its structure: [34.177–194]). On a regional level, the alliances of the *koina* ('confederations') had an important role, particularly the Achaean and Aetolian Leagues, which steered the military and diplomatic activities of their members. For instance, Boeotia supervised military training in the member *poleis*, and Achaea reimbursed their expenses for the military defence of their own territories (on the power relationships [25.347–351]; cf. [25.429–432 T15] on an agreement between the cities of Orchomenus and Chaeronea for the joint fulfilment of military obligations to the league).

The military clauses in bilateral and multilateral *symmachiai* (full military alliances) essentially continued traditions of the Classical period, although they do exhibit striking diversity. They often contain detailed provisions regarding the type of military aid to be provided, the payment of summoned confederate troops after 30 days (StV III 480, ll. 35–40: treaty between Aetolia and Acarnania, detailed schedule of deadlines), and the sharing out of spoils (StV III 511 = [12.208–213, no. 11]: treaty between Lyctus and Malla, decided by lot in proportion to the ratio of combatants). Although treaties with kings were often asymmetrical, they did not differ greatly in formal aspects (StV III 549: treaty between Philip V and Lysimachia). Monarchs, however, were often in a position to bring cities under their control without entering into reciprocal relationships as allies. Even where such agreements were made, they were often concluded with royal underlings rather than the king himself (SEG 36, 973: accord between Euromus and Zeuxis) [24.150–174].

E. EARLY ROME AND ITALY

The Roman tradition distinguished between formal treaties (*foedera*) of friendship and other forms of relations between states, including the establishment of 'friendship' (*amicitia*) without a treaty (Dig. 49,15,5,2) [15.1–67, 111–152]. It was possible to distinguish between unequal treaties made with communities that had surrendered to Rome, peace treaties founded on alliances, and symmetrical treaties between communities that had never been at war (Liv. 34,57,7–9). This distinction, however, is unlikely to have been a formal one. In historical times, the authority to enter into a *foedus* with other states rested solely with a voting assembly known as the *comitia* (Pol. 6,14; Cic. Balb. 34f.; Sall. Iug. 39), although the specific conditions were established by the Senate or by commanders in the field. As in Greece, the swearing of oaths accompanied the ratification of treaties. The sources offer abundant information regarding the religious aspects of concluding treaties, but they are often unreliable in reference to early Rome. The rite of the *fetiales* (a guild of priests) was used at the ratification of treaties well into the late Republican period and beyond – if for nothing else, then at least as an antiquarian reenactment (Varro, Ling. 5,86; [31. no. 8, l. 85]; Gell. NA 16,4; Suet. Claud. 25) [41.82–108].

As with the Greeks, the earliest Roman alliances are legendary (cf. Liv. 1,13 on Romulus). Nevertheless, there may have been a documentary tradition behind the texts of the early treaties of friendship with Carthage between 508 and 279 BC (Pol. 3,22–25) and of the *foedus Cassianum* of 493, which founded the alliance with the Latins (Dion. Hal. Ant. Rom. 6,93; Cic. Balb. 53), because the provisions that survive in written form for these treaties are strikingly archaic. Among the notable features of the early treaties are the close attention paid to the division of spoils (equally divided between the Romans and Latins, but remaining with the Carthaginians in cities they cede to the Romans), and rules governing the transfer of prisoners of war from allied territories to the territory of those who were party to the treaty. Antiquarian evidence (Paul. Fest. p. 276L) suggests that the Romans did not always have overall operational command of the allied Latin forces in the early period, but there is no hint of this in the annalistic tradition.

By the end of the Samnite Wars (343–290 BC), Rome had established a system of bilateral alliances, which were mostly imposed on its defeated opponents ([7]; a more sceptical view: [33]). This system enabled Rome to exercise control over Italy, and to impose military obligations on Italic cities (*socii*, 'allies' or *foederati*, 'those allied by treaty'). Evidence of exact content, however, is scanty. It is unclear whether there was a full-fledged *foedus* ('treaty') for every Italic community, and treaty conditions appear to have differed markedly. Most treaties contained non-reciprocal obligations imposed on the allies 'to preserve in friendship the dignity of the Roman people' (*maiestatem populi Romani comiter conservare*) and 'to have the same friends and enemies as the Roman people'. The later juristic tradition drew a distinction between this and the category of the *foedus aequum* ('equitable treaty'), which lacked such obligations (Cic. Arch. 6; Cic. Balb. 46; Dig. 49,15,7,1) [3]; [16]. The opposite term *foedus iniquum* ('inequitable treaty'), frequently used in modern scholarship, is not reliably attested in the ancient sources. Personal rights of the *socii* also varied (cf. e.g. Diod. Sic. 37,15,2 on Samnite communities that possessed the right of marriage with Roman men or women).

F. ROMAN REPUBLIC, 3RD CENT.–1ST CENT. BC

During the middle Republican period that ended with the Social War (91–87 BC) and the granting of Roman citizenship to citizens of Italic communities south of the Po, the *formula togatorum* ('register of those who wear the toga') indicates that the Italic *socii* ('allies') [9.545–548]; [21.57–85]; [2] probably provided up to two thirds of the Roman fighting force (Pol. 2,23f.; App. Pun. 8; Vell. Pat. 2,15) [9.677–686]; [21.148–173]. Some of the allies (the *socii navales*) provided ships for the fleet and made financial contributions instead of (or in addition to) army troops [21.105–117]. The Italic allies were entitled to a portion of the spoils of war. Moreover, with few exceptions and unlike the *stipendiarii* ('those serving for pay') of the provinces, they did not pay Roman taxes. But the spoils from the growing empire beyond the Mediterranean were not divided up in this way. The abolition of direct personal taxation in Rome itself (167 BC) was not imitated by the Italic confederates, because they needed to fund their respective military contributions.

Rome probably began to negotiate alliance treaties with communities outside Italy as early as the middle of the 3rd century BC (SEG 41, 545: mention of an early treaty with Pharos in Illyria; Cic. Verr. 2,3,13; 2,5,49–51; 2,5,56; 2,5,133: *civitates foederatae*, 'allied polities' in Sicily) as part of its process of expansion. Complementing the textual evidence for this are epigraphic sources from the Greek east, ranging in date from the treaty concluded in Aetolia in 211 BC (StV III 536) to the treaty with Mytilene around 25 BC (Sherk 73). The treaties with Maronea (167 BC; IThrakAig. 168; SEG 35, 823), Astypalaea (105 BC, Sherk 16B) and the Lycaean League (46 BC; SEG 55, 1452) are preserved largely intact [18.13–53, 731–751]; [35.67–74]. Although the *civitates foederatae* constituted a more privileged category of communities under Roman rule, their treaty conditions varied considerably, as did those in Italy. With regard to military terms, however, there was relative uniformity. In addition to mutual support in case of attack, these terms might require preventing a hostile third-party from crossing one's territory or taking measures against the smuggling of military supplies and mercenaries. Even towards the end of the Republic period, Rome was still relying on local fighting forces in many provinces (cf. [29] on the example of Sicily). Its dependence on local elites for provincial administration and tax collection lasted into the Imperial period. Not all communities with their own *foedera* ('treaties') were particularly important (Epidaurus: IG IV² 1 63; Thyrrheum in Acarnania: Syll.³ 732). On the other hand, a considerable number of communities were simply made Roman *socii* ('allies') by a declaration of the Senate, without the conclusion of a treaty. This could even happen to kings, upon whom the title *amicus et socius populi Romani* ('friend and ally of the Roman people') was bestowed (e.g. Ariovistus in 59 BC: Caes. B Gall. 1,43,4; Cass. Dio 38,34,3). As far as the Romans at least were concerned, this also meant acceptance of Roman supremacy. Even so, both categories were considered 'free polities' (*civitates liberae*). It is confusing for the modern observer that Roman usage also applied the term *socii* to dependent provincial communities.

G. IMPERIAL PERIOD

During the Imperial period, the right to conclude alliance treaties on behalf of Rome effectively became reserved for the emperor and his representatives (R. Gest. div. Aug. 26,4; ILp 244, ll. 1f.), although Augustus and his immediate successors continued to pay lip service to Republican traditions. Later legal texts were subject to far simpler ratification processes than under the Republic (Dig. 2,14,5; Gai. Inst. 3,94) [41.111–114]. The establishment of Roman standing armies on the Empire's external frontiers, as well as more orderly provincial organization, gradually eroded the autonomy of communities in the Empire, and no new treaties with communities are attested after the reign of Augustus. Old treaties of alliance remained valid in the legal sphere in their outdated form (e.g. Plin. Ep. 10,93; OGIS 530, ll. 2–4: Amisus in the Roman province of Bithynia et Pontus), and sometimes underwent antiquarian revival even in Italy (ILS 432; 5004). Within the Empire, however, they were no longer of any real military significance. Meanwhile, Rome continued to rely on auxiliary forces provided by frontier peoples and client kings (general principle: Suet. Aug. 47f.; Tac. Ann. 4,5). It is often unclear, however, whether such arrangements were regulated by formal treaties [27.54].

In the late Imperial period, the term *foederati* ('allied by treaty') came to be used mainly of the 'barbarian' tribes that provided troops to Rome for payment under the terms of their alliance provisions. These tribes sometimes settled within the territory of the Empire on the condition of *hospitalitas* ('being a guest'; i.e. billeting). The Roman military was increasingly reliant on such forces [22.416–437]. Until the 6th century, the title *foederatus* could denote a privileged relationship of equals with the imperial power (Procop. Pers. 3,11,3). For the earlier period, however, it has been shown that even in the 4th century, the term *foedera* ('treaties'), which Rome often initiated from a position of power after military victories, had no such connotation. No alliance conditions survive in detail from the late centuries of the Roman Empire. Alliances were often limited in time, and concluded on an individual basis with tribal chiefs [40]; [36.539–549]; [37]; [19.107–115]; [28]; [20].

☞ Diplomacy; Empire; Oath

BIBLIOGRAPHY

[1] E. BALTRUSCH, Symmachie und Spondai. Untersuchungen zum griechischen Völkerrecht der archaischen und klassischen Zeit (8.–5. Jahrhundert v.Chr.), 1994   [2] D.W. BARONOWSKI, The formula togatorum, in: Historia 33, 1984, 248–252   [3] D.W. BARONOWSKI, Sub umbra foederis aequi, in: Phoenix 44, 1990, 345–369   [4] H. BECK / P. FUNKE, An Introduction to Federalism in Greek Antiquity, in: H. BECK / P. FUNKE (eds.), Federalism in Greek Antiquity, 2015, 1–29   [5] H. BECK / P. FUNKE (eds.), Federalism in Greek Antiquity, 2015   [6] H. BECK / A. GANTER, Boiotia and the Boiotian Leagues, in: H. BECK / P. FUNKE (eds.), Federalism in Greek Antiquity, 2015, 132–157   [7] J. BELOCH, Der italische Bund unter Roms Hegemonie, 1880   [8] E. BICKERMAN, Remarques sur le droit des gens dans la Grèce classique, in: RIDA 4, 1950, 99–127   [9] P.A. BRUNT, Italian Manpower, 225 B.C.–A.D. 14, 1971   [10] P.A. BRUNT, The Hellenic League against Persia, in: P.A. BRUNT, Studies in Greek History and Thought, 1993, 47–81   [11] G.L. CAWKWELL, Cyrene to Chaeronea. Selected Essays on Ancient Greek History, 2011   [12] A. CHANIOTIS, Die Verträge zwischen kretischen Städten in der hellenistischen Zeit, 1996   [13] T. CORSTEN, Von Stamm zum Bund. Gründung und territoriale Organisation griechischer Bundesstaaten, 1999   [14] J.-C. COUVENHES, La symmachie comme pratique du droit international dans le mond grec, in: J.-C. COUVENHES (ed.), La symmachia comme pratique du droit international dans le monde grec d'Homère à l'époque hellénistique, 2016, 13–49   [15] W. DAHLHEIM, Struktur und Entwicklung des römischen Völkerrechts im dritten und zweiten Jahrhundert v.Chr., 1968   [16] L. DE LIBERO, 'Ut eosdem quos populus Romanus amicos atque hostes habeant'. Die Freund-Feind-Klausel in den Beziehungen Roms zu griechischen und italischen Staaten, in: Historia 46, 1997, 270–305   [17] G.E.M. DE STE. CROIX, The Origins of the Peloponnesian War, 1972   [18] E.S. GRUEN, The Hellenistic World and the Coming of Rome, 1984   [19] P. HEATHER, Goths and Romans 332–489, 1991   [20] P. HEATHER, The Late Roman Art of Client Management. Imperial Defence in the Fourth Century West, in: W. POHL et al. (eds.), The Transformation of Frontiers from Late Antiquity to the Carolingians, 2000, 15–68   [21] V. ILARI, Gli Italici nelle strutture militari romane, 1974   [22] P. KEHNE, 1000 Selected International Treaties of Graeco-Roman Antiquity, in: BNP Index Lists and Tables, 2010, 350–451   [23] J.E. LENDON, Thucydides and the 'Constitution' of the Peloponnesian League, in: GRBS 35, 1994, 159–177   [24] J. MA, Antiochos III and the Cities of Western Asia Minor, 1999   [25] E. MAKKIL, Creating a Common Polity. Religion, Economy, and Politics in the Making of the Greek Koinon, 2013   [26] G. PANESSA, Philiai. L'amicizia nelle relazioni interstatali dei Greci, vol. 1, 1999   [27] L.F. PITTS, Relations between Rome and the German 'Kings' on the Middle Danube in the First to Fourth Centuries AD, in: JRS 79, 1989, 45–58   [28] W. POHL (ed.), Kingdoms of the Empire. The Integration of Barbarians in Late Antiquity, 1997   [29] J.R.W. PRAG, Auxilia and Gymnasia. A Sicilian Model of Roman Imperialism, in: JRS 97, 2007, 68–100   [30] K. RAAFLAUB, Forerunners of Federal States. Collaboration and Integration through Alliance in Archaic and Classical Greece, in: H. BECK / P. FUNKE (eds.), Federalism in Greek Antiquity, 2015, 434–451   [31] J. REYNOLDS, Aphrodisias and Rome, 1982   [32] P.J. RHODES, A History of the Classical Greek World, 478–323 BC, 2006   [33] J. RICH, Treaties, Allies and the Roman Conquest of Italy, in: P. DE SOUZA / J. FRANCE (eds.), War and Peace in Ancient and Medieval History, 2008, 51–76   [34] K. SCHERBERICH, Koine Symmachia. Untersuchungen zum Hellenenbund Antigonos' III. Doson und Philipps V. (224–197 v.Chr.), 2009   [35] C. SCHULER, Ein Vertrag zwischen Rom und den Lykiern aus Tyberissos, in: C. SCHULER (ed.), Griechische Epigraphik in Lykien. Eine Zwischenbilanz, 2007, 51–79   [36] I. SHAHÎD, Byzantium and the Arabs in the Fourth Century, 1984   [37] H. SIVAN, On foederati, hospitalitas and the Settlement of the Goths in AD 418, in: AJPh 108, 1987, 759–772   [38] B. SMARCZYK, The Hellenic Leagues of Late Classical and Hellenistic Times and Their Place in the History of Greek Federalism, in: H. BECK / P. FUNKE (eds.), Federalism in Greek Antiquity, 2015, 452–470   [39] K. TAUSEND, Amphiktyonie und Symmachie. Formen zwischenstaatlicher Beziehungen im archaischen Griechenland (Historia Einzelschriften 73), 1992   [40] H. WOLFRAM, Zur Ansiedlung reichsangehöriger Föderaten, in: MIÖG 91, 1983, 5–35   [41] K.-H. ZIEGLER, Die Völkerrecht der römischen Republik, in: ANRW I.2, 1972, 68–114.

GEORGY KANTOR

Armament

A. Greek
B. Roman

A. GREEK

A.1. Attack weapons
A.2. Protective armour
A.3. Lightly armed infantry
A.4. Macedonia and the Hellenistic kingdoms

The Greek battlefield was dominated by the hoplites. The precise date at which hoplite tactics emerged is a matter of debate. At all events, the term – which modern scholarship understands as meaning heavily armed infantry, arranged in rank and file generally at least eight ranks deep, and armed with the hoplite shield and javelin – is a modern construct, as is the term → phalanx.

A.1. Attack weapons

The hoplite's main offensive weapon was his spear (*doru*). Its shaft, made of ash, was more than two metres long, and its forward tip was usually iron, while the sharp rear tip (*sauroter*) was bronze. It appears that the hoplite was able to use the spear with either an overhand or an underhand grip. His most important defensive weapon was a round shield (*aspis*), 80 cm in diameter (sometimes called the 'Argive shield'). This was made of wooden elements, which were glued together before the assembly was hollowed out on the lathe to give it a dished shape. Originally, the *aspis* had a bronze rim, but from about 510 BC onwards, its entire exterior surface was covered with a thin bronze sheet. It had two grips: the *porpax*, for the forearm, and the *antilabe* at the edge for the hand.

The cavalry used a larger array of spears as their main weapons. The cavalry spear resembled that of the hoplites, with its small, leaf-shaped tip and its *sauroter* ('rear tip'). It was generally used in conjunction with a pair of javelins. During the 4th century, the *palton*, a light spear with a cherrywood tip adopted from the Persians, came into ever wider use. *Palta*, used in pairs, served as fighting and throwing weapons. The *xyston* ('spear with polished shaft') appeared in the late 4th century, and throughout the Hellenistic period, it remained the most widely used cavalry spear. Its shaft was also made of wild cherrywood, but rather than a metal shoe at the end, it had a second spear tip.

The sword was a secondary weapon for foot soldiers and cavalrymen alike. The most widely used sword type had a cruciform grip and a straight, double-edged, leaf-shaped blade tapering towards the tip. A second type was the single-edged sabre with a curved blade. The rear of this blade was curved forward, and most of the weapon's weight was near the tip, the concave side forming the cutting edge. During the Hellenistic period, sabres of this type with grips in animal shapes (usually birds) were manufactured for issue to units of mounted guards. A third type of sword resembled the medieval falchion (*fauchon*). The rear of its heavy, single-edged blade could be either flat or slightly concave. The blade had a pronounced convex curve and broadened markedly towards the tip. These last two sword types came into use in the late 6th century, and may have been of Near Eastern ancestry. During the Hellenistic period, foot soldiers fighting in the tight formation of the phalanx had space only to use a dagger.

A.2. Protective armour

The helmet was the second most important piece of defensive equipment. Assorted helmets very similar to one another are often furnished with a spectrum of deceptive geographical names, usually in reference to the region in which they were first discovered. Open helmets played an increasing role from the 5th and 4th centuries onwards. The only geographical descriptors possibly used by the Greeks themselves were Corinthian and Boeotian (in conjunction with *pilos*, 'helmet'). The cavalry of the 4th century preferred open helmets, particularly of the Boeotian type. The chronological typology established for the evolution of Greek helmets fails for the Hellenistic period, as particular classes of troops increasingly began to use their own types of helmets. This development is related to the growing tendency for authorities to issue military → equipment, replacing the tradition of private acquisition.

At first, hoplites were equipped with a cuirass with a bell-shaped lip (German *Glockenpanzer*, 'bell armour') running around the bottom to deflect spear thrusts at the upper thighs. This cuirass was decorated with rudimentary anatomical details. This developed organically into the muscle cuirass, in which the front and rear bronze plates were modelled in imitation of the musculature of the human torso. The composite cuirass, which appeared in the first half of the 6th century, was made of assorted materials, usually with iron or bronze plates or scales that were often covered with leather or stiffened linen to prevent rust. The first iron armour appeared around the middle of the 4th century, along with chainmail, a Celtic invention, in the wake of the Galatian invasions.

The flanks were protected by a double layer of flaps or straps (*pteruges*, 'wings'), the second layer covering the gaps in the first. These were usually made of stiffened leather, sometimes also metal. Most had a coloured band and fringes on the lower ends. The *pteruges* formed an integral part of the design of the cuirass, and were affixed to its lower edge in the composite version.

Foot soldiers' legs were protected with greaves. Structures to protect the arms, thighs and ankles were developed in the third quarter of the 6th century to counter the threat from Persian archers. As the tactic of attacking at a run developed, protection was sacrificed in favour of mobility, and these defensive structures disappeared, except in the west. Greaves and body armour were generally abandoned for the sake of greater mobility in the first quarter of the 4th century. Cavalrymen never used leg protection, because it would have prevented the lower thigh from maintaining contact with the horse. Instead, riders wore boots.

A.3. Lightly armed infantry

The light infantry (*psiloi* or Hellenistic *euzonoi*) carried bows, catapults or javelins. Archers from Crete used bows produced there, while other formations imported Scythian armaments. Bronze spear tips appear to reflect this division: the larger Cretan type had a tongue for the shaft, a boss in the centre and a retrograde hook, whereas the smaller Scythian type had a socket and three wings. However, they were more diverse in materials as well as shapes during the Archaic period than later.

Slingers initially used stone projectiles. Lead seems to have started coming into use in the early 4th century. Cast elements sometimes bore pictorial symbols, typically a lightning flash. Slogans were also inscribed (e.g. 'Take that!'), as were names of kings or commanders, frequently abbreviated. The 'bolt-discharging engine' (*kestrosphendone*) had a considerable impact in the Third Macedonian War (171–168 BC).

The javelin was a weapon with a shorter range. Javelin throwers (*peltastai*) were sometimes equipped with the *pelte* ('light shield') to defend themselves; Aristotle defines this as a shield without a frame (Aristot. fr. 498 Rose). These shields were often made of non-metallic materials in the Archaic and Classical periods, and they had cutouts to improve the field of vision, giving them a sickle-like appearance. They were also decorated with an apotropaic eye (or eyes) – all these features are indicative of Thracian origins.

A.4. MACEDONIA AND THE HELLENISTIC KINGDOMS

The chief offensive weapon used by the Macedonian infantry in the phalanx of the Hellenistic period was the pike (*sarisa*, *sarissa*), distinguished by its great length. Polyaenus mentions *sarisai* 16 ells (7.92m) long (Polyaenus, Strat. 2,29,2), and Polybius reports that in his day, the *sarisa* is usually 14 ells (6.93m) in length, diminished from the original 16 (Pol. 18,29,1–3). Theophrastus declares that in his time (late 4th century), the longest *sarisai* are 12 ells long, corresponding to the height of a wild cherry tree (Theophr. Hist. pl. 3,12,1f.). The *sarisa* was made of ash (Stat. Theb. 7,269) and had a small iron point (Grattius, *Cynegeticon* 117–120).

Macedonian shields appeared in two sizes. The larger was about 74 cm across and heavily concave in shape. It was used by the Macedonian regiment of *chalkaspides* ('[soldiers] with brazen shields'). The second type was 66 cm across and almost flat. Asclepiodotus (*Taktika* 5,1) describes it when recommending the 'Macedonian bronze shield, 8 hands across and not excessively hollowed'. These Hellenistic *peltai* were covered with bronze on the front, and the forces carrying them were called *peltastai*, even though they fought in the phalanx formation. Grips differed from those on the hoplite shield. In 228 BC, Cleomenes III of Sparta equipped his phalanx 'in the Macedonian manner'. Each man held his *sarisa* in both hands and carried his shield on a band apparatus (*ochane*), not a handle (*porpax*) as on the hoplite shield (Plut., *Cleomenes* 11,2).

A third type of foot soldier emerged in the early 3rd century: the *thyreophoros*, named after the oval shield (*thyreos*, from the Greek *thyra*, 'door', probably a nickname inspired by its size). It was made of plywood covered with felt, and was fitted with a bronze rim and a shield buckle. According to one school of thought, Hellenistic armies adopted the *thyreos* in the wake of Pyrrhus' Italian campaigns (280–275) or following the Galatian invasions of Greece in 281 BC. It was certainly associated with the expansion of the (Celtic) La Tène cultures. From then on, the armies of the Greek mainland states were generally equipped as *peltastai* (in the Hellenistic sense of the term) or *thyreophoroi*. It was around this time that the Greek and Macedonian cavalry also first began to use shields.

☞ Equipment

BIBLIOGRAPHY
[1] H. BAITINGER, Die Angriffswaffen aus Olympia (Olympische Forschungen 29), 2001   [2] P. DINTSIS, Hellenistische Helme, 1986   [3] E. Jarva, Archaiologia on Archaic Greek Body Armour, 1995   [4] A. SCHWARTZ, Reinstating the Hoplite. Arms, Armour and Phalanx Fighting in Archaic and Classical Greece, 2009   [5] N.V. SEKUNDA, Military Forces. A. Land Forces, in: P. Sabin et al. (eds.), The Cambridge History of Greek and Roman Warfare, vol. 1, 2007, 325–357   [6] N.V. SEKUNDA, The Antigonid Army, 2013   [7] A. SNODGRASS, Early Greek Armour and Weapons, 1964   [8] A. SNODGRASS, Arms and Armour of the Greeks, 1967.

NICHOLAS SEKUNDA

B. ROMAN

B.1. Preliminary remarks and source survey
B.2. Offensive weapons
B.3. Defensive weapons

B.1. PRELIMINARY REMARKS AND SOURCE SURVEY

A distinction is made in Roman military armament between offensive and defensive weapons. Three main types of sources are available [5.18–20]; [2.1–47]. First and foremost are the literary and epigraphic testimonies that record the purpose and use of Roman armaments. Secondly, information is available through the study of pictorial sources, which may be categorized as official and private representations. One example of an official monument is the Trajan Column in Rome [16]; [9.46–48], while private monuments include soldiers' gravestones (e.g. [20]). A third type of source, original finds (*militaria*), is the most important type of source for reconstructing Roman armaments.

B.2. Offensive weapons

B.2.1. Long-range combat
B.2.2. Close combat

Offensive weapons fall into two categories: weapons for long-range combat (catapults, bows and arrows and pole weapons, *pilum*, *plumbata*) and weapons for close combat (swords and daggers).

B.2.1. Long-range combat

Roman catapults could hurl projectiles (*glandes*) up to 300 m. Projectiles were usually made of lead (40–70 g) in the shape of a double cone or an acorn. They were often inscribed with lettering, for instance denoting an army unit. Catapults were used from the Republican period to Late Antiquity. Auxiliary units called *funditores* ('hurlers' or 'slingers'), from specific regions (e.g. the Balearics), are attested as using such weapons in the late Republican and early Imperial periods [9.202f.]; [10]; [18]; [6.209–211].

The best-known bow design was the reflex composite bow, which was made of various organic materials (e.g. bones, horn, sinews) glued together for increased elasticity. Such bows could fire feathered wooden arrows with iron tips (the most familiar being three-winged) distances up to 200 m. All troop types used bows and arrows from the Republican period until Late Antiquity, but specialist units called *sagittarii* ('archers') are also attested [5.29f.]; [4]; [6.211–213].

Pole weapons essentially comprised a metal tip (usually iron), a wooden shaft and a metal shoe. They were used throughout Roman history, mainly by auxiliary units, as throwing weapons in long-range combat (spear) or as thrusting weapons in close combat (lance). Scholars have made many attempts to establish a typology of these widespread weapons according to the designs of their tips, but as yet without satisfactory results [2.53f., 76–78, 151–154]; [6.169–171]; [15].

The *pilum* is one of the best-known weapons of the Roman army. It consisted of an iron tip on a long, flexible shank made of untempered iron, fitted to a wooden shaft via a tongue or sleeve mounting. The shaft in turn fitted into an iron sleeve shoe. The total length was approximately 1.5–2 m. The *pilum* was mainly used by legionaries, and it amassed considerable penetrative power when thrown (range approx. 25–30 m). It was probably an Italic invention, and its heyday in use lasted from the Republican period to the middle Imperial period, although refined versions of the *pilum* are still found dating to Late Antiquity [3]; [5.25f.]; [6.166–169]; [9.197–200].

The *plumbata* was a throwing spear with a double-winged tip and a lead sleeve around the shaft. It was used in Late Antiquity by infantry, who threw these weapons by hand. The *plumbata* also goes by the name *mattiobarbulus* [2.200–202]; [6.237]; [17].

B.2.2. Close combat

The sword is probably the best-known Roman weapon alongside the *pilum*. A distinction can be made, for the Republican and early/middle Imperial periods, between the short sword (*gladius*, 35/40–60 cm) for the infantry (especially legionaries) and the long sword (*spatha*, ≥ 60 cm) for the auxiliaries (especially mounted). It seems that only long swords continued in use after the middle of the 3rd century. Literary references to *semispathae* ('half swords') are difficult to corroborate through archaeology.

The Republican short sword (*gladius hispaniensis*) had definite Iberian and possible Italic origins. In the Augustan period, it was superseded by the Mainz type of *gladius* (broad, curved blade, up to 60 cm long; cf. fig. 1). The more standardized Pompeii-type *gladius* (with parallel blade edges and a maximum length of 50 cm) emerged by the mid-1st century AD at the latest, and became the regular form of short sword until the 2nd century. The Republican long sword may have been identical to the long sword of Celtic origin (Fontillet-Nauportus type). These forms began to be superseded by the new standard type (Newstead type) in the decades around the mid-1st century AD; only its greater length (≥ 70 cm) distinguished it from the Pompeii type. The long swords used by all classes of troops in the 2nd and 3rd centuries were either of the Straubing-Nydam type, with narrow, tapering blades, or the Lauriacum-Hromówka type, with broad, parallel blades and short tips. During Late Antiquity, long swords of the Illerup-Wyhl (long, narrow blades) and Osterburken-Kemathen types (heavy, broad blades) came into use, and these blurred into early medieval forms.

In general, foot soldiers wore their sword on their belt on the right side (centurions on the left side), and cavalrymen wore their sword on the left side. From at least the 2nd century onwards, it became usual to affix the sword to a separate shoulder strap (the *balteus*; → Equipment B.) [2.54–56, 78–83, 130–134, 154–163, 202–205]; [5.30–32]; [9.177–193]; [11]; [12].

In addition to the sword, the other melee weapon used by the infantry of the Roman army was the dagger (*pugio*). However, it seems to have been employed only rarely in battle. This weapon type can be derived from Iberian antecedents, and it appears to have become part of a Roman soldier's standard equipment around the time of Caesar. Late Republican daggers were kept in a simple, minimally decorated frame sheath and had either a two-disc pommel or one with a cruciform end (total length 15–28 cm). Daggers of the were kept in undecorated frame sheaths (Künzing type). It is possible that these long daggers served as replacements for the short swords that fell out of use from the 2nd century onwards (see above). Daggers were no longer in use in Late Antiquity [5.34–36]; [6.163–166]; [9.193–196].

B.3. Defensive weapons

B.3.1. Helmets
B.3.2. Shields
B.3.3. Body armour
B.3.4. Arm and leg protectors

The defensive weaponry of the Roman army, that is, armament for protection of the person, comprised helmets, shields, body armour (muscle armour, mail armour, scale armour, segmented armour) and arm and leg protectors.

B.3.1. Helmets

The helmet (*cassis*) was a key piece of the Roman soldier's equipment from the earliest times. Its design can be traced back to Italic (bronze) and Celtic (iron) helmet types. The best account of the further development and typology of the helmet has been provided by continental (French and German) scholarship. The only Roman helmets known from the Republican period are those of the infantry. Middle and late Republican helmets are of the Montefortino type, made of bronze with a fixed central knob. The Coolus-Mannheim type (bronze with smooth cap) also arose in the Caesarean period. The direct descendant of the Montefortino type was the Hagenau type of the Augustan period, made of bronze with neckguard, cheek pieces and a fixed central knob. This was used by the legionary infantry until the late 1st century AD. The iron Weisenau type of helmet also developed in the Augustan period based on late Celtic antecedents (cf. fig. 2). This helmet, which until the mid-1st century was worn by all troop classes, and thereafter until the late 2nd century was worn by the infantry alone, exhibits numerous variants (e.g. entirely bronze, or decorated with bands around the cap). From the 3rd century onwards, it was replaced by the Niederbieber type (iron or bronze forms), which had much wider cheek pieces and crossed protective reinforcements on the cap.

Special iron helmets for cavalry began coming into use in the mid-1st century. The bowls of these helmets were designed to resemble coiffures (real hair or made from a separate bronze plate). Replacing these helmet forms from the 2nd century onwards were richly decorated bronze cavalry helmets of pseudo-Attic and pseudo-Corinthian types. Besides the helmets so far described, which were undoubtedly intended for use in

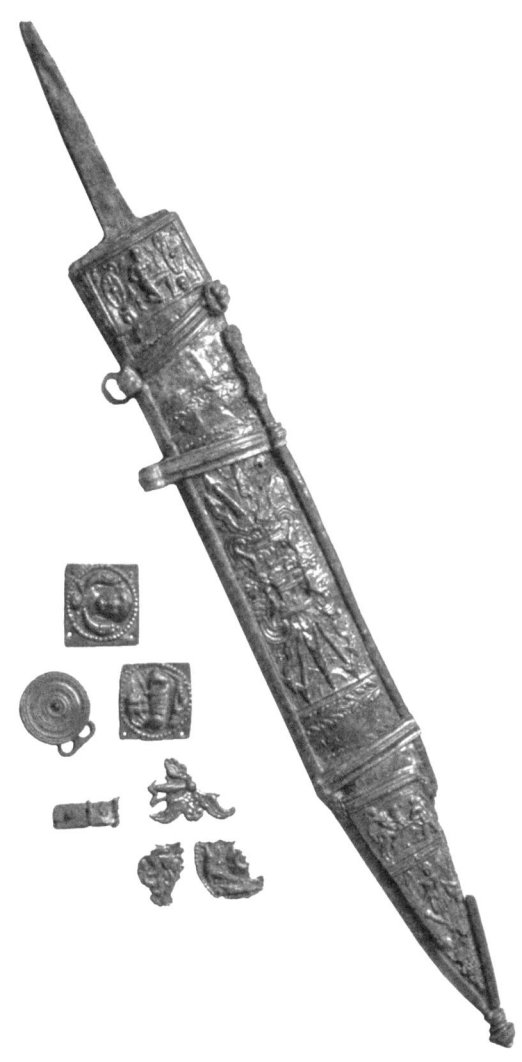

Fig. 1: Mainz-type *gladius*, in its sheath, with corresponding belt (mid-1st cent. AD, from a ditch at the legionary camp of Vindonissa, modern Windisch, Switzerland). Taken together, the reliefs on the sheath (prisoners among trophies; Jupiter's thunderbolt; cavalry battle; tropaeum) and belt attachments (Tiberius above cornucopia; Lupa with the twins; animal hunt; Jupiter's thunderbolt; lotus ornamentation) can be read as a complete programme of imperial ideology: 'with the gods for emperor and Rome'.

early Imperial period (total length 25–35cm) were usually kept in sheaths made of two plates, joined with riveted iron mountings and richly decorated. German-language scholarship distinguishes between the older Mainz type with a broader blade shape and a sheath made of two iron plates, and the later Vindonissa type with a narrow blade and a wooden sheath with an iron plate on the front. English-language scholarship, on the other hand, divides 1st-century daggers into Types A, B and C. From the mid-2nd century onwards, daggers steadily grew in size (28–40 cm), and they

Fig. 2: Iron helmet of the Weisenau type (mid-1st century AD, from the legionary camp at Vindonissa, modern Windisch, Switzerland). This helmet displays all the characteristic Weisenau elements (helmet plume holder; bowl with 'eyebrows'; neck rib and neckguard; ear cutouts; cutout cheek pieces; non-ferrous decorative fittings), and can be regarded as exemplary of the type.

battle, face-mask helmets began to appear from the Augustan period onwards (e.g. Kalkriese). Although these may have been usable in combat in the 1st century, they were surely used only in parades and tournaments from the 2nd century onwards. 'Alexander mask' helmets and mask helmets of Near Eastern type are also known.

Entirely new helmet designs for both infantry and cavalry were introduced by the time of the Tetrarchy at the latest. The antecedents for these types lay in the Sassanid territories of the east. These were iron comb helmets in several parts, with a bowl in two halves, a noseguard and an attached neckguard. The more simply designed comb helmets of the Dunapentele-Intercisa type may have been intended for foot soldiers, and the more lavishly decorated Deurne-Berkasovo type for the cavalry. Appearing at the very end of the history of Roman helmets were the conical *spangenhelm* segmented helmets that were in use from the 4th/5th centuries onwards in a tradition that merged seamlessly into the helmet forms of the Early Middle Ages [7]; [8]; [1.140–162, 205–214].

B.3.2. SHIELDS

Roman soldiers' shields were generally made either of several curved staves of wood or several layers of plywood. The basic composition had a covering of multiple layers of rawhide, leather and felt or fabric. The edges were protected with bronze rims. The shield front was often painted or decorated with metal plate designs (e.g. thunderbolts). There was a grip, usually horizontal, in the middle of the inside of the shield, and this was protected on the exterior by a shield boss in iron or bronze. When not in use, the shield was protected from the weather in a leather case (*tegimentum*), which sometimes bore sewn unit insignia.

Roman shields of the Republican period were mostly inspired by Celtic antecedents, with Germanic influences also felt from the Imperial period onwards. Beginning in the middle Republican period, legions used an elliptical, convex shield almost the height of a man (*scutum*), which was made of glued sheets of wood with a spindle-shaped boss. Under the Principate, this was gradually superseded by a convex rectangular shield with a round shield boss, sometimes set on a square iron plate. This shield form remained the standard design until the 3rd century. Elliptical forms with round bosses became the norm from the 3rd century onwards and remained in use until Late Antiquity. At all periods, auxiliaries' shields could be either rectangular, hexagonal, oval or round. These consisted of bentwood spars covered in leather, with metal rims and (usually) round bosses. Finally, there were also special shields called *parma*, small in size and round, which were mainly used by standard-bearers [2.61–63, 91–94, 137–139, 179–182, 216–218]; [14].

B.3.3. BODY ARMOUR

With few exceptions (e.g. scouts (*exploratores*)), all Roman soldiers probably owned body armour. The various designs are briefly presented below. Soldiers probably wore the *subarmalis*, a padded fabric or felt undergarment, under all forms of armour, to dampen blows and prevent the armour from chafing the skin [1.98]; [9.163].

The breastplate (*pectorale*) was used in the early to middle Republican period, and comprised a metal plate (bronze?) that was worn around the chest to protect the most important internal organs [1.99]; [2.63–65].

Muscle armour (*thorax*) in chased bronze was reserved for those of officer rank, including the emperor. This armour type is known only from a very few original finds. It was based on Hellenistic and Etruscan antecedents, and was worn throughout the entire Roman era from the middle Republic to Late Antiquity [1.103f.]; [9.164].

Mail armour (*lorica hamata*) or mail shirts, made of forged and riveted rows of iron rings, was adopted from Celtic antecedents, and from the late Republican period onwards it was the most widespread form of armour used by Roman soldiers of all unit classes. The mail armour of the early Imperial period was worn with doubled shoulder protection, held together over the chest with a double hook. The construction became simplified from the 2nd century onwards, and the mail shirt was worn without the extra shoulder piece. One or two non-ferrous flaps served to fasten the front of the shirt. Mail armour was still used in Late Antiquity [1.99f.]; [5.49]; [9.165].

Scale armour (*lorica squamata*) originated in the Near East and seems only to have come into use among the Roman legions in the mid-1st century AD. It consisted of innumerable metal scales that were threaded in rows on an organic underlay. Scale armour was used by all troop types until Late Antiquity [1.100f.]; [5.49f.]; [9.169f.].

Segmented armour (*lorica segmentata*), made of several iron segments connected together but permitting movement, was an original Roman invention and was probably only worn by the (legionary) infantry. It first appeared during the Augustan period. The contemporaneous Kalkriese type is distinguished primarily by the design of the bronze elements. The Corbridge type, first developed in the Claudian period, was identified on the basis of a mass archaeological find at Corbridge, Northumberland, and is one of the best-known forms of armour used by Roman soldiers. The Newstead type superseded it in the mid-2nd century, characterized by special fastening hooks for the armour plates. Scholars have recently identified a further Alba Iulia type for the 3rd century, although as yet it is known only from a limestone statue. No segmented armour is known to survive from Late Antiquity [1.102f.]; [5.45–48]; [9.166–169].

Another form of armour was lamellar armour, made of leather or metal strips sewn together longitudinally. This armour type is known only from the Near East. It seems never really to have been adopted as Roman army equipment.

There are also rare cases of 'hybrid armour' types: combinations of scale armour with a mail shirt or segmented shoulder armour with a mail shirt. These combinations may only have been used in exceptional instances. There has been speculation about the existence of leather armour until very recently, but this can now be ruled out [1.101f., 104]; [9.163f., 170f.].

B.3.4. ARM AND LEG PROTECTORS

Original finds of solid metal greaves are very rare. They were most likely worn by legionaries and perhaps also by cavalrymen. An arm guard (*manica*) was constructed from several iron elements that moved relative to one another. It was probably worn as an accessory to segmented armour from the 1st century AD onwards [1.104f.]; [9.171f.].

☞ **Equipment**

BIBLIOGRAPHY

[1] M.C. BISHOP, Body Armor, in: Y. LE BOHEC et al. (eds.), The Encyclopedia of the Roman Army, vol. 1, 2015, 98–106 [2] M.C. BISHOP / J.C.N. COULSTON, Roman Military Equipment. From the Punic Wars to the Fall of Rome, ^{2}2006 [3] A. BONGARTZ, pilum, in: Y. LE BOHEC et al. (eds.), The Encyclopedia of the Roman Army, vol. 2, 2015, 746–750 [4] J. COULSTON, Bow, in: Y. LE BOHEC et al. (eds.), The Encyclopedia of the Roman Army, vol. 1, 2015, 113–114 [5] E. DESCHLER-ERB et al., Römische Militärausrüstung aus Kastell und Vicus von Asciburgium (Funde aus Asciburgium 17), 2012 [6] M. FEUGÈRE, Les armes des Romains, 1993 [7] M. FEUGÈRE, Casques antiques, 1994 [8] M. FEUGÈRE, Helmet, in: Y. LE BOHEC et al. (eds.), The Encyclopedia of the Roman Army, vol. 2, 2015, 475–478 [9] T. FISCHER, Die Armee der Caesaren. Archäologie und Geschichte, 2012 [10] C. FLÜGEL, glandes, in: Y. LE BOHEC et al. (eds.), The Encyclopedia of the Roman Army, vol. 2, 2015, 443–445 [11] C. MIKS, Studien zur römischen Schwertbewaffnung, 2007 [12] C. MIKS, Sword, gladius, in: Y. LE BOHEC et al. (eds.), The Encyclopedia of the Roman Army, vol. 3, 2015, 948–970 [13] A. NABBEFELD, Römische Schilde. Studien zu Funden und bildlichen Überlieferungen vom Ende der Republik bis in die späte Kaiserzeit, 2008 [14] A. NABBEFELD, Shield, in: Y. LE BOHEC et al. (eds.), The Encyclopedia of the Roman Army, vol. 3, 2015, 872–880 [15] L. PERNET, Spear, in: Y. LE BOHEC et al. (eds.), The Encyclopedia of the Roman Army, vol. 3, 2015, 911–915 [16] D. RICHTER, Das römische Heer auf der Trajanssäule, 2004 [17] R. VERMAAT, plumbatae, in: Y. LE BOHEC et al. (eds.), The Encyclopedia of the Roman Army, vol. 2, 2015, 754–757 [18] T. VÖLLING, Funditores im römischen Heer, in: Saalburg Jahrbuch 45, 1990, 24–58 [19] T. VÖLLING, Plumbata – Mattiobarbulus. Bemerkungen zu einem Waffenfund aus Olympia, in: Archäologischer Anzeiger, 1991, 287–298 [20] M. WIELAND, Vom Grabstein zum Pflasterstein. Eine neue Soldatengrabstele mit bildlicher Darstellung von der Hohe Straße in Köln, in: H.-J. SCHALLES / A.W. BUSCH (eds.), Waffen in Aktion. Akten der 16. Internationalen Roman Military Equipment Conference (ROMEC) (Xantener Berichte 16), 2009, 269–281.

ECKHARD DESCHLER-ERB

Army

A. Greek
B. Hellenistic period
C. Roman
D. Late Antiquity

A. Greek

A.1. Warfare in the Bronze Age
A.2. The catastrophe
A.3. The 'Dark Ages'
A.4. Rise of the hoplites
A.5. The Classical period
A.6. The Macedonian phalanx

Throughout its long history, from the 2nd millennium BC to the final conquest of the Hellenistic world by Rome in the 2nd century, the Greek army underwent a series of fundamental innovations and revolutions. The early stages of this development must be traced through archaeological finds and limited written sources. Even so, the material does permit an outline reconstruction of the history of this process.

A.1. Warfare in the Bronze Age

The first military conflicts of proto-Greek armies in the Middle Bronze Age (c. 2000–1600 BC) involved clashes between infantry armies of archers, and lancers fighting in close formation. The archers thinned the ranks of the enemy, and infantry battles unfolded readily, with phases of single combat. → Chariots, where used, were ponderous ceremonial vehicles fitted with disc wheels and drawn by slow draught animals that were ill-suited to warfare. Carts may also have been used in 'mopping up' operations after the main battle.

The first great revolution in ancient warfare came in the 17th century BC, with the introduction of war horses, spoked wheels and light, two-wheeled war chariots that carried archers armed with composite bows. These fast-moving shooting platforms enabled archers to operate with impunity outside the range of enemy shooters. This left the archers free to incapacitate enemy infantry. By around 1600 BC, war chariots were dominating the battlefields of the Near East. Pharaoh Thutmosis III, for instance, was able to deploy a thousand or more chariots in his victory at Megiddo in 1456. In the 13th century, the Hittite King Muwattalli II turned the tables, sending about 3,500 war chariots to his confrontation with Ramesses II at Qadesh. Although the Mycenaean palace states were never able to send chariots into battle on quite the scale of the Hittites or Egyptians, the societies that gave birth to the armies of Greece still possessed the same elements as the great kingdoms: a powerful and centralized monarchy with wealthy, well organized and tightly controlled bureaucracies. Linear B documents from Pylos suggest that the men in the imperial chariot corps of the king (*wanax*) and the charioteers answerable to a local 'city chief' (*basileus*) formed loyal aristocracies. Equipped with this new weapon, the Greek armies now assigned lesser roles to their infantries: pursuing enemies and besieging and attacking cities.

A.2. The catastrophe

A number of developments put an end to Bronze-Age civilization across Greece and much of the Near East. The most radical change was related to the introduction of offensive infantry formations, which were able to counter the king's chariot attacks. This became possible thanks to the invention of the first true slash-and-thrust sword, which superseded the composite bow as the primary weapon of the Late Bronze Age (1600–1150). The Naue II sword type signals the historic change from chariot to infantry warfare in the late 13th and early 12th centuries, the period known as 'the catastrophe', which gave rise to armoured foot soldiers. Various types of armour reflect this transition: chest and back armour, greaves, small round shields and short spears all indicate the new importance of close combat. The infantry no longer relied on large shields as protection against projectiles. The warrior vase and stela from Mycenae, for example, show non-professional Mycenaean infantry around 1200 in possession of standard equipment and assuming a relatively tight formation in order to fight the enemy at close quarters with a close combat weapon [11.190]. Apparently this is how the monarchies reacted to the attacks and devastation brought by infantry armies that were roaming the eastern Mediterranean, such as the assaults made by the 'Sea Peoples' that were repelled by Ramesses III in Egypt around 1179. The royal army seems to have been composed more of fighters drawn from less civilized regions than of bondsmen conscripted from palace estates.

A.3. The 'Dark Ages'

The years 1150–700 – the period beginning with the 'catastrophe' and leading through the 'Dark Ages' to the Geometric period – marked the era of long-range combat for Greek armies. The early phase of this era was characterized by skirmishers armed with swords and spears replacing war chariots. There was no continuity of body armour from the Late Bronze Age to the Dark Ages, probably as a result of the poverty of this period. The most important change came with the transition from bronze to iron weapons in the Proto-Geometric (1050–900) and Geometric periods (900–700). The simple spear remained in use without interruption, but iron points came into use from 1000 BC onwards. The round shield with metal boss was also in continuous use. Sub-Mycenaean and Proto-Geometric warriors armed with round shields and spears, and later with iron swords, engaged in a type of warfare that was highly mobile and focused on single combat. There was no need for a throwing spear, but individual skirmishers and forward detachments might be brought to and from the battlefield in a horsedrawn cart. Homer's portrayal of the battles of heroic figures such as Achilles, Hector and Ajax may reflect memories of this obscure period of Greek warfare.

The javelin came into general use during the Geometric period, although fighters in the 9th century still kept the spear as a thrusting weapon. Kings, by now in a much less wealthy and powerful position than before, relied on foot soldiers as the key offensive element of their armies. These soldiers were lightly armed and loosely organized. In place of chariots, the aristocracy now rode on horseback as cavalry. This mobile form of warfare, operating across great distances, employed short throwing spears as the primary weapon alongside swords.

A.4. RISE OF THE HOPLITES

The revolution that took place in the late 8th and early 7th centuries BC was driven by the most noteworthy development in the entire history of the Greek military: the rise of the hoplite → phalanx. The invention of the highest importance for this development was that of the double-gripped concave shield (*aspis*), one metre in diameter, with a central forearm grip (*porpax*) and a hand grip (*antilabe*). The helmet of 'Corinthian style', hammered from a single bronze plate, was a masterly accomplishment of Greek metallurgy. It provided unprecedented protection to the head and face, although it did limit its wearer's field of view. These new armour elements – combined with existing elements of armament and tactics, such as the simple spear and a specific variant of mass combat – triggered developments that have long been associated with the rise of the *polis*. The *aspis* and the Corinthian helmet only make sense in the context of mass combat, where the protruding left side of a soldier's broad shield offers some lateral protection to the vulnerable right side of his neighbour. Effectiveness in battle now depended on a relatively fixed and rigidly organized style of combat that required every soldier to maintain his position in the battle array. The non-professional character of the citizen militia and the association between battle and agricultural labour distinguished the *polis* army from all preceding Greek armies. Most of its soldiers were small-scale farmers, but with sufficient resources at their disposal to afford their own equipment. For the first time now, there developed a general awareness that the fate of the community depended on each citizen's acceptance of his personal role in battle.

The egalitarian nature of hoplite warfare helped shape the social and political institutions of the *polis*. Non-noble peasant citizen soldiers fought shoulder to shoulder with their social superiors, and their contribution was equally important to the successful military defence of the *polis*. It was not long before these peasant citizen soldiers were demanding status in political matters comparable to their social superiors. Whether through the intervention of a tyrant or through direct concessions, the hoplites ultimately broke the aristocratic monopoly on high office that had characterized the politics and lawmaking of the early Greek republics. Indeed, the army turned the whole idea of *arete* around: from an emphasis on combat for individual honour and renown, to an ideal in which the individual subordinated his own glory to that of the *polis*.

A.5. THE CLASSICAL PERIOD

The first two centuries of *polis* warfare primarily consisted of clashes between hoplite armies of rival states fighting over contested frontier zones. The first conflicts may have included the war between Chalcis and Eretria over the Lelantine Plain (c. 710–650), and the major conflict between Sparta and Argos over the Thyreatic Plain, the whole of Cynuria and the island of Cythera in the south (c. 546 BC). Certainly, these wars developed into ritual battles, in which one *polis* marched its army across the other's border to fight for lands it had previously occupied. The defence of one's home territory and the injured collective pride of the *polis* motivated states to seek satisfaction in direct confrontation with the enemy army. During this early phase, as the Greek world evolved in isolation from the Near East, *polis* armies perfected the battle tactics of the heavy infantry. As a result, when Greek liberties and autonomy first came under threat from Persian aggression in the 5th century, Athens won a commanding victory at Marathon in 490 BC, and the Hellenic League defeated the Medians at Plataeae in 479. Indeed, so successful was the *polis* infantry against the greatest empire the world had ever seen that the Persians went on to recruit Greek mercenaries for their own wars whenever possible (Isoc. Or. 4,168). One striking example is the force of 10,000 soldiers under the command of the Spartan general Clearchus, who came to the aid of Cyrus the Younger against his brother Artaxerxes at Cunaxa in 401.

However, the Peloponnesian War (431–404) between Athens and Sparta changed the nature of Greek warfare, sending the status of the peasant citizen-soldier into decline. There were several reasons for this. For one thing, at the beginning of the Archidamian War (431–421), Pericles persuaded the Athenians to remain behind their city walls and refuse the Peloponnesian army's

Fig. 1: Frieze from the Monument of the Nereids at Xanthus, Lycia (relief, c. 400 BC; British Museum, London). This relief from the western pediment of a sculptural tomb in the shape of a Greek temple shows a row of hoplites besieging a city, while the defenders, not shown here, are attempting a counteroffensive to break the siege. This part of the frieze shows the attackers. They hold their broad shields by the *antilabe* on the rim, as they approach the fortification in close formation. The depiction suggests that hoplites were used in a wider range of settings in the Classical period – including situations far removed from the standard open infantry battle.

challenge to a decisive hoplite battle. Another dramatic change came with the steady professionalization of the Greek army, the use of mercenaries and the emergence of the *peltastai* ('light armed footsoldiers'), armed with a light shield and javelin. Armies also now began to fight during all seasons of the year, in a wide range of settings, under conditions that diminished the effectiveness of the traditional hoplite units. In 427, for instance, inhabitants of the scattered mountain villages of Aetolia succeeded in defeating the hoplite army of the Athenian general Demosthenes with their lightly armed soldiers trained in guerrilla tactics. Around 394, during the Corinthian War, the superior speed and manoeuvrability of his *peltastai* enabled the Athenian general Iphicrates to annihilate 600 Spartan hoplites (Diod. Sic.14,91,2f.). This shows how profoundly the character of warfare and the nature of the Greek army were changing during the 4th century. The hoplites' traditional aura of invincibility suffered perhaps its heaviest blow with the defeat of the Spartan army at Leuctra in 371. Here, the Theban generals Epaminondas (→ Generals of note, F.) and Pelopidas displayed their tactical brilliance by setting up their left wing at a depth of 50 shields and making use of a special corps of 300 elite hoplites, the Sacred Band (→ Elite troops; cf. fig. 1).

A.6. THE MACEDONIAN PHALANX
The changes in warfare heralded in the Peloponnesian War (→ Wars of note H.) also shaped the rise of the last of the great Greek armies: the Macedonian. Since the 7th century, members of noble families and clans (*hetairoi*) had provided the cavalry, the main wing of the Macedonian army. In the 5th century, Alexander I founded his realm's first heavy infantry (*pezetairoi*). However, it would require the political and military brilliance of Philip II (→ Generals of note, M.) to shape the peasants and herdsmen of the nation into the renowned Macedonian phalanx. The first task for Philip, who in his youth had completed his military studies while a hostage of Pelopidas in Thebes, was to establish a strong state with defined boundaries. Gold and silver from the mines of the Pangaeum mountains, recently acquired, enabled him to pay for the training of his infantry in the use of the *sarisa*, a pike 4–6 m in length, and the maintenance of a formation up to 16 ranks deep. He also increased his army's effectiveness by deploying *peltastai* ('light armed footsoldiers') and assorted lightly armed troops to protect the vulnerable flanks and rear of the phalanx. Unlike the hoplite phalanxes of the *polis*, which had been developed to defend frontier zones, Philip's phalanx was a professional army of conquest that fought all year round. The climax of his fight for hegemony in Greece came at Chaeronea in 338. There, he pulverized the Sacred Band before launching the decisive attack by *hetairoi* cavalry under the command of his son Alexander III (Polyaenus, Strat. 4,2,2), the future Alexander the Great.

The tactics that put an end to the liberties and autonomy of the *polis* on the plain of Chaeronea presaged Alexander the Great's triumph (→ Generals of note, B.) over the Persian Empire: the use of cavalry as the key offensive strike force, with the → phalanx in a supportive role tying up the enemy infantry. Alexander and his successors of the

Hellenistic period marked the return of the Greek army to the figure of the divine monarch as general. The professional Macedonian phalanx dominated the battlefields of the eastern Mediterranean until the Roman legions rose to global dominance in the 2nd century. The superior mobility of the Roman maniple and the skills of legionaries armed with the *gladius* ('sword') crushed the Greeks at Cynoscephalae in 197 and Pydna in 167.

☞ Armament; Cavalry; Conscription; Mercenaries; Society and army; State and army; Strategy

BIBLIOGRAPHY
[1] P.A. CARTLEDGE, The Birth of the Hoplite, in: P.A. CARTLEDGE, Spartan Reflections, 2001, 153–166 (first published as La nascita degli opliti e l'organizzazione militare, in: S. Settis (ed.), I Greci, vol. 2, 1996, 681–714) [2] R. DREWS, The End of the Bronze Age. Changes in Warfare and the Catastrophe ca. 1200 B.C., 1993 [3] P. DUCREY, Warfare in Ancient Greece, 1986 [4] P.A. GREENHALGH, Early Greek Warfare. Horsemen and Chariots in the Homeric and Archaic Ages, 1973 [5] V.D. HANSON, The Other Greeks. The Family Farm and the Agrarian Roots of Western Civilization, 1999 [6] V.D. HANSON, The Western Way of War, 2000 [7] D. KAGAN / G.F. VIGGIANO (eds.), Men of Bronze. Hoplite Warfare in Ancient Greece, 2013 [8] J. KROMAYER / G. VEITH, Heerwesen und Kriegführung der Griechen und Römer, 1928 [9] C. MANN, Militär und Kriegführung in der Antike, 2013 [10] W. RÜSTOW / H. KÖCHLY, Geschichte des Griechischen Kriegswesens von der Ältesten Zeit bis auf Pyrrhos, 1852 [11] A.M. SNODGRASS, Early Greek Armour and Weapons, 1964 [12] H. VAN WEES, Greek Warfare. Myths and Realities, 2004.

GREGORY F. VIGGIANO

B. HELLENISTIC PERIOD

B.1. Composition and structure
B.2. Use of unfree people for labour
B.3. Size and costs

All the armies of the Hellenistic kingdoms were descended from that of Alexander the Great (→ Generals of note, B.). Although Alexander's army was the model for the Diadochi, the geographical extent and peculiarities of their kingdoms, as well as their varying military traditions, caused them to develop differently. Moreover, unlike the Roman army, the Hellenistic armies had no system of fixed command and tactical division; they were very flexible in regard to composition, size and subdivision. Yet, three elements were common to all these armies. First, they were larger than the citizen armies of the Classical period (see above). Second, they employed a large proportion of professional soldiers (mercenaries and *klerouchoi*, 'those receiving land allotments') of highly diverse backgrounds. Third, they restored the phalanx to the dominant position in the battle array.

B.1. COMPOSITION AND STRUCTURE

B.1.1. Antigonids
B.1.2. Seleucids
B.1.3. Ptolemies

B.1.1. ANTIGONIDS
The Antigonid army was the most homogeneous of the Hellenistic armies, with its large proportion of Macedonian soldiers bound to the king by obligation of military service. Complementing these were confederates, mainly from Crete and the Balkans (Thracians, Illyrians, Paeonians), who were tied to the king by treaties of alliance, and mercenaries (mostly Cretan) who were recruited on contracts of long or short term. The latter two groups served mainly as specialists in long-range combat, as slingers, javelin throwers or archers, and they provided the manpower for the occupation of garrisons (IG XII 644; SEG 51, 640bis).

The army of Macedonians in compulsory service comprised a small nucleus of professional soldiers who formed the guard of infantry (*hypaspistai*, 'shieldbearers', later *argyraspides*, 'silver shieldbearers') and cavalry (*basilike ile*, 'royal guard'), the elite group of 5,000 *peltastai* ('light armed footsoldiers'; with the 2,000-strong *agema* detachment), recruited from across Macedonia, and the great majority of reservists recruited *ad hoc* on a territorial basis. The Macedonian cavalry bore the name *hetairoi* ('peers' or 'the noble class') from the time of Alexander the Great onwards (FGrH 72 F4). Serving with them were light cavalry (*prodromoi* or *sarisophoroi*; → Cavalry A.). The maximum size of the Macedonian cavalry in a general mobilization ran to 3,000 horsemen under Perseus at the Battle of Pydna in 168 BC (Liv. 42,51,10; Plut. *Aemilius Paullus* 13, here 4,000 horsemen). The phalanx was called the *pezetairoi* ('foot soldiers'), and sometimes numbered over 18,000 men. Little or nothing is known of the tactical units. The organization of the infantry (in descending order of size into *strategiai, chiliarchiai, speirai, tetrarchiai* and *lochoi*) is known from a military decree (→ Rank) of Amphipolis and a letter of Philip V (ISE II 114 and 110). The most important cavalry units were the *hipparchia, ile, lochos, tetrarchia* and *oulamos* [6.213–220]; [9.32–84]; [13].

It was Philip II who laid the foundations of the Antigonid navy (Generals of note M.). Citizens of several coastal cities, including Pydna, Amphipolis and Cassandrea, were required to serve as crew aboard ships, their assets probably being subject to a special census (Diod. Sic. 19,69,3; SEG 49, 722, Z. 11; Liv. 28,8,14; [9.27f.]).

B.1.2. SELEUCIDS
The Seleucid army comprised Greek-Macedonian military settlers (*katoikoi*) who occupied a plot of land (*kleros*), mercenaries (*misthophoroi*) and

allies (*symmachoi*) who fought in their own contingents (e.g. Cretans, Galatians, Cilicians, Cappadocians, Jews, Arabs), and indigenous subjects required to perform military service [1.190–200].

Military settlements established for strategic reasons are attested above all in Asia Minor (in Lydia, Mysia and Phrygia) and northern Syria. There is no evidence for them in eastern parts of the empire, such as Persis [4.158–166]; [5].

The phalanx, also known as the company of *pezetairoi* ('foot soldiers') or *sarisophoroi* ('pike bearers'), consisted of the shieldbearers – 'silver' (*argyraspides*), 'gold' (*chrysaspides*) and 'bronze' (*chalkaspides*) – and the *peltastai* ('light armed footsoldiers'). Of the tactical units of the phalanx, only two minor ones are known: *tagma* as the general term for a subdivision or mercenary unit (ISmyrna 573,46) and *semaiai* (Pol. 10,49,7), probably the smallest, numbering 16 men [2.66f.]. The cavalry comprised the royal guard (*basilike ile/hetairoi*) of Greek-Macedonian cavalry and the guard of Near Eastern horsemen (*agema*), each 1,000 men strong, as well as the 4,000–6,000 regular cavalry and (beginning in the reign of Antiochus III) cataphracts. The tactical units appear to correspond to those attested by the military authors (*chiliarchia*, *hipparchia*, *ile* and *oulamos*) [2.67–75]. The Seleucids also had specialist mounted units, such as the camel riders (→ Camels) (App. Syr. 34; Liv. 37,40,11) and Near Eastern archers (App. Syr. 32; Liv. 35,48,3).

Until soon after 162 BC, the Seleucids had a large number of Asian → elephants, which were used in almost all major battles. Seleucus I is said to have received about 500 animals from the Indian King Chandragupta (Str. 15,2,9; 16,2,10; Plut. *Alexander* 62), and his successors were able to obtain up to 150 more animals (Pol. 11,34,10–12: Antiochus III). After the Romans had the entire herd slaughtered (App. Syr. 46,239f.; Pol. 31,2,9–11), no new animals were obtained. Also peculiar to the Seleucid army were the chariots adopted from the Achaemenid army. Despite repeated mishaps, these continued to be regularly used until the Battle of Magnesia in 190/89 BC (Liv. 37,42,1) [2.75–84].

It appears that with the exception of Antiochus III, the Seleucids maintained no cohesive naval units in the Mediterranean. However, a permanent war fleet safeguarded Seleucid interests in the Persian Gulf (Ichara/Failaka; [1.197–199]; disagreeing to some extent [3.98–100]).

B.1.3. PTOLEMIES

The Ptolemaic army was a multiethnic entity that originally consisted mostly of Greek-Macedonian immigrants either serving as mercenaries (*misthophoroi*), mainly in garrisons within and outside Egypt, or settled in Egypt with a plot of land (*kleros*) as *klerouchoi* ('those receiving land allotments') or cavalry *katoikoi* ('settlers'). Depending on rank, cavalrymen received *kleroi* of 100 or 80 *arourai* (for members of numbered hipparchies) or 70 *arourai* (for members of ethnic hipparchies), while infantrymen received 25 or 30 *arourai*. Egyptian soldiers (*machimoi*) also served in the army from the outset, traditionally holding 5 *arourai* of land.

Virtually the only way of assessing Ptolemaic army units is through the officers who commanded them. The tactical cavalry units, in descending order of strength, were the *epitagma*, *telos*, *ephipparchia*, *hipparchia*, *epilarchia*, *ile* and *lochos*, and the infantry units were the *chiliarchia*, *pentakosiarchia*, *syntagma* and *taxis*. There were also elite units, such as the *agema* and the royal guard ('life guards', 'sabre bearers', etc.), and many other (specialist) units ([11.56–95] on the cavalry; [7.116–153]).

The Ptolemies made changes to their military organization in response to several internal Egyptian revolts and the invasion by Antiochus IV in 170–168 BC. First, they increased the intake of Egyptian soldiers into the newly installed garrisons in the Delta and in Middle and Upper Egypt, and into the *klerouchia* ('land allotments'), which had initially been dominated by Greek-Macedonian immigrants. Second, they instigated various reforms. Prior to the Battle of Rhaphia, new 'eponymous' officers were appointed (see → Rank A.; Pol. 5,64). In the late 3rd and early 2nd centuries BC, probably in the course of a streamlining of light and heavy cavalry, the ethnic hipparchies were abolished and incorporated into the numbered hipparchies. Regiments (*laarchiai*) were created for the *machimoi* between 204 and 194 BC, each commanded by a *laarches*, and the internal structure of the infantry was modified: the *chiliarchia* disappeared, four *syntagmata/semeia* replaced the *pentakosiarchia*, and they were further subdivided into two *hekatontarchiai*, each of two *pentakosiarchiai*. Finally, in the early 180s, an *epistrategos* was appointed with supreme military and civil authority over Upper Egypt ([11.69–71] (on the cavalry); [7]).

Ptolemy II (308–246 BC) had a fleet of more than 300 warships built (Ath. 5,203d), with the primary aims of establishing a thalassocracy in the Aegean and eastern Mediterranean and of securing the India trade. The king, and to some extent his wealthy friends, took responsibility for maintaining the fleet, which represented a major burden for the royal treasury (see below), even though crews were recruited from the lowest echelons of society, especially Egyptians [7.71–73]; [15.22–32].

Under the first four Ptolemies, the army also included about 70–100 elephants. All the animals were Asian at first, before African elephants were introduced under Ptolemy II [7.153–155].

B.2. Use of unfree people for labour

The use of unfree people (→ Slavery) as weapon assistants and retinue servants is attested for all the Hellenistic armies. Together with soldiers' families, this workforce comprised the baggage train, the *aposkeue*. Their primary function was as porters, caring items for soldiers and animals. The sources accordingly refer to them using terms such as *therapontes* ('squires'), *hypaspistai*, *hoplophoroi*, *skeuophoroi* ('weapon porters'), *hippokomoi* ('grooms') and *paides* ('servants'). As in all premodern armies, constant efforts were made to cut the numbers of the accompanying escort, and with it the supply train needing provisions (Frontin. Str. 4,1,6; SB XVI 12221) [10]; [16.88–112].

B.3. Size and costs

The sizes and compositions of the various armies varied greatly, and with them the associated costs, so that only a partial impression of these is available or can be estimated. In peacetime, the Seleucid army had a total strength of 80,000–90,000 men: about 70,000–80,000 soldiers (c. 35,000 regular soldiers, 15,000 mercenaries and 20,000–30,000 garrison troops) and about 10,000 sailors. A further 20,000–30,000 (or more) men could be recruited for major expeditions. Annual costs in peacetime were about 7,000–8,000 talents, rising perhaps in excess of 9,000–10,000 in wartime, and thus swallowing up about 45% (57% in wartime) of the entire state budget. The Ptolemaic army had 63,000–78,000 men regularly under arms (36,000 regular soldiers, 8,000–12,000 garrison troops, 1,000 mercenaries, 5,000–6,000 Egyptians and 45,000–50,000 sailors), rising to 160,000–175,000 in times of war. About 34% of the state budget was thus committed to the army in peacetime, 78% in wartime. The higher costs borne by the Ptolemies arose chiefly because their navy was between three and six times as large as the Seleucids', and from the fact that, unlike the Seleucids (or Antigonids), they had recourse neither to a citizen militia nor to allied forces [1.189–205]; [7.66–83]. The vast financial resources that kings were prepared to spend on their armies reflect their importance.

In Macedonia in times of war, up to 10,000 phalangites were generally recruited, or about 3,000 per district. Except in dire emergencies, recruitment was always confined to three districts out of four [8.455f.]. At most between 20,000 and 30,000 Macedonians were called to arms, more than 10% of them horsemen. There were also contingents of allies and mercenaries [6.214f.].

☞ **Colonies; Elephants; Fleet; Mercenaries; Rank; Siege warfare**

BIBLIOGRAPHY
[1] G.G. APERGHIS, The Seleukid Royal Economy. The Finances and Financial Administration of the Seleukid Empire, 2004 [2] B. BAR-KOKHVA, The Seleucid Army. Organization and Tactics in the Great Campaigns, 1976 [3] E. BIKERMAN, Institutions des Séleucides, 1938 [4] L. CAPDETREY, Le pouvoir séleucide. Territoire, administration, finances d'un royaume hellénistique (312–129 avant J.-C.), 2007 [5] F. DAUBNER, Seleukidische und attalidische Gründungen in Westkleinasien. Datierung, Funktion und Status, in: F. DAUBNER (ed.), Militärsiedlungen und Territorialherrschaft in der Antike, 2011, 41–63 [6] R.M. ERRINGTON, Geschichte Makedoniens. Von den Anfängen bis zum Untergang des Königreiches, 1986 [7] C. FISCHER-BOVET, Army and Society in Ptolemaic Egypt, 2014 [8] M.B. HATZOPOULOS, Macedonian Institutions under the Kings, vol. 1: A Historical and Epigraphic Study, 1996 [9] M.B. HATZOPOULOS, L'organisation de l'armée macédonienne sous les Antigonides. Problèmes anciens et documents nouveaux, 2001 [10] M. HOLLEAUX, »Ceux qui sont dans le bagage«, in: REG 39, 1926, 355–366 [11] S. SCHEUBLE-REITER, Die Katökenreiter im ptolemäischen Ägypten, 2012 [12] N. SEKUNDA, Military Forces. A. Land Forces, in: P. SABIN et al. (eds.), The Cambridge History of Greek and Roman Warfare, 2007, 325–349 [13] N.V. SEKUNDA, The Antigonid Army, 2013 [14] E. VAN'T DACK, La littérature tactique de l'antiquité et les sources documentaires, in: E. VAN'T DACK, Ptolemaica Selecta. Études sur l'armée et l'administration lagides, 1988, 47–64 [15] E. VAN'T DACK, Sur l'évolution des institutions militaires lagides, in: E. VAN'T DACK, Ptolemaica Selecta. Études sur l'armée et l'administration lagides, 1988, 1–46 [16] K.-W. WELWEI, Unfreie im antiken Kriegsdienst, vol. 2: Die kleineren und mittleren Staaten und die hellenistischen Reiche, 1977 [17] J.K. WINNICKI, Das ptolemäische und das hellenistische Heerwesen, in: L. CRISCUOLO / G. GERACI (eds.), Egitto e storia antica dall'ellenismo all'età araba. Bilancio di un confronto. Atti del colloquio internazionale Bologna, 31 agosto–2 settembre 1987, 1989, 213–230.

SANDRA SCHEUBLE-REITER

C. ROMAN

C.1. Monarchical and early Republican periods
C.2. The manipular army
C.3. The emergence of a professional army
C.4. The army of the high Imperial period
C.5. Constantine and the Late Roman army

C.1. Monarchical and early Republican periods

Servius Tullius' role in the development of a Roman citizen army was hampered by the stubborn presence in Latium of clan forces, whose commanders were primarily interested in booty. Pressure from the Sabellian tribes and enmity with some Etruscan cities in all likelihood laid the ground for hostilities beginning in the second half of the 5th century. The first appearance of the census in 443 BC indicates the establishment of a censitary army recruited from landowners, its infantry organized in the form of the hoplite phalanx [2]. Only the *iuniores*, aged between 17 and 45, fought on the battlefield. The *seniores* between 46 and 60 formed a reserve force to defend the city of Rome. At this period, the legion probably comprised 4,000 footsoldiers, possibly divided into 40 centuries, with ten centuries for each of the four topographical *tribus* created by Servius Tullius. It is probable that there were 18 equestrian centuries at this period, making a total of 1,800 cavalrymen.

C.2. THE MANIPULAR ARMY

The Romans' military originality really began to show itself during the Samnite Wars. It was probably then that the increasing size of the infantry provoked the foundation of a second, then third censitary class. Soldiers of the second class carried a sword, a shield, a lance, spears and a helmet, but wore no breastplate. Those of the third class had the same equipment with the exception of the spears. Their shields were oval, to provide better protection to the whole body in the absence of the breastplate.

Hoplite combat proved unsuitable for uneven terrain that precluded open battlefield fighting. Greater flexibility was achieved by dividing the legion into maniples, each composed of two centuries of 60 men. The maniples were arrayed in three ranks: in the front, the *hastati* armed with lances; behind them the *principes*, whose name derived from their former position in the first rank of the Archaic phalanx; then the third rank of *triarii*. Behind these came the more lightly armed *rorarii* and the *accensi*, who were only called up and armed in emergencies. It is possible that these last two categories of soldiers came from the fourth and fifth censitary classes. They were probably introduced by Appius Claudius while he was censor in 312 BC. Every legion had 300 cavalry, divided into ten *turmae* ('units'). Three decurions commanded each *turma*. This system made it possible for the three battle ranks to alternate. The round shield now replaced the oval for all infantrymen, and it only offered protection if the soldiers maintained tight ranks. Legionaries, who underwent regular training, were guided by a plethora of visual and acoustic signals on the battlefield. Rome already had two legions by 362 BC, and by 311 there were four – two per consul.

Through its expansion in Italy, Rome concluded treaties with the peoples and cities there, requiring them to provide contingents of soldiers. The → oath sworn for incorporation placed the soldier wholly at the disposal of the holder of *imperium* ('command'). Perhaps inspired by a Campanian model, the censor for 312 BC, Appius Claudius, created an equestrian class in honour of an elite group of horsemen, each of whom now received state support for the upkeep of his horse, which became known as an *equus publicus* ('public horse'); admission to the 18 equestrian centuries was exclusively reserved for these horsemen. Membership qualified them to hold magistracies and military commands, initially as military tribunes, of whom there were six per legion. The further division of the legion into constituent units also required there to be enough officers, if full tactical efficiency was to be guaranteed. Each legion had 60 centurions, selected by the military tribunes from the most outstanding soldiers. Over the course of the 4th century, the evolving conditions of war led to the introduction of a stipend, which was financed through taxation. The manipular order depended more on the age differences among the soldiers than on a strict distinction between censitary classes. The Roman army was housed in camps, which seem to have fulfilled a double function from the outset, guaranteeing the safety of the army on campaign while also instilling awe in adversaries.

The First Punic War (264–241 BC; → Wars of note K.) compelled the Romans to develop their naval forces. The need for a permanent military presence overseas emerged during the Second Punic War (218–201 BC), and developed further in the course of establishing new provinces where Rome began to recruit auxiliaries. The inevitably lengthy timeframes of some military operations in remote regions necessitated the extension of the terms of office for the magistrates who were charged with carrying out these operations. The censitary army was evolving, especially on a logistical level. Legionaries, for instance, were frequently called upon to perform duties of supply and administration.

C.3. THE EMERGENCE OF A PROFESSIONAL ARMY

The effects of changes in agricultural production in Italy on the recruitment of legions have been exaggerated. So too has the impact on the military of the enlistment of *proletarii* ('citizens of the lowest class') by Marius (Generals of note K.) during the Jugurthan War, as this was no more than sporadic, with limited numbers involved. Even the Social War, despite causing the mobilization of a considerable number of army personnel and the granting of Roman citizenship to the Italic tribes, may not have provoked the permanent abolition of census criteria in the recruitment process [4]. Armies were now developing ever closer relationships with their commanders, whose ambitions delivered the mortal blow to republican institutions [1]. The process of professionalization was completed under the principate of Augustus, who set the term of army service at 20 years, a condition to which the legions henceforth adhered. The number of legions was held unchanged at 28 until its reduction to 25 in AD 9, in the wake of the annihilation of legions XVII, XVIII and XIX in the defeat of Varus' forces in the Teutoburg Forest. In 27 BC, a ten-year consular *imperium* gave Augustus command of all provinces of Gaul, Spain and Syria, while the others remained under senatorial administration. At least 20 legions were stationed in the provinces of the *princeps*, all commanded through legates of senatorial rank, except the legions in Egypt, which were assigned to equestrian prefects. A legion comprised between 5,200 and 6,000 Roman citizens, divided into ten cohorts of 600 men apiece. A century was composed of 80 footsoldiers. The maniples now ceded their tactical preeminence to the cohorts. Every legion was assigned a contingent of 120 cavalry. The legions were each commanded by a legate who was a senator of praetorian rank appointed by the emperor. Alongside the legate were a *tribunus laticlavius* ('broadstriped tribune') of the senatorial class, and five *tribuni angusticlavii* ('narrow-striped tribunes') of the equestrian class. There was also a camp prefect in charge of managing the army camp. He would have served as *primus pilus*, that is, centurion in charge of the first century of the first cohort, prior to his elevation to the equestrian class.

In Rome itself, nine praetorian cohorts of 500 Roman citizens under the command of equestrian prefects acted as the imperial guard, while three urban cohorts, each likewise with a troop strength of 500 and commanded by a consular prefect, performed policing duties. Seven cohorts of 500 *vigiles* ('watchmen') had the specialist task of providing police and fire protection at night. They were under the command of an equestrian prefect, and their recruits were freedmen, lest they give the appearance of an extraordinary troop of regular soldiers in occupation of the city. The *princeps* also introduced an old-age pension for demobilized veterans. In AD 6, military difficulties compelled Augustus to extend army service in the praetorian cohorts to 16 years and in the legions and urban cohorts to 25 years, and then to establish a veterans' fund financed by a five-percent inheritance tax imposed on Roman citizens. Regular exchanges defused tensions between the provincial troops and the garrisons of the capital. Thus, praetorians might continue their careers as centurions in the legions. The cohorts of *vigiles* were each headed by a former *primus pilus* of a legion who was now continuing his career as a tribune of the *urbaniciani* ('troops garrisoned in the city') and praetorians [13].

The *alae* ('auxiliary forces') consisted of 16 *turmae* ('units') of 30 horsemen under the command of a *duplicarius* ('double pay') and a decurion. The cohorts comprised six centuries of 80 infantry, a total of 480 men. The *cohortes equitatae* ('equestrian cohorts') combined six centuries of 80 infantry and four *turmae* of 30 cavalry. From the Flavian period onwards, *cohortes milliariae* are also attested: they had approximately twice the strength of the older cohorts, which now came to be known as *cohortes quingenariae*. The *alae milliariae* comprised 24 *turmae* of 30 cavalry, the *cohortes milliariae* ten centuries of 80 infantry, and the *cohortes milliariae equitatae* the same ten infantry centuries plus eight cavalry *turmae* [12].

The imperial naval forces were stationed at Misenum on the Tyrrhenian Sea and at Ravenna on the Adriatic. Like the auxiliary troops, sailors were mainly recruited from *peregrini* ('foreigners'). Both served for 25 or 26 years. They (and their children) were granted Roman citizenship on discharge from military service [16].

C.4. THE ARMY OF THE HIGH IMPERIAL PERIOD

The key change that took place during the empire's final territorial conquests in the high Imperial period was the army's adaptation to a new geopolitical context, in which the majority of troops were stationed on the empire's borders in permanent camps. The border defences referred to today as the *limes* took very different forms depending on the terrain and the nature, threatening or otherwise, of nearby tribes. Contiguous ramparts and ditches were the exception rather than the rule, and roads were important features everywhere and at all periods. Beginning in the 3rd century, pressure at the borders exposed the Roman military's inability to fight wars on multiple fronts. Instead of redeploying entire units, the army began to use mixed detachments drawn from units called *vexillationes* ('temporary military detachments'). The quest for greater mobility also led to the development of a cavalry corps proper, although recent scholarship has cast doubt on its significance prior to the 5th and 6th centuries. Between 240 and 285, the contingent of legionary horsemen rose from 120 to 726. Caracalla's bestowal of Roman citizenship on most of the freemen of the empire in 212 eroded the traditional distinction between legionaries and auxiliaries. In 262, Gallienus replaced the legates and tribunes of senatorial rank with equestrians, many of whom had previously served as centurions and were promoted on the basis of their military experience.

The work of reconstruction and new fortification that began in the reign of Probus (276–282) was only completed under Valentinian and Valens (364–378). Laws passed under Diocletian and Constantine I made the call-up of soldiers' sons compulsory. Landowners were also required to provide recruits to the army or pay the state a tax in lieu. Even so, the shortage of recruits within the empire that had set in during the reigns of Aurelian (270–275) and Probus led to increasing reliance on barbarians.

C.5. Constantine and the Late Roman army

It was Constantine I who created the Late Roman army, which was now divided into two categories of troops: the *comitatenses* ('court troops') and the *limitanei* ('border troops') (→ Borders). Compelled to mobilize a larger army by his confrontations first with Maxentius and later with Licinius, Constantine brought in Germanic tribesmen whom he incorporated into elite units. In the wake of his victory at the Battle of the Milvian Bridge in 312 (→ Battles of note G.), he abolished the Praetorian Guard, which had intervened on Maxentius' side, and replaced it with eleven *scholae palatinae* ('Palatine Guards'), each comprising 500 horsemen, along with the *protectores domestici* ('Domestic Protectors'). Around AD 360, these augmented imperial → guards began to be referred to as a single Palatine Guard. Some soldiers were rewarded for loyalty with the title *comitatenses* and with certain privileges, while the remainder were first called *ripenses* or *riparienses* ('troops stationed on a riverbank'), then after 363 *limitanei*. The defining characteristic of the latter was that these soldiers were answerable to regional *duces* ('commanders'), while the *comitatenses* were under the command of two *magistri militum* ('masters of soldiers') appointed by the emperor: one *magister peditum* for the infantry and, subordinate to him, one *magister equitum* for the cavalry.

Following the loss of two thirds of the Roman army routed by the Goths at the Battle of Adrianople in 378, recourse to barbarian fighters became indispensable. In 382, Theodosius I granted the Goths the status of *foederati* ('allied by treaty'). They provided contingents of soldiers, receiving financial support and provisions from the emperor in return. However, they remained under the authority of their own commander. The Roman army was becoming increasingly indistinguishable from its adversaries. Seeking to stem the barbarian threat in the 5th century, Rome in the West was left with no other option than to play off the various *foederati* against one another. The loss of North Africa created a deficit in resources that was impossible to offset well enough to maintain an army. In the East, by contrast, the Byzantine Army maintained the presence of Roman armed forces in the region [15].

☞ Legion; Military service; Society and army; State and army; Veterans

BIBLIOGRAPHY
[1] H. AIGNER, Die Soldaten als Machtfaktor in der ausgehenden römischen Republik, 1974   [2] J. ARMSTRONG, War and Society in Early Rome. From Warlords to Generals, 2016   [3] D.J. BREEZE, The Roman Army, 2016   [4] F. CADIOU, L'armée imaginaire. Les soldats prolétaires dans les légions romaines au dernier siècle de la République, 2018   [5] J.B. CAMPBELL, War and Society in Imperial Rome 31 BC–AD 284, 2002   [6] P. COSME, L'armée romaine. VIIIe s. av. J.-C.–Ve s. ap. J.-C., ^{2}2012   [7] A. EICH, Die römischen Kaiserzeit. Die Legionen und das Imperium, 2014   [8] P. ERDKAMP (ed.), A Companion to the Roman Army, 2007   [9] P. FAURE, L'aigle et le cep. Les centurions légionnaires dans l'Empire des Sévères, 2013   [10] T. FISCHER, Die Armee der Caesaren. Archäologie und Geschichte, 2012   [11] A. GOLDSWORTHY, Die Legionen Roms. Das große Handbuch zum Machtinstrument eines tausendjährigen Weltreichs, 2004   [12] I. HAYNES, Blood of the Provinces. The Roman Auxilia and the Making of Provincial Society from Augustus to the Severans, 2013   [13] L. KEPPIE, The Making of the Roman Army. From Republic to Empire, ^{2}1998   [14] Y. LE BOHEC, Die römische Armee, 2009   [15] Y. LE BOHEC, Das römische Heer in der späten Kaiserzeit, 2010   [16] M. REDDÉ, Mare nostrum. Les infrastructures, le dispositif et l'histoire de la marine militaire sous l'Empire romain, 1986   [17] J.P. ROTH, The Logistics of the Roman Army at War (264 BC–AD 235), 1999   [18] M.A. SPEIDEL, Heer und Herrschaft im Römischen Reich der Hohen Kaiserzeit, 2009.

PIERRE COSME

D. Late Antiquity

D.1. Reorganizations by the soldier-emperors
D.2. Reforms of Diocletian
D.3. Constantine's introduction of two categories of troops
D.4. Integration of foreign ethnicities into the army
D.5. Army strength and organization
D.6. Changing tactics
D.7. Developments in the Eastern and Western Empires

In the middle of the 3rd century AD, persistent wars on multiple fronts severely undermined the strategy of concentrating all forces along a linear line of defence (the *limes*) and the practice of deploying temporary detachments (*vexillationes*) to troublespots. A far-reaching reform of the military was needed to counter the new threats. Gallienus, Diocletian and Constantine I created new military structures that endured, albeit with many adaptations, until the early 7th century. Surveys of these developments, not all details of which are clear, are offered in [9]; [13. vol. 1, 607–686]; [2]; [16]; [18]; [32]; [36]; [1]; [15] and [22].

D.1. Reorganizations by the soldier-emperors

The soldier-emperors and the tetrarchs led their armies into battle in person, so they needed a large and powerful military retinue. Septimius Severus had already boosted the strength of the emperor's mounted guard, the *equites singulares Augusti*, from 1,000 to 2,000. Together with the Praetorian Guard, they formed the nucleus of the emperor's 'attendants', the *comites*. Large detachments were drawn from the legions to form new 'field legions'. Constant campaigning required these field legions to be deployed continuously, so that many detachments never returned to their units of origin, but were constituted in their own right as independent formations with new names [12. vol. 1, 218–222]. In other cases, the parent unit and the detachments kept the same name, as in the example of the *legio V Macedonica*. This legion was originally stationed in Dacia ripensis. Around AD 400, while there was indeed still a *legio V Macedonica* in four garrisons on the Danube, there was also a second *legio V Macedonica* stationed in Memphis, and a third legion by the same name in the army of the *magister militum per Orientem* ('Master of Soldiers in the East'). The latter two legions had been sent to the east as detachments in the 290s and had stayed there [33]; [3]. Along some sections of the frontier, the old legions with a regular strength of 6,000 men were divided into two, each part retaining the traditional name but distinguished by the suffixes *seniores* and *iuniores* (first attested 356 in AE 1977, 806; [29]; [18.24–34]; otherwise [23]).

Mounted enemies and the need for greater mobility demanded a significant expansion of the cavalry. Gallienus implemented the necessary changes [27]. The systematic nature of the nomenclature for the new mounted units and a new → rank system (Jerome, *Contra Iohannem Hierosolymitanum episcopum* 19) suggest that the raising of a field army of cavalry was the result of a planned reform, even if the first epigraphic evidence for the new *equites Dalmatae* (AD 268: [25]), *equites Mauri* (AD 272 at the latest: [28.123–136]) and *equites stablesiani* (late 3rd century: [28.391–396]) postdates Gallienus. The byname *Illyriciani* attached to some of these formations shows that they were originally raised in the Danube Plain and the Balkans, the territories of Gallienus' powerbase (Zos. 1,40,2; SHA Gall. 14,4). Gallienus' successors, notably Aurelian, formed these cavalry units, along with the *equites promoti Domini Nostri* ('Advanced Cavalry of Our Ruler'), as the Praetorian cavalry were now known, and the *comites Domini Nostri* ('Attendants of Our Ruler'), the new name of the *equites singulares Augusti*, into a mobile field army.

Besides the new field army, which functioned as the emperor's personal military retinue (*comitatus*) while also providing a powerful reserve behind the *limes* ('fortified boundary line'), the *legiones* ('legions'), *alae* ('auxiliary forces') and *cohortes* ('cohorts') continued to serve in their permanent camps on the frontier. They retained their traditional nomenclature and rank, and operated as garrison troops, their main roles being to patrol the *limes* and maintain internal order. Officer roles were no longer filled by young careerists of the equestrian and senatorial classes, but by professional soldiers.

D.2. REFORMS OF DIOCLETIAN

Diocletian and his co-emperors continued these reforms. One important step was the separation of civilian and military authority, which began to make itself felt across the whole empire from about AD 308 onwards. Governors handed over their military authority to *duces* ('commanders'), who kept command of major frontier sections. The appointment of about 30 supraregional military commands (*ducatus*) was intended to reorganize the frontier zones according to military criteria. It is impossible to establish in detail which measures were instigated by Diocletian himself and which by other tetrarchs or by Constantine I. It seems likely that the consolidation of frontier protection (including the building of fortifications) was Diocletian's initiative, while the permanent establishment of a mobile field army probably only took place under Constantine. The dissolution of the Praetorian Guard after Constantine's victory over Maxentius (AD 312) created space for a new type of *comitatus* ('imperial retinue') (→ Battles of note G.). Some authors of the period, such as the Christian Lactantius (De mort. pers. 7,2), accuse Diocletian in particular of having militarized the mechanisms of state and quadrupled the strength of the army. However, this is a polemical distortion of the facts, particularly given that it was Diocletian himself who founded the civilian branch of government. Units may have doubled in number, but this was because many were divided. There were 33 legions at the death of Septimius Severus (211), and about 70 by 305 [13. vol. 1, 59f.; vol. 3, app. II tab. IX], whereas the *Notitia Dignitatum* (c. AD 400–430) lists at least 190. However, the new units were significantly smaller [4]. Although in theory the cavalry units were probably still supposed to be 500 strong (Lydus, Mag. 1,46; P. Cair. Masp. III 67321, mid-6th century), papyri attest that they were considerably understaffed (300–400 men; [17. vol. 1, 217–231]). The sizes of Late Antique legions in particular cannot be given more accurately than as vague estimates (of between 750 and 1,200 men), because the divided units had no standard strengths [13. vol. 2, 680–682]; [18.67–73]; [30.169–173]; [26.96–98].

D.3. CONSTANTINE'S INTRODUCTION OF TWO CATEGORIES OF TROOPS

The creation of two categories of troops emerged soon after Constantine became sole emperor (324). Soldiers of the mobile field army were first referred to as *comitatenses* ('court troops') in 325 (Cod. Theod. 7,20,4), while soldiers of the frontier army commanded by a *dux* ('commander') or *comes rei militaris* ('military attendant') were known as *limitanei* ('border troops') or *ripenses* ('riverbank troops') by 363 at the latest. For the most part, the frontier army continued to be made up of *alae* ('auxiliary forces') and *cohortes* ('cohorts') along with some units of *equites* ('cavalry'), stationed in garrisons along the *limes* ('fortified boundary lines'). The new elite units of cavalry (now called *vexillationes*: [12. vol. 1, 243–279]; [27]) and infantry (now *auxilia*: [12. vol. 1, 131–173]; [18.53–56]) that had hitherto formed part of the emperor's *comitatus* ('imperial retinue') were now incorporated into the more combat-capable and more highly privileged (Cod. Theod. 7,13,7; 7,20,4) field army. Legions were found in both troop categories [30]. Units of the *limitanei* that were later promoted to the *comitatus* were called *pseudocomitatenses* (Cod. Theod. 8,1,10; 365).

Constantine delegated his supreme command of the field army to a *magister equitum* ('master of cavalry') and a *magister peditum* ('master of infantry') for the cavalry and infantry respectively (Zos. 2,33). The term *magister militum* ('master of soldiers') later came to be applied to both. The division of the empire among the sons of Constantine led to the creation of several *comitatus*. These remained in existence as field armies even after the deaths of Constantine II and Constans. Constantius II assigned them regional spheres of action and put them under supreme commands defined by territory, which corresponded approximately to the territories of the civilian praetorian prefectures. For instance, there was a *magister militum per Orientem* as from 351, a *magister militum per Galliam* as from 355 and a *magister militum per Illyricum* as from 359. Two further army divisions commanded by *magistri militum praesentales* ('Masters of Soldiers in the (Imperial) Presence') also resided at each imperial court.

Scholae palatinae – five in the Western Empire, seven in the Eastern, each 500 men in strength – replaced the defunct Praetorian Guard as the palace guard. The *scholae* were under the authority of the *magister officiorum*, a court official whose post was also created under Constantine [8]. The palace guard and the divisions of a field army that accompanied the emperor were called the *palatini*. The *palatini* also came to be regarded as a unit category in their own right, beginning probably in the reigns of Valentinian I and Valens (Cod. Theod. 8,1,10; 365). Constantine had transferred the Praetorians' function as a cadet school and elite training facility for staff officers to the newly created corps of the *protectores* and the even more elite body of *protectores domestici* that was soon sequestered from it (Cod. Theod. 12,1,38; ca. 346). The latter were commanded by a high-ranking *comes domesticorum equitum* ('attendant of the domestic cavalry') and a *comes domesticorum peditum* ('attendant of the domestic infantry) [7]. High-ranking *protectores* and *domestici* were seconded to the staffs of the highest military commands to support and monitor commanders there (Cod. Theod. 7,21,3; 396).

By the 5th century, the *protectores* and *domestici* had lost their military relevance and the *scholae palatinae* had degenerated into ceremonial units. Around 466, Leo I responded by establishing the *excubitores* ('sentinels') as his new palace guard. This unit, 300 strong (Lydus, Mag. 1,16), was commanded by a *comes excubitorum* ('attendant of the sentinels'), who was a powerful figure given his presence at court. Justin I, Tiberius II and Maurice all attained the imperial throne from this position.

The division of forces into the three categories of *comitatenses* ('court troops'), *limitanei* ('border troops') and *palatini* ('palace troops') continued (e.g. Cod. Iust. 4,65,35; 530) until the empire gave way to Germanic successor states in the West (476) and a completely new military system was founded in the East in the form of the thematic system (7th century). Procopius' polemical accusation (*Anekdota* 24,12–14) that Justinian eliminated the status of the regular troops finds no support in other sources.

D.4. INTEGRATION OF FOREIGN ETHNICITIES INTO THE ARMY

The AD 382 compact (*foedus*) with the Goths marked the start of a new chapter, not only in the relationship between the empire and the Germanic tribes, but also in the concept of defending the empire. In return for provisions and the right of settlement, the Goths undertook to defend the imperial frontier as *foederati* ('allied by treaty'). Unlike in previous agreements (treaty of 332), they were no longer answerable to the Roman army (although they did appear on its payroll), but rather to their own Gothic king, so that they were operating as allies [25]. An increasing Germanic presence within the Roman army was also making itself felt in other ways [6.134–154]. Beginning in the time of Constantine I, many served in the *vexillationes* ('elite cavalry units') and *auxilia* ('elite infantry units') of the field army, and from the mid-4th century onwards, Germanic aristocrats succeeded in attaining senior positions in the army. For example, the Frank Merobaudes, as *magister militum praesentalis* ('Master of Soldiers in the (Imperial) Presence'), became consul in 377 and 383, while two other Frankish *magistri militum*, Bauto (d. 387) and Arbogast (d. 394) functioned as advisors and powers behind the throne. The Vandal Stilicho (d. 408) was first in a series of Germanic *magistri militum* who *de facto* ruled the Western Empire in the 5th century. Attempts to do the same in the Eastern Empire by figures such as the Goth Gainas (d. 400) and the Alan Aspar (d. 471) failed, and the balance of power between the civilian government and the military was preserved. Supply of the army and recruitment remained in the hands of the civilian *praefecti praetorio*, to whom military commanders had to submit their requirements on a monthly basis [17]. This mechanism prevented the military from decoupling from civil institutions, whereas the greater 'barbarization' of the army in the West created a fateful distance between the population and the military. Even the ascent of many Germanic figures into the ranks of the generals failed to bridge the gap between them and the Roman elite. As a result, by the 5th century, a politically influential military nobility and a wealthy senatorial aristocracy were facing off in an atmosphere of mistrust.

D.5. ARMY STRENGTH AND ORGANIZATION

An organizational plan of the Late Roman army, with a register of its constituent units (including their shield patterns) and deployment, is available in the *Notitia Dignitatum*, a systematically organized list of the civil and military offices of the Roman Empire. It reflects the status quo in the Eastern Empire at about AD 400, while the sections dealing with the Western Empire underwent several redactions up to AD 430. Overall, the *Notitia* lists 338 units of *limitanei* ('border troops') for the East (although the section on the two Libyae is lost), and shows these to have been commanded by twelve *duces* ('commanders') and two *comites limitis* ('boundary attendants'). There were also 156 units of *comitatenses* ('court troops'), under the authority of the two *magistri militum praesentales* ('Masters of Soldiers in the (Imperial) Presence') and the *magistri militum per Orientem, per Thracias* and *per Illyricum*. Finally, there were the guard units: eight *scholae palatinae* ('palace guards'), the *domestici pedites* ('domestic infantry') and the *equites* ('cavalry'). The army in the eastern half of the empire thus comprised over 500 units. Assuming an average nominal strength of 400 men per unit, there would have been an estimated 200,000 men under arms.

The details the *Notitia* provides on the western half of the empire produce a similar figure. Here, there were 169 *comitatenses*, no fewer than 316 *limitanei* and, as in the East, eight *scholae palatinae* along with the *domestici pedites* and *equites*. There were eleven *duces* and five *comites* for the frontier troops in the West, along with two *magistri militum praesentales* and seven *magistri militum* for the field armies. The total number of units listed is 485, so that the same procedure of estimation as in the East again yields a result of around 200,000 men. Accordingly, there were probably only a few more soldiers serving throughout the whole empire in AD 400 than the 350,000 estimated for the early Principate. However, the lists of the *Notitia* also show that the picture was constantly changing. Nine tenths of the *alae* ('auxiliary forces'), *cohortes* ('cohorts') and *numeri* ('divisions') of the 2nd century AD have disappeared from the troop lists of the *Notitia*. The *comitatenses* at this point made up about one fifth of the entire army.

D.6. CHANGING TACTICS

The overall profile of the army, along with its tactics, changed dramatically after the Severan period, when armoured infantry still formed the backbone of the armed forces [6.107–117]. Although outnumbered by infantry regiments two to one, the cavalry now came increasingly to the fore, especially in the *limitanei* ('border troops'), since mounted units were more efficient for patrol duty. The armoured *equites catafracti* ('armoured cavalry') grew in importance and size from the late 3rd century onwards, and in the early 4th century, a new type of cavalry emerged in the *clibanarius* [5], which had both rider and mount fully armoured.

Changes in armament and fighting techniques also led gradually to transformations in the organization of units. In the Severan period, some legionaries were still armed with javelins and long thrusting lances (*lancearii, contarii*). Under the soldier-emperors, selected horsemen began to be armed and trained as *catafractarii* ('armoured cavalry') in the cavalry units. This change was reflected in the ranking system by AD 400 at the latest: in place of the *sesquiplicarius* and *duplicarius*, the *catafractarius* was now the service rank above the simple *eques* ('cavalry soldier') [34]. Combining a range of weapon types within a single unit represented a radical departure from the old principle that all soldiers within a unit had the same weapons and that it was only possible to combine different classes of weapons by using multiple units of different types in concert. The only exception to this rule had been the *cohortes equitatae* ('equestrian cohorts'), composed of one third cavalry and two third infantry. By 400, soldiers with different arrays of weaponry were found within a single unit. The *Strategicon* traditionally attributed to the Emperor Maurice (c. 600) illustrates the outcome of this process of development, presenting every mounted unit as essentially a mixed array of soldiers with different weapons. Any unit was thus now able to conduct a range of different tactical actions autonomously.

The *civitates* ('citizens') were responsible for the supply of recruits, and with the expansion of large-scale land ownership in the late 4th century, landowners were also required to contribute [31]; [6.128–154]; [35]. Veterans' sons were also subject to compulsory service by virtue of their status. Following the Gothic settlement in the last quarter of the 4th century, it was permitted, indeed desired, to have one's service obligation commuted to a monetary payment by the procedure of *adaeratio* (monetary payment in lieu of a service obligation), because the Goths and other *gentes* ('tribes') outside the borders of the empire were providing plentiful troops (Amm. Marc. 20,8,13). Prisoners of war were also taken into the army, sometimes in special units bearing the names of their former tribes in their titles (Ennod. *Panegyric on Theoderic* 6,6,2–4; Zos. 2,15,1). Stationed far from home, such 'ethnic' units would also be augmented by local recruits, so that their ethnic character would be no more than nominal within a generation. Most soldiers of 'barbarian' backgrounds and career soldiers probably served in the *comitatenses* ('court troops'), where frequent deployments hampered the development of local roots at a garrison town. By contrast, the stationary *limitanei* ('border troops') were generally augmented from the local population and the sons of soldiers, so that military families developed. Some papyrus dossiers (e.g. of Fl. Abinnaeus, mid-4th century, and Fl. Taurinus, 5th century [20.260]) suggest that the rules governing service duration and the mechanisms of advancement were far from rigid. Service terms well in excess of 20 years were commonplace. Promotions took place at irregular intervals, which provided occasions for corruption [19].

D.7. DEVELOPMENTS IN THE EASTERN AND WESTERN EMPIRES

In the Western Empire, the military crises of the 5th century meant that the primary task of army chiefs was to keep the field armies fit for deployment. The *limitanei* ('border troops') were often abandoned to their fate. A striking picture of disintegrating military structures is available in Eugippius' *Vita S. Severini* 20, which describes the situation on the Danubian *limes* ('boundary line') in Rhaetia and Noricum around AD 470–480. In terms of numbers and fighting capacity, the soldiers who remained there amounted to little more than skeleton guard details in their permanent camps, where civilian populations also resided, having long since sought refuge behind the walls. Cut off from routes of supply and communication (→ Infrastructure) with their army commands, they were thrown back on their own resources.

Despite some turmoil, the situation in the Eastern Empire remained stable on the whole. However, the tripartite command structure – local *duces* (or *comites*) for the *limitanei*, *magistri militum* for the *comitatenses* and the two *magistri militum praesentales* for the elite imperial units – proved ineffective in responding to invasions, since the complexities involved in coordinating this structure made it difficult to respond quickly. Anastasius I therefore decreed in AD 492 (Cod. Iust. 12,35,18) that all *comitatenses*, *palatini* and *foederati* belonging to a *ducatus*, along with the *limitanei*, should be at the command of the *dux*. This had the effect of strengthening regional military commands at the expense of the central military authority. Justinian went further still, abolishing the Diocletianic separation of powers in military frontier regions and putting civil and military power once again in the hands of a single official (*dux et Augustalis*). Large-scale military actions were carried out by the imperial expeditionary force, some units of which might possibly remain stationed in the province concerned [21].

A bundle of papyri from the frontier garrison of Syene, dating from the late 6th century (known as the Patermuthis Archive, see [14]), provides useful information on the position of the *limitanei*. These troops continued to perform their military duties organized in the old, traditional units (Cod. Iust. 12,35,15f.), and – despite integrating into local society – they were certainly not 'farmer-soldiers'. It can be seen here that the structures created in the Roman Empire in the 3rd and 4th centuries were still essentially in place in the Eastern Empire until the early 7th century. The Late Roman army system finally vanished only when the Near Eastern provinces were lost to the Arab Caliphate. The thematic system then replaced it in the remaining territories of the empire, marking the genesis of the Byzantine military [10]; [11.107–110].

☞ **Rank**

BIBLIOGRAPHY
[1] B. CAMPBELL, The Army, in: CAH 12: The Crisis of Empire, A.D. 193–337, 2005, 110–130   [2] J.-M. CARRIÉ, L'esercito. Trasformazioni funzionali ed economie locali, in: A. GIARDINA (ed.), Società romana, vol. 1: Istituzioni, ceti, economie, 1986, 449–488–760–771   [3] D.N. CHRISTODOULOU, Galerius, Gamzigrad, and the Fifth Macedonian Legion, in: JRA 15, 2002, 275–281   [4] T. COELLO, Unit Sizes in the Late Roman Army (BAR International Series 645), 1996   [5] J.W. EADIE, The Development of Roman Mailed Cavalry, in: JRS 57, 1967, 161–173   [6] H. ELTON, Warfare in Roman Europe, AD 350–425, 1996   [7] M. EMION, Des soldats de l'armée romaine tardive. Les protectores (IIIe–VIe siècles ap. J.-C.), 2 vols., 2017   [8] R.I. FRANK, Scholae Palatinae, 1969   [9] R. GROSSE, Römische Militärgeschichte von Gallienus bis zum Beginn der byzantinischen Themenverfassung, 1920   [10] J.F. HALDON, Administrative Continuities and Structural Transformation in East Roman Military Organisation ca. 580–640, in: M. KAZANSKI / F. VALLET (eds.), L'armée romaine et les barbares du IIIe au VIIe siècles, 1993, 45–53   [11] J.F. HALDON, Warfare, State and Society in the Byzantine World, 1999   [12] D. HOFFMANN, Das spätrömische Bewegungsheer und die Notitia Dignitatum, 2 vols. (Epigraphische Studien 7/1–2), 1969–1970   [13] A.H.M. JONES, The Later Roman Empire 284–602. A Social, Economic and Administrative Survey, 3 vols., 1964   [14] J.G. KEENAN, Evidence for the Byzantine Army in the Syene Papyri, in: BASP 27, 1990, 139–150   [15] Y. LE BOHEC, L'armée romaine sous le Bas-Empire, 2006   [16] A.D. LEE, The Army, in: CAH 13: The Late Empire, A.D. 337–425, 1998, 213–237   [17] F. MITTHOF, Annona militaris. Die Heeresversorgung im spätantiken Ägypten. Ein Beitrag zur Verwaltungs- und Heeresgeschichte des Römischen Reiches im 3. bis 6. Jahrhundert n.Chr., 2 vols. (Papyrologica Florentina

32), 2001 [18] M.J. Nicasie, Twilight of Empire. The Roman Army from the Reign of Diocletian until the Battle of Adrianople, 1998 [19] F. Onur, The Anastasian Military Decree from Perge in Pamphylia. Revised 2nd Edition, in: Gephyra 14, 2017, 133–212 [20] B. Palme, Imperial Presence. Government and Army, in: R.S. Bagnall (ed.), Egypt in the Byzantine World, 300–700, 2007, 244–270 [21] R. Rémondon, Soldats de Byzance d'après un papyrus trouvé à Edfou, in: Recherches de Papyrologie 1, 1961, 41–94 [22] M. Rocco, L'esercito romano tardoantico. Persistenze e cesure dai Severi a Teodosio I, 2012 [23] R. Scharf, Seniores-iuniores und die Heeresteilung des Jahres 364, in: ZPE 89, 1991, 265–272 [24] R. Scharf, Equites Dalmatae und cunei Dalmatarum in der Spätantike, in: ZPE 135, 2001, 185–194 [25] R. Scharf, Foederati. Von der völkerrechtlichen Kategorie zur byzantinischen Truppengattung (Tyche Suppl. 4), 2001 [26] O. Schmitt, Stärke, Struktur und Genese des comitatensischen Infanterienumerus, in: BJ 201, 2001, 93–111 [27] H.G. Simon, Die Reform der Reiterei unter Kaiser Gallien, in: W. Eck et al. (eds.), Studien zur antiken Sozialgeschichte. Festschrift für Friedrich Vittinghoff, 1980, 435–452 [28] M.P. Speidel, Roman Army Studies, vol. 1, 1984 [29] R.S.O. Tomlin, Seniores – Iuniores in the Late-Roman Field Army, in: AJPh 93, 1972, 253–278 [30] R.S.O. Tomlin, The Legions of the Late Empire, in: R.J. Brewer (ed.), Roman Fortresses and Their Legions, 2000, 159–181 [31] M. Whitby, Recruitment in Roman Armies from Justinian to Heraclius (c. 565–615), in: A. Cameron (ed.), The Byzantine and Early Islamic Near Eastern States, Resources, and Armies, 1995, 61–124 [32] M. Whitby, The Army, c. 420–602, in: CAH 14: Late Antiquity. Empire and Successors, A.D. 425–600, 2000, 288–314 [33] C. Zuckerman, Legio V Macedonica in Egypt. CPL 199 revisited, in: Tyche 3, 1988, 279–287 [34] C. Zuckerman, Le camp de Ψῶβθις/Sosteos et les catafractarii, in: ZPE 100, 1994, 199–202 [35] C. Zuckerman, Two Reforms of the 370s. Recruiting Soldiers and Senators in the Divided Empire, in: REByz 56, 1998, 79–139 [36] C. Zuckerman, L'armée, in: C. Morrisson (ed.), Le monde byzantin, vol. 1: L'Empire romain d'Orient (330–641), 2004, 143–180.

Bernhard Palme

Artillery

A. Preliminary observations
B. Sources
C. Hellenistic period to Principate
D. Roman Imperial period and Late Antiquity

A. Preliminary observations

Artillery in the armies of Greco-Roman Antiquity comprised military apparatuses designed to be used at long range and, generally, to be operated by several soldiers (i.e. projectile weapons). On the equipment and other armament of the Roman army, see → Equipment B. and → Armament B. Ancient artillery included pieces that fired piercing projectiles (*catapultae/scorpii*), and others that hurled impact projectiles like stones (*ballistae*). It must be remembered, however, that the terms used in ancient sources to denote the various categories of artillery often do not correspond unambiguously to one specific type.

B. Sources

B.1. Textual sources
B.2. Pictorial sources
B.3. Archaeological sources

Information on long-range weapons in Greco-Roman Antiquity is derived from textual and pictorial sources and from archaeological finds.

B.1. Textual sources

A comprehensive theoretical literature on artillery survives from Classical Antiquity. It was already possible in the early 20th century to use this to make the first reconstructions of ancient artillery pieces [7].

– Biton, a Hellenistic author who dedicated his work to King Attalus I of Pergamum (c. 230–197 BC), described heavy bows as they were used in the early years of ancient artillery (see below) [2.164]; [6.61–103].

– Philo of Byzantium wrote his works in the 3rd/2nd centuries BC in the vicinity of Alexandria and Rhodes. His treatise *Belopoieka* is chiefly concerned with possible standard sizes and modular relationships in the construction of artillery pieces for piercing or impact projectiles. He also examined experimental catapult constructions like repeaters [2.164]; [6.105–184].

– Hero of Alexandria's treatise *Belopoieka*, probably written in the late Hellenistic period, offers a comprehensive survey of the history of the artillery of his day, along with brief descriptions of the weapons then in widespread use [2.164f.]; [6.17–60].

– Marcus Vitruvius Pollio, known as Vitruvius, lived in the 1st century BC and worked under Caesar and Augustus as an engineer specializing in the construction of war machines. His work *De architectura* (10,10–12) contains a description of the types of artillery pieces used at the time, including details of their construction and proportions [2.165]; [6.185–205].

– Pseudo-Hero is an otherwise unknown author who was formerly identified with Hero of Alexandria (see above), but in reality probably wrote in Late Antiquity. One fragment by him (*Cheiroballistra*) survives, describing the construction of a small torsion crossbow that was probably fired by hand [2.165]; [6.206–233]. The fragment also contains medieval copies of the ancient illustrations.

B.2. Pictorial sources

The surviving pictorial representations of ancient artillery are usually public rather than private. One example of a private image is the relief of a bolt-shooter on the tombstone of Gaius Vedennius

Moderatus of Rome (CIL VI 2725, 1st cent. AD; cf. fig. 1) [2.155, fig. 38]; [3.91, fig. 48, 1]. Public depictions include the reliefs on the Trajan Column (AD 112/13; cf. fig. 2) [2.156, fig. 39]; [3.91, fig. 48, 2]. The medieval copies of the technical diagrams from the *Cheiroballistra* by Pseudo-Hero are also worthy of mention [1.176, fig. 3].

Fig. 1: Tombstone of Gaius Vedennius Moderatus (Rome, 1st century AD). As a legionary of the legio XVI Gallica specializing in artillery, Vedennius was seconded to the Praetorians. He served nine years in this assignment, by the end as a reservist recalled to duty. After this he was honoured by Vespasian. On the side of the stone is a detailed front view of the torsion frame of a bolt-shooter. Two washers for the rope skeins are clearly visible emerging from the top and bottom of the frame, with the bolts holding them secure. The torsion frame is clad in metal plates, with the aperture for the firing channel in the centre.

Fig. 2: Detail from the spiral relief on the Trajan Column (image 25, scene 69; Rome, AD 112/13; plaster cast, 1861). Two legionaries working in a field fortification are operating a bolt-shooter with an iron torsion frame. The two metal washers for the rope skeins at the sides are clearly visible, as is the slide in which the bolt was placed and a mobile footboard allowing the weapon to be aimed at the target.

B.3. ARCHAEOLOGICAL SOURCES
Original finds have included parts of torsion frames, revolving washers, bolts and, very rarely, complete arrows and stone projectiles (see below).

C. HELLENISTIC PERIOD TO PRINCIPATE
Ancient artillery began around 400 BC with catapults that were cocked by hand (*gastraphetes*) and launched piercing projectiles shaped like oversized bows. These were quickly replaced beginning in the mid-4th century BC with torsion catapults. The latter derived their propulsion power from two skeins of rope (hair or sinew) tightly pulled forward, each with a lever arm sitting on it. Washers (*modioli*) and bolts attached to a torsion frame rotated the skeins of rope. Piercing projectiles or stones served as ammunition. Hellenistic, Republican and Early Imperial weapons were characterized by a thin wooden torsion frame reinforced with metal plates (see above, fig. 1) and long arrow projectiles feathered with bird feathers. Examples of original finds include components from up to seven catapults found at Ephyra (Greece, 167 BC), large pieces of the torsion frame of a catapult from Ampurias (Spain, early 1st cent. BC) and parts from at least two catapults from Cremona (Italy, AD 69). Most notable in the last of these finds is a protective plate from the bronze torsion frame, which bears an inscription of the *legio IV Macedonica* detailing the weapon's manufacture (AD 45) and responsibility for it within the legion (ILS 2283) [1.172–182, 185–194, pl. 90]; [2.154–159]; [5.201–204].

All large armies of the Mediterranean region in the Hellenistic period had catapults, which they used primarily in → siege warfare. The Roman army also began using artillery pieces in the 3rd century BC. Artillery was a firm fixture of the Roman's fighting force from at least the time of Caesar's campaigns. They were used systematically not only during sieges, but also on the battlefield. However, it appears that only the legions and the Praetorian Guard had catapults before the middle of the Imperial period [2.158–160]; [4.230].

D. ROMAN IMPERIAL PERIOD AND LATE ANTIQUITY
Beginning in the late 1st century AD, with its first verifiable use during the Dacian Wars (illustration on the Trajan Column), a new form of catapult was developed by the Roman army. This catapult had a broad torsion frame made of iron (see above, fig. 2), and its upper strut was shaped like a bow (bow strut). Artillery pieces of this type used relatively short piercing projectiles with wood lamellae as flights. This weapon type remained in use until Late Antiquity. Examples of finds include parts of a torsion frame from Orşova (Romania, after AD 378), a washer from Pityus (Abkhazia/Georgia, 4th cent. AD) and parts of a bronze

washer from Morocco (4th cent. AD) [1.207–215]; [2.160]; [3.206–208, fig. 132]; [5.204f., fig. 147].

In addition to these twin-armed catapults, there were also single-armed versions with a torsion spring fitted horizontally (called the *onager*). Although this type of artillery piece seems to have been known already in the Hellenistic period and under the Roman Principate, it is only well attested in connection with the Roman army of Late Antiquity [2.160f., Abb. 44].

Artillery continued to be mainly operated by legionary forces in the middle and late Imperial periods. However, there is also regular reference to its use by auxiliary units. In particular, it seems to have been very common for artillery pieces to be used to defend military installations in Late Antiquity [2.162].

☞ Army; Battle; Strategy; Training

BIBLIOGRAPHY
[1] D. BAATZ, Bauten und Katapulte des römischen Heeres (Mavors 11), 1994 [2] D. BAATZ, Catapult, in: Y. Le Bohec et al. (eds.), The Encyclopedia of the Roman Army, vol. 1, 2015, 154–166 [3] M.C. BISHOP / J.C. COULSTON, Roman Military Equipment. From the Punic Wars to the Fall of Rome, ²2006 [4] T. FISCHER, Die Armee der Caesaren, 2012 [5] L. GUILLAUD, Militaria de Lugdunum. Étude de l'armement romain et de l'équipement militaire à Lyon, Iᵉʳ s. av.–IVᵉ s. ap. J.-C. (Monographies Instrumentum 62), 2019 [6] E.W. MARSDEN, Greek and Roman Artillery. Technical Treatises, 1971 [7] E. SCHRAMM, Die antiken Geschütze der Saalburg, 1918.

ECKHARD DESCHLER-ERB

Auxiliaries

A. Roman auxiliaries in the Republican period
B. Auxilia in the early Principate
C. Service conditions
D. Auxiliary unit numbers in the army of the Imperial period
E. New units
F. The auxilia of Late Antiquity

A. Roman auxiliaries in the Republican period

As soon as the Romans began fighting wars with enemies from outside Italy, they began finding it necessary to augment their citizen army and the forces of their Italic allies with troops from a wide variety of backgrounds. The status and origins of these auxiliaries (*auxilia*) changed over the centuries that followed, but they remained a key element of the Roman army until the last years of the Roman Empire.

As Rome's territorial ambitions in Italy expanded during the Republican period, the Roman army was reinforced with two similarly organized *alae sociorum* ('auxiliary forces of allies'). When these forces entered battle with foreign adversaries that were sometimes differently organized and used unfamiliar tactics, deficits came to light in the Roman citizen army. Seeking to remedy their weaknesses in cavalry, light infantry and slingers, the Romans deployed auxiliaries of three types. First, allies were drawn from beyond the ranks of the Italic *socii*, from such sources as Syracuse, Numidia and Aetolia. Second, mercenaries like Cretan archers were recruited. Third, defeated tribes such as the Ligures, and at a later time peoples of Spain and Gaul, were required to provide troops. For his Macedonian campaign of 171 BC, for example, Publius Licinius Crassus' army included 2,000 Ligures, Cretan bowmen, and Numidian cavalry and → elephants (Liv. 43,35).

Auxiliaries were attached to the provincial armies in the 1st century BC. In Gaul, archers from Crete, slingers from the Balearics and Numidians served in the Roman army (Caes. B Gall. 2,7), and Caesar augmented his forces further with Gaulish and Germanic mercenaries. Pompey deployed auxiliaries from the East during the Roman Civil War. Soon after, soldiers from Hispania and Lusitania served in the East in the army of Brutus and Cassius. In all but official name, therefore, the late Republic already had a standing army.

Augustus, emerging victorious from the Civil Wars, recognized the need for a professional standing army (Cass. Dio 52,27). The legions underwent a process of evolution over the course of his reign. Although no authoritative sources survive to prove it, the same is probably true of the *auxilia*.

The basic organization of the auxiliary units at this period can be traced as follows: the infantry was organized into cohorts on the model of the legions. The crucial innovation, however, concerned the cavalry, and consisted in the banding together of 16 *turmae* ('units') into a single *ala* ('auxiliary force'). Sometimes, four *turmae* were also placed alongside one cohort, creating the mobile *cohors equitata* ('mounted cohort'; cf. tab. 1).

B. Auxilia in the early Principate

Augustus continued the Republican practice of using *auxilia* ('auxiliaries') of different backgrounds. Those from defeated peoples fell into two categories. Some, like the Gaulish and Spanish *auxilia*, were used throughout the empire, while others, such as the Dalmatians, Pannonians and Germanic tribes from the right bank of the Rhine, tended to serve close to their home territories and under their own commanders. (In AD 9, however, the auxiliaries raised in Pannonia and Dalmatia were stationed away from those regions in the wake of the Bellum Batonianum).

Tab. 1: Strength and organization of units. Underscored figures are taken from military treatises of the period.

Type	centuriae	turmae	total
cohors quingenaria	<u>6</u> × 80 men = 480 men		480 men
cohors quingenaria equitata	<u>6</u> × 80 men = 480 men	4 × 30 men = <u>120</u> men	600 men
cohors milliaria	<u>10</u> × 80 men = 800 men		800 men
cohors milliaria equitata	<u>10</u> × 80 men = 800 men	8 × 30 men = 240 men	1040 men
ala quingenaria		<u>16</u> × 32 men = <u>512</u> men	512 men
ala milliaria		<u>24</u> × 32 men = 768 men	768 men

It is uncertain whether all auxiliaries were paid stipends at this early stage, or only those serving far from their homelands. Client kingdoms, such as Thrace, Commagene, Judaea and Mauretania, maintained their own armies, and were required to provide troops when necessary. There were always certain allies, particularly city-states in the east, that were able to provide troops in times of war. Augustus increased the numbers of *auxilia*, such that Tiberius had 14 *alae* ('auxiliary forces') and 70 cohorts in his army in AD 6–9 (Vell. Pat. 2,113). Tacitus describes the strength of the *auxilia* in AD 23 as about the same as that of the legions, that is, about 130,000 men, including the troops of the client kingdoms (Tac. Ann. 4,5).

As evidence from archaeology and sculpture accumulates, it becomes ever clearer that the auxiliaries of the Principate differed from those of the Republican period (→ Representations of war A.). There were no longer units of slingers, but archers were increasingly numerous. The tribes of Gaul and Hispania succeeded the Numidians as the heart of the cavalry. Equipment was now more standardized, with chain and scale armour prevailing. A flat shield of an oval or hexagonal shape was the norm, although at least two cohorts bore the *scutum* shield of the legionaries. Footsoldiers were armed with the *gladius* sword, cavalrymen with the *spatha* long sword. The former carried two spears each, to be used either as thrusting or throwing weapons. The latter, operating from the security of the saddle, had a lance and a number of projectile weapons.

Augustus set a minimum term of legionary service as a qualification for honourable discharge. In AD 5, this was twenty years, with a further five to be served in the reserve. There is no record of the minimum term of military service in the *auxilia* for this early period, but it would be strange if the auxiliaries were not also expected to serve for at least 25 years from the foundation of the Principate onwards. While legionaries received a monetary gift at discharge, the auxiliaries' main reward was exemption from taxes ([5.250f.]; Suet. Aug. 40,3). A privileged few were granted Roman citizenship (→ Military diploma). Evidence of auxiliaries' receiving citizenship after serving for 25 years first begins to accumulate under Tiberius. Of course, all such auxiliaries were recruited under Augustus. This award was made on an individual basis, in the expectation that the recipient would further extend his term of service [2].

Source material showing the further development of the *auxilia* improves over the century that followed. The armies of the client kingdoms were absorbed into the Roman army when those kingdoms became provinces. In the case of Thracia, this took place in two phases. Following the revolt of AD 26, Thracian units were stationed away from their home territory. After 46, when Thracia became a Roman province, Thracians began to appear regularly in non-Thracian units. Along the Rhine, the process was more gradual. Before the advent of the Flavian emperors, units recruited locally appear to have served on the Rhine. One exception, as a result of their unusual treaty conditions, was the Batavians. However, individual Germanic auxiliary soldiers also appear regularly in non-Germanic units. Such connections broke down after the suppression of the Batavian rebellion led by Iulius Civilis (AD 70) – but clearly not in the case of the Batavi.

Unit titles were generally uncomplicated. They were named after the place they were raised, or the tribe that had originally provided the unit. One final group received permanent names only in the reign of Tiberius: mostly unnumbered *alae*, and mainly from Gaul. To distinguish them, they were named after specific commanders [4], or sometimes after the province in which they served.

Under Augustus, commanders of auxiliary units were young senators (two per unit), *equites* (knights), *primipilares*, centurions and tribal chiefs. Only in the reign of Claudius was a three-tier command hierarchy established, the so-called *tres militiae*: *praefectus cohortis* (*prima militia*) – *tribunus militum legionis* (*secunda militia*) – *praefectus alae* (*tertia militia*). At first, the highest-ranking of these three was the legionary tribunate, but it was soon superseded by the command of the *praefectus alae* (→ Rank B.). Once the *cohortes milliariae* (cohorts of 1,000 men), commanded by tribunes, had been founded towards the end of the reign of Nero, this tribunate developed into an alternative *secunda militia* [9]. At the end of the 1st century, commanders of all units were of equestrian rank. Hadrian conferred on the *ala milliaria* (i.e. *ala* 1,000 strong), which was probably established under Vespasian, the rank of an elite unit, and established the *quarta militia* for its commanders. The system, however, always remained flexible, and patronage could override the usual career route. One and the same military position could be occupied by either a legionary tribune or a cohort tribune, whether the unit concerned was 1,000 strong or not (on the latter: [3]).

C. Service conditions

Augustus founded the *aerarium militare* ('military treasury') in AD 6 to pay out allowances and apparently also stipends to serving soldiers (Suet. Aug. 49,2). The precise rate of pay for auxiliaries is not known. One payment receipt for an *eques* ('cavalry soldier') of an auxiliary cohort is preserved from the year AD 38. This records him receiving the same sum as a legionary. Auxiliary infantry generally received rather less pay, cavalrymen of an *ala* ('auxiliary force') rather more [12].

Beginning in the mid-1st century, an imperial constitution (*constitutio*) granted auxiliary soldiers of at least 25 years' seniority (as well as their children and descendants) citizenship and the right to a legally valid Roman marriage (*conubium*). They could obtain a personal copy of this conferral of rights in the form of a document that is now known as a → military diploma. From the early 2nd century onwards, this conferral was made to auxiliaries on their honourable discharge from service. As a result, a greater number of citizenship constitutions has been preserved from this period, making for a fuller source basis. Entire units seem to have started receiving citizenship (and other distinctions and honorific titles) *en bloc* in the reign of Vespasian. The title concerned, however, and the date of its conferral are rarely preserved in full. The example of the *cohors I Brittonum milliaria Ulpia torquata pia fidelis civium Romanorum* of AD 106 is an exception (CIL XVI 160). Sometimes, too, such awards are recorded only once, and sometimes with rather surprising idiosyncrasies. Hadrian in AD 121, for instance, granted Roman citizenship not only to the serving cavalrymen of the *ala I Ulpia contariorum milliaria*, but also to their fathers, mothers, sisters and brothers [6]. Furthermore, some units only appear in a single citizenship constitution.

D. Auxiliary unit numbers in the army of the Imperial period

At no point is the exact number of auxiliary units in the Roman army of the Imperial period recorded, and it is not easy to determine. There is occasional confusion over whether units with the same name serving in neighbouring provinces at different dates are identical or not (e.g. the *cohors I Flavia civium Romanorum* in Syria and Syria-Palaestina). Other units are referred to at different times by different parts of a certain name, even on one and the same diploma. One such case concerns the *ala Augusta* in Mauretania Tingitana in AD 88 (CIL XVI 159), later known as the *ala I Augusta Gallorum civium Romanorum*. Its honorific title is not found in the list of units for the year 153, but it is recorded as part of the name of the recipient (RGZM, no. 34). There are also examples of units that as yet had no number in the 1st century, but had clearly received one by the reign of Hadrian, e.g. the *cohors (I) Cilicum*, *cohors (I) Ubiorum* and *ala (VII) Phrygum*. The last of these appears to have been the seventh *ala* ('auxiliary force') in Syria [7].

It is, however, possible to calculate how many *alae* ('auxiliary forces') and *cohortes* ('cohorts') were extant in Hadrian's reign (see table 2). Omitting units never attested after their date of raising, and assuming that 70% of all cohorts were partly made up of cavalry, the paper strength of the *auxilia* ('auxiliaries') around AD 129 comes to almost 220,000 men, of whom about 74,000 were cavalry soldiers. Of these, at least 20,000 were serving in special units of archers, including about 4,500 mounted. More individual specialist units were then recruited after the accession of Trajan, e.g. the *alae milliariae* of *contarii* (armed with the *contus* lance) and *dromedarii* (camel riders; → Camels) and a 1,000-strong cohort of *gaesati* (armed with the Gaulish lance, the *gaesum*). There was also specialist training elsewhere in the use of weapons like the slingshot and the *contus* ('pike') [14.89f.]. During the 2nd century, units began to be accommodated in their own permanent *castella* ('forts'), which adhered to a standard architectural plan, but with scope for variation according to terrain and deployment requirements.

E. New units

Much as during the Republican period, Rome in the 2nd century still had supplementary forces, as the relevant sources show [13]. Although many client kingdoms had by now been absorbed into the empire, there were still allied city-states in the east. Local → militias were transformed into regular auxiliary units and incorporated into the Roman army. This, at least, is the best explanation for findings like the presence of the *cohors I*

Tab. 2: Units in the reign of Hadrian (after: [8], updated 2021).

Province	Date	ala milliaria	ala	cohors milliaria	cohors
Dacia Porolissensis	128		3	3+(3)	2+(3)
Dacia superior	129	(1)	(2)		(10)
Dacia inferior	129		1+(2)+vex+?1	(1)	4+(4)
Moesia inferior			5		10+(2)
Thracia	127				(3)
Macedonia	127				(1)
Moesia superior	129		1+(1)		5+(7)+?2
Pannonia inferior	127	1	(5)	(2)	3+(8)
Dalmatia	129				(3)
Pannonia superior	129	(1)	(4)	(3)	(5)
Noricum	129	(1)	(2)	(2)	(4)
Raetia	127	(1)	3	3	10+(1)
Germania superior	129		3	1	12+(8)
Germania inferior	127		5+(1)		15+(2)
Britannia	127	1	6+(3)+?1	4+(1)	20+(14)+?5
Mauretania Tingitana	129		2+(3)	(1)	3+(6)
Hispania	129		(1)		(2)
Mauretania Caesariensis	128/31	1	(3)		3+(7)+?2
Africa	127		2		8+(1)+?1
Sardinia	127				(1)
Cyrenaica	127				(1)
Aegyptus	129		(3)		(11)
Syria Palaestina	129		(3)	(2)	(10)
Arabia	?126	1	1		5+(1)+?3
Syria	129		2+(5)	?1	11+(12)+?1
Cappadocia	129		(4)	(3)	(12)+?1
Galatia	129		(1)		(1)
Cilicia	129				(1)
Lycia et Pamphylia	129				(1)
Bithynia	129				(1)
Totals					
attested		4	34+vex	11	111
inferred		(4)	(43)	(18)	(143)
possible			?2	?1	?15

() – units that are attested in the province before and/or after the selected date during the reign of Hadrian, but not at that actual date
? – units that are attested in the reign of Trajan or in the reign of Hadrian up to the selected date, but not after it

Aelia Athoitorum in Thracia in 155 (AE 2004, 1907) or the *cohors I Helvetiorum* in Germania superior in 148 (CIL XIII 6472). Allies like the *Palmyreni sagittarii* were called up for specific campaigns, then granted citizenship in return [15]. Field armies also contained *nationes* ('local peoples') (Ps.-Hyg. De Mun. Cast. 29). Some only served in one specific war, while others were assimilated as *numeri* ('military units'), such as the *Brit(tones) Triput(ienses)* attested on the Upper Germanic frontier at Hesselbach in 146 (CIL XIII 6514; [11]). The *numeri* were mostly smaller units with vague service conditions.

It remains unclear to what extent these additional units, mostly cohorts, may have functioned as replacements for war losses prior to the crisis of the 3rd century. A citizenship *constitutio* of August 11, AD 193, which was granted to the auxiliaries of Pannonia inferior (RMD V 446; 447), shows that five cohorts had been added to the garrison of the province, although it seems that only one cohort had been lost in the wars under Marcus Aurelius. This had the effect of raising the number of cohorts in the province to 17. Three of these new cohorts, including the *cohors milliaria Maurorum*, are still attested there during the reign of Gordian

III. Five of the six *alae* ('auxiliary forces') stationed in Pannonia inferior are also mentioned. Of those, the *ala I Flavia Britannica milliaria* and the *ala I civium Romanorum* were in Apamea in Syria in AD 252 [1].

F. THE AUXILIA OF LATE ANTIQUITY

Caracalla's conferral of citizenship on all free-born inhabitants of the Roman Empire in AD 212 effaced once and for all the main distinction between the auxiliaries and the legions. All future distinctions – with the exception of the names – would be apparent only in the organization and function of the units. The reforms to the army carried out in the Severan period were not enough to avert the military crisis of the 3rd century, in which civil wars became entangled with foreign armed conflicts. Rates of losses to sometimes long-established units were now high. New units, whether made up of 'barbarian' mercenaries, settlers or recruits, still comprised legions, *alae* ('auxiliary forces') and *cohortes* ('cohorts'), replacing the lost units, but there were now increasing numbers of *numeri* ('military units'), including cavalry units called *cunei* ('divisions').

The distinction between *legiones* ('legions') and *auxilia* ('auxiliaries') was only finally abandoned in the early 4th century, in the wake of the complete reorganizations by Diocletian and later Constantine. In their place, there arose a field army of *palatini* ('palace troops') and *comitatenses* ('court troops'), stationed mainly at strategically important locations, while *limitanei* ('border troops') and *ripenses* ('riverbank troops') manned the frontiers. These latter units could be legions, *equites* ('cavalry'), *alae* ('auxiliary troops') and so forth, but there remained the possibility of promotion to the field army. Some units dating back to the early years of the Roman Empire are still listed in the *Notitia Dignitatum*, especially in provinces less prone to invasion and civil war, such as Britannia (Not. Dign. Occ. 40), Cappadocia (Not. Dign. Or. 38) and Mauretania Tingitana (Not. Dign. Occ. 26). From this point on, the term *auxilia* denoted a new type of infantry unit, probably of 500 men, presumably established by Constantine. The *Notitia Dignitatum* has 65 units of *auxilia palatina* in the army of the western *magister peditum praesentalis* (Not. Dign. Occ. 5) and 43 in the five eastern field armies (Not. Dign. Or. 5–9).

☞ Army; Legion; Military diploma

BIBLIOGRAPHY

[1] J.C. BALTY / W. VAN RENGEN, Apamea in Syria. The Winter Quarters of Legio II Parthica, 1993 [2] F. BEUTLER, Claudius und der Beginn der Militärdiplome – einige Gedanken, in: H. LIEB / M.A. SPEIDEL (eds.), Militärdiplome. Die Forschungsbeiträge der Berner Gespräche von 2004 (Mavors 15), 2007, 1–14 [3] A.R. BIRLEY, The Cohors I Hamiorum in Britain, in: Acta Classica 55, 2012, 1–16 [4] E. BIRLEY, Alae Named after Their Commanders, in: Ancient Society 9, 1978, 257–273 [5] E. BIRLEY, Before Diplomas, and the Claudian Reform, in: W. ECK / H. WOLFF (eds.), Heer und Integrationspolitik. Die römischen Militärdiplome als historische Quelle, 1986, 249–257 [6] W. ECK / A. PANGERL, Vater, Mutter, Schwestern, Brüder ... 3. Akt, in: ZPE 166, 2008, 276–284 [7] P. HOLDER, Two Commanders of Ala Phrygum, in: ZPE 140, 2002, 287–296 [8] P. HOLDER, Auxiliary Deployment in the Reign of Hadrian, in: J.J. WILKES (ed.), Documenting the Roman Army. Essays in Honour of Margaret Roxan (Bulletin of the Institute of Classical Studies Suppl. 81), 2003, 101–145 [9] D.L. KENNEDY, Milliary Cohorts. The Evidence of Josephus BJ III.4.2 (67) and of Epigraphy, in: ZPE 50, 1983, 253–263 [10] M. PETITJEAN, Pour une réévaluation de l'essor de la cavalerie au IIIe siècle, in: C. WOLFF / P. FAURE (eds.), Les auxiliaires de l'armée romaine. Des alliés aux fédérés, 2016, 491–525 [11] M. REUTER, Studien zu den numeri des Römischen Heeres in der Mittleren Kaiserzeit, in: Bericht der Römisch-Germanischen Kommission 80, 1999, 357–562 [12] M.A. SPEIDEL, Roman Army Pay Scales, in: M.A. SPEIDEL (ed.), Heer und Herrschaft im Römischen Reich der Hohen Kaiserzeit, 2009, 349–380 [13] M.A. SPEIDEL, Actium, Allies, and the Augustan Auxilia. Reconsidering the Transformation of Military Structures and Foreign Relations in the Reign of Augustus, in: C. WOLFF / P. FAURE (eds.), Les auxiliaires de l'armée romaine. Des alliés aux fédérés, 2016, 79–95 [14] M.P. SPEIDEL, Emperor Hadrian's Speeches to the African Army. A New Text, 2006 [15] O. ȚENTEA, Some Remarks on Palmyreni sagittarii. On the First Records of Palmyrenes within the Roman Army, in: I. PISO (ed.), Scripta classica. Radu Ardevan sexagenario dedicata, 2011, 371–378.

PAUL HOLDER

Avoidance of military service

A. Refusal to serve and conscientious objection
B. Desertion

A. REFUSAL TO SERVE AND CONSCIENTIOUS OBJECTION

Avoiding the obligation of military service was always regarded as a serious offence, and it was punished accordingly, although the specific punishments varied from case to case (death penalty, confiscation of assets, life imprisonment, corporal punishment, enslavement; Val. Max. 6,3,3f.; Cic. Caecin. 99; Frontin. Str. 4,1,20; Dig. 49,16,4,10). According to Arrius Menander, the death penalty ceased to be applied during the Imperial period (Dig. 49,16,4,10).

Men regularly mutilated their fingers to avoid military service (e.g. Amm. Marc. 15,12,3; Cod. Theod. 7,13,4). Fathers who attempted to spare their sons military service by this means were severely punished (Suet. Aug. 24,1; Dig. 49,16,4,11f.). The paucity of source material means that little can be said in detail about the motives behind the avoidance of military service or, among active soldiers, desertion. Occasionally, some writers and philosophers express antipathy towards war (Prop. 2,7,13; Tib. 1,10; Colum. prooem. 7; Tac. Hist. 3,81), but lack of criteria precludes investigating whether pacifism played a part in their reasoning [6]. During the Republican period, the attempt to avoid recruitment and military service was probably motivated in many cases by personal financial problems. That the first evidence of avoidance begins to appear in the 3rd century BC is unlikely to be a coincidence [7]. Rome at this period was fighting more and more wars outside Italy – with the result that serving men were often away from home for long periods and unable to maintain their farms, driving them and their families into poverty. The first recorded instance of avoidance of military service dates from 275 BC. Men in that year refused to obey their conscription by the consul following the landing in Italy of Pyrrhus of Epirus and his army (Val. Max. 6,3,4). With the devastating Roman defeats of 280 and 279 BC fresh in their minds, they were probably anticipating certain death (→ Recruitment). A general war-weariness in the aftermath of the gruelling First Punic War (264–241 BC) afflicted the first years of the Second Punic War (218–201 BC): according to Livy, over 2,000 conscripts avoided service for four years. They were struck off the list of citizens, with the consequence that they became taxable and had to serve as footsoldiers until the enemy was driven from Italy (24,18,7–9). The usual punishment of enslavement was not applied, probably because there was an urgent need for soldiers. Similar problems arose in the course of mobilization for the Third Macedonian War (169 BC; Liv. 43,14,2–4), and also in 151 BC during recruitment for the theatre of war in Hispania (Pol. 35,4,6). Added to this was an obvious unfairness in carrying out conscriptions: according to Republican recruitment practice, only some of those obliged to serve were actually conscripted (Ps.-Sall. Rep. 1,8,6). Concern for one's own life and → cowardice no doubt also played a significant part. Active soldiers may have been provoked to desert as a result of disciplinary problems, a history of crimes or misdemeanours, or tempting promises from the enemy (e.g. the offer made by Arminius to the soldiers of Germanicus: Tac. Ann. 2,13,2f.).

Christians sometimes objected to military service for religious reasons. St. Maximilian of Tebessa and the committed Christian Vitricius refused to serve because of the evils associated with the military (Musurillo 244–249; Paul. Nol. 18,7 (PL 41,240C)). However, the spread of Christianity did not lead to a mass boycott of military service [6].

B. DESERTION

B.1. Desertio and emansio
B.2. Defection

B.1. DESERTIO AND EMANSIO

Legal attitudes to abscondment or absence from the unit without leave differed according to the severity of the offence. The Roman jurists made a distinction between *desertio* ('desertion') and *emansio* ('staying away beyond furlough'), although the nature of the sources makes clear differentiation difficult. Standards for assessment likely varied over time and perhaps even from officer to officer (cf. Dig. 49,16,4,13f.). Criteria for rulings included the duration of absence, willingness of return, the specific circumstances that gave rise to the absence and the motivations of the deserter. Absence without leave was carefully described in army books (P. Dura. 100 = RMR 1 col. 22 l. 8; P. Mich. 455a = RMR 53 verso l. 6f.).

The legal sources dating from the late 2nd and early 3rd centuries AD indicate that a sophisticated procedure was in place for determining the level of punishment for desertion. Besides the duration of absence, consideration was given to time served and rank attained, the situation in which the soldier deserted and his conduct while absent from the unit. There was also the matter of whether this was a first or repeat offence, whether the accused deserted alone or with others and whether he had been apprehended or had returned voluntarily (Dig. 49,16,3,2f.; 49,16,4,15–5,5; 49,16,13,6). A soldier deserting for the first time was sometimes reinstated with his rights intact (Dig. 49,16,5,3). Recruits were forgiven a first abscondment (Dig. 49,16,3,9), but if they offended again, they were punishable. Deserters who committed a crime (e.g. theft or assault) during their desertion were punished as repeat offenders (Dig. 49,16,5,2). They could expect capital punishment (Dig. 49,16,5,3). In times of peace, a cavalryman deserting for the first time could expect demotion (probably to infantryman), and an infantryman disciplinary transfer. Those who deserted together were demoted and transferred to separate units (Dig. 49,16,3,9).

In wartime and in military emergencies, desertion was without exception subject to the death penalty (Tac. Ann. 13,35,5; Dig. 49,16,3,4; 49,16,5,1). The same fate awaited those avoiding military service by hiding out in the city of Rome (Dig. 49,16,5,3).

Soldiers sometimes exceeded their permitted period of furlough. This put them under suspicion of being an *emansor* or *desertor*. If the suspect could prove that he had embarked on his return journey in good time, and that only adverse circumstances, such as illness or powers beyond his control, had prevented his timely arrival, he escaped punishment. If, on the other hand, he was responsible for his own delay, the punishment depended on the duration of his absence. The tardy soldier in this case had to present evidence proving his innocence (Dig. 49,16,14 pr.; cf. 49,16,4,15).

B.2. DEFECTION

The gravest form of desertion was defection to the enemy (Dig. 49,16,7). An individual taken captive by the enemy and failing to return despite having the opportunity to do so was also regarded as a defector (*perfuga, transfuga*). Any soldier returning home from captivity was automatically suspected of defection, so that every individual case had to be investigated in detail. If the suspect was unable to prove that he had been captured rather than defecting, his history of conduct was admitted as evidence towards the verdict (Dig. 49,16,5,6). To the Romans, a *transfuga* was an enemy and no longer a member of the *exercitus Romanus* ('Roman army'). If captured, he could therefore expect, having first been formally expelled from the soldier class, the same fate as a traitor: generally torture and the death penalty without honour (Dig. 49,16,7; cf. 49,16,3,12). Anyone caught in the process of defecting was executed (Dig. 49,16,3,11). A deserter could be reprieved in certain circumstances. Hadrian pardoned a *transfuga* who had captured bandits (*latrones*) and reported other defectors (Dig. 49,16,5,8). A defector reinstated with former rights intact received neither pay nor *donativa* ('irregular monetary payments') for the period of his absence, unless the emperor gave a special dispensation. If a soldier could prove that he had not deserted, he received his full pay in arrears (Dig. 49,16,15; vgl. 49,16,10,1).

☞ **Military law**

BIBLIOGRAPHY

[1] J.H. JUNG, Die Rechtsstellung des römischen Soldaten. Ihre Entwicklung von den Anfängen Roms bis auf Diokletian, in: ANRW II.14, 1982, 977–990 [2] T. KISSEL, Kriegsdienstverweigerung im römischen Heer, in: Antike Welt. Zeitschrift für Archäologie und Kulturgeschichte 27/4, 1996, 289–296 [3] S.E. PHANG, Roman Military Service. Ideologies of Discipline in the Late Republic and Early Principate, 2008, esp. 148–150 and 209–212 [4] C. SCHMETTERER, Die rechtliche Stellung römischer Soldaten im Prinzipat (Philippika. Marburger altertumswissenschaftliche Abhandlungen 54), 2012, 28–31 [5] G. WESCH-KLEIN, Soziale Aspekte des römischen Heerwesens in der Kaiserzeit (HABES 28), 1998, 160–178 [6] L. WIERSCHOWSKI, Roma naturaliter bellicosa? – Kriegsdienstverweigerung und Fahnenflucht im Römischen Reich, in: Osnabrücker Jahrbuch Frieden und Wissenschaft 4, 1997, 131–153 [7] C. WOLFF, Déserteurs et transfuges dans l'armée romaine à l'époque républicaine, 2009.

GABRIELE WESCH-KLEIN

Bandits

Banditry was ubiquitous in Classical Antiquity. Robber bands and individual criminals were as commonplace in city centres as in the countryside. The outlaw was a very popular hero figure, particularly in the ancient novel (e.g. Apuleius' *Metamorphoses*) and in poetry. These genres constitute our most important sources of information alongside inscriptions [6.7f.]; [8.192]; [9]. Greek *poleis* and the Romans tried all conceivable means to combat banditry, which was virtually a mass phenomenon. Besides municipal and private initiatives, such means sometimes even included the deployment of regular army troops.

The Greek word *leisteia* denoted all forms of banditry and *leistai* the bandits themselves. Many of the fortifications in the territories of the Greek *poleis* were manned with municipal garrisons charged with fighting not only external, but also internal threats. The Hellenistic city-states and kingdoms also sought to keep the phenomenon in check. Garrisons (*phrourai*) and fortresses (*phrouria*) were set up to provide protection in rural areas, and *strategoi* and *peripoloi* (patrols, also attested in Classical Athens) were entrusted with punitive actions [3]. Some time after 80 BC, for example, a certain Apollodorus assembled a group of young men to fight the bandits who were plaguing the environs of Berenice in Cyrenaica (SEG 28, 1540). There is evidence of similar actions in Athens in 272–271 (SEG 24, 154), and in Hyettus in Boeotia, where soldiers of the Achaean League were committing all manner of banditry (*leisteia*) in the countryside around Heraclea Trachinia during their campaign against the city [1.21]; [3.117–119].

The Roman Empire enjoyed an interlude of relative internal peace from the mid-1st century AD to the reign of Marcus Aurelius. There are no surviving reports of large-scale banditry from this period, which may indicate that the phenomenon had been brought under a measure of control [8.194]. There is some indication that the Marcomannic Wars (AD 166–180) represented a significant watershed. This turbulent period yields evidence of the *latrones Dalmatiae atque Dardaniae* (SHA Aur. 21,7), and there are inscriptions of around the same date from the middle and lower Danube Basin that refer to 'those killed by bandits' (*interfecti a latronibus*) [7]; [11]; [12]. The generic Latin term for 'bandits' was thus *latro* (a word of Greek origin with the meaning of 'mercenary'). Other words used included *praedo* ('plunderer', from *praeda*, 'booty taken from an enemy', synonymous with *praemium*) [4]; [6.5, 14–32]; [10]. The Latin word for a 'robber band' is *factio*; *latrocinium* denotes 'banditry'. Bandits were not called *hostes* ('enemies'), a term reserved for foreign peoples waging war on Rome (Dig. 50,16,118). Some of these bands became notorious, such as the Bulla Felix (apparently a nickname, highly reminiscent of Sulla Felix!), which conducted a two-year campaign of plunder across the whole of Italy in 205–206 [6.111–123]. However, various tribes that caused trouble in the Roman provinces also earned themselves the name of 'bandits'. Examples include the Brisei in the borderlands between Macedonia and Thracia, who were eventually annihilated by the *procurator* of Moesia inferior, M. Valerius Maximianus, during the reign of Marcus Aurelius (AE 1956, 124 = 1959, 183), and intruders into Roman territory (*latrunculi*) in Pannonia inferior during the reign of Commodus (CIL III 10312 = RIU 5,1131) and in the province of Scythia in AD 337–340 (CIL III 12483 = ILS 724).

Military *stationes* ('stations'), as well as *burgi* ('forts') and *praesidia* ('fortifications'), were set up throughout the territories of the empire to curtail the activities of bandits (Tert. Apol. 2,8) – not only in the frontier provinces and zones [5], but also in Asia Minor and Egypt, where the presence of bandits is attested everywhere [1]; [2]; [13].

☞ Policing

BIBLIOGRAPHY

[1] C. BRÉLAZ, La sécurité publique en Asie Mineure sous le Principat (Ier–IIIème s. ap. J.-C.). Institutions municipales et institutions impériales dans l'Orient romain, 2005 [2] C. BRÉLAZ, L'adieu aux armes. La défense de la cité grecque dans l'empire romain pacifié, in: P. DUCREY / C. BRÉLAZ (eds.), Sécurité collective et ordre public dans les sociétés anciennes (Entretiens sur l'Antiquité Classique 54), 2008, 155–196 [3] A. CHANIOTIS, Policing the Hellenistic Countryside. Realities and Ideologies, in: P. DUCREY / C. BRÉLAZ (eds.), Sécurité collective et ordre public dans les sociétés anciennes (Entretiens sur l'Antiquité Classique 54), 2008, 103–153 [4] M. CLAVEL-LÉVÊQUE, Brigandage et piraterie. Représentations idéologiques et pratiques impérialistes au dernier siècle de la République, in: DHA 4, 1978, 17–31 [5] J. FRANCE / J. NELIS-CLÉMENT (eds.), La statio. Archéologie d'un lieu de pouvoir dans l'empire romain, 2014 [6] T. GRÜNEWALD, Bandits in the Roman Empire. Myth and Reality, 2004 [7] P. KOVÁCS, Interfectus a latronibus intrusis. Beiträge zum Tod eines Freigelassenen aus Scarbantia, in: E. NEMETH (ed.), Violence in Prehistory and Antiquity, 2018, 301–317 [8] R. MACMULLEN, Enemies of the Roman Order. Treason, Unrest, and Alienation in the Empire, 1966 [9] W. RIESS, Apuleius und die Räuber. Ein Beitrag zur historischen Kriminalitätsforschung, 2001 [10] B.D. SHAW, Bandits in the Roman Empire, in: Past & Present 105, 1984, 3–52 [11] R. VARGA / A.-I. PÁZSINT, The Reflection of Personal and Collective Tragedies in the Ancient Sources. 1. Personal Tragedies in Roman Epigraphy, in: Journal of Ancient History and Archaeology 5(4), 2018, 22–31 [12] C. WOLFF, Interfecti a latronibus, in: M. BĂRBULESCU (ed.), Funeraria Daco-Romana, 2003, 205–214 [13] C. WOLFF, Les brigands en Orient sous le Haut-Empire romain, 2003.

FLORIAN MATEI-POPESCU

Battle

A. Introduction
B. Pitched battle
C. Classical Greece
D. Hellenistic period
E. Roman Republic
F. Imperial period
G. Late Antiquity
H. Wounded and fallen

A. Introduction

No ancient source makes a clear distinction between a battle and a skirmish (*diaplektizomai*: Plut. Luc. 31,6; Lucian. Anach. 11; *leve proelium*: Liv. 35,3,3; 39,2,8). The Greek noun *akrobolismos* ('discharge of [long-distance] weapons') was sometimes also used to denote a skirmish (Pol. 14,8,4; Arr. *Acies* 25). A battle, in general, was a one-day encounter at a specific location. Battles reported as lasting several days are either exceptional cases or exaggerated accounts (e.g. Asculum, only two days: Plut. Pyrrh. 21,5–9; Orchomenus, two days: Plut. Sull. 21,1–4; App. Mithr. 199–202; Macrinus' three-day battle at Nisibis: Hdn. 4,15).

Clausewitz wrote that 'the "decision by weapons" ... for any operation of war, large or small, was like the cash payment for a financial transaction' [2.25]. Paradoxically, ancient theorists advised avoiding battles – the cornerstone of traditional military history – wherever possible, because they tended to be decided by luck rather than by skill or numbers (e.g. Polyaenus, Strat. 1 pr. 3; Veg. Mil. 3,3,3; 3,3,12; 9,3; 9,8; 22,12f.; 26,4–6; 26,31f.).

The concept of the decisive battle, a precursor to Clausewitz' *Vernichtungsschlacht* ('battle of annihilation'), arose in the 18th century and became a favourite topic of military historiography in the 19th and 20th centuries [4]; [5]; [11]; [6]. No Greek or Latin technical term corresponds to this notion or distinguishes it from general expressions for deciding a war or campaign by a battle (e.g. Pol. 3,111,2; Liv. 35,3,5). Whether a battle was decisive or not depended on the strategic and political context of the confrontation, the goals for the warring parties, the losses of men and materiel, and the will of the defeated party to keep fighting or that of the victor to press home the victory.

Variants of the general terms for 'battle' (Greek *mache*; Latin *pugna/proelium*; cf. as an exception Isid. Orig. 18,1,8) justify Clausewitz' concept of the *Waffenentscheidung* ('decision by weapons'). A battle was a contest (Greek *agon*, Latin *certamen*), a test with weapons, in which the victors proved themselves superior (*dis volentibus*, 'if the gods are willing'; Paus. 4,17,3). In Hellenistic usage (especially Polybius, e.g. 1,87,10; 4,12,14), the word *kindynos* ('hazard', 'venture'), when used with reference to a battle, emphasizes the uncertainty of the outcome. A naval battle in Greek was *naumachia* (Hdt. 6,14,1; Thuc. 1,13,4); in Latin *navale proelium/certamen* (Gell. NA 10,6,1; Veg. Mil. 4,44,1).

In the case of the traditional 'pitched' battle, victory was a matter of honour, an aspect that recent scholarship has sometimes neglected. The way in which a → general achieved victory was important, lest his reputation suffer. The use of force in direct confrontation was synonymous with valour (*arete/virtus*), but victory by deception was shameful (e.g. Isid. Orig. 18,2,1; Thuc. 4,86,6; Xen. Hell. 6,5,16; Iust. 14,1,12; cf. Sall. Iug. 42,3). Similarly, war between comparable peoples and civilized states represented a competition for rank and *imperium* (the right to rule), involving certain constraints on conduct – as distinct from the more brutal struggles for life and death against 'barbarian' tribes (cf. Cic. Off. 1,38; Liv. 22,58,3; 30,32,2). Victory in pitched battle compelled the vanquished party to admit defeat and broke their will to continue the war (Ennius in Serv. Aen. 11,307; Pol. 13,3,3; Liv. 42,47,8; Claud. *De sexto consulatu Honorii* 248f.).

Pre-state warfare, which was often characterized by surprise attacks, ambushes and feigned withdrawals, had no standard practices, but differed from culture to culture. In general, peoples before the formation of states paid little heed to their own heavy losses, even though bloody conflicts and massacres were a possibility, depending on the purpose the war and the strength of the adversary. There is also evidence for ritualized, formal confrontations that were relatively low in bloodshed. Duels between heros (Greek *monomachia*, 'single combat') in the no-man's-land between opposing armies functioned either as preludes to battle or as proxy battles in place of deploying full forces.

In the single combat of the *monomachia*, the day, hour and venue for the duel were often agreed in advance (z.B. Liv. 1,24,2), making this a battle 'by appointment' (Pol. 13,3,5; Liv. 42,47,5) that might be announced as part of a declaration of war (z.B. Plut. Publ. 16,1). Such a practice was known to the Germanic Cimbri (Plut. Mar. 25,2–4), the Samnites (Liv. 8,23,8–10) and even the Tibareni of Pontus (Schol. Apoll. Rhod. 2,1010–1014). As in the case of a simple challenge to battle, the unwritten rules for a battle by appointment required both sides to march up without attacking or harassing the other. It was also impermissible for either party to draw advantage from arriving at the agreed theatre first (Ambr. Off. 1,29). Ranged weapons were not prohibited, either in single combat or in pitched battle, but ruses of war such as feigned retreats, while permissible in a duel, jeopardized one's honour if used in a pitched battle [7].

Night combat (Greek *nyktomachia*, e.g. Thuc. 7,44; Latin *nocturum proelium*, Liv. 42,47,5), a form of surprise attack, belonged more to the spheres of siege warfare, the localized raid and guerrilla warfare than to the pitched battle, where its use was regarded as dishonourable (Pol. 4,8,11; 4,25,3; Plut. Alex. 31,10f.; Dion. Hal. Ant. Rom. 3,8,2) [8. vol. 2, 162–170]. The kind of night attacks on fortified enemy camps that were feasible for smaller units posed countless technical and tactical difficulties for large field armies.

B. Pitched battle

Most battles cannot be reconstructed historically. Only in a very few cases are (necessarily makeshift) attempts possible. Marathon, Leuctra, Cannae and Adrianople spark new discussions on an almost annual basis. Ranke's *wie es eigentlich gewesen* (the 'how it actually happened' principle), desirable as it is for the history of ancient battles, is unattainable for many reasons, not least the inadequacy of the sources [1]. Still, many a modern scholar is undeterred from a career as a wargamer and armchair general. The following remarks concern particular aspects of battle, not tactics (see in general on the pitched battle [10]; [13]).

Differences in topography (or relative position) can contribute greatly to a defeat on land or at sea (Pol. 5,21,6). A judicious choice of venue could make the impossible possible, even more effectively than valour (Pol. 9,13,8; Veg. Mil. 3,26,11). A general could build his plan around the nature of the terrain (Caes. B Civ. 3,43,1f.; cf. Cato in Liv. 34,14,1), although finding a favourable location was sometimes simply a matter of luck (Onas. Strat. 21,4). Frontinus (Str. 2,2) and Vegetius (Mil. 3,13) devoted entire chapters to the choice of the correct venue for battle. Confrontations arising from more or less accidental discovery of or by the enemy made it impossible to choose the location. Any topographic advantage in these cases depended on chance or adaptive manoeuvres.

The choice of venue depended on the strategic context of the battle and the respective strengths and weaknesses of both armies. Mountain passes and junctions were frequent battle sites: Thermopylae (480, 279, 191 BC), Mantinea (418, 362, 207 BC), Chaeronea (338, 245, 86 BC) and Issos (333 BC, AD 194). It was an accepted principle that flat ground benefited armies with strong cavalry, while infantry had an advantage over cavalry on rugged or rising terrain (Pol. 1,30,8–11). In the age before the advent of gunpowder, defenders in a battle were not able to take up positions behind fortifications and fire from trenches.

When forces of equal size met, it was advisable to position one or both flanks against a river, natural obstacle or rough ground, to prevent an envelopment attack. However, a river or ditch at an army's rear was an obstacle to withdrawal, and hence to be avoided (Pol. 2,33,7f.). Even so, some generals did choose such a position deliberately, in order to instill a frenzy of desperation in cases where morale and discipline were in doubt – one example being that of the Spartans at the Battle of the Great Foss during the Second Messenian War (probably second half of 7th century BC; Aristot. eth. Nic. 1116a36–b1 mit Schol. 1116b30).

Armies with heavy infantry preferred flat ground. The Greek hoplite phalanx was cumbersome in manoeuvres or about-face. It developed as a formation for non-professional soldiers with the aim of operating as a single, cohesive mass in a frontal collision with the enemy (*mache ek tou phanerou*). The Spartans became skilled at flanking manoeuvres in the late 5th century BC (Mantineia, 418 BC; Nemea, 394 BC). The Macedonian innovation of reducing the individual soldier's armour while considerably lengthening his spear (*saris(s)a*) did not greatly alter the character of the phalanx. However, the combined forces of the Hellenistic period exhibited a degree of flexibility, with increased use of light infantry and an enhanced tactical role for the cavalry. Variable ground conditions sometimes disrupted the cohesion of the phalanx (Aristot. Pol. 5,1303b12), but this was true of any formation of heavy infantry. Polybius' further remarks on the inferiority of the phalanx to the supposedly more flexible Roman legion are misleading (Pol. 18,31,2–7). The Romans also preferred to fight on level ground (*iusti/aequi loci*, e.g. Caes. B Civ. 3,56,1; 3,73,5; Liv. 9,19,15f.; Tac. Ann. 2,5,3).

C. Classical Greece

The origins of the → phalanx are obscure. A hoplite phalanx of the Classical period comprised a rectangular block of ranks in tight formation, at least eight men deep, the depth varying from *polis* to *polis* and according to the general's preference. Depth could be reduced against a numerically superior enemy in order to lengthen the battle line and thus prevent encirclement (e.g. the Athenians at Marathon: Hdt. 6,111–112,1). This, however, could be dangerous (Onas. Strat. 21,1f.). The phalanx was primarily designed for direct attacks and lacked mobility when an about-face or other manoeuvre was required. On the one hand, its depth deterred a frontal cavalry attack, while on the other it served to conceal the limited fighting ability of the non-professional hoplites. They carried a twin-handled round shield (*aspis*) with a diameter of about 90 cm, designed chiefly to protect the fighter's left side (Thuc. 5,71,1), and a lance (*dory*) no less than 2.40 m in length. The design of the round shield encouraged the mutual support of fighters in the ranks, whose cohesion the sources regularly emphasize.

The emergence of the phalanx coincides with that of the *polis*. It enabled *poleis* to send citizens who were performing military service only for a short time to fight in wars that generally did not last long. Despite the widespread distribution of hoplite armour, the phalanx did not appear simultaneously in all parts of the Greek world, and some parts the phalanx never reached at all (e.g. Aetolia and Acarnania). In the larger *poleis* of the Greek mainland, the phalanx supplanted the cavalry and light infantry until changes came in the 5th century. For a long time Sparta had no regular company of archers and no cavalry. Only in 424 BC were these hastily assembled to defend the country against coastal attacks by the Athenians (Thuc. 4,55,2). One company (*lochos*) of 600 Laconian Scirites (*skiritai*) performed the light-infantry functions of reconnaissance and flank protection (Thuc. 5,67,1; Xen. Lac. Pol. 12,3; Xen. Cyr. 4,2,1). Even at Marathon in 490, Athens had no archers, and in 424 it still lacked regular field units of light infantry (Thuc. 4,94,1). Meanwhile, a more fluid style of warfare with light infantry, cavalry and hoplites working in concert was the norm on the peripheries of the Greek world.

No source explains the preference for a depth of eight rather than the usual ten ranks in the Classical hoplite phalanx [8. vol. 1, 134–143]. When allied troops fought together, every *polis* decided the depth of its own units. Thebes often chose a depth of 25 or even 50 ranks (e.g. at Leuctra, 371 BC). The phalanxes of each *polis* also acted separately when allies joined formations, probably leaving a small gap between the contingents of the individual cities. The front of an allied battle formation should thus not be imagined as a single phalanx. Disputes occured among allied units over which contingent should take up the right flank of the formation, the traditional position of honour (e.g. at Plataeae, Hdt. 9,26–28,1; 9,46). The obscure origins of this tradition must be connected somehow with the lack of protection on the right side, as well as with the tendency of phalanx advances to veer to the right (Thuc. 5,71,1). The commander's position was at (or near) the front rank of the right flank, which consisted of the top-rated hoplites – hence the tradition that the right flank constituted the main offensive wing of the phalanx.

Prior to the 4th century BC, the cavalry was not a regular support set up on the flanks of the hoplite phalanx. Whether or not light infantry took part in pitched battles before the 4th century is unclear. Nor were hoplite battles invariably preceded by skirmishes between the opposing light infantry, as was the standard practice by the Hellenistic period (cf. Ael. *Taktika* 17; Arr. Tact. 15).

D. HELLENISTIC PERIOD

The reforms to the Macedonian army under Philip II (→ Generals of note, M.) set the tone for battle formations of the Hellenistic period and beyond. These formations reflect the growing importance of the cavalry and light infantry since the late 5th century BC. The greater ethnic diversity of combatants (whether → mercenaries or allies) and the preferred weapons of these diverse fighters introduced new elements to the battlefield, for the size and resources of the Hellenistic kingdoms far exceeded those of individual *poleis*.

The transition from hoplites (citizen-soldiers of the *polis*) to phalangites (soldiers of the Hellenistic phalanx) demanded changes in armour and weaponry. However, the hoplites did not disappear entirely. The Macedonian *hypaspistai* (footsoldiers armed with long spear and shield) are generally regarded as hoplites, and some *poleis* were still sending hoplite armies into the field. Philip II equipped the hoplite phalanx with new weapons and a new structure. The *pelte*, a round shield (diameter somewhat over 60 cm) that hung from a strap (*telamon*) around the neck, superseded the Classical shield (*aspis*, approx. 90 cm diameter), and the *saris(s)a*, a lance 3.60 m in length (or more – its length varied in the Hellenistic period) that was wielded in both hands, supplanted the Classical spear (the *dory*, approx. 2.40 m long; cf. → Armament). The hoplite phalanx's traditional depth of eight ranks was doubled to 16, and sometimes increased to as many as 32 as circumstances dictated. The greater length of the *sarissa* and the five lance tips that protruded from each rank of the phalanx front, exceeding the potential thrusting range of the hoplite lance (*dory*), made the Hellenistic phalanx an unstoppable force in frontal combat against a hoplite phalanx or a Roman legion.

Like the hoplite phalanx, the Macedonian phalanx had subunits with subordinate officers. The extreme system of subunits and their officers laid out in the tacticians' treatises, however, are probably no more than theoretical. Macedonian organization was already continuing to evolve under Alexander the Great (→ Generals of note, B.). Later terminology differed in the Diadochic armies of the Antigonids, Seleucids, Ptolemies and others. Following the Battle of Pydna (168 BC), the Seleucid, Ptolemaic and Pontic armies began to develop units imitating Roman equipment and manipular organization [3]; [9].

How best to use the composite forces of the Hellenistic army was a perpetual problem. The varied types of different units invited creativity in battle planning. Any 'typical' scenario for the formation of Hellenistic field armies had exceptions. The Macedonian phalanx, which was just as cumbersome as that of the hoplites, needed protection on its flanks. Often, a hoplite unit was positioned at either or both sides of the Macedonian phalanx, and light infantry were placed at either or both sides of the hoplites. The cavalry defended both flanks. If → elephants were deployed, they were mostly stationed in front of the heavy infantry, alternating with light footsoldiers, as additional protection for one or both flanks, or as a reserve. Skirmishes involving opposing units of light infantry prior to the conflict between the main forces became a standard feature of Hellenistic battles. Once the main conflict began, the skirmishers withdrew to the flanks of their respective armies, from where they could continue to aim volleys of projectiles at the enemy's main units.

The traditional preference for a stronger right wing in the battle formation was linked with the model of Epaminondas, in which the attack was confined to one wing only. A tendency towards having one offensive and one defensive wing developed from the time of Alexander to the ends of his successors' reigns (e.g. Demetrius at Gaza: Diod. Sic. 19,82,4). The task of the Macedonian phalanx at the centre was to deal with the enemy's heavy infantry, while the cavalry on one wing (often the right) would exploit a gap in the opposing battle lines to attack the enemy phalanx in the flank and from behind. Alexander leading the cavalry of his entourage (*hetairoi*) became the model here. The wedge of the new Macedonian cavalry did not attempt to break through where the enemy's heavy infantry was massed together, but made use of a gap that appeared in the course of the battle (e.g. Arr. Anab. 3,13,2).

As the Hellenistic period wore on, the cavalry's initial prominence as the key impact force faded, and the attack capabilities of the *sarissa* phalanx once again increased in importance. Some tried to make the phalanx more flexible. At the Battle of Sellasia in 222/21 BC, Antigonus III Doson deployed Illyrian units and his own phalanx troops alternately in an attack on a hill (Pol. 2,66,5). The intent of Antiochus III Megas for his main phalanx at the Battle of Magnesia ad Sipylum (190 BC; → Battles of note, E.) – whether it was offensive or defensive – is unclear. The phalanx numbered 16,000 and consisted of units 32 ranks deep and 50 men wide. Two elephants were positioned in the gaps between these units (Liv. 37,40,1–4; App. Syr. 162–168).

→ Artillery, a key element of siege warfare since its invention in the early 4th century BC, now began to appear sporadically on the battlefield. Before the Roman invention of the *carroballista* (a specialist, heavy, twin-armed torsion catapult) around AD 100, the limited mobility of the human arm restricted the use of artillery on the battlefield – except where siege machinery already in place was moved to hilltops or behind fortifications so that its firing range could be exploited without exposing it to capture. The earliest attested case involves Onomarchus deploying non-torsion stone catapults on hilltops to fire down on the army of Philip II (Polyaenus, Strat. 2,38,2). Alexander organized covering artillery fire for his withdrawal from Illyria across the River Eordaicus (Arr. Anab. 1,6,8). He secured his crossing of the Iaxartes in Sogdiana in a similar way in the face of Scythian resistance (Arr. Anab. 4,4,4; cf. Curt. 7,9,3–7). Thereafter, artillery features mainly in the defence of fortified lines – essentially siege scenarios. For the Antigonids, Philip V used artillery to reinforce his battle lines against Publius Villius and Titus Quinctius Flamininus at the Battle of the Aous (Liv. 32,5,13; 32,10,11). Perseus did the same against Aemilius Paullus at the River Elpeus (Liv. 44,35,8f.; 44,35,21f.).

E. ROMAN REPUBLIC

E.1. Phalanx
E.2. Manipular legion
E.3. Cohort legion

E.1. PHALANX
The formations of the earliest Roman armies are beyond reconstruction. Hoplite equipment reached Italy about 650 BC. The Etruscans deployed a 'phalanx', but the retention of their traditional battleaxes, single-edgedswords and helmets suggest that theirs was a looser formation than that of the Greeks. The Romans took up the *aspis* ('shield'; Latin *clipeus*) and *dory* ('spear'; Latin *hasta*) along with the phalanx formation under Etruscan influence, and Livy's comparison (8,8,3) is with the Macedonian version rather than with the hoplite army. Rome also adopted the practice of 'static battle' from the Etruscans (Poseidonius in Ath. 6,273f.; cf. Diod. Sic. 23,2,1f.), suggesting a link between the Roman phalanx and the evolution of the older, more flexible form of warfare as the Roman state emerged.

The constitution attributed to Servius Tullius (traditionally dated to the mid-6th century BC) organized citizens by class according to their property into centuries (*centuriae*), laying down specific military functions for each century. Every man provided his own equipment. The accounts by Livy (1,43) and Dionysius of Halicarnassus (Dion. Hal. Ant. Rom. 4,16–18), although not identical, both record combined fighting units of heavy and light infantry (slingers and stone throwers) as well as cavalry. In the first four classes of infantry, there were two age groups: the *seniores* charged with defending the city were distinguished from the *iuniores* who served in the field. The first class, with full hoplite equipment, was stationed at the front line, while the second class, which lacked the breastplate, carried the elongated-shield (*thyreos/scutum*) rather than the *clipeus*. The spears in classes 1–4 were *hastae*. Livy's class 4, however, has no *scutum*, but does carry a javelin (*verutum*). Class 5 had no armour and consisted of slingers and stone throwers, but not archers.

Members of the cavalry ('horsemen', *equites*) came from the wealthiest families. The poorer citizens in class 5 were known as *rorarii* (*ferentarii/levis armatura* in some sources), later *velites*.

E.2. MANIPULAR LEGION

In the Roman Republic (founded in 509 BC according to the traditional dating), the two consuls, who were elected for a one-year term, from at least 311 BC onwards each commanded an army of two legions (each comprising 5,000 infantry and 300 cavalry), which were recruited as required. More and larger legions could also be raised. The → legion (*legio*), the most important organizational component of the army, was never a tactical unit. The manipular legion evolved out of the phalanx. It comprised 30 maniples (*manipuli*), each in turn made up of two centuries (*centuriae*) of 60 men apiece (not the same as the *centuriae* of the Servian constitution above), which could act independently. The manipular legion, tactically more flexible and manoeuvrable than the unwieldy unified phalanx, offered a direct system of reserves to relieve fighters at the front. In later times, the Hellenistic phalanx was also sometimes subdivided into smaller units (e.g. at Sellasia).

Livy (8,8,3) connects the transformation of the phalanx into the manipular legion with the introduction of the soldier's stipend (*stipendium*; traditionally 405 BC; → Pay) and the replacement of the hoplite shield (the *aspis/clipeus*) with the large, oval shield known as the *scutum* (*thyreos*), which had one handle and a protruding boss (*umbo*). The gradual transition to the manipular legion did not wholly eliminate phalanxes, which are still occasionally attested in later times. The origins of the Roman *pilum*, a heavy throwing spear with limited range but considerable penetrating power, are much discussed (Celtic? Samnite? Hispanic? Indigenous Roman?). It is unclear exactly when it was first used (by 250 BC at the latest: Pol. 1,40,12). The renowned Roman short sword, the Hispanic *gladius*, does not appear in the archaeological record before about 200 BC (cf. Liv. 31,34,3–5). In all likelihood, therefore, the Roman legionary for quite some time remained a spearman rather than a swordsman.

Livy (8,8–10) gives his excursus on the manipular legion immediately before his account of the Battle of Vesuvius (near the the River Veseris; 340 BC), while Polybius' account (6,21–25) refers to the early 2nd century BC. Both describe a battle array of three ranks (*triplex acies*), divided by age group and weaponry. All three ranks carried the *scutum*. The *hastati* ('lancers' carrying the *hasta*, a short stabbing spear), the best of the young soldiers, formed the first *acies* ('line of battle') with gaps between their maniples that were covered by the *principes*, the second *acies* made up of older, stronger soldiers. If the attack of the *hastati* failed to decide the battle, they withdrew through the gaps between the maniples of the *principes*, and the *principes* advanced almost simultaneously to renew the assault. There is no record of this substitution procedure being reversed, where the *hastati* advanced to relieve the *principes*, as is sometimes assumed. Vegetius' description of the *principes* as the first line of battle (Mil. 1,20,3; 2,15,3; 2,15,9; 3,14,5) is either his own innovation or a misunderstanding; at all events, it has no basis in earlier sources.

These two ranks, which were also called the *antepilani*, formed up in front of the third *acies* ('line of battle'), the *triarii* or *pilani*. These were the oldest soldiers, divided into maniples of two half centuries. They functioned as a general reserve and tactical bulwark (*probole*). The *triarii* still carried the *hasta* – as distinct from the *pilum* of the *antepilani*. If the *principes* failed, they – along with the *hastati* – withdrew through the gaps between the maniples of the *triarii*, and battle continued with a single front of all three groups in phalanx formation. There is general support for the formation of the maniple in a chessboard array (Pol. 15,9,8; cf. Asclepiodotus, *Taktika* 11,7), although there is no record of the term *quincunx* ('five twelfths') being used for it.

The three successive waves of battle as described by Livy have led to endless speculation over how the manipular legion worked. There is no dispute over the component elements of the *triplex acies* (e.g. Pol. 14,8,5; Liv. 30,8,5). But did the Romans really take the field with gaps in their battle lines that were large enough for maniples to pass through? The sources as they stand do not permit a conclusive answer, although Polybius' account of Gaius Flaminius' battle with the Gauls (Pol. 2,33,7f.) lends support to Livy's scenario. Discussions of the gaps between the ranks of footsoldiers (Pol. 18,30,5–10; Veg. Mil. 3,14,6f.; 3,15) assume the width needed for a legionary fighting with a sword – a phenomenon of the Second Punic War (?). The theoretical scheme of Vegetius is flawed, and that of Polybius' is propaganda. In his descriptions of Roman combat, Polybius generally ignores the *pilum*. He mentions it only in one excursus (Pol. 6,23,8–11) and in connection with the battle of 250 BC (Pol. 1,40,12). Its omission from his comparison of the legion and the phalanx (Pol. 18,28–32) is particularly glaring. The space between soldiers in a legion was probably identical to the *pyknosis* ('close order') of the Hellenisticphalanx: 90 cm between the ranks and the soldiers within them, leaving the individual soldier rather less than one square metre of space.

In a *manipulus* of 120 soldiers, 20 men lined up side by side in each of six ranks, one behind the other. The depth of the formation was the same as the breadth of the marching column (→ March). This reflected the *contubernium* ('tent-companionship') of the Republican period. At some point in the Imperial period, the number of ranks increased to eight, a development attested only in Pseudo-Hyginus Gromaticus (Mun. Cast. 1). Each *centuria* of a *manipulus* had its own commander, the *centurio*. He was called *prior* or *posterior* depending on his seniority of service. The two centuries took the field side by side, and the *centurio prior* commanded the century on the right-hand side, with responsibility for the whole maniple (Pol. 6,24,1f.; 6,24,8). One officer from the rear ranks, the *optio* ('adjutant'), served each century, very much like the *ouragos* of a phalanx. The *primipilus*, the senior *centurio* of the legion, commanded the first *centuria* of the *triarii* (Liv. 8,8,16; cf. Pol. 6,35,12). Each *manipulus* also had a → standard (*signum*), the emblem of the unit's identity with religious connotations of divine presence. The *signa* also served as visual guides in manoeuvres and as gathering points visible from afar during combat.

Over time, the flexibility and adaptability of the manipular legion became obvious, as formal pitched battles like the Battle of Vesuvius (near the River Veseris; Liv. 8,8–10) gave way to less formal battles and conflicts outside Italy. The use of single or multiple maniples to attack the enemy's flanks (rather than as support in frontal attacks) began with the experiments of Scipio Africanus at Baecula (Pol. 10,39,1–8; Liv. 27,18; → Generals of note, O.) and Ilipa during the Second Punic War (Pol. 11,22–23,7; Liv. 28,14–15,14), where the manoeuvre came close to a semilunar formation (*lunata acies*), also known to the tacticians as the 'pincer movement' (*forceps/forfex*; Asclepiodotus, *Taktika* 11,1,5 and 7; Ael. *Taktika* 37,7).

E.3. COHORT LEGION

As the frequency of formal pitched battles with other state-like entities decreased after the Second Punic War, the inefficiency of heavy legionary infantry in combat with 'barbarians' and insurgent forces outside Italy became clear, since these opponents often avoided the pitched battle (*aperta proelia*, cf. Plut. Sert. 12,5; Plut. Pomp. 17,2). A new tactical trend took hold that would endure until the end of the Roman Empire: a preference for light infantry, cavalry and ranged weapons [6]. In view of the clear inferiority of the Roman and Italic cavalry to that of the Numidians and others in the war against Hannibal, Rome increasingly began to rely on fighters from outside Italy (whether as confederates or → mercenaries), and on their specialist skills, as cavalrymen, light infantry, slingers and bowmen. The last appearance of the cavalry of the Italic allies (*socii*) was at the end of the 2nd century BC (Sall. Iug. 95,1). The timeframe for the elimination of the legionary cavalry is disputed, but it had essentially lost all relevance by the Imperial period. The *velites* also vanished, around 100 BC or shortly thereafter (Sall. Iug. 46,7; 105,2; cf. Frontin. Str. 2,9,3).

The reorganization of the → legion is traditionally linked to the so-called Marian Reforms of the late 2nd century BC (→ Generals of note, K.). Notably, this saw the manipular legion transformed into the cohort legion, which is described most clearly in the works of Julius Caesar. In a typical cohort battle, one legion in tripartite battle array (*triplex acies*) opened hostilities with volleys of javelins (*pila*). These were thrown at a run while storming into the pitched battle, which was fought with the sword (*gladius*; e.g. Caes. B Gall. 1,25). Experiments with combinations of maniples began during the Second Punic War. The need for a larger tactical unit for fighting barbarian tribes suggests (to many scholars) that the wars in Spain were the testing ground for the development of the cohort (*cohors*).

A *cohors* combined the maniples of *hastati*, *principes* and *triarii* into a single tactical unit. The 30 maniples of a legion now became ten *cohortes*, known by their numbers I–X, with 60 centurions. The practice of assigning soldiers to maniples by age ceased. The *triarii*, hitherto limited to 600 men per legion, were reinforced to reach the strength of the regular maniples at 120 men each (1,200 in total). A cohort thus in theory comprised 360 men, but in practice might number between about 200 and 600.

F. IMPERIAL PERIOD

The establishment by Augustus of a professional standing army made no difference to the formations of the legions, but as permanent units, they now acquired individual identities. The reform of the *cohors I* from six to five *centuriae* at double strength, archaeologically attested only in the Flavian period (AD 68–96), had no clear tactical relevance. Augustus and the Julio-Claudian emperors also established formal units of → auxiliaries (*auxilia*) out of the continuous recruitment of non-Roman fighters for light infantry, cavalry and specialist units (shooters, slingers). In the end, the *auxilia* grew to match the entire strength of the legions in size. In AD 200, Roman legionaries and non-Roman auxiliaries were using the same weapons. This included the use by the legionaries of the *spatha* (a longer sword of Germanic origin). The short Roman sword (*gladius*) now disappeared (cf. → Armament). An assumption that the cavalry units grew between the 2nd century AD and Late Antiquity is disputed. The infantry continued to outnumber the cavalry.

During the Imperial period, smaller field deployments and sieges superseded large-scale battles, chiefly because adversaries generally avoided major confrontations (*aequi loci*). The sources do not go into detail even about major battles, discussing civil wars against other Roman armies more than conflicts with 'barbarians' or battles occasioned by unplanned encounters (which were not *iustae pugnae*, 'proper battles'). In his treatment of Idistaviso, for instance, Tacitus describes the deployment by Germanicus, but not his formation (Tac. Ann. 2,16,3; cf. → March). Legions, made up of Roman citizens, were expensive to maintain and costly to replace. As the trend towards greater mobility and firepower in frontier engagements intensified, auxiliaries acquired a more significant role in combat. The legions now provided the tactical bulwark (*probole*), on the basis of which the *auxilia* went on the attack. There is a parallel here with the role of the *triarii* as described by Livy (8,8), as a base from which the *hastati* and *principes* attacked, and to which, if necessary, they returned for support.

The scenario given in Arrian's *Acies contra Alanos*, for a battle against the Sarmatian Alans (in AD 135), contains the most detailed description of a battle formation in the Imperial period. The *legio XV Apollinaris* and a *vexillatio* of the *legio XII Fulminata* took the field in the manner of a phalanx, eight ranks deep, between two hills. Differences of weapons used are again seen within the legions. The first four ranks carried long spears (*conti/hastae*?), the next four *lanceae* (originally Celtic spears). There is no mention either of *pila* or of *cohortes* of the legions. *Auxilia* held the hills, with the infantry in front, archers and javelin throwers behind. Fighting at the legions' rear, the archers on foot came first, followed by the legionary artillery, and finally the mounted archers. One cavalry unit formed up behind each flank at a right angle to the front, to forestall any attempt to outflank the lines. Arrian's description of the defensive formation evokes a phalangic *probole* ('bulwark') against the assault of the Alan cataphracts, with an overwhelming bombardment from ranged weapons [14]; [15].

G. Late Antiquity

Battle formations between about AD 284 and 400 suffer from a lack of detail in the sources, which display a predilection for rhetorical descriptions and/or archaizing terminology (e.g. Ammianus Marcellinus, Vegetius). Although later sources, including Procopius and Pseudo-Maurice, reflect on some earlier events, they convey Byzantine rather than classical Roman tactics and organization. During the 3rd century, the redeployment of many units, their fragmentation through the creation of – often permanent – *vexillationes*, their diminishing size and the introduction of new types of units all gave rise to an increasingly heterogeneous organization (cf. Army D.). By the 4th century, a legion numbered just 1,000–1,200 men, and the Late Roman *contubernium* ('occupants of a tent') may have shrunk back to just six men. The legion now lost its traditional supreme status within the army in the face both of the increasing number of *auxilia* units (many of them cavalry) and of the new prestige of the mobile reserve forces that belonged to the emperor's entourage: the *comitatenses* ('court troops'), who were now regarded as the best fighting troops. By the 6th century, the word *legio* was an archaic curiosity (Procop. Aed. 3,4,16).

The description of the Battle of Strasbourg in AD 357 (Amm. Marc. 16,12,19–63; Lib. Or. 18,54–61) permits an approximate reconstruction of Julian's formation against the Alamanni. The cavalry was still protecting both flanks of the heavy infantry, which formed up in *duplex acies* ('double battle line'). The sole legion mentioned here (*primani*) was set up as a reserve, and was known in soldiers' slang as the *castra praetoria* ('praetorian camp'). All three Roman battle ranks were in phalanx formation, shields interlocked in the tactical formation of the *testudo* ('tortoise'). Vegetius' comments on legionary formation (Veg. Mil. 1,20,11–21; 2,15f.; 3,14–17) have some points in common with Julian's approach at Strasbourg, with Arrian's *Acies* and even with Livy (8,8). His blurring of earlier sources with practices of his own day and with some of his own theoretical ideals produces inconsistencies that render a precise description of the Late Roman formation impossible. The heavy infantry formed the centre, flanked on either side by cavalry in full panoply and armed with the *conti* ('pikes'). The light cavalry and mounted archers took up positions at either end of the battle line (Veg. Mil. 3,16,1).

H. Wounded and fallen

Battles generally ended with one party retiring from the battlefield. In Classical Greek practice, abandoning the theatre of battle, whether in a rout or by elective withdrawal, amounted to an admission of defeat. Requesting permission to collect the fallen for burial marked the formal end of the battle. The Athenian tactical victory at Solygea turned into a defeat when Nicias failed to collect all the dead before he withdrew (Thuc. 4,44; Plut. *Nicias* 6,5f.). Possession of the fallen continued to be a sign of victory under the Diadochi (e.g. Diod. Sic. 19,31,3f.; cf. 19,85,1–3).

When encroaching darkness made it necessary to suspend hostilities in a battle still underway, the → generals had three options: continue fighting the next day, move to a more favourable location in the immediate vicinity, or retreat elsewhere to find a better opportunity. In a more dramatic – but also more common – scenario, one army experienced a major breach in its ranks or found itself outflanked. If a general in such a situation was unable to rally his troops, call up reserves or find relief in some other way, the order and cohesion of his army would collapse. This could lead to a loss of morale and the flight of his forces. Battle order and morale alike are extremely fragile, even among highly disciplined soldiers. Order and cohesion can evaporate in the heat of battle for both attackers and defenders. It was sometimes necessary to reestablish the battle formation in order to launch a new attack.

Defeat had a psychological impact, both on the army and on its commanders. Ultimately, battles are won in the mind (*psychai*). Morale is of the highest importance (Xen. Cyr. 3,3,19; Xen. An. 3,1,42; Pol. fr. 58 Büttner-Wobst; Veg. Mil. 3,26,10). Armies sometimes disintegrated psychologically at the battle line and took flight even before the first substantial contact with the enemy, as in Archidamus III's victory in the 'tearless battle' of 368 BC [8. vol. 2, 203–205]. Rumours, irrational terror or false information could even cause an army to panic before forming ranks [12]. Even when an army achieved success in individual battles, heavy losses sometimes dissuaded them from continuing a campaign, or produced a 'Cadmean victory' (better known since the 19th century as a 'Pyrrhic victory'; Hdt. 1,166,2; Plut. *Pyrrhus* 21,9f.; Plut. Mor. 10A; Malchus fr. 18,2,39–41 Blockley).

Fleeing the battlefield led to terrible losses, particularly on the defeated side, when retreating soldiers turned their backs to the enemy and discarded their weapons, having lost the mutual support of their comrades within the formation (Veg. Mil. 3,21,3–5; cf. Onas. Strat. 32,5–8; Frontin. Str. 2,6,2–6; 4,7,16). This partly explains the great difference in the number of deaths between victors and vanquished. There are abundant (rough) modern estimates of comparative losses. For the period between 479 and 371 BC, Greek losses in battle may have amounted to 14% on the losing side and 5% on the winning. Between 334 and 45 BC, estimates suggest 37% and 5.5% respectively. At Cannae in 216 BC, Hannibal won a victory but lost 11% of his army. Quite apart from a tendency on the part of victors (and sources) to exaggerate enemy losses and play down their own, correct numbers of those fallen in battle are difficult to ascertain. Victors often killed enemy wounded who were not important enough to earn a ransom or serve as a political pawn. Moreover, 30% of the wounded may have died days later.

The only Greeks to publish lists of fallen combatants were the Athenians of the 5th century BC. The sole comparable Roman list appears on the monument commemorating the Dacian Wars at Adamklissi (ILS 9107). Given the meticulous nature of Roman bookkeeping, the Roman death figures may be somewhere close to accurate, particularly for the Imperial period. From 310 BC onwards, despite sources like Valerius Antias (1st century BC), who was notorious for inflating the number of enemies killed in battle, some potentially reliable information is preserved. For example, the *aediles* received fairly exact reports on the number of *signa* taken from the enemy. Moroever, there was a rule for how many enemy dead had to be registered for a commander to be celebrated as *imperator*, although the sources disagree as to what the exact threshold was (6,000 dead: Diod. Sic. 36,14; 3,000: Cass. Dio 37,40,1f.; 10,000: App. Civ. 2,44,176f.). Similarly, a law of 62 BC stipulated that a minimum of 5,000 enemy fighters had to be killed for a commander to be granted a triumph (Val. Max. 2,8,1; cf. Oros. 5,4,7: the same rule dated to 143 BC). Yet, the validity and very existence of such rules are matters of scholarly debate (cf. → Consequences of war).

The burial of the fallen was obligatory for reasons of morale and religious scruple (Onas. Strat. 36,1f.). In the Greek hoplite battles, the defeated commander's request that the bodies of his fallen soldiers be returned marked the formal admission of defeat. In other cases, a defeated army was compelled to leave its dead behind. They might be cremated or left to decay. Not burying the dead was shameful. Greek practices varied in this regard. The fallen at Marathon and Plataeae were cremated and buried *in situ*. After the mid-5th century BC, cremated remains were transferred to Athens for burial. The Spartans performed burials on the battlefield or brought their dead to friendly territory. The Romans generally incinerated their fallen on the battlefield (e.g. Liv. 27,2,9). Only senatorial families could demand the return of their relatives' ashes to Rome (App. Civ. 1,43,195).

Greeks and Romans alike commemorated → victories with public monuments or ceremonies, but there were no such arrangements to commemorate those who died in war. The Greeks sometimes erected a *tropaion* ('trophy', 'monument') on the battlefield at the place where the enemy line broke, and in the case of naval battles, on the mainland near the site. Between the mid-5th century BC and the 4th century an obsession with setting up *tropaia* spread. In Athens, beginning in the mid-5th century BC at the latest, those who died in war were given a public burial. This practice, however, was not standard for all places. Commemoration of fallen individuals was usually a private matter, the prerogative of their families or legal heirs. Only two public monuments to fallen Romans are known: the Tomb of Germanicus in the Mausoleum of Augustus, with commemorations of those who died at the Battle of the Teutoburg Forest (Tac. Ann. 3,4–6; → Battles of note J.), and the Domitianic/Trajanic monuments at Adamklissi.

☞ Armament; Army; Auxiliaries; Cavalry; Death; Elephants; General; Infantry; March; Military literature; Siege warfare; Standard; Strategy

BIBLIOGRAPHY
[1] R. Bichler, Probleme und Grenzen der Rekonstruktion von Ereignissen am Beispiel antiker Schlachtenbeschreibungen, in: M. Fitzenreiter (ed.), Das Ereignis. Geschichtsschreibung zwischen Vorfall und Befund, 2009, 17–34 [2] C. von Clausewitz, Vom Kriege, 1832 (2010 online) [3] J.-C. Couvenhes, L'armée de Mithridate VI Eupator d'après Plutarque, Vie de Lucullus, VII, 4–6, in: H. Bru et al. (eds.), L'Asie Mineure dans l'Antiquité. Échanges, populations et territoires, 2009, 415–438 [4] Y. Harari, The Concept of »Decisive Battles« in World History, in: Journal of World History 18, 2007, 251–266 [5] F. Lammert, Die römische Taktik zu Beginn der Kaiserzeit und die Geschichtschreibung (Philologus, Suppl. 33/2), 1931 [6] C. Nolan, The Allure of Battle, 2017 [7] S. Oakley, Single Combat in the Roman Republic, in: Classical Quarterly 35, 1985, 392–410 [8] W. Pritchett, The Greek State at War, 5 vols., 1971–1991 [9] N. Sekunda, Hellenistic Infantry Reform in the 160's BC, 2001 [10] O. Stoll, Aus Können wird Wissen. »Amplius prodest locus saepe quam virtus« (Veg. mil III 26, 11). Landschaft in der militärwissenschaftlichen Fachliteratur der Antike, in: Marburger Beiträge zur Antiken Handels-, Wirtschafts- und Sozialgeschichte 33, 2015, 87–130 [11] R. Weigley, The Age of Battles, 1991 [12] E. Wheeler, Polla kena tou polemou. The History of a Greek Proverb, in: Greek Roman and Byzantine Studies 29, 1988, 153–184 [13] E. Wheeler, Taktik, in: H. Sonnabend (ed.), Mensch und Landschaft in der Antike. Lexikon der Historischen Geographie, 1999, 533–539 [14] E. Wheeler, The Legion as Phalanx in the Late Empire, Part I, in: Y. Le Bohec / C. Wolff (eds.), L'armée romaine de Dioclétien à Valentinien Ier, 2004, 309–358 [15] E. Wheeler, The Legion as Phalanx in the Late Empire, Part II, in: Revue des études militaires anciennes 1, 2004, 147–175.

EVERETT L. WHEELER

Battles of note

A. Actium
B. Adrianople
C. Cannae
D. Carrhae
E. Magnesia ad Sipylum
F. Marathon
G. Milvian Bridge
H. Pharsalus
I. Salamis
J. Teutoburg Forest

A. ACTIUM
On September 2, 31 BC, a naval battle near Actium, at the entrance of the Ambracian Gulf on the western coast of northern Greece, decided the military conflict between the two leaders of the Roman Civil War, Imperator Caesar (as 'Octavian', Caesar's heir, was known at this point) and Mark Antony (main sources: Vell. Pat. 2,84f.; Flor. Epit. 2,21,4–9; Plut. *Marcus Antonius* 61–68; Cass. Dio 50,11–35). The Roman Senate had declared war in 32 BC, but only on Antony's closest ally, Cleopatra VII of Egypt (Cass. Dio 50,4,4f.). The historical record for the Battle of Actium is fragmentary and heavily coloured by the perspective of the victor, who sought to portray Mark Antony as cowardly, irrational and 'un-Roman' (portraying Cleopatra and Antony's other allies as barbarians).

After the declaration of war, Imperator Caesar and his close friend Marcus Vipsanius Agrippa were anxious to prevent Antony from bringing the conflict to Italy. Antony had taken up positions in the Ambracian Gulf and its hinterland. He commanded the Roman forces of the east empire along with Rome's eastern allies, and the surviving sources deliberately exaggerate the sharp distinction between 'east' and 'west' (cf. e.g. Suet. Aug. 17,2; Cass. Dio 50,6,3–6; 50,11,2; 51,2,3; SEG 32, 833). Imperator Caesar and Agrippa disrupted their adversary's supplies, landed on the Greek coast north of Actium and prevented Antony's fleet from escaping by occupying the island of Leucas, ten kilometres south of Actium. Their army and the allied western forces advanced from the north. According to Plutarch, a total of 180,000 infantry, 24,000 cavalry and the crews of some 750 ships faced off against each other. These soldiers came from countless regions of Europe, North Africa, Asia Minor and the Near East (Prop. 4,6,19; Plut. *Marcus Antonius* 61f.; Cass. Dio 50,6,3–6).

At first, the two sides were fairly well balanced with only minor differences between them (Antony had more infantry, but fewer ships). The first encounters brought no decisive result, but Antony's position was deteriorating. There was no longer any possibility for his fleet to make its escape, and his soldiers were suffering from fevers and hunger. Cases of desertion were frequent. Antony offered his opponents a land battle several times without success. Some of his advisors recommended that he withdraw to Macedonia and abandon the fleet, but Cleopatra, who herself had provided 60 ships (Oros. 6,19,9; 6,19,11; cf. Flor. Epit. 2,21,5), won the argument with her insistence on a naval battle. Antony decided to use some of his ships to break the blockade and sail back to Egypt with his war chest. The land army would then pull back into Asia Minor under the command of Publius Canidius Crassus. It seems that Antony planned to postpone the decisive battle to a later date and another location, in the hopes of finding conditions better suited to his cause (but see [3]).

Antony therefore had the war chest secretly brought on board Cleopatra's ships at night. He also ordered the mainsails brought aboard; these would be useful for fast sailing in open seas, but not for a naval battle. On the morning of September 2, Antony's warships took up a tight, crescent-shaped formation at the entrance to the gulf to await their opponent's attack, which they hoped to neutralize with their larger ships, fitted with towers full of armed men. But Imperator Caesar and Agrippa, who lined up their fleet immediately in front of Antony's ships, did not attack. Instead, they began pulling back. Around noon, one of Antony's squadron of vessels launched a unilateral attack. Antony moved up with it to maintain his battle order. In doing this, he was also forced to widen the gaps between his vessels to avoid being outflanked. This is the moment when the smaller ships of Imperator Caesar attacked, their rapid incursions doing damage to the rudders and tillers of Antony's larger ships. When a gap appeared in the battle line, Cleopatra took flight. She had clearly waited for this opportunity to escape, with her 60 ships carrying the war chest grouped at the centre of the formation but behind the front. Antony duly lost the battle and sailed off after the queen.

Antony managed to salvage some of his ships and his war chest. His vast land army initially remained loyal, but his failure to act in the battle's immediate aftermath and the manner in which he left most of his ships to their fate ruined his reputation. The land army surrendered seven days later. Poetry and art elevated Actium to the foundation myth of the Principate. Rather than setting up an army camp there, Imperator Caesar founded the city of Nicopolis (Cass. Dio 51,1,3), where he erected an immense victory monument (AE 2002, 1297) and ordered annual games to commemorate the victory. He also declared a public holiday and set the battle date as the start of a new reckoning of years according to the 'Actian Era'.

☞ Civil war

BIBLIOGRAPHY
[1] J. BLEICKEN, Augustus. Eine Biographie, 1998, 276–288 [2] J.M. CARTER, The Battle of Actium. The Rise & Triumph of Augustus Caesar, 1970 [3] C. LANGE, The Battle of Actium. A Reconsideration, in: CQ 61, 2011, 608–623 [4] D. LASPE, Actium. Die Anatomie einer Schlacht, in: Gymnasium 114, 2007, 509–522 [5] W.M. MURRAY / P.M. PETSAS, Octavian's Campsite Memorial for the Actian War, 1989 [6] J. OSGOOD, Caesar's Legacy. Civil War and the Emergence of the Roman Empire, 2006 [7] C. SCHÄFER, Kleopatra, 2006, 222–230.

MICHAEL A. SPEIDEL

B. ADRIANOPLE
The Battle of Adrianople, fought on August 9, 378, is one of the most famous and best-documented military encounters of Late Roman history. Northeast of the Thracian city of Adrianople roughly 200 km west of Constantinople, a mixed but predominantly Gothic army drawn from the Thervingi and Greutungi peoples under the command of the Gothic chieftain Fritigern inflicted a devastating defeat on the Roman army led by Emperor Valens (364–378), who died in the battle. Ammianus Marcellinus' almost contemporary *Res gestae* supplies the most detailed account, which is supplemented by other (mostly later) sources. In Ammianus' narrative, the battle reaches its catastrophic climax in the last book, which characterizes it as a massacre exceeded only by the Battle of Cannae (216 BC; → Battles of note C.). Modern historiography has traditionally seen it as a harbinger of the fall of the Roman Empire and a turning point in the history of warfare, but more recent analyses have variously questioned or downplayed its importance.

The battle marked the culmination of events that began in 376, when Valens granted permission to Gothic groups fleeing the Huns to settle in Roman territory, anticipating that this would boost Rome's military power. Mistreatment by Roman provincial authorities, however, caused the Goths to rebel. In 378, when regional Roman troops failed to quell the plundering despite reinforcements, Valens returned from Syria with additional forces, intending to coordinate action against the Goths on the Thracian Plain. His nephew and western co-emperor Gratian undertook to bring in further units from Gaul, although confrontations along the Rhine delayed their departure (Amm. Marc. 31,4,1–11,2; 31,11,6; Eunap. fr. 42; Zos. 4,20,5–22,3). Valens transferred command of an elite battle group to the *magister peditum* ('master of foot soldiers') Sebastianus, and it enjoyed some success in executing small, irregular missions designed to tie up the Goths and exacerbate their logistical difficulties (Amm. Marc. 31,11,2–5; 31,12,1; Eunap. fr. 44,1; 44,3f.; Zos. 4,22,4–24,6). When Roman scouts (*exploratores*) reported a group of 10,000 Goths north of Adrianople, Valens advanced and had a camp built near the city. Modern estimates suggest that the Roman force numbered 15,000–20,000 men, including numerous elite units. The Romans assumed that the Gothic fighting force was weak, and Fritigern's efforts to negotiate, which Valens rebuffed, confirmed this assumption (Amm. Marc. 31,12,1–4; 31,12,8f.).

Some senior officers urged Valens to wait for Gratian, but he decided to settle the matter immediately. With the benefit of hindsight, it is easy to attribute his fateful decision to hasty misjudgement or unwillingness to share the glory of victory, but seizing the opportunity to engage a numerically inferior foe was wholly consistent with Roman tactical military doctrine. Blame really lay with Roman → reconnaissance, which failed to spot a separate troop of Gothic cavalry and underestimated the size of the Gothic army. After a long forced march in summer heat across difficult terrain, by August 9 the Roman troops were tired, hungry and dehydrated, which left them unprepared for combat. Early in the afternoon, Valens found the main Gothic army, mostly infantry, fortified within a wagon circle. While waiting for his Gothic cavalry, Fritigern managed to buy time by sending emissaries, while harrying the Romans with bushfires (Amm. Marc. 31,12,4–7; 31,12,10–15; Zos. 4,23,5–24,1). Ammianus' lively portrayal of the battle, inspired by classical descriptions, conveys only an outline of the phases of the hostilities (31,12,16–13,11; cf. Jer. Chron. s. a. 378; Oros. 7,33,13–15; Socr. 4,38,7–9; Sozom. Hist. eccl. 6,40,3). Overconfident Roman troops involved themselves in fighting too soon and without orders, while negotiations were still in progress, and this led to uncoordinated thrusts. Just when units on the Romans' left flank were making inroads, the Gothic cavalry suddenly materialized, tying up the supporting Roman cavalry in combat and overwhelming the left wing. A Gothic attack on all fronts now drove the Roman army into narrow confines where its troop strength and reserves could make no impression. Some Roman units fought on, but others withdrew from the battlefield. The carnage and pursuit continued until nightfall. Two thirds of the Roman soldiers are said to have died along with many officers (Amm. Marc. 31,13,18f.). There are contradictory reports as to whether Valens died in the battle or only in its wake (e.g. Amm. Marc. 31,13,8f.; 31,13,12–17; Socr. 4,38,7–10; Sozom. Hist. eccl. 6,40,3–5; Philostr. VS 9,17; Zos. 4,24,2).

The wider historical context shows that the Roman defeat was not a result of some long-term or systematic decline in the quality of troops or fighting operations. Scholars have also disposed of an old theory that identified Adrianople as the crucial turning point from the infantry-based armies of Classical Antiquity to the mounted warfare of the Middle Ages. The heavy losses of experienced troops caused a near-term shortage of personnel and necessitated the establishment of new units. Valens' successor Theodosius I (379–395) resorted to guerrilla tactics, but was also unable to overcome the Goths. In 382, he granted them permission to settle in the Balkans as 'allies' (*foederati*) on condition that they provided troops to Rome for military service. The Goths retained an unparalleled level of autonomy within the empire, which over the ensuing decades became a source of political and military instability.

BIBLIOGRAPHY
[1] D. BRODKA, Einige Bemerkungen zum Verlauf der Schlacht bei Adrianopel (9. August 378), in: Millennium 6, 2009, 265–280 [2] T.S. BURNS, The Battle of Adrianople. A Reconsideration, in: Historia 22, 1973, 336–345 [3] J. DEN BOEFT et al., Philological and Historical Commentary on Ammianus Marcellinus XXXI, 2017 [4] N. LENSKI, Initium mali romano imperio. Contemporary Reactions to the Battle of Adrianople, in: Transactions of the American Philological Association 127, 1997, 129–168 [5] N. LENSKI, Failure of Empire. Valens and the Roman State in the Fourth Century A.D., 2002 [6] U. WANKE, Die Gotenkriege des Valens, 1990.

PHILIP RANCE

C. CANNAE
The battle fought at Cannae in northern Apulia on August 2, 216 BC was one of the most important of the Second Punic War (218–201 BC). It dealt Rome a devastating defeat, with a powerful resonance in subsequent tradition that impedes modern reconstructions of the actual events. The Roman mentality refused to accept any explanation of the defeat that fundamentally called into question the Roman political and social order. Roman historians accordingly exonerated some who were to blame, invented heroes and identified a scapegoat. This approach can already be seen in embryonic form in the histories of Polybius. Airbrushing is even more evident in Livy and the works of later Roman historians (Pol. 3,100–118; Liv. 22,40–58) [7].

Throughout 217 BC, Quintus Fabius Maximus avoided fighting a pitched battle against the Carthaginian army that had invaded Italy under the command of Hannibal. Dissatisfied with this strategy, the Senate voted to provoke a battle to decide the war. Two new consuls were elected, Gaius Terentius Varro and Lucius Aemilius Paullus, in the expectation that they would act in concert (Pol. 3,106,1; 3,107,8; Liv. 22,33–36; App. Hann. 17; Plut. *Fabius Maximus* 14). New levies boosted the army in Italy to twice its usual strength. Soldiers were required to swear an oath not to abandon their ranks out of fear or to save themselves. Numerical superiority made them confident. The Romans also believed that they at last understood their enemy (Hannibal) and his way of operating. They had, after all, inflicted a defeat on him just days before the battle.

According to the traditional account (Pol. 3,113–117; Liv. 22,45–50; App. Hann. 19–25; Plut. *Fabius Maximus* 15f.), the two consuls, Aemilius Paullus and Terentius Varro, alternated as commanders on a daily basis, which supposedly hampered leadership of the army on the eve of battle. Terentius Varro had supreme command on the day of the battle, and he led the army to the south bank of the River Aufidus (Ofanto), terrain supposedly difficult for the Roman cavalry (Varro later became the scapegoat). The largest army ever fielded by the Romans was designed to annihilate the Carthaginian invaders led by Hannibal: 70,000 infantry and 6,000 cavalry. A further 10,000 soldiers remained in the marching camp as a reserve. The battle order chosen was a conventional one:

heavy infantry in the centre, cavalry on both wings. However, the Roman commanders opted for an extraordinarily deep formation, apparently intending thereby to make the best use of their numerical superiority.

Hannibal placed his Celtic and Iberian allies in the centre, in a semicircular formation convex towards the enemy. To their left and right stood the Libyan heavy infantry, divided into two equal units of 5,000 men each. Cavalry on the wings awaited orders to attack, those on the left wing being particularly strong in numbers. The job of the left wing was to rapidly and decisively alter the starting position in Hannibal's favour, which their quick victory soon enabled them to do. They then reinforced the cavalry on the right wing, putting the remainder of the Roman cavalry to flight. Meanwhile, the Roman infantry was attacking the Celtic and Iberian semicircle, which was slowly pulling back, drawing the mass of Roman soldiers on with it. As the legionaries pursued the enemy into the Carthaginian centre, the Roman formation broke, only to be attacked on both unprotected flanks by the Libyan heavy infantry, and in the rear by the Carthaginian cavalry. Completely encircled, the Roman army was destroyed.

According to Livy, the Romans lost 47,000 infantry and 2,700 cavalry. Over 19,000 soldiers were taken captive. Only a few horsemen and footsoldiers succeeded in escaping. Most of the Roman commanders also fell, including one of the two consuls, several former consuls, two quaestors, two thirds of the military tribunes, 80 senators and many *equites*. Hannibal's losses, conversely, were comparatively light: 200 cavalry and 5,500 infantry. Despite Rome's catastrophic defeat, however, Hannibal did not march on Rome. Presumably he did not think the time was yet right. His overwhelming victory by this unexpected and risky encirclement of the enemy has fuelled many a military imagination down to recent history.

☞ Generals of note, G. Hannibal; Wars of note, K. Punic Wars

BIBLIOGRAPHY
[1] G. DALY, Cannae. The Experience of Battle in the Second Punic War, 2003   [2] A. GOLDSWORTHY, Cannae. Hannibal's Greatest Victory, 2007   [3] D.B. HOYOS, Hannibal. Rome's Greatest Enemy, 2005   [4] I. KERTÉSZ, Die Schlacht bei Cannae und ihr Einfluss auf die Entwicklung der Kriegskunst, in: H. GERICKE (ed.), Miszellen zur Wissenschaftsgeschichte der Altertumskunde 38, 1980, 29–43   [5] P. KUSSMAUL, Der Halbmond von Cannae, in: MH 25, 1978, 249–257   [6] J. SEIBERT, Hannibal, 1993, 191–198   [7] M.A. SPEIDEL, Halbmond und Halbwahrheit. Cannae, 2. August 216 v.Chr., in: S. FÖRSTER et al. (eds.), Schlachten der Weltgeschichte. Von Salamis bis Sinai, ³2003, 48–62 (editor's note: in: M.A. Speidel, Heer und Herrschaft im Römischen Reich der Hohen Kaiserzeit, 2009, 653–666).

MICHAEL A. SPEIDEL

D. CARRHAE

D.1. Course of the battle
D.2. Aftermath of the battle

In the battle fought in the plain of Carrhae on June 9, 53 BC, the Parthians succeeded in annihilating a Roman force under the supreme command of the triumvir Marcus Licinius Crassus, and in stopping the Roman advance to the conquest of Mesopotamia.

The two main witnesses to these events, Plutarch (*Crassus* 17–33) and Cassius Dio (40,16–27), do not always agree. It is difficult to establish the sources on which they rely, and the degree of their reliance on Livy [2]; [3]; [9]. Crassus' plan of conquest followed a strategy similar to that of Lucullus' Parthian campaign of 69 BC. On the pretext of settling dynastic squabbles, the aim was to occupy Mesopotamia as far as the Euphrates, and thus to challenge the Parthians' control over territories they had seized from the Seleucid Empire in the 2nd century. The Roman invasion force amounted to seven legions – eleven if the auxiliary contingents are included (Flor. Epit. 1,46,2f.) [9]. Crassus began by marching his troops southwards along the Euphrates. His hopes of obtaining reinforcements in the form of mounted units from King Artavastes II of Armenia were thwarted by an attack launched by the troops of the Parthian king Orodes II (Plut. Crass. 22).

D.1. COURSE OF THE BATTLE
Early in 53 BC, the Roman forces were attacked by the Parthians under Surena, who had replaced the governor of Mesopotamia, Silaces. This battle took place on the banks of the River Belich, where the Romans had taken their horses and draught animals for water. The attack put a stop to the Roman advance. In this context, Plutarch (*Crassus* 23f.; 26) emphasizes the roaring of the Parthian war drums as an instrument of psychological warfare [10]. He agrees with Cassius Dio, the other main source on these events, that the incessant arrow attacks from the Parthian cavalry prevented the Roman infantry from moving into close combat, while the opposing bowmen profited from favourable weather conditions.

Crassus had initially positioned his troops in the long ranks customary for heavy infantry, with cavalry cover on the flanks. He then had them close ranks into a formation described by Plutarch as a 'hollow square of four fronts' (*Crassus* 23,3). Besides Crassus himself, contingents at Carrhae were commanded by the quaestor Cassius Longinus and Crassus' son Publius Crassus, the latter in charge of 1,300 Celtic (and probably Germanic) cavalry, 500 archers and eight cohorts of legionaries.

The Parthian's opening strategy was to break the Roman lines with an attack by their armoured cavalry, the cataphracts. Faced with their opponent's tight formation, however, they fell back on a tactic of encirclement using mounted archers. The Romans attempted a counterattack but were driven back by the rain of Parthian arrows (Cass. Dio, 40,22,2), at which point they sent the Gaulish cavalry under Publius Crassus into the fray. They rode against the Parthian archers, seeking to slash the bellies of their enemies' horses, a favourite battle tactic of theirs (Plut. *Crassus* 25). This distraction manoeuvre was intended to give respite to the legionaries and auxiliaries so that they could close ranks once again, tightening the hollow square formation still further. This would allow them to protect each other with their overlapping shields. Publius Crassus, supported by the tribunes Censorinus and Megabacchus, had his cavalry – closely followed by the infantry – set off in pursuit of the Parthian bowmen, which brought them into an encounter with the Parthian armoured cavalry. But before the Roman contingent was able to reform, the Parthians halted and confronted them with a wall of cataphracts, while their archers resumed their bombardment.

Surprised by this manoeuvre and harried by the rain of arrows, the Romans felt compelled to fall back to a nearby hill, where the enemy promptly surrounded them. The legionaries then adopted the defensive square 'tower formation'. Seeing the hopelessness of the situation, Publius Crassus and Censorinus had themselves stabbed to death and Megabacchus took his own life. The Parthians broke through the Roman ranks, took 500 prisoners and had the commanders beheaded. Publius Crassus' head was put on a pike and presented thus to his father. By sunset, the Parthians' armoured cavalry were overrunning the Roman infantry.

Plutarch's account devotes much space to the early phases of the battle, but literary decorum prevents him from giving a lengthy description of the later stages. From his description of the positioning of the opposing forces, however, it is clear that the Romans' initial plan was to win a battle of attrition [1]. Yet, they failed to recognize that, like other 'barbarians' (Just. Epit. 41,2,8), the Parthians were militarily able to sustain hostilities for long periods.

As darkness fell, the Parthians, unaccustomed to fighting at night, withdrew (Cass. Dio, 40,24, 1f.). Crassus was in a state of shock and unresponsive, leading some commanders to make the extraordinary decision to assemble even centurions and other officers for consultation – Plutarch may be distinguishing here between *primipili* and regular centurions (Crass. 27,5). This emergency committee ultimately ordered a retreat. After the prefect of the cavalry, Ignatius, commanding a contingent of 300 horsemen, informed the garrison at Carrhae of the outcome of the battle and began pulling his men back to the Euphrates, Coponius, commander of the garrison, went out to rescue the survivors and bring them to the city. Meanwhile, the legate Vargunteius, with 2,000 men in his retinue, became disorientated in darkness. The enemy encircled him on a hilltop, and his contingent was overpowered; no more than two dozen of his men managed to escape to the city. According to Cassius Dio (40,23,1), the Osroeanians, under their king, Abgar II, now cancelled their alliance with Rome and turned on their former confederates. The Parthians broke into the Roman camp and their commander, Surena, besieged Carrhae (Plut. *Crassus* 27f.; Cass. Dio, 40,25f.).

D.2. AFTERMATH OF THE BATTLE

Some days later, Crassus was killed in a skirmish. The few survivors on the Roman side were deported, and the Parthians took possession of the legions' standards as a visible symbol of the Roman defeat. The Battle of Carrhae marks a watershed in the Roman policy of expansion. Rome's legions had hitherto been regarded as invincible, but their advance had now been stopped by an opponent whose military capacity and resilience had clearly been underestimated.

The Battle of Carrhae changed public perceptions of military defeats in Rome. Caesar still cited revenge for the disgrace suffered at Carrhae as a motive for the planned Asian campaign that was prevented by his murder. Mark Antony later expressed the same idea. But by at least the time of the campaigns of Gaius Caesar and Germanicus, efforts were underway to portray the Parthian War as a private enterprise on the part of Crassus, who was driven by the thirst for glory and money. Historians of the late Augustan period did not shrink from manipulating the facts, asserting that the law assigning supreme command (*provincia*) to Crassus did not authorize a campaign against the Parthians. Ultimately, Crassus found himself cast as a negative stereotype: a commander greedy for wealth and renown, but militarily incompetent (Ov. Fast. 5,580–586; Prop. 4,6,81–85) [7]; [8].

BIBLIOGRAPHY

[1] G. BRIZZI, Note sulla battaglia di Carre, in: G. BRIZZI, Studi militari romani, 1983, 9–30   [2] B.A. MARSHALL, Crassus. A Political Biography, 1976   [3] K. REGLING, Crassus' Partherkieg, in: Klio 7, 1907, 357–394   [4] G.P. SAMPSON, The Defeat of Rome. Crassus, Carrhae and the Invasion of the East, 2008   [5] F. SMITH, Die Schlacht bei Carrhä, in: HZ 115, 1916, 237–262   [6] D. TIMPE, Die Bedeutung der Schlacht von Carrhae, in: MH 19, 1962, 104–129   [7] G. TRAINA, La resa di Roma. Battaglia a Carre, 9 giugno 53 a.C., 2010   [8] G. TRAINA, Le sconfitte dei Romani, in: Aevum 84, 2010, 177–185   [9] G. TRAINA, Carrhes, 9 juin 53 av. J.-C. Anatomie d'une bataille, 2011   [10] G. TRAINA, Harmonie barbare? Tambours des

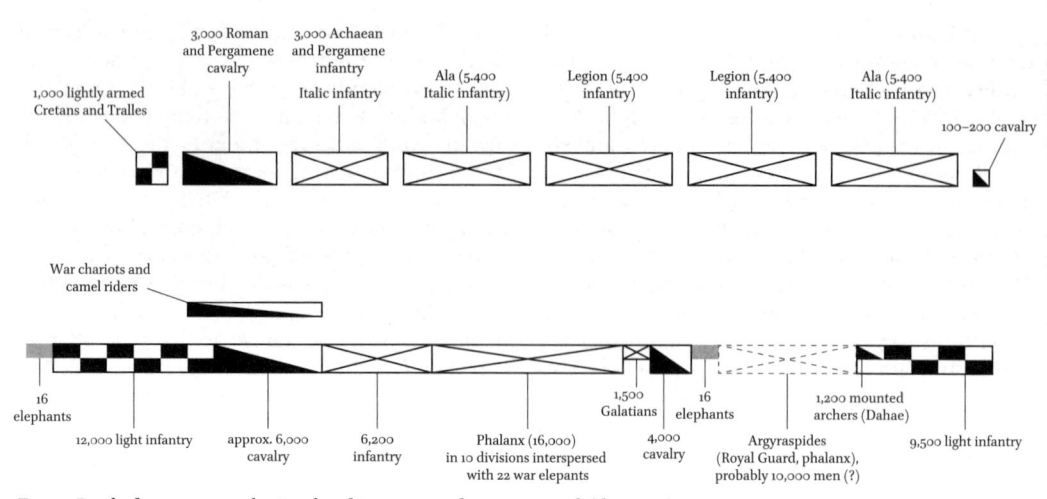

Fig. 1: Battle formation at the Battle of Magnesia after Liv. 37,39f. (diagram).

Parthes à la bataille de Carrhes, in: A. GONZALES / M.T. SCHETTINO, Les sons du pouvoir des autres, 2017, 91–102.

GIUSTO TRAINA

E. MAGNESIA AD SIPYLUM

Late in the autumn of 190 BC, the army of the Seleucid Antiochus III confronted Roman, Italic and Pergamene troops commanded by L. Cornelius Scipio and Eumenes II of Pergamum at Magnesia on the River Hermus, in Lydia in Asia Minor. [3]; [2] (cf. fig. 1).

The Roman battle force consisted of two legions in the centre and two units (*alae*) of Italic confederates and Latins on the wings (5,400 men each). Three thousand Pergamene infantry formed the right flank, combining with Achaean *peltastes* (lightly armed footsoldiers), 3,000 cavalry (including 800 from Pergamum) and lightly armed Cretans and Tralles (500 men each). The left wing, along the River Phrygius, was formed of a small detachment of Roman cavalry (four *turmae*). Some 2,000 Macedonians and Thracians guarded the Roman → camp, and 16 African elephants stood in reserve (Liv. 37,39,7–13).

At the centre of the numerically superior Seleucid army was the phalanx, totalling 16,000 men in ten divisions, all equipped with long spears. Elephants carrying towers, each containing four armed men, formed up between the divisions. The right wing consisted of 1,500 Galatian infantry, the royal cavalry (3,000 armoured horsemen called cataphracts, and 1,000 Median horsemen (*agema*)), the *argyraspides* (heavy phalanx), 1,200 mounted Dahae archers and light infantry (3,000 Cretans and Tralles, 2,500 Mysian archers, 4,000 Cyrtian slingers and Elymaean archers). More infantry occupied the left (including 1,500 Galatians, 2,000 Cappadocians), along with cavalry (3,000 cataphracts, 1,000 Syrian, Phrygian and Lydian horsemen, an unknown number of Tarentines and 2,500 Galatian cavalry) and light infantry (1,000 Neocretans, 1,500 Carians and Cilicians, 1,500 Tralles, 4,000 Pisidian, Pamphylian and Lycian *peltastes*, 4,000 Cyrtian slingers and Elymaean archers). In front of the left wing were → chariots fitted with scythes, and Arabian archers riding camels (Liv. 37,40,1–41,1; App. Syr. 32.).

Eumenes had the Cretan archers, javelin throwers and light infantry advance in loose formation against the scythed chariots. The hail of projectiles and shouts of the attackers frightened the horses pulling the chariots and unsettled the Arabian camel cavalry and the light infantry behind them. The cavalry attack led by Eumenes plunged into the now disordered left wing, and the Seleucid auxiliary contingents took flight. Meanwhile, the Roman legions in the centre were advancing on the phalanx, bombarding it with spears, stones and arrows.

Antiochus III led his cataphracts in a concentrated attack on the Roman auxiliaries on the left wing, driving off the Roman cavalry and attacking the allied soldiers frontally and on the flank. At first, the allies took flight, but they rallied. Antiochus hoped to involve his cavalry in the main battle in the centre, but instead witnessed the collapse of the Seleucid phalanx under enemy fire. The Roman cavalry pursued the fleeing troops. Antiochus gave up the battle for lost and fled, leaving 50,000 Seleucid infantry and 3,000 cavalry dead on the battlefield. The Roman side lost 300 infantry and 24 horsemen, along with 25 Pergamenes. Many Romans were wounded (Liv. 37,41,1–44,2; App. Syr. 11,31–36).

Antiochus III suffered greatly for his alliance with the Greek Aetolians and his landing in Greece in 192/91 BC. Not only was he severely punished with defeat at the Battles of Thermopylae and Magnesia and with the destruction of his military power in Asia Minor [1]. Colossal reparation payments were also imposed on him by Rome, and he was furthermore required under the terms of the Treaty of Apamea (188 BC) to relinquish power in Asia Minor and retreat beyond the Taurus mountains. At first, Rome did not fill the resultant power vacuum in Asia Minor directly, but by assigning territories to its allies Pergamum and Rhodes [4.18–27]. The victory at Magnesia ad Sipylum, however, enabled ambitious Roman politicians to consolidate Rome's power in Asia Minor through the 2nd century BC and the first half of the 1st.

BIBLIOGRAPHY
[1] J.D. GRAINGER, The Roman War of Antiochos the Great, 2002 [2] A. HIRT, Magnesia. Entscheidung am Sipylos. Phalanx, Elefanten und Streitwagen gegen römische Legionäre, in: G. MANDL / I. STEFFELBAUER (eds.), Krieg in der antiken Welt, 2007, 215–237 [3] J. KROMAYER, Antike Schlachtfelder in Griechenland. Bausteine zu einer antiken Kriegsgeschichte, vol. 2: Die hellenistisch-römische Periode. Von Kynoskephalae bis Pharsalos, 1907, 125–227 [4] A.N. SHERWIN-WHITE, Roman Foreign Policy in the East, 168 B.C. to A.D. 1, 1984.

ALFRED MICHAEL HIRT

F. MARATHON
The Battle of Marathon, fought on the coastal plain in northeastern Attica between the Athenian citizen contingent and a Persian force in 490 BC, formed part of the Persian Wars. According to Herodotus, the most important source on these events, the Persian King Darius took Athens' and Eretria's participation in the Ionian Revolt as a pretext to launch a punitive expedition against the two cities. His real intention, however, was to secure control of as much of Greece as possible (Hdt. 6,43f.; 6,94, cf. Plut. *Aristides* 5). Herodotus' account accords a prominent role to the former tyrant of Athens, Hippias (Hdt. 5,96; 6,102; 6,107–109; 6,121), suggesting that Darius' strategic goal was to reinstate him. A failed first assault led by Mardonius in 492 was followed in 490 by a naval expedition commanded by Datis and Artaphernes, which proceeded from the west coast of Asia Minor against the Aegean islands and then Attica. The destruction of Eretria and the abduction of its population were followed in early autumn by the landing at Marathon. The numbers of Persian ships and soldiers are a matter of speculation. Herodotus states (6,95) that Datis was in command of 600 triremes. This would imply a total army strength of 120,000, which is implausible from a logistical standpoint. In all likelihood, he fielded only about 10,000 infantry and an unknown number of cavalry (12,000–15,000 according to [4]; [9]).

The Athenian hoplites under the polemarch Callimachus and the ten *strategoi* ('commanders') had made camp in the southwest of the Plain of Marathon, near the Sanctuary of Heracles, where they controlled a road to Athens. The exact location of the sanctuary is disputed. Although Herodotus gives no indication of their strength, the figures of 9,000 (Paus. 10,20,2) or 10,000 men (Just. Epit. 2,9) given by other historians are plausible. A contingent from Plataeae reinforced the Athenians (Hdt. 6,108). The events immediately running up to and during the battle cannot be reliably reconstructed. Most scholars (most recently [7]) rely on Herodotus, who of course represents an Athenian perspective. Other authors, such as Nep. Milt., Lys. 2,21–26, Paus. 1,14,5 and Pl. Menex. 240C–241C, contribute individual details at most. The two armies faced off for several days. The Athenians may have been hoping for the arrival of Spartan reinforcements, although some [6] think this an Athenian invention. Hdt. 6,109f. reports differences of opinion among the Athenian commanders; the Philaid Miltiades in particular urged battle against the Persians. According to Hdt. 6,111f., the Athenians reinforced the wings of their army to prepare for the fight, and attacked at a run over a distance of eight stadia (approx. 1.5 km; cf. Aristoph. Vesp. 1081–1083). Many scholars since [2] have dismissed this as legend in view of the heavy weight of the hoplite armour, but [7] takes Herodotus at his word, arguing that this weight has been exaggerated (arguing a shorter running distance [8]; [9]). At all events, the outcome of the battle confirms that the strengths of the Persian army, cavalry and ranged weapons (especially the archers) were not used to advantage. The victorious Greek wings were able to encircle the Persian centre and put it to flight. Assorted heroes are said to have helped the Athenians in this endeavour (Heracles, Theseus and Echetlus: Paus. 1,15,3; cf. Plut. *Theseus* 35). Several thousand Persians are reported to have died while attempting to board their ships. Some 192 Athenians were killed, Callimachus among them. The subsequent attempt by the Persians to threaten Athens by circumnavigating Attica was abandoned.

The victory at Marathon, which in military terms merely deferred further conflict (*pace* e.g. [1]), was widely glamourized in Athens (see [5]). Miltiades and especially Cimon acclaimed the victory to consolidate the status of the Philiads in the city (on the *stoe poikile* Paus. 1,15,1–4; Aeschin. In Ctes. 186; Nep. Milt. 6,3; Plin. HN 35,8,57). It was also extolled by the *polis* itself, which proclaimed its service to Greece in epitaphs (esp. Lys. 2,21–26; Pl. Menex. 240C–241C), monuments, victory songs (Simon. frg. 88A Diehl) and embellishments of the battle history (Thuc. 1,73; for a critical reaction to this: Theopomp. FGrH 115 F 153). These legendary embellishments include the story, which appears only belatedly in the sources, of the 'Marathon runner' (Plut. Mor. 347c; Lucian. Laps. 3). According to this story, a messenger ran from Marathon to Athens bringing word of the victory, and collapsed dead in the Agora there having done his job.

☞ Generals of note, I. Cimon; Wars of note, J. Persian Wars

BIBLIOGRAPHY
[1] R.A. BILLOWS, Marathon. How One Battle Changed Western Civilization, 2010 [2] H. DELBRÜCK, Geschichte der Kriegskunst, vol. 1, 2000, 58–59 [3] N.A. DOENGES, The Campaign and Battle of Marathon, in: Historia 47, 1998, 1–17 [4] J. FISCHER, Die Perserkriege, 2013 [5] M. JUNG, Marathon und Plataiai. Zwei Perserschlachten als lieux de mémoire im antiken Griechenland, 2006 [6] M. JUNG, Spartans at Marathon? On the Origin and Function of an Athenian Legend, in: K. BURASELIS / E. KOULAKAKIOTIS (eds.), Marathon the Day after, 2013, 15–37 [7] P. KRENTZ, The Battle of Marathon, 2010 [8] F.E. RAY, Land Battles in 5th Century B.C. Greece. A History and Analysis of 173 Engagements, 2012, 59–68 [9] M. ZAHRNT, Marathon, das Schlachtfeld als 'Erinnerungsort', einst und jetzt, in: K.-J. HÖLKESKAMP / E. STEIN-HÖLKESKAMP (eds.), Die griechische Welt. Erinnerungsorte der Antike, 2010, 114–127.

LEONHARD BURCKHARDT

G. MILVIAN BRIDGE
The Battle of the Milvian Bridge, fought on October 28, AD 312, brought Constantine I victory over his rival for the imperial throne, Maxentius. The victor's ensuing triumph as sole ruler of the Roman Empire, which furthered the rise of Christianity, rapidly caused great historical significance – to some extent spiced with legend – to be ascribed to the battle. The military campaign resulted from shifting power relations in the collegial system of imperial sovereignty known as the Tetrarchy (293–c. 313). From 306 onwards, both protagonists were *de facto* regional rulers in the west of the Roman Empire: Constantine in Gaul, Britain and Spain, Maxentius in Italy and Africa. Although both were sons of *augusti*, they were strictly speaking usurpers, having attained their status by acclamation from local troops rather than by lawful nomination by senior members of the imperial college. Whereas rulers of the eastern part of the empire generally recognized Constantine to some degree, they repeatedly tried to depose Maxentius and restore a legitimate *augustus* to power in the west. This tense coexistence of the two western regimes continued for more than five years, underscored by Constantine's marriage to Maxentius' sister Fausta.

The greatest threat to Maxentius came from Licinius, who had been the lawful western *augustus* since 308, and who was seeking to enforce his claim to Maxentius' territories with support from the east. By late 311, Licinius, now also the senior ruler in the eastern provinces, was in a position to eliminate Maxentius. Constantine, who saw his own position under threat from Licinius' westward expansion, decided to preempt Licinius' plan. He raised an army in Gaul and advanced into Italy early in 312. Most of Maxentius' forces were ordered towards the Julian Alps to confront Licinius. Constantine won decisive victories near Turin and Verona, with few cities offering resistance (Paneg. 4(10),19–26; 12(9),5–13; Zos. 2,15,1f.). He spent several months securing control over Northern Italy, while Maxentius remained in Rome preparing for a siege. Yet, as Constantine approached Rome along the *via Flaminia*, Maxentius suddenly decided to confront him on the battlefield. Later sources explain his decision by invoking God's will or Maxentius' superstitious belief in prophecies, but dwindling support in the capital may have forced him to accept an open battle (Paneg. 12(9),16; Lactant. De mort. pers. 44,7–9; Zos. 2,16,1).

Reports of the battle are shot through with propaganda, legend and pure invention. They also differ greatly, and overall offer no basis for tactical analysis (Paneg. 4(10),28–30; 12(9),16f.; Euseb. HE 9,9,2–8; Euseb. VC 1,37f.; Lactant. De mort. pers. 44; Epit. Caes. 40,7; Aur. Vict. Caes. 40,23; Zos. 2,15,3–17,1). The name of the battle is taken from the stone bridge that carried the *via Flaminia* over the Tiber into Rome, the site of the drama's finale. The battle proper took place on the plain to the northeast. Because the bridge had been destroyed in anticipation of a siege, Maxentius had a temporary structure built alongside it, either of timber struts or floating on pontoons (the sources disagree as to its construction and purpose). There is no reliable information regarding the sizes, formations or tactics of the opposing armies. Maxentius' troops were gradually forced back towards the river as the battle proceeded. Their attempt to flee back to Rome caused congestion on the wooden bridge, and when Constantine's soldiers stormed it, panic broke out. The bridge collapsed, and the men of Maxentius' army who remained on the north bank were captured or killed. The Praetorian Guard, loyal supporters of Maxentius, faced the enemy with resolution. Maxentius himself drowned attempting to cross the Tiber. Constantine entered Rome the following day.

The victory won Constantine control over the symbolically important city, along with unchallenged hegemony in the western provinces, thus effectively spelling the end of the Tetrarchy that had governed the empire for two decades. Constantine thus built for himself the political and military foundation from which he would later oust Licinius and establish himself as sole ruler of the entire empire (in AD 324). He also abolished the Praetorian Guard and its cavalry corps (the *equites singulares*). Christian historians and apologists later defamed Maxentius as a tyrant and persecutor of Christians, and portrayed the battle as a key episode in Constantine's so-called conversion to Christianity. Most famously, they disseminated the story, which Constantine himself allegedly told and which survives in various versions, that a heavenly vision and/or dream sent by God on the eve of the battle inspired him to have an apotropaic Christian symbol placed on his soldiers' shields or on the standards (*lobarum*; Euseb. VC 1,28–32; Lactant. De mort. pers. 44). This retrospective reinterpretation of the conflict obscures the ambiguity of Constantine's religious intentions, which only resolved into a preference for Christianity at a later date. The depiction of the battle on the Arch of Constantine in Rome, which was built to commemorate the battle in AD 312–315, alludes to divine assistance, but displays no Christian symbolism.

☞ **Generals of note, J. Constantine**

BIBLIOGRAPHY
[1] A. ALFÖLDI, Cornuti. A Teutonic Contingent in the Service of Constantine the Great and Its Decisive Role in the Battle at the Milvian Bridge, in: Dumbarton Oaks Papers 13, 1959, 169–184 [2] T. BARNES, Constantine. Dynasty, Religion and Power in the Later Roman Empire, 2011 [3] H. BRANDT, Constantin und die Schlacht an der Milvischen Brücke – im Zeichen des Kreuzes, in: E. STEIN-HÖLKESKAMP / K.-J. HÖLKESKAMP (eds.), Erinnerungsorte der Antike. Die römische Welt, 2006, 277–288 [4] W. KUHOFF, Ein Mythos in der römischen Geschichte. Der Sieg Konstantins des Großen über Maxentius vor den Toren Roms am 28. Oktober 312 n.Chr., in: Chiron 21, 1991, 127–174 [5] M.P. SPEIDEL, Maxentius and His Equites Singulares in the Battle at the Milvian Bridge, in: Classical Antiquity 5/2, 1986, 253–262.

PHILIP RANCE

H. PHARSALUS

The Battle of Pharsalus is named after the city in Thessaly close to where it took place on August 9, 48 BC (pre-Julian calendar). The exact site of the battlefield beside the River Enipeus was long a subject of debate [9]. At all events, this pitched battle between the armies of Julius Caesar and Pompey heralded the end of the first phase of the Civil War that had begun in January of 49. Caesar was the victor, spectacularly reversing a balance of military power that had shifted against him as a result of his defeat at Dyrrhachium a month earlier. Although the Battle of Pharsalus did not immediately end the war, which dragged on through a series of military campaigns until March of 45, it can be fairly called the decisive battle, in that it unexpectedly provoked Pompey to flee. In the wake of the confrontation, the most illustrious general of his day absconded to Egypt, where, looking very much like the defeated party, he was promptly killed by order of the young King Ptolemy XIII, who was attempting to curry favour with the victor (28 September, 48). Given these events, this battle resounded as one of the most famous of Antiquity, and subsequent generations often cited it as one of the most remarkable and dramatic moments in Roman military history (Cass. Dio 41,55,1; 56,1; 60,1). Appian used it as an example of a circumstance when fortunes turn [2]; [11.262f.]. During the reign of Nero, Lucan made this battle the subject of Book VII of his poetic epic on the *Bellum civile*, and later manuscripts even go so far as to mistitle the whole epic *Pharsalia*.

That we know so much about these events and the battle itself is partly due to the lasting significance of the episode in Roman historical consciousness. But above all we owe our knowledge to the accounts given by contemporary witnesses. The modern reconstruction of the course of the battle (recent syntheses e.g. in [6]; [8]; [3]) is mainly based on the account Caesar himself provides in his commentaries on the Civil Wars (Caes. B Civ. 3,85–99). The other, rather more detailed descriptions, all of which are of a later date (Plut. *Caesar* 42–45; Plut. *Pompeius* 68,5–72; Cass. Dio 41,53–61; App. Civ. 2,70–82), for the most part rely on him, although it is generally supposed that Plutarch and Appian also drew on other eye-witness reports, such as that of Asinius Pollio, who was present at the battle (Plut. *Caesar* 46,2f.; App. Civ. 2,82; cf. also Suet. Iul. 30,4).

According to Caesar's account, a ruse of war brilliantly enacted during the battle won him the victory, even though he was initially hampered by considerable numerical inferiority. Pompey's forces outnumbered his two to one (Caes. civ. 3,88,3–5 und 3,89,2f.). Pompey also had a much larger cavalry, which he justifiably believed gave him a critical advantage (Caes. B Civ. 3,86,3f. and 3,94,5). At the last moment, Caesar noticed that his opponent's battle plan had the cavalry supported by archers and slingers on the left wing commanded by Pompey and L. Domitius Ahenobarbus (Caes. B Civ. 3,88,6). Caesar therefore took a number of cohorts out of his third line to create a fourth, which he positioned out of sight behind his own cavalry on the right flank as a reserve (Caes. B Civ. 3,89,4). He thus thwarted the breakthrough of Pompey's cavalry, which, after easily overrunning Caesar's (Caes. B Civ. 3,93,3f.), found itself confronted with this unexpected defensive line and was put to flight. Pompey's left flank and rear lines were left unprotected, which allowed Caesar's right wing to attack in a turning manoeuvre (Caes. B Civ. 3,93,5–8; 3,94,4). Caesar now replaced his first line with fresh troops from the third, who, fighting exhausted opponents, again succeeded in breaking their formation (Caes. B Civ. 3,94,1f.). The battle ended with the capture of Pompey's camp (Caes. B Civ. 3,95f.) and the return of the survivors (Caes. B Civ. 3,97f.).

As Caesar describes it, his victory relied on a manoeuvre that he improvised in response to the circumstances given (Caes. B Civ. 3,89,4; 3,94,3). Modern commentators often cite this as proof that Caesar, although outclassed by Pompey as a strategist, surpassed him as a tactician, this being the key to his superiority as a general [10.95]. However, it is worth considering the narrative strategy evident in Lucan's *Bellum civile*, which consistently praises Caesar's perceptivity while emphasizing Pompey's lack of awareness [4.260–264]; [5.72–77, 115–117]. From this perspective, it is striking that Caesar's verdict on his opponent emphasizes a clear contrast in the two men's attitudes on the battlefield. At Pharsalus, Pompey immediately sought refuge in his camp after his cavalry suffered their first setback (Caes. B Civ. 3,94,5), whereas previously at Dyrrhachium, in the face of similar difficulties, Caesar had defied the enemy to the end (Caes. B Civ. 3,69,4). Of course, it must not be forgotten that Caesar's telling of the story of the Battle of Pharsalus is first and foremost a general's self-portrait.

☞ Civil war; Generals of note, C. Caesar; Generals of note, N. Pompey

BIBLIOGRAPHY
[1] E. BALTRUSCH, Caesar und Pompeius, 2004 [2] G.S. BUCHER, Fictive Elements in Appian's Pharsalus Narrative, in: Phoenix 59, 2005, 50–76 [3] G.S. BUCHER, From Defeat at Dyrrachium to Victory at Pharsalus, in: K.A. RAAFLAUB (ed.), The Landmark Julius Caesar, 2017, 297–303 [4] L. GRILLO, Scribam ipse de me. The Personality of the Narrator in Caesar's Bellum Civile, in: AJPh 132, 2011, 243–271 [5] L. GRILLO, The Art of Caesar's Bellum Civile. Literature, Ideology, and Community, 2012 [6] Y. LE BOHEC, César, chef de guerre, 2001 [7] J. LOSEHAND, Die letzten Tage des Pompeius, 2008 [8] S. MATTHEWS, Pompey versus Caesar, 49–45 BC, in: M. WHITBY / H. SIDEBOTTOM (eds.), The Encyclopedia of Ancient Battles, 2017 (pt. 5: The Imperial Roman Republic, no. 55; https://doi.org/10.1002/9781119099000.wbabat0055) [9] J.D. MORGAN, Palaepharsalus. The Battle and the Town, in: AJA 87, 1983, 23–54 [10] N. ROSENSTEIN, General and Imperialist, in: M. GRIFFIN (ed.), A Companion to Julius Caesar, 2009, 85–99 [11] T. STEVENSON, Appian on the Pharsalus Campaign. Civil Wars 2.48–91, in: K. WELCH (ed.), Appian's Roman History. Empire and Civil War, 2015, 257–275.

FRANÇOIS CADIOU

I. SALAMIS

The island of Salamis, about 2 km off Piraeus, and the bay of the same name which is enclosed between the island and the mainland, were the setting for one of the most famous naval battles of Antiquity, with a historical resonance extending into modern times. It has been portrayed as a victory of the Greek *poleis*, fighting for their freedom from a position of grave numerical inferiority, over the powerful Persians, who were seeking to engulf Greece in their (despotic) embrace. All such interpretations derive exclusively from Greek sources (survey in [3]), and their sweeping exaggerations have as little basis in reality as the notion that the Persian fleet was completely annihilated. However, the facts of the battle's outcome are beyond dispute: together with the land battle at Plataeae, the naval battle at Salamis represented the turning point in the war against the Persian army under Xerxes, and in the medium term it ushered in the rise of Athens as a naval power in the eastern Mediterranean.

The initial strategic positions and the course of the battle are also broadly undisputed. After conquering central Greece and taking Athens, the Persians hoped to cap their campaign of 480 BC with a decisive victory over the naval forces of the Hellenic League before winter set in [1.108f.]. The Greek camp, meanwhile, was split. Most favoured a withdrawal to the Isthmus of Corinth, but the Athenian Themistocles pushed for a naval engagement since this offered the only chance of recapturing his evacuated city. Themistocles eventually won the argument by pointing out the advantages of surprising the Persian fleet – much reduced by storms and conflicts off Artemisius (Hdt. 7,190; 8,7,1) – in the Straits of Salamis and dictating the terms of combat.

On the night of September 27, 480 BC, the Persian naval force was en route from Phalerum heading into the Straits of Salamis with the aim of intercepting the Greek fleet, which was supposedly in retreat. A large contingent (of Egyptian ships, Diod. Sic. 11,17,2; Aesch. Pers. 368; but otherwise Hdt. 8,100) was ordered to round Salamis and sail to the Straits of Megara to cut off the Greeks' escape to Corinth via the Bay of Eleusis [5.82]. In fact, however, the Greek triremes had positioned themselves in the Bay of Salamis in line side by side. Following a brief backpaddling manoeuvre exploiting the morning breeze, they rowed at full speed at the arriving Persian units (Aesch. Pers. 364). When the Persians turned through 45 degrees, they were also attacked in the flank by the Corinthians posted off the island of Pharmacussa. More Persian units were moving up, which prevented a retreat into the Saronic Gulf. Only after Phoenician and Anatolian captains had stabilized the situation could the intact portion of the Persian fleet pull back to Phalerum at the end of the day. From a Persian perspective, the position was sobering, but not catastrophic. After all, two large squadrons of at least 200 units had not even seen battle yet, and by no means were all the contingents that had been attacked destroyed. Significantly, according to Herodotus (8,96,1; 8,108,1), the Greeks were expecting hostilities to resume with a new attack by the Persian fleet [1.110]; [5.84].

The fact that no such attack ever came was the real surprise. It handed the Hellenic League a strategic victory, albeit one that was partly influenced by external factors. Xerxes, for instance, receiving word of unrest in Babylon, decided to withdraw much of his still-intact navy to the coast of Asia Minor and leave an army under Mardonius to winter in Thessaly (Hdt. 8,107). It was only when that army was defeated at Plataeae, while almost simultaneously the remainder of the Persian fleet was destroyed at Mycale, that the Persians ended their war of aggression, and the significance of Salamis became apparent.

The battle quickly acquired the aura of legend (Simonides, Pindar), dominated by the Athenian interpretation. In this way, it rivalled the victory of the hoplites at Marathon [4]. Eight years after Salamis, Aeschylus turned the victory into the key experience of Greek identity under the divinely ordained leadership of Athens. For Herodotus (7,138f.) Athens at Salamis became the saviour of Greece. Near Eastern and Persian sources, on the other hand, fail to mention the battle, and it left no noticeable shockwaves within the structure of the Persian Empire.

☞ **Wars of note, J. Persian Wars**

BIBLIOGRAPHY
[1] G. CAWKWELL, The Greek Wars. The Failure of Persia, 2007 [2] J.F. LAZENBY, Aischylos and Salamis, in: Hermes 116, 1988, 168–185 [3] J. MALYE, La véritable histoire de la bataille de Salamine, 2014 [4] K. RUFFING, Salamis. Die größte Seeschlacht der alten Welt, in: Grazer Beiträge 25, 2006, 1–32 [5] R. SCHULZ, Feldherren, Krieger und Strategen. Krieg in der Antike von Achill bis Attila, ²2013 [6] B. STRAUSS, The Battle of Salamis. The Naval Encounter that Saved Greece, 2004.

Fig. 2: Tombstone of the centurion Marcus Caelius of Bononia (now Bologna; Lorraine limestone, 1.37m tall). This funerary monument, discovered near modern Xanten in 1620, shows a relief of the highly decorated Marcus Caelius, who fell in the 'Varian Disaster' at the age of 53 ½. He is depicted in half length inside an *aedicula*. To his left and right are busts of his two freedmen. The inscription provides the earliest known reference to the *bellum Varianum*, and probably refers to the devastating Roman defeat of AD 9.

RAIMUND SCHULZ

J. TEUTOBURG FOREST

J.1. Name
J.2. Political background
J.3. Events
J.4. Classification
J.5. Aftermath
J.6. Reception

J.1. NAME

The title 'Battle of the Teutoburg Forest' gained widespread currency in the modern age as the name of the attack by Germanic tribal groups on three Roman legions somewhere on the right bank of the Rhine in the autumn of AD 9. The long-term consequence of this attack was the end of Roman rule in Germania. The term has its origins in the rediscovery of Tacitus' *Annales* in 1507. Tacitus locates the key events in the *saltus Teutoburgiensis*, although he does not himself name those events after the location (Tac. Ann. 1,60,3). The usual term at the time was *bellum Varianum* (CIL XIII 8648; cf. fig. 2), or, often, *clades Variana* (the 'Varian Disaster'; e.g. Plin. HN 7,150; Tac. Ann. 1,57,5; Suet. Aug. 23,1). Both terms adopt the name of the defeated general.

J.2. POLITICAL BACKGROUND

The Romans began conducting major offensives eastwards from the Rhine as far as the Elbe in 12 BC. Political and military cooperation with Germanic groups, the archaeological record of a network of Roman military bases and the beginnings of civil administration all indicate that Rome intended to exercise permanent rule in these territories. In AD 7, when the seasoned P. Quinctilius Varus succeeded his brother-in-law Tiberius in command, he inherited a largely stable situation [4]; [7.83–177]; [13.637–646]; [15.216–218].

J.3. Events

This was not a battle, but an ambush on a marching Roman army. A subterfuge on the part of Germanic tribal groups drew the legions into difficult terrain that was little known to the Romans. A forested landscape honeycombed with river valleys offered no space for open battle. Over a period of four days, the legions (*legio XVII–XIX*), along with six cohorts and three *alae* (auxiliary forces), were annihilated as they continued to march (Vell. Pat. 2,117,1). Varus ultimately took his own life (in detail Cass. Dio 56,18–22; also the account in Tac. Ann. 1,63–69; [14]; [15.100–124]; alternative reconstruction in: [6]). In addition to the ambush of the marching army, further attacks on Roman soldiers stationed on the right bank of the Rhine are known or must be assumed.

J.4. Classification

The nucleus of the attacking force consisted of Germanic auxiliaries who had accompanied the Roman march before absconding shortly before the ambush. Their leader was Arminius. As the commander of a tribal contingent in the Roman army, this chief of the Cherusci had been granted citizenship and equestrian rank by Rome. Scholars disagree over whether Arminius' legal status meant that the Cheruscan unit was a regular body of Roman troops. If it was, then its abscondence would be a case of mutiny, a far cry from nationalist interpretations [12]; [13]; [15.119–124].

J.5. Aftermath

The main participants were the Germanic tribes of the western low mountain range, with the attackers gaining further support after their initial success. However, not all Germanic groups joined the uprising against Rome, and even the Cheruscan leadership was split. Following the ambush, Rome stabilized its defensive lines on the Rhine, and in AD 11, it resumed offensive maneuvres on the right bank. Late in AD 16, however, the new emperor Tiberius revoked the command of his adoptive son Germanicus, who had repeatedly taken his forces deep into Germanic lands at excessive risk, and ordered his troops back to the Rhine. While it is unlikely that this action reflected a change in Rome's conception of its external policy, the recall of the troops proved over time to mark the *de facto* end of Rome's attempts at conquest. Writing in the early 2nd century, Tacitus was already able to call Arminius *liberator Germaniae* ('liberator of Germania'), a title that explicitly included the successful resistance to Germanicus' attempts at reconquest in AD 13–16 (Tac. Ann. 2,88,2; [7.179–198]; cf. now in general [3]).

J.6. Reception

German Humanists already anachronistically declared the ambush to be the birth of the German nation, poetically elevating it to the status of the 'Battle' of the Teutoburg Forest. Adaptations of this theme in art, literature and music, which have been produced up to the present day, tell us primarily about the times in which they were made, while gradually obscuring our view of the actual historical events [2]; [14]; [15.174–201, 223f.]; [1. vol. 3]. The search for the location of the incident has always formed part of this reception process. The modern name 'Teutoburg Forest' given to the range of hills formerly known as the Osning became established in the 16th century on the basis of the topographical descriptions provided by Tacitus. Ahead of the bimillennium of the 'battle' in 2009, Kalkriese (near Osnabrück) was presented as the location of the Varian Disaster. Occasional objections to this interpretation – that the written record on the catastrophe fails to fit this region and the findings made here, and that a numismatic dating is not possible for this period using the range of methods currently available – are reinforced by the latest archaeological discoveries. These suggest that the site was a Roman marching camp for perhaps half a legion, and they are no longer compatible with the elaborate scenarios of what happened in this valley that transfixed laypeople and professionals alike for more than two decades ([10]; [11]; [14]; [1. vol. 2]; criticism in [8]; [9]; [15.150–173, 220–223]; cf. [13.625–637]). It is noticeable that, in consequence of these developments, the terms 'Battle of the Teutoburg Forest' and 'Varian Disaster' have come to denote more widely all the theatres of conflict in the context of AD 9, or even more generally the entire final phase of the Roman occupation of Germania.

Bibliography

[1] 2000 Jahre Varusschlacht, vol. 1: Imperium, pub. LWL-Römermuseum Haltern am See; vol. 2: Konflikt, pub. der Varusschlacht im Osnabrücker Land GmbH – Museum und Park Kalkriese; vol. 3: Mythos, pub. Landesverband Lippe, 2009 (Ausstellungskataloge) [2] E. BALTRUSCH et al. (eds.), 2000 Jahre Varusschlacht, 2012 [3] S. BURMEISTER / S. ORTISI (eds.), Phantom Germanicus. Spurensuche zwischen historischer Überlieferung und archäologischem Befund, 2018 [4] W. ECK, Consilium coercendi intra terminos imperii. Motivationswandel in der augusteischen Expansionspolitik?, in: S. SEGENI (ed.), Augusto dopo il bimillenario. Un bilancio, 2018, 128–137 [5] S. JAMES / S. KRMNICEK, The Oxford Handbook of the Archaeology of Roman Germany, 2020 [6] W. JOHN, P. Quinctilius Varus, in: RE 24/1, 1963, 907–984 [7] K.P. JOHNE, Die Römer an der Elbe, 2006 [8] P. KEHNE, Neues, Bekanntes und Überflüssiges zur Varusschlacht und zum Kampfplatz Kalkriese, in: Die Kunde n.s. 59, 2008, 229–280 [9] P. KEHNE, Der Kalkriese-Wall doch ein römisches Bauwerk, und alter

Wein in neuen Schläuchen, in: P. HENRICH et al. (eds.), Non solum ... sed etiam. Festschrift für Thomas Fischer, 2015, 223–231 [10] G.A. LEHMANN / R. WIEGELS (eds.), Römische Präsenz und Herrschaft im Germanien der augusteischen Zeit. Der Fundplatz von Kalkriese im Kontext neuerer Forschungen und Ausgrabungsbefunde, 2007 [11] M. REDDÉ / S. VON SCHNURBEIN (eds.), Alésia et la bataille du Teutoburg. Un parallèle critique des sources, 2008 [12] D. TIMPE, Arminius-Studien, 1970 [13] D. TIMPE, Die »Varusschlacht« in ihren Kontexten, in: HZ 294, 2012, 593–652 [14] R. WIEGELS, Kalkriese und die literarische Überlieferung zur clades Variana, in: R. WIEGELS, Kleine Schriften zur Germanienpolitik in der Kaiserzeit, 2016, 64–107 [15] R. WOLTERS, Die Schlacht im Teutoburger Wald. Arminius, Varus und das römische Germanien, 2017.

REINHARD WOLTERS

Booty

A. Concepts and categories
B. Plunder and the taking of booty
C. Spolia opima and the distribution of booty
D. The imperator and the state: quantitative values

A. CONCEPTS AND CATEGORIES

Compared to other aspects of warfare, booty has inspired relatively little interest among modern historians. It is documented much more thoroughly in the Roman world than the Greek, a result of Rome's rigorous public administration. The following discussions exclude plunder for purposes of army supply. That was widespread everywhere as a military practice, and we have no specific information about it (e.g. Liv. 31,33,4–6).

The legitimacy of plundering and robbing the vanquished was never questioned; on the contrary, it was constantly affirmed (Xen. Cyr. 7,73; App. Civ. 5,128; Amm. Marc. 24,1,15 etc.). Polybius (8,24,9–13), for instance, compared the *exodia* ('expedition'), the hunt for *leia* ('booty'), with the *kynegia* ('hunt'), the hunt for game. War booty was distinguished from robbery only by the legitimacy of the state (cf. Cic. Pis. 24,57). The words *harpage* ('pillaging') and *direptio* ('pillaging') denote destructive plunder, and have no exclusive military connotation. To Rome, at least, war was in theory a 'demand for reparations' (*repetitio rerum*), which distinguished it from robbery, although the Romans did have a reputation as plunderers (Sall. Hist. 4,69 M,5). *Imperatores* ('generals') regularly returned goods seized in war to their original owners (e.g. Liv. 3,10,1; 5,16,5–7; 10,36,16–18).

The Latin language developed a specific vocabulary for booty in connection with warfare: *praeda* ('booty'), *spolia* (arms stripped from an enemy), *manubiae* (money obtained by sale of booty). These terms denoted objects and purposes alike.

Greek, on the other hand, had a number of words that, although used in the context of warfare, were not limited to it: *leia* (*leie*) ('booty'), *laphyra* ('plunder'), *skyla* (arms stripped from an enemy); occasional additions to the list being *andrapoda* ('captives'), *chremata* ('treasures') and *aichmalota*, which often denoted 'prisoners' and, by reason of its etymology ('those taken by the spear'), was also used of booty.

Leia in general meant movable property and livestock (Xen. Hell. 1,3,2). This word seems occasionally to have been used of the booty as a whole, but it must be remembered that the tithe paid on the *leia* only covered the sale of ordinary booty, not weapons or valuables (Xen. Hell. 4,3,21). *Leia* was broadly synonymous with the Latin *praeda*. Some of this type of booty might be consumed *in situ*, but it was often bulky and therefore sometimes had to be sold for the sake of the army's mobility (Liv. 10,17). *Praeda* in the literature can also have the general meaning of 'booty', although not before the time of Augustus (Liv. 45,33,5).

Laphyra, related to *lambano*, denoted what was taken from the vanquished, but was used particularly of weapons. Polybius (4,26,7) describes the Achaeans' declaration of war on the Aetolians as *to laphyron epekeryxan kata ton Aitolon* ('they decreed plundering against the Aetolians'). In Sparta, responsibility for selling the *leia* lay with the *laphyropolai* ('sellers of plunder/booty'), who also sold the *aichmalota* ('prisoners') (Xen. Lac. 13,11; Hell. 4,1,26). *Laphyropoleo* denoted the sale of booty (Xen. An. 6,6,38; Pol. 5,16,5), including captives (Str. 4,6,7). The closest Latin term in the strict sense of goods stripped from an enemy is *spolia* (*spoliare*), which was never used of the entire booty, but rather referred to weapons, the *ornamenta urbium* (i.e. statues and images) and sacred objects (Liv. 42,63,11).

Skyla (rarely *skyleuma*), which appears almost always in the plural, was a specific term for weapons (especially defensive weapons) taken from the bodies of the enemy dead (cf. *skylos*). The word is an almost exact synonym of the Latin *spolia*, which also included Gaulish torques (Flor. Ep. 1,8,2; Liv. 24,42,8). The semantic field largely coincides with that of *laphyra*, but in a very specific way. Stripping weapons was a privilege of war granted to the victor in single combat or, in a pitched battle, to the general or the *polis*. The weapons were the most prestigious category of goods, particularly suited to offering to the gods. In Latin, *praeda* and *spolia* were complementary and even mutually exclusive (Liv. 29,35,5). When Papirius Cursor called the valuable weapons of the Samnites *praeda*, he was denying them any military value (Liv. 9,40,4–7).

There was no Greek equivalent for *manubiae*. Almost half the instances of its occurrence are in Cicero or commentaries on him, that is, at a period in history when the legal meaning of the term had evidently long since been lost (Gell. NA 13,25). *Manubiae* were not directly taken into possession, but were either put into use or kept for future use. They came into being by converting the *spolia* into money. They were entirely subject to the authority of the army commander, who ruled on their use [9]; [10].

In Roman practice, the army commander had some leeway in regard to assigning the various categories. He could expand the range of *praeda* to inspire his men with the temptation of gains (Liv. 7,16,4). Conversely he could also classify a city's valuable objects as *spolia*.

Alongside the specific vocabulary, there were also more general terms, such as *hopla* ('weapons') or *skeue* ('equipment'), equivalent to the Latin *impedimenta*.

Captives usually comprised a category of their own (Liv. 7,27,8; 25,25; Plut. *Marcus Antonius* 19). In the Roman world, they were often called *captivi* ('captives'), *dediti* ('surrendered') or *capita* ('heads', 'persons') and managed separately (Pol. 10,17,6; Cic. Att. 5,20,5; Liv. 41,11,8). This distinction, however, was not a general rule. Captives were sometimes considered part of the *leia/praeda* (Liv. 31,30,3 and 42,3; 32,26,6; 41,4,8). At all events, 'free' people taken captive had to be distinguished from slaves, who were counted among the material objects (Liv. 31,40,4f.; 38,34,6). In 406 BC, Callicratidas at Methymna forbade his men to sell Greeks (Xen. Hell. 1,6,14). During the conquest of Phocaea in 190, the praetor could guarantee protection only to free people (Liv. 37,32,10–14). The Greeks often practised extortion. In 210, Sulpicius Galba developed an interest in this practice and indulged in it himself, 'such being their [the Greeks'] custom' (Pol. 9,42,5–8).

There was no special word for booty from a royal or state treasury. It was called *pecunia/ chremata*, 'money [of the state]'.

B. PLUNDER AND THE TAKING OF BOOTY

The actual procedure for taking booty is seldom described. A victory on the battlefield was customarily followed by plunder of the surrounding lands (Xen. Hell. 1,2,3; Liv. 44,45,3f.). The soldiers laid waste to the land and took possession of money (*chremata*), captives (*andrapoda*) and *leia* (Xen. Hell. 1,2,4). Bona's [2] assumption that *direptio* ('plundering') implied a *solutio* ('dissolution') of the soldier's oath as described in Gell. NA 16,4,2 is in error. In fact, the personal acquisition of *res* ('goods') obtained by force was permitted not by their plunder, but by their distribution.

Plunder of cities came generally as a result of their conquest by force, but cities that had surrendered were also frequently plundered in line with the *deditio* ('surrender') formula (Liv. 1,38,1f.). Tacitus' description of the taking of Cremona emphasizes the wave of violence. The most detailed description is that of the conquest of Jerusalem (Jos. BI 6,85,403–406; 9,2,418). Polybius' (10,15–17) ethnological description of the capture of Cartagena delivers a detailed report. As soon as the soldiers had established themselves on the walls, a detachment opened the gates. Scipio then let loose most of the troops to massacre whoever they could find (e.g. also Liv. 31,23,7; 39,34,2; 42,63,10; Tac. Ann. 12,17,1). He then called a halt to the bloodbath and ordered the plunder. The *praeda* was gathered, and a detachment guarded the booty until it was distributed. It is clear that the massacre phase played a significant role in legitimizing the plundering, for it was also enacted in cities that had surrendered (App. Ib. 9,52; Jos. BI 3,10,10,539–541).

Taking the enemy captive took place in various situations. It was rather rare on the battlefield, and more frequent during plunder of the countryside and the conquest of cities. In such circumstances, women and children, who were generally spared, were also taken in order to be sold. There is no mention of the 'unsaleable' elderly or sick, but it must be assumed that they were killed (App. Ib. 11,63).

The defeated sometimes denied the victors their booty by destroying all valuables and even killing their own people (Liv. 21,141–144; 41,18,3f.; App. Ib. 13,77). Nothing could be done with remains left in this way (App. Ib. 2,12). Livy (41,11,1–6) describes the collective suicide of the population of Nesactium as a barbaric 'outrage' (*facinus*). In fact, the suicide denied the victor what were legitimate captives. From the moment a city was taken, its people belonged to the victor, and it was somewhat unconventional to frustrate this.

The Homeric heroes took possession of enemies they had killed. This behaviour, no doubt derived from an Archaic reality, is also expressed in iconography. The image of the robbed corpse is found on reliefs, such as the frieze on the Siphnian Treasury at Delphi and at the Mausoleum of Glanum. The gathering of booty was a proof of victory, albeit an ambivalent one (Liv. 2,7,1–3; 40,50,1–5).

It was important to take booty in order to display it (Liv. 10,39,13). The Romans developed the practice of the *caedes* ('slaughter'), the pursuit and massacre of the enemy (Liv. 44,42,1–5; 27,49,8; Plut. *Aemilius Paullus* 22,3–7). Massacres were less frequent in the Greek world, but they are well attested (cf. Thuc. 1,106; Diod. Sic. 15,72,3; Xen. Hell. 5,3,3f.) [4].

In single combat, booty was removed at the scene (*spolia provocatoria* or simply *spolia*, cf. Val. Max. 3,2,24). The weapons that filled the Temple of Apollo at Thermus doubtless came from such encounters. In Rome, it was customary for aristocrats to take possession of personal booty (Liv. 6,20; Plin. HN 7,29,103; Liv. 45,39,16); Flamininus suffered an accusation for not having any (Plut., *Titus* 23). This practice was long-lived (Pol. 6,39,1–4). Soldiers and centurions were forbidden to step out of their lines. To do so required authorization from their commander, who released them from their oath, thus allowing them to take possession of the weapons (cf. Pol. 6,38,4; Val. Max. 3,2,23).

Following a battle, frequently the next day, the infantry collected the weapons under the command of their general. The Greeks and Romans alike appear to have developed a selection process at an early date. The Greeks used selected weapons to build a temporary *trophaeum* ('memorial of victory') (Xen. Hell. 2,4,7; Cic. Div. 2,69). The Romans, who did not build *trophaea* on the battlefield [8], collected the weapons designated for the → triumph and piled the rest into *aggeres* ('mounds', 'piles') (Tac. Hist. 2,70,5), which were sometimes set alight (Liv. 45,33,1f.; Plut. *Marius* 22,1–5: sole description of the ritual!). Tradition traced the custom of the pyre of weapons back to Tarquinius Priscus (Liv. 1,37,5; Serv. Aen. 8,562). This pyre (*acervum*) is associated more often with *arma* than with *spolia*, that is, with offensive weapons, which consisted largely of wood. A vow to Vulcan was frequently made in connection with the weapons pyre, in a practice also known to the Gauls (Flor. Epit. 1,20,5). Where weapons were of little value and it would be laborious to prepare them for reuse, they were also abandoned (Plut. *Sulla* 22).

In the Greek world, weapons taken as booty for a votive offering were sometimes placed under the control of the *polis*, or else a prince might use them for his own purposes, as for example Perseus did, distributing the finest Roman weapons among his officers (Liv. 42,61,2). Among the Romans, the *imperator* ('general') had sole disposal rights over the *spolia*. Q. Lutatius Catulus kept the choicest *spolia* from Vercellae at his own house (Plut. *Marius* 23). Their public display certainly included an inscription [3].

C. SPOLIA OPIMA AND THE DISTRIBUTION OF BOOTY

In theory, the *spolia opima* (*opima*: 'abundant', 'honourable') comprised the weapons taken by the Roman commander from the enemy commander he had killed in person (CIL X 809 = D. 64). Tradition cites only three examples (Prop. 4,10): Romulus, Cornelius Cossus (437 or 428 or 426 BC) – much disputed (Liv. 4,20,5–11) – and M. Claudius Marcellus (222 BC). Later came the controversial case of Crassus junior in 31 BC. Prior to the personal intervention by Augustus, there seems to have been no fixed definition of the *spolia opima* (cf. Liv. 23,46,13f.; Paul. Fest. 202–204L). Festus makes clear that this booty was won *classe procincta* ('with the army equipped for battle'). Polybius entirely ignores this ritual, even in the case of Marcellus (Pol. 2,34,6–9). The decisive detail for these procedures was the killing of a commander who had broken treaties, almost always with mention of a vow previously sworn. The *spolia opima* differed from the *spolia provocatoria* (*provocatoria*: 'of a challenger') in that the victor was acting in the name of his *auspicia* ('auspices', 'signs of approval by divination') as a representative of Rome.

Nothing is known of the rules governing the distribution of booty in the Greek world. In Rome, the distribution of the *praeda* among the men and the public treasury (but cf. Liv. 7,16,3) was the responsibility of the *imperator*. The senate and people did not interfere, or where they did (Veii or Epirus), the magistrate still remained liable for the consequences of his decision. Within the bounds of custom, he was free to determine the extent of the *praeda* and *spolia*, to distribute the *praeda* among the troops and the public treasury, to determine the portion of *spolia* to be put on public display and for his own personal appropriation as *manubiae*, and to decide what to do with the captives. Royal and state treasuries of defeated opponents, on the other hand (and as in the case of Capua these could include private riches of senators; Liv. 26,14,8), were administered by the quaestor, although this did not necessarily prevent the army commander from making use of them in the course of his duties.

The subject of Cato the Elder's oration *De praeda militibus dividenda* is not so much the pouring in of wealth to the public treasury as the exorbitant appropriation by army commanders (Cic. Cato frg. 173; 203 ORF[2]; Gell. NA 11,18,18). Shatzman [9] has pointed out that no case was ever brought for misconduct in the distribution of booty – a fact also highlighted by M. Servilius Pulex (Liv. 45,37,6). The troops expected at least some of the *praeda*, and it is thus unsurprising that the soldier's stipend was introduced after an occasion when this expectation was not met (Liv. 4,49; 4,59f.). The sole surviving description of a division of booty with subsequent distribution of the *praeda* among the men is that of Polybius in his account of the conquest of Carthage.

Polybius (2,31,3f.) summarizes the distinction between the battlefield *spolia* and the *praeda* earmarked for the troops in the year 225 BC: The consul had the *skyla/spolia* gathered in and sent to Rome. He returned the *leia/praeda* taken from the Gauls to their rightful owners, then released the territory of the Boii to his soldiers for plunder.

The distinction according to which plunder focused on utilitarian goods, and particularly consumables, also occurred in the Greek world, albeit less strictly (Xen. Hell. 2,1,19).

The traders who accompanied the army (Pol. 11,32,2; 14,7,2f.; Sall. Iug. 44,5; Caes. B Gall. 6,37,2; Bell. Afr. 75,2f.; Liv. 38,23,10) were crucial to the booty economy, disencumbering soldiers and buying up captives *en bloc*.

The *trophaeum*, the exhibition of the booty in a sanctuary in the name of the polity (Thuk. 2,13: the *skyla Medika*) and the weapons pyre all presupposed public control of the *spolia*. The Romans consecrated the *spolia* in the name of the *imperator*. Q. Lutatius Catulus exhibited the booty from Vercellae in a pillared hall for this purpose. There is no record of what was done with the remains of the weapons pyre. It is unlikely that they were simply left behind if the metal they contained was valuable. They may have been the source of the metal needed for the *aediculae aereae* ('bronze sanctuaries') [1].

The *spolia* that included the objects of value enabled the commander to reward deserving soldiers, whether by giving them objects from the booty (Sil. 15,251–267) or by having small valuables rapidly made for them (Liv. 39,31,18; Jos. BI 7,1,3,14f.). He could also offer additional rewards as an incentive to his men (Liv. 2,20,12). Rewards also came from public funds, senatorial donations, *praeda* designated for the public treasury, *manubiae* or even an officer's personal assets (Cic. Verr. 2,3,186; Val. Max. 4,3,10; 8,14,5). Soldiers thus honoured were said to be *spoliis decorati* ('adorned with *spolia*') (Liv. 29,27,3; → Honours).

Conversely, it was rare for an *imperator* to distribute the weapons among his soldiers (Cass. Dio 42,48,2). Bearing the weapons of a defeated foe was regarded as an ill omen, as illustrated by the examples of Flaminius at Lake Trasimene and Fulvius Flaccus in the year 121 BC. However, the slaves who served as *volones* ('volunteers') with T. Sempronius Gracchus were equipped with weapons taken from enemies (Liv. 25,6,21; 20,4). The Greeks seem to have harboured no such misgivings (Liv. 46,61,2).

The *praeda/leia* was sometimes assigned entirely or in part to the body of soldiers. The promise of the *praeda (praeda (omnia) militibus concessa* ('[all] the booty having been given up to the soldiers'), or similar) functioned as a powerful motivation. On the other hand, it was regarded as an abuse of power to reserve the entire *praeda* for the public treasury – its other legitimate recipient. Lucius Aemilius Paullus Macedonicus thus found himself in a quandary after Pydna, having no target to offer his men for plunder. He solved the problem by granting them Epirus. The *praeda* went to the men if they had obtained it by force with their own hands. The men serving under Caecina Alienus in AD 69 cited this point: *expugnatae urbis praedam ad militem, deditae ad duces pertinere* ('when a city has been conquered, the booty goes to the soldier; when it has surrendered, it goes to the commander') (Tac. Hist. 3,19,6).

D. THE IMPERATOR AND THE STATE: QUANTITATIVE VALUES

Soldiers were prohibited from acquiring silver and gold. Hannibal took this principle into account after taking the small camp at Cannae (Liv. 22,52,5). Aulus Gellius (NA 16,4,2) quotes from Cincius a soldier's oath from 'olden days', forbidding the appropriation of more than one piece of silver per day. Any distribution of money took place *praedae nomine* ('in the name of booty') (Caes. B Gall. 8,4,1).

The following was the procedure at Cartago Nova (Pol. 10,15,8–16,5): the *praeda* comprised the equipment of the Carthaginian soldiers and the movable goods of the citizens and artisans. The detachment responsible for the plunder collected the booty in the public square, and the soldiers slept beside it grouped by maniple (cf. Liv. 7,27,13–17). The next day, the tribunes conducted the distribution among the legions and the men, including those indisposed. Fairness in distribution contributed to a commander's good reputation, as in the cases of Scipio Africanus, Caesar and Julian (Amm. Marc. 24,4,26f.).

This procedure, which Gruen [5] calls the 'distribution routine', has been called into question by Ziolkowski [11]. Yet the examples he cites show above all that the *imperatores* strove to remedy any abuses of the marauding soldiery. Manlius Vulso twice corrected a situation by arranging a just distribution (Liv. 38,23). The authority of the *imperator* was crucial in keeping the soldiers' natural greed under control (cf. Plut. *Pompeius* 10; Caes. B Civ. 1,21; Caes. B Gall. 2,33,1). From the soldiers' perspective, whatever they had obtained by force belonged to them (Diod. Sic. 38,8). This did not necessarily contradict a desire for fair distribution.

Scene XLV – 116 on the Trajan Column without doubt shows the distribution of booty. The men are carrying the same heavy sacks as during the plunder of the Dacian city, and – contrary to what would be expected at a *contio* ('public meeting'), Trajan is shown seated. The *praeda* is heavy and unwieldy. The soldiers are *praeda onusti/graves* ('burdened/heavy with booty'), which would slow their progress (Liv. 38,15,14), necessitating the immediate sale of whatever could not be consumed.

In rare cases, captives were allotted to soldiers. Usually, though, they were reserved for officers and soldiers of merit. There was also room for sharing out the proceeds from the sale of captives, if many soldiers were involved. It is also reasonable to assume that the remaining captives from Cartago Nova, whom Scipio handed to the tribunes, would have been sold and the proceeds given to the troops (Pol. 10,19,8). Caesar distributed captives *praedae nomine* on one occasion (Caes. B Gall. 7,89,5).

We have no full tally of a haul of booty. All available figures refer just to one category, such as the Persian *skyla* that comprised a portion of the 500 talents available in 431, less than the annual income of the Delian League (Thuc. 2,13). Polybius (2,62) estimated a maximum of 300 talents each in booty from Megalopolis and Mantinea. Lysander in 396 took a sum of 70 talents from the camp of Tissaphernes (Xen. Hell. 3,4,24) and 100 talents from the Battle of Coronea (Xen. Hell. 4,3,21). More figures are available for the Romans, but no data about the *manubiae*, the *pecunia* managed by the quaestor (Cic. Fam. 2,17,4), the unsold *spolia*, the *praeda* released for consumption during the campaign, or – naturally – the plunder carried out for immediate subsistence. Cato is said to have promised his men one pound of silver during the campaign in Hispania (Plut. *Cato maior* 10,4). Essentially, what remained for the public treasury was the sale of the *praeda* and the captives. We have two overall estimates: the sum given by Pliny (HN 33,17,56) for Aemilius Paullus – 300 million *sesterces*, between 11,000 and 12,000 talents – and the takings from the conquest of Tarentum (Plut. *Fabius Maximus* 22). Manlius Vulso was able to display about 3,300 talents in his triumphal procession (according to Liv. 39,5,7–14; 7,1f.). These cases clearly constituted remarkable quantities of booty.

☞ **Consequences of war**

BIBLIOGRAPHY

[1] M. ABERSON, Temples votifs et butin de guerre dans la Rome républicaine, 1994 [2] F. BONA, Osservazioni sull'acquisto della 'res hostium' a seguito di 'direptio', in: SDHI 24, 1958, 237–268 [3] G. COLONNA, Un 'trofeo' di Novio Fannio, comandante sanita, in: M.G. MARZI COSTAGLI (ed.), Studi di antichità in onore di Guglielmo Maetzke, vol. 2, 1984, 229–241 [4] Y. GARLAN, Guerre et économie en Grèce ancienne, 1999 [5] E.S. GRUEN, The Hellenistic World and the Coming of Rome, 1984 [6] G. HELLENKEMPER SALIES, Kriegsbeute oder Handelsgut? Das Wrack von Mahdia und seine Fracht, in: Gymnasium 103, 1996, 321–332 [7] H. MÜLLER, Zur Erschließung antiker Kriegskosten, in: Marburger Beiträge zur Antiken Handels- Wirtschafts- und Sozialgeschichte 26 (2008), 2009, 185–207 [8] G.-C. PICARD, Les trophées romains. Contribution à l'histoire de la religion et de l'art triomphal de Rome, 1957 [9] I. SHATZMAN, The General Authority over Booty, in: Historia 21/2, 1972, 177–205 [10] M. TARPIN, Les 'manubiae' dans la procédure d'appropriation du butin, in: M. COUDRY / M. HUMM (eds.), 'Praeda'. Butin de guerre et société dans la Rome républicaine / Kriegsbeute und Gesellschaft im republikanischen Rom (Collegium Beatus Rhenanus 1), 2009, 81–102 [11] A. ZIOLKOWSKI, 'Urbs direpta', or How the Romans Sacked Cities, in: J. RICH / G. SHIPLEY (eds.), War and Society in the Roman World, 1993, 69–91.

MICHEL TARPIN

Borders

A. Greek
B. Roman

A. GREEK

A.1. *Polis* boundaries: Introduction
A.2. *Poleis*: Border protection

A.1. POLIS BOUNDARIES: INTRODUCTION
(Cf. surveys [58]; [20]; [47]; [6]; [21]; on the history of scholarship [18]; on the terminology, most recently [7].)

Boundaries between the territories of the Greek commonwealth by no means always consisted of linear borders marked with pillars, boundary stones (inscribed or otherwise), herms etc. Even in the Classical period, frontier zones (*methoria*, *eremiai*) of variable width were commonplace. Thucydides, for instance, describes such zones between Attica and Boeotia (2,18,1f.), Corinth and Epidaurus (8,10,3) and Argos and Sparta (5,41,2). They were sometimes inhabited and/or put to economic use by one or both sides. Often, though, they were located in natural landscapes, such as mountain ranges, which as liminal zones (*eschatia*) in the 'wilderness' were endowed with mythical and ritual meaning (seminal [62]; recently also [42] and critical [53]; an example of mythical significance in [4]). The 'frontier situation' between many Greek colonies (*apoikia*) and indigenous populations represents a special case (on which, comprehensively, [1]). It was typical of early history in particular to assert territorial claims by actions such as placing a sanctuary in a border zone (classic account [52. cap. 2]; cf. [13]; [9]), although recent research has established that such actions were often oriented towards interaction rather than delimitation. Examples include the sanctuary of Messon on Lesbos, that of Artemis Limnatis on the border between Laconia and Messenia, and that of Zeus Atabyrios on Rhodes at the tripoint where the territories of Ialysus, Lindus and Camirus met (cf. several articles in [3]; [42.36–38]). In Attica, the *deme* ('political districts') system for the political organization of the citizenry reconstituted by Cleisthenes still drew on this practice to accentuate territorial sovereignty in the early 5th century [48].

In terms of ritual and cult, borders near temples were also marked with images or altars to liminal deities, such as Zeus, Apollo Horios or Hermes (Nilsson, GGR 205; [57.216f., 221f.]), or by practices like the Spartan border-crossing ritual (*diabateria*) [10]. There is strong evidence for the physical marking of *polis* territorial borders by the placement of boundary stones (*horoi*) at least from the Classical period onwards (e.g. Plut. *Aristides* 11,8 (before 479); Xen. Hell. 4,4,6; IPArk 14 = BCH 39 (1915), 55, from 369 BC; e.g. Paus. 10,4,1), but it probably happened before this (Hom. Il. 21,403–405; one example circa 700 BC mentioned in IG VII, 52 and Paus. 1,44,1; Hdt. 6,108,5; cf. in general [57.216f.]; [46]). The same is probably true of stelae announcing borders in inscriptions. Paus. 8,25,1 tells of a stela with an inscription 'of great antiquity' marking the border between the small Achaean cities of Psophis and Thelphusa. A story told in Str. 3,5,5 and Plut. *Theseus* 25,3 presupposes the same practice: there was a stela, they report, on the border between Attica and Megara, which in olden days announced to travellers from the Peloponnese, 'This is not [any longer] the Peloponnese, but Ionia', and *vice versa* on the other side. Reliable evidence for the existence of such frontier stelae accumulates from the Classical period onwards (e.g. Dem. Or. 7,39; Syll.³ 933; IG VII, 2792). Finally, this period and even more the Hellenistic period yield frontier treaties or arbitration verdicts between polities that define exact linear borders in relation to natural landmarks, geomorphology, roads, buildings or artificial markers such as boundary stones or walls. They also contain precise stipulations that regulate rights of way and use for purposes of grazing or → hunting [20.93–129]; [54]; [14. esp. 153–159]; [31]; [55.71–177]; [26]; [34].

A.2. *POLEIS*: BORDER PROTECTION

A.2.1. Patrols etc.
A.2.2. Structural installations

A.2.1. PATROLS ETC.
Border disputes were ubiquitous, and at all periods they were one of the chief causes of wars (cf. generally Thuc. 1,122,2 and Aristot. pol. 1330a15–23 and [2]; [57]; [13]). There were centuries of discord, for instance, between Athens and the Boeotians over the borderlands in the Cithaeron and Parnes mountain ranges (Hdt. 5,74; 6,108; Thuc. 5,3,5) and Oropus [50. esp. 487–511], between Megara and Eleusis/Athens over the 'Sacred Meadow' (*hiera orgas*; Thuc. 1,139,2; IG II³, 292 = R&O 58 with commentary), between Argos and Sparta over Cynuria, particularly its fertile northern part, the Thyreatis (Hdt. 1,82; Thuc. 5,41,2; cf. [20.201–204] and [51]), Triphylia and other borderlands between Elis and Arcadia [56], and between Delphi and its neighbours over the coastal plain of Crisa (which triggered the Third Sacred War) and the pastures on Parnassus (Hell. Oxyrh. 21,3; Xen. Hell. 3,5,3 with [20.132–142]). In the 4th century BC, Athens was the first *polis*, with others following suit, to establish a magistracy (the *strategos epi ten choran* ('commander over the territory'), similar names elsewhere) responsible for protecting the borders [15.127f.]. Many places also created a border guard of *peripoloi* ('patrols') – sometimes called (*h*)*orophylakes* ('border guards') – who regularly patrolled the *chora* ('territory') and borders. Attestations for Attica in the 5th and 4th centuries include Thuc. 2,13,6–8; 4,67,2; 8,92,2; Aeschin. 2,167; IG II³, 292 = R&O 58, l. 21 (352/1); Aristot. Ath. pol. 42,4; for elsewhere Thuc. 6,45,1 and 7,48,5 (Syracuse), 4,55,1 (Sparta); in general Aristoph. Av. 1170–1250 and 1366f. The practice became universal in the Hellenistic period (cf. only [11] and [15.127–138]). In Athens from at least the Classical period onwards, border defense was the responsibility of the *ephebes* (18–20-year-olds registered for service) stationed in frontier forts, who in their 'hoplite oath' (R&O no. 88 with comm.) swore to protect the borders of Attica [49.35–49]; [45.90–95]. The use of young men as border guards is also attested on Crete [15.135f.] and probably happened elsewhere as well [11.210–214]; [16.64–69]. During the Hellenistic period, there is evidence to suggest that outsiders were sometimes settled in border regions specifically to protect the border [20.35f.].

A.2.2. STRUCTURAL INSTALLATIONS
The first records of permanent structural installations for border protection appearing on a broad basis date from the Classical period. Prior to this, and even thereafter, temporary remedies were more commonplace – embankments, palisades, ditches and the like constructed *ad hoc* to counter immediate dangers from attackers. Examples include the wall built across the Isthmus of Corinth to defend against the Persians in 480 BC (Hdt. 8,71; 8,74; 9,8f.) and the redoubts with which the Thebans hoped to thwart King Agesilaus of Sparta as he sought to invade their *chora* in 378 (Xen. Hell. 5,4,38; more examples in Diod. Sic. 15,68,3 and [38.167–172]). Yet defensive walls are occasionally attested even from the late Archaic period, like that built at Thermopylae by the Phocians in fear of the Thessalians 'long ago' (Hdt. 7,176,5), or the embankment that Miltiades the Elder, countering the Thracians, had put up across the isthmus of Thracian Chersonesus, which was later renovated on several occasions (Hdt. 6,36,2; Plut. *Pericles* 19,1; Xen. Hell. 3,2,8–10). Disagreements over dating have surrounded the great 'Dema', an earthwork in Attica running roughly along the border between Eleusis and Athens, from the Parnes massif to the

Aegaleos. Estimates have varied from the 8th century BC to the 3rd, but most scholars today agree on the 4th (on the debate [43], survey of research: [43.11–13]). Frontier fortifications with guard garrisons are attested in 5th-century Attica (Thuc. 2,13,6), including at Eleusis (perhaps even older), Oenoe, Panactum (both c. mid-5th cent.) and – from the Decelean War onwards – Cape Sunium, Thoricus, Oropus and probably Rhamnus and Phyle. Others were added in the 4th and 3rd centuries (survey in [45.130–180]; [36]; [37]; [43.7–11]; [19]). Sparta also probably maintained frontier fortresses in the 4th century and manned them on a temporary basis (Xen. Hell. 6,5,24 on the year 370; cf. [29]), as did Argos [65.42f.]; [5.425–428], Megara (notably the fortress of Aegosthena on the border with Boeotia [60]; but cf. [17.157–162]), Hellenistic Achaea [5.429–431], Clazomenae [32] and other *poleis* of Asia Minor [35]. (See also below and in [38.157–197]; history of research in [23.127–133].)

It is clearly apparent that, from the 4th century onwards and through the Hellenistic period, many communities were investing in complex border security systems involving fortresses, observation towers and signalling systems to warn of incursions. Yet some such installations may date back to the Archaic or even the Mycenaean periods (with literature [19.31ff.]). The classic example is Attica, where fortresses like Panactum and Phyle are recorded as now having been permanently manned by *ephebes* and mercenaries for purposes of border control. Dozens of other fortified installations formerly seen as watch towers and signal posts came to be regarded as part of a comprehensive system for defending the territory and the (northern) border of Attica. Historians generally attribute this development to an intensifying 'defence mentality' (particularly [45]). Some scholars, however, dispute the existence of such a system, citing among other things that many of these fortifications offered no strategic benefits against invading armies. They propose instead that these fortifications served as refuges (→ Acropolis) and border posts guarding against marauders. Moreover, many structural remains interpreted as signal towers or the like may equally have been farmsteads. The dates of many of these edifices are also controversial, as is the attribution (Boeotian or Athenian?) of fortresses like the present-day Gyphtokastro (ancient Eleutherae?) (on the debate [43.15–33]; [39.516–523]; [17]; [44]; [24] and [19]). The existence of similar border security systems has also been suggested for the Late Classical period and later in Megaris [60], in Boeotia [25] (perhaps with Archaic antecedents?), in the northeastern Peloponnese [27], in Phocis at the time of the Third Sacred War [41.340–354]; [59. esp. 305–324], in Mantinea [40] and perhaps on the Cimmerian Bosporus [63]. Note, however, the arguments of [23.263–294], to the effect that the many fortifications in the *chora* of Eretria served not as border protection, but as refuges and protection for rural settlements.

Information about border protection in the Hellenistic kingdoms is sparse and as yet barely investigated. Philip II (→ Generals of note, M.) secured frontier zones by establishing fortified cities and forts and by planting military settlers whom he transferred from conquered territories (Just. Epit. 8,6,1, probably from Theopomp.; Dem. 4,48; cf. [22]; [30.236–241]). Alexander the Great proceeded in the same way along his empire's borders to the north (with Central Asia) and east (with India), after encircling Media with a ring of Greek cities 'as defence against the barbarians' ([8.247–249]; the quotation in Pol. 10,27). In the Ptolemaic kingdom, the borderlands in northern Sinai seem to have been secured with fortresses and garrisons along a line from Pelusium after the loss of Syria in the early 2nd century BC [61], and likewise the southern border with Nubia [64.87–99]. Seleucus I and his successors made extensive use of the strategy of founding cities to consolidate and secure their authority across the kingdom. For border protection, they planted military settlers and built fortresses and fortified towns in vulnerable borderlands in Central Asia and northern Syria (bordering the Ptolemies) in the 3rd century ([28.155–160]; [12.158–165]; in general [33] on the emphasis placed on borders in the Seleucid Empire).

☞ **Fortification**

BIBLIOGRAPHY

[1] Confini e frontiera nella grecità d'Occidente. Atti del Trentasettesimo Convegno di Studi sulla Magna Grecia, Taranto, 3–6 OTTOBRE 1997, 1999 [2] S.L. AGER, Interstate Arbitration in the Greek World 337–90 BC, 1996 [3] S.E. ALCOCK / R. OSBORNE (eds.), Placing the Gods. Sanctuaries and Sacred Space in Ancient Greece, 1994 [4] C. ANTONETTI, I confine della Megaride. Incontri cultuali e culturali, in: E. OLSHAUSEN / H. SONNABEND (eds.), Stuttgarter Kolloquium zur Historischen Geographie, vol. 4: Grenze und Grenzland, 1994, 539–551 [5] C. BALANDIER, Étudier l'organisation défensive d'une région et son évolution, in: R. FREDERIKSEN et al. (eds.), Focus on Fortifications. New Research on Fortifications in the Ancient Mediterranean and the Near East, 2016, 417–434 [6] H. BERTHELOT et al. (eds.), Vivre et penser les frontières dans le monde méditerranéen antique, 2016 [7] I. BOEHM, Pur concept, élément naturel ou réalité édifiée de main d'homme? À propos du vocabulaire de la frontière en grec ancient, in: Cahiers des études anciennes 52, 2015, 19–45 [8] A.B. BOSWORTH, Conquest and Empire. The Reign of Alexander the Great, 1988 [9] S. BUJSKIH, Die kolonialen Heiligtümer der archaischen Zeit in Olbia, in: S. CONRAD (ed.), Pontos Euxeinos. Beiträge zur Archäologie und Geschichte des antiken Schwarzmeer- und Balkanraumes, 2006, 265–274 [10] P.F. BUTTI DI LIMA, Sui sacrifici spartani ai confine, in: M. SORDI (ed.), Il confine nel mondo classico,

1987, 100–116   [11] P. CABANES, Recherches épigraphiques en Albanie. Péripolarques et periploi en Grèce du Nord-Ouest et en Illyrie à la période hellénistique, in: Comptes rendus des séances de l'Académie des inscriptions et belles-lettres, vol. 135, 1991, 197–221   [12] L. CAPDETREY, Le pouvoir séleucide. Territoire, administration, finances d'un royaume hellénistique (312–129 avant J.-C.), 2007   [13] A. CHANIOTIS, Habgierige Götter, habgierige Städte. Heiligtumsbesitz und Gebietsanspruch in den kretischen Staatsverträgen, in: Ktema 13, 1988, 21–40   [14] A. CHANIOTIS, Die Verträge zwischen kretischen Poleis in der hellenistischen Zeit, 1996   [15] A. CHANIOTIS, Policing the Hellenistic Countryside. Realities and Ideologies, in: C. BRÉLAZ / P. DUCREY (eds.), Sécurité collective et ordre public dans les sociétés anciennes, 2008, 103–153   [16] A. CHANKOWSKI, L'entraînement militaire des éphèbes dans les cités grecques d'Asie Mineure à l'époque hellénistique, in: J.-C. COUVENHES / H.-L. FERNOUX (eds.), Les cités grecques et la guerre en Asie Mineure à l'époque hellénistique, 2004, 55–76   [17] F.A. COOPER, The Fortifications of Epaminondas and the Rise of the Monumental Greek City, in: J.D. TRACY (ed.), City Walls. The Urban Enceinte in Global Perspective, 2000, 155–191   [18] A. CORCELLA, La frontiera nella storiografia sul mondo antico, in: Confini e frontiera nella grecità d'Occidente. Atti del Trentasettesimo Convegno di Studi sulla Magna Grecia, Taranto, 3–6 ottobre 1997, 1999, 43–82   [19] K.F. DALY, On When and Where to Find Athenian Forts, in: K.F. DALY / L.A. RICCARDI (eds.), Cities Called Athens. Studies Honouring John McK. Camp II, 2015, 23–60   [20] G. DAVERIO ROCCHI, Frontiera e confini nella Grecia antica, 1988   [21] G. DAVERIO ROCCHI, Systems of Borders in Ancient Greece, in: S. BIANCHETTI et al. (eds.), Brill's Companion to Ancient Geography. The Inhabited World in Greek and Roman Tradition, 2016, 58–77   [22] J.R. ELLIS, Population-Transplants under Philip II, in: Makedonika 9, 1969, 9–16   [23] S. FACHARD, La défense du territoire. Étude de la chôra érétrienne et de ses fortifications, 2012   [24] S. FACHARD, Eleutherai as the Gates to Boeotia, in: Revue des études militaires anciennes 6, 2013, 81–106   [25] J. FOSSEY, The Development of some Defensive Networks in Eastern Central Greece during the Classical Period, in: S. VAN DE MAELE / J. FOSSEY (eds.), Fortificationes antiquae, 1992, 109–132   [26] K. FREITAG, Überlegungen zur Konstruktion von Grenzen im antiken Griechenland, in: R. ALBERTZ et al. (eds.), Räume und Grenzen. Topologische Konzepte in den antiken Kulturen des östlichen Mittelmeerraums, 2007, 49–70   [27] G. GAUVIN, Les systèmes de fortifications de Kléonai et de Phlionte à la période classique-hellénistique, in: S. VAN DE MAELE / J. FOSSEY (eds.), Fortificationes antiquae, 1992, 133–146   [28] J.D. GRAINGER, Seleukos Nikator. Constructing a Hellenistic Kingdom, 1990   [29] M. GUINTRAND, Les fortifications dans le système défensif lacédémonien à l'époque classique, in: R. FREDERIKSEN et al. (eds.), Focus on Fortifications. New Research on Fortifications in the Ancient Mediterranean and the Near East, 2016, 435–445   [30] N.G.L. HAMMOND, The Western Frontier of Macedonia in the Reign of Philip II, in: N.G.L. HAMMOND, Collected Studies, vol. 2, 1993, 223–241 (originally 1981)   [31] K. HARTER-UIBOPUU, Das zwischenstaatliche Schiedsverfahren im achäischen Koinon, 1998   [32] E. KOPARAL, Border Forts of Klazomenai. Cinderesi Fortification, in: R. EINICKE et al. (eds.), Zurück zum Gegenstand. Festschrift für Andreas E. Furtwängler, vol. 2, 2009, 501–507   [33] P.J. KUSMIN, Land of the Elephant Kings. Space, Territory, and Ideology in the Seleucid Empire, 2014   [34] E. KYRIAKIDIS, Borders and Territories. The Borders of Classical Tylissos, in: Cambridge Classical Journal 58, 2012, 115–144   [35] G. LABARRE, Phrourarques et phrouroi des cités grecques d'Asie Mineure à l'époque hellénistique, in: J.-C. COUVENHES / H.-L. FERNOUX (eds.), Les cités grecques et la guerre en Asie Mineure à l'époque hellénistique, 2004, 221–248   [36] H. LAUTER et al., Attische Festungen. Beiträge zum Festungswesen und zur Siedlungsstruktur vom 5. bis zum 3. Jh. v.Chr., 1989   [37] H. LAUTER, Some Remarks on Fortified Settelements in the Attic Countryside, in: S. VAN DE MAELE / J. FOSSEY (eds.), Fortificationes antiquae, 1992, 77–91   [38] A.W. LAWRENCE, Greek Aims in Fortification, 1979   [39] H. LOHMANN, Die Chora Athens im 4. Jahrhundert v.Chr. Festungswesen, Bergbau und Siedlungen, in: W. EDER (ed.), Die athenische Demokratie im 4. Jahrhundert v.Chr. Vollendung oder Verfall einer Staatsform? Akten eines Symposiums, 3.–7. August 1992 (Bellagio), 1995, 515–548   [40] M. MAHER / A. MOWAT, The Defense Network in the Chora of Mantineia, in: Hesperia 87, 2018, 451–495   [41] J. MCINERNEY, The Folds of Parnassos. Land and Ethnicity in Ancient Phocis, 1999   [42] J. MCINERNEY, On the Border. Sacred Land and the Margins of the Community, in: R.M. ROSEN / I. SLUITER (eds.), City, Countryside, and the Spatial Organization of Value in Classical Antiquity, 2006, 33–59   [43] M. MUNN, Defense of Attica. The Dema Wall and the Boiotian War of 378–375 B.C., 1993   [44] M. MUNN, Panakton and Drymos. A Disputed Frontier, in: H. LOHMANN / T. MATTERN (eds.), Attika. Archäologie einer 'zentralen' Kulturlandschaft, 2010, 189–200   [45] J. OBER, Fortress Attica. Defense of the Athenian Land Frontier, 404–322 B.C., 1985   [46] J. OBER, Greek horoi. Artifactual Texts and the Contingency of Meaning, in: D.B. SMALL (ed.), Methods in the Mediterranean. Historical and Archaeological Views on Texts and Archaeology, 1995, 91–123   [47] E. OLSHAUSEN / H. SONNABEND (eds.), Stuttgarter Kolloquium zur Historischen Geographie, vol. 4: Grenze und Grenzland, 1994   [48] J. PAGA, The Monumental Definition of Attica in the Early Democratic Period, in: M.M. MILES (ed.), Autopsy in Athens. Recent Archaeological Research on Athens and Attica, 2015, 108–125   [49] C. PÉLÉKIDIS, Histoire de l'éphébie attique des origines à 31 avant Jésus-Christ, 1962   [50] B. PETRAKOS, Οι επιγραφές του Ωρωπού, 1997   [51] M. PIÉRART, Argos, Philippe II et la Cynourie (Thyréatide). Les frontières du partage des Héraclides, in: R. FREI-STOLBA / K. GEX (eds.), Recherches récentes sur le monde hellénistique, 2001, 27–43   [52] F. DE POLIGNAC, La naissance de la cité grecque. Cultes, espace et société, VIIIᵉ–VIIᵉ siècles, ²1995   [53] I. POLINSKAYA, Liminality as Metaphor. Initiation and the Frontiers of Ancient Athens, in: D.B. DODD / C.A. FARAONE (eds.), Initiation in Ancient Greek Rituals and Narratives, 2003, 85–106   [54] D. ROUSSET, Les frontières des cités grecques. Premières réflexions à partir du recueil des documents épigraphiques, in: Cahiers du Centre Gustave Glotz 5, 1994, 97–126   [55] D. ROUSSET, Le territoire de Delphes et la terre d'Apollon, 2002   [56] J. ROY, The Frontier between Arkadia and Elis in Classical Antiquity, in: P. FLENSTED-JENSEN et al. (eds.), Polis & Politics. Studies in Ancient Greek History Presented to Mogens Herman Hansen, 2000, 133–156   [57] M. SARTRE, Aspects économiques et aspects religieux de la frontière dans les cites grecques, in: Ktema

4, 1979, 213–224 [58] M. SORDI (ed.), Il confine nel mondo classico, 1987 [59] C. TYPALDOU-FAKIRIS, Villes fortifiées de Phocide et la IIIe guerre sacrée, 356–346 av. J.-C., 2004 [60] S. VAN DE MAELE, Le réseau mégarien de défense territoriale contre l'attique à l'époque classique (V^e et IVe s. av. J.-C.), in: S. VAN DE MAELE / J. FOSSEY (eds.), Fortificationes antiquae, 1992, 93–107 [61] H. VERRETH, The Border between Egypt and Syria from the 7th Century B.C. until the 7th Century A.D., in: P. VAN NUFFELEN (ed.), Faces of Hellenism. Studies in the History of the Eastern Mediterranean (4th Century B.C.–5th Century A.D.), 2009, 199–216 [62] P. VIDAL-NAQUET, Le chasseur noir et l'origine de l'éphébie athénienne, in: P. VIDAL-NAQUET, Le chasseur noir. Formes de pensées et formes de société dans le monde grec, ^{2}1983, 151–176 [63] A. WASOWICZ, Le système de défense des cités grecques sur les côtes septentrionales de la mer noire, in: P. LERICHE / H. TRÉZINY (eds.), La fortification dans l'historie du monde grec, 1986, 79–103 [64] J.K. WINNICKI, Ptolemäerarmee in Thebais, 1978 [65] F.E. WINTER, Greek Fortifications, 1971.

SEBASTIAN SCHMIDT-HOFNER

B. ROMAN

B.1. The boundaries of Rome
B.2. Republican period
B.3. The *limes*
B.4. The evolution of the borders in the Principate
B.5. Military organization on the borders in the 2nd century
B.6. Changes in the 3rd century
B.7. The Roman borders in Late Antiquity
B.8. Impacts of the Roman border

B.1. THE BOUNDARIES OF ROME

To the Romans, the concept of the boundary (*finis, terminus*) was associated on the one hand with land ownership, and on the other with the expansion of the territory of the Roman people (*imperium*) and its defence. Although modern cartography tends to represent the separation between Roman and neighbouring territories using lines, this procedure does not reflect realities in an empire whose borders lacked material presence on the ground and were not defined clearly or unambiguously, particularly where peripheries ran out into deserts. The empire's borders also moved a great deal over the course of history. Above all, though, the idea of a geographically delineated Roman territory does not correspond to the mentality of those 'sons of the wolf' to whom Jupiter had promised an 'empire without limit [sc. in time or space]' (*imperium sine fine*; Verg. Aen. 1,279). This mentality is also expressed in the testament of Augustus. In it, the emperor celebrates his having extended the borders (*fines*) of all Roman provinces in the context of a programme of global expansion whose power politics require no ideological justification (R. Gest. div. Aug. 26,1).

B.2. REPUBLICAN PERIOD

Under the Republic, Roman territory was not secured by a system of fortifications, but by the raising of a citizen army in response to threats. For hostilities outside the borders of the *res publica*, a formal declaration of war was made using a legal formula by the *pater patratus*, who having uttered the ritual formula hurled a javelin dipped in blood into enemy territory. This ceremony, which dated back to very early times, was still sometimes enacted even in the Imperial period, notably by Augustus fighting Cleopatra (Cass. Dio 50,4,5) and by Marcus Aurelius against the Marcomanni (Cass. Dio 72,33,3). By now, however, it was performed in a purely symbolic spirit, and in Rome itself rather than at the border.

The rapid rise of Rome after the Second Punic War (218–201 BC) gave the Republic footholds outside Italy in a number of territories that were not interconnected. For instance, Hispania, parts of which Rome had conquered, was separated from the Apennine peninsula by the territory between the Pyrenees and the Alps. The Senate also exerted control over a number of cities and states that were tied to it by treaties of alliance, such as Massilia (modern Marseille) and the Numidian kingdom. In such cases, real borders blurred with the sphere of influence of the city or state, which extended far beyond Roman territory in the strict sense. The latter, in fact, was very limited, given that the allied tribes of Italy (*socii*) remained formally autonomous until the Social War. Writing in the 2nd century BC, Polybius describes this situation thus: 'Besides which, it was now clear to all as self-evident and inescapable fact, that from now on, all must comply with the Romans and obey their commands' (3,4,3). This political situation, combining direct territorial conquests with a mosaic of theoretically independent client states that *de facto* were reduced to vassalage, was tightened still further by the *imperatores* of the Republic's final century, especially Pompey (→ Generals of note, N.) in the east. It continued into the Imperial period at least until the reign of Trajan, who in AD 106 conquered the Nabataean kingdom, a Roman ally but formally still independent.

B.3. THE *LIMES*

The Latin word *limes* is commonly used today to denote the border of the Roman Empire and its system of fortifications. However, the usage is modern, and the term should be used with caution. The word first occurs in the vocabulary of land surveyors surveying land ownership, in which context it denoted a cross-path between fields. Towards the end of the 1st century AD, the term became current in military language in frontier regions of the empire, denoting roads or tracks laid to penetrate the interior of Germania following forest clearance operations (Frontin. Str. 1,3,10; Tac. Ann. 1,50; 2,7; Tac. Germ. 29,4). The first attested use in the sense of a 'border' occurs in Tacitus in connection with the campaigns of Agricola (Agr. 41). In the 3rd century, the *Itinerarium Antonini* uses expressions such as *a limite, id est a vallo* ('from the *limes*, i.e. from the ramparts'; 71,464 Cuntz), referring to Hadrian's Wall, and *limitem Tripolitanum* of the desert road from Tacape to Leptis Magna (10,73 Cuntz). Even so, the word remains rare in inscriptions until the 3rd century. It now described frontier zones that were geographically defined (CIL VIII 22765), and particularly in Africa it was gradually taking on the sense of 'military sector' (AE 1985, 849). The term evolved further in Late Antiquity, frequently coming to mean a 'defensive zone', bringing it close to the modern sense (CIL III 12483). It thus denoted both an administrative concept and, in a stricter sense, a military system.

B.4. THE EVOLUTION OF THE BORDERS IN THE PRINCIPATE

B.4.1. Types of borders
B.4.2. The linear defensive systems in Britannia and Germania
B.4.3. The borders in the east

B.4.1. TYPES OF BORDERS
Incessant conquest in the early Principate left the borders of the empire in a state of constant flux. There was never any intention of establishing defensive systems on the peripheries of the rapidly expanding imperial territory. Thus, Augustan policy in Germania was shaped by the general project of gaining control over part of Europe. The assorted military bases found there must be recognized as bases for further conquest, not as markers of territorial borders. The abandonment of this policy under Tiberius brought consolidation at the Rhine frontier, until a new phase of expansion in the early 70s AD, which in Germania superior led to the construction, in several stages, of a definitive defensive line (the 'Upper Germanic-Rhaetian Limes') in the reign of Antoninus Pius. The conquest of Britain that began in the reign of Claudius, and that of North Africa beginning under Augustus, also took place in several stages, each of which left material traces of a military occupation, even if a border in the strict sense was not established at every stage. Relative stabilization of the territorial limits of the empire began only under Hadrian (AD 117–138). The power of Rome began its decline only at the watershed of the years AD 254–260.

Borders, therefore, in their course and organization served both offensive and defensive requirements. They represented the material manifestation of Roman policy at a particular moment in history. In examining them, account must be taken of the different geographical zones and the different theories at work. There were (1) 'open' borders, comprising series of fortified installations along the boundary of the territories under direct Roman control. Good examples of this type are the borders in Dacia and North Africa. Next were (2) borders along rivers, which, in the case of major arterial rivers (Rhine, Danube), offered a natural defence. Finally, there were (3) long, linear fortifications functioning as defensive barriers (e.g. Hadrian's Wall or the Upper Germanic-Rhaetian Limes) and exemplifying Roman military expertise in this area. These are rarer and only began to be built at a late date, from the early 2nd century AD onwards. The different structural types were not mutually exclusive. For instance, the Rhaetian Limes, a linear barrier, meets the frontier of the River Danube downstream of Eining (Lower Bavaria).

The Roman borders were never organized in a uniform way. In North Africa, where 'usable' regions that were farmed and inhabited sat right next to sparsely populated desert in the south, there was no significant threat. Consequently, except at some closely defined locations, it was never considered necessary to build a continuous barrier preventing nomadic tribes from invading the territory. Indeed, in these geographical regions, where it was more important to control roads that lacked alternative routes and sources of water than entire zones of semidesert, the very definition of a 'border' becomes hazy. The empire also developed an interest in treaties of alliance with tribes outside its territory, as exemplified by the treaties with the Baquates, who protected Mauretania Tingitana from the east with no defensive system.

B.4.2. THE LINEAR DEFENSIVE SYSTEMS IN BRITANNIA AND GERMANIA
In Britain, the building of Hadrian's Wall severed the north of the island from the remainder, thereby creating zones that developed separately within mutually alien worlds that scarcely influenced one another. The structure, which the Romans called the *vallum Aelium* ('the wall of Aelius') and which they began constructing in AD 122, superseded a first defensive line of four forts built in the reign of Domitian along a military road (the Stanegate) that cut across the Pennine isthmus and facilitated rapid movement between east and west. Extending from Wallsend (Newcastle upon Tyne) to Bowness-on-Solway, the Wall is 113km in length. The structure is not technically uniform along its whole length.

Initially, the *vallum Aelium* was built with a walled section 4.4 m high and 10 Roman feet (3 m) deep, enough to permit a guards' walkway. This first section, beginning in the east, was constructed along a length of 78.5 km. It comprised a masonry shell over a core of earth and uncut rocks. Continuing for a further 49.5 km westwards was a turf wall 6 m wide. A system of pits and traps ahead of the Wall has recently been excavated in the Ouseburn area of Newcastle. A ditch 9 m wide was dug in front of the wall, except where natural defences rendered it superfluous. Gates were placed in the wall at intervals of one Roman mile (1,482 m), each being guarded by a milecastle fortlet built of stone or turf. Each milecastle contained a barracks for – probably – eight men. Two turrets built entirely of stone were interspersed between the forts. At this stage, the forts were still behind the wall.

Even before the project was completed, a major modification was undertaken. Large forts were now built directly on the wall at intervals of approximately 12.2 km. At the same time (or very soon afterwards), a ditch was dug behind the new defensive installation, flanked on both sides by an earth embankment called a *vallum*. The forts were accessible only via bridges secured by colossal gates. The reasons for this construction are disputed. At each end of the defensive system, series of fortifications were built to defend against attacks from the sea. At least three *castella* were built beyond the wall to the west, to detect any hostile approach in time and protect local allied populations.

Soon after the death of Hadrian (AD 138), his successor, Antoninus Pius, shifted the border considerably farther north to the line between the River Clyde and the Firth of Forth. He had a new wall built on this line, although the name Antonine Wall, which is generally applied to it today, is a modern one. Latin inscriptions invariably call it *opus valli* ('the work of the wall'). This structure was about 60 km long, and for most of its length it runs along the edge of the chain of hills to the south, making it clearly visible from the north. The wall consisted of a stone base with a turf wall on top, except at its eastern extremity, where clay bricks were mostly used. It is estimated to have been 3 m high and 6 m wide at ground level. To the north, the ground formed a glacis about 20 m high that was probably fortified. Pitfalls have been found during excavations at various locations, especially around Rough Castle. Initially, camps were established about every 13 km along the wall. These were fortified facilities capable of housing a complete unit of auxiliaries. Fortlets protected northward exits at intervals of one Roman mile. Larger forts replaced some of these in a second phase of development. As the new Roman Wall was built, it was celebrated with the placing of assorted stone slabs called 'distance slabs', each decorated and inscribed, bearing the name of the emperor and that of the unit that had built the wall section concerned.

The expansion of the Roman Empire that had come to a halt at the Rhine since the reign of Augustus continued in the south of Germania under Vespasian and his immediate successors. As a result, a coherent chain of fortifications gradually developed east of the Rhine, increasingly coming to form a fixed border from the highlands of the Taunus to the Danube.

In the first phase, towards the end of the 1st century AD and early in the 2nd, the Upper Germanic-Rhaetian *limes* appears to have amounted to no more than a border road (*limes*), along which wooden towers were built at irregular intervals (between 200 m and 1,000 m). During the reign of Hadrian, wooden palisades were then built along the ditch on the side facing the enemy. Dendrochronological studies have confirmed this sequence, dating the cutting of the wood used for the pillars to the winter of AD 119/20. A third phase began around 145/46, when the wooden towers were replaced with stone turrets, as many inscriptions attest (CIL XIII 6511; 6514; 6518). The architecture of this complex of installations varied in detail from one section to another.

The shift eastward in the front line took place in stages beginning shortly before 160 ('Anterior Limes'). In its first phase, this section of the *limes* was equipped with a simple walkway and wooden towers. Later, as several recent dendrochronological datings have shown, wooden palisades were added too, before stone turrets gradually began to replace the wooden towers from about AD 180 onwards. According to the dating of the wooden structural elements in the foundations, a final phase of construction attested only in Rhaetia took place in AD 206/07, when a stone wall was built.

Along the Danube, a long section of which marked the border of the Roman Empire, defence was assured by a series of riverside camps. Several architectural inscriptions from the reign of Commodus (180–192) record that he had the entire riverbank (*ripa*) fortified with fortlets (*burgi*) and redoubts (*praesidia*), to prevent covert crossings of the river (RIU 1127–1136). By contrast, where the Romans took lasting control of territory north of the Danube in Dacia, the new province was protected neither by a system of fortifications directed outwards nor even by military roads along the border, but merely by a network of fortlets that blocked access.

B.4.3. THE BORDERS IN THE EAST

In the Near East, meanwhile, Rome was facing another powerful empire: the Parthians. In this region too, geography determined how the border would be managed. Towards the southeast, the terrain is dominated by a desert zone that is difficult to cross, which made building a continuous, linear defensive system unnecessary. Most potential routes of invasion were in the north, in northern Syria along an extension of the axis formed by the Euphrates flowing to the southeast. The most important Roman defensive bases were built in this area, while the course of the river itself in the southern borderlands made it unsuitable as a line of defence.

More than 1,000 km beyond contiguous Roman provincial territory in the Red Sea, two Latin inscriptions discovered on the Farasan Islands (AE 2005, 1639 and 1640 = AE 2007, 1659) show that Rome in this sector controlled the shipping that carried the empire's commercial traffic with India, southern Arabia and East Africa, but that it was also vulnerable to piracy. In the Black Sea, meanwhile, the empire held the Crimea, a territory that was rich in grain but geographically cut off from the provincial territories of Moesia inferior and Cappadocia. The territory of Egypt was sufficiently protected by its vast encircling deserts, except in the south, towards the lands of the Nubian kingdoms. Here, the Roman army functioned as more of a → policing and administrative force than a purely military one. This adaptation to local conditions suggests that the Romans adopted different military approaches at their various borders.

B.5. Military organization on the borders in the 2nd century

The stationing of the most important Roman army units, the legions, in the 2nd century AD offers ample evidence of the relative military importance of the different border sections. Seen in global perspective, the army was concentrated near the borders, with no strategic reserve in the empire's interior. Germania, where up to eight legions – no less than a third of the entire army – had been stationed at the end of the reign of Augustus, now had no more than four. The heaviest military concentration was now along the Danube downstream from Vienna, where ten legions were distributed among five provinces. The empire's eastern front had eight legions, Britannia three, and Hispania, Egypt and Africa one each. Except along the Danube front, these units always had their headquarters behind the border proper, while auxiliary forces were stationed directly along the *limes*. The *auxilia* doubled the overall strength of the forces to an estimated 300,000 men. In view of the dimensions of such a vast territory, this may seem a small number, but it sufficed against threats that were limited to the local level. The forces in Hispania had no combat mission at all. The legions in Alexandria and Jerusalem performed the obvious function of maintaining internal order in those populous and unruly cities. The African legion, along with its auxiliaries, had the job of controlling an immense and thinly populated region.

Until the 2nd century, this system for the most part worked well, provided that the empire did not face serious simultaneous threats on multiple fronts. Where necessary, the high command would move forces along the empire's northern border, so that troops were temporarily withdrawn from one sector to reinforce another. Growing threats during the reign of Marcus Aurelius necessitated the levying of two new legions, the *II Italica* and *III Italica*, which were ultimately stationed at Lauriacum (Lorch, Upper Austria) and Regensburg on the Danube to protect a section of border that was coming under increasing pressure (Rhaetia/Noricum). Septimius Severus recruited three more new legions, called the 'Parthian' legions (*legio I, II* and *III Parthica*), two of which went to occupy the newly established border province of Mesopotamia, while the third (*legio II Parthica*) became the first legion ever to be stationed in Italy, near Rome itself, where it served regularly as the imperial → guard.

B.6. Changes in the 3rd century

The increasing threat had its roots in changes underway in the Germanic world, which had begun to emerge in connection with the Marcomannic Wars of Marcus Aurelius, and in the resurgence of Rome's eastern rival, the Persian empire of the Sassanids in the early 3rd century. These twin foci of pressure on two fronts that were very far apart caused a general political, economic, social and moral crisis in the empire, and led within just a few years to breaches made by the enemy at various sections of the border.

The date of AD 260, traditionally seen as the year in which the Upper Germanic-Rhaetian Limes was breached, is now once more a subject of debate, for it seems that the part of Rhaetia downstream of Eining was already invaded in AD 254. An inscription in Augsburg (AE 1993, 1231) shows that the Iuthungi had overwhelmed Roman defences around 260 and penetrated as far as Italy before returning north with their booty and captives and being apprehended by Roman troops from Rhaetia and Germania. The exact circumstances of this breach of the Germanic border, which led to territorial losses east of the Rhine, remain for the most part obscure. Rather than a sudden and unexpected breach in 260, as traditionally imagined, scholars now tend to prefer a scenario in which the border was abandoned gradually and partially, perhaps in connection with a series of agreements or even alliances with the Alemanni or individual Alemannic groups. At all events, the border was certainly breached by force, and Rome never relinquished its historic claims to the territory it lost.

At about the same time, in AD 259/60, Gothic groups from north of the Black Sea succeeded in taking a fleet into the Aegean and laying siege to Athens. Also in the year 260, the taking prisoner of the Roman Emperor Valerian by the Persian King Sapor I was a political event of the first magnitude, in the wake of which borders in the Near East fell and Antioch was captured. The ensuing years were marked by a sequence of sometimes fierce attacks, attempts at reconstruction and abandonments of territory. For instance, Roman troops left Dacia during the reign of Aurelian (AD 270–275). Even so, and in spite of acknowleged losses, Roman defences were largely restored, and the military reforms of Diocletian (284–305) and Constantine (306–337) brought consolidation.

B.7. The Roman borders in Late Antiquity

The military system of the Principate, in which troops at the border were moved from one location to another to carry out an offensive or to respond to a threat, buckled in the face of the number and severity of (often simultaneous) attacks. The remedy proposed was to restructure the army. It was now divided into two main categories: the border troops proper and the mobile strike force available to the emperor as a strategic reserve. This comprehensive reorganization was carried out in several stages, apparently quite complex in terms of details, but largely completed by about 325 (Cod. Theod. VII 20,4). Simultaneously, a major administrative reform, including far-reaching modifications to the command structure (→ General), was taking place. These changes continued throughout the 4th century, and the remodeled army is visible in its final form in the *Notitia Dignitatum*.

The elite troops, initially called *comitatenses* ('court troops'), were assigned to the task of confronting serious threats to any region of the empire. Regular border protection was delegated to the *ripenses* ('riverbank troops'; later *limitanei*, 'border troops' in some zones), commanded by a *dux* ('commander'), who bore responsibility for a particular section of a province. The *Notitia Dignitatum* contains a list of the garrisons stationed along the border. This border force was considerably smaller in strength than the general reserve army. Indeed, the strength of each of the various units seems to have been considerably reduced compared with their numbers under the Principate.

One major innovation of this period was the great many city walls, road guardhouses and even hilltop fortresses that were positioned behind the border inside imperial territory, which served as places of resistance or protection against potential attack. Admittedly, it cannot be stated with confidence that these defensive bases were permanently manned with regular troops. At this period, the defence of the Roman border involved neither an aggressive external policy as in the early Principate, nor a systematic development of linear defensive barriers (with the exception of Hadrian's Wall, which was still in use); rather, Roman border defense comprised a mix of forward defensive installations to counter minor, regular threats, a network of fortifications in the hinterland, and a mobile strategic reserve. Furthermore, barbarians were increasingly settling in imperial territory (as *laeti* ('foreign bondmen') or *foederati* ('allies')), receiving land in exchange for compulsory defensive aid.

Border defence was also accompanied by new principles of military architecture. Military buildings were now more strongly built and more numerous, but also considerably smaller than during the Principate. Despite various crises, this system remained essentialy intact until the early 5th century, when it finally collapsed on several fronts in the west, while the Eastern Empire continued to thrive.

B.8. Impacts of the Roman border

The establishment of fixed borders, particularly during long periods of peace, as for instance in Germania in the 2nd century AD, had lasting historical and cultural consequences, as zones of symbiotic coexistence with the army developed behind the border. Largely dependent on the army's presence, these regions diverged markedly from the purely 'civilian' provinces of the empire's interior. Rome profoundly and permanently altered the settlement history of these territories. Many settlements (*canabae* ('hovels') or *vici* ('hamlets')) that developed near military camps and through contact with soldiers evolved into cities destined for considerable historical significance (e.g. Mainz, Koblenz, Bonn, Cologne, Nijmegen, Vienna, Budapest, Belgrade). The presence of troops diverted the flow of commerce to border areas, sometimes over considerable distances, contributing to a productive connection between economy and society in the provinces. Spanish oil and Gaulish wine found their way to the fortified establishments on the Rhine. The military population, accustomed to a Mediterranean diet, brought a range of plants hitherto unknown in these regions which duly became naturalized there, e.g. pears, cherries, peaches and coriander. These economic changes affected entire regions, and contributed to their agricultural and industrial growth. Soldiers also introduced new cultural practices (e.g. the baths, the public life of Roman society, new societal structures, their native language). With these factors in mind, by the end of Antiquity, the border constituted an enormous gulf between spaces internal and external to the empire, a dichotomy that was still palpable in the early modern period.

☞ Camp; Fortification; Maps; Rear; Strategy

BIBLIOGRAPHY
[1] D. BAATZ (ed.), Der römische Limes. Archäologische Ausflüge zwischen Rhein und Donau, ⁴2000   [2] D.J. BREEZE, Handbook of the Roman Wall, ¹⁴2006   [3] D.J. BREEZE, The Antonine Wall, 2006   [4] D.J. BREEZE, The Frontiers of Imperial Rome, 2011   [5] P. DYCZEK, The Lower Danube Limes in Bulgaria, 2008   [6] B.H. ISAAC, The Limits of Empire. The Roman Army in the East, 1990   [7] S. JILEK, Frontiers of the Roman Empire. Grenzen des römischen Reiches. The Danube Limes, a Roman River Frontier. Der Donaulimes, eine römische Flussgrenze, 2009   [8] D. KENNEDY / D. RILEY, Rome's Desert Frontier from the Air, 1990   [9] Y. LE BOHEC et al. (eds.), The Encyclopedia of the Roman Army, 3 vols., 2015   [10] E.N. LUTTWAK, The Grand Strategy of the Roman Empire, 1976   [11] D. MATTINGLY et al., Frontiers of the Roman Empire. African Frontiers. Die Grenzen in Afrika. Les frontières africaines, 2013   [12] G. MOOSBAUER / R. WIEGELS (eds.), Fines imperii – imperium sine fine? Römische Okkupations- und Grenzpolitik im frühen Principat, 2011   [13] C.S. SOMMER, Trajan, Hadrian, Antoninus Pius, Marc Aurel …? Zur Datierung der Anlagen des raetischen Limes. With an English Summary, in: Bericht der Bayerischen Bodendenkmalpflege 52, 2011, 137–180   [14] C.R. WHITTAKER, Frontiers of the Roman Empire. A Social and Economic Study, 1994.

MICHEL REDDÉ

Camels

The word 'camel' (Greek *kamelos*, Latin *camelus*) is used of single-humped (*Camelus dromedarius*: Arabian camel or dromedary) and twin-humped (*Camelus bactrianus*: Bactrian camel) even-toed ungulates. The use of camels as draft and riding animals was widespread in Arabia, Syria and Egypt. These animals were also quickly put to military use in these regions.

Both male and female camels were put to service (Ael. NA 4,55; Plin. HN 11,261). According to Vegetius (Mil. 3,23), camels were only useful in sand deserts; they withstood thirst and could find a path even when it was hidden under windblown sand, but in other respects they were not effective in combat. Indeed, because camels are less receptive to drilling than horses, and are even averse to it (see below on Cyrus II), they are ill-suited to tactical deployment. The camel's size, however, offers an advantage to archers and lancers who are able to fight from its saddle (see Hdn. 4,14,3; 4,15,2).

In view of their limitations, therefore, camels were used only on select occasions, in dry, sandy regions of the Near East and in Near Eastern armies. In 546 BC, Cyrus II in advance of the decisive battle at Sardeis against Croesus supposedly ordered his warriors to ride the camels of his train (Hdt. 1,80; Polyaenus, Str. 7,6; see also Ael. NA 11,36). There were also said to be Arabian camel riders among the troops sent to Greece by Xerxes I in 480 BC (Hdt. 7,86,2; 7,184,4). According to Diodorus Siculus (2,54), the Arabs put two archers back to back on camels so that they could shoot at attackers ahead and pursuers behind simultaneously. The Seleucids (App. Syr. 34; Liv. 37,40,13: Arabian archers called *dromades* with long swords at the Battle of Magnesia in 190 BC), Mithridates VI (Amm. Marc. 23,6,56; Plut. *Lucullus* 11) and the Parthians (Hdn. 4,14,3; 4,15,2: armoured troopers with long spears riding camels in the army of Artabanus in 217 BC) also used camel riders in their battles. Palmyra was particularly renowned for its camel cavalry.

The Romans too used camels in their eastern provinces [3]. The *ala I Ulpia dromedariorum (Palmyrenorum) milliaria* was founded in the reign of Trajan, its presence recorded in Syria and Arabia [7.257f.]. Camels may even have been used at the Danube frontier during Marcus Aurelius' Marcomannic Wars [8.258]. Small squadrons known as (*turmae*) *dromedarii* ('camel units') were also incorporated into auxiliary units in Egypt, Syria and Arabia, particularly in the *cohortes equitatae* ('equestrian cohorts') [3.365]. For instance, 19 *dromedarii* of the *cohors I Augusta praetoria Lusitanorum equitata* camped between Thebes and Syene in the 2nd century AD (RMR 64,16), and there are records of up to 36 *dromedarii* in the *cohors XX Palmyrenorum milliaria equitata* at Dura-Europus (P. Dura 101; see also P. Dura 82; 89; 100; 102). The guard for the governor of Arabia included *dromedarii* alongside *equites singulares* (CIL III 93). According to Not. Dign. Or. 31,48; 31,54; 31,57, there were three *alae dromedariorum* ('troops of camel riders') in the Thebaid around AD 400: the *III, II Herculia* (cf. P. Panop. Beatty 2,29; 168f.) and the *I Valeria*. The *ala II Herculia* at least dated back to the reign of Diocletian, or even before [6.358, 378–380, 513f.]. The *ala Antana dromedariorum* was in Palaestina around AD 400 (Not. Dign. Or. 34,33). Justinian's cuts to the number of camel riders were said to have contributed significantly to the weakening of the Roman army (Procop. Arc. 30,15f.). There is, however, little or no record of camels in active service, and they were probably mostly used in escort and (express) courier operations and patrols, and as a kind of desert police force [2.345]; [3.365]. According to Pseudo-Hyginus, camels were a fixture of Roman military camps, whether they were used in battle or as draft animals (Mun. Cast. 29). They were either purchased (P. Gen. I 35) or requisitioned (P. Flor. II 278).

In all likelihood, the camel's main task was the transportation of supplies. The camels that belonged to the tithe of the war booty of Pausanias following the Battle of Plataeae in 479 BC may thus have come from the train of the Persian army (Hdt. 9,81,2), like the camels attacked by lions at night in Thessaly (Hdt. 7,125; see also 7,83) and those captured by Agesilaus at Sardeis in 395 BC (Xen. Hell. 3,4,24). Alexander the Great (Curt. 4,7,12; 5,6,9; 9,10,17; Str. 15,2,10), the Antigonids (Diod. Sic. 20,73) and the Romans (Tac. Ann. 15,12; Ps.-Hyg. Mun. Cast. 29) also used camels in their army trains. At the Battle of Carrhae in 53 BC, the Parthians' mounted archers received supplies via camels that carried loads of projectiles (Plut. *Crassus* 25).

☞ Army, C. Roman; Army, D. Late Antiquity; Supply

BIBLIOGRAPHY

[1] D. AGUT-LABORDÈRE / B. REDON (eds.), Les vaisseaux du désert et des steppes. Les camélidés dans l'Antiquité (Camelus dromedarius et Camelus bactrianus) (Maison de l'Orient et de la Méditerranée), 2020 [2] H. CUVIGNY, La route de Myos Hormos. L'armée romaine dans le désert Oriental d'Égypte, vol. 1: Praesidia du désert de Bérénice, 2003 [3] E. DABROWA, Dromedarii in the Roman Army. A Note, in: V.A. MAXFIELD / M.J. DOBSON (eds.), Roman Frontier Studies 1989. Proceedings of the XVth International Congress of Roman Frontier Studies, 1991, 364–366 [4] O. FIEBINGER, Dromedarii, in: RE 5.2, 1905, 1712–1713 [5] H. GOSSEN, Kamel, in: RE 10.2, 1919, 1824–1831 [6] A.M. KAISER, Militärorganisation im spätantiken Ägypten (284–641 n.Chr.), 2012 [7] P. WEISS / M.P. SPEIDEL, Das erste Militärdiplom für Arabia, in: ZPE 150, 2004, 253–265 [8] E.L. WHEELER, The Army and the Limes in the East, in: P. ERDKAMP (ed.), A Companion to the Roman Army, 2007, 235–266.

SANDRA SCHEUBLE-REITER

Camp

A. Greek
B. Roman

A. Greek

A.1. A construction more or less impermanent
A.2. Greek castrametation

A.1. A CONSTRUCTION MORE OR LESS IMPERMANENT

Unlike the permanent structure of a fortress, which was generally found within the confines of the town it served to protect, the camp was a temporary edifice that functioned as the field headquarters of an army. Given the logistics involved in military operations, Greek armies needed to construct camps – which could range from simple bivouacs to walled compounds – so that the armed engagment could take place on a plain that offered both armies, which were usually phalanxes, enough space to form ranks.

The Battle of Marathon (→ Battles of note, F.) in September 490 BC offers a good example of this strategic practice in action. Prior to the battle, the Athenians and Plataeans took up a position near the Sanctuary of Heracles (Hdt. 6,108), at the foot of Mount Agrieliki southwest of the Bay of Marathon. They delayed their attack for several days, reconnoitring the Persian camp, which had been built as a bridgehead for landing the forces brought by the Persian fleet. These forces lay at anchor, protected from the north wind in the lee of Cape Cynosura. The camp built by the Greeks thus allowed them to assess the enemy's positions ahead of the battle. The sanctuary in the area offered the perfect location for a camp. Archaeologists used to be confident of the location of the Persian camp, placing it on the strip of dunes at Schinias. However, the area where relatively dense pine woods stand today was until the 19th century a marsh almost ten kilometres across, which the dunes separated from the coast [5]; [7].

When a camp was meant to last, a dry wall would be built to encircle it. In the *Iliad*, the Achaeans make camp outside Troy in wooden huts, and at some point, the ships pulled ashore were protected with stone entrenchments [3]. The Spartans became masters of the art of entrenchment. Xenophon devotes Chapter 12 of his *Lakedaimonion Politeia* to military camps, attributing the following precept to Lycurgus: 'Recognizing that the angles of a square are not usable, he availed himself of circular camps, except where a hill offered protection or the camp had a wall or river behind it' (12,1). When taking Decelea in 413 BC, the Spartans made use of an Athenian fortification, perhaps renovating it, and they developed the strategy of *epiteichismos* ('fortification'), that is, capturing and holding bases on enemy territory [8]. The Athenians adopted the same strategy at Pylos in 425 when they fortified a temporary camp [4].

The literary sources offer no detailed descriptions of camps. Where they do mention them, it is invariably in passing, generally describing a period of waiting before battle, or occasionally recounting how a defeated party's camp was taken after a battle and the baggage of the fleeing army confiscated as booty (cf. → Supply A.). Following his victory at Issus (November 333) and the flight of Darius III, Alexander the Great (→ Generals of note, B.) took possession of the Great King's retinue. The nomadic nature of the Achaemenid state meant that this was very substantial indeed, comprising not only great riches but also members of the royal family – including Sisygambis, Darius' mother, whom Alexander treated with great courtesy [1].

Archaeology, meanwhile, has enabled the rediscovery of 'fortified military camps', especially in Attica [6]. The sites date from between about 325 and about 250 BC, a period during which Attica suffered numerous invasions. During the Chremonidean War (268–261), Ptolemaic troops built the sites of Koroni and Patroklou charax.

The most frequent Greek terms denoting an army's fortified or unfortified field camps in the textual sources are *stratopedeia* and *stratopedon* ('encampment', 'army ground'). According to McCredie [6.104], the word *parembole* ('camp', 'enclosure') more precisely described the fortified character of a camp built on a longer-lasting basis, especially in connection with a siege or an *epiteichismos* (establishment of a permanent garrison in enemy territory; see Thuc. 7,18,1). This distinction can be seen in two passages by Diodorus Siculus. The first tells how Alexander, son of Polyperchon, 'made camp near Piraeus' (*plesion tou Peiraios katestratopedeusen*), complying with Cassander's order to lay siege to the fortress of Munichia, which was held by Nicanor (Diod. Sic. 18,68,2). The second passage, describing Polyperchon's siege of Megalopolis (Diod. Sic. 18,70,4), declares that Polyperchon 'took up his position near the city and built two camps' (*plesion tes poleos estratopedeuse dyo themenos parembolas*).

A.2. GREEK CASTRAMETATION

Modern scholars generally cite a famous passage from Polybius (6,42) about Roman castrametation ('the practice making of a military camp') to draw a fundamental distinction between the Greeks and Romans: 'The Greeks, when making camp, consider it most important to adapt the camp to the natural contours of the terrain, firstly to avoid the work of entrenching, and secondly in the conviction that defences made by hand cannot offer protection to match that of natural obstacles. Thus, in planning their camps, they are compelled to adopt the shape to fit the nature of the ground, and in consequence to arrange the various parts of the army in different and incongruous ways. This changeability breeds uncertainty as to one's own position and that of each division within the camp. The Romans, on the other hand, prefer to accept the hard labour of digging entrenchments and other defensive works for the reward of convenience in having always the same type of camp (*parembolen*), which never varies and is well known to all.' It is clear that Polybius considered the Roman practice superior to the Greek.

A different tradition, however, maintained that the Romans at first built disorderly camps, and it was only in imitation of Pyrrhus, the first to structure his camps in a regular way, that they converted to their classical camp design (Frontin. Str. 4,1,14; Liv. 25,14,5–12). The existence of this tradition, it is argued, reveals traces of a Greek debate of the late 3rd and early 2nd centuries BC concerning the origins of the art of building military camps – a debate that excluded the Romans, even though they were in the process of conquering Greece [2]. This is plausible, and undermines the assumption that the Greeks had no understanding of the art of building and fortifying camps. The Greeks had their own techniques of castramentation long before they were conquered by the Romans.

☞ Battles of note, F. Marathon; Fortification; Supply; Wars of note, A. Campaign of Alexander

BIBLIOGRAPHY
[1] P. BRIANT, Histoire de l'Empire perse, de Cyrus à Alexandre, 1996 [2] D. BRIQUEL, Les Romains. Des imitateurs en matière d'armement? Le débat sur l'origine du camp romain, in: P. SAUZEAU / T. VAN COMPERNOLLE (eds.), Les armes dans l'Antiquité. De la technique à l'imaginaire, 2007, 541–555 [3] G.S. KIRK, La guerre et le guerrier dans les poèmes homériques, in: J.-P. VERNANT (ed.), Problèmes de la guerre en Grèce ancienne, 1969, 121–155 [4] P. LAFARGUE, La bataille de Pylos. 425 av. J.-C., Athènes contre Sparte, 2015 [5] H.G. LOLLING, Zur Topographie von Marathon, in: MDAI(A) 1, 1876, 67–94 [6] J.R. MCCREDIE, Fortified Military Camps in Attica, (Hesperia Supplement 11), 1966 [7] G. SOTERIADES, Ἀνασκαφαὶ καὶ ἔρευναι ἐν Μαραθῶνι, in: PAAH, 1935, 84–158 [8] H.D. WESTLAKE, The Progress of Epiteichismos, in: CQ 33, 1983, 12–24.

JEAN-CHRISTOPHE COUVENHES

B. ROMAN

B.1. *Castrum*, *castra* and *castellum*: Roman army camps and forts
B.2. Structures inside legionary and auxiliary *castra* and *castella*
B.3. Fortress and fort types of the early and middle Imperial period

B.1. *CASTRUM*, *CASTRA* AND *CASTELLUM*: ROMAN ARMY CAMPS AND FORTS

B.1.1. Marching camps
B.1.2. Legionary fortresses and auxiliary forts and fortlets
B.1.3. Walls and ditches
B.1.4. Towers
B.1.5. Gates
B.1.6. Roads

In Latin, *castrum* in the singular originally meant a fortified place or structure, *castra* in the plural an encampment of soldiers' tents. Both came to denote 'camps' of varying degrees of permanence, from temporary marching camps and siege camps to the enduring structures that in English are generally called '[legionary] fortresses'. Distinct from both were the '[auxiliary] forts' and 'fortlets' (*castella* or *praesidia*), which, although similar in design, were generally much smaller. Archaeologists have studied numerous fortresses and forts from the early to middle Imperial-period, but only a few examples from the Republican period. Such structures only began to multiply dramatically in the reign of Augustus, as the professional standing army began to undertake lengthier occupations, and to make use of permanent camps in border regions.

B.1.1. MARCHING CAMPS

Roman camps were carefully planned. Manuals for their construction must have been available, and we also know of training camps for entrenchment work. Known, too, are the marching camps that Roman armies built every evening, complete with walls and ditches, using wooden palisade stakes that they carried with them. Troops put up their leather tents in the compound inside. These camps were always built according to the same pattern.

The first literary record of Roman marching camps is found in Polybius (6,26–32), writing in the 2nd century BC. The basic forms of these camps generally corresponded to the regular design of more permanent camps at the time. They included polyhedral ground plans adapted to the terrain, as well as oblong installations with rounded ends (the 'playing card' model).

B.1.2. LEGIONARY FORTRESSES AND AUXILIARY FORTS AND FORTLETS

The first fortresses and *castella* were built of wood and earth in the north, in Britannia and on the Rhine and Danube. As a linear border defence was definitively established from the mid-1st century AD onwards, legionary fortresses were increasingly built of stone. The → auxiliaries, originally closely associated with the legions, were now increasingly operating as independent units, with their own auxiliary forts. They guarded the borders, while the legions were kept in readiness for larger operations. From the Flavian period onwards, stone began to supersede wood and earth in auxiliary installations. One common feature of the *castra* and *castella* of the Republic and those of the Principate, however, arose by virtue of their purpose. They were not intended strictly as secure fortresses in which a numerically inferior force could hold off a superior attacker. Rather, they were relatively lightly fortified barracks, from which troops conducted mobile and offensive operations, and ideally functioned as a precaution against surprise attacks and protection for the unit's baggage and supplies. With good reason, [9] applies a term from old Austrian military language to the Roman fort[ress]; they were not secure fortresses, but *'fortifizierte Casernements'* ('fortified cantonments'). Most elements of Roman fortification were not genuine Roman inventions. In many cases, the Romans adopted aspects of the highly developed Hellenistic fortification tradition, but combined them in innovative ways, leading to the emergence of something distinctly Roman.

B.1.3. WALLS AND DITCHES

Defensive walls in various wood and earth designs were particularly prevalent across the northwestern provinces during the Principate. All such walls made from perishable materials also had wooden parapets with crenellations. None appears to have exceeded a maximum height of 4–5 m. The first instance of a military camp with external and internal construction in solid stone based on the 'playing card' groundplan was the Praetorian camp in Rome, built in AD 21–23. The stone design gradually became the standard for permanent legionary camps and fortresses in the provinces. Later, beginning in the Flavian period, auxiliary forts also began to be encircled with stone defences. Squared rubble walls were generally whitewashed and painted with red lines to mimic ashlar masonry. It appears to have been obligatory to place a cut stone ledge around the exterior of the defensive walls at the level of the walkway. Only rarely do physical finds make it possible to ascertain the height of these walls. For legionary fortresses, it was approximately 5–6 m, and for auxiliary forts approximately 4–5 m. Ramps or wooden staircases were built at various places along the rear of the defensive walls (whether the latter were built in wood and earth or stone), to enable rapid deployment in emergencies.

B.1.4. TOWERS

Towers were often built into these wall structures, at corners and set at intervals along their length. The only evidence for them in excavations is the postholes of their weight-bearing vertical beams (four in towers along a wall, five or six in corner towers). Wooden towers were always incorporated into the wall, that is, they never protruded from the wall façade. They were at least three storeys high.

Like wooden towers, stone towers at corners and along walls were also integrated into the *agger* ('mound') in legionary fortresses and auxiliary forts, jutting out from the wall façade only slightly, if at all.

B.1.5. GATES

Castra and *castella* usually had four gates, each flanked by towers. The *porta praetoria* ('praetorian gate') was in the centre of the narrow end facing the enemy, the *porta decumana* ('gate of the tenth') on the narrow end opposite. The two gates in the long side walls were usually placed not centrally, but some distance closer to the *porta praetoria*. These side gates were called the *porta principalis dextra* ('right main gate') and *porta principalis sinistra* ('left main gate'). There were special cases on Hadrian's Wall. Where the front of a fort, including its *portae principales*, jutted out from the wall into enemy territory, additional gates were sometimes placed in the *retentura* in the rear: the *porta quintana dextra* and/or *sinistra*.

The stone gateways of legionary camps were sometimes very complex in design with several thoroughfares. Their designs often corresponded to those of contemporary city gates. Entirely different gateway designs occurred, often within the same installation, in both legionary fortresses and auxiliary forts, and no fixed rules are discernible.

Stone architectural inscriptions, sometimes with bronze lettering, were incorporated into the walls at all four gateways of legionary fortresses and *castellae*. One, or frequently several encircling V-shaped ditches were dug to hamper access.

B.1.6. ROADS

A continuous roadway called the *via sagularis* ('road of the cloak') ran around the inside of the perimeter wall. The internal space was divided by a system of roads that crossed at right angles. The main axis was the *via principalis*. This divided the camp into two generally unequal areas, the smaller of which to the front was called the *praetentura*, the larger to the rear the *retentura*. The *via praetoria* met the *via principalis* in front of the main entrance to the central building. The road leading from the rear gate, the *porta decumana*, into the heart of the camp was called the *via decumana*. Apart from these roads, *castra* and *castella* also had smaller lanes. Wooden and stone conduits for water and waste water were sunk into the gravelled and paved roadway.

B.2. STRUCTURES INSIDE LEGIONARY AND AUXILIARY *CASTRA* AND *CASTELLA*

B.2.1. Staff quarters (*principia*)
B.2.2. Living quarters of the commander (*praetorium*)
B.2.3. Tribune houses
B.2.4. Barracks
B.2.5. Multipurpose buildings (*tabernae*)
B.2.6. Baths
B.2.7. Exercise halls
B.2.8. Granaries (*horrea*)
B.2.9. Field hospitals (*valetudinaria*)
B.2.10. Workshops (*fabricae*)
B.2.11. Storerooms and other rooms
B.2.12. Water supply and latrines

Timber framing was prevalent at first in camps intended for a longer life span in the northern and northwestern provinces. It was gradually superseded by masonry techniques using squared rubble, with architectural details such as ledges and columns added in worked ashlar. Some building types, such as barracks, continued to be constructed with timber framing on squared rubble bases until the 3rd century AD. The timber used in these wattle-and-daub buildings was not meant to be visible, but was plastered over and whitewashed. Some such timber-framed buildings have been shown to have had their bases painted red. Timber-framed barracks sometimes had an end section, including baths with hypocaust heating, built entirely of solid stonework. Recent findings have established that the interior buildings of camps, such as the *praetoria* and barracks, were two storeys high, considerably higher than previously believed.

B.2.1. STAFF QUARTERS (PRINCIPIA)

The general's tent put up in the centre of the camp was called the *praetorium* in the Republican period. The first archaeological evidence of a spatial division of this structure into two, the *praetorium* as living quarters and the *principia* as the working area, dates only from the Augustan period. The exact date of this separation cannot currently be determined.

Fortresses and forts of the Imperial period had at their centre the *principia*, a large complex of buildings around a central courtyard. Its origins in the forums of civic urban spaces are obvious. Inscriptions and literary evidence show that it was called the *principia*, in linguistic terms a *plurale tantum* ('occurs only in the plural'). This central complex preserved its basic form throughout the Imperial period, but did evolve somewhat over time. The main entrance of the *principia* was in the centre on the *via praetoria*. The entrance to the *principia* was emphasized in various ways in the architecture. The rear of the *principia* comprised a row of rooms with a hall (*basilica*) running all the way across in front of them. Like the *basilica* in a forum, this also contained *tribunales*, or speakers' platforms. Altars and statues of emperors have also been found here. To the rear were the *aedes* (sanctuary) where the unit's standards were kept, and a cellar (of wood or stone) *aerarium*, the strongroom for its funds. Rooms adjoining the *aedes* could be used as orderly rooms, archives or other administrative spaces, and from the 2nd century AD onwards they could be heated. From the mid-1st century AD onwards, suites of rooms also began to appear behind the side porticos, and inscriptions or relevant finds reveal these to have been used as *armamentaria*, or armouries. There were also more offices and archives in these side wings. There is also evidence of *officia*, private offices of senior officers, and of *scholae*, assembly rooms and cult spaces for particular ranks or positions, within the *principia* complex.

B.2.2. LIVING QUARTERS OF THE COMMANDER (PRAETORIUM)

The *praetoria*, the living quarters of camp commanders, resembled Mediterranean townhouses. *Praetoria*, located beside or behind the *principia*, had many rooms and several courtyards. Dining rooms (*triclinia*) and baths can be identified. Their internal fittings (architectural decoration, wall paintings, etc.) also attest to high levels of comfort.

B.2.3. TRIBUNE HOUSES

The houses of military tribunes in legionary fortresses, the senatorial *tribunus laticlavius* ('broad-striped tribune'), the five or six equestrian *tribuni angusticlavii* ('narrow-striped tribune') and probably the *praefectus castrorum* ('camp commander') also represented adaptations of Italic townhouses, albeit in much more modest form. These tribune houses were traditionally located in the *scamnum tribunorum* ('tribunes' bench') in the *praetentura* on the *via principalis*, where the tribunes' tents had already been pitched in the marching and field camps of the Republican period.

B.2.4. BARRACKS

Soldiers in legionary fortresses and auxiliary forts were housed in elongated barracks (*centuria*) with covered porticos running along their length. These evolved from the tents of the Republican-period marching and field camps. They had no antecedents in civilian architecture. Each *contubernium* ('group occupying a tent') had two rooms at its disposal in the infantry barracks. The rear room for sleeping and living contained four beds (double-stacked bunks?) and a hearth, and was called the *papilio*. The front room was a weapons and equipment store known as the *arma*. These names derived from the Republican tradition: *papilio* means 'tent' and the *arma* was originally the plot of land in front of the tent where weapons and marching gear were stowed. Hearths and fireplaces have been found in the *papiliones* as regularly as they have been absent from the *armae*. It is assumed that smoke was conducted out through a chimney built of clay and wood, with a ceramic chimneypot in the roof.

Recent excavations have shown that cavalrymen lived under the same roof as their horses. Soldiers' accommodations were accordingly different in design here. There was a single (heatable) living room for three troopers, with an adjoining stable for three horses.

The centurions occupied the end buildings of the barracks, which offered considerably more comfortable living conditions. Baths, underfloor heating and wall paintings, for instance, have often been found in these quarters, along with multiple living rooms and bedrooms. Some *castra* and *castella* also had larger rooms at the opposite end of the barracks. These structures may have housed junior officers, the *optio* ('adjutant'), *tesserarius* ('guard commander') and *signifer* ('standard bearer'). They also contained offices. From the Augustan period onwards, the design of centurions' houses can be seen to diverge considerably from that of the other barracks. End buildings began to be built of solid wood or stone, whereas the *contubernia* were of much flimsier design (e.g. timber-framed).

The end buildings for cohorts 2–10 were generally built at the end of the barracks facing the defences, that is, on the enemy side. In emergencies, the centurions were evidently responsible for ensuring that their centuries moved without delay to occupy their allotted section of wall or other emergency position.

The centurions' houses of the 1st cohort faced on to the *via principalis* and were located next to the *principia*. Forming a kind of guard for the legion commander, this cohort was clearly responsible for his safety while also functioning as a quick-response reserve under his direct command. The houses of the 1st cohort's centurions differed from those of the other centurions not just in their orientation, but also in that they were much larger and more comfortable. Even so, they were still smaller than the tribunes' houses. There were also clear distinctions within the *cohors prima*: the house of the *primipilus* ('chief centurion') was generally the largest and finest of the five.

B.2.5. MULTIPURPOSE BUILDINGS (TABERNAE)

Rows of simpler buildings are regularly found along the main roads inside legionary camps, and these were probably the *tabernae* attested in the literature and inscriptions. Here, the army train was presumably housed: stable boys, muleteers, cart drivers, and others. There were probably also orderly rooms, stables and sheds for draught and pack animals, carts and artillery pieces. A letter from Vindonissa reveals that the *tabernae* had sequential numbers, making them easy to find, and that an indigenous woman was operating a tavern in one of them [4.263, 316].

B.2.6. BATHS

During the Principate, it may be assumed that bathing was possible in tubs and basins made of wood and metal, but that this happened in buildings whose design does not necessarily identify them as bathhouses. Military baths began to appear in legionary fortresses in the reign of Nero, as soon as buildings began to be constructed in stone. Their location within the camp was usually to the right in the *praetentura*. Baths also became an indispensable fixture of auxiliary forts in the Flavian period. However, the simpler baths for auxiliary units were rarely located within the camp. More usually, they were outside it, in the *vicus* ('hamlet').

B.2.7. EXERCISE HALLS

There is literary evidence of exercise halls (→ Training) in which riders and infantrymen could practise swordfighting and shooting, but there are almost no archaeological findings [9.80f.]. The sole exercise hall identified at an auxiliary fort is at Birdoswald (Banna) on Hadrian's Wall.

B.2.8. GRANARIES (HORREA)

Ancient sources indicate that the provisions distributed to Roman legionaries consisted mostly of unground wheat, which soldiers had to grind themselves using hand mills (→ Supply). Each man received at least 650 g per day. This clearly implies that the chief task of military logistics in the Roman period was to keep large stores of grain in camps and forts – about a year's supply. Legionary fortresses and auxiliary forts thus had their characteristic *horrea* ('granary') with an elevated floor for airing. Loading ramps were built at the ends of the *horrea*. Stone granaries were always buttressed to distribute the outward pressure of the grain on the walls. For obvious reasons, *horrea* were invariably located near to gateways, shortening the distance to be covered by transport carts.

B.2.9. Field hospitals (valetudinaria)
Valetudinaria were an invention of the Augustan period, with no civilian antecedents in the Mediterranean (→ Medical corps). In legionary fortresses, the *valetudinarium* was a rectangular complex built around a peristyle courtyard with garden. One side formed the reception area, containing operating theatres, storerooms and perhaps kitchens or other functional rooms. In the other three wings, small sickrooms and probably rooms for staff lined both sides of central corridors. It is presumed that auxiliary forts also had field hospital buildings, but none has yet been found clearly identifiable.

B.2.10. Workshops (fabricae)
Legionary fortresses and auxiliary forts often contain complexes of small rooms grouped around a courtyard or corridor. Troughs, ovens and other finds make clear that these were *fabricae*, workshop buildings, chiefly for metalworking.

B.2.11. Storerooms and other rooms
Castra and *castellae* also contained amongst the *horrea* and *tabernae* an assortment of buildings of variable design, whose functions are unclear. These are often described as storerooms, but some may equally have been specialist workshops. Armouries (*armamentaria*) at legionary fortresses and auxiliary forts were not always located in the side wings of the *principia*. Sometimes they were housed in buildings of their own.

B.2.12. Water supply and latrines
A supply of running water and disposal of sewage were matters of course at permanent legionary fortresses and auxiliary forts. Findings of wells in *castra* and *castellae* are therefore a rarity, other than one well in the *principia*. Tanks of water (for extinguishing fires?), baking ovens and latrines were often built into the earth embankments abutting the inside of the defensive walls on the *via sagularis*.

B.3. Fortress and fort types of the early and middle Imperial period

B.3.1. Legionary and double-legionary fortresses
B.3.2. Vexillation fortresses
B.3.3. Auxiliary forts

B.3.1. Legionary and double-legionary fortresses
Building standards for legionary fortresses (approx. 20 ha in area) became established from the reign of Tiberius (AD 14–37) onwards. By the mid-1st century AD at the latest, fortified camps were largely standardized installations, usually on an elongated rectangular ground plan with rounded ends (the 'playing card' pattern). These early forts usually had a defensive perimeter wall built in wood and earth, and buildings inside it constructed in timber-framed wattle-and-daub. Where the relevant infrastructure was available, the Romans began to rebuild legionary fortresses in stone at about the time of Nero. There is occasional evidence of double-legionary fortresses (40 ha and more), but Domitian (AD 81–96) banned this innovation after a rebellion against him broke out at the double-legionary fortress of Mainz (Mogontiacum).

B.3.2. Vexillation fortresses
Smaller camps built for detachments (*vexillationes*) from legions are known in English as 'vexillation fortresses'. Archaeologists in Britain in particular have identified fortresses that were clearly occupied by legionaries, but that are too small to have held an entire legion. They are usually half the size of a legionary fortress (i.e. 10 ha), and they also exhibit evidence of the presence of auxiliary units, especially cavalry. No single-legionary fortresses have been found dating from the Augustan period in Germania, only double-legionary and vexillation fortresses. Only during the reign of Tiberius, as Rome consolidated its territory and established the Rhine frontier, did construction of a series of classic single-legionary fortresses begin, at Vindonissa.

B.3.3. Auxiliary forts
Depending on the unit concerned (500 or 1,000 men, infantry or cavalry), forts for cohorts and *alae* ('auxiliary forces') measured between 2 and 6 hectares in area. Fortlets for *numeri* ('military units') and other detachments were considerably smaller (<1 ha).

☞ **Administration; Auxiliaries; Fortification; Infrastructure; Legion; Supply**

Bibliography
[1] R.J. Brewer (ed.), Roman Fortresses and Their Legions. Papers in Honour of George C. Boon, FSA, FRHistS, 2000 [2] A.W. Busch, Militär in Rom, 2011 [3] D.P. Davison, The Barracks of the Roman Army from the 1st to 3rd Centuries A.D. (BAR Int. Ser. 427), 1989 [4] T. Fischer, Die Armee der Caesaren. Mit Beiträgen von R. Bockius, D. Boschung und T. Schmidts, 2014 [5] A. Johnson, Roman Forts of the 1st and 2nd Centuries in Britain and the German Provinces, 1983 [6] A. Johnson, Römische Kastelle des 1. und 2. Jahrhunderts n.Chr. in Britannien und in den germanischen Provinzen des Römerreiches, 1987 [7] S. Johnson, Late Roman Fortifications, 1983 [8] J. Krohmayer / G. Veith, Heerwesen und Kriegführung der Römer und Griechen (HdAW 4,3,2), 1928 (unchanged new edition 1963) [9] H. von Petrikovits, Die Innenbauten römischer Legionslager

während der Prinzipatszeit (Wissenschaftliche Abhandlungen der Rheinisch-Westfälischen Akademie der Wissenschaften 56), 1975.

THOMAS FISCHER

Cavalry

A. Greek
B. Roman

A. Greek

A.1. Armament
A.2. Organization and tactical deployment
A.3. Hellenistic period

Cavalry is the combat arm that fights mounted, usually on horseback. Greek cavalry generally played a secondary role in the Archaic and Classical periods. It only became decisive for winning battles under Philip II (c. 382–336 BC; → Generals of note, M.) and his son Alexander the Great (356–323 BC; → Generals of note, B.).

A.1. Armament

The arming (especially defensive) of cavalry varied enormously through history and according to local tradition and troopers' personal preferences. According to Xen. Eq. 12,11f., the ideal armament for a cavalryman in the early 4th century BC consisted of a single-edged concave sabre (*machaira* or *kopis*) and two javelins (*palton*) with shafts of cornel wood (*Cornus mas*). The double-edged sword (*xiphos*) Xenophon declares less suitable, along with the lance (*kamax*), whose greater length rendered it more brittle and difficult to handle. For body protection, he recommends a breastplate with leather flaps, a helmet and a protector he calls a 'hand' (*cheir*), probably some kind of glove, for the left arm. The head, chest and thighs of the horse should also be protected (Xen. Eq. 12,1–10). It thus appears that there was no standard armament, a supposition supported by pictorial evidence on vases and funerary reliefs, and by literary and epigraphic sources [13.50–56].

Rather than carrying javelins or lances, the Macedonian cavalry, also known as the king's *hetairoi* ('companions'), began in the wake of the Battle of Chaeronea in 338 BC to use the *sarissa*, a long spear (length 4.5 m) that was primarily used as a thrusting weapon, although it could also be thrown. Macedonian troopers between 432 and 335 BC, Antigonid cavalry and perhaps Athenian cavalry of the Hellenistic period also carried a shield [10.97].

A.2. Organization and tactical deployment

A.2.1. Archaic and Classical periods
A.2.2. Hellenistic period

A.2.1. Archaic and Classical periods

Cavalry as a cohesive formation probably did not exist as such in the Homeric period or, perhaps, some of the Archaic (but [16.21–58]). To Homer, horses are a luxury that only aristocrats can afford. Reflecting this, horsemen (*hippeis*) comprised their own social, that is, aristocratic class. It appears that horses were used only to ride to the battle site. Fighting was done on foot. The first depictions of riders fighting on horseback appear on Attic and Corinthian vases of the late 7th/early 6th centuries BC [15.67]. Athens, the *poleis* on the Peloponnese and many other Greek polities generally had only small cavalry units, and it seems that the Peloponnesian *poleis* had none at all for some generations in the 5th century BC [15.67]. Tellingly, however, much greater importance was attached to cavalry from the outset in regions that offered more favourable geographical conditions for horse breeding, such as Thessaly (cf. Hdt. 5,63; Pl. Men. 70b; Pl. Leg. 625d; Arist. fr. 498 Rose), Boeotia (Hdt. 9,68–69; Thuc. 4,72,4; Xen. Hipp. 7,3), Syracuse (Pind. Nem. 1,15–19; Hdt. 7,158; Thuc. 6,64,1) or Macedonia [6.79–130]. The evolution of cavalry differed from region to region, but in many cases we know very little about numbers and organization. This is true even of regions with famous cavalry traditions, such as Thessaly and Boeotia.

We are best informed when it comes to the Athenian cavalry [5]. By 430 BC, Athens had built a cavalry of 1,000 men in addition to 200 *hippotoxotai* (mounted archers; Thuc. 2,13,8). They were recruited from the second Solonic census class, the *hippeis*, and were divided into two *hipparchiai*, each commanded by a *hipparchos*. These in turn were each divided into five *phylai*, each headed by a *phylarchos* and in turn comprising ten *dekades* each under a *dekadarchos* (Aristot. Ath. pol. 61,4f.; Xen. Hipp. 1,7f.; 9,3). To qualify to serve in the cavalry, horsemen had to submit to a muster by the council (Aristot. Ath. pol. 49,2). Although service in the cavalry was reserved to the upper classes, Athens still paid some costs for maintenance and equipment, amounting to an annual subsidy of 40 talents in the 4th century BC (Xen. Hipp. 1,19).

The cavalry played a similar role to the light infantry in phalanx tactics (Asclepiades 7). This usually consisted of protecting the heavy infantry from attacks by enemy cavalry, attacking the enemy's flanks with projectiles and securing supply lines while disrupting the enemy's [13.121–163]. Troopers had a particularly important part to play in *pararrhexis* ('breaching' a battle line), mopping up the breached phalanx (Hdt. 9,96,1f.) and pursuing the fleeing enemy (Xen. An. 3,1,2). Horsemen with their greater mobility were also charged with defending border regions and plundering neighbouring territories (Thuc. 2,31,3; 4,95,2). Light cavalry units, such as the *hippotoxotai* and *prodromoi* (mounted scouts) were mainly used for → reconnaissance and as skirmishers.

On the whole, the military role of the Archaic and Classical cavalry was a subordinate one. The ratio of cavalry to infantry at this period was frequently only 1:10 or even less [13.124f.]. There were several reasons for this. The geography of many Greek territories offered only limited scope for horse breeding (Hom. Od. 4,601–608; Pl. Leg. 1,625d; Str. 8,8,1). The great expense of breeding and keeping horses also meant that owning a horse was something only a small, privileged elite could afford. Even the enlargement of the Macedonian cavalry under Philip II (see below) only became possible as the Macedonian Empire expanded and acquired new territory. Horsemen received land in payment for their service rather than a monetary stipend. There were also practical factors at work. Not all ground was suitable for the deployment of cavalry, particularly given that horses were not shod (Xen. Eq. 4,4f.). Moreover, the absence of saddles and stirrups made it difficult for riders to sit securely on the horse (Xen. An. 3,2,19). Where footsoldiers were able to retreat to difficult terrain in an encounter with enemy cavalry, they could avoid engaging the cavalry altogether (Thuc. 4,44,1f.; Diod. Sic. 18,15,4f.). Ancient authors also strongly emphasize how important → discipline and regular → training were for cavalry deployment, and nonetheless how difficult the animals were to control in battle (Xen. Hipp. 1,3–7; 1,13; 8,1–6). There was also a sense that fighting on horseback was less demanding than serving as a hoplite, for riders with javelins were mainly fighting at longer range. An Athenian who preferred fighting on horseback to fighting in the phalanx might even be regarded as a coward, while a horseman who volunteered to fight in the phalanx was proving himself a man of notable valour (Lys. 14,7; 16,13; cf. [13.180–229]). Among the Spartans at the Battle of Leuctra in 371 BC, while the wealthy provided the horses, those riding them were the 'weakest of body' (Xen. Hell. 6,4,11).

A.2.2. HELLENISTIC PERIOD

During the 4th century BC, the evolution of hoplite tactics (→ Phalanx) and the concomitant increase in the importance of light infantry and cavalry gradually gave rise to more complex warfare, a form of combined-arms combat. Philip II and Alexander the Great perfected this. They began deploying the cavalry as a tactical unit, and often won their battles through targeted cavalry actions. With this purpose in mind, Philip II between 359 and 336 BC not only enlarged his cavalry from 600 to 1,800 or 3,300 men (Diod. Sic. 16,4,3; 17,17,4f.; see above), but also armed them with long thrusting spears (*sarissai*; see above) and deployed them in a wedge formation for attacks (Aelianus, Tact. 18,4; Asclepiades 7,3; Arr. Tact. 16,6), for instance at Chaeronea in 338 BC (Diod. Sic. 16,86,3f.; Polyaenus, Strat. 4,2,2; 7). Following suit, the first Hellenistic kings also sought to deploy as many horsemen as possible in battle, for the cavalry was now seen as the army's key to victory, with the infantry far behind (Pol. 3,117,5) [11]. Troopers were now recruited from across the entire Mediterranean world [9]. The Ptolemaic army, for example, had cavalry units named after ethnic groups. These were without doubt originally made up of riders from the regions concerned, and even later in their history they preserved the typical ethnic armament and dress [10.65–69]. In another practice inherited from Philip II and Alexander the Great, horsemen were often settled permanently within the Hellenistic kingdoms as *klerouchoi*, with a plot of land (*kleros*) as their most important benefit (→ Colonies). They came to form the military and social elite in the regions they settled (Ptolemies: [10]; Antigonids: [8.29–54], [4.146–182]; Seleucids: [2.20–48], [3.78–90]).

☞ **Armament; Colonies; Guards; Infantry; Phalanx; Reconnaissance**

BIBLIOGRAPHY

[1] J.K. ANDERSON, Ancient Greek Horsemanship, 1961 [2] B. BAR-KOCHVA, The Seleucid Army. Organization and Tactics in the Great Campaigns, 1976 [3] E. BICKERMAN, Institutions des Séleucides, 1938 [4] R.A. BILLOWS, Kings and Colonists. Aspects of Macedonian Imperialism, 1995 [5] G.R. BUGH, The Horsemen of Athens, 1988 [6] T. DONAGHY, Horse Breeds and Breeding in the Greco-Persian World, 1st and 2nd Millennium BC, 2014 [7] R.E. GAEBEL, Cavalry Operations in the Ancient Greek World, 2002 [8] M.B. HATZOPOULOS, L'organisation de l'armée macédonienne sous les Antigonides. Problèmes anciens et documents nouveaux, 2001 [9] M. LAUNEY, Recherches sur les armées hellénistiques, 2 vols., 1949–1950 [10] S. SCHEUBLE-REITER, Die Katökenreiter im ptolemäischen Ägypten, 2012 [11] S. SCHEUBLE-REITER, Zur Organisation und Rolle der Reiterei in den Diadochenheeren. Vom Heer Alexanders des Großen zum Heer Ptolemaios' I., in: H. HAUBEN / A. MEEUS (eds.), The Age of the Successors and the Creation of the Hellenistic Kingdoms (323–276 BC), 2014, 475–500 [12] P. SIDNELL, Warhorse. Cavalry in Ancient Warfare, 2006 [13] I.G. SPENCE, The Cavalry of Classical Greece, 1993 [14] W.W. TARN, Hellenistic Military and Naval Developments, 1930 (Ndr. 1975) [15] H. VAN WEES, Greek Warfare. Myths and Realities, 2000 [16] L.J. WORLEY, Hippeis. The Cavalry of Ancient Greece, 1994.

SANDRA SCHEUBLE-REITER

B. Roman

B.1. The emergence of an equestrian elite
B.2. Cavalry of the *socii* and mounted auxiliaries
B.3. Cavalry units' equipment and functions
B.4. New role of cavalry after AD 200

B.1. The emergence of an equestrian elite

The first known illustrations of riders in Italy date back to the late 8th century BC, but it is not always easy to determine if these are mounted warriors or infantrymen riding to war or back home. A contingent of 300 riders (100 for each of the three original *tribus*) was probably in existence at Rome from the beginning of the Monarchical period onwards, recruited from the wealthiest families (given that they had to provide their own equipment). L. Tarquinius Priscus and later Servius Tullius are said to have increased the numbers of cavalry in the 6th century BC. To the three original centuries of cavalry, each already duplicated as *priores* and *posteriores*, the kings supposedly added another twelve, giving 18 centuries, a total of 1,800 riders [7]. Whereas infantrymen had to take part in 16 campaigns, cavalrymen were required to serve in just ten. Perhaps imitating Campanian or even Corinthian practices, the censor for 312 BC, Appius Claudius, established an equestrian order (*ordo equester*) to honour a cavalry elite, whose members received a payment (called the *equus publicus*, 'public horse') defraying the costs of equipping and keeping their mount. From now on, only those so honoured could be accepted into the 18 cavalry centuries and apply for magistracies. Other Roman citizens did, however, serve in the cavalry at their own expense alongside these *equites* [5]; [9]; [17].

B.2. Cavalry of the *socii* and mounted auxiliaries

The treaties signed with subjugated Italic tribes also required those tribes to provide contingents of cavalry to the Roman army as part of the *formula togatorum*. These allied troopers were organized into *turmae* ('units') of 30 men each, under commanding officers of the same tribal origin as the soldiers. These *turmae* were in turn organized into *alae* ('auxiliary forces') commanded by Roman officers, the *praefecti sociorum* ('commanders of allied forces'). Rome began recruiting cavalrymen not just from its Italic allies, but from all around the Mediterranean and as far afield as Gaul on similar systems. These were now called *auxilia externa*, to distinguish them from forces raised in Italy. Rome's priorities were to increase its authority over these peoples and to reinforce its own armies to confront its enemies, but also to acquire light troops who specialized in certain forms of combat, such as Mauri cavalrymen after the Second Punic War (218–201 BC). Although the lion's share of Rome's mounted troops now came from the *socii* and *auxilia*, the cavalry provided by Roman citizens themselves probably did not dwindle in military significance after the late 2nd century BC as much as previously thought [2]; [8].

During the Principate, the urban and Praetorian cohorts were mostly made up of infantry, but they also contained cavalry, including roughly 300 *speculatores Augusti* ('imperial scouts'). There was also a mounted Imperial guard of about 500 Germanic troopers. Augustus abolished it after the destruction of Varus' legions in Germania in AD 9, but it was reformed before being abolished again by Galba in AD 68. Trajan then recruited a new guard, drawing on auxiliary forces stationed along the empire's borders. These troopers, called the *equites singulares Augusti* ('imperial mounted guards'), were based successively in two barracks in what is now the Lateran district of southeastern Rome. They served for between 27 and 29 years until AD 138, when the term was reduced to 25 years. They were organized into *turmae*, each under the command of a *decurio*. The highest-ranking of these held the rank of *princeps*. At the apex of the hierarchy was one tribune (two beginning in the reign of Septimius Severus), who answered to the Praetorian Prefect [14]; [15].

The use of mounted auxiliaries increased under the Principate, particularly as a result of the recruitment of many Batavians and Gauls. They were stationed to oversee either their own home territories or, on the contrary, a sector far away, to help pacify it [11]. Among the Africans, this was how the Mauri horsemen commanded by Lusius Quietus were used: they played a decisive role in the army of Trajan fighting the Dacian Wars. The *alae* comprised 16 *turmae* of 30 troopers each, commanded by a *duplicarius* and a *decurio*. The cohorts were made up of six centuries of 80 infantrymen each, a total of 480 men. There were also mixed *cohortes equitatae* ('equestrian cohorts'), which combined six centuries of 80 footsoldiers with four *turmae* of 30 cavalrymen.

Beginning in the Flavian period, there are also records of cohorts designated *milliaria*, which, as the name suggests, were around double the strength of the traditional cohorts, which now came to be known as *cohortes quingenariae*. The *alae milliariae* comprised 24 *turmae* of 30 troopers each, the *cohortes milliariae* ten centuries of 80 infantry. The mixed *cohortes milliariae equitatae* had the same ten infantry centuries augmented by eight cavalry *turmae*. These were elite units. The Roman army had only about ten of them, no more than one per province. The stipend paid to auxiliary and legionary troopers may have been seven sixths of the pay of an infantryman in a legion. It is possible that Septimius Severus and later Caracalla used these successive recalculations of the stipend to bring the pay of auxiliary troops gradually into closer alignment with that of legionaries. They likely took note of the narrowing difference in status between these two components of the army, and of the difficulties in recruiting auxiliaries after the expansion of Roman citizenship [4]. Each auxiliary unit bore at least one number and the name of the tribe from which it was originally recruited, or sometimes of its first commander. That name might be further supplemented with an epithet referring to the emperor who created the unit, terms describing outstanding qualities of the unit, or the name of the province in which the unit was stationed. Evidence from military diplomas shows that auxiliary units were numbered by province and in sequence according to their recruitment [3]; [13].

B.3. Cavalry units' equipment and functions

In general, auxiliary units were mostly stationed in the outlying regions of the empire. Fortifications along the borders in Europe were more developed than in Africa or the east, where deserts offered natural protection and where the auxiliary cavalry surveyed routes and monitored population movements at the borders. Mounts were chosen using methods similar to those used for selecting recruits. Horses were sometimes brought in from distant regions that had good reputations for the quality of their animals, for example Cappadocia. A unit commander first had to apply to the governor in order to replace a specific horse, which he had to identify clearly. Mounts were always allocated to specific riders and marked to distinguish them. This first allocation of mounts, approved by the governor's office, probably included a thorough veterinary examination. The horses concerned were then put through intensive training, before being entered in the registers of the unit under the names of the riders to whom they were assigned. On the same principle as when issuing weapons, riders probably had to pay a deposit, which may have been set by the financial procurator of the province. Sometimes, however, the provision of mounts was treated in the same way as a tax in kind [6].

Like the artillery, the cavalry usually only intervened in support of the infantry. Horses made easy targets, and those deployed in the front ranks in battle required more frequent replacement than others. If horses were easy targets, it follows that their riders were also exposed when riding in the front rank. The evolution of the cavalry therefore required increasing numbers of officers who were competent in this field, especially to compensate for losses. The preference for Illyrian horsemen that took hold under Septimius Severus intensified still further between the reigns of Gallienus and Aurelian. Illyricum was renowned for its equestrian tradition and its wealth of practical expertise in the field. The training of troopers differed from that of footsoldiers in that horsemanship demanded more technique. Scholars have highlighted the lack of stirrups as a probable limitation on the effectiveness of ancient cavalry. However, it appears likely that troopers were perfectly capable of launching attacks, given that their enemies also lacked stirrups. Because of their longer and tougher training programme, cavalrymen were exempt from some burdensome fatigue details that infantrymen were obliged to undertake – as Hadrian's speech to the African army at Lambaesis attests. In stressing technical military issues in this speech, the emperor emphasized the distinction between infantry and cavalry more strongly than that between legionaries and auxiliaries. The presence at his side of the tribune of the *equites singulares Augusti* may stem from his desire to find the best auxiliary troopers in order to recruit them [16].

B.4. New role of cavalry after AD 200

Beginning in the 3rd century, the quest for greater mobility also brought innovative developments to the cavalry. The need to combat Germanic tribes, Sarmatian nomads and the heavy cavalry of the Sassanids raised the profile of the mounted units, challenging the tradition that the heavy legionary infantry was the key component of the Roman army. The legionary cavalry increased from 120 men to 726 between AD 240 and 285, those 726 being divided into 22 *turmae* per unit, but without severing their connection with the unit itself. The *equites promoti* were legionary infantrymen promoted to the cavalry. Whereas the deployment of light cavalry had hitherto been restricted to monitoring duties on borders, the next innovation – introduced in the reign of Severus Alexander (222–235) – was the use of armoured cavalry (cataphracts). To the *numeri* of Mauri and Dalmatian horsemen who had been part of the Roman army since the 2nd century, Severus Alexander added mounted archers from Osroene, Palmyra and Emesa. On the Rhine around 256, Gallienus probably combined mounted vexillations drawn from legions, *alae* and the *numeri*. In doing so, he was likely bringing together soldiers who had been mobilized since the end of the Severan period. It was simply impossible to conjure up a mounted force, especially given that such a force required long training. These cavalrymen, who were stationed in Milan from 259 onwards, functioned as a reserve to counter both the 'Gallic Empire' and the Alemanni. However, the various detachments seem only to have been temporarily separated from their original units, and the force also included infantrymen.

Modern historians disagree as to the status of the Roman cavalry. At all events, the ratio of cavalry to infantry units shifted from 1:10 to 1:3 between the 2nd and 4th centuries. The career of the soldier Aurelius Gaius during the Tetrachy testifies to the importance of cavalrymen and lancers in the Roman army of the late 3rd century. His was a classic legionary's career. He was a *discens equitum* ('trainee calvaryman') before becoming *eques legionis* ('cavalry soldier attached to a legion') and *lanciarius* ('lancer'), despite having been recruited to the infantry. These changes in direction reveal both the importance of the cavalry and the absence of a distinction in the legion between infantrymen and troopers under the Tetrarchy. In 312, Constantine abolished the Praetorian Guard and the *equites singulares Augusti* ('imperial mounted guard'), and instead created eleven *scholae palatinae* ('Palace Guards'), each comprising 500 troopers. His decision to reclassify his forces as *comitatenses* ('court troops') and *ripenses* or *riparienses* ('riverbank troops'), later called *limitanei* ('border troops'), led to the first ever appointment of a supreme cavalry commander, in this case of the *comitatenses*. This commander, the *magister equitum* ('master of cavalry'), was subordinate to the supreme commander of the infantry, the *magister peditum* ('master of foot soldiers') [12]; [10].

☞ Auxiliaries; Legion; Rank, B. Roman; Rank, C. Late Antiquity

BIBLIOGRAPHY
[1] M. BIANCARDI, Cavalleria romana del Principato nelle province occidentali dell'Impero, 2004 [2] F. CADIOU, Cavalerie auxiliaire et cavalerie légionnaire dans l'armée romaine au Ier s. a. C., in: C. WOLFF / P. FAURE (eds.), Les auxiliaires de l'armée romaine. Des alliés aux fédérés. Actes du sixième Congrès de Lyon (23–25 octobre 2014), 2016, 53–78 [3] C. CICHORIUS, Ala [2], in: RE 1/1, 1893, 1224–1270 [4] I. HAYNES, Blood of the Provinces. The Roman Auxilia and the Making of Provincial Society from Augustus to the Severans, 2013 [5] M. HUMM, Appius Claudius Caecus. La République accomplie, 2005 [6] M. JUNKELMANN, Die Reiter Roms, 3 vols., ⁴2008 [7] N. LUBTCHANSKY, Le cavalier tyrrhénien. Représentations équestres dans l'Italie archaïque, 2005 [8] J.B. MCCALL, The Cavalry of the Roman Republic. Cavalry Combat and Elite Reputations in the Middle and Late Republic, 2002 [9] C. NICOLET, L'ordre équestre à l'époque républicaine (312–43 av. J.-C.), 2 vols., 1974 [10] M. PETITJEAN, Pour une réévaluation de l'essor de la cavalerie au IIIe siècle, in: C. WOLFF / P. FAURE (eds.), Les auxiliaires de l'armée romaine. Des alliés aux fédérés. Actes du sixième Congrès de Lyon (23–25 octobre 2014), 2016, 491–525 [11] D.B. SADDINGTON, The Development of Roman Auxiliary Forces from Cesar to Vespasian, 49 BC–AD 79, 1982 [12] P. SOUTHERN / K.R. DIXON, The Roman Cavalry, 1992 [13] J. SPAUL, Ala 2. The Auxiliary Cavalry Units of the Pre-Diocletian Imperial Roman Army, 1994 [14] M.P. SPEIDEL, Die equites singulares Augusti. Begleittruppe der römischen Kaiser des zweiten und dritten Jahrhunderts, 1965 [15] M.P. SPEIDEL, Riding for Caesar. The Roman Emperors' Horse Guards, 1994 [16] M.P. SPEIDEL, Emperor Hadrian's Speeches to the African Army. A New Text, 2006 [17] M. STEMMLER, Eques Romanus – Reiter und Ritter. Begriffsgeschichtliche Untersuchungen zu den Entstehungsbedingungen einer römischen Adelskategorie im Heer und in den comitia centuriata, 1997.

PIERRE COSME

Chariot

War chariots in Classical Antiquity functioned as mobile platforms for archers or for warriors armed with throwing spears. These vehicles were charged with supporting the infantry, softening up the enemy battle lines with frontal attacks and bombardments, performing flanking manoeuvres and pursuing enemies who fled the battlefield. Scythed chariots, used by the Achaemenids, were deployed to weaken the cohesion of enemy battle lines. They achieved maximum effect only on flat, even terrain.

Battle wagons (Akkadian *narkabtu(m)*) with four disc wheels are attested in Mesopotamian illustrations as early as the 3rd millennium BC (Standard of Ur). The draught animal here is the horse, which probably came into use with two-wheel chariots around 2000 BC (more rarely used was the donkey). The Kingdom of Mitanni is believed to have had a key influence on the development of chariots, not least because some specialist vocabulary related to chariots is of Hurrian origin. Texts from the second half of the 2nd millennium BC from Nuzi (Iraq) describe the use of chariots in local hostilities and record their equipment. The war chariot spread rapidly through the Near East. It was imported into Egypt (*wrrt, mrkbt*) from the Levant in the mid-2nd millennium BC as a technological innovation in conjunction with general chariot building, the bentwood technique and horse conditioning. Maintaining a chariot unit required a logistical infrastructure of workshops and stables, trained charioteers, experienced cartwrights and horse trainers (as at Pi-Ramesses/Qantir). Obtaining specific timbers and horses, as well as arming, armouring and supplying the chariot unit, represented a significant additional cost for the Pharaonic state (cf. P. Anastasi 1). Chariots were also an important component of the land army of the Hittites. Texts from the Hittite Empire (including a text of the 15th century BC written by the Mitannian horse-trainer Kikkuli) give exact instructions for the specialist training of chariot horses [4].

There are illustrations of war chariots found in Greece (SpBZ, EZ). They were first mentioned in Linear B texts from Knossos, Pylos and elsewhere. Chariots (*to harma*) are mentioned in the Homeric *Iliad*, where their use, however, is limited to the aristocratic elite travelling to the battlefield (Hom. Il. 19,392ff.). The influence of Greek topography and the growing importance of the heavy infantry (hoplite phalanx) led to the gradual disappearance of chariots from Greek literature [3]. According to Greek sources, scythed chariots were used by the Persians at the battles of Cunaxa (401 BC; Xen. An. 1,7,10; 1,8,10) and Gaugamela (332 BC; Arr. Anab. 3,8,7; 3,13,5), and by the Seleucids at Magnesia in 189 BC.

In Italy, most chariot components and terracottas, and most illustrations on vases and other materials, come from Iron-Age Etruria. All these seem to suggest that, as in Greece at that period, chariots were not directly used in battle. Rather, two-wheeled chariots were used – as in Greece – as transport platforms for conducting the warrior elite to the theatre of battle. War chariots are not mentioned by Livy or Dionysius of Halicarnassus in their literary descriptions of the battles of early Roman history [1].

Depictions of chariot burials (burial together with one's chariot) using two-wheeled chariots dating from the La Tène period are widespread across Western and Central Europe [2]. The sources report that chariots were used by the Gaulish Senones at the Battle of Sentium in 295 BC (Liv. 10,28,8f.), and by the Celtic groups who invaded Italy in 225 (Pol. 2,23,4). By the mid-1st century BC, the Celtic war chariot was still used only in Britain, where Caesar's troops encountered them on several occasions (Caes. B Gall. 4,24,1; 4,32,5; 4,33; 5,9,3; 5,15,1; 5,19,1; called *essidum* or *covinnus*). *Covinnarii* (chariot warriors) were deployed against Agricola's auxiliaries at the Battle of Mons Graupius in AD 83 (Tac. Agr. 35,2; 36,3).

BIBLIOGRAPHY
[1] J.H. CROUWEL, Chariots and Other Wheeled Vehicles in Italy before the Roman Empire, 2012 [2] C.F.E. PARE, Wagen und Wagenbau, Wagengrab, in: RGA 33, Wagen und Gewichte–Wielandlied, 2006, 62–68 [3] R. PLATH, Der Streitwagen und seine Teile im frühen Griechischen. Sprachliche Untersuchungen zu den mykenischen Texten und zum homerischen Epos, 1994 [4] T. RICHTER, Der Streitwagen im Alten Orient im 2. Jahrtausend v.Chr. Eine Betrachtung anhand der keilschriftlichen Quellen, in: S. BURMEISTER / M. FANSA (eds.), Rad und Wagen. Der Ursprung einer Innovation. Wagen im Vorderen Orient und Europa, 2004, 507–514 (with additional bibliography).

ALFRED MICHAEL HIRT

Civil war

A. Greek
B. Roman

A. GREEK

A.1. Stasis
A.2. Occurrence and characteristics
A.3. Causes
A.4. Civil wars outside *stasis*

A.1. STASIS

There is no generally accepted definition of civil war, but in essence it amounts to violence within a polity, and thus to an extreme form of social disintegration. Unlike in external wars or pogroms, the enemy is not characterized as an alien or outsider. As a result, internal conflicts are often notably brutal, since the opposing side must be held at fault for breaching a taboo, and the internal opponent must thus be treated as a traitor and malefactor [12].

The typical Greek form of civil war was the *stasis*, which scholars understand to mean the collapse of a *polis* into (almost invariably) two enemy factions, in which the conflict between the two often escalated violently. It must be noted, however, that not every *stasis* was a civil war, nor is every internal dispute called a *stasis* in the sources. Other expressions used included *metabole* (Aristot. Pol. 1305b), *tarache* (Pol. 1,71,8), *diaphora* (SEG 49, 1171), *krisis* (Syll.³ 426) and *emphylios polemos* (Pol. 1,65,2). The widespread fear of *stasis* that was prominent in the Archaic period and continued to shape Greek discourse for centuries is striking [18]; [26].

A.2. OCCURRENCE AND CHARACTERISTICS

The tally of *staseis* directly attested in literary and epigraphic sources runs into the hundreds. The entire world of the *poleis* was affected, from Southern Italy [1] to the Seleucid Empire. Given that neither large *poleis*, such as Athens, Corinth (Xen. Hell. 4,4,1–14), Syracuses (Diod. Sic. 19,6–8) or Rhodes (Xen. Hell. 4,8,20–31), nor smaller polities like Corcyra (Thuc. 3,70–85) or Nacone (SEG 30, 1119) were spared, the tendency towards *stasis* and the fear of it may be seen as a structural feature of the *polis*, even a characteristic of Ancient Greek society [11]. Given the fragmentary record and the frequent attempts by affected communities to end such conflicts through *amnesia*, it must also be assumed that the numbers were even greater. The large number of exiles in the Greek world also seems to suggest this (see Diod. Sic. 18,8,5). Despite the basically bipolar structure of these conflicts, there was always an abundance of non-participant citizens. Only in cases of extreme violence did it become impossible to adopt a neutral position. Such an escalation was by no means inevitable. A *stasis* often simmered for a long time, paralysing municipal institutions, but only flaring up in violence when a trigger occurred. Internal and external conflicts were often interconnected, as opposing factions appealed to different external allies ([13.180ff.]; [20]; [9.359]; cf. Pol. 18,15,2f.). The risk of revolution thus rose considerably in *poleis* under siege (Aen. Tact. 10; 11; 17). When violence did break out, it ranged from outbursts of stone-throwing and beatings, to the assassination of individual leaders, to bloody massacres. Particularly in cases where the weaker faction succeeded in withdrawing to a defensible position such as an acropolis (e.g. Pol. 4,53,9), hostilities sometimes assumed the proportions of a full-scale war, with mercenaries often involved.

From an early date, civil disputes were associated with the emergence and removal of tyrannies. Herodotus describes the establishment of the Peisistratid *tyrannis* in Athens as the result of several *staseis* (Hdt. 1,59,3; Aristot. Ath. Pol. 13,4f.), and although its authenticity and interpretation are controversial, the 'stasis law' of Solon (Plut. Solon 20) also seems to belong to this context. Indeed, the emergence of a 'tyranny' [24] or 'oligarchy' [22] often cloaked the (actual or putative) dominance of one party, the legitimacy of which the opposing party naturally contested. The reforms of both Solon and Cleisthenes can only be understood in the context of what was virtually endemic *stasis* in Athens. The establishment of the Athenian democracy can thus be interpreted as an attempt to prevent internal conflicts from escalating. Even so, the years after 415 BC saw renewed *stasis* in Athens, which escalated into violence in 404/03 [16] and was only brought to an end through an amnesty [27] (Xen. Hell. 2,3,11–2,4,43).

A.3. CAUSES
The causes of *staseis* were already a subject of debate in Antiquity. Two approaches in particular have set the tone for these debates ever since: first, the assumption that the real causes were power struggles and rivalries within the elite [14]; [9.308ff.]; [21.95ff.]; and second, the position – by no means unique to Marxist scholarship – ([23]; [8]; cf. [7.509ff.]) that such conflicts had their roots primarily in socioeconomic tensions (see Aristot. Pol. 1266a). Sources discussing *staseis* often report demands for the cancellation of debts (*chreon apokope*; e.g. Diod. Sic. 32,26,3) and land reforms (*ges anadasmos*; e.g. Plut. Agis 8,1), and they explain conflicts in terms of (context-dependent) dichotomies, such as 'rich versus poor', 'democrats versus oligarchs', 'young versus old' or 'Romophiles versus Macedonophiles' [3]. In the Classical and Hellenistic world of multipolar power politics, existing factions regularly found themselves able to seek support from powers that were themselves rivals. It would seem, therefore, that the foreign policies of *poleis* only rarely played a causative role. At the same time, the importance of socioeconomic factors in conflicts should not be underestimated, particularly in regard to the return of exiles who were previously dispossessed (Plut. *Aratus* 12,1; SEG 36, 752). Divisions among the elite, however, seem to have been at least a necessary precondition for a *stasis* (see Aristot. Pol. 1305b; Hell. Oxyrh. 20,1f.; FGrH 87 F 108c). The underlying reason why many *poleis* were so susceptible to civil strife was that the urban elites were unable to establish peacably their own internal hierarchies. In an essentially agonal honour society like that of Greece, this could create tensions that escalated rapidly, combining with other conflicts and dragging the entire citizenry to ruin (see Plut. Mor. 823e–825f).

Various measures were implemented to prevent or resolve crippling conflicts in *poleis*. These included establishing cults of Homonoia [17]; [25], requiring oaths of citizenship (IOSPE 1² 401; ICret. I ix, 1), proclaiming an *amnesia* (SEG 25, 447) and above all appointing external judges and arbitrators, a practice widely attested from the late 4th century BC onwards (e.g. OGIS 7; SEG 1, 132; StV III, no. 45; IG XII 9,4) [6]; [4.131ff.]. However, the sources do report cases where even a sacred oath was broken (e.g. Liv. 41,25,4). If reconciliation failed, only three options remained: the killing of all relevant supporters of the opposing party, which provoked vengeance, their banishment [10], which led to constant fear of the exiles' return, or the cessation of violence as a result of external pressure on the *polis*.

A.4. CIVIL WARS OUTSIDE *STASIS*
Although *staseis* were still widespread during the Hellenistic period (e.g. Diod. Sic. 19,63; Pol. 4,54,6; Str. 13,1,66; ICret. I xix, 3A; Syll.³ 684), a second form of conflict can be observed emerging in the Greek world in the period after Alexander the Great, one that is more readily definable than *stasis* as civil war. The Seleucids (Pol. 4,48; Just. Epit. 40,1f.) and later the Ptolemies (Liv. per. 59; Just. Epit. 39,4f.) in particular faced frequent attempts at usurpation that esclated into military conflicts [5]. Indeed, the Wars of the Diadochi up to the death of Seleucus I may be interpreted as civil wars within the Macedonian elite of Alexander's empire. These conflicts, which were generally fought out by regular troops in territorial states, were of a character quite different from outbreaks of violence within a city, in which organization, if any, was at most paramilitary.

The Maccabean Revolt exibited features of a civil war between a pro-Seleucid and a Hasmonaean group vying for control of the office of high priest [2]. However, the categorization of bloody conflicts like the Carthaginian mercenary uprising (Pol. 1,65–88) or the 'Ephesian Vespers' (App. Mithr. 4,23) is more problematic, because internal violence in these cases was not directed against fellow citizens.

Civil wars in the Hellenistic monarchies died with the monarchies, but the fear, at least, of civil war persisted even into the Imperial period, even as the number of actual cases dwindled dramatically under the sway of the *pax Augusta*. The fear of civil strife was certainly present in the political discourse of the Imperial period (see Aristid. Or. 24,41; FGrH 100 F 3), and even in Late Antiquity, Greek authors often classified violent unrest associated with Christological controversies (Sozom. Hist. eccl. 2,20) or circus riots (see *Peri politikes epistemes* 5,103–106) as *stasis*, and described it accordingly.

☞ Mutiny

BIBLIOGRAPHY
[1] S. BERGER, Revolution and Society in Greek Sicily and Southern Italy, 1992 [2] C. BERNHARDT, Die jüdische Revolution, 2017 [3] H. BÖRM, Stasis in Post-Classical Greece. The Discourse of Civil Strife in the Hellenistic World, in: H. BÖRM / N. LURAGHI (eds.), The Polis in the Hellenistic World, 2018, 53–83 [4] A. CASSAYRE, La justice dans les cités grecques. De la formation des royaumes hellénistiques au legs d'Attale, 2010 [5] B. CHRUBASIK, Kings and Usurpers in the Seleukid Empire. The Men who Would Be King, 2016 [6] A. DÖSSEL, Die Beilegung innerstaatlicher Konflikte in den griechischen Poleis vom 5.–3. Jahrhundert v.Chr., 2003 [7] A. EICH, Die politische Ökonomie des antiken Griechenland (6.–3. Jahrhundert v.Chr.), 2006 [8] A. FUKS, Social Conflict in Ancient Greece, 1984 [9] H.-J. GEHRKE, Stasis. Untersuchungen zu den inneren Kriegen in den griechischen Staaten des 5. und 4. Jahrhunderts v.Chr., 1985 [10] B. GRAY, Stasis and Stability. Exile, the Polis, and Political Thought, c. 404–146 BC, 2015 [11] M.H. HANSEN, Stasis as an Essential Aspect of the Polis, in: M.H. HANSEN / T.H. NIELSEN (eds.), An Inventory of Archaic and Classical Poleis, 2004, 124–129 [12] S. KALYVAS, The Logic of Violence in Civil War, 2006 [13] R.P. LEGON, Demos and Stasis, 1966 [14] A.W. LINTOTT, Violence, Civil Strife and Revolution in the Classical City, 1982 [15] D. LOENEN, Stasis, 1953 [16] N. LORAUX, The Divided City, 2002 [17] A. MOULAKIS, Homonoia, Eintracht und die Entwicklung eines politischen Bewußtseins, 1973 [18] J.J. PRICE, Thucydides and Internal War, 2001 [19] W. RIESS, Performing Interpersonal Violence, 2012 [20] E. RUSCHENBUSCH, Untersuchungen zu Staat und Politik in Griechenland vom 7.–4. Jh. v.Chr., 1978 [21] W. SCHMITZ, Die griechische Gesellschaft, 2014 [22] M. SIMONTON, Stability and Violence in Classical Greek Democracies and Oligarchies, in: Classical Antiquity 36, 2017, 52–103 [23] G. DE STE. CROIX, The Class Struggle in the Ancient Greek World. From the Archaic Age to the Arab Conquests, 1981 [24] D. TEEGARDEN, Death to Tyrants! Ancient Greek Democracy and the Struggle against Tyranny, 2014 [25] G. THÉRIAULT, Le culte d'Homonoia dans les cités grecques, 1996 [26] R.L. WEED, Aristotle on Stasis, 2007 [27] A. WOLPERT, Remembering Defeat. Civil War and Civic Memory in Ancient Athens, 2002.

HENNING BÖRM

B. ROMAN

B.1. The quest for *concordia*
B.2. The civil wars of the late Republic
B.3. Civil war and the evolution of *imperium* into empire
B.4. The Year of Four Emperors
B.5. Usurpations and civil wars

B.1. THE QUEST FOR *CONCORDIA*
The founding murder of Remus by Romulus shaped the conceptual world of the Romans to such a degree that they dedicated a Temple of Concord (Concordia) in the Forum out of fear of internal strife [2.171–207]. This act was in fact intended to bring an end to the conflict that had lasted from the foundation of the Republic in the early 5th century until the year 367 BC, within a Roman citizenry split into two factions: the patricians and the plebeians.

B.2. THE CIVIL WARS OF THE LATE REPUBLIC
This invocation of Concordia did not prevent Rome from being riven by many more civil wars over the course of its history. The killings of Tiberius and Gaius Sempronius Gracchus in 133 and 121 BC respectively brought violence to the heart of Roman political life. Yet the trigger for the cycle of civil wars that sent the Republic to its doom is generally identified as the coup d'état of L. Cornelius Sulla, who in 88 BC became the first Roman magistrate to lead his legions into the city across the boundary of the *pomerium* (MRR 2, 39f.).

Although the demographic history of Italy in the last two centuries BC is always controversial, the theory of a mass proletarization of the legions giving rise to indiscipline among soldiers has now been abandoned [4]. Testing this theory requires ceasing to see Roman legionaries simply as *clientes* who needed to be trained, and understanding them also as citizens who needed to be persuaded. This restores to the civil wars a far more political dimension. Herein, incidentally, lies the importance of studies devoted to the milieu and staff of the *imperatores* [11]. For instance, members of the same family are sometimes found taking different sides in order to ensure that the family will have a representative in the victorious camp whatever the outcome. The inescapable fact remains that in spite of ever closer ties between armies and their commanders, generals who sought to take power by force always had to justify themselves before their soldiers. Legionaries did not form private armies *per se*, as some have hastily claimed, but remained citizens who attached great importance to the arguments of the magistrate or promagistrate to whose appointment they had contributed. Attesting to this are the numerous speeches that protagonists in the civil wars delivered to them at the moment of confrontation with the adversary. It may, of course, be objected that such appeals to soldiers' civic sensibilities concealed less noble motives. Yet it remains interesting to note that those civic sensibilities were still taken into account. Despite the ill repute in which ancient authors held soldiers of the 1st century BC, the civil wars did not originate in their demands, but in the rivalries stoked by the ambitions of *imperatores* in whose hands extraordinary powers and riches were concentrated.

Until the death of Caesar, in fact, soldiers never initiated civil war themselves. It was always their commanders who chose to launch hostilities. At the end of the war between Caesar and Pompey, the army did become a political force that was aware of its own interests and willing to defend them against the civilians in the respective camps. On several occasions after Caesar's murder, his former soldiers and veterans of their own volition enforced a reconciliation with his heirs. They did so at the end of the Siege of Perugia and outside Brindisi in 40 BC (MRR 2, 379). Conversely, there was no attempt at reconciliation between the two armies that collided at Actium. This reflected the circumstances of the armies' ongoing recruitment, whereby the two sides were drawing on two geographically distinct populations [2]. The crisis of the Roman Republic was thus in the first place a crisis of the Roman aristocracy [16]. The expansion of Roman rule across much of the Mediterranean destroyed the equilibrium among the assorted noble groups that traditionally vied for power. Those magistrates entrusted with the conduct of the military operations that were most lucrative in terms of booty accumulated far more prestige, and financial and personnel resources, than their rivals. The competition for the consulate, always fought with enormous vigour, increasingly now took on overtones of violence.

Historians have recently undertaken a revision of another aspect of the civil wars, namely, the status of the political ideologies in these confrontations, or, more specifically, the opposition of the *populares* ('[the men] of the people') and *optimates* ('the best [men]') [10]. The focus in these conflicts was generally not so much the defence of a political ideology as the will to power. This is evident in many situations, such as the allocation of new citizens to the *tribus* in 88 BC, the right to supreme command in the war against Mithridates, which was claimed by both Marius and Sulla, the campaign conducted by Caesar to secure a second consulship in 49 BC, and Octavian's intimidation of the supporters of Mark Antony in 32 BC. The justifications offered in these cases were so vague – the defence of the *res publica*, say, or that of Italy – that all the proponent's supporters would unite behind them along with a fair number of the opponent's.

What remained, then, of the binary opposition of the *populares* and *optimates* after 88 BC? Arguably a certain relationship to the institutions. *Populares* tended to rely on an alliance between the people's tribunes and the *imperator*, *optimates* on one between the *imperator* and the Senate. After the experience with the Gracchi revealed the limits of the political power of a people's tribune with no army, some *imperatores* began to ally with people's tribunes in order to take greater control over political life. As the first instigator of a civil war in the city of Rome, Sulla was also the first to consider how such a war could be prevented. His strategy was to limit the power of the people's tribunes and conduct a purge, which has gone down in history under the title of 'proscription'. Sulla published the names of Roman senators and *equites*, whose estates he confiscated and whom he condemned to death by issuing rewards for their murder. Their descendants were also legally excluded from political life [13].

The victory of Julius Caesar seemed finally to bring about the personalized manifestation of power that came from combining dictatorship with the consulate. However, he failed to take into account the nostalgic character of the oligarchy, who murdered him on the Ides of March 44 BC. The heirs of the late dictator consequently turned on the oligarchs in question by reviving the instrument of proscription. In the end, Augustus' stroke of genius was without doubt to merge the positions of *imperator* and tribune into a personal union, and to assume both *imperium* and the authority of the tribunate.

B.3. CIVIL WAR AND THE EVOLUTION OF *IMPERIUM* INTO EMPIRE

A clear line of development is apparent between the conflicts in which Sulla and the Marian party faced off, and the wars that followed them. The former remained for the most part confined to Italy, although they spilled over somewhat into the Iberian Peninsula, Sicily and Africa. The latter spread across the entire Mediterranean, which to Romans meant that they took on a global dimension. They even drew in other kingdoms, as they joined the clienteles of various *imperatores* in their campaigns of conquest. The most important examples here were in Africa and Egypt. Juba I of Numidia, a client of Pompey, lost his kingdom and his life when Caesar defeated the sons of Pompey in 46 BC. Juba's kingdom was relegated to the status of a province, and Caesar could now claim to have triumphed over 'Africa'. Yet the boundaries between civil war and external war subsequently blurred even further. When Octavian justified his final battle with Mark Antony by declaring war – on the pretext of defending Italy – only on the Queen of Egypt, Cleopatra VII, he was undoubtedly seeking to lend a civil war the aura of a war against foreign enemies. Admittedly, those best informed were not wholly deceived by the unanimity Octavian affected here. Yet those least receptive to the patriotic arguments of Octavian's faction were also those to whom the new conquests in the east, especially the prize of Egypt now coming into view, offered the best prospects of enrichment. The clear interests of most senators who remained in Italy thus led them to follow Octavian rather than Mark Antony. Moreover, this civil war also offered *de facto* better opportunities for seizing booty than earlier wars of conquest. Herein lay its unique character.

The civil wars of the 1st century BC thus contributed to forging the unity of a Roman world that was expanding beyond the boundaries of its provinces. They fostered certain innovations in the fields of logistics and administration that would become advantages of the imperial regime. Examples include the recruitment of Roman citizens in the provinces and the stationing of armies in Rome itself. Caesar's heir and successor, as Augustus, ruled his provinces in just the same way as Pompey had led his provinces in Hispania between 55 and 49 BC: by dispatching legates. A *lex Pompeia de provinciis* of 52 BC introduced a system of regulations for the public provinces, a measure originally intended as a weapon against Caesar. Although Augustus put an end to the civil wars, his powers, which stemmed from the Republican tradition, were not hereditary at first. The method of their transfer constituted one of the challenges of the new regime. The *imperator* held his position neither by divine right nor as an embodiment of the state.

B.4. The Year of Four Emperors

Following the death of Nero, whom an uprising by the governors of the provinces of Gaul, Iberia and Africa and the defection of the Imperial Guard and Senate drove to suicide in June AD 68, the Julio-Claudian house had no suitable successor to offer. Even so, there was never any question of restoring the Republic, as some senators still seem to have considered after the assassination of Caligula in AD 41. On the contrary, the extinction of the Julio-Claudian Dynasty reopened the field for a power struggle within the Roman aristocracy [12]. For Tacitus (Hist. 1,4), the successive coups by Galba, Otho, Vitellius and Vespasian revealed the 'secret of empire' (*imperii arcano*): the provincial legions could force the emperor of their choice on the garrison of Rome. Still, the decisive battles fought twice in the Po Valley served as a reminder that Italy and Rome remained the centre of the empire, and the most important prize in any struggle for power in it [8].

B.5. Usurpations and civil wars

Unlike the civil wars of AD 68/69, the decisive battles that followed the murder of Commodus, in AD 193 and 197, were not fought in Italy. Nonetheless, strategic gravity undoubtedly proved the key determinant of factional loyalties, as it had in the wake of Nero's death. Clodius Albinus' receptive response to the acclamation of Septimius Severus probably arose from the great remoteness of Britannia from Italy, whereas Upper Pannonia profited from its proximity to Italy and the importance of its garrison. Mention should also be made of the many senators who were in Italy and Rome in the spring of 193, and who were thus aware that nothing could prevent Septimius Severus' advance on the imperial capital [7].

The 3rd century confronted the imperial power in brutal fashion with the consequences of wars that broke out simultaneously on multiple fronts. As a result, a plethora of usurpers now found their way to Rome. Soldiers tended to abandon an emperor who was no longer in a position to fulfil his task of defending the empire. When they realized that the one issuing orders in the emperor's name was more sympathetic to their concerns than the emperor was, they quickly joined him. A usurper in this position would then seek to enforce his claim in Rome and the rest of the empire in order to found a dynasty. The Tetrarchy founded by Diocletian offered only a temporary solution to this problem [7]. Beginning in the late 4th century, commanders of *foederati* ('allies') were installing and deposing emperors as they saw fit, until the empire vanished altogether from the west.

☞ **Generals of note, C. Caesar; Generals of note, K. Marius; Generals of note, N. Pompey; Mutiny**

Bibliography

[1] L. de Blois, The Roman Army and Politics in the First Century B.C., 1987 [2] H. Botermann, Die Soldaten und die römische Politik in der Zeit von Caesars Tod bis zur Begründung des Zweiten Triumvirats, 1968 [3] D. Briquel, Romulus, jumeau et roi. Réalités d'une légende, 2018 [4] F. Cadiou, L'armée imaginaire. Les soldats prolétaires dans les légions romaines au dernier siècle de la République, 2018 [5] J.B. Campbell, The Emperor and the Roman Army, 31 BC–AD 235, 1984 [6] J.B. Campbell, War and Society in Imperial Rome, 31 BC–AD 235, 2002 [7] M. Christol, L'Empire romain du IIIe siècle. Histoire politique (de 192, mort de Commode, à 325, concile de Nicée), ^{2}2006 [8] P. Cosme, L'année des quatre

empereurs, 2012 [9] P. ERDKAMP (Hrsg.), A Companion to the Roman Army, 2007 [10] J.-L. FERRARY, Optimates et populares. Le problème du rôle de l'idéologie dans la politique, in: H. BRUHNS (ed.), Die späte römische Republik. La fin de la République romaine. Un débat franco-allemand d'histoire et d'historiographie, 1997, 221–231 [11] M.-C. FERRIÈS, Les partisans d'Antoine. Des orphelins de César aux complices de Cléopâtre, 2007 [12] E. FLAIG, Den Kaiser herausfordern. Die Usurpation im Römischen Reich, 1992 [13] F. HINARD, Les proscriptions de la Rome républicaine (Collection de l'École française de Rome 83), 1985 [14] A. KEAVENEY, The Army in the Roman Revolution, 2007 [15] L. KEPPIE, The Making of the Roman Army. From Republic to Empire, ²1998 [16] C. MEIER, Res publica amissa. Eine Studie zu Geschichte und Verfassung der späten Republik, 1980 [17] R. SYME, Die römische Revolution. Machtkämpfe im antiken Rom, 2006.

PIERRE COSME

Civilians

A civilian is defined as either a citizen (*cives*) or a non-soldier. The negative definition of this category is particularly apt for Greco-Roman Antiquity: a civilian was anyone who was not a soldier. In Classical Greece and the Roman Republic, citizenship was also linked to military service. Every male citizen was also a soldier – even if he was not serving permanently, for the armies of the Greek *poleis* and the Roman Republic were based on the concept of the militia. The negative definition here is accordingly problematic. It would mean that civilians were essentially women, children and non-citizens. The definition is much easier in the case of the Hellenistic royal armies and especially the professional army of the Roman Imperial period and Late Antiquity. Here, everyone who was not a soldier was a civilian [3]; [6]. Our focus will therefore be on this period.

A. Numerical relationship
B. Civilians directly involved with the military
C. Coexistence of civilians and soldiers
D. Legal definition
E. Veterans

A. NUMERICAL RELATIONSHIP

The numerical relationship between civilians and soldiers differed markedly between the Greek *poleis* (i.e. here Athens, for which the best information is available) and the Roman Imperial period. An estimated 15% of the total population of Athens was under arms in the 5th and 4th centuries BC. They were fighting in wars for an average of two years out of every three, and experienced no periods of peacetime longer than ten years. By contrast, while the Roman army of the Imperial period was very large by the standards of Classical Antiquity – estimates suggest 400,000–450,000 strong –, only 5–7.5‰ of the entire population was under arms. By way of comparison, most western countries today have between 3 and 5‰ of their populations in active service, and during the Cold War the figure was comparable with the Roman Imperial period. The distribution of soldiers also differed from province to province, and from the time of Augustus onwards (27 BC–AD 14), most of the military was stationed on the empire's borders. Soldiers were often a negligible presence in the interior of provinces, except where a major army road passed through. Relating the strength of the army to the territory of the entire empire, each individual soldier equated to an area of more than 10km². There were fewer than 34 soldiers for each kilometre of the imperial frontier – again, far fewer than in most western countries today. Furthermore, the population of the Roman Empire suffered little from war. Many soldiers never experienced a single battle throughout their careers [16].

B. CIVILIANS DIRECTLY INVOLVED WITH THE MILITARY

Although warfare was dominated by large pitched battles in Greco-Roman Antiquity, hostilities always affected the civilian population. The → supply of armies passing through or fighting nearby led to attacks, the requisitioning of provisions and transport animals, plunder and repression. Civilians on the losing side were often abused and sold as human booty or as → slaves. Meanwhile, civilians were also found in every army's train of followers, satisfying the very wide range of the fighting force's needs.

Among the Romans in particular, supply was often arranged via civilian traders, who were invariably the first to settle in the surroundings of newly constructed Roman camps. Illegitimate consorts and children of Roman soldiers, who until after the reign of Septimius Severus (AD 193–211) were forbidden to marry, were often the next to establish themselves. Unlike their subordinates, senior Roman officers were permitted to marry, if they were not already married by the time they took command – which represented just one step in their career of political advancement (the *cursus honorum*). Their wives were also allowed to live in the permanent camps, as vividly attested by letters from the auxiliary fort of a cohort at Vindolanda on Hadrian's Wall (Tab. Vindol. II 291–294).

The Roman army had civilian employees working alongside the soldiers. These *salariarii* were mostly salaried → specialists. The first category warranting mention are those providing medical care. The range of tasks performed by Roman soldiers meant that there was much more to treat than just war wounds and injuries resulting from battle. Performing manual work around the camp and guard duty and security details in the provinces, woodcutting, foraging, quarry work, burning lime and building roads, Roman soldiers were vulnerable to many and varied injuries in the course of their work. Medical services were thus of great importance, and not just after military engagements. Civilians are regularly attested in the ranks of Roman military physicians. Their status meant that they were not required to obey all rules that applied to soldiers, and they signed up only for a limited period. It would therefore seem that they were able to negotiate their pay and working conditions. Such a *medicus* would certainly benefit from working with the Roman army, for example in that his income would be secure and he would acquire a wealth of experience that would not easily be gained as a civilian. As with other civilian employees, it seems that the army was particularly prone to turn to civilian medics when it experienced a shortage of its own military staff. A lack of military specialists was probably the chief reason for non-medics likewise to be appointed to the army. Temporary increases in demand may also have stimulated the recruitment of civilians in some other specialist functions, for example as translators for Dacian or artisans in the army workshops [17.43f.].

C. Coexistence of civilians and soldiers

C.1. Attacks by soldiers on civilians
C.2. Soldiers as guarantors of peace and order
C.3. Legal provisions

C.1. Attacks by soldiers on civilians

Even in times of peace, and in provinces where no army (either friendly or hostile) was passing through, there was always a palpable influence of the army on everyday life in the interior of the Roman Empire, whether from the burden of taxes, the various methods of recruitment, the necessary supply activities that were organized and coordinated on an empire-wide basis, or military traffic and transportation. Given that only about 5–7.5‰ of the total population was serving in the army, however, it is not possible to claim that society was militarized or that the Roman army and its soldiers were omnipresent, except in certain provinces with a military presence above the average or an unusual geographical profile, such as Egypt, where all traffic was funneled through the Nile Valley.

Even so, interaction between civilians and soldiers in the Roman Imperial period did not enjoy a particularly good reputation. Doubtless, this is partly a function of some bias in the sources. Juvenal (Sat. 16) describes Roman soldiers as a violent mob against which civilians dared not even defend themselves in court, given that various laws furnished soldiers with privileges (→ Military law). He writes that, of course, no civilian would dare to strike a soldier, and should a soldier strike a civilian, the latter would make no complaint, because the court would be made up of the soldier's officers. The court might well issue a just verdict, but the entire unit would then mobilize against the plaintiff, and the original offence that led to the complaint would suddenly pale into insignificance.

In general, attacks by Roman soldiers on civilians are attested frequently. Such evidence is found chiefly in documentary sources, especially inscriptions and papyri. These must, however, be treated with caution, for such documents were not written with the intention of describing general conditions in the empire, and as a rule they refer only to a particular time and place. Complaints of wrongful treatment of civilians by Roman soldiers are particularly prevalent from the 2nd and 3rd centuries AD. Many of them are directed at soldiers travelling through an area. Unsurprisingly, regions of the empire crossed by major roads that the Roman army used for troop movements or soldiers' official travel were disproportionately affected by illegitimate (and legitimate) requisitions.

Many edicts issued by emperors and governors addressed such attacks by soldiers on civilians, including illegitimate requisitions and abuses of power, which occurred at all periods. Every provincial governor had to ensure that civilians were not harassed and that soldiers did not demand more in the way of supplies than they were entitled to. An edict of the governor of Egypt, issued around AD 133–137, remarks that the army was hated for its greed and lawlessness. Soldiers roamed the land without warrants, requisitioning boats, livestock and people in excess of allowances, either by force or even through official channels. The governor now ordered that only soldiers who could prove their identity with letters of accreditation were permitted to receive goods and services (Sel. Pap. II 221). Such letters of accreditation would include the official permit to use the *cursus publicus*, that is, to travel at public expense [10].

Evidence from Asia Minor also shows soldiers having to be restrained from illicit activity. Around AD 187–191, the *proconsul Asiae* instructed two senior military commanders to ensure that their soldiers behaved properly in the future while travelling through the province (SEG 48, 1514). At first glance, then, it would seem that Juvenal was right. Soldiers at all periods were also known for using force where necessary to achieve their aims – drawing, of course, on part of their repertoire of professional skills.

C.2. Soldiers as guarantors of peace and order

At second glance, however, a different picture emerges. For one thing, it must be remembered that complaints and grievances are much more likely to produce a written record than everyday coexistence that works well. Moreover, the inscriptions from Asia Minor and the Egyptian papyri also show that civilians were very well aware of the functionality of the state, and put their trust in the protection of state institutions. Communities asked soldiers and officers to deliver messages and asked for the army to be stationed in their territory. Cities honoured officers as benefactors. The grounds for such honours were seldom recorded in writing, but in the case of *praefectusalae* ('auxiliary force commander') Marcus Sulpicius Felix, a statue of whom was put up in Mauretania Tingitana in AD 144, it was because he and his soldiers had kept the inhabitants of the city of Sala, which endowed the statue to him, safe from attacks and livestock thefts. His deployment of guards, it was said, enabled the people to work safely in the woods and fields. He also directed building work that was done on the city's fortifications, supporting its grain supply from his unit's private resources. Furthermore, he even acted personally as a judge (AE 1931, 36). All of this, of course, he certainly did with the permission or even by order of the emperor. Having the military stationed in one's own territory thus afforded some protection, for instance against robbers and highwaymen. These, of course, were also civilians, but military action against them was generally seen in a positive light.

C.3. Legal provisions

A more critical problem were cases where the guilt of a civilian party against whom the military acted was not clearly established. Some of the attested attacks on civilians in connection with illegitimate requisitions probably arose from failures of the Roman administration and military logistics – not that this diminishes or legitimizes the attacks *per se*. If soldiers lacked supplies to which they were entitled, the danger of attacks and even mutiny was particularly high. Here, too, it was the responsibility of governors to prevent such shortages from occurring in the first place. Quite apart from the illegitimate commandeering of supplies, the legitimate services and duties that civilians were required to provide were themselves unpopular. This was particularly the case if they were to benefit a military that was, after all, notorious for using violence where necessary to achieve its aims.

That soldiers did not always force themselves on civilians to obtain their (supposed) due, however, is apparent from the complaints lodged by soldiers against civilians, a category of document that is particularly prevalent in law collections dating from the 3rd century AD [16.499, note 5]. Here, soldiers were explicitly refraining from the use of force. The legal advantages that soldiers enjoyed in court may have offered an inducement to pursue complaints through official channels. Roman soldiers were generally entitled even to go over their most senior officers' heads and appeal to the emperor [4]; [14]; [16]; [11].

D. Legal definition

Attempts were made to distinguish soldiers clearly from civilians through legal advantages – and disadvantages (→ Military law). Particularly striking in this context is the prohibition on marriage, which banned soldiers from contracting legally valid marriages and starting families. Of course, this was often unenforceable for those who served in excess of twenty years, but soldiers' illegitimate partners and children suffered legal discrimination.

The jurists of the Severan period (193–235) also highlighted the ban on a soldier's acquiring land in the province where he was stationed – mirroring the prohibition on public officials' purchasing land in the province of their posting (Dig. 18,1,62 pr; 49,16,9; 49,16,13 pr-2). However, this rule, which may have dated back to Augustus (the earliest attestation is from the mid-2nd century AD; BGU V 1210 col. X 243), did not prohibit land purchases in other provinces. This suggests that the consideration behind the ban was the irreconcilability of military life and agriculture, since soldiers would only be able to manage estates in distant provinces through agents. Another perhaps equally important motivation may have been the prevention of abuse by military authorities. Soldiers and public officials alike would be well positioned to put pressure on civilians in matters relating to land purchase. There also seems to have been a ban on soldiers' leasing land in the province where they were stationed. If a soldier bought land unlawfully and no objection was raised prior to his honourable discharge (*missio honesta*), he was allowed to keep the land. Nor was there a ban on inheriting land in the province of one's posting. Finally, Septimius Severus allowed soldiers to buy land back from the *fiscus* in cases where their fathers had been forced to mortgage it because of tax debts. Soldiers were still forbidden to buy or lease land in Late Antiquity. They were not expected to work in the fields, but to devote themselves entirely to defending the empire. That real life differed markedly from legal theory on this point, especially in Late Antiquity, is evident above all from the papyrological record in Egypt.

The common feature of all these special regulations imposed on the military was the exclusion of soldiers from civilian life. Legally speaking, soldiers were not allowed to start families, which meant that they were not able to integrate deeply into civil society. The ban on land purchase prevented them from settling down in the province where they were stationed and pursuing a civilian livelihood there. Privileges granted to soldiers in court proceedings could easily poison relations between soldiers and civilians. The privilege of holding and freely disposing his own assets (even during the lifetime of his father) also tended to weaken a soldier's ties to his family. Officially, at least, their special legal status largely cut soldiers off from the civilian world [9.942-947]; [17.67-70]; [11.36-38].

E. Veterans

→ Veterans enjoyed a special status among civilians. The *missio honesta*, honourable discharge from military service, gained former soldiers a series of privileges that were intended to set them apart from the – already abundantly privileged – class of Roman citizens. Still, the Egyptian papyri in particular show that demarcation between veterans and civilians in regard to privileges was not always straightforward. The most important of such privileges were tax exemptions and the waiving of obligations to perform liturgies (compulsory public services). Naturally, this sometimes strained relations with the local civilian population. Documentary sources also attest to constant and lively confrontations with assorted branches of the civil administration. Although veterans were entitled to no special treatment in the courts, governors and senior officials appear to have exerted pressure for their concerns to be dealt with quickly. Yet the right to appeal to the provincial governor even in the most trivial of cases was also available to any civilian. Although veterans were generally in a good social and economic position, they very rarely succeeded in making the leap to the *honoratior* class in their cities of residence, and thereby gaining access to the high municipal offices reserved to it [12]; [13].

☞ Society and army

BIBLIOGRAPHY
[1] R. Alston, Soldier and Society in Roman Egypt. A Social History, 1995 [2] J.B. Campbell, The Emperor and the Roman Army, 31 BC–AD 235, 1984 [3] J.-M. Carrié, Le soldat, in: A. Giardina (ed.), L'homme romain, 1992, 127–172 [4] W. Dahlheim, Die Armee eines Weltreiches. Der römische Soldat und sein Verhältnis zu Staat und Gesellschaft, in: Klio 74, 1992, 197–220 [5] M. Debrunner Hall, Eine reine Männerwelt? Frauen um das römische Heer, in: M.H. Dettenhofer (ed.), Reine Männersache? Frauen in Männerdomänen der antiken Welt, 1996, 207–228 [6] W. Eck, Milites et pagani. Die Stellung der Soldaten in der römischen Gesellschaft, in: A. Corbino et al. (eds.), Homo, caput, persona. La costruzione giuridica dell'identità nell'esperienza romana, 2010, 597–630 [7] W. Eck, Septimius Severus und die Soldaten. Das Problem der Soldatenehe und ein neues Auxiliardiplom, in: B. Onken / D. Rohde (eds.), In omni historia curiosus. Studien zur Geschichte von der Antike bis zur Neuzeit. Festschrift für Helmuth Schneider, 2011, 63–77 [8] J.H. Jung, Das Eherecht der römischen Soldaten, in: ANRW II.14, 1982, 302–346 [9] J.H. Jung, Die Rechtsstellung der römischen Soldaten. Ihre Entwicklung von den Anfängen Roms bis auf Diokletian, in: ANRW II.13, 1982, 882–1013 [10] A. Kolb, Transport und Nachrichtentransfer im Römischen Reich, 2000 [11] C. Kreuzsaler, Zwischen Privilegierung und Diskriminierung. Die Sonderstellung der Soldaten im römischen Recht, in: B. Palme (ed.), Die Legionäre des Kaisers. Soldatenleben im römischen Ägypten, 2011, 27–39 [12] S. Link, Konzepte der Privilegierung römischer Veteranen, 1989 [13] F. Mitthof, Soldaten und Veteranen in der Gesellschaft des römischen Ägypten (1.–2. Jh. n.Chr.), in: G. Alföldy et al. (eds.), Kaiser, Heer und Gesellschaft in der Römischen Kaiserzeit. Gedenkschrift für Eric Birley, 2000, 377–405 [14] B. Palme, Zivile Aufgaben der Armee im kaiserzeitlichen Ägypten, in: A. Kolb (ed.), Herrschaftsstrukturen und Herrschaftspraxis. Konzepte, Prinzipien und Strategien der Administration im römischen Kaiserreich, 2006, 322–239 [15] W.K. Pritchett, The Greek State at War, vol. 2, 1974 [16] M.A. Speidel, Soldaten und Zivilisten im Römischen Reich. Zu modernen Rekonstruktionen antiker Verhältnisse, in: M.A. Speidel, Heer und Herrschaft im Römischen Reich der Hohen Kaiserzeit, 2009, 473–500 [17] G. Wesch-Klein, Soziale Aspekte des römischen Heerwesens in der Kaiserzeit, 1998.

Anna-Maria Kaiser

Colonies

A. Concept
B. Greek colonies
C. Roman *coloniae*

A. Concept

An accurate definition is even more vital than usual in considering this topic. Contemporary usage has the term denoting territories mostly outside Europe, ruled in the early and late modern periods by European powers. The word 'colony', although derived from the Latin *colonia*, thus comes to mean variously 'a settlement in a new country; a group of people settling in a new location and forming a community that is subject to their place of origin or somehow related to it', or 'the territory populated by such a community'. The creation of colonies formed part of the policy of Western colonialism, which may be defined as 'a political-economic phenomenon whereby various European nations explored, conquered, settled, and exploited large areas of the world' (*Encyclopedia Britannica*). In this sense, then, 'colony' refers to a distant region controlled and exploited by an imperial power. 'Colonialism' is directly and inextricably bound up with the systematic military and economic subjugation of foreign countries between the 15th and 20th centuries.

When used in the context of Greco-Roman Antiquity, the term 'colony' has a range of meanings and functions. In the Ancient Greek world, it is used to translate the Greek *apoikia* ('settlement away from the homeland'). An *apoikia* was a full-fledged, independent *polis* founded by another *polis*, its 'mother city' (Greek *metropolis*). *Apoikiai* spread over a period of centuries between the 8th and early 6th centuries BC, and the process was a key element in the migration of Greeks into many regions of the Mediterranean and later farther afield. Yet this process was quite different in nature from early and late modern colonization, and indeed from the founding of colonies by the Romans. The early Greek world knew no colonialism in the sense defined above for modern Europe. The process is better described as a form of migration than part of some centrally ordained programme of imperial expansion, even where the foundation of an *apoikia* was an organized undertaking.

B. Greek colonies

Especially before 500 BC, most Greek colonies were not ruled from a distant *metropolis* ('mother city', i.e. founding city). The relationship between the *apoikia* and the *metropolis* was friendly but otherwise variable and partly dependent on distance. Sometimes it was close, as between Thasos and the Thracian mainland. It was always a relationship between two formally independent cities. Sometimes, the colony became more important than the mother city, as in the case of Cyrene, an *apoikia* of Thera. The Greek *poleis* differed greatly in how many *apoikiai* they founded. Miletus founded more colonies than any other city, whereas Athens was quite undistinguished in this respect. Mention should also be made of the founding of *emporia*, smaller trading posts – a different but related phenomenon.

C. Roman *coloniae*

C.1. Veterans' colonies
C.2. Titular colonies

Roman *coloniae* differed from Greek *apoikiai* in almost every respect. Their history began at the dawn of the Monarchical period and lasted throughout the Republic and into the Principate. The character of these settlements changed drastically over the centuries. The early colonies were small, comprising around 300 families of Roman citizens. They were located in newly conquered territories on the initiative of Rome as an occupying power, because there was no standing army to take control. The first such colonies appeared mostly along the coasts of Italy. Larger colonies of 2,000–3,000 families began to be founded in the 2nd century BC, e.g. Placentia (Piacenza) and Cremona in Northern Italy. During the final phase of the Roman Republic, the founding of colonies became a means of obtaining land for distribution to Roman *plebs* and discharged veterans.

Under the Principate, the decision to found a *colonia civium Romanorum* lay with the emperor. Colonies were established in the provinces, and were sometimes entirely new settlements; but more frequently, existing cities were required to accept a group of incomers to function as the ruling elite while requisitioning the best estates for themselves. This process served both to provide land and to establish military security. The new settlers were discharged army veterans, whose presence was intended not to fill a vacuum – a lack of soldiers in active service – but to place regional centres of loyal Roman citizens in locations of strategic importance. These is no shortage of sources attesting that local provincial populations found such impositions of settlers a very heavy burden and a matter of severe grievance. During provincial uprisings against Roman rule, *coloniae* often became targets of the most intense animosity, such as in the late 3rd century BC in Northern Italy (Placentia und Cremona), AD 60/61 in Britannia (Camulodunum/Colchester), 69 in Germania (Colonia Agrippinensis/Cologne) and 132–136 in Judaea/Palaestina (Aelia Capitolina/Jerusalem).

C.1. Veterans' colonies

Until the mid-1st century AD, all *coloniae civium Romanorum* were settled with a nucleus, at least, of veterans. The free citizens of the province also became Roman citizens. It is often assumed that veterans in the provinces formed a Latin-speaking element and thus an important instrument of the Romanization of many territories, particularly insofar as they disseminated the Latin language and Roman law and customs. But rarely is there any evidence to support this. Berytus did have its well-known Roman legal schools. Yet the opposite effect is also attested. A veteran colony in a non-military province could very quickly become demilitarized. In the Roman east, this generally fostered a tendency towards Hellenization, as is notably clear in the example of Corinth.

Among the specifically Roman features of colonies in the provinces, mention should be made of the special Italic legal status (*ius italicum*) that was granted to certain *coloniae*. This involved financial advantages, especially exemption from direct taxation of land and persons, and a greater degree of autonomy in the relationship between a city and provincial governors.

The effect of Latinization and Romanization achieved by the foundation of colonies has perhaps been exaggerated. Literary, epigraphic and numismatic findings from cities of the Near East give a vivid impression of the influence that a

Roman administrative and military presence had on local environments. Ultimately, however, that influence remained limited. The Greek language continued to be dominant, at least numerically, in the abundant texts found in several *coloniae*. Although inscriptions clearly attest to a Latin presence in official and administrative spheres, they do not justify the assumption that these cities differed markedly in social respects from other cities in the region. One genuine long-term effect of the foundation of veteran colonies in the Roman provinces, however, was that these cities became fertile soil for the recruitment of legionaries, who went on to serve in their own or other provinces.

C.2. TITULAR COLONIES

The final phase in the history of the founding of Roman colonies was the bestowal of the title of colony on provincial cities. Veteran colonies were either founded from scratch, or formed out of existing cities, which received colonial status and underwent reorganization, with veterans from Roman legions settled there and granted land. These veterans constituted a new local elite imposed on existing communities. By contrast, titular colonies came about through political reorganization and a change to the city's status – without the settlement of veterans or other outsiders. This was a crucial difference. Establishing a veteran colony caused a major disruption to the social and economic life of a community and the imposition of a foreign elite – both of which were part of the occupation of subjugated territories. Awarding colonial status to a provincial city with no accompanying veteran settlement, on the other hand, brought the local population nothing but benefits. All free male citizens of the colony were collectively granted Roman citizenship, and the city gained preferential relations with the provincial authorities, as well as superior status to other urban centres in the province.

Writing in the 2nd century AD, Aulus Gellius described the essence of colonial status in a famous passage. The status of a colony, he wrote, was 'considered preferable and advantageous by reason of the greatness and majesty of the Roman people, of which these colonies appear as it were to be small effigies and in a sense simulacra' ('potior tamen et praestabilior existimatur propter amplitudinem maiestatemque populi Romani, cuius istae coloniae quasi effigies parvae simulacraque esse quaedam videntur'; Gell. NA 16,13,9).

The first awards of titular colonial status took place in the 1st century AD, and the process continued until the late 3rd century. The last true veteran colonies were founded in the reign of Hadrian. Finally, mention must be made of one more development: the changes made to the status of cities under Septimius Severus and his successors, to reward or punish their conduct during the civil wars. To sum up, the Greek colonial tradition, unlike early modern and modern colonization that took place primarily for purposes of economic exploitation, was a form of organized migration, not imperialism. Roman colonies were a means of furthering the integration of the expanding empire.

☞ **Veterans**

BIBLIOGRAPHY

[1] F. DE ANGELIS, Colonies and Colonization, in: G. BOYS-STONES et al. (eds.), The Oxford Handbook of Hellenic Studies, 2009, 48–64 [2] J. BOARDMAN, The Greeks Overseas. Their Early Colonies and Trade, ^{4}1999 [3] G. BRADLEY / J.P. WILSON (eds.), Greek and Roman Colonization. Origins, Ideologies and Interactions, 2006 [4] C. BRÉLAZ (ed.), L'héritage grec des colonies romaines d'Orient. Interactions culturelles dans les provinces hellénophones de l'empire romain, 2017 [5] W. BROADHEAD, Colonization, Land Distribution, and Veteran Settlement, in: P. ERDKAMP (ed.), A Companion to the Roman Army, 2007, 148–163 [6] M.H. CRAWFORD, The Roman History of Roman Colonisation, in: J.H. RICHARDSON / F. SANTANGELO (eds.), The Roman Historical Tradition. Regal and Republican Rome, 2014 [7] T.J. DUNBABIN, The Western Greeks, 1948 [8] T.J. DUNBABIN, The Greeks and their Eastern Neighbours, 1957 [9] W. ECK, The Presence, Role and Significance of Latin in the Epigraphy and Culture of the Roman Near East, in: H. COTTON et al., From Hellenism to Islam, 2009, 13–42 [10] P.M. FRASER, Cities of Alexander the Great, 1996 [11] C.J. FUHRMANN, Ius italicum, in: R.S. BAGNALL et al. (eds.), The Encyclopedia of Ancient History, 2012, 3555–3556 [12] C.J. FUHRMANN, Policing the Roman Empire. Soldiers, Administration, and Public Order, 2012 [13] A.J. GRAHAM, Colony and Mother City in Ancient Greece, ^{2}1983 [14] A.J. GRAHAM, Collected Papers On Greek Colonization, 2001 [15] J. HALL, Colonization, in: G. SPEAKE (ed.), Encyclopedia of Greece and the Hellenic Tradition, 2000, 361–364 [16] B. ISAAC, The Greek Settlements in Thrace until the Macedonian Conquest, 1986 [17] B. ISAAC, The Limits of Empire. The Roman Army in the East, ^{2}1992 (ch. 7) [18] B. ISAAC, Caesarea-on-the-Sea and Aelia Capitolina. Two Ambiguous Roman Colonies, in: C. BRÉLAZ (ed.), L'héritage grec des colonies romaines d'Orient. Interactions culturelles dans les provinces hellénophones de l'empire romain, 2017, 331–343 [19] B. ISAAC, Latin in Cities of the Roman Near East, in: B. ISAAC, Empire and Ideology in the Graeco-Roman World, 2017, 257–284 [20] L.J.F. KEPPIE, Colonisation and Veteran Settlement in Italy, 47–14 B.C., 1983 [21] L.J.F. KEPPIE, Colonisation and Veteran Settlement in Italy in the First Century A.D., in: Papers of the British School at Rome 52, 1984, 77–114 [22] I. MALKIN, Religion and Colonization in Ancient Greece, 1987 [23] J.C. MANN, Legionary Recruitment and Veteran Settlement during the Principate, 1983 [24] F. MILLAR, The Roman Coloniae of the Near East. A Study of Cultural Relations, in: H. SOLIN / F.M. KAJAVE (eds.), Roman Policy in the East and Other Studies in Roman History. Proceedings of a Colloquium at Tvärmine, 1987, 1990, 7–57 [25] R. OSBORNE, Early Greek Colonization? The Nature of Greek Settlement in the West, in: N. FISHER /

H. van Wees (eds.), Archaic Greece. New Approaches and New Evidence, 1998, 251–269 [26] E.T. Salmon, Roman Colonization under the Republic, 1969 [27] G. Tsetskhladze (ed.), Greek Colonisation. An Account of Greek Colonies and Other Settlements Overseas. 2 vols., 2006 [28] G. Tsetskhladze / F. De Angelis (eds.), The Archaeology of Greek Colonisation, 2004 [29] F. Vittinghoff, Römische Kolonisation und Bürgerrechtspolitik unter Caesar und Augustus, 1952.

BENJAMIN ISAAC

Communications

☞ Transmission of orders

Conscientious objection

☞ Avoidance of military service

Conscription

Compulsory military service for citizens with assets above a certain threshold was a cornerstone of the Roman commonwealth. Only when Marius recruited men from among the *capite censi* for the Jugurthan War (111–105 BC) did those without property break into the Roman ranks (Sall. Iug. 86,2). The situation changed once more when the first *princeps*, Augustus, created a standing army, whereupon general conscription began to wane in importance. Even so, it was never abolished. Under the Republic, conscription probably applied up to the age of 46. The age limit for recruitment in the Imperial period appears to have been about 35, although older men and → veterans were called up in times of crisis (e.g. Liv. 22,11,8; Cass. Dio 56,23,2f.). Inscriptions show that most recruits of the Imperial period were between 17 and 25 when first admitted to the army, with most being around 17–18. However, there were younger soldiers too. C. Sempronius Gracchus set the minimum age for army service at 17, but his law did not remain in force for long (Plut. *Gracchi* 26,1; cf. Ascon. 68b). Factors taken into account for recruitment to the army in the Imperial period included not only good physical condition, but also an orderly family background and a minimum level of education (Tac. Ann. 4,4,2). Fitness for service was tested by examination (*probatio*). According to Vegetius, farmers were the most suitable candidates because of the toughness they acquired through their work (Mil. 1,3; 1,7; 2,19). Priests were exempt from military service (exception: threat from the Gauls; App. Civ. 2,150 (627); Plut. *Camillus* 41,6).

The municipal law of Urso (*lex coloniae Genetivae Iuliae* §62 and 66), dating from 44 BC, stipulated exemptions not just for the *pontifices* and *augures* and their children, but also for the *apparitores* of the magistrates for the duration of their service [1]. Presumably the magistrates themselves were also exempt.

Generally, there were enough volunteers available during the Imperial period, especially given that *peregrini* also performed military service. Accordingly, the death penalty for evading military service tended to fall into disuse (Dig. 49,16,4,10; Aristid. 26,71; 26,75–78). Where heavy losses were suffered or epidemics occurred, situations could arise in which recruitment had to be compulsory (Cass. Dio 56,23,2f.). Levies were sometimes undertaken as a punitive measure (e.g. Hdn. 4,9,4–6; SHA Carac. 6,2f.; cf. Cass. Dio 78,22,1–23,3). The young men of dependent peoples, where fit for service, were also conscripted under compulsion, as Rome skimmed off such peoples' military strength (e.g. Tac. Hist. 4,14,1–3; Agr. 31,1).

Conversely, military service was not open to all. The unfree were excluded in the Republican and Imperial periods, although Rome reacted to its disastrous defeat at Cannae (→ Battles of note C.) by recruiting slaves (Liv. 22,57,11). This principle also ceased to be followed strictly during the final decades of the Republic (App. Civ. 2,103 (427); 5,131 (544); Caes. B Civ. 1,24,2). When circumstances required it, Augustus recruited slaves whose owners had to manumit them. They then performed military service on poorer conditions than the freeborn (Suet. Aug. 25,2; Cass. Dio 55,31,1). Marcus Aurelius is also said to have recruited slaves (SHA Aur. 21,6). Slaves who were captured while attempting to escape the army faced the death penalty (Dig. 49,16,11). A ruling by Trajan shows a specific case in which such a judgment took into account whether slaves had volunteered or been offered as substitutes (Plin. Ep. 10,29f.). Men whose condition (i.e. whether they were free or not) was uncertain were also excluded from military service (Dig. 49,16,8). Likewise excluded were exiles, offenders who had not yet been convicted or had not yet served their sentence, and those who were ransomed from the enemy when the ransom had not yet been reimbursed. If such people accepted the levy or joined up, they could expect the severest punishments (Dig. 40,12,29 pr.-1; 49,16,2,1; 49,16,4,1–4). *Infames* were excluded, but after their punishment was served and the *infamia* was lifted, they could join up (Dig. 49,16,4,4; 49,16,4,7). Freedmen could become soldiers in the Imperial period, unlike in the classical heyday of the Republic. While they are frequently attested as members of naval crews and the urban Roman *vigiles*, there were objections to the admission of *libertini* to the legions and *auxilia*. Emergencies constituted another exception (Liv. 22,11,8), and matters were more fluid in the last decades of the Republic, when freedmen were frequent recruits (Cass. Dio 56,23,3).

☞ **Military service**

BIBLIOGRAPHY
[1] M.H. CRAWFORD (ed.), Roman Statutes, vol. 1 (Bulletin of the Institute of Classical Studies, Suppl. 64), 1996, 393–454 (no. 25) [2] G. FORNI, Il reclutamento delle legioni da Augusto a Diocleziano (Pubblicazioni della Facoltà di Lettere e Filosofia dell'Università di Pavia 5), 1953 [3] J.H. JUNG, Die Rechtsstellung des römischen Soldaten. Ihre Entwicklung von den Anfängen Roms bis auf Diokletian, in: ANRW II.14, 1982, 884–913 [4] G. WESCH-KLEIN, Soziale Aspekte des römischen Heerwesens in der Kaiserzeit (HABES 28), 1998, 161–163.

GABRIELE WESCH-KLEIN

Consequences of war

A. Greek
B. Roman

A. GREEK

A.1. Demographic consequences of war
A.2. Political consequences of war
A.3. Economic consequences of war

Consequences of war differed in nature and duration. The present article will focus on key issues in the spheres of demographics, politics and economics, and will not attempt to examine the full spectrum of discussions on this subject. It will exclude religious and cultural consequences, which seem to follow a different logic. We shall confine ourselves to a few revealing examples, while always bearing in mind regional developments and peculiarities, of which our sparse sources often divulge nothing. Furthermore, → war itself underwent profound changes between the Archaic and Hellenistic periods, and the consequences of the various conflicts that affected the Greek world accordingly belonged to specific historical contexts.

A.1. DEMOGRAPHIC CONSEQUENCES OF WAR

War had effects on the demographics of civic communities, whether of the victor or the vanquished. Military losses are difficult to assess on the basis of the sources, and the absence of systematic data sets essentially limits any statistical approach to analyzing trends. At sea, the sources do not indicate losses of men, but of ships. On land, the death rate in hoplite battles seems to have been quite limited – an average of 5% losses to troop strength for victors and 14% for the defeated [18], although this would not include subsequent losses arising from wounds [9]. Civilian losses were also taken into account. These occurred during sieges, which were capable of leading to veritable massacres of the civilian population. Such massacres might be selective or otherwise, and were sometimes limited to ruling families, although this would generally be followed by the enslavement of the remaining population. Well-known examples include Sybaris (in 511 BC), Mytilene (427) and Melos (416). Diodorus Siculus' (17,46,3f.) description of the demographic consequences of the Siege of Tyre in 332 is notorious: 'All but a few [of the Tyrians] were killed fighting, more than seven thousand in total. The king sold the women and children into slavery, and all the men fit for military service, two thousand at least in number, were crucified. So many captives were there, that although most had been taken to Carthage, there still remained more than thirteen thousand'.

Defeated Greek cities sometimes suffered tragic demographic consequences. The displacement of parts of the population for variable periods of time was a heavy burden on a community's human resources. The inhabitants of Megalopolis fled to Messene during the war with Cleomenes in 223 BC (Plut. *Cleomenes* 24,1). In 219 BC, over 5,000 Eleans, bringing with them a quantity of property and a vast tally of slaves and cattle, took refuge in the fortress of Thalamae (Pol. 4,75,2–8). Because Elatea failed to achieve an alliance with the Romans during the Second Macedonian War, its inhabitants had to abandon their city and live in exile in Stymphalus for eight years before the Romans agreed to their resettlement (c. 198–190 BC; IHG, no. 123). Sometimes, a population displacement became permanent exile with no hope of return. Others would then take over the economic resources of the original territory. In 431 BC, the Athenians condemned the population of Potidaia to such a fate. The Spartans did the same to the people of Samos in 404, as Philip II did to the inhabitants of Methone in 354. In none of these cases were those driven out permitted to take their property with them, except that the Potidaians were allowed to take a cloak and money for travel, and two cloaks for their wives. The Samians and Methonians were only granted one piece of clothing.

Victors too felt the demographic effects of war. Early in the 5th century, the Spartan state suffered an *oliganthropia* ('shortage of people') caused partly by losses in warfare. Dwindling numbers of *homoioi* ('peers'), however, were also linked with the socioeconomic phenomenon of land concentration, and after 369 BC with the consequences of the loss of Messenia (→ Sparta). At Athens during the Classical period, a funerary oration (*epitaphios logos*) was given in honour of soldiers killed in battle, who were buried in a common grave at the public cemetery (*demosion sema*). On Thasos around 350 BC, military magistrates had to issue a kit of weapons to male orphans of citizens killed in battle when they reached the age of majority, and female orphans were given a dowry when they reached the age of 14.

A.2. POLITICAL CONSEQUENCES OF WAR

There were also political consequences of war. Beginning in the Archaic period, a city wishing to preserve its autonomy (*autonomia*) and freedom (*eleutheria*) had to be able to raise a citizen army within its urban confines and eject an enemy from territory it declared inviolable. According to our sources, the raiding campaigns conducted by one community in the lands of another for purposes of seizing booty had no visible political consequences. In the context of 'land shortage' (*stenochoria*), however, such conflicts in the Archaic period sometimes revolved around the control of disputed borderlands. The Lelantine Plain on Euboea witnessed a war that broke out between Chalcis and Eretria in 710, and spiralled into a full-scale and much wider conflict, which Thucydides (1,15) briefly discusses. Following two wars of highly uncertain date (the first either c. 735–c. 715 BC or c. 700–c. 690; the second 685–672, 681–668 or 670–657), the conquest of Messenia by the Spartans led to the extinction of Messene, a city culturally very close to its neighbour. Some of the population became helots in the Spartan *homoioi* community, which from now on controlled the two plains on the Pamisos (Stenyklarus and Macaria). Another group went into exile in Italy, Sicily or Cyrenaica, forming the Messenian diaspora to which Epaminondas turned in 369 BC to revive the city. Even in 546 BC, during the conquest of Phocaea by the Persians under Cyrus the Great, wealthy families had time to escape, and fled to their colonies, helping to secure their future (Hdt. 1,164–167).

The defeated were more affected by political turmoil than the victors. At the time of the Delian League (478–404), Athens adopted a policy of repression in its wars with rebellious allies. Measures consisted of forcible readmission to the league and a new calculation of the *phoros* ('tribute', 'tax'), exaction of war reparations, destruction of city walls, foundation of a *klerouchia* ('land allotment'), imposition of an Athenian resident (*episkopos*, 'overseer') and reorganization of the political regime. Having won the Peloponnesian War (431–404), the Spartans also imposed on Athens' former allies, who had now joined the Peloponnesian League, a new political regime (*dekarchia*) and a governor (*harmostes*) with a Spartan garrison under his command. At Athens, the rule of the Thirty Tyrants (404–403) took effect only thanks to the support of the Spartan Lysander. Likewise, the regime of Demetrius of Phalerum was supported by the Macedonian Cassander. In the late 4th and early 3rd centuries BC, the Antigonids revived the *tyrannis* ('tyrants') in several cities on the Peloponnese, and stationed garrisons there. In Asia Minor, the kings developed a policy of diverse relationships with the Greek cities in their territories, ranging from alliances to assorted forms of subordination (subsumption, subjugation, incorporation) [6].

War also affected the political world in the form of peace treaties. Unlike truces (*ekecheiria, anoche*), treaties (*syntheke, spondai, homologia*) put a real end to conflict, and representatives of both parties had to acknowledge them. They were bilateral or – particularly under the hegemonies of the Classical period – multilateral in character. They were egalitarian in design, often with a symmetrical clause structure on which each party had to swear an oath invoking the gods as witnesses. Still, the broader contexts reveal that there were frequently disparities between the parties to the treaty. Until the 4th century, peace treaties were limited to the duration of some number of years, no more than a century, and they included the right to review the clauses on a regular basis if an interested party demanded this. Thucydides (5,18) describes the chief characteristics of this type of agreement on the basis of the treaty known as the Peace of Nicias that ended the first phase of the Peloponnesian War. During the 4th century, there emerged an ideal of general → peace (*koine eirene*), and various parties implemented it, from the King's Peace of 386 to the Corinthian League of 337. In the Hellenistic period, various monarchs who were constantly at war guaranteed peace as it was experienced by the Greek cities. Peace here was thought of as a mere interruption, a digression from the normal condition, which was war. Kings often demanded a tribute (*phoros, syntaxis*) from the Greek cities and imposed a garrison (*phrouron*), which the city was obliged to maintain (*epistathmeia*). Royal letters, which were copied into stone inscriptions to mark the publication of municipal honorary decrees, attest that cities sought privileges in the form of exemption from tributes, the garrison or its maintenance [4].

A.3. ECONOMIC CONSEQUENCES OF WAR

A.3.1. Effects on agriculture
A.3.2. Effects on other economic sectors

A.3.1. EFFECTS ON AGRICULTURE

According to the pattern of the 'old strategy' [16], a war between two communities, generally over a border dispute, took place on the territory of one of the participants in the form of a battle between two hoplite armies on the principle of an agon ('struggle', 'contest'). After invading the *chora* (the rural territory of a *polis*), the hostile army had to provoke a battle, which served as the decisive criterion for determining a victor. To this end, invaders might attack harvests, farms and villages. If the defenders still did not react, but were forced to open negotiations, attackers would regard this as a kind of moral victory.

In this pattern of behaviour, harm to agriculture was not motivated by vengeance (*sylon*), but by the desire for methodical devastation of the agricultural resources of the city under attack. The army might do further damage in the countryside. This is particularly apparent in the model of the 'Periclean strategy', in which the *chora* was surrendered to Peloponnesian troops on the understanding that the latter would 'devastate' it (Thuc. 4,2,1). When the Peloponnesians invaded in 430, 'they felled fruit trees and burned barns', as Diodorus Siculus recounts (12,45,1). Even under the 'new strategy', which took hold in the 4th century, evidently in reaction to previous attacks, and which consisted in a more active defence of the territory by the citizen militias, the pressure exerted by depredations was far from negligible. The Hellenistic period also provides many examples of territories devastated by enemy forces. The *chora* of Argos was plundered by Cleomenes III in 223 BC (Pol. 2,64), and those of Athens and Alabanda by Philip V in 201/00 (Pol. 16,24,8; 16,27,1; Liv. 31,14,9f.). The advice given by tacticians to army leaders that they should keep their troops away from their adversaries' fields confirms this to have been a widespread practice. Philo of Byzantium (D 6f.; [2]; [15]), for instance, suggests not destroying the *chora*, but imposing a siege so that the fields will still be intact after capitulation.

All this destruction had an effect on the agrarian economy that is much debated by modern historians. Hanson sought to classify in greater detail the list of destructive campaigns as it is currently available [17]. According to him, sources (especially literary) are prone to exaggerate phenomena and statistics. He has attempted to show how difficult it would be to destroy a territory, and to estimate the time and energy necessary for an army to do so in an effective way – without risking a counterstrike by a response force. This highly pragmatic analysis by a scholar (and owner of a Californian ranch) is now generally accepted [14]. Even so, it also shows that such campaigns of destruction were sometimes not insignificant. On the one hand, they had a psychological impact that should not be underestimated, potentially causing lasting damage to citizens' morale. On the other, their physical consequences were sometimes devastating. It should not be forgotten that such damage took place in the context of a fragile agrarian economy in which harvests were modest, and which was vulnerable to the slightest (especially climatic) change. Theophrastus makes clear that when war caused the abandonment of the terraced fields in the Cretan city of Arcadia in the western foothills of the Lasithi range, this caused wells to dry up and the city to disappear (Theophr. Hist. pl. 31,53; [8]). Shortages in the workforce needed for agriculture also occurred in the wake of wars, whether through demographic losses or the disappearance of slave labourers, as wars offered slaves an opportunity for escape. Around 219 BC, the city of Larisa lacked workers 'because of war', and the fields were not worked to the full (Syll.^{3} 543 = [1. no. 75]). The economic impact of war on agriculture is thus not to be underestimated. In peacetime, cities were keen to protect territories (*phylake tes choras*) and agricultural resources by constructing systems of fortresses and fortlets of the kind seen in Attica [10]; [22]; [21] and elsewhere in the Greek world.

A.3.2. EFFECTS ON OTHER ECONOMIC SECTORS

Other economic sectors may also have been affected by war, but we lack the sources to assess this. What is certain is that Athens emerged from the Peloponnesian War (→ Wars of note H.) less degraded than was long supposed. Damage had been done to the fields of Attica, and the mines of the Laurium were flooded in 413 – extraction work can only have revived slowly after 404. However, we know too little about Athenian minting to be able to date its resumption (c. 395?), which was accompanied by minor changes in design. The eye of Athena, previously depicted frontally (almond shape), now appeared in profile. At all events, the Athenian economy seems to have mitigated the impact of the Peloponnesian War entirely, especially by the 380s/370s BC, and even enjoyed a new boom.

Matters proceeded differently elsewhere and at other periods. The Hellenistic kings attempted to help population groups that had suffered notable hardship in war. In Asia Minor, emissaries from an unknown city asked an official of Antiochus III for help [20. no. 36]. Their city had been burned down during a war, and many citizens had lost everything. They requested exemption from taxes and the dispatch of new colonists. The official granted them a seven-year period of tax exemption with reduced taxes thereafter. The city was also excused from receiving garrisons, stationing soldiers and paying other dues. Samothrace faced a similar problem in the late 3rd century, when parts of its Thracian territories (*peraia*) remained uncultivated, probably because of attacks by Thracian tribes. The Samothracians asked the Ptolemaic commandant to support them with the construction of a fort (*ochyroma*), and to help citizens retain land and work it (IG XII, 8 156 B,

I. 17–23). They also promised to set aside part of the resultant harvests for offerings to secure the health of the royal family.

Finally, war hampered trade, which was a highly risky operation during times of armed conflict. In 386 BC, Lysias, addressing problems with the Athenian grain supply arising from the Corinthian War, disparaged the base character of the merchants. Of these *emporoi*, he asserted, 'They are so thrilled at the disasters that befall your city that they strive to learn of them before anyone else, or else they even invent stories themselves, whether of the sinking of ships in the Black Sea, their capture by the Lacedaemonians on their outward voyage, the blockade of your trading ports or the cancellation of contracts of supply' (Lys. 22,11–16). It may also be recalled that in 340 BC, Philip II was threatening the Bosporus and Hellespont when he intercepted a convoy of 230 merchant ships loaded with grain coming from the Strait of Kerch. Since 180 of these ships were destined for the port of Piraeus, the action provoked an Athenian move to support Byzantium and Perinthus. During the Hellenistic period, pirates, who readily became privateers in times of war, and royal fleets put constant pressure on merchant convoys. Around 302 BC, Archestratus of Macedonia, an officer of Demetrius I Poliorketes, was honoured at Ephesus for having protected a convoy of grain ships en route for the city (OGIS I,9).

Persistent conflicts often required Greek cities to look for foreign grain to supplement their own production. The economic significance of acts of beneficence must also be emphasized. These might come from citizens of the city itself or from outside, frequently kings or dynasts. Communities of citizens constantly complained of their desperate tax situation, their burden of debt, the militarization of their territories and their dwindling populations. Can a link be established between these complaints and the famous claim of Polybius (36,17,5–7) that a decline in population was underway around the middle of the 2nd century BC? It has been assumed that Polybius was referring either to a strictly regional phenomenon or to the oliganthropic perspective of a wealthy citizen elite that was concentrating citizenship in its own hands – or that his observations owed more to ideology than reality [11.268]; [3.25–27]. Yet even if Polybius did exaggerate its scale, a degree of local depopulation may well have occurred in connection with the wars against the Romans, for instance in Boeotia [13.208f.]. Abundant caution, however, is required here. A demographic decline, which in regard to Classical Antiquity is impossible to quantify, would not mean the disappearance of civic communities. We may tentatively agree with S. Alcock, when she argues in the case of Achaea, for instance, for a 'virtually ubiquitous decline in site numbers in the Hellenistic and Roman [...] epochs' [3.56] – although it must be kept in mind that this conclusion derives from a dozen or so surveys whose chronologies remain unproven [23.370]. While the Roman military presence may well have had a negative impact on the economic development of Greek cities between the early 2nd century and 146 BC, it must be said that the six decades through to 88 BC were a time of peace, autonomy and relative prosperity for the cities of the Peloponnese, Attica and Central Greece.

Bibliography

Sources
[1] The Hellenistic World from Alexander to the Roman Conquest. A Selection of Ancient Sources in Translation, edited by M. Austin, ²2006 [2] Philon von Byzanz (Philo Mechanicus), On Sieges, translated with introduction and commentary by D. Whitehead, 2016.

Secondary literature
[3] S.E. Alcock, Graecia capta. The Landscapes of Roman Greece, 1993 [4] T. Boulay, Arès dans la cité. Les poleis et la guerre dans l'Asie mineure hellénistique, 2014 [5] A. Bresson, La cité marchande, 2000 [6] L. Capdetrey, Le pouvoir séleucide. Territoire, administration, finances d'un royaume hellénistique (312–129 avant J.-C.), 2007 [7] C. Chandezon, Guerre, agriculture et crises d'après les inscriptions hellénistiques, in: J. Andreau et al. (eds.), Économie antique. La guerre dans les économies antiques, 2000, 231–252 [8] A. Chaniotis, War in the Hellenistic World. A Social and Cultural History, 2005 [9] J.-N. Corvisier, Guerre et société dans les mondes grecs (490–322 av. J.-C.), 1999 [10] J.-C. Couvenhes, Les garnisons de l'Attique du IVe siècle au Ier siècle av. J.-C. par les inscriptions, 2000 (unpublished doctoral thesis) [11] J.K. Davies, Cultural, Social and Economic Features of the Hellenistic World, in: F.W. Walbank et al. (eds.), CAH 7, pt. 1: The Hellenistic World, ²1984, 257–320 [12] P. Ducrey, Le traitement des prisonniers de guerre dans la Grèce antique, ²1999 [13] R. Étienne / D. Knoepfler, Hyettos de Béotie et la chronologie des archontes fédéraux entre 250 et 171 av. J.-C. (BCH Suppl. 3), 1976 [14] L. Foxhall, Farming and Fighting in Ancient Greece, in: J. Rich / G. Shipley (eds.), War and Society in the Greek World, 1993, 134–145 [15] Y. Garlan, Recherches de poliorcétique grecque, 1974 [16] Y. Garlan, Guerre et économie en Grèce ancienne, 1989 [17] V.D. Hanson, Warfare and Agriculture in Classical Greece, ²1999 [18] P. Krentz, Casualties in Hoplite Battles, in: GRBS 26, 1985, 13–20 [19] M. Launey, Recherches sur les armées hellénistiques, 2 vols., ²1987 [20] J. Ma, Antiochos III and the Cities of Western Asia Minor, 1999 [21] R. Oetjen, Athen im dritten Jahrhundert v.Chr. Politik und Gesellschaft in den Garnisonsdemen auf der Grundlage der inschriftlichen Überlieferung, 2014 [22] G.J. Oliver, War, Food, and Politics in Early Hellenistic Athens, 2007 [23] D. Rousset, La cité et son territoire dans la province d'Achaïe et la notion de 'Grèce romaine', in: Annales. Histoire, Sciences Sociales, March–April no. 2, 2004, 363–383 [24] G. Shipley, The Greek World after Alexander, 323–30 BC, 2000.

JEAN-CHRISTOPHE COUVENHES

B. Roman

B.1. Political consequences
B.2. Economic and social consequences
B.3. Cultural consequences
B.4. Consequences to demographics and urban planning

'Having subjugated the Etruscans and Samnites, and defeated the Celts of Italy in many battles, the Romans now attacked the rest of Italy [...]. Their wars with the Samnites and Celts had already made them true masters in the art of warfare' (Pol. 1,6,6). From the perspective of Polybius, an observer not unacquainted with military matters, the Romans used war as an instrument of expansion. They themselves regarded it consistently as a state of emergency with implications for political, societal and economic life. As victors, they benefited from the consequences of war. Economic benefits came to individuals who were directly involved (Artem. 2,31), as well as to society as a whole. The Romans also benefited from the processes of cultural change that war stimulated. This discussion will summarize the full spectrum of these aspects as they took shape in the Republican and Imperial periods.

Given the often inexact and partisan nature of our sources, it is impossible to describe the precise effects of a military conflict, not least because wars themselves are part of a complex network of causes and effects. For example, archaeologists and historians have in part refuted Arnold Toynbee's account of the economic and social decline of Southern Italy in the wake of Hannibal [21].

B.1. Political consequences

The most important consequence of Roman wars of conquest was the incorporation of new territories into the Roman political and administrative system. Although they were often the result of long-term developments, many processes of radical political transformation in Roman history were accompanied by military action. The outbreak of the Punic Wars (→ Wars of note K.) marked the advent of Roman imperialism; the Social Wars (91–88 BC) marked the shift from an alliance among city-states to a legally and adminstratively unified political territory. The defeat at Carrhae (→ Battles of note D.; 53 BC) and the 'Varian Disaster' in the Teutoburg Forest (→ Battles of note J.; AD 9) were severe setbacks to the Roman policy of conquest. The → Civil Wars accompanied the transition from Republic to Principate. Finally, the Battle of Adrianople in AD 378 (→ Battles of note B.) may be thought of as a key moment in the process of the Roman Empire's decline and fall.

Nor were wars without their domestic consequences. In the Republican period, a military victory was a welcome springboard to political ascent through the *cursus honorum* ('course of honours'). Examples include Lucius Aemilius Paullus after his victory at Pydna (168 BC) and the rise of Sulla following his triumph over Jugurtha (105 BC). Even Caesar (→ Generals of note, C.) needed first to conquer Gaul (59–50 BC) in order to gain the necessary backing to take on Pompey (→ Generals of note N.) and the Senate. Meanwhile, a battle lost could also bring wide-ranging political consequences. The death of Crassus after the Battle of Carrhae (53 BC) affected the equilibrium of the First Triumvirate, and brought the struggle for power between Caesar and Pompey to a head (Plut. *Caesar* 28,1; Flor. Ep. 2,13,13). The failure of his Parthian campaign (36 BC) tarnished the aura of Mark Antony in Rome to the advantage of his rival, Caesar the Younger (Octavian). The campaigns of Germanicus failed to offset the catastrophe of the Teutoburg Forest (→ Battles of note J.), leading Tiberius to abandon plans to conquer Germania and establish the frontier of the empire along the Rhine and Elbe. The disastrous defeat (and capture) of Valerian at Edessa (AD 260) exposed the east of the Empire to the threat of Sapor I and created an unstable political situation in which new contenders for the imperial throne emerged. Valens' defeat at Adrianople, which contemporaries already saw as a historic watershed, accelerated the process whereby foreign tribes were integrated into the Roman Empire. It also demonstrated that the death of an emperor on the battlefield created a dynastic vacuum that was difficult to manage, as had already been seen in the cases of Decius at the Battle of Abrittus in AD 251 (Iord. Get. 18,103; Zos. 1,23,3) and Julian after the failure of the Siege of Ctesiphon (AD 363: Amm. Marc. 25,3,23).

Wars could also lead to restructuring in the military and administrative spheres. Examples include in the decentralization of the *dilectus* ('levy' of troops) in the wake of the Social Wars (Caes. B Gall. 7,1,1), and the reorganization of the magistracies after the Second Punic War (Liv. 23,32,1–4), when the praetors lost responsibility for the legal system and instead took on army commands [2].

B.2. Economic and social consequences

B.2.1. Economic consequences
B.2.2. War as a source of wealth
B.2.3. Social consequences

B.2.1. Economic consequences

A lack of reliable data on troop strengths and pay levels, the extent of monetary rewards to soldiers and war → booty hampers the task of reliably estimating the economic consequences of individual wars. In general, it may be assumed that expenditures rose during wars, for troops needed to be recruited and equipped, and the farther a campaign ventured and the longer it lasted, the greater the costs it incurred. The costs of the Armenian campaign in the reign of Nero (AD 58–63) are estimated at 13 million sesterces (Plin. HN 7,129). When the Marcomannic War dragged on in AD 180, Marcus Aurelius had exhibition pieces from the imperial palace sold off to avoid putting a further burden on the empty treasuries of the provinces (SHA Aur. 17,4f.). The military expedition against the Parthians under Macrinus in AD 218 swallowed up 200 million sesterces (Cass. Dio 79,27,1). The Persian campaign of AD 502–506 led to confiscations affecting the province of Egypt (J. Styl. 54; 70; 77).

Deficits caused by military expenditure often led to reforms in the financial and fiscal systems. Following the Roman defeat at Cannae in 216 BC (→ Battles of note C.), a doubling of the *tributum*, the direct tax levied to defray the costs of the war, was justified with the need to prevent economic collapse in consequence of the war (Liv. 23,31,1f.). The Senate drew on all available resources, including the private assets of its own members.

Negative impacts of war included enemy occupation of commercial hubs and supply lines. This is particularly noticeable in wars fought at sea, which the sources suggest often went hand in hand with piracy (R. Gest. div. Aug. 25,1; Liv. per. 123; Vell. Pat. 2,73,3). In 42 BC, for instance, the fleet of Sextus Pompeius plied the Mediterranean to cut Rome off from its grain supply (App. Civ. 5,72). Ships of the usurper Heraclianus lay off the North African coast to prevent vessels from departing for Rome (AD 412/13: Sozom. Hist. eccl. 9,8,7), and the Vandals under Geiseric adopted the same tactic soon afterwards (Sid. Apoll. Carm. 5,388–392; Victor Vitensis 1,41f.; Procop. Vand. 1,5,22–24).

The chief source for financing the army in the Imperial period was the provinces. The case of Gaius Valerius Marianus, magistrate of the city of Tridentum, illustrates this. The city had to donate corn supplies to furnish the *legio III Italica* stationed there with provisions (CIL V 5036 = ILS 5016). Major military actions could cause the economic collapse of an entire province [19]. They could even cause an epidemic, if a food shortage occured. The gathering of large contingents of troops in Syria in the run-up to the Persian campaign (AD 363) of Emperor Julian triggered a famine in Antioch (Iul. *Misopogon* 369 A–370 C; → Wars of note I.).

Even minor enemy troop movements sometimes had grave consequences for local economic life, for soldiers were allowed to undertake campaigns of plunder. Plunder (Onas. Strat. 6,11; Tac. Agr. 38,1) and the destruction of crops (Cic. Manil. 6,16) were commonplace among enemy forces in transit. Italy was no exception, as it suffered from these during the march of Hannibal through Southern Italy after the Battle of Cannae (Liv. 23,14–20), at the time of the Social Wars (*vastitas Italiae*: Sall. Iug. 5,1), during Sulla's march on Rome (App. Civ. 1,57) and in the events of the 'Year of the Four Emperors' in AD 69 (Tac. Hist. 3,19,6 and 3,26,5). Besides the tactic of → scorched earth and the quest for booty, feelings of hatred and revenge also surfaced here, playing out for instance in the devastation caused by Vitellius' armies commanded by Valens and Caecina on the march to Rome in AD 69 (Tac. Hist. 1,63ff.; 2,12; 2,56).

B.2.2. WAR AS A SOURCE OF WEALTH

Rome's wars of conquest generated enormous incomes in the form of booty, tribute and other payments (Liv. 34,46,2f.: M. Porcius Cato's booty from Hispania; Amm. Marc. 17,9,6: unrest in the army of Julian when pay and gifts were not forthcoming on the campaign against the Franks in AD 358). Tigranes II was only able to retain control of Armenia by paying a tribute of 6,000 talents, in addition to donations of 50 silver drachmae to every ordinary soldier, 1,000 to every centurion and one talent of silver to each of the tribunes (Plut. *Pompeius* 33,5f.). Rising incomes from wars of conquest and the increasing circulation of money benefited both the Roman public treasury (Liv. 10,46,5; following victories over the Samnites) and individual commanders (Quintus Fabius Maximus Rullianus after the Battle of Sentinum in 295 BC: Liv. 10,31,3), who could then distribute their gains among their soldiers as they wished ([17]; but cf. [7]). This in turn had an impact on economy and society. Revenues from the victory over the Macedonians at Pydna (168 BC) amounted to 120 million sesterces in silver and gold alone (Liv. 45,40,1), and made it possible to suspend the *tributum* until the consulate of Hirtius and Pansa (43 BC: Val. Max. 4,3,8; Plut. *Aemilius Paullus* 38,1). Vast fortunes poured into Rome from the conquests of Pompey (→ Generals of note, N.), with the revenues of the public treasury almost doubling (Plut. *Pompeius* 45).

As Roman territory expanded, extraordinary revenues from wars of conquest were replaced by the taxation of the conquered populations. In the mid-2nd century BC, incomes from war booty and tributes amounted to roughly two fifths of public revenue, but by the end of the Republican period, taxes raised in the provinces already made up most of it. The improved economic conditions, as well as the importing of valuable raw materials (Plin. HN 12,20 mentions the ebony brought to Rome for the triumph of Pompey in 61 BC), benefited mainly the wealthier strata of society. This widened the gulf between rich and poor and set in motion the mechisms of *luxus* and *luxuria* that, for conservatives, lay at the root of the decline in traditional morals.

Revenues were often ploughed back into war, whether through the recruitment of mercenaries (Caes. B Civ. 3,4,6: Pompey ahead of the Battle of Pharsalus), or in the form of *donativi* (supplementary monetary payments) to troops to encourage their fighting spirit and assure commanders of the devotion of their men. The kind of relationship this fostered, akin to that between patron and client, formed the basis of the military successes of figures such as Sulla (Plut. *Sulla* 12), Pompey (Str. 11,14,10; Plut. *Pompeius* 45), Caesar (Suet. Caes. 38,1; App. Civ. 2,29; Cass. Dio 42,49,4f.) and Octavian (Plut. *M. Antonius* 16; App. Civ. 3,42; [3]; [11]). It was also a way of securing the experience of *veteres milites* ('veterans') forged in long years of military campaigning [4]. Resources for new military campaigns were also sometimes acquired in recently conquered regions, as in the case of the gold and silver mines of Transylvania, which fell into Roman hands during the Dacian campaign (→ Wars of note C.), and the income from which Trajan used to finance his Parthian War of AD 114–117 [9].

War gains were also invested in construction and infrastructure projects (roads and aqueducts), and in the development of new branches of industry, like weapons and the manufacture of military equipment in the late Imperial period (Not. Dign. Or. 11,18–39; Not. Dign. Occ. 9,16–39; Cod. Theod. 7,6,4f.; 10,22,1). However, the relentless influx of funds from victories in war also had negative consequences. Authorities tried to counter the resultant currency debasement with measures like the Diocletianic Price Edict of AD 301, which also regulated trade with the military.

The issue of → veterans and their maintenance, which had immediate social and economic effects, was intimately related to war and its consequences. A *veteranus* was anyone who had been honourably discharged from the army and was thereby entitled to a settlement, comprising a piece of farmland (*missio agraria*) and a monetary payment (*missio nummaria*). From the end of the Second Punic War onwards, the grant of land was made only occasionally and was limited to small parcels corresponding to the term of service. With Sulla (App. Civ. 1,96), it began to take on a more systematic form, and it can be said to have become firmly established under Caesar (→ Generals of note, C.), the (Second) Triumvirate and Augustus. Augustus laid down specific rules for the allocation of land and money to veterans after the Battle of Actium (→ Battles of note A.; R. Gest. div. Aug. 16f.; Cass. Dio 54,25,5) [3]. The years of the → Civil Wars had created a crisis of small-scale land ownership, with farmers required to stay away from their mostly small farms more and more often to perform military service. Meanwhile, the use of slaves in the fields of large-scale landowners was increasing, and slaves were increasingly abundant as a result of the many campaigns of conquest. In AD 6, Augustus established the *aerarium militare* ('military treasury'), a fund for meeting the necessary expenditure (R. Gest. div. Aug. 16–17,2; Cass. Dio 55,25,2). This he financed initially out of his own private fortune, before later imposing taxes on profits from auctions (*centesima rerum venalium*) and inheritances (*vicesima hereditatum*). Besides the land grant and payment, veterans also enjoyed other privileges (*emerita*: Suet. Aug. 24,2; Dig. 49,16,3,8; 49,16,5,7) – dependent on rank, term of service and type of deployment – mostly consisting in exemption from certain taxes, duties or civic service obligations (Dig. 49,18,5). The sums set by Augustus were revised upwards under Caracalla from 20,000 sesterces for Praetorians and 12,000 for legionaries (Cass. Dio 55,23,1) to 25,000 and 20,000 sesterces respectively (Cass. Dio 78,24,1; [12]). Over time, the land grant became less important than the monetary payment, until Hadrian abolished the former altogether and instead defined *missio agraria* as the settlement of entire companies of veterans. These functioned not only as battle-hardened troops to defend the localities where they were settled, but also as drivers of urban development in hitherto underdeveloped regions. In civilian life, colonists either performed the same roles they had in the military (as surveyors, surgeons, smiths etc.), moved into manufacturing raw materials or products for the army – as *vestiarius* ('clothier'), *gladiarius* ('cutler'), *naupegus* ('boat builder') and so forth – engaged in commerce, or went into arable or livestock farming.

B.2.3. SOCIAL CONSEQUENCES

War stimulated social mobility and societal advancement for some of the population. The long absence of men called up to serve in the Punic Wars, for example, brought greater social leeway and visibility to wives. This provoked harsh criticism from conservatives, such as Cato the Elder, who saw the changing status of Roman wives as an indication of moral decline, which these conservatives blamed on the increase of prosperity and the Hellenization of Roman society as a result of wars in the east (see below). The debate over the repeal of the *lex Oppia*, which restricted women's wealth, was indicative. The law had been passed in 215 BC after the Battle of Cannae (→ Battles of note C.), and in their struggle to abrogate it, Roman women for the first time exerted pressure on constitutional bodies to improve their legal status (195 BC: Liv. 34,1–8).

Another significant component of war booty comprised the people taken captive in conflict (→ Prisoners). It was from this group that the great majority of → slaves were recruited. Numbers given in ancient sources cannot be taken at face value, but may convey an impression of the scale of the phenomenon: 69,000 captives were said to have come from the wars in Central Italy in 297–293 BC (Liv. 10,14–46); 18,000 from the campaigns of Scipio Africanus in 204–202 BC (→ Generals of note, O.; App. Lib. 65; 94; 108f. etc.); one single consular army supposedly took over 5,000 prisoners during the campaign in Istria in 177 BC (Liv. 41,11,8); 10,000 Romans entered captivity at Carrhae (→ Battles of note D.; Plut. Crassus 1). When the Romans had defeated an enemy, they soon faced the task of deciding what to do with those taken prisoner. The general could make them his private slaves, gift them to his soldiers or take them to Rome to display in the triumphal procession. Anyone not taken into the ranks of the 'volunteers' (*volones*) in the army (as during the Second Punic War: Liv. 23,32,1) would end up on the busy slave market. According to Strabo (14,5,2), up to 10,000 slaves a day were sold on the market on Delos, most destined for Italy. There they were put to work *en masse* in the fields of large-scale landowners, who were in a position to buy vast expanses of farmland from the *ager publicus*, while small-scale landowners suffered increasing impoverishment under the burdens of military service, tax and ultimately the loss of their land (Plut. *Tiberius Gracchus* 8; App. Civ. 1,7).

B.3. CULTURAL CONSEQUENCES
Through their wars of conquest, the Romans imbued the cultures of defeated peoples with their own ways of living and thinking, and not least with the Latin language, which stood alongside Greek as a *lingua franca* of educated people throughout the empire. The language of the victors also slowly but surely supplanted local languages (in Hispania this was already happening in the first centuries of the Imperial period: Str. 3,2,15). The use of members of foreign tribes as *auxilia* gave them the chance to learn and disseminate Latin. Thus, Jugurtha, who fought alongside Romans as an auxiliary at Numantia (Sall. Iug. 101,6), and Arminius, who would destroy Roman troops in the Teutoburg Forest (→ Battles of note J.; Tac. Ann. 2,9), both spoke the language of the Romans.

The encounter with the cities of Magna Graecia during the Punic Wars (→ Wars of note K.) and the wars of conquest that followed them had a lasting impact not only on Rome's economic life, but also on its cultural life. Conservatives saw the resultant Hellenization (Sall. Catil. 5,8; Liv. 39,6,7; Val. Max. 9,1,3; Plut. *Marcellus* 21) as the root of *luxuria* ('extravagance'), *avaritia* ('greed') and *ambitio* ('excessive desire to please'), and as responsible for moral decline and the abandonment of the *mos maiorum* ('ancestral custom'), adherence to which had made military success possible (Flor. Epit. 1,13,23). At the same time, the spread of eastern cults, such as those of the *Magna Mater* Cybele and Mithras (Cic. Har. resp. 24; Plut. *Pompeius* 24) had spawned religious syncretism that manifested itself, for instance, in the cult of Isis. The destruction of Jerusalem in AD 70, and even more so the suppression of the rebellion led by Bar Kochba in AD 132–135 (→ Wars of note B.), would also bring consequences that went far beyond the devastation of the Jewish territory, the depopulation of its capital (Cass. Dio 69,15,1f.) and the expulsion of the Jews from Palestine. These events spelt the end of Messianic expectations that an independent Jewish state would soon be restored, and they marked the advent of the diaspora [20].

Roman popular beliefs linked wars of uncertain outcome or problematic character with *prodigia* – omens (generally bad) like earthquakes and other afflictions. L. Coelius Antipater listed a series of such events throughout Italy associated with the Roman defeat at Lake Trasimene in 217 BC (Cic. Div. 1,35,78 = F 20b Beck/Walter, F 14b Cornell), and Livy (22,1,8–20) counts no fewer than 20. Various natural disasters were also reported for the year 49 BC, as civil war broke out between Caesar and Pompey (Cass. Dio 41,14,3).

The Roman wars of conquest had a positive effect on the development of science and technology. Hitherto unexplored regions were charted in the course of military operations. The growth in new geographical knowledge arising from the campaigns of Caesar in Gaul, Britain and Germania was enormous (Cic. Prov. 22; Caes. B Gall. 1,1ff.; 5,12–14; 6,13–28). Pliny the Elder credits the information he gives about the region of Pontus to the detailed report made by Domitius Corbulo during his campaign against the Parthians (AD 58–63: Plin. HN 6,23), and he mentions the geographer 'Dionysius' (actually Isidorus of Charax), whom Augustus sent to the east to gather information ahead of the campaign to be led by Gaius Caesar (Plin. HN 6,141). Technical innovations for military purposes also found their way into civilian use (→ Innovation). One example is the *centones*, blankets soaked in vinegar, which were used in the field to prevent siege machinery from being set on fire, and which the *vigiles* ('firewatchers') later started using in firefighting (Cod. Theod. 14,8,1). The army also served as a training ground for many specialist occupations. For instance, the *librator* ('surveyor') of the legate of Moesia, Calpurnius Macer, who is mentioned in two letters of Pliny the Younger from AD 112, learned his civilian trade from his time in the army (Plin. Ep. 10,41,3; 10,42).

B.4. Consequences to demographics and urban planning

It is impossible to capture the demographic consequences of war in Antiquity in figures. The sources contain numbers of war dead, which may be more or less accurate. Indications of deaths not directly connected to hostilities – among the civilian population, prisoners of war, women and slaves – are hardly more reliable, depending on the duration of the conflict and the size of the territory concerned. Other factors to be considered include declines in birth rates caused by warfare, and victims of epidemics. For example, the epidemic that broke out during the Parthian campaign among the troops of Avidius Cassius in Seleucia in AD 165 spread rapidly throughout Asia Minor, Egypt, Greece and Italy, including Rome (Amm. Marc. 23,6,24; SHA Verus 8,1). There is no assessable evidence in the sources as to individual psychological consequence, in the sense of post-traumatic stress disorder, of which no mention is made.

The wars of conquest had an indirect impact on the Roman cityscape, triggered by the resulting influx of resources. Most of the temples built in the Republican period were financed from war booty (*ex manubiis*). Victorious generals often had existing buildings renovated and inscriptions put up to commemorate the event. One was Marcus Fulvius Flaccus, who had a hand in the conquest of the Volsinii in 264 BC, and who financed renovations to the Temples of Fortuna and Mater Matuta at the foot of the Capitoline Hill. Shields and standards were also hung from temple columns (Liv. 40,51; Plin. HN 34,20). Commanders who were granted a → triumph had statues built (Plin. HN 34,20–32) or *tabulae* put up recounting their feats (L. Aemilius Regillus after the Battle of Myonnessus in 190 BC: Liv. 40,52,5f.; T. Sempronius Gracchus after the conquest of Sardinia: Liv. 41, 28,8f.). Triumphal arches (*fornices*) were built to celebrate Roman victories – no fewer than three, for instance, by order of Lucius Stertinius, two in 196 BC outside the Temples of Fortuna and Mater Matuta following his return from Hispania ulterior, and a third in the Circus Maximus (Liv. 33,27,3f.). Scipio Africanus had one built on the Capitol in 190 BC before setting off for the east, and Quintus Fabius Maximus commissioned one for the *via Sacra* following his victory over the Allobroges (120 BC: Cic. Planc. 17; [14]).

War trophies decorated buildings in the city of Rome, like the Corinthian columns from the Olympeium at Athens, installed by Sulla in the Temple of Jupiter on the Capitol (Plin. HN 36,45). Exotic booty items, which were often included in triumphal processions, excited onlookers' imaginations while also serving as inspirations. Such was the illustration of the Lighthouse of Pharos exhibited by Caesar at his triumph of 47 BC (Flor. Epit. 2,13,88), and later used by Claudius as the model for his *portus* at Ostia (Suet. Claud. 20,3). The temple treasure looted by Titus at Jerusalem (which probably included the *menorah*) was put on display in the *Templum Pacis* consecrated by Vespasian in AD 75 (Jos. BI 7,158–162).

In many cases, revenues from war booty were donated to finance public buildings and monuments, either by commanders themselves, or by the Senate, which was responsible for the most prominent public areas of the imperial capital. The Senate regularly had old monuments removed to make way for new ones (Plin. HN 34,30). The institution of the triumphal procession also had an impact on the architectural landscape of Rome, for triumphs produced a concentration of victory monuments at the most prominent locations they passed (Liv. 33,27,3f. on the *fornices* – 'triumphal arches' – of Lucius Stertinius).

Bibliography

[1] G. Alföldy, Römische Sozialgeschichte, ⁴2011 (¹1975) [2] T.C. Brennan, The Praetorship in the Roman Republic, 2 vols., 2000 [3] P.A. Brunt, Italian Manpower, 225 B.C.–A.D. 14, 1971 [4] F. Cadiou, L'armée imaginaire. Les soldats prolétaires dans les légions romaines au dernier siècle de la République, 2018 [5] B. Campbell, The Roman Army, 31 BC–AD 337. A Sourcebook, 1994 [6] B. Campbell / L.A. Tritle (eds.), The Oxford Handbook of Warfare in the Classical World, 2013 [7] M. Coudry, Partage et gestion du butin dans la Rome républicaine. Procédures et enjeux, in: M. Coudry / M. Humm (eds.), Praeda. Butin de guerre et société dans la Rome républicaine. Kriegsbeute und Gesellschaft im republikanischen Rom, 2009, 21–79 [8] D. Favro, The Street Triumphant. The Urban Impact of Roman Triumphal Parades, in: Z. Çelik et al. (eds.), Streets. Critical Perspectives on Public Space, 1994, 151–163 [9] C. Howgego, The Supply and Use of Money in the Roman World 200 B.C. to A.D. 300, in: The Journal of Roman Studies 82, 1992, 1–31 [10] L. Keppie, Colonisation and Veteran Settlement in Italy, 47–14 B.C., 1983 [11] R. Laignoux, Des guerres à prix d'or. Multiplication et cérémonialisation des distributions exceptionnelles à la fin de la République, in: M. Redde (ed.), De l'or pour les braves! Soldes, armées et circulation monétaire dans le monde romain, 2014, 199–227 [12] Y. Le Bohec, L'armée romaine sous le Haut-Empire, ²1998 (¹1989) [13] C. Nicolet, Le métier de citoyen dans la Rome républicaine, ²1988 (¹1976) [14] I. Östenberg, Staging the World. Spoils, Captives, and Representations in the Roman Triumphal Procession, 2009 [15] D.S. Potter (ed.), A Companion to the Roman Empire, 2006 [16] N. Rosenstein / R. Morstein-Marx, A Companion to the Roman Republic, 2006 [17] I. Shatzman, The Roman General's Authority over Booty, in: Historia 21, 1972, 177–205 [18] P. Southern, The Roman Army. A Social and Institutional History, 2006 [19] D.C. Stathakopoulos, Famine and Pestilence in the Late Roman and Early Byzantine Empire. A Systematic Survey of Subsistence Crises and Epidemics, 2004 [20] G. Stemberger, Das klassische Judentum. Kultur und Geschichte der rabbinischen Zeit, ²2009 (¹1979) [21] A. Toynbee, Hannibal's Legacy. The

Hannibalic War's Effects on Roman Life, 1965 [22] G. TRAINA, Carrhes, 9 juin 53 avant J.-C. Anatomie d'une défaite, 2011.

IMMACOLATA ERAMO

Costs of war

A. Greek
B. Roman

A. GREEK

A.1. Introduction
A.2. Costs of land troops
A.3. Costs of navies
A.4. Total costs and financing

A.1. INTRODUCTION

The following discussion of the costs of war will limit itself to expenses for equipping and maintaining military units. It will not address reparation payments or economic costs arising from soldiers' absence from their ordinary occupations, the deportation and murder of people, or depredation, plunder or destruction. Because Classical *poleis* did not maintain standing armies, their costs for war primarily consisted of expenses for equipment and maintenance during hostilities. These varied, and they were borne by different people or groups from one *polis* to another and at different times throughout history. However, the sources frequently offer only snapshots – in the Classical period relating chiefly to conditions in Athens, and in the Hellenistic period relating to the major kingdoms. Distinctions must also be made between the different troop types (infantry, cavalry and navy).

A.2. COSTS OF LAND TROOPS

It appears that footsoldiers generally provided their own equipment during the Archaic and Classical periods (the same may have been true of mercenaries: [11]), so individual costs varied greatly. Soldiers were probably only provided with armour in exceptional cases (Thuc. 6,72,4). The exact cost of a full suit of armour remains unknown (see also Aristoph. Pax 1236f.). Hellenistic kings sometimes set great store by equipping their soldiers as splendidly as possible (cf. Ath. 5,194), which increased costs considerably. Maintenance costs for infantrymen in the Archaic period appear to have been limited to food provisions, donations and a share of the booty. Participation was more or less voluntary, often arising from relationships of amity and loyalty, and it was not directly recompensed (Hom. Od. 2,291f.; 3,363). Without doubt, the share of the booty offered a strong incentive to take part in a campaign, for booty was generally distributed according to performance (cf. Hdt. 9,81). Tyrants were readily resorting to the use of mercenaries (Hdt. 1,61,4; 1,64,1f.) already in the Archaic period, but nothing is known of exactly how they were paid. A fixed stipend only emerged during the 5th century BC (the *misthos*, later the *opsonion*), and varied between 2 obols and 1 drachma per day (Dem. Or. 4,28: 2 obols; Xen. An. 1,3,21: 1–2 dareikoi/month). Pay was distributed in arrears at month end (Xen. An. 1,3,21; 7,6,1) or at the end of the campaign (Arr. Anab. 3,19,5), although advance payments may well have been possible. One-off bonuses were also paid, for instance after a victory in battle (Xen. An. 1,4,13; Plut. *Dion* 31). On occasion, some of the stipend was withheld to prevent desertion (Thuc. 8,45,2). There was an increasing tendency, especially in the heavily manned naval forces, to recruit mercenaries who received a bounty in advance and a discharge payment on release (Arr. Anab. 3,19,5). It seems likely that the *misthos* replaced not only the booty and donations, but also the regular provision of food. Certainly, Athenian naval crews after 470 BC had to cover these costs themselves out of the *misthos*. However, it seems that allowances were later paid along with the *misthos*, partly in monetary form (the terminology is not always clear, but frequent terms used are *sitarchia*, *siteresion* (maintenance), *sitos* (feed for riders) or *trophe* (food)) [8.82–90]. The supply of provisions for large armies and the army train was managed in many different ways. It is generally unclear how much this process cost and who was responsible to pay it [7.206–209].

Some heavily armed soldiers required a servant and received double wages (Thuc. 3,17,4). Mounted troops seem to have received triple wages, because they also had to take care of their horses (Dem. Or. 4,28). Cavalry was thus relatively expensive, and except in Thessaly and Boeotia, it was only introduced comparatively late in Greece (in Athens 457 BC; in Sparta only 424 BC: Thuc. 4,55,2; cf. Xen. Hell. 6,4,11; the Sicilian tyrants appear already to have had large cavalry units before this: Hdt. 7,158). Senior ranks might receive triple or quadruple pay (Xen. An. 7,2,36; 7,6,1; cf. Aristot. Ath. pol. 42,3). In a system already practised by Sicilian tyrants in the 4th century BC (Diod. Sic. 14,78,1–3) and established in the Ptolemaic and Seleucid kingdoms in the Hellenistic period, soldiers were given land (a *kleros*), with larger parcels generally going to cavalrymen [10.83]. The fact that, over time, land in Egypt could also be bequeathed to women, placed an indirect financial burden on the Ptolemies, for landless men in these situations could no longer be recruited as soldiers. The number of garrison troops apparently increased over the course of the Hellenistic period [10.92], raising operating costs in turn. → Mercenaries were the first choice for this type of operation, and they probably had their equipment provided to them [7.206].

A.3. COSTS OF NAVIES

Navies created much bigger costs than land armies. It was expensive not only to build fleets, but also to maintain them. Aristot. Ath. Pol. 22,7 has often been cited as evidence that building one trireme cost one talent (but critical: [4.48–56]), and there were other fixed expenses in the cost of wharves and dockyards (Isoc. Or. 7,66: the cost of building Athenian dockyards was at least 1,000 talents) and in the cost of securing crews. The trireme superseded the pentecontor as the standard warship around the turn of the 6th/5th centuries. Because triremes required a much larger crew (200 men as against 80), the cost per ship increased. As a result, few private individuals owned triremes, and only tyrants, *poleis* or leagues could afford to maintain large navies. The introduction of the *misthos* (see above) may have been associated with this switch to triremes (earliest evidence: IG XII 9, 1273f. = SEG 41, 725; c. 525–500 BC; [9]), as perhaps the only possible way to recruit enough sailors. Sailors in the Peloponnesian War (→ Wars of note H.) initially received 1 drachma per day (later cut to 3 obols: Thuc. 6,31,3; 8,45,2; raised again to 4 obols: Xen. Hell. 1,5,6f.). This meant that the costs for long naval sieges were considerable (cf. the Siege of Samos in 440 BC; ten months, 60 ships: approx. 1,400 talents; IG I^3 363 = [6.55]; cf. Nep. Timoth. 1,2; [2.9–12]).

During the Hellenistic period, larger ships were put into service (e.g. the quinquereme with a crew of 270). This meant a considerable increase in costs if the number of vessels remained the same. Ptolemy II Philadelphus had 122 ships larger than triremes (Ath. 5,203d, including two with thirty banks of oars). The design of fortifications, siege technology and artillery also increased in importance during the Hellenistic period (cf. e.g. Diod. Sic. 20,85; 20,91). The actual costs of these measures cannot be quantified.

A.4. TOTAL COSTS AND FINANCING

The costs of individual elements occasionally make it possible to estimate the total costs of wars. The Peloponnesian War, for instance, appears to have cost the Athenians about 40,000 talents [5.262]. Ancient sources also sometimes make direct reference to total costs. The campaign of Artaxerxes II against Euagoras, for instance, is said to have cost more than 15,000 talents (Isoc. Or. 9,60).

Costs of war were met in different ways. During the Archaic period, polities used their own amassed wealth (Hom. Il. 18,291f.) or imposed the costs on the populace (Hom. Od. 19,196–198). Following the introduction of the *misthos*, booty seems no longer to have been shared out, meaning that it was now available for financing campaigns. Where booty and reserves were not sufficient, special taxes could be raised (*eisphorai*; Thuc. 3,19,1). Politicians and generals were often highly inventive when it came to finding new sources of money and cutting costs (Xen. Hell. 1,1,22: construction of a customs station; Aristot. Oec. 2,20b; 2,29a: special levy; 2,29d: shift in payment deadlines; 2,30: deception). If such measures did not suffice, precious metals in temples were accessed (Thuc. 2,24,1; 8,15,1; Pol. 10,27) or plundered (see e.g. Hdt. 3,57f.; 8,111f.; [3.268f.]). Wealthy allies helped out on occasion, as when the Persians aided the Spartans in the Peloponnesian War. Frequently, though, it was citizens who acted to defray costs. In 483/82 BC, wealthy Athenians became trierarchs for a year, taking on the costs of equipping one trireme each. Private individuals also took on maintenance costs in Lindus and elsewhere [3.257f.]. For shipbuilding in particular, there was a frequent need not only for money, but also for diplomatic skill, if sufficient quantities of usable timber were to be obtained (e.g. Hdt. 5,23,3; Xen. Hell. 6,1,11).

Ideally, of course, ongoing expenses could be covered by requisitions in enemy territory, so that in propitious circumstances, wars financed themselves (in terms of ongoing expenses at least) and might even make a profit. The shining example of this was the campaign of Alexander the Great (→ Generals of note, B.), who set out with a treasury of just 70 talents and 200 talents of debt (Plut. *Alexander* 15), but eventually carried off at least 180,000 talents from the Achaemenid Empire (Diod. Sic. 17,80,3; Str. 15,3,9; cf. Just. Epit. 12,1,3 and [1]). The considerable residue of this fortune remained available to Alexander's successors, the Diadochi, to finance their own wars.

☞ Booty

BIBLIOGRAPHY

[1] F. DE CALLATAŸ, Les trésors Achéménides et les monnayages d'Alexandre. Espèces immobilisées et espèces circulantes?, in: REA 91, 1989, 259–274 [2] C.W. FORNARA, On the Chronology of the Samian War, in: JHS 99, 1979, 7–19 [3] V. GABRIELSEN, Warfare and the State, in: P. SABIN / H. VAN WEES (eds.), The Cambridge History of Greek and Roman Warfare, 2007, 248–272 [4] V. GABRIELSEN, Die Kosten der athenischen Flotte in klassischer Zeit, in: F. BURRER / H. MÜLLER (eds.), Kriegskosten und Kriegsfinanzierung in der Antike, 2008, 46–73 [5] V. HANSON, A War like No Other. How the Athenians and Spartans Fought the Peloponnesian War, 2005 [6] R. MEIGGS / D. LEWIS, A Selection of Greek Historical Inscriptions to the End of the Fifth Century BC, 1969 [7] N.V. SEKUNDA, War and Society in Greece, in: B. CAMBELL / L.A. TRITLE (eds.), The Oxford Handbook of Warfare in the Classical World, 2013, 199–215 [8] M. TRUNDLE, Greek Mercenaries. From the Late Archaic Period to Alexander, 2004 [9] H. VAN WEES, 'Diejenigen, die segeln, sollen Sold erhalten'. Seekriegführung und -finanzierung im archaischen Eretria, in: F. BURRER /

H. MÜLLER (eds.), Kriegskosten und Kriegsfinanzierung in der Antike, 2008, 128–150 [10] E. VAN'T DACK, Sur l'évolution des institutions militaires lagides, in: A. CHASTAGNOL et al. (eds.), Armées et fiscalité dans le monde antique, 1977, 77–105 [11] D. WHITEHEAD, Who Equipped Mercenary Troops in Classical Greece?, in: Historia 40, 1991, 105–113.

PETER FRANZ MITTAG

B. ROMAN

B.1. Costs in the Republic
B.2. Costs in the Principate

Although Rome is recorded as having been involved in over 140 major military conflicts with domestic or external enemies during the Republican period (509–27 BC) and under the Principate (until AD 238) [8.189–193], not a single literary source gives reliable details of how much wars cost (even Liv. 45,40,1f., lacks specifics). Where ancient historians do touch on the costs of war, they do so mostly in regard to how much the *aerarium* contained before (Plin. HN 33,17 (55)) or after a war (Liv. 28,9,16–17) or at the accession of an emperor who went on to wage a war (Cass. Dio 74,8,3). More often, vague mention is simply made of the extraordinary expense of a war leading to the emptying of the *aerarium* (Val. Max. 5,6,8). The following discussion will thus take 'costs of war' to mean the sum of specific costs (e.g. for clothing, → armament, animals and equipment, army → supply and → pay), leaving as unanswerable the question of what portion was taken up by material assets requisitioned from the populace. There will be no discussion of costs incurred at the beginnings and ends of wars (e.g. → infrastructure, losses, embassies, ransom payments, settlements, → triumphs), or of those borne by the cities and inhabitants of the empire as a result of the state of war.

B.1. COSTS IN THE REPUBLIC
Little is known of the costs of war in the early Republic [1]; [9.4–41], but given that most conflicts at this period were local, involving no major troop movements, they were probably less than in the middle or late Republic. Soldiers of the early militia army also provided their own equipment, so that war costs were shared among the participants themselves (Liv. 1,43; Dion. Hal. Ant. Rom. 4,16–18). The first evidence for soldiers' kit being funded from the *aerarium* dates from the Second Punic War (218–201 BC; → Wars of note K.; Liv. 27,10,13, see also 44,16,1–4 (Third Macedonian War, 171–168): dispatch of 6,000 togas and 30,000 tunics to the war zone; at Pompeii, the price of a tunic was 15 sesterces (HS), although the dating is uncertain, see CIL IV 9108). During wartime, the *aerarium* was funded partly by a special contribution (*eisphora/tributum*) payable by the populace eligible for military service; ideally, this would be repaid from the booty (Dion. Hal. Ant. Rom. 4,19,1–4; 19,16,3).

Soldiers' pay was an essential component of the costs of war, and it was paid from public funds, probably beginning with the Siege of Veii (406–396 BC; Liv. 4,59,11)) – although at this date the payment may have been in kind, for the minting of Roman coins had not yet begun [3]. The first indication of how much a soldier was paid per month dates from the mid-2nd century BC (Pol. 6,39,12–15). Deductions were made for grain, clothing and additional weapons. Professionalization of the army became apparent in the 2nd century, although it probably began at the time of the Second Punic War. Altered → recruitment practices and the abolition of the link between military service and personal assets (Sall. Iug. 86,2f.; Plut. Marius 9,1) now demanded higher public expenditure. This is seen particularly clearly in the Senate's new expectation arising from the law introduced by C. Sempronius Graccus in 123 BC that the state should provide clothing for Roman soldiers (Plut. C. Gracchus 5,1). Besides the costs of pay and supplies, the cavalry represented a major cost of war. Sources from the late Republic show that some riders received publicly subsidized cavalry horses (Cic. Phil. 6,13). But because it was expensive to acquire, train and keep such animals, the Romans also sought → cavalry from among the *socii* ('allies') (Pol. 6,26,7) and mercenaries (Caes. B Gall. 7,13,1), who had to be paid. According to Varro (Ling. 8,71), a 'public horse' in the 1st century BC cost about 1,000 asses (see also P. CZ I 59093: 800 drachmae, but privately purchased). Rome first felt the need for its own navy during the First Punic War (264–241 BC) at the battle for Sicily. Costs for the construction and maintenance of Roman warships are rarely recorded (Plut. *Lucullus* 13,4: 3,000 talents during the Third Mithridatic War, 74–63 BC; Cic. Flacc. 30: 4.3 million sesterces (HS) for naval defences around Italy). How much was spent on the construction of dockyards and on wages is unknown.

Ascertaining exact costs of war in Republican Rome from literary sources ranges from difficult to impossible. Scholars therefore sometimes draw on numismatic evidence, assuming military causes behind abrupt changes in mint quantities or coin typologies [13]. Yet this approach is poorly suited to quantifying costs of war, for an increased need for money says nothing about how that money was used [2.405f.].

Although no total costs of war are recorded – surprisingly so for the Republic, given that the public finances were much more widely known at that period than in the Imperial period (Plut. Cato *minor* 18,5; [14.8f.]) –, the central authorities must have been able to estimate them in advance. That a basis existed for anticipating expenditures is hinted at, for example, by the remark that the triumvirs still lacked 200 million drachmae for war preparations even after proscriptions (App. Civ. 4,31), and the suggestion that costs of war were met from public funds (Liv. 27,10,11–13; 40,35,3ff.; Diod. Sic. 29,21), augmented where necessary by calculated special contributions (Liv. 23,48,9–49,4; 24,11,7–9; 26,35,1–3; 39,7,4f.; App. Civ. 5,67; Dion. Hal. Ant. Rom. 4,19,1–4; Cass. Dio 46,31,3). Other means of covering costs of war included financial donations from third parties (Jos. BI 15,6,7; Pol. 23,14,9), revenues from booty (App. Civ. 2,102; Liv. 26,14,8; 38,9,13; Plut. *Lucullus* 37,3f.; Jos. BI 1,8,8; Vell. Pat. 2,56,2), fines and tributes (Bell. Afr. 90; Liv. 33,29,12; Str. 11,14,10).

B.2. COSTS IN THE PRINCIPATE

The operation of the standing army of the Imperial period was no longer confined to times of war. Beginning in the reign of Augustus, it was permanently involved in protecting and shaping the Roman Empire (Cass. Dio 52,27). Unlike the Republican militia army, this professional force required constant financing in wartime and peacetime alike, as well as the maintenance of administrative structures in order to ensure its supplies and logistics (criticisms of the high cost of the military at the time: SHA Probus 23; Tac. Hist. 1,89). Although literary sources still lack exact costs of war for the Imperial period (Eutr. 8,13), occasional indications of payments suggest that calculations were being made as to the expected cost of military actions (e.g. Cass. Dio 79,27,1). Given the meticulous bureaucracy that kept detailed records of all military matters in the Imperial period (RMR; [15]), it seems likely that costs of war were also ascertained in advance and – if we are to believe Strabo (2,5,8; 4,5,3) – even subjected to cost-benefit analysis. According to his account, the only reason why the Roman Conquest of Britain had not yet taken place as he was writing was that the costs of such a war and of supplying the soldiers would have been uneconomical compared with the revenues from customs duties [11.71f.].

Within this professional army, not all legions took part in a war. Still, it was essential to ensure that they were reliably paid, especially those going into battle. Titus showed this when he interrupted the conquest of Jerusalem during the First Jewish War (AD 66–73/74; → Wars of note E.) to pay the *stipendium* (Jos. BI 5,9,1). Soldiers' pay was an important means of securing imperial power, such that the basic annual pay rate increased several times, from 900 sesterces (HS) for a legionary under Augustus to 7,200 HS under Maximinus Thrax [12.350]. Modern estimates of the cost of paying a legion for a year in the 1st century AD range from 158 million HS (including officers) [5.4] to about 184 million HS [15.213], the difference partly arising from the use of different legions as a basis for calculation. Given that actual troop strengths would be increased in times of war, these are certainly minimum estimates. Here again, deductions were made to cover costs of clothing, weapons and provisions (Tac. Ann. 1,17; P. Gen. Lat 1 = RMR 68), probably amounting to around 40 percent of a legionary's gross pay in the first century AD [12.360].

Besides payments for wages, other costs were incurred in wartime, such as money for → infrastructure and transport (perhaps 30 million HS [5.4]), mercenaries' pay, *donativa*, animals and war material [15.217–219], the question arising in the latter case whether production or purchase would be more economical. At the very least, supplies of arrowheads, spearheads and projectiles would need to be secured during a war, and these 'single-use' weapons were probably manufactured by the army's own craftsmen working on site. Weapons requiring more complex manufacture, on the other hand, were probably procured [15.177–198]. The contribution of public finances to this is difficult to assess, for the sources also show weapons being privately acquired or held by soldiers as their own private property (P. Giss. Apoll. 6; perhaps P. Princ. II 57; SB XVI 12609 (= ZPE 36 (1979), 109–11)). Wierschowski suggests that the total value for a soldier's equipment was 200–300 *denarii*, and he estimates that the value of the entire army's personal weapons and equipment was between 60 and 90 million *denarii* [15.202]. Also to be considered was the material value of the cavalry. The price of a public cavalry horse awarded to a soldier is recorded as 125 *denarii* for the 3rd century (P. Dura 56a). Papyri from Egypt give prices for horses between 72 and 2,800 (perhaps even 5,000) drachmae in the Imperial period [4.296–300]. Wierschowski, who assumes a total of 100,000 horses, accordingly estimates that the Imperial-period cavalry was worth at least 12.5 million *denarii* [15.219].

The city of Rome alone could not supply an army of 40,000–60,000 soldiers (Tac. Hist. 2,87; 3,33) along with its train in wartime. Thus, the provinces along the marching route were required to provide goods for sale or to make special contributions [10.256]; [6.164–262], as, for example, in Egypt, where Caracalla's Parthian campaign requisitioned → camels (BGU I 266) and quantities of money and grain (P. Oxy. XLIII 3091; P. Stras. VII 688; P. Yale III 137). Other means of financing wars included levies made by the provinces (Vell. Pat. 2,39,2) and donations by the emperor (Tac. Ann. 15,18,2), but these were exceptional cases.

☞ **Administration; Supply**

Bibliography

[1] J. ARMSTRONG, Breaking the Rules? Irregularities in the Recruitment of the Early Roman Army (509–c. 450 BC), in: E. BRAGG et al. (eds.), Beyond the Battlefields, 2008, 47–66 [2] J.-P. BOST, Guerre et finances de Marc Aurèle à Maximin (161–238), in: J. ANDREAU et al. (eds.), Économie antique. La guerre dans les économies antiques, 2000, 399–415 [3] A.M. BURNETT, The Beginnings of Roman Coinage, in: AIIN 36, 1989, 33–65 [4] H.-J. DREXHAGE, Preise, Mieten, Pachten, Kosten und Löhne im römischen Ägypten bis zum Regierungsantritt Diokletians, 1991 [5] T. FRANK (ed.), An Economic Survey of Ancient Rome, vol. 5, 1959 [6] A. JÖRDENS, Statthalterliche Verwaltung in der römischen Kaiserzeit, 2009 [7] R. MACMULLEN, The Roman Emperors' Army Costs, in: Latomus 43, 1984, 571–580 [8] H. MÜLLER (ed.), 1000 & 1 Talente. Visualisierung antiker Kriegskosten, 2009 [9] M.M. SAGE, The Republican Roman Army, 2008 [10] M.A. SPEIDEL, Auf kürzestem Weg und gut verpflegt an die Front, in: M.A. SPEIDEL, Heer und Herrschaft im Römischen Reich der Hohen Kaiserzeit, 2009, 255–271 [11] M.A. SPEIDEL, Geld und Macht. Die Neuordnung des staatlichen Finanzwesens unter Augustus, in: M.A. SPEIDEL, Heer und Herrschaft im Römischen Reich der Hohen Kaiserzeit, 2009, 53–84 [12] M.A. SPEIDEL, Roman Army Pay Scales, in: M.A. SPEIDEL, Heer und Herrschaft im Römischen Reich der Hohen Kaiserzeit, 2009, 349–380 [13] W. SZAIVERT, Kriegskosten. Eine Spurensuche in der antiken Numismatik, in: F. BURRER et al. (eds.), Kriegskosten und Kriegsfinanzierung in der Antike, 2008, 161–173 [14] W. SZAIVERT / R. WOLTERS, Löhne, Preise, Werte, 2005 [15] L. WIERSCHOWSKI, Heer und Wirtschaft, 1984 [16] R. WOLTERS, Nummi Signati, 1999.

STEFANIE SCHMIDT

Cowardice

Greek had a number of words denoting concepts of cowardice with a range of nuances. These included *deilia* ('state of being filled with dread'), *kakia* ('[moral] badness'), *anandria* ('want of manhood') and *apsychia* ('swoon'/'want of spirit'/'faintheartedness'). Latin expressed 'cowardice' in terms of *ignavia* ('listlessness') and *timiditas* ('timidity'). Cowardice was thought of as an inner disposition that expressed itself in certain behaviours. According to Aristotle, it consisted of a shortage of confidence and an excess of fear (Eth. Nic. 1115b33–1116a3; 1109a,1–9). As is also clear from his usage, the concept related to actual dangers, especially the danger of death, so that the terminology was not used in a wider sense, as it is today (e.g. 'cowardly decisions'). This shortage of courage, to which was attached an aura of unseemliness, was particularly glaring in a military context and expressed itself in specific physical manifestations. Homer describes the symptoms: a change in complexion, shrinking in unease, chattering teeth and rapid heartbeat (Il. 13,276–283). Other typical behaviours Homer describes are 'cowering down' (*kataptossein*) and fleeing in panic. In Sparta, *tresas* ('runaway') was the technical term for 'coward' (e.g. Plut. *Agesilaus* 30). Yet fleeing – like any other way of avoiding battle – can be induced by many factors other than cowardice. The behaviour in itself thus admits a range of possible interpretations.

As far as can be ascertained, legislative texts recognize this ambiguity. The *Digest*, for instance, describes grounds for declaring an *emansio* (absence without leave) pardonable (Dig. 49,16, 4,15). As for an accusation of desertion, factors such as rank and number of deserters had a bearing on the severity of punishment (Dig. 49,16,5pr.; see [5.147–150]). In general, though, what counted most of all was behaviour. Cowardice is seldom given as a motivation (cf. Cod. Theod. 7,18,4,3). By contrast, Attic law certainly did make a connection between cowardice and behaviours such as desertion (*lipotaxion*), refusal to perform military service (*astrateia*) and discarding one's shield. Lysias (14,5) cites a law requiring fellow soldiers to pass judgment 'on anyone who, out of cowardice (*deilias heneka*), deserted the ranks and retreated while the others fought on' (on the distinction between *astrateia* and *lipotaxion* [3]; [4]; [1.143f.]). Aeschines reports Solon's having stipulated that anyone refusing military service should be punished on par with deserters and cowards, since there had been prosecutions for cowardice (In Ctes. 175). Andocides (1,74) also mentions a ship that was kept away from battle. In this instance, cowardice was not seen as the motivating factor, but as an additional behaviour. Nevertheless, doubts have sometimes been raised as to whether there really were prosecutions for cowardice, or whether accusations were always made on the basis of specific failings [7]. Roman law stipulated the death penalty for desertion or, in the case of mass desertion, the *decimatio* [5.120–129]. The main punishment in the Greek world was ostracism, that is, exclusion from public life (Sparta: Plut. *Agesilaus* 30, Xen. Lac. Pol. 9,1–6, according to Lycurg. Leocr. 129f. – though probably exaggerating – death; Athens: Aeschin. In Ctes. 176; Dem. Or. 59,27).

Being closely interwoven with issues of honour, status and reputation, but at the same time governed by a degree of subjectivity (as is clear from the terminological confusion that was exploited for political purposes on Corcyra, Thuc. 3,82f.), the concept of cowardice was readily available for rhetorical use: for purposes of mockery (e.g. the 'shield-dropper' Cleonymus [6]), discrediting opponents (especially political ones) [2.128–142] or motivational paraenesis [8.31–75]. Because cowardice implied a want of manhood, the term was heavily gendered [9.40–44]. Cowards were often

called 'women' or compared to women (e.g. Hom. Il. 7,96). Another stereotype was that of the archer, fighting from afar and shunning close combat like a 'coward' (Hom. Il. 11, 385–390; Eur. Herc. 157–161).
☞ Honour; Valour

BIBLIOGRAPHY

SOURCES
[1] LYSIAS, Selected Speeches, 1989.

SECONDARY LITERATURE
[2] M. CHRIST, The Bad Citizen at Classical Athens, 2006 [3] D. HAMEL, Coming to Terms with λιποτάξιον, in: GRBS 39, 1998, 361–405 [4] M.H. HANSEN, Lysias 14 and 15. A Note on the γραφή ἀστρατείας, in: G.W. BAKEWELL / J.P. SICKINGER (eds.), Gestures. Essays in Ancient History. FS Alan Boegehold, 2003, 278–279 [5] S. PHANG, Roman Military Service. Ideologies of Discipline in the Late Republic and Early Principate, 2008 [6] I.C. STOREY, The 'Blameless Shield' of Kleonymos, in: RhM 132, 1989, 247–261 [7] T. THALHEIM, Δειλίας γραφή, in: RE 8, 1901, 2384 [8] J. WISSMANN, Motivation und Schmähung. Feigheit in der Ilias und in der griechischen Tragödie, 1997 [9] J. WISSMANN, Cowardice and Gender in the Iliad and Greek Tragedy, in: D. MUNTEANU (ed.), Emotion, Genre and Gender in Classical Antiquity, 2011, 35–55.

JESSICA WISSMANN

Customs of war

A. General customs
B. Declarations of war and commencement of hostilities
C. Treatment of the vanquished

A. GENERAL CUSTOMS
There were no legal documents regulating warfare in Ancient Greece. Instead, generally accepted standards of behaviour prevailed, which were understood by different groups to varying degrees. Thucydides (4,97,2) mentions 'the laws of the Hellenes' (*tanomima ton Hellenon*). Polybius (5,11) criticizes Philip V of Macedon for the damage done in his name to temples and statues, for sanctuaries were regarded as inviolable – in contrast to legitimate economic damage done in accordance with the 'laws of war' (*hoitou polemou nomoi*). Herodotus (7,136) has the Persian king Xerxes, whose heralds were killed by the Spartans in defiance of all convention, speak of 'the laws of all humanity' (*ta panton anthropon nomima*). The motivation underlying these unwritten laws was fear of divine retribution. Sophocles' Antigone emphasizes the obligation on all people to obey 'the unwritten and immutable statutes of the gods' (*agrapta kasphale theon nomima*; Soph. Ant. 454f.).

The early Greek states maintained at least three forms of relation: no relation at all, war or amity. Various kinds of individual or group violence could occupy the space between the first two of these – anything short of all-out war (*phaneros polemos*). The most frequent was *syle*. This word denoted an act of retribution for damage or culpability attributed to members of a foreign polity. In Archaic and Classical Greece, judicial compensation was only possible within the boundaries of the individual *polis*. Raids were still causing wars even in the Hellenistic period (Pol. 22,4,15).

B. DECLARATIONS OF WAR AND COMMENCEMENT OF HOSTILITIES
A herald was sent to convey a formal declaration of war to an enemy (Pol. 4,5,8; 4,26,7; 4,36,6; 4,53,2). Every polity had such an official, (*keryx*). He was untouchable as a person (Hdt. 7,136), being under the protection of Hermes, messenger of the gods, whose staff (the *kerykeion*) he carried as a symbol of this status. In Sparta, this office was held by the Talthybiad clan (Hdt. 6,60; 7,134). The Argives appointed two heralds (Xen. Hell. 4,7,3). As soon as two states entered into war against each other, they communicated only through heralds (Thuc. 2,1).

Emissaries (*presbeis*) who were commissioned to carry messages or negotiate conditions were not inviolable. The herald was therefore usually sent before them, to obtain approval for sending an emissary. Various forms of truce (*sponde*, literally 'drink-offering', because ceremonial libations were poured when it was concluded; cf. Diod. Sic. 3,71,6) were negotiated between combatant polities. An armistice applied during all Panhellenic festivals (Isoc. Or. 4,43). Prior to the Olympic Games, the Elians first declared an armistice in Elis, then sent messengers to all other polities to announce the same there (Thuc. 5,49).

On a local level, there were sacred months in which important religious festivals requiring an armistice took place. An inscription of 367/66 BC in Athens (R&O 35) protests against the arrest in Aetolia, 'contrary to the general laws of the Greeks', of two messengers announcing the *spondai* ('truces') for the Eleusinian Mysteries of Demeter and Kore, after the Aetolian League had already accepted the truce. The month of Karneios was sacred to the Dorians. The festivities of the *Karneia* prevented the Spartans from sending a fighting force to Marathon (→ Battles of note F.; 490 BC) and an appropriately large body of men to Thermopylae (480). The *Hyakinthia* also delayed their deployment to Plataeae (479; Hdt. 6,106; 7,206; 9,11). The dates of these ceremonial armistices were open to manipulation. For instance, the Argives (who were Dorians) marched into Epidaurus on the 27th day of the month prior to the *Karneia*, then declared every further day on which they plundered Epidaurian territory still to be the 27th day of this preceding month (Thuc. 5,54,3). The Spartans invaded Argos as its populace declared a sacred armistice not on the usual day, but at the moment the invasion was to begin (Xen. Hell. 4,7,2).

Following hostilities, one side was left in possession of the battlefield. At some point, it became customary for the victor to build a monument to victory (*tropaion*) there. The oldest surviving *tropaion* is at Marathon (although it was built long after the battle there). Sending a herald to collect the dead for burial amounted to an admission of defeat (Diod. Sic. 17,68,4; Just. Epit. 6,6,9). The victor sometimes set conditions for the release of the bodies. After Lysander's defeat and death outside Haliartus, the Spartan king Pausanias agreed to leave Boeotia after the retrieval of their fallen (Xen. Hell. 3,5,24).

Following their defeat at the Battle of Delium (424 BC), the Athenians sent a herald to the Boeotians to obtain the release of their dead, but this was refused, because the Athenians had occupied and fortified the temple at Delium, thereby contravening the 'laws of the Hellenes' (*ta nomima ton hellenon*; Thuc. 4,97–101). More than 17 days passed before the Boeotians finally drove the Athenians out of Delium and allowed them to take their dead home. Besides the fear of divine wrath, combatants also obeyed established customs of war in the hopes that their enemies would do the same.

C. Treatment of the vanquished

The treatment of prisoners of war depended on the conditions negotiated prior to capitulation. The Athenians, surrendering on Sicily in 413 BC, trusted in the condition that they would not be killed or caused to die as a result of captivity or starvation. However, the Syracusans had not taken into account the sheer number of prisoners (7,000) coming into their care. They kept the Athenians in quarries, where many did indeed die (Thuc. 7,82,2; 7,87).

When a city surrendered after a siege, negotiating lenient conditions was particularly difficult. When Methone surrendered to Philip II, the condition was that its citizens were allowed to take only one cloak with them as they left the city. Philip destroyed the city and distributed its goods among the Macedonians (Diod. Sic. 16,34,5). Prior to the capitulation of Potidaea, the Athenian generals agreed that the men could leave the city with one cloak each, the women with two, but also sufficient money for their journey (Thuc. 2,70,3). Athenians later chastised the generals for the generosity of these concessions. When Mytilene capitulated, its populace had to accept that Athens would decide its fate. They were permitted to send an embassy to Athens, but the besieging army was admitted into the city. The Athenians' first decision was to kill all adult males and sell the → women and children into slavery. Although this decision was later reversed, over a thousand Mytileneans who had organized the secession from the Delian League had already been executed (Thuc. 3,28,1; 3,36,2; 3,50,1). When Plataeae conceded defeat to the Spartans, it was agreed that no one would be punished unlawfully. The men were then killed and the women sold as slaves (Thuc. 3,52,3–68,3). When the Melians capitulated, they accepted the condition that their fate would be decided by the Athenians, who opted to kill all adult males and sell the women and children into slavery (Thuc. 5,116,4). In 223 BC, when Mantinea surrendered to the forces of the Macedonian king Antigonus Doson and the Achaean League, the leading citizens were put to death, other men sent as prisoners to Macedoni and the remainder along with woman and children enslaved. Of the money thereby earned, two thirds went to the Macedonians and one third to the Achaeans. According to Plutarch, while this was commensurate with the 'law of retribution' (*ton tes amynes nomos*), it was not in keeping with the Greek spirit (Plut. *Aratus* 45,4f.).

☞ Law of war; Military law

Bibliography
[1] W. Kendrick Pritchett, The Greek State at War, pt. 5, 1991 [2] K.A. Raaflaub (ed.), War and Peace in the Ancient World, 2007.

Nicholas Sekunda

Death

A. Introduction
B. Battles
C. Burial grounds near camps

A. Introduction

Although no comprehensive account of soldiers' funeral rites is yet available, the case studies published suggest that they did not differ from civilian rites, although naturally a soldier's place of origin and the local customs of where they were buried need to be taken into account. Besides a basic set of common and shared ritual customs, burial places also attest that local practices were followed. The necropolis at Mainz-Weisenau, for example, shows no distinction between the graves and burial rites of soldiers from elsewhere and the local dead [15]; [16]. The large necropolis of the Adriatic fleet at Classe (Ravenna) [10] also indicates that burial practices for the dead orgininating from various regions of the empire were very similar. Even so, some differences in practice did surface, particularly during the first century of the Principate. For instance, funerary stelae of soldiers from the east buried in Italy took on an Italic appearance, while soldiers from Italy buried at Mainz were given portrayals that were not usual in their homeland. The same is apparent at the necropoleis in Nijmegen and Haltern, although the latter also displays the peculiarity of having male graves concentrated in one area and most females graves in another. It has been established at Nijmegen that soldiers' graves contain few if any grave goods – generally no more than a jug and a little everyday pottery – while the civilian burials follow the Gaulish and Germanic customs of having relatively abundant grave goods. In this burial ground, dating from the early years of the Principate, legionaries were thus tending to follow the customs of Italy rather than those of the northern provinces. Grave types and attested rituals, however, are largely the same.

This alignment may date from the days of the permanent army camp, which naturally tended towards standardization in burial customs that then continued outside in the civilian burial grounds. The situation was certainly different in the Republican period, when the dead were buried by their comrades in situ. This was unlike the military necropoleis of the Imperial period, which were laid out along the roads leading to the camps and left no visible archaeological trace. As can be inferred from the inscriptions, these camp burial grounds were not 'military cemeteries' in the modern sense, but 'ordinary' burial grounds in which anyone active in the camp might be buried, whether a soldier or not. The rites were the same as for civilians, and were dictated more by local custom than by the fact that the deceased had belonged to the military.

B. Battles

Funeral ceremonies and burial sites associated with battlefields were a different matter. Here, mass graves were prepared for soldiers who had fallen in battle [9.173–176]. Famous episodes in literature even describe collective funerals carried out by the Romans as soon as they could return to the battlefield (Tac. Ann. 1,61f.). Generally, the same rites were practised in military as in civilian life, apart from this creation of mass graves and grave mounds (Liv. 10,27,2; 9f.; Suet. Cal. 3,6; Tac. Ann. 1,62) and the parades (*decursiones*) that had to be carried out in accordance with the rites of the *funus militare* ('military funeral'; the term is from Liv. 3,43,7). We know of funerals with military honours for emperors and *caesares* [12] and from mythological descriptions (Verg. Aen. 11,59–99). Livy describes the rituals of the military funeral arranged by Hannibal for T. Sempronius Gracchus on his death in 212 BC (Liv. 25,17,4f.). As a sign of respect, Hannibal is said to have ordered his troops to perform a parade before the pyre built at the entrance to the Carthaginian camp. It involved Iberian troops performing their cultural dances, while units from other ethnicities in the Punic army conducted their respective traditional marchpasts and movements. According to a different tradition, Gracchus was buried in the camp in the presence of the army and the populace of Beneventum. Livy's account corresponds to what we know of imperial funerals. Here too, *equites* ('cavalry') or legionaries paraded around the pyre, possibly performing a Pyrrhica (Hdn. 4,2,9). The emperor's body was borne by soldiers, sometimes military tribunes. The pyre of Augustus was lit by centurions. All these practices probably replicated customs of the *funus militare*.

In certain circumstances, monuments were put up at the site of a battle to mark the place of the funeral ceremonies. The deceased who were buried at these collective ceremonies were denied the usual mortuary cult, since they were being buried far from home. Lamenting this, some (as in the case of the centurion Marcus Caelius at Xanten: CIL XIII 8648; ILS 2244; cf. [13]) built cenotaphs, at which friends likely gathered for annual ceremonies. Empty graves have also been discovered at Haltern am See (Westphalia). There are a number of possible explanations for why these graves were left unoccupied, but one is that they represented modest cenotaphs for soldiers, fallen in the area, whose bodies had not been retrieved [2.70]. Unlike in the case of M. Caelius, however, no stelae exist to answer this question. In the

Republican period, when battles were still being fought close to Rome, the bodies of fallen soldiers were sometimes brought back to the city. Attesting to this in the period of the Civil Wars is the funerary inscription of Sergius Mena (ILLRP 969), who died in battle in the year 90 BC and was buried at Rome. To address unease among conscripts triggered by such funeral ceremonies, a senatorial decree contemporaneous with Mena required the dead to be buried where they fell, and their bodies not to be brought back to Rome (App. Civ. 1,43,195).

In the wake of the battle in the Teutoburg Forest (→ Battles of note, J.), an altar was built in memory of Drusus, probably at the place where he died. It was destroyed by Germanic tribes in AD 16, along with the grave mound built shortly before by order of Germanicus for those fallen in the 'Varian Disaster' (Tac. Ann. 2,7,3f.). Germanicus had the Altar of Drusus restored, and took part in the ensuing *decursio* ('military pageant') along with his men. The *Drususstein* ('Stone of Drusus') at Mainz is located within the burial ground of the camp; it is almost certainly this cenotaph to Drusus. One of the better-preserved grave mounds is the Tropaeum Traiani of Adamklissi (AD 107/08), dedicated to Mars Ultor. It commemorates the victory over the Dacii and Sarmatae, but it was also intended to honour the soldiers who died in this war: the names of over 3,000 legionaries and auxiliaries are inscribed on the walls of the mausoleum (→ Wars of note C.) [1]; [14].

C. BURIAL GROUNDS NEAR CAMPS

The only distinction between municipal burial grounds and those at military camps was that in the latter case, relations, friends and associations generally did not tend the graves. The social world of these burial grounds was in constant flux. Soldiers were often deployed elsewhere, and only comrades-in-arms would take responsibility for a grave and the annual funerary cult. For this reason, soldiers automatically paid half their *donativa* ('supplememtary monetary payments') into a fund administered by the *signifer* ('standard bearer') to pay for their funerals (Veg. Mil. 2,20). Junior officers had associations charged with funeral management. Anyone who died was entitled to a payment of 500 *denarii* for his funeral ceremonies, which would be carried out by comrades-in-arms or kin. Veterans on discharge from the military were able to join a veterans' association that would deal with their funeral when necessary.

Some soldiers' graves, regardless of whether or not those buried there died in active service, show evidence of military culture. Tombs frequently bear funerary poems, generally composed in imitation of the works of Roman poets (cf. [4]). At Aquincum and Ulcisia Castra in Pannonia inferior, and at Raphia in Syria Palaestina, three inscriptions connected to soldiers' funerals have been found using the same funerary poem, written by a certain Lupus [5].

☞ Battle; Religion

BIBLIOGRAPHY
[1] G. AMIOTTI, Il 'monumento ai caduti' di Adamclissi (avec la bibliographie), in: M. SORDI (ed.), Dulce et decorum est pro patria mori. La morte in combattimento nell'antichità, 1990, 207–213 [2] S. BERKE, Die römische Nekropole von Haltern, in: S. BERKE / T. MATTERN (eds.), Römische Gräber augusteischer und tiberischer Zeit im Westen des Imperiums, 2013, 58–92 [3] S. BERKE / T. MATTERN (eds.), Römische Gräber augusteischer und tiberischer Zeit im Westen des Imperiums, 2013 [4] A. BOWMAN et al., Vindolanda Tablets Online, Inventarnummer 85.137, n.d. [5] W. ECK, Judäa – Syria Palästina. Die Auseinandersetzung einer Provinz mit römischer Politik und Kultur, 2014, 284–295 (first in: ZPE 184, 2012, 117–125) [6] H. VAN ENCKEVORT / E.N.A. HEIRBAUT, Soldaten und Zivilisten. Frührömische Gräber aus Nijmegen, in: S. BERKE / T. MATTERN (eds.), Römische Gräber augusteischer und tiberischer Zeit im Westen des Imperiums, 2013, 109–122 [7] S. GIORCELLI, Il funus militare, in: F. HINARD (ed.), La mort au quotidien dans le monde romain, 1995, 235–242 [8] A. KOLB / J. FUGMANN, Tod in Rom. Grabinschriften als Spiegel römischen Lebens, 2008 [9] P. KRENTZ et al., War, in: P. SABIN et al. (eds.), The Cambridge History of Greek and Roman Warfare, vol. 1, 2007, 147–185 [10] C. LEONI et al., Scavi in aree umide. Le necropoli di Classe. Ravenna, in: J. SCHEID (ed.), Pour une archéologie du rite. Nouvelles perspectives de l'archéologie funéraire (Collection de l'École française de Rome 407), 2008, 89–104 [11] M.L. RICCI et al., Motivi dell'oltretomba virgiliana nei Carmina latina epigrafica, in: Atti del Convegno virgiliano di Brindisi nel bimillenario della morte, 1983, 199–234 [12] J.-C. RICHARD, Les aspects militaires des funérailles impériales, in: Mélanges d'archéologie et d'histoire 78, 1966, 313–325 [13] H.-J. SCHALLES / S. WILLER (eds.), Marcus Caelius. Tod in der Varusschlacht, 2009 [14] B. TURNER, War Losses and Worldview. Re-Viewing the Roman Funerary Altar at Adamclisi, in: AJPh 134, 2013, 277–304 [15] M. WITTEYER, Grabbestattung und Beigabenausstattung in der Gräberstraße von Mainz-Weisenau, in: A. HAFFNER / S. VON SCHNURBEIN, Kelten, Germanen, Römer im Mittelgebirgsraum zwischen Luxemburg und Thüringen. Archäologische und naturwissenschaftliche Forschungen zum Kulturwandel unter der Einwirkung Roms in den Jahrhunderten um Christi Geburt, 2000, 320–343 [16] M. WITTEYER / P. FASOLD, Des Lichtes beraubt. Totenehrung in der römischen Gräberstraße von Mainz-Weisenau, 1995

JOHN SCHEID

Descriptions of war

A. Monuments with Greek inscriptions: Greek and Hellenistic periods
B. Monuments with Latin inscriptions
C. Greek literature
D. Latin literature

A. Monuments with Greek inscriptions: Greek and Hellenistic periods

A.1. Monuments with inscriptions
A.2. Legal texts
A.3. Honorific decrees
A.4. Lists and accounts
A.5. Votive inscriptions
A.6. Funerary inscriptions
A.7. The long life of inscriptions

A.1. Monuments with inscriptions

Unlike historical texts (cf. → Descriptions of war C.; → Sources B.2.), inscriptions on stone rarely offer complete military narratives. Nevertheless, they are important sources in the field of Ancient Greek warfare. For one thing, they lend weight to inferences drawn from historical narratives, and for another, they contain information of a different kind than what historical narratives report, although few inscriptions describe a war from its outbreak to its end. The pervasive effects of warfare on life produced many inscriptions that implicity or explicitly address war (→ Consequences of war). Inscriptions on objects and those recorded in literary sources (e.g. by Pausanias) portray almost all aspects of war: military organization and alliances; defensive measures; causes of war; participants' ideologies; the processes of a campaign (e.g. → equipment, tactics, → pay); the outcomes of battles; → consequences of war; and memories of people and events. Epigraphic sources thus preserve information about political, economic, social and cultural aspects of war. Like all written documents, however, they cannot be taken as direct expressions of historical reality. The motives and prejudices of the people who commissioned a monument must be taken into account along with those of the people (and groups) who were to read the inscriptions.

The content of an inscription communicated its message in conjunction with the object on which it was inscribed and the venue where it was placed. The form and appearance of the object bearing the inscription – which was often, but by no means always, a stela – and any accompanying decoration (e.g. a relief or statue) contributed to the sense and reception of the text (→ Representations of war). The expressive content worked together with the narrative content [3]. In an era when few could read, the visual impact of an inscription may even have been greater than the impact of its words [8]. The physical venue of the text was similarly important. The location chosen for exhibition (cemeteries, sanctuaries, public places, gymnasia) and the objects and rituals of the environment would influence how people read and/or viewed the words of the inscription.

A.2. Legal texts

Legal decrees offer a wide range of testimonies regarding ancient warfare. The Decree of Themistocles, for instance, gives a vivid description of the Athenians' preparations in response to the Persian threat (ML 23). Edicts that address alliances between two or more parties are particularly frequent. The stelae into which they were chiselled supply legal details as well as the treaty text and/or the oath sworn (→ Alliances). Defensive alliances secured both parties military support if attacked, either for a specified time or indefinitely. Offensive alliances laid out the militray aims of the treaty partners. Agreements made by leagues of *poleis* were more complex, including information on the leadership and organization of the leage and/or giving lists of members (R&O 22; 76; Austin 50).

Some inscriptions give the → oaths that soldiers reportedly swore before the battle or as part of a battle ritual. These reveal what was considered to be the ideal mentality for combatants (→ Esprit de corps). The oath of the *ephebes*, for instance, drew on concepts of shame, loyalty and competition (R&O 88). An oath could also help facilitate reconciliation between groups. Eumenes I and his → mercenaries, for example, swore an oath after a rebellion (Austin 230).

Epistles, especially from kings, complemented legal texts in the Hellenistic period. These would have been first written on organic material, then transferred to stone and thereby transformed into public monuments. They described the purported reasons for war and/or peace, settled disputes, outlined conditions of reconciliation and affirmed and strengthened personal and political relationships (Austin 6; 38; 53; 66; 175).

A.3. Honorific decrees

Honours for individuals or groups were decided or declared by elections and announced in public inscriptions. They were part of a system intended to encourage loyalty and preparedness, particularly among the elite. These inscriptions became more common from the 4th century BC onwards, especially under the Hellenistic kings, as politics became more personal and *poleis* were eager to gain the goodwill of powerful rulers. Inscriptions give various reasons for honours, which might include valorous deeds in battle, military service in a broader sense or financial or logistical support to the city in wartime (R&O 2; 4; Austin 54f.; 62; → Honours; → Honour). A certain Phanocritus was even acknowledged for passing on information that was not acted upon (R&O 19). Those honoured received the distinction of an inscription along with privileges such as a golden crown, a statue, tax exemptions and citizenship.

A.4. LISTS AND ACCOUNTS

Thanks to the use of inscriptions for recording the public finances and records of Greek city-states, information concerning wars has been preserved that could never be obtained from historical narratives (→ Infrastructure). The considerable and persistent expenditures of war are documented in stone, from the maintenance of armies to the costs of a defeat – or indeed of a victory (→ Costs of war). Although sporadic inscriptions cannot be used to determine precisely how much a war cost, seen as a whole the epigraphic corpus attests to the complexity of administrative and financial aspects of military affairs. For example, inscriptions record the preparations for a major expedition (ML 78) and the financial contributions for a joint campaign (R&O 57). They also document the costs incurred for building and maintaining → fortifications [7.26, 116f.]. Naval inventories reveal how complex and costly it was to maintain → fleets and shed light on fluctuations in their size and strength [10.12–24]. Inscriptions also record reparation payments (R&O 67).

A.5. VOTIVE INSCRIPTIONS

There are also inscriptions on votive gifts presented to the gods after military successes, including statues, buildings and booty – all as fruits harvested from war, offered in thanksgiving (→ Religion). Individuals or *poleis* financed these votive offerings and the texts that accompanied them. Kings often commissioned such works in the Hellenistic period. Texts were often quite short, simply naming the donor and the god (or gods) to whom the monument was dedicated, generally along with the deity worshipped at the sanctuary concerned [2.61]. Longer inscriptions might mention the battle site, the participants in the battle, the name of the artist, technical terms related to the offering – e.g. *aparche* ('firstlings'), *akrothinia* (offering from → booty) or *dekate* (tenth part of the booty, i.e. tithe) – and comments on the battle or on the object donated (Austin 231).

Giving thanks to the gods for a victory derived from the belief that the gods played a fundamental role in military successes. A victory granted by the gods was thereafter considered just. The Athenians, for example, claimed that the first military victory of their Cleisthenic democracy had extinguished the *hybris* of the Boeotians and Chalcidians (ML 15). Under the *do-ut-des* ('I give, so that you may give') system of Greek religion, the act of making an inscription was meant to secure ongoing divine approval for such military activities. Votive inscriptions gave visible expression to the donor's piety, while also publicizing their heroic deeds and close relationship with the gods. In the Hellenistic period, votive gifts bolstered the legitimacy of monarchical authority (Austin 231). A votive inscription reached a particularly large audience if it was placed in a sanctuary of Panhellenic reach.

A.6. FUNERARY INSCRIPTIONS

Inscriptions on gravestones, whether privately or publicly commissioned, document the human price of war (→ Death). They attest to heavy losses, as well as to the mourning and suffering brought about by the loss of often young relatives and friends (IG I^3 1194bis). Some mortuary inscriptions also supply information about the ideology of wars. Funeral epigrams to the fallen and those who died away from the battlefield recall notable feats in battle to honour the dead, highlight their service to the community and/or emphasize their leadership qualities.

The simplest texts of this kind are found on Spartan gravestones, which were inscribed 'in war' (IG V,1 701–710; 918; 921; 1124; 1125; 1320; 1591). Other funerary inscriptions were more substantial and creative (IG I^3 503/4), but the outcome of the event referenced was always less important than the outstanding qualities of the deceased, especially courage and valour (*arete*). The language of these inscriptions, sometimes composed in sophisticated metrical verse, served to praise the dead, comfort the bereaved and inspire the living to emulate the example of the deceased hero (IG I^3 1194bis).

Public lists giving the names of fallen combatants made the military force appear as a community collective. The format of these lists sometimes reflected the political structure of the society. In democratic Athens, for example, names were given without patronymics and listed by *phyle*. Accompanying epigrams honoured the dead, and in some city-states they elevated them to the status of heroes (Sim. fr. 531). At the same time, these texts carefully transferred renown (*kleos*) from the deceased to the community for which they fought. Events in which the community enjoyed success or suffered failure were woven into a long history of conflicts and framed by ideological principles such as Grecian freedom. Thus, commemoration was not confined to victories, but also extended to catastrophes, which were ascribed to supernatural forces (IG I^3 1163d–f) or portrayed as part of an ongoing struggle (*agon*) [5.104–108].

A.7. THE LONG LIFE OF INSCRIPTIONS

As physical objects, inscriptions were subject to modification and assorted revisions over time. To some extent, they were living documents. Their words might be augmented, emended ('improved') or removed as perspectives changed or new information came to light. The name of the Spartan general Pausanias, for example, was effaced from the Serpent Column at Delphi (ML 27). Conversely, *polis* names were steadily added to the prospectus of the Second Athenian League (R&O 22).

An object bearing an inscription might 'attract' other monuments that dealt with similar events or were erected to compete with or surpass it. This was a phenomenon associated mainly (but not exclusively) with burial grounds [5.66–76] and Panhellenic sanctuaries [12]. For example, countless burials of fallen Athenians surrounded a monument to the Marathonomakoi (→ Battles of note, F.), and donations given by Spartans and Arcadians occupied the same space at Delphi. Although many monuments were meant to be permanent [2.33], they could be damaged or destroyed through natural or human forces [4]. Some inscriptions even stipulated that other existing inscriptions should be destroyed (R&O 44).

☞ Sources, C. Latin inscriptions

BIBLIOGRAPHY

SOURCES

[1] Schenkungen hellenistischer Herrscher an griechische Städte und Heiligtümer, pt. 1: Zeugnisse und Kommentare, edited by K. Bringmann and H. von Steuben, 1995 [2] Choix d'inscriptions de Delphes, traduites et commentées, edited by A. Jacquemin et al., 2012.

SECONDARY LITERATURE

[3] N.T. ARRINGTON, Inscribing Defeat. The Commemorative Dynamics of the Athenian Casualty Lists, in: Classical Antiquity 31, 2011, 179–212 [4] N.T. ARRINGTON, The Form(s) and Date(s) of a Classical War Monument. Re-evaluating IG I3 1163 and the Case for Delion, in: Zeitschrift für Papyrologie und Epigraphik 181, 2012, 61–75 [5] N.T. ARRINGTON, Ashes, Images, and Memories. The Presence of the War Dead in Fifth-Century Athens, 2015 [6] M.M. AUSTIN, The Hellenistic World from Alexander to the Roman Conquest. A Selection of Ancient Sources in Translation, ²2006 [7] A. CHANIOTIS, War in the Hellenistic World. A Social and Cultural History, 2005 [8] J. ELSNER, Visual Culture and Ancient History. Issues of Empiricism and Ideology in the Samos Stele at Athens, in: Classical Antiquity 34, 2015, 33–73 [9] V. GABRIELSEN, Die Kosten der athenischen Flotte in klassischer Zeit, in: F. BURRER / H. MÜLLER (eds.), Kriegskosten und Kriegsfinanzierung in der Antike, 2008, 46–73 [10] B. LOVÉN, The Ancient Harbours of the Piraeus, vol. I.1: The Zea Shipsheds and Slipways. Architecture and Topography, 2011 [11] P. LOW, Remembering War in Fifth-Century Greece. Ideologies, Societies, and Commemoration beyond Democratic Athens, in: World Archeology, 2003, 98–111 [12] M. SCOTT, Delphi and Olympia. The Spatial Politics of Panhellenism in the Archaic and Classical Periods, 2010

NATHAN ARRINGTON

B. MONUMENTS WITH LATIN INSCRIPTIONS

B.1. Republican period
B.2. Imperial period
B.3. Monuments outside Rome
B.4. Monuments not built by emperors

B.1. REPUBLICAN PERIOD

War was always a self-evident reality for Rome. Being a Roman citizen meant being a soldier, too, from the very foundation of the Roman state onwards. *Civis* ('citizen') and *miles* ('soldier') were not binary opposites, but complementary aspects of a single person. This unity only broke down as a result of the creation of the standing army under Augustus. Now *civis* and *miles* could evolve into the contrastive pair, 'civilian and soldier' [5]. Even so, this had no bearing on the general view of the military or Rome at war, for the military, and above all victory in war, had deep roots in the Roman mentality. Accordingly, there was never any truly negative view of war, and particularly not of the army. They carried positive connotations, especially when Rome emerged victorious. Public monuments taking war as their theme or referring directly or indirectly to it, or even partially verbalizing it through inscriptions, were therefore very much a matter of course in the Roman world.

A distinction must be drawn between public and private monuments that communicated the subject of war to society. The earliest known monument publicly announcing a victory was the *columna rostrata*, put up at the *rostra* on the Forum in Rome. It bore an *elogium* ('inscription') describing the naval victory of C. Duilius, consul for 260 BC, over Carthage at Mylae, and the booty won there (ILLRP 319). Some Republican *imperatores* ('generals') used booty to sponsor temples at Rome, where booty was also put on display. One such general was L. Mummius, consul for 146 BC, who celebrated his army's destruction of Corinth and his victorious return from Achaea by commissioning a temple dedicated to Hercules Victor (ILLRP 122; vgl. [1]). Victory monuments were also constructed in other cities of Italy and in the provinces: the same Mummius, for example, had monuments built in Cures Sabini, in Nursia and Parma (CIL IX 4966 = ILLRP 328; CIL IX 4540 = ILLRP 329; CIL XI 1051 = ILLRP 330) and in Italica (CIL II 1119 = ILLRP 331). Conversely, Delphi honoured M. Minucius Rufus with a statue in the Sanctuary of Apollo, celebrating his victory over the Gauls, Scordisci and Bessi (CIL I² 692 = Syll.³ 710). *Imperatores* of the late Republic were even more emphatic in displaying their military success to the Roman people. Pompey, for instance, commissioned a theatre for himself, in which he depicted with statues the peoples he had subjugated.

Augustus made the distinction of being victorious the sole prerogative of the *princeps*, so that arches commemorating a triumph could now be built only for emperors at the behest of *Senatus populusque Romanus* (SPQR). Augustus' Parthian Arch displayed the standards that had been returned. These were probably also mentioned in the dedicatory inscription. This arch also bore the *fasti* ('registers') listing all *triumphatores* ('military victors') through to AD 19, as a sign of Rome's victorious character (Inscr. It. XIII 1, 1b). Later victory arches include those built for Claudius over the *via lata* (CIL VI 40416 = ILS 216), for Titus in the Circus Maximus (CIL VI 944 = D. 264; the arch on the Velia was posthumous, though furnished with reliefs of the triumph over the Jews, CIL VI 945 = 31211 = ILS 265) and for Septimius Severus and his family in the Forum Romanum (CIL VI 1033 = 36881 = ILS 425). The Arch of Constantine commemorated the victory over Maxentius (CIL VI 1139 = 31245 = ILS 694). In all these cases, the statements emphasized in the inscriptions about the emperor's success in victory and defeat of enemies are reinforced by the monumental nature of the arches and reliefs.

B.2. IMPERIAL PERIOD

Like the Republican *imperatores*, the emperors also commemorated their victories with monumental edifices. Augustus, for instance, had the Temple of Mars Ultor built in his forum (see CIL VI 8, VIII 3, 40311: the reconstruction is generally accurate, even if the wording is too hypothetical), and made it the focus of all military activity. Statues there accordingly immortalized all generals who defeated → enemies of Rome by the emperor's command [10]. Vespasian followed Augustus' example with the Templum Pacis, in which the booty from Jerusalem was put on display, and the Amphitheatrum Flavium ('Colosseum'), which was probably built *ex manubiis* ('with money obtained from the sale of booty') (CIL VI 40454a). Trajan surpassed them all with his own forum, also built with booty, this time from the Dacian Wars. The legions that had taken part in those wars were commemorated in inscriptions on the architrave of the porticos. But most notably, the events of the two wars were depicted along the 200 metres' length of the spiral relief on the Trajan Column. The inscription above the entrance to the column records only the excavation work necessary to built the forum in this location, and mentions nothing of the wars (CIL VI 960 = ILS 294). The connection with the wars was probably made – for the entire complex – in the lost inscription above the entrance to the forum, which identified the whole site as the location of the Dacian triumph.

B.3. MONUMENTS OUTSIDE ROME

Rome's victorious character and triumphs over its enemies also needed monumental expression outside Rome. Augustus had an imposing victory monument built near Actium, in the city of Nicopolis, which he founded and whose very name was intended to uphold the memory of the triumphant naval battle of 31 BC. The monument was consecrated in 29 BC to Neptune and Mars, patrons of the marine victory ([12]; AE 1999, 1448; 2002, 1297), and the ships' prows at the front of the monument document the type of → victory won. SPQR also had built, on a hilltop near what is now Monaco where the Alpine chain meets the sea, the Tropaeum Alpium, announcing victory for Augustus over the Alpine peoples *ductu auspiciisque* ('under [his] guidance and command'), and its site is just as significant topographically as Nicopolis. Its inscription lists by name the 49 defeated *gentes Alpinae* ('Alpine peoples') (CIL V 7817; cf. Plin. HN 3,136f.; [7]). Following a 'victory' over Germanic tribes on the right bank of the Rhine, Germanicus had a victory monument built on the battlefield, *superbo cum titulo: debellatis inter Rhenum Albimque nationibus* ('bearing the proud inscription: "having subdued entirely the peoples between the Rhine and the Elbe"'; Tac. Ann. 2,22,1). For Germanicus himself, three commemorative arches were built after his death: one in Rome (→ Honour), one on the *mons Amanus* in Syria, and a third on the bank of the Rhine near Mainz. The last of these in particular was intended to show what triumphs he had achieved in Germania, triumphs to which the inscription on the arch in Rome also refers. The attic of the arch on the Rhine would show Germanicus depicted with the standard lost by Varus and won back by him [13.54–57, Fragment I, l. 26ff.]. After the first victory of Claudius' army in Britain, SPQR had a triumphal arch built for him at Gesoriacum (Boulogne), the imperial army's point of departure for the island.

B.4. MONUMENTS NOT BUILT BY EMPERORS

Victorious generals also announced success in battle on the emperor's behalf. The proconsul Cossus Cornelius Lentulus, for example, ordered a monument built at Leptis Magna, after defeating the Gaetuli in Africa *auspiciis Imp. Caesaris Augusti* ('by command of the Emperor Caesar Augustus') between AD 6 and 8 (IRT 301; cf. AE 1961, 107; cf. a monument to Victoria Augusta, also built at Leptis Magna, by order of proconsul Dolabella following the death of Tacfarinas: AE 1961, 108). At Vetera (near Xanten), the *legio VI Victrix* under the legate of the army of Germania inferior, Marius Celsus, marked the place at which they had defeated the last remnants of the rebel Batavi with a monument. The victory was dedicated to Vespasian and Titus (AE 1979, 413). A triumphal arch was built somewhat prematurely at Dura-Europus by the *legio III Cyrenaica* as Trajan's Parthian War was still being fought [8]; [9]. Either a legion or SPQR also had a monumental arch built for Hadrian at the end of the Bar Kochba Revolt, at Tel Shalem in the province of Judaea [6]. One of the victorious generals in this conflict, Poblicius Marcellus, legate of Syria, also had a 'victory monument' built commemorating his success after returning to his home city of Aquileia, although the text of the inscription does not make this clear. For Marcellus and his contemporaries, mention of the *ornamenta triumphalia* ('triumphal honours') sufficed to connect him personally with the victory (AE 1934, 231 = IAquileia 499; cf. [2.83]). At Augsburg, Simplicinus Genialis, *agens vice praesidis* ('acting governor') of Rhaetia, had a bronze statue of *dea sancta Victoria* constructed on a massive plinth, probably at the place where he had defeated Germanic hordes on April 24 and 25, AD 260 (AE 1993, 1231). Also in Rhaetia, the *dux* ('commander') Aurelius Senecio had a *templum* built for Victoria Augusta in AD 310 to celebrate a victory (CIL III 5565 = 11771).

Poblicius Marcellus at Aquileia was no longer acting as an imperial official, but as a private individual, albeit a direct participant [4.166f.]. Others built monuments to victories of the emperors without even having taken part in a war. Some of these were generic monuments dedicated to Victoria Augusta (e.g. CIL VIII 2351f.; AE 1941, 49), while others were more specific: the citizens of Uchi Maius evoked all victorious wars of Caracalla with a statue of 'Victoria Parthica Britannica Germanica Maxima Augusta' in their city (CIL VIII 26243; similarly Althiburus: AE 1913, 46). At Tamugadi, a former *centurio* ('centurion') of the *legio III Augusta* and the *XXX Ulpia* had two statues of Victoria Parthica built *ex testamento* (as directed by his will), an indication of the importance of this war in his life (CIL VIII 2354 = ILS 305). Many former participants in conflicts who did not have specific monuments built nevertheless remembered to request that mention be made in inscriptions beneath honorific statues or on tombs to the honours they had received from an emperor during a war: *ornamenta triumphalia* ('triumphal honours') and *dona militaria* ('military decorations') (see e.g. AE 1956, 124; → Honours). Such monuments, which frequently carry illustrations of the honours concerned (e.g. CIL III 14187,4 = [11.111, pl. XX]), bear particularly eloquent testimony to the importance attached to wars and perceptions of war in the societies of the Roman Empire [3].

☞ **Borders, B. Roman; Military service; Sources, C. Latin inscriptions**

BIBLIOGRAPHY
[1] M. ABERSON, Temples votifs et butin de guerre dans la Rome républicaine, 1994 [2] W. ECK, The Bar Kokhba Revolt. The Roman Point of View, in: JRS 89, 1999, 78–86 [3] W. ECK, Monumente der Virtus. Kaiser und Heer im Spiegel epigraphischer Denkmäler, in: G. ALFÖLDY et al. (eds.), Kaiser, Heer und Gesellschaft in der römischen Kaiserzeit. Gedenkschrift für Eric Birley, 2000, 483–496 [4] W. ECK, Hadrian, the Bar Kokhba Revolt, and the Epigraphic Transmission, in: P. SCHÄFER (ed.), The Bar Kokhba War Reconsidered, 2003, 153–170 [5] W. ECK, Milites et pagani, in: A. CORBINO et al. (eds.), Homo, caput, persona. La costruzione giuridica dell'identità nell'esperienza romana, 2010, 597–630 [6] W. ECK / G. FOERSTER, Ein Triumphbogen für Hadrian im Tal von Beth Shean bei Tel Shalem, in: JRA 12, 1999, 294–313 [7] J. FORMIGÉ, Le Trophée des Alpes (La Turbie), 1966 [8] S. GOULD, III. Inscriptions I. The Triumphal Arch, in: P.V.C. BAUR et al. (eds.), The Excavations of Dura Europos. Preliminary Report, vol. 4, 1933, 56–65 [9] S. GOULD, XV Supplementary Inscriptions. I. An Addition to the Inscriptions of the Arch of Trajan, in: M.I. ROSTOVZEFF et al. (eds.), The Excavations of Dura Europos. Preliminary Report, Bd. 6, 1936, 480–482 [10] V. KOCKEL, Forum Augusti, in: LTUR 2, 1995, 289–295 [11] C. MAREK, Stadt, Ära und Territorium in Pontus-Bithynia und Nord-Galatia, 1993 [12] W.M. MURRAY / P.M. PETSAS, Octavian's Campsite Memorial for the Actian War, 1989 [13] Á SÁNCHEZ-OSTIZ, Tabula Siarensis. Edición, traducción y comentario, 1999

WERNER ECK

C. GREEK LITERATURE

C.1. Introduction
C.2. Homer
C.3. Individuals – army
C.4. Causes of war
C.5. Consequences of war
C.6. Battle descriptions

C.1. INTRODUCTION

Dating back to the beginnings of Greek literature in the 7th century BC, war was always a central theme of all genres. Authors' personal experiences in a world shaped by conflict were often combined with literary references, especially to the 'book of war' by the poets' poet, Homer's *Iliad*, such that historical and literary contexts blur together. The concept of a 'description of war', which either defines an entire literary work as the dominant element or fulfills a function in the conception of the text as a subordinate element, is understood to include descriptions of actual fighting and all that goes with it, but also analyses of the causes and effects of war [13.22].

War was characterized by ambivalence, as Hesiod expressed in his exposition of the twin personifications of discord (Erides; Op. 11–46), one positive and one negative [5.142–144]. On the one hand, it afforded an individual (Hom. Il. 1,492; 7,189–191; 16,65) or a community (Thuc. 2,41,4f.) the possibility of earning renown (*kleos*), honour (*time*) and lasting memory (Hdt. Prooemium), and was for this reason desirable. On the other hand, war was an evil (Hom. Il. 19,221–224; cf. Hdt. 1,87,4; Aristoph. Ach.; Aristoph. Pax) and Ares was the deity whom Zeus loved the least (Hom. Il. 5,891). War, elevated to divine rank through personification, determined the course of history in interaction with the opposed principle of peace (and amity; Emp. (31 B 17 Diels/Kranz); cf. Hom. Il. 18,467–608 (Achilles' shield): war and peace as basic forms of human existence), as a general metaphysical principle (Heraclitus (22 B 80 Diels/Kranz)), and as 'father of all things' (Heraclitus (22 B 53 Diels/Kranz)). War created hierarchies in the world, between immortals and mortals, between the free and the enslaved [13.23]. The frequent use of war metaphors to describe the relationship between the sexes [10.169–173] made war – for Ares was a lover of Aphrodite (Hom. Od. 8,256–366) – a cosmic, life-bestowing principle. As a 'violent teacher' (Thuc. 3,82,2), war – the 'father of the war cry that invites people to the dance of lances' (Pind. fr. 78 [6]; [7.283–285]) – lays bare the egotistical, animalistic nature of humanity concealed beneath the carefully nurtured veneer of civilization. As a vicious chef in Aristophanes' *Peace* (180–288), 'War' with his assistant 'Tumult' (Kydoimos; cf. Hom. Il. 5,593) wields his pestle to pulverize cities in a mortar, a fitting allegory for the Spartan and Athenian commanders Brasidas and Cleon [14.114]. The simple choir of Acharnian charcoal-burners will never accept the immoderate drinker and bringer of havoc as a guest in their house (Aristoph. Ach. 979–987).

C.2. Homer

While Homer's *Iliad* takes war as its central theme, the *Odyssey* explores the many different → consequences of war for an individual (Odysseus; fate of a warrior returning home), his family (Penelope, Telemachus: plight of a supposed 'war widow'; maintaining power over the *oikos*, 'household'; initiation of the son in a fatherless family) and society (→ Civil war).

In the *Iliad*'s descriptions of combat, Homer – as befits the overarching concern of the epic to sing the 'renown of the hero' – lays bare the interdependence of the individual and the collective. He sometimes directs the focus of the narrative on individual 'champions' (*promachoi*) fighting at the front line, and on their heroic combat (*aristeia*), and sometimes broadens it to the entire contingent [12]; [19]; [16.47–49]. The course of a battle following the paraenesis of the commander falls into two phases: the actual hostilities, comprising the single combat of the *promachoi* and the ensuing melée of the soldiery, followed by flight and pursuit, in which → chariots might be used. Comparison with the battle paraeneses of Callinus (fr. 1 [2]) and Tyrtaeus (fr. 10 [2]) suggests that the armies of the *Iliad*, structured in phalanxes or 'ranks' (*stichoi*) and regional divisions, reflect realities of the 7th century BC, in which relationships of personal dependency (*hetairoi*) may have played a part [19.670f.], and in which the Classical hoplite phalanx remained unknown.

'War' in the Homeric epics is furnished with a plethora of epithets evoking suffering, cruelty and destruction, with the word 'death' frequently in close proximity. About 75% of Homer's similes in descriptions of war – often referencing untamable nature or the animal world – are found in the *Iliad* [9.39]. Where these draw on everyday occurrences, they bring the epic battle narrative into the experiential horizon of the recipient.

Post-Homeric literature is dominated by intertextual references to literary techniques, motifs and themes of the Homeric epics – occasionally repudiatory (e.g. Sappho fr. 16 [1]), but usually approbatory. The Trojan War became the model for conflict between Greeks and barbarians. Herodotus, for example, makes a clear reference to Homer with Xerxes' visit to Troy, which is accompanied by an omen presaging disaster (7,43). Attic tragedy [21] from the time of the Peloponnesian War (→ Wars of note H.; 431–404 BC) uses events from the Trojan War to reflect current events on a mythical level, the reference to the present being created through the use of 'bridges', words or concepts taken from contemporary discourse (esp. Eur. Hec.; Eur. Tro.). Even for Thucydides, who is critical of Homer's poetic glorification (1,21; 1,22,4: *mythodes*) of the Trojan War (1,9–11; cf. already Hdt. 7,20), the *Iliad* is still the literary reference text for his account of the Athenians' catastrophic defeat on Sicily (7,75; 7,81–87) [22].

C.3. Individuals – army

The grave consequences that an individual's motives and decisions can bring for the collective (Achilles' deep resentment and withdrawal from the fight) are central to subsequent descriptions of war. Ajax's suicide had consequences that threatened the very existence of his retinue and family (Soph. Aj.). Philoctetus' refusal to bury his grudge against the Greeks and thus to end the Trojan War brings further suffering – even for those who were not part of the injustice done to him (Soph. Phil.). Xerxes' ambition leads to the defeat of the Persians (Hdt. 7,8; Aesch. Pers. 739–752). Alcibiades' unbridled thirst for glory, together with his rivalry with Nicias, drives the Athenians into disaster on Sicily (Thuc. 6,15), whereas, in Xenophon's portrayal of himself in the *Anabasis*, his rational decisions and selfless actions rescue the Greeks. Aristophanes shifts the perspective in his plays about war. The heroes of his battles are not the generals like Lamachus, but the little people fighting for the good of the city, while the *strategoi* and emissaries are only concerned with their own advantage (Aristoph. Ach. 595–597).

C.4. Causes of war

In analyzing the causes of war, a depersonalization can be observed in the transition from Homer to Thucydides [13.80–84]. The issue according to the immediate reception of Homer was the guilt (Eur. Hec.; Eur. Tro.) or innocence of Helen (Gorgias and Isocrates, *Helena*). Stesichorus (*Palinodes*, fr. 192f. [3]) invented a new literary tradition, whereby Zeus whisked away his daughter Helen to Egypt, and the Trojan War was fought over a mere phantom (Eur. Hel.). Although Herodotus refers to the various stories of female abduction in an aetiology of the conflict between Greeks and barbarians, he suspends judgment on their historicity, and begins his account with Croesus, who he says committed historically verified 'unjust acts' against the Greeks (1,5,3f.). Attic comedies place blame for the outbreak of the Peloponnesian War on Pericles, for using the Megarian Psephism to pick a fight (Aristoph. Ach. 515–556; Cratinus, *Nemesis, Dionysalexander*). Plato's verdict is likewise damning (Gorg. 515e, 519a): Pericles, he suggests, corrupted the people with his excessive complaisance (cf. Aristoph. Equ.). For Thucydides, according to whom this accusation can fairly be made only of Pericles' successors (2,65), the Megarian Psephism was merely the pretext (*prophasis*). The true cause (*aitia*), he argues, was Athenian expansionism (1,23) and both sides' fear of waning power (1,140f.; 5,91).

C.5. Consequences of war

Beginning with Homer's *Odyssey*, military conflict was depicted as leading to the breakdown of family and societal structures, and especially of recognized social and political norms (*kathestotes nomoi*). Thucydides describes the → consequences of war in a narrative of escalating effects: The uprooted rural populace, penned in between the Long Walls, finds refuge from distress by settling in the sanctuaries (2,16f.). The great pestilence leads the people to fully disregard all religious burial rites (2,52,4). When the external pressure from war is compounded with an internal crisis such as a state of civil war (*stasis*), this – catalyzed by the innate human characteristics of ambition and greed – leads to the complete breakdown of all social and religious norms (3,82; already 3,81,4).

C.6. Battle descriptions

Greek authors often wrote descriptions of war from their own personal army experience, either as officers (Sophocles, Thucydides, Xenophon; Polybius wrote a military instruction book: *Tactica*) (→ Military literature) or as common soldiers (Aeschylus), and they wrote for a public whose lives were determined by military experiences [11]; [18]. It is therefore unsurprising that works of both poetry and prose contain detailed descriptions of army organization (Hom. Il. 2,484–877; Hdt. 7,55; 6087; Thuc. 5,72; Xen. An. 1,8), the execution of battles, feats of engineering (Hdt. 7,22: canal through Athos, 7,115: road building in Thrace), army administration (especially supplies; Hdt. 4,83), military tactics (e.g. of the Scythians, Hdt. 4,120–128), and peculiarities and innovations in fighting technique, necessitated for instance by difficult terrain (mountains, rivers; Xenophon [17]). Descriptions of hostilities demand an internal plausibility that stands up to comparison with reality. Homer's *Iliad* already passes this test. The agreements with Thucydides' battle descriptions (3,97f.; 4,32–37; 4,43; 6,69f.) with respect to the phases of battle and terminology are indicative of the historicity of Homer's portrayals of combat [12.227f.]. Thucydides undertakes this kind of plausibility check through archaeology when considering the dimensions of the war (1,2–20). He is well aware that 'communicative memory' degenerates over time into historically unreliable 'cultural memory' (cf. on the tyrannicide 6,54–59), and that a battlefield thus becomes a venue of memory beset with ideology (especially in epitaphs and panegyric orations: e.g. Lys. 2,34–47; Isoc. Or. 4,85–99).

In large-scale descriptions of battles where authors were not personally present, they combine and condense eye-witness reports and oral traditions together with information about military and topographic conditions using the principle of probability (*eikós*), thereby describing each event as it 'must' or 'might' have been (Thuc. 1,22,1: *ta deonta*). They follow the narrative model of the *Iliad*: paraenesis of the commander – battle in its various phases – flight, plunder and consequences of the event. The course of the battle as it unfolds often implicitly questions the cogency of the tactics outlined in the commander's paraenesis [11.394–396]. There is frequent use of counterfactuals to analyse military processes in hypothetical modes [11.396–400]. In terms of literary technique, survey of the battle by the omniscient narrator is used alongside focus on the action of an individual. Given that descriptions of battles never stand in isolation, but are always embedded in an overall narrative (Aristot. Poet. 1450a15, *systasis ton pragmaton*), they serve as a lens through which the narrative focuses on what is crucial to the work's overall message. Xenophon (An.), for example, develops his concept of the ideal ruler using the example of how he leads an army [20]. Thucydides uses battle descriptions to illustrate a spiral of violence and brutality. Literary references in a battle description serve to criticize and engage with predecessors or contemporaries, while at the same time applying the technique of *mise en abyme* to elevate and reflect upon the event in question against a less contoured background.

Poetic descriptions of historical battles are found in encomiastic lyric poetry strongly influenced by Homer. Homeric battle metaphors (list in [15.190–205]) are often reworked in describing military events. In the *Wasps* of Aristophanes (Vesp. 1071–1090), the chorus of old men recount their own heroic deeds, in an audacious collage of the most significant battles of the Persian Wars (→ Wars of note, J.; [4.400]), casting themselves as a swarm of Athenian wasps (cf. Hom. Il. 16,259f.). In *Lysistrata* (Aristoph. Lys. 1247–1272), the fighting of the Spartans led by Leonidas is amplified through the Homeric wild boar metaphor (cf. Hom. Il. 20,168f.), and the Athenians at Artemisium are like gods as they lay the foundations of liberty (Aristoph. Lys. 1249–1253; Pind. fr. 77 [6]).

☞ Sources, A. Literary sources

BIBLIOGRAPHY

SOURCES
[1] Poetarum lesbiorum fragmenta, edited by E. Lobel and D. Page, 1955 [2] Iambi et elegi graeci ante Alexandrum cantati, vol. 2: Callinus, Mimnermus, Semonides, Solon, Tyrtaeus, Minora Adespota, edited by M.L. West, 1972 [3] Poetarum melicorum Graecorum fragmenta, vol. 1, edited by M. DAVIES, 1991 [4] ARISTOPHANES, Wasps, edited, introduction and commentary by Z.P. Biles and S.D. Olson, 2015 [5] HESIOD, Work and Days, edited by M.L. West, 1978 [6] PINDARUS, Pindari carmina cum fragmentis: Fragmenta. Indices, edited by H. Maehler, 1989 [7] PINDARUS, Pindari dithyramborum fragmenta, edited by S. Lavacchia, 2000

SECONDARY LITERATURE
[8] R. BUXTON, Similes and Other Likenesses, in: R. FOWLER (ed.), The Cambridge Companion to Homer, 2004, 139–155 [9] M.W. EDWARDS, The Iliad. A Commentary, vol. 5, bks. 17–20, 1991 [10] J. HENDERSON, The Maculate Muse, 1991 [11] P. HUNT, Warfare, in: A. RENGAKOS / A. TSAKMAKIS (eds.), Brill's Companion to Thucydides, 2006, 385–413 [12] J. LATACZ, Kampfparänese, Kampfdarstellung und Kampfwirklichkeit in der Ilias, bei Kallinos und Tyrtaios, 1977 [13] H. MÜNKLER, Gewalt und Ordnung. Das Bild des Krieges im politischen Denken, 1992 [14] H.-J. NEWIGER, Metapher und Allegorie, 1957 [15] W.C. SCOTT, The Oral Nature of the Homeric Simile, 1974 [16] M. STOEVESANDT, Feinde – Gegner – Opfer. Zur Darstellung der Troianer in den Kampfszenen der Ilias, 2004 [17] O. STOLL, Terror im Gebirge. Xenophon und die Anforderungen transkultureller Kriegführung, in: Göttinger Forum für Altertumswissenschaft 16, 2013, 277–345 [18] L. TRITLE, Warfare in Herodotus, in: C. DEWALD / J. MARINCOLA (eds.), The Cambridge Companion to Herodotus, 2006, 209–223 [19] H. VAN WEES, Homeric Warfare, in: I. MORRIS / B. POWELL (eds.), A New Companion to Homer, 1997, 668–693 [20] B. ZIMMERMANN, Macht und Charakter. Theorie und Praxis von Herrschaft bei Xenophon, in: Prometheus 18, 1992, 231–244 [21] B. ZIMMERMANN, Zur Pathologie des Krieges in der griechischen Literatur des 5. Jahrhunderts v.Chr., in: H. HECKER (ed.), Krieg in Mittelalter und Renaissance, 2005, 107–123 [22] B. ZIMMERMANN, Vergangenheit(en) bei Thukydides, in: RFIC 139, 2011, 28–42

BERNHARD ZIMMERMANN

D. LATIN LITERATURE

D.1. Rhetoric of descriptions of war
D.2. War and the military as seen by Latin authors

Ever since Homer, Herodotus and Thucydides, war had been the dominant subject of ancient narrative literature (epic and historiography). For Tacitus, violent wars, conquests of cities and defeated kings gave enough grandeur and significance to the past for it to be remembered as history, whereas periods of peace and tranquillity paralysed the pen (Ann. 4,32; on the factors lending grandeur to a war see Liv. 21,1,1–3). The epic that Cn. Naevius wrote around 200 BC concerned the First Punic War (*Bellum Poenicum*). Prose histories, which began with the Second Punic War against Hannibal and culminated in Livy's *Ab urbe condita*, as well as Q. Ennius' epic in hexameters *Annales*, also placed Rome's wars on centre stage. Later came the prose monograph devoted to one particular military conflict (Coelius Antipater, *Bellum Punicum*; Sall. Iug.). Civil wars offered their own challenges and opportunities for rhetorically and poetically enhanced descriptions of war, as exemplified in the works of L. Cornelius Sisenna (FRH 16), Sallust (Catil.), Lucan (the epic *Bellum Civile*) and Tacitus (Hist.) [10]. Florus' historical sketches (Epit.) consist almost entirely of descriptions of war. War and descriptions of battles also play an important role in Virgil's multifaceted epic, the *Aeneid* (Aen. 1,1 *arma virumque cano*; [7]), as they do in the *Histories of Alexander the Great* by Q. Curtius Rufus, the writings of Tacitus [1]; [2] and the history of Ammianus Marcellinus, himself a former soldier (Amm. Marc. 31,16,9). Omnipresent non-literary manifestations of war also had an influence on the self-image of the 'Sons of Mars' as a community – dedications of booty, victory monuments and inscriptions, and the → triumph.

D.1. RHETORIC OF DESCRIPTIONS OF WAR
Rhetorical theory assigns to battle description the goals of depicting events as occurring simultaneously or in rapid succession by the skilful aggregation of images, and of eliciting emotions through clarity and versimilitude (Quint. Inst. 8,3,67–70,

taking of a city; [12. § 810. 813,2]). For the sake of *variatio*, historiographic descriptions of war tend to combine various rhetorical and stylistic elements, such as terse, monumental statements in the style of a general's address to the Senate [5], novelistic miniatures, exemplary individual actions and trenchant statements, *descriptiones* of complex series of events (battle, siege) and general's orations [8]. Individual elements in turn obey structural rules that serve to orient the reader, shaping the chaotic reality of a mass battle into a clear and logical narration ([6.18, 26]; cf. for Sallust [21. cap. X], for Livy [22.158–163. 197–204]). Recurring components form the framework for the actual battle descriptions, especially in 'annalistic' reports (i.e. organized year by year), e.g. assigning the task to the general, religious acts, exact details of army numbers, numbers of fallen and quantities of booty, formal ending of the war, and triumph. In general, similar processes can be described with varying degrees of narrative detail within a single work (cf. Caes. B Gall. 4,4,6 with 5,28 and 7,57–62).

Overall, the lexis, semantics, grammar and rhetoric of war descriptions were not intended simply to portray events as exactly or effectively as possible in textual form. They also influenced the patterns of perception through which experiences were predisposed and charged with meaning. On the Roman side, the valour associated with stamina and implacability (*virtus*) was always central. Because the Romans tended to see qualities of military leadership in a general's strengths of character rather than in his tactical virtuosity, descriptions of war also covered his actions before and after the battle [16]. The psychology of the combatants was another recurring theme, particularly for Livy. Accounts of single combat and outstanding individual feats (e.g. Enn. Ann. 391–398 Skutsch; Cato FRH 3 frg. 4,7a; Claudius Quadrigarius FRH 14 frg. 10b; Caes. B Gall. 5,44; Liv. 4,20,6) emphasized not only the valour, but also and especially the → discipline of Roman participants (e.g. Cato FRH 3 frg. 4,6; cf. Sall. Catil. 9,4). Livy used the example of the Romans' war with the city of Veii to develop a typology of various species of war (*genera militiae*; Liv. 5,6,9), from the raid to the *bellum iustum* ('just war'), and from the battle of a clan squad to salaried, year-round war service [4.125].

Roman epic poets and historians tended to avoid in their descriptions of war the kind of technical language that was permissible in military treatises and *commentarii*. Even so, factuality and artistic rhetorical design should not be taken as mutually exclusive in descriptions of war ([18]; but [15. vol. 2, 307–312]). Authors and their readership often shared expertise and practical experience, but did not regard stylizations, exaggerations or impossibilities as defects in war narratives [6].

The *Commentarii* of Caesar are a unique case, with their pathos of factuality and sobriety [4.81–122]. His *De bello Gallico* in particular [11]; [19] presents the war as the product of a considered, rational military mind that is always equal to emerging crises [17]; [23]. Even here, though, there is no lack of rhetorical exaggeration and stereotyping.

D.2. WAR AND THE MILITARY AS SEEN BY LATIN AUTHORS

Uniform opinions on 'war' and 'the military' are not found in Latin literature. Both could be assessed very differently even from an early date. Plautus, for instance, put a caricature of a pompous and stupid (admittedly Greek) officer on the comic stage (Mil.). Ennius praised the achievements of Roman customs and men in war, but also forcefully described the consequences: 'After foul Discord has broken open the ironclad doors and doorposts of war, wise counsel is driven from the field, the matter being decided by force; a good speaker is despised, a coarse warrior loved,.... Amends they seek with the sword, striving for sway and proceeding by might pure and simple' (Ann. 225f.; 248–253 Skutsch; on the uncertain context and the interpretation [9.151–193]). Among the accomplishments of King Numa was supposedly that he made the Romans, whom war had brutalized, peaceful, by weaning them off the use of weapons (Liv. 1,19,1f.). Yet this kind of lament for the suffering caused by war never implied a categorical pacifism, as a study of Virgil illustrates. Once himself a victim of civil war in Italy, he articulated the Romans' mission of rule and order in striking language (Aen. 6,851–853) and portrayed the bitter struggles for a new homeland in Latium as necessary and right (on the Augustan discourse see [13]). This corresponds to the abundance of good reasons for war cited by Latin authors [14.40f.].

For many authors, the obvious and discursively clear distinction between external war and civil war was of great importance. The latter was generally painted in bleak colours (cf. Sisenna FRH 16 Frg. 131; Hor. Epod. 7; 16; Luc.; Caes. B Civ. is primarily directed at his own party). In 44 BC, Cicero attempted to encapsulate the notion of external war by means of philosophical and formal legal categories and arguments with reference to (admittedly inconsistent) Roman practice, delimiting it by defining *officia* and *iura belli* (Off. 1,34–40). He distinguished, for instance, between hegemonic wars and wars fought for survival, and classified enemies variously as *hostes*, *perduelles* or *barbari* (Off. 3,107). The sole purpose of war was peace (Off. 1,80), albeit only peace that was just – from the Roman perspective, i.e. the *pax* defined by Rome's security and authority. Cicero was far from being motivated by any notion of justification [3]. Sallust saw war in the 'good old days' as a field for pursuing the 'desire for glory' (*cupido gloriae*) (Catil. 7,3-7). Of the Christian Latin authors, the first to formulate a consistent judgment on war was Augustine [20].

☞ **Sources, A. Literary sources**

BIBLIOGRAPHY
[1] H. ALLGEIER, Studien zur Kriegsdarstellung bei Tacitus, 1957 [2] R. ASH, Tacitus and the Battle of Mons Graupius, in: J. MARINCOLA (ed.), A Companion to Greek and Roman Historiography, 2009, 434-440 [3] H. BOTERMANN, Ciceros Gedanken zum »gerechten Krieg« in de officiis 1,34-40, in: AKG 69, 1987, 1-30 [4] H. CANCIK, Antik - Modern. Beiträge zur römischen und deutschen Kulturgeschichte, 1998 [5] E. FRAENKEL, Eine Form römischer Kriegsbulletins, in: Eranos 54, 1956, 189-194 [6] S. GERLINGER, Römische Schlachtenrhetorik. Unglaubwürdige Elemente in Schlachtendarstellungen, speziell bei Caesar, Sallust und Tacitus, 2008 [7] R.F. GLEI, Der Vater der Dinge. Interpretationen zur politischen, literarischen und kulturellen Dimension des Krieges bei Vergil, 1991 [8] B. HAMBSCH, Feldherrnrede, in: G. UEDING (ed.), HWRh 3, 1996, 225-238 [9] R. HÄUSSLER, Das historische Epos der Griechen und Römer bis Vergil, pt. 1, 1976 [10] T.A. JOSEPH, Tacitus the Epic Successor. Virgil, Lucan, and the Narrative of Civil War in the Histories, 2012 [11] C.S. KRAUS, Bellum gallicum, in: M. GRIFFIN (ed.), A Companion to Julius Caesar, 2009, 159-174 [12] H. LAUSBERG, Handbuch der literarischen Rhetorik, ³1990 [13] A. LUISI, L'idea di guerra nei poeti elegiaci di età augustea, in: M. SORDI (ed.), Il pensiero sulla guerra nel mondo antico, 2001, 173-193 [14] K.L. NOETHLICHS, Krieg, in: RAC 22, 2008, 1-75 [15] H. PETER, Die geschichtliche Litteratur über die römische Kaiserzeit bis Thedosius I und ihre Quellen, 2 vols., 1897 [16] H. PLÖGER, Studien zum literarischen Feldherrnporträt römischer Autoren des 1. Jahrhunderts v.Chr., 1975 [17] A.M. RIGGSBY, Caesar in Gaul and Rome. War in Words, 2006 [18] J.P. ROTH, Siege Narrative in Livy. Representations and Reality, in: S. DILLON / K.E. WELCH (eds.), Representations of War in Ancient Rome, 2000, 49-67 [19] M. SCHAUER, Der Gallische Krieg. Geschichte und Täuschung in Caesars Meisterwerk, 2016 [20] R. SCHULZ, Augustinus und der Krieg, in: Millennium 4, 2008, 93-110 [21] R. SYME, Sallust, 1964 [22] P.G. WALSH, Livy. His Historical Aims and Methods, 1963 [23] K. WELCH / A. POWELL (eds.), Julius Caesar as Artful Reporter, 2009

UWE WALTER

Desertion

☞ **Avoidance of military service**

Diplomacy

A. Introduction
B. Greece and the Hellenistic period
C. Rome

A. INTRODUCTION

The Greeks and Romans of Antiquity had no terminology that encompassed in a single word the multifaceted concept of diplomacy and the actions and principles that today are subsumed under it. Moreover, neither Greek nor Roman society knew the profession of the 'career diplomat'. There were no permanent international diplomatic institutions. Nevertheless, both the Greeks and the Romans recognized the necessity of peaceful communication between states, particularly in situations with a potential for conflict. Consequently, both sides in such a situation would seek ways and means to achieve 'diplomatic' dialogue.

One core principle of diplomacy between polities was that interactions between the states should be largely free from violence. It was accepted everywhere as a matter of course that heralds and messengers enjoyed diplomatic immunity. Even if they belonged to a hostile state, they were protected against attack. It is often stated without qualification that concepts of international law were unknown to the Greeks and Romans, but the immunity of diplomatic messengers is a clear indication of the existence of a rudimentary *ius gentium* ('law of nations'). The personal safety of emissaries is the foundation of diplomatic communication. Without it, there is no diplomacy.

Even if the procedures of ancient diplomacy were free from violence, however, they were not necessarily directed at finding solutions to conflicts. The basic aim of all diplomats is to further the interests of their own state, not to improve relationships within the international system as a whole. If such furtherance can be found in signing a peace treaty with an enemy, diplomacy can certainly achieve its goal through negotiations leading to → peace. Yet it can be employed equally well to recruit military allies, to threaten or intimidate another party or to deceive and confuse them, to drag out a conflict rather than end it, to deflect blame for a dispute on to someone else and, in general, to manoeuvre and manipulate. Thus, diplomacy is perfectly well suited to further military aims, and it can do so at least as easily as it can promote peace.

B. GREECE AND THE HELLENISTIC PERIOD

The history of ancient Greece is primarily one of wars, but it is also a history of attempts to mitigate the damage done by violence between polities. If Strabo (10,1,12) is to be believed, one of the first attested conflicts between *poleis*, the Lelantine

War (c. 700 BC), was fought under a contractual agreement by both sides to limit the use of ranged weapons. Over time, the Greeks developed ever more complex peace treaties. They even experimented in the 4th century BC with wider security structures that were intended to be valid for all *poleis* through the institution of a 'general peace' (*koine eirene*) [15]; [25]. The whole of Greek history is peppered with evidence of third party interventions intended to help settle disputes by peaceful means [24]; [2]; [21].

B.1. Aims of diplomacy

B.1. Aims of diplomacy
B.2. Instruments of diplomacy

Diplomatic negotiations pursued many specific goals. Some were concerned with further development of friendly relations between polities, while others were intended to optimize the power of one *polis* and its ability to endure amid the anarchy of the wider political arena. Examples of the former type in the Greek world include religious embassies aimed at securing the inviolability (*asylia*) of sacred sites and the recognition of festivals, delegations seeking a monarch's charity, emissaries from monarchs to cities who brought letters with the ruler's answer or decision, and reciprocal embassies between *poleis* transmitting declarations of amity and kinship and assorted honours and privileges, such as communal citizenship. Of primary importance to the present context, however, is the interplay between diplomatic and military aims. States at war seek their own advantage, and this also applies to diplomacy. The political arrangements and formal structures that went hand in hand with war – alliances, declarations of war, truces and treaties – were achieved by diplomatic means. Military actions almost inevitably demanded diplomatic activity, whether in advance, concurrently or afterwards.

Alliances in Greek Antiquity could be strictly defensive (*epimachia*) or both defensive and offensive (*symmachia*, 'fighting with the same friends and against the same enemies'). Not all *symmachiai* were meant to be permanent. The shining example of an 'eternal' alliance is the one led by Athens in the 5th century BC: the Delian League. Its members dropped blocks of iron in the sea and swore to remain allies until the iron floated back to the surface (Aristot. Ath. Pol. 23,5; cf. Hdt. 1,165). The cleaving of the Greek world into a bipolar system in the 5th century BC, with the Athenians and Spartans respectively leading leagues of states bound in *symmachia*, created the dangerous conditions that culminated in the Peloponnesian War (431–404 BC).

Although the Greeks had no formal concept to match the Roman idea of 'just war' (*iustum bellum*), they did believe in the importance of divine and mortal sanction. A good part of diplomacy leading up to conflicts was geared towards shifting as much blame as possible on to the opposing party and their failings. In 432/31 BC, when the Spartans finally decided to go to war, they did it by presenting the Athenians with an unfulfillable ultimatum: 'The Lacedaemonians desire peace. There can be peace if you grant autonomy to the Greeks' (Thuc. 1,139,3). Given that fulfilling this ultimatum would have meant the dissolution of the Athenian empire, the Spartans can hardly have expected that Athens would agree. Rather, the condition was formulated in order to focus blame for the outbreak of war on Athenian imperialism.

B.2. Instruments of diplomacy

An announcement by a herald (*keryx*) might be sufficient to launch a war or signal readiness for a truce. A more permanent end to hostilites, however, required the diplomatic services of properly appointed ambassadors (*presbeis*). These were typically selected for the occasion at hand, for which they sometimes lacked any special qualification. Frequently, they were relatives of senior dignitaries of their own *polis*. Hellenistic kings were often represented by their 'friends' (*philoi*). Such emissaries had wider powers than a regular herald when negotiating an alliance, a truce (*anoche, ekecheiria, spondai*) or a treaty (*spondai, synthekai*). Even so, agreements negotiated by the representatives of a *polis* could be disowned by that *polis*, as an Athenian delegation learned in the late 6th century BC. The emissaries were sent to Sardis to negotiate an alliance with Persia, and they accepted the Persian conditions of a symbolic subjugation by making an offering of earth and water. When they returned to Athens, however, their countrymen greeted them with fury and contempt (Hdt. 5,73).

The fact that *philoi* of a Hellenistic king often appeared as his representatives on diplomatic missions emphasizes one important aspect of Greek diplomacy: the weight of personal relations of all kinds. The general absence of permanent institutions of diplomacy in Antiquity was offset by extensive relational networks that included individuals as well as polities. Polities interacted within a framework of fictitious emotional connections – whether benevolent or hostile – and much Greek diplomacy proceeded in this way. Cities, alliances and kings fostered reciprocal relationships of 'amity' (*philia*) and 'kinship' (*syngeneia*) that could be solidified through the bestowal of intermarriage rights (*epigamia*) or through royal marriage alliances [20].

Friendship on a personal level could be established by the bestowal of *proxenia*, a concept not easily translatable, which in Ancient Greece approximated the position of a permanent ambassador or consul [22]. A Greek *proxenos* was not a citizen of the polity whose interests he upheld. Rather, he represented the interests of the other polity to his own fellow citizens. The Athenian aristocrat Cimon was a *proxenos* of the Spartans, and accordingly he took on the role of defender of Spartan interests among his fellow Athenians – an often thankless task that ultimately led to his banishment by ostracism in 461 BC.

In addition to direct bilateral or multilateral negotiations conducted by representatives of parties in conflict, the Greeks also often called on third parties to function as mediators or arbitrators in disputes between polities. Third-party arbitration is a thread running through the whole of Greek history. There is clear evidence of diplomatic missions being sent by *poleis* great and small to resolve conflicts among other *poleis*. Emissaries from Rhodes, Byzantium, Cyzicus and Aetolia, for instance, tried in 219/18 BC to negotiate a peace between Antiochus III and Ptolemy IV (Pol. 5,63; 5,67). Fifty years later, the Rhodians offered to arbitrate on a disagreement between Perseus of Macedonia and Rome – with fatal consequences, as will be seen below (C.) (Liv. 44,14; 45,3; Pol. 28,17; 29,10; 29,19).

C. ROME

C.1. Roman concepts of relations between states
C.2. Values and instruments of Roman diplomacy
C.3. Imperial period
C.4. The 'just war' in Christianity

C.1. ROMAN CONCEPTS OF RELATIONS BETWEEN STATES

Events involving Rhodes in 168 BC offer a glaring example of the chasm between Roman and Greek concepts of diplomacy. The Romans reacted with nothing short of fury to a form of diplomatic contact that was routine in the Greek world at the time, and the Rhodians almost found themselves embroiled in war with Rome. The Roman reaction seems to have been a manifestation of an intrinsic characteristic of Roman 'national' identity: never in their history of dealings with other peoples, whether in war or diplomacy, did the Romans entertain the possibility that they might be in the wrong. Their diplomatic customs concerning war, such as the *ius fetiale* or the practice of *deditio* (see below), grew out of the conviction that any war of Rome was by definition a just one (*iustum bellum*; cf. → Law of war).

If the available sources are to be believed, Roman declarations of war, at least in the first centuries of the Republic, were worked out to the last detail and composed in accordance with proper ritual to ensure that every war fulfilled the criteria of the *iustum bellum*. The *fetiales*, the college of fetial priests, had the job of performing the necessary rituals. These culminated in the actual declaration of war, which in early times was accompanied by the hurling of a spear into enemy territory (unless this was an invention of Octavian's; see Liv. 1,24; 1,32; Dion. Hal. Ant. Rom. 2,72). In an anarchic international system, the final court of appeal was the gods (hence also the importance of oaths in alliances and treaties), and Roman declarations of war called on them to support the lawful Roman position. It was even justifiable to drive an unwilling opponent into a corner to force a battle, as the Romans did with Perseus of Macedonia in 171 BC, although some Romans did express misgivings about such vexatious conduct by their own state (Liv. 42,47; Pol. 36,2). Ironically, Rome's emphasis on the just war sometimes gave rise to hypocritical and contorted *casus belli* that earned the criticism even of admirers like Polybius (32,13,8f.; fr. 99 B–W).

The Romans developed a brusque form of diplomacy that relied on duress and coercion as a natural outcome of their uncompromising military attitude [10]. In 191 BC, the Aetolians made diplomatic contact with Rome in an anxious attempt to achieve lenient peace conditions. Misled by their inadequate knowledge of Roman customs and language, Polybius tells us, the Aetolian representatives unwittingly offered the consul, M. Acilius Glabrio, a complete *deditio*, that is, unconditional capitulation. They still believed themselves in a position to negotiate further, but were swiftly disabused by the Roman general, who had them shackled at the neck and curtly informed them that he could do with them as he pleased (Pol. 20,9f.).

The Roman Senate, however, often displayed considerable patience, particularly with the Greeks in the 2nd century BC [14]. Beginning around 200 BC, the Senate offered annual audiences to many communities throughout the Mediterranean, which frequently sought Roman support in disputes with their neighbours. If no Roman interests were affected, the Romans generally responded by sending senatorial emissaries (*legati*) to carry out local soundings and submit recommendations (like the Greeks, the Romans had no resident ambassadors).

C.2. VALUES AND INSTRUMENTS OF ROMAN DIPLOMACY

The Romans, like the Greeks, conducted their relations with external powers on the analogy of personal relationships. The customs of Roman society guided their diplomatic approach. Friendship (*amicitia*), loyalty (*fides*) and the patron-client relationship (*patrocinium, clientela*) each played a role. Scholars debate whether *clientela* or *amicitia* was the dominant element, but there is no doubt that Rome expected appropriate gratitude and a measure of deference from its 'friends' (*amici*) [4]; [7]. The Rhodians in 168 BC failed to consider the parameters of their diplomatic relationship with Rome. Formally speaking, they were not 'confederates' (*socii*), but *amici*, and Rome expected them to behave as such. The Hellenistic rulers learned this lesson thoroughly. Ptolemy XII of Egypt went to great lengths to win the status of an *amicus et socius populi Romani*, apparently paying exorbitant bribes to both Caesar and Pompey (Suet. Caes. 54; Cass. Dio 39,12,1). Although in the end Egypt gained nothing from its friendship with Rome, other kings on the peripheries of the Roman Empire, including Herod the Great of Judaea and Juba of Mauretania, benefited from mutually advantageous diplomatic relationships with Rome as 'client kings' or 'friendly kings' [6].

Before Rome rose to become the Mediterranean superpower, its military and diplomatic activities on the Italian peninsula produced a cascade of treaties (*foedus*, plural *foedera*) with those it defeated. The nearest at hand, furnished with the most privileges, were its neighbour communities in Latium. Some of these became integrated into the Roman state, and their citizens received Roman citizenship, while others were granted the *ius Latii*, a set of rights and obligations for the 'Latins' that was eventually extended to favoured non-Latins too. Beyond Latium, a more restricted form of Roman citizenships (*civitas sine suffragio*) was granted, and this was slowly extended to (or imposed upon) a plethora of Italian communities as the Romans conquered them. Other ethnicities of Italy were tied to Rome as *socii*. Common to all these *foedera* was the obligation to serve in the Roman army. In the wake of the Social War of the early 1st century BC, the Romans were compelled to extend citizenship to their Italian confederates. Thereafter, they wielded the privilege with greater generosity. The talisman of Roman citizenship was one of the forces that held the *imperium* together in the *Pax Romana* (cf. → Empire).

C.3. IMPERIAL PERIOD

Many forms of diplomatic communication known under the Republic continued in the Imperial period, including the sending of delegations to the Senate or the emperor, and formal embassies sent to distant countries. However, the 'international' character of the discourse had changed. Although there were still no permanent diplomatic representatives or ambassadors, provincial governors furnished with an imperial mandate were available for contact with representatives of external powers. The Romans continued to pay close attention to the symbolism of diplomacy.

The emperor, for example, would never agree to a direct conversation of equals with the ruler of the Parthian Empire, the only high culture of the period capable of standing up to Rome. Such communication would have implied that the authority of the two rulers was evenly matched – an admission neither side was prepared to make. When Augustus negotiated with the Parthians for the return of the lost standards of Crassus, he did so through intermediaries like his stepson Tiberius. He then celebrated his diplomatic victory as if it had been a military one. He had coins minted, showing a grovelling Parthian handing back the standards (Suet. Tib. 9; Cass. Dio 54,8; cf. R. Gest. Div. Aug. 29; → Standard).

Diplomatic relations with important powers beyond the frontiers of the empire – Germanic tribes in the north and the Iranian empires in the east – reinforced the defensive ring around imperial territory. Such relations were pursued in order to support a *modus vivendi* that fulfilled Roman interests as far as possible [18]. Rome elevated some tribes to the status of military allies and partners (*foederati*). This policy proved counterproductive in AD 378, when the Gothic *foederati* rebelled, defeating Roman forces at Adrianople and killing Emperor Valens (Amm. Marc. 31; → Battles of note, B.). In the east, there were recurrent wars with the Persians. Roman-Persian relations reached a nadir in AD 260, when Emperor Valerian was captured and held prisoner. At the diplomatic level, however, many treaties were drafted to put an end to this sequence of wars. The treaty between Justinian and the Sassanid Emperor Chosroes (Xusrō) I (AD 562), which was recorded by Menander Protector, gives comprehensive details regarding both sides' embassies, negotiations and incessant diplomatic posturing and manoeuvring ([9.164–177], M20 = Menander frg. 20 Blockley).

C.4. THE 'JUST WAR' IN CHRISTIANITY

The idea of just war was a crucial topic throughout Roman history. The adoption of Christianity as the empire's official religion had a great impact on the concept of the *iustum bellum*, and on the structure of Christianity itself (→ Religion). A Roman Emperor simply could not afford 'to turn the other cheek' when facing a rebellion from within or an attack from without. Constantine himself supplied the precept for the new way of thinking when he announced his vision at the Milvian Bridge: a cross of light in the sky, with the message 'In this sign thou shalt conquer!' (*In hoc signo vinces*). The paradox of combining a pacifist religion with a militarized society was resolved through the concept of just war. The statements of Augustine (5th century) on just war and the enabling of Christians to fight as soldiers still form the basis for the Catholic doctrine of just war today.

Bibliography
[1] F.E. Adcock / D.J. Mosley, Diplomacy in Ancient Greece, 1975 [2] S.L. Ager, Interstate Arbitrations in the Greek World, 337–90 BC, 1996 [3] C. Auliard, La diplomatie romaine. L'autre instrument de la conquête. De la fondation à la fin des guerres samnites (755–290 av. J.-C.), 2006 [4] E. Badian, Foreign Clientelae (264–70 BC), 1958 [5] E. Baltrusch, Außenpolitik, Bünde und Reichsbildung in der Antike, 2008 [6] D. Braund, Rome and the Friendly King. The Character of the Client Kingship, 1984 [7] P.J. Burton, Friendship and Empire. Roman Diplomacy and Imperialism in the Middle Republic (353–146 BC), 2011 [8] E. Caire / S. Pittia (eds.), Guerre et diplomatie romaines (IVe–IIIe siècles), 2006 [9] B. Dignas / E. Winter, Rom und das Perserreich. Zwei Weltmächte zwischen Konfrontation und Koexistenz, 2001 [10] A.M. Eckstein, Rome Enters the Greek East. From Anarchy to Hierarchy in the Hellenistic Mediterranean, 230–170 BC, 2008 [11] C. Eilers (ed.), Diplomats and Diplomacy in the Roman World, 2009 [12] A. Giovannini, Les relations entre états dans la Grèce antique. Du temps d'Homère à l'intervention romaine (ca. 700–200 av. J.-C.), 2007 [13] B. Grass / G. Stouder (eds.), La diplomatie romaine sous la République. Réflexions sur une pratique, 2015 [14] E.S. Gruen, The Hellenistic World and the Coming of Rome, 1984 [15] M. Jehne, Koine Eirene. Untersuchungen zu den Befriedungs- und Stabilisierungsbemühungen in der griechischen Poliswelt des 4. Jahrhunderts v.Chr., 1994 [16] C. Koehn, Krieg – Diplomatie – Ideologie. Zur Außenpolitik hellenistischer Mittelstaaten, 2007 [17] M. Lang et al. (eds.), Staatsverträge, Völkerrecht und Diplomatie im Alten Orient und in der griechisch-römischen Antike, 2010 [18] A.D. Lee, Information and Frontiers. Roman Foreign Relations in Late Antiquity, 1993 [19] P. Low, Interstate Relations in Classical Greece. Morality and Power, 2007 [20] S. Lücke, Syngeneia. Epigraphisch-historische Studien zu einem Phänomen der antiken griechischen Diplomatie, 2000 [21] A. Magnetto, Gli arbitrati interstatali greci, vol. 2: Dal 337 al 196 a.C., 1997 [22] C. Marek, Die Proxenie, 1984 [23] E. Olshausen / H. Biller (eds.), Antike Diplomatie, 1979 [24] L. Piccirilli, Gli arbitrati interstatali greci, vol. 1: Dalle origini al 338 a.C., 1973 [25] J. Wilker (ed.), Maintaining Peace and Interstate Stability in Archaic and Classical Greece, 2012

Sheila L. Ager

Discipline

A. Greek
B. Roman

A. Greek

A.1. Age of Heroes
A.2. Farmers as citizen-soldiers
A.3. The art of war in the *polis*
A.4. Discipline in Sparta
A.5. Discipline in Athens

Discipline in the Greek military can only be explained in the context of the emergence of the *polis* and the hoplite phalanx. For discipline and battle tactics in the age prior to the *polis*, the 'Dark Ages' (1100–800 BC), inferences must be made from Homer's *Iliad*. The first historical sources coincide in date with the advent of the phalanx.

A.1. Age of Heroes

Homer's heroes, who it may be assumed resemble warriors in the pre-phalangic era, live up as best they can to the ideal of *arete* (literally 'bestness', male virtue, valour) and seek to avoid shame. In their quest for *arete*, warriors like Achilles and Hector aspire to a quasi-divine renown (*kleos*), fighting among the greatest of the heroes far ahead of the ordinary battle lines. Hector, for example, explains to his wife Andromache why he must meet Achilles out on the battlefield and cannot remain behind the walls of Troy (Hom. Il. 6,440–445): 'Wife, I am aware of all this too, but my shame facing Trojan men and deep-robed Trojan women would be profound if I shrank from the fighting like a coward. My heart won't allow me, for I've learned always to be valorous [i.e. to display *arete*] like a noble and to fight among the foremost of the Trojans, striving for glory for my father and myself'. Nestor reminds Patroclus of the advice Achilles received from his father when about to embark for Troy: 'Old Peleus instructed his son Achilles always to be the best and distinguished above all others' (Hom. Il. 11,784). The heroic ideal is best illustrated in the single combat between two heroes, with their peers sitting and watching – for example, in the battle between Hector and Ajax (Hom. Il. 7,1ff.). In all such cases, military discipline (*eutaxia*) is synonymous with moral conditioning.

In large battles, any man who shrinks from the front line of the raging fight like a coward (*kakos*) incurs great shame. Thus, Nestor in the *Iliad* (4,297–300) drives the cowards back into the midst of the battlefield 'so that all, even those unwilling, would have to fight'. Ordinary infantrymen are expected not to avoid battle entirely or to run away when danger looms in war. The battle is fought between individuals, but sometimes also between entire armies. Men like Thersites, a common soldier, can expect rapid correction for unbefitting conduct in the form of a thrashing with their superior's staff – though even heroes face reproof if they lurk in the background out of → cowardice or neglect of duty (Hom. Il. 4,370). Agamemnon, for instance, chides the men around Odysseus for their reticence (Hom. Il. 4,340ff.): 'Why do you stand aside, cowering and waiting on others? It would befit you two to take your place among the foremost troops, and face the fire of battle! You're always first to heed my call to eat, when we Achaeans make a banquet for the elders! You're happy enough then to gorge on roast meat, and quaff honeyed wine by the cupful, to your hearts' content. But now you'd rather stand idly by and watch, even if ten Achaean squadrons were ahead of you, battling the relentless bronze'.

The immediate reward for earning *arete* is recognition among peers and honour (*time*) in physical form: booty after the sharing out of the gains. In the longer term, the hero's aim is to win renown (*kleos*), the fruit of the good reputation of heroic courage and an intimation of immortality in heroic song. For the Homeric warriors, the struggle for *arete* as part of the quest for *time* and *kleos* – not to mention avoiding the opposite, an ignominious (*aischros*) and inglorious (*dysklees*) reputation – sufficed to maintain discipline.

A.2. FARMERS AS CITIZEN-SOLDIERS

During the Archaic period (900–700 BC), still before the introduction of the hoplite system, warfare was dominated by horsemen and owners of large estates, as social elites. New battle techniques were then introduced in the 8th century, ushering in a new concept of *arete* and the democratization of combat. Wealthy farmers now made up the majority of the fighting force. This group was distinct from the elite, but excluded poorer groups who could not afford the new equipment. The crucial determining feature of the hoplite was that he was a free citizen, defending his own land and the territory of his *polis*. According to the new canon of values, the hoplite was defending his fatherland and its greater good. Aristotle, for instance, contrasted the soldiers of Persia with the farmer-soldiers of Greece as follows: 'Their lords compel them to fight...; their generals and officers, who beat them if they give ground, do likewise, as do the commanders who have them form up in front of trenches, and suchlike ... – they all coerce them. But a man should be brave not under compulsion, but for the nobility of it'. (Arist. Eth. Nic. 1116a 29–33).

As for tactics, the key manoeuvre when an army was advancing into battle was to reform the marching column into a phalanx eight rows deep. This demanded a new kind of discipline. All fighters had to hold their position in the array, without advancing further or turning to take flight. As soon as the formation was in place, the primary duty of those at the rear was to plug gaps as others fell in front of them. The soldier's job was to risk his own life and safety for the greater good of the *polis*. As Tyrtaeus explained, 'A man is not good in war if he has not suffered the sight of bloody slaughter and had the courage to stand up close to strike his foe. This is valour and renown, the finest thing and the dearest prize a youth can attain. This sense of pride is common to all, to city and to people, when a man stands unflinching and unwavering in the front line, banishing all thought of shameful flight, risking with forbearance and courage all this life has promised him, and with words that inspire stands side by side with his comrades. Thus and only thus can a man be good in war. Quickly then he turns the enemy ranks to flight and holds back the waves of battle with steadfast arm. Should he fall in the vanguard, losing his life in the battle, to the honour of his people, his city, and his father – with his breast pierced many times through the bronze of his armour and his shield run through by spears – then young and old will weep for him with a yearning and pain felt by all throughout the city' (Tyrt. 9D,10–28).

Positioning in the phalanx was uncomplicated, demanding little of commanding officers. All *poleis* sought to retain as many hoplites as possible, but farmers able to afford full equipment were few in number. Self-discipline was the highest priority for these farmer citizen-soldiers, but since they attached great importance to their personal freedom, their commanders had limited scope for disciplining them.

Herodotus contrasts this with the observation that Persian commanders literally had to whip their troops to battle (Hdt. 7,103,4; 7,223,3). By contrast, declares Aristotle (Eth. Nic. 1116a 29–33; cf. Pol. 1327b 23–33), 'The courage of citizens is the best, since it most resembles true courage. Citizen soldiers, it seems, accept danger firstly because of the legal penalties and the stigma attached to cowardice, secondly for the honours valour earns. Hence, the bravest in contests appear to be those who disdain cowards and honour courageous men'. Given the importance attached to fighting spirit and courage, the citizen of the *polis* resembles the Homeric hero.

A.3. THE ART OF WAR IN THE *POLIS*

The art of war and tactics were essentially identical in Athens, which resembled other Greek city-states, and Sparta with its professional army. As in the world of the Homeric heroes, the *polis* regarded discipline as essential to the status of a citizen and synonymous with moral conditioning. To the early legislators of the two cities, Lycurgus in Sparta and Solon in Athens, only citizens and landowners could be members of the army. The Greeks equated military education with athletic training, which was associated with the gymnasium (e.g. weapon-throwing and war dances). For most Greek men, training thus took place in the private sphere. In Sparta, by contrast, the citizen belonged to the city, not to himself. As Plutarch describes it, 'The Spartans' military training lasted into the years of maturity. No man was permitted to live as he wished. Their city, like a military camp, always imposed a military regime and duties in public service, for they belonged wholly to their country and not to themselves' (Plut.

Lycurgus 24,1). By contrast, Athenian citizens emphasized their personal freedom and initiative. They thus regarded miltary exercises as practised in Sparta an intrusion into personal liberty. In the words of Pericles, in his famous funeral oration, 'In education, our rivals [sc. the Spartans] strive with relentless discipline for manly valour, beginning in childhood. Whereas we in Athens live without compulsion, and yet we are no less equal to the dangers that face us' (Thuc. 2,39,1).

A.4. Discipline in Sparta

The Spartans were notorious for the violence with which they instilled discipline in their own citizens and other free Greeks under their command (Plut. *Themistocles* 11,3; Thuc. 8,84,2f.). Spartan officers, for instance, were permitted to use their cane (*bakteria*) to strike idlers or recalcitrant subordinates. Perhaps the best-known example is the treatment meted out by the Spartan regent Pausanias to non-Spartan Greeks of the Hellenic League after the Persian War (Thuc. 1,95,1). The allies from other *poleis*, notably the Ionians, rejected Pausanias because of his cruelty (he was regarded as *biaios*, 'violent'), preferring Athenian commanders. His disciplinary methods went beyond the mere use of blows (*plegai*); he also forced soldiers to stand wearing an iron anchor round their neck (Plut. *Aristides* 11). The custom of making soldiers stand holding their shields was a well-attested form of punishment for lack of discipline in Sparta (*ataxia*; cf. Xen. Hell. 3,1,9).

Failure to obey an order from a Spartan king was treated as an act of cowardice. Thucydides describes how, during the Battle of Mantinea (418 BC), two Spartan officers refused to carry out an order from King Agis II, causing a fatal gap to appear in the phalanx (Thuc. 5,72,1): 'But it happened, despite [Agis'] having given the command unexpectedly at the very beginning, that both Aristocles and Hipponoidas refused to go to the appointed place, and in the meantime the enemy attacked. For this the two were subsequently banished from Sparta, as it was thought they had disobeyed out of cowardice'. Other acts that typically incurred disciplinary consequences included throwing away one's shield and fleeing the battlefield. In Athens and Sparta alike, penalties for such offences would involve at least the withdrawal of some civic rights (*atimia*, 'dishonour').

In Sparta, cowards were called 'runaways' (*tresantes*) and they were subject to social exclusion. Xenophon, in his *Constitution of the Lacedaemonians* (9,4f.), describes the consequences of → cowardice (*deilia*): 'In other states, when a man turns out to be a coward, the only consequence is that he is called a coward. He visits the same market as the brave man, sits with him, attends the same gymnasium, should he so wish. But in Lacedaemon, anyone would be ashamed to have a coward with him at table, or to face him in a wrestling match'.

'He is often last to be chosen when teams are picked for a ball game. He is consigned to the dishonourable place in the chorus. In the streets, he is obliged to give way. If he has taken a seat, he must give it up, even to a younger man. At home, he must support his unmarried female relatives, and explain to them why they are old maids. He must make the best of a hearth with no wife, and make reparations even for that. He cannot expect to walk around with a smile on his face, or to behave like a man with an untainted reputation, without being beaten for it by his betters'.

A.5. Discipline in Athens

In his *Constitution of the Athenians* (61,2), Aristotle describes the powers of the city's military: 'When in command of a force, they are empowered to punish breaches of discipline with imprisonment, exile, or the imposition of a fine, but the last of these is not usual'. In 394 BC, for instance, the Athenians banished Simon for disobedience, when he failed to appear on time as a group was drafted to be sent to Corinth. Lysias (3,45), in his oration denouncing Simon, declared, 'I will [...] mention but one thing, which you should hear as proof positive of his bare-faced temerity. At Corinth, where he arrived after our battle with the enemy and the expedition to Coronea, he fought with the taxiarch Laches, and gave him a thrashing. And when the citizens set out with the entire army, he alone stood out as the most insubordinate and cowardly, and he was the only Athenian whom the herald banished from the country by order of the generals'.

In conclusion, the Greeks regarded military discipline as a moral and strategic duty. However, the egalitarian nature of the *polis* set limits to the use and extent of military drill and military punishment.

Bibliography

[1] P.A. Cartledge, The Birth of the Hoplite, in: P.A. Cartledge, Spartan Reflections, 2001, 153–166 (first published as La nascita degli opliti e l'organizzazione militare, in: S. Settis (ed.), I Greci, vol. 2/1, 1996, 681–714) [2] R. Drews, The End of the Bronze Age. Changes in Warfare and the Catastrophe ca. 1200 B.C., 1993 [3] P. Ducrey, Warfare in Ancient Greece, 1986 [4] P.A. Greenhalgh, Early Greek Warfare. Horsemen and Chariots in the Homeric and Archaic Ages, 1973 [5] V.D. Hanson, The Other Greeks. The Family Farm and the Agrarian Roots of Western Civilization, 1999 [6] V.D. Hanson, The Western Way of War, 2000 [7] S. Hornblower, Sticks, Stones and Spartans. The Sociology of Spartan Violence, in: H. van Wees (ed.), War and Violence in Ancient Greece, 2009, 57–82 [8] D. Kagan / G. Viggiano (eds.), Men of Bronze. Hoplite Warfare in Ancient Greece, 2013 [9] J. Kromayer / G. Veith, Heerwesen und Kriegführung

der Griechen und Römer, 1928 [10] C. MANN, Militär und Kriegführung in der Antike, 2013 [11] W. RÜSTOW / H. KÖCHLY, Geschichte des Griechischen Kriegswesens von der Ältesten Zeit bis auf Pyrrhos, 1852 [12] A. SNODGRASS, Early Greek Armour and Weapons, 1964 [13] H. VAN WEES, Greek Warfare. Myths and Realities, 2004.

GREGORY F. VIGGIANO

B. ROMAN

B.1. Discipline – the foundation of the Roman military
B.2. Offences against discipline and their punishment

B.1. DISCIPLINE – THE FOUNDATION OF THE ROMAN MILITARY

Pliny the Younger praised Trajan as *conditor* ('founder') and *firmator* ('establisher') of military discipline (Ep. 10,29). An inscription from Timgad praises Septimius Severus as *conditor Romanae disciplinae*, 'founder of Roman discipline' (CIL VIII 17870 = ILS 446). In AD 249, Decius was celebrated as *reparator disciplinae militaris*, 'restorer of military discipline' (CIL III 12351 = ILBulg 7 = ILS 8922 = IDR 2, 639 = AE 1891, 46). These three stood in a long sequence of Roman commanders and rulers who strove to preserve and improve discipline in the *exercitus Romanus* ('Roman army'). Valerius Maximus saw strict military discipline and the absolute obedience of the individual as a particular glory and bulwark of the Roman Empire (2,7 pr.; likewise 6,1,11; Liv. 8,7,16; Jos. BI 3,5,1 (§71); SHA Alex. 53,5). It was the guarantee of bountiful peace and the source of Rome's greatness. It had made it possible to achieve dominion over Italy and to make Rome the capital of the whole world (2,8 pr.). The founder of discipline in the Imperial period was Augustus, who in establishing the standing army also laid the foundations for its reliability and successful deployment [10]. Beginning with Hadrian, who took great pains to sharpen discipline (SHA Hadr. 10,3; Veg. Mil. 1,27), the personification of discipline began to attract cultic veneration (AE 1979, 388 = RIB 3, 3298; [4]). The mounted guard of the governor of the province of Africa proconsularis, for instance, dedicated an altar to her: *disciplinae militari Augustor(um) aram ded(icaverunt) Q(uinto) Anicio Fausto co(n)s(ule) eq(uites) sing(ulares) pr(ovinciae) Af(ricae)* (AE 1957, 1222 = 1971, 507 = 1973, 629; Lambaesis, AD 198).

Roman discipline was a virtue inherited from the *maiores* ('ancestors'), and it had to be upheld (Sall. Iug. 44,3; 55,1). The term discipline included both correction as implemented by the commander and the soldiers' conduct in general. It encompassed physical performance, strength in battle, and mental readiness for unconditional subordination and absolute obedience [4]; [8]. Discipline intensified not only soldiers' strike capabilities, but also their cohesion, as they were obliged to rely on one another in battle. It also generated confidence in the combat abilities of the individual. Hierarchical structures, standing orders and daily employment nurtured obedience and countered uncertainty and anxieties.

B.2. OFFENCES AGAINST DISCIPLINE AND THEIR PUNISHMENT

The annalistic historians are clear: generals were required to prioritize the nurturing and intensification of discipline above all else. Postumius Tubertus and Manlius Torquatus are said to have executed their own sons for fighting the enemy in defiance of an order from their fathers. The fact that they fought and won changed nothing: unconditional obedience and collective discipline were more important than a courageous individual initiative (432 and 340 BC; e.g. Liv. 4,29,5f.; 8,6,14–7,22; Diod. Sic. 12,64; Val. Max. 2,7,6; Frontin. Str. 4,1,40f.). Imperial law also prescibed the death penalty for actions contrary to orders in wartime (Dig. 49,16,3,15). Good commanders always made sure to restore discipline that had been lost under their predecessors. One such was P. Cornelius Scipio Aemilianus Africanus (Val. Max. 2,7,1; Frontin. Str. 4,1,1; Flor. Epit. 1,34,11; Liv. Per. 57), conqueror of Numantia (133 BC), and another was Q. Caecilius Metellus during the Jugurthine War (111–105 BC; Sall. Iug. 44f.; Val. Max. 2,7,2; Frontin. Str. 4,1,2; Eutr. 4,27). Generations later, Augustus (Suet. Aug. 24,1: *militarem disciplinam severissime rexit*; *senatus consultum de Cn. Pisone* 52 [1]: *militarem disciplinam a divo Augusto institutam*) wrote a treatise about discipline (Dig. 49,16,12,1; Veg. Mil. 1,8; 1,27; [10]). Vespasian, charged with putting down the Jewish Revolt, is said to have inculcated new discipline at once (Suet. Vesp. 4,6). Formulaic as these examples may be, they show how Romans over the centuries conceived of the ideal commander, and that generals were judged by their ability to manage discipline – the *certissima Romani imperii custos*, 'the most reliable guard of the Roman Empire' (Val. Max. 6,1,11). Subordinate to commanders, centurions and decurions bore responsibility for upholding discipline in units, and they used their *vitis* ('[staff made from a] vine branch') to enforce it (Tac. Ann. 1,18,1; Dig. 49,16,13,4). The oath a soldier took on enlistment included the promise of obedience (Pol. 6,21; [11.142]). Nevertheless, preserving discipline was a daily challenge that sometimes caused conflicts.

The chapter of the *Digest* that deals with breaches of discipline, *De re militari*, 'Concerning Military Affairs' (49,16), is mostly derived from the work of jurists of the Severan period, but older sources show that the principles it formulates were used earlier. According to Arrius Menander, all breaches of discipline were military crimes (Dig. 49,16,6 pr.). He makes explicit mention of *segnitas* ('sloth'), *contumacia* ('obstinacy') and *desidia* ('sitting idle'). Typical offences against discipline included refusal to obey, ignoring a command, unbecoming conduct, failure to provide assistance, assault on a comrade, causing bodily harm to a comrade, sale or loss of weapons, insurgency, treachery, cowardice (e.g. Dig. 49,16,3,15–18; 49,16,6,1 and 49,16,14,1; cf. Frontin. Str. 4,1,38; 4,5,17), corruption (e.g. Tac. Ann. 1,17,4; 1,35,1; Tac. Hist. 1,46,1–3; O. Krok. 99f.) and attacks on the civilian population (e.g. Sall. Iug. 44,5 [3]).

Punishments depended on the severity of the offence, the status of the soldier and the specific circumstances. Modestinus supplies us with a list of military penalties. They ranged from corporal punishment to hard labour through compulsory transfer, to demotion, and even to dishonourable discharge (Dig. 49,16,3,1). The death penalty was in place for crimes against superior officers, the severity of the offence rising with the rank of the aggrieved party (Dig. 49,16,6,1f.). The death penalty was also applied for the betrayal of secrets (Dig. 49,16,6,4) and for being the first to flee the field of battle (Dig. 49,16,6,3; cf. Dion. Hal. Ant. Rom. 9,50,6f.). If a superior officer encountered danger and was killed, those who failed to protect him could expect execution (Dig. 49,3,22). Drunkenness and debauchery earned reduction in rank (Dig. 49,16,6,7), for soldiers and officers alike were expected to lead a simple life (e.g. Frontin. Str. 4,1,5; 4,1,7; Suet. Vesp. 8,3; SHA Hadr. 10,3; SHA Avid. 5,3–5).

The extent to which psychological problems jeopardized discipline cannot be known. There are some indications of mental distress and anxiety. For instance, anyone who feigned illness to avoid battle forfeited his life (Dig. 49,16,6,5). The legal sources are familiar with the concept of soldiers' committing suicide out of 'disgust at life' (*taedium vitae*). Suicide and self-mutilation were considered the gravest breaches of discipline (Dig. 49,16,6,7). Soldiers who attempted suicide were executed. If reasonable grounds were evident (severe illness, intolerable pain, psychological motives), this was commuted to dishonorable discharge (Dig. 28,3,6,7; 29,1,34 pr.; 49,16,6,7; cf. 29,5,1,23; Paulus, Sent. 5,38,6).

Occasionally, punishments to the body were delivered to enforce discipline, such as the severing of one or both hands. The jurists do not discuss these punishments, which in itself indicates their rarity (e.g. Frontin. Str. 4,1,16; Caes. B Gall. 8,44,1; Amm. Marc. 29,5,22; 29,5,31; SHA Avid. 4,5). Soldiers and officers guilty of a breach of discipline were sometimes publicly shamed by having to stand outside the headquarters in undignified attire (e.g. Suet. Aug. 24,2; Frontin. Str. 4,1,26–28). The *decimatio* was a collective punishment, entailing the selection by lot of every tenth man for execution (Pol. 6,38). The *vicesimatio* and *centesimatio* (SHA Opil. 12,2), attested nowhere else, may be inventions. The first mention of a *decimatio* for → cowardice and the loss of military standard and weapons dates from 471 BC (Liv. 2,59,11; Dion. Hal. Ant. Rom. 9,50,7; Frontin. Str. 4,1,34); another occurred around 300 BC (Frontin. Str. 4,1,35). The *decimatio* was sometimes mitigated. For instance, centuries whose positions were breached by the enemy suffered only the loss of three men each (Frontin. Str. 4,1,36). According to Plutarch, it was Crassus who revived this ruthless punishment (10,3). Caesar (Cass. Dio 41,35,5) and Mark Antony (Frontin. Str. 4,1,37; cf. Plut. *Marcus Antonius* 39,7; Cass. Dio 49,27,1) also practised the *decimatio*, as did the future Augustus (Cass. Dio 49,38,4; cf. Suet. Aug. 24,2). The last to order a *decimatio* seems to have been Galba (Suet. Galba 12,2; Tac. Ann. 3,21,1; Tac. Hist. 1,37,3; 1,51,5; Cass. Dio 63,3,1f.).

The abundance of offences discussed may give the impression that indiscipline was widespread. However, the opposite was probably the case. This becomes clear from a detailed study of the individual offences and the abolition of the collective *decimatio*.

☞ Education; Honour; Military law; Military service

BIBLIOGRAPHY
[1] W. ECK et al., Das senatus consultum de Cn. Pisone patre, 1996 [2] V. GIUFFRÈ, Militum disciplina e ratio militaris, in: ANRW II.13, 1980, 234–277 [3] P. HERRMANN, Hilferufe aus römischen Provinzen. Ein Aspekt der Krise des römischen Reiches im 3. Jhdt. n.Chr. (Berichte aus den Sitzungen der Joachim-Jungius-Gesellschaft der Wissenschaften e.V. 8,4), 1990 [4] G. HORSMANN, Untersuchungen zur militärischen Ausbildung im republikanischen und kaiserzeitlichen Rom (Wehrwissenschaftliche Forschungen 35), 1991 [5] J.H. JUNG, Die Rechtsstellung des römischen Soldaten. Ihre Entwicklung von den Anfängen Roms bis auf Diokletian, in: ANRW II.14, 1982, 963–1008 [6] Y. LE BOHEC, Decimatio, in: BNP 4, 2004, 150–151 [7] Y. LE BOHEC, Disciplina, in: BNP 4, 2004, 537–539 [8] O. MAUCH, Der lateinische Begriff Disciplina. Eine Wortuntersuchung, 1941, 72–80 (Diss. Basel 1939) [9] C. SCHMETTERER, Die rechtliche Stellung römischer Soldaten im Prinzipat (Philippika. Marburger altertumskundliche Abhandlungen 54), 2012, 25–33 [10] M.A. SPEIDEL, Augustus' militärische Neuordnung und ihr Beitrag zum Erfolg des Imperium Romanum, in: M.A. SPEIDEL, Heer und Herrschaft im Römischen Reich der Hohen Kaiserzeit (MAVORS 16), 2009, 19–51 [11] M.A. SPEIDEL, Pro patria mori ... La doctrine du patriotisme romain dans l'armée impériale, in: Cahiers Centre Gustave Glotz 21, 2010, 139–154 [12] G. WESCH-KLEIN, Soziale Aspekte des römischen Heerwesens in der Kaiserzeit (HABES 28), 1998,

147–156 [13] M. ZIÓŁKOWSKI, Il culto della disciplina nella religione degli eserciti Romani, in: Rivista storica dell'Antichità 20, 1990, 97–107.

GABRIELE WESCH-KLEIN

Dogs

The ancient sources make sporadic reference to the use of dogs in warfare. These references mostly relate to a mythical past, or else to people living in the geographical peripheries of Greece and Rome [2]; [1].

According to Polyaenus (2nd century AD), Alyattes II of Lydia in the early 6th century BC made successful use of dogs in battle against Cimmerian horse nomads invading Asia Minor. Large, aggressive dogs attacked the Cimmerians and put some of them to flight (Strat. 7,2,1). The inhabitants of Castabala and Colophon in Asia Minor also kept war dogs, which fought in the first rank, were eager to fight, showed unflinching loyalty and needed no pay (Plin. HN 8,143; Ael. NA 7,38). According to Claudius Aelianus, dogs from Magnesia attacked the enemy ranks and broke through them (VH 14,46). Like the Magnesians, the Paeonians of Thrace were also said to have used dogs in war (Poll. 5,47). Herodotus reports three episodes of single combat between men, horses and dogs during a conflict between the Paeonians and the Greek colonists of Perinthus (5,1).

According to Claudius Aelianus (NA 7,38), the Hyrcanians also used dogs for military purposes. Purportedly, the Caspii even equipped their dogs with armour, although the only source for this is the epic *Argonautica* of Valerius Flaccus (6,105–115). An unknown ruler of the Libyan Garamantes supposedly led 200 dogs into battle against his opponents on his return from exile (Plin. HN 8,142). A Byzantine excerpt of Appian (Rom. 4,12) describes dogs as the 'bodyguards' (*doryphoroi*) of an Allobrogian emissary who was meeting Gn. Domitius Ahenobarbus during the latter's campaign in Southern Gaul in 121 BC. The only source to mention Gaulish war dogs is Strabo, who wrote his *Geographia* in the reigns of Augustus and Tiberius. He claimed (probably citing the historian Poseidonius, c. 135–50 BC) that animal hides, slaves and dogs were among the many goods traded from the British Isles to Gaul. The Gauls interbred the British dogs with their own, not only for → hunting, but also for war (Str. 4,5,2; cf. Grattius, *Cynegetica* 174–181). Dogs could also be used for defence. According to Pliny the Elder (HN 8,143), dogs defended the wagon fort of the Germanic Cimbri (probably at the Battle of Vercellae in 101 BC).

An episode related by Claudius Aelianus probably represents an exception rather than evidence of how war dogs were regularly used. An Athenian is said to have taken his dog to the Battle of Marathon, and he and his 'fellow soldier' were immortalized in a painting in the *stoa poikile* (HN 7,38). Philip II of Macedon made use of dogs' tracking abilities when pursuing the Thracian Arbelians (or Orbelians), who were hiding in difficult, mountainous terrain (Polyaenus, Strat. 4,2,16). According to Zonaras (8,18, Dindorf, p. 227), M. Pomponius used dogs to catch indigenous Sardinian 'bandits' hiding in caves and forests around 231 BC.

BIBLIOGRAPHY
[1] J.M. COOK, Dogs in Battle, in: T. DORN (ed.), Festschrift Andreas Rumpf, 1952, 38–42 [2] D. KARUNANITHY, Dogs of War. Canine Use in Warfare from Ancient Egypt to the 19th Century, 2008 [3] F. ORTH, Hund, in: RE 8/2, 1913, 2566–2567

ALFRED MICHAEL HIRT

Education

A. Introduction
B. Sparta and Athens
C. Hellenistic period
D. Roman Republic and Principate
E. Late Roman Empire

A. INTRODUCTION

Military education in Greco-Roman Antiquity was part of the general education that enabled the youngest men of the city-states to become full members of the citizen body (Aristot. Ath. Pol. 42). This continued to be the case for as long as there were citizen armies – that is to say, throughout the Greek Archaic and Classical periods, and the Roman Monarchical and Republican periods. During the Hellenistic period, and particularly under the Roman Principate, as standing armies came into being, states gradually revised their systems for providing young recruits with effective military → training. There is no direct information on the armies of the Hellenistic kings, which were mainly made up of → mercenaries, but many details are preserved of the → recruitment system and military education of the Imperial Roman armies. The situation did not change as radically as might be expected through Late Antiquity or the early Byzantine period – except in relation to the units of *foederati* ('allies'), who, although integrated into the army, preserved their own fighting styles and command structures. Even this, however, was not entirely new, for foreign units of *numeri* and *nationes* with their own commands and variegated fighting styles had already been deployed in early Roman history, albeit on a very small scale.

B. SPARTA AND ATHENS

In → Sparta, the ritual of the *krypteia* ('hidden attack') formed part of military education (Plut. *Lycurgus* 28). This involved young men, each armed only with a small dagger, being sent out alone into the territory of a city, particulalry in harsh winter conditions, to practise guerrilla warfare against the helots. The young men were expected to use survival tactics including deception and theft. Only after completion of this ritual could they be admitted to the ranks of the hoplites (*hoplitai*). This procedure followed the state military schooling system, the *agoge* (Xen. Lac. 4,1–7), in which seven-year-old boys were separated from their families to be educated and trained by the state. From the age of 14 onwards, their education was strictly military. The aim was to nurture soldiers and future *homoioi* ('equals') for the Spartan phalanx. The *agoge* dwindled in importance through the 4th century, but Cleomenes III revived it around 230, before Philopoemen finally abolished it in 188 BC [21.6, 87, 112–114]; [4.47]; [17.406f.].

Although military service had been mandatory in Athens for men between the ages of 18 and 60 since the Archaic period, most information on this educational tradition dates from the 4th century. Young recruits were registered in every *demos* (Arist. Ath. Pol. 42,1) before beginning their basic military training. Working under the supervision of two trainers and educators, they learnt the hoplite fighting tactics, the use of bow and sling, and how to throw a javelin (Arist. Ath. pol. 42,3). They were then sent to various guard posts or border fortresses (e.g. Panactum, Decelea, Rhamnus) and to garrisons in the rural demes (e.g. Eleusis). There they continued their military education in areas brimming with all kinds of dangers. Thucydides makes several references to the military duties of the eldest and the youngest that differed from those of the *hoplitai* (Thuc. 1,105,4; 2,13,7).

The *ephebes* (men over 18 registered for service) were also called *peripolos* ('those on patrol'). This period of duty lasted two years, as Aeschines reports of his own experience (Aeschin. Leg. 167) and as epigraphic sources confirm (inscription of the *ephebes* of the Cecropis *phyle*, registered 334 BC, discharged 332 BC). Sometimes, the *ephebes* even wore a striking black coat and swore an → oath alongside the oath of the Athenian soldiers when they faced 'barbarians' (attested in an inscription of the mid-4th century (R&O, 440–457, no. 88f.); on the organization of the Athenian hoplites cf. also [21.85–105, 106–128]). The *ephebeia* was thus tantemount to a term of professional military service for young members of the citizenry, lasting two years and mainly served in frontier regions. As theirs was not a standing professional army, but a hoplite army made up of citizens, the *ephebes'* duties during their military education were confined to policing and guard duties on the border. Their mission was to prevent unauthorized entry and to protect sanctuaries near the border, tasks of considerable importance to the physical and ritual demarcation of the territory. This time of life as *ephebes* was a transitional period for youth who were becoming adult warriors. It was a period of military training and initiation that could not be accomplished in the urban, civilized world of the city, but only in the wilderness of the borderlands [16.64f.]

The training and education of cavalrymen was generally managed in a similar way in Archaic and Classical Greece, as Xenophon's reports from Athens show. Young recruits to the cavalry first had to learn to mount their horses at a leap, then to stay safely on the horse's back, then to throw the javelin. Instruction was supposed to be entrusted to a professional trainer, but all cavalry regiment commanders (*phylarchos*) were also expected to supervise the process (Xen. Hipp. 1,5f.; 1,17f.). It must be remembered that, just as in the Roman Republic, horsemen (*hippeis*) occupied an elite position in society and in the economy, and they only came to play a vital role in battle at a later date, from the 4th century BC onwards.

In Classical Greece, contact with other *poleis* was sometimes used to expand a soldier's military education. Illustrative of this is the famous case of the Theban hero Epaminondas (→ Generals of note, F.), who learned a great deal from Spartan military discipline when he served in the Spartan army with his Theban detachment beginning in 385 BC. The military experience he gained, and the army reforms that he himself implemented at Thebes – the 'oblique order' (*loxe phalanx*) and the attack on the left wing – contributed to the decisive victory over the Spartans won by the Thebans under Cleombrotus at Leuctra in 371, and to their victory over the allied armies of Sparta and Athens at Mantinea in 362 BC. His example shows just how important a thorough knowledge of the fighting techniques and capabilities of the enemy was in military education [21.61–82].

C. HELLENISTIC PERIOD

There are not many sources that give information about military education in the various parts of the army within the Hellenistic monarchies. Armies by this time often consisted of men from different backgrounds. Such soldiers, notably Cretans, mainland Greeks and members of warrior peoples of Asia Minor, probably had some military training before they were enlisted. Information is preserved on the training of *ephebes* in the Greek cities of Asia Minor during the Hellenistic period. Outside Athens and Sparta, scholars long regarded the institutions of the *ephebeia* as purely sporting facilities for aristocrats, since it was assumed that citizen armies no longer existed by this period. This, however, in no way corresponds to historical reality. The *poleis* continued to maintain citizen armies throughout the entire Hellenistic period, and they even fought small battles among themselves, as attested in epigraphic records all over the Hellenistic world. The *ephebeia* remained a citizen institution and continued to play an important role in the military education of young *polis* members.

Following the Athenian example (see above), the *ephebeia* spread throughout the Greek world as an institution for the military training of young men between 18 and 20 years of age. The Gymnasiarchical Law of Beroea reveals in detail the military training of young men in a Hellenistic city (SEG 27, 261; 43, 381; I. Beroia 1). It was divided into two groups: *epheboi* aged between 18 and 20, and *neoi* ('young men') aged up to 22. They had to practise shooting with the bow and throwing the javelin daily. This is clear enough evidence that young Macedonians from Beroea were receiving military education as young adults [5] (on the citizen armies and the armies of the various Hellenistic city leagues, as distinct from those of the Hellenistic monarchies, see [4.18–43]). The same was happening in Drerus on Crete, where another ephebic oath is preserved in an inscription (SIG³ 521; SEG 46, 1210; [3.195–201, no. 7]; commentary and brief survey of the Hellenistic *ephebeia* in [4.46–56]). The importance of the training of *ephebes* is also seen in the growing numbers of gymnasia (training centres for *ephebes*) that were being built in many Hellenistic cities, and that were regarded as typical features of a Greek *polis*.

D. ROMAN REPUBLIC AND PRINCIPATE

Under the Roman Republic, military education probably took place after → recruitment under the supervision of the centurions, for the army was not yet professionalized. Young members of senatorial families served as military tribunes (*tribuni militum*) for proconsuls, and thus received their training in the provinces (Sall. Catil. 7,4–6). The most talented members of influential families were even made legates (*legati*) to proconsuls, with several legions under their command. Caesar, for instance, had many *legati* over the course of his long war in Gaul. Few of them, however, distinguished themselves as officers. One who did was Marcus Petreius, who defeated Catilina at Pistoria in 62 BC, and thereafter served as legate to Pompey in Spain (Sall. Catil. 59,6: *Homo militaris, quod amplius annos triginta tribunus aut praefectus aut legatus aut praetor cum magna gloria in exercitu fuerat*; 'A military man, who served with great distinction in the army for more than thirty years, as tribune, prefect, legate and praetor').

As already mentioned, more is known about military education during the early Imperial period (in general: [9]). Many recruits (to the legions and *auxilia* alike) may have already possessed useful military skills and knowledge before enlisting in the Roman army. Exactly when official military training began in the process of enlistment is not known. The first admission phase was the *probatio* ('probation') by the governor of the province in which the new soldier had been recruited [7.3–30]; [11.47, 73f., 87f.]. The potential recruit was questioned on his geographical and social origins at the provincial headquarters (*examinatio*; *origo parentum*), and his physical condition was evaluated [18.213–234]; [19]. Once officially accepted as a recruit (*tiro*), he received a payment (*viaticum*) covering the cost of travelling to his unit (usually) in the same province (BGU 423; RMR 70).

On arrival, recruits had their names entered in the register of their unit (RMR 87), and they were assigned to their respective *centuria* (RMR 74).

They were now officially soldiers (*milites*). When some recruits were sent by imperial order to a different province after the *probatio* (as e.g. the *tirones Asiani* in the abovementioned papyrus RMR 74), the governor of that province assigned them to the units of his provincial army [18.213–234]. It is not known whether any specific training was already given during the *probatio* period, which may have lasted several (perhaps four) months.

Official military education was conducted under the supervision of a centurion and specially assigned soldiers and *principales*. It began when the recruit arrived at the unit, if not before. According to Vegetius, young soldiers needed twice as much training as experienced men (Veg. Mil. 2,23,1f.). Recruits first learned the marching step, and hence to march in formation. Another important element of training was to learn the signals given on the trumpet (*tuba*) and horn (*cornu*). This training continued in peacetime, to guarantee soldiers' ability to follow commands given acoustically if war should break out (cf. Veg. Mil. 2,22 [6.44]; on musicians and musical instruments in the Roman army cf. [1]; → Music). Naturally, training in combat and use of weapons also formed part of the educational programme (Veg. Mil. 1,11–17) [11.113].

Epigraphic sources reveal that some soldiers were classified as *discentes* ('trainees') (e.g. CIL III 3565 = ILS 2393). These soldiers were receiving specialist training, and the position for which they were being trained is often indicated [2. passim, esp. 166]; [12.265f.], e.g. *discens equitum* ('trainee cavalryman'; CIL VIII 2882 = ILS 2331; CIL V 944; CIL V 8278 = ILS 2333), *discens aquiliferum* ('trainee eagle-bearer'; CIL VIII 18302 = ILS 2344), *discens armaturae* ('trainee weapons instructor'; CIL XIII 6824 = IDRE I 195; AE 1989, 482), *discens me(n)sore* ('trainee surveyor'; AE 2004, 1258), *discens libratorum* ('trainee surveyor'; AE 1973, 646), *discens capsariorum* ('trainee medical orderly'; CIL VIII 2553; 18047), *discens lanciariorum* ('trainee javelin-thrower'; AE 1993, 1575), *discens epibeta* ('trainee marine'; CIL III 14567 = ILS 9225 = IMS IV 31: a soldier of the *legio VII Claudia*, who was learning sailing in the small legionary flotilla on the Danube).

Soldiers of both infantry and cavalry were expected to learn to swim in full kit (cavalrymen together with their horses; Veg. Mil. 1,9f.). A striking funerary inscription in verse, probably for a member of the *equites singulares Augusti*, has the deceased declare, 'best and bravest of a thousand Batavian men, I succeeded, with Hadrian as judge, in swimming across the wide waters of the deep Danube in full battle kit' (*inter mille viros primus fortisque Batavos / (H)Adriano potui qui iudice vasta profundi / aequora Danuvii cunctis transnare sub armis*; CIL III 3676 = ILS 2558 = CLE 427) [10].

This famous case, which Cassius Dio (69,9,6) also mentions, illustrates the high level of military skill that soldiers in the Roman army possessed – as a result of their official education, their traditional training, or both.

Tacitus tells of a cohort of Usipetes (*cohors Usiporum*) recruited in Germania superior and augmented with a *centurio* and several experienced soldiers 'who were integrated into the company to instill military discipline and functioned as their examples as well as their instructors' (*qui ad tradendam disciplinam inmixti manipulis exemplum et rectores habebantur*, Tac. Agr. 28,1). Unfortunately, we do not know exactly how training was managed when new legions were recruited (which happened 16 times from AD 39 onwards), with the exception of reorganized units such as the *legio IIII Flavia Felix* or *legio XV Flavia* under Vespasian. It can be assumed, however, that it must have been a 'long and complicated process' [14. passim, esp. 2 (new ed.)]. In all likelihood, experienced junior officers and soldiers from other legions were transferred to form the core of a newly recruited legion, as was the case with the *legiones Parthicae* in the reign of Septimius Severus [18.187–189].

The Roman army included auxiliary units – regular (*alae* and *cohortes*) and irregular (*numeri* and *nationes*) – as well as legions that were recruited from eastern peoples, for example Syrians, Ituraeans, Commagenes, Palmyrenes and Nabataeans (cohorts from Petra, *cohortes Petraeorum*, formerly regiments of the royal Nabataean army, which were organized and trained in the Hellenistic manner). These often placed strong emphasis on the military expertise and training traditionally inculcated from childhood in their home communities, that is, long before they joined the Roman army (survey of the 'Oriental' units in [20. passim, esp. 87–95], on fighting styles and military equipment, which differed slightly from the Roman standard). This was particularly true of mounted archers (*hypotoxotai*), for whom the central Roman command had high praise, and apparently also in the case of the Moorish cavalry units (*alae* and *numeri*) who had fought for Roman since the days of the Republic. Thus, military education that differed from that of the Roman tradition mostly took place before recruits were inducted into the Roman army.

E. LATE ROMAN EMPIRE

For the Principate, it is possible to get a relatively good impression of how new recruits and newly recruited units were trained and brought to the requisite level of experience and discipline. Conversely, no direct information on educational practices exists for the Dominate, particularly the transitional period of the reigns of Diocletian and Constantine, when many new units were being created. It seems, however, that much of the old system was retained. Vegetius' treatise, for instance, refers not only to the earlier Roman military tradition, but also to his own day. The military oath he quotes, for example, contains a reference to God, Christ and the Holy Spirit (*iurant autem per Deum et per Christum et per sanctum Spiritum*, Veg. Mil. 2,5,3) [13.181–193]. The *protectores domestici* ('Domestic Protectors') played an important role in the later Roman Empire, having received training and education with the Imperial Guard. On completion of their educational phase, the best of them were posted to the headquarters of the *magistri militum* ('Masters of Soldiers'), *duces* ('Commanders') or *comites rei militaris* ('Associates in Military Affairs'), to support and even monitor commanding officers [15.92f.]. In the Eastern Empire from the reign of Justinian onwards, recruitment focused on martial peoples like the Isaurians, who were already trained according to their local traditions when they entered the Roman army [8.21]. This, however, did not replace the basic training given to new recruits, the purpose of which was to integrate them into the squad.

☞ Discipline; Motivation; Recruitment; Training

BIBLIOGRAPHY

[1] C.-G. ALEXANDRESCU, Blasmusiker und Standartenträger im römischen Heer, 2010 [2] G. ALFÖLDY, Epigraphica Hispanica XII. Eine neue Inschrift aus Tarraco Dispensator census Sarmatici oder discens armaturae, in: ZPE 87, 1991, 163–167 [3] A. CHANIOTIS, Die Verträge zwischen kretischen Städten in der hellenistischen Zeit, 1996 [4] A. CHANIOTIS, War in the Hellenistic World. A Social and Cultural History, 2005 [5] A.S. CHANKOWSKI, L'entraînement militaire des éphèbes dans les cités grecques d'Asie Mineure à l'époque hellénistique. Nécessité pratique ou tradition atrophée?, in: J.-C. COUVENHES / H.-L. FERNOUX (eds.), Les cités grecques et la guerre en Asie Mineure à l'époque hellénistique, 2004, 39–56 [6] R.W. DAVIES, Peace-time Routine in the Roman Army, 1967 (Theses, Durham University: http://etheses.dur.ac.uk/8075/) [7] R.W. DAVIES, Service in the Roman Army, 1989 [8] J.F. HALDON, Recruitment and Conscription in the Byzantine Army c. 550–990. A Study on the Origins of the Stratiotika Ktemata, 1979 [9] G. HORSMANN, Untersuchungen zur militärischen Ausbildung im republikanischen und kaiserzeitlichen Rom, 1988 [10] P. KOVÁCS, 'Eques super ripam Danuvii' – Notes on CIL III 3676, in: Acta Archaeologica Academiae Scientiarum Hungaricae 69, 2018, 311–320 [11] Y. LE BOHEC, The Imperial Roman Army, 1994 [12] P. LE ROUX, L'armée romaine sous les Sévères, in: ZPE 94, 1992, 261–268 [13] A.D. LEE, War in Late Antiquity. A Social History, 2007 [14] J.C. MANN, The Raising of New Legions during the Principate, in: Hermes 91, 1963, 483–489 (repr. J.C. Mann, Britain and the Roman Empire, 1996, 1–7) [15] B. PALME, Feldarmee und Grenzheer. Das römische Militär in der Spätantike, in: G. MANDL / I. STEFFELBAUER (eds.), Krieg in der antiken Welt, 2007, 85–113 [16] F. DE POLIGNAC, Cults, Territory, and the Origins of Greek City-State, 1995 (trans. J. Lloyd) [17] K. SCHNEGG, Sparta. Geschlechteregalität oder -eliminierung, in: G. MANDL / I. STEFFELBAUER (eds.), Krieg in der antiken Welt, 2007, 401–419 [18] M.A. SPEIDEL, Heer und Herrschaft im Römischen Reich der Hohen Kaiserzeit, 2009 [19] M.A. SPEIDEL, Recruitment and Identity. Exploring the Meanings of Roman Soldiers' Home, in: Revue internationale d'histoire militaire ancienne 6, 2017, 35–50 [20] O. ȚENTEA, Ex Oriente ad Danubium. The Syrian Units on the Danube Frontier of the Roman Empire, 2012 [21] P. VIDAL-NAQUET, The Black Hunter. Forms of Thought and Forms of Society in the Greek World, 1986 (trans. A. Szegedy-Maszak)

FLORIAN MATEI-POPESCU

Elephants

Macedonian Greek troops first faced elephants (Greek *elephas*; Latin *elepha(n)s* or *elephantus*, rarely *barrus*) at the Battle of Gaugamela (331 BC). The Persian army is reported to have had 15 of the animals. A gift of 30 elephants from the Indian prince Taxiles, and the seizure as booty of the elephants of Porus following the Battle of the Hydaspes, enabled Alexander the Great to integrate them into his own army (Arr. Anab. 4,27,8f.; 5,3,5).

Elephants were deployed in numerous pitched battles over the ensuing two centuries. The practice reached its height during the Wars of the Diadochi (Pisidia 319; Paraetacene and Gabiene 317; Gaza 312; Ipsus 301) and the Syrian Wars between the Seleucids and Ptolemies (Rhaphia 217; Panium c. 200 BC). When King Pyrrhus crossed to Southern Italy with his army, he also brought some 20 elephants, which he deployed with success against Roman forces (Heraclea 280 and Asculum 279). However, the elephants were not decisive at the Battle of Beneventum in 275.

The Carthaginians also used elephants against the Roman ranks in the First Punic War (Agrigentum 262, Africa 256, Panormus 250). Hannibal took elephants over the Alps at the beginning of the Second Punic War. The few animals that survived the ordeal were used in the pitched battle on the Trebia in 218. The Carthaginian general also used elephants in sieges and battles for roads – for example, against Roman positions in an attempt to relieve Capua in 212, and in skirmishes near Venusio in 210.

When Roman armies advanced into the Greek east, they encountered elephants again, this time in the Macedonian and Seleucid armies (Lyncestis 199, Cynoscephalae 197, Thermopylae 190, Magnesia 189), but by now the terrorizing effect of the animals on battle-hardened Roman soldiers and commanders had long since evaporated. Any tactical benefit of using elephants in pitched battles depended on their intimidating enemy troops and horses, and this depended

Fig. 1: War elephant (interior of a ceramic bowl, 3rd cent. BC). This bowl, from Capena (Italy), shows a war elephant with a driver and a tower-like superstructure with two armed soldiers. A baby elephant holds the war elephant by the tail with its trunk. The illustration may recollect the Roman victory over Pyrrhus at the Battle of Beneventum (275 BC). Several sources (Flor. Ep. 1,13,12f.; Plut. *Pyrrhus* 25; Zon. 8,6) tell the story that a young elephant and its mother within Pyrrhus' army broke through Pyrrhus' own lines, contributing to his defeat.

largely on the elephants' size and exotic strangeness. The animals were deployed with the intention of disrupting the cohesion of the opposing ranks and scattering the enemy force. Beginning in the 3rd century BC, elephants began to be fitted with tower structures (cf. fig. 1), with archers riding them, in order to amplify the effect of ranged weapons on the enemy. Thanks to their size and strength, elephants could also be used in sieges.

Most ancient battle descriptions state that elephants were usually positioned ahead of the army's battle lines (often in the centre, sometimes also – or only – on the flanks). More rarely, they were held in reserve behind the army's lines. However, the impact of elephants in battle could be double-edged, especially when enemy infantry or volleys of arrows and stones caused the animals to panic and run blindly back into 'friendly' lines. Asclepiodotus (*Taktika kephalaia* 11) gives a detailed description of the organization of Hellenistic elephant units. Each elephant had its own name, and elephant drivers were called *elephantistes*, *magister* or simply *indi*.

In the Hellenistic period, armies in the Mediterranean region initially received their supplies of elephants from India. Ptolemaic Egyptians, however, apparently hunted African elephants on expeditions to Meroë and acquired them from trading posts on the Red Sea, bringing them to Memphis to train for use in battle (e.g. P. Petr. 2,20; OGIS 54 and 86). During his campaign across the Hindu Kush, the Seleucid Antiochus III acquired 150 elephants from the Indian prince Sophagesenus (Pol. 11,34). The Seleucids kept their elephants at Apamea on the Orontes in Syria, and probably also at Babylon (*Astronomical Diaries*, vol. 1, no. 273B). Campaigning Carthaginians used African forest elephants, as did Roman commanders. During their extended campaign of wars and sieges in Hispania, the Romans used elephants imported from Numidia against the Numantines (153, 134–133). They also used them in Gaul against the Allobroges (121). The last use of elephants in warfare for the time being was at the Battle of Thapsus in 46 BC: Metellus Scipio sent elephants obtained from King Juba of Numidia into battle against Caesar. After this, the Romans' use of elephants was almost entirely confined to animal baiting and pulling triumphal chariots.

The military career of the elephant was then revived by Emperor Caracalla, who sought to portray himself as the second Alexander. In AD 216/17, he went so far as to deploy a Macedonian phalanx against the Parthians. He also brought elephants for use in the battle (Cass. Dio 78,7,4). The Sassanids, Rome's new enemy in the east, likewise returned to the use of elephants when besieging Nisibis (AD 337, 350) and Amida (359). They again deployed elephants at the battle against the army of Emperor Julian outside Ctesiphon in AD 363.

BIBLIOGRAPHY

[1] M.B. CHARLES / P. RHODAN, Magister Elephantorum. A Reappraisal of Hannibal's Use of Elephants, in: CW, vol. 100, no. 4, 2007, 363–389 [2] P. RANCE, Elephants in Warfare in Late Antiquity, in: Acta Antiqua Academiae Scientiarum Hungaricae 43, 2003, 355–384 [3] H.H. SCULLARD, The Elephant in the Graeco and Roman World, 1974 (with further bibliography) [4] T.R. TRAUTMANN, Elephants and Kings. An Environmental History, 2015 [5] M. WELLMANN, Elefant, in: RE 5, 1905, 2248–2257

ALFRED MICHAEL HIRT

Elite troops

The category of elite troops, widespread in modern terminology, was also familiar in Antiquity (Diod. Sic. 19,30,5f.; 19,41,2). It was defined, subjectively to some degree, by various complementary and often related criteria (fighting qualities and specialities, background, proximity to power, etc.). The weight attached to each of these criteria differed from case to case. Members of elite troops were often identified by specific markers that showed their distinctive identuty and prestige. In general, elite status in warfare for the Greeks and Romans was associated with high societal status and wealth. This encouraged the participation ofaristocrats and citizens who owned mounts and could afford to equip themselves properly for the cavalry, the hoplite phalanx or the Republican legion. The demands and increasing diversification of warfare quickly led to the inclusion of other social categories and to increased hierarchy in the fighting force.

The heroes and *promachoi* ('fighters at the front') of Homeric narrative and Archaic sources – the troops of Ajax and the Myrmidons of Achilles (Hom. Il. 16,200–277) [5] – were succeeded from the 6th century BC onwards by outstanding small infantry units – *logades* ('selected') and *epilektoi* ('chosen'). These were formed temporarily, although some cities and leagues (→ Alliance) created permanent regiments [1]. They included the 300 Spartiates who fell at Thermopylae in 480 BC (Hdt. 7,205ff.) and the Sacred Band of Thebes, which existed from 378 to 338 BC (Plut. *Pelopidas* 18). Conversely, mercenaries were also sometimes used, despite occasional criticisms of this practice. This was at least in part motivated by their military capabilities (Aristot. Eth. Nic. 3,8,6–9; Xen. Hell. 6,1,5f.). The armies of Philip II and Alexander III (the Great) of Macedon included not only the famous Macedonian phalanx, but also distinguished infantry and cavalry units. Among the 1,800 *hetairoi* ('comrades') recruited from the aristocracy, the *agema* was prominent, a royal squadron of 300–400 elite horsemen (Arr. Anab. 5,12,2). Likewise, the *pezetairoi* ('comrades on foot') included the notable 3,000 *hypaspistai* ('shieldbearers'), who later evolved into the *argyraspides* ('silver shieldbearers'; Plut. *Eumenes* 16), versatile infantrymen deployed to protect the king. As the organization of the Hellenistic armies confirm, functioning as royal guard and proximity to the king now became the defining criteria of elite forces (Liv. 40,6,2f.).

In Rome from the 3rd century BC onwards, the elite troops were the *extraordinarii* (selected allied cavalry and infantry; Pol. 6,26,6–8) together with soldiers of the *cohortes praetoriae* ('Praetorian Guard') assembled for this purpose. *Imperatores* of the 1st century BC recruited experienced foreign horsemen, while some legions earned for themselves special status (Caes. B Gall. 1,40,15). Although the legionaries, who were in all cases citizens, retained their prestige in the professional army of Augustus, the imperial (Praetorian) 'guard' now became the new elite military force. The *cohortes praetoriae*, now a standing force, numbered 5,000 (later 10,000) soldiers. Until the end of the 2nd century AD, they were composed of citizens, mostly Italic, and they enjoyed better service conditions as well as the prestige of their connection with the emperor, the more so as they exercised an important political role [3]. The mutinies that took place in the year AD 14 revealed legionaries' envy of the *cohortes praetoriae* (Tac. Ann. 1,17,6; 1,27,1), illustrating the important role of military ethos and psychology. Ambitious individuals sometimes took advantage of rivalries fostered by special interests, competition and → esprit de corps (Hdn. 2,10,2–9). It should be noted that being highly valuable to the military did not always earn elite status or treatment. The *Germani corporis custodes* ('Germanic Bodyguards') and the *equites singulares Augusti* ('Imperial Mounted Guards') – members of the mounted imperial guard recruited mainly on the Rhine and Danube – did not enjoy the same privileges as the Praetorians [6]. Every branch of military service also had its own internal hierarchies (e.g. the *alae milliariae* ('milliary troops') were the elite troops within the auxiliary cavalry). Embodying a different form of excellence were the centurions who had risen from the ranks, but this was a path only a few navigated successfully, with service in the elite units a more reliable route to glittering prospects of advancement (in later centuries, occasionally even as far as the imperial throne). During the 2nd and especially the 3rd centuries, the best troops were brought together in the *comitatus*, the mobile imperial corps

(AE 1981, 777). After various adaptations throughout the 3rd century, the Tetrarchs and then Constantine reorganized the elite forces completely. The *scholae palatinae* ('Palace Guards') replaced the Praetorian Guard in AD 312 [4]. Other units and functions emerged (e.g. *auxilia palatina* ('elite palace units'), *antesignani* ('troops in front of the standard'), *protectores domestici* ('domestic protectors') and *bucellarii* (elite escort troops, lit. 'biscuit eaters')), some surviving as late as the 6th century. There was also now increasing use of the military capabilities of barbarians.

☞ Guards

BIBLIOGRAPHY
[1] V. ALONSO / K. FREITAG, Prolegomena zur Erforschung der Bedeutung der Eliteeinheiten im archaischen und klassischen Griechenland, in: Gerión 19, 2001, 199–219 [2] S. BINGHAM, The Praetorian Guard. A History of Rome's Elite Special Forces, 2013 [3] M. DURRY, Les cohortes prétoriennes, 1938 [4] R.I. FRANCK, Scholae palatinae. The Palace Guards of the Later Roman Empire, 1969 [5] M. SEARS, Warrior Ants. Elite Troops in the Iliad, in: CW 103/2, 2010, 139–155 [6] M.P. SPEIDEL, Riding for Caesar. The Roman Emperors' Horse Guards, 1994

PATRICE FAURE

Emotions

A. Introduction
B. Anger
C. Fear
D. Panic
E. Confidence
F. Shame
G. Pity
H. Love and friendship

A. INTRODUCTION
Attempts to understand the emotions that were connected to war in Antiquity face a range of difficulties. It is obviously necessary to infer the nature of such emotions from the texts that describe them. Yet texts are subject to literary conventions – some according to genre, others more general in character – that invariably refract the emotional experiences they report, even as some texts are themselves capable of influencing how emotions are felt and perceived. It must also be recognized that emotions have a history. It must not be assumed that popular classifications implicit in modern languages precisely reflect the conception of emotions in Ancient Greece or Rome [7]. For instance, the assertion by Aristotle that it is 'impossible to be afraid [*phobeisthai*] and angry [*orgizesthai*] at the same time' (Rhet. 1380a 33) serves as a useful warning of potential dissonances between the Greek word *orge* and the modern 'anger'.

The Greeks and Romans had a cognitive concept of emotions insofar as, according to the classical understanding, emotions entailed or even (for the Stoics) represented judgments – as opposed to the modern tendency to separate the emotions and intellect. They generally thought that people feel anger, fear, compassion, love and hate for specific reasons. In part, this was because Greece and Rome had a rhetorical culture in which orators aroused or soothed emotions through argument. This way of thinking also influenced the way Greeks and Romans told stories – as illustrated, for instance, by the practice of including speeches in historical texts.

As a final point, the boundary between military and civilian life in the Greek and Roman world was not clearly marked, as both societies (at least in some phases of history) were built on citizen armies and were dominated by almost uninterrupted warfare. Much classical literature is about conflict – Ovid asserted that every lover is a soldier (*militat omnis amans*: Ov. Am. 1,9,1), and the citizens assembled in a theatre probably all had military experience. The absence of a strict distinction between comradeship in the field and friendship at home may even have assuaged the emotional traumas of war [5].

B. ANGER
The oldest work of Greek literature, the *Iliad*, gives vivid portrayals of many emotions associated with war. It begins with the wrath of Achilles, insulted (or feeling himself insulted) by Agamemnon. Then it explores his grief (and perhaps a measure of guilt) at the death of his friend Patroclus. Both emotions are extreme. Achilles' initial wrath, denoted by the emphatic *menis* rather than the more usual *cholos*, corresponds closely to the definition of *orge* in Aristotle's *Rhetoric* (*orge* itself does not occur in the Homeric epics): 'Let us then define anger as a longing, accompanied by pain, for revenge, real or apparent, for a slight, real or apparent, affecting one or a friend, when such a slight is unwarranted'. (Aristot. Rhet. 1378a 31–33). Achilles reacts in precisely this way to the insult from a man who, in his opinion, is in no position to belittle him, given that Achilles is in no way subordinate to Agamemnon. His reaction is thus a striving for revenge, which he achieves by withdrawing from the fight until Agamemnon must approach him to ask for help. This, Achilles calculates, will force Agamemnon to feel the very humiliation (*antipathein*) that he inflicted on Achilles (cf. Aristot. Rhet. 1382a 14f.). Aristotle

refers explicitly to the wrath of Achilles. There can be no doubt that he developed his discussion of the subject on the model of the *Iliad*.

After Hector kills Patroclus, Achilles returns to the thick of battle with well-nigh unearthly energy and butchers Trojans. Finally, he kills Hector and desecrates his corpse, apparently in a hopeless attempt to make up for his own loss – until he is finally persuaded to release Hector's body to Priam. It has been argued that this second phase entails a diversion of Achilles' rage from Agamemnon to Hector, and so wrath remains the key theme of the epic from beginning to end [10]. Yet a scholiast is found already making the following comment on Achilles' turn of mind: 'Of the two emotions that lay claim to Achilles' soul, anger [*orge*] and pain [*lype*], one gains the upper hand... For his feelings for Patroclus are stronger, and it is therefore necessary for him to abandon his wrath [*menis*] and take vengeance upon his enemies' (schol. bT ad Hom. Il. 18,112f.). Whether the scholiast's interpretation is correct or not, it reminds us not to place too much trust in modern intuition. Hatred for an enemy for the suffering he caused may well have been understood as an emotion quite different from the wrath elicited by an attack on one's → honour.

Homer's heroes are portrayed as *promachoi* ('fighters in the front rank'), who engage in single combat rather than fighting in tight, disciplined formations like the hoplite phalanx or the Roman legion. The epics are stories of individuals, whose personal feelings and passions dictate the narrative. In Virgil's *Aeneid*, Turnus is driven by furious wrath (*furiis*; Verg. Aen. 12,946). He burns with anger, and sparks fly from his eyes (*ardentis*; 12,101). Aeneas, for his part, uses wrath to rouse himself to battle (*se suscitat ira*; 12,108). When Iuturna then directs Turnus' chariot away from single combat, Aeneas sees this as a breach of treaty. Feelings of wrath rise in him (*adsurgunt irae*; 12,494) and he gives free rein to his rage (*irarumque omnis effundit habenas*; 12,499).

The grounds for Aeneas' wrath point to one of the most frequent justifications for extreme retribution against an enemy: breaking a pact. According to Thucydides (3,36,2), the Athenians during the Peloponnesian War (431–404 BC) voted 'out of wrath' (*hypo orges*) to exterminate the Mytileneans for having defected, despite being allies of Athens. Isocrates retrojects this motif on to the destruction of Troy. 'Because a woman was abducted, all Greeks were so incensed,... that they would not cease from war until the city was completely destroyed' (Isoc. Or. 4,181). Polybius reports that the Carthaginians first sued for peace, then seized a Roman convoy. Later, when Scipio sent emissaries to retrieve it, the Carthaginians ambushed their ship on their return voyage. The wrath (*orge*) of Scipio at this scurrilous breach of trust led him subsequently to enslave the populations of cities he conquered (Pol. 15,1,2; 15,4,2; cf. 2,58,8 on the fate of Mantinea; cf. also Liv. 23,25,6; 28,25,12f. on 'just wrath', *iusta ira*).

Although wrath was sometimes justified, its unpredictable character made it problematic. During the Peloponnesian War, the Spartan king Archidamus noted that wrath would overcome the Athenians if they saw their lands devastated by the Spartans. 'They will then use very little reason, and a great deal of passionate feeling [or 'wrath': *thymos*] – so that they will no longer be able to fight effectively' (Thuc. 2,11,6–8). In his speech against the massacre of the Mytileneans, Diodotus declared, 'I believe that two things above all hamper good decision-making: haste and wrath. The one invites thoughtlessness, the other clumsiness and rashness' (Thuc. 3,42,1; cf. 2,22,1; 2,59,3; 4,122,5; 8,27,6). Xenophon describes a general who, in a fit of rage (*orgistheis*), sent his troops out against a city, with the result that he himself was killed and his men massacred (Xen. Hell. 5,3,5f.). Almost echoing Socrates, Xenophon opines, 'An attack on an opponent in wrath and without judgment [*gnome*] is entirely a mistake, for wrath lacks forethought, whereas intelligent insight seeks both to avoid harm to oneself and to cause it to the enemy' (Xen. Hell. 5,3,7). As part of the general Stoic rejection of emotions, Seneca declares wrath to be a trait typical of barbarians, and one that makes them vulnerable in spite of their abilities (Sen. Dial. 3,9).

C. Fear

The effects of fear are opposite to those of anger. It leads soldiers to flee rather than attack, and when citizens contemplate starting a war, fear makes them think twice. It is not in itself a symptom of → cowardice. According to Aristotle, a person would be 'either mad or insensitive to pain were he to fear nothing, "neither earthquake nor the waves of the high seas", as is said of the Celts' (Aristot. Eth. Nic. 1115b 23–28; Aristotle calls this state of mind *aphobia* ('fearlessness'), the vice opposite to fearfulness; cf. Xen. Mem. 4,6,10).

When in the *Iliad* Achilles approaches Hector for the last, decisive trial of strength, Hector flees. Yet he is not portrayed as a coward. Not to fear Achilles would be foolhardy. Achilles too feels fear (*deisas*: Hom. Il. 21,249), when he is caught in the surging waters of the River Scamander. Only exaggerated fear is contemptible, for it overestimates threat and thus betrays a cowardly character. Hector chastises Polydamas for just such fearfulness (*deos*: Hom. Il. 12,246).

In his explanation of the ultimate causes of the Peloponnesian War, Thucydides argues, 'The real motive [*prophasis*] ... was that the Athenians had grown powerful and had instilled fear into the Spartans, compelling the latter to make war' (Thuc. 1,23,6) – a rational fear given the spectacular rise of the Athenian Empire, and not one that in any way undermines the legendary courage of the Spartans.

Like anger, then, fear rests on a judgment – in this case, about the capacities and intentions of the enemy. When the Peloponnesian generals notice that their men are fearful ahead of a sea battle having previously been defeated by the Athenians (Thuc. 2,86,5), they respond by explaining why this fear is irrational. 'The previous sea battle, Peloponnesians, offers no justifiable cause to be afraid [*to ekphobesai*]' (2,87,1). The defeat, they declare, was caused by poor preparations, bad luck and lack of experience (2,87,2). The *strategoi* ('commanders') warn that 'fear excludes presence of mind [*phobos gar mnemen explessei*]' (2,87,4), and they remind the men of their numerical advantage, encouraging them to sail into battle with confidence (*tharsountes*: 2,87,8). If fear can defeat reason, it must also be susceptible to rational arguments.

D. Panic

Unlike fear, which arises from the perception of a plausible danger, panic (it was believed that the word derived from an unexpected manifestation of the god Pan) was understood as an 'irrational terror', associated with noise and confusion, such as can suddenly seize a military camp, especially at night [1.88f.]. It arose despite the absence of any evident cause (cf. Jos. BI 5,7–9; Paus. 10,23,5–8; Cornutus, *Theologia* 27: 'Attacks of panic are sudden and irrational', akin to frightened sheep; cf. Aen. Tact. 4; Pol. 20,6,12; Longus 2,25,3f.). In panic, a noise or movement is imagined to be a sign of real danger. This is contagious, and cannot be stopped with rational arguments. The term *ekplexis* ('shattering', 'paralysis') suggests a shock reflex, and indeed expressions denoting shaking (e.g. *phrike*) can also be used of an involuntary reaction akin to fear – although both words are also used synonymously with *phobos* ('fear'; see above) [4]. When the Stoics considered these feelings of panic, they labeled them as *propatheiai* ('pre-emotions'), that is, instinctive reactions which, like shuddering upon contact with cold water or jumping at a sudden noise, occur regardless of reason (Sen. Dial. 4,2,6).

E. Confidence

Just as fear arose when the enemy was perceived to be stronger, so confidence (*tharsos*) – which Aristotle makes the opposite emotion to fear – grew from the knowledge that the adversary was weak and had fewer allies than oneself (Aristot. Rhet. 1383a 22–25). Confidence was aroused through inference and comparison. However, an excess of confidence could be dangerous. According to Xenophon, Socrates said, 'Confidence [*to thárros*] leads to complacency, indifference [*rathymia*] and ruthlessness, whereas fear makes men more attentive, compliant and orderly. This can be inferred from what happens aboard ships. Whenever the sailors have no fear, they brim with lack of discipline. But when they are in fear of a storm or an enemy, they not only obey all orders, but also silently await instructions, just like members of a chorus' (Xen. Mem. 3,5,5f.; cf. Xen. Equ. 7,7; Isoc. Or. 7,6).

It is important to note that *tharros/tharsos*, like fear, was understood as an emotion, and not synonymous with courage. Courage was, as Aristotle explained, a virtue born of a habitual disposition (the same kind of disposition as produced cowardice). 'Confidence' is therefore a misleading translation of the term, suggesting as it does a calm sense of security. *Tharros* was much closer to an emotion of superiority, almost arrogance, which motivated someone to go to battle with courage or to pursue the enemy. It was an agonistic emotion, typical of contests and competitions, and its natural home was the battlefield. Of the emotions (*pathe*) discussed by Aristotle, *tharros* was probably the most specifically related to war.

F. Shame

Shame was also capable of inducing a warrior to overcome his fear. When Hector challenges the Greeks to single combat, the Achaean heroes are torn between the shame of refusing and the fear of fighting him (Hom. Il. 7,93). Later, when Hector is terrified by the onrushing Achilles, he refuses to seek refuge behind the walls of Troy out of shame at having endangered his people when Achilles returned to the battlefield (Hom. Il. 22,105; in both passages, the verb is *aideisthai* ('to be ashamed', 'to have self-respect')). Demosthenes tried to motivate the Athenians to fight Philip of Macedon by evoking the shame they would feel (*aischynesthai*) were they not to inflict on Philip the same suffering he would inflict on them given the chance (Dem. Or. 1,24; cf. 4,42). In his funeral oration, Lysias expresses certainty that the Athenians at Marathon could have taken on the Persians alone – out of shame at the barbarians' being in their country (Lys. 2,23).

Sometimes, however, fear keeps the upper hand. Homer tells how Nestor, encircled by Trojan enemies, proposes flight (*phobos*) to Diomedes (Hom. Il. 8,139). Although Diomedes worries that Hector will boast of having scared him off, he bows to Nestor's good judgment and flees. A scholiast here remarks (schol. Hom. Il. b ad 8,139), 'A timely withdrawal brings no shame [*ouk aischynei*]'; and

Agamemnon too asserts, 'No stigma [*ou tis nemesis*] attaches to avoiding disaster' (Hom. Il. 14,80).

G. PITY

Aristotle defines pity as 'a kind of pain kindled by the advent of a destructive or painful evil that afflicts someone who does not deserve it, and which one might expect oneself (or those close to one) to suffer, and this when it seems near at hand' (Aristot. Rhet. 1385b 13–16; cf. Aristot. Rhet. Alex. 34,4–6; Soph. Phil. 1318–1320). Pity was the opposite of wrath, for it elicited mercy rather than punishment. The Athenians boasted of their capacity for pity, and Isocrates called them 'the most compassionate and gentlest-spirited of all Greeks' (Isoc. Or. 15,20; cf. Dem. Or. 24,171; Pl. Mx. 244E; Lys. 12,14). Much later, Libanius, tutor to Emperor Julian, wrote, 'To my mind, the cardinal point on which the Greeks differ from the barbarians is that, where the latter resemble animals in their disdain for compassion, the former are easily disposed to compassion and the mastery of their wrath' (Lib. Or. 19,13). Similarly Apsines in his treatise on rhetoric (307 Spengel/Hammer) declares that 'those capable of pity differ from the uncompassionate just as men differ from animals'.

However, because pity was a moral emotion that took into account the merit of the sufferer and not just suffering in itself, sympathy for a defeated enemy was conditional at best. It would readily be withheld if there was suspicion that the enemy had caused his own misfortune, for instance through betrayal or an unwarranted attack. The victor's reaction here would be wrath, not leniency. In the *Iliad*, a warrior sometimes begs for mercy, but it is never forthcoming [3.71f.]. When Alastorides falls to his knees and pleads with Achilles to show pity, Homer observes that he is a fool, for since the death of Patroclus, Achilles is no longer gentle of spirit (Hom. Il. 20,467; cf. Achilles' answer to Lycaon: 21,74–106).

In the Mytilene debate, Cleon warns the Athenians against inappropriate pity (*oiktos*), for the Mytileneans are now permanent enemies and would show no compassion if the tables were turned (Thuc. 3,40,2f.; cf. Men. Mis. 716–718 Arnott). The small city of Plataeae, which lay in Boeotian territory but was allied with Athens in the Peloponnesian War, was destroyed by the Spartans and Thebans in 431 BC. Its populace asked the Spartans to show 'temperate pity' (*oiktoi sophroni*: Thuc. 3,59,1), but the Thebans replied, 'Deserving of pity are those who have suffered something undeserved, whereas those who suffer rightly, like these men, on the contrary deserve scorn' (Thuc. 3,67,4). Plataeae was rebuilt in 386, but Thebes destroyed it again in 373. In Isocrates' account in the *Plataikos*, the Plataeans urge the Athenians to take revenge on Thebes. Towards the end of their oration, they declare that it is not fitting (*eikos*) for an entire city destroyed in such an unlawful manner to receive no pity whatsoever, given that every individual who has suffered unjust (*para to dikaion*) misfortune should be pitied (Isoc. Or. 14,52).

When Antigonus Doson of Macedon conquered the city of Mantinea during the war against the Achaean League (223 BC), he sold its populace into slavery. Polybius criticizes the historian Phylarchus for having elicited inappropriate pity for the Mantineans with his descriptions of women baring their breasts and tearing their hair, and of men weeping and wailing like their wives while being taken away (Pol. 2,56,7). He comments (Pol. 2,58,9–12), 'Did they not deserve some far graver and more extreme punishment – so that, even if they suffered as Phylarchus tells it, we should not expect the Greeks to have heaped pity upon them, but rather to have offered praise and approval for those who acted to avenge their iniquity?' Polybios explains, 'Phylarchus simply recounts most of the calamities without suggesting the causes or the nature of such causes, without which it is impossible, in relation to any event, either to feel legitimate pity [*eulogos*] or appropriate anger [*kathekontos*]' (Pol. 2,56,13; cf. Cass. Dio 51,15,2).

H. LOVE AND FRIENDSHIP

War is not only a crucible of hostile emotions. It also nurtures intensive devotion among comrades. Achilles' grief and desire for vengeance are aroused by the death of his closest comrade, Patroclus, whom, in his own words, he loved more than life itself (Hom. Il. 18,80–82), and whose loss pains him more than that of his own father or son (Hom. Il. 19,321–324). Alexander the Great displayed similar grief at the death of his beloved companion Hephaestion, no doubt partly in imitation of Achilles (Plut. *Alexander* 72,3; Arr. Anab. 7,14; cf. Virgil's magnificent portrayal of Nisus' affection for Euryalus, Verg. Aen. 9,168–459).

There is no need to interpret such relationships as homoerotic or pederastic, in the style of the 'Sacred Band' of Thebes (Deinarch. 1,72f.; Plut. *Pelopidas* 18f.; cf. Pl. Symp. 178E–179A; Xen. Symp. 8,32–34), but there is equally no reason to draw a sharp distinction between the Greek *philia* and *eros* or between the Latin *amicitia* and *amor*. Close relationships between men in war were expressed in terms that resemble those for passionate love. Very occasionally, usually in the context of civil wars, such devotion was even capable of crossing the battle lines. Lucan celebrates the brief fraternization of the troops of Caesar and Pompey as they prepare to do battle (*rupit amor leges*: Luc. 4,175), and conjures an image of universal concord (4,169–253; a more realistic picture in Caes. B Civ. 1,74; App. Civ. 2,42–44). Yet this transient fellowship contrasts with more frequent descriptions of fratricidal hatred, as between Eteocles and Polyneices (e.g. Aeschylus, *Seven Against Thebes*; Statius, *Thebaid*) or Romulus und Remus. These stories express in mythical form the deadly enmity that could arise even between closely related ethnic groups as a result of competing ambitions, class conflicts and political antagonism.

BIBLIOGRAPHY
[1] P. BORGEAUD, The Cult of Pan in Ancient Greece, 1988 [2] S. BRAUND / G.W. MOST (eds.), Ancient Anger. Perspectives from Homer to Galen, 2004 [3] W. BURKERT, Zum altgriechischen Mitleidsbegriff, 1955 [4] D. CAIRNS, A Short History of Shudders, in: A. CHANIOTIS / P. DUCREY (eds.), Unveiling Emotions, vol. 2, 2013, 85–107 [5] J. CROWLEY, Beyond the Universal Soldier. Combat Trauma in Classical Antiquity, in: P. MEINECK / D. KONSTAN (eds.), Combat Trauma and the Ancient Greeks, 2014, 105–129 [6] R.A. KASTER, Emotion, Restraint, and Community in Ancient Rome, 2005 [7] D. KONSTAN, The Emotions of the Ancient Greeks, 2006 [8] N. ROSENSTEIN, War and Peace, Fear and Reconciliation at Rome, in: K.A. RAAFLAUB (ed.), War and Peace in the Ancient World, 2007 [9] N. SHERMAN, Stoic Warriors. The Ancient Philosophy behind the Military Mind, 2005 [10] O. TAPLIN, Homeric Soundings. The Shaping of the Iliad, 1992

DAVID KONSTAN

Empire

A. Greek
B. Roman

A. GREEK

A.1. Definition and theory
A.2. Athens
A.3. Macedonia

A.1. DEFINITION AND THEORY
Empires form when states subjugate outside communities or former states to their own sphere of influence. Explanations of the phenomenon tend to emphasize either internal 'metrocentric' motives, including aggressive militarism and economic interests, or 'pericentric' factors [11.27–30]. To [12], socialization and political culture in some states create aggressive impulses, as also discussed in debates on militarism in the Hellenistic monarchies and the Roman Republic (see below, B.). According to pericentric theories, the imperial state is compelled to impose order in response to a threat to its security or instability on its peripheries. Empires tend to disintegrate if they do not evolve from conquering states into stable territorial polities in which distinctions between citizens and subjects of the empire are abolished [9.112–126]. Marcher states or peripheries of empires are particularly prone to form new empires through processes of secondary state formation and ethnogenesis [13.50–93].

A.2. ATHENS
Ancient Greek had no word for 'empire', let alone 'imperialism'. The word *arche* denoted the rule of one *polis* over another, and that of a king or governor over his territory. Herodotus (5th cent. BC) provides the first attestation of the theory of a succession of empires: from the Assyrians to the Medians, then the Persians (Hdt. 1,95; 1,130); later were added the Macedonians and Romans [14]. The Greeks, on the periphery of the Near East, underwent a process of secondary empire formation: in the Athenian Empire of the 5th century, which adopted strategies from Persian rule [10], and the empires of Alexander the Great and his successors (Diadochi), which were even more directly shaped by Persian institutions and ideologies.

Athens established itself as the dominant sea power after the Persian invasion of Greece (480/79), and it organized the *poleis* of the Aegean into a maritime league with its council and headquarters (*synhedrion*) on Delos (Delian League). Only a few of Athens' allies could afford to maintain a fleet. Instead, they paid an annual tribute (*phoros*) into the league's treasury on Delos. The treasurers (*hellenotamiai*) were Athenians, and the treasury was moved to Athens in 455/54. By the outbreak of the Peloponnesian War, contemporaries were talking of Athens' 'rule' (*arche*) over its allies, who at the zenith of the league numbered over 250 members. This Athenian rule had established a virtual monopoly over instruments of coercion, and Athens used them to restrict its allies' autonomy and suppress revolts (Thuc. 1,99). Given that those subjugated in this process differed little from the Athenians, what was forming in this process might properly be called a territorial state rather than an empire [8]. Even so, Athens in the 5th century fits most criteria for the definition of an empire [5.351–356]: there were phases of aggressive expansion and imperial overstretch, for example the expeditions to Egypt and Sicily, but there were also periods of consolidation, for example when, following the reverses of the 5th century, Pericles restructured the empire and curtailed its ambitions. Athens' widely distributed coinage (guaranteed by its abundant silver mines), its regulation of markets and law, its preference for democracies and its policing of the seas all promoted the political and economic integration of the Aegean world.

→ Sparta only became able to break the power of Athens when it built its own → fleet, and it was only able to do that with Persian money – proving that an empire founded on tribute was indispensable for waging war on this scale. The Persian prince Cyrus took command in Sardeis, and in 405 BC he transferred to the Spartan commander Lysander authority (*arche*) over several cities, including their tax revenues (*phoroi*; Plut. Lys. 9,2; Xen. Hell. 2,1,11). After the defeat of Athens, Sparta's 'empire' beyond the Peloponnese depended largely on Lysander's personal initiative, and this would soon prove incompatible with the Spartan social and political order [1.99–101].

Over the decades that followed, the Persian Empire repeatedly launched brief interventions in the Greek world aimed at preventing a new empire from forming. In 379/78, when Athens founded a second maritime league (Athenian League), the conditions of treaties with the island *poleis* explicitly forbade Athens to extract annual tributes from them. Instead, the league council was empowered to authorize payments (*syntaxeis*) in support of Athens' *de facto* war expenses.

A.3. MACEDONIA
Philip II and Alexander (→ Generals of note, M.; → Generals of note, B.) took advantage of the foundation of a Corinthian League in 338/37 to recruit troops for their campaign against Persia without imposing levies on the *poleis*. For the most part, Philip financed his imperialism through his timber resources, silver mines and, especially, the spoils from his campaigns of conquest. In 334, Alexander declared the Greeks of Asia Minor 'exempt from tribute' (*aphorologetos*, cf.. Arr. Anab. 1,18) and instead demanded that allied *poleis* provide war contributions (*syntaxeis*). The immense treasures seized by Alexander in Damascus, Memphis, Babylon, Susa and Persepolis enabled him to enrich his followers without having to pay much attention to financial matters. Alexander's campaign in the east towards Central Asia and India reveals that his objectives were not limited to plunder and revenge for the Persian destruction of Athens. Victories were part of his self-proclaimed godhead. He set out to match or outdo Cyrus, founder of the Persian Empire, and mythical conquerors of old. This psychology of limitless conquest has much in common with Schumpeter's definition of imperialism. Yet Alexander also adopted Persian administration and expanded his own imperial elites to include members of the Persian nobility. This culminated in the mass wedding at Susa and the addition of an elite corps of non-Greek *epigonoi* ('descendants') to his army [2.60–64].

Following Alexander's death, and after the wars among his successors (323–271), only two large Macedonian successor realms became established: those of the Seleucids and the Ptolemies. The Macedonian Antigonids meanwhile exercised hegemony over parts of Greece. Scholarly debate over Hellenistic imperialism has focused intensely on the issue of whether these realms were striving for limitless conquest like Alexander, or whether they sought only to achieve a balance of power to cement their regional base [2.158–163]. Traditionally, the Ptolemies are seen as representing the 'balance of power' approach, but they too showed interest in expanding beyond Egypt [3]. Essential as the idea of victory was to the ideology of the kingdom [4], recent research does suggest that the Seleucids were seeking to establish the territorial legitimacy of their realm, and were supporting this by founding new cities [6]. Through interaction among communities of equal status – 'peer-polity interaction' – the major kingdoms gained many shared characteristics of territoriality, court politics, fiscal centralization and military rivalry [7]. Seeking to maximize the revenues they needed for maintaining their professional land and sea forces, they imposed royal taxes on privileged urban areas and temple precincts wherever possible. In their relations with the Greek cities, the Hellenistic monarchs adopted a rhetoric of beneficence, liberty and protection. Some of them took over confederative institutions in Asia Minor and the Aegean, in order thereby to integrate the *poleis* into their realms.

The eastern Macedonian realms thus fell into line with an imperial tradition of the Near East. At the same time, realms of the Greek world in particular were reorganized and expanded in part as a result of the traditional process whereby confederations evolved into empires.

BIBLIOGRAPHY
[1] A. ANDREWES, Spartan Imperialism?, in: P.D.A. GARNSEY / C.R. WITTAKER (eds.), Imperialism in the Ancient World, 1978, 91–102 [2] E. BALTRUTSCH, Außenpolitik, Bünde und Reichsbildung in der Antike, 2008 [3] C. FISCHER-BOVET, Army and Society in Ptolemaic Egypt, 2014 [4] H.-J. GEHRKE, Der siegreiche König. Überlegungen zur hellenistischen Monarchie, in: AKG 64, 1982, 274–277 (English in: Luraghi, N. (ed.), The Splendors and Miseries of Ruling Alone, 2013, 73–98) [5] P. KEHNE, Das attische Seereich (478–404 v.Chr.) und das spartanische Hegemonialreich (nach 404 v.Chr.). Griechische Imperien?, in: M. GEHLER / R. ROLLINGER (eds.), Imperien und Reiche in der Weltgeschichte, pt. 1, 2014, 329–362 [6] P.J. KOSMIN, The Land of the Elephant Kings. Space, Territory, and Ideology in the Seleucid Empire, 2014 [7] J. MA, Hellenistic Empires, in: P.F. BANG / W. SCHEIDEL (eds.), Oxford Handbook of the State in the Ancient Near East and Mediterranean, 2013, 324–360 [8] I. MORRIS, The Greater Athenian State, in: I. MORRIS / W. SCHEIDEL (eds.), The Dynamics of Ancient Empires, 2009, 99–177 [9] H. MÜNKLER, Imperien. Die Logik der Weltherrschaft – vom Alten Rom bis zu den Vereinigten Staaten, 2005 [10] K.A. RAAFLAUB, Learning from the Enemy. Athenian and Persian 'Instruments of Empire', in: J. MA et al. (eds.), Interpreting the Athenian Empire, 2009, 89–124 [11] W. SCHEIDEL, Studying the State, in: P.F. BANG / W. SCHEIDEL (eds.), The Oxford Handbook of the Ancient State in the Near East and the

Mediterranean, 2013, 5–41 [12] J. Schumpeter, Zur Soziologie der Imperialismen, 1919 [13] P. Turchin, Historical Dynamics. Why States Rise and Fall, 2003 [14] J. Wiesehöfer, The Medes and the Idea of the Succession of Empires in Antiquity, in: G.B. Lanfranchi et al. (eds.), Continuity of Empire (?). Assyria, Media, Persia, 2003, 391–396.

Andrew Monson

B. Roman

B.1. Italy before the Social War
B.2. The acquisition of provinces
B.3. The Late Republican period
B.4. The systematic expansion of the empire under Augustus
B.5. Definition of the imperial borders through the 3rd century
B.6. Reasons for the expansion of the empire

B.1. Italy before the Social War

The idea that communal political and societal action took place within the context of a 'city-state' was taken for granted in the Roman Republic. Despite this, however, processes leading to the formation of what would later be called an empire took hold at a very early date – from the moment Rome outgrew the scale and functional boundaries of a city-state. As long as conquered territories and populations remained directly connected to the original centre on the Tiber, and the populace remained part of the *populus Romanus*, these processes can still be seen as merely the expansion of the urban entity, even if they worked against its specific functionality. However, even the incorporation of territories in the *ager Romanus* (the rural area surrounding Rome), no longer directly connected with the rural environs of Rome, visibly disrupted the dimensions of a city-state on the Italian mainland. Still, the Roman leadership was long content to let most of the other subjugated city-states and tribes in Italy continue to exist as political units, merely binding them to Rome as *socii* ('allies') by a treaty of confederation (*foedus*) with variable conditions. These polities remained internally autonomous, but politically speaking they were aligned entirely towards Rome, yet with no part in the decision-making process there. Militarily speaking, they were entirely dependent on Rome. From 275 BC onwards, all Italic polities from the toe of the boot to the Apennines in the north were united under Roman leadership according to this model. The system remained in place until the Social War of 90/89 BC. The idea of the limited city-state still prevailed, legally and politically.

B.2. The acquisition of provinces

Rome had in fact already taken the decisive step away from this concept when it moved beyond the Italian mainland during its first war with Carthage, which was fought over Sicily. In 264 BC, Rome consented to be drawn into the conflict between Messina, under mercenary control, and Syracuse. Very quickly this escalated into war with Carthage. The war lasted over 20 years and was waged as far afield as Punic Africa (→ Wars of note, K.). Victory over Carthage in 241 brought all of Sicily under Roman control, with the exception of the kingdom of Hieron of Syracuse. There was no move yet to establish a province, in the sense of direct government by a Roman official (the later 'provincial governors'), although Rome was certainly aware that the political and legal relationships with the communities on Sicily were of a different character from those in Italy. For the time being, a quaestor based at Lilybaeum represented Rome's (mostly economic) interests. It was only in 227 BC, when Carthage was forced to cede its remaining islands of Sardinia and Corsica, that Rome found itself compelled to devise a new form of political organization for its new territories outside Italy. Two additional praetors (ordinary magistracies) were appointed, and for the duration of their terms of office, they were assigned Sicily and Sardinia/Corsica – now called *provincia* (see *Lex Acilia*: FIRA I^2 no. 7, ll. 69, 72/79) – as their respective areas of responsibility. Because *provincia* referred to a territory that was precisely defined (as is the nature of an island), the term eventually came to take on the sense of the modern concept of 'province', that is, a political and administrative subunit within the larger political unit under Roman rule. However, Rome constructed no special administrative apparatus for controlling these subjugated territories, and no Roman troops were permanently stationed there. Instead, much as in Italy, the existing communities were for the most part allowed internal autonomy. Where necessary, though, they were required to perform certain duties for Rome. Rome did not even create its own state organization for collecting taxes. Providing auxiliary troops for the central political authority on demand was obligatory.

Although Hannibal's campaign meant that the second war with Carthage (218–201) was mainly fought in Italy, Rome did over the course of those two decades expand into the Iberian Peninsula, where the long conflict had its roots. Little by little, through ongoing confrontations with Carthaginian commanders, tribes that had owed allegiance to Carthage were linked with Rome by treaties or subjugation. After the peace settlement with Carthage in 201 BC, Rome set about organizing the Iberian territories in a similar way to

Sicily and Sardinia. Two new provinces, Hispania citerior and ulterior, were created, again under a praetor appointed year by year. This brought the total number of Roman praetors to six. Over the decades that followed, the territories of both provinces expanded steadily, mostly as a result of wars with individual tribes, and in spite of many reverses and defeats. Prospects of → booty and a → triumph at Rome were powerful motivations for many governors. The conquest of the entire Iberian Peninsula was completed only in the first decade of the Augustan period, when Agrippa and several Augustan legates achieved the conquest of its north and northwest. The peninsula was ultimately divided into three provinces.

Rome had already come into conflict with tribes across the Adriatic along the Illyrian coast before the second war with Carthage. Conflict with the Hellenistic kingdoms beyond, however, arrived only as a result of the attempt by King Philip V of Macedon, allied with Hannibal, to expand his territory as far as the Adriatic. Immediately after the Second Punic War (218–201 BC) Rome sided with Greek cities that felt threatened by Philip. From this point on, and with a shifting assortment of allies, Rome was a party to conflicts in Greece and Macedonia that ultimately brought down the Macedonian kingdom in the wake of the Battle of Pydna in 168 BC. During the wars between Rome and Macedonia in the 190s, the Seleucid Antiochus III made a military foray from Asia Minor into Europe, triggering the Roman army to move against him. After suffering a string of heavy defeats in Europe and Anatolia, Antiochus was finally forced, under the terms of the Peace of Apamea in 188 BC, to surrender the Seleucid possessions in Asia Minor. Yet, Rome made no more effort to organize these territories under direct rule than it had in Macedonia. Instead, it handed them to its allies Pergamum and Rhodes. Rome subsequently made its presence felt in the eastern Mediterranean as a regional 'peacekeeper' (Popillius Laenas; Liv. 45,12).

It was only after its third war against Carthage (149–146), which led to the destruction of the city, that Rome decided to create new provinces. The former Carthaginian heartlands became the province of Africa under the direct authority of a governor, while the remaining western peripheries were handed to Rome's ally, King Micipsa of Numidia. Another victory was won at almost exactly the same time (150–148) over Macedonia and the Achaean League, the final defeat of which came with the destruction of Corinth in 146. Rome now established the province of Macedonia, which also included vanquished Greece. Soon after this, the last king of Pergamum, Attalus III, bequeathed his kingdom to Rome, on condition that Pergamum and the Greek *poleis* remained free. Rome accepted the bequest, although Ti. Sempronius Gracchus' plan to use it to finance internal Roman reforms probably played a part in this decision. However, an uprising followed in the wake of the king's death in 133, so that Rome was only able to establish its new province of Asia after a military campaign. A few decades later, in 96 BC, a Ptolemy also left his kingdom – of Cyrenae – to Rome. Crete was conquered in 67 BC and established as the province of Creta. In 74 BC, the kingdom of Bithynia also became a Roman province by bequest.

B.3. THE LATE REPUBLICAN PERIOD

The extraordinary command granted in 67/66 BC to Pompey (→ Generals of note, N.) in the eastern Mediterranean to counter Mithridates of Pontus, with whom Rome had been at war since 88 BC, marked a watershed. The successful prosecution of this war brought a far-reaching reorganization of the east. Pontus, now conquered, was added to the province of Bithynia. Where there were no cities (i.e. autonomous communities), Pompey created them so that they could control territory without the need for Rome to set up its own small-scale administrative structures. The last remnant of the Seleucid Empire was organized as the province of Syria, from where Rome intended to uphold its interests in the east. The Hasmonean kingdom to the south was destroyed; it was only permitted to live on as an ethnarchy. As with other small princedoms, it was put under the supervision of the governor of Syria, thus drawing them into the Roman sphere of influence. Many Greek *poleis* were released from suzerainty and revived as autonomous communities under Roman overlordship.

Caesar (→ Generals of note, C.) conducted his military operations in Gaul largely to compete with Pompey. He started out from Gallia cisalpina (Italy north of the Po) and Gallia transalpina (the future province of Gallia Narbonensis). Northern Italy had been a Roman province since the war with Hannibal; Transalpine Gaul since 123 BC. By 51 BC, Caesar had conquered the rest of Gaul as far as the Rhine. At first, it was organized as a single province with 60 *civitates*, that is, self-governing tribes.

B.4. THE SYSTEMATIC EXPANSION OF THE EMPIRE UNDER AUGUSTUS

The ensuing civil wars, which spread throughout the Mediterranean, showed clearly that all affected regions now belonged to Rome's sphere of influence, even though not all were yet under direct Roman rule. The end of the civil war in 30 BC brought the incorporation as a province of Egypt, but Augustus, like Pompey and Mark Antony before him, still left many kingdoms and princedoms along the eastern frontier intact, as buffers between Rome and the Parthian Empire. The only such kingdom to be converted into a Roman province was Galatia in the Anatolian interior, on the death of its king Deiotarus in 25 BC. Farther east, the kingdoms of Cappadocia and Commagene lived on. Judaea was provincialized in AD 6 and attached to the province of Syria. It finally became a province in its own right after the suppression of the Jewish Revolt in AD 70.

Augustus shifted the focus of Roman military expansion to the Rhine and Danube. Security interests along the borders were important, as was the link between the west and east of the empire. Economic interests, which were of some significance in the east, were less of a priority. The Alpine lands were conquered in 16–15 BC, clearing the way for the start of offensives in the Balkans between the Sava and Danube in 13 BC, and on the Rhine in 12 BC. Both offensives seem to have fulfilled their objectives in 8/7 BC with the foundations of the provinces of Illyricum inferius (= Pannonia) and Germania. The tribes of Pannonia and Dalmatia rose up in AD 6 in a widespread revolt aimed at casting off Roman rule, but a massive military response in the summer of AD 9 eradicated the threat. Tiberius, as supreme commander, was forced to break off subjugating the Marcomannic kingdom to deal with the situation. Shortly afterwards, Germanic tribes destroyed most of the Roman army stationed on the Rhine in the ambush in the *saltus Teutoburgiensis* (Teutoburg Forest) (→ Battles of note, J.), but Augustus immediately set about recovering the lost province. It was Tiberius' decision in AD 16 to cease regarding Germania on the right bank of the Rhine as part of the empire after the troops were withdrawn. This would be the last time until the second half of the 3rd century AD that a Roman province of long standing was relinquished.

B.5. DEFINITION OF THE IMPERIAL BORDERS THROUGH THE 3RD CENTURY

New provinces continued to be added after Augustus, but the succession of wars of conquest that had been almost uninterrupted since the late 3rd century BC now came to an end. Despite the standing army created by Augustus, wars of conquest now became exceptional events. After the death of King Archelaus in AD 18, Tiberius annexed his kingdom of Cappadocia and it became a province. Considerable expansions of the territory under direct Roman control took place in the reign of Claudius, but almost always without major army involvement. Following internal unrest in Northwestern Africa, he transformed the client kingdom of Mauretania into the two provinces of Mauretania Caesariensis and Mauretania Tingitana (AD 41). The Lycian federation also suffered internal problems and became the province of Lycia, and the Kingdom of Thrace, which had long since been a Roman satellite, was transformed into the province of Thracia (both AD 43). Only the conquest of the island of Britannia, which began in AD 43, required the massive intervention of legions and auxiliaries for its launch and completion. By the reign of Domitian, the area of the island under Roman control had slowly expanded as far as Scotland, until the emperor called a halt to the conquest phase in AD 85.

The only intensive phase of offensive military engagement is associated with the name of Trajan. Like Domitian, he identified the Danube front as the empire's vulnerable point. He accordingly waged two wars, in AD 101/02 and 105/06, to subdue the Dacian kingdom to the north of the river and turn the territory into an advance bastion to relieve the pressure on the Danube border. It is unclear whether Trajan also planned a war with the Parthian Empire in advance. He may have had such a plan, as suggested by the fact that he annexed the Nabataean kingdom in AD 106 and turned it into the province of Arabia, even though the Nabataean dynasty was far from extinct. The war with the Parthians, however, which began in 113/14 with Roman successes and an attempt to establish two new provinces beyond the established Euphrates border, ended in disaster before Trajan's death. Hadrian did not continue his predecessors' aggressive policies.

Not until AD 199 during the reign of Septimius Severus was the empire successfully expanded beyond the Euphrates, and an admittedly small province of Mesopotamia was established that would endure until the 7th century. Soon, though, the idea of imperial expansion was no longer in keeping with the times. More and more, the military priority was to preserve what was held and to repel attacks from peoples outside the empire. This approach even led occasionally to the abandonment of imperial territory, for example the Decumates Agri (Decumatian Fields) in Germania superior to the east of the Rhine, and the province of Dacia, which was surrendered north of the Danube in the reign of Aurelian (270–275), although nominally living on as two provinces, which were now south of the river.

Over the course of more than 450 years, Rome thus established a realm encompassing about five million km², an area occupied today by 32 nation states (not counting the European microstates). This empire, spanning the entire Mediterranean world at its maximum extent under Trajan (discounting the small expansion under Septimius Severus), remained essentially unaltered in dimension until the late 5th century, although it found itself threatened on many fronts from the mid-3rd century onwards.

B.6. Reasons for the expansion of the empire

The external process by which the parts of the empire were acquired gives only partial insight into the motivations and driving forces behind the creation of this empire. Over such a long period, causes and reasons naturally changed. Real and imaginary threats certainly played a part, particularly in regard to Carthage. During the 2nd and 1st centuries BC, aristocratic rivalries and internal power struggles lay behind many campaigns of conquest, along with the prospects of booty, which often served as a motivating factor for ordinary soldiers too. Pompey and Caesar, while seeking to reinforce their own personal positions within the aristocratic elite, were also driven by their perceptions of how the Roman realm might be organized in the long term – one indication of this being their determination to strengthen communitarian structures in the provinces. It was Caesar who established communities of citizens in the provinces on a large scale for the first time. Under Augustus, geopolitical considerations became a higher priority. This is why he refrained from further expansion in the east, and instead sought to establish external borders on the Rhine and Danube, which would provide greater security. He certainly did not attempt to translate into concrete policies the idea being voiced in the Roman public sphere during this period (and not only in the lines from Virgil's *Aeneid*, 6,851–854), namely, the idea of a universal empire, a global oecumene under Roman leadership.

What Augustus did initiate was a tighter administration of the empire, as shown by the design of the provinces in Gaul and on the Iberian Peninsula. This did not lead to a more 'rational' structure overall, for instance in the size of provinces – as a comparison between the sizes of the provinces of Cyprus and Hispania citerior makes abundantly clear. The priority was still dominion rather than effective management by officials of the central government. The same is true of levels of taxation, which were mostly kept as they had been, or as they were set, when the province in question was created. In regard to policies of citizenship and settlement in the provinces, Augustus generally upheld the Caesarean line, as did most of his successors, although the distinction between Roman citizens and peregrines was still preserved in law and politics until the *constitutio Antoniniana* of AD 212. Despite the advice supposedly given by Augustus to keep the empire within its existing bounds (*consilium coercendi intra terminos imperii*; Tac. Ann. 1,11,4), expanding the empire remained a powerful motivation for a number of his successors. For many Romans, the traditional Roman aristocratic mindset made it one of the key obligations of the *principes* ('rulers') to display *virtus imperatoria* ('imperial power') and thus to prove himself *propagator imperii* ('propagator of the empire'; e.g. AE 1969/70, 697; CIL VI 40500: *propagator orbis terrarum*, 'propagator of the world'). At the same time, this imposed on the lord of the earthly sphere the duty to ensure the safety and security of its inhabitants and uphold peace within the empire, as expressed, for instance, in the titular epiclesis *ho ges kai thalasses kai pantos anthropon ethnous despotes* ('lord of land and sea and of the entire human race'; e.g. TAM V 2, 1234).

Regarding motivations for the expansion of Roman territory (particularly in the Republican period), scholars debate this topic fiercely under the heading of 'imperialism' (which is sometimes taken as more defensive, sometimes more offensive). Those who consider this word to be a useful heuristic tool and those who reject it find little or no common ground. Yet it is perfectly possible to analyse the issues of territorial expansion and empire formation without using the word, with the proviso that the perspective in doing so cannot be global, but can only address the politics of shorter periods and individual factors.

Bibliography

[1] E. Baltrusch, Außenpolitik, Bünde und Reichsbildung in der Antike, 2008 [2] B. Bleckmann, Die römische Nobilität im Ersten Punischen Krieg, 2002 [3] J. Bleicken, Der Preis des Aelius Aristides auf das römische Weltreich, 1966 [4] C.B. Champion (ed.), Roman Imperialism. Readings and Sources, 2004 [5] W. Eck, Provinz. Ihre Definition unter politisch-administrativem Aspekt, in: W. Eck, Die Verwaltung des römischen Reiches in der Hohen Kaiserzeit, vol. 2, edited by R. Frei-Stolba / M.A. Speidel, 1998, 167–186 [6] W. Eck, Consilium coercendi intra terminos imperii: Motivationswandel in der augusteischen Expansionspolitik?, in: S. Segenni (ed.), Augusto dopo il bimillenario. Un bilancio, 2018, 128–137 [7] A. Eich, Der Wechsel zu einer neuen grand strategy unter Augustus und seine langfristigen Folgen, in: Historische Zeitschrift 286, 2009, 561–611 [8] D. Flach, Der sogenannte römische Imperialismus, in: Historische Zeitschrift 222, 1976, 1–42 [9] W. Harris, Imperialism in Republican Rome, 1979 [10] A. Heuss, Der erste Punische Krieg und das Problem des römischen Imperialismus. Zur politischen Beurteilung des Krieges, 1949 (reprinted in: Gesammelte Schriften, vol. 2, 1995, 1066–1147) [11] K. Hopkins, Conquerors and Slaves, 1978 [12] D. Hoyos (ed.), A Companion to Roman Imperialism, 2012 [13] S.P. Mattern, Rome and the Enemy. Imperial Strategy in the Principate, 2002 [14] J.W. Rich, Fear, Greed, and Glory. The Causes of Roman War Making in the Middle Republic, in: C.B. Champion (ed.), Roman Imperialism. Readings and Sources, 2004, 46–67 [15] R. Schulz, Feldherren, Krieger, Strategen. Krieg in der Antike von Achill bis Attila, 2012.

Werner Eck

Enemies

Enmity, like friendship, is a cultural constant that is present – whether latent or immediate – at all periods among all peoples. It arises from conflicts of interest or essential differences, it expresses itself in antipathy or hate, and it leads to verbal and physical confrontations. The parties in dispute agree as to the value of the disputed object and the form of conflict resolution, if both sides are prepared to use force. Enemies exist along a spectrum of intensity, from opponents, competitors and rivals, to enemies of the country, sworn enemies, hereditary enemies and arch-enemies. Enmity can exist between individuals or between groups – it divides people, but as a force that builds community it also unites people. This is seen in wars that establish political power, and that create, sustain and annihilate states. In many cases, wars also lead to cultural exchange, as opponents learn from one another.

A. Concept of enemy
B. The Jews
C. The Christians
D. The Greeks
E. The Romans

A. Concept of enemy

As a concept, 'enemy' is determined by vantage point. The enemy is always the other. No one calls themselves or their friends an enemy if they are in conflict with a third party. The concept of an enemy, entirely dependent on perspective, presupposes an observer who identifies himself negatively with the enemy, but also classifies himself by placing himself on par with the enemy, albeit in opposition. Thus, the enemy is Evil and the observer is Good.

Since we see Antiquity from the classical perspective, we regard the Persians as the enemies of the Greeks and the Carthaginians as the enemies of the Romans, not *vice versa*. We speak of the Persian Wars and the Punic Wars, named after the enemies of the Greeks and Romans, although the Greeks and Romans were themselves enemies to the Persians and Carthaginians. To us, the Greeks and Romans have enemies, but are not enemies themselves. The same applies to the Jews, whom we see from the perspective of the Bible. The concept of enemy becomes unserviceable if we take neither side in a third–party dispute. This is true for wars of the Ancient Near East, such as the Battle of Qadesh, for the war between Croesus and Cyrus, and for the Trojan War, which Homer describes without resort to any concept of enemy. Both sides speak the same language and worship the same gods.

Similarly, in internal wars among Greek *poleis*, the wars of the Romans in Italy, and the wars among and between the Celtic and Germanic tribes, it is generally not clear who the 'enemy' is. It may be the aggressor – if we deny its *casus belli* and take sides on the question of guilt, but this would not necessarily reflect the conditions of the time fairly. An impartial account of history will avoid the word 'enemy', consigning it to the sphere of war propaganda, for instance in → eve-of-battle speeches.

All peoples of Antiquity – Egyptians, Assyrians, Chaldaeans, Hittites, Persians, Scythians, the Carthaginians in Africa, the peoples of Western and Northern Europe – had enemies and were themselves their enemies' enemies. Yet we can only perceive the contrasting image of the enemy that invariably underlies a war from the internal partisan perspective of those peoples who left records that enable this. They are chiefly the Jews and Christians, the Greeks and the Romans.

B. The Jews

'Enemy' in Hebrew is *ojeb*. The word strictly means 'opponent in a legal dispute', 'personal adversary', but its sense is mostly political and military [18.118ff.]. The Septuagint translates it as *echthros*, the Vulgate as *hostis*. The word appears well over a hundred times in the Old Testament. It shows an Israel surrounded by enemies, but also riven by internal tensions. History confirms the portrayal [23]; [4]. There were wars with the prior inhabitants of the Promised Land, the Canaanites, and with all neighbours, with the Midianites, Ammonites and Philistines, with the Edomites, Moabites, Amalekites and Jebusites. Claims to power, always effective, were intensified by the exclusivity of the Jews, whose religion did not permit table fellowship or intermarriage with other peoples and demonized foreign deities. For the Moabites, the people most closely related to the Israelites, this prohibition applied to the tenth generation (Dt 23,4). Threatened by enemies and following their example, the Israelites furnished themselves with kings (Jdg 9,6ff.; 1 Sam 8,5; Dt 17,14), and they adopted the war chariot from the Canaanites and Philistines (Jos 17,16ff.; 1 Sam 13,5).

When the kingdom was divided after the reigns of Saul, David and Solomon, half a century of war ensued between the northern Kingdom of Israel and the southern Kingdom of Judah. Israel then had to contend with the Aramaeans of Syria, before being defeated by the Assyrians in 721 BC. Judah fought with Egypt, then also with the Assyrians and Babylonians, who – led by Nebuchadnezzar – took Jerusalem in 587 BC and transported many Jews into the Babylonian Captivity.

The Bible gives a theological explanation of these hostilities. The enemies of Israel are also the enemies of God. The seizure of land in Canaan is made by order of Yahweh. He is the Lord of Battle (Ps 46,10), and the angels are his heavenly host (Gn 32,3; Dt 4,19; 2 Chr 18,18). They too have war chariots at their disposal (Is 66,15). The enemies of Israel are booty, for they are also enemies of God, who promises their annihilation. He will 'cut off' the Amorites, Hittites, Perizzites, Canaanites, Hivites and Jebusites (the inhabitants of Jerusalem) (Ex 23,22f.). In a divine rapture, Deborah announces, 'So let all your enemies perish, O Yahweh!' (Jdg 5,31). The prophet Samuel instructs Saul to annihilate the Amalekites, but when Saul spares their livestock, he incurs Yahweh's wrath (1 Sam 15). The psalms show the singer surrounded by enemies, and swearing merciless revenge (Ps 137). God will destroy them 'for their wickedness' (Ps 94,23). His right hand dashes the enemy to pieces (Ex 15,6; Nm 10,35).

When Israel triumphs, it attributes its victory to God's favor well earned. When it is defeated, this is punishment for having broken God's commandments. In such cases, enemies are the rod of Yahweh, as Jeremiah (15,1ff.; 17,4ff.; 19,7ff. et al.) portrays it, the 'scourge' of God, in the words of Isaiah (10,26; 28,18f.). Yahweh, Jeremiah proclaims (51,20ff.), is the 'hammer and weapon of war' that will 'break in pieces' the nations: 'man and woman, [...] old and young, [...] the young man and the maid'. The Bible revels in atrocities committed against the enemies of Israel, who include pregnant women and infants (Nm 21,21ff.; Nm 31,14ff.; Jos 10,28ff.; Jdg 1,6; 1 Sam 18,27; 2 Sam 3,14; 2 Kg 8,12; 15,16; Ps 137,9). Assyrian reliefs exhibit similar brutality, with enemies impaled on spikes – for instance, on the Palace of Tiglath-Pileser III at Nimrud.

The term 'enemy' became ambivalent with reference to the Jews, insofar as they themselves were branded as 'enemies of all others' in the long history of anti-Semitism [17]; [25]. Diodorus Siculus (34/35,1,1ff.) highlights the Jews' xenophobic laws and their antipathy towards all other peoples, whom they regard as 'enemies' (*polemioi*). Tacitus (Hist. 5,5,1) similarly accuses them of 'antagonistic hatred towards all others', *adversus omnes alios hostile odium*. This Judophobia also lies behind discrimination against the early Christians, who Tacitus (Ann. 15,44,4) says were 'convicted of hatred of the human race' (*odio generis humani convicti*) in the reign of Nero.

C. THE CHRISTIANS

The 'old evil' enemy in the New Testament is the Devil (Mt 13,25ff.). Presumably the injunction in the Sermon on the Mount, 'Love your enemies!' (Mt 5,44), is not intended to include him. In both instances, Matthew uses the same word: *echthros*, rendered by Jerome in the Vulgate as *inimicus*, which can denote either a civilian or a military enemy (see below). Jesus did not espouse a consistent pacifism. 'I did not come to bring peace, but a sword', he says (Mt 10,34). As his capture looms, he orders his disciples to buy swords. They do it and use them. Peter's strike (Joh 18,10f.) at the servant of the High Priest is aimed not at his ear, but at his head (Lk 22,36ff.; 50). Jesus orders the disciples (Lk 19,27) to bring his enemies (*echthroi, inimici*) who do not recognize his kingdom, and slaughter them before his eyes (*katasphaxate!*).

For Paul, the enemies of God are the pagans and the Jews (*echthroi*, Rom 5,10; 11,28), not to mention the 'enemies of the cross' in general, whom damnation awaits (Phil 3,18f.). Early Christians sometimes refused military service, but sometimes performed it. In the tradition of Constantine from AD 312 onwards, and of Theodosius from 394, Christ was a reliable helper in battle when fighting the enemies of the true faith – as argued by Eusebius and Gregory of Nazianzus, Ambrose and Augustine. They adopted Cicero's theory of 'just war', adding in the legitimacy of the war of faith. Theodoret (Hist. eccl. 5,41) espoused ancient bellicism – according to which peace bred slackness but war strengthened the spirit – and augmented it with the Christian notion that war laid bare the worthlessness and transience of all earthly goods. To the Church Fathers, the enmity of the barbarians was less wicked than that of the Devil, which is to say heresy – for the barbarians merely threatened the body, while the Devil took aim at the soul [10.528ff., 565].

D. THE GREEKS

D.1. Enmity within Greece
D.2. Enmity with barbarians
D.3. Enmity with Persia
D.4. Enmity with Rome

The Greek *echthros* is an adjective in Homer, derived from *to echthos* or *he echthra* – 'hatred' or 'rancour'. It is used in the sense of 'hated [by]' or 'repugnant [to]', of people (Il. 9,312) and things (Il. 9,378), not specifically of adversaries in war. As the noun 'enemy', Hesiod (Op. 342) contrasts it with *philos* – 'friend', but in the general sense of opponent. For the enemy in battle, *echthros* can be used as well as the more incisive *polemios*, from *polemos* – 'war', as in Herodotus (1,87,3). The adversary is *enantios* or *hypenantios*. The opponent in a general sense is *antagonistes*. Derived from *agon*, the sporting contest, the word is used of rivals, opposing parties in law, competitors and enemies in war, as in Xenophon (Cyr. 1,6,8).

D.1. Enmity within Greece

Homer in the *Iliad* exhibits a wide array of motifs in dealings with enemies. The Trojan War was an honour conflict. The abduction of Helen injured the Achaeans' honour. Returning her would have averted war, but that was incompatible with the honour of the Trojans. Beyond this, the Achaeans' interest in war was limited to obtaining weapons as booty – before the motive of revenge took effect, which called Achilles to battle. Whereas his adversary Hector declared that, should he be victorious, he would release the body of Achilles for burial (Il. 7,84), Achilles in victory dragged Hector's body three times each morning around the grave mound of Patroclus, at which he had slaughtered twelve Trojan nobles as sacrifices to the dead (Il. 23,175; 24,15ff.). How different the attitudes of Glaucus and Diomedes! When they met in battle, they affirmed that their fathers were friends. They exchanged weapons and promised to spare one another (Il. 6,119ff.). The intention of meeting the enemy in a manner befitting a noble soldier is signalled by the ban on ranged weapons, as attested in an Archaic inscription at the Temple of Artemis Amarynthia on Euboea (Str. 10,1,12).

Enmity between a Greek *polis* and its neighbours was the norm in the Classical period. Plato (Leg. 626a–d) says as much, and history confirms it. Peace was an empty word, war the state of nature. There was no appeal to the gods, only to the natural law of the stronger [7.45ff.], according to the Athenians in Thucydides' Melian dialogue (5,84ff.; 116). In this case as in others (e.g. Plataeae 427, Orchomenus 363, Olynthus 348 BC), the men of the conquered city were killed and the women and children enslaved [2.270ff.]. Otherwise revenge would surely follow [15]. Given neighbours' ambitions of expansion and annexation, war was fought for the independence that enabled a city to fight at its own discretion. Peace was better than war, but victory was better than peace. The Spartans declared war on the Messenians annually, in order to continue keeping them as helots, i.e. state slaves (Plut. *Lycurgus* 28).

Where peace was the aim of war, the enemy had to be spared. Philip II thus sent the Athenians who were taken captive after his victory at Chaeronea (338 BC) home without conditions (Just. Epit. 9,4,4). The Pan-Hellenic idea was to overcome enmity among the Greeks. Efforts in this direction date far back. Thus, a truce – the *hieromenia* – was in force during the games at Olympia, Delphi, Nemea and on the Isthmus, and it included the period of gathering and dispersing (Xen. Hell. 4,7,2f.). If the peace of the gods was not strictly observed, there was certainly belief in divine retribution. To limit damage done in war, no olive trees were to be cut down and no houses destroyed. Victory monuments (*tropaia*) were to be built of perishable wood, so that strife would not be perpetuated (Diod. Sic. 13,24,5; Cic. Inv. 2,70). Still, this was the effect of the votive gifts at Delphi, where monuments to Spartan victories over Athens stood peacefully alongside monuments to Athenian victories over Sparta, all of them in thanks to Apollo (Paus. 10,9).

D.2. Enmity with barbarians

Plato thought in Pan-Hellenic terms (Resp. 470a–d; Plt. 262d). Although conflicts among Greeks were normal to him, he insisted that weapons of defeated Greeks should not be put on display in temples, for this would be a 'defilement' (*miasma*). An enemy's women, children and elderly should be spared, and booty should not exceed the value of a year's harvest. War among Greeks was not *polemos*, but *stasis*, i.e. → civil war. For Plato, what connected the Greeks was not language, culture and religion, but kinship. The Greeks were a vast family to him, amicable 'by nature'. This biological criterion distinguished them from the 'barbarians', who were alien and hostile. Humankind comprised two races, Greeks and barbarians, however much the former disagreed and however diverse the latter might appear. Greeks and barbarians were 'enemies by nature' (*polemioi physei*), and war (here *polemos*) was the natural state between them. This, however, had its benefits: enemies without fostered harmony within. To this end, the enemy was interchangeable. Isocrates (4,157; 4,184; 12,163) in animosity against the Persians invoked the unity of the Greeks and sought help from Philip of Macedon, whereas Demosthenes saw the same Philip as the arch-enemy, appealing for Hellenic unity against him in his *Philippic Orations* – and even accepting support from Philip's enemy, Persia (Plut. *Demosthenes* 14; 23). My enemy's enemy is my friend.

The enemies that Plato considered catalysts of Greek unity were divided into the 'barbarians' of the west and the east. The arch-enemies in the west were the Carthaginians, the point of dispute being Sicily. In his letters to the relatives of Dion at Syracuse, Plato does not counsel accommodation with the Carthaginians occupying the west of the island, but declares that they should be expelled or enslaved (Ep. 7,333a; 7,336a; 8,353a). This centuries-old dispute ended only in 241 BC, when the Romans made the island a protectorate. The Carthaginians, for their part, harboured no comparably hostile feelings towards the Greeks. Conflicts with the Greeks did not prevent them from minting coins inspired by Greek models, using the Greek language or tolerating a Greek colony within their city. They had a high regard for Greek art, and supported Grecian cults in their territories (Diod. Sic. 14,77,5; 32,25).

D.3. Enmity with Persia

The arch-enemy in the east was Persia from the moment in 546 BC when Cyrus II took control of the cities of Ionia. Plato's *Menexenus* offers testimony to the implacable hostility of the Greeks towards Persia. The Athenians here are defending freedom against the arch-enemy, the Persian king (243b), for hatred of the barbarian is innate in them (*physei misobarbaron*) because they are Hellenes of pure descent (245d). Persophilic attitudes, *medismos*, amount to treason. Securing freedom against Persians want to 'enslave' Greece also determines the view of the enemy in Isocrates' *Panegyricus*, his oration to Philip of Macedon (Or. 5) and his two open letters to him. Isocrates demands a war of vengeance. The legend of the Oath of Plataeae comes from his time. According to the Athenian orator Lycurgus (81), as well as Cicero (Rep. 3,15), Diodorus Siculus (11,29) and Pausanias (10,35,2), the Greeks on the eve of battle in 479 BC swore to leave untouched the temple destroyed by the Persians as an eternal exhortation to revenge. This was propaganda in support of an enemy stereotype: disrepair of temples was often blamed on the Persians, as can be inferred from Pausanias (1,1,5; 2,31,6; 10,35,2).

Like the Carthaginians, the Persians exhibit no signs of categorical hostility towards the Greeks. The Achaemenid Empire was a multiethnic society, in which Greeks played a prominent role, as physicians, sculptors and seafarers and as fellow soldiers and mercenaries. The Persians had a high regard for Greek art and Greek literature (Gell. NA 4,17). Darius venerated Apollo both Delian (Hdt. 6,97) and Clarian (Gadatas inscription). Xerxes accorded to Themistocles, victor at Salamis and supposedly his deadly enemy, princely asylum (Plut. *Themistocles* 29). In the other direction, Herodotus, Aeschylus and Xenophon all treat the Persians sympathetically.

Just as Philip II spared the defeated Athenians in a pan-Hellenic spirit, so Alexander was lenient to surrendering Persians in a cosmopolitan spirit. He enslaved no prisoners, built no victory monuments and – contrary to the advice of his teacher Aristotle – did not regard the barbarians as enemies, but rather, as their king, made them the equal of the Greeks (Str. 1,67; Plut. Mor. 329c–d). He married a Persian woman and reinstalled the defeated Indian Porus as a client king. Alexander's death was mourned in Persia, whereas Greece breathed a sigh of relief and hastened to resume the autonomy of the *poleis*. The cultivation of nationalistic stereotypes of enemies was not Alexander's or the Diadochi's way.

D.4. Enmity with Rome

From the Greek point of view, the Romans too were barbarians and enemies. During the Roman advance into the east, resistance developed there, which Polybius (5,104) portrays as represented by the Aetolian *strategos* Agelaus. In an oration of 217 BC, he urges Philip V to regard the Greeks as blood relatives and treat them accordingly, for only the unity of all Greeks can repel the danger from the barbarians of Italy who are moving in over Greece like a dark cloud from the west, threatening the freedom that allows them to take up hostilities as they choose. When the Aetolians nevertheless defected to the Roman side, the Acarnanian Lyciscus (in 211/09) warned against the 'cloud from the west' and the alien tribe of Roman barbarians (Pol. 9,32–39), who were 'enemies' (*echthroi*; 9,37,9). A third speech, by the Rhodian Thrasycrates (207 BC), repeated the appeal against Rome (Pol. 11,4–6; [5.32ff.]). As long as Greeks were fighting Romans in Greece, the Romans, being aliens to the country, were the enemy.

E. The Romans

E.1. Just war
E.2. Domestic political enemies
E.3. The emperor as victor
E.4. Bellicism
E.5. Enmity with the Germani

According to Cicero (Off. 1,37), the original Latin word for an enemy in the warlike sense was *perduellis*, as someone with whom one makes *bellum* – 'war' (*perbellis*). The Classical Latin word for an enemy of the people is *hostis*. At first, this word denoted a 'stranger', the *peregrinus* or *extraneus*. It is still used in this sense in the Twelve Tables (2,2; 3,7). *Hostis* is related to *hospes* – 'guest' – and indeed also to the English word 'guest'. The term *hostis*, where weapons are involved, contrasts with terms for opponents where only words are used, such as in court or when seeking office. Terms like *adversarius* and *competitor* are used here. *Inimicus* had multiple meanings. It could denote an internal political enemy (escalatable to *inimicissimus*), or deadly external political enemies in war, such as the Celtiberians and Cimbri (Cic. Off. 1,38). *Inimicus* became the source of the French *ennemi* and from there the English 'enemy' (and 'inimical'). Late Antique *hostilitas* – 'hostility' – in Cassiodorus (Var. 1,50,1) is what the fire-spewing Vesuvius is exhibiting towards the inhabitants of Campania.

E.1. Just war

The *Digests* (50,16,118) offer the following definition by the legal scholar Sextus Pomponius from the 2nd century AD: *hostes hi sunt, qui nobis aut quibus nos publice bellum decrevimus, ceteri latrones aut praedones sunt* ('Enemies are those who conduct, or with whom we conduct, a publicly declared war. All others are robbers or bandits'). The distinction between enemies and robbers made here depends on a formal declaration of war that is made and announced *publice*. This condition is emphasized in expressions like *hostis legitimus* (Cic. Off. 3,107f.) and *hostis iustus* (Gell. NA 5,6,21). The preconditions were a senate vote, a popular resolution of the centuriate committees, and originally a declaration of war to the adversary with an ultimatum demanding retribution, because a 'just war', a *bellum iustum*, could only be fought to make good damages incurred or to expel enemies (Cic. Rep. 3,35), in defence of the home or allied territory. Carthage and Numantia, Cicero declares, were destroyed because they posed a chronic threat. By contrast, he felt shame at the fate of Corinth, finding its destruction by Mummius in 146 BC to be disproportionate (Cic. Off. 1,35; 3,46). War with the Greeks, while sometimes justified, ran counter to respect for their culture. This was exemplified in the war against Pyrrhus. When a deserter advised the Roman senate to poison the king, the Romans sent him back to the Greeks in chains. Pyrrhus returned prisoners without ransom – after all, he was not a merchant (Cic. Off. 1,38f.). The gesture earned the Aeacid respect in Rome.

According to the law of war (*ius bellicum*), there were obligations towards the 'legitimate' enemy. Retribution had to be proportionate, and good faith had to be upheld, even with an enemy: *fides est conservanda*, as when Regulus, released on word of honour in 250 BC, returned to Carthaginian captivity. Emissaries were inviolate and the defeated were to be treated mercifully. When an enemy laid down his weapons and entrusted himself to the *fides* of the general, he must be accepted, even if the wall-breaker had already made the breach – according to Cicero (Off. 1,33ff.; 3,107; Gell. NA 3,8). A general who conquered a city and brought it into a confederacy with Rome became its patron. The Romans gave their Italic opponents citizenship. In Virgil (Aen. 6,853), Jupiter warns the Romans *parcere subiectis et debellare superbos* ('to spare the defeated and crush the arrogant'). Abuse of prisoners was punishable (Diod. Sic. 24,12,3).

In this spirit, Augustus claimed 'never [to have] inflicted unjust war on any people' (*nulli genti bello per iniuriam inlato*), and to have preferred to spare rather than destroy all those who could be forgiven with confidence. Thus, he declared, he had brought about 'peace through victory' (*parta victoriis pax*; R. Gest. div. Aug. 26; 13). Augustus here followed the principle formulated by Cicero: every war should be fought such that it serves the cause of peace. The Pax Romana also benefited the defeated enemy. According to Cato, sparing the defeated imposed an obligation of gratitude on them (Diod. Sic. 31,3,4). Leniency was in everyone's interests.

The legal classification of grounds for war was linked to a moral classification of adversaries. Thus, just as the Romans arranged themselves in hierarchies, they did the same with their enemies. External enemies fell into two categories. Cicero (Off. 1,38) distinguishes between wars against other cultural groups, such as Italics, Carthaginians and Greeks, in which hegemony alone was at stake, and wars against perfidious or brutal barbarians, in which – it would appear – existence itself was under threat, as with the illiterate Celts and Cimbri. But that was simply ideology, since the Celts were interested in gold (Liv. 5,48), the Cimbri in land (Plut. Marius 11).

E.2. DOMESTIC POLITICAL ENEMIES

A third class of opponents were robbers [21.192ff.], even if they saw themselves as worshippers of Mars and warriors, as in Apuleius (Met. 5,11; 5,22; 7,10f.). Augustine (Civ. 4,4) recounts from Cicero (Rep. 3,24) the anecdote of Alexander and the captured pirate, who claimed to be doing on a small scale what Alexander was doing on a large scale, for states were nothing but oversized bands of robbers. Cicero, however, took care to explain the difference. The *latro*, *praedo* or *pirata* was an enemy of all, a *communis hostis omnium* (Cic. Off. 3,107), and a stranger to the *ius bellicum*. Harsher measures were permissible against him. The same was true of rebels. Pompey had 5,000 slaves loyal to Spartacus killed (Plut. Crassus 11). A victory over robbers, rebels or insurgent slaves brought no particular renown – and certainly not a triumph, but at most an *ovatio*, a ceremonial entry on foot (Gell. NA 5,6,20f.).

In the course of the civil war of the 'Roman Revolution', the term *hostis* began to be used not just of enemies of the people, but of political opponents, whose right of protection as *cives Romani* was denied. Although this was without legal foundation [22.1242], it culminated in the proscriptions of 82/81 and 43 BC. Sallust (Catil. 52) reports that Cato also declared the Catilinarians *hostes*. Fighting domestic enemies was regarded as shameful. Even victors in a civil war, *bellum civile*, received no triumph. Augustus therefore dressed up his defeat of Mark Antony as a victory over a foreign enemy, Cleopatra (Hor. Carm. 1,37), much as Pompey had done in his victory over Sertorius (Plin. HN 7,96), as Caesar did in his war against Cato Uticensis in Africa (Suet. Caes. 37; Liv. Epit. 115), and as Vespasian would later do through his coins after his *civium bellum* (Tac. Hist. 4,72,1) against Iulius Civilis. This was an alteration of the enemy's image.

Anyone who jeopardized the order of the state or the law, or engaged in treachery or high treason, was regarded as *hostis publicus*, an enemy of the state. In the Imperial period, this essentially meant usurpers or those suspected of usurpation, such as Magnentius in AD 353 (Cod. Theod. 10,8,4 with Seeck; [10.106]), Gildo in 398 (Symmachus, Ep. 4,5; Dessau ILS 795) and Stilicho in 408 (→ Generals of note, P.; CTh. 7,16,1). One thus condemned must die and suffer the *damnatio memoriae*. His assets were confiscated.

E.3. THE EMPEROR AS VICTOR

During the Imperial period, the claim to world dominion softened the concept of an 'enemy'. Apart from the Parthians and Persians, who were sometimes acknowledged as equals, opponents of Rome were illiterate 'barbarians', whose *superbia* ('pride') and wildness seemed to rule out any lasting peace, and who, given the backwardness of their civilizations, ought to welcome being subjugated and Romanized (Plin. HN 16,4). They were seen as troublesome neighbours, rather than true enemies. The prommise of Anchises in Virgil (see above, E.1.) justified war against them, but also required that they be treated with mercy.

The belief that the emperor was ordained by fate to achieve victory was rooted in his institutionalized charisma. Augustus, on his return from Egypt on August 28, 29 BC, had Victoria atop the globe put up in the Curia Iulia. The statue had come to Rome in 209 BC following the conquest of Tarentum, and its subject became the tutelary goddess of the senate, affording the emperor – according to Symmachus (Relat. 3,3) in AD 384 – eternal invincibility. Emperors used all means of public relations to portray themselves as victors. This is seen in the bynames added to their inscriptions and coins. The elder Scipio and Pompey had already been called *invicti*, and this byname later became attached to Trajan, Commodus and the soldier-emperors. It was further heightened into *invictissimus* and *victor omnium gentium* [33]. Names of enemy peoples appear in generals' → victory titles. The earliest of these are purely geographic, like the bynames Africanus for Publius Cornelius Scipio, victor over Hannibal in 202 BC (Liv. 3,45), and Asiaticus for his brother Lucius Cornelius Scipio, who defeated Antiochus III in 190 BC (Liv. 37,58). A tribe's name marked out Publius Servilius 'Isauricus' as a victor in 76 BC, and the emperors later adopted the custom. Germanicus, adoptive nephew of Augustus, received his byname from the senate, which also dubbed the son of Claudius 'Britannicus' [20]. Titus and Vespasian refused the byname Judaicus (Cass. Dio 66,7,2). Trajan called himself Germanicus, Dacicus and Parthicus, and later emperors added Adiabenicus, Alamannicus, Alanicus, Arabicus, Armeniacus, Francicus, Gothicus, Palmyricus, Persicus, Sarmaticus and Vandalicus. Sometimes, an emphatic Maximus was added. Enemies were everywhere.

Names of subjugated enemy peoples were listed on victory monuments. On his Pyrenaean Tropaea, Pompeius referred to a total of 876 hilltop fortresses (*oppida*) that had been stormed, from the Alps to the limits of Hispania ulterior (Plin. HN 7,96). Statues of 14 personifications of peoples defeated by Pompey decorated his theatre (Plin. HN 36,41). Augustus listed 46 defeated Alpine tribes on his colossal Tropaeum Alpium, above what is now Monaco (Plin. HN 3,136).

Roman victory iconography, as seen on coins and reliefs, humiliates the defeated enemy by showing him in mourning (*iudaea capta* coins), bound (Adamklissi), in chains (Mainz Relief), begging for protection (Bronze, Paris, Bibliothèque Nationale), being dragged into captivity by Romans (Trajan Column) or ridden over (Worms tombstones, Mainz, Cologne), or else by portraying executions, as on the Marcus Aurelius Column. In the last of these cases, the miscreants' executioners are pro-Roman Germans [28].

In prominent instances, enmity was given a mythological expression. Pyrrhus, who bore the name of Achilles' son and saw himself as a descendant of him and his father Aeacus, was in a sense continuing the Trojan War when he landed in Italy in 280 BC to free the Greeks there from the yoke of the Romans, descended from the Trojan Aeneas (Paus. 1,12,1). His coins promoted this story [19.132]. Rome's hereditary enmity towards Carthage was also founded in the Homeric tradition. Its roots lay in the legend of Dido. In his first Roman national epic, the *Bellum Poenicum*, dealing with the First Punic War, the poet Naevius, who had himself fought in the war, had Aeneas, en route from Troy to Latium, make a detour via Carthage. There, he fell in love with and then abandoned Queen Dido, who hurled after him a curse of eternal hatred. Ennius took up this motif between the Second and Third Punic Wars, then Virgil (Aen. 4,625) did so in the reign of Augustus, by which time this image of the enemy was long since obsolete.

Republican Rome was more implacable towards Carthage than towards any other enemy, and yet Rome's arch-enemy Hannibal was portrayed with the utmost respect [3.381ff.]. Livy (30,30) calls Hannibal and Scipio 'by far the most splendid leaders' of their age, and has them express their mutual admiration on the eve of the Battle of Zama (30,20). Pliny (HN 34,32) knew of three statues of Hannibal in Rome, and Valerius Maximus (5,1 ext. 6) praised Hannibal's *humanitas* and *clementia*. Homer was even still relevant to Kritoboulos of Imbros. When Mehmed II visited the grave of Achilles at Troy in 1462, Kritoboulos declared the Turks, as descendants of the 'Teucri' – after

Teucer, the first King of Troy – the hereditary enemies of the Greeks in Byzantium [1.225].

E.4. BELLICISM

A positive connotation was sometimes also attached to enmity in Rome. Bellicism, for instance, which ascribes to war an educational and purifying effect, emphasizes that threats from the outside reinforce internal cohesion and keep all forces strong, since otherwise they become slack. Enmity was *materia virtutis* (a cause or occasion for virtue). In 149 BC, as the senate mulled a third war against Carthage and the elder Cato reiterated his *Ceterum censeo Karthaginem esse delendam* (Aur. Vict. Vir. ill. 47,8; Flor. Epit. 2,15), Scipio Nasica contradicted him with the observation that Rome needed a whetstone (*cos*), in order to remain sharp and able to defend itself (Oros. 4,23,9f.). When Carthage was finally destroyed in 146 BC, and no external enemy remained as a threat, Sallust argued that decadence increased in the form of civil war, which began with the Gracchi in 133 BC (Sall. Iug. 41). Augustine (Civ. 1,30; 2,18) agreed. Propertius (4,1,138) made playful use of the motif of the useful enemy in his love poetry. While the emperor fought for Rome, the poet wielded the weapons of *militia Veneris* ('the warfare of Venus') with the beloved, himself an *utilis hostis* ('a useful enemy') for the arrows of Amor.

The enemy was also useful in a quite different sense, insofar as conflict created contacts that triggered learning processes. Wars have always brought cultural exchange [11]. This is particularly true of the Romans, who were diligent students not only of the Greeks, but of all their neighbours, adopting and refining useful things from them (Pol. 6,25,11; Cic. Rep. 2,30; Cic. Tusc. 2,1,5). From the Greeks they adopted writing, coinage and temple architecture, from the Etruscans religious and political ceremonies, from the Celts forms of clothing and chariots, and from the Carthaginians types of ships and theories of agriculture. They adopted equipment of war from various peoples (Ath. 273e–f), and from the Germans, albeit belatedly and hesitantly, they adopted furs and trousers (Cod. Theod. 14,10,2–4; 15,14,14). By the same token, the Germans owed practically their entire civilization to the Romans [9].

E.5. ENMITY WITH THE GERMANI

The relationship between the Romans and Germans was a fateful one. The *metus Cimbricus* ('Cimbric panic') recapitulated the *metus Gallicus* of 386 BC and the *metus Punicus* of 216 [31], the Germanic tribes reviving the trope of the terror from the north. Enmity dominated the two centuries on either side of Christ's birth, palpably so in Tacitus (Germ. 33). At the same time, Tacitus displays a positive regard for Arminius, whom he does not brand an enemy, traitor or rebel, but holds up as *liberator Germaniae* (Ann. 2,88). He also ascribes a searing speech against Roman imperialism to the Briton Calgacus (Agr. 30). The Roman authors treat the enemies of Rome not with hatred, but rather with respect. Other examples include Viriathus in Lusitania and Decebalus in Dacia, the two Batos in Dalmatia and Tacfarinas in Africa.

Along the empire's borders, Germanic raids alternated with Roman punitive expeditions from the 1st century BC to the 6th century AD. Many tens of thousands of Germans were settled in the empire after Agrippa brought the Ubii across the Lower Rhine. The law classified the Germanic *barbari* simply as foreign to the empire. Caesar recruited Germanic cavalry and the Julio-Claudian emperors kept a Germanic bodyguard [29]. More and more Germanic → mercenaries were engaged [32]; [30]; [10.380ff.]. After Constantine, Germanic *magistri militum* ('Masters of Soldiers') acquired key positions [6]. The Visigoths who annihilated the Eastern Roman army at Adrianople in 378 were not enemy invaders: they had crossed the Danube with the emperor's permission in 376 (Amm. Marc. 31,4). They became legal settlers on imperial soil in 381. The court rhetorician Themistius (Or. 16) reflected Roman universalism in voicing the emperor's concern for those foreign to the empire. Marriage alliances occurred, several around AD 400 with the imperial house, and the last years of the Western Empire were dominated by a Roman-Germanic military aristocracy [13.66ff.]. Germans taken into the empire operated alternately as imperial confederates and independent enemy actors. In 410, when Honorius denied the Goth Alaric promotion to *magister militum*, Alaric responded by sacking Rome. Odoacer, who deposed the last Western Roman Emperor in 476, was an officer of the empire.

The Church Fathers offer contrasting views of the Germans. Ambrose (Epist. 19; 24; 30) and Prudentius (*contra Symmachum* 2,816f.) regard them as barbarians more akin to beasts than people. Orosius (7,39) is more benevolent in his assessment, and Salvian (Gub. 4,21; 5,36; 5,57; 7,24ff.) even depicts them as children of nature, not yet spoiled by civilization. For Procopius (Goth. 4,30ff.), the Gothic King Totila was a beacon of light in the 'fight for Rome'. In general, the Germans were not seen as enemies to be fought, but as neighbours to be civilized and proselytized. Admittedly, there was sporadic concern about the growing importance of the Germans in the empire. This surfaced in spontaneous actions, such as the massacre of Gothic *adcrescentes* (trainees for military service) in Asia Minor following the catastrophe of Adrianople in AD 378 (Amm. Marc. 31,16,8), the massacre of the Gothic inhabitants of Constantinople in 400 (Zos. 5,19,4), the toppling of Stilicho in 408

(Zos. 5,32ff.) and the palace revolt at Constantinople in 471 (Chron. min. 2,90; Procop. Vand. 1,6,27). Even so, there was no dominant anti-Germanic image used to depict Germans as the enemy, still less any fundamentally anti-Roman sentiment among the Germans. The friend-enemy relationship was no longer a stable category. With the failure either to exclude or to include the Germans, the unity of the empire disintegrated in the 5th century.

BIBLIOGRAPHY
[1] F. BABINGER, Mehmed der Eroberer und seine Zeit, 1953 [2] J. BURCKHARDT, Griechische Kulturgeschichte, vol. 1, 1898 (repr. 1956) [3] K. CHRIST, Zur Beurteilung Hannibals (1968), in: K. CHRIST (ed.), Hannibal, 1974, 361–407 [4] M. CLAUSS, Geschichte des Alten Israel, 2009 [5] J. DEININGER, Widerstand gegen Rom in Griechenland 271–86 v.Chr., 1971 [6] A. DEMANDT, magister militum, in: RE, Suppl. 12, 1970, 553–790 [7] A. DEMANDT, Der Idealstaat. Die politischen Theorien der Antike, 1993 [8] A. DEMANDT, Vandalismus. Gewalt gegen Kultur, 1997 [9] A. DEMANDT, Römisches Erbe im deutschen Kulturgut, in: A. DEMANDT, Sieben Siegel. Essays zur Kulturgeschichte, 2005, 66–77 [10] A. DEMANDT, Die Spätantike. Römische Geschichte von Diocletian bis Justinian, 2007 [11] A. DEMANDT, Feindliche Übernahme, in: Kulturaustausch. Zeitschrift für internationale Perspektiven 57, 2007, 18–21 [12] A. DEMANDT, Römer und Germanen. Versuch einer Bilanz, in: H. SCHNEIDER (ed.), Feindliche Nachbarn. Rom und die Germanen, 2008, 271–289 [13] A. DEMANDT, Der spätrömische Militäradel, in: A. DEMANDT, Zeitenwende. Aufsätze zur Spätantike, 2013, 52–84 [14] A. DEMANDT, Germanen und Römer zwischen Konfrontation und Integration, in: A. DEMANDT, Zeitenwende. Aufsätze zur Spätantike, 2013, 512–529 [15] H.-J. GEHRKE, Die Griechen und die Rache, in: Saeculum 38, 1987, 121–149 [16] R.S. HARTIGAN, Saint Augustine on War and Killing, in: Journal of the History of Ideas 27, 1966, 195–204 [17] I. HEINEMANN, Antisemitismus, in: RE, Suppl. 5, 1931, 3–43 [18] E. JENNI, Ojeb – Feind, in: Theologisches Handwörterbuch zum Alten Testament, vol. 1, 1971, 118–121 [19] D. KIENAST, Pyrrhos, in: RE 24, 1963, 108–165 [20] P. KNEISSL, Die Siegestitulatur der römischen Kaiser, 1969 [21] R. MACMULLEN, Enemies of the Roman Order, 1996 [22] T. MOMMSEN, Römisches Staatsrecht, vol. 3, 1887 (repr. 1952) [23] M. NOTH, Geschichte Israels, 1950 (²1954) [24] B. SCARDIGLI / P. SCARDIGLI (eds.), Germani in Italia, 1994 [25] P. SCHÄFER, Judeophobia. Attitudes toward the Jews in the Ancient World, 1997 [26] H. SCHNEIDER (ed.), Feindliche Nachbarn. Rom und die Germanen, 2008 [27] A. SCHULTEN, Hostis, in: RE 8,2 (series 1), 1913, 2515–2516 [28] K. SCHUMACHER / H. KLUMBACH, Germanendarstellungen, vol. 1: Darstellungen aus dem Altertum (Kataloge des Römisch-Germanischen Zentralmuseums zu Mainz 1), 1935 [29] M.P. SPEIDEL, Germanen in der kaiserlichen Leibwache zu Rom, in: B. SCARDIGLI / P. SCARDIGLI (eds.), Germani in Italia, 1994, 151–158 [30] M.P. SPEIDEL, Ancient Germanic Warriors, 2004 [31] D. TIMPE, Kimberntradition und Kimbernmythos, in: B. SCARDIGLI / P. SCARDIGLI (eds.), Germani in Italia, 1994, 23–60 [32] M. WAAS, Germanen im römischen Dienst, 1971 [33] S. WEINSTOCK, Victor, in: RE 8,A,2 (series 2), 1958, 2485–2500

ALEXANDER DEMANDT

Equipment

A. Greek
B. Roman

A. GREEK

A.1. Equipment of the hoplite armies
A.2. Clothing and shield
A.3. Tendency for uniformity in the Hellenistic period

A.1. EQUIPMENT OF THE HOPLITE ARMIES
Originally, the Greek citizen-soldier was responsible for obtaining all his → armour, clothing and equipment. In the field, he carried his weapons, and his slave took care of his personal equipment. In more impoverished regions of Greece, the hoplites had to carry their own baggage, unless they could find a younger relative who was not yet of age for military service to accompany them (Xen. An. 4,3,11). These 'porters' (*skeuophoroi*) transported their rations in a woven container (*gylios*, Aristoph. Ach. 1097–1101) on a yoke that was kept in balance by the weight of mattresses, a water bottle and a cooking pot on the other end. It was recommended to bring a small first-aid kit, a file for sharpening weapons and a whittling knife with which experts could repair broken spear shafts (Xen. Cyr. 6,2,32).

Hoplites usually ate alone or with their tent companions (*syskenoi*). Every tent team brought along a mule to carry the tent, into which leather casings and other heavy equipment of the group were packed. Less wealthy soldiers, who had no slaves, had to assign one of the *syskenoi* to take care of the mule (Xen. An. 5,8,5). Xenophon recommended loading every pack animal with an axe and scythe for obtaining fodder (Xen. Cyr. 6,2,34).

The Greeks did not know a simple method of creating fire. It had to be centrally organized, brought by every army. The Spartan army had an officer with the title of 'fire-carrier' (*pyrophoros*, Xen. Lac. Pol. 13,2; Hdt. 8,6,2). Although his duties were chiefly religious in nature, he was also responsible for guarding the flame. King Agesilaus thus enhanced his personal reputation when he sent ten men with fire in cooking pots to a regiment that would be spending the night on a mountain, but whose food porters had forgotten to take fire with them (Xen. Hell. 4,5,4).

A hoplite and his personal slave could only carry rations for a few days or weeks. For longer campaigns, it was necessary to organize markets at which soldiers could obtain provisions. A joint central supply system is known from the year 479 BC, when an attempt was made to bring Greek allied forces at Plataeae supplies from the Peloponnese, transported through the mountains by 500 pack animals (Hdt. 9,39). We do not know how league commanders assembled these 500 animals and their drivers (many of whom died when the Persians attacked the convoy), or where the money for the provisions came from.

Later, reports tell us that convoys of ox carts accompanied armies. At the first Battle of Mantinea (418 BC), men too old for the battlefield looked after the Spartan convoy (Thuc. 5,72,3). The main task of the convoy of carts was probably to bring provisions, but Xenophon also recommended equipping every cart with a shovel and a pickaxe in case substantial earthworks had to be made (Xen. Cyr. 6,2,33f.).

The Macedonian infantry as reorganized by Philip II beginning in the winter of 359/58 BC frowned upon vehicles. Troops carried their own weapons, in addition to their baggage and their 30 days' ration of flour. Every *dekas* (unit of – probably – 16 men) had its own assigned servant, who was expected 'to carry the grinders and ropes' (Frontinus, Strat. 4,1,6). The use to which grinders were put is obvious; that of the ropes was probably in tent construction. Each of Philip's cavalrymen had a groom assigned to him. The custom of bringing at least one such personal servant was also known from before.

A.2. Clothing and shield

Originally, every soldier provided his own clothing, but there were already tendencies towards uniformity. In his listing of household objects, Xenophon distinguishes between clothing for war and for festival days and everyday apparel (Xen. Oec. 9,6). He also explains why he reserves his finest clothing for battle. If the gods grant victory, he says, it is appropriate to wear one's best clothes to befit the occasion – and if he dies, it is right to meet his fate well dressed (Xen. An. 3,2,7). The most expensive dye was purple, the preferred colour for uniforms. The Spartan army wore purple uniforms and bronze shields (Xen. Lac. 11,3). Xenophon traces this practice back to Lycurgus; accordingly, it goes back at least to the 5th century, if not earlier. He describes the army of the Spartan King Agesilaus in 394 BC as 'entirely bronze, entirely purple' (Xen. Ages. 2,7). Plutarch reports that a dark red tunic would terrify inexperienced opponents while also helping to conceal one's own wounds (Plut. Mor. 238F). Spartan warriors were buried in their purple uniforms with an olive bough (Plut. *Lycurgus* 27,1). It was said that in 401 BC, all 10,000 Greek mercenaries in the army of Cyrus the Younger wore bronze helmets, purple tunics and greaves for their parade at Tyriaeum (Xen. An. 1,2,16), but we do not know if these were their private property, or if Cyrus issued them.

During the Classical period, it remained the responsibility of the individual citizen-soldier to buy his own shield along with his other weapons and equipment. Meanwhile, this period also provides our first information about uniform shield devices. The earliest comes from a fragment by Bacchylides (b. c. 524–521), whose last poem dates from 452. It urges attention be paid to the Mantineans, and 'how they wear the trident of Poseidon on their beautifully worked bronze shields'. Poseidon was the patron god of Mantinea.

More prosaically, the Spartans used the letter lambda as their shield device. The first evidence for this comes from a fragment by the Attic comedian Eupolis contained in the lexicon of Photius (s.v. *lambda*): 'The Lacedaemonians painted a lambda on their shields, the Messenians a mu'. It has been suggested that this fragment was related to the first Battle of Mantinea (418 BC), but the Messenians did not fight in that battle. Painting the shield with the initial letter of the *polis* became the dominant custom, probably in imitation of the Spartans. The Sicyonians put the letter sigma on their shields (Xen. Hell. 4,4,10). This practice of painting the symbol or inital of the relevant city-state on shields seems to have become much more widespread by the time of the second Battle of Mantinea (362 BC). Xenophon reports that the Arcadian allies of the Thebans painted clubs on their shields 'as if they were Thebans' (Xen. Hell. 7,5,20). The club was the emblem of Hercules, the patron of Thebes. Archaeology yields evidence for shield devices of other *poleis*.

A.3. Tendency for uniformity in the Hellenistic period

With the rise of the Hellenistic monarchies, weapons, equipment and clothing began to be centrally manufactured and issued when war broke out. Alexander the Great distributed 25,000 sets of armour to his army in India (Diod. Sic. 17,95,4). This process had begun with the rise to power of the Sicilian tyrants. Diodorus Siculus (14,43,2f.) reports that Dionysius I of Syracuse had 140,000 shields, daggers and helmets and 14,000 breastplates made in 399 BC. In addition to production for their own use, the Hellenistic monarchies also held weapons in reserve in their arsenals to be issued to potential allies. Philetaerus of Pergamum gave 600 bronze round shields (*peltai*) to the city of Cyme as a gift – 50 for each of the 12 *phylai*. The city's inhabitants inscribed them with his name [2]. In 188 BC, Ptolemy V Epiphanes gifted 6,000 bronze *peltai* to the Achaean League (Pol. 22,9,3). After the sea battle of Salamis off Cyprus (306 BC), Demetrius Poliorketes (→ Generals of note, E.) presented the Athenians with a gift of 12,000 complete suits of armour from the booty (Plut. *Demetrius* 17,1) – more than enough for every citizen of Athens. Archaeological finds of lead stamps in the Athenian Agora from this period onwards prove that military equipment was being stored centrally and issued to soldiers, rather than being individually bought by them [1]. Even armies of citizen-soldiers were acquiring a uniform appearance.

Such weapons stores were sometimes enormous. In 172 BC, prior to the outbreak of the Third Macedonian War, the Macedonian King Perseus was accused of having accumulated a quantity of grain that would supply 30,000 infantry and 5,000 cavalry for ten years, and money to pay 10,000 mercenaries for the same length of time. His armouries were said to contain enough weapons for armies three times this size (Liv. 42,12,8–10). Five years later, the 'newly made purple clothing' of the soldiers of the Macedonian elite infantry regiment (the *agema*) on the eve of the Battle of Pydna in 168 BC was described – presumably as just issued (Plut. *Aemilius Paullus* 18,3). Purple seems to have remained in favour as the military colour, at least for footsoldiers.

The first indication of uniform clothing for cavalry is given by Diodorus Siculus (17,77,5). After the death of Darius in 330 BC, he reports, Alexander the Great distributed Persian cloaks with purple braids to his officers. The Alexander Sarcophagus shows horsemen identifiable as members of Alexander's elite cavalry, wearing saffron yellow Macedonian cloaks with purple braids. It then became standard in the Hellenistic period for elite cavalry regiments of all armies to wear capes in these colours [4]. Similar tendencies towards uniform apparel are observable in other institutions and regiments of the Hellenistic courts. The *philoi* or 'bodyguards' wore purple cloaks and tunics, the 'royal pages' white (or sometimes black) capes.

☞ **Armament, A. Greek; Military service**

BIBLIOGRAPHY
[1] J.H. KROLL, An Archive of the Athenian Cavalry, in: Hesperia 46, 1977, 83–140 [2] G. MANGANARO, Kyme e il dinasta Philetairos, in: Chiron 30, 2000, 403–414 [3] A. SCHWARTZ, Reinstating the Hoplite. Arms, Armour and Phalanx Fighting in Archaic and Classical Greece (Historia Einzelschriften 207), 2009 [4] N.V. SEKUNDA, The Ptolemaic Guard Cavalry Regiment, in: Anabasis, Studia Classica et Orientalia 3, 2012, 93–108

NICHOLAS SEKUNDA

B. ROMAN

B.1. Clothing/Uniform
B.2. Other equipment

Our knowledge of the equipment of Roman troops comes largely from three types of source. The first are written sources (literary or epigraphic), notably numerous papyri from Egypt and writing tablets from Vindolanda. Secondly, there are pictorial sources, classifiable in turn as public (e.g. Trajan Column) and private art (e.g. soldiers' tombstones). Finally, the third source type is material finds in archaeology.

B.1. CLOTHING/UNIFORM

B.1.1. Introduction
B.1.2. Underclothing
B.1.3. Tunic and trousers
B.1.4. Belts
B.1.5. Cloaks
B.1.6. Footwear and other accessories

B.1.1. INTRODUCTION
In general, the Roman army was not uniformed in the modern sense [5.97], but presumably the soldiers within the same unit had more or less the same clothing and equipment, for reasons of operational fitness alone. It is also likely that there were some identifying marks for particular units and ranks within the army [6.152f.]; [1.266f.]; [5.97f.].

The archaeological sources are limited in regard to clothing and uniform, because the organic materials from which these items were made (wool, linen, leather) have only rarely been preserved. There are only a few finds from Central Europe, preserved mostly immersed in damp strata (wells and bogs). A few remains of value for research have, however, been obtained from arid zones (e.g. Egypt) [8.241f.]. Items of clothing were mostly made of wool or linen. Silk was used only rarely, and only for the highest ranks. Leather seems to have been used for trousers and perhaps for some cloaks [2.204]; [8.249], but otherwise its main uses were in belts and shoes. Fur and felt were utilized for headgear, and felt may also have been added as padding under body protectors (→ Armament B.).

The Roman army was characteristically very colourful in appearance [8.254f.]. However, many items of clothing were not dyed, so the natural tones of the textiles used, ranging from beige to light brown, were dominant.

B.1.2. UNDERCLOTHING
The sources are almost entirely silent on the question of whether soldiers wore underwear under

their clothing, and if so, what it was like. Written sources mention a piece of clothing called a *subligaculum*, indicating some kind of undertrouser or apron. But there is no indication of how it was used, in the military or elsewhere [6.155]; [7.190f.].

B.1.3. TUNIC AND TROUSERS

The tunic was the quintessential basic Roman garment. Most tunics in the military were probably made of wool. The military tunic was always worn with a belt. Two basic forms are known: one sleeved and one sleeveless (see fig. 1). The sleeveless tunic was the earlier type, found in the Republican period. It comprised two panels of fabric sewn together, with cutouts for the head and arms. Short-sleeved tunics then began to appear early in the Imperial period. These were cut in a T shape and, like their sleeveless antecedents, they reached to just above the knee. The long-sleeved tunic, in combination with trousers (see fig. 2), became the standard type from the 3rd century onwards. Decorative elements and stripes can be

Fig. 1: Legionary of the 1st century AD (drawing by Graham Sumner). The illustration shows a legionary in work clothing, with a sleeveless tunic and a pickaxe (*dolabra*) in his right hand.

Fig. 2: Soldiers of Late Antiquity (drawings by Graham Sumner). The men here are shown in long garments with appliqué decorations, and in trousers. The soldier to the left is equipped with chain armour, helmet, shield and two javelins. The soldier to the right is in a woollen cape (*paludamentum*) fastened with a fibula, and wears a felt cap (*pilleus pannonicus*).

observed as applications to tunics from the earliest days of their use through to Late Antiquity, and these functioned not merely as adornments, but also as rank insignia [8.243–246]; [2.114]; [6.154–156]; [1.110f., 224f.].

Trousers were originally considered barbaric, and the Roman army did not wear them. The military began using a form of knee-length trouser (*feminalia*) in the Imperial period. Long trousers (*braccae*) became standard equipment by the 3rd century at the latest (cf. fig. 2). To date, only woollen trousers have been identified, but it is not impossible that leather was also used [2.115]; [8.248f.]; [5.100].

B.1.4. BELTS

A dagger was hung from a leather waist-belt. The belt also served as support for any armour (→ Armament B.). It could be used to fasten and puff up the tunic. Fabric padding was placed under the belt [2.115]; [5.100]. The military belt had enormous symbolic significance, becoming synonymous with the soldier class [5.102, 106]. Until the middle Imperial period, its name in Antiquity was *balteus*. Only in Late Antiquity did the now more familiar term *cingulum* come into use [2.115]; [1.106].

The military belt always had some kind of fastening (hook, buckle, button), and it was often decorated with metal plaques. Infantry belts of the early Imperial period began to be extended with aprons made of leather straps with metal fittings. Little is known of the appearance of belts in the Republican period. They probably had hook-and-eye fastenings and decorative plaques [1.67f.]. Thorn buckles, decorative plaques of various designs, and button fastenings became typical of the early and middle Imperial period [1.106–110]; [2.115–126]. Often two belts were worn crossed, or else one was worn in combination with a shoulder holster for the sword [5.100]. *Cingula* with ring and frame buckles began to appear in the 3rd century [1.182–184], but belts with thorn buckles and decorative plaques reasserted themselves in Late Antiquity [1.218–224]; [2.128–134].

B.1.5. CLOAKS

The Roman soldier used his cloak not just as protection against the weather, but also as a sleeping mat or blanket in the field [2.135]. Virtually nothing is known of the design of cloaks in the Republican period, although some variant of the classical toga is conceivable for the early and middle Republic [7.71f.]. Beginning in the late Republic and dominating the picture into Late Antiquity, we know of the *paludamentum*, *sagum* and *paenula*.

The *paludamentum* was the cape of high-ranking officers. This rectangular woollen cape was of good quality. It fastened with a fibula over the right shoulder (see fig. 2), or it could be slung over the arm as a hip cape [8.247]; [2.135f.]. The *sagum* was very similar, and much used by lower-ranking soldiers in particular. It was a rectangular (later also semicircular) woollen cloak of coarser design, also fastened at the right shoulder [6.157]; [8.247]; [2.135]. The main defining feature of the semicircular *paenula* (made of wool, perhaps also leather) was its hood. The *paenula* was sewn shut over the chest and could be fastened all the way up to the chin by means of hooks and eyelets. It was in use from the late Republican period until about AD 200 [7.73–80]; [6.157].

B.1.6. FOOTWEAR AND OTHER ACCESSORIES

Caligae were the main form of footwear. These were three-layered, nailed sandals (80–90 nails per sole) made of cow leather, with an upper cut into tongues and tied with laces [6.158f.]; [9]. The *caligae* were worn by the lower ranks and remained in use from the late Republic to the middle Imperial period [9]. During the Republican period and early to middle Imperial period, higher-ranking soldiers wore a closed-toed boot called the *calceus*. This type of footwear was adopted by all categories of troops by the 3rd century at the latest [7.191–193].

Personal equipment also included a woollen scarf (*focale*) that was generally worn in inclement weather, but that probably also protected the throat area against chafing from armour [8.250].

Although the sources are unclear, it seems likely that soldiers used other headgear apart from helmets. The *pilleus pannonicus*, a flat-topped felt cap, is known to have been used in Late Antiquity at least (see fig. 2) [2.137].

B.2. OTHER EQUIPMENT

Apart from weapons and clothing, the Roman military needed a great deal of other equipment for use in troop movements and ongoing operations at temporary bases and permanent camps and forts [2.238–243]; [4.517]. Much of this was indistinguishable from tools used in civilian life, but a few objects specific to the military are worthy of mention here.

The *dolabra* was the classic Roman pickaxe. This was an all-purpose entrenching tool with a blade running parallel to the handle on one side, and a pick or adze-shaped point at right angles to it on the other (see fig. 1). Non-ferrous blade guards were often made to protect axe blades [1.117f., 185–187]; [4.518].

Scholars use the word *tribuli* ('caltrops' = MLat *calcatrippa*, 'trip-traps') to denote the small, multi-pronged iron devices that were scattered in front of a fortification or buried in ditches to hamper advances [3.1023].

Pegs, usually made of iron, were used to anchor the leather tents (*papilio*) used by the army on campaign [6.207–209]. In the late Republic and early Imperial period, these pegs were sharpened iron rods with a ring in the thickened head. A design with unciform eyelets superseded these in the late 1st century [4.518f.].

☞ Military service

Bibliography

[1] M.C. Bishop / J.C.N. Coulston, Roman Military Equipment. From the Punic Wars to the Fall of Rome, ²2006 [2] T. Fischer, Die Armee der Caesaren. Archäologie und Geschichte, 2012 [3] C. Flügel, tribuli, in: Y. Le Bohec et al. (eds.), The Encyclopedia of the Roman Army, vol. 3, 2015, 1023–1024 [4] J. Harnecker, Implements, in: Y. Le Bohec et al. (eds.), The Encyclopedia of the Roman Army, vol. 2, 2015, 517–519 [5] S. Hoss, Der Gürtel als Standeszeichen der römischen Soldaten, in: Mannheimer Geschichtsblätter 19, 2010, 97–110 [6] M. Junkelmann, Die Legionen des Augustus. Der römische Soldat im archäologischen Experiment, 1986 [7] G. Sumner, Roman Military Dress, 2009 [8] G. Sumner, Clothes, in: Y. Le Bohec et al. (eds.), The Encyclopedia of The Roman Army, vol. 1, 2015, 241–257 [9] C. Van Driel-Murray, Military Footwear, in: Y. Le Bohec et al. (eds.), The Encyclopedia of the Roman Army, vol. 2, 2015, 653.

Eckhard Deschler-Erb

Esprit de corps

The emergence in the 7th century BC of the hoplites (*hoplitai*) [3.714f.], heavily armed soldiers, and their fighting formation, the → phalanx, dramatically altered the nature of warfare. These developments fuelled an esprit de corps in the common soldiery of the Archaic Greek world, as hoplite tactics spread throughout the Aegean by 600 BC. This fighting formation saw the right side of every soldier protected by the shield of his comrade. Surviving a battle depended on the joint efforts of all phalanx members. They knew each other, many being relatives or close friends, and they went on campaign together – just as they appeared in the agora together as citizens of their *polis*. No further measures to ensure esprit de corps were therefore required. It developed quite naturally from the structures of the *polis* and the specific battle formation [8]. Particularly during the Persian Wars, the phalanx and the heightened esprit de corps of the hoplites proved highly effective, with the Greeks winning crucial battles despite numerical inferiority – motivated by the need to defend their home *poleis* and the Grecian world [1.132–154]. This system was refined to its utmost in → Sparta. Spartan society being wholly militarized, esprit de corps was so much the stronger: soldiers had shared the same way of life together since childhood [1.89–94]. A similar esprit de corps must also have prevailed among marine soldiers, particularly when the Athenians faced the Persians in naval battles. They had to be able to rely on each other in the daily exercise of their duties aboard warships, for victories and fights for survival alike.

The sources do not permit examination of esprit de corps within the Theban army that won hegemony for its *polis* in the Grecian world before the Macedonian kingdom under Philip II (→ Generals of note, M.) entered the fray. As the importance of the Archaic and Classical phalanx on the battlefield gradually waned, Theban esprit de corps was heavily dependent on soldiers' common origins. This was presumably also true of the Macedonian army during Philip's campaigns in the Balkans and Greece, and on Alexander the Great's campaign in the east (→ Generals of note, B.).

Following the partitioning of Alexander's empire and the emergence of the Hellenistic monarchies, establishing the existence of an esprit de corps becomes ever more difficult, for the Hellenistic armies were chiefly made up of → mercenaries (*misthophoroi*), local contingents (*enchorioi*) and a nucleus of soldiers of Macedonian origin (*Makedones*). Esprit de corps presumably rested on soldiers' common origins, their loyalty to their immediate superiors (*xenologoi*) – who mostly came from the same country as their contingents – and the guarantee of payment as agreed with the king and the generals accompanying him (*hegemones*). Alongside this active army (*syntagma*), a non-active army (*epitagma*) of → veterans settled in military colonies (*klerouchoi, katoikoi, katoikountes*) helped the king with the defence of the frontiers. Their esprit de corps would depend on their shared interest in defending the property and land they had received from the king [7.3–75].

Initially, the Roman → legions exhibited the same esprit de corps as the Greek phalanx, since they drew their fighters from the same social strata of heavily armed Roman citizens. The rapid professionalization of the Republican army that was deployed in various regions of the Mediterranean reinforced this esprit de corps. As members of the same century or maniple (*commanipularis*), soldiers were very close. The Roman field camp system during military deployments encouraged interreliance among the soldiers, who called themselves *contubernales* ('tent comrades') or *fratres* ('brothers[-in-arms]') [5]. This became fully institutionalized with the establishment of a professional army by Augustus after 27 BC. Long years of service and the life spent together in legionary camps and auxiliary forts created what became the first explicitly military corps in an ancient society [6]. Imperial propaganda used every available means to emphasize that even the emperor was a 'comrade-in-arms' (*commilito*) [2.32–59]. Soldiers retained this esprit de corps even after being discharged, notably in the many Roman veteran colonies across the empire [9.129–135].

The same esprit de corps lived on in the Roman army of Late Antiquity, now heightened still further in imperial propaganda (Amm. Marc. 14,10,11–14: *commilitones mei fidissimi*, 'my most faithful comrades-in-arms') [4.61–66], but such expressions then disappeared almost entirely from epigraphic practice. There is, however, no reason to suppose that close relationships among comrades in the army diminished in Late Antiquity. On the contrary, the Christianization of the army will have intensified esprit de corps still further. Fellow soldiers identified themselves as 'soldiers of Christ' (*milites Christi*). This began under Theodosius I, and gained momentum particularly after AD 395, rooted in the military metaphors of the Epistles of Paul (Phil 2,25; 2 Tim 3–5). A reference to God and Christ had probably already become part of the military oath (*sacramentum*; cf. Veg. Mil. 2,5,3: *iurant autem per Deum et per Christum et per sanctum Spiritum*) in the reign of Theodosius. The Christian basilicas built in all fortifications in the early 5th century played their part in building the morale of frontier troops and heightening their esprit de corps [4.181–193].

BIBLIOGRAPHY

[1] H. BENGTSON, Griechische Geschichte. Von Anfängen bis in die Römische Kaiserzeit, ^{6}1982 [2] J.B. CAMPBELL, The Emperor and the Roman Army 31 BC–AD 235, 1984 [3] H.-J. GEHRKE, Hoplitai (Hoplites), in: BNP 6, 2005, 480–481 [4] A.D. LEE, War in Late Antiquity. A Social History, 2007 [5] J.E. LENDON, Contubernalis, commanipularis, and commilito in Roman Soldiers' Epigraphy. Drawing the Distinction, in: ZPE 157, 2006, 270–276 [6] R. MACMULLEN, The Legion as a Society, in: Historia 33, 1984, 440–456 [7] P.M. MEYER, Das Heerwesen der Ptolemäer und Römer in Ägypten, 1900 [8] M. RAUSCH, Das Zeitalter der Hopliten. Bauern, Bürger und Soldaten im archaischen und klassischen Griechenland, in: G. MANDL / I. STEFFELBAUER (eds.), Krieg in der antiken Welt, 2007, 32–56 [9] O. STOLL, 'De honore certabant et dignitate'. Truppe und Selbstidentifikation in der Armee in der Römischen Kaiserzeit, in: O. STOLL, Römisches Heer und Gesellschaft. Gesammelte Beiträge 1991–1999, 2001

FLORIAN MATEI-POPESCU

Eve-of-battle speech

The practice of giving an exhortation before battle, which was a commonplace in Antiquity (Thuc. 5,69; Caes. B Gall. 2,20,1; 2,21,1; Caes. B Civ. 3,90,1; Cic. Orat. 66), made it essential that a general have good rhetorical abilities (Pl. Ion 540d–e; Xen. Mem. 3,3,10–15; Onas. Strat. 1,13; 1,16) [2]; [14]. The basic arguments, most of which are already found in Homer [6]; [11], remained the same, and were adapted to the circumstances. Frequent themes included the enemy's failings (breach of an agreement, treaty or customary law; refusal to negotiate); the favour of the gods (Onas. Strat. 4,1–4); defending the homeland (or wives, children, property); the enemy's inferiority or superiority in numbers, weapons and strategic position (Veg. Mil. 3,9,13; 3,12,3f.); warning against complacency; future rewards and punishments; and the general's skill in warfare and his 'kinship' with the soldiers (general as comrade and father figure).

Speeches on the eve of battle fall into categories of occasion that are not mutually exclusive: addresses at the start of a campaign (e.g. Archidamus: Thuc. 2,10,3–11; Cleomenes III: Pol. 2,64,1; Hannibal: Liv. 21,21,3–6); general assessments of a situation one or more days before the battle; speeches on the day of battle as the troops formed up (Liv. 30,32,4f.); and exhortation of the army after it had formed up. Speeches after battle fell into two types depending on the occasion: the gathering of troops after a defeat (Thuc. 7,5,3f.; Onas. Strat. 36,3; Veg. Mil. 3,25,10; cf. App. Civ. 4,119f.), or the ceremony after a victory at which honours were bestowed for valour (Pol. 6,39,1f.), which in the Imperial period became an occasion for an *adlocutio* (an address by the emperor to the troops) if the emperor was present.

Audiences for generals' speeches varied in size. Opinions differ as to whether it was possible for a general to address an entire army formed up for battle [3]; [4]; [5]; [6]; [7]; [14]. Quite apart from the size and composition of the audience, much depended on the strength of the speaker's voice and the weather conditions. Modern estimates of the number of people who could have heard a speech clearly range from 1,200 (after forming up) to 30,000 (gathering not formed up). Audibility (*akoe*) and timing (*kairos*) were recognized as limiting factors for a passionate speech before a formed-up force (*De scientia politica dialogus* 4,1f. Mazzucchi).

In the most prevalent type of inspirational speech to an army in formation, a general would walk along the first rank of troops, giving brief encouragement to the individual units, essentially corresponding to a Homeric *epipolesis* ('marshalling'). Otherwise, some generals gave their eve-of-battle address to the officers, who were then responsible for encouraging their own units. They sometimes received instructions for where to lay particular emphasis in their arguments (Hdt. 9,42,1; 9,44,1; Thuc. 2,10,3; Xen. An. 1,7,2).

Despite the practical importance of the eve-of-battle speech, its place in the ancient rhetorical and historiographic tradition is unclear. Besides the aforementioned marshalling inspection (*epipolesis*), Homer offers the earliest examples of general topics for increasing battle motivation. Herodotus has generals, as one would expect, making encouraging speeches, but Thucydides established the model for later historians (Pol. 12,25b; Lucian. Hist. conscr. 42; 47; [12]; [13]) by claiming to reproduce actual speeches – or at least what 'must have been' said on a particular occasion (Thuc. 1,22) – and using them as instruments of interpretation and analysis [5]; [10].

Parakletikos logos ('hortatory speech') and *epipolesis* became established as technical terms in the 2nd century AD. The surviving *protreptikoi* ('exhortations') of Lesbonax of Mytilene are essentially eve-of-battle exhortations. It may be that eve-of-battle speeches had by this date become exercises at the schools of rhetoric, as part of the archaizing tendency of the Second Sophistic. Roman commanders must surely have been giving encouraging speeches, but as the composition of the Roman officer corps evolved away from the learned senatorial elite towards men of equestrian and non-equestrian rank, formal eve-of-battle speeches rooted in the rhetoric and values of the Classical Greek *polis* and the Roman Republic became less attractive [8]; [9]. Anyone capable of addressing an entire army would furthermore have been subject to close scrutiny. Syrianus Magister (if he was active in the 6th century and not in the 9th or 10th) wrote the lone ancient manual on the eve-of-battle speech, the *Demegoriai protreptikai* (Latin *Rhetorica militaris*). This work brings together topics for speeches under various categories, but offers few contemporary references and shows only slight interest in the practical purposes of the motivational address [1].

☞ Military literature; Motivation; Transmission of orders

BIBLIOGRAPHY

SOURCES
[1] SIRIANO, Discorsi di Guerra, edited by I. Eramo, 2010.

SECONDARY LITERATURE
[2] J. ALBERTUS, Die ΠΑΡΑΚΛΗΤΙΚΟΙ in der griechischen und römischen Literatur, 1908   [3] E. ANSON, The General's Pre-Battle Exhortation, in: Greece & Rome 57, 2010, 304–318   [4] J. CAMPBELL, The Emperor and the Roman Army 31 BC–AD 235, 1984   [5] M. CLARK, Did Thucydides Invent the Battle Exhortation?, in: Historia 44, 1995, 375–376   [6] C. EHRHARDT, Speeches before Battle, in: Historia 44, 1995, 120–121   [7] M.H. HANSEN, The Battle Exhortation in Ancient Historiography. Fact or Fiction?, in: Historia 42, 1993, 161–180   [8] J. HARMAND, L'Armée et le soldat à Rome, 1967   [9] M. HARTO TRUJILLO, Las arengas militares en la historiografía latina, 2008   [10] J. IGLESIAS ZOIDO (ed.), Retórica e historiografía. El discurso militar en la historiografía desde la Antigüedad hasta el Renascimiento, 2010   [11] E. KEITEL, Homeric Antecedents to the 'Cohortatio' in the Ancient Historians, in: Classical World 80.3, 1987, 153–172   [12] R. LEIMBACH, Militärische Musterrhetorik. Eine Untersuchung zu den Feldherrnreden des Thukydides, 1985   [13] O. LUSCHNAT, Die Feldherrenreden im Geschichtswerk des Thukydides (Philologus Suppl. 34.2), 1942   [14] W.K. PRITCHETT, The General's Exhortations in Greek Warfare, in: Essays in Greek History, 1994, 97–109

EVERETT L. WHEELER

Family

☞ Marriage

Fleet

A. Concept and historical dimension
B. History and deployment

A. Concept and historical dimension

The construction and deployment of large numbers of specialized warships under a unified command was a formative development of the ancient Mediterranean that over time spread to neighbouring seas (Black Sea, Red Sea, North Atlantic and West African waters), but which otherwise originated in no other region of the ancient world. Naval deployments took place in military and political contexts, and for colonial and exploratory purposes [10.61–81]. Publicly owned commercial or fishing fleets, on the other hand, were largely unknown in Antiquity (probably existing only under the Ptolemies and on Rhodes; [1.170]). The transition from privately owned vessels to a state navy was fluid, and the process was not irreversible [21.273]. It went hand in hand with long-term political changes, and took place only under certain conditions: a favourable geographical setting with access or proximity to harbours, sea routes, bases and resources, which made the use of warships politically necessary, economically viable and ecologically possible; a level of organization that was capable of financing and providing technical and logistical support over a long period of time for the costliest instrument of war; and finally, a society with the maritime disposition to focus all its efforts on the building, manning and deploying of military fleets. Also essential was the catalyst of internal and external political exigencies, usually a rivalry with a potential or actual opponent, often not limited to maritime spheres of influence. The construction and deployment of military fleets (usually near the coast) were almost always closely interrelated with developments on land. An independent naval command would have been seen as too costly and politically risky. Accordingly, no admiralty with a high-seas fleet acting independently ever came into being. Instead, command of naval and land army forces remained connected under common leadership [18.100]; [10.103]. The construction and deployment of war fleets usually extended deeply into the political and societal structure of the state. The history of ancient fleets is thus always an important aspect of general political and economic history, and can only be analysed in this context.

B. History and deployment

B.1. Origins in the Bronze Age to c. 1000 BC
B.2. Mediterranean fleets of the Archaic period
B.3. The transition to state fleets during the Persian Wars
B.4. The Athenian navy and democracy
B.5. The Peloponnesian War and its consequences
B.6. Eastern Mediterranean fleets in the Hellenistic period
B.7. Roman and Carthaginian fleets in the Punic Wars (284–201 BC)
B.8. Roman naval policy in the east, and the rise of piracy
B.9. Fleets of the late Republic in the Civil Wars
B.10. Fleets under the Principate
B.11. 3rd century AD to Late Antiquity

B.1. Origins in the Bronze Age to c. 1000 BC

Written and archaeological sources already attest to the use by the Middle Bronze Age of specialized ships [18.82] that were sent on major expeditions, to guard coasts and merchant vessels, to transport soldiers, and as part of amphibious operations. Egyptian ships (*kbnyt*, *kbn*) were sent into action in the Red Sea (Punt expeditions), the Nile Delta and off the coast of the Levant as far afield as Cyprus [1.92–94]. Units from Levantine city-states visited Crete, southern Anatolia and the Aegean, which was crossed by flotillas belonging to the Minoan and Mycenaean palace cultures. Although the structures necessary for controlling large areas of sea were lacking, overseas settlements and harbour installations (Kommos in southern Crete) point to authorities' efforts to provide stops for their own ships within a network of regularly frequented sea routes. The 'Sea Peoples' who pushed out of the Aegean and farther west in the Mediterranean (Sardinia) as far as the Nile Delta had specialized vessels that destabilized the coasts of Egypt and Asia Minor [9.47, 125]. Their experience in military technology and their nautical traditions were an important factor behind the rise of the Phoenician ports that shaped naval history from the 10th century BC onwards [28.36f.]. While conditions for naval construction developed only slowly at first in the context of the small *polis* societies in Greece after the collapse of the Mycenaean palace polities, the regents of Tyre and Sidon exploited maritime experience in the Levant to launch expeditions as far as Spain, and from the Red Sea to Somalia and Arabia (Ophir?), with ships capable of deep-sea nagivation ('Tarsis ships'). It seems likely that, besides their round-bellied *gayloi* [10.86f.], the Phoenicians also had double-banked pentoconters, which they used as all-purpose vessels for voyages of discovery and colonization [10.66f., 124–126]; [8.83].

B.2. Mediterranean fleets of the Archaic period

The founding of Carthage created a second centre of Phoenician seafaring in the west, which used its navy to expand its political influence. In the Levant, by contrast, the Phoenician city-states were compelled to put their warships at the disposal of dominant land powers after the king of Tyre fled the Assyrians in 701 BC. In 525, the Phoenicians offered much of their attacking fleet in support of the Persian King Cambyses in his conquest of Egypt (Hdt. 3,19; [8.89]). Along with units from Cyprus and southern and western Anatolia, it formed the nucleus of a permanent navy under supreme Persian command – an unprecedented and innovative turning-point in the history of the Near Eastern kingdoms (cf. [28.44], according to which the Persians henceforth provided the ships and the dependent coastal communities provided the oarsmen and captains). Earlier, a pharaoh, probably Necho (or his predecessors) added a triple-banked type of vessel to his fleet (trireme; cf. fig. 1) (Hdt. 2,159,1; [21.276]) that had probably been developed in Phoenicia [8.85]; [11.35]. The trireme made the ship and its ram bow a decisive weapon. Although it did not supplant the old technique of boarding, it made well-practised manoeuvres a recipe for success in tactical naval warfare. The deployment of the naval ram demanded a larger company of oarsmen and longer training. It was more expensive to build and suffered more wear and tear [27.153f.]; [20.109]. Accordingly, only powers with sufficient financial muscle, material resources, docks and harbours – as well as plenty of willing oarsmen – were able to afford many such warships. In Greece, these conditions were met only where a tyrant was able to concentrate the resources of a maritime *polis*, such as Samos under Polycrates, who provided the Persians with 100 pentaconters and 40 triremes, and Corinth under the Bacchiads, whose engineer Ameinocles was said to have built triremes for the Samians [11.34f.]. These *poleis* have yielded evidence of harbour installations with artificial piers ([21.274f., 283];

Fig. 1: Lenormant Relief (marble, 4th century BC; excavated on the Athenian Acropolis by the archaeologist François Lenormant in 1852). This relief fragment, now in the Acropolis Museum in Athens, shows the longitudinal section of an Athenian trireme of the 4th century BC. Only the uppermost bank of oarsmen is visible, but the two rows of oars visible below them running parallel to the rowers of the first bank indicate that the warship was also powered by two more banks of oarsmen lower in the body of the ship. The exact arrangement and coordination of the oarsmen continues to be a subject of debate, but the illustration on this relief was nonetheless used for the successful reconstruction of a usable trireme in the 1990s. With the depiction of the fully committed oarsmen arranged in parallel ranks from top to bottom, the artist evidently hoped to show not only the perfection of the ship's construction as a whole, but also the professional skills of the rowers, whose extensive training enabled them to synchronize their strokes precisely. This contributed greatly to the swiftness of the Athenian triremes, and constituted their tactical superiority in battle.

Hdt. 3,45). While the construction of small trireme fleets was driven by the need to protect commercial shipping (Thuc. 1,13,5; [20.106]) and by clashes with colonies (Corcyra) or with the Phoenicians in the Aegean and the Gulf of Corinth, it was conflicts with Carthage that forced the tyrants of Syracuse to launch similar programmes in the west from the mid-5th century onwards. Other *poleis*, such as Miletus, Phocaea, Aegina, Carthage and Massilia continued for the most part to rely on pentoconters, because they were deemed more suitable for use in long-distance trade, colonization and the fight against competitors in distant waters (naval battle at Alalia) [10.124f.]. It is possible that in such contexts the concept first developed of maritime supremacy (thalassocracy), in the sense of control over maritime spaces, their coasts and sea routes, as enforced by warships ('long ships') (Hdt. 3,122,3; Thuc. 1,13,6; [12]; [21.282]; [20.105, 108]).

B.3. THE TRANSITION TO STATE FLEETS DURING THE PERSIAN WARS

Ships were generally owned by noble elites or tyrants [20], but when larger fleets were deployed (the threshold appears to have been about 60), the institutions of the *polis* may have become involved, especially for tasks such as building new vessels, technical improvements, work on harbour installations and paying oarsmen [28.41]. In terms of organization, experiments were tried with various models and assignments of responsibilities (the naucrary (*naukraria*) in Athens and *aeinautai* ('perpetual sailors') in Eretria; [20.106f.]). In Asia Minor, city rulers provided ships and/or oarsmen to the Persians [28.44], but also undertook private expeditions [20.108]. The decisive breakthrough in the development of 'state fleets' probably came only during the Persian Wars, at which time the terms *nautikos stratos* and *nautikon* for 'naval force' gained currency [20.109]. The expeditionary fleets of the Athenians (20 pentoconters) and Eretrians that were sent out in the course of the Ionian Revolt may have gone with the assent of the popular assembly, as may the rebel fleets at the Battle of Lade. The first clear evidence comes from Herodotus, who reports that the Thasians had used their mining revenues to build 'long ships' [20.103]; [23.286], which were then transferred to the Persian naval base at Abdera (Hdt. 6,46). In 483 BC, Themistocles arranged the construction of 100 or 200 triremes (to join the existing pentoconters) at Athens, and completed the expansion (begun in 494) of harbour and armament installations at Piraeus (Thuc. 1,90–93; Plut. *Themistocles* 19; [5]; [3.256f.]). Financing for this was secured by leasing the silver mines of the Laurium and receiving donations from wealthy citizens, but the ships belonged to the *polis*. This meant that Athens now had the strongest navy (alongside Syracuse with 200 triremes; Hdt. 7,158; [14.139f.]) in the Greek world. In 481, when Xerxes advanced on central Greece with about 100,000 men and 600 ships, a coalition of *poleis* intent on resistance formed at Corinth (Hellenic League). It handed command to Sparta, including command over the naval forces, even though Athens was providing at least half of the triremes. After indecisive engagements north of Euboea, the Greek ships struck back at the Persian fleet in the Bay of Salamis (→ Battles of note I.) in 480. Given the lateness of the season, Xerxes withdrew his vessels to the Anatolian coast, where a year later (almost simultaneously with the Greek land forces' victory at Plataeae), they were almost completely destroyed by the Greeks at the Battle of Mycale.

B.4. THE ATHENIAN NAVY AND DEMOCRACY

The outcome of the Persian Wars was fundamental for the development of the fleet, especially since in the west the tyrants of Syracuse were able not only to repel a Carthaginian expeditionary force, but also (at Cumae in 474 BC) to break Etruscan naval dominance of the Tyrrhenian Sea (Diod. Sic. 11,51; Pind. Pyth. 1,70f.; [19.132f.]). In the medium term, many coastal *poleis* now sought to transfer their warships into public ownership following the example of Athens and Thasos. The Ionian ports won new freedom of action after the Persian withdrawal, but stayed on the lookout for allies in fear of Persian retaliation. In 478/77, the Athenian Aristides took over supreme command of the Hellenic League fleet, and began to sign new treaties with the Greeks of Asia Minor and the island and coastal *poleis* of the Aegean. Rhodes followed, along with a number of cities on Cyprus. The members of the maritime league agreed to supply ships and crews, or else make financial contributions (*phoroi*) for the construction and maintenance of the fleet. The money went into a joint treasury on Delos, also the venue for meetings of the (hence now 'Delian') league's assembly (*synhedrion*), and the ships gathered at Piraeus. Because the navy was commanded exclusively by Athenian *strategoi* ('commanders'), while the *synhedrion* met rarely and the aims of the league (revenge against Persia) were formulated rather vaguely, Athens was quickly able to make use of the league's fleet in pursuit of its own interests. The naval operations of Cimon (→ Generals of note, I.) combined the expansion of the Athenian sphere of influence with attacks on Persian bastions outside the Aegean. The destruction of the Persian naval base with 200 warships at the mouth of the River Eurymedon (in Pamphylia) in 465 BC finally elevated Athens to the status of prime maritime power of the eastern Mediterranean.

Athenian naval policy was possible only because of the city's unusual material resources (silver mines) and its extraordinary abundance of citizens. By the same token, it had a profound effect on the internal situation of the *polis*, especially on the relationship between the noble elites and the remainder of the citizenry. While the wealthy faced an obligation of one year to cover the equipping of the body of the ships and the payment of wages [18.91], the fleet had to be manned with a colossal number of oarsmen, mostly from the class of (propertyless) *thetes* (paid laborers). It seems that slaves and, in emergencies, foreigners were also used from the outset (200 triremes required about 40,000 men) [3.257]. Constant naval war and leadership of the far-flung league system created a dynamic that further catalyzed the development of democracy. While the *thetes* were making indispensable contributions to successes in foreign policy by rowing the warships, the *boule* (council) was having to develop a budget mentality to finance the fleet, and the popular assembly was dealing with far more complex topics of naval league policy than in other *poleis*. Meanwhile, the profits that were flowing into Athens facilitated not only the maintenance of a standing fleet, but also the financing of the cost-intensive institutions of democracy (courts, council). The expansion of the fleet thus went hand in hand with the development of the democratic constitution. The fleet was regarded as a military instrument of democracy and guarantor of freedom in the face of the Persian 'barbarians'. The success of the fleet was also able to reconcile the aristocracy with the 'perfected' democracy, as long as Aristocrats were able to satisfy their urge for renown and recognition as *strategoi*.

Another cornerstone of internal peace was the economic growth that the naval policy brought. The city and Piraeus now became the leading commercial centre of the eastern Mediterranean, putting old port cities like Corinth and Aegina in the shade. For this reason, even after the further transfer of control of powers to the popular assembly by Ephialtes and Pericles, Athens continued to pursue its aggressive foreign policy, with naval expeditions into eastern Mediterranean waters, to Egypt (with 200 triremes) and against the Phoenician cities on Cyprus. The structures were able to absorb catastrophic defeats (like the loss of the fleet in the Nile Delta), and even the enormous costs involved did nothing to change the basic imperialist direction, which was only curtailed eastwards by the (informal) accord with Persia (Peace of Callias) regarding respective spheres of interest. Meanwhile, the Athenians were further consolidating their influence in the Delian League, dissolving the league constitution and moving its treasury to Athens in 454. From then on, the city staged the league members' annual delivery of *phoroi* (financial contributions) as a demonstration of power, and it documented the income on public lists. The process of turning the league's territories into a single Athenian territory was also advanced by the introduction of a common currency, an increase in the number of officials working in league territories, the establishment of citizen colonies and the issuance of decrees against rebel members. Confiscations and the incorporation of ships from dissident members at times increased the fleet's strength to 300 triremes, at least 60 of which were always operational [3.261–263]. It may have been during this period that the concept of thalassocracy developed and was refined to describe Athenian hegemony. The Athenian Thucydides (along with other writers) was so impressed by this development that he described early Greek history according to the criteria of naval power and fleet organization.

B.5. The Peloponnesian War and its consequences

B.5.1. Success and failure of the Athenian naval policy
B.5.2. New developments of the 4th century BC

B.5.1. Success and failure of the Athenian naval policy

During the 440s BC, some coastal *poleis* began deliberate expansions of their naval forces in imitation of, or in competition with, the Athenians. Corinth catapulted itself to the status of second-strongest Greek maritime power, with a fleet of 150 triremes as against the 100 triremes of Corcyra. For the building and manning of their ships, the Corinthians encroached on the sphere of the Delian League. When Athens retaliated (alliance with Corcyra, 'Megarian Psephism' and attack on the Corinthian colony of Potidaea), Corinth together with Megara and Aegina succeeded in persuading the Peloponnesian League to declare war, leading to a prolonged period of open hostilities ('Peloponnesian War'; → Wars of note, H.). During the first phase, the fleet of the Delian League enjoyed successes against the tactically inferior forces of their opponents (naval battles of the *strategos* Phormio, Sphacteria) and kept supplies flowing into their city from overseas. Fortunes turned as a result of Brasidas' extensive campaign breaking into the northern Aegean, where, with the help of King Perdiccas II of Macedonia and the gold mines in the Pangaeum mountain range, he began to build his own fleet. Although the Spartan authorities were not yet prepared to follow through on these naval ambitions, the threat to the Delian League's unprotected flank, along with a failed diversionary attack, sufficed to induce the

Athenians to sue for peace (Peace of Nicias) in 421. However, in 415, a naval expedition comprising around 300 units (135 of them triremes) set off to curb the influence of Syracuse on Sicily and curtail the flow of grain to the Peloponnese. When the Spartan Gylippus brought reinforcements to the Syracusans and increased the striking power of the Syracusan ships' prows, the latter destroyed almost all the Athenian triremes in the narrow entrance to the Great Harbour. The Sicilian expedition ended just as calamitously as did the expedition to Egypt. Even so, the Athenians quickly (412) replaced their annihilated fleet by building new ships. With Persian subsidies enabling Sparta to construct a trireme fleet of comparable size, hostilities now, with the exception of Spartan forays into Attica, shifted into Ionian waters, where the war was ultimately decided in Sparta's favour by the destruction of the last Athenian fleet at Aigos Potamos in 405.

B.5.2. NEW DEVELOPMENTS OF THE 4TH CENTURY BC

Within a few years, following the dissolution of the Delian League and the reduction of the Athenian fleet to twelve units, → Sparta took control of the league's former territory. That control, however, collapsed in 394 BC in the naval battle with the new Persian fleet (commanded by the Athenians Conon and Pharnabazus) off Cnidus. Persia, with fleets numbering up to 300 units, now established hegemony in the eastern Mediterranean, and allowed Athens to establish a new fleet, as a counterweight to reviving Spartan ambitions. Their defeat at the hands of Sparta had not undermined the Athenians' concept of sea power as a key component of their identity and guarantee of their security, but rather strengthened it. In 379 BC, the Athenians succeeded in combining a number of alliances into a Second Athenian (maritime) League opposed to Sparta. Although its organization was designed to safeguard the alliance against a one-sided dependence (they paid fixed matricular contributions called *syntaxeis*), the Athenians were still able within a few years to recapture the position of leading maritime power in Greece. However, the rising costs of war in other spheres (siegecraft, mercenaries, cavalry) placed limits on the size of the navy. Although nominally Athens was able to raise its tally of warships to 349 following the reorganization of state finances under Eubulus, they were operating exclusively in the Aegean in smaller flotillas that never comprised more than 30 units. Naval forces operated by powers with limited experience of warfare at sea (Thebes, Thessaly) remained a rarity.

As in the early Archaic period, new approaches to fleet construction now emerged wherever political structures enabled the concentration of resources and fundamental military exigencies demanded investments in naval power. For example, Dionysius I (who was named supreme commander of the Syracusan forces in 406) and his successor, because of conflict with Carthage and perhaps also in reaction to new Phoenician-Carthaginian constructions (Plin. HN 7,207f.; Diod. Sic. 16,44,6; [22.358]), ordered larger ships to be built. These ships were given between one and three additional ranks of oarsmen ('polyremes') and a reinforced prow that was designed in imitation of the frontal ram that had proved itself in battle against the Athenian triremes (see above; Diod. Sic. 14,41,3; 14,42,2; 14,44,7; Ael. VH 6,12; [13.78–85]). More naval soldiers (especially archers) could be stationed on these vessels' wider decks, and it was also possible to install on these ships a catapult (*gastraphetes*) that had been invented at Syracuse. These new technologies made it possible to sweep over the triremes, lying lower in the water, from above, and to attack fortified harbour installations in combination with land troops. Dionysius hereby ushered in a new form of naval deployment that would shape maritime warfare during the Hellenistic period. However, it spread slowly across the Grecian world, once again because of the greater costs in terms of men and materials. Of the old *poleis*, only Athens (330 onwards) could afford a slow conversion of its fleet to the new vessels [13.142]. Alexander the Great only resorted to these new technologies when the military situation required the use of naval-based catapults (at the Siege of Tyre in 332). The ships built in the course of his Indian campaign were used to transport troops and explore the waters leading to the Persian Gulf. The new vessels built for the conquest of Arabia were the first to take up the trend towards polyremes (Diod. Sic. 18,4,4; [13.144]), but they were not involved in any direct engagements at sea.

B.6. EASTERN MEDITERRANEAN FLEETS IN THE HELLENISTIC PERIOD

These new developments only came to full fruition in the eastern Mediterranean under the Diadochi. Resourced with the riches of the Persian war chest, driven by a competitive martial ethos and in possession of the most populous and resource-rich territories in the east, the Ptolemies and Antigonids introduced an unprecedented gigantism to their military shipbuilding that reflected their authoritarian ideal and a changed overall strategic situation. Whereas the *poleis* of the Classical period had established themselves as maritime powers through the hegemonic evolution of alliance systems, the control of trade routes and the absorption of rival navies, the Hellenistic kings now sought to combine their extensive territories with the control of maritime domains in the eastern Mediterranean, just as the Persians had done and Alexander had briefly tried to do. Crucial to this ambition was the conquest of fortified coastal *poleis* and harbours, and the polyremes – designed to take naval soldiers and catapults – were ideally suited for this, even if they were not always successful (failed attack on Rhodes by Demetrius I Poliorketes (→ Generals of note, E.) in 305/04 BC, Diod. Sic. 20,85–88). Invariably, too, fleets of polyremes [13.205] were a means of showing off monarchical power. Naval battles could end old hegemonic ambitions and traditions of maritime power (victory of Cleitus over the Athenians at Amorgos in 322; [22.362]) and found new ones (Antigonid victory over the Ptolemies off Cos in 255, Ephesus and Andros circa 245 BC). At first, the permanent war fleet of the Ptolemies dominated the waters of the eastern Mediterranean as far as the northern Aegean, but their victory off the coast of Andros in 245 enabled the Antigonids to establish naval supremacy in the Aegean, which was only challenged by medium-sized powers (Pergamum, Rhodes), pirates and Ptolemaic allies. Meanwhile, the Ptolemies concentrated their efforts in Syrian waters and the Red Sea (Plut. *Aratus* 24,4; [13.197–200]; [24.53]; [4.114f., 186]). Overshadowed by Hellenistic struggles for hegemony, *poleis* with maritime experience were able to preserve their independence if they performed functions that the great battle fleets could not. Rhodes, for instance, established itself as a protector (*phylake*) of commercial traffic, with a specialist fleet, owned partly by the state and partly by the nobility, of 40 triremes and biremes (*triemiolia* [*naus*], *hemiolia* [*naus*] and a few polyremes). As the hegemon of an alliance system (Nesiotic League 188–167), Rhodes was able to exercise limited maritime power in the Aegean [2.56–111]; [14.133f.].

B.7. ROMAN AND CARTHAGINIAN FLEETS IN THE PUNIC WARS (284–201 BC)
In the west, Carthage and the Roman Republic followed the trend towards polyremes, but avoided the Hellenistic monarchies' gigantism in regard to hulls and ranks of oarsmen. As a result of its gruelling wars with Syracuse, Carthage had developed a modular construction method involving prefabricated components [16.267], which made it possible to build warships of a standard design relatively economically, and to assign crews flexibly to different parts of the fleet. Because the main threats to its existence in the 5th and 4th centuries were on land, the Roman Republic at first confined itself to establishing citizen colonies (*coloniae maritimae*) and deploying a flotilla of 20 units organized by two officials (*duoviri*) (Liv. 9,30,3f.; 38,2–4; [23.382f.]; [14.2f.]). Only gradually did it integrate the maritime forces of the colonies of Magna Graecia into its system of Italic confederates. The first Roman battle fleet was not built until the war over Sicily (supposedly in 60 days (Pol. 1,20f.; [14])) of the year 260 BC). It comprised 20 triremes and 100 quinqueremes. In battle, they sought to capitalize on their advantages in frontal ramming and boarding in opposition to the lighter, tactically skilful Carthaginian vessels (cf. fig. 2). The later tradition construed much as invention born of necessity, which in reality was the pragmatic adoption of existing technologies (the wondrous 'boarding gangways' (Pol. 1,22) were probably boarding hooks fired by catapults). In the wider context, the war was not decided by these technologies, but by Rome's greater resources and integrative Italic alliance system, which made it possible to absorb the losses of larger fleets and always keep a quantitative advantage over the opposing naval forces.

Unlike the navies of the *poleis*, the Roman fleet was not sponsored by contributions from wealthy citizens except in emergencies; nor was it financed from taxes or (monarchical) state treasuries. Its usual sources of funding were confederations and war booty. Using oarsmen from the *socii* ('allies'), the *coloniae maritimae* (Roman colonies near the sea), the lowest property class of the citizenry (*proletarii*), the ranks of freedmen and (in emergencies) slaves and prisoners of war [22.364f.] enabled the Republic to establish (alongside the fleet) large militia armies on land. Unlike the mercenary armies maintained by Carthage, these militia armies did not constitute any additional financial burden [22.366f.]; [16.268f.], and they prevented the mentality and constraints of naval policy from interfering with internal affairs and influencing them too strongly. Unlike at Athens, then, consolidating and expanding territorial power was always the prime strategic objective, and naval policy had to adapt accordingly. After the First Punic War (→ Wars of note, K.), turning the islands of the Tyrrhenian Sea into provinces, forging alliances with Massilia and Saguntum, and establishing land bases in Illyria enabled Rome to create a strategic headwind with the aim of choking off any Carthaginian ambition for revenge and securing control of maritime routes. During the Second Punic War, Roman fleets of up to 100 units were able to prevent Carthaginian and Macedonian forces from joining up, and to block support for Hannibal from overseas, while also exporting the war to Hispania and North Africa – thereby ultimately winning it for Rome.

B.8. ROMAN NAVAL POLICY IN THE EAST, AND THE RISE OF PIRACY
The Roman advance into the Greek east that began around 200 BC was shaped by an understanding of the importance of maritime spaces. It was only

Fig. 2: Part of a ram bow (bronze, 3rd century BC). This end piece of the ram bow, terminating towards the right, was found at a depth of 80m near the Aegadian Islands off the western tip of Sicily in 2020. It carries an inscription dedicated to the god Baal, and therefore belonged to a Carthaginian warship that probably encountered Roman units during a naval battle (241 BC) of the First Punic War. Scrape marks indicate that it came into direct contact with the ram bow of a hostile ship, and that it was torn off its wooden support during the battle. The reason for the peculiar design of the ram bow (as distinct from a harpoon-shaped tip) was the desire for a successful impact on the hull of the enemy ship to do as much damage as possible and cause the vessel to sink rapidly.

when Philip V of Macedon threatened to take control of the grain supply from the north shore of the Black Sea that Rome intervened on behalf of the Athenians, Rhodians and Pergamenes, all of whom were concerned about the freedom of maritime trading routes. However, Rome sent only small fleets, which were designated to the transportation and supply of land forces. Working in conjunction with the Pergamene and Rhodian fleets, both of which comprised up to 40 vessels, they were able to defeat the heavy polyremes of the Macedonian navies [13.222–224]; [14.138]. Pergamene and Rhodian ships also paved the way for victory on land in the war against Antiochus III (192–188). Against Perseus, there was only a brief deployment of a fleet of 38 ships [14.139]. After this, the Romans began to curtail the sea power of their allies by banning timber exports from Macedonia and opening up the free port of Delos. Yet, they did not establish a sea presence of their own in the form of a permanent war fleet. This maritime power vacuum was gradually filled by the rise of the pirates of the eastern Mediterranean. By the late 2nd century, they were already beginning to establish a quasi-state organization along the metal- and timber-rich coasts of Cilicia Trachea, complete with armament factories, wharves and arsenals, and to build fleets of over 100 triremes and biremes that were able to operate over great distances all year round (App. Mith. 12; [18.110]; [14.147]). The pirates limited the influence of the Hellenistic monarchies, while also satisfying the demands of large Roman landowners for slaves. Consequently, Roman countermeasures like the naval expedition of Marcus Antonius Orator in 102 BC only received hesitant support or were thwarted by domestic political objections (*lex de Cilicia Macedoniaque provinciis*, 100 v.Chr.). It was only when Cilician pirates in conjunction with Mithridates VI of Pontus began to threaten the province of Asia inland, and when in cooperation with pirates farther west they began to disrupt the grain trade to such an extent that Rome experienced severe shortages, that younger politicians were able to achieve a change of course. In parallel with the establishment of provinces in the coastal regions and islands that were important to maritime trade – with the exception of Egypt – (Bithynia and Cyrene 75–74; Crete 67; Syria 63), the *lex Gabinia* granted an extraordinary command to Cn. Pompeius (Pompey). It gave him proconsular powers in any province within 75 km of the Mediterranean coast, provided him with funds from state and provincial treasuries and revenues from tax farmers for the construction of 500 ships, and conceded to him the right to nominate 25 legates of praetorian rank. Armed with these powers, Pompey divided the entire Mediterranean into operational zones, using political arrangements and the coordination of his main fleet and smaller fleets to break the sea power of his opponents and force the Cilician pirates to surrender.

B.9. FLEETS OF THE LATE REPUBLIC IN THE CIVIL WARS

Many of the pirates who had become clients of Pompey (→ Generals of note, N.) became an important support when in 49 BC he cut off Caesar (→ Generals of note, C.) in Italy from the grain supply and moved to attack him with superior naval forces. Caesar reacted by building up to 150 new vessels, securing Hispania and breaching the blockade of the Strait of Otranto. With these measures he was able to thwart his opponent's maritime strategy and force a decisive encounter on land. As the adversaries moved farther away from the norms of aristocratic coexistence, so also did their naval deployments become detached from the security interests of the state as a whole, becoming instead instruments of power for individuals who sought to impose their own absolute rule. Following the death of Caesar, the Civil Wars, whose theatre expanded to fill the entire Mediterranean, saw an unprecedented massing of naval forces. These amounted to over 1,000 vessels of assorted types, which were used both to supply and transport land forces, and to cut off opponents from supplies. Central to these conflicts were great naval battles, such as that fought off Naulochus between Agrippa and Sex. Pompeius (cf. fig. 3), and ultimately the Battle of Actium, in which Mark Antony and Cleopatra faced Agrippa and Octavian. These battles decided the balance of power, initially in the west and then in the entire Mediterranean, and paved the way for Octavian's rise to unchallenged power [19.270f.].

B.10. FLEETS UNDER THE PRINCIPATE

As the whole Mediterranean came under unified rule, the conditions of naval deployment changed fundamentally once more. Since there was no longer any maritime opposition, Augustus was able to abandon the costly and material-intensive polyremes and instead organize a permanent navy, based on the light units that had fought at Actium, as a regular arm of the imperial army, serving the interests of the empire and its *princeps*. Several small fleets of about 50 vessels (mostly triremes), manned at first by provincials before Roman citizens began to serve alongside them in the 70s AD, were established under the command of equestrian prefects. Stationed in Italy, the *classis Misenatium* ('Fleet of Misenum', in the Bay of Naples) and *classis Ravennatium* ('Fleet of Ravenna') were deployed to protect the grain supply, maintain communications, and transport and supply troops [15.56]. Fleets operating in the peripheral seas continued an imperial tradition founded by Caesar when he defeated the 220 ships of the Celtic Veneti (Caes. B Gall. 3,14f.; [14.153]) and (for his 54 BC invasion of Britain) performed the first amphibious landing in the history of the Atlantic (Caes. B Gall. 4,20–26; Vell. Pat. 2,46,1; Plut. Caes. 23; [19.258f.]). Under Augustus (R. Gest. div. Aug. 26), the naval operations of Drusus and Tiberius on the Rhine and in the North Sea combined the tasks of supplying land forces and exploring waterways and seas. In 25 BC, a war fleet supported the advance of Aelius Gallus into southern Arabia (Str. 16,4,23). When land expansion was abandoned there, it was repurposed as a naval task force operating in the Red Sea and later occupying fortified anchorages farther south (on the Farasan Islands). There were also small flotillas in Syria (from the Flavian period onwards), Alexandria, Carthage (late 2nd century AD), the Black Sea (as from the reign of Nero), and in the north (as from AD 43 under Claudius) that the *classis Britannica* (the fleet of the province of Britannia) stationed at Boulogne and Dover, alongside the monoremes and biremes of the Rhine and Danube fleets (*classis Germanica, Pannonica, Moesiaca*).

Fig. 3: Denarius of mint master Q. Nasidius (44/43 BC; RRC 483/2; 3.81g; diameter: 20.23mm). This reverse side of a denarius shows a Roman warship in full sail. A ram bow is suggested to the right. The star in the field to the left of the sail is interpreted either as a mark of success or as a nautical symbol. According to the inscription (legend), Quintus Nasidius had the coin minted, probably during the years 44–35 BC. Nasidius was an admiral and the son of a noted naval commander (*praefectus classis*?) of Sextus Pompeius, who controlled much of the Tyrrhenian Sea from Sicily in the 40s BC. The coin was intended to document Pompeius' claim to maritime power and the military strength of his fleet, which harried the coasts of Italy. The depiction of the ship with all sails set and oarsmen in action may be a reference to the speed of the fleet.

B.11. 3RD CENTURY AD TO LATE ANTIQUITY

Not all flotillas had their own independent military assignments; many supported land forces operating near the coasts ([18.130]; Cass. Dio 78,18; Tac. Agr. 30) and patrolled fluvial and maritime frontier regions. They were therefore not in a position in the 3rd century AD to offer effective opposition to the Ostrogoths, who began advancing from the Black Sea region into the Aegean, or the Frankish groups that were operating in the Mediterranean from Spain. Decisive success here came only through a combined counterattack by several provincial fleets (under the *praefectus Aegypti*) and land forces [19.345]; [14.156f.]. As fighting against barbarian intruders intensified in the late 3rd century, larger naval groups began to be created again (as previously after Pompey's campaign against the pirates). Pretenders to the imperial throne (like Carausius [14.155]) used such fleets in support of their attempts to seize power, and they ultimately had a crucial part in deciding control over the Mediterranean (naval battle between Constantine and Licinius on the Bosporus in AD 324; Zos. 2,23f.; Anon. Vales. 5,21–28; [23.391]). After the founding of Constantinople, as after Actium, warships shrank in size to light monoremes, and maritime forces were transferred to the Propontis in order to prevent seaborne invasions and secure the grain supply from Egypt [19.364]. Smaller fleets in the west now concentrated on protecting the grain trade between Africa and Italy and the grain supply from Istria to Split, Milan and Ravenna [17.572–641]. The division of the armed forces to the detriment of the west accelerated as Germanic groups succeeded in establishing themselves in imperial territories in Italy, Gaul, Hispania and North Africa. After taking Carthage and commandeering the provincial fleet stationed there (AD 439), the Vandals controlled North African waters as far as the Tyrrhenian Sea, with up to 120 ships, and they advanced as far as Ostia [14.157f.]. The degree to which the distribution of power on land depended on the use of naval forces was demonstrated one last time when a combined invasion fleet of the Eastern and Western Empires, comprising about 1,400 vessels (dromons and transport ships), was repelled with heavy losses off Carthage by Vandal fireships and boarding ships (Procop. Vand. 3,6,18; [19.415f.]; [14.158]). The Western Empire never recovered from this blow. Only in the first third of the 6th century was the political unity of the Mediterranean restored one final time, as the campaigns of Justinian achieved the reconquest of North Africa, Italy and parts of southeastern Spain. However, the Arab advance in the east, requiring the recall of Roman troops from their western bridgeheads, spelt the end of even that unity.

☞ State and army

BIBLIOGRAPHY
[1] D. FABRE, Seafaring in Ancient Egypt, 2004   [2] V. GABRIELSEN, The Naval Aristocracy of Hellenistic Rhodos, 1997   [3] V. GABRIELSEN, Warfare and the State, in: P. SABIN et al. (eds.), The Cambridge History of Greek and Roman Warfare, vol. 1: Greece, the Hellenistic World and the Rise of Rome, 2007, 248–272   [4] J.D. GRAINGER, Hellenistic and Roman Naval Warfare 336 BC–31 BC, 1993   [5] L. KALLET-MARX, Money, Expense, and Naval Power in Thucydides' History 1–5,24, 1993   [6] H. KOPP, Das Meer als Versprechen. Bedeutung und Funktion von Seeherrschaft bei Thukydides, 2017   [7] M. LADEWIG, Rom. Die antike Seerepublik. Untersuchungen zur Thalassokratie der res publica populi romani von den Anfängen bis zur Begründung des Principat, 2014   [8] A.B. LLOYD, Saite Navy, in: G.J. OLIVER et al. (eds.), The Sea in Antiquity, 2000, 81–115   [9] S. MCGRAIL, Boats of the World. From the Stone Age to Medieval Times, 2001   [10] S. MEDAS, La marineria cartaginense. Le navi, gli uomini, la navigazione, 2000   [11] F. MEIJER, A History of Seafaring in the Classical World, 1986   [12] A. MOMIGLIANO, Sea-Power in Greek Thought, in: A. MOMIGLIANO, Secundo contributo alla storia degli studi classici, 1960, 57–67   [13] W.M. MURRAY, The Age of Titans. The Rise and Fall of the Great Hellenistic Navies, 2012   [14] M. PITASSI, The Roman Navy, Ships, Men and Warfare 350 BC–AD 475, 2012   [15] B. RANKOV, Military Forces, in: P. SABIN et al. (eds.), The Cambridge History of Greek and Roman Warfare, vol. 2: Rome from the Late Republic to the Late Empire, 2007, 30–75   [16] L. RAWLINGS, The Carthaginian Navy. Questions and Assumptions, in: G.G. FAGAN / M. TRUNDLE (eds.), New Perspectives on Ancient Warfare, 2010, 253–287   [17] M. REDDÉ, Mare nostrum. Les infrastructures, le dispositif et l'histoire de la marine militaire sous l'Empire romain, 1986   [18] J. ROUGÉ, Ships and Fleets of the Ancient Mediterranean, 1981   [19] R. SCHULZ, Feldherren, Krieger und Strategen. Krieg in der Antike von Achill bis Attila, ^{3}2018   [20] L. SCOTT, Were There Polis Navies in Archaic Greece?, in: G.J. OLIVER (ed.), The Sea in Antiquity, 2000, 93–115   [21] P. DE SOUZA, Towards Thalassocracy? Archaic Naval Developments, in: N. FISHER / H. VAN WEES (eds.), Archaic Greece. New Approaches and New Evidence, 1998, 271–293   [22] P. DE SOUZA, Naval Forces, in: P. SABIN et al. (eds.), The Cambridge History of Greek and Roman Warfare, vol. 1: Greece, the Hellenistic World and the Rise of Rome, 2007, 357–367   [23] P. DE SOUZA, War at Sea, in: B. CAMPBELL / L.A. TRITLE (eds.), The Oxford Handbook of Warfare in the Classical World, 2013, 369–394   [24] C.G. STARR, The Influence of Sea Power on Ancient History, 1989   [25] C. STINBY, The Roman Republican Navy. From the Sixth Century to 167 B.C., 2007   [26] H.D.L. VIERECK, Die römische Flotte. Classis Romana, 1996   [27] H.T. WALLINGA, Ships and Sea Power before the Great Persian War. The Ancestry of the Ancient Trireme, 1993   [28] H.T. WALLINGA, The Ancestry of the Trireme 1200–525 BC, in: R. GARDINER / J.S. MORRISON (eds.), The Age of the Galley. Mediterranean Oared Vessels since Pre-Classical Times, 1995, 36–48

RAIMUND SCHULZ

Fortification

Although the art of fortification dates far back through history, we will confine ourselves here to Classical and Hellenistic Greece, to Rome, which to some extent adopted Greek traditions of fortification while also making important changes, and to the Byzantine heirs to Rome. The recording of knowledge in this field from the 4th century AD onwards produced an abundant technical literature, and this can be traced through a whole series of Greek and Latin treatises into the Byzantine period. As a subject, fortification has political, military and architectural aspects. The ways in which a city-state like Athens protected itself against attack differed from those employed by an empire like Rome in terms of means, spatial dimensions and strategy.

    A. Greece
    B. Rome
    C. Late antiquity

A. GREECE

The debate over whether fortifications are necessary or not is a very old one. Plato explicitly addresses it when he has the Athenians (Leg. 778c–779a) declare that the real fortification of a city like Sparta is its men and not its walls, which encourage weakness. Here we find echoes of debates about the policy pursued by Themistocles after the Persian Wars, which resulted in the construction of the walls of Piraeus (Thuc. 1,93,3–8) and then the Long Walls. These linked the city of Athens with the harbour and formed a highly effective fortification that provided access to the sea, making it possible to prevent siege. Pericles' → strategy in view of this fortification is described in detail in the speech he made to the Athenians in 432 on the eve of the Peloponnesian War (Thuc. 1,143,5; 2,13,2): avoiding engagement with the Spartans on open ground, defending the city rather than the territory, evacuating the population of Attica, and relying on the wider empire thanks to the fleet, thereby expanding the strategic theatre. Aristotle would later call city walls the symbol of the self-determination of a *polis* (Pol. 1330b–1331a). However, his comments also took into account the technological advances of his time, which was in general dominated by more powerful → artillery, siege engines and poliorcetics (→ Siege warfare).

Fortifications consisted of a variety of elements that became ever more complex and elaborate over time [1]; [10]. The practice of seeking out the optimum topographical position continued from the Archaic period, but for the fortification of towns, that optimum position was no longer necessarily an → acropolis on a height. The acropolis model involved a winding and often elongated layout adapted to the summit that was sometimes difficult to defend. Structures like these required enormous quantities of materials and the mobilization of a large number of people. Diodorus Siculus, for example (14,18,2–8), reports that Dionysius I put 60,000 men to work building the fortifications at Syracuse, and that they constructed a wall 5,400m long in a period of 60 days.

In most cases, fortifications were built of stone, which was generally but not exclusively delivered in rectangular shape and could be assembled in a variety of ways. Over time, this time-consuming and costly technology gave way to a double-walled construction enclosing a core of earth and rubble. Bricks were still often used, however, because they were cheap and easy to build with and offered good resistance to battering rams. They were usually placed on a base consisting of several rows of stones. Ramparts consisted of battlements and embrasures fitted with covers to prevent water from entering. A walkway ran along these ramparts, generally taking up the entire depth of the fortification wall. Some curtain walls were probably protected with a wooden superstructure covered with tiles. In most cases, they were not particularly high (average 4m).

Additional defensive structures important to a defensive system, in that they protruded in front of the wall and made it possible to fire projectiles (arrows or catapults) along the outside of the fortification, consisted of towers of various designs. These almost always projected out, and were usually square or rectangular in shape, although they sometimes had rounded corners or were polygonal, semicircular or circular. Corners of curtain walls were consistently fitted with such towers, which very often contained arrow slits.

From the Hellenistic period onwards, more fortifications began to be built on serrated or zigzag ground plans, offering an economical solution by increasing the number of defensive angles [9]. Access to the wall itself could also be prevented by building an outer wall (*proteichisma*), which kept attackers at bay by artificially deepening the ditch. Over time, the ditch steadily grew in scale, often reaching 10m in depth and only becoming passable when filled in. The ditches of the Euryalus Fortress at Syracuse were 22m wide and 7–9m deep (ditch B). Architects like Philo of Byzantium also advised spreading an assortment of obstacles on the slope ahead of the ditch (ditches, traps, 'Spanish riders' (a line of interconnected, spiked poles), etc.), although archaeologists have yet to find any, except during the excavations at Roman Alesia, which clearly show Rome's debt to the Hellenistic tradition [3]. More ditches, sometimes a considerable distance from the walls, completed the defensive installation.

Particular attention was paid to the gates, always the weak point of a defensive system. Elaborate architecture was used to avoid standardization and ensure that attackers were unclear as to the construction. Even so, a number of general rules were followed: the principle of flanking, which involved putting towers near to the aperture, which was kept as narrow as possible; the use of multiple chicanes; and often the construction of a second gate that would trap attackers who had broken through the outer defensive line in a courtyard. Numerous sally ports in the walls (often in the corners of stairway structures) made it possible to leave the main gates locked and, if needed, to increase the feed-through of troops moving out.

Besides city walls, which often attained large dimensions, we also know a great many lesser structures that served to protect small garrisons, for example, at Cydna. However, the defensive mechanisms of these installations were no different from those described above.

B. ROME

The widespread diffusion of fortification technologies on Sicily and in Magna Graecia explains how they were already known in the Roman world in the 3rd century BC, even though other architectural traditions were still dominant in Central Italy. In terms of defence, Rome no longer felt any threat on its own soil after the Second Punic War, or at least after the incursions of the Cimbri and Teutones in the late 2nd century BC, and this had a bearing on the upkeep of fortifications. The *urbs* ('city') itself offers a good example: the old Servian Wall was never replaced, and by the time of Augustus all that remained of it were ruins across which the city had sprawled in all directions. Even those cities that still had walls in the 1st century BC did not necessarily retain defensive installations capable of withstanding a serious siege. The civil wars in the final years of the Republic, however, led many towns and cities to construct new defences, often by refurbishing their old walls.

Paradoxically, new city walls began to be built (in Northern Italy and Narbonensis) at the very moment when peace was restored after the civil war and the end of the Republic. [2]. In most cases, these were privileges for newly founded Roman colonies like Fréjus, or cities honoured with special status, such as Nîmes and Autun, the new capital of the Haedui. Walls in such instances represented a civic honour, and attest more to the status of the city than any concern for its defence. Not all cities were entitled to the honour, so that Augst (Augusta Raurica), for example, although it was a colony of the Raurici, only received a wall (which was never finished) at a very late date. At Nîmes, an inscription dating from 16 BC explains that the construction was made by order of the *princeps* (CIL XII 3151). The gates of Fréjus still clearly exemplify the Hellenistic legacy, and certain traditional techniques (zigzag ground plan, abundance of tower designs, protrusion of towers) are visible on the city walls of Nîmes. However, city gates of this period exhibit a distinctly new, monumental appearance that tends towards ostentation, manifested in the size of their passageways, their height and their architectural decoration. The same kind of display is found in prestigious walls of the Imperial period, such as those of Autun and Cologne and the Porta Nigra in Trier.

Rome's real defensive installations in this period, however, were in the provinces (→ Borders), and here we must consider the technologies of military architecture unearthed by archaeology and described by authors such as Pseudo-Hyginus and Vegetius. These authors were essentially interested only in field fortifications that were built for one night or a few days. According to Pseudo-Hyginus (49), the key element was the ditch, which was always dug, even on secure terrain, 'in order to maintain → discipline'. A rampart was only built in unsafe locations. For Vegetius, on the other hand, the rampart was the main element, and a ditch was only dug where it was not posisble to build a proper wall. The 'normal' form of defence was a wall of evenly cut turf strips that were held together by the grass roots and put together like bricks (*caespites*). A palisade (*vallum*) made of stakes (*valli*) or caltrops made of sharpened wooden spikes (*tribuli lignei*) was then built along the top. Only where no turf was available or the ground was not firm enough would a ditch be dug to pile up a raised earth embankment (*agger*). Happily, archaeology is bringing more and more details to light [6]; [5]; [11].

Walls made of turf strips have numerous advantages. They use material that is immediately available nearby, and they can be built quickly. This is also the most frequent structural form we see legionaries using on the reliefs of Trajan's Column commemorating the conquest of Dacia or on reliefs in Roman Britain. With a height of a dozen feet (approx. 3.60m) and a slight slope to improve stability, walls generally stood on a base 6m deep. A rampart (*lorica*) and battlements (*pinnae*), often comprising lattice panels, were fixed along the crest using anchored wooden supports. The battlement walkway was about six feet wide, the minimum necessary for two men to pass each other.

Along the Rhine frontier, earth embankments with wooden cladding were preferred. This technique facilitated vertical façades and less depth, but required more wood. The cladding was held in place using posts anchored in the ground at intervals of 1.20/1.50m. Most frequently, these were four-sided oak posts. Walls were usually 3m deep. Wooden planks were fixed behind the posts to cover the core material dug from the ditch. As in the turf embankments, ramparts and battlements were fixed to the foremost posts, jutting out in front of the battlement walkway. Occasionally, most notably on the Saalburg, it has been possible to demonstrate the existence of walls with dry stone facings and a latticed wood interior construction, structurally reminiscent of Celtic building (*murus Gallicus*).

Towers belonging to turf or wood-and-earth walls were also built of wood, and were placed along the curtain wall without ever protruding in front of it. Their main function consisted in housing the small artillery pieces with which the Roman army was equipped (*ballistae*) and controlling the wall with their firing range, which was superior to those of the classic projectiles (javelins, arrows). Gates of this period were often complex constructions, with the actual portal often – particularly during the Augustan period – placed behind the curtain wall to form a protective redan.

The ditches dug in front of the wall functioned as obstacles to the enemy as well as sources of material for building the *agger*. Individual installations differed greatly in form, size and number. With few exceptions, they were dry ditches rather than moats. The simplest and commonest ditch was dug in a V-shape and positioned immediately in front of the wall, although often dug one behind the other, especially in Roman Britain.

Fortifications of this kind were built at legionary camps until the 70s AD, and even at auxiliary forts until the first quarter of the 2nd century, when they were superseded by stone constructions. Turf, earth and wood, however, continued to be used in temporary fortifications. In general, these purely military defensive systems, which also tended to be used in Roman → camps, proved largely adequate against adversaries unacquainted with the sophisticated siege techniques of the east. The new stone constructions should not be seen as indicative of any growing threat; rather, they simply attest to a shift towards more stable → borders [7]. This shift sometimes manifested itself in a simple replacement of the curtain wall, with the embankment retained to reinforce the stone wall, which tended to be rather shallow (0.90–1.50m) and no higher than the preceding walls – 3.60m (12 feet) seems to have been the norm. These new masonry walls were often painted white with red joints to imitate cut stones. The stone towers of the Imperial period seem to have been no taller than their wooden predecessors. They were almost invariably square (except at the corners), and they never jutted out in front of the wall, although they often extended behind the wall. Gates were often highly monumental in design. Embrasures were placed on both storeys of the building.

C. LATE ANTIQUITY

The increasing threats arising in the 3rd and 4th centuries, the sometimes violent invasions and the reorganization of the military necessitated review of these models, and a return to considerably stronger fortification systems [11]. From the time of the Tetrarchy onwards, the borders of the empire were furnished with smaller, more easily defensible fortresses. They were also appreciably reinforced, with higher and longer defensive walls with protruding towers that enabled better defence of the wall, and with many architectural designs indicative of a return to the principles of Hellenistic military architecture. The same section often exhibits adjoining square, round, horseshoe and polygonal designs, with no indication that this is a result of repairs or construction at different times. Gates became systematically smaller and were reinforced with an inner gate. Larger and deeper ditches were often built, dug well away from the walls.

A striking number of cities (although not all) in the hinterland of the *limes* ('boundary'), often deep in the heartlands of provinces, built their own fortifications between the mid-3rd and early 5th centuries. A city wall was built at Mainz, for example, as early as 254, while Saint-Bertrand-de-Comminges did not build its wall until the late 4th century. In many cases, these new walls failed to enclose the entire built-up area; this does not necessarily indicate a shrinking of the inhabited urban space, but may suggest special protection for a privileged or central zone. The idea of 'reduits' or 'refuges' may be defended in some cases, but not in general. The defensive principles of these new installations were no different from those of the more strictly military structures. This often makes it difficult to distinguish the two, especially given that soldiers (when stationed there) and civilians lived alongside each other in cities of this period, as shown by the barracks in the centre of Arras. Citing the *spolia* (blocks of older monuments) reused in their foundations, the older academic tradition tended to classify these new city walls as structures put together hastily in the face of a threat. Scholars today take a different view, pointing out the ostentatious character of defensive walls such as those of Le Mans, which are decorated very meticulously with coloured geometric motifs, and also the fact that these monuments symbolized the status of the city through the protection they offered it, especially as older public monuments (theatres, baths, fora etc.) increasingly lost their importance. The finest example is surely the wall built around the imperial capital during the reign of Aurelian (270–275), a gigantic structure almost 19km long, whose monumental gates were also an adornment to the city. The only comparable structure is the city wall of Constantinople built in the reign of Theodosius II. The Theodosian Walls guaranteed the security of the New Rome until its fall in 1453.

Also associated with these great defensive installations (forts of the *limes* and fortified towns) were the hilltop fortifications that began to proliferate in some areas, such as the Mosel Valley between Trier and Koblenz. Rather than mere refuges in the strict sense, these small installations, adapted to the terrain and often built of dry stone or wood, should be seen as bases and watchtowers. Moreover, more classical forms of territorial occupation were not out of the question, as can be seen at Mayen in the Eifel, where the unfortified *vicus* ('district') continued to be inhabited, while a small, probably Germanic garrison was set up on the nearby Katzenberg hill in the second quarter of the 4th century [4].

BIBLIOGRAPHY
[1] J.-P. ADAM, L'architecture militaire grecque, 1982 [2] M.-G. COLIN, Les enceintes augustéennes dans l'Occident romain (France, Italie, Espagne, Afrique du Nord) (École antique de Nîmes 18), 1987 [3] Y. GARLAN, Recherches de poliorcétique grecque (Bibliothèque des Écoles Françaises d'Athènes et de Rome 223), 1974 [4] A. HUNOLD, Die Befestigung auf dem Katzenberg bei Mayen und die spätrömischen Höhenbefestigungen in Nordgallien (Römisch-Germanisches Zentralmuseum Monographien 88), 2011 [5] A. JOHNSON, Roman Forts of the 1st and 2nd Centuries in Britain and the German Provinces, 1983 [6] M.J. JONES, Roman Fort-Defences to A.D. 117 (British Archaeological Reports 21), 1975 [7] J. LANDER, Roman Stone Fortifications. Variation and Change from the First Century A.D. to the Fourth (British Archaeological Reports. International Series 206), 1984 [8] Y. LE BOHEC et al. (eds.), The Encyclopedia of the Roman Army, 3 vols., 2015 [9] P. LERICHE / H. TRÉZIN (eds.), La fortification dans l'histoire du monde grec. Actes du colloque international 'la fortification et sa place dans l'histoire politique, culturelle et sociale du monde grec', Valbonne, December 1982, 1986 [10] A.W. McNICOLL, Hellenistic Fortifications from the Aegean to the Euphrates, 1997 [11] M. REDDÉ et al., L'architecture de la Gaule romaine, vol. 1: Les fortifications militaires (Documents d'archéologie française 100), 2006

MICHEL REDDÉ

Garrison

A. Greek
B. Roman

A. Greek

A garrison (*phroura*, *phrourion*) in Greek Antiquity [7.23–30] was a small to medium-sized unit of troops that was mainly stationed at fixed locations or towns in wartime to establish temporary military security or exert political pressure. Distinguishing a garrison from a simple 'guard' (*phylake*) is not always easy. Wars occurred very frequently, so that garrisons were ubiquitous. Since they generally shared similar structures, a selection of details must be made so that specific features can be described. During the Archaid period and as described later by Herodotus, garrisons were used exclusively for the abovementioned military purposes, except that a Spartan garrison sometimes served in support of the *tyrannis* ('tyrants') at Athens. According to Thucydides, garrisons in the main were still of the same character during the Peloponnesian War and the events leading up to it. But the Delian League, founded in 476 BC, added functions intended to restore or consolidate the political authority of Athens. In the case of Samos, for example, in addition to the establishment of democracy and the placement of hostages, a garrison was also stationed at the *polis* (Thuc. 1,115,3). Fortifications were also frequently demolished [8.32–36].

The political function of these garrisons was subsequently expanded. The mere presence of a garrison may often have been sufficient for the given purpose, but on a number of occasions it proved necessary to exert stronger influence on the forcibly restored city. The commander (*phrourarchos*) represented the physical presence of the Athenian power, and was accordingly furnished with the requisite perogatives, which went beyond the purely military. Two inscriptions (IG I^3 14f.) show that he participated in drawing up the new constitution of Erythrae in Asia Minor, and had a role in its judicial system [8.39f.].

Following the defeat of Athens in the Peloponnesian War (the expansion of the Attican village of Decelea into a fortress by Sparta goes beyond the definition of a garrison), the overseas possessions of Athens were lost, and with them the garrisons. However, Spartan garrisons commanded by *harmostai* ('governors') had already begun taking their place during the war [3.141]. Even Athens itself at first received a Spartan garrison in support of the oligarchic system, but it (along with the oligarchy) was soon abolished. The *harmostai* subsequently took care to ensure that the Greek cities concerned remained within the Spartan territory established after 404 BC, the successor to the Delian League, and accordingly arranged for internal conditions friendly towards Sparta, namley, oligarchies rather than democracies. In 386, however, direct Spartan rule ended quickly, leaving military garrisons as simply the usual instrument of warfare amid the shifting fortunes of the chaotic period that followed. Not even in the Second Athenian League did they resume their former role [2].

Garrisons acquired a new function under Alexander the Great. He left garrisons along his ever-extending campaign route through Persia as far as India, to protect connections homeward. They were not stationed in existing cities. Rather, their functions were secured by the foundation of new cities on a large scale.

The unrelenting wars of the first phase of the Hellenistic period [4] saw garrisons revert to their exclusively military role [5.79–250]. Three notable locations in Greece acquired their specific functions from the Macedonian garrisons, which served to control Greece as possession of territories changed: Acrocorinth, Munichia (Piraeus), and Euboean Chalcis. In the words of Philip V, these were the leg irons of Greece (Plut. *Aratus* 16,5), and they were disbanded by T. Quinctius Flamininus' proclamation of the freedom of Greece at the Isthmian Games of 196 BC, although they later came and remained under Roman rule.

Phrourarchs (commanders of garrisons) are occasionally encountered in Ptolemaic Egypt. Examples include the garrisons of Herodes of Pergamum, which served a military function in the reign of Ptolemy VI, garrisons that served as border guards at Syene (= Aswan) (OGIS 111,16), and other garrisons assigned to control external possessions [1.220–224] – in all cases tending to exercise authority in the civilian sphere beyond their military role.

BIBLIOGRAPHY
[1] R.S. BAGNALL, The Administration of the Ptolemaic Possessions outside Egypt, 1976 [2] M. DREHER, Hegemon und Symmachoi. Untersuchungen zum Zweiten Athenischen Seebund, 1995 [3] M. DREHER, Athen und Sparta, 2012 [4] H.-J. GEHRKE, Geschichte des Hellenismus, ^{4}2008 [5] W. HUSS, Ägypten in hellenistischer Zeit, 332–30 v.Chr., 2001 [6] S. LAUFFER, Alexander der Große, ^{5}2005 [7] V. ROSENBERGER, Besatzung in der Antike, in: G. KRONENBITTER et al. (eds.), Besatzung. Funktion und Gestalt militärischer Fremdherrschaft bis zum 20. Jahrhundert (Krieg in der Geschichte 28), 2006, 23–36 [8] W. SCHULLER, Die Herrschaft der Athener im Ersten Attischen Seebund, 1974 [9] K.-W. WELWEI, Phrourarchos, in: BNP 11, 2007, 194.

WOLFGANG SCHULLER

B. ROMAN

B.1. Definitions
B.2. Instruments of imperial policy
B.3. Functions of the provincial army

B.1. DEFINITIONS

The Duden dictionary defines *Besatzung* ('garrison' or 'occupation') as 'troops in a (besieged) fortress; troops that occupy a foreign territory'. However, definitions in modern international law of a 'garrison' as a physical military presence and of 'occupation' as a state of military control are based on conditions that would have been irrelevant to premodern entities such as the Roman Empire. Whatever happens in practice today, there exist universally accepted norms prohibiting unprovoked military aggression and the permanent occupation of a territory under the *de facto* rule of a foreign armed force. When such incidents occur despite these norms, efforts are made to remedy the situation in accordance with moral criteria. Although Rome knew the concept of the *bellum iustum*, this was not a moral category, but a ritual and formal one with its origins in the *ius fetiale*. Military conquest, the subjugation of foreign peoples, and the permanent military occupation and absorption of conquered territories were not seen as morally problematic. Just as the enslavement of an individual was fully acceptable in the private sphere, so occupation and foreign rule were a natural consequence of victory in the military sphere.

B.2. INSTRUMENTS OF IMPERIAL POLICY

Like other states of the ancient world, Rome subjugated foreign territories with the intent of acting as rulers of these territories, aiming especially to use military authority to assert political, military, legal and economic control. For an imperial power to survive and function well, it must effectively integrate subjugated foreign peoples. The Roman Empire developed several means to achieve this. The first was the practice of founding Roman settlements (*coloniae*; → Colonies) in the newly conquered regions. The second was the gradual granting of Roman citizenship to the subjugated population, beginning with the social elites. When such measures were implemented successfully and achieved the desired result for the Roman Empire, as in the provinces of Asia, Macedonia, Dalmatia, Achaia, Gaul and Hispania Baetica, no further regular military presence was needed, or at most a very limited number of smaller units were left in place. Such a situation can no longer be described as an occupation – a fact most clearly illustrated by the fact that over time many emperors came from the provinces.

The long–term development of the Roman system must also be taken into account. There were no significant fighting forces in the provinces before the Second Punic War (218–201). Thereafter, the provinces were occupied with troops recruited by force who served for at least six years. During the 1st century BC, Rome began to maintain standing armies in an increasing number of its provinces beyond the Mediterranean. Under the Principate from the reign of Augustus onwards, professional provincial armies were stationed at permanent locations.

The question, therefore, is: Should the permanent military presence of tens of thousands of men in large, long–standing provinces, such as Britannia, Pannonia superior and inferior or Syria, be called an occupation? Or, more precisely, how long after the initial conquest may this state of affairs be called an occupation? At what point is it permissible to speak of a regular garrison that is stationed in a province and recruits its soldiers locally? The answer depends on the actual functions of these troops in their respective provinces.

B.3. FUNCTIONS OF THE PROVINCIAL ARMY

The Roman provincial army had a range of roles. The first was as the equivalent of an internal police force (→ Policing). This was especially important because, unlike modern states, the Roman Empire had no such regular institution. Troops acted in this capacity even during major uprisings, for example in Britain (Boudicca), Germania (Frisii, Batavi), Africa and Judaea. In these circumstances, the army could plausibly be described as an occupying force. Moreover, the army might be stationed in a frontier region to enable possible imperial expansion or to provide defence against hostile threats and attacks. These are not functions normally associated with an occupying force. Yet, scholars have not been able to agree on what Rome's actual priorities were. According to the traditional view, the primary task of the army in the Imperial period was to protect the empire's borders against external enemies. Another view advanced today is that stationing troops served multiple purposes, such as facilitating mobility and transport (along rivers), ensuring readiness for further expansion, and performing internal policing functions (see above). There is far less emphasis in contemporary scholarship on the protection of borders as the key function. One important aspect of scholarly discussion is the interpretation of Roman military organization in the frontier provinces. Traditionally, this was equated with the so-called *limes* ('boundary') system, that is, the practice of using garrisons to occupy defensive lines. Today, however, some hold a different view on the nature of this organization. Meanwhile, clear differences have been identified between the west and east of the empire. Units were far more frequently stationed in cities in the eastern provinces than in the west.

The army in the Roman provinces was reorganized in the late 3rd and early 4th centuries. This process is well documented, but exactly what the changes were intended to achieve is a subject of lively debate. Usually, smaller units were spread across several bases in the provinces, with some located on the borders and others in the interior. Can this really be called an 'occupation'? There is room for doubt, but the provinces were undoubtedly 'garrisoned'.

☞ State and army

BIBLIOGRAPHY
[1] A. CAMERON (ed.), The Byzantine and Early Islamic Near East, vol. 3: States, Resources and Armies, 1995 [2] J.P. GRANT / J. CRAIG BARKER, Parry & Grant Encyclopaedic Dictionary of International Law, ³2009 [3] B. ISAAC, The Limits of Empire. The Roman Army in the East, 1992 (rev. ed.) [4] A.H.M. JONES, The Later Roman Empire 284–602, vol. 1, pt. 2, ch. XVII [5] L. KEPPIE, The Making of the Roman Army. From Republic to Empire, 1984 [6] Y. LE BOHEC, The Imperial Roman Army, 1994 [7] Y. LE BOHEC (ed.), The Encyclopedia of the Roman Army, 2015 [8] E. LUTTWAK, The Grand Strategy of the Roman Empire, 2016 (rev. ed.) [9] G. WEBSTER, The Roman Imperial Army of the First and Second Centuries A.D., ³1985 [10] C.R. WHITTAKER, Rome and its Frontiers. The Dynamics of Empire, 2004.

BENJAMIN ISAAC

General

A. Concept
B. The social status of generals
C. Training
D. Duties of generals
E. Evolution of the function of the general
F. Generals and politics

A. CONCEPT
The usual classical terms for a supreme military commander or an officer in charge of a field army – the Greek *strategos* and the Latin *dux* – are nearly synonymous with the modern term 'general'. Yet, titles varied from one period to another, and according to circumstance and polity. Greek also had *hegemon* (often the title of a commander of an alliance), *polemarchos* and *archon*. Latin frequently used titles of Roman magistracies, such as *dictator*, *consul*, *proconsul* and *imperator*. The function and status of the command rather than the size of the fighting force defined the general, who was expected to be equally competent in operations on land and sea.

As in other societies that predate the emergence of states, the roots of Greek and Roman command lay in the institution of clan chiefdom, which often combined civil, religious and military functions. Status within the community was based on feats in battle and/or lineage, and correlated with the possession of sufficient wealth to afford military equipment and the spare time to train. All this enabled a clan chief to assemble troops for war from his clan, to organize his retinue and supporters, and to ally himself with other leading figures. Success in battle and individual daring heightened personal prestige, and with it the renown of the warrior and his family – as well as augmenting his wealth from booty and the acquisition of slaves. These characteristics were common to the Homeric heroes and the chiefs of the Roman *gentes*.

B. THE SOCIAL STATUS OF GENERALS
From Antiquity until the 18th century, most but not all generals came from royal or aristocratic families. In monarchies, the king often took on the role of general, while under non-monarchical forms of government, senior elected officials shouldered military responsibilities for limited periods of time alongside their civil duties. In empires, provincial governors or satraps had their own armies, or rulers delegated supreme command to trusted individuals. Constitutional developments, political machinations, the exigencies of war, coups and civil wars created opportunities for non-aristocrats. Examples in 5th and 4th-century Athens include Cleon, a product not of the hereditary landowning aristocracy but of the mercantile class, and Iphicrates, the son of a shoemaker. In Sparta, Brasidas and Lysander held extraordinary commands, since the usual general of the *polis* was one of its two kings.

From the late 5th century until the Hellenistic period, an era of mercenaries, appointment as a general was no longer dependent on citizen status. Mercenary recruiters could become generals, and wandering generals-for-hire sought appointments after wars ended. Sparta's reputation for military excellence increased demand for Spartan generals, especially in Magna Graecia [11]. At Rome, C. Marius, a *novus homo* ('new man') from outside the traditional senatorial elite, took the consulship (*cos.* 107, 104–100, 86 BC) as well as numerous military commands. The Roman Empire was capable of recognizing and promoting talent from beneath the senatorial class. Vespasian, an *eques Romanus* ('Roman cavalry soldier') by background (*cos.* 51), won the imperial throne in the civil war of AD 68–70. It now became possible for reliable military performers (*viri militares*) to plan careers as officers. By the 3rd century, rising through the ranks to positions of senior command had become normal [6], and within another century after that, even 'barbarians' were becoming Roman generals, albeit as holders of Roman citizenship (e.g. the Vandal Stilicho and the Alan Aspar).

C. TRAINING

The commonplace criticism that generals in Antiquity were amateurs incapable of strategic thinking is fallacious. The first state-operated military academies date only from the 18th century, so virtually all generals before the 19th century were amateurs. In general, the Greeks and the Romans of the Republican period took it for granted that the qualifications for military command were high birth and ancestors who had excelled in battle. In other words, outstanding military aptitude (*arete*) was inherited. In practice, sons of aristocrats learned basic combat techniques from their fathers or other relatives, and through athletic training; but until the 4th century BC, acquiring the skills of a general depended on experience in the field and an innate talent for organization and leadership [9]. Philip II of Macedon, possibly following Persian practice, employed pages at court to train officers, including some future generals. The Seleucids had a similar educational institution at Apamea in Syria (Str. 16,2,10). In the Roman Republic, a ten-year period of military service was required before a candidate could take political office leading to a possible future army command. There was also an apprenticeship system, whereby a young man whose father, other relative or family friend held a senior military command served on the general's staff or as a 'companion' (Latin *comes*). In the 4th century AD, the titles *protectores* and *domestici* often denoted staff officers training for higher positions. After AD 300, written information was also available in treatises on the art of military command (cf. → Military literature) [10].

D. DUTIES OF GENERALS

The duties of a general differed according to the constitution of the state, the historical period, and the complexity, nature and strategic aims of the war. In the Grecian world before the advent of the phalanx, decisions about war and the aims of war were matters to be decided by the 'state', if the general was not himself the ruler. Generals bore little responsibility in the brief wars of this era for training, organizing (by regions or tribes/clans) or supplying armies. Their duties were limited to assembling their forces, leading them personally into battle and demonstrating superior skills in single combat – for purposes of personal renown and the inspiration of their men.

The development of the phalanx between about 700 and 500 BC established the general's position in the first ranks of the right wing of his battle formation, where his role continued to include leading the fight by personal example.

Once the hoplite army was in formation, generals were typically engaged in single combat with only scant opportunities for ordering manoeuvres of troops. The individual members of the army remained responsible for their own training, equipment and provisions. The *polis* decided how to organize the composition of the phalanx. In the colonies on the fringes of the Greek world and on Sicily, the light infantry and cavalry played a larger role than it did in the leading *poleis* on the Greek mainland (cf. e.g. Gelon of Syracuse, Hdt. 7,158,4), implying that more developed command functions were needed.

The Greeks' confrontation with the leading non-Greek military power, Persia (499–478 BC), along with the effects of Athenian imperialism, brought farther-reaching changes in the art of war. This process continued through the 4th century [2]. Although greater troop strengths, long campaigns in distant, unknown territories, and operations on both sea and land allowed generals more freedom for independent judgment, the same factors further complicated operational systems such as supply, equipment and pay. All this now required strategic thought. On a tactical level, the increased use of mercenaries, cavalry and light infantry brought about developments in fighting techniques that utilized combinations of troop types, attention to topography and mastery of siege technologies, which ultimately came to include artillery.

Training in arms and for the unit's manoeuvres increased in importance. War was becoming more technical and more complex than in the days of the typical hoplite engagement on an open plain. Battles were now planned, and demanded not just valour, but also management, with the option of altering plans during the fight by drawing on tactical reserves. Cunning, surprise and deception, long since practised in minor engagements, now came into use in large pitched battles, making it possible for smaller armies to defeat larger forces, while taking fewer losses. The new word *strategema*, originally denoting 'trickery', now stood for an instance of brilliant generalship. Although the gods continued throughout Antiquity to be seen as the final arbiters of victory in war, a new, more rational and secular approach began to teach that the gods would help those who helped themselves (Xen. Cyr. 1,6,5f.). Manuals in the new field of military theory – many bearing the title *Strategika* – offered instruction in all the duties of a general.

E. EVOLUTION OF THE FUNCTION OF THE GENERAL

The developments mentioned above, which altered existing conceptions of the qualities and responsibilities of a general, exerted a profound influence on the western military tradition in two respects. For one thing, the practice of fighting pitched battles in which warriors honourably demonstrated their valour and strength in a 'fair fight' – in other words, the approach represented by Homer's Achilles – was rejected by generals who employed deceit, cunning and/or the avoidance of battle – in other words, the approach represented by Odysseus. Intelligence and creativity were now sought after. Every general was expected to devise stratagems for war (Thuc. 5,9,4f.; Xen. Cyr. 1,6,27–38, Xen. Eq. mag. 5,9–11; Xen. Ages. 6,5–8). To be sure, the two categories were not mutually exclusive. Guileful generals like Hannibal (→ Generals of note, G.) were not above fighting pitched battles, and Scipio Africanus the Elder (→ Generals of note, O.) won renown by combining both approaches with success. Even so, generals and polities alike chose to portray themselves as honourable exponents of the Achillean approach.

Secondly, the early 4th century saw a new distinction between the duties of a general and the tasks of ordinary fighters (Xen. An. 3,1,37; Plut. Mor. 187B; Frontin. Str. 4,7,4): A general now exercised higher functions (*strategika*) than the mere techniques of battle (*taktika*). Previously, generals had been distinguished by their insignia, armour or symbolic weapons. This manifested itself in a range of leadership styles, such as the flashy commander – the *miles gloriosus* – or, in contrast, the general who shared the ordeals of his men, inspiring them by enduring hardships with confidence and forging a 'kinship' with those he led. Such a distinction was already apparent in the 7th century BC (Archilochus fr. 114 West). What was new now was the general's responsibility for all aspects of a military enterprise. As the 'manager' of the battle, he was not actively to participate in it, lest his being killed or wounded lead to defeat [1]. Targeting the enemy commander sometimes became the tactical goal (e.g. Alexander the Great at Gaugamela against Darius III, 331 BC). However, the general's duty to provide leadership in the first battle line, particularly in times of crisis when his troops needed to rally, prevented him from remaining altogether on the sidelines. Hellenistic kings, as embodiments of the unity of the state, often took personal command in major military operations. They sought to emulate the charismatic leadership of Alexander the Great, which entailed active participation in battle. Generals would take personal part (and die) in battle until the 19th century. The degree of such participation varied according to the character of the general and the situation [13].

The generals of the Hellenistic period and the Roman Republic continued on this path that orginated in the 4th century. Hellenistic generals, however, had to deal with multiethnic fighting forces and assorted weapon types. Roman generals had to contend with the constitutional problem that their commands were designated for a limited time – although later the *prorogatio* ('extension') of commands allowed some flexibility. Nevertheless, Roman generals often hurried to finish a campaign before their term in office ended, rather than allowing a successor to take credit for the victory. The Romans took pride in *fides* ('fidelity') as their defining quality, and the demonstration of *virtus* ('virtue'; a dimension of the Achillean approach) motivated Roman generals as much as it did ordinary soldiers. Although the Romans generally preferred formal pitched battles, in which superior Roman weaponry and legionary discipline gave them an advantage (cf. Pol. 1,37,7), it is not true, as some have claimed, that the Romans were innocent in matters of military deception until they were taught by Hannibal during the Second Punic War (218–202 BC) [12]. Even a victory won by trickery did not disqualify a general from the accolade of a triumph, provided that other criteria were also met. The craft of generalship was by no means the main criterion.

Rome produced many 'great' generals (e.g. Scipio Africanus the Elder and Younger, Fabius Maximus Cunctator, C. Marius (→ Generals of note, K.), Cn. Pompeius (Pompey; → Generals of note, N.), C. Iulius Caesar (→ Generals of note, C.)), each of whom exhibited brilliance in one or more aspects of generalship, even if the Roman military system, which limited time in office, in many respects regarded generals as replaceable [4]. We can discern no specifically Roman type of generalship as distinct from Roman strategy or tactics. Roman generals were battle managers. Much like their Hellenistic counterparts, they often surveyed developments in battle from the rear, but they also led armies into battle. The example of Alexander the Great provided a new model. From the 3rd century BC there were attempts to define the ideal general, in which descriptions of character blended with analyses of military accomplishments. The recurring themes of strength versus cunning and aptitude versus luck emerged together with the expectation that a good general display foresight (Greek *pronoia* / Latin *providentia*), prompt analysis (Greek *anchinoia* / *coup d'oeil*) and good timing (*kairos/occasio*). Historians and biographers preserve some aspects of these discussions, which Lucian (already; Lucian. Dial. mort. 25) and later Julian (*Caesares*) satirized [13]. Cicero's definition of the good general is found in his treatise *De imperio Cn. Pompei* [5].

F. GENERALS AND POLITICS

Sources adequate for a detailed military analysis are lacking for the Principate and the empire of Late Antiquity. This is precisely what Augustus intended with his strict control over the army and its commanders. Renowned generals (such as Agricola, Domitius Corbulo (→ Generals of note, D.), Trajan, Avidius Cassius, Aurelian, Constantine I (→ Generals of note, J.), Belisarius) are known more for their successes than for their brilliance in tactics or strategy. What counted most was management, administration and the defence of borders. No great progress or change in generalship is evident. It was during these periods that the political role of the general came particularly to the fore.

Rulers faced an ever-present political threat from victorious generals or from large forces under an ambitious commander (Aristot. Pol. 1329a,12f.). The lack of a standing army did not necessarily prevent commanders from attempting to seize power. The first Greek tyrant, Cypselus of Corinth, took power as *polemarchos* ('warleader') in about 657 BC, and Peisistratus, a former Athenian *strategos* ('commander'), resorted to mercenaries in 546 BC, although any involvement of these tyrants with the emergence of a hoplite class and the phalanx is dubious. On Sicily, known for its military tyrants, Gelon used his position as cavalry commander to take power at Gela in 491 BC. Dionysius I, a man of low birth and a battle veteran, secured election as *strategos* at Syracuse in 409 BC, and rose to become tyrant through demagogy and the use of mercenaries. The death of Alexander the Great ushered in the first great era of generals who transformed their military status into hereditary monarchies. Some of the Diadochi enjoyed more success in this enterprise than others. The extensive Seleucid Empire endured not only dynastic wars and intrigues, but also rebellions in the provinces; the satraps of Media proved problematic, as in the revolts of Molon against Antiochius III (c. 220 BC) and of Timarchus against Antiochus V (164–160 BC)

In the late Republican period, Rome's destiny was sealed by the demands imposed by the empire and internal political turmoil. Commands extended in time, and geographical range enabled ambitious and charismatic politicians who were governors of provinces (e.g. Iulius Caesar) to build armies that owed more loyalty to them than to the Roman state. L. Cornelius Sulla, the first general to capture the city of Rome with his army (in 88 and 82 BC), may have been responsible for the politicization of the military [8]. The Principate established by Augustus then dressed up a military dictatorship as the Republic restored. Thereafter, the *princeps* was always the sole commander, to whom all victories and successes were ascribed, even where they were actually achieved by his proxies wielding command in the provinces. Popular or unusually effective generals were suspected of harbouring greater ambitions (e.g. Germanicus and Tiberius, Corbulo and Nero). It remained vital for a distant emperor to maintain contact with his armies to assure them of his patronage, whether through *donativa* ('supplementary monetary payments'), support to veterans, or occasional visits – besides promoting the ruler cult.

Augustus and Tiberius had actual experience as generals, but later emperors' practical experience as military commanders varied. Army recognition lent legitimacy to an emperor's rule, but the provincial armies did not always adhere to the decisions made by the Praetorian Guard at Rome. Thus Tacitus' 'secret of the empire' ('that emperors could be made elsewhere than at Rome', Tac. Hist. 1,4,2) led to the civil wars of the years 68–70, 192–194 and 196–197. There were also attempted usurpations by provincial governors.

During the 3rd century, constant barbarian threats at the borders and the political problems associated with establishing legitimate rule brought about an era of soldier-emperors: generals as emperors [6]. This trend lasted into the 4th century. The dynasties of Constantine I and Theodosius I, both of whom were originally soldier-emperors, brought only temporary stability. In the 5th century, generals (many of 'barbarian' background) wielded the real power behind the thrones of young or weak monarchs. While the Western Empire disintegrated and disappeared, even emperors of the East who were in a position to lead campaigns as field generals ceased to do so. The political power of the provincial armies had evaporated, and emperors were now often chosen in palace revolutions. A monarch's physical absence from Constaninople was an invitation to a coup [7]. Heraclius was the last Roman emperor to come to power with the help of a provincial army, and he was also the last to wage war on the battlefield against an external enemy.

☞ Battle; Eve-of-battle speech; Military literature; Strategy

BIBLIOGRAPHY
[1] P. BESTON, Hellenistic Military Leadership, in: H. VAN WEES (ed.), War and Violence in Ancient Greece, 2000, 315-335 [2] J. BOËLDIEU-TREVET, Commander dans le monde grec au Ve siècle avant notre ère, 2007 [3] J. CAMPBELL, The Emperor and the Roman Army 31 BC–AD 235, 1984 [4] E. GABBA, Il generale dell'esercito romano nel I secolo a.C., in: M. SORDI (ed.), Guerra e diritto nel mondo greco e romano, 2002, 155–162 [5] J. GRUBER, Cicero und das hellenistische Herrscherideal, in: Wiener Studien 101, 1988, 244–258 [6] K.-P. JOHNE et al. (eds.), Die Zeit der Soldatenkaiser, 2008 [7] W. KAEGI, Byzantine Military Unrest, 471–843. An Interpretation, 1981 [8] A. KEAVENEY, The Army in the Roman Revolution, 2007 [9] A. LEWIN, Storia militare e cultura militare nei primi due secoli dell'Impero, in: L. TROIANI / G. ZECCHINI (eds.), La cultura storica nei primi due secoli dell'Impero Romano, 2005, 129–144 [10] C. PETROCELLI (ed.), Onasandro. Manuale per l'esercizio del comando, 2008 [11] E. WHEELER, The Hoplomachoi

and Vegetius' Spartan Drillmasters, in: Chiron 13, 1983, 1–20 [12] E. WHEELER, Sapiens and Stratagems. The Neglected Meaning of a Cognomen, in: Historia 37, 1988, 166–195 [13] E. WHEELER, The General as Hoplite, in: V. HANSON (ed.), Hoplites. The Classical Greek Battle Experience, 1991, 121–170 [14] E. WHEELER, The General's Métier. The Lists of 'Great Captains' and Criteria for Selection, in: C. WOLFF (ed.), Le métier de soldat dans le monde romain, 2012, 417–449

EVERETT L. WHEELER

Generals of note

A. Aëtius
B. Alexander
C. Caesar
D. Corbulo
E. Demetrius Poliorketes
F. Epaminondas
G. Hannibal
H. Julian
I. Cimon
J. Constantine
K. Marius
L. Marcus Aurelius
M. Philip of Macedon
N. Pompey
O. Scipio Africanus
P. Stilicho

A. AËTIUS

Flavius Aëtius was the supreme military commander in the Western Roman Empire (*magister utriusque militiae*) from 433 to 454. He was probably born at Durostorum in the early 390s, the son of a military man named Gaudentius and a wealthy Italic noblewoman (Iord. Get. 176). In his youth he served as a → hostage, with Alaric (before 408) and later with the Huns (Greg. Tur. Franc. 2,8). While a hostage, he learned the use of weapons and riding. Gaudentius was briefly *comes Africae* (the official in charge of Roman Africa; 399–401), but then seems to have fallen out of favour at court, as nothing further is heard of him or Aëtius until Iohannes Primicerius (423–425) seized the throne. While his father served as *magister militum* ('Master of Soldiers'), Aëtius now became *cura palatii* ('Manager of the Palace'). Iohannes faced conflicts on multiple fronts, including an uprising in Gaul that cost Gaudentius his life (*Chronica Gallica* 452, 100). There were also difficulties in Africa, where the emperor tried in vain to keep the *comes Africae* Bonifatius in check.

When the Eastern Empire attempted to restore Valentinian III in the west, Iohannes sent Aëtius to recruit Hun mercenaries (Greg. Tur. Franc. 2,8). Aëtius was successful, but his return to Ravenna came too late, three days after the Eastern Roman army had toppled Iohannes' government (425). He attacked the eastern army, but the sides were evenly matched. In a compromise Aëtius was given command as *comes* (*rei militaris* or *domesticorum*) in exchange for the dismissal of the Hun army (Philostorgius 12,14). From 425 onwards, Aëtius campaigned frequently against Goths and Franks in Gaul. He attained the rank of *magister militum per Gallias* in 429 (CIL VI 41389; Prosp. s.a. 429). In 430, he organized the assassination of the *magister utriusque militiae* Felix at Ravenna, while he remained in the field until 431, in Rhaetia and Noricum (Prosp. s.a. 430; Hydatius, *Chronica* 93–95).

The western imperial court was helpless, having already committed itself to a campaign against the invading Vandals in North Africa. Aëtius took Felix's command, and in 431 promptly returned to battle against the Franks in Gaul. By 432 the court recalled Bonifatius from North Africa and gave supreme command of the western army to him in place of Aëtius. The two warlords met at Rimini in the winter of 432/33. Aëtius was defeated. Bonifatius died of his wounds. Aëtius managed to flee to the Huns by way of Dalmatia. He then returned to Italy at the head of a Hun army and demanded his restoration as *magister utriusque militiae*. He held that position until his death in 454 (Prosp. s.a. 432, *Chronica Gallica* 452, 112). By 435, he had also acquired the title of *patricius* ('patrician'), at roughly the same time as a treaty was signed with the Vandals (*Annales Ravennates* s.a. 435).

Aëtius turned his military attention back towards Gaul in 436–437, and with the help of the Huns, he was able to destroy the First Kingdom of Burgundy at Worms (Merobaudes, *Panegyricus* 2,5–7). He also suppressed the activities of the *bagaudae* (a class of peasants) in the Loire region. War broke out with the Goths in Aquitania in 436 and lasted until 439. Aëtius' junior colleague Litorius succeeded in breaking the Gothic siege of Narbonne, but afterwards he suffered an ignominious defeat that resulted in the annihilation of Aëtius' Hun auxiliaries. Aëtius signed a treaty with the Goths in 439. That same year, the Vandals took Carthage (Sid. Apoll. Carm. 7,297–309).

The 440s were a peaceful decade, during which Aëtius settled Alans near Valence and in Armorica, and Burgundians in Sapaudia (*Chronica Gallica* 452, 124; 127f.). He returned to the battlefield in 448 to face the Franks of Belgica, defeating them in an ambush at Vicus Helena (Sid. Apoll. Carm. 5,210–218). After that, he adopted a Frankish prince as his son and comrade-in-arms (Priscus Frg. 16).

The greatest challenge of Aëtius' career came in 451, when Attila marched his army of Huns and assorted other tribes into Gaul. Aëtius succeeded in fielding an army of imperial troops and allies in Gaul. The Battle of the Catalaunian Fields (near

Troyes) was probably the largest land battle of the 5th century (Iord. Get. 197). Its outcome is unclear, but there were heavy losses on both sides, and Attila was forced to retreat for the first time. Attila then invaded Northern Italy in 452, and this time Aëtius was not in a position to organize an adequate defence (Prosp. s.a. 452). Aquileia and Milan were sacked. Attila finally withdrew after his army was weakened by disease and the Eastern Roman Emperor, Marcianus, invaded his home territories in Pannonia (Hydatius, *Chronica* 154). A rift later developed between Valentinian III and Aëtius, when the latter insisted on the marriage of their respective children (Prosp. s.a. 454). The emperor personally murdered Aëtius in the imperial palace at Rome towards the end of September 454 (John of Antioch, Frg. 201).

Like Stilicho and Constantius [III], Aëtius was one of a series of generals who dominated the court of the Western Roman Empire. Unlike them, however, he cemented his position by directly challenging the imperial court by force on several occasions. He was generally regarded as a successful commander, but his strategy of focusing on Gaul while neglecting North Africa placed a heavy financial burden on the Western Roman treasury. In calling Aëtius (along with Bonifatius) the 'last of the Romans', Procopius glossed over the harm done by Aëtius to the substance of the Western Roman state.

BIBLIOGRAPHY
[1] M.A. McEvoy, Child Emperor Rule in the Late Roman West, 2013 [2] T. Stickler, Aëtius, 2002 [3] J.W.P. Wijnendaele, Bonifatius, 2015 [4] J.W.P. Wijnendaele, The Early Career of Aëtius and the Murder of Felix, in: Historia 66, 2017, 468–482 [5] G. Zecchini, Aezio, 1983.

JEROEN WIJNENDAELE

B. Alexander
Alexander III ('the Great', 356–323 BC), son of Philip II and Olympias, ruled the Macedonians from 336 to 323 BC. Under his leadership, the Macedonian army destroyed the Persian Empire and conquered Western Asia as far as the Indus Valley. This established Alexander's renown during his lifetime and has been the foundation of his reputation ever since. Alexander received a military education from an early age, and played a significant role at the Battle of Chaeronea (Diod. Sic. 16,86,2f.; Plut. *Alexander* 9). However, he also received a philosophical education. Following his father's murder, he had to defend the throne against threats both internal and external. Unrest in Thrace and Greece was quelled – sometimes with great brutality – with the help of the army newly organized and superbly trained by Philip. Most rival claimants to the throne were killed.

Philip effectively laid the political and military groundwork for the attack on the Persian Empire. Due to its long duration and vast extent, this Asian campaign placed heavy demands on the leadership abilities of Philip's successor, Alexander, who took it over unhesitatingly. Great battles had to be won (Granicus 334 BC, Issus 333, Gaugamela 331, Hydaspes against Porus 326), guerrilla-style small battles had to be managed (especially in Bactria and Sogdiana 329–327), sieges needed to be overcome (Tyre and Gaza 332, fortresses in Bactria and India), naval battles had to be endured, and combined-arms combat needed to be organized. Alexander was resoundingly successful in performing these tasks thanks to his tactical flexibility, speed, charisma and personal courage. To secure legitimacy and followers, he systematically cultivated his image as a youthful hero who was the equal of Achilles (Diod. Sic. 17,17,3; 17,97,3; Plut. *Alexander* 15) and Heracles (e.g. Diod. Sic. 17,46,6; Arr. Anab. 2,18,1; 5,26,5), the son of Zeus-Ammon (visit to the Ammon oracle in 332: Arr. Anab. 3,3f.; Diod. Sic. 17,49,2–51,4; Plut. *Alexander* 26f.; Curt. 4,7,25; Iust. 11,11) and the successor to the Achaemenids as King of Asia (Gordium episode: Arr. Anab. 1,24,3–2,4,6; Plut. *Alexander* 18; Curt. 3,1,12–18; Iust. 11,7; negotiations with his opponent Darius III: Arr. Anab. 2,14f.; 2,25; cf. Curt. 4,5,1–9; Iust. 11,12). Alexander did not shrink from personal bravery on the front lines, and the sources repeatedly credit this as the decisive factor in major battles (cf. fig. 1). However, he paid for this approach to combat with frequent wounds, several of them serious (gravest of all during the siege of the citadel of the Mallians in the Indus Valley: Arr. Anab. 6,9,1–11,8; Diod. Sic. 17,98,4–99,4; Plut. *Alexander* 63; Curt. 9,4,30–5,20; Iust. 12,9). His competence as a *strategos* ('military commander'), however, is a source of disagreement. [9], like [8], considers him an irresponsible gambler, haphazardly stumbling from victory to victory, whereas [3] regards him as a unique military genius. More level-headed and probably more realistic assessments, such as those of [2] or [7], recognize great qualities in Alexander, especially in his tactical abilities, his compelling charisma and his ambitious drive (Greek *pothos*, 'longing'), combined with brutality, increasingly tyrannical behaviour and self-aggrandizement.

It is clear that the Macedonian army, which was recruited locally, was a fighting force without equal in its day, combining as it did heavy infantry – the phalanx armed with the *sarissa* long spear – with an offensive cavalry and a competent corps of engineers. Alexander could count on a highly experienced and well trained officer corps, drawn mainly from the Macedonian nobility. Individual officers repeatedly exercised independent commands to great effect. Despite enormous burdens, the army remained loyal except on two occa-

Fig. 1: *Alexander Mosaic* (2nd century BC). This floor mosaic from Pompeii, covering an area of almost 14 square metres and comparatively well preserved, is probably based on an early Hellenistic painting, and shows the turning point in one of the two battles Alexander fought against Darius III (Issus or Gaugamela). Alexander is portrayed as a dynamic, unflinching and decisive warrior seeking personally to turn the battle in his favor, while his cowardly and impotent adversary is turning to flee with no concern for his own losses. This depiction corresponds to the clichés attached to both men in the Greek (and Roman) public sphere. A small army of courageous, free soldiers with a charismatic leader takes on a gigantic army led by a general of mediocre abilities. This reading of the image is underscored by the detail that Alexander is fighting without a helmet or other head protection, while the protective armour worn by Darius and his soldiers is no help to them against Alexander's attack. The two protagonists here embody a commonplace view of the relationship between Greeks and barbarians that became still more entrenched as a result of Alexander's campaign: courage and forward-driving self-confidence on the one hand, timidity and moral cowardice on the other. This has no basis in history.

sions: the mutiny on the Hyphasis in 326 and the mutiny at Opis in 324. Part of the reason for this loyalty was that Alexander allowed his soldiers a generous share of the booty that was won during the campaign. The loyalty of this fighting force and their readiness to follow their auspicious king almost anywhere were crucial factors behind the campaign's success. Even so, there were several intrigues and conspiracies that took place for various reasons, mainly among the nobles, particularly during hostilities in Bactria and Sogdiana. Alexander acted against these, sometimes viciously.

Alexander died in June 323 without a succession plan. Conflicts broke out among the *hetairoi* (the noble class), all of whom sought power, wealth and honour. In the course of these events, Alexander became the consummate military, propagandistic and political model for the Diadochi ('Successors'), the Hellenistic kings and, later, certain Roman Emperors.

☞ Wars of note, A. Campaign of Alexander; Mutiny

BIBLIOGRAPHY
[1] A.B. BOSWORTH, Alexander and the East, 1998 [2] H.-J. GEHRKE, Alexander der Große, ^{6}2013 [3] N.G. HAMMOND, The Genius of Alexander the Great, 1997 [4] W. HECKEL, The Conquests of Alexander the Great, ^{2}2012 [5] R. LANE FOX, Alexander the Great, 2004 [6] J. ROISMAN (ed.), Brill's Companion to Alexander the Great, 2003 [7] H.-U. WIEMER, Alexander der Große, ^{2}2015 [8] W. WILL, Alexander der Große, 1986 [9] G. WIRTH, Alexander der Große, ^{9}1995.

LEONHARD BURCKHARDT

C. CAESAR
Ever since Antiquity, Gaius Iulius Caesar has been regarded as an exceptional general and often compared with Alexander the Great, as he was by Appian (Civ. 2,149–154) and above all Plutarch, who paired him with the Macedonian in his *Parallel Lives*. For Plutarch, Caesar outshone not only the great Roman commanders of the past (Fabius Maximus, Scipio Africanus, Scipio Aemilianus, Metellus), but also those of his own time (Sulla, Marius, Lucullus, Pompey) (Plut. *Caesar* 15,3f.). This remarkable assessment in one of our main sources on Caesar concurs with the distinctive praise reserved for him by other authors of the Imperial period (Vell. Pat. 2,47; Plin. HN 7,25; 7,27; Suet. Iul. 55,1; App. Civ. 2,149).

The image of Caesar as the Roman general *par excellent* has been a correspondingly powerful influence on modern historiography. Yet this reputation is based above all upon the authority accorded to Caesar's own *commentarii* on the *Bellum Gallicum* and *Bellum civile*, both of which have been much read and admired since the end of the Middle Ages [13]; [8]. A revision of this traditional exaltation of Caesar's military genius has, however, been observable for some years. A number of more recent works endeavour to show that the military culture and practice of Caesar were well within the bounds of normality for his time [7]; [6]; [2].

Born into a patrician family, Caesar – like the other Roman autocrats – received in the course of his schooling a military education based on the reading of relevant military literature, intensive physical training and actual military service, which he performed in 81 BC in Asia as *contubernalis* ('tent comrade') of the praetor Marcus Minucius Thermus (Suet. Iul. 2), and briefly in 78 BC under the command of P. Servilius Vatias on Sicily (Suet. Iul. 3,1). Even at this stage, he was already distinguishing himself with his fighting spirit, which won him the *corona civica* ('Civic Crown') at the siege of Mytilene in 81 (Suet. Iul. 2). He was also demonstrating clarity of decision-making, as when he carried out retribution against pirates who had taken him prisoner around 75 BC (Suet. Iul. 4; 74; Plut. *Caesar* 2,5–7), and when shortly afterwards he boldly – as a private citizen – recruited auxiliaries in the province of Asia to stop the incursion of Mithridates' troops (Suet. Iul. 4,2). Caesar was thus able in the course of these years of apprenticeship to acquaint himself with various aspects of Roman warfare (combat on land and sea, sieges).

He was elected military tribune for the year 72 (Suet. Iul. 5; Plut. *Caesar* 5,1), although we do not know whether he took part in operations in Italy against Spartacus. In 61, as propraetor of Hispania ulterior, he led the victorious operations against the Callaeci (Suet. Iul. 18 and 54; Plut. *Caesar* 12,1). In the wake of this victory, his soldiers acclaimed him as *imperator* (Plut. *Caesar* 12,4), and he considered demanding a triumph, but he ultimatley decided against this, so that he could take part in the consular elections for the year 59. Contrary to a view sometimes held in modern times, it was Caesar's incontestable and varied experience that enabled him as proconsul of Illyria and Gallia (cisalpina and transalpina) to embark in the spring of 58 on the series of campaigns for which he is best known. After concluding these in 51, he resumed them from January 49 to March 45 in an almost unbroken sequence of campaigns during the Civil War. From this point, the career and image of Caesar become that of a victorious, almost invincible general, to the point where authors ancient (Plut. *Caesar* 15,2) and modern [10] sometimes suggest that the experience gained during his extensive and lengthy proconsulate in Gaul marked a watershed that renders the superiority of Caesar's forces in the Civil Wars explicable. On the tactical and above all strategic levels, however, historians today downplay Caesar's originality and portray him as merely innovative [11].

Considered alongside the Roman generals to whom historians have often sought to compare him, Caesar exhibits a distinctiveness that derives primarily from other factors. First, his deeds are recorded in more detail in the sources – beginning with his own account, which generally portrays him as a genius who was idolized by his troops [4]; [5]. Second, unlike Lucullus, who was relieved of his command against Mithridates, Crassus, who lost his life at Carrhae, and Pompey, who was put to flight in defeat at Pharsalus, Caesar was always associated with the winning side, even though he often faced difficulties. When Suetonius or Appian look back on Caesar's military accomplishments as a general, they insist that his few defeats were not his fault, but should be attributed to unfavourable circumstances or errors by his legates and soldiers (Caes. B Gall. 1,22; Suet. Iul. 25; 36; App. Civ. 2,150). It is this tendency in our sources above all that gives Caesar – one of the most capable generals of his era – the aura of exceptionality that is still associated with his name to this day.

BIBLIOGRAPHY
[1] E. BALTRUSCH, Caesar und Pompeius, 2004   [2] G. BRIZZI, Eloquentia militarique aut aequavit praestantissimorum gloriam aut excessit (Suet. Caes. 55). Cesare soldato. Strategia e imagine, in: G. URSO (ed.), Cesare. Precursore o visionario? Atti del convegno internazionale Cividale del Friuli, 17–19 settembre 2009, 2010, 85–103   [3] M. GELZER, Caesar. Der Politiker und Staatsmann, 2008 (reprint of the 1983 edition)   [4] A.K. GOLDSWORTHY, 'Instinctive Genius'. The Depiction of Caesar the General, in: K. WELCH / A. POWELL (eds.), Julius Caesar as Artful Reporter. The War Commentaries as Political Instruments, 1998, 193–219   [5] A.K. GOLDSWORTHY, Nostri – Caesar, the Commentaries and Understanding the Roman Army, in: A. MORENO HERNÁNDEZ, Julio César. Textos, contextos y recepción. De la Roma clásica al mundo actual, 2010, 45–59   [6] Y. LE BOHEC, César, chef de guerre, 2001   [7] L. LORETO, Pensare la guerra in Cesare, in: D. POLI (ed.), La cultura in Cesare. Atti del convegno internazionale di studi (Macerata-Matelica, 30 aprile–4 maggio 1990), 1993, 239–343   [8] M. MCLAUGHLIN, Empire, Eloquence, and Miliatry Genius. Renaissance Italy, in: M. GRIFFIN (ed.), A Companion to Julius Caesar, 2009, 335–355   [9] C. MEIER, Caesar, 1982 (reprinted 2018)   [10] D. POTTER, Caesar and the Helvetians, in: G.C. FAGAN / M. TRUNDLE (eds.), New Perspectives on Ancient Warfare, 2010, 305–329   [11] N. ROSENSTEIN, General and Imperialist, in: M. GRIFFIN (ed.), A Companion to Julius Caesar, 2009, 85–99   [12] W. WILL, Caesar, 2009   [13] J. WINTJES, From 'Capitano' to 'Great Commander'. The Military Reception of Caesar from the Sixteenth to the Twentieth Centuries, in: M. WYKE (ed.), Julius Caesar in Western Culture, 2006, 269–284.

FRANÇOIS CADIOU

D. Corbulo

Corbulo (Cn. Domitius Corbulo; d. AD 66 or 67) was a Roman senator chiefly known for his command in Nero's Armenian war. Tacitus portrays him as the model of a Roman general. This portrayal and the detailed reports of his deeds (Tac. Ann. 12,44,1–51,4; 13,6,1–9,3; 13,34,2–41,4; 14,23,1–26,2; 15,1,1–18,3; 15,24,1–31; Cass. Dio 62,19,1–23,5; 63,1,2–7,2) offer an exemplary view of the conditions in which army leaders of the early and high Imperial period operated.

Under the Principate, supreme command of all troops lay with the emperor, but local command (generally associated with provincial governorships) was delegated to high-ranking senators. They functioned as *legati Augusti pro praetore* ('legates of the empror, acting on behlf of the praeter'): they were bound by instructions, subject to recall at any time and generally replaced after a few years. However, because they were deployed far from Rome, they often had to act independently.

Corbulo came from a many-branched senatorial family and completed a long career as a senator, which led him to the consulship (c. AD 39). This at last made senior command positions available to him. Under Claudius, he received the regular command of the army district of Germania inferior. His harsh measures there provoked the Chatti to war. Claudius recalled him with honour in AD 47 (he received the *ornamenta triumphalia*), whereupon the Chatti laid down their arms. The *quondam duces* ('commanders of old'), however, are said to have praised Corbulo warmly (Tac. Ann. 11,20,1; Cass. Dio 61,30,5 – i.e. the generals of the republic, who were able to act with much more discretion). It was part of the senatorial canon of values to demonstrate *virtus* ('vigour'), and many commanders complained that the emperor would rein them in purely out of jealousy at their successes. In fact, he legitimized himself through his supposedly outstanding *virtus*. Yet, senatorial ambition easily led to unnecessary wars that could spin out of the emperor's control. Moreover, if the soldiers transferred their obedience from the emperor to a successful commander, the empire might quickly be threatened with civil war. Internal stability demanded strict supervision of able commanders.

Late in AD 54, Corbulo received a major, extraordinary command in the east, after a conflict with the Parthians over Armenia had gone awry. The new and still young emperor Nero clearly needed successes. Corbulo proceeded with caution – large-scale losses would not have been easy to replace. Thanks to rigorous discipline and the technical brilliance of the Roman army, he was able to drive the Parthians out of Armenia by AD 59. However, the peace terms dictated from Rome proved to be a failure, so the war continued.

During this war, Corbulo and the legate of Syria, C. Ummidius Durmius Quadratus, pursued different plans, which led to disputes between them. The same happened when Corbulo himself became legate of Syria, with Cn. Caesennius Paetus in charge of operations. Lack of coordination was a major factor in Paetus' serious defeat in AD 62. This arose because all commanders were of equal rank, answerable to the emperor alone, so that no overall regional command was established. While this reduced the emperor's risk of being overthrown through misuse of the military command structures, it hampered efficiency. The emperor could have resolved the situation by taking the field in person and coordinating operations, as would often happen later. Nero, however, was not ready for this.

Not until AD 63 did Corbulo receive an enlarged command with access to all the resources of the eastern part of the empire, and this enabled him to impose a peace settlement on the Parthians that satisfied Nero's wishes. He retained command until the peace terms were implemented.

Corbulo's destiny now depended on whatever political role he might be able to play using his army. By the time of the Pisonian Conspiracy (AD 65) if not before, Nero's regime was under threat. There was a clear expectation that Corbulo would attempt a coup with the help of his troops. Nero thought he had to preempt an uprising. He therefore summoned Corbulo and forced him – isolated from his troops – to commit suicide. The regime of Nero collapsed shortly afterwards in spite of – or because of – such excessively harsh actions against Corbulo and other generals.

Corbulo's memory was long honoured. Yet, he never came to be regarded as one of the greatest generals of Antiquity. Nor, indeed, did any other commanders of the Imperial period. None of them was able to make major independent decisions, for they had to operate within a system that strictly limited their opportunities for individual distinction. But this may have been one of the main factors that gave the empire its stability and endurance.

Bibliography

Sources
[1] PIR,² D 141 (E. Groag).

Secondary literature
[2] M. Heil, Die orientalische Außenpolitik des Kaisers Nero, 1997 [3] R. Syme, Domitius Corbulo, in: JRS 60, 1970, 27–39 [4] F.J. Vervaet, Domitius Corbulo and the Senatorial Opposition to Nero, in: AncSoc 32, 2002, 135–193 [5] F.J. Vervaet, Domitius Corbulo and the Rise of the Flavian Dynasty, in: Historia 52, 2003, 436–464.

MATTHÄUS HEIL

E. Demetrius Poliorketes

Demetrius I Poliorketes (c. 336–283/82 BC) was a key figure in the Wars of the Diadochi. Of all the Diadochi, his rule best illustrates the territorial instability of early Hellenistic monarchies and the importance of military prowess.

As the elder son of the Diadoch Antigonus I Monophthalmos, Demetrius was soon a linchpin of his father's rule. He married the much older Phila in about 320 BC to cement the alliance with her father Antipater. From 314 onwards, Demetrius chiefly appears as a general. Resoundingly defeated at the hands of Ptolemy at Gaza (312), he made a name for himself as an army commander in the years that followed. His military successes culminated in a naval victory over the Ptolemaic fleet at Salamis on Cyprus (306) and the conquest of the strategically important island [6]. Spurred on by this triumph, Antigonus and Demetrius became the first of the Diadochi to adopt the title of king (Diod. Sic. 20,53; Plut. *Demetrius* 17f.). They then moved against Rhodes, which was sympathetic towards Ptolemy. Demetrius' siege of Rhodes (305–304) made a great impression. Diodorus Siculus (20,81–88; 20,91–100) stresses his energetic fighting, particularly his technological innovations. Demetrius placed siege engines and artillery pieces on ships in order to attack from the sea. The *helepolis*, a gigantic siege tower, is described as a technological marvel (Diod. Sic. 20,91f.; Plut. *Demetrius* 20). These new siege engines won Demetrius the byname *Poliorketes* ('Besieger of Cities'), although it is disputed how new they truly were. What certainly was new was the idealized image of a king who excelled through his knowledge of military technology [4]. Rhodes, however, could not be taken, and Demetrius agreed to peace terms so that he could transfer his military activities to Greece, where he succeeded over the ensuing years in establishing a hegemony.

The key turning point in Demetrius' life was the Battle of Ipsus (301), at which the Antigonids were overcome by a coalition of the other Diadochi. Antigonus fell, but Demetrius escaped. He still had a powerful fleet, but he had lost almost all his territorial possessions. As a king without a kingdom, he embarked on feverish activity. Naval operations against Lysimachus kept his troops happy until the loose coalition of the Diadochi fell apart and he succeeded in engineering an alliance with Seleucus and establishing himself in Cilicia. Coins from this period indicate his claims to mastery of the seas and victoriousness in battle (despite Ipsus). It is even possible, according to one particularly controversial theory, that the Winged Victory (Nike) of Samothrace was a victory monument of Demetrius, thus forming part of his pictorial programme [1].

Fig. 2: Gold stater of Demetrius Poliorketes (probably from Euboea, after c. 290 BC; 8.56g; diameter: 18mm). The obverse shows Demetrius with diadem and bull horns, while the inscription ΔΗΜΗΤΡΙΟΥ ΒΑΣΙΛΕΩΣ ('of King Demetrius') on the reverse frames a rider with lance and wearing a causia that identifies him as a Macedonian.

Following the death of Cassander (297), Demetrius shifted his activities westward, taking Athens and reestablishing a hegemony over Greece. Called to help in disputes over succession among the sons of Cassander, Demetrius had Alexander V murdered and himself proclaimed king by the Macedonian army (294) – not least because he was related to the royal house through Phila. The gain of Macedonia, however, was offset by the loss of most of the eastern possessions. A hymn from Athens (Duris of Samos FGrH 76 F 13 from Ath. 6,253D–F), one of the most important testimonies to the Hellenistic ruler cult, also dates from this period, having been composed about 291/90 [2]. It praises Demetrius as a god and calls for military action against the Aetolians (cf. fig. 2 on Demetrius as king of Macedonia).

Demetrius was not satisfied with what he had achieved. He ordered an enormous armament programme, once more emphasizing innovations in military technology. Of special note were his ships with sixteen rows of oarsmen (Plut. *Demetrius* 43). Unsettled by his rearmament, the other Diadochi allied against Demetrius. When Demetrius fell seriously ill and Pyrrhus invaded Macedonia, much of the army deserted. Demetrius left his son Antigonus II Gonatas behind in Europe and crossed into Asia Minor with the remainder of his forces. After initial successes, the position became increasingly precarious. Already under military pressure, the army had to contend with supply shortages and sickness. Demetrius moved on to Cilicia, but with little success. He fell ill, and parts of his demoralized army defected to Seleucus. Demetrius was forced to surrender into Seleucid captivity (285), where he died a few years later, probably around 282 [5].

Bibliography

[1] J.C. Bernhardt, Das Nikemonument von Samothrake und der Kampf der Bilder, 2014 [2] A. Chaniotis, The Ithyphallic Hymn for Demetrios Poliorketes and

Hellenistic Religious Mentality, in: P.P. IOSSIF et al. (eds.), More than Men, Less than Gods. Studies on Royal Cult and Imperial Worship, 2011, 157–195 [3] E. MANNI, Demetrio Poliorcete, 1951 [4] I. PIMOUGUET-PÉDARROS, La Cité à l'épreuve des rois. Le siège de Rhodes par Démétrios Poliorcète (305–304 av. J.-C.), 2011 [5] P. WHEATLEY, The Lifespan of Demetrius Poliorcetes, in: Historia 46, 1997, 19–27 [6] P. WHEATLEY, The Antigonid Campaign in Cyprus, 306 BC, in: Ancient Society 31, 2001, 133–156.

JAN B. MEISTER

F. EPAMINONDAS

The Theban Epaminondas (d. 362 BC) performed important military and political functions, and helped his home *polis* briefly attain the leading position in Greece (Theban Hegemony, 371–362 BC). The year of his birth is not known. He seems to have come from a noble but not altogether wealthy background, and to have enjoyed a good education (Diod. Sic. 15,39,2; Plut. *Pelopidas* 3; Paus. 9,13,1; Nep. Epam. 2,1). Probably his first political appearance was as spokesman for the Thebans at the peace negotiations of 375/74 (Diod. Sic. 15,38,3, partly related to the peace of 371; see [9.57–64]), where he vehemently defended the hegemony of his *polis* over Boeotia. In 371, a similar assembly led to the isolation of Thebes at the peace congress in Sparta (Plut. *Agesilaus* 27f.), which denied Thebes admission to the Common Peace because of Thebes' refusal to accept the autonomy clause. Here too, Epaminondas, who is said to have possessed great gifts of rhetoric, supposedly played a key role (Diod. Sic. 15,55,1–4; Nep. Epam. 6,4; Paus. 9,13,2). The ensuing invasion of Boeotia by Sparta and its allies under King Cleombrotus led to the Battle of Leuctra, which gave rise to certain innovations on the part of the victorious Thebans.

Although Epaminondas was only one of seven Boeotarchs of the confederacy, history assigns him a leading role in the Theban military effort, and in particular gives him credit for victory in the battle (Din. 72f.; Diod. Sic. 15,39,2; 55,1–56,3; Paus. 9,13,6–14,1; Plut. *Pelopidas* 23; Nep. Epam. 8,3; cf. Tod 2, no. 130; Plut. Mor. 542b-c; Frontin. Str. 4,2,6; Polyaenus, Strat. 2,3,2). Besides the superiority of the Boeotian cavalry, whose attack at the beginning of the battle threw the Spartan ranks into disarray (Xen. Hell. 6,4,11–13; cf. Frontinus, Strat. 2,2,12), their victory was chiefly due to the reinforcements given to the left wing of the Theban phalanx and an energetic advance on the enemy's royal wing by the Sacred Band led by Pelopidas (Xen. Hell. 6,4,11–13; Diod. Sic. 15,55,2–4; Plut. *Pelopidas* 23; [1.193–220]; [6.55–69]; [7.260–263]). This hitherto unfamiliar formation later became known as the oblique order (*loxe phalanx*; Arr. Tact. 26,3; Ascl. 10,21). Epaminondas used this formation to maximize the resources of the numerically inferior Boeotian troops, employing a rapid, powerful attack to put severe pressure on the best units of the enemy forces (cf. Polyaenus, Strat. 2,3,15). With the loss of 1,000 Lacedaemonians – including Cleombrotus and 400 Spartiates – (Xen. Hell. 6,4,15; Plut. *Agesilaus* 28), and with the confidence of its allies waning, Sparta forfeited its hegemony in Greece.

In the course of several campaigns commanded by Epaminondas over the following years on the Peloponnese, Thebes succeeded in separating Messene from the Spartan federation, weakening the Peloponnesian League and strengthening Sparta's enemies. However, several attacks on Sparta itself failed (Xen. Hell. 7 pass.; Din. 73; Pol. 9,8; Diod. Sic. 15,62,3f.; 65f.; Plut. *Pelopidas* 24; Plut. *Agesilaus* 30f.; 34; [6.70–109]; [10]). Thebes' success was based in part on the quality of the Boeotian hoplites, who were well-schooled through many conflicts with Sparta (anecdotal: Plut. *Agesilaus* 26), but also on the effectiveness of their alliance policies and the leadership capabilities of Epaminondas. When he was prosecuted for extending his command beyond the year's end after the first campaign on the Peloponnese in 370 BC, he won the trial by invoking his military successes (Paus. 9,14,4–7; App. Syr. 212–218; Plut. *Pelopidas* 24f.; Plut. Mor. 194a–b; 540d–f; Ael. VH 13,42; Nep. Epam. 7,3–8,5; [2.75–111]; [5]).

His domestic political position was thus not unchallenged, but his prestige was so great that he continued usually to be elected Boeotarch. Epaminondas is portrayed as the driving force behind Thebes' quest for hegemony, although according to [3] this only developed gradually after Leuctra. He fell at the Battle of Mantinea (Xen. Hell. 7,5,18–25; Diod. Sic. 15,82–88; Paus. 9,15,4f.; Plut. *Agesilaus* 35; Nep. Epam. 9,1–4), which in itself went according to plan and brought a Boeotian victory. Even so, the death of Epaminondas marked the end of the Theban hegemony. Xenophon (Hell. 7,5,18–21) portrays Epaminondas as a gifted but overly ambitious soldier concerned with cementing his legacy [4.259–265], while Diorodus Siculus (15,88,1–4) sees him as the outstanding man of his generation who combined in himself 'all the virtues'. Certainly, the charismatic Epaminondas had a gift for identifying the strengths and weaknesses of friend and foe alike, deploying his forces wisely and not shying away from unconventional solutions [8]. He could do nothing, however, to eliminate the main flaw in Theban policy: the degree to which expansion depended personally on him.

☞ Sparta

BIBLIOGRAPHY

[1] J.K. ANDERSON, Military Theory and Practice in the Age of Xenophon, 1970 [2] H. BEISTER, Untersuchungen zu der Zeit der thebanischen Hegemonie, 1970

[3] H. Beister, Hegemoniales Denken in Theben, in: H. Beister / J. Buckler (eds.), Boiotika, 1989, 131–153 [4] S. Brown Ferrario, Historical Agency and the 'Great Man' in Classical Greece, 2014 [5] J. Buckler, Plutarch on the Trials of Pelopidas and Epameinondas (369 BC), in: CPh 73, 1978, 36–42 [6] J. Buckler, The Theban Hegemony, 371–362 BC, 1980 [7] G.L. Cawkwell, Epaminondas and Thebes, in: CQ 22, 1972, 254–278 [8] V.D. Hanson, Epaminondas the Theban and the Doctrine of Preemptive War, in: V.D. Hanson (ed.), Makers of Ancient Strategy, 2010, 93–117 [9] M. Jehne, Koine eirene, 1994 [10] J. Roy, Thebes in the 360s BC, in: CAH 6, ³1994, 187–208.

LEONHARD BURCKHARDT

G. Hannibal

Hannibal (247/46–183 BC), son of Hamilcar Barcas (ca. 270–229), took over the Carthaginian command in Iberia in 221. His action there against Saguntum provoked the Romans to military intervention against the resurgent Carthage in 218. His ensuing march across the Alps into Italy, and his series of victories in Italy lasting until 216 established Hannibal's fame as a military genius. After 216, Rome's delaying strategy in Italy and successes outside Italy put him increasingly on the defensive. A Roman invasion forced Hannibal to return home, where he was defeated at Zama by P. Cornelius Scipio in 202. As suffete (a chief administrative position in Carthage) in 196, Hannibal's energetic reforms earned him influential enemies. In Rome he was accused of conspiring with Antiochus III. In 195, Hannibal fled from a Roman investigative commission, going to the court of the Seleucid king. Following the latter's defeat by Rome, Hannibal went in 189/88 via Armenia to Prusias I of Bithynia, who in 183 suffered defeat at the hands of Rome's ally Eumenes II of Pergamum. Facing a hopeless situation, Hannibal escaped the extradition demanded by Rome through suicide [3].

Our view of Hannibal is distorted beyond recognition by Roman and Roman-influenced reporting. This is true of the suspect oath 'never to be a friend to the Romans', which the nine-year-old Hannibal's father supposedly made him swear (Pol. 3,11,5–7). It is also true of the claim that Hannibal was pursuing conflict on his own initiative against the will of the Carthaginian leadership (Pol. 3,8) – a claim that Fabius Pictor was clearly using to mask Rome's provocation of the Saguntum crisis. It extends likewise to the downright demonization of the enemy in the annalistic tradition, to the point of accusing him of cannibalism (Liv. 21,4,9; 23,5,11–13). At the same time, the distortion also includes the assessment of Hannibal as an exceptional military talent, which quite clearly was meant to explain Rome's defeats and add lustre to its victory [2]: only the best could successed in forcing Rome to the edge of the abyss, but even the best – according to this interpreted view of history – failed in the end because of the superior *virtutes* of the Romans.

When attempting to reconstruct the historical Hannibal, therefore, we must rely on an assessment of the historical event. The idea of confronting the enemy in their own country was not new, and in view of Roman maritime supremacy, there was probably no alternative to the land march. Still, crossing the Alps in order to join up with the Celts of Northern Italy to pursue further action was anything but conventional. Besides charisma, this demanded extraordinary organizational and logistical abilities. It compelled the Roman leadership to abandon for a time the idea of invading Africa. At the River Trebia (218), at Lake Trasimene (217) and at Cannae (216), Hannibal proved himself to be an original planner of battles, who repeatedly demonstrated the ability to outmanoeuvre superior enemy armies by skilful exploitation of terrain, the strengths of his own forces and the personal weaknesses of his opponents. On the evening after Cannae, Rome seemed to have been thoroughly defeated, but Hannibal rejected the idea of attacking the city, recognizing his limited capacities to impose a siege [9]. Instead, he tried to establish strategic alliances (Philip V, Hieronymus) and attract Italic allies (Capua, Tarentum). But he could find no way of luring the Romans, who had learned from the damaged they suffered, back to the battlefield. Nor could he undermine the loyalty of the *socii* of Central Italy to Rome. Thus it was that time, Roman successes in other theatres, and bad luck (as in Hasdrubal's failed attempt to reinforce Hannibal in 208/07) worked against Hannibal.

Even if Hannibal's genius and tragic failure are in large part a product of Roman self-portrayal, his extraordinary tactical gifts are beyond dispute. His battles, especially Cannae, have continued to be models for instruction into the modern age (Schlieffen Plan). One may also see him as a kind of personification of what did not happen – a development of the ancient world without an all-conquering Rome – and as an example of how a failure to achieve world-changing success can sometimes earn one a place among the 'greatest of all'.

☞ Generals of note, O. Scipio Africanus; Wars of note, K. Punic Wars

Bibliography
[1] G. Brizzi, Carthage and Hannibal in Roman and Greek Memory, in: D. Hoyos (ed.), A Companion to the Punic Wars, 2011, 483–498 [2] M.P. Fronda, Hannibal. Tactics, Strategy, and Geostrategy, in: D. Hoyos (ed.), A Companion to the Punic Wars, 2011, 242–259 [3] L.-M. Günther, Hannibal [4], in: BNP 5, 2004, 1127–1129 [4] D. Hoyos, Hannibal. Rome's Greatest Enemy, 2008 [5] E.

MacDonald, Hannibal. A Hellenistic Life, 2015 [6] J. Seibert, Forschungen zu Hannibal, 1993 [7] J. Seibert, Hannibal, 1993 [8] B.S. Strauss, Masters of Command – Alexander, Hannibal, Caesar, and the Genius of Leadership, 2012 [9] K. Zimmermann, Hannibal ante portas. Warum verzichtete Hannibal 216 v.Chr. auf den Marsch auf Rom?, in: K. Brodersen (ed.), Vincere Scis, Victoria Uti Nescis. Aspekte der Rückschauverzerrung in der Alten Geschichte, 2008, 49–60 [10] K. Zimmermann, Interpretatio als Mittel der Auseinandersetzung im Zweiten Punischen Krieg, in: L.-M. Günther / B. Morstadt (eds.), Phönizische, griechische und römische Gottheiten im historischen Wandel, 2015, 31–46.

KLAUS ZIMMERMANN

H. Julian
Flavius Claudius Julianus (331/32–363), the last emperor (361–363) of the Constantinian dynasty, was an army commander, theosopher and man of letters. He became renowned as the last non-Christian Roman emperor, called 'the Apostate'. His return to paganism formed part of a reformist agenda that aimed to restore the greatness of Rome by reviving old virtues. This also found expression in his actions as a military leader. The key sources on his role as a general were written by friends or admirers, especially Libanius, Ammianus Marcellinus and Eunapius, and therefore portray him sympathetically as a hero emperor.

Julian, who grew up in isolation in the eastern part of the empire, spent the early 350s studying Neo-Platonist philosophy. In 355, his cousin, Constantius II (337–361), awarded him the rank of a *Caesar* and appointed him his representative in Gaul. Given that Julian had no experience in warfare or public life, and was unfamiliar with the west, it seems likely that Constantius' plan was to place him as a dynastic figurehead in provinces that had recently been plagued by usurpation and barbarian raids. Over the ensuing five years (356–361), Julian commanded successful operations in eastern Gaul, mainly against the Alamanni, but also against the Franks, to secure the border and assert Roman control over the Rhine Valley (Julian. Ep. ad Ath. 277–280; Lib. Or. 18,31–90; Amm. Marc. 16,2–4; 16,7,1–3; 16,11f.; 17,1–3; 17,8–10; 18,2; Zos. 3,1,2–7,8). His most notable victory came over an alliance of Alamannic kings near Argentoratum (Strasbourg) in AD 357 (Lib. Or. 18,52–67; Amm. Marc. 16,12; Zos. 3,3,3–5). A series of punitive expeditions across the Rhine was intended to recapture Roman spheres of influence, subjugate tribal groups through terror and secure natural resources. Julian's rapid transformation from arcane scholar to victorious general raises difficult historical questions. In his early campaigns (356–357), he was guided by experienced officers and played only a minor role within a more comprehensive strategy driven by Constantius or his generals (Julian. Ep. ad Ath. 277D–278A; Lib. Or. 18,42f.; Eunap. fr. 16,2; Zos. 3,2,2). Sources sympathetic to Julian exaggerate his role and successes, and blame colleagues, subordinates and extraordinary circumstances for tactical errors. Ammianus in particular attempts to provide Julian with a military résumé in Gaul to compare with that of Julius Caesar. While his aggressive warfare did strengthen his political position, it is doubtful whether his victories made any special or lasting contribution to bringing peace to the border.

Responding to reports that Constantius had ordered their transfer to the east, Gaulish units mutinied early in AD 360 and acclaimed Julian as *Augustus*. Any underlying conspiracies here remain obscure. Julian embarked on a civil war with Constantius early in 361 and led a force down the Danube to occupy Illyria. After some initial skirmishing, Constantius' death in November obviated further bloodshed and handed Julian absolute power. Early in 363, following elaborate preparations, he set off for a major campaign against the Sassanid Empire. His objectives remain unknown, but would obviously have included weakening the Persians' offensive power and enhancing his imperial prestige with a triumph in the east. Julian's rapid advance along the Euphrates accompanied by a fleet met with little resistance, but the flooded terrain and heat in southern Mesopotamia slowed his progress. Although he succeeded in defeating a Persian force outside Ctesiphon, Julian failed to take the city and apparently lacked an alternative strategy. The Persians' scorched earth tactic forced the Roman army to retreat up the Tigris. Persian attacks on the rear and flanks of the Roman army intensified, and Julian was fatally wounded in a skirmish on June 26. His successor, Jovian, withdrew the army under humiliating conditions (Lib. Or. 18,213–276; Amm. Marc. 23,2–25,7; Zos. 3,12–33).

Julian's military leadership was more successful in the west, when he was conducting operations with a clear purpose against tribal groups near the border. The cohesion, resources and technology of the Sassanid Empire presented a far greater strategic challenge, and Julian's great offensive was hampered by the Persians' tactical retreats, the harsh environmental conditions and logistical difficulties. Julian was a controversial figure, both during his lifetime and after his death. His character, motivations and achievements were received with striking partiality whether for or against. Although his real actions are difficult to separate out from the literary depictions of him, it seems that his education and temperament led him to embrace a mission of imperial renewal and a romantic vision of conquest in which he emulated Alexander or Trajan. Even taking into account the panegyric tone of some of the sources, it seems fair to say that Julian's military career was marked by a personal willingness to put himself in danger (e.g. Amm. Marc. 24,2,14–17; 24,4,3–5; 24,5,6; 24,5,11; Zos. 3,20,2f.; 3,27,2), to intervene decisively in events (Lib. Or. 18,56–59; Amm. Marc. 16,12,38–41; 24,6,4–6) and to enforce discipline (Amm. Marc. 24,3,2; 24,5,10; 25,1,7–9; Zos. 3,3,4f.; 3,19,2) – all expressions of a personal regard for leadership that was conscious of tradition.

☞ Wars of note, I. Julian's Persian War

BIBLIOGRAPHY
[1] J.F. DRINKWATER, The Alamanni and Rome 213–496 (Caracalla to Clovis), 2007 [2] T. GNOLI, Le guerre di Giuliano imperatore, 2015 [3] D. HUNT, Julian, in: CAH 13, 1998, 44–77 [4] G. KELLY, Ammianus Marcellinus. The Allusive Historian, 2008 [5] R. KLEIN (ed.), Julian Apostata, 1978 [6] O. LAGACHERIE, Libanios et Ammien Marcellin. Les moyens de l'héroïsation de l'empereur Julien, in: REG 115, no. 2, 2002, 792–802 [7] S. LORENZ, Imperii fines erunt intacti. Rom und die Alamannen 350–378, 1997 [8] M. MARCOS, A Tale of Two Commanders. Ammianus Marcellinus on the Campaigns of Constantius II and Julian on the Northern Frontiers, in: AJPh 136, no. 4, 2015, 669–708 [9] K. ROSEN, Julian. Kaiser, Gott und Christenhasser, 2006.

PHILIP RANCE

I. CIMON

Historically speaking, Cimon (c. 510–450 BC) was an exponent of the dynamic expansion of Athens in the first two centuries after the foundation of the Delian League. In terms of the organization of the Athenian *polis*, he espoused the unity of political and military leadership that would be practised until the time of the Peloponnesian War. His career illustrates the range of opportunities that were available to Athenian aristocrats in the democracy of the 5th century, but also how precarious their leading position was if they lost the confidence of the *demos*. In later tradition, Cimon was falsely made an exponent of a 'conservative', pro-Spartan, anti-democratic political line [5].

As the son of the victor at Marathon, Miltiades, and a Thracian princess, and as the husband of an Alcmaeonid, Cimon by birth found himself in the circles of the late Archaic aristocracy. Yet, he fought bravely as a fleet soldier at Salamis (Plut. *Cimon* 5,2–4). Cimon, along with Aristides, played a key role in the hegemonic shift at Byzantium in 478 BC, when Athens displaced Sparta from leadership in the war against the Persian Empire. He was also instrumental in the founding of the Delian League (Plut. *Cimon* 6,1–3). All the major offensive operations of the league between 476 and 463 BC took place under his command. This included ejecting the Persians from important positions, and expanding and consolidating the Athenian sphere of power and interest (Thrace, northern Aegean, sea route to the Hellespont; Plut. *Cimon* 7f.; Thuc. 1,98–101; [8.83–91]; on the chronology [6.37–50; 87–114]). Probably as *strategos* in each case, he led the conquest of Eion on the Strymon and the island of Skyros, oversaw the incorporation of the city of Carystus on Euboea into the league, led the conquest of the Thracian Chersonesus, and directed the siege of Thasos, which had seceded from the league. Cimon advanced the program to establish lasting Athenian power by founding *klerouchoi* (colonies for those receiving land allotments) on conquered lands (Eion; Skyros; Chersonesus), accelerating the development of Athens into an island-like fortress ('Long Walls') and enhancing the city's symbolic status (e.g. the transfer of the supposed bones of Theseus). Cimon overcame the new challenge of waging constant war at the head of a coalition through circumspect dealings with loyal allies, but he also urged them to provide nothing but money or empty ships. In this way, through the development of their own practical experience and resources, Athens attained an increasing military superiority (Plut. *Cimon* 11).

Cimon's only known tactical innovation grew out of the new conditions of warfare. Whereas the crucial factor at the Battle of Salamis had been the manoeuvrability of the triremes, the Delian League's combined offensive operations demanded both dominance at sea and operational capacity on land. Accordingly, the triremes, 'which Themistocles had constructed for the greatest possible speed and mobility [...] now received from Cimon a broader structure and a linking bridge between the decks, so that they would be a more powerful fighting force with more hoplites' (Plut. *Cimon* 12,2; cf. [3.168–175]). Whether this was also indicative of the distance between Cimon and the thetic democracy (the *thetes* were the lowest social class in Athens) is a matter of dispute (affirmative [7.320–322]); in any case, the innovation proved its worth in the sea/land battle on the Eurymedon River in Pamphylia, in which Athens was victorious (probably 466 BC; Thuc. 1,100,1; Plut. *Cimon* 12,5–13,3).

Cimon's political effort to keep Sparta from resisting Athen's expansion despite tense relations, and even to place the rival under an obligation of gratitude, failed in 462 BC, when the Spartans, severely pressured by a helot revolt, nevertheless rebuffed a relief force that Cimon had organized from Athens. Cimon, whose reputation had already faded, was banished by ostracism in 461 BC.

Still, Cimon clearly remained loyal to Athens, negotiating a five-year peace with Sparta after his return (451 BC), and once again promoting Athenian imperial policy as commander of the Cyprus campaign of 450/49 BC (Thuc. 1,112,2–4; [4]). Cimon died of an illness before the end of this operation, which overall did not achieve its strategic aims. But Athen's continued to follow the policy that Cimon established of combining naval dominance with the besieging and conquest of cities, culminating in the Sicilian Expedition of 415 BC.

☞ Sparta; Wars of note, J. Persian Wars

BIBLIOGRAPHY

SOURCES
[1] PLUTARCH, Life of Kimon, with Translation and Commentary, edited by A. Blamire, 1989.

SECONDARY LITERATURE
[2] S. HORNBLOWER, A Commentary on Thucydides, vol. 1: Books I–III, ²1997   [3] J.S. MORRISON / J.F. COATES, Die athenische Triere, 1990   [4] S.T. PARKER, The Objectives and Strategy of Cimon's Expedition to Cyprus, in: AJPh 97, 1976, 30–38   [5] E. STEIN-HÖLKESKAMP, Cimon, in: BNP 3, 2003, 338–339   [6] M. STEINBRECHER, Der delisch-attische Seebund und die athenisch-spartanischen Beziehungen in der kimonischen Ära, 1985   [7] B. STRAUSS, Democracy, Kimon, and the Evolution of Athenian Naval Tactics in the Fifth Century BC, in: P. FLENSTED-JENSEN et al. (eds.), Polis and Politics, 2000, 315–326   [8] K.-W. WELWEI, Das klassische Athen, 1999.

UWE WALTER

J. CONSTANTINE

Flavius Valerius Constantinus (c. AD 272–337), also known as Constantine I or Constantine the Great (306–337), was one of the most experienced and successful generals of Roman history. His military policies had a lasting impact on the organization, deployment and operational duties of the Late Roman army. Accounts of his role as a field commander are few, and what does survive is distorted in various ways by official panegyric, Christian propaganda and pagan invective. Constantine was born the son of an army officer, Flavius Constantius (later called Chlorus), in the garrison town of Naissus. When his father was named *Caesar* in the west (293–305), Constantine remained in the entourage of the eastern emperor Diocletian (284–305). He took part in campaigns against the Sarmatae and Persians in the 290s, and attained the rank of tribune (Euseb. VC 1,19; Lactant. De mort. pers. 18,10; Anon. Vales. 2f.). Later, under the command of his father, by now the western *Augustus* (305–306), he took part in a campaign against the Picts. Following the death of Constantius at Eboracum (modern York) in AD 306, his troops acclaimed Constantine as *Augustus*. This reflects the positive view held by many of dynastic succession, but it also undermined the collegial system of the Tetrarchy. Over the following six years, Constantine consolidated his *de facto* rule in Gaul, Britain and Spain. From his capital, present-day Trier, he undertook intensive campaigning against the Franks and Alamanni, established a fortified bridgehead at Cologne and secured the imperial frontier (e.g. Paneg. 6(7),10–13).

In 312, Constantine led an army across the Alps to eliminate the regime of his rival Maxentius (306–312) in Italy and Africa. Following initial victories at Turin and Verona, Constantine inflicted a decisive defeat on Maxentius at the Battle of the Milvian Bridge (→ Battles of note, G.). He then entered Rome, making him the undisputed ruler of the Western Empire (Paneg. 4(10),19–30; 12(9),5–17; Euseb. HE 9,9; Euseb. VC 1,37f.; Lactant. De mort. pers. 44; Zos. 2,15–17,2). A unification with the eastern emperor Licinius disintegrated with the outbreak of two civil wars. During the first (316–317), Constantine won two battles at Cibalae and Mardia and occupied the western Balkans. In 324, he resumed hostilities, winning further victories at Adrianople and in a naval bettle in the Hellespont. His final victory over Licinius came at Chrysopolis, making him sole and undisputed ruler (Anon. Vales. 15–18; 23–28; Zos. 2,18–20; 2,22–28). Besides these internal conflicts, Constantine also undertook campaigns against the Sarmatae (323, 334) and Goths (332), and he reorganized the defences along the middle and lower reaches of the Danube. Towards the end of his reign (337), he planned a major campaign against the Sassanid Empire. Although his founding of Constantinople (324) had no direct military consequences, the city developed into the strategic center of the Eastern Empire by virtue of its transcontinental location.

The sources for Constantine's campaigns permit no detailed analysis of his tactics, but they point to a leadership style rooted in the display of outstanding courage and personal command of the cavalry (e.g. Anon. Vales. 3; 24; Zos. 2,18,3f.; 2,22,3–7). Constantine' influence on the evolution of the Late Roman army was far-reaching. He formalized the operational separation between the *limitanei*, units stationed along the borders that were responsible for security procedures, and the *comitatenses*, a standing field army. The latter were stationed near cities in the interior of the empire and served as mobile action forces and a strategic reserve. In this connection, Constantine was responsible for the foundation of many new *comitatenses* units. His large-scale troop discharges after the civil wars formed the basis for the veterans' privileges in the Late Roman legal system. Later sources (Zos. 2,33,3; Lydus, Mag. 2,10) also attribute to Constantine the establishment of the senior command positions of the *magister peditum* ('master of foot soldiers') and the *magister equitum* ('master of cavalry'), although the earliest known holders of these ranks (342) postdate his reign (Amm. Marc. 14,10,2). The military responsibilities of the Praetorian prefects thus shifted to primarily administrative duties (recruitment, supplies, armaments) under Constantine, reflecting a stricter separation of civilian and military authority and career structures.

Constantine's unification of the empire under his sole authority enabled a harmonization of regional differences that had emerged through the separate imperial jurisdictions of the Tetrarchy. In particular, there was a standardization and empire-wide application of a new regimental hierarchy in the new unit types (*scholae*, 'guards', *auxilia palatina*, 'palace auxiliaries', and *vexillationes*, 'temporary military detachments'). Christian historians and apologists retrospectively interpret Constantine's military accomplishments, especially his victory at the Milvian Bridge, in the light of his subsequent 'conversion' to Christianity (Euseb. VC 1,28–32; Lactant. De mort. pers. 44). His new imperial role as arbiter of Christian orthodoxy embroiled the army in ecclesiastical politics and the suppression of pagan and non-Orthodox groups and institutions. Although later authors claim that Constantine strove to introduce Christian practices into the army (e.g. Sozom. Hist. eccl. 1,8,10f.), its institutional Christianization was a longer-term process that was only completed in the late 4th/early 5th centuries.

BIBLIOGRAPHY
[1] T. BARNES, Constantine. Dynasty, Religion and Power in the Later Roman Empire, 2011 [2] M. COLOMBO, Constantinus rerum nouator. Dal comitatus dioclezianeo ai palatini di Valentiniano I, in: Klio 90, 2008, 124–161 [3] H. ELTON, Warfare and the Military, in: N.E. LENSKI (ed.), The Cambridge Companion to the Age of Constantine, 2006, 325–346 [4] D. HOFFMANN, Das spätrömische Bewegungsheer und die Notitia Dignitatum, 2 vols., 1969–1970 [5] M.J. NICASIE, Twilight of Empire. The Roman Army from the Reign of Diocletian until the Battle of Adrianople, 1998 [6] M. ROCCO, L'esercito romano tardoantico. Persistenze e cesure dai Severi a Teodosio I, 2012.

PHILIP RANCE

K. MARIUS

C. Marius was born into a Roman equestrian family from Latium. Thanks to his great military successes, he rose as a *homo novus* ('new man', first in his family to attain senatorial rank) to become consul on seven occasions. He is regarded as one of the greatest generals of the late Republican period, as well as an important military reformer. After serving with distinction in the war against Numantia (134 BC) under Scipio Aemilianus, Marius embarked on the *cursus honorum* ('course of honors', sequential order of public offices), becoming military tribune, quaestor (probably 123), people's tribune (119) and praetor (115). As propraetor in Hispania ulterior, he again showed his military prowess (Plut. *Marius* 6). It may have been through a patron-client relationship that Marius became legate to the consul Q. Caecilius Metellus (109) in the war against the Numidian king Jugurtha. Noble generals who were sometimes corrupt had hitherto led this war (113–105) with little competence. Rome had suffered several defeats and the reputation of the elite was tarnished. Marius, by contrast, distinguished himself several times in combat, which led the reluctant consul to approve him for candidacy for the consulship. He was elected consul (107) in opposition to the discredited elite. Moreover, contrary to convention, he had himself named commander of the campaign against Jugurtha by the popular assembly (Sall. Iug. 73). He recruited volunteers for the war, some from the wealthless classes that were not usually called upon for military service. The ancient tradition (Sall. Iug. 86; Plut. *Marius* 9) and with it some modern scholars regard this as an extraordinary innovation, but this view should be put into perspective. Numerous wars across the entire Mediterranean had pushed Rome's military system to its limits in terms of both quality and quantity. It was probably for this reason that the census threshold was lowered, thereby increasing the number of citizens available for recruitment. The opening of the legions to all *cives* ('citizens') may thus only have been a final step (see [4]; [7] et al.; *contra* [5]; [6]). Even so, the consequences were profound. For landless and small-scale peasants, military service sometimes lasting several years could provide an income through pay and booty that would be lost if they were discharged. The Roman militia thus began to evolve into a professional army. Generals, who became *patroni* ('patrons') to the soldiers as a result of the long period of service, were obliged to compensate them, which was only possible through allocations of land. Marius and several generals after him attempted to implement this. Because in most cases the senate vehemently opposed it, veteran welfare became one of the most contentious problems of the Roman Republic.

Following extensive recruitment and drills, Marius crossed over to Africa. In a desert war characterized by interruptions to the supply lines, the securing and conquest of permanent sites, long marches and small skirmishes, he drove Jugurtha from Numidia. In 105 BC, Marius' ally Bocchus of Mauretania delivered Jugurtha to Marius' legate Sulla. Marius celebrated a triumph on January 1, 104. By this time, he had already been elected consul for 104 *in absentia*, with the expected ten-year interval disregarded, and he was entrusted with the task of leading the fight against the Germanic Cimbri and Teutones tribes. These tribes had defeated several Roman armies in the years since 113, most recently and devastatingly at Arausio (Orange) (MRR 1, 555). Other reforms were introduced at this time, if not before: Marius divided the legion into ten cohorts; in place of the maniple, cohorts became the legion's most important subunits and were able to operate independently. Here too, he seems to have been completing a process that was already underway [1]. The armaments of the legion were standardized: the legionary was equipped with *pilum* ('javelin'), *gladius* ('sword') and *scutum* ('shield'). The legions were provided with a legionary eagle, and they may have been assigned numbers (MRR 1, 558). The baggage train was reduced, and soldiers now had to carry much of their own burden (*muli Mariani*, Frontinus, Strat. 4,1,7; Plut. *Marius* 13). These changes made the army more flexible, helped the legions expand collectively, and made better use of reserves.

Because the Cimbri and Teutones had split up and turned towards Iberia, Marius – who was elected consul in every year through to 100 BC – had time to train his forces. In 102, a cautious wait-and-see strategy won him a victory at Aquae Sextiae against the Teutones (and Ambrones), and in 101 he won a victory together with Catulus fighting against the Cimbri at Vercellae (Northern Italy). Although the *optimates* (members of the ruling classes) played down his military achievements, he was now generally seen as the saviour of Rome against the Germanic threat.

As consul in 100 BC (he had previously tried in 103), Marius, in conjunction with the popular people's tribune Saturninus, pursued a settlement policy for his veterans, although its success was limited. He distanced himself, however, from the veterans' acts of violence, and he ultimately pushed through the *senatum consultum ultimum* ('final decree of the Senate') issued against them. Marius was active in the field once again in the Social War (91–88), fighting the Marsi with some success. His attempt to use a popular resolution brought by the tribune Sulpicius to win the command against Mithridates failed as a result of Sulla's coup d'état. Marius was forced to flee, but after a period of exile and civil war, he and L. Cornelius Cinna marched their armies into Rome in 87. Marius then had himself elected consul a seventh time. He died a few days after taking office, having conducted a bloody persecution of his enemies.

☞ **Armament; Veterans**

BIBLIOGRAPHY
[1] M.J.V. BELL, Tactical Reform in the Roman Army, in: Historia 14, 1965, 404–422   [2] T.F. CARNEY, A Biography of C. Marius, ²1970   [3] R.J. EVANS, Gaius Marius, 1994   [4] E. GABBA, Republican Rome, the Army and the Allies, 1976   [5] M. LABITZKE, Marius. Der verleumdete Retter Roms, 2013   [6] C.A. MATTHEW, On the Wings of Eagles, 2010   [7] L. THOMMEN, Gaius Marius – oder: Der Anfang vom Ende der Republik, in: E. STEIN-HÖLKESKAMP / H.-J. HÖLKESKAMP (eds.), Von Romulus zu Augustus, 2000, 187–199   [8] V. WERNER, Quantum bello optimus, tantum pace pessimus, 1995.

LEONHARD BURCKHARDT

L. MARCUS AURELIUS
Marcus Aurelius, the Roman emperor, was born M. Annius Catilius Severus at Rome in AD 121. He ruled the Roman Empire as emperor from 161 to 180 (jointly with Lucius Verus from 161 to 169). Although he is generally known as the 'philosopher on the imperial throne', his activities as emperor were largely determined by difficult wars [4]. He spent long years with the soldiers on the northern front, sharing their privations and dangers (SHA Aur. 2,6 with M. Aur. 1,6 and SHA Aur. 22,5). Like every Roman emperor, he had to cultivate his relationship with the army if he did not wish to see his power disintegrate or his own life put in danger. This was especially true for Marcus Aurelius in the light of initial military setbacks and the long and difficult wars that followed them. Because he was extraordinarily successful in those wars and on the battlefield in general, Marcus Aurelius was regarded by his contemporaries as one of the greatest of Roman generals [6]; [7].

Marcus was born into one of the leading families of his day, and through the education he received as befitting his social status he also gained considerable abilities in riding and handling weapons (Cass. Dio 72,36,2). However, his real interest lay in philosophy, so that when he came to the throne, he had virtually no practical military experience and had never seen the border regions for himself. Even when his predecessor, Antoninus Pius, decided to share supreme command of the Roman army with him in AD 147, Marcus still was not required to leave Rome.

Marcus' relationship with war and the military was driven above all by his concern for the empire and his powerful sense of duty (e.g. Fronto, *ad Antoninum Imperatorem* 4,1,3 (van den Hout 105); Fronto, *De bello Parthico* 1 and 10 (van den Hout 220 and 225)). War threatened in Britain soon after he came to the throne. On the Rhine and Danube, the Germanic Chatti tribe invaded the provinces of Germania superior and Rhaetia. At the same time, M. Sedatius Severianus, governor of the province of Cappadocia, suffered a heavy defeat at the hands of the Parthians. One legion (*legio IX Hispana*?) was annihilated. Marcus sent his co-emperor Lucius Verus to the east to combat the Parthians, but retained supreme military command over the entire operation at Rome (SHA Aur. 8,14; 20,2). The war led to the occupation of Armenia and northern Mesopotamia, although the former provinces established by Trajan were not restored (Armenia: CIL III 6052 = 13627; AE 1910, 161 = ILS 9117; SEG 15, 839; see also Cass. Dio 71,3,11f.; 72,4,1f.; SHA Aur. 21,2; Mesopotamia: Cass. Dio 71,1,2f.; Hdn. 3,1,3; 4,7; 9,1; SHA Sept. Sev. 9,9). Dura-Europus on the Euphrates was also occupied and the province of Syria annexed (Lucian, *Quomodo historia concribenda sit* 20; 24; 28).

Soldiers returning home from the east brought with them an epidemic, which, along with the war

Fig. 3: Relief on a monument honouring Marcus Aurelius (marble, c. AD 176–180). The emperor is seen during the Marcomannic Wars subjugating Germanic enemies, who kneel before him and plead for mercy with hands raised. The image symbolized Marcus Aurelius' great victories in the north.

now breaking out in the north and the incursions of Marcomanni, Quadi and Sarmatae as far as Italy, claimed countless lives, while tens of thousands more were abducted into slavery by the invaders (Cass. Dio 72,11,2; 72,13,2–4; 72,16,2; 72,20,1; 73,2,3; 73,3,2; SHA Aur. 21,10). Both emperors began by moving to the Danube front and setting up a barricade along the southern foothills of the Alps (*praetentura Italiae et Alpium*) [2]; [9]. On the way back to Rome, Lucius Verus died of a stroke. The wars and losses led to severe tax shortfalls, so much so that in the summer of 169, Marcus was compelled to raise more funds to finance the war by means of an extraordinary auction of imperial assets (SHA Aur. 17,4f.; 21,9; Epit. Caes. 16,9f.; Eutr. 8,13). With only a few interruptions, including one to put down a rebellion in the east in AD 175, Marcus now spent the remaining years of his life with his troops, at war on the Danube (cf. fig. 3). He had already created two new legions at the beginning of the war in the north (*legio II Italica* and *legio III Italica*), and these were later stationed in the provinces of Noricum and Rhaetia. There were also rumours that he intended to create two new provinces, Marcomannia and Sarmatia, on the far bank of the Danube, where Roman troops were occupying territory (SHA Aur. 24,5; 27,10; cf. Cass. Dio 72,20,1f.; 72,33,4²) [5]. Coins and major monuments celebrated his military successes in Rome, with reliefs and inscriptions in his honour, 'because he surpassed all the valorous deeds of the greatest emperors before him [and] destroyed or subjugate the most warlike of peoples' (CIL VI 1014 = 31225 = ILS 374).

BIBLIOGRAPHY

[1] M. van Ackeren (ed.), A Companion to Marcus Aurelius, 2012 [2] G. Bigliardi, La praetentura Italiae et Alpium alla luce di nuove ricerche archeologiche, in: Aquileia Nostra 78, 2007, 297–312 [3] A.R. Birley, Marcus Aurelius. A Biography, ²1987 [4] A.R. Birley, The Wars and Revolts, in: M. van Ackeren (ed.), A Companion to Marcus Aurelius, 2012, 217–233 [5] T. Fischer, Archaeological Evidence of the Marcomannic Wars of Marcus Aurelius, in: M. van Ackeren (ed.), A Companion to Marcus Aurelius, 2012, 29–44 [6] J. Fündling, Marc Aurel. Kaiser und Philosoph, 2008 [7] M.A. Speidel, Marcus Aurelius. Der pflichtbewusste Philosoph in der Gewalt der Umstände, in: S. Förster et al. (eds.), Kriegsherren der Weltgeschichte. 22 historische Portraits, 2006, 79–92 (reprinted in: M.A. Speidel, Heer und Herrschaft im Römischen Reich der Hohen Kaiserzeit, 2009, 167–180) [8] M.A. Speidel, Der Philosoph als Imperator. Marc Aurel und das Militär, in: V. Grieb (ed.), Marc Aurel. Wege zu seiner Herrschaft, 2017, 49–74 [9] J. Šašel, Opera Selecta, 1992, 388–396.

MICHAEL A. SPEIDEL

M. Philip of Macedon

M.1. Biography
M.2. Military history

M.1. Biography

(in general: [5.40–97]; [7]; [9]; [15]; [14]; [19] and for the older literature [4])

Born about 382 BC as the third son of the Macedonian king Amyntas III (reigned c. 393–370) and a princess from the upper Macedonian territory of Lyncus, Philip spent some of his youth as a → hostage with the Illyrians and at Thebes, where he is said to have received important inspiration for his subsequent military innovations. After his elder brother, King Perdiccas III, fell in battle (along with an alleged 4,000 Macedonians) against the expansionist Illyrians under King Bardylis in 359 (Diod. Sic. 16,2,5), Philip was made king. He was able to avert attacks by the Paeonians and Thracians by making standstill payments, while rivals to the throne achieved no success. With a reconstituted army, he then attacked the Illyrians in 358, and inflicted a devastating defeat on them, driving them out of upper Macedonia. Over the years that followed, he consolidated and expanded the authority of the Macedonian monarchy in the region by establishing fortified settlements, building fortresses and contracting strategic marriages (e.g. with Olympias, a daughter of the Molossian king).

From this point on, Philip pursued an unprecedented policy of expansion. A key motive for this was the constant need to prove his suitability as a military leader and king in opposition to potential aristocratic rivals in what was still a structurally weak monarchy. Another motive was the need to supply, through booty and increased territorial possessions, the considerable finances required to maintain the army, conduct an extravagent court and satisfy the demands of his powerful backers. He completed his efforts to control the Macedonian heartlands on the Thermaic Gulf by conquering the cities of Pydna in 356 and Methone in 354. Along the Thracian border, he brought Amphipolis (357) and Crenides (356) under his control, founding the city of Philippi on the site of the latter. This won him access to the precious metal deposits of the Pangaeum and other natural resources. Still in the 350s, Philip made princedoms and coastal cities of Thrace as far as the River Hebrus into dependencies. In 353, he answered a call for help from the Aleuadae of Larisa in Thessaly against the dynasts of Pherae, who were allied with the Phocaean League. He suffered a defeat here so crushing that it led to a mutiny in his army. However, he triumphed against the Phocaeans and Pheraeans in 352 at what became known as the Battle of Crocus Field, which was part of the Third Sacred War against the Phocaeans, in which Philip acted as an ally of Thebes. This victory won him the office of *archon* of the Thessalian League, and with it access to its powerful cavalry. In 349, Philip preempted an emerging coalition consisting of Athens – which had technically, but without consequence, been at war with Philip since Amphipolis –, the Thracian king Cersebleptes and the Chalcidian League led by Olynthus. He accomplished this by attacking the Chalcidice and Olynthus, which he took and destroyed after a long siege in 348. The so-called Peace of Philocrates with Athens (346) was no more than an aside, for only a few weeks later, Philip subjugated the Phocaeans, with whom he remained in a state of war because of the Third Sacred War. Athens now became Philip's chief adversary in southern Greece. At the Battle of Chaeronea in 338, Philip defeated a southern Greek alliance led by Athens and Thebes, which saw itself as wronged by Philip's action against the Phocaeans. Philip organized his rule in central and southern Greece in the form of the League of Corinth, functioning as its hegemon.

During the 340s, alongside these events, Philip (in person or through his generals) imposed direct or indirect rule on the regions of Thrace that were still independent, as far as the Haemus Mountains and beyond in the north, and as far as the Black Sea in the east. He did the same in the south with Illyria and Epirus, where Philip could count on the support of his close allies, the Molossian kings. In 337, a campaign to 'liberate' (Diod. Sic. 16,91f.) Persian Asia Minor began, but in the summer of 336, Philip was assassinated at the celebration marking his daughter's wedding (most recent thorough discussion of the possible background to this in [20.181–186]).

M.2. MILITARY HISTORY
(in general [9.405–449]; [19])

Under Philip, the Macedonian army was professionalized and became the strongest army of the time. Starting from 10,000 infantry and 600 cavalry in 358 BC (Diod. Sic. 16,4,3), its overall strength is said by ancient sources to have tripled or even quadrupled by 336 (discussion in [9.407–409]). In addition to this, there was an ever-increasing number of non-Macedonian contingents from dependent communities, most prominently the Thessalian cavalry, which Philip kept in his army not least for purposes of discipline. Initially, the army was mainly composed of fighting recruits (apparently organized by region), although a growing number of them became professional soldiers as a result of the permanent state of war. Later, as Philip acquired sufficient funds, mercenaries were also hired (Dem. Or. 2,17; Diod. Sic. 16,8,7 etc.; cf. [9.438–444]). Philip provided the Macedonian infantry with new equipment (see below) and put them through regular training to develop their stamina and improve their fighting formations (Diod. Sic. 16,3,1; Polyaenus, Strat. 4,2,10). It is uncertain whether Philip or a predecessor gave the foot soldiers the title *pezetairoi* ('foot soldiers'). According to Anaximenes, *Philippika* (FGrH 72 Frg. 4), this was meant to motivate them by putting them on par with the cavalry, who were known as *hetairoi* ('nobles'). Nor is it certain whether all infantrymen held this title or if the *pezetairoi* were an elite unit (as in Dem. Or. 2,17 in 349 and Theopomp, FGrH 115 Frg. 348). Likewise unclear is the relationship between the *pezetairoi* and the *astetairoi* or the elite and lifeguard unit of the *hypaspistai* ('shieldbearers') – if these even existed in Philip's time. Here as elsewhere, a fundamental problem is the question of how much of the far better documented arrangements in the army of Alexander the Great can be attributed to Philip (on the debate over the infantry [9.405f., 705–713]; [10.148–151]; [6]; [1]).

The introduction under Philip of a lance (*sarisa*) about 5 m long had a considerable impact. It possessed great penetrative power and was far superior in offensive operations to the traditional weapons of the phalanx [13.2515–2529]; [2]; [17]; [18]. The remaining weaponry was light and enabled great mobility. Although the chronology of these reforms is uncertain, some may – according to the traditional view (Diod. Sic. 16,3,1) – indeed date back to 359/58, which provides a possible explanation for Philip's surprising successes against the Illyrians and the rivals to his throne in 358 [2]. It is also likely that during Philip's reign the cavalry were already being trained in new tactics such as wedge formations and attacks on opposing flanks, and that this is why they were becoming so much more significant in battle ([9.413f.]; cf. also [15.376]). Philip later invested heavily in siege technology, and probably became the first to use new torsion catapults [8.201–244]; [12]; [16]. He was also able to establish a small fleet, but for the Persian campaign he was still reliant on Athens and other *poleis* [11]. From a psychological perspective, the success of the Macedonian army may be attributed not only to the material advances and the euphoria of the ongoing series of victories, but also to Philip's personal charisma, his exemplary commitment in the field and his comradely approach – all of which set standards of behaviour for Alexander ([10.64–70]; but cf. [14.359–366]). The same factors made the army an important catalyst for the internal unification of what had, before Philip, been a hopelessly fragmented Macedonia [3].

☞ Generals of note, B. Alexander

BIBLIOGRAPHY
[1] E.M. ANSON, Philip II and the Creation of the Macedonian Pezhetairoi, in: P. WHEATLEY / R. HANNAH (eds.), Alexander & His Successors. Essays from the Antipodes, 2009, 88–98 [2] E.M. ANSON, The Introduction of the Sarisa in Macedonian Warfare, in: AncSoc 40, 2010, 51–68 [3] J.R. ELLIS, The Dynamics of Fourth-Century Macedonian Imperialism, in: Ancient Macedonia 2, 1977, 103–114 [4] R.M. ERRINGTON, Review-Discussion. Four Interpretations of Philip II, in: AJAH 6, 1981, 69–88 [5] R.M. ERRINGTON, Geschichte Makedoniens. Von den Anfängen bis zum Untergang des Königreichs, 1986 [6] A. ERSKINE, The πεζέταιροι of Philip II and Alexander III, in: Historia 38, 1989, 385–394 [7] J. FÜNDLING, Philipp II. von Makedonien, 2014 [8] Y. GARLAN, Recherches de poliorcétique grecque, 1974, 202–244 [9] G.T. GRIFFITH, Part Two, in: N.G.L. HAMMOND / G.T. GRIFFITH, A History of Macedonia, vol. 2: 550–336 B.C., 1979, 203–674 [10] N.G.L. HAMMOND, The Macedonian State. Origins, Institutions, and History, 1989 [11] N.G.L. HAMMOND, The Macedonian Navies of Philip and Alexander until 330 B.C., in: Antichthon 26, 1992, 30–41 [12] P.T. KEYSER, The Use of Artillery by Philip II and Alexander the Great, in: Ancient World 15, 1994, 27–49 [13] F.K. LAMMERT, Sarisse, in: RE 1/2, 1920, 2515–2529 [14] R. LANE FOX, Philip of Macedon. Accession, Ambitions, and Self-Presentation, in: R. LANE FOX (ed.), Brill's Companion to Ancient Macedon. Studies in the Archaeology and History of Macedon, 650 BC–300 AD, 2011, 335–366 [15] R. LANE FOX, Philip's and Alexander's Macedon, in: R. LANE FOX (ed.), Brill's Companion to Ancient Macedon. Studies in the Archaeology and History of Macedon, 650 BC–300 AD, 2011, 367–391 [16] E.W. MARSDEN, Macedonian Military Machinery and Its Designers under Philip and Alexander, in: Ancient Macedonia 2, 1977, 211–223 [17] C. MATTHEWS, The Length of the Sarissa, in: Antichthon 46, 2012, 79–100 [18] N. SEKUNDA, The Sarissa, in: Acta Universitatis Lodziensis, Folia Archaeologica 23, 2001, 13–41 [19] N.V. SEKUNDA, The Macedonian Army, in: J. ROISMAN / I. WORTHINGTON (eds.), A Companion to Ancient Macedonia, 2010, 446–471 [20] I. WORTHINGTON, Philip II of Macedonia, 2008.

SEBASTIAN SCHMIDT-HOFNER

N. POMPEY
Cn. Pompeius emerged as one of the outstanding generals of the late Roman Republic. Pliny the Elder, in the eulogy he devotes to him in Book 7 of the *Naturalis historia*, recalls that the young Pompey twice won the supreme honour of a triumph (in March 81 and December 71), 'proving himself a general before having been a soldier' (*totiens imperator ante quam miles*; Plin. HN 7,96). This wording emphasizes the degree to which the career of this most famous *imperator* of his time [3] went against all established rules. Technically, eligibility for military command was earned through holding a magistracy, which itself required first completing military service (*militia*) as a simple soldier or *contubernalis* ('tent companion') of a general. Pompey, however, was able to bypass this course of promotion thanks to the civil war of 83–82 BC. After serving during the Social War (Plut. *Pompeius* 3,1) with his father Cn. Pompeius Strabo (*cos.* 89), he launched a spectacular personal initiative in the spring of 83, despite not yet being even a simple Roman *eques* ('cavalry soldier'): he recruited a private army from among his clients in Picenum and put it at the disposal of Sulla (Plut. *Pompeius* 6). The senate then assigned a series of extraordinary commands to him as *privatus cum imperio* (citizen granted temporary command), in Sicily (82), Africa (81/80), Italy (78) and Spain (77–72). These earned him his first two triumphs and the byname *Magnus* ('the Great'), which Plutarch reports he was long reluctant to use officially (Plut. *Pompeius* 13). This fame, together with his reputation as a general of unmatched ability, which were bestowed on him at an early age and under extraordinary circumstances, explain his election as consul in 70 BC despite never having been even a senator [7]; [5].

Following this, he maintained his exceptional position by withdrawing from public life, and instead taking ever more extensive extraordinary commands through plebiscitary laws, first against the pirates in the Mediterranean (67), then against Mithridates in the east (66–62). The climax of his fame, symbolized in his triumph of September 61, also marked the end of the main phase of his military activity; after this, he would not campaign again until the Civil War (49/48), which was shaped by his premature surrender of Italy and his final defeat at the Battle of Pharsalus in Thessaly.

He was murdered at Alexandria soon afterwards. This failure against Caesar has paradoxically led some modern authors to grant him first place among *imperatores* – a position which, in the eyes of his contemporaries, he had held up to this point (Cic. Deiot. 12). A tradition hostile to Pompey, probably originating from his rivals, portrayed him as an opportunist who readily adorned himself with the accomplishments and victories of others (Plut. *Pompeius* 22,2 and 31,7; Plut. *Crassus* 11,7f.). Less detailed than the reports about Caesar, the surviving accounts of his various campaigns offer no more than highly fragmentary insights into his strategic and tactical ideas, which modern authors often underestimate [8]. Yet his resounding success against the pirates in 67, which took him only three months rather than the anticipated three years (Plut. *Pompeius* 28,2), suggests remarkable powers of organization and strategy. Even if Caesar ultimately proved the better tactician at the Battle of Pharsalus, an analysis of the campaign in Greece in 48 shows Pompey again proving his superiority on the strategic level [4], as he had previously done at Brundisium (Plut. *Pompeius* 63,1). The sources also emphasize the physical courage of Pompey, who prior to 63 often fought on the battlefield in person (Plut. *Pompeius* 7,2f.; 12; 19,2f.; 35,3), and who was known for his skill in handling weapons, the result of training that he continued until he was advanced in age (Plut. *Pompeius* 1,3; 41,4; 64,1f.; App. Civ. 2,49).

For all the evident breaches of the *mos maiorum* ('ancestral custom') in his career, and despite a record tarnished by his defeat in the Civil War (Plut. *Pompeius* 83f.; App. Civ. 2,71), the impression remains that Pompey combined in himself, to a greater extent than any of his contemporaries, all the qualities the Romans expected of a great general. This was summarized by Cicero in his January 66 oration *De imperio Cn. Pompei* ('On the Command of Cn. Pompeius'): 'knowledge of military affairs, valour, authority and good fortune' (*scientiam rei militaris, virtutem, auctoritatem, felicitatem* (Cic. Manil. 28), as well as 'industry in business, fortitude amid dangers, energy in acting, rapidity in executing, wisdom in foreseeing' (*labor in negotiis, fortitudo in periculis, industria in agendo, celeritas in conficiendo, consilium in providendo*; Cic. Manil. 29; trans. C.D. Yonge).

☞ Generals of note, C. Caesar

BIBLIOGRAPHY
[1] M. DINGMANN, Pompeius Magnus. Machtgrundlagen eines spätrepublikanischen Politikers, 2007 [2] M. GELZER, Pompeius, 2005 (reprint) [3] A. GOLDSWORTHY, In the Name of Rome. The Men Who Won the Roman Empire, 2003 [4] N. ROSENSTEIN, General and Imperialist, in: M. GRIFFIN (ed.), A Companion to Julius Caesar, 2009, 85–99 [5] R. SEAGER, Pompey the Great. A Political Biography, ²2002 [6] T. STICKLER, Pompeius, 2010 [7] J. VAN OOTEGHEM, Pompée le Grand, bâtisseur d'Empire, 1954 [8] G. WYLIE, The Genius and the Sergeant. Sertorius versus Pompey, in: C. DEROUX (ed.), Studies in Latin Literature and Roman History, 1992, 145–162.

FRANÇOIS CADIOU

O. SCIPIO AFRICANUS

O.1. Early career and campaign against Carthage
O.2. Later career and legacy

O.1. EARLY CAREER AND CAMPAIGN AGAINST CARTHAGE

P. Cornelius Scipio (236–183 BC, cos. 205 and 194 BC) was a Roman noble who became the most important and successful Roman general of the Second Punic War (218–201 BC). While still a young man, Scipio fought in the Battle of the Ticino against Hannibal's army (218), and he is said to have saved the life of his father, consul and commander of the Romans there (Pol. 10,3; Liv. 21,46,8–10; Cass. Dio frg. 57,30). Later, as military tribune, he led the units of men who had survived the defeat at Cannae (216; Liv. 22,53; App. Hann. 114 and MRR 1,251). He must already have had some military experience and considerable prestige by 210, when – far younger than was customary and ahead of the regular career path – he was given supreme command of Roman forces in Spain (Pol. 10,6,10; Liv. 26,18,2–19,9; App. Ib. 68f.; Val. Max. 3,7,1a; Sil. 15,1–151; Cass. Dio frg. 57,39f.; Zon. 9,7), taking the place of his father and uncle, who had fallen there. He may have been selected for this position because he was able to enter directly into their network of relationships with local tribes and the army.

In 209, after consolidating his position and thoroughly training his troops, Scipio took Carthago nova (Cartagena), the wealthy epicentre of Carthaginian Iberia, in a tactically brilliant surprise attack (Pol. 10,6–16; Liv. 26,42,2–46,10; App. Ib. 74–88; Frontin. Str. 2,11,5; Sil. 15,180–250; Zon. 9,8 and MRR 1,287). Thanks to abundant booty (Pol. 10,16; Liv. 26,47,1–10; App. Ib. 90) and an enhanced reputation among the Iberians, Scipio and the Romans thereafter won the initiative in the Hispanic theatre. Following arduous confrontations, countless skirmishes, diplomatic manoeuvring and several major battles, most notably Baecula in 208 (Pol. 10,38f.; Liv. 27,18,1–18; Sil. 15,410–492; App. Ib. 95; Eutr. 3,15; Oros. 4,18,7; Zon. 9,8) and Ilipa in 206 (Pol. 11,20–24; Liv. 28,13,6–15,13; Sil. 16,78–114; App. Ib. 96–109; Zon. 9,8, cf. MRR 1,299 with 301, note 4), they were finally able to expel the Carthaginians from the Iberian Peninsula.

Scipio was elected consul for 205 on the basis of this success and his popularity, even though he had not yet reached the required age (MRR 1,301).

He was given the jurisdiction of Sicily, and – in the face of opposition from prominent figures like Fabius Maximus (Liv. 28,40,1–3; App. Hann. 228f.; App. Lib. 26–29; Plut. *Cato maior* 3; Plut. *Fabius Maximus* 25f.; Sil. 16,597–700; Zon. 9,11) – permission to take the war to Africa. The crossing took place in 204, after extensive preparations (Liv. 29,1,1–8; Val. Max. 7,3,3; App. Hann. 230; Zon. 9,11) and a large influx of volunteers, and with the support of Rome's confederates. Several defeats and the capture of its ally, King Syphax of Numidia, compelled Carthage to recall Hannibal from Italy. Despite this reinforcement given to the enemy forces, Scipio won the decisive battle of the war at Zama (202 BC; Enn. ann. 314f.; Pol. 15,9–16; Liv. 30,32,1–35,15; Nep. Hann. 6f.; Frontin. Str. 2,3,16; Plut. *Fabius Maximus* 27; Flor. Epit. 2,6,58–61; Vir. Ill. 42,6; 49,14; App. Lib. 165–206; Eutr. 3,23; Oros. 4,19,2f.; Zon. 9,14). The battle was decided by the greater fighting capacity of the Italic infantry and the superiority of the Roman and Numidian cavalry, which routed the Carthaginian riders stationed on the wings, and then encircled and destroyed the centre. Scipio here was copying the tested and proved tactics of Hannibal. In general, he showed himself capable of responding with flexibility to various military situations and orchestrating the different troop types effectively. He probably led with great charisma, and he undertook careful preparations for his campaigns in terms of diplomacy, logistics and the education and training of his men (Liv. 30,3,1ff.). In this way he made optimum use of Rome's resources.

O.2. LATER CAREER AND LEGACY

Scipio's outstanding achievements in the war against Carthage earned him a distinguished political career after the war (*cos.* for the second time 194, *ces.* 199/98, *princeps senatus* from 199) and the byname Africanus. According to Livy, he was the first Roman to be named after a defeated people (30,45,6f.; cf. Pol. 10,3; Liv. 21,46,8–10; App. Hann. 236). Although he was denied major military commands after this, he did accompany his brother Lucius (*cos.* 190) as legate on the latter's campaign against the Seleucid king Antiochus III (MRR 1,358), which culminated in the victory at Magnesia ad Sipylum. Scipio's role here was as an advisor and diplomat negotiating with several monarchs (including Philip V of Macedon, Prusias of Bithynia and Antiochus III) and Greek powers, and achieving favourable outcomes for Rome by virtue of his prestige and skill (e.g. Liv. 37,25,8f.). He did not take part in the battle itself, because of illness (Liv. 37,37,6; App. Syr. 150).

His spectacular career outside established norms and his successes earned him bitter enemies among the Roman elite, the most prominent being Cato the Elder. These differences spawned lawsuits against his brother L. Scipio (in 187) and him personally (in 184) (Pol. 23,14; Cic. Prov. 18; Liv. 38,50–54; Diod. Sic. 29,21; Val. Max. 3,7,1e; 4,1,8; 5,3,2 b/c; 8,1, damn. 1; Vir. Ill. 49,17; 53,2; 57,1; Gell. NA 4,18,3–5; 6,19; 12,8,1–4; Cass. Dio frg. 63,65,1; App. Syr. 205–212; Plut. *Cato maior* 15; 18; Mor. 196E/F; 540E–541A; [3]). As a result of these lawsuits, he retired to his country estate at Liternum (Liv. 38,52,1–3; Zon. 9,20), where he died in 183 (cf. fig. 4).

Subsequent historiography and informative literature showers Scipio with praise, emphasizing not only his great popularity (Pol. 23,14, cf. 10,4f.; Liv. 29,14,6–12; Plut. *Fabius Maximus* 25), but also his courage, intellect, magnanimity and flexibility as a general. Polybius explicitly refuses to call him a mere darling of fortune owing his success to Tyche (10,2; cf. Liv. 26,29,5, where Scipio is renowned for his *fortuna*), while Livy sees him as the 'leader cho-

Fig. 4: Bust of Scipio Africanus (bronze, 1st century AD). This bronze bust of an elderly man wearing a toga may possibly depict Scipio Africanus as a seasoned *nobilis*. Although the head certainly has individual traits, it also exhibits qualities that were readily attributed to the Roman nobility, such as dignity (*dignitas*), severity (*severitas*) and sincerity (*fides*). Scipio, who often clashed with his peers and survived such conflicts thanks to his outstanding military accomplishments, is thus shown here as an experienced nobleman, and yet one who, despite his enormous achievements, blends seamlessly into the canon of values recognized by his own and later ages.

sen by fate for the war' against Hannibal (*fatalis dux huiusque belli*; Liv. 22,53, cf. 38,53,11). Inevitably, he became stylized as an embodiment of the Roman attitude and the 'invincible' hero (*memoria optimi et invictissimi viri memoria*, Cic. Rep. 6,9, cf. 6,13f.), who alone was the equal of Hannibal (e.g. Sil.). His undoubted military achievements, which represented a significant step towards Roman expansion in the Mediterranean world, lent themselves to such idealization, as did his extraordinary career.

☞ **Battles of note, C. Cannae; Battles of note, E. Magnesia ad Sipylum; Generals of note, G. Hannibal; Wars of note, K. Punic Wars**

BIBLIOGRAPHY
[1] G. BRECCIA, Scipione l'Africano. L'invincibile che rese grande Roma, 2017 [2] R.A. GABRIEL, Scipio Africanus. Rome's Greatest General, 2008 [3] E.S. GRUEN, The »Fall« of the Scipios, in: I. MALKIN / Z.W. RUBINSOHN (eds.), Leaders and Masses in the Roman World, 1995, 59–90 [4] D. HOYOS, Mastering the West. Rome and Carthage at War, 2015 [5] G. MANZ, Roms Aufstieg zur Weltmacht. Das Zeitalter der Punischen Kriege, 2017 [6] K.-H. SCHWARTE, Publius Cornelius Scipio Africanus. Eroberer zwischen West und Ost, in: K.-J. HÖLKESKAMP / E. STEIN-HÖLKESKAMP (eds.), Von Romulus zu Augustus, ²2010, 106–119 [7] H.H. SCULLARD, Scipio Africanus. Soldier and Politician, 1970 [8] K. ZIMMERMANN, Rom und Karthago, ³2013.

LEONHARD BURCKHARDT

P. STILICHO
Flavius Stilicho was the most powerful *magister militum* ('Master of Soldiers') of the Western Roman Empire from 395 to 408, and the *de facto* head of the imperial government. His father, a Vandal, had served as a cavalry officer under Valens (Claud. Stil. 1,36–39; Oros. 7,38,1). His mother was a Roman. Sources hostile to him accordingly branded him *semibarbarus* (Jer. Ep. 123,16). Stilicho rose rapidly in the army of the Eastern Empire under Theodosius I. An inscription in the city of Rome records his career from Praetorian tribune to commander of the imperial life guards at the court, and master of the cavalry and infantry (*tribunus praetorianus, comes domesticorum, magister equitum peditumque*, CIL VI 1730). His first major achievement was a diplomatic mission to Persia (before 384), where he may have taken part in negotiations towards the partition of Armenia (Claud. Stil. 1,51–68). Soon after this, he married Theodosius' adoptive daughter Serena. In 388, Stilicho accompanied Theodosius to war against Magnus Maximus. His first military office is attested from the early 390s, as *magister militum* in Thracia against 'barbarians' (Claud., *In Rufinum* 1,310–322). Stilicho served as *magister militum praesentalis* ('Master of Soldiers in the (Imperial) Presence') in the emperor's war against Eugenius in 394 (Zos. 4,57,2).

Following Theodosius' death early in 395, Stilicho functioned as head of the Western Roman government for the child emperor Honorius (Philostorgius 11,3). However, he also claimed that the late emperor had entrusted him with care of Honorius' brother Arcadius, and thus with the government of the Eastern Roman Empire (Ambr. Obit. Theod. 5). The east never accepted this claim, which led to a period of 'cold war'. Before the end of 395, Stilicho had command of both parts of the Roman army, western and eastern, which had fought on the Frigidus as recently as 394 (Claud., *In Rufinum* 2,4–6). He took advantage of the rebellion of Alaric to send this army to Greece. Before any real battle could take place, however, Constantinople demanded the return of the eastern army and his withdrawal from the eastern sphere of responsibility (Claud., *In Rufinum* 2,208–210). In 396, Stilicho travelled to the Rhine front, where he renewed treaties with allied barbarian tribes (Claud., *In Eutropium* 1,405–411). It may have been at this time that he also sent troops against Irish and Pictish raiding groups in Britain.

Stilicho moved against Alaric again in 397, attacking the Peloponnese from the sea (Zos. 5,7,1–3). However, he was forced to abandon this campaign after a few skirmishes. The *magister militum* of Africa, Gildo, had transferred with his diocese from the western court to the eastern, and was now withholding grain deliveries to Rome (Claud., *In Gildonem*; Symmachus, Ep. 4,5). Stilicho immediately returned to Italy, arranged grain supplies from Gaul and Spain and dispatched an elite force to North Africa, which succeeded in putting down Gildo's rebellion early in 398 (Oros. 7,36,2–13). The legal texts of this period indicate serious recruitment problems: laws were frequently being passed to make the profession of soldier more attractive, alongside others threatening harsh punishments for deserters. These problems reached their climax in the early 5th century.

Towards the end of 401, Alaric crossed the Alps and marched into Italy (Claud. Get. 151–153). He overcame minor resistance at the Timavo, then laid siege to the court at Milan. Stilicho was away fighting a war in Rhaetia, but he brought this conflict to an end, concluded new treaties with neighbouring 'barbarians' to acquire auxiliaries, then recalled imperial troops from Gaul and Britain (Claud. Get. 414–420). He fought Alaric at Pollentia in April 402. The battle ended in a standoff, with Alaric withdrawing with sufficient forces intact, while Stilicho succeeded in seizing Alaric's war chest and wife (Claud., *Panegyricus dictus Honorio Augusto sextum consuli* 281–298). A battle at Verona produced another stalemate, but this time Alaric was forced to retreat into the Balkans. Finally, Stilicho signed a treaty with Alaric granting him a command in Illyricum (Olympiodorus Frg. 6).

Late in 405, Stilicho faced his greatest challenge: the invasion of Italy by the Gothic king Radagaisus. His barbarian army plundered widely in the north and pushed down as far as Tuscany (Oros. 7,37,4–16). Stilicho needed months to gather imperial troops and allied tribal warriors, who helped him to eliminate some of Radagaisus' forces through attrition or subjugation. He won a comprehensive victory over Radagaisus' main army at Florence in August 406 (Zos. 5,26,3–5). This enabled him to incorporate thousands of Goths into the army of the Western Empire (Olympiodorus Frg. 9).

Warriors of Radagaisus caused a panic as they fled to Gaul, and the situation was soon exacerbated by Alans, Vandals and Suebi who crossed the Rhine (406/07). This led to a seizure of power by Constantine III in Britain, and early in 407 he took the last field army there across to Gaul (Zos. 6,2,2). Thus began the political crisis that would lead to Stilicho's fall. A counterattack in Gaul failed to stop Constantine. Meanwhile, Alaric marched on Noricum and demanded additional payments (Zos. 5,29,5). Stilicho succeeded in convening the senate and addressing both threats. However, when word reached him of the death of the Eastern Roman Emperor Arcadius in May 408, he decided to travel to Constantinople and intervene in the succession. This was a step too far for his enemies at the western imperial court. They organized a massacre of the officers and officials close to Stilicho at Ticinum (Zos. 5,32). Stilicho went to Ravenna to negotiate with Honorius, but was forced to surrender. He was arrested and executed in August 408 (Olympiodorus Frg. 5,1).

For all his faults, Stilicho had a clear understanding of the problems facing the Western Roman Empire, and he was able to defuse those problems for twelve years. His death unleashed chaos from which the western half of the empire would never truly recover.

BIBLIOGRAPHY
[1] A. CAMERON, Claudian, 1970 [2] T. JANSSEN, Stilicho, 2004 [3] S. MAZZARINO, Stilicone, 1942 [4] M.A. MCEVOY, Child Emperor Rule in the Late Roman West, 2013 [5] J.W.P. WIJNENDAELE, Stilicho, Radagaisus and the So-called Battle of Faesulae, in: Journal of Late Antiquity 9.1, 2016, 267–284.

JEROEN WIJNENDAELE

Guards

A. In the service of the ruler
B. Protecting the emperor and his representatives
C. From Rome to Byzantium

The modern concept of a unit called a guard primarily refers to the function of protecting prominent figures. Equivalent terms in Antiquity were many and varied, and often quite explicit (*somatophylakes*, *corporis custodes*, literally: 'bodyguards' etc.). There was similar variety in the deployment, recruitment and identity of guard units, the reputation of which rested on their military ability, prestige and close connection to the centre of power.

A. IN THE SERVICE OF THE RULER

A.1. Beginnings among tyrants and kings
A.2. Macedonian and Hellenistic rulers
A.3. The security of the Roman magistrates and *imperatores*

A.1. BEGINNINGS AMONG TYRANTS AND KINGS

Special guard units began to emerge within and beyond the Greek world in the 7th and 6th centuries BC. On a much more modest scale than the 10,000 'immortals' and *melophoroi* ('apple-bearers') of the Achaemenid king (Hdt. 7,83,1), many Greek tyrants had guard units made up of outsiders and locals. In some cases, these guards even brought the tyrants to power and helped them keep it, as in the case of the *korynephoroi* ('club bearers') of Peisistratus in Athens in 561 BC (Hdt. 1,59,4f.) [16.396–398]. There is mention in Central Italy in the late 6th century BC of armed escorts or life guards to kings such as Lars Porsenna and Tarquinius Superbus called *satellites* (Liv. 2,12,8). These soldiers had great symbolic value in the eyes of the Greeks, and were considered one of the defining characteristics of a *tyrannis*. Aristotle accordingly contrasts the guard of the threatened tyrant, composed of foreign mercenaries, with the royal guard composed of willing citizens, finding the latter more acceptable (Aristot. Pol. 1285a) [11]; [24]. In Sparta, for instance, a king going to war in the Classical period would be surrounded by a unit of elite citizen soldiers known as the *hippeis* (Hdt. 6,56 mentions 100 men, but there were usually about 300; Thuc. 5,72,4). Although these were foot soldiers, their name ('riders') betrays an old, originally aristocratic mounted specialism.

A.2. Macedonian and Hellenistic rulers

Cavalry did in fact enjoy an elevated status in the ancient guard units. Particular value was attached to their deployment together with infantry units in the armies of Philip II of Macedon (382–336 BC; → Generals of note M.) and Alexander the Great (356–323 BC; → Generals of note B.). Guard members, sometimes known as *doryphoroi* ('lancers'), also belonged to special corps. Also part of the cavalry of the *hetairoi* ('companions') under Alexander – traditionally chosen from among the Macedonian nobility to accompany and advise the king and fight with him – was a 'royal squadron' (*ile basilike*) charged with his protection. This unit, which may have been cut from 400 to 300 men, was also known by the name *agema* (Arr. Anab. 4,24,1), and it formed a highly prestigious bodyguard. The same term was also used to specify 500 footsoldiers among the 3,000 royal *hypaspistai* ('shield bearers'), themselves regarded as highly valuable soldiers and successors to Philip's *pezetairoi* ('companions on foot'; Theop. FGrH. 115 Frg. 348). The *argyraspides* ('silver shieldbearers') who succeeded them also continued after the death of Alexander (Plut. Eumenes 16,6–8) [14]. Finally, the *somatophylakes* ('bodyguards', who actually performed a variety of tasks for the king) were originally seven, later eight very close colleagues of Philip and Alexander (and included Lysimachus and Ptolemy).

The existence of a royal guard was justified by genuine threats at court, and also by the military and ideological foundations of the Macedonian and Hellenistic kingdoms, which existed in an almost permanent state of war and expected the ruler's active participation in battle. The guard units of the Diadochi and their successors adapted the Argead legacy to the particularities of their respective kingdoms [18]. A comprehensive reconstruction of the organization of the royal guards is not possible due to the fragmentary or vague state of the sources. Much familiar terminology, however, is contained in these sources. Infantry guards, consisting either of *hypaspistes* (Pol. 4,67,6) or of *argyraspides* (Pol. 5,79,4), are attested for the Antigonids, the Ptolemies and the Seleucids, as are assorted cavalry squadrons called *agema* or *ile basilike* (*regia* or *sacra ala* in Liv. 37,40,11; 42,58,9) [1.58–75]; [13.32–73]. Collective terms could be used to describe the entire body of a king's or court's forces (Pol. 15,25,3). The composition of the guard troops varied in terms of diversity and elitism. The Ptolemaic guards seem to have exhibited a degree of ethnic diversity [9.148–153], whereas inscriptions containing military regulations show that the *hypaspistai* of the Antigonids were physically, morally and socially elite, recruited according to census criteria (SEG 49, 722; 855).

Guards are also attested in other kingdoms that came under Roman influence and later Roman rule between the 2nd century BC and the 1st century AD. These corps combined the Greek-Macedonian tradition and the use of mercenaries with the Roman military model that would now come to prevail (Pol. 30,25,3). Herod (37–4 BC), for instance, had *doryphoroi* as well as Thracian, Germanic and Celtic mercenaries, including 400 Gauls from the guard of Cleopatra, gifted to him by Octavian (Jos. Ant. Iud. 15,217; 17,198).

A.3. The security of the Roman magistrates and *imperatores*

Units for assuring the security of magistrates and *imperatores* gradually (but not exclusively) began to emerge in the Roman Republic, which was receptive to Hellenistic influences and conducted far-flung and long-lasting campaigns [25]. During the 3rd and 2nd centuries BC, the protection of such figures was probably one of the responsibilities of the *extraordinarii*, selected from among the best infantry and cavalry soldiers of the confederate forces (Pol. 6,26,6–8; 6,31,2–4). P. Cornelius Scipio Africanus (235–183 BC; → Generals of note, O.) may have been the first to have a *cohors praetoria* ('praetorian guard'), an escort made up of better-paid, specialist elite soldiers (Fest. Lindsay p. 249, I. 7; → Elite troops). From then on, generals' entourages might consist of oustanding soldiers as well as relations, clients and friends. This process culminated in the 1st century BC with the appearance of ever more hardened, awe-inspiring guards for *imperatores* and legates. Marius (→ Generals of note, K.) and Sulla had their own guards (App. Civ. 1,100), and shortly thereafter Caesar in Gaul surrounded himself with 400 Germanic mounted fighters (Caes. B Gall. 7,13,1) (→ Generals of note, C.). This unit, reinforced with Gaulish cavalry and Spanish infantry, protected him throughout the Civil Wars. After his death, when the *cohortes praetoriae* were enlarged to become elite – and not necessarily guard – units (Cic. Fam. 10,30,1), Mark Antony and Octavian employed Spanish and German guards (Suet. Aug. 49,1; Cass. Dio 47,48,2). Following the Battle of Philippi (42 BC), 8,000 veterans were divided between the two *imperatores* (App. Civ. 5,3), who now had permanent *cohortes praetoriae*. They continued to increase in number to the point where Octavian was compelled to discharge some of them after the victory at Actium (31 BC). Some soldiers were settled in colonies, while others went on to serve, for double pay, in the first imperial *cohortes praetoriae* after 27 BC (Cass. Dio 53,11,5).

B. Protecting the emperor and his representatives

B.1. Evolution of an imperial guard
B.2. Functions and reforms
B.3. Service and recruitment

B.1. Evolution of an imperial guard

The establishment of a permanent personal guard could not be based solely on models from the Republican period, but also had to reflect the monarchical and military nature of the Principate (Cass. Dio 53,11,5). The Praetorian Guard founded in 27 BC was an elite force (→ Elite troops) that in the reign of Tiberius comprised at least nine cohorts, each probably with 500 men (Tac. Ann. 4,5,5) [7]; [15]; [3]. Augustus (27 BC–AD 14) also kept a squadron of Germanic cavalry in his service – the *Germani corporis custodes* ('Germanic Bodyguards') – functioning as his life guard [2]. The advantages they offered derived in equal measure from their riding skills, their lack of involvement in the political intrigues at Rome and their loyalty to their lord. All these units reflected the power and extraordinary nature of the *princeps* [25]. Other motivations for creating these units were the sense that protection was needed in light of the civil wars that had only recently concluded, and the fear of reactions that might be triggered by the new regime. For fear of creating a shock effect, Augustus stationed only three cohorts in the city of Rome among the locals, and sent the others to cities in Italy (Suet. Aug. 49,1; Suet. Tib. 37,1). The Germanic cavalry were also barracked in the peripheries of Rome, at Trastevere, before Augustus discharged them as a precaution after the defeat in the Teutoburg Forest (→ Battles of note, J.) in AD 9 (Cass. Dio 56,23,4).

The Germanic cavalry returned, however, under Tiberius (AD 14–37), and soon all Praetorian cohorts were brought together in a single camp. In 2 BC, Augustus had placed them under the command of two *praefecti praetorio* ('praetorian prefects') recruited from the equestrian order (Cass. Dio 55,10,10). A barracks occupying an area of 18 hectares was then built in AD 23 on the initiative of L. Aelius Seianus, the sole prefect under Tiberius (Tac. Ann. 4,2,1). Its remote location on the Viminal Hill (where part of the defensive walls, integrated into the Aurelian Walls, is still visible today) testifies to an attempt at restraint, but the very existence of the *castra praetoria* ('praetorian barracks') rooted the Praetorian Guard in the urban, military and political landscape of Rome [6]; [17]; [4].

B.2. Functions and reforms

The Praetorian cohorts, which aside from a few hundred horsemen mainly consisted of infantry, were responsible for the safety and security of the emperor and his family in residence on the Palatine Hill. They were also tasked with maintaining order (Tac. Ann. 14,61,1) and conducting special operations such as political assassinations (Hdn. 3,12,11). They accompanied the court when it left the city on journeys or expeditions, they served as a reserve, and they occasionally intervened in conflicts, especially civil wars (Tac. Hist. 2,14,4). The number and strength of the cohorts fluctuated in the 1st century AD, particularly during the crisis of AD 68/69, before stabilizing at ten cohorts (CIL VI 1009). Besides the Praetorians, there are also references to the little-known *statores Augusti* ('imperial attendants') and the close protection unit of the *speculatores Augusti* ('imperial scouts'). The *Germani corporis custodes*, on the other hand, were abolished once and for all by Galba in 68 (Suet. Cal. 12,2), before Domitian or Trajan established the *equites singulares Augusti* ('imperial mounted guards'). This cavalry unit numbered 1,000 men in the 2nd century. It was commanded by a tribune and stationed on the Caelian Hill [22]; [23]. Its members were selected from among the best auxiliary cavalrymen across the entire empire.

Soldiers were also entrusted with ensuring the safety and security of representatives of imperial power in the provinces [20]. The terminology, which is mostly preserved in the form of inscriptions dating from the 2nd and 3rd centuries, was largely based on that of the imperial guard. Provincial governors had a *stratura* (AE 2007, 1257) made up of *equites singulares* ('mounted guards') and often commanded by a *centurio* ('centurion')(CIL VIII 21034). There are also records of *pedites singulares* ('infantry guards') and *stratores* ('grooms') (CIL XIII 8203). *Singulares* ('guards') were in the service of more senior officers (AE 1969/70, 583), while other functionaries and dignitaries could call upon military escorts (Plin. Ep. 10,27). Finally, the function of *protector* emerges in the epigraphic record in the Severan period in connection with the guards of governors and the Praetorian Prefect (AE 1979, 448) [21]; [19].

B.3. Service and recruitment

Although all guard troops performed security duties, their specialties, service conditions and recruitment differed. Until AD 193, Praetorians were Roman citizens, and mainly Italic (Tac. Ann. 4,5,5). They were treated as elite soldiers with shorter terms of service (16 years) and higher pay than other soldiers, which sometimes caused tension, especially with the legions (Tac. Ann. 1,17,6; 1,27,1). They enjoyed excellent opportunities for advancement in the Praetorium, extending to the *evocatio* (extension of service) and the rank of a *centurio* (in the cohorts of the urban garrison or in the legions with the prospect of becoming *primus pilus*; CIL III 7334). Some of them rose to become Roman tribunes (commanders of city watch, Praetorian or urban cohorts; CIL V 930) or pursued an equestrian career (procurators and senior prefects, including Praetorian Prefect; CIL VI 41141). The *Germani corporis custodes* and *equites singulares Augusti* were also counted among the elite units, but they were of less prestigious backgrounds and status than the Praetorians. The former, Germans without citizenship, were adopted into the *familia Caesaris* in the service of the ruler. The *equites singulares Augusti* mainly came from the Danube and Rhine region (and were therefore occasionally known as the Batavi after the Germanic tribe that provided many of their recruits). Their fate was better: they became Roman citizens and could achieve promotion to *decurio* ('decurion') or *centurio* in their own units, in auxiliary units or in the legions (AE 2006, 1013 = AE 2010, 1167; CIL II^2 14/2, 1031) [8]. This mobility facilitated contact between urban and provincial units, and promoted the integration of soldiers of the guard units into the Roman army.

C. From Rome to Byzantium

C.1. An ambiguous institution
C.2. The guards of Late Antiquity

C.1. An ambiguous institution

The rise and subsequent fall of Sejanus in AD 31 displayed the power and yet also the vulnerability of the Praetorian Prefects, who were furnished with important military, judicial and advisory privileges. The division of the office among multiple prefects was intended to limit their influence, but some of them, sometimes as sole prefects, came to be seen as so threatening that they were murdered by order of the emperor (Hdn. 1,12,3–1,13,6; 3,10,5–3,12,12 on Cleander and Plautian). Their power derived from the importance of the Praetorian Guard. Although serving as the emperor's bodyguard and as a bulwark of the regime, the Praetorian Guard also represented a threat and destabilizing factor. The loyalty of the Praetorians was based on a fragile equilibrium that was maintained by the granting of gifts and privileges, and also by the personality and decisions of the emperor.

The Praetorians, in fact, played a crucial role in many changes of emperor, particularly in the 1st century AD (e.g. in AD 41: murder of Caligula and accession of Claudius). This role, however, was challenged by provincial troops in AD 68–69 and 193. In the events of 193, the murder of Pertinax and the defeat of Didius Julianus – whom the Guard had put on the throne because he offered the highest *donativum* ('monetary payment') – resulted in the Praetorians being punished by Septimius Severus, whose first priority was to consolidate his own position (Hdn. 2,5f.; 2,13). He dismissed those responsible and replaced them with legionaries who had helped him seize power. The *cohortes praetoriae* ('Praetorian Guard') now numbered 10,000 men, while the *equites singulares Augusti* ('Imperial Mounted Guards') were increased to 2,000 horsemen and acquired a second tribune and a second barracks on the Caelian Hill (remains are located beneath the Lateran Basilica). The new form of recruitment for the Praetorians continued into the 3rd century and inaugurated a change in the social and cultural composition of the Guard, most of whose members were by now Illyrian (CIL VI 2602). At the same time, the increasing mobility of the emperors, who were now forced to travel to multiple fronts, brought about a corresponding mobility in the nucleus of the guard troops, who were combined with other elite detachments in the mobile imperial units (*comitatus*). To distinguish the centurions and tribunes serving in this army, the honorific title *protector Augusti* came into use in the second third of the 3rd century (CIL III 327) [5]. The military challenges of the years 240–280 promoted the social advancement of the Praetorian Prefects and strengthened their influence. Some of them even rose to become emperor (Macrinus, reigned 217–218; Philippus Arabs, 244–249). During this period, the ruler's safety was under serious threat from enemies (Decius' death in battle 251; Valerian's captivity 260) and attempts at usurpation, some of which were supported by the guard troops themselves.

C.2. The guards of Late Antiquity

According to the system introduced by Diocletian, the mobile guard troops joined the two (later four) *comitatus* of the Tetrarchs, while others remained at Rome (AE 1981, 777; Zos. 2,9,1–3). However, the victories of Constantine (306–337) in AD 312 and 324 spelled the end of the *equites singulares Augusti* and the *cohortes praetoriae* (Zos. 2,17,2), which were dissolved and replaced by the *scholae palatinae* ('Palace Guards') [10]. This new elite cavalry originally comprised five units of 300 or 500 men each, which were commanded by tribunes, but under the authority of the *magister officiorum*. An important, albeit not exclusive role was played by Germanic recruitment. Forty *candidati* (named for their 'bright white' garments) were chosen from among the *scholares* ('Imperial Guards') to form the emperor's life guard. The subdivision of the *scholae palatinae* – which comprised *scutarii* ('Shield Guards'), *armaturae* ('Armored Guards') and *gentiles* ('Foreign Guards') – had to be adapted to suit the political changes of the 4th century. There were probably five schools in the west and seven in the east around AD 400 (Not.

Dign. Occ. 9,4–8; Not. Dign. Or. 11,4–10). The main theatre of operations for the imperial guard was no longer Rome, but the new centres of power in the Late Antique empire, such as Milan and Constantinople. Even so, their close association with the emperor still earned the *scholares* prestige and better career prospects, and the same applied to the *protectores domestici* ('Domestic Protectors'). Closely connected with the emperor and court, this group of soldiers (which included the historian Ammianus Marcellinus and the Emperor Jovian) increasingly behaved like a guard, taking on a range of assignments under the command of the *comes domesticorum* ('Commander of the Domestic Protectors'). The *scholae palatinae*, who were known as *obsequium* ('Obedience') in the 5th century, were dissolved in the west and gradually reduced to a ceremonial role in the east. Leo I (457–474) created a new imperial guard corps of 300 *excubitores* ('sentinels'; cf. *exkoubitai*), soon commanded by the influential *comes excubitorum* (*domestikos ton exkoubiton*). Justin I (518–527) held this post before taking the throne. During the 5th and 6th centuries, prominent figures such as Belisarius (d. 565) also had their own guards (Procop. Goth. 7,1,18f.), often known as *bucellari* ('escort troops'; cf. *bukellarioi*) [12].

Over the thousand or more years of their history, the ancient guard units fulfilled not only their assorted designated functions (protection, combat, maintenance of order, special assignments), but also an important psychological and ideological role as a symbol of the power of the people they guarded, who were chiefly rulers. Their esprit de corps (often expressed in special insignia), their changing ability to create problems for those in power (especially if they were weak), their privileges and the careers of some of their members reflect their proximity to the ruler's circle as well as their status as → elite troops. In their partial openness to non-citizens and foreigners, the guard troops illustrate the diversity of the societies, military cultures and political regimes of Antiquity, in which every soldier – regardless of his specialization – had the task of ensuring the safety of his lord and master. (See the many articles on the subject in [25].)

☞ Elite troops; Esprit de corps

BIBLIOGRAPHY

[1] B. BAR-KOCHVA, The Seleucid Army. Organization and Tactics in the Great Campaigns, 1976 [2] H. BELLEN, Die germanische Leibwache der römischen Kaiser des iulisch-claudischen Hauses, 1981 [3] S. BINGHAM, The Praetorian Guard. A History of Rome's Elite Special Forces, 2012 [4] A.W. BUSCH, Militär in Rom. Militärische und paramilitärische Einheiten im kaiserzeitlichen Stadtbild, 2011 [5] M. CHRISTOL, La carrière de Traianus Mucianus et l'origine des protectores, in: Chiron 7, 1977, 393–408 [6] J.C. COULSTON, 'Armed and Belted Men'. The Soldiery in Imperial Rome, in: J.C. COULSTON / H. DODGE (eds.), Ancient Rome. The Archaeology of the Eternal City, 2000, 76–118 [7] M. DURRY, Les cohortes prétoriennes, 1938 [8] P. FAURE, De Rome à Salone. T. Flavius Lucilius, cavalier de la garde impériale, in: ZPE 172, 2010, 223–238 [9] C. FISCHER-BOVET, Army and Society in Ptolemaic Egypt, 2014 [10] R.I. FRANCK, Scholae palatinae. The Palace Guards of the Later Roman Empire, 1969 [11] V. GABRIELSEN, The Impact of Armed Forces on Government and Politics in Archaic and Classical Greek Poleis. A Response to Hans van Wees, in: A. CHANIOTIS / P. DUCREY (eds.), Army and Power in the Ancient World, 2002, 83–98 [12] J.F. HALDON, Byzantine Praetorians. An Administrative, Institutional and Social Survey of the Opsikion and Tagmata, c. 580–900, 1984 [13] M.B. HATZOPOULOS, L'organisation de l'armée macédonienne sous les Antigonides. Problèmes anciens et documents nouveaux, 2001 [14] W. HECKEL, The Three Thousand. Alexander's Infantry Guard, in: B. CAMPBELL / L.A. TRITLE (eds.), The Oxford Handbook of Warfare in the Classical World, 2013, 162–178 [15] L. KEPPIE, The Praetorian Guard before Sejanus, in: Athenaeum 84, 1996, 101–124 [16] L. DE LIBERO, Die archaische Tyrannis, 1996 [17] R. SABLAYROLLES, La rue, le pouvoir et le soldat. La garnison de Rome de César à Pertinax, in: Pallas 55, 2001, 127–153 [18] N.V. SEKUNDA, The Macedonian Army, in: J. ROISMAN / I. WORTHINGTON (eds.), A Companion to Ancient Macedonia, 2010, 446–471 [19] M.A. SPEIDEL, Protectors and Assassins. Caracalla's Guards on the Day He Died, in: C. WOLFF / P. FAURE (eds.), Corps du chef et gardes du corps dans l'armée romaine, 2020, 421–431 [20] M.P. SPEIDEL, Guards of the Roman Armies. An Essay on the Singulares of the Provinces, 1978 [21] M.P. SPEIDEL, The Early Protectores and Their Beneficiarius Lance, in: AKB 16, 1986, 451–454 [22] M.P. SPEIDEL, Die Denkmäler der Kaiserreiter. Equites singulares Augusti, 1994 [23] M.P. SPEIDEL, Riding for Caesar. The Roman Emperors' Horse Guards, 1994 [24] H. VAN WEES, Tyrants, Oligarchs and Citizen Militias, in: A. CHANIOTIS / P. DUCREY (eds.), Army and Power in the Ancient World, 2002, 61–82 [25] C. WOLFF / P. FAURE (eds.), Corps du chef et gardes du corps dans l'armée romaine, 2020.

PATRICE FAURE

Heroism

A. Introduction and definition
B. Greece
C. Rome

A. Introduction and definition

Heroism denotes the crystallization of exemplary qualities in individuals real or fictional. It is not limited to the military sphere, but the most famous heroes in Antiquity were indeed warriors, whose actions in battle were seen as an expression of masculinity, defiance of death, fighting strength and sometimes patriotism. It is not such actions in themselves that define heroism, but the relationship between the actions and the value system of the reference group. Heroism does not imply cultic veneration, but rather the memorial celebration of deeds in textual and pictorial tributes and rituals.

B. Greece

B.1. Heroism in Homer
B.2. Heroes of the *polis*
B.3. Kings as heroes

B.1. Heroism in Homer

The most vigorous and influential formulation of ancient heroism came from Homer ([7]; [15.61–165]; [9.20–38]; comparison with epic heroes in other cultures [10]). The heroes of the *Iliad* stand out from the multitude of humanity by virtue of their physical beauty, illustrious ancestry, wealth and intelligence, but above all by their outstanding deeds in battle. As leaders of divisions of troops, they far surpass ordinary soldiers and the poet's contemporaries in bodily size and strength (Hom. Il. 5,302–304; 12,381–383), and they distinguish themselves in particular through their valour and disdain for death. Although the *Iliad* certainly acknowledges the mass fighting of armies, the poet's attention is focused on combat between individual, named heroes. The Homeric concept of the hero includes no magnanimous renunciation of 'unfair' methods in warfare. Only rarely do heroes announce an attack in advance, and most spears are thrown without prior warning. Nor are these heroes 'noble' in the sense of treating their adversaries with respect. Generosity towards enemies killed is rare, whereas scorn for the fallen is the rule [8.160–162].

Heroism in war is relevant to status in Homer. The best warriors are honoured with costly gifts, the best portions of meat and prestigious seating positions. Even the aged Nestor, highly regarded as a counsellor in the army of the Greeks, boasts of his youthful heroism in battle (Hom. Il. 11,670–761). One visible manifestation of heroic deeds was the armour captured from an enemy that the victor would display in a prominent place. The ideal death for the Homeric hero was in battle. Faced with the choice of falling gloriously in the prime of his youth or living a peaceful life into old age, he would opt for the former [7.136f. with examples]. An honourable funeral and a grave mound visible from afar secured the hero's legacy of renown.

The Homeric epics do not, however, glorify heroic deeds in battle without qualification. The *Iliad* recounts Achilles' thirst for blood in a critical tone, and in the underworld he confides to Odysseus that he would willingly be a poor day labourer if only he could still be alive (Hom. Od. 11,488–491) – undermining the mystique of the heroic death in battle. Nevertheless, Homeric heroism with its exhibition of strength and valour in single combat remained an influential factor in warfare throughout Antiquity [9]. For Homer, heroism stands in contrast to the ways of ordinary men and women, and a failure of valour leads to the revocation of masculinity (Hom. Il. 2,235). On the other hand, there is a distinction drawn between heroes and the gods. The Homeric heroes enjoy the support of gods and are honoured like gods (Hom. Il. 11,58; Hom. Od. 5,36) – but the poet does not mean by this cultic veneration through sacrifice or other religious acts performed for actual gods [7.22–29].

B.2. Heroes of the *polis*

Heroic single combat dominates the depiction of war in Greek art (→ Representations of war A.). Representations of battle lines are rare. Reliefs and vase paintings tend to show duels, which can be mythological encounters between heroes of the past (identified by name inscriptions or iconographic attributes) or combat between anonymous hoplites [11]. Yet, influential as the Homeric epics were, the actual practice of warfare limited the scope for individual heroism in battle. The typical military scenario both on land and at sea consisted of encounters between groups of men, which rendered outstanding accomplishments in single combat virtually impossible, and in any case imprudent. Rather than individual heroes, there were heroic collectives, most notably the 300 Spartiates led by Leonidas, who refused to retreat while defending Thermopylae against the army of Xerxes and were finally surrounded and slaughtered (480 BC) (→ Sparta). Some aspects of Herodotus' description of this conflict (7,223–227) recall the Homeric epics: a fight breaks out over the body of Leonidas, the Persians are repelled four times, and the bravest men in battle are accorded special attention. The focus, however, is on the collective effort, not individual participants. It is unclear whether Leonidas' decision to hold out at Thermopylae was motivated by the strategic aim of allowing most of the army to retreat, or by the desire to set an example of Spartan courage in the face of death (cf. [1.34–39]). The latter motive dominates ancient and post-ancient reception alike, and the '300' are still to this day received as heroes who willingly accepted death in battle for their homeland. Other famed heroic collectives of the Classical period are the Athenian Marathonomakoi, who became symbols not only of patriotism and fighting strength, but also of moral purity (on the reception [8]), and the Theban 'Sacred Band', who were almost entirely wiped out after fighting bravely at the Battle of Chaironeia (338 BC) against Philip II (→ Generals of note, M.).

The Homeric heroism of the lone warrior fighting the enemy's best soldier ahead of the battle line now gave way to a new heroism, that of the hoplite persevering in the battle line and defying all enemy attacks (e.g. Tyrt. 8,21–34 G.-P.). When the Spartiate Aristodemus, the only one of Leonidas' hoplites to return alive from Thermopylae to Sparta, who had been stripped of his honorific civic rights as a suspected coward, broke out of formation at the Battle of Plataeae (479 BC), stormed at the enemy and was killed, the Spartans denied him honours. It was argued that he had performed his deeds solely out of personal motivations, not in the service of the *polis* (Hdt. 7,229–231; 9,71). Persistence on the battlefield also informed the concept of → victory. Regardless of losses in battle, the party controlling the battlefield was regarded as the victor (Hdt. 1,82; Diod. Sic. 19,31). When commanders fought in person, which they did often, but not always, they performed no heroic deeds in single combat, but offered the soldiers an example of brave conduct in the battle line [16].

The concept of collective heroism is also expressed in the commemoration of the fallen. Until the early 5th century, it was commonplace for notably brave warriors to be buried in prominent graves. After the Battle of Plataeae, for instance, the Spartans made graves for the Spartiates and Helots, but they also made a third for the burial of the greatest heroes of the battle. In later times, however, egalitarian tendencies came increasingly to the fore. The lists of the fallen that many *poleis* published give the names of the dead, but no individual commendations, and eulogies refrain from describing individuals' deeds in battle. The focus was on the collective effort made on behalf of the *polis*. The Homeric concept of surpassing all others in outstanding accomplishments was transferred from the individual to the group – a tendency that is particularly evident in armies made up of contingents from different *poleis*. Prior to the Battle of Plataeae, the Tegeatae and Athenians argued over who should take the place of honour on the left wing (Hdt. 9,26f.). After the Battle of Salamis (480 BC), the Aeginetans were placed ahead of the Athenians as the bravest (Hdt. 8,93).

B.3. KINGS AS HEROES

A new phase of heroism began with Alexander the Great (→ Generals of note, B.), who often fought in the front line during battles and sieges, deliberately emulating the Homeric heroes, especially Achilles [9.115–139]. The literary record shows the decisive phase of the Battle of the Granicus (334 BC) as a sequence of duels (Arr. Anab. 1,15). Alexander here created a model for the Hellenistic kings. They would legitimize their rule through war, in which military success alone was not sufficient – personal deeds were also required (essential: [5]). In extreme cases, this led to duels between the enemy generals. Eumenes and Neoptolemus fought each other at the Battle of the Hellespont (321 or 320 BC), on horseback at first, then on foot, until Eumenes killed his opponent and – firmly in the Homeric tradition – removed his armour (Diod. Sic. 18,31; Plut. *Eumenes* 7). But the epitome of the heroic Hellenistic commander was Pyrrhus of Epirus, whose name and mythical genealogy connected him with Achilles and his son, and who sought out illustrious opponents for duels in battle (Plut. *Pyrrhus* 7,4f.; 16,8–10; 24; 30,5f.). Nor was it only kings who associated themselves with the heroic ideal: commanders of league armies did, too. Philopoemen, for example, the *strategos* of the Achaean League, killed the Spartan tyrant Machanidas with his own hands at the Battle of Mantinea (207 BC).

The main opportunity for ordinary soldiers to distinguish themselves visibly came during sieges (e.g. Pol. 7,17).

C. ROME

C.1. Exempla
C.2. Single combat
C.3. Centurions
C.4. Generals

C.1. EXEMPLA

Roman tradition asserted that in early times, there were many heroic figures who saved the city through their personal efforts in critical situations and thereby enabled the expansion of Roman power. After the expulsion of the kings from Rome, Horatius Cocles was said to have single-handedly defended a bridge across the Tiber against the army of the Etruscan king Lars Porsena, until his comrades tore down the bridge and thwarted the invasion of the city (Pol. 6,55; Liv. 2,10f.; on the statue in Rome, Plin. HN 34,22). Marcus Furius Camillus reputedly conquered Rome's powerful rival Veii in 396 BC, and later, with the Gauls ready to capture Rome, saved the city by his personal heroism and drove away the enemy (on the evolution of the Camillus legend cf. [13.382–407]). According to legend, Publius Decius Mus won the Battle of Sentinum for the Romans in 295 BC by ritually devoting himself to death, then attacking the enemy alone and dying in their midst (Liv. 10,26–30). According to a modern understanding, these exempla are constructs, but in the Roman mind they were part of their history and manifestations of typically Roman virtues, such as the spirit of sacrifice and the will to fight.

C.2. SINGLE COMBAT
Loose Roman battle formations and the suitability of legionaries' weapons for single combat created opportunities for notable individual victories in battle. Tradition records challenges that took place before battles and also spontaneous single combat during the fighting. Unlike in the Greek phalanx, it was regarded as acceptable and glorious in the Roman legion for individual soldiers to break out of formation and seek single combat [12]. In the early Republican period, T. Manlius Torquatus was said to have accepted a challenge from a gigantic Gaul, whom he defeated in a duel after he first obtained permission from his commanding officer (Liv. 7,9f.). Single combat is also attested during the Roman Civil Wars. During the war in Spain in 45 BC, the Pompeian Antistius Turpio and the Caesarian Q. Pompeius Niger fought 'as did once Memnon and Achilles' (Bell. Hisp. 25,3–5). Members of the Roman senatorial aristocracy were also among those who reportedly distinguished themselves in duels [12.393–396], e.g. Scipio Aemilianus as a young military tribune (Pol. 35,5,1f.; 151/50 BC). According to Polybius (6,54,4), the funeral ceremonies of aristocrats and the continuously updated memories of past heroic deeds inspired Romans to seek out single combat in battle. However, the Romans had no tradition of the duel as a proxy battle, that is, single combat between two heroes replacing a battle.

C.3. CENTURIONS
Among the Roman legions, heroism came into particular focus with the centurions [9.213–222], who are often mentioned by name in reports of battles and sieges. At Pharsalus (48 BC), the centurion Crastinus Caesar reportedly promised before battle to exhibit supreme valour, and he kept his promise during the battle to the point of giving up his life (Caes. B Civ. 3,91; 3,99). Two centurions of a besieged army contingent left their fortifications and attacked the enemy (54 BC; Caes. B Gall. 5,44). At the siege of Gergovia (52 BC), the centurion Marcus Petronius emulated Horatius Cocles, confronting the enemy alone and giving his comrades time to save themselves (Caes. B Gall. 7,50). He was praised for his valour, but he was also expressly reprimanded for his impetuousness in venturing too far ahead contrary to orders. Discipline, Caesar indicates, is just as important as heroic courage (Caes. B Gall. 7,52). This illustrates the conflicting nature of centurion heroism. On the one hand, it served to boost troops' morale in critical situations, and it served a functional purpose for the Roman army. On the other hand, there was a risk that it might rob generals of tactical control. According to Polybius, a centurion should not initiate hostilities except when objectively necessary, but he should persevere to the point of death once hostilities were underway (Pol. 6,24,9).

C.4. GENERALS
In the the Roman army there were numerous awards (→ Honours) for valiant fighters, whether simple soldiers or officers and generals. The highest and rarest military honour was the *spolia opima* ('rich spoils'), the dedication of weapons taken from an opposing general by the commander who killed him with his own hands [4]. There are only three instances of such an event in the Roman tradition, the last being that of Marcus Claudius Marcellus, who defeated the Insubrian king Viridomarus in 222 BC (Plut. *Marcellus* 8). On the whole, however, the obligation for Roman generals to display soldierly self-discipline, strength of character and renunciation of a luxurious life in the camp was stronger than any imperative to fight on the front line. Under normal circumstances, generals only took up arms in crisis situations [6.150–163]. Typical Roman practice is evident in Onasander's insistence that generals should not jeopardize the overall success of the battle to strive for personal glory, and so they they should oversee the whole battle rather than fight in the first rank (Onas. 33). When heroism in battle was discussed, it was emphasized that such deeds were done in the service of the *res publica*. This is reflected in political discourse. Senators involved in heated debates sometimes bared their chests to show off their scars earned in battle, thereby drawing attention to their military prowess. Marcus Servilius Pulex did so, for example, when in 167 BC the people at first denied Aemilius Paullus a triumph. Pulex recalled his 23 victories in single combat with enemies of Rome (Liv. 45,39; Plut. *Aemilius Paullus* 31). This was not a demand to be honoured for his military feats, but a move to assert senatorial authority and discredit a political opponent who could display no such evidence of valour [3.123–136].

During the late Republican period, the Hellenistic ideal of a charismatic general beloved of the gods also took root in Rome. Sulla had himself described as the favourite of Aphrodite on the victory monument at Chaeronea, and at Rome he accepted the byname Felix ('the Fortunate') as a reference to his victorious nature as seen in the good luck in battle that constantly smiled upon him. Pompey (→ Generals of note, N.) presented himself publicly in ways that recalled Alexander the Great – for instance, wearing a cloak during a triumphal procession that was said to have belonged to the world-conquering Macedonian himself (App. Mithr. 577). Although there are anecdotes of personal feats in combat performed by these generals (Plut. *Sulla* 21), the basis of their military self-portrayal was not personal heroism, but overall success in battle.

A victorious nature was essential to the legitimacy of Roman emperors, but unlike with the Hellenistic kings, there was no expectation that they would display personal heroism. They generally did not take the battlefield in person, even if they commanded the troops. All this changed, however, with Maximinus Thrax (235–238), who joined the Roman army as a simple soldier and embarked on a swift ascent through his military career. Maximinus did fight personally in battles, and most of his successors did likewise. The old heroic ideal exerted a powerful influence again in Late Antiquity [9.290–309], the most notable illustration being the emperor Julian, who on his Persian campaign (AD 363) killed prominent enemy figures with his own hands and removed their armour – in conscious emulation, according to Ammianus Marcellinus (24,4,5), of Manlius Torquatus and other heroes of the distant past.

Military heroism looms large in the surviving written and pictorial sources of Antiquity, but it did not go unchallenged. Greek and Latin literature alike contain passages and even entire works in which individuals portraying themseves as war heroes are lampooned. Notable examples include Lamachus in Aristophanes' comedy *The Acharnians* (ll. 1072–1226; 425 BC), and the eponymous *miles gloriosus* ('The Vainglorious Soldier'), an oafish, braggart soldier in Plautus' play (c. 206–204 BC).

☞ Cowardice; Emotions; Honour; Valour

BIBLIOGRAPHY
[1] A. ALBERTZ, Exemplarisches Heldentum. Die Rezeptionsgeschichte der Schlacht an den Thermopylen von der Antike bis zur Gegenwart, 2006 [2] L. DE BLOIS, The Roman Army and Politics in the First Century before Christ, 1987 [3] E. FLAIG, Ritualisierte Politik. Zeichen, Gesten und Herrschaft im Alten Rom, 2003 [4] H.I. FLOWER, The Tradition of the Spolia Opima. M. Claudius Marcellus and Augustus, in: Classical Antiquity 19, 2000, 34–64 [5] H.-J. GEHRKE, Der siegreiche König. Überlegungen zur hellenistischen Monarchie, in: AKG 64, 1982, 247–277 [6] A.K. GOLDSWORTHY, The Roman Army at War, 100 BC–AD 200, 1996 [7] F. HORN, Held und Heldentum bei Homer. Das homerische Heldenkonzept und seine poetische Verwendung, 2014 [8] M. JUNG, Marathon und Plataiai. Zwei Perserschlachten als »lieux de mémoire« im antiken Griechenland, 2006 [9] J.E. LENDON, Soldiers and Ghosts. A History of Battle in Classical Antiquity, 2005 [10] D.A. MILLER, The Epic Hero, 2000 [11] S. MUTH, Gewalt im Bild. Das Phänomen der medialen Gewalt im Athen des 6. und 5. Jahrhunderts v.Chr., 2008 [12] P.S. OAKLEY, Single Combat in the Roman Republic, in: CQ 35, 1985, 392–410 [13] U. WALTER, Memoria und res publica. Zur Geschichtskultur im republikanischen Rom, 2004 [14] H. VAN WEES, Status Warriors. War, Violence, and Society in Homer and History, 1992 [15] H. VAN WEES, Greek Warfare. Myths and Realities, 2004 [16] E.L. WHEELER, The General as Hoplite, in: V.D. HANSON (ed.), Hoplites. The Classical Greek Battle Experience, 1991, 121–170.

CHRISTIAN MANN

Honour

A. Introduction
B. Greece
C. Republican Rome
D. Late Republic and Imperial period

A. INTRODUCTION

Modern sociology sometimes treats the concept of honour as a basic value of Mediterranean societies. Although this could also be said of the ancient Mediterranean world as whole and its concept of military honour specifically, it is important to distinguish the story of how people thought from the study of historical realities, lest we repeat the topos of a 'western model of war', whose superiority is based on the central place of honour among the Greeks and Romans, in contrast to a supposedly 'Oriental' model based on deceit and perfidy.

B. GREECE

The Homeric epics already convey their own concept of honour (*time*). The epic hero distinguishes himself in combat and his death in battle assures him of everlasting renown. Some heroes, such as Achilles, exhibit a notably strict 'code of honour'. Jean-Pierre Vernant describes the Greeks' as a 'civilization of honour, in which every man throughout his life is defined in terms of what others see and say about him; in which the greater the glory celebrated in him, the more he exists, and in which only he whose fame endures continues to exist instead of sinking into oblivion' [10]. This concept of honour underlies the contrast between Achilles the hero, whose honour is founded on deeds in battle, and Odysseus, the ingenious, artful fighter, for whom the outcome is all that counts. In the later culture of the *polis*, honour (*time*) was expressed in the community's recognition of the individual. The contrast between *time* and shame/disgrace (*aidos*) was fundamental to the canon of values in Greek society. This concept of honour also spread beyond Greek civilization, particularly in the Roman world, by virtue of the ideals of *paideia* ('education') [3]; [4].

An honour-based canon of virtues was especially important in Sparta, as illustrated by the poetry of Tyrtaeus (fr. 10 West). Horace later transformed Tyrtaeus' key idea into the aphorism *dulce et decorum est pro patria mori* ('It is sweet and decorous to die for one's country'; Carm. 3,2,13). Spartan soldiers sometimes took their own lives after losing their honour, as the example of Pantites illustrates. Sent as an emissary by Leonidas to Thessaly, he was not at his post for the Battle of Thermopylae (480 BC) in time. He hanged himself on his return to Sparta (Hdt. 7,232). The military superiority of the Spartans was rooted in their honour – a 'beautiful death' was preferable to a life of shame (Xen. Lac. 9,1). The dilemma faced by Leonidas – to do battle and die honourably or to save himself dishonourably – became a popular topic for the *suasoriae* (rhetorical exercises in deliberation) at the rhetorical schools of the Roman period (Sen. Suas. 2). Moreover, persisting in a hopeless battle while preserving one's honour was also seen as a possible way to achieve an unexpected victory. Spartan tradition preserved a report of the Battle of the Sagra River (c. 560/50 BC), at which the Locrians defeated the numerically superior Crotoniates: 'But while they strove to die with honour, they had the good fortune to win victory, and there was no other reason for their victory but their desperation' (Just. Epit. 20,3,4). Facing the threat of danger during the Battle of Arginusae (August 406 BC), the Spartan navarch Callicratidas declared that 'Sparta would be no worse off if he were killed, but to flee would be a disgrace' (Xen. Hell. 1,6,32). The generals of the Greek city-states could potentially suffer punishment for dishonouring the *polis*. In his speech against the *strategos* ('commander') Lysicles, who was one of those responsible for the defeat at Chaeronea in 338 BC, the orator Lycurgus called him a 'living monument to the disgrace and dishonour of the land of our fathers'. These words convinced the jury to impose the death penalty (Diod. Sic. 16,88,1f. = Lycurg. fr. 77 Conomis).

The concept of soldierly honour in the Greek *polis* often referred to the citizen's deployment as a hoplite [12]. Plato attributed the idea that one must 'endure and face danger without fearing death or any evil more than disgrace' to Socrates, who had served as a hoplite in the Peloponnesian War. The same motivations that led him to remain at his post during the war later inspired him in facing the accusations of the Athenians (Pl. Ap. 28d–e). Especially important was the topos of the warrior's shield as a symbol of his honour. Returning home from battle without one's shield might incur an accusation of desertion. In a verse fragment in elegiac distichs (fr. 5 West = 8 Tarditi), Archilochus, although not worried over the loss of his shield, since he was able to save his life, still needed to insist that the shield remained 'unblemished' (*amometon*). Also befitting this list of examples is the story of Epameinondas, who it was said could only die in peace when he knew that his shield had been saved, and with it his honour safeguarded (Cic. Fam. 5,12,5).

The concept of honour in Greek *paideia*, conveyed through the lens of the Homeric heroes, also echoes in the literature about Alexander the Great. The decision by Demetrius Poliorketes to surrender to Seleucus (286 BC) was seen as dishonourable, because Demetrius could equally have chosen to die honourably (*honeste*: Just. Epit. 16,2,6). Plutarch, in the *synkrisis* ('comparison') of his *Parallel Lives* of Demetrius and Mark Antony (6,2), describes the latter's suicide as cowardly, lamentable and dishonourable (*deilos men kai oiktros kai atimos*), and he concedes that Antony's behaviour was just as discreditable as Demetrius', and yet he censures Demetrius more, because Antony did not go so far as to hand his physical person over to the enemy.

C. REPUBLICAN ROME

One key aspect of the ancient concept of honour was conduct in battle. Polybius (13,3,2–7) praises the traditional practice of fighting with the same weapons on the battlefield, which he ascribes to the Romans, while declaring that the Greeks abandoned this element of the military code in favour of strategems. In the introduction to *De viris illustribus*, Cornelius Nepos states that Greeks and Romans have different views on what is proper and appropriate, but he does not discuss the military aspect of this in any detail.

To be sure, a Roman of Polybius' day would have seen the success of his commonwealth as arising not simply from its logistical and technological superiority, but above all from its superior concept of honour. Carlin Barton has attempted to explain Rome's military success by appealing exclusively to the Roman categories of honour and shame [1]. She relies chiefly on Livy as the most instructive source in this regard, since his work depicts Roman victories and defeats as episodes in an unending theatrical spectacle, which is how Roman history is presented by Livy. However, a category such as honour, fundamental as it may be in sociology, cannot suffice to explain Rome's military successes – and still less its failures in moments of dishonour. While Barton undeniably displays a degree of interpretative acumen, her approach remains simplistic and derives from a superficial reading of the sources.

The sources offer numerous examples of Roman generals preferring to die rather than act dishonourably. Because it was an act contrary to *fides* ('fidelity'), breaking a promise was seen as dishonourable. One well-known, if legendary, example is the case of Marcus Atilius Regulus, who, held captive by the Carthaginians during the First Punic War, was sent to Rome to conclude a peace treaty. Although he spoke out in Rome against the Carthaginian demands, he kept his promise to the enemy and returned to Carthage, where he was brutally put to death (Liv. Per. 18,5). There is a hostile legend going back to the Augustan period that Mark Antony lacked any sense of honour and therefore lacked credibility (Sen. Suas. 7,7).

Many examples are recorded in which harsh punishments are demanded for soldiers who surrendered to the enemy or withdrew from combat – unless the move was made for tactical reasons (*maiore dedecore quam periculo*: Just. Epit. 31,8,6, Battle of Magnesia 190 BC). In 137 BC, when the troops of Gaius Hostilius Mancinus faced great difficulties during the Siege of Numantia, Mancinus was forced to negotiate a treaty with the city. When his plea to the Senate to confirm the treaty was unsuccessful, the consul was sent back to Numantia naked and in chains as a demonstration of the agreement's invalidity (Plut. *Tiberius Gracchus* 7). When he came back to Rome, Mancinus was deprived of citizenship (Cic. De or. 1,181). During the war against Jugurtha in 110 BC, the consul Spurius Postumius Albinus returned to Rome, transferring command to his brother Aulus. Defeated by Jugurtha, Aulus concluded a peace treaty with him that required Roman soldiers to be put under the yoke. This unleashed fierce outrage in Rome.

For a commander to abandon his men was considered dishonourable. In 105 BC, when the general Marcus Aurelius Scaurus fell into the hands of the Cimbri, he could have saved himself if he had surrendered to the enemy. But out of consideration for his *verecundia* ('sense of shame'), and to avoid the disgrace of surviving his own soldiers, he did not avail himself of this opportunity (Granius Licinianus 33,1–5). It was also seen as dishonourable for a defeated Roman general to surrender to an armed enemy. When Roman troops were massacred during the uprising of the Eburones under Ambiorix, the legate Lucius Aurunculeius Cotta, although gravely wounded, rejected the suggestion of his colleague Titurius Sabinus to suspend hostilities in order to negotiate with Ambiorix. Cotta stated that he was reluctant to surrender 'to an armed enemy' (Caes. B Gall. 5,36,3). The accusation that he dishonourably abandoned his men after the Battle of Actium in order to rush to Cleopatra's side was levelled against Mark Antony (Plutarch, *Demetrii cum Antonio comparatio* 3; 6).

Ethical considerations of this kind likewise influenced Roman political thought, which offered a multifaceted concept of *honos* (to Mathieu Jacotot, a 'fluid term and a theoretical concept, a political idea and a moral value, a literary figure and an ideological background' [7]). *Honos* can by used synonymously with *gloria* (in both military and social senses). The concept of military honour involved *fides*, fidelity to an ally, and the refusal to vacate a territory. A soldier who fought with honour received a monetary payment, an honorific wreath or other military decoration, which was also called *honos* and was regarded as a reward for having demonstrated *virtus* ('valour'; Cic. Brut. 28; cf. the speech of Metellus in Sall. Iug. 49,4). The word *honos* also occurs in honorific inscriptions from the Middle Republican period, such as those of L. Caecilius Metellus (221 BC: Plin. HN 7,139f.) and P. Cornelius Scipio (son of Scipio Africanus? c. 175–140 BC; CIL I², 10 = ILLRP 311).

The Middle Republican period provides the first evidence for a cult of Honos [2]. In 233 BC, Q. Fabius Maximus Verrucosus dedicated a temple to Honos in Rome near the Porta Capena. M. Claudius Marcellus later dedicated it to Virtus in 208 BC. Much of the booty from the conquest of Syracuse was deposited there (Liv. 25,40,1–3), including the *sphaira* ('[celestial] globe') of Archimedes (Cic. Rep. 1,21). The father of Marcellus had previously dedicated a temple to Honos and Virtus at Clastidium in 222 BC. Cicero mentions a similar dedication by C. Marius (Sest. 116).

D. LATE REPUBLIC AND IMPERIAL PERIOD

The greatest disgrace in this period was to lose the standard (Jos. BI 6,225), and to capture the enemy's standard was correspondingly honourable. In 20 BC, when Augustus secured the return of the legion standards that had been lost to the Parthians by Crassus, Decidius Saxa and Mark Antony, along with the return of Roman prisoners of war, the propaganda focused mainly on the standards, especially in their sacred dimension. Conversely, Horace three years previously (Carm. 3,5,5–12) had written disparagingly of those captured at Carrhae, alleging that they had allowed themselves to be married to Parthian women and therefore were living 'dishonourably' (*turpis*) among enemies. At the ceremonies to celebrate their recovery, the standards were first put on show in the Temple of Jupiter Feretrius, before being transferred in AD 2 to the newly built Temple of Mars Ultor in the Forum of Augustus (Ov. Fast. 5,585–589: *signa, decus belli*) [9].

Late Republican and Imperial historiography offers numerous examples of honourable actions by Roman soldiers and officers [8], whose courage and sense of sacrifice in the face of danger are emphasized (e.g. Cass. Dio 68,14,2: incident from the Dacian War). At the rhetorical schools, death in battle for the *patria* ('homeland') functioned as a standard theme in the rhetorical exploration of the difference between *honestum* and *turpe* ('honourable conduct' and 'disgraceful conduct'; Cic. Top. 84). In the final phase of the Civil War, senior commanders of Pompey's forces in Africa chose to commit suicide, an act for which Cato the Younger became the prime example in the literary tradition. Defeated Roman officers often made the same choice to avoid the shame of being killed by the enemy or falling into enemy hands. Among many notable examples is Quinctilius Varus and his staff, whose suicide Cassius Dio describes as 'terrible, yet unavoidable' (Cass. Dio 56,21,5). In this way, responsibility for military failures was diverted from the collective to the individual. That Varus, defeated at the Battle of the Teutoburg Forest, was placed on a par with Crassus was no accident. Nor is it accidental that the commonplace of Crassus' military ineptitude emerged during the principate of Tiberius.

The Roman sense of honour was often contrasted with the lack of such a sense among barbarians. This served to justify the severity of punishments that were inflicted for dishonourable conduct (Tac. Hist. 4,76). During the Imperial period, a legionary who allowed himself to be captured by the enemy faced execution or dismissal from the army. Numonius Vala, a legate under Varus, abandoned his men and fled on horseback; but he died 'as a deserter' (Vell. Pat. 2,119,4), which means that he was executed. Captured soldiers whose families bought their freedom from Germanic captivity could not return to Italy. Although they retained their other rights and their property according to the *ius postliminii* (right to return to Rome and resume rights as a citizen), Emperor Tiberius restricted their settlement to the provinces, invoking a provision for banishment that was originally intended to deal with minor cases of *maiestas* ('treason'). Titus spared the life of a legionary who had fled captivity with the Jewish rebels and returned to his unit, 'but since he considered him unworthy of remaining a Roman soldier because he had allowed himself to be captured alive, he took his weapons and expelled him from the legion, a humiliation worse than death' (Jos. BI 6,362).

The concept of honour influenced soldiers' behaviour. Even harmless jokes could trigger violent reactions. In AD 69, when Vitellius and his troops stood at the gates of Rome and plebeians jokingly took weapons from some legionaries, the result was a massacre of the population (Tac. Hist. 2,88,2). Within units, there were cases of discrimination with regard to honour. For instance, in the legions raised in the east of the empire, Fronto wrote a kind of memorandum to Marcus Aurelius in which he made reference to *Graecanici milites* ('soldiers of the Greek type'), which he associated with cowardice in the face of the enemy. 'As the height of dishonour' (*praeter huiuscemodi dedecora*), they took flight as soon as they set eyes on the Parthians in battle (Fronto, *Principia historiae* 13).

In Late Antiquity, the military concept of honour was transferred to other spheres. When Valerian was taken captive by the Parthians in AD 260, Lactantius notes with satisfaction that this persecutor of Christians died in enemy territory, 'for this put so shameful an end to a shameful life' (*quam pudendam vitam in illo dedecore finivit*, Lactant. De mort. pers. 5,6). Conditions of peace treaties were sometimes felt to be dishonourable, as in the case of the treaty with the Parthians signed by Emperor Jovian shortly after the death of Emperor Julian in AD 363. Ammianus Marcellinus, who as a historian takes a highly critical view of Jovian, speaks disparagingly of 'the dishonourable conditions that were brought about by dire need, even though both parties had sworn the traditional oaths,' which, as Ammianus argues in reference to examples from history, would have sufficed to render the treaty null and void (Amm. Marc. 25,9,11).

☞ Cowardice; Valour

BIBLIOGRAPHY

[1] C.A. BARTON, Roman Honor. The Fire in the Bones, 2001 [2] G. BRIZZI, Honos et Virtus, Fortuna Huiusce Diei. Idéologies et propagande au dernier siècle de la République, in: Y. LE BOHEC (ed.), État et société aux deux derniers siècles de la République romaine. Hommage à François Hinard, 2010, 13–22 [3] D.L. CAIRNS, Aidōs. The Psychology and Ethics of Honour and Shame in Ancient Greek Literature, 1993 [4] D.L. CAIRNS, Honour and Shame. Modern Controversies and Ancient Values, in: Critical Quarterly 51, 2011, 23–41 [5] H. DREXLER, Honos (1961), in: H. DREXLER, Politische Grundbegriffe der Römer, 1988, 55–72 [6] P. HORDEN / N. PURCELL, The Corrupting Sea. A Study in Mediterranean History, 2000 [7] M. JACOTOT, Question d'honneur. Les notions d'honos, honestum et honestas dans la République romaine antique, 2013 [8] J.E. LENDON, Empire of Honour. The Art of Government in the Roman World, 1997 [9] G. TRAINA, Carrhes. 9 juin 53 av. J.-C. Anatomie d'une bataille, 2011 [10] J.-P. VERNANT (ed.), L'uomo greco, 1991 [11] F.J. VERVAET, Honour and Shame in the Roman Republic, in: H.J. KIM et al. (eds.), Eurasian Empires in Antiquity and the Early Middle Ages. Contact and Exchange between the Graeco-Roman World, Inner Asia and China, 2017 [12] S. YOSHITAKE, Arete and the Achievements of the War Dead. The Logic of Praise in the Athenian Funeral Oration, in: D. PRITCHARD (ed.), War, Democracy, and Culture in Classical Athens, 2010, 359–377.

GIUSTO TRAINA

Honours

A. Republican period
B. Changes from the Augustan period onwards
C. Distinguishing decorations by recipient's military rank
D. Citizenship as reward
E. Awards in the form of monetary gifts

A. REPUBLICAN PERIOD

Fighting for the *res publica* as a soldier was legally speaking a matter of course for all citizens of the Roman Republic. To be a *civis Romanus* ('Roman citizen') also meant serving in the army. It is no coincidence that what was in this period the most important popular assembly, the *comitia centuriata* ('Centuriate Assembly'), was organized by military categories and met outside the *pomerium* (the boundary around the city of Rome) in the Field of Mars. No one could escape the hardships of army service and its draconian punishments. A measure of balance was achieved in that outstanding military deeds and exceptional dedication by individual participants in warfare received official recognition from the general, the army as a whole or the Senate, and in that all participants could expect a share in the spoils at the end of a victorious campaign (on the principles Pol. 6, 39). Plin. HN 16,7f. and 22,6–13, as well as Gell. NA 5,6, describe the various decorations that honoured military successes and deeds of exceptional valour.

Men so honoured were most often recognized publicly for their outstanding military performances with *coronae* (chaplets, crowns). The *corona civica* ('Civic Crown') was the decoration for those who had saved an entire military unit or an individual citizen in battle by risking their own lives. It was made of sprays of oak. The *corona obsidionalis* ('Siege Crown') was a wreath of grasses (*corona graminea*), awarded to a man who had freed an army from a siege that would otherwise have led to its destruction. Both *coronae* were bestowed immediately by the army (Plin. HN 22,9). The other honours were made of metal and were presented by the general or commander. They included the *corona muralis* ('Wall Crown') and *corona vallaris* ('Rampart Crown') awarded to the first to storm a wall or rampart. The *corona aurea* ('Gold Crown') was in the shape of a wall defended by towers, while the *corona rostrata* ('Beaked Crown', as in the curved 'beak' or prow of a ship) was a wreath decorated with a ship's prow denoting the destruction of an enemy fleet. Pliny (HN 16,7) mentions that M. Terentius Varro received this honour during Pompey's campaign against the pirates, and M. Vipsanius Agrippa received it after the victory over Sicily (PIR[2] V 674, p. 360). In almost all cases during the Republican period, it was the general who awarded these honours (on the award formula Cic. Verr. 2,3,187), regardless of the military rank of the recipient. In the first half of the 2nd century BC, a certain Spurius Ligustinus, who began as an ordinary legionary and rose to the rank of *primipilus* ('Chief Centurion'), received honours on 34 occasions during campaigns on the Iberian Peninsula and in the eastern Mediterranean, including six *coronae civicae* (Liv. 42,34,11; cf. the legendary story of Siccius Dentatus, Dion. Hal. Ant. Rom. 10,37,3; Plin. HN 7,102; Val. Max. 3,2,24).

Besides the *coronae*, *phalerae* (metal discs worn on the breastplate), *hastae* ('spears'), *torques* ('necklaces'), *fibulae* ('brooches'), *catellae* ('small chains'), *vexilla* ('standards') and *armillae* ('armlets') were also bestowed (Cic. Verr. 2,3,18; Dion. Hal. Ant. Rom. 10,37,3; Liv. 39,31,18f.; Sall. Iug. 85,29). These *dona* (gifts, decorations) were mostly made of silver or gold, but in army culture their symbolic value as indicators of *virtus* was probably of greater import, which also applied after the recipient returned to civilian life (Val. Max. 8,14,5). Attesting to this are the countless tombstones of the Imperial period that not only name such honours, but also depict them. Decorated soldiers like Spurius Ligustinus were also frequently promoted to a higher rank by their commander. The general often gave a portion of the spoils gathered after the victory to soldiers while still in the battle area. In many cases, this would mainly consist of slaves (Dion. Hal. Ant. Rom. 9,16,8; Cic. Att. 5,20,5; Pol. 10,16f.). A general's actions in this respect could be a crucial factor in ensuring his troops' loyalty to him. Sometimes, monetary gifts were distributed to participants in a campaign before or during the triumph. In 187 BC, Fulvius Nobilior gave *dona militaria* to senior Roman and allied officers before his triumph. Ordinary soldiers were each given 25 *denarii*, centurions were given double, and cavalrymen received triple (Liv. 39,5,17). Cn. Manlius Vulso observed the same increments at his triumph of the same year, after also doubling the *stipendium* ('pay'; Liv. 39,7,2). Those who had received honours from the general were allowed to wear them at the triumph and other ceremonial processions (Pol. 6,39), and later to display them in their homes. The *spolia opima*, the armour of the enemy general, were of special value. The person under whose auspices the battle had been fought would later dedicate them to the gods (Val. Max. 3,2,1; 3,2,3–6). Although there were large contingents of confederates serving alongside Roman citizens in the Roman army, the sources suggest that no categorical distinction was yet made between Romans and *socii* ('confederates') when it came to the bestowal of honours and rewards. This is highly significant given the very different practice that prevailed from soon after Augustus until the early 3rd century [9].

The general had a special status as holder of *imperium* ('command') and the *auspicia* (the right to take auspices). He generally claimed part of the spoils for himself, but even more important than this, his troops might proclaim him *imperator* ('[Victorious] Commander') on the battlefield. After this, he was entitled to apply to the Senate to enter the city in triumph and to make a sacrific to Jupiter on the Capitol. Until the Senate gave its approval, he and his legions had to wait outside the *pomerium*, for if he crossed the sacred boundary of the city, he would lose his *imperium*.

B. Changes from the Augustan period onwards

Augustus' creation of the monarchical system of government fundamentally altered the context and conditions for awarding honours and rewards. The army was now once and for all transformed into a standing army, for whose members – except equestrian and senatorial officers and commanders – military service became a profession that lasted two or more decades. A special military status whereby soldiers had to remain unmarried was also established. Being a soldier excluded members of the military from the ordinary sphere of citizenship. A dichotomy of soldier – civilian (*miles* – *paganus*) developed. However, unlike during the Republican period, the existence of the army was not fundamentally predicated on permanent deployment in war. It was no longer a wartime army, but a peacetime one [1]. Certainly, wars of conquest (and later, increasingly, of defence) were still fought from time to time. To a far greater extent than before, however, army life was shaped by the condition of peace. The potential for → booty at the end of a conflict, which had long been a key ingredient in the → motivation of many soldiers during the Republic (before the welfare of → veterans came increasingly to the fore), would now play no part in the life of most members of the military. Nonetheless, the principle that the booty from a conquered city belonged to the soldiers was still recognized, according to Tac. Ann. 3,19,2, in the → civil wars of AD 69. Where possible, that principle also became reality, as after the conquest of Jerusalem in AD 70, when most the soldiers took abundant spoils (cf. Jos. BI 6,317).

Besides the increasing professionalization associated with a standing army, a second factor came into effect that fundamentally influenced the character of the entire *exercitus Romanus* ('Roman army'). Beginning in the reign of Augustus, a far greater distinction than before began to be made, particularly in regard to honours and rewards, between the → legions, in which exclusively Roman citizens served, and the → auxiliary units, most of whose recruits came from the *peregrini* ('foreigners') of the provinces. The *cives Romani* ('Roman citizens'), who were mainly legionaries, were already of a markedly different status from auxiliaries under Augustus. Not only did they receive higher pay, but they were also given land or a lump cash payment at the end of their service. Auxiliaries received less pay and no settlement. Still, they did not remain unrewarded at the end of their army careers. Their reward came in the form of the bestowal of Roman citizenship on them and – until AD 140 – on any children born to them while performing military service (see → Military diploma). This change of status normally took place at the end of their term of service; it was not dependent on any achivements in battle, although this is often claimed to be the case (see the clear argument of [9]). Augustus already restricted financial emoluments to the legionaries. At his triumph in 29 BC, he had 1,000 *sesterces* paid out of the war booty to his former soldiers already settled in colonies (R. Gest. Div. Aug. 15). A *donativum* ('supplementary monetary payment') issued in 8 BC in the name of his two adoptive sons, Gaius and Lucius, was given only to the soldiers of the Rhine legions (Cass. Dio 55,6,4). In his will, Augustus left 1,000 *sesterces* to every Praetorian, 500 to every urban soldier, and 300 to every legionary and soldier in the *cohortes civium Romanorum* ('Roman Citizens' Cohorts'; Suet. Aug. 101; Tac. Ann. 1,8,2). This illustrates the different grades of importance attached to the various types of troops, as expressed materially through levels of pay and *donativa*.

The *donativa* were payments made to soldiers on special occasions and were independent of regular pay. They evolved into a considerable supplement to the regular compensation, at least under certain rulers, and they were restricted sometimes to all legionaries and sometimes to particular units. The most commonly rewarded soldiers were the Praetorians, which is not surprising given their importance to the security of the imperial power. Tiberius paid the Praetorians 1,000 *denarii* after the elimination of Sejanus (Suet. Tib. 48,2), and Hadrian spoke generally about the generous size of the Praetorians' pay and the *praemia* ('rewards'), meaning by this the *donativa*: *ut et stipendior(um) his et praemior(um) honor praecipuus habeatur* ('that it [sc. the dignity of the Praetorians] be explicitly reflected in both pay and rewards'; [5.247]). Occasions for *donativa* were many and varied. After Augustus' death, Tiberius doubled the amount that his predecessor had left in his will to soldiers with Roman citizenship, thereby effectively marking out the beginning of his reign as an event requiring a monetary gift to the military (Suet. Tib. 48,2; Tac. ann. 1,36,3). Immediately after his own acclamation by the Praetorians, Claudius gave each of them 15,000 *sesterces*, setting a precedent for later emperors (Suet. Claud. 10,4). In AD 68, the soldiers in Rome swore an oath to Galba when their commanders promised them a *donativum* above the norm (Suet. Galba 16,1; 17). The failure to keep this promise was one of the key factors leading to Galba's murder (Tac. Hist. 1,5,1; 1,19,3; 1,25,2; 1,37,5; 1,41,2). Trajan also paid a gift to soldiers (Plin. Pan. 25,2; 41,1), as did Marcus Aurelius and Lucius Verus (Cass. Dio 74,8,4). None of the emperors could afford not to promise the soldiers a *donativum* at their accession. Pertinax not only provided a *donativum* of his own, but also made good the unfulfilled financial promises of Commodus (Cass. Dio 74,5,4; SHA Pert. 4,6; 7,5). After Pertinax' death, two pretenders sought to obtain power by outbidding each other in monetary offers to the Praetorians, with Didius Iulianus finally winning with 25,000 *sesterces*. This shows the degree to which a genuine obligation to make a monetary payment could be perverted (Cass. Dio 74,11). It also became acceptable to appoint a successor by this method (SHA Hadr. 23,11), and the marriage of Antoninus Pius' daughter Faustina to his adoptive son Marcus Aurelius was marked by a monetary gift to troops (SHA Pius 10,2). Even the death of his wife was an occasion for Antoninus Pius to make a *donativum* to the troops (SHA Pius 8,1). Because the size of *donativa* increasingly became aligned with higher levels of pay, the amounts grew steadily throughout the 3rd century. Under Diocletian, the *donativa* became regular payments, losing the character of a reward, although this process had already begun under Augustus. The payments were politically necessary because the military was the guarantor of the position of whoever was in power.

C. Distinguishing decorations by recipient's military rank

Unlike the *donativa*, which were still awarded in the Imperial period after victories on the battlefield, but generally not for reasons directly related to combat, the decorations proper that had developed during the Republican period were usually linked to military successes and individual deeds in battle. On some occasions, however, they were used to mark non-military accomplishments. This is illustrated in an extreme way by Nero, who awarded honours after the exposure of the Pisonian Conspiracy in AD 65, bestowing them on people of wildly divergent social status, from consular rank to Imperial freedmen (Tac. Ann. 15,72,1; IRT 346; ILS 9505; [2]; [7]).

All the *coronae* and lesser *dona militaria* known from the Republican period were still awarded by the emperors, at least until the early 3rd century. The *Constitutio Antoniniana* and the establishment of legal equality for all members of the army deprived the *dona militaria* of their significance as a distinguishing emblem of reward for the legions [8]; [5.248f.]. In contrast with the past, however, distinctions of all types were no longer granted to anyone who had performed a qualifying military feat, regardless of his rank in the army. Instead, the various honours were bestowed with far more consideration than before to the individual's status within the military hierarchy, and firmer correlations between status and reward evolved over the course of the 1st century AD. Part of the reason for this was that from the Augustan period onwards, all officers above the rank of centurion were exclusively drawn from the *ordines* ('social ranks') of the senators and *equites* (members of the equestrian order). There was no room for granting rewards totally independent of rank in a hierarchy so strongly bound up with social criteria. Even under the Republic, rank had increasingly begun to exert influence on the awarding of decorations. Furthermore, the original link between the individual honour and a specific action in battle was abandoned completely. It was no longer necessary, for instance, to be the first to breach a fortified wall in order to receive the *corona muralis*. Only the *corona civica* maintained its association with a specific action, namely, saving a citizen. An interdependence developed between rank, type of honour and especially the number of honours awarded, which tended to be regular, but always allowed for variation [8.64].

A greater degree of regularity is seen in the reign of Vespasian, and then especially in the reigns of Domitian and Trajan – although this only becomes apparent because of the increasing number of sources. Recipients belonging to the *ordo senatorius* now begin to display clear gradations according to their rank in the Senate. Fourfold *dona* are only found awarded to *consulares*: *hastis puris IIII, vexillis IIII, coronis IIII* (AE 1968, 145), *coron(a) mural(i), item vallar(i), item classic(a), item aurea, item hast(is) puris IIII, item vexill(is)*, with the *coronae* remaining an equal group (CIL VI 41142; 41146; cf. CIL V 6976; XI 1833) – in a few cases that we know of, they were also awarded twice at this level (CIL II 14,1,124; VI 1444: *hastis puris VIII, vexillis VIII, coronis muralib(us) II, vallaribus II, classicis II, auratis II*). Praetorians generally received the honours three times (ILS 1029; 8977), *praetores* twice or once (ILS 1025). The highest honours bestowed on senators were the *ornamenta triumphalia*, replacing the celebration of a → triumph, which was no longer possible. This award was invariably associated with a *statua triumphalis* in the Forum of Augustus. *Ornamenta triumphalia* were usually awarded only to *consulares*, but Claudius made the award to legionary legates after the conquest of Britain (Suet. Claud. 17,1; Suet. Vesp. 4,2). Hadrian awarded the last *ornamenta triumphalia* to three *consulares* after the end of the Bar Kochba

Revolt [3]. The only instances of an agglomeration of multiple *coronae* for people of other social stations involve tribunes of the Praetorians (ILS 1326; CIL VI 41143) or the urban cohorts, and a few *praefecti praetorio* of the 2nd century. This reflects the prestige of these positions, which in the case of the Praetorian Prefects had largely come to match that of the senatorial class.

For military men of equestrian rank (*praefectus cohortis, tribunus legionis, praefectus alae*), a strict system of rewards comparable to that of the *ordosenatorius* never developed. The *dona* granted to them were dependent on the flexibility of equestrian duties and the personal idiosyncrasies of the individual emperor. This led to great diversity in the numbers of honours granted and their various combinations [8.158–183]. The honour given to M. Valerius Maximianus is remarkable: *ab Imp(eratore) Antonino Aug(usto) coram laudato et equo et phaleris et armis donato quod manu sua ducem Naristarum Valaonem interemisset* ('publicly praised by Emperor Antoninus Augustus (i.e. Marcus Aurelius) and given a horse, *phalerae* and weapons, for having killed Prince Valao of the Naristi by his own hand'; AE 1956, 124). Variation in *dona* is relatively less for centurions: there was never an award of more than one *corona* and several *torques, armillae* and *phalerae* (ILS 2080; AE 1937, 101). Below the rank of centurion, from the *evocati Augusti* to the ordinary *milites*, the usual practice was to award multiple *torques, armillae* and (mostly) *phalerae*, sometimes in combination with a *corona aurea*. Most known cases date from the 1st century AD [8.210–217].

Besides *dona* awarded to individuals, entire units were sometimes recognized with honorific titles. Claudius did this, honouring the *legiones* VII and XI with the honorific bynames *pia* ('reverent') and *fidelis* ('trustworthy') to go with the gentile name (Cass. Dio 60,15,4). Domitian honoured the entire army of Germania inferior as *exercitus Domitianus pius fidelis*. Military diplomas (e.g. RMD V 336; AE 2004, 1911) show that the central element of this title, *exercitus Germanicus pius fidelis*, continued to be used throughout the 2nd century [4.42–47]. Auxiliary units could also receive honorific bynames of this sort. An *ala Silianacivium Romanorum* ('Silius' auxiliary unit of Roman citizens') bore the honorific descriptors *torquata* and *armillata* (ILTun 720). Some units were also known as *victrix* ('conqueror'; e.g. CIL XVI 165; AE 2009, 1798), others simply *torquata* or *bis torquata*. In such cases, a *torques* (or a second one) or an *armilla* would be awarded to the unit, which would affix it to its standard [8.218–232].

D. CITIZENSHIP AS REWARD
Special decorations included granting citizenship to groups of soldiers for their accomplishments in battle. The soldiers of the *legio II Adiutrix*, for instance, who had earlier served in the navy, were made citizens by Vespasian: *quod se in expeditione belli fortiter industrieque gesserant* ('for conducting themselves vigorously and diligently on expeditions of war'; CIL XVI 10; RMD IV 205). Trajan did the same for an entire auxiliary unit even before their regular term of service had ended: *pie et fideliter expeditione Dacica functis ante emerita stipendia civitatem Romanam dedit* ('to those who served loyally and faithfully on the Dacian Campaign, he has granted Roman citizenship before their completion of service'; CIL XVI 160; RMD V 343), as did Hadrian: *ante emerita stipendia civitatem Romanam dedit*, followed by the unique rider, *cum parentibus et fratribus et sororibus* ('with their parents, brothers and sisters'; RMD V 357; AE 2008, 1749f.; AE 2010, 1858). Although in rare cases like these, auxiliaries could receive honours in association with their units for services in war, no *dona* to individual auxiliaries are recorded after the reign of Augustus. The only definitive case, that of an *eques* ('cavalry soldier') of the *ala Parthorum et Araborum ... donis donatus*, probably dates from the very earliest days of the Principate, and it is not known which *dona* was meant here (AE 1976, 495).

For ordinary *milites* ('soldiers') and *centuriones* ('centurions') in particular, the distinction *obvirtutem* ('in recognition of valour') quickly came to consist of promotion to a higher rank, as in the case of a certain Ti. Claudius Maximus, who had killed Decebalus (AE 1969/70, 583), or one Furius Octavius Secundus, whom Hadrian promoted for his gallantry in the war in Judaea (ILS 2080). Pay was also sometimes increased (Tac. Ann. 2,9,3), as during the Republican period, or an extra monetary gift could be granted (AE 1952, 153).

E. AWARDS IN THE FORM OF MONETARY GIFTS
Formal *dona* effectively disappear from the record after the Severan period. In their place, monetary gifts proliferate, although the record provides little or no detail. Caracalla honoured a *primipilaris* ('chief centurion') with 75,000 *sesterces*, (*ob*) *alacritatemvirtu(tis)* ('in recognition of eagerness in valour'; CIL III 14416). 'Payments' like this may have become common practice, particularly with the increasing numbers of fighting *foederati* ('allies') who were not (yet) part of Roman society. Even so, honorific gifts that distinguished their recipients within their social environments did not disappear entirely. As the few testimonies suggest, they continued to be awarded occasionally. ILS 2434 mentions a *milestorquatus etduplarius* (cf. AE 1982, 274), who according to [11] was rewarded with a *torquis* ('necklace') and also received double rations of the *annona* ('annual

income'; cf. Veg. Mil. 2,7). Others seem to have been honoured with special clothing [12]. Such phenomena do not, however, appear to point to any formal system of military honours. They are still seen in use in Late Antiquity, probably on the personal initiative of the general, such as the armlets and necklaces that Narses and Belisarius gave to soldiers to reward valour during the campaigns in the reign of Justinian (Procop., *bella* 7,1,8; 8,31,9). Julian's *coronae obsidionales* at the Siege of Maogamalcha, on the other hand, were probably a nostalgic revival, much like the *dona militaria* with which the Senate of Rome honoured the *magister militum* ('Master of Soldiers') Aetius under Valentinian III. We still know of this honour today thanks to an inscription from the city of Rome (CIL VI 41389).

☞ Pay

BIBLIOGRAPHY
[1] B. DOBSON, Wartime or Peacetime Army, in: W. ECK / H. WOLFF (eds.), Heer und Integrationspolitik. Die römischen Militärdiplome als historische Quelle, 1986, 20–25 [2] W. ECK, Neros Freigelassener Epaphroditus und die Aufdeckung der Pisonischen Verschwörung, in: Historia 25, 1976, 381–384 [3] W. ECK, The Bar Kochba Revolt. The Roman Point of View, in: JRS 89, 1999, 78–86 [4] W. ECK, La romanisation de la Gérmanie, 2007 [5] W. ECK et al., Edikt Hadrians für Prätorianer mit unsicherem römischen Bürgerrecht, in: ZPE 189, 2014, 241–253; ZPE 191, 2014, 266–268 und ZPE 206, 2018, 199–201 [6] W. ECK / H. WOLFF (eds.), Heer und Integrationspolitik. Die römischen Militärdiplome als historische Quelle, 1986 [7] M. GIOVAGNOLI, Il presunto sepolcro del liberto di Nerone Epaphroditus. Nuovi dati dall'archivio Gatti, in: ZPE 204, 2017, 241–245 [8] V. MAXFIELD, The Military Decorations of the Roman Army, 1981 [9] V. MAXFIELD, Systems of Reward in Relation to Military Diplomas, in: W. ECK / H. WOLFF (eds.), Heer und Integrationspolitik. Die römischen Militärdiplome als historische Quelle, 1986, 26–43 [10] C. RICCI, Dai dona ai donativa. Fine dello scambio simbolico tra comandante e soldati?, in: C. MASSERIA / D. LOSCALZO (eds.), Miti di guerra, riti di pace. La guerra e la pace. Un confronto interdisciplinare, 2011, 235–240 [11] M.P. SPEIDEL, Late Roman Military Decorations I. Neck- and Wristbands, in: AntTard 4, 1996, 235–243 [12] M.P. SPEIDEL, Late Roman Military Decorations II. Gold-Embroidered Capes and Tunics, in: AntTard 5, 1997, 231–237 [13] H. WOLFF, Die römische Bürgerrechtspolitik nach den Militärdiplomen, in: M.A. SPEIDEL / H. LIEB (eds.), Militärdiplome. Die Forschungsbeiträge der Berner Gespräche von 2004, 2007, 345–372.

WERNER ECK

Hostages

It was common practice in Antiquity to demand and give hostages (Greek singular *homeros*, Latin *opses/obses*). Their primary function was as a pledge guaranteeing agreements between opposing parties, so they were also referred to as *pistis* ('surety'; Latin *pignus*) [9]. The issue of hostages arose most often in connection with truces, negotiations and treaties. A victor might make the provision of hostages a condition for commencing negotiations, and include this in the terms of the treaty [5]; [11].

When hostages were exchanged, this meant that the parties recognized each other as equals. Giving hostages unilaterally in the context of a treaty meant accepting subordinate status. Leaving aside the taking hostage of Roman officials or soldiers and discounting civil wars, Republican Rome was forced to hand over hostages on only three occasions (and the first two are legendary): the young people delivered up to Porsenna in 508, who included Cloelia (Liv. 2,13,4–11; 9,11,6; Val. Max. 3,2,2; Plut. *Poplicola* 18,3–19,8; Dion. Hal. Ant. Rom. 5,31,4–35,2; Plin. HN 34,13,28; Flor. Epit. 1,4,7; Oros. 2,5,3); the *equites* ('equestrians') handed to the Samnites following the episode of the Caudine Forks in 321 (Liv. 9,5,5f.; 9,5,12; 9,12,9; 9,14,14–16; App. Samn. 1,4; 1,6; Gell. NA 2,19,8; 17,2,21; Oros. 3,15,6); and the soldiers turned over to the Gaulish Tigurini in 107 (Liv. Per. 65,5f.; Caes. B Gall. 1,14,6f.; Oros. 5,15,24) [4]; [5]; [11]. Imperial Rome occasionally handed over hostages (between Corbulo and Vologaeses I in AD 63; Tac. Ann. 15,28) or exchanged hostages (with the Persians for a short period in AD 363; Amm. Marc. 25,7,13) during negotiations, but only in the Late Roman Empire did it deliver hostages unilaterally (Zos. 5,42,1; 5,44,1; 5,45,4; Flavius Aëtius: PLRE II 21f.).

The Greeks in the 5th century BC were willing to entrust their hostages to a third party [11], but the Romans guarded their own hostages, usually in Rome itself (Tac. Ann. 14,26), and later in Constantinople (Iord. Get. 271; 281) or Italy (Liv. 32,2,4; 32,26,5). In the Republican period, decisions regarding hostages were made by the senate, and later the emperor made such decisions [2]; [5]; [8]; [10]; [11].

The status of hostages differed depending on whether the cessation of conflict led to a *deditio* ('surrender') or a *foedus* ('treaty'). In either case, hostages were inviolable, provided that the treaty was honoured and they did not attempt to escape (Liv. 25,7,14 on the Tarentine hostages of 212 BC) ([5]; [11]; disputing the inviolability [1]). Their living conditions seem to have been good. They clearly enjoyed a degree of freedom. The escape of the future Demetrius I of Syria was only discovered after four hours (Pol. 31,15,6) [6]; [11]; [3]. However, ancient authors discuss only illustrious hostages, and they are also pro-Roman in their attitudes.

The Romans demanded a varying number of hostages, mainly young men (aged from 10–18 to

30-45) and close relatives of members of the leadership. Female hostages were relatively rare (Suet. Aug. 21,4; Tac. Ann. 15,30) [5]; [8]; [10]; [11]; [1]. The duration of time hostages spent as captives varied, and they were not always released immediately when all conditions of the treaty were met. They were sometimes exchanged. The Treaty of Apamea stipulated that exchanges should take place once every three years (Pol. 21,42,22; Liv. 38,38,15; App. Syr. 39), but no general conclusions can be drawn from this case [5]; [7]; [11].

When hostages remained in captivity for long periods, they sometimes came under Roman cultural influence and became to some degree 'Roman' themselves. However, there was no deliberate Roman policy to this effect (Pol. 26,1,5f.; Liv. 41,20,1; 41,20,9-13; Diod. Sic. 29,32 on Antiochus IV of Syria) [6]; [11]; [1].

☞ Peace; Prisoners

BIBLIOGRAPHY
[1] J. ALLEN, Hostages and Hostage-Taking in the Roman Empire, 2006 [2] D. ÁLVAREZ PÉREZ-SOSTOA, El confinamiento de los prisioneros de guerra y rehenes en la Roma republicana, in: Veleia 26, 2009, 153-171 [3] D. ÁLVAREZ PÉREZ-SOSTOA, Escipión Emiliano, Polibio y Demetrio I Sóter, in: Historia Antigua 22, 2009, 107-115 [4] D. ÁLVAREZ PÉREZ-SOSTOA, Conflits autour des otages romains pendant les guerres civiles, in: H. MÉNARD et al. (eds.), La pomme d'Éris. Le conflit et sa représentation dans l'Antiquité, 2012, 383-397 [5] S. ELBERN, Geiseln in Rom, in: Athenaeum 78, 1990, 97-140 [6] M.J. MOSCOVICH, Hostage Princes and Roman Imperialism in the Second Century B.C., in: EMC 27, 1983, 297-309 [7] S. NDIAYE, Le recours aux otages à Rome sous la République, in: DHA 21/1, 1995, 149-165 [8] C. RICCI, Principes et reges externi (e loro schiavi e liberti) a Roma e in Italia, in: RAL 7/3, Serie 9, 1996, 561-592 [9] P. ROOS, Οἱ ὁμηρεύοντες. On the Terminology of Ancient Hostages, in: S.-T. TEODORSSON (ed.), Greek and Latin Studies in Memory of Cajus Fabricius (Studia Graeca et Latina Gothoburgensia 54), 1990, 158-164 [10] B. SCARDIGLI, Germanische Gefangene und Geiseln in Italien (von Marius bis Konstantin), in: B. SCARDIGLI / P. SCARDIGLI (eds.), Germani in Italia, 1994, 117-150 [11] C. WALKER, Hostages in Republican Rome, 2005 (http://chs.harvard.edu/publications.sec/online_print_books.ssp).

CATHERINE WOLFF

Hunting

From the Greek Archaic period onwards, hunting was one of the primary activities through which a man could demonstrate his courage and fortitude. From the earliest times, the hoplite armies hunted while on campaigns, not only in the form of organized hunts - mainly in order to obtain food, but also to prove their capabilities and improve their cohesion as a body of men. The Pseudo-Xenophon treatise *Cynegeticus* (1,17f.; 12,1-9) describes hunting as an outstanding method of military → training and one of the best preparations for long and arduous military expeditions.

In the Hellenistic period, hunting was an important aspect of the image that a king would project of himself. It served as proof of his valour in the tradition of Alexander the Great (→ Generals of note, B.), who had conducted many hunts during his campaigns in Asia, chiefly in pursuit of lions. Hellenistic kings on royal hunts were invariably accompanied by their closest followers and members of the royal guard (Pol. 32,15 on the hunting tradition of the Macedonian kings and the hunt organized for Scipio Aemilianus) [3]. The kings of Ptolemaic Egypt devoted a great deal of money and energy to hunting and capturing → elephants, which were needed in the army, especially in the war with the Seleucid Empire. The Seleucid rulers had direct access to Indian elephants, and the Ptolemies sought to offset their disadvantage by hunting African elephants. These hunts were led by the king's *strategoi* ('military commanders') and began in the far southeast of Egypt, on the Red Sea coast near Ptolemais (Str. 16,4,7f.; 16,4,15; Diod. Sic. 3,18,4; 3,36,3; CIG 4836b; 5127; OGIS 82; 86) [8.135-138].

The army of the Roman period was much involved in hunting, the main purpose being to send wild animals to the arena. *Venationes* (Latin: 'hunts'; 'pursuits') were an important element of the public circus and gladiatorial games (*munera*), and they required a considerable number of animals, especially at Rome, as required by the emperor himself [4]. There is evidence, for example, of a *venatio Caesariana* at Montana, Moesia inferior, in AD 147, ordered by Tiberius Claudius Ulpianus, *tribunus cohortis I Cilicum*, along with *vexillationes* ('military detachments') of the *legiones I Italica* and *XI Claudia for example, of a venatio* and the military fleet on the Danube (*classis Flavia Moesica*). Bears and bison (*bisontes*; cf. fig. 1) were captured, then brought to Rome for the nonacentennial celebrations in the spring of 148 (AE 1987, 867; 1999, 1327; Paus. 9,21,3; 10,13,1) [7]. *Immunes venatores* (hunters who were exempted from certain other duties) of the *legio XI Claudia* are attested in the same region in AD 155 (CIL III 7449). The *immunes venatores for example, of a venatio* of the *cohors VI praetoria* are in turn mentioned at Rome in 241; one of them was also *custos vivari(i) cohh(ortium) praett(oriarum) et urbb(anarum)*, keeper of the animal enclosures (ILS 2091). Another *immunis venator* is attested in the fortress of the *legio II Parthica* at Albano Laziale (AE 1968, 101; 1975, 160).

At Xanten, an *ursarius* ('bear hunter') of the *legio XXX Ulpia Victrix* is attested (CIL XIII 8639). At Cologne, a centurion of the *legio I Minervia*

HUNTING

Fig. 1: Hunt scene from the mosaic at the Villa Romana del Casale, Piazza Armerina, Sicily (detail; first half of 4th century AD). The detail shows several servants dragging a captured bison towards a ship. The hunt for, or capture of wild animals was a suitable subject for a floor mosaic in a rural villa, and illustrated the *virtus* ('valour') of the owner. The mosaic of the 'Great Hunt' encompasses a geographical space that includes the entire *orbis terrarum* ('whole world') from Mauretania to India, with Italy at the centre. The catching of bison (*bisontes*) during an imperial hunt (*venatio Caesariana*) and the transfer of the animals to Rome is mentioned, for instance, in the aforementioned inscription from Montana in the province of Moesia inferior.

p.f. caught 50 bears in six months (ILS 9241). At Birdoswald (Banna) on Hadrian's Wall, mention is made of *venatores Banniess(es)* ('hunters of Banna'), probably members of the *auxilia* of *cohors I Aelia Dacorum* (RIB I 1905), while at Vindolanda (Chesterholm) in the early 2nd century AD, the *venatores* ('hunters') of the prefect Flavius Cerialis, a passionate hunter, were probably soldiers of the *cohors VIIII Batavorum* (Tab. Vindol. III 615) [2.147–151].

At the same time, soldiers also hunted for food. In Egypt towards the end of the 1st century AD, an auxiliary of the unit stationed in the fortress at Bir Umm el-Fawakhir wrote in a letter to a colleague that he and his comrades hunted animals and birds every day. All these hunts were by order of army officers. In fact, army law forbade soldiers to join unofficial hunting expeditions [5.191–193]. Hunting sometimes formed part of military → education, as can be seen from a section in Iulius Africanus that gives instructions for capturing lions in the wilderness (*Kestoi* 1,14, written 228–231). A detachment of the *legio III Augusta* stationed at Lambaesis in Numidia was sent to the El-Agueneb region to catch lions (CIL VIII 21567).

Besides textual sources, there are also pictorial materials that attest to the hunting activities of the Roman army. Outstanding among these is the impressive mosaic of the 'Great Hunt' in the Roman villa of Piazza Armerina, dating from the first two decades of the 4th century (see fig. 1) [11]; [8].

The army continued to hunt and capture wild animals in Roman Late Antiquity (Urb. Tact. 10, on the reign of the Emperor Anastasius). Inscriptions and epigraphic sources like the aforementioned 'Great Hunt' mosaic complete the picture. Several units of *ursarienses* are thus attested [4]. Around the middle of the 4th century, farmers of the Faiyum sought help from a cavalry unit located nearby to catch gazelles that had destroyed some of their crops [1.44–46, no. 6]. The *duces limitis* ('border commanders') on the Euphrates frontier in the 5th century received orders (in 414 and 417) to supply wild animals for the imperial *venationes* (Cod. Theod. 15,11,1f.).

BIBLIOGRAPHY
[1] H. BELL et al., The Abinnaeus Archive. Papers of a Roman Officer in the Reign of Constantius II, 1962 [2] A. BIRLEY, Garrison Life at Vindolanda. A Band of Brothers, 2002 [3] P. BRIANT, Chasses royales macédoniennes et chasses royales perses. Le thème de la chasse au lion sur la chasse de Vergina, in: DHA 17, 1991, 211–255 [4] C. CHIRIAC et al., Un vétéran d'un numerus dans une épitaphe latine tardoantique de Tomis, in: Pontica 47, 2014, 439–450 [5] R.W. DAVIES, Service in the Roman Army, 1989 [6] C. EPPLETT, The Capture of Animals by the Roman Military, in: Greece & Rome 48, 2001, 210–222 [7] D. KNOEPFLER, Pausanias à Rome en l'an 148?, in: REG 112, 1999, 500–509 [8] H.I. MARROU, Sur deux mosaïques de la villa romaine de Piazza Armerina, in: Christiana tempora. Mélanges d'histoire, d'archéologie, d'épigraphie et de patristique, 1978, 258–285 [9] P.M. MEYER, Das Heerwesen der Ptolemäer und Römer in Ägypten, 1900 [10] H.H. SCULLARD, The Elephant in the Greek and Roman World, 1974 [11] S. SETTIS, Per l'interpretazione di Piazza Armerina, in: MEFRA 87, 1975, 873–994 (923–987, Mosaiken).

FLORIAN MATEI-POPESCU

Infantry

A. Greek infantry: *peltastes*, archers and slingers
B. Support for the legions: the *velites*

A. Greek infantry: *peltastes*, archers and slingers

The advent of hoplite warfare in the Greek world during the Archaic period [6] did not fully displace fighting units of unarmoured light infantry armed with bows, projectiles or spears. The sources do, however, frequently neglect these soldiers, because they were recruited from the lowest strata of society and because ranged warfare was considered less honourable than direct confrontation. The Persian Wars (→ Wars of note, J.) further reinforced this attitude, as ranged warfare came to be identified with the Persian (or Scythian, in the case of the archers) enemy [13]. The best-known Greek light infantryman was the *peltastes* ('light armoured footsoldier'), the name deriving from the characteristic crescent-shaped leather or wicker shield known as the *pelte*. The *peltastes* began to appear on vase paintings in the 6th century BC, but his tactical significance did not crystallize until the Peloponnesian War (→ Wars of note, H.) [1]. When the war broke out in 431, Athens already had a corps of mounted archers and 6,000 archers on foot. Despite this, the Athenian hoplites commanded by the *strategos* ('commander') Demosthenes in 426 proved incapable of keeping pace with the Aetolians in their mountainous terrain, and consequently the Athenians fell victim to their spears. The following year, Demosthenes together with his colleague Cleon learned their lesson from this defeat, and they successfully deployed 800 *peltastes* and 800 archers against the Spartans on the island of Sphacteria. At Lechaeum (c. 390 BC) during the Corinthian War, the isolation of the Spartan hoplites made them vulnerable to attacks by the Athenian *peltastes*, who were commanded by the *strategos* Iphicrates. This battle technique developed mostly during the 4th century, although without challenging the primacy of the hoplites. The light infantry functioned primarily as a support. At Lechaeum, it should be noted, it was the intervention of Callias in command of the Athenian hoplites that proved decisive. Hoplite equipment was tending to become lighter, as greaves and breastplates were replaced by a linen tunic. Archers and slingers were never sent into battle alone, but – like the *peltastes* – they were generally deployed at the beginning of a confrontation to disrupt enemy lines, or at the end, to pursue those fleeing the battlefield [12]. A slinger could fire a lead bullet over 300 metres. The bow, on the other hand, remained a fragile instrument that was susceptible to drying out and disintegrating. It was also difficult to handle. Its effectiveness in naval battles, however, where enemy soldiers were unable to scatter, was fearsome. Depending on the situation, light infantry might be placed ahead of the wings, behind them or even on them. The strategic use of light infantry made managing military operations more complex, which explains the proliferation of treatises on military theory from this time and throughout the Hellenistic period. Not only is Philip II generally regarded as the inventor of the Macedonian hoplite phalanx, but he also ensured that a light infantry made up of archers, slingers, javelin throwers and *hypaspistes* ('shield carriers'; also armed with lances) were integrated into his army as protection for the flanks of the phalanx (→ Generals of note, M). Such soldiers were frequently → mercenaries, recruited from regions that specialized in these battle techniques. *Peltastes* were brought from Achaea, the Balearic Islands, Thessaly and Thrace, and archers were brought from Crete [4].

B. Support for the legions: the *velites*

In the Roman Republic, the distinction between heavy and light infantry at first related to the division of Roman citizens into censitary classes. Livy and Dionysius of Halicarnassus attributed this division to Servius Tullius alone, but it is more likely the result a gradual development that began in the mid-5th century. Light infantry were recruited from the lowest censitary classes. The legionaries of the 20 centuries of the fourth class were armed only with lances and spears. The 30 centuries of the fifth class provided slingers, trumpeters (*tubicines*), whose job was to give signals to set out, attack or retreat, and buglers (*cornicines*), who were entrusted with conveying orders from the command level to standard-bearers of the maniples (→ Specialists B.). The fifth class also provided a special form of light infantry: the *velites* ('light armoured soldiers'), reminiscent to a degree of the Greek *peltastes*. There were 1,200 of these per legion, and they were equipped with a small round shield called a *parma*, a helmet and a sword. They were recruited from among the youngest and poorest citizens of Rome, and their role was to initiate hostilities at the start of battle by skirmishing from the front row. Later in the battle, they could withdraw into the spaces that opened up between the maniples. They were also sent on reconnaissance missions and put to use for ambushes and pursuits. The first evidence of their existence dates from 211 BC, and they seem to have disappeared again around the end of the 2nd century BC or the beginning of the 1st. They testify to a close link between heavy and light infantry – one of the → innovations of the Roman army [8].

From the 3rd century BC onwards, the Roman army became the army of an empire, incorporating contingents of non-Roman soldiers, Italic *socii* ('allies') and later *auxilia externa* ('outer auxiliaries') from the provinces. Their equipment did not differ markedly from that of the citizens serving in the legions. These contingents cannot therefore be entirely counted among the lightly armed specialist forces such as the Balearic or Aetolian slingers, Cretan archers or Numidian javelin throwers. Incidentally, the engraved slingshot bullets found at the site of the Siege of Perugia in 41 BC demonstrate that legionaries were perfectly capable of operating these projectile weapons.

Under the Principate, the manipular legion, which was reorganized into cohorts, was essentially composed of heavy infantry. Lightly armed troops were now mainly recruited from among the *peregrini* ('foreigners') in the auxiliary units [7]. The quingenarian *alae* ('troops') consisted of 16 *turmae* ('units') of 30 riders each, and the milliary *alae* consisted of 24 *turmae*. Quingenarian cohorts comprised six centuries of 80 infantrymen each, and the milliary cohorts comprised ten. There were also mounted cohorts that combined eight mounted *turmae* and six infantry centuries to form a unit totalling about 600 men, or twice as many for milliary cohorts. Light infantry and light cavalry were generally positioned ahead of the legions or on their flanks. Their tasks were to provoke the enemy to battle through skirmishing and to protect the flanks of the heavy infantry.

Estimating the strength of these auxiliary units is a difficult matter, and estimating the proportion of light troops is even more difficult. This is partly because it is not always possible to link a particular weapon with a legionary or an auxiliary. It has been shown, however, that many auxiliaries were indeed heavily armed. At the forefront, defending the border – as at the Battle of Mons Graupius in Caledonia – they sometimes even took the field alone. During the 2nd century AD, new units of an ethnic character appeared with the classification *numeri* or *nationes*, and they continued to practise their own methods of battle. As with the auxiliary forces, however, it is impossible to determine the proportion of light troops. The same applies to the new units that emerged from the reforms of the Roman army during the reigns of Diocletian and Constantine [18].

☞ Armament; Auxiliaries

BIBLIOGRAPHY
[1] J.G. BEST, Thracian Peltasts and Their Influence on Greek Warfare, 1969 [2] M.C. BISHOP / J.C.N. COULSTON, Roman Military Equipment. From the Punic Wars to the Fall of Rome, 1993 [3] G. BRIZZI, Il guerriero, l'oplita, il legionario, 2002 [4] P. DUCREY, Guerre et guerriers dans la Grèce antique, 1985 [5] M. FEUGÈRE, Les armes des Romains de la République à l'Antiquité tardive, 1993 [6] V.D. HANSON, The Western Way of War, 1989 [7] I. HAYNES, Blood of the Provinces. The Roman Auxilia and the Making of Provincial Society from Augustus to the Severans, 2013 [8] L. KEPPIE, The Making of the Roman Army. From Republic to Empire, ²1998 [9] J. KROMAYER / G. VEITH, Handbuch der Altertumswissenschaft, sec. 4, pt. 3, vol. 2: Heerwesen und Kriegführung der Griechen und Römer, 1928 [10] Y. LE BOHEC, Die römische Armee. Von Augustus zu Konstantin dem Großen, 1993 [11] Y. LE BOHEC, Das römische Heer in der späten Kaiserzeit, 2010 [12] J.E. LENDON, Soldiers and Ghosts. A History of Battle in the Classical Antiquity, 2005 [13] F. LISSARAGUE, L'autre guerrier. Archers, peltastes, cavaliers dans l'imagerie antique, 1990 [14] P. SABIN, The Face of Roman Battle, in: JRS 90, 2000, 1–17 [15] P.F. STARY, Zur eisenzeitlichen Bewaffnung und Kampfweise in Mittelitalien, 1981 [16] G. ULBERT, Römische Waffen des 1. Jahrhunderts n.Chr., 1968 [17] T. VÖLLING, Funditores im römischen Heer, in: Saalburg Jahrbuch 45, 1990, 24–58 [18] C. WOLFF / P. FAURE (eds.), Les auxiliaires de l'armée romaine. Des alliés aux fédérés, 2016.

PIERRE COSME

Infrastructure

A. Definition
B. Harbours
C. Ship canals and trackways
D. Roads, bridges and communication
E. Purposes and technologies of Roman road-building and other construction

A. DEFINITION

Material infrastructure built and/or used by the military included structures such as roads, bridges, canals, harbours, permanent and temporary camps and forts, duty stations and supply bases (→ Camp; → Supply). Such infrastructure only began to appear on a large scale under the Romans, who from the 3rd century BC onwards began to make systematic provision for a military supply network in support of soldiers who were passing through as well as those stationed in camp. However, this only developed into what can be called infrastructure with the emergence of the standing army of the Roman Imperial period. The Greek and Hellenistic periods, with their expeditionary armies, produced only sporadic elements of architectural infrastructure, and never though large-scale, systematic planning. Such elements included above all naval ports and canals, but also permanent camps, frontier posts and supply facilities for some permanent garrisons, such as those of the military monarchies of the Hellenistic kingdoms, with their professional armies and occasional standing units deployed to exercise control over conquered regions or to secure frontiers. In the Greek *poleis* and kingdoms of the Diadochi, military education and → training took place in the gymnasia of the Ephebes, which could thus be said to have been military infrastructure, but they evolved more and more into civilian training facilities over the course of the Hellenistic period (→ Education). Walls and fortifications that served to protect cities, smaller settlements and military bases from attack formed part of a long tradition; they became ever more important as a result of the advances in siege technology from the 4th century BC onwards (→ Fortification; → Borders).

B. HARBOURS

Constructing artificial harbours was only found necessary when the Greek *poleis* began to intensify their commercial traffic [4]. The military made use of these facilities, which were originally built for economic purposes. Harbours dedicated to military usage (e.g. Piraeus, Rhodes, Aegina, Thasos, Cnidus) or sections of harbours [3] devoted to the military were established from the mid-6th century BC onwards to serve → fleets of warships and supply vessels. Pioneering structural alterations included breakwaters and piers, as on Delos (8th century BC). It was not until the Hellenistic period that large harbour basins began to be dredged out. The earliest securely attested harbour facility (530 BC) was the one on Samos; it boasted a jetty approximtely 300 m long with boathouses for the war fleet of Polycrates (Hdt. 3,45; 60,3). As was the case with the harbour at Athens during the Persian Wars (499–479 BC), the harbour at Samos was integrated into the city's fortifications. The Athenians developed the Piraeus peninsula into a commercial and military harbour, connecting it with the city by means of the 'Long Walls.' The war fleet was stationed in the two smaller bays to the east (Munichia and Zea), where equipment was stored and maintained in over 250 boathouses [5], and where, after 347/46 BC, the Arsenal (Skeuotheke) of Philo was also stored. Large military harbours also had workshops, warehouses, and sometimes administrative buildings, such as later at Carthage and Alexandria. In the last of these, the offshore island of Pharos was linked to the mainland by an artificial causeway (1,316 m long), creating two new harbour basins. Between 299 and 279 BC, a lighthouse approximately 135 m tall was built in the harbour entrance to the east of the island, becoming the model for this type of building (Str. 17,1,6–10; Plin. HN 36,83). At Carthage, the harbour basin, which had been dredged out in the 3rd century BC, was connected to the sea via a canal. The circular military harbour behind the rectangular merchant harbour had over 200 boathouses (Str. 17,3,14).

From the 2nd/1st centuries BC onwards, the Romans developed the use of hydraulic concrete and highly sophisticated engineering to the point where they could build harbours and anchorages wherever they saw fit in pursuit of military, political, or economic goals. Commercial harbours began to appear in Italy and the provinces, some of which were also used by the military, since there were no standing navies as yet. New naval bases founded from the time of Augustus onwards (Misenum, Ravenna, Aquileia, Alexandria) were of vital importance to the Imperial army and its supply, as were the many river ports of the provincial fleets along the Rhine and Danube (cf. fig. 1) and in Gaul, Britain, the Black Sea and on the Euphrates (→ Fleet; → Supply). The first dedicated Roman military harbour, Portus Iulius, was established by Agrippa on Lake Avernus near Cumae in 37 BC, but it was abandoned between 27 and 20 BC in favour of the better location of Misenum at the northern end of the Bay of Naples. Misenum became the home of the largest maritime base of the Imperial period, for the *classis praetoria Misenensis* (comprising approx. 80 ships and up to 10,000 soldiers). It consisted of inner and outer harbour basins connected by a canal, and two curved breakwaters (100 and 180 m long). Augustus also had another naval harbour constructed (along with the port suburb of Classis) four Roman miles from Ravenna at the mouth of the *fossa Augusta*, which was a canal

Fig. 1: Detail from the spiral relief on the Trajan Column (Rome, AD 112/13; plaster cast taken 1934–1940). This section of the Trajan Column illustration shows soldiers loading barrels in a Roman harbour on the bank of the Danube. The scene dates from the first Dacian Campaign of AD 101.

leading to the Po. This site had been founded as a base in 38 BC (App. Civ. 5,80; Suet. Aug. 49,1; Tac. Ann. 4,5,1) [23.145–319]; [7]; [25].

C. SHIP CANALS AND TRACKWAYS

Canals and trackways built to aid the advance of armies date back to the Archaic period. In the 6th century BC, Periander of Corinth attempted – initially in vain – to make the Isthmus of Corinth navigable for his warships by building a canal. Later, he was more successful constructing the Diolkos, a grooved trackway approximately 8 km long that connected the Saronic and Corinthian gulfs at the narrowest point [16.10–15]. Historians attest to the ongoing importance of this Diolkos in many subsequent naval wars of the Greeks and Romans [20]. Similar trackways are believed to have been built in the harbour of Alexandria and the harbours of Rhodes [4.660].

The Persian king Xerxes, remembering the catastrophic storm of 492 BC, had a ship canal built across the Athos peninsula in 480 BC for his campaign against the Greeks (Hdt. 7,22–24; Thuc. 4,109). In Egypt, the first canal linking the Nile with the Red Sea, an ancestor of the Suez Canal, was built by order of Pharaoh Necho around 600 BC. It was later restored and expanded by Darius I of Persia, by several Ptolemaic rulers and by the Emperor Trajan (preparing for his Parthian War of AD 113–117) [26]. Later sources testify to continued maintenance and use through to the 5th century AD [12.417–423].

The Romans built numerous canals to augment their extensive transport network, which consisted of a system of roads that allowed for transportation in coordination with navigable rivers and lakes. Aemilius Scaurus reputedly had navigable canals built between Modena and Parma in the 2nd century BC (Str. 5,1,11). Consul Marius had a canal built in the Rhône Delta that extended from Arles to the Mediterranean in 104/03 BC (the *fossa Mariana*), the purpose of which was to counteract the disruption of shipping caused by silting (Str. 4,1,8; Plin. HN 3,34; Plut. Marius 15). Horace (Sat. 1,5) documents the 28 km towing canal along the *via Appia* in the Pontine Marshes in the 1st century BC. Drusus was said to have had canals constructed between the Lower Rhine and the North Sea in 12 BC as part of the expansion in Germania (Tac. Ann. 2,8; Suet. Claud. 1). The 34 km *fossa Corbulonis* ('Canal of Corbulo') was built by order of the legate Cn. Domitius Corbulo between the Maas and the Rhine in AD 47 (Tac. Ann. 11,20). Lucius Antistius Vetus, commander of Germania superior, planned a canal for supplying the army, which would have joined the Mosel with the Saône to connect the Mediterranean with the Atlantic, but it was never built (Tac. Ann. 13,53). Emperor Vespasian had the rivers Orontes and Karasu united in a single river bed north of Antioch in an effort to improve the city's transportion links to the hinterland and the Euphrates (AE 1983, 927). Emperor Trajan had a canal 3 km long and 14 m wide built by the Danube during the Dacian Wars (AD 101–102 and 105–106) (AE 1973, 475), as a means of bypassing the cataracts at the Iron Gates (near Đerdap) [8.329–333].

D. ROADS, BRIDGES AND COMMUNICATION

Political and geographical conditions in Greece, where up to 80% of the terrain is mountainous, with 15,000 km of coasts, and a maximum distance to the sea from inhabited areas of just 45 km, invariably made the primary medium of transportation the sea. Nevertheless, and especially in Attica [18], a rather dense network of mule tracks and single-track regional roads with simple, natural routes criss-crossed the countryside [10]; [18]. Since we know of these largely from war histories such as Xenophon's *Hellenika* (for the years 411–362 BC), it is clear that they were put to military use [9]. The Athenian fortification programme that culminated in the 4th century BC may also have stimulated road-building [17.130–132].

Among the more spectacular projects were the bridge built over the Hellespont by order of Xerxes in 480 BC (Hdt. 4,85ff.), and the monumental causeway built by order of Alexander the Great when he besieged the island of Tyre in 332 BC. Alexander used this causeway to connect the island of Tyre to the mainland in order to deploy his siege towers (Arr. Anab. 2,18f.).

The Hellenistic kingdoms used and improved the networks of roads and communications developed by the Assyrians and Persians. The territorial states of the Neo-Assyrian Empire (9th–7th cents. BC) and later the Persian Empire (from the reign of Cyrus II onwards; 550–530 BC) constructed imperial roads with distance markers and waystations for the use of the military and government officials. They also founded state courier services [6]; [22.202–208]. Such systems are still attested in the reign of Antigonus I (Diod. Sic. 19,57,5) and in Ptolemaic Egypt (P. Hib. 110). Public roadbuilding in Macedonia appears to have been highly developed from the time of Archelaus (413–399 BC) (Thuc. 2,100,2), and distance markers testify to the existence of the east-west link, the future *via Egnatia*, in the 4th century BC.

Rome drew inspiration from these examples as it began to establish a territorial state in the course of its expansion. To this end, Rome embarked on a systematic program of road–building in order to connect newly acquired regions with the centre of the empire and secure them militarily. The building of the major public roads largely reflects the progress of Roman expansion, beginning in Italy and continuing westwards and eastwards. The roads facilitated the movements of troops and supplies, enabling legions to reach battlegrounds quickly and supplies to reach the legions efficiently [24]. Sometimes entirely new roads were laid in unknown territories; in other cases, existing links were paved or repaired, as for example during the war against King Perseus of Macedon (Liv. 44,4,12; 9,10f.).

Emperor Augustus also established a public transport system (*vehiculatio, cursus publicus*) to ensure the rapid transfer of military staff and officials, especially messengers. At first, this comprised a courier service of alternating messengers. However, Augustus soon developed it into an efficient transport system by providing conveyances at regular intervals along main roads for travellers to use in rotation (Suet. Aug. 49,3; AE 1976, 653). However, this infrastructure was not a public mail service, as it lacked regular schedules and was not available for private use. The system conveyed only military and civilian officials, as well as goods for the army and the court (gold, silver, clothing and equipment). Its basis was the Roman road network, along which waystations and changing stations (*mansiones, mutationes*) were established. The financing was obtained through a service obligation laid on the populace (*munus*), who were required to provide vehicles and animals, run waystations, and provide accommodation free of charge, in exchange for compensation determined by the governor [13]; [15].

E. Purposes and technologies of Roman road-building and other construction

Major road connections were fundamental for transportation–related engineering in Rome. The significance of these road connections for the army is documented in the term *viae militares* [27]. These did not constitute their own legally defined type of road (like *viae publicae* and *viae privatae*), but a terminological variant of the *viae publicae*, which ran on public land, were not privately financed, and were used for public transportation [21]. Emperor Nero had waystations and changing stations built along the *viae militares* in Thrace for soldiers and officials (*militantes*) (e.g. CIL III 6123) [14].

The firmness of Roman roads was founded on their drainage technology. The road bed of a *via publica* consisted of several layers of foundations (limestone rubble; timbers in marshy areas) paved with stone slabs or gravel. Paving was often partial, especially in the environs of towns. The width

Fig. 2a: Detail from the spiral relief on the Trajan Column (Rome, AD 112/13; plaster cast taken 1934–1940). This section of the Trajan Column shows the famous Trajan Bridge between the Roman camp at Drobeta on the north bank of the Danube (now Romania) and the village of Kostol (Serbia) on the south bank. The bridge, composed of stone pillars and a wooden arch stretching 1.1 km, was built under the direction of the architect Apollodorus of Damascus in AD 103–105.

Fig. 2b: Trajan Bridge on the Danube. The photo shows some of the remains still visible today at Kostol (Serbia).

of a *via publica* corresponded to the needs of traffic, so that ideally two carts could pass each other. Grooves or steps carved into the stone helped overcome extreme inclines. This often necessitated difficult work on rock faces or the construction of tunnels or bridges, especially because the goal in Roman road-building was to achieve as direct and straight a route as possible regardless of difficulties in the terrain. The 81 km of frontier road (*limes*) in Germania superior attests to this [2]. Overcoming natural obstacles, such as mountains and rivers, also had symbolic significance for the Romans. The use of the most expert technical competence even for building temporary bridges on a campaign demonstrated Roman military power to the enemy. Caesar's bridge over the Rhine (Caes. B Gall. 4,17), or the Danube bridge built during Trajan's Dacian Wars (Cass. Dio 68,13; Procop. Aed. 4,6,11ff.; cf. figs. 2a and b), were constructed in service of military advances that were intended to display an impressive show of force. Finally, road-building could function as an instrument of strategy. According to Frontinus (Str. 1,3,10), Domitian had roads built 120 miles into the territory of the Germanic peoples in order to destroy their refuges in the forests.

Many roads were built by soldiers, but this was not the rule: in principle, the populace was required to do the construction as well as the maintenance of roads [21]; [1.224–226]. Other types of construction completed the military infrastructure both inside and outside camps, including facilities for water supply, baths, granaries (*horrea*) and workshops for making bricks and other necessities (→ Armament; → Production system; → Camp; → Supply) [19.23–34]; [28]. From the reign of Diocletian onwards (AD 284–305), equipment was made in state-run factories (*fabricae*) at 35 locations across the empire (Not. Dign. or. 11,18ff.; Not. Dign. occ. 9,15ff.). These facilities were major complexes for hundreds of workers, and consisted of workshops, storehouses and barracks [11].

☞ State and army

BIBLIOGRAPHY
[1] C. ADAMS, War and Society, in: P. SABIN et al. (eds.), The Cambridge History of Greek and Roman Warfare, vol. 2: Rome from the Late Republic to the Late Empire, 2007, 198–232 [2] G. ALFÖLDY, Die lineare Grenzziehung des vorderen Limes in Obergermanien und die Statthalterschaft des Caius Popilius Carus Pedo, in: E. SCHALLMAYER (ed.), Limes imperii romani. Beiträge zum Fachkolloquium 'Weltkulturerbe Limes' November 2001 in Lich-Arnsburg (Saalburg-Schriften 6), 2004, 7–20 [3] K. BAIKA, Early Naval Bases and Military Harbour Infrastructure in the Mediterranean, in: A. HAFNER et al. (eds.), Die neue Sicht. Unterwasserarchäologie und Geschichtsbild. Internationaler Kongress für Unterwasserarchäologie. Zürich 21.10.–24.10.2004, 2006, 176–192 [4] D.J. BLACKMAN, Sea Transport, pt. 2: Harbours, in: J.P. OLESON (ed.), The Oxford Handbook of Engineering and Technology in the Classical World, 2008, 638–670 [5] D.J. BLACKMAN / B. RANKOV, Shipsheds of the Ancient Mediterranean, 2013 [6] P. BRIANT, From the Indus to the Mediterranean. The Administrative Organization and Logistics of the Great Roads of the Achaemenid Empire, in: S.E. ALCOCK et al. (eds.), Highways, Byways, and Road Systems in the Pre-Modern World, 2012, 185–201 [7] P.A. GIANFROTTA, Harbour Structures of the Augustean Age in Italy, in: A. RABAN / K.G. HOLUM (eds.), Caesarea Maritima. A Retrospective after Two Millennia, 1996, 65–76 [8] K. GREWE, Tunnels and Canals, in: J.P. OLESON (ed.), The Oxford Handbook of Engineering and Technology in the Classical World, 2008, 319–336 [9] F. GSCHNITZER, Straßen, Wege und Märsche in Xenophons Hellenika. Ein Beitrag zur Verkehrsgeographie Griechenlands in klassischer Zeit, in: E. OLSHAUSEN / H. SONNABEND (eds.), Zu Wasser und zu Land. Verkehrswege in der antiken Welt (Stuttgarter Kolloquium zur Historischen Geographie des Altertums 7, 1999), 2002, 202–208 [10] T. HOWE, Transport, Greece, in: The Encyclopedia of Ancient History, 2013, 6823–6828 [11] A. JAMES, The fabricae, in: J.C. COULSTON (ed.), Military Equipment and the Identity of Roman Soldiers, 1988, 257–331 [12] A. JÖRDENS, Statthalterliche Verwaltung in der römischen Kaiserzeit. Studien zum praefectus Aegypti, 2009 [13] A. KOLB, Transport und Nachrichtentransfer im Römischen Reich, 2000 [14] A. KOLB, Mansiones and cursus publicus in the Roman Empire, in: P. BASSO / E. ZANINI (eds.), Statio Amoena. Sostare e vivere lungo le strade romane, 2016, 3–8 [15] L. LEMCKE, Imperial Transportation and Communication from the Third to the Late Forth Century. The Golden Age of the cursus publicus, 2016 [16] M.J.T. LEWIS, Railways in the Greek and Roman World, in: A. GUY / J. REES (eds.), Early Railways. A Selection of Papers from the First International Early Railways Conference, 2001, 8–19 [17] H. LOHMANN, Antike Straßen und Saumpfade in Attika und der Megaris, in: E. OLSHAUSEN / H. SONNABEND (eds.), Zu Wasser und zu Land. Verkehrswege in der antiken Welt (Stuttgarter Kolloquium zur Historischen Geographie des Altertums 7, 1999), 2002, 109–147 [18] H. LOHMANN, Roads IV: Greece, in: BNP 12, 2008, 620–622 [19] R. MACMULLEN, Soldier and Civilian in the Later Roman Empire, 1963 [20] G. RAEPSAET / M. TOLLEY, Le Diolkos de l'Isthme à Corinthe. Son tracé, son fonctionnement, in: BCH 117, 1993, 233–261 [21] M. RATHMANN, Untersuchungen zu den Reichsstraßen in den westlichen Provinzen des Imperium Romanum, 2003 [22] M. RATHMAN, Der Princeps und die viae publicae in den Provinzen. Konstruktion und Fakten eines planmäßigen Infrastrukturausbaus durch die Reichszentrale, in: A. KOLB (ed.), Infrastruktur und Herrschaftsorganisation im Imperium Romanum. Akten der Tagung in Zürich 19.–20.10.2012, 2014, 197–221 [23] M. REDDÉ, Mare Nostrum. Les infrastructures, le dispositif et l'histoire de la marine militaire sous l'Empire romain, 1986 [24] J.P. ROTH, The Logistics of the Roman Army at War (264 B.C.–A.D. 235), 1999 [25] T. SCHMIDTS, Stützpunkte der römischen Flotten in der Kaiserzeit, in: T. FISCHER (ed.), Die Armee der Caesaren. Archäologie und Geschichte, 2012, 354–365 [26] H. SCHÖRNER, Künstliche Schifffahrtskanäle in der Antike, in: Skyllis 3, 2000, 28–43 [27] M.A. SPEIDEL, Heer und Straßen – Militares viae, in: R. FREI-STOLBA (ed.), Siedlung und Verkehr im Römischen Reich. Römerstrassen zwischen Herrschaftssicherung und Landschaftsprägung. Akten des Kolloquiums

anlässlich des 65. Geburtstags von Prof. H.E. Herzig, Bern 26.–29.6.01, 2004, 331–344 (again in: Heer und Herrschaft im Römischen Reich der Hohen Kaiserzeit (MAVORS 16), 2009, 501–513) [28] M.A. SPEIDEL, Herrschaft durch Vorsorge und Beweglichkeit. Zu den Infrastrukturanlagen des kaiserzeitlichen römischen Heeres im Reichsinneren, in: A. KOLB (ed.), Infrastruktur und Herrschaftsorganisation im Imperium Romanum. Akten der Tagung in Zürich 19.–20.10.2012, 2014, 80–99.

ANNE KOLB

Innovation

A. Introduction: Innovation and the military
B. Organizational innovations
C. Innovations in strategy and tactics
D. Innovations in military technology
E. Innovations in the ancient military – causes and effects

A. INTRODUCTION: INNOVATION AND THE MILITARY

The concept of innovation first came into scholarly use in the study of economics, where it denotes 'the introduction of a new product on the market, or of a new production process' [5.884]. Economic historians now use the term in general to refer to new ventures that are intended to raise productivity or efficiency in an enterprise or a society. Such innovations are generally inspired by technological developments and advances. In many cases, innovations result from purposeful action by individuals, groups of people or enterprises. Research into innovation considers those innovations that have a positive impact. In economics, such an impact might be a productivity increase, cost reductions, improvements to products already introduced or the introduction of new products for which demand exists and which accordingly can achieve a breakthrough in the marketplace.

The term 'innovation' is also gaining ground outside the sphere of economics. In the political field, there is a close kinship between reformist policies and innovations. Organizational innovations, for instance, are intended to increase the efficiency of institutions and to bring about desirable effects on general wellbeing and an overall improvement in the performance of a society. The implementation of political reforms can thus be seen as a process of social innovation. Innovations often represent reactions to changes in enterprises or societies. How such challenges are met determines to a certain extent the continued existence of the enterprises, institutions and societies concerned [50].

Because disputes between cities, peoples and monarchies in the ancient world were often resolved through military conflict, the military was immensely important to the political processes by which groups pursued their interests. The primary purpose of innovation in the military sphere was to improve the combat effectiveness of armies and navies, thereby achieving superiority over enemy forces. Even so, besides offensive warfare aimed at advancing one's political interests, mention must also be made of defense and the protection of one's community or political soverignty against attacks.

According to much recent research, the fighting methods of ancient armies barely changed from the Archaic period to Late Antiquity. Soldiers fought in battle formations using handheld weapons such as swords. The only ranged weapons were bows and arrows, javelins and slingshot projectiles. The cavalry, being on horseback, was more mobile than the infantry units; but with few exceptions, the cavalry played a rather insignificant role in combat. Battles were usually won by deploying the infantry. According to this view, the real turning point in military history came only with the development of firearms in the Late Middle Ages and early modern period [47.688f.]. Works on the technological history of the early modern period call the advent of firearms a 'revolution in the profile of war' [41.312–348]. Even modern scientific literature tends to neglect technological developments in the ancient military [10].

Despite this neglect, due consideration must be given to the constant innovations of the Greek and Roman militaries in the organization of armies, in strategy and tactics, and especially in military technology. A simple comparison between the citizen militias of the Greek *poleis* of the Classical period and the Roman legions of the Principate makes the profound transformation of the ancient military abundantly clear. Scholars now pay greater attention to such "military innovations" ([17.361]; likewise [47.689]). The driving forces behind innovations were sometimes purely military, but more often they were also social, political and technological. As elsewhere, so also in regard to the ancient military: innovations can only be properly understood if their contexts are sufficiently taken into account.

B. ORGANIZATIONAL INNOVATIONS

B.1. Greece
B.2. Hellenistic period
B.3. The Roman Republic
B.4. Principate
B.5. Late Antiquity

Organizational changes in the military affected the formation of armies, the ranks of officers, the recruitment of soldiers, the financing of the draft, the care of wounded and incapacitated soldiers

(→ Medical corps) and the social welfare of soldiers and veterans.

B.1. GREECE

The military contingents of the Greek *poleis* usually consisted of citizens' militias, with military service mandatory for citizens. According to their wealth, citizens were required to fight either as hoplites, in which case they provided their own equipment and weapons, or as light infantrymen. The only way for cities to strengthen their citizen's militias was to recruit → mercenaries (Thuc. 7,27,1f.). Mercenary armies began to play an increasingly prominent role in the struggles for hegemony in Greece after the Peloponnesian War (431–404 BC) [8.48f.]; [28.17f.].

The professionalization of warfare in the late 5th century BC led to the creation of elite corps of especially well trained troops [23.202]. Thucydides mentions such a unit at Argos comprising 1,000 soldiers (Thuc. 5,67,2). The Arcadians disagreed over the pay for such a force (Xen. Hell. 7,4,22; 7,4,33). The 'Sacred Band' of elite soldiers of Thebes was famous in Antiquity (Plut. *Pelopidas* 19). As time went on, the practice of relying on a militia army required more and more extensive military training for citizens. Such training took place in the context of the Ephebia at Athens in the 4th century BC (Aristot. Ath. pol. 42,2–5).

The total restructuring of the Macedonian armed forces is attributed to Philip II (→ Generals of note, M.) [8.51–54]; [7]; [20.6f.]; [28.20f.]. The reorganization of the Macedonian military came in response to a series of crushing defeats in battle against the Illyrians. Philip adopted the phalanx formation and equipped the infantry with weapons better suited for war (Diod. Sic. 16,3,1f.). The traditionally strong Macedonian cavalry was transformed into the elite force of the *hetairoi* ('peers'), in which the Macedonian nobility fought.

B.2. HELLENISTIC PERIOD

The foreign-policy objectives of the Ptolemies, whose ambitions extended far beyond Egypt, and the competition between the Hellenistic monarchies for dominance in the Syrian region in particular, demanded strong armies. It was necessary to recruit Macedonians and Greeks to serve in these armies. In order to secure enough soldiers for Egypt's needs, Ptolemy I switched to a new system of maintenance for his soldiers. He gave the Greeks and Macedonians who served in his army land they could cultivate, in order to gain their loyalty [44.474]; [49.124f.]. Through these soldiers, the Greek language and culture spread widely throughout Egypt.

B.3. THE ROMAN REPUBLIC

During the Republican period, the Senate made decisions regarding the raising and deployment of legions and their assignment to the various provinces. In conducting war, however, control of the troops was in the hands of the consuls, who were given *imperium*, that is, power of command over one or more legions. The Roman army itself was a militia. Roman citizens were required to do military service, the duration of which depended on what was needed for the particular situation. On principle, only citizens who owned proprty served as legionaries. Citizens without property, the *proletarii*, were not fit for military service and did not bear arms. Legions formed up for battle in three ranks (Liv. 8,8,3–8), which were in turn divided into maniples.

Rome's alliance system was a crucial factor behind its military strength. Unlike Athens, for instance, which exacted tribute from allied *poleis* in the 5th century, Rome required its allies (*socii*) to provide military contingents when war broke out. After the Samnite Wars, when the cities and peoples of Italy were contractually bound to Rome as *socii*, the Republic was able to draw on the entire military potential of the Apennine Peninsula for a war – a potential that certainly matched that of the Hellenistic monarchies (Pol. 2,24). Such a unifying of military power coordinated through unparalleled political organization and integration was without precedent in the history of the ancient world.

This early military organization underwent many changes throughout the wars of the 3rd and 2nd centuries. Most of these changes were probably part of long-term developments. Cohorts, for instance, superseded maniples as the army's most important tactical unit [24.63–67]. Based on an observation made by Sallust, C. Marius is responsible for the practice of recruiting citizens without property to serve in the military (Sall. Iug. 86,2f.; → Generals of note, K.). This, however, in no way represented a shift to a professional army. Conscription remained the normal means for recruiting soldiers into the legions until the outbreak of the → Civil War in 49 BC [6.391–415].

Alongside these developments, important changes also came to the political dimension of Roman warfare. Following Roman defeats at the hands of the Cimbri and Teutones, C. Marius remained consul – contrary to established law – from 104 to 100 BC without interruption. He was therefore able to prepare the legions for battle through continuous → training and to wage war according to his own strategic convictions. Through the intervention of plebeian tribunes in 67 and 66 BC, Pompey (Cn. Pompeius; → Generals of note, N.) was granted large-scale *imperia* of long duration in operational territories extending beyond individual provinces, in order to ensure success in war (Cic. Manil. 27–50). Caesar (→ Generals of note, C.) followed this example: in 59 BC, he had himself assigned, by statute and by senatorial decree, to several provinces including Gallia Transalpina for five years. These *imperia* not only gave the general new and previously unknown political power, but also freed his campaign from the instabilities caused by rapid turnover in commanders. It is significant that Cicero formulated his thoughts on the ability of the Romans to respond to new situations with new measures in his speech on Pompey's command (Cic. Manil. 59–63).

B.4. PRINCIPATE

The establishment of a new political system, the Principate, went hand in hand with a comprehensive reform of the Roman military [3.541–563]; [14.81–89]; [25.376–387]; [24.146–154]; [26.207–209]; [28.40–43]; [34.246–271] (key sources are R. Gest. div. Aug. 16f.; Suet. Aug. 49,1f.; Cass. Dio 54,25,5; 55,23,1f.). The crucial historical factor behind this reform was the fact that the power base of Caesar the Younger during the politically difficult phase after the murder of the dictator C. Iulius Caesar and throughout the civil wars until his victory over Mark Antony at Actium (31 BC; → Battles of note, A.) depended in large part on the loyalty of the veterans and soldiers of his legions. It was for this reason that Caesar the Younger took the title of *imperator* and began, late in 40 BC, to call himself Imperator Caesar. Following the political realignment of 27 BC, it was essential to secure the bond between the soldiers and the *princeps*, who had received the honorific name Augustus. What had to be prevented at all costs was the deployment of the legions against the *princeps* as the result of an internal conflict. At the same time, the Roman army still had to meet the needs of an expansionist foreign policy and defend the → borders of the Roman Empire effectively. These requirements demanded the elimination of the structural weaknesses that had plagued the Roman military in the last years of the Republic.

The foundation for the new system was laid in the proconsular *imperium* granted to Augustus in 27 BC, which was first awarded for the limited term of ten years and later repeatedly extended. This gave the *princeps* almost sole authority over the legions, so that wars were fought under his *imperium* and his auspices. In this way, the system of the late Republic, with military power divided among several promagistrates, each with his own *imperium* and answerable to the Senate, was superseded by the virtually exclusive *imperium* of the *princeps* over the military. Within this system, command of the individual legions was delegated to legates. The legions, each of which received a number and an epithet, and thus its own identity, were stationed in permanent legionary camps, mostly along the borders. This configuration of *imperium* had implications for the honours that accompanied military success. The *princeps* was understood to be present in the legion in the form of his image, and only he was entitled to celebrate a triumph after a military victory.

Difficulties with the → recruitment of troops were solved with a new regulation governing soldiers' terms of service. A term of 16 years was now set, after which soldiers remained as reservists for four years, liable to call-up for service in the legions in case of a military emergency. → Pay was almost doubled in comparison with the late Republic (to 900 *sesterces*). The centurions, indispensable to the professional leadership of the maniples, received a considerably higher rate. On discharge, soldiers were entitled to receive land, although a monetary payment replaced this during Augustus' reign, because of a shortage of land for the settlement of → veterans. The payment on discharge from military service (3,000 *denarii* or 12,000 *sesterces*) was roughly equivalent to 14 years' pay. These provisions, which served to ensure the material security of veterans, corresponded to the tradition of popular politicsin the late Republic. The grants to veterans were financed through a new institution of the Roman administration, the *aerarium militare* ('military fund'). At the start, money from Augustus' private fortune was paid into the fund. Later, the *aerarium militare* received revenues from an inheritance tax and an auction tax.

Also in the reign of Augustus, regular corps of → auxiliaries were established: the *auxilia* and the *alae* ('wings', i.e. divisions of cavalry). Soldiers for the *auxilia* were recruited from among the provinces, and Roman prefects were appointed to command the units. It is reported that about the same number of soldiers did military service in the *auxilia* as in the legions (Tac. Ann. 4,5,4).

The measures introduced by Augustus were as a whole unprecedented, and undoubtedly highly innovative. The Augustan reform of the Roman military created a professional army of long-serving soldiers who were well trained through constant drills and fiercely loyal to the current *princeps*. This was an army that, despite increasing pressure on the imperial borders, proved capable of preserving the cohesion of the Roman Empire until the end of the 3rd century.

Another important change to military organization implemented by Augustus was the permanent stationing of army units in the city of Rome. The task of the Praetorian Guard was to safeguard the authority of the *princeps* in his capital. The Praetorians were also an elite unit of the Roman army [35.44–47].

B.5. Late Antiquity

The Roman military was completely reorganized during the reigns of Diocletian and Constantine (→ Generals of note, J.) between 284 and 337 [8.119–124]; [9.120–130]; [12.303–325]; [28.50–54]; [16.272–278]. The reforms of Diocletian went far beyond simply establishing the Tetrarchy that replaced the single *princeps* with four rulers called Augusti and Caesares. They also addressed almost all areas of administration, including the financial and tax systems, the reorganization of the provinces and the establishment of dioceses. Key changes affecting military organization were the separation of civilian and military authority and the division of the army into units responsible for securing the borders (*limitanei*) and mobile units (*comitatenses*). Securing the frontiers along the Rhine and Danube was entrusted to the *ripenses* ('riverbank troops'; Cod. Theod. 7,20,4). Zosimus was critical of this division into unit classes (2,34). The 'commanders' of the border units were called *duces*. The army commanders were the *magistri militum* ('Masters of Soldiers'). Germanic figures were able to rise to these positions from the late 4th century onwards.

Meanwhile, the numerical strength of the army was greatly increased, although Lactantius' assertion that the number of soldiers more than quadrupled (De mort. pers. 7,2) has been rightly refuted [12.305]. This new organization of the Roman army was the result of a long evolution that began in the reign of Gallienus [12.305]. According to [9], Constantine was 'not a dramatic innovator' [9.129]. The Roman army was certainly effective after these reforms. The main problems of the 4th and 5th centuries arose from the frequent usurpations resulting from internal conflicts, and from the fact that Germanic occupants of the position of *magister militum* met with fierce resistance from the Roman elites.

C. Innovations in strategy and tactics

C.1. Greece
C.2. Strategy and tactics in the army of the Roman Republic
C.3. Securing the borders under the Principate

C.1. Greece

Fundamental to land warfare in Late Archaic and Classical Greece was the formation of the → phalanx [8.22–30]; [7]; [15.155–161]; [19.680f.]; [28.5–9]; [51.192–213]; [43.32–37]; [45.60–71]; [46.49–74], a close-order array of heavily armed hoplites, equipped with helmets, armour, leg protectors and shields. Their weapons were a heavy spear not suited for throwing, and a sword. Soldiers were usually formed eight ranks deep. The hoplite phalanx was one of the most important innovations of ancient military history, shaping the course of battle in the Age of Hoplite Warfare [39.25]. It is, however, unclear at exactly what date the hoplite phalanx became generally established. In the war over the Lelantine Plain on Euboea, the belligerents are said to have forgone the use of ranged weapons and agreed to confine themselves to close combat (Str. 10,1,12; cf. Archil. fr. 3). Homer and Tyrtaeus both mention phalanx warfare (Hom. Il. 13,130–135; Tyrt. fr. 11,29–34). The Chigi Vase (7th cent. BC), which portrays combat between hoplites, is regarded as one of the earliest pictorial references to the phalanx [8.26]; [46. fig. 30]. The necessary precondition for the emergence of the hoplite phalanx was the existence of a social class of *polis* citizens capable of meeting the costs of the equipment. The ability of smiths to make bronze chest armour, helmets and greaves for the hoplites is well attested for the Archaic period. Thucydides gives a thorough description of the phalanx in battle (5,66–73 on the Battle of Mantinea). The requisite coordination in the forward march was achieved through the rhythm of accompanying → music (Thuc. 5,70; cf. also the Chigi Vase).

It became clear during the Peloponnesian War (→ Wars of note, H.; 431–404 BC) that in certain conditions light infantry could outperform a company of hoplites in combat. In the summer of 426 BC, light Aetolian infantry defeated a troop of Athenian hoplites under the command of Demosthenes (Thuc. 3,97f.; cf. also Thuc. 4,32–36 on the fighting on the island of Sphacteria). After this, the *poleis* started to deploy light infantry with increasing frequency [8.48]; [28.19]; [43.130]. *Peltastai* ('light armed footsoldiers') commanded by the Athenian general Iphicrates almost annihilated a unit of Spartan hoplites at Corinth (Xen. Hell. 4,5,11–18).

Epaminondas (→ Generals of note, F.) and Pelopidas of Thebes introduced an innovation in combat formation at the Battle of Leuctra (371 BC) [8.50]; [43.140–142]. By reinforcing the left wing of the phalanx, the Thebans broke the Spartan troops on that side, then attacked the enemy ranks from the flank (Xen. Hell. 6,4,3–15; Plut. *Pelopidas* 23). The concentrated attack on one wing became part of the combat repertoire for Hellenistic generals, employed for instance by Demetrius (→ Generals of note, E.) before the Battle of Gaza in 312 BC (Diod. Sic. 19,82), and later by Roman commanders, for example in the battle against Philip V at Cynoscephalae (197 BC) (Pol. 18,23).

The deployment of a powerful fleet, first urged by Themistocles and then justified in detail by Pericles, brought about a complete transformation in Athenian military strategy in the 5th century BC

[8.32–40]; [15.185–191]; [28.12–15]. The primary aim of war was no longer to win victory on land, but to attain naval supremacy, which, it was believed, would make Athens nothing short of invincible (Thuc. 1,142f.; 2,62). The model for this strategy of extensive naval operations may have been the creation of a large → fleet by the Tyrant of Samos, Polycrates, in the Late Archaic period (Hdt. 3,39,3; Thuc. 1,13,6; 3,104,2).

Among the innovations that Philip II introduced to the Macedonian military [36.369] was new weaponry for the infantry, the *pezetairoi* ('footsoldiers'), in the form of the *sarisa*, a pike over five metres long. The Macedonian phalanx, which fought in a dense formation with several rows one behind the other, was far superior to the hoplite phalanx of the Greek *poleis*. It was under Philip II and Alexander the Great (→ Generals of note, B.) that the cavalry acquired a significant role in the Macedonian army. Its task was to bring the battle to a head by attacking the opponent's ranks [8.52–54]; [17.356f.]; [28.20]. The hallmark of Macedonian tactics in battle was close cooperation between the phalanx and the cavalry, as seen at the Battle of Gaugamela (Arr. Anab. 3,14,1–3).

The permanent state of war maintained by Philip II allowed Demosthenes to call his force a 'standing army' (*dynamin synestekuian*; Dem. Or. 8,11). Adding weight to this observation is his statement that Philip did not fight only in the summer, as the Spartans did, for example. In no season did Philip remain idle (Or. 9,48–50).

C.2. STRATEGY AND TACTICS IN THE ARMY OF THE ROMAN REPUBLIC

There are a number of indications that the Romans adopted the phalanx formation in the early Republican period, and that the Roman army fought in this formation [8.76f.]. However, the Romans quickly abandoned the single battle formation of the phalanx, probably still in the 4th century, and divided their legions into maniples [8.83f.]; [15.210–214]; [24.19]; [43.184f.]. Following this innovation, the Roman army in battle formation consisted of three ranks: the *hastati* (originally 'spearmen'), the *principes* (literally 'leaders', the second rank in the formation) and the *triarii* (the third rank in the formation) (Liv. 8,8,5–13), the *hastati* and *principes* each consisting of 15 maniples. These maniples were not formed up as a single uninterrupted battle line. Gaps were left between the maniples of the *hastati*, with the maniples of the *principes* standing behind covering those gaps.

This formation had considerable advantages over the Greek phalanx. Units enjoyed greater mobility, could adapt with flexibility to the conditions of the terrain, and had sufficient space for close combat with a sword. Light infantry could retreat quickly into the gaps between the maniples after the battle began, and the *principes* and *triarii* could intervene in the fighting without difficulty whenever necessary.

When Roman forces came face to face with the rigid formation of the *sarisa*-armed Macedonian phalanx at Cynoscephalae (197 BC) and at Pydna (168 BC), the Roman tactics proved vastly superior (Pol. 18,24–26; 18,29–32; 29,17).

Another innovation was the standardization of the design of a Roman field camp [21.75–104]; [24.36–38], which followed strict rules and was implemented in essentially the same way in many different wars (Pol. 6,27–31). Pyrrhus was said to have expressed admiration for a Roman → camp and its organization (Plut. *Pyrrhus* 16). The example of the camp and the precise regulations for guard duty (Pol. 6,33–36; Veg. Mil. 1,21–24) make another fact clear, which Livy mentions in his discussion of whether Alexander the Great could have defeated the Romans (Liv. 9,17,10): Roman warfare relied on clear precepts that were binding upon commanders. These *perpetua praecepta* ('perpetual precepts'), which were developed into an *ars* ('art'), summarized the experience and collective expertise of all Roman commanders. In this way, leadership of a Roman army was no longer dependent on the abilities or intuitions of a particular general. As Livy concedes, the Romans might lose an occasional battle (9,18,9), but throughout the entire Republican period, such losses never led to defeat in a war.

The classic example of an opponent scoring a victory over a Roman army is the Battle of Cannae (→ Battles of note, C.; 216 BC). Hannibal's cavalry succeeded in outflanking the Roman legions and attacking them from behind [43.209–211]. This strategy of a pincer attack followed by the encirclement of the enemy was unprecedented in ancient warfare, and it was virtually never used again.

C.3. SECURING THE BORDERS UNDER THE PRINCIPATE

Although Augustus sought to expand the Roman Empire with great determination, Roman historians (Suet. Aug. 21,2; Tac. Ann. 1,3,6) suggest that his efforts to enlarge Roman territory ceased towards the end of his life [26.165–185]. This assessment may be influenced by the policies of later *principes*, but with the exception of a few territorial gains, especially in Britain, and in Dacia and Arabia during the reign of Trajan, it cannot be denied that the main phase of expansion was essentially complete in the 1st century AD. After this phase, the main task was securing the borders, which called for a defensive strategy. Offensive actions, such as those against the Parthian Empire and later the Persians, did not lead to the permanent annexation of short-term conquests, so in the long run proved unsuccessful.

Traditional forms of warfare no longer suited this new strategic priority. Wars to win territory or subjugate peoples were now waged within limits of time and space. However, such campaigns proved ineffective in repelling incursions and invasions by foreign tribes or peoples, who were classified as barbarians and proved unreliable when it came to adhering to the provisions of treaties. To keep the barbarians at bay, it became necessary to fortify the borders (SHA Hadr. 12,6). This led to a fundamental revision of military strategy. The purpose was no longer to defeat an opponent in battle, but to prevent invasion in the first place, by building forts and border fortifications. First the Rhine, then the Danube frontiers were secured by constructing forts. When Domitian conquered territories to the east of the Rhine, it became necessary to build a continuous border fortification. In Germania superior, the *Limes* ('boundary') was a fortification line consisting of watch towers and a palisade fence. From the late 2nd century onwards, it consisted of a palisade, embankment and ditch, and stone towers. Early in the 2nd century, the province of Britannia was also secured with a border fortification, Hadrian's Wall. The further advance of this line to the north through the wall of Antoninus Pius (Antonine Wall) was short-lived. In North Africa, forts protected cities and roads in the areas that bordered on the desert. The Romans also conducted large-scale operations to secure their → borders in the Near East. Cities in frontier zones were fortified by the construction of walls and towers (Amm. Marc. 23,5,2). Auxiliary units were generally stationed in the forts along the *limes*, so that legions and auxiliary units now performed different military tasks (summary [8.118f.]; [40]; [52]). The defensive strategy during the crisis of the 3rd century manifested itself in the construction of walls around Rome in the reign of Aurelian (AD 271–280).

In the east of the empire, the Romans in their conflicts with the Parthians [22.60–68] and (after AD 224) Persians found themselves confronting armies whose → cavalry units were especially formidable because their horses wore armour in battle (Plut. *Crassus* 24; Heliodorus, *Aethiopica* 9,15; Amm. Marc. 24,6,8). This forced the Romans to supply their own riders and horses with armour. There is epigraphic evidence from the reign of Hadrian of a unit of armoured cavalry called the *ala catafractata* ('armoured unit') (ILS 2735; Veg. Mil. 3,23,3), but it is uncertain whether the horses of this unit were also protected with armour.

D. INNOVATIONS IN MILITARY TECHNOLOGY

D.1. Warfare and craftsmanship in Greece
D.2. Classical Greece and Hellenistic period
D.3. Roman Republic and Principate
D.4. Late Antiquity

D.1. WARFARE AND CRAFTSMANSHIP IN GREECE

It is impossible to exaggerate the importance of innovation for the development of the military. Improvements to existing weapons and the introduction of new weapons fundamentally influenced warfare from the dawn of Antiquity. One innovation in metallurgy was of relevance to all ancient warfare: the processing of iron in the period following the fall of the Mycenaean palace cultures. Although bronze continued to be the preferred material for making armour until the Classical period, swords and other weapons were increasingly forged from iron from the 'Dark Ages' onwards [15.144–147].

Homer already describes the warrior's dependence on his weapons and armour. When Achilles, having given his weapons to Patroclus, lost them as a result of the latter's death, he was no longer capable of returning to battle. In this predicament, his mother, the goddess Thetis, asked Hephaestus for weapons for her son. The making of these weapons is a key scene of the *Iliad* (18,79–84; 18,136f.; 18,369–617; 19,10–23). What Homer portrays in the story of a single hero was true in general for all hoplites of the Archaic period. They depended on smiths to supply them with weapons and bronze armour [46.50–59]. The Corinthian helmet, made of thin bronze plate, was particularly important, since it protected the head against injury [15.158]. As the great workshop of Cephalus at Athens shows, the manufacture of weapons, armour, and shields was a highly specialized craft by the last years of the Peloponnesian War (Lys. 12,4; 12,19).

D.2. CLASSICAL GREECE AND HELLENISTIC PERIOD

D.2.1. Strategy and tactics of naval warfare
D.2.2. The catapult and siege technology
D.2.3. The use of war elephants

D.2.1. STRATEGY AND TACTICS OF NAVAL WARFARE

The basis for Athenian power in the Greek world was the construction of a type of ship that was suitable for naval warfare [48.224–226]. The Greeks likely followed the Phoenician example when they began to build warships with ram bows and multiple banks of oars. According to Thucydides, the first triremes were built at Corinth (1,13). Triremes, 'three-oared' vessels, had three ranks of rowing benches one on top of another. The purpose was to sink an enemy ship by ramming it. Triremes were propelled forwards by about 170 oarsmen, who gave the ship the impact force necessary for ramming. The Athenian fleet comprised mainly triremes from the time of the Persian Wars onwards. It played a decisive role in the naval victory at Salamis (480 BC) and thereafter guaranteed Athenian hegemony in the Aegean (→ Fleet) [8.32–40]; [15.186–189].

D.2.2. THE CATAPULT AND SIEGE TECHNOLOGY

The invention of the catapult at Syracuse in the early 4th century represents a decisive turning point in the history of ancient military technology [2]; [15.192–202]; [28.48–64]; [42]; [53.346–350]. This weapon was first built in preparation for the campaign of Dionysius I against the Carthaginians (Diod. Sic. 14,42,1). The Spartan king Archidamus recognized the importance of the invention, as evidenced by his remark that 'the valour of men is no more!' (Plut. Mor. 191e; 219a). The catapult greatly increased the range and power of the missile compared with the bow. The effect of a projectile was no longer dependent on human musclepower.

Dionysius I fostered innovations in military technology through his strong support for technicians brought from Italy, Greece, and even Carthage (Diod. Sic. 14,41,3). Based on experiences with Carthaginian siege technology in previous campaigns (Diod. Sic. 13,54,7; 13,55,2), those innovations included the building of siege equipment, especially siege towers, which were put to use in the Siege of Motya (396 BC) (Diod. Sic. 14,50,4; 14,51,1; 14,51,7). Catapults, which the Carthaginians had never seen before, were said to have caused considerable alarm on this campaign (Diod. Sic. 14,50,4).

It was Philip II of Macedon who made consistent use of the new developments in military technology to take cities rapidly. For instance, the Thessalian Polyidus developed new siege equipment, and Diades and Charias worked as technicians in the army of Alexander the Great (Vitr. De arch. 10,13,3). These were practitioners who were able to write treatises about the construction of siege equipment (Vitr. De arch. 7 praef. 14). Vitruvius attributes to Diades the invention of the mobile siege tower (*turres ambulatoriae*), and makes reference to the content of a treatise about the 'ram' (10,13,3–8). Moreover, the *Laterculi Alexandrini* identifies Diades as the technician who, serving under Alexander, was responsible for the sieges of Tyre and other cities [13.30]. Thanks to advances in siege technology, Alexander was able to conquer the strategically important cities along the coasts of Asia Minor and the Levant at great speed.

Demetrius Poliorketes is also said to have been greatly interested in technical innovations. The construction of warships and siege equipment apparently fascinated him. His ships with fifteen and sixteen rows of oars, like his siege towers, astonished even his enemies (Plut. *Demetrius* 20). For the Siege of Rhodes in 305/04 BC, Demetrius had a colossal siege tower called 'Helepolis' built [27.58–70]. Given these circumstances, Vitruvius is justified in calling the Siege of Rhodes primarily a competition between the technicians working for both sides (Diod. Sic. 20,91,1–8; Vitr. De arch. 10,16,3–8).

The Greek world noticed and sometimes reflected on the transformations in warfare brought about by technological innovations. In his *Third Philippic* of 341 BC, Demosthenes discussed in detail the changes to the military in Macedonia, referring specifically to the Macedonians' ability to besiege cities (Or. 9,50). Aristotle reacted to the invention of catapults and siege equipment by demanding that the *poleis* redouble efforts to build fortifications and defensive walls, and criticized failures to do so (Pol. 1330b).

In the 4th century BC, the early two-armed catapult was developed into the torsion catapult, in which tension was created using two vertical spools of sinew skeins. Stones as well as arrows were used as projectiles, with stone catapults primarily used in sieges. Because it proved difficult when constructing catapults to achieve the range and power desired, technicians in the 3rd century – encouraged by the Ptolemies – began experiments that ultimately produced a formula for the dimensions of the the individual components of a catapult [29.24–43]; [30.105–184].

One mathematician in particular, Archimedes, made a crucial contribution to the defence of Syracuse with the construction of new defensive weapons when the Romans besieged the city in 212 BC. Above all, he developed catapults capable of hurling stones of considerable weight over great distances. These caused the Romans heavy losses. In the end, only treachery delivered Syracuse to the Romans (Plut. *Marcellus* 14–19).

D.2.3. THE USE OF WAR ELEPHANTS

Another development in Hellenistic warfare came about during Alexander's campaign in India, when the Greeks and Macedonians found themselves facing an army that included elephants in its ranks (Arr. Anab. 5,9,1; 5,15,4–7; 5,17,2–7) (→ Elephants). The Diadochi began putting elephants to military use in increasing numbers in the generation immediately after Alexander [28.27f.]; [37.419–421]. Before the Battle of Gaza (312 BC), Demetrius

Poliorketes (→ Generals of note, E.) positioned 30 Indian elephants with light infantry in front of his left wing, and another 13 elephants in front of his right (Diod. Sic. 19,82,3f.). At the Battle of Ipsus (301 BC), it is reported that 400 elephants were deployed on Seleucus' side and 75 in the forces of Antigonus (Plut. *Demetrius* 28). Later, the Ptolemies made use of African elephants captured in Ethiopia and shipped to Egypt (Diod. Sic. 3,36,3; 3,40,4). Pyrrhus brought elephants to Italy with his army (Plut. *Pyrrhus* 17; Plin. HN 8,16). Following the Hellenistic example, the Carthaginians used elephants in their battle against M. Atilius Regulus in the First Punic War (Pol. 1,33f.). Although these animals had the capacity to cause devastating destruction, an elephant attack could be repelled effectively, as had been seen at the Battle of Gaza (Diod. Sic. 19,83,2; 19,84,1–4). Vegetius offered a thorough description of how to defend against elephants (Veg. Mil. 3,24). The inclusion of a demand to surrender war elephants in the peace treaty with Antiochus (Liv. 38,38,8) illustrates the importance the Romans attached to them. The Romans, however, only rarely used elephants in battle themselves, as they did at Cynoscephalae in 197 BC (Pol. 18,23; Liv. 33,8,3) and in a battle with the Allobroges in 121 BC (Oros. 5,13,2).

In the 4th century BC and throughout the Hellenistic period, the development of military technology, especially in relation to siegecraft and catapult construction [8.26]; [30], was stimulated through technical writings on the subject. The relevant chapters of Vitruvius give an impression of the Hellenistic literature (De arch. 10,10–16).

D.3. ROMAN REPUBLIC AND PRINCIPATE
As soon as the Romans began fighting wars outside Italy, they started to adopt weaponry from other peoples to increase the effectiveness of their legions. An important example of this is the introduction of the Spanish sword in the early 2nd century BC. This sword was ideal for both thrusting and slicing and caused terrible injuries, as seen in the Second Macedonian War (Pol. 6,23,6f.; Liv. 31,34,1–5). Evidence suggests that Roman legions used the catapult during Caesar's campaigns in Gaul and under the Principate [11.698f.] (*tormenta*: Caes. B Gall. 2,8,4; 4,25,1f.; 7,41,3; 7,81,5; 8,40,5; cf. also Vitr. De arch. 1 praef. 2; 10,10–12; Tac. Ann. 15,9,1; Tac. Hist. 3,23). Archaeological findings at the battlefield on the Harzhorn (AD 235/36) indicate that catapults were used there [31]; [32.93–97]. The catapult was made more mobile by mounting it on a cart drawn by horses, as a relief on the Trajan Column illustrates [2.342]; [29.174–198, pl. 9–13]. According to Vegetius (Mil. 2,25,2–4), each legion had 55 of these *carroballistae*, and every one was operated by eleven soldiers [11.699]; [31.246–248].

When the need came to justify the construction of catapults during the Roman period, it was argued that they served primarily to defend against attacks and to deter potential enemies, and therefore they helped secure peace (Hero *Belopoeica* 71–73 Wescher).

The Romans only began waging true naval warfare after 264 BC in their conflict with Carthage. Because their experience of fighting wars at sea was limited, having previously fought only within Italy, and after they were defeated by the Carthaginians in a naval battle, the Romans moved during the initial phase of the First Punic War to develop a new form of maritime warfare (Pol. 1,22f.). The primary aim was no longer to sink enemy ships by ramming them, but to board these ships and fight man to man as on land [43.195–201]. As in the Hellenistic fleets, a tendency existed for the Romans to build ever larger warships, as was the case with Mark Antony's fleet. Antony had large vessels built with tall towers. The fleet was manned with many soldiers, including archers, whose task was to prevent enemy ships from approaching. However, Antony's warships proved inferior to the fast and manoeuvrable smaller craft of Caesar the Younger at the Battle of Actium in 31 BC (→ Battles of note, A.) (Cass. Dio 50,18,4–6; 50,23,2f.; 50,32,2–8; Plut. *Antonius* 66).

D.4. LATE ANTIQUITY
Inventions in the field of military technology are the subject of a treatise from Late Antiquity (*Anonymus de rebus bellicis*) whose author is unknown, and which is dated to the period between AD 337 (death of Constantine) and 378 (Battle of Adrianople) [4]; [1.1–6]. The *praefatio* emphasizes the usefulness (*utilitas*) of the proposals submitted to the *sacratissimi principes* ('most sacred emperors'), and asserts that useful inventions, including innovations in military technology, do not depend on lineage, wealth or literary erudition, but on a natural disposition towards *ingenium*. Besides new approaches in military technology, this text also discusses problems of public finance. The author sees a close correlation between the two fields, because expenditure for the military far exceeded the empire's ability to pay. The struggle against the barbarians who were constantly assailing the borders demanded the deployment of new, more efficient weaponry that could be operated by just a few soldiers (praef. 7–9). The author gives a detailed description of a four-wheeled horse-drawn cart on which arrow catapults are installed (7), various types of scythe chariots (12–14), a bridge for crossing rivers that can be quickly constructed using inflated animal hides (16), and a warship propelled by paddle wheels driven by animal muscle power (17). Appended

to the text are a number of precise drawings to facilitate the construction of this equipment (6,4) [1.15–17, figs. I–XII]. Whatever assessment one may give to these innovations in weapons technology, it is striking that the treatise attempts to use new military technology to overcome a crisis that was both military and political [1.49].

This anonymous treatise is not the only source showing interest in military technology in the 4th century. Ammianus Marcellinus, who also offers a thorough description of Roman siege equipment (Amm. Marc. 23,4) [30.249–265], calls Valentinian I an 'inventor of new weapons' (*novorum inventor armorum*, Amm. Marc. 30,9,4). Confirming the anonymous author's observation on the inventions of the barbarians (Anon. de rebus bell. praef. 4), Procopius' report of the Siege of Petra on the Black Sea in AD 551 [1.46] has Huns fighting on the Roman side building a new kind of battering ram that helped in the conquest of the city (Procop. Goth. 4,11,27–34).

E. Innovations in the ancient military – causes and effects

There were crucial innovations throughout the history of ancient warfare in the organization of armies, in strategy and in military technology. Such developments were of different kinds. In many cases, innovations were outcomes of long-term processes closely linked to social, economic and political changes. This is true, for instance, of the introduction of the hoplite phalanx in the Archaic period, the development of the manipular army in the Roman Republic, and the reorganizations of the military in the Republican period and in Late Antiquity. At the same time, far-reaching changes in the miltary also came about through the initiatives and influence of specific individuals. Philip II created a military in Macedonia that was far superior to the militias of the Greek city-states, and Augustus established a professional army that was not only able to defend the borders of the Roman Empire and secure internal peace, but also proved to be a crucial factor in processes of social integration and cultural development.

Technological innovations – iron processing in the 'Dark Ages', the manufacture of bronze chest armour and helmets in the Archaic period, and above all the introduction of the catapult in the Late Classical period – contributed significantly to changes in warfare, which were carried forward by Hellenistic technicians through their inventions and writings. With catapults, gunstone catapults and siege equipment such as tall siege towers, cities and fortresses could be captured in short order. Specialist literature, replete with detailed and precise descriptions, spread knowledge of technical innovations far and wide. Some individual rulers vigorously promoted military innovations, such as Dionysius I of Syracuse, Philip II of Macedon, Demetrius Poliorketes and the Ptolemies of the 3rd century BC. As is clear from comments made by Aristotle, Demosthenes, Diodorus Siculus and Ammianus Marcellinus, the importance of such innovations for warfare and military success was already recognized in Antiquity. Military innovations often involved adopting technical achievements from other peoples or civilizations. This applies, for example, to the large siege equipment for which Carthaginian precursors existed, and to the Spanish sword.

Innovations in ancient military practice and technology had far-reaching consequences for warfare, and hence also for political developments and power relations in the Mediterranean world. In particular, the political success of Athens, Macedonia and later Rome, which in each case relied on military superiority, was largely due to their capacity for innovation.

☞ **Army; Equipment; Fortification; Production system**

Bibliography

Sources
[1] A Roman Reformer and Inventor. De rebus bellicis, trans. and intro. by E.A. Thompson, 1952.

Secondary literature
[2] D. Baatz, Catapult, in: BNP 3, 2003, 9–16 [3] J. Bleicken, Augustus. Eine Biographie, 1998 [4] H. Brandt, Anonymus de rebus bellicis, in: BNP 1, 2002, 711 [5] K. Brockhoff, Innovation, in: Vahlens Großes Wirtschaftslexikon, vol. 2, 1987, 884–885 [6] P.A. Brunt, Italian Manpower 225 BC–AD 14, 1971 [7] L. Burckhardt, Phalanx, in: BNP 10, 2007, 907–908 [8] L. Burckhardt, Militärgeschichte der Antike, ^{3}2020 [9] B. Campbell, The Army, in: CAH 12, 2005, 110–130 [10] A. Chaniotis, War in the Hellenistic World, 2005 [11] G. Davies, Roman Warfare and Fortification, in: J.P. Oleson (ed.), The Oxford Handbook of Engineering and Technology in the Classical World, 2008, 691–711 [12] A. Demandt, Die Spätantike. Römische Geschichte von Diocletian bis Justinian 284–565 n.Chr., ^{2}2007 [13] H. Diels, Antike Technik, ^{2}1920 [14] W. Eck, Augustus und seine Zeit, ^{4}2006 [15] A. Eich, Die Söhne des Mars. Eine Geschichte des Krieges von der Steinzeit bis zum Ende der Antike, 2015 [16] H. Elton, Military Forces, in: P. Sabin et al. (eds.), The Cambridge History of Greek and Roman Warfare, vol. 2, 2007, 270–309 [17] Y. Garlan, Hellenistic Science. Its Application in Peace and War. War and Siegecraft, in: CAH 7/1, 1984, 353–362 [18] Y. Garlan, Guerre et économie en Grèce ancienne, 1989 [19] Y. Garlan, Warfare, in: CAH 6, 1994, 678–692 [20] H.-J. Gehrke, Geschichte des Hellenismus, 1990 [21] K. Gilliver, Auf dem Weg zum Imperium. Eine Geschichte der römischen Armee, 2003 [22] A.K. Goldsworthy, The Roman Army at War 100 BC–AD 200, 1996 [23] S. Hornblower, The Greek World 479–323 BC, ^{4}2011 [24] L. Keppie, The Making of the Roman Army. From the Republic to Empire,

1984 [25] L. Keppie, The Army and the Navy, in: CAH 10, 1996, 371–396 [26] Y. Le Bohec, Die römische Armee. Von Augustus bis zu Konstantin d. Gr., 1993 [27] O. Lendle, Texte und Untersuchungen zum technischen Bereich der antiken Poliorketik, 1983 [28] C. Mann, Militär und Kriegführung in der Antike, 2013 [29] E.W. Marsden, Greek and Roman Artillery. Historical Development, 1969 [30] E.W. Marsden, Greek and Roman Artillery. Technical Treatises, 1971 [31] G. Moosbauer, Torsionsgeschütze. Antike Wunderwaffen, in: H. Pöppelmann et al. (eds.), Roms vergessener Feldzug. Die Schlacht am Harzhorn, 2013, 242–248 [32] G. Moosbauer, Die vergessene Römerschlacht. Der sensationelle Fund am Harzhorn, 2018 [33] J.P. Oleson (ed.), The Oxford Handbook of Engineering and Technology in the Classical World, 2008 [34] K. Raaflaub, Die Militärreformen des Augustus und die politische Problematik des frühen Prinzipats, in: G. Binder (ed.), Saeculum Augustum, vol. 1: Herrschaft und Gesellschaft, 1987, 246–307 [35] B. Rankov, Military Forces, in: P. Sabin et al. (eds.), The Cambridge History of Greek and Roman Warfare, vol. 2, 2007, 30–75 [36] J.P. Roth, War, in: P. Sabin et al. (eds.), The Cambridge History of Greek and Roman Warfare, vol. 1, 2007, 368–398 [37] P. Sabin, Battle. A. Land Battles, in: P. Sabin et al. (eds.), The Cambridge History of Greek and Roman Warfare, vol. 1, 2007, 399–433 [38] P. Sabin et al. (eds.), The Cambridge History of Greek and Roman Warfare, 2 vols., 2007 [39] M.M. Sage, Warfare in Ancient Greece. A Sourcebook, 1996 [40] E. Schallmayer, Der Limes. Geschichte einer Grenze, 2006 [41] V. Schmidtchen, Technik im Übergang vom Mittelalter zur Neuzeit 1350–1600, in: W. König (ed.), Propyläen Technikgeschichte, vol. 2: Metalle und Macht 1000–1600, 1992, 207–598 [42] H. Schneider, Krieg und Technik im Zeitalter des Hellenismus, in: Berichte zur Wissenschaftsgeschichte 19, 1996, 76–80 [43] R. Schulz, Feldherren, Krieger und Strategen. Krieg in der Antike von Achill bis Attila, 2012 [44] J. Serrati, Warfare and the State, in: P. Sabin et al. (eds.), The Cambridge History of Greek and Roman Warfare, vol. 1, 2007, 461–497 [45] H. Sidebottom, Der Krieg in der antiken Welt, 2008 [46] A.M. Snodgrass, Arms and Armor of the Greeks, 1999 [47] P. de Souza, Greek Warfare and Fortification, in: J.P. Oleson (ed.), The Oxford Handbook of Engineering and Technology in the Classical World, 2008, 673–690 [48] B. Strauss, Battle. B. Naval Battles and Sieges, in: P. Sabin et al. (eds.), The Cambridge History of Greek and Roman Warfare, vol. 1, 2007, 223–247 [49] E. Turner, Ptolemaic Egypt, in: CAH 7/1, 1984, 118–174 [50] R. Walter, Innovationsgeschichte. Einführung, in: R. Walter (ed.), Innovationsgeschichte, 2007, 7–11 [51] E.L. Wheeler, Battle. A. Land Battles, in: P. Sabin et al. (eds.), The Cambridge History of Greek and Roman Warfare, vol. 1, 2007, 186–222 [52] C.R. Whittaker, Les frontières de l'Empire romain, 1989 [53] A.I. Wilson, Machines in Greek and Roman Technology, in: J.P. Oleson (ed.), The Oxford Handbook of Engineering and Technology in the Classical World, 2008, 337–366.

Helmuth Schneider

Intelligence

☞ Reconnaissance

Language

A. Multilingualism in ancient armies
B. The case of Egypt
C. Consequences of multilingualism

A. MULTILINGUALISM IN ANCIENT ARMIES

Many languages came into contact in the cosmopolitan armies of the great states of Antiquity. Around AD 400, soldiers from roughly 50 satellite peoples belonged to the Roman army, not counting the barbarians living beyond the borders of the empire. A distinction must therefore be made between the official state languages of the cultures running the army, spoken by the high command and senior officers, and the regional languages of the soldiery (who consisted of local recruits, mercenaries, allies, recruits from vanquished armies, prisoners of war, defectors and outsiders of uncertain ethnic affiliation). The official languages (Punic until the fall of Carthage, then Greek and Latin alone) also functioned as administrative and cultural languages, and as *linguae francae*. This was particularly true of Greek, which was omnipresent as a commercial language in the Near East and in the ports of the west (although Caesar was able to use Greek as a secret language in Gaulish territories; B Gall. 5,48,4). With the exception of some dialects of Aramaic, regional languages were not written down.

Multilingualism was widespread, but the combinations of languages in leadership circles differed from those in the army at large. At the top of the hierarchy, men spoke two or three official languages, which would be familiar to a greater or lesser degree to ordinary soldiers, whose native languages were regional ones. Roman generals spoke Latin and Greek, Hannibal spoke Punic, Greek and Latin, and the Numidian princes of Hannibal's day spoke Libyan, Punic and – some at least – Latin and Greek. Alexander spoke two dialects of Greek: Attic, the everyday language of his social class, and Macedonian, his mother tongue, into which he lapsed at moments of high excitement (Plut. *Alexander* 51,6). Before they merged into the *koine*, Greek dialects briefly enjoyed high status in Egypt during the 3rd century BC: speakers of these Greek dialects, members of a select military elite, were able to use them to distinguish themselves from the Hellenized natives [3].

To alleviate the problem of multilingual confusion, orders were given in one official language: Greek in the Greek armies of the Hellenistic period (Ascl. 12,11), and Latin in the Roman army – including in the Byzantine Empire, even though Greek became the official language again in the 5th century (Maur. Strat. 3,5). The *Strategikon* indicates that heralds (*mandatores*) who convey orders had to master Latin, Greek and, if possible, Persian (12B,7).

Verbal communication, which was essential for maintaining troop morale at critical moments, posed greater problems. A general who wished to address his men directly would need to have his speech repeated by the requisite number of interpreters, but such a system proved impractical in critical situations (Pol. 1,67,3–11). Alternatively, the bilingual commanders of foreign-language units were available as intermediaries, but their loyalty could not always be relied upon.

We know little of the status and training of army translators. Two translators (who monitored each other) were used for diplomatic negotiations, even if the senior generals had one or even two languages in common (as Scipio and Hannibal, for instance, shared Latin and Greek). This was done partly as a precaution, and partly for reasons of patriotic pride. Although the literature makes frequent reference to professional and occasional translators in the army, they rarely appear in documentary sources. In most cases, they would probably be native speakers (from among the Trogodytes, Dacii and Germani, for instance) who had learned Greek or Latin. In the Roman army, translators who appear in inscriptions belonged to the legions and served as soldiers, with the sole possible exception of the *salariarius* ('salaried man') in IDRE II 273.

B. THE CASE OF EGYPT

The abundance of documentary papyri from Egypt means that studies on the use of language in the military, not least in the Roman military, tend to focus more on this region. Beginning in the 2nd century AD, most recruits to the *exercitus Aegyptiacus* ('Army of Egypt') were locals. Legally the soldiers were *Aigyptioi*, but they were Hellenized and probably bilingual, having learned Egyptian at home and Greek at school. They used Greek in private documents (letters, bills, contracts they drew up themselves), since the Egyptian language was no longer in use outside temple contexts. The only people to write Latin of their own accord were officers and soldiers who were originally from Italy or from provinces where Latin was used as an administrative language (Dacians newly arrived in Egypt spoke Latin). Although there is evidence to suggest that some Greek-speaking soldiers made efforts to learn Latin (Fournet 445; O. Did. 417, a letter laboriously put together using a glossary), knowledge of Greek made learning Latin unnecessary for an Egyptian soldier of no particular ambition. The case of Claudius Terentianus, son of Claudius Tiberianus, a veteran settled at Caranis, who in correspondence with his father switched readily between Greek and Latin, remains unique and unexplained [2.593–597].

Latin was prescribed as a written language among the Egyptian troops for official documents, since these were addressed to the imperial administration (personnel registers, accounting documents), for official architectural and monumental inscriptions, and for registering the birth of soldiers' children, in order to secure Roman citizenship for them after their fathers' discharge from military service (P. Mich. VII 436, *testatio*, written AD 138 at the Pselchis camp in Lower Nubia). The fact that the officer Flavius Abinnaeus wrote a petition to the emperor in Latin around AD 340 may be attributed to convention rather than to strict regulations. Petitions to the prefects of Egypt could be submitted in Greek, and communication between a unit commander and his subordinates (letters, reports) also took place in Greek.

C. Consequences of multilingualism
The socio-linguistic contacts that came about through military life can be seen primarily in loanwords. The soldiers' written Greek is peppered with technical terms taken from Latin, especially names of military ranks and functions, as well as expressions from administrative terminology. Specialist jargon sometimes included new words coined from the soldiers' language (the commonly used expression *sermo castrensis*, 'camp language', is modern and disputed). The incorporation of soldiers from enemy peoples was accompanied by the reception of new technologies (weapons, manoeuvres), which went along with borrowings from the languages of peripheral areas – many examples are found in Byzantine military literature [5.251–257]. Enemy battlecries were also appropriated (Arr. Tact. 44,1).

Although the use of Greek as an administrative language of the Roman army was permitted in Hellenized provinces, in some situations soldiers had to be able to utter (alone or in chorus) Latin words or formulae, especially in ritualized communication with officers. Nightwatchmen's passwords were Latin (Veg. Mil. 3,5,4), and had to be transcribed into Greek on the *tesserae* (tiles showing the password) so that Greek-speaking soldiers could read them (cf. fig. 1). They were limited in number so that soldiers with no Latin could memorize them more quickly. The oath of loyalty spoken at the morning report in reply to the order of the day was also in Latin (Rom. Mil. Rec. 47,6, Dura Europus, c. AD 230). In the Byzantine army, an attack was announced by one officer shouting *parati!* ('Ready!'), then a second shouting *adiuta* ..., then the troops in chorus shouting ... *Deus!* ('God help us!'; Maur. Strat. 12B,16,42).

The ritual use of Latin was intended to kindle a feeling of Roman identity in the soldiers, thereby fostering loyalty and cohesion. Further strengthening this professional identity, each recruit was given a Latin name. However, changes to given names (which are also attested in the Ptolemaic army) were not applied systematically. They were widely used among the Egyptians at garrisons in the Arabian Desert in the 2nd century AD, but Thracians and Dacians kept their given names from their own regional languages. Bilingual (Latin and Aramaic) inscriptions of Palmyrene soldiers indicate equally strong ties to their adopted identity and their ethnic roots [2.247–260].

☞ Military service

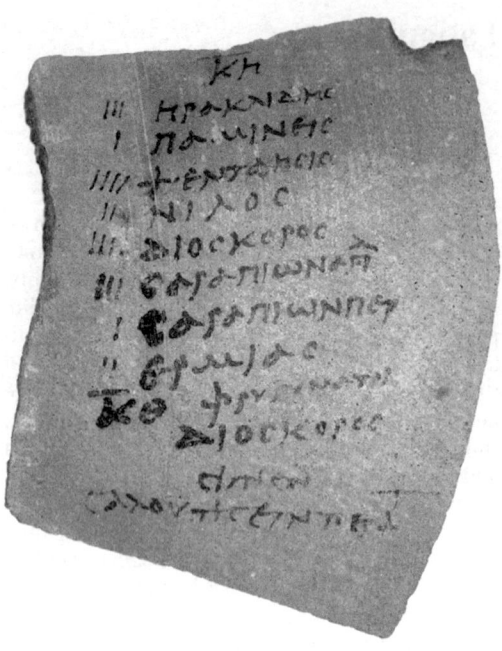

Fig. 1: O. Claud. II 331 (Mid-2nd century AD). List of watches in Greek, with the number of reliefs in Latin numerals. A second hand below has added in Greek script the Latin words (signen for the Latin signum): saloutis einperat(oris) ('the health [of the] emper[or]').

Bibliography

Sources
[1] Maurikios, Das Strategikon des Maurikios, edited by G.T. Dennis and E. Gamillscheg, 1981.

Secondary literature
[2] J.N. Adams, Bilingualism and the Latin Language, 2003 [3] W. Clarysse, Ethnic Diversity and Dialect among the Greeks of Hellenistic Egypt, in: A.M.F.W. Verhoogt / S.P. Vleeming (eds.), The Two Faces of Graeco-Roman Egypt. Greek and Demotic and Greek-Demotic Texts and Studies Presented to P.W. Pestman, 1998, 1–13 [4] M. Coltelloni-Trannoy, Guerre et circulation des savoirs. Le cas des armées numides, in: J.C. Couvenhes et al. (eds.), Pratiques et identités culturelles des armées hellénistiques du monde méditerranéen, 2011, 307–335 [5] G. Dagron / H. Mihăescu, Le traité sur la guérilla (De velitatione) de l'empereur

Nicéphore Phocas (963–969), 1986 [6] J.-L. FOURNET, Langues, écritures et culture dans les praesidia, in: H. CUVIGNY (ed.), La route de Myos Hormos. L'armée romaine dans le désert oriental d'Égypte, vol. 2, 2003, 427–500 [7] H. GALLEGO FRANCO, Intérpretes militares en el limes del Danubio, in: Aquila legionis 4, 2003, 27–43 [8] W. HERAEUS, Die römische Soldatensprache, in: ALLG 12, 1902, 255–280 [9] T.G. KOLIAS, Tradition und Erneuerung im Frühbyzantinischen Reich am Beispiel der militärischen Sprache und Terminologie, in: F. VALLET / M. KAZANSKI (eds.), L'armée romaine et les barbares du IIIe au VIIe siècle, 1993, 39–44 [10] L.C. PÉREZ CASTRO, Naturaleza y composición del sermo castrensis latino, in: Emerita 73/1, 2005, 73–96 [11] P. RANCE, The De Militari Scientia or Müller Fragment as a Philological Resource. Latin in the East Roman Army and Two New Loanwords in Greek: palmarium and *recala, in: Glotta 86, 2011, 63–92 [12] B. ROCHETTE, Les armées d'Alexandre le Grand et les langues étrangères, in: AC 66, 1997, 311–318 [13] B. ROCHETTE, Sur le bilinguisme dans les armées d'Hannibal, in: Les Études Classiques 65, 1997, 153–159 [14] C. WIOTTE-FRANZ, Hermeneus und Interpres. Zum Dolmetscherwesen in der Antike, 2001.

HÉLÈNE CUVIGNY

Law of war

A. Greek
B. Roman

A. GREEK

A.1. Introduction
A.2. Religious support for actions
A.3. Diplomacy and treaties

Detailed discussions of various aspects of the subject matter examined here may be found in [13]; [1]; [10]; [4]; [17]; [9] and [12].

A.1. INTRODUCTION
There was no true 'law of war' in Greek Antiquity. No generally recognized agreements existed, or any supranational institutions with the authority to enforce them. Relations between states increasingly existed within a sphere of anarchy dominated by the 'law of the strongest' [8].

It was generally understood that the victor was entitled to treat the vanquished as it chose. This could include the destruction of settlements, the annexation of territory, the execution of men of fighting age and the enslavement of women and children. In early Greek history, however, wars were also expressions of rivalry between neighbouring *poleis*. The aim in this case was victory, not the annihilation of the enemy. Such wars contained ritual elements and were regulated by traditional norms (→ Phalanx). In addition, gaps in the source material and the tendency to idealize the past help explain why we rarely hear of the annexation or destruction of defeated polities or the enslavement of defeated populations [7]; [17.115–117, 124]. The extreme example of Troy in the *Iliad* may in part be explained by Near Eastern influence on Greek epic.

When methods of warfare changed drastically in the 5th century [14], reports of the brutal assertion of the victor's 'rights' became frequent. War now became much crueller and more 'total' [15]. Traditional norms and treaties were only respected if they promised an immediate advantage. Attempts to facilitate diplomatic negotiations, moderate or sometimes prevent warfare and forestall its most brutal outcomes were on the one hand put under the protection of the gods, and on the other hand were enforced by the dominant powers.

A.2. RELIGIOUS SUPPORT FOR ACTIONS
The support of the gods was of supreme importance, particularly in war. Although the concept of 'just war' was less developed than it would be at Rome [5], all participants attempted to prove that right was on their side. This is already evident in the *Iliad* (Hom. Il. 7,400–402), which contains a description of the agreement necessary for a truce and an alternative solution to the conflict (3,264–301) [16.122–126]. The history of the run-up to the Peloponnesian War (→ Wars of note H.; 431–404 BC) illustrates the same imperative (Thuc. 1,140–142). → Sparta later explained its initial failures in terms of its not having respected existing treaties at the outbreak of hostilities (Thuc. 7,18).

For a long time, the moral authority of the Oracle at Delphi exerted broad influence. Its call for moderation ('not too much', *mede agan*) also had an impact on war. The Amphictyones ('people of the surroundings') charged with the protection and administration of the sanctuary were forbidden to destroy any of their allied *poleis* or to interrupt their water supply (Aeschin. Leg. 2,115).

A 'sacred → peace' was regularly proclaimed for the 'great games' (e.g. Olympia, Delphi), in order to guarantee safe arrival and departure and undisturbed proceedings [6.116–118]. Sparta's army was prohibited from moving out during certain festivals and phases of the moon. Argos declared one month of truce during the Karneia (a religious festival). Admittedly, rules like these were often manipulated to benefit the 'celebrant' side, whereas others ignored such rules or neutralized them with countermeasures [17.118f.]. There was a general feeling that armies should avoid sanctuaries (Hdt. 9,65; Thuc. 4,97), but this rule was also frequently broken (Hdt. 5,78–81).

The Greeks defined this kind of 'general feeling' as a Hellenic, general, universal, divinely ordained or unwritten law or norm (Aristot. Rhet.

1,10,3; 1,13,1f.) [13.52–58]. Such norms had no political authority, but a high moral one. They touched on many aspects of interstate relations that were important during wartime, such as the protection of sanctuaries, *proxenoi* (comparable to modern consuls), emissaries and heralds, asylum and the burial of the fallen [4.88–134].

It was customary after a battle to declare a truce to retrieve the dead. Refusal of this 'right' was unusual. The Thebans justified their refusal after the Battle of Delium (424 BC) by asserting that the Athenians had disregarded the 'customs of the Hellenes' that forbade 'infringement of sanctuaries in an invaded country' (Thuc. 4,97–101). In Sophocles' tragedy, Antigone grants her brother Polyneices a minimal funeral despite a royal prohibition, because divine laws overrule the authority of the king (Soph. Ant. 450–460). In the absence of supreme secular authorities, recourse was made to the highest deities. Heralds were accorded the protection of Zeus [1.152f.]. The mistreatment of Persian emissaries by Athens and Sparta resulted in divine punishment. Allegedly, the Persian king refused to free the Spartans from their guilt and thus violate the universal norms of humankind, so he executed the heralds sent to him by the Spartans to atone for the death of Persian heralds (Hdt. 7,133–137).

A.3. DIPLOMACY AND TREATIES

A formal declaration of war was commonplace, but not essential [1.202f.]. If one wanted to avoid war, it was customary to send emissaries to demand satisfaction or to seek mediation or arbitration through a third party who was recognized by both sides [9.177–184]; [2]. Diplomatic negotiations of this kind are already attested in the *Iliad* (3,205–224; 11,122–125; 11,138–142; cf. Hom. Od. 21,11–21), and they played an important part in the run-up to the Peloponnesian War (Thuc. 1,139; 1,145). The main purpose of → alliances was to avoid war or else to ensure support in the event of war [1.203–207]; [9.240–244]. The concept of neutrality was known, but for a group to be recognized as neutral depended on the goodwill of the belligerents and on the specific constellation of powers [3]. The famous case of Melos (416/15) serves as an example of neutrality, although a problematic one (Thuc. 5,84–116).

Under the strain of almost permanent wars for supremacy in Greece in the late 5th and 4th centuries, and under pressure from the Persian king, attempts were finally made by Greek polities to stabilize the situation by means of ambitious systems of treaties, with the aim of securing a 'common peace' (*koine eirene*) (→ Peace) and thus restricting the right to wage war [11]. However, all these initiatives failed, because they served the interests of a major power and were exploited by its proxy (Sparta) for its own ends. Peace (of any meaningful duration) would only be guaranteed after 338 BC, when the kings of Macedon, Philip II and Alexander the Great, put an end to the liberty of the Greeks under the pretence of an alliance (the 'Hellenic League').

☞ Customs of war; Diplomacy; Military law

BIBLIOGRAPHY

[1] F. ADCOCK / D. MOSLEY, Diplomacy in Ancient Greece, 1975 [2] S.L. AGER, Interstate Arbitrations in the Greek World, 337–90 B.C., 1996 [3] R.A. BAUSLAUGH, The Concept of Neutrality in Classical Greece, 1991 [4] D.J. BEDERMAN, International Law in Antiquity, 2001 [5] S. CLAVADETSCHER-THÜRLEMANN, Polemos dikaios und bellum iustum, 1985 [6] W. DECKER, Sport in der griechischen Antike, 1995 [7] P. DUCREY, Le traitement des prisonniers de guerre dans la Grèce antique, ²1999 [8] A.M. ECKSTEIN, Mediterranean Anarchy, Interstate War, and the Rise of Rome, 2006 [9] A. GIOVANNINI, Les relations entre États dans la Grèce antique, 2007 [10] V. ILARI, Guerra e diritto nel mondo greco-ellenistico fino al III secolo, 1980 [11] M. JEHNE, Koine Eirene, 1994 [12] P. LOW, Interstate Relations in Classical Greece, 2007 [13] C. PHILLIPSON, The International Law and Custom of Ancient Greece and Rome, vol. 1, 1911 [14] D. PRITCHARD, Athenian Democracy at War, 2018 [15] K.A. RAAFLAUB, War and the City. The Brutality of War and Its Impact on the Community, in: P. MEINECK / D. KONSTAN (eds.), Combat Trauma and the Ancient Greeks, 2014, 15–46 [16] K.A. RAAFLAUB, Greek Concepts and Theories of Peace, in: K.A. RAAFLAUB (ed.), Peace in the Ancient World. Concepts and Theories, 2016, 122–156 [17] H. VAN WEES, Greek Warfare. Myth and Realities, 2004.

KURT A. RAAFLAUB

B. ROMAN

B.1. Introduction
B.2. Outbreak of war. Just war. Declaration of war
B.3. Prisoners. Defectors. Land. Goods
B.4. Agreements made in war. Surrender of a polity
B.5. Peace agreement
B.6. Hostages

B.1. INTRODUCTION

The law of war is understood to be the law that must be observed when one side wages war against another, that is, the law that pertains in the relationship with the enemy. Discussions at Rome revolved around whether a war was only justified if the aggressor had a just cause, how war was to be declared and how spoils (especially prisoners and their right to return home: *ius postliminii*) were to be dealt with, and how peace was to be concluded such that it was binding on the entire community. These are issues of international law today. The Romans essentially saw things the same way, but they designed their own rules, initially taking into account the legal opinions of other communities in Latium and Italy, but adopting ever more ruthless positions over time. → Civil wars, on the other hand, were illegal in communities with constitutions like Rome (Cic. Off. 2,26–29), since the purpose of the constitution was to regulate the management of internal disputes, with violence only permissible within strictly controlled limits. It is worth observing, nonetheless, that victors in civil wars were wont to confer retrospective legality on their illegal actions, perhaps in order to establish a new constitution, but at the very last to create a pretence of a new rule of law.

Distinct from the Roman law of war (or, more accurately, the general ancient law of war in its Roman manifestation) was Roman military law. The latter was an internal Roman legal system that only became established as a specialized legal field over the course of the Imperial period. It concerned legal relations between and among Roman military personnel: recruitment, service law, disciplinary law, military criminal law, soldiers' special private law in cases involving property acquired in military service (*peculium castrense*), and marital and inheritance law (*testamentum militis*).

B.2. OUTBREAK OF WAR. JUST WAR. DECLARATION OF WAR

The Romans attached great importance to waging war justly (Cic. Rep. 3,35) [1]; [8]; [10]; [6.115–155]. War could be fought without compunction against foreign peoples with whom no agreements had ever before been made [14.186–191]. Regardless of war or peace, it was recognized that Romans were entitled to appropriate such people's worldly goods on Roman territory, and that conversely Roman property was available for foreign seizure on foreign territory – even to the extent of Romans there being enslaved (Pompon. Dig. 49,15,5,2; Paulus, Dig. 49,15,19 pr.; contrary Proc. Dig. 49,15,7 pr.; Pol. 2,8,10. Ulp. Dig. 49,15,24 merely ignores the by-now rare circumstance), although the Romans made no use of the right to enslave such foreigners in times of peace (disputed: [18]). However, if Rome and the other polity had already had dealings, established an informal *amicitia* ('friendship') or *societas* ('fellowship') or concluded a formal *foedus* ('treaty') [20.93–117], attacking the other party was only justified (*bellum iustum*) if it had done Rome a great wrong, such as renouncing an alliance with Rome, supporting a warring enemy of Rome, allowing raids from its own territory into Roman territory or that of an ally, or doing harm to representatives of Rome and refusing to make recompense, even in defence against an attack [1.17f.].

When Rome wished to declare a just war of aggression against a polity with which it had dealings, certain formalities established by one of the early kings had to be observed (Gell. NA 16,4,1). The priests of the *fetiales* had developed the requisite rites (Liv. 1,32,3–14) and claimed the sole right to perform them for many centuries. In historical times, their college comprised 20 life members – exclusively patricians until the *lex Ogulnia* (300 BC) – expandable by cooptation. They were responsible for all business with other peoples, including trade treaties. After the king (later the magistrate responsible) had made a ceremonial approach to the *verbenarius* (the fetial priest responsible for the sacred herbs), the latter plucked a plant from the ground on the Capitoline Hill and used it to designate from among the group of his colleagues the executive priest (*pater patratus*) for the task of declaring war. Other members accompanied the *pater patratus* (Varro in Non. 12, 850 Lindsay). The senate dispatched this delegation to the border of the enemy poilty's territory, where the *pater patratus* used set formulae to invoke Jupiter and other gods and to demand the righting of the wrong at issue and the extradition of those responsible for it. He repeated this in a slightly amended form after crossing the border, when encountering the first member of the enemy polity, then again before its gates, and finally in its marketplace. If he achieved satisfaction through an agreement for recompense, or by some other resolution of the dispute, the delegation would withdraw peacefully, taking with it any extradited culprits. If the other side demanded time for consultations, the *pater patratus* would grant a stay of 30 days, but would repeat his demand every ten days. If the deadline passed without resolution, he would wait for three more days, then formally appeal to the gods as witnesses to the wrong suffered and issue a threat that Rome would now consult on appropriate measures for asserting its rights – meaning war. Upon his return to Rome, the senate would debate his report. If war was the decision, a law of the Centuriate Assembly *de bello indicendo* ('on the proclamation of war') confirmed it – at least indirectly – by stipulating the powers of the general. The *pater patratus* then made his way back to the border of the enemy territory, pronounced the declaration of war, explained the reason for it and initiated hostilities by hurling a spear across the border (Liv. 1,32,5–14; Dion. Hal. Ant. Rom. 2,72) [12]; [14]; [11.97–117]; [17.18–51, 69–73]; [13].

The old rite of declaring war was only practicable for as long as Rome was waging war only in its immediate vicinity. As it expanded its range, the senate began to appoint its own emissaries from among its members, entrusting them with negotiations for atonement prior to a declaration of war [4.171–180]; [19.103f.]. As is still apparent in evidence from the reign of Marcus Aurelius, however, the *fetiales* continued to play an important role, although perhaps no longer on every occasion [13]. They certainly no longer did so in the empire once Christianized [8.311]. By about 275 BC, there was no longer any need for anyone to travel far to make the final declaration of war. At this time, a captive from Tarentum was coerced into buying a plot of land by the *circus Flaminius*, which was henceforth once and for all declared enemy territory. From this time onwards, the *pater patratus* hurled the spear into this plot of land, from a boundary pillar (*columna bellica*) put up next to the Temple of Bellona, where the spear was kept. Thus it was that Augustus – a fetial priest like other emperors after him – declared war on Cleopatra in 32 BC: according to the old rite, but in Rome. Marcus Aurelius did likewise to launch the Second Marcomannic War in AD 178 (Cass. Dio 50,4,5; 72 (71),33,3).

B.3. Prisoners. Defectors. Land. Goods

When a foreign polity was overcome in war, the victor was entitled to kill or enslave everyone, including women and children (Marcian. Dig. 1,5,5,1). The Roman general decided their fate. Those enslaved he either shared out among his colleagues or sold (Florent. Dig. 1,5,4,2f.). He was also entitled to allow the people their freedom, resettle them, or impose Roman colonists on them. The last of these measures became increasingly frequent from the 3rd century BC onwards, seen often when legal institutions at Rome were involved, and invariably where mass enslavement was subsequently revoked [15.71–105]. Beginning with Marcus Aurelius' victories over the Marcomanni, defeated enemies and their families were often settled in desolate regions as semi-free peasants bound to the soil, a status later called *laeti*. They were required to provide → auxiliaries or defend borders directly themselves. Anyone who defected promptly to the Romans remained free (Celsus, Dig. 41,1,51 pr.). If an enslaved person managed to escape Roman control into his free homeland, or if that homeland bought his freedom, he was again considered a free foreigner (Gai. Dig. 41,1,7 pr.; Inst. Iust. 2,1,17).

Roman citizens who fell into enemy hands during wartime could also be killed and survivors enslaved (Pompon. Dig. 49,15,5,1; Ulp. Dig. 49,15,24). They thereby lost all their legal rights. If the person was married, the marriage was dissolved. Children over whom a captive had paternal authority were no longer subject to any *potestas* ('legal authority'). The captive's assets went into trusteeship *in absentia* (Ulp. Dig. 4,6,15 pr.; 26,1,6,4; Paul. Dig. 42,4,6,2; Diocl. Cod. Iust. 8,50,3f.). If he died in captivity, he was legally succeeded as if he had died at capture. If he succeeded in returning to Roman or allied territory, however, he benefited from the right to return home (*ius postliminii*, 'right of return behind the threshold'; Dig. 49,15; Cod. Iust. 8,50; [3]). In such a case, his rights revived, where possible: property rights and paternal *potestas* were reestablished retrospectively, guardianship was revived from that point on, but marriage and rights linked to possessions were not. If anyone had bought the freedom of the captive, the individual who gained freedom by crossing the border remained in that person's *potestas* until the purchase price had been repaid to him, unless the purchaser was a close relative or waived the requirement. The right of return was lost if it had been waived by a subsequent peace treaty (Tryph. Dig. 49,15,12 pr.), for instance because the Roman government considered those involved to have fallen into captivity through → cowardice. Even if such individuals succeeded in escaping, they remained slaves of the former enemy and were extradited. The redeemer of the ransomed captive had a right of lien. No such peace conditions are preserved, but Liv. 22,61,4 reports on a similar case.

Conquered land belonged to the victorious state (Liv. 3,71,7; Dion. Hal. Ant. Rom. 9,59; 10,37,4f.; Pompon. Dig. 49,15,20,1). Personal property including slaves of the enemy, on the other hand, in principle belonged to whoever took them as → booty (*praeda*; Gai. inst. 4,16; Paul. Dig. 41,2,1,1). The Romans were unique in that the general forbade his soldiers to take booty until he gave a sign granting permission to plunder the vanquished. Even then, they were required to deliver anything particularly valuable (later everything) to the general. The general set aside what he reserved for the state treasury and his own triumphal procession, and distributed the remaining booty among all the soldiers according to a specific ratio [2], so that those entrusted with tasks behind the battlefield and those who were sick also got their share (Pol. 10,15,8–16,9). Sometimes, he sold the booty and divided the takings (*manubiae*), minus the portion set aside for Rome [16.63–74]. It was said of enemies, by contrast, that they seized booty in disorderly fashion immediately after the battle ended, so that Romans who had fled could reassemble and strike back, if possible (Pol. 10,17,1–5). By the 2nd/3rd centuries AD at the latest, war booty belonged in principle to the Roman state (Mod. Dig. 48,13,15). Valuable items captured by the enemy but then returned to Roman territory belonged to their former owners again by virtue of the *ius postliminii* (Fest. s.v. p.). Anyone who had bought a slave who had originally been Roman before being captured by the enemy would find themselves in dispute with that slave's former owner, a situation that an imperial *constitutio* of the late 2nd century sought to resolve (Tryph. Dig.

49,15,12,7–9) [3.282–297]. Anyone was entitled to take foreign property on Roman soil in wartime (Celsus, Dig. 41,1,51,1).

B.4. AGREEMENTS MADE IN WAR. SURRENDER OF A POLITY

The authority to conclude temporary truces (*induciae*; Paul. Dig. 49,15,19,1) and other agreements during a war, such as partial capitulations, lay with the general (Ulp. Dig. 2,14,5, if he indeed wrote *pro pace*) [20.119–165]. If an entire polity was defeated, it could avert total destruction by surrendering to the unconditional authority of the victor (*deditio*, 'surrender'; *deditio in potestatem*, 'surrender to the authority'; *deditio in fidem*, 'surrender to the trust') [4.5–52]. Such a surrender was originally decided in a question and answer ritual involving the Roman general and the representatives of the defeated party (Liv. 1,38,1f.). This put an end to the polity's independence, but its former citizens remained free, albeit stateless (*dediti*) and without citizenship. Their status in private law was also limited to the terms of the *ius gentium* ('law of nations'). Their offspring (*dediticii*) remained in this status. Rome often restored the former citizenry in order to bind these people to itself contractually according to Rome's own conditions. It later also made use of the *deditio* in peacetime to conclude an alliance with a foreign polity on terms favourable to Rome [4.52–109].

B.5. PEACE AGREEMENT

Generals also made peace agreements, and they did so by oath, that is, a *sponsio* ('promise') confirmed by a curse placed on their own polity in the event of a breach of the treaty (see Gai. inst. 3,94). The Roman state was originally bound by such agreements, but from the 4th/3rd centuries BC onwards only if the senate voted to ratify it. For the final treaty (*foedus*), which was in principle intended to be permanent, the *fetiales* had to be consulted. Furthermore, the people were entitled – at least in later centuries – to reject a peace treaty [19.90–94, 97–99]. For example, if a general and his staff, facing a hopeless situation and seeking to save thier men, promised peace under oath in exchange for free passage without weapons, the senate and people could reject the agreement and, having informed the *fetiales*, they could repudiate any commitment to the terms of the treaty, provided that those who had concluded the treaty were handed over to the enemy. The popular assembly could even decide that the only one to be extradited was the supreme commander. It made no difference if the enemy signatory refused to accept those extradited. Rome considered itself entitled to continue the war, including with those previously spared [8]. For a peace treaty to be valid, all that was required was the oath of the magistrate authorized by the senate and people, although from the outset it was customary for the terms to be recorded in writing. The original document, on a wax tablet, papyrus or wooden shield, was kept in a temple, and bronze inscriptions were put up for public viewing [19.98f.]. Provided that the obligations laid down in the peace treaty were fulfilled, neither side was entitled to resume the war. Breach of treaty was a just *casus belli* ('cause for war'), but the other side might well be satisfied with less.

B.6. HOSTAGES

→ Hostages (*obsides*) were often provided to guarantee a *deditio* or a treaty binding on both sides to put a temporary or permanent end to a war. [5]; [7]; [9]. These were usually young relatives (even females) of the elite of the polity involved (Suet. Aug. 21,2; Tac. Germ. 8,1) [6.175–185]. They stood bail for adherence to the conditions. In Rome, they were sacrosanct, but their legal status was otherwise precarious (Ulp. Dig. 28,1,11; Marcian. Dig. 49,14,31). During the Imperial period, they were treated leniently [7.244–247], often even preferentially (Marcian. Dig. 49,14,32) [5.110–124]. If the other side breached the treaty, it was permissible to kill hostages, but this was abandoned under the Principate. In any case, they were often spared.

☞ **Customs of war; Diplomacy; Military law**

BIBLIOGRAPHY

[1] S. ALBERT, Bellum iustum. Die Theorie des 'gerechten Krieges' und ihre praktische Bedeutung für die auswärtigen Auseinandersetzungen Roms in republikanischer Zeit, 1980 [2] F. BONA, Osservazioni sull'acquisto delle res hostium a seguito di direptio, in: SDHI 24, 1958, 237–268 [3] M.F. CURSI, La struttura del postliminium nella republica e nel principato, 1996 [4] W. DAHLHEIM, Struktur und Entwicklung des römischen Völkerrechts im dritten und zweiten Jahrhundert v.Chr., 1968 [5] S. ELBERN, Geiseln in Rom, in: Athenaeum 78, 1990, 97–140 [6] N. GROTKAMP, Völkerrecht im Prinzipat. Möglichkeit und Verbreitung, 2009 [7] P. KEHNE, Geiselstellungen im römischen Völkerrecht und der Außenpolitik des Prinzipats, in: Marburger Beiträge zur antiken Handels-, Wirtschafts- und Sozialgeschichte 30, 2012, 2013, 199–254 [8] D. LIEBS, Bellum iustum in Theorie und Praxis, in: Ars iuris. Festschrift für Okko Behrends zum 70. Geburtstag, 2009, 305–318 [9] D. LIEBS, Geiseln als Bürgen unter Justinian, in: Der Bürge einst und jetzt. Festschrift für Alfons Bürge, 2017, 49–60 [10] M. MONTOVANI, Bellum iustum. Die Idee des gerechten Krieges in der römischen Kaiserzeit, 1990 [11] J. RÜPKE, Domi militiae. Die religiöse Konstruktion des Krieges in Rom, 1990 [12] E. SAMTER, Fetiales, in: RE 6/2, 1909, 2259–2265 [13] F. SANTANGELO, The Fetials and Their Ius, in: BICS 51/1, 2008, 63–93 [14] C. SAULNIER, Le rôle des prêtres fétiaux et l'application du 'ius fetiale' à Rome, in: Revue historique du droit français et étranger,

4th ser., 58/2, 1980, 171–199 [15] H. VOLKMANN, Die Massenversklavungen der Einwohner eroberter Städte in der hellenistisch-römischen Zeit, ²1990 [16] A. WATSON, The Law of Property in the Later Roman Republic, 1968 [17] A. ZACK, Studien zum römischen Völkerrecht, 2001 [18] A. ZACK, Fragen an Sextus Pomponius. Quellen- und sachkritische Untersuchungen zu Pomponius 37. lib. ad Muc. D. 49,15,5, in: Göttinger Forum für Altertumswissenschaft 14, 2011, 47–119 [19] K.-H. ZIEGLER, Das Völkerrecht in der römischen Republik, in: ANRW I.2, 1972, 68–114 [20] K.-H. ZIEGLER, Fata iuris gentium. Kleine Schriften zur Geschichte des europäischen Völkerrechts, 2008.

DETLEF LIEBS

Legion

A. Monarchical and Republican periods
B. Imperial period
C. The legions of the Imperial period

A. MONARCHICAL AND REPUBLICAN PERIODS

A.1. Early forms and phalanx
A.2. The manipular order
A.3. The 'Marian Reforms'

Despite many changes and reforms, the legion was the core unit and backbone of the Roman army from its beginnings to the 4th century AD. The name 'legion' meant 'the pick [of the crop]' (*legio*; Varro, Ling. 5,89). In all periods, serving in this unit was in principle (if not always in practice) reserved to freeborn Roman citizens. Surveys of the variegated – and not always adequately documented – history include [4]; [5]; [6]; [12]; [13]; [15]; [16]; [17]; [19]; [22]; [23]; [24]; [25]; [34].

A.1. EARLY FORMS AND PHALANX

The beginnings of the Roman military, and thus of the legion, are largely obscure because of the sporadic and unreliable source material. It is suggested that the army in Rome's early history developed out of the king's bodyguard, the nobles and their retinues, and that it ultimately comprised about 3,000 warriors, with each of the three *tribus* ('tribes') of the early Monarchical period providing a fighting force of about 1,000 men, under the command of a *tribunus militum* ('military tribune'). At some unknown point in time (but well before the mid-5th century BC), the Romans adopted the Greeks' phalanx tactics, no doubt chiefly as a result of confrontations with the Greek-influenced Etruscans (on the use of these tactics by legions even much later in history see [35]; [37]).

A new division of the Roman people into five property classes, which was further subdivided into *centuriae* (Liv. 1,42,4–43,13; Dion. Hal. Ant. Rom. 4,15–18), is traditionally attributed to the penultimate king Servius Tullius, but it probably happened later. This division was done on the basis of citizens' registered assets, and it determined what weapons citizens were required to obtain for their army service (*classis*). The wealthiest served in the → cavalry, which may have numbered 300 men at first (Liv. 1,13,8), but which Servius Tullius supposedly expanded to a force of 1,800 (Liv. 1,43,9; Pol. 6,20,9; Dion. Hal. Ant. Rom. 4,18,1). Those without property (*infra classem*) were excluded from military service in the legion. The remainder served in the legion in different positions according to their assets and equipment. Serving in the legion was thus both an obligation as a Roman citizen and a privilege for those in possession of assets above a certain threshold. The introduction of this system expanded the legion's recruitment base beyond the previous system based on the three *tribus*. Weapons largely corresponded to Greek models, essentially comprising shields, swords, lances and helmets [3.48–64]; [4.79f.]. Because cavalrymen and lightly armed personnel were counted with the infantry, the term *legio* at this early date denoted the entire mobilized army.

A.2. THE MANIPULAR ORDER

Late in the 4th century BC, before or during the war with the Samnites, the Romans created a more flexible military structure that was also suitable for mountainous terrain. It involved three battle lines and smaller constituent units, called maniples (*manipuli*), each consisting of two *centuriae* and able to operate independently (Liv. 8,8,3–8,8,14). The word *legio* by now denoted a unit perhaps up to 5,000 men strong and divided into 30 maniples, in which soldiers were armed with a shield (*scutum*), a javelin (*pilum*) or a lance (*hasta*: Liv. 1,43,2) and a sword (*gladius*; Pol. 6,23. Dion. Hal. Ant. Rom. 14,9,2) [3]. According to Roman tradition, army soldiers also began to receive → pay in 406 BC (Diod. Sic. 14,16,5; Liv. 4,59,11–60,8).

The best description of the Roman army of this period is supplied by Polybius (6,19–25). Although his account relates to the 3rd and 2nd centuries BC, it is also valid for some time prior to this. He describes the Roman army as comprising four legions, with two each under the command of the two serving consuls. The consuls appointed the senior officers of the legion, six *equites Romani* ('Roman cavalry'), who served under their supreme command as *tribuni militum* (Pol. 6,12,6). Both *centuriae* of each maniple were commanded by one *centurio* and his deputy, the *optio* ('adjutant'). Finally, these officers also appointed a standard-bearer for each *centuria* (Pol. 6,24).

In battle, the legion formed up in three ranks behind the lightly-armed *velites* (lightly armed

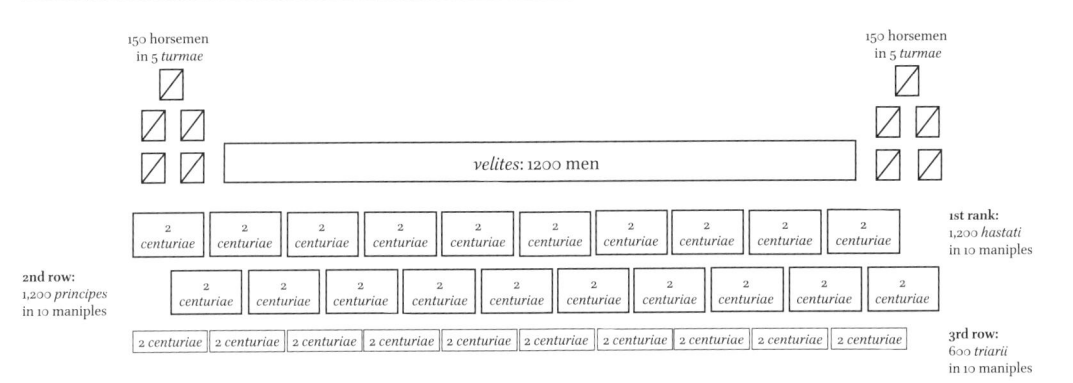

```
                150 horsemen                                                                                        150 horsemen
                in 5 turmae                                                                                         in 5 turmae
                   ◨                                                                                                   ◨
                ◨  ◨                                                                                                ◨  ◨
                ◨  ◨                          velites: 1200 men                                                     ◨  ◨

              ┌────┬────┬────┬────┬────┬────┬────┬────┬────┬────┐                                          1st rank:
              │ 2  │ 2  │ 2  │ 2  │ 2  │ 2  │ 2  │ 2  │ 2  │ 2  │                                          1,200 hastati
              │cent│cent│cent│cent│cent│cent│cent│cent│cent│cent│                                          in 10 maniples
              └────┴────┴────┴────┴────┴────┴────┴────┴────┴────┘
2nd row:        ┌────┬────┬────┬────┬────┬────┬────┬────┬────┬────┐
1,200 principes │ 2  │ 2  │ 2  │ 2  │ 2  │ 2  │ 2  │ 2  │ 2  │ 2  │
in 10 maniples  │cent│cent│cent│cent│cent│cent│cent│cent│cent│cent│
                └────┴────┴────┴────┴────┴────┴────┴────┴────┴────┘
                  ┌──┬──┬──┬──┬──┬──┬──┬──┬──┬──┐                                                         3rd row:
                  │2c│2c│2c│2c│2c│2c│2c│2c│2c│2c│                                                         600 triarii
                  └──┴──┴──┴──┴──┴──┴──┴──┴──┴──┘                                                         in 10 maniples
```

Fig. 1: Formation of the manipular legion (diagram). In each rank, a gap was left between the maniples. Thus, the second rank formed up behind the first so as to cover the gaps in the first, and the third rank covered the gaps in the second. There were also 1,200 lightly armed infantry assigned to the maniples (Pol. 6,24,4).

→ infantry). The first rank consisted of the 1,200 *hastati* ('spearmen'), divided into ten maniples of 120 men each. Behind them, also in ten maniples of 120 soldiers each, stood 1,200 more experienced *principes* ('leaders'), bearing the same arms as the *hastati*. The third rank comprised the *triarii* (the third rank) or *pili* ('javelin men'), who were armed with javelins (*pilum*), and fought in ten maniples of 60 men each. The *triarii* were the oldest and most experienced fighters (cf. fig. 1) [31].

In wartime, Rome's allies provided the same number of foot soldiers and a further 900 cavalry to augment the Roman cavalry of 300 men (30 horsemen in each of ten *turmae*; Pol. 6,20,9). The allies' weaponry was the same as the Romans' (Pol. 3,87; 18,28). There were established plans to be followed for building → camps (*castra*), and marching (Pol. 6,27–36; 6,40f.) duties were regulated in detail.

Legionary soldiers were required to be Roman citizens between 16 and 45 years of age (Pol. 6,19,2; Gell. NA 10,28,1). They were often farmers, and originally they only served in the army between spring and autumn on a campaign-by-campaign basis. According to Polybius, though, a cavalryman's overall term of service was ten years, and an infantryman's term was 16 years, in emergencies extended to 20 (Pol. 6,19,2). At least from the time of the Punic Wars onwards (→ Wars of note, K.), citizens of military age were expected to serve for up to six years (and more), often without interruption and increasingly in distant lands. Over time, therefore, the legions evolved so that they increasingly took the form of a standing force, especially when soldiers' pay facilitated legionaries' long absences from home (Pol. 6,39).

A.3. THE 'MARIAN REFORMS'

Further changes of a substantial nature are attributed to C. Marius (*cos.* 107 BC; → Generals of note, K.), although many of the changes probably resulted more from gradual developments than from a general reform imposed all at once. Under Marius, the eagle (*aquila*) became the most important standard of every legion (Plin. HN 10,5). When Marius needed recruits for his war against Jugurtha in Africa, he acted 'contrary to law and tradition' by accepting men without property as volunteers (Sall. Iug. 86,2f.; Plut. *Marius* 9). Although this earned him the censure of classical authors, he was not the first to resort to such actions in times of crisis (the senate, for example, did so in the wake of the defeat at Cannae; → Battles of note, C.). From that time on, the only legal qualifications needed to serve in the Roman legions were Roman citizenship and free birth (even these two conditions were occasionally overlooked in emergencies). This once again enlarged the recruitment base for the legions, which once again expanded shortly afterwards, when the *civitas Romana* was granted to the Italic *socii* ('confederates') in 88 BC.

Furthermore, replacing the old manipular order, six *centuriae* (i.e. three maniples) were now combined into one *cohors*. This seems likely to have happened before Marius (at least occasionally, and chiefly among the → auxiliaries; Pol. 11,23,1; Sall. Iug. 38; 46; 49,6), but Marius made the cohort the most important subunit in the legions. Each legion now consisted of ten cohorts of 480 men each (cf. fig. 2).

Every soldier was now equipped with *pilum* and sword. The legion formed up in three battle lines, with four cohorts in the front rank and three in the two ranks behind. Cohorts of the legion could operate independently, alone or in groups (e.g. Caes. B Gall. 2,5,6 and Caes. B civ. 3,52,2; Tac. Ann. 1,60). This remained unchanged for much of the Imperial period (e.g. AE 2006, 1800c, Z. 3–6; AE 1911, 233; AE 1984, 915; AE 1990, 893; AE 1998, 1115b; RIB 1343), although there are indications that the strength of the first cohort may have been doubled [31]. Legions proliferated in the last years

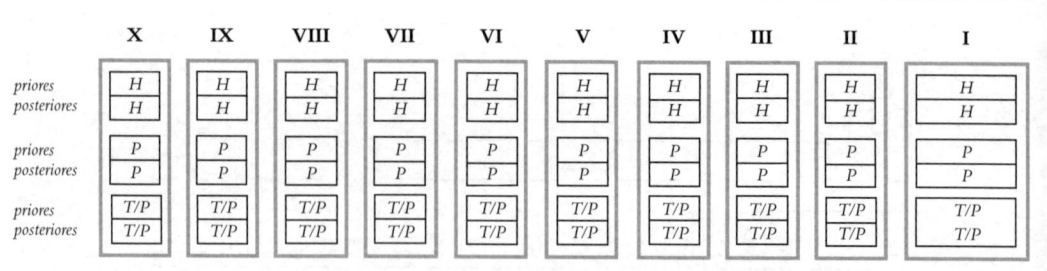

	X	IX	VIII	VII	VI	V	IV	III	II	I
priores	H	H	H	H	H	H	H	H	H	H
posteriores	H	H	H	H	H	H	H	H	H	H
priores	P	P	P	P	P	P	P	P	P	P
posteriores	P	P	P	P	P	P	P	P	P	P
priores	T/P	T/P	T/P	T/P	T/P	T/P	T/P	T/P	T/P	T/P
posteriores	T/P	T/P	T/P	T/P	T/P	T/P	T/P	T/P	T/P	T/P

Fig. 2: The ten cohorts of a legion (diagram). The first cohort is shown here at double strength and with just five centuriae (Ps.-Hyg. Mun. Cast. 3) [31]. The division of the hastati, principes and pili into centuriae of priores and posteriores reflects the older manipular order of two centuries (see e.g. RIB 2032; IDR II 325; 327).

of the Republic, so much so that about 60 legions confronted each other at the Battle of Actium (31 BC; → Battles of note, A.) [16.145].

B. Imperial period

B.1. Modernizations under Augustus
B.2. Tally and structure
B.3. Deployment and evolution

Thanks in particular to a greater abundance of archaeological and documentary → sources, more information survives from the first three hundred years of the Imperial period than from the centuries before and after. Augustus modernized the Roman army in several stages, but essentially preserved its traditional structure and equipment [28.22–35]; [30]. He did not conduct a genuine, coherent reform, as appearances might suggest in view of the state of the Imperial army at his death in AD 14. Rather, the new army was the result of a variety of innovations scattered throughout the long years of his reign. The key innovation lay in the permanent transformation of the *exercitus Romanus* into a standing professional army. Admittedly, the Roman army had been increasingly evolving in this direction since the time of the Punic Wars (→ Wars of note, K.), but it was Augustus' spectacular closure of the Gates of Janus on January 11, 29 BC, with the celebration of the *Augurium Salutis* (i.e. the proclamation of peace at all the borders of the empire), and yet with the legions still mobilized, that gave a clear signal that the permanent and uninterrupted existence of an army would be a hallmark of the new order of the Roman state [30.80].

B.1. Modernizations under Augustus

Various specific modernizations were needed. Augustus began by cutting the number of legions to 28 immediately afterc Actium in 31 BC, and he posted the remaining units (together with most of the → auxiliaries) to the 'unpacified' frontier provinces (Suet. Aug. 17,3; 49,1; Cass. Dio 51,4,1–5,1; 54,25,5f.; 55,23,1; Oros. hist. 6,19,14). On the eve of the Germanic Wars in 13 BC, he regularized the minimum terms of service, pay, and discharge bonuses for all classes of troops and ranks within the units, his aim being to create a contract of service with reliable conditions (Suet. Aug. 49,2; Cass. Dio 54,25,5f.; [28.19–51, 408–414]). The right to serve in a legion (*ius militandi in legione*: CPL 102) was still reserved to freeborn Roman citizens of good standing. It was a serious crime to impersonate a soldier (Dig. 49,16,2,1; 49,16,4,1–9; 49,16,16; Veg. Mil. 1,7,1f.), a rule that was strictly enforced even during forced levies (*dilectus*; Plin. Ep. 10,29f.; [7] = AE 2013, 2182). Most legionaries, however, reported as volunteers for a term of military service that lasted around 25 years in all.

Ordinary legionaries received → pay of 225 *denarii* per year until AD 83/84, when it was raised to 300 *denarii* (until AD 197) [28.350, 427]. Soldiers of higher rank received half as much again or double pay. The pay of centurions and senior officers was even higher. From the time of Augustus onwards, ordinary soldiers also regularly received a discharge bonus upon honourable discharge, in the form of either land or cash (R. Gest. div. Aug. 3). The value of the bonus was set at 12,000 *sestertii* (= 3,000 *denarii*) for ordinary legionaries in AD 5 (Cass. Dio 55,23,1; [22]; [28.415f.]). It is possible that this bonus remained unchanged until the reign of Caracalla (AD 211–217), when ordinary legionaries received 20,000 *sestertii* (= 5,000 *denarii*; Cass. Dio 78,24,1). The rank of the recipient determined the level of these payments. The *aerarium militare* ('military treasury') was set up in AD 6 to fund the cash payments of the discharge bonuses (R. Gest. div. Aug. 16f.; Suet. Aug. 49,2; on which [28.65f., 74f.]). The new army was a considerable drain on public finances, which affected both the size of the military and the financial structure of the empire ([28.41–44, 54–62]; cf. also [8]).

That the legions were spread out across many thousands of kilometres at the empire's borders meant that special measures were needed to ensure standards of conformity in training (→ Education) and fighting techniques. To this end, Augustus created a set of written rules, the *Disciplina Augusti* [28.26–35]. In their → oath (*sacramentum*), legionaries of the Imperial period swore to fight and if necessary die for the Roman state, and to obey their supreme commander, the emperor [14]; [29]. The Roman emperors and their families relied on the loyalty of the legions, as the army remained a key political factor in the Roman Empire throughout the Imperial period. The introduction of cults venerating the emperor in the Roman army served to promote such loyalty [28.45f., 521f.]; [32].

B.2. TALLY AND STRUCTURE
A survey of the legions during the reign of Augustus is found in Cassius Dio 55,23. At Augustus' death (AD 14), Rome had over 25 legions (Tac. Ann. 4,5; the three legions XVII, XVIII and XIX had been destroyed in the 'Varian Disaster' in the Teutoburg Forest in AD 9). They increased in number to 33 by the early 3rd century (see below, C.; the inscription CIL VI 3492 = ILS 2288 gives a list from the early 3rd century), with new legions generally being raised in conjunction with planned or actual creations of new provinces [21]. Each legion had its own number, name, standard and animal emblem. They all had their own treasuries and city-like permanent camps built according set regulations, which became the epicentre of soldiers' daily lives and routines [12.82–93]; [19.111–136]; [28.519–526].

A legion of the Imperial period comprised about 5,000 (max. 6,000) infantry and 120 cavalry, under the command of a senator of praetorian rank bearing the title *legatus legionis* ('legionary legate'). At his side were six younger military tribunes, one of senatorial rank (*tribunus laticlavius*, 'broad–striped tribune') and five *tribuni angusticlavii* ('narrow–striped tribunes') from the *ordo equester* (*equites Romani*) [1]. The commander also had a mounted life guard (*equites singulares*) drawn from the ranks of the legion's cavalry, and a staff of soldiers. Commanding each 80-strong *centuria* (Ps.-Hyg. Mun. Cast. 1) was a *centurio* ('centurion') [9]. Each legion had about 480 of the higher-ranking soldiers (*principales*) who received one and a half times or twice the regular pay [28.384]. These were exempt from the heavy duties of the ordinary soldiers. The same privilege (*immunitas*) was also extended to a larger group of ordinary soldiers (*immunes*) who worked as → specialists in various capacities in the administration or medical corps or as pioneers, etc. [28.439–449].

According to surviving inscriptions, legionaries at first came mostly from Northern Italy, southern Gaul, the south and east of the Iberian Peninsula and (in legions stationed in the east) the Roman colonies of Asia Minor. However, growing numbers of soldiers later began to be recruited from the provinces in which the legions were stationed and from the wider environs of the camp [2]; [10]; [11.62f., 113ff.]. In the early Imperial period, legions would relocate every few decades, but increasingly, especially from the early 2nd century onwards, they began to be established at permanent locations. By far the majority of these locations were in the north: in Britain, and on the Rhine and Danube. A much smaller group was stationed along the eastern borders of Anatolia and the Middle East. Three, and later two legions were stationed in North Africa (cf. Map 1).

B.3. DEPLOYMENT AND EVOLUTION
The deployment of the legions in their heavy infantry role is described in detail by authors such as Flavius Josephus (*Bellum Iudaicum*) for the time of the First Jewish War (AD 66–70; → Wars of note, E.), and Flavius Arrianus (*Ektaxis kata Alanon*) for a campaign against the Alani that he led or planned in AD 135. It became less and less usual for entire legions to be deployed as a single unit from the 2nd century onwards. It was much more common for legionaries to be formed into detachments of various strengths, and to assemble expeditionary forces consisting of detachments from a number of legions, and from auxiliary and allied units [26]; [28.255–271]. After the many wars of the 3rd century, some of these detachments never returned to their units of origin. Instead, they lived on as formations in their own right, with their own particular name or the same name as their unit of origin [15.218–222]. These developments in the Roman army of the late period (→ Army, C.) gradually but considerably reduced the strength of the orginal legions. At the same time, these offshoots along with numerous new units, especially during the reign of Diocletian (AD 284–305), greatly increased the number of legions [25.1350f.]. These developments also ushered in another important innovation of the 3rd century: the establishment of a new field army, which served as the escort troop (*comitatus*) for the emperor and as a mobile reserve. Legions founded in Late Antiquity served in this field army, as did the main legions in their established camps along the imperial borders, where they maintained their traditional ranks and duties.

C. THE LEGIONS OF THE IMPERIAL PERIOD
The list below gives the names, bynames and symbols of the legions of the first three centuries of the Imperial period, up to the reign of Diocletian. Included are their dates of foundation (where after 31 BC) and the dates of their dissolution or destruction (where before AD 284). Where these dates are missing, the foundation and end dates lie outside these limits. However, the list does

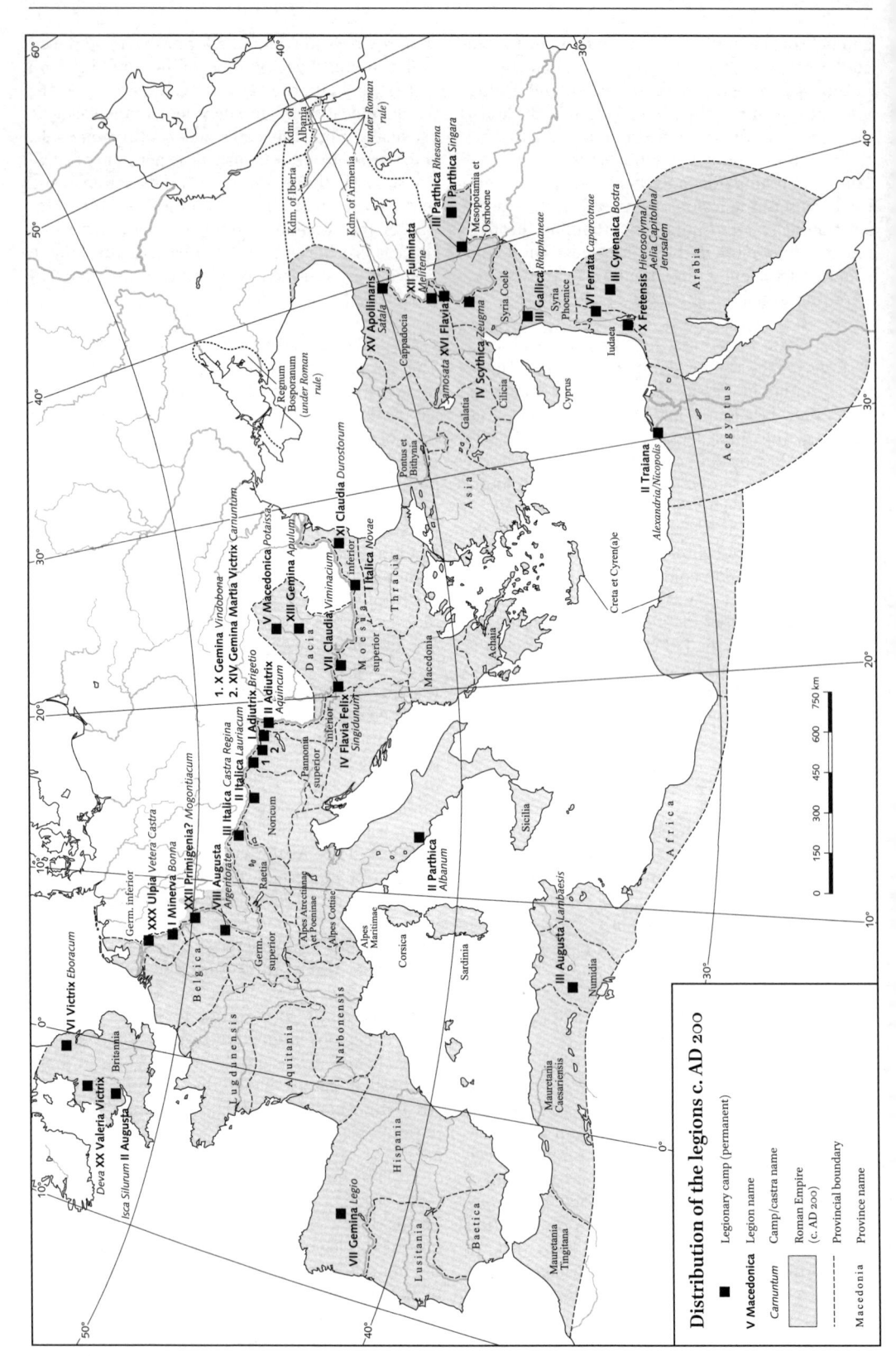

Map 1: Distribution of the legions c. AD 200

not reflect the tally of legions at any particular moment in the Imperial period, because several units did not exist throughout the entire period. Emperor bynames of the late 2nd and 3rd centuries that did not endure are not listed here. On the history of the individual legions and their changing locations, see especially [16]; [18]; [25]. Useful summaries are found in [5]; [20]; [34].

Legio I Germanica – founded AD 9/10, dissolved by Vespasian AD 70. Symbol: bull?

Legio I Adiutrix – founded by Galba AD 68. *Pia fidelis* as of AD 105/06. Symbols: Capricorn, Pegasus.

Legio I Italica – founded by Nero AD 66/67 for his planned eastern campaign. Symbols: boar, bull.

Legio I Macriana – founded AD 68 by L. Clodius Macer, who revolted against Nero while governor of Africa. Dissolved by Galba that same year. *Liberatrix* as of foundation. Symbol: unknown.

Legio I Minervia – founded by Domitian AD 83, probably for the war against the Chatti. *Pia fidelis Domitiana* as of AD 89. *Domitiana* cut AD 96. Symbol: Capricornus.

Legio I Parthica – founded by Septimius Severus AD 195 [28.188]. Symbol: unknown.

Legio II Adiutrix – founded by Vespasian AD 69/70. *Pia fidelis* from then on. Symbols: Capricornus, Pegasus.

Legio II Augusta – Symbols: Capricornus, Pegasus.

Legio II Italica – founded by Marcus Aurelius AD 165/66. Called at first *legio II pia* (CIL III 1980). *Fidelis* as of the early 170s [18.147]. Symbol: she-wolf with twins.

Legio II Parthica – founded by Septimius Severus AD 195 [28.188]. *Pia fidelis felix aeterna* probably by 215 (AE 1993, 1572 and 1579). Symbol: centaur.

Legio II Traiana Fortis – founded by Trajan AD 105. *Germanica* as of AD 213 [25.1489]. Symbol: Hercules.

Legio III Augusta – *Pia vindex* as of AD 193. Symbols: Capricornus, Pegasus.

Legio III Cyrenaica – Symbol: unknown.

Legio III Gallica – Symbol: bull.

Legio III Italica – founded by Marcus Aurelius AD 165/66. Appears originally to have been named *Legio III concors* (CIL III 1980, although here wrongly given as *Concordia*). Symbol: stork.

Legio III Parthica – founded by Septimius Severus AD 195. *Pia* as of 240s? Symbol: centaur.

Legio IIII Flavia – founded by Vespasian AD 70. *Felix* as of foundation? Symbol: lion.

Legio IIII Macedonica – dissolved by Vespasian AD 70. Symbol: bull, Capricornus.

Legio IIII Scythica – Symbol: Capricornus [16.206]; [27.327].

Legio V Alaudae – dissolved or destroyed in the Flavian period. Symbol: elephant.

Legio V Gallica – dissolved by Augustus after the defeat in 16 BC? Symbol: unknown.

Legio V Macedonica – *Pia constans* by AD 170 (AE 1972, 454), *pia fidelis* by 211 (CIL III 12645). Symbol: bull.

Legio VI Ferrata – *Fidelis constans* as of AD 195 (cf. CIL VI 210; [25.1592]). Symbols: bull, she-wolf with twins.

Legio VI Victrix – *Pia fidelis Domitiana* as of AD 89. *Domitiana* cut AD 96. Symbol: bull.

Legio VII – *Claudia pia fidelis* as of AD 42. Symbols: bull, lion.

Legio VII – founded by Galba AD 68. *Gemina* as of AD 69. *Pia felix* as of reign of Septimius Severus. Symbol: unknown.

Legio VIII Augusta – *Pia fidelis constans Commoda* as of AD 187. *Commoda* cut AD 192. Symbol: bull.

Legio IX Hispana – destroyed in eastern Anatolia AD 161? Symbol: bull?

Legio X Fretensis – Symbols: bull, boar, dolphin, trireme.

Legio X Gemina – *Pia fidelis Domitiana* as of AD 89. *Domitiana* cut AD 96. Symbol: bull.

Legio XI – *Claudia pia fidelis* as of AD 42. Symbols: Neptune, she-wolf with twins?

Legio XII Fulminata – *Certa constans* as of AD 175. Symbol: thunderbolt.

Legio XIII Gemina – Symbol: lion.

Legio XIIII Gemina – *Martia Victrix* as of AD 61. Symbol: Capricornus.

Legio XV Apollinaris – Symbol: griffin [36.265–267].

Legio XV Primigenia – founded by Gaius (Caligula) AD 39. Symbols: Capricornus, bull.

Legio XVI Gallica – dissolved by Vespasian AD 70. Symbol: lion.

Legio XVI Flavia – founded by Vespasian AD 70/71, thereafter *firma*. Symbol: lion.

Legio XVII – destroyed in the Varian Disaster of AD 9. Symbol: unknown.

Legio XVIII – destroyed in the Varian Disaster of AD 9. Symbol: unknown.

Legio XIX – destroyed in the Varian Disaster of AD 9. Symbol: unknown.

Legio XX – *Valeria victrix* as of AD 61? Symbols: Capricornus, boar.

Legio XXI Rapax – dissolved by Domitian AD 89? [18.58]. Symbol: Capricornus.

Legio XXII Deiotariana – formed 25 BC out of an indigenous unit of the Kingdom of Galatia. Probably destroyed in the Bar Kochba uprising c. AD 132/33 (→ Wars of note B.) [25.1795]. Symbol: unknown.

Legio XXII Primigenia – founded by Gaius (Caligula) AD 39. *Pia fidelis Domitiana* AD 89 onwards.

Domitiana cut AD 96. Symbols: Capricornus, Hercules, bull.

Legio XXX Ulpia Victrix – founded by Trajan AD 105. *Pia fidelis* as of AD 196/97. Symbols: Neptune, Jupiter, Capricornus.

☞ Army, C. Roman; Recruitment; State and army, B. Roman Republic; State and army, C. Imperial period

BIBLIOGRAPHY
[1] G. ALFÖLDY, Die Generalität des römischen Heeres, in: G. ALFÖLDY, Römische Heeresgeschichte. Beiträge 1962–1985, 1987, 3–18 [2] G. ALFÖLDY, Das Heer in der Sozialstruktur des Römischen Kaiserreiches, in: G. ALFÖLDY et al. (eds.), Kaiser, Heer und Gesellschaft in der Römischen Kaiserzeit, 2000, 33–57 [3] M.C. BISHOP / J.C.N. COULSTON, Roman Military Equipment. From the Punic Wars to the Fall of Rome, ²2006 [4] L. BURCKHARDT, Militärgeschichte der Antike, ³2020 [5] B. CAMPBELL, Legio, in: BNP 7, 2005, 356–371 [6] P. COSME, L'armée romaine, VIIIe s. av. J.-C.–Ve s. ap. J.-C., 2012 [7] W. ECK et al., Edikt Hadrians für Prätorianer mit unsicherem römischen Bürgerrecht, in: ZPE 189, 2014, 241–253; ZPE 191, 2014, 266–268 und ZPE 206, 2018, 199–201 [8] A. EICH, Der Wechsel zu einer neuen grand strategy unter Augustus und seine langfristigen Folgen, in: HZ 286, 2009, 561–611 [9] P. FAURE, L'aigle et le cep. Les centurions légionnaires dans l'Empire des Sévères, 2013 [10] G. FORNI, Il reclutamento delle legioni da Augusto a Diocleziano, 1953 [11] G. FORNI, Esercito e marina di Roma antica, 1992 [12] A.K. GOLDSWORTHY, The Complete Roman Army, 2011 [13] J. HARMAND, L'armée et le soldat à Rome de 107 à 50 avant notre ère, 1967 [14] O. HEKSTER, Fighting for Rome. The Emperor as a Military Leader, in: L. DE BLOIS / E. LO CASCIO (eds.), The Impact of the Roman Army (200 BC–AD 476), 2007, 91–105 [15] D. HOFFMANN, Das spätrömische Bewegungsheer und die Notitia dignitatum, 2 pts., 1969–1970 [16] L. KEPPIE, The Making of the Roman Army, 1984 [17] W. KUBITSCHEK, Legio. Der späteren Zeit, in: RE 12,2, 1925, 1829–1837 [18] Y. LE BOHEC (ed.), Les légions de Rome sous le Haut-Empire, 2000 [19] Y. LE BOHEC, L'armée romaine sous le Haute-Empire, ⁴2018 [20] J. LENDERING, www.livius.org, 2020 [21] J.C. MANN, The Raising of New Legions during the Principate, in: Hermes 91, 1963, 483–489 [22] J.C. MANN, Legionary Recruitment and Veteran Settlement during the Principate, 1983 [23] H.M.D. PARKER, The Roman Legions, ²1958 [24] A. PASSERINI, Legio, in: E. DE RUGGIERO (ed.), Dizionario epigrafico di antichità romane, vol. 4, 1949, 549–614 [25] E. RITTERLING, Legio, in: RE 12,1–2, 1924–1925, 1186–1829 [26] R. SAXER, Untersuchungen zu den Vexillationen des römischen Kaiserheeres von Augustus bis Diokletian, 1967 [27] M.A. SPEIDEL, Legio IV Scythica, in: Y. LE BOHEC (ed.), Les légions de Rome sous le Haut-Empire, 2000, 327–337 [28] M.A. SPEIDEL, Heer und Herrschaft im Römischen Reich der Hohen Kaiserzeit, 2009 [29] M.A. SPEIDEL, Pro patria mori ... La doctrine du patriotisme romain dans l'armée impériale, in: Cahiers du Centre Gustave Glotz 21, 2010, 139–154 [30] M.A. SPEIDEL, Actium, Allies, and the Augustan Auxilia. Reconsidering the Transformation of Military Structures and Foreign Relations in the Reign of Augustus, in: C. WOLFF / P. FAURE (eds.), Les auxiliares de l'armée romaine. Des alliés aux fédérés, 2016, 79–95 [31] M.P. SPEIDEL, The Framework of an Imperial Legion, in: R.J. BREWER (ed.), The Second Augustan Legion and the Roman Military Machine, 2002, 125–143 [32] J. STÄCKER, Princeps und Miles. Studien zum Bindungs- und Nahverhältnis von Kaiser und Soldat im 1. und 2. Jahrhundert n.Chr., 2003 [33] G. WEBSTER, The Roman Imperial Army, ³1985 [34] G. WESCH-KLEIN, Legions, History and Locations of, in: R. BAGNALL et al. (eds.), The Encyclopedia of Ancient History, vol. 7, 2013, 3996–4005 [35] E.L. WHEELER, The Roman Legion as Phalanx, in: Chiron 9, 1979, 303–318 [36] E.L. WHEELER, Legio XV Apollinaris. From Carnuntum to Satala – and beyond, in: Y. LE BOHEC (ed.), Les légions de Rome sous le Haut-Empire, 2000, 259–308 [37] E.L. WHEELER, The Legion as Phalanx in the Late Empire (pt. 1), in: Y. LE BOHEC / C. WOLFF (eds.), L'armée romaine de Dioclétien à Valentinien Ier, 2004, 309–358 (pt. 2 in: Revue des études militaires anciennes 1, 2004, 147–175).

MICHAEL A. SPEIDEL

Looting

☞ Booty; Scorched earth

Maps

A map is a graphic representation of spatial knowledge, using the technique of illustration to scale, and a standardized idiom.

The standard Greek word for 'map' is *pinax* (literally 'board', 'writing tablet'), and the Latin word is *forma* (literally 'form', 'figure'). Both words have broad ranges of meaning, so that only context can determine whether the few potentially relevant ancient sources are talking about 'maps' or about other, related concepts, such as 'drawings', 'diagrams', 'pictures', or '(geographical) lists' [5]. In some cases, such as the 'Map of Agrippa', the meaning is indecipherable, so there is considerable debate among scholars [1]; [2]. The term *tabula* (familiar from the *tabula Peutingeriana*, 'Peutinger Table' for example) is seldom encountered in Antiquity (Cic. Att. 6,2,3; Prop. 4,3,37). *Ges periodos* (literally 'circuit of the Earth'), which is usually used of early geographic literature, can also mean 'map' (cf. Aristoph. Nub. 206; Hdt. 4,36; Aristot. Mete. 2,5). Although *mappa* ('cloth', 'towel') is known from medieval and modern *mappaemundi* ('world maps'), it did not yet convey this meaning in Antiquity. According to LSJ 391, the Greek *diagramma* meant 'figure [marked out by lines]', 'geometrical proposition', 'horoscope', 'list', 'register', 'inventory', 'ordinance', 'regulation'. The specific sense of 'map' is first attested in the letters of Emperor Julian (10 [403 C] Bidez-Cumont). The Latin term *orbis terrarum* (literally 'disc of the world') is only rarely – and by no means exclusively – used of ancient maps (cf. e.g. Vitr. De arch. 8,2,6). To sum up: the ancient languages had no single unambiguous word for 'map'.

No maps corresponding to the above definition survive from Antiquity [6]; [4]. Only the *oikumene* maps created in scholarly contexts (especially those of Ptolemy) paid any attention to the problem of scale (projection). What do survive and are attested, however, are maplike objects, such as diagrams, sketches, land registry drawings, landscape pictures and climate charts [7]. There are several reasons for the 'maplessness' of Antiquity. Besides the 'hodological perspective' as the 'master model' of spatial awareness in the ancient world (which rendered ancient maps redundant in practice) [6], there were also the technical difficulties posed by the copying process, the costliness of papyrus and the sophisticated norm set by ancient cartographic works such as Ptolemy's *Geography* [8]; [9].

The maps used in Antiquity had no practical use (for orientation, travel, navigation, learning, etc.), but instead fulfilled purposes of propaganda (*Map of Agrippa*), aesthetics (*Dura-Europus Stages Map* on a Roman shield), tourism (*Vicarello Cups*) and especially scholarship (maps of Hecataeus of Miletus, Eratosthenes of Cyrene and Ptolemy of Alexandria).

The extent to which maps were drawn and used in military contexts is debated (*contra*: [4]; *pro*: [10]). Evidence that might suggest the use of maps for military purposes is sparse or late, and therefore of limited value (cf. esp. Plin. HN 6,40: *situsque depicti*; Veg. Mil. 3,6: *itineraria picta*, in both cases unclear whether maps, illustrated itineraries or landscape drawings are meant). As a rule, generals did not have maps that were strategically or tactically useful. There was no expectation of cartographic awareness. Geographical information was obtained only during campaigns, through → reconnaissance [3]. Nevertheless, there is evidence of the presence of *mensores* ('surveyors') in Roman armies, and they would have the ability and expertise to translate topographical information into map form [10]. For orientation in space, and thus as a 'substitute' for drawn maps, ancient armies made use of itineraries, which probably at least recorded distinctive landmarks, stations along the way (*mansiones*, permanent camps, supply points, etc.) and travel times or distances, all mainly in tabular form (particularly instructive is SHA Alex. 45,2f.).

Neither ancient military leaders nor civilian administrations recognized, let alone exploited, the potential of maps [11].

BIBLIOGRAPHY
[1] P. ARNAUD, Observations sur l'original du fragment de carte du pseudo-bouclier de Doura-Europos, in: REA 90, 1988, 151–161 [2] P. ARNAUD, Une deuxième lecture du 'bouclier' de Doura-Europos, in: Comptes rendus des séances de l'Académie des inscriptions et belles-lettres, in: Comptes rendus des séances de l'Académie des inscriptions et belles-lettres, vol. 133, no. 2, 1989, 373–389 [3] A.C. BERTRAND, Stumbling through Gaul, in: The Ancient History Bulletin 11, 1997, 107–122 [4] K. BRODERSEN, Terra Cognita, ³2003 [5] S. GÜNZEL / L. NOWAK, Karten Wissen, 2012 [6] P. JANNI, La mappa e il periplo, 1984 [7] F. PRONTERA, Karte (Kartographie), in: RAC 20, 2001, 187–229 [8] M. RATHMANN, Kartographie in der Antike, in: D. BOSCHUNG et al. (eds.), Geographische Kenntnisse und ihre konkreten Ausformungen, 2003, 11–49 [9] M. RATHMANN, Orientierungshilfen für antike Reisende in Bild und Wort, in: E. OLSHAUSEN / V. SAUER (eds.), Mobilität in den Kulturen der antiken Mittelmeerwelt, 2014, 411–423 [10] R.K. SHERK, Roman Geographical Exploration and Military Maps, in: ANRW II.1, 1974, 534–562 [11] R. TALBERT, Cartography, in: BNP 2, 2003, 1138–1143.

KLAUS GEUS

March

A. Introduction
B. Greece
C. Rome
D. Speed and performance

B. Greece
 B.1. Formations
 B.2. Square
 B.3. Regular march
 B.4. Hellenistic period

A. Introduction

Marches varied according to conditions and location, but there was a fixed repertoire of types: the regular march (Xen. Hell. 3,1.22), the combat march (App. Ib. 86,373), and the deployment march (approaching the enemy with the army in formation or ready for it). A combat march could either be part of the movement of the force, or part of the battle (Sall. Iug. 101,2; Tac. Ann. 1,51,2; Arr. An. 3,16,3). Combat and deployment marches were also used as stratagems, to deceive the enemy about the size of an army or to conceal a general's true intentions (Caes. B Gall. 8,8; Amm. Marc. 24,1,3).

The placement of the general field kit and the kits of individual units differed according to the type of march. In a combat march, the kit was protected to some degree, and in the deployment march it was often left behind. The march type also determined whether soldiers could be unburdened and ready to fight (*expediti*). The regular march enabled speed, whereas protective measures could slow down a combat march. Varied topography and the weak cohesion of battle formations ruled out the possibility of deploying an army in full formation and ready to fight across a broad front over any great distance (cf. Pol. 2,27,4; 12,20,2f.; Arr. An. 1,13,4f.).

The length of a march and the cultural context of the style of warfare and of the rules of war at a particular period determined the form of the march. In the case of full-scale declared wars among the Greek mainland *poleis* before the 5th century BC, there is no evidence of a marching army protecting its flanks or of scouts engaged in tactical reconnaissance. Ambushes and surprise attacks violated unwritten, but generally accepted rules. However, none of this applied to a 'war without herald' (*polemos akeryktos*, 'undeclared war') or to conflicts between colonies and peoples outside the Greek warfare system. The Romans, too, even in the Middle Republican period, neglected security on marches and found themselves ambushed, for example at the Caudine Forks (321 BC) and at Lake Trasimene (217 BC). In classical Athenian practice, as documented for the Peloponnesian War (431–404 BC), hoplites were required to bring only three days' worth of rations, suggesting short campaigns and relative proximity to the army base.

B. Greece

B.1. Formations

The Greek tacticians (Asclepiodotus 10,22–11; Ael. Tact. 36f.; Arr. Tact. 28f.) make no distinction between marching and battle formations, so that the battle orders for attack and defence appear in the same discussions as marches. They consist of the oblique, crooked, curved, convex and concave phalanx.

Armies marched in one column or several (Ael. Tact. 36,6; Arr. Tact. 28,6: *monophalangia, diphalangia, triphalangia, tetraphalangia*). A marching column had a narrow vanguard (of one to eight men) and might be several kilometres long – although if it was too long, this caused problems when its head or tail required reinforcement (Onas. 6,2–5). For battle, this column (or these columns) had to form up into one or more ranks, much wider than deep, in order to maximize the fighting potential of the force. It was generally rectangular. Various factors might influence the width of a marching column (e.g. city or camp gates, road width, cf. Veg. Mil. 3,11,4). The arrangement of troops in a column was not haphazard. In general, the width of a marching column corresponded to the anticipated depth of the battle line, to make it easier to transition the column into a line. The Romans followed the same principle.

B.2. Square

In order to cross open ground, and frequently when withdrawing or in cases where an army lacked sufficient cavalry, a hollow rectangle (*plaision*) could be formed to counter potential attackers from all four quarters, protecting the kit placed in the centre of the formation. This rectangle was also called the 'square' (*tetragonon*) or the 'brick' (*plinthion*) (Asclepiodotus 11,6; 11,8; Ael. Tact. 37,8f.; 39,1; Arr. Tact. 29,7f.; 30,2). Whether the formation was a square or an oblong was immaterial: the *plaision* and *plinthion* seem to have been interchangeable. Sometimes, each of the four sides had its own commander (Xen. An. 3,2,37).

This hollow rectangle is first attested during the Peloponnesian War (→ Wars of note, H.) (Brasidas, 423 BC; Thuc. 4,125,2f.). At the first Battle of Syracuse (415 BC) during that war, Nicias had half his army form up as a reserve in a square (*plaision*), eight men deep on each side – the same depth as the other half formed up for battle. The square enclosed the train (Thuc. 6,67,1). The *plaision* appears in Macedonian practice during combat marches or withdrawals, with no reference made to any enclosed kit (Alexander's campaign against the Getae, 335 BC: Arr. Anab. 1,4,2). It was difficult to maintain the shape of the *plaision*, which slowed its progress. Topographical oddities and obstacles (such as rivers) disrupted the formation. The need to harmonize the soldiers' marching tempo with the train, the beasts of burden and the ox carts posed further difficulties (cf. Xen. Oec. 8,4; Xen. Cyr. 6,3,2f.; Xen. An. 7,3,37f.).

B.3. REGULAR MARCH

Details of regular marches are rarely given. For long marches across country by day, Greek custom (*Hellenikos nomos*) demanded that the head of the column was made up of the unit type best suited to the terrain – whether hoplites, *peltastai* ('light armed footsoldiers') or cavalry. At night, the slowest type of unit would lead the march, to avoid loss of cohesion and prevent units from losing their way or colliding (Xen. An. 7,3,37f.). Column widths were variable, but two men side-by-side seems to have been the most typical formation (Xen. Hell. 3,1,22; 7,4,22; Xen. An. 2,4,22). The lateral distance between men was probably the same as in the Hellenistic period: four ells (six feet: Pol. 12,19,7).

With the possible exception of Sparta (cf. Xen. Oec. 8,4), regular marches of the Classical period may have been less organized and cohesive than theoretical and idealized accounts suggest. Hoplites were not required to carry their own shields while marching. They each had at least one servant (a helot, for the Spartans) to carry their shield and other equipment. Servants were never allowed to stray far from their hoplites for fear of an unexpected attack. This suggests a rather varied practice of organization. Hoplites only took physical charge of their heavy shield (*aspis*) when advancing to fight.

B.4. HELLENISTIC PERIOD

Apart from the writings of tacticians, little is recorded about how Macedonian and Hellenistic marching practices worked. We know the distances and speeds of the marches of Alexander the Great (→ Generals of note, B.), but not his marching formations. Alexander changed the order of units for leading the march and the battle order on a daily basis (Arr. Anab. 1,28,3; 5,13,4). Advancing on the Granicus (334 BC), it was a mounted guard, mixed with light infantry, that led the way. The main cavalry units were on the wings, and the kit was behind the phalanx units, which Arrian enigmatically calls the 'double phalanx' (*diplen phalanga*, Arr. Anab. 1,13,1), probably meaning parallel columns (*paragoge kata syzeuxin*).

C. ROME

C.1. Manipular legion
C.2. Agmen quadratum
C.3. Combat marches: Tacitus, Josephus, Arrian

C.1. MANIPULAR LEGION

The Romans distinguished between regular route marches and combat marches. Polybius (6,40,4–9) describes the route march of a consular army comprising two legions with Italic confederate allies (*socii*). It consisted of a single marching column in *epagoge* (literally 'leading against,' = marching in a column) with the units following one after another. The *extraordinarii* (selected allied cavalry and infantry) headed the column, followed by the right-wing *socii* (*dextra*), with their beasts of burden behind them. Then came the two legions, with the kit of the first legion borne between it and the second, followed by the kit of the second legion and that of the left wing (*sinistra ala*) of the socii, who brought up the rear. The cavalry (600 men for each ala of the socii, 300 per legion) marched behind the infantry units to which they belonged, or else flanked the beasts of burden to protect or drive them. There is no reliable information recorded for the width of the infantry column. Six men apparently marched abreast (probably equalling the depth of a centuria formed up for battle), if the road allowed it. The order of maniples in the legion column (also not recorded) presumably followed the order of the battle formation: hastati ('spearmen', the first rank), principes ('leaders', the second rank), *triarii* (the third rank). No mention is made of the protective troops at the column's flanks, head and rear.

If a manipular legion faced an immediate threat, and if the open terrain permitted it, the marching army would form three parallel columns (*triphalangia*), duplicating the *triplex acies* ('triple line of battle') of the battle formation – *hastati*, *principes* and *triarii*, each formed up in their own column. The kit of each maniple preceded it (Pol. 6,40,10–14). The placement of the *hastati* depended on the direction of the perceived danger. It was placed on the nearside of the three columns if the army was marching leftwards and a threat was observed to the left, and it was placed on the offside if the army was marching rightwards and the threat emerged on that side. The *hastati* never formed the middle column, which belonged to the *principes*.

Caesar's combat march against the Nervii (Caes. B Gall. 2,19,1–4) was headed by six battle-ready (*expeditae*) veteran legions with a vanguard of cavalry, archers and slingers. All the kit was in the rear, with two legions of new recruits forming the rearguard. It is not clear whether the formation was an *epagoge* or a *paragoge* (marching side by side) – with units side by side. It may be that the hedges in this territory prevented a wide formation in an *acies* ('line of battle'), in which case either an *epagoge* or parallel columns in *orthia paragoge* (several marching columns formed up alongside) would seem likely. When an army marched into battle in relatively close proximity to the enemy, the *triplex acies* would probably mean the fully formed-up *paragoge* (Caes. B Gall. 1,49,1; 1,51,1), but a march across country in *triplex acies* (Caes. B Civ. 1,41,2; cf. Caes. B Gall. 4,14,1: march of eight (Roman) miles, i.e. 12 km) probably meant a cohort version of the *triphalangia* (march in three phalanxes) mentioned by Polybius, perhaps in *orthiaparagoge*.

C.2. AGMEN QUADRATUM

The most frequently mentioned Roman combat march, the *agmen quadratum* ('square formation'), poses numerous problems for researchers. Polybius does not use the term, and the specialized combat march he describes (6,40,10–14) in no way resembles a rectangle, as would be expected from the term. Some clarity emerges from the second sense of *agmen* as a rectangular block of troops, not merely a marching column. The *agmen quadratum* of Antiochus III (Liv. 36,10,4) may well be a Latin translation of the Greek *plinthion* ('brick'), just as, in the other direction, the march in rectangular formation (*plinthion*) conducted by Licinius Lucullus when he was pressed by Pallantian cavalry (App. Ib. 55,232; 151 BC) suggests a Greek translation of *agmen quadratum*. This does not mean, however, that the two formations were identical.

While descriptions of the *plinthion* include heavy infantry forming all four sides of a hollow rectangle, detailed accounts of the *agmen quadratum* point to a looser formation of vanguard, rearguard and flank protection, generally speaking in the shape of a diamond, which surrounded the main marching formation, although the sides did not join up. On C. Marius' march to Cirta (106 BC), which is explicitly called an *agmen quadratum* (Sall. Iug. 100,1f.), the cavalry was positioned on the right flank under L. Cornelius Sulla. Aulus Manlius was on the left flank with slingers, archers and a cohort of Ligurians. Battle-ready (*expediti*) maniples led by tribunes marched ahead and behind.

Although he does not use the term, Tacitus describes the *agmen quadratum* in the diamond shape on two occasions. Both passages are probably describing units in *orthia paragoge* rather than fully formed up in an *acies*. On Germanicus' Germanic campaign responding to the uprising on the Rhine (AD 14), the cavalry and the auxiliary cohorts led the combat march, followed by the *legio I Germanica*, with the kit behind. The *legiones XXI Rapax* and *V Alaudae* formed the left and right flanks, while the *legio XX* together with other auxiliary units formed the rearguard (Tac. Ann. 1,51,2). Flanks here were protected not by auxiliaries, but by legions. When the Armenian pretender Tiridates threatened Corbulo's advance towards Artaxata (AD 57), the latter positioned the *legiones VI Ferrata* and *III Gallica* on his left and right flanks respectively.

C.3. COMBAT MARCHES: TACITUS, JOSEPHUS, ARRIAN

Tacitus, Josephus and Arrian together give four descriptions of combat marches. None corresponds to the diamond model of the *agmen quadratum*, and strictly speaking one is a deployment march. At Idistaviso (AD 16), Germanicus took the field with Gaulish and Germanic auxiliaries (doubtless cavalry), supported by infantry archers, leading the troops. He himself followed them up with four legions, two Praetorian cohorts and one unit of elite cavalry (perhaps the *Germani corporis custodes*), then four more legions accompanied by lightly armed auxiliaries. Mounted archers (probably the *ala I Augusta Parthorum*) continued the column, with auxiliary cohorts bringing up the rear. The exact composition of the army is speculative. No information survives regarding kit or flank protection.

Josephus (Jos. BI 3,115–126; 5,47–49) and Arrian (*Acies contra Alanos* 1–10, AD 135) both offer more detailed accounts. Vespasian had lightly armed infantry and archers (but not cavalry) conduct reconnaissance before the arrival of the main column. It was headed by a group of heavily armed infantry and cavalry (not legionaries). *Metatores/mensores* ('surveyors') followed. Given the three legions present, these probably numbered about 180 men. Road-builders (*hodopoioi*), whose numbers are not given and who were probably detailed from the legions, accompanied the *metatores*, tasked with repairing the roads or removing obstacles. Vespasian's personal kit and that of the senior officers went ahead of him in the column accompanied by a mounted escort. His own place was with the *equites* ('cavalry') and *pedites singulares* ('infantry guards'), augmented by an additional escort of *lancearii* ('lancers'). After this marched the entire legionary cavalry, 360 strong (120 per legion), followed by the siege convoy with mobile, mule-drawn towers (*helepoleis*) and the → artillery. Behind these marched the legions, beginning with the legionary legates, the *praefecti castrorum* ('camp commanders'; wrongly given as *praefecti cohortis* in Josephus) and the tribunes, then the three *aquilae* (one per legion) accompanied by the trumpeters, and finally the legionaries in ranks of six men abreast, each led by a centurion (*primus pilus*?). The legions' kits and the soldiers' servants followed. Auxiliary cohorts brought up the rear, with a rearguard of mixed infantry and cavalry (probably *auxilia*) accompanying them.

Arrian's account of a march against the Alani, who were threatening to invade Cappadocia, provides the most detailed of all descriptions of Roman marching formations, down to details on the placement of particular units. His army was an expeditionary force, part of the Cappadocian provincial army, which he commanded as governor. It did not represent the entire garrison of the province. It cannot be known whether some units had been assigned as detachments combating the Bar Kochba Revolt in Palaestina (AD 132–136), or whether they were left in place to avoid leaving the frontier undefended or to guard Arrian's marching camp. Only one *vexillatio* (temporary detachment) of the *legio XII Fulminata* took part, and of the four known units of the *cohortes equitatae* (mixed cavalry and infantry), only the cavalry appear (*coh. I Germanorum, I* and *IV Raetorum, III Ulpia Petraeorum*). Provincial militias also served: *hoplitai* ('hoplites') from Trapezus and Armenia minor, javelin throwers (*lonchophoroi*) from Rhizus and the Colchian coast and two units of archers (infantry and mounted) from Armenia minor (who are missing from the description of the *agmen*).

The middle of the column began with Arrian's *equites singulares*, which indicates his own position, and they were followed by the legionary cavalry of the *XV Apollinaris* and the artillery. A unit of javelin throwers (*akontistai*) preceded the *legio XV Apollinaris*. The legionary legate Vettius Valens, the *praefectus castrorum*, tribunes and the centurions of the *primi ordines* of *cohors I* accompanied the legion's eagle (*aquila*). Then came the legion itself, in ranks of four. Next was the *aquila* of the *XII Fulminata* with its tribunes and centurions. This legion also marched in ranks of four. Parts of the provincial militias now followed, then the infantry of the *cohors Apuleia* (or perhaps the *cohors I Lepidiana*), whose prefect, Secundinus, also commanded the provincial militias. The kit completed the column, with the *ala I Ulpia Dacorum* under its prefect as rearguard. The cavalry of the *cohors I Italica* and the *ala II Gallorum*, formed up in single ranks and commanded by the prefect of the *ala II Gallorum*, protected the flanks of the legions, the provincial militias and the kit.

Arrian's description of the battle formation shows the significance of the differences in column widths. The infantry adopted phalanx formation, eight men deep, arranged by weapons (the first four ranks with long pikes, Greek *kontoi* = Latin *hastae*, the second four with *lanceae*). The differentiation of the weapons of manipular legions probably ceased with the emergence of the cohort legion and the replacement of the *triarii hasta* with the *pilum*. The new system of organization and tactics that now developed would last into Late Antiquity (e.g. Maur. Strat.): a 4/8 formation with a *contubernium* (group occupying a tent) of eight men superseded the Republican 3/6 system with a *contubernium* of six.

D. SPEED AND PERFORMANCE

Speed and the ability to achieve strategic surprise by covering long distances rapidly were cardinal virtues in the art of warfare. Caesar's *celeritas* ('speed') is proverbial in modern commentaries [4]. However, importance was not attached to speedy progress in all marching situations. When provisions had to be obtained, the tempo slackened. When invading, plunder and the destruction of enemy property might form part of the campaigning strategy, which slowed progress. The speed and direction of a march could thus be influenced not just by weather, terrain, condition (or absence) of good roads and the size of the force (small units moved more quickly than large armies), but also by strategic aims.

Scholars agree that an ancient army could march roughly 30 km per day if weather conditions were good. However, theorists advised against fighting on the same day as a long march, lest fatigue affect the outcome (Onas. 6,9; Veg. Mil. 3,11,6–9). The reforms of the Macedonian army by Philip II required soldiers to carry more of their own equipment and provisions with the aim of cutting down on the baggage train and non-military personnel. Training for marches of about 55 km per day thus became possible (Frontin. Str. 4,1,6).

Reports of extraordinary marches (forced marches) sometimes elicit scepticism [3]. Feats achievable over one or two days cannot be sustained over longer periods, since people and animals alike need to recuperate. Greek lacks a specific term for forced marches. Thucydides (6,66,1; 415 BC) called a day's march of about 50 km from Symaethum to Syracuse a 'long march' (*makra hodos*). This involved untrained Syracusan troops hurrying back to their city to repel an Athenian attack. A general estimate puts Greek and Hellenistic forced marches at about 65 km per day: in 490 BC, 2,000 Spartans took three days and three nights to march from their home city to Marathon, a distance of around 225 km (Hdt. 6,10; Isoc. Or. 4,87). The marches of Alexander the Great involved too many variables (sizes and types of units, terrain, weather etc.) for generalizations to be possible (→ Wars of note, A.) [2].

The Romans distinguished between the normal march (*iustum iter*) and the forced march (*iter magnum/duplicatum*; Caes. B Gall. 3,76,4).

Although the 30 km covered in five hours of *gradus militaris* ('miltary step') as described by Vegetius could be classified as a *iustum iter*, Vegetius himself did not use this term. As mentioned above, numerous variables influenced the length of a day's march. The *iustum iter* is better understood in terms of time, as a distance coverable in four to five hours, rather than as a specific measure of distance. Cato boasted of a victory in Hispania won by accomplishing a four-day march in two days (Frontin. Str. 3,1,2).

☞ Battle; Education; Military literature; Reconnaissance; Representations of war; Supply; Training; Vehicles

BIBLIOGRAPHY
[1] J. ANDERSON, Military Theory and Practice in the Age of Xenophon, 1970 [2] D. ENGELS, Alexander the Great and the Logistics of the Macedonian Army, 1978 [3] G. HORSMANN, Untersuchungen zur militärischen Ausbildung im republikanischen und kaiserzeitlichen Rom, 1991 [4] J. KROMAYER / G. VEITH (eds.), Heerwesen und Kriegführung der Griechen und Römer, 1928 [5] F. LAMMERT, Marsch, in: Real-Encyklopädie der klassischen Altertumswissenschaft 14.2, 1930, 165–177 [6] F. LAMMERT, Die römische Taktik zu Beginn der Kaiserzeit und die Geschichtschreibung, in: Philologus, Supplement 33.2, 1931 [7] A. MORIN, L'ordre de marche de l'armée romaine, in: Revue des études anciennes 104, 2002, 145–162 [8] L. PÉREZ CASTRO, Los agmina romanos y los significados de pilatum agmen y quadrato agmine, in: Emerita 74.1, 2006, 1–6 [9] T. STEINWENDER, Die Marschordnung des römischen Heeres, 1907 [10] F. STOLLE, Das Lager und Heer der Römer, 1912 [11] E. WHEELER, The Legion as Phalanx in the Late Empire, I, in: Y. LE BOHEC / C. WOLFF (eds.), L'Armée romaine de Diolétian à Valentinien Ist, 2004, 309–358 [12] E. WHEELER, The Legion as Phalanx in the Late Empire, II, in: Revue des Études militaires anciennes 1, 2004, 147–175.

EVERETT L. WHEELER

Marriage

A. Women
B. Soldiers' families

A. WOMEN

A.1. Unmarried status
A.2. Privileges for auxiliaries

A.1. UNMARRIED STATUS

From the time of Augustus onwards, the *disciplina militaris* (the customary lifestyle of a soldier) demanded that soldiers of the Imperial *exercitus Romanus* ('Roman army') should be unmarried, probably to cement the military's authority over them [9]; [11]. This prohibition, however, applied only to legal marriages, and did not exclude the foundation of lasting partnerships or families (e.g. Cass. Dio 56,20,1f.). Only equestrian and senatorial officers were exempt from the ban on marriage, probably because they only spent a few months of the year with the army, and increasing the numbers of legitimate children – particularly of the senatorial class – was desirable. According to Suet. Aug. 24, however, Augustus only reluctantly permitted his legates to visit their wives, and only during the winter months, that is, outside the campaigning season. Soon, though, it appears to have become customary for officers and other senior mandate holders to bring their wives and children along to the camp where they were stationed (e.g. Tab. Vindol. 291; CIL XIII 7565 = AE 1966, 263; cf. Tac. Ann. 3,33f.).

If a man was married at the time of his enlistment to the Roman army, the marriage was suspended, and any children he and his wife produced during the period of suspension were classified as illegitimate. It seems that the marriage could resume without further ado by mutual agreement when the man's term of service ended. If the wife wished to marry another, however, the existing marriage had to end in a formal divorce [1].

According to Cassius Dio, Claudius (AD 41–54) softened the legal consequences of the marriage ban by granting soldiers the privileges of married men (60,24,3). This must have applied only to soldiers who were Roman citizens. Precisely what privileges they were accorded remains open to debate. Claudius either exempted them from the provisions of the Augustan marriage laws that applied to men between the ages of 25 and 60 – that is, he granted them rights equivalent to those of married men – or else he bestowed the *ius trium liberorum* ('the right of three children') on them, giving them equal status with married men who could show that they had at least three legitimate children. This would have freed soldiers from all disadvantages (especially regarding inheritance) that unmarried status – and hence the impossibility of calling legitimate children their own – would have brought them.

A.2. PRIVILEGES FOR AUXILIARIES

To those serving in the → auxiliary forces, Claudius granted citizenship and *conubium* (the right to marry) on completion of their full term of service – and not necessarily only on their honourable discharge. Thus, under Roman law, soldiers who continued to serve after their regular term were permitted to be married. These privileges began to be granted only on discharge from the end of the 1st century AD onwards.

The *ius conubii* ('the right of marriage'), the right to conclude a marriage valid under Roman law with a woman, applied either to the woman with whom the soldier was living in a sexual union at the time of the granting of the marital privilege, or to a woman he might marry in the future. Children conceived before as well as during an auxiliary soldier's active term and acknowledged by him as his children also received citizenship. Women with whom soldiers lived in sexual unions were called *uxores* ('wives'), as is clear from the very first → military diploma known to us (December 11, AD 52; CIL XVI 1). This provoked regular debate, for strictly speaking *uxor* meant a wife in the legal sense. Perhaps the *ius conubii* was at first granted only to women who were married to soldiers according to their own tribal law, and this criterion became watered down over time. However this may be, the use of the word implies that, from the outset, only permanent and monogamous relationships with respectable women who fit the image of a Roman wife were considered eligible for legalization. According to Gaius, the *conubium* once granted permitted marriage both to a *peregrina* ('foreigner') and to a woman with Latin legal status, and thus conceivably a freedwoman (→ Slavery) (Gai. Inst. 1,57).

Before the end of the year AD 140, Antoninus Pius drastically curtailed the now customary award of citizenship to children and offspring. He appears to have done this because he considered it to violate the principle of equal treatment: unlike auxiliaries, for instance, soldiers serving in the legions would never enjoy the benefit of having *civitas Romana* ('Roman citizenship') granted to children whom they fathered with non–citizens during their term of service [5] (on the reasons why: [12]). Antoninus Pius' reform also had the effect of reviving the perhaps fading allure of the auxiliary unit: earning citizenship by serving in an auxiliary unit was a redundant incentive to young men who were already Roman citizens thanks to the privileges granted to their fathers. The change introduced by Antoninus Pius henceforth limited the award of citizenship to children whom the soldier had already fathered before enlistment – and even this applied only if the father registered his paternity with the governor with credible supporting evidence. It should be noted that the specialist literature on this subject generally talks about children born before the soldier's enlistment for → military service, but the phrase applied to recipients in the diplomas is *ex se procreatos* ('begotten from himself'). Thus, the criterion was the time of conception, not birth. It was long assumed that only decurions and centurions could claim citizenship for children they had fathered while civilians, but it is now clear that all auxiliaries of whatever rank were entitled to this privilege for their children [2]; [4].

Until the reform of AD 140, auxiliaries and men serving in the fleets had received equal treatment in regard to the granting of *civitas*. This now also changed, since the *classici* ('sailors') continued to earn citizenship for children fathered during their term of active service. It was probably after the late autumn of AD 154 that this unequal treatment ended for soldiers serving in the provincial fleets (last attested: RMD 169). From this point on, their rights were the same as those of the auxiliaries. The privileges of soldiers serving in the Praetorian fleets stationed at Ravenna and Misenum were also curtailed after AD 152 and before 158 (CIL XVI 100; RMD 171). Although they still received citizenship for children born during their active service, this only applied if fathered with *mulieribus quas secum concessa consuetudine vixisse* ('women with whom they were living in a permissible relationship'), and if the father could prove this. It is noteworthy that women here are correctly defined as life-partners and not as quasi-wives (*uxores*). It is not clear what is meant by 'permissible relationship' (*concessa consuetudo*). Concubinates may be meant, and perhaps also marital relations concluded under foreign law. It is also possible that fleet soldiers now had to have permanent relationships approved by their commanding officers. Certainly, the range of qualifying women and mothers was narrowed, curtailing the traditional rights of fleet soldiers without entirely abolishing them. There was probably reluctance to remove entirely the privileges of marine soldiers stationed in Italy.

Rulers were less open to quasi-marital relationships among members of the *cohortes urbanae* ('urban guard') and Praetorians (→ Guards). It is clear that during their term of service, burdened with heavy responsibilities, they were expected to focus wholly on their work and not, for instance, devote themselves to a family. On honourable discharge, all they received was the *ius conubii* with a non-citizen. Children born of such a union received citizenship but the woman herself did not (e.g. RMD 213; 302f.; 474f.) [8]. Diplomas issued to *equites singulares* ('mounted guards') attest to practices of this kind befitting *auxilia* in regard to the award of citizenship and *conubium* (e.g. RMD 158; 198; 453f.).

Privileges granted to men serving in the abovementioned units applied neither to legonaries nor to Roman citizens belonging to other units. Whereas for *peregrini* ('foreign') soldiers the bestowal of *conubium* represented a necessary accompaniment to their elevation to Roman citizenship, citizen soldiers, as *cives Romani*, were still subject to the restrictions applicable to this population group with regard to the status of a wife in a legally valid marriage.

Until a few years ago, a remark by Herodian (3,8,5) led most scholars to assume that in AD 197, Septimius Severus permitted soldiers to marry [9]. However, a military diploma issued in AD 206 shows this to be a dubious assumption – for it shows Septimius Severus granting the *conubium* to auxiliaries and the *civitas Romana* to decurions and centurions of the auxiliary units for the children born to them as *ordinati*, that is, as officers, and recognized by them as such (*quos ordinati susceperunt*) [2]; [11]. Accordingly, the bestowal of a privilege on a child depended on the rank of his father at the time of birth. This measure is probably to be explained in connection with Septimius Severus' army policy. His aim must have been to reward centurions and decurions of the *auxilia* and to bind them closely to his dynasty [3]. It is to be hoped that further fortuitous finds will make clear which specific measure Herodian refers to and precisely what the first Severan emperor ordered. Septimius Severus was probably responding to peoples' lived realities when he equated life partnerships between soldiers and women to concubinates. Because the concubinate possessed neither the standing nor the effect of a marriage, and because children born of a concubine were illegitimate, it was possible in substance to maintain the ban on marriage and the illegitimacy of children born to soldiers. Marriage may have been permitted at some later date. Various legal testimonies seem to point in this direction, referring as they do to married soldiers (e.g. Dig. 23,2,35; Cod. Iust. 2,11,15; 12,35,5).

B. SOLDIERS' FAMILIES

B.1. Partners' origins and status
B.2. Quasi-marital relationships
B.3. Illegitimacy of children

B.1. PARTNERS' ORIGINS AND STATUS

The ban on soldiers marrying did not mean sexual abstinence, as the discussions above amply indicate. A number of options were available to soldiers seeking a partner, besides dealing with prostitutes. Sources in many cases convey the impression that, despite the ban on marriage, soldiers were interested in permanent relationships and a family life at home outside their camps. As a rule, the surroundings of camps would contain civilian settlements of various sizes where a suitable woman could be found. A soldier also had the option of acquiring a slave to satisfy his requirements (e.g. P. Mich. VIII 476). She would then remain dependent on him as her patron, even as a freedwoman.

Women sometimes followed their men over great distances. Lollia Bodicca, for instance, went with the centurion T. Flavius Virilis, whom she must have met and fallen in love with during his service in Britain, to North Africa (CIL VIII 2877 with p. 1740 = ILS 2653). Conversely, soldiers would bring from far away women they had met on detachment, for instance M. Tertinius Gessius probably found his companion Tertinia Amabilis of Nicomedia during Caracalla's Parthian campaign (CIL XIII 1897). Permanent relationships were fostered by the tendency, which increased from the late 1st century AD onwards, to post forces at the same location for long periods. We may assume that soldiers' partners and children would generally live in settlements outside the camps, often reliant on the support of their male partner and father (e.g. P. Princ. II 57; P. Mich. VIII 471 = CPL 254). → Veterans frequently settled close to their former unit, thus creating an environment in which soldiers felt comfortable. This encouraged the formation of soldier families. Soldiers often found companions among the sisters and daughters of their comrades. Sons of soldiers growing up outside the gates of the camp would often follow in their fathers' professional footsteps, particularly given the high prestige involved. A soldier's life also offered them a regular income, opportunities for advancement, plentiful food and good medical care for decades to come.

B.2. QUASI-MARITAL RELATIONSHIPS

Despite the ban on marriage, or in order to evade it, soldiers often entered into quasi-marriages with women; in other words, they received a *dos* ('dowry') from their 'brides' as if concluding a legal marriage. The quasi-wife, however, had no claim to the restitution of the *dos* if the couple separated or her partner died, for such a recognition would suggest that the partnership was viewed as a marriage (M. Chr. 1,5–3,10; 6,18–27). Technically, relationships between soldiers and women fell under the *lex Iulia de adulteriis* ('Julian law concerning adultery') in terms of moral provisions: incest, *stuprum* ('lewdness'), *adulterium* ('adultery'), pandering and similar offences incurred *infamia* ('disgrace') and dishonourable discharge from the military (Dig. 3,2,2,3; 48,5,12 pr.-1; Cod. Iust. 2,11,15; cf. Dig. 49,16,4,7). Women of dubious reputation (*quae stupro cognitae*) could receive nothing from a soldier's testament (Dig. 29,1,41,1; 34,9,14).

B.3. ILLEGITIMACY OF CHILDREN

Some soldiers – although we do not know how many – felt an obligation to their illegitimate children. Surviving from the first half of the 2nd century AD, for instance, are questions submitted to the governor of Egypt from men who had become fathers during their military service and wanted to be legally recognized as such in order to spare their children the status of illegitimacy. The prefect's answers are clearly in line with the existing ban on marriage. A soldier could neither father legitimate children (M. Chr. 4,1–15) nor become the legal father of sons and daughters conceived during his military service (M. Chr. 3,11–22).

Because children conceived *in militia* were illegitimate and thus not legally related to their natural fathers, they were disadvantaged in relation to inheritance law. This also generated questions, and presumably no shortage of them, for in AD 119, the Prefect of Egypt sought the advice of the emperor on this question (BGU 140 = M. Chr. 373 = FIRA I² 78). Hadrian ruled that the legal situation in question was not harsh, because an act had been committed contrary to the *disciplina militaris*, and so the prarents' quasi–marital relationship was in breach of the law. Nevertheless, he decided to bestow a favor on the soldiers in the form of a more philanthropic interpretation of the law. He admitted the children concerned to the third class of the order of succession (*unde cognati*) for inheritance purposes. This placed them after children conceived within a legal marriage and heirs of the second class (*unde legitimi*). Classification as *unde cognati*, however, lays bare the whole dilemma, because technically this class of succession assumed descent in wedlock, a fact that must have escaped Hadrian's attention [1.159]; [10.81].

Several documents survive from Egypt composed during the reign of Hadrian, drafted on behalf of soldiers to certify with witnesses the birth of a child, specifying the child's name, date of birth and mother. The fathers explain that they had these documents created because of the constraints placed upon them (P. Diog. 1 = CPL 159 = AE 1937,112; BGU VII 1690 = CPL 160; P. Mich. VII 436 = CPL 161). Documenting paternity was important so that, after their honourable discharge, they could prove that children born to them were their natural offspring, as P. Diog. 1 (AD 127) explicitly states. Furthermore, after Hadrian's ruling on the inheritance rights of illegitimate children, it was vital to prove descent.

Even before Hadrian's recognition of inheritance rights for children conceived during military service, soldiers were able to designate such children as heirs because of the wide-ranging freedoms granted to them in composing a *testamentum militis*, in which they were allowed to designate non-citizens and Latins in full measure (Gai. Inst. 2,109–111; Dig. 29,1,1 pr.; 29,1,24; 29,1,40 pr.; 37,13,1,1). Unlike legitimate children, illegitimate children had to pay inheritance tax (M. Chr. 4,1–15).

☞ Camp; Civilians; Military diploma; Rear; Society and army; Veterans

BIBLIOGRAPHY
[1] O. BEHRENDS, Die Rechtsregelungen der Militärdiplome und das die Soldaten betreffende Eheverbot, in: W. ECK / H. WOLFF (eds.), Heer und Integrationspolitik. Die römischen Militärdiplome als historische Quelle (Passauer Historische Forschungen 2), 1986, 116–166 [2] W. ECK, Septimius Severus und die Soldaten. Das Problem der Soldatenehe und ein neues Auxiliardiplom, in: B. ONKEN / D. ROHDE (eds.), In omni historia curiosus. Studien zur Geschichte von der Antike bis zur Neuzeit. Festschrift für Helmuth Schneider zum 65. Geburtstag (Philippika. Marburger altertumskundliche Abhandlungen 47), 2011, 63–77 [3] W. ECK, Die kaiserliche Bürgerrechtspolitik im Spiegel der Militärdiplome. Ein Thema Hartmut Wolffs, in: Passauer Jahrbuch 55, 2013, 9–24 [4] W. ECK / A. PANGERL, Eine Konstitution für die Truppen von Dacia superior aus dem Jahr 142 mit der Sonderformel für Kinder von Auxiliaren, in: ZPE 181, 2012, 173–182 [5] W. ECK / P. WEISS, Die Sonderregelungen für Soldatenkinder seit Antoninus Pius. Ein niederpannonisches Militärdiplom vom 11. Aug. 146, in: ZPE 135, 2001, 195–208 [6] J.H. JUNG, Das Eherecht der römischen Soldaten, in: ANRW II.14, 1982, 302–346 [7] C. KREUZSALER, Zwischen Privilegierung und Diskriminierung. Die Sonderstellung der Soldaten im römischen Recht, in: B. PALME (ed.), Die Legionäre des Kaisers. Soldatenleben im römischen Ägypten (Nilus, Studien zur Kultur Ägyptens und des Vorderen Orients 18), 2011, 27–39 [8] H. LIEB, Die constitutiones für die stadtrömischen Truppen, in: W. ECK / H. WOLFF (eds.), Heer und Integrationspolitik. Die römischen Militärdiplome als historische Quelle (Passauer Historische Forschungen 2), 1986, 322–346 [9] S.E. PHANG, The Marriage of Roman Soldiers (13 B.C.–235 A.D.). Law and Familiy in the Imperial Army (Columbia Studies in Classical Tradition 24), 2001 [10] C. SCHMETTERER, Die rechtliche Stellung römischer Soldaten im Prinzipat (Philippika. Marburger altertumskundliche Abhandlungen 54), 2012, 56–82 [11] M.A. SPEIDEL, Les femmes et la bureaucratie. Quelques réflexions sur l'interdiction du mariage dans l'armée romaine, in: Cahiers du Centre Gustave Glotz 24, 2013, 205–215 [12] P. WEISS, Die vorbildliche Kaiserehe. Zwei Senatsbeschlüsse beim Tod der älteren und der jüngeren Faustina, neue Paradigmen und die Herausbildung des 'antoninischen' Prinzipats, in: Chiron 38, 2008, 1–45, especially 30–37.

GABRIELE WESCH-KLEIN

Medical corps

(For Greek medical corps, see → Specialists, A. Greek).

A. General healthcare
B. Medical personnel
C. Valetudinaria
D. Therapeutic baths

A. GENERAL HEALTHCARE
Marching camps of the Republican period already had hospital tents, which were supposed to be pitched in secluded locations (Hyg. Mun. Cast. 4). The transformation of the *exercitus Romanus* ('Roman army') into the first professional army in the ancient world brought with it the establishment of a permanent army medical corps and, as camps were developed into permanent structures, hospital buildings. Possibly following through on plans or actions initiated by his adoptive father C. Iulius Caesar, Augustus set up a medical service, which was consolidated over a considerable

length of time. Maintaining a medical service for legionaries and auxiliaries was a major accomplishment in both humanitarian and cultural terms. It must also be remembered, however, that educated and trained soldiers were valuable resources that were well worth preserving and protecting. When there was a shortage of soldiers, levies were required, and this could cause unrest in the population. Those responsible for mustering troops paid attention from the start to the physical and mental conditions of the future soldiers. Consequently, one may assume that men were generally in good health when they first enlisted into the armed forces. Just as important as medical care were preventative measures taken to prevent infection, such as providing clean water and food and regular cleaning of camps and building interiors. The military author Vegetius explicitly advises that camps be built in locations with a healthy climate, to ensure a supply of clean water and to protect soldiers against wet, frost and blazing sunshine, while at the same time toughening their resilience by means of daily → training (Mil. 3,2). The baths found at all legionary camps and even small auxiliary forts during the Imperial period, with their typical sequence of cold and hot pools, both supported physical hygiene and also – together with regular open-air training and exercise – contributed to the toughening process. Finally, a nutritious diet played an important role in soldiers' good physical condition. In all probability, civilian populations living near the camps were allowed access to the military baths at certain times. Given that soldiers were in constant contact with these people and often lived with partners and children outside the camp gates, this should be understood not only as a contribution to general cleanliness, but also as a means of protecting soldiers against illness.

The commander's duties included inspecting the sick men of his unit (Dig. 49,16,12,2; Veg. Mil. 3,2). On the one hand, this was intended to prevent the feigning of illness (Dig. 49,16,6,5), and on the other, it reflected a spirit of care for soldiers. According to Vegetius, officers and senior commanders were responsible for the care and provisioning of sick soldiers (Mil. 3,2). For commanders to concern themselves with the sick and wounded was a tradition dating back to the Republic (Liv. 33,36,7). Mark Antony, for example, would visit the wounded after battles to bolster their morale (Plut. *Antonius* 43,1). It was accordingly seen as one of the virtuous acts of a 'good ruler' to minister to sick or wounded soldiers, and visits to the infirmary were part of this (Vell. Pat. 2,114,1f. (Tiberius); Tac. Ann. 1,71,3 (Germanicus); Plin. Pan. 13,3 (Trajan); SHA Hadr. 10,6; Alex. 47,2).

Responsibility for the health of soldiers lay with unit physicians and their assistants. They offered help with battle wounds, accidents and ailments both chronic and acute. Daily reports gave the numbers of those sick (e.g. O. BuNjem 2f.; 5–15). One such report of the *cohors I Tungrorum* records 31 of a total of 296 men unfit for action, which constitutes a sickness rate in excess of 10% (Tab. Vindol. II 154 ll. 22–25). Those affected were classified as *aegri* ('sick'), *volnerati* (= *vulnerati*, 'wounded') and *lippientes* ('inflamed in the eyes'). Eye infections were common in the Roman world and spread rapidly through camps. Exposure to bright sunlight or strong winds could also cause eye problems. Soldiers stationed at the fort of Künzing on the Rhaetian *limes* ('boundary') in the Imperial period suffered from trichuriasis (whipworm infection) [13]. Soldiers sometimes fell ill from overexertion, from unaccustomed or spoiled food (App. Ib. 6,9,54; probably fish poisoning: P. Mich. VIII 477f.) or from deficiencies. The garrison of a fort in Friesland probably fell victim to scurvy, and their Frisian allies recommended a remedy from Britain that was also said to cure throat infections and snakebite (Plin. HN 25,6,20f.; [5]; [4]; [9]). Like anyone else, soldiers fell prey to infectious diseases and contributed to their spread, as exemplified in the major epidemic during the reign of Marcus Aurelius (e.g. SHA Aur. 13,3–6; 17,2; 21,6; Ver. 8,1–4; Amm. Marc. 31,6,24).

Treatment and care were free of charge to soldiers, or at least no evidence to the contrary survives. Men who were no longer fit to serve were granted the *missio causaria*, premature honourable discharge for urgent reasons – like the men of the *legio II adiutrix* in AD 70: *causari, qui militaverunt in leg(ione) II adiutrice pia fidele qui bello inutiles facti ante emerita stipendia exauctoritati sunt et dimissi honesta missione* ('causari [sc. soldiers] who served in the *legio II adiutrix pia fidelis* who were made unfit for battle before reaching honourable discharge and were released with honour'; CIL XVI 10; see also Dig. 3,2,2,2; 49,16,13,3). According to Dig. 29,1,4, deafness and muteness were among the conditions qualifying for premature discharge. A ruling given by Gordian III shows that it was possible for a man to return to military service once he had recovered, subject to thorough assessment (Cod. Iust. 12,35,6).

Sick soldiers and officers did not always entrust themselves to the medical arts alone, as offerings to deities amply attest. Even medics sought the blessing of deities who would be able of restore health. Aid was sought from Aesculapius, Hygieia and Apollo in particular. The *valetudinaria* ('infirmaries') probably had small sanctuaries, although no archaeological evidence of these has yet been found [3].

B. Medical personnel

During the Republican period, soldiers helped their wounded comrades as best they could. In many cases there were likely men skilled in healing among the combatants. Generals also brought with them personal physicians, who must have helped soldiers as circumstances permitted. The sick and wounded were brought to civilian settlements to be cared for (Caes. B Civ. 3,75,1; Bell. Alex. 44,4; Bell. Afr. 21,2; Frontin. Str. 2,11,2). Even after the establishment of the medical corps, the help given by fellow soldiers was still important, for there would never be enough specialist personnel available to provide immediate medical care to all the wounded after a major engagement. Following the decisive battle between Otho and Vitellius at Bedriacum (AD 69), the soldiers cared for their comrades in tents (Tac. Hist. 2,45,3). The wounded were treated on the edges of the battle. Those who were not able to leave the field by themselves were carried. Once they had received first aid, soldiers were taken to civilian settlements or the nearest field hospital. If the enemy attacked during a withdrawal, the wounded were sent ahead and efforts were made to secure their transport (Caes. B Civ. 3,75; Tac. Ann. 1,64,4).

The medical personnel of the *exercitus Romanus* ('Roman army') consisted of physicians (*medici*), attendants (*capsarii*, from *capsa*, the unit's cylindrical document chest) and orderlies (*qui aegris praesto sunt*). All belonged to the *immunes* (those exempted from other duties) (Dig. 50,6,7). In North Africa, records reveal, there were *marsi*, men trained in the treatment of snakebites and scorpion stings (CIL VIII 2564 = 18052 = AE 1978, 889 = ILS 470; CIL VIII 2618 = 18096; AE 1992, 1872 = 1917/18, 29; [19]). Most military physicians had probably been general physicians before – only in the case of one of the Praetorian cohorts of the city of Rome do inscriptions record two specialists: one *medicus chirurgus* ('surgical physician') (AE 1945, 62) and one *medicus clinicus* ('sick–bed physician') (CIL VI 2532 = ILS 2093). Galen mentions an eye doctor of the *classis Britannica* ('Britannic fleet') (XII 786 Kühn). Like others, military physicians were sometimes moved to different locations. M. Ulpius Telesphorus, for instance, was first stationed with the *ala Indiana Gallorum* at Echzell in Germania superior as *medicus alae* ('physician of the troops'), before moving to the province of Mauretania Tingitana to work with the *ala III Asturum*. He later worked as a civilian physician (CIL XI 3007 = ILS 2542).

A hierarchy existed among unit medics. Alongside the *miles* ('soldier') *medicus*, in the fleets at least, we know of physicians who called themselves *duplicarii* ('double pay') (CIL VI 3910 = 32767; 32769 = ILS 9222; X 3441–44; 3599; XI 29; 6944; AE 1984, 337; 1995, 1350). Higher pay undoubtedly meant greater responsibility – perhaps these *duplicarii* were the senior naval physicians. As for the legions and auxiliary forces, we know of *medici ordinarii*, physicians probably of the rank of centurion (CIL III 4279; 5959; 6532; VII 690 = RIB 1618; CIL VIII 18314 = ILS 2432; CIL XIII, 11979 = ILS 9182; [18]; [19]). They may conceivably have functioned as their unit's senior physicians. Among the military medics were also *salariarii* ('salaried'), civilians employed for a fixed term who negotiated their salary and working conditions. Unlike their colleagues on the military career path, they were exempt from various restrictions, including the ban on matrimony. Like regular soldiers, they were not required to perform *munera civilia* ('civil duties') while working for the *exercitus Romanus* (Cod. Iust. 10,53,1).

How many physicians were assigned to a unit remains unclear because of a lack of source material. Auxiliary units of about 500 men probably had just one medic. One may therefore assume approximately one physician for every 500 soldiers. Given that orderlies were able to treat some of the sick and wounded themselves, such a ratio of physicians to potential patients seems plausible. One *medicus* served 250 men of the *vigiles* ('watchmen'). This more favourable ratio is probably explained by the fact that the *vigiles* were spread throughout the city of Rome, so that physicians had to travel longer distances. Medics in the Praetorian fleets were assigned to individual triremes, but they may have been required to care for crews of other vessels as well.

Since there are records of *discentes capsarii* ('student attendants'), it is likely that units trained the requisite attendants themselves. This was probably also the case for other medical personnel (e.g. orderlies), and suitable men may perhaps have been trained as physicians. Some medics were probably called into service as needed, and so were able to fulfil other roles within the unit (assignment to the *valetudinarium*: PSI XIII 1307 = C. P. Lat. 108 = RMR 51 l. 20; Tab. Vindol. II 155 l. 6).

Like the adjutant of the infirmary (*optio valetudinarii*), physicians and orderlies were *immunes*, exempt from heavy physical labour in the course of their service (Dig. 50,6,7). A unit's entire medical corps was answerable to the *praefectus castrorum* ('camp commander'): *praeterea aegri contubernales, et medici a quibus curabantur, expensae etiam ad eius industriam pertinebant* ('his remit also included sick comrades, the physicians treating them and related expenses'; Veg. Mil. 2,10). This proves that physicians were counted as artisans. In Lambaesis during the Severan period, the *valetudinarium* personnel of the *legio III Augusta* formed a college (CIL VIII 2553 = 18047 = ILS 2438). It had a *librarius* ('secretary') in charge of accounting for the field hospital, and *pecuarii* ('cattle men') who may have been assigned to the field hospital to take care of the pack and draught animals required for transporting the sick. Their main work certainly involved caring for the animals that belonged to the unit, particularly sick and injured beasts of burden and mounts. The Roman army also had its own *medici veterinarii* (CIL III 11215; VI 37194 = ILS 9071 = AE 1910, 27; Tab. Vindol. I 81; II 310 = AE 1990, 670a = 1991, 1163; horse specialist: CIG 5117 = IGRR I 1373 = SB V 8541).

C. VALETUDINARIA

The legionary camp of Haltern (Germania inferior), located on the River Lippe in connection with the occupation of Germanic territories on the right bank of the Rhine between 7/5 BC and AD 9, is the earliest camp known to have been equipped with a field hospital [9]. Building such a facility here in particular made sense given the prevailing lack of infrastructure, the sometimes hostile climate and the permanent risk of bloody conflict with an invading army. Thanks to medical instruments that have discovered, it has been possible to prove beyond doubt the existence of *valetudinaria* ('infirmaries'), although this does not prove that every legionary camp of the Imperial period had one. The *valetudinarium* was not a firm fixture inside the legionary camp. Often, field hospitals have been found in the *praetentura* (the front area), sometimes also in the *retentura* (the rear area) or in the middle zone [12]; [5]. Archaeological proof of field hospitals is trickier for auxiliary forts, but it may be assumed that at least the larger forts had such facilities [5]; [19]. Smaller *castella* ('forts') did not have dedicated *valetudinaria* – a room functioning as an infirmary would suffice. Garrisons at smaller sites undoubtedly received medical help from staff at the nearest larger fort. No field hospitals have yet been identified serving the fleets or the *vigiles* ('watchmen') of the city of Rome. Sick *vigiles* were probably cared for in their *stationes* ('posts') or with their relatives, who in most cases lived nearby. An *optio convalescentium* ('adjutant of convalescents') supervised their care (CIL VI 1057; 1058 = 31234 = ILS 2157).

The *valetudinaria* exhibit a typical ground plan. A complex of four wings was grouped around a rectangular inner courtyard. Each wing had a long central corridor, to the sides of which lay the wards, which were sometimes heated. The corridor afforded good ventilation and light. Short cross-passageways were inserted after every second or third ward. It is uncertain whether these were also meant to provide air and light, or whether they offered specially protected entrances to the wards [12]; [5]; [9]. Each ward could hold several patients. Near the entrance area, there would be one or two larger rooms that in all likelihood served as treatment or operating rooms. Archaeologists have identified latrines, bathhouses and cookhouses at some field hospitals [12]; [5].

The level of expertise among military physicians was probably high. Galen praises a remedy for headache learned from the military physician Antigonous (XII 557, 580, 773 Kühn) and the eye ointment of the *ocularius* ('eye expert') of the Britannic fleet, Axius [15]. He also mentions anatomical studies by military physicians (XIII 604 Kühn). Medical treatises, such as that by the medic Celsus, writing in the reign of Tiberius, attest to the high standards in the treatment of wounds (*de medicina* 5,26,21–24; 7,5,1–5; 7,33). Wine deliveries are recorded for the *valetudinarium* at the camp of Aquincum (e.g. AE 1933, 120; 1995, 1259d–e; 1996, 1260f.; [14]). Wine was put to all kinds of uses as medicine (e.g. as an analgesic and antiseptic). Wine mixed with horehounds, a tried and tested remedy for bronchial ailments, was prescribed at the Scottish legionary camp of Carpow ([20]; Diosc. mat. med. 5,58). Respiratory infections and diarrhea were treated with Aminean wine at the legionary camp of Caerleon in Britannia (Wales) [21]. Wine also formed the basis for the preparation of medicines. Where possible, the herbs required were cultivated locally. The field hospital of the legionary camp at Novaesium (Neuss) in Germania inferior had its own herb garden [7]; [8]. At the Augustan legionary camp of Haltern, an apothecary's chest was found bearing the inscription *ex radice Britan(n)ica* ('from Britannic root'), meaning that a remedy from Britannia was being used, probably the same one Frisians recommended for the treatment of a sick Roman soldier [4].

D. THERAPEUTIC BATHS

Therapeutic baths were built for army personnel in provinces where large contingents were stationed. Inscriptions and seal stamps indicate that, as from the 1st century AD, troops stationed in a province would produce and supply building materials and do the building work for such military baths.

Soldiers stationed in the province of Germania inferior sought cures at Aquae Granni (Aachen). Their colleagues in Germania superior sought cures at Aquae Mattiacorum (Wiesbaden) and Aquae (Baden-Baden). Rhaetian soldiers sought cures in the thermal spa now known as Bad Gögging, where construction began with the arrival of the *legio III Italica* at Castra Regina (Regensburg) [10]. Soldiers garrisoned in Britannia could go to the therapeutic baths at Aquae Sulis (Bath). In the Pannonian provinces, the hot springs at Aquae Iasae (Varaždinske Toplice, Pannonia superior [11]) and Aquincum (Budapest, Pannonia inferior) promised recovery. Military baths were open to all serving in the army regardless of troop type or rank. We know nothing about the rules governing a therapeutic stay and its duration, or about how bathing cures proceeded and how successful they were.

→ Camp; Military service

BIBLIOGRAPHY

[1] R.W. DAVIES, The Medici of the Roman Armed Forces, in: Epigraphische Studien, vol. 8, edited by Landschaftsverband Rheinland, Rheinisches Landesmuseum Bonn, 1969, 83–99 [2] R.W. DAVIES, Some More Military Medici, in: Epigraphische Studien, vol. 9, edited by Landschaftsverband Rheinland, Rheinisches Landesmuseum Bonn, 1970, 1–11 [3] P. DYCZEK, A sacellum Aesculapii in the valetudinarium at Novae, in: N. GUDEA (ed.), Roman Frontier Studies. Proceedings of the XVIIth International Congress of Roman Frontier Studies, 1999, 495–500 [4] A.P. FITZPATRICK, Ex radice Britannica, in: Britannia 22, 1991, 143–146 [5] A. JOHNSON, Römische Kastelle des 1. und 2. Jahrhunderts n.Chr. in Britannien und in den germanischen Provinzen des Römerreichs, trans. by G. Schulte-Holtey; ed. by D. Baatz, in: Kulturgeschichte der Antiken Welt 37, 1987, 179–188 [6] T. KISSEL, Untersuchungen zur Logistik des römischen Heeres in den Provinzen des griechischen Ostens (27 v.Chr.–235 n.Chr.), in: Pharos 6, 1995, 238–250 [7] K.-H. KNÖRZER, Römerzeitliche Heilkräuter aus Novaesium (Neuß/Rh.), in: Sudhoffs Archiv für Geschichte der Medizin und Naturwissenschaft 47, 1963, 311–316 (continuation: [8]) [8] K.-H. KNÖRZER, Römerzeitliche Heilkräuter aus Novaesium (Neuß/Rh.), in: Sudhoffs Archiv für Geschichte der Medizin und Naturwissenschaft 49, 1965, 416–422 [9] E. KÜNZL, Die medizinische Versorgung der römischen Armee zur Zeit des Kaisers Augustus und die Reaktion der Römer auf die Situation bei den Kelten und Germanen, in: B. TRIER (ed.), Die römische Okkupation nördlich der Alpen zur Zeit des Augustus. Kolloquium Bergkamen 1989 (Bodenaltertümer Westfalens 26), 1991, 185–202 [10] H.U. NUBER, Ausgrabungen in Bad Gögging. Römisches Staatsheilbad und frühmittelalterliche Kirchen, 1980 [11] H. VON PETRIKOVITS, Aquae Iasae, in: ArhVest 19, 1968, 89–93 (reprinted in: Beiträge zur römischen Geschichte und Archäologie, vol. 1: 1931–1974 (BJb, Beihefte 36), 1976, 479–483) [12] H. VON PETRIKOVITS, Die Innenbauten römischer Legionslager während der Prinzipatszeit (Abhandlungen der Rheinisch-westfälischen Akademie der Wissenschaften 56), 1975, 98–102 (116–117, 147) [13] W. SPECHT, Eine interessante Erdprobe aus einer Abortgrube im Römerkastell Künzing, in: Saalburg Jahrbuch 21, 1963–1964, 90–94 [14] G. ULBERT, Römische Holzfässer aus Regensburg. Mit einem tierkundlichen Beitrag von J. Boessneck, in: Bayerische Vorgeschichtsblätter 24, 1959, 6–29 [15] M. WELLMANN, Axius [2], in: RE 2/2, 1896, 2633 [16] G. WESCH-KLEIN, Soziale Aspekte des römischen Heerwesens in der Kaiserzeit (HABES 28), 1998, 71–87 [17] G. WESCH-KLEIN, Gesundheit spendende Gottheiten des römischen Heeres, in: C. WOLFF / Y. LE BOHEC (eds.), L'armée romaine et la religion sous le Haut-Empire romain. Actes du quatrième congrès de Lyon, 26–28 octobre 2006, 2009, 99–120 [18] J.C. WILMANNS, Der Arzt in der römischen Armee der frühen und hohen Kaiserzeit, in: P.J. VAN DER EIJK et al. (eds.), Ancient Medicine in Its Socio-cultural Context. Papers Read at the Congress at Leiden University, 13–15 April 1992 (Clio Medica 27), vol. 1, 1995, 171–187 [19] J.C. WILMANNS, Der Sanitätsdienst im römischen Reich, 1995 [20] R.P. WRIGHT, Roman Britain in 1962. II: Inscriptions, in: JRS 53, 1963, 160–167 (no. 51) [21] R.P. WRIGHT, Roman Britain 1965. II: Inscriptions, in: JRS 56, 1966, 217–225 (no. 51).

GABRIELE WESCH-KLEIN

Mercenaries

A. Definition and concept
B. Greece up to the Peloponnesian War
C. From the Peloponnesian War to Alexander
D. Hellenistic period
E. Rome

A. DEFINITION AND CONCEPT

Mercenaries wage war for pay on behalf of foreign powers as temporary or permanent professional soldiers, with no direct political or military interest. They are distinguished not only from the militia soldiers who long dominated the military in the ancient world, but also from professional soldiers who fought for their own community, and from confederates who fought alongside foreign states on the basis of treaties of alliance. There is no term in Greek or Latin that accurately reflects this definition and the concepts underlying it. Most of the terms used describe one aspect of the phenomenon, and they are often ambiguous. *Epikouros*, 'helper', could be used in Greek classical historiography in the sense of a soldier working for pay, but terms such as *misthophoros*, 'one serving for pay', and *xenos*, 'foreigner', were used more frequently. *Misthotos*, 'hireling', was also sometimes used in this sense. In the Hellenistic period, the simple *stratiotes*, 'soldier', could also mean 'mercenary'. The commonest Latin term was *mercenarius*, 'one hired for pay', from which the modern English word derives. Motives for serving as a mercenary were many and varied, but generally economic (in general on this subject [4]; [5]; [34]; [35]; [20]; [23]; [12]; [17]).

B. GREECE UP TO THE PELOPONNESIAN WAR

Mercenaries were occasionally encountered in the Archaic period, hired by foreign powers or local potentates. According to Hdt. 2,152 (see also Pl. Lach. 187b; cf. Hdt. 2,163; 3,4; 11; [11.19f.]), Egyptian pharaohs such as Psammetichus engaged Ionian or Carian hoplites, as did Croesus of Lydia (Hdt. 1,77). Antimenides, brother of the poet Alcaeus, may have served in Babylon (Alc. 350 Lobel/Page, but cf. [10]). Tyrants such as Peisistratus of Athens (Hdt. 1,61; 1,64), Polycrates of Samos (Hdt. 3,45; 3,54) and Gelon of Syracuse (Diod. Sic. 11,72,3; see in general [23.7ff.]) used mercenaries to bolster their illegitimate authority, although the earlier view of research that mercenaries were an essential structural feature of early tyranny is overstated ([6.41ff.]; see also [7.55f.]). There is no evidence for the existence of mercenaries in Greece in the late 6th and 5th centuries BC.

C. FROM THE PELOPONNESIAN WAR TO ALEXANDER

C.1. Peloponnesian War
C.2. Growth of the mercenary industry after the Peloponnesian War

C.1. PELOPONNESIAN WAR

Demand for foreign troops began to grow again during the Peloponnesian War (→ Wars of note, H.). Although this war was mainly fought with militiamen, its long duration, wide geographical range and variety of theatres – together with a lack of home-grown soldiers – compelled several powers over time to employ mercenaries. Several remarks by Thucydides show that the belligerents were using mercenaries (e.g. 3,73; 3,85; 4,129,2; 5,4,6; 7,27-30). Many of these were specialists in a particular kind of weapon, such as *peltastai*, who fought in open formation with a *pelte* (a light wood or wicker shield), javelin, thrusting spear and sword, and who for the most part came from Thrace (Thuc. 7,27; [4]). Other specialist soldiers were archers who came from Crete (Thuc. 6,43). Thuc. 1,35 (cf. 1,121; 1,143) and Xen. Hell. 1,5,4ff. make clear that the fleets of Greek *poleis* needed not only citizen oarsmen (who probably remained in the majority), but also considerable contingents of foreign oarsmen, whose primary motivation was pay.

C.2. GROWTH OF THE MERCENARY INDUSTRY AFTER THE PELOPONNESIAN WAR

The mercenary industry underwent a striking expansion after the Peloponnesian War (431–404 BC). The most conspicuous indication of this was the rebellion of Cyrus the Younger, who sought to overthrow the Persian king, his own brother Artaxerxes, with the support of an army of Greek mercenaries (401–400 BC). Xenophon's report of this campaign, the *Anabasis*, offers a unique insight into the inner life of a mercenary army. It consisted mainly of hoplites recruited under false pretence by local agents working for Cyrus. In all, about 12,000 hoplites and 2,000 peltasts gathered ([19.298], cf. in general [22] and Burckhardt in [29]). They came from all over Greece, but Arcadians, Athenians and Spartans seem to have been particularly numerous (cf. also Hdt. 1,77,4) [28.303–306]. The chief interest for most participants was pecuniary, but some were motivated by difficulties in their home country, exile or a thirst for adventure. Although Cyrus failed, the campaign of the 'Ten Thousand' showed that the heavily armed hoplites were capable of instilling terror, as they were generally superior in fighting power to other infantrymen of the period. After this, the Persian king, his satraps and lesser monarchs began recruiting more and more hoplites to reinforce their armies. At the Battle of the Granicus (334 BC), for instance, up to 20,000 Greek mercenaries reportedly fought in service of the Persian king or his satraps (Arr. An. 1,14,4; see also 12,8; cf. also Diod. Sic. 16,41ff. on Artaxerxes II; cf. in general [30]).

The Greek *poleis* continued to use mercenaries after the Peloponnesian War. At Athens, they provided a complement to the regular militia units. They were used on overseas campaigns, on smaller operations as guards (e.g. at the fortresses of Attica [18]) and as oarsmen. Specialist units such as the *peltastai* were also maintained. In an outcome that defied expectations, a mercenary peltast unit in conjunction with regular units commanded by Iphicrates took advantage of favourable terrain to defeat a Spartan army at Lechaeum near Corinth in 390 BC (Xen. Hell. 4,5,9–17). Even so, Athens continued to rely mainly on citizen-soldiers in their most significant conflicts and in all major battles [7.76–153]. So too did the Spartans and the other Greek *poleis*. It is true that Sparta recruited the remnants of Cyrus' army returning to western Asia Minor in 400 BC to use in war against the Persian king. Still, militia units bore the brunt of battle in Sparta's wars. The only powers to rely primarily on mercenaries were tyrants such as Dionysius of Syracuse and Iason of Pherae, as they sought to consolidate power they had won by irregular means (in general Aristot. pol. 1306b20ff.). It should be noted that genuine *condottiero* figures also emerged in the 4th century BC – professional generals who, sometimes independently of *polis* structures, raised armies to fight for the highest bidder (one example: [6.197–199], others e.g. Polyaen. Str. 2,1,27; Plut. *Agesilaus* 36). These, however, remained the exception that proved the rule [25.34ff., 59ff.].

The history of the Third Sacred War (356–346 BC), on the other hand, shows that polities did on occasion fight wars with armies consisting almost entirely of mercenaries – as in this particularly flagrant case the Phocians did, after they had robbed the treasury of Delphi (sources: [23.133–142]; see also [5.186–195]). The appearance of mercenaries and the specialization of troop types burdened army leadership with greater responsibility, as armies that had been recruited in various ways and were driven by different motivations had to be guided, equipped, paid, and maintained in unity. This led to increase in the professionalization of the officer class, just as with the ordinary soldier. Nevertheless, Aristotle (Eth. Nic. 1116a16–b23) still considered the citizen a more suitable soldier for the *polis* than the mercenary, whose valour could not match that of a committed militiaman. In general, authors were sceptical of mercenaries. Isocrates (8,44f.), for example, calls them homeless and criminal. Aeneas Tacticus (12,1–5 etc.) regards them as a potential danger to every *polis*, even the *polis* for which they fight. Demosthenes (4,24) accuses them of faithlessness and lack of commitment. Only Xenophon (Hell. 6,1,5f.) breaks this image, in his depiction of the multilayered speech of Iason of Pherae. In it, Iason declares that, instead of citizen-soldiers, he prefers mercenaries, who are physically strong men with good military training and experience, whom he drills so that they meet his exact needs, with the result that his army is superior to all others. On the whole, remarks by authors of the period amount to ideologically biased reactions to the increased presence of mercenaries in the Aegean world. They generally insinuate that the heavy use of mercenary forces is a disruptive factor that is difficult to reconcile with traditional *polis* structures.

The army of Alexander the Great (→ Generals of note, B.) that invaded Persia included relatively few mercenaries (Diod. Sic. 17,17,3), its main body comprising half of the Macedonian levy. Nevertheless, Alexander's men were in practice all professional soldiers, making their livelihood from battle.

D. HELLENISTIC PERIOD

D.1. Ptolemies and Seleucids
D.2. Relationship between mercenaries and the employer

Mercenaries comprised a significant component of the armed forces of the Diadochi and the subsequent Hellenistic monarchies (in general and discussing many aspects [29]). However, the state of the sources hampers precise quantitative and qualitative assessments of the phenomenon, for authors who wrote of mercenaries from outside the Greco-Roman cultural sphere exhibit a double prejudice: against barbarians and against mercenaries [3.38ff.]. To make matters worse, it is sometimes difficult to distinguish domestic recruits from mercenaries in the Hellenistic armies. What is clear is that the power of Hellenistic kings and potentates depended on professional soldiers, but they cannot all be called mercenaries. Military success was an important source of legitimacy for rulers, who accordingly relied on an effective standing army. After the death of Alexander, they first looked for their recruits chiefly among Macedonians and Greeks, whom they were more disposed to trust than their own local populations, and who were trained in the usual fighting techniques of heavy infantry units. This was most straightforward for the Antigonids, who ruled Macedonia and thus found themselves in control of one of the main sources of mercenaries. Yet their armies also included mercenaries, who were mostly hired from neighbouring regions, although Gauls and Cretans were sometimes employed (e.g. the army of Perseus before the Third Macedonian War: Liv. 42,51,6–11; [31.104–113]).

D.1. PTOLEMIES AND SELEUCIDS

At first, the Ptolemies relied primarily on Greek and Macedonian soldiers, who were taken from Alexander's army or migrated from their homelands. They provided the heavy infantry, whereas hired mercenaries typically fought as light infantry (for the following [11.116–195]). Soldiers were paid either in cash or in land, the latter mainly applying to the cavalry. Mercenaries later seem to have served in garrisons abroad with notable frequency (Pol. 5,63,11). At Rhaphia, 8,000 Greek mercenaries fought alongside the phalanx that was recruited locally (Pol. 5,65,3). Towards the end of the 3rd century BC, there was an increasing tendency to recruit Egyptians and Greeks who resided in Egypt, and the papyri often call these soldiers *misthophoroi*. The dividing line between regular troops and mercenaries blurs here. One particular challenge for the Ptolemaic Dynasty was to equip a fleet, which by the 3rd century was the most efficient instrument for enforcing its foreign policy. According to [11.71f., 76], the requisite oarsmen were recruited from the lowest social classes of Egypt, but the costs of the navy nevertheless represented the largest item of Ptolemaic military expenditure.

The Seleucid army also relied in part on mercenaries. According to [2.51], 12,500 mercenaries fought at the Battle of Rhaphia, and 10,700 fought at Magnesia, mainly Greeks, Cretans, Cilicians and Carmanians. The regular Seleucid phalanx consisted mainly of Greek and Macedonian *klerouchoi* (those who received land allotments), who – as in the other Hellenistic kingdoms – had been systematically settled in conquered territory ([12.142ff.]; [2.22ff., 56f.]). Even so, it was necessary to augment them with mercenaries recruited abroad.

D.2. RELATIONSHIP BETWEEN MERCENARIES AND THE EMPLOYER

The contract concluded between the Attalid Eumenes I and his mercenaries after a revolt (OGIS 266) in the 3rd century BC exemplifies the problems mercenaries and their employers faced in their mutual relationship. Eumenes made numerous guarantees to his mercenaries who were stationed at two of his garrisons. These guarantees included the payment of grain and wheat at an agreed price, the settlement of full pay for time served even after the completion of service, the waiving of the intercalary month, the right to take property without taxation on leaving service, and tax exemption for a particular year. He also promised to provide for the dependants of mercenaries, who of course ran the risk of death. For their part, mercenaries guaranteed their loyalty to Eumenes and his successors, and they pledged not to conspire against him and to report any conspiracies. There was also a ban against mercenaries contacting outsiders on their own initiative. Conquests and spoils due to Eumenes were to be handed over to him, and in general the mercenaries promised to serve him with zeal. Each side assured the other of their goodwill and adherence to the promises made.

Obviously, the loyalty of recruited soldiers was not to be taken for granted. For the employer, attempts by potential adversaries to woo mercenaries away were a problem. → Mutinies were also not unusual. The king could never be sure of the loyalty of his troops. Discipline always had to be enforced, and military competence was an urgent necessity for kings and their entourages. Despite these concerns, monarchs were by no means immune to the temptation to alter conditions of remuneration, deployment and service time. Moreover, financial straits often forced their hands, as financing a standing army was a heavy burden for the royal treasury. Even so, if all promises were kept, lasting ties between mercenaries and their employers could develop. The specific conditions under which someone served as a mercenary depended on the negotiating position of each party. According to [13], → pay often corresponded to the wage levels for physical labour in civilian life. As in the Classical period (on which [14], on the modalities also [3.99ff.]), pay seems normally to have been disbursed in cash. The opportunity to plunder occupied territories and defeated enemies was often an attractive motivation for mercenaries, tantamount to a component of their pay package.

In general, there was high demand in the Hellenistic world for men who were fit to fight, and the presence of the military was ubiquitous. This much is emphasized by the stereotype of the *miles gloriosus* ('vainglorious soldier'), who takes the leading role – albeit in a thoroughly peaceful context – as a mercenary returned home in a Greek-inspired drama by Plautus. The mercenary recruiter also seems to have been a familiar figure (Pol. 33,18,12; Diod. Sic. 18,61,4f.). Cape Taenarum on the southern tip of the Peloponnese functioned as a recruitment centre where mercenaries could find work, at least in the second half of the 4th century. Over time, however, fewer and fewer mercenaries in the Hellenistic kingdoms came from Greece. The Ptolemies were not alone in turning more to local populations for mercenaries, although even these populations would have been trained in Macedonian fighting techniques. The phalanx armed with the *sarissa* remained the monarch's most valuable military asset until the end of the Hellenistic period. According to [11], though, it was the Greek and Macedonian mercenaries in the Ptolemaic kingdom who were the drivers of Hellenization in the territories conquered by Alexander.

E. ROME

Unlike Carthage (see [1.190ff.; 222], which, however, rightly moderates the earlier view that Carthage was almost entirely dependent on mercenaries), the Roman Republic used few mercenaries until its late period, employing them mainly as specialists, for example slingers from the Balearic Islands or archers from Crete (e.g. Plut. *Gracchus* 16,3f.). According to Liv. 24,49,7f., however, the Romans did poach Celtiberian mercenaries (*mercenarii*) from the Carthaginians in the Iberian theatre during the Second Punic War (218–201 BC) (though at 25,33,1 Livy calls them *auxilia*, cf. Pol. 10,6,1; on the recruitment of Celtiberian mercenaries see [8.662–667]). The expansion of theatres of war and the proliferation of conflicts compelled some generals to recruit local units and specialist auxiliaries. For example, Caesar in Gaul had available Numidians, probably light infantry, Cretans, presumably archers (*sagittarii*), and Baliares, presumably slingers (*funditores*) (Caes. B Gall. 2,7,1). Again, however, it is difficult to distinguish clearly between auxiliaries and mercenaries, although the terms *auxilia* and *socii* are not to be taken literally, for they either belonged to the regular forces or were not directly employed by Rome. The same applied in the Imperial period, especially after Augustus had systematically integrated the *auxilia* into the army. The status of mercenaries was never high, if there was any status at all. Consequently, the phenomenon has yet to be studied in its own right (outdated [15]). Aelius Aristides praises Rome for not trusting mercenaries (*xenois*) (Aristid. 26,74). Indications that more mercenaries were being recruited start to appear in greater numbers in the 3rd century AD [32]. Rome had to turn increasingly to soldiers from outside the empire in Late Antiquity, as it sought to address growing resistance to levies and the strain put on its demographic base by the empire's military needs.

☞ **Society and army**

BIBLIOGRAPHY

[1] W. AMELING, Karthago, 1993 [2] B. BAR-KOCHBA, The Seleucid Army, 1976 [3] L. BARAY, Celtes, Galates et Gaulois, mercenaires de l'Antiquité. Représentation, recrutement, organisation, 2017 [4] J.G.P. BEST, Thracian Peltasts and Their Influence on Greek Warfare, 1969 [5] M. BETTALLI, I mercenari nel mondo greco, vol. 1: Dalle origini alla fine del V sec. a. C., 1995 [6] M. BETTALLI, Mercenari. Il mestiere delle armi nel mondo greco antico, 2013 [7] L. BURCKHARDT, Bürger und Soldaten. Aspekte der politischen und militärischen Rolle athenischer Bürger im Kriegswesen des 4. Jahrhunderts v.Chr., 1996 [8] F. CADIOU, Hibera in terra miles, 2008 [9] P. DUCREY, Armée et pouvoir d'Agamemnon et Alexandre, in: A. CHANIOTIS / P. DUCREY (eds.), Army and Power in the Ancient World, 2002, 51–60 [10] L. FANTALKIN / E. LYTLE, Alcaeus and Antimenidas. Reassessing the Evidence for Greek Mercenaries in the Neo-Babylonian Army, in: Klio 98, 2016, 90–117 [11] C. FISCHER-BOVET, Army and Society in Ptolemaic Egypt, 2014 [12] G.T. GRIFFITH, The Mercenaries of the Hellenistic World, 1935 (reprint 1968 and 2014) [13] J.A. KRASILNIKOFF, Aegean Mercenaries in the Fourth to Second Centuries BC. A Study in Payment, Plunder and Logistics of the Ancient Greek Armies, in: CeM 43, 1992, 23–36 [14] J.A. KRASILNIKOFF, The Regular Payment of Aegean Mercenaries in the Classical Period, in: CeM 44, 1993, 77–95 [15] F. LAMMERT, Mercenarii, in: RE 15,1, 1931, 972–974 [16] F. LAMMERT, Μισθοφόροι, in: RE 15,2, 1932, 2074–2078 [17] M. LAUNEY, Recherches sur les armées hellénistiques, 2 vols., 1949–1950 [18] H. LAUTER, Attische Festungen, 1989 [19] J.W.I. LEE, A Greek Army on the March. Soldiers and Survival in Xenophon's Anabasis, 2007 [20] C. MANN, Militär und Kriegführung in der Antike, 2013 [21] L. MARINOVIC, Le mercenariat grec au IVe siècle avant notre ère et la crise de la polis, 1988 (translated from Russian by J. and Y. Garlan) [22] G.B. NUSSBAUM, The Ten Thousand. A Study in Social Organization and Action in Xenophon's Anabasis, 1967 [23] H.W. PARKE, Greek Mercenary Soldiers, 1933 (reprint 1970) [24] W.K. PRITCHETT, The Greek State at War, 5 vols., 1971–1991 [25] W.K. PRITCHETT, The Greek State at War, vol. 2, 1974 [26] L. RAWLINGS, The Ancient Greeks at War, 2007 [27] J. ROP, Greek Military Service in the Ancient Near East, 401–330 BCE, 2019 [28] J. ROY, The Mercenaries of Cyrus, in: Historia 16, 1967, 287–323 [29] P.-A. SÄNGER / S. SCHEUBLE-REITER (eds.), Söldner und Berufssoldaten in der griechischen Welt, 2022 [30] G. SEIBT, Griechische Söldner im Achämenidenreich, 1977 [31] N. SEKUNDA, The Antigonid Army, 2013 [32] M.P. SPEIDEL, The Rise of Mercenaries in the Third Century, in: M.P. SPEIDEL, Roman Army Studies, vol. 2,, 1992, 71–81 [33] M. TRUNDLE, Identity and Community Among Greek Mercenaries in the Classical World, 700–323 BCE, in: Ancient History Bulletin 13, 1998, 28–38 [34] M. TRUNDLE, Greek Mercenaries. From the Late Archaic Period to Alexander, 2004 [35] M. TRUNDLE, The Business of War. Mercenaries, in: Oxford Handbook of Classical Warfare, 2013, 330–351.

LEONHARD BURCKHARDT

Military diploma

A. Definition, key data, inventory
B. Design
C. Manufacture
D. Recipients, privileges
E. Witnesses
F. Developments and disruptions
G. Significance
H. Related documents, *honesta missio*

A. DEFINITION, KEY DATA, INVENTORY

Since Theodor Mommsen, the term *diplomata militaria* has been used to designate bronze documents from a large and strictly defined group: two-part certificates (*diplomata*, from the Greek *diploma*, '[something] doubled, folded together') of the Roman Imperial period that were routinely issued to soldiers of various (non-legionary) troop types. They contained constitutions detailing privileges bestowed by the emperor on certain fixed occasions (usually discharge from service) or, rarely, on special occasions (for → valour). These privileges were typically Roman citizenship (*civitas*) and the right to marry foreign women (*conubium*), or the latter alone. Thus, military diplomas were not themselves certificates of discharge, but they often served to certify honourable discharge, the *honesta missio*. The earliest known military diploma is from the reign of Claudius and is dated to December 11, AD 52 (CIL XVI 1). After a gap lasting from the 260s to AD 298, the practice continued until the last surviving document, dated to January 7, AD 306 (RMD I 78).

Military diplomas were part of normal proceedings for administration and military affairs. Estimates suggest that over 300,000 were manufactured and issued between about AD 50 and the mid-2nd century [3.57f.]. Their design remained essentially unchanged. The documents were made at Rome. The hallmark of this type of document is that it was made of metal, initially brass, later bronze. Thanks to this peculiarity, the diplomas survive in relatively large (and still increasing) numbers, in variable states of preservation from small fragments to fully intact diplomas. By 1955, the corpora (CIL XVI Suppl.) listed 189 military diplomas, and a further 201 were added by 1994 (RMD III). Numbers soared after the collapse of the Eastern Bloc. Unregulated excavations brought large numbers of military diplomas into the international art trade from the Balkans. Most were immediately published, and this led to a quantum leap in the state of knowledge. Over 1,000 examples are currently extant – but this represents not even one half of one percent of the supposed original total. Since 1978, the inventory has been available in the volumes of the RMD, kept constantly up to date and furnished with commentaries. Because of the information they contain, military diplomas are a key source for numerous aspects of the imperial, administrative and military history of the Roman Imperial period.

B. DESIGN
Roman military diplomas contain the full text of the relevant imperial constitution published at Rome on a large bronze *tabula* with a list of all recipient soldiers of the unit concerned. Alongside the text indicating the privileges, the personal document specifies the individual recipient, sometimes giving details of his unit and other privileged members of his family, all with exact personal data. The constitutions were in the first place published on the Capitol (list in RMD IV app. III) – on walls of buildings such as the Tabularium (e.g. RMD V 329), at locations such as behind *Casa Romuli* (the 'Hut of Romulus') (CIL XVI 23) and on the plinths of assorted monuments, although archaeological evidence no longer survives for constitutions on plinths of monuments such as the *Apollo magnus* (the colossus of Apollo by the sculptor Calamis, taken as spoils by Lucullus (RMD VI 482f.) [25.239ff.]). Some time between AD 88 and the autumn of 90, because of a lack of space and probably following the thwarted rebellion of L. Antonius Saturninus in 89, the publication of constitutions was limited to the wall behind the Temple of Divus Augustus near the statue of Domitian's patron goddess Minerva. Finally, a formula on the documents certifies the transcription. As from 89/90, the text read as follows: *Descriptum et recognitum extabula aenea* [*aerea* after February AD 138], *quae fixa est Romae in muro post templum Divi Augusti ad Minervam* ('transcribed and checked against the brazen [bronze] tablet that is put up at Rome on the wall behind the Temple of Divus Augustus beside the Minerva').

The principle of the two-part document (a document with a locked, sealed text and an accessible duplicate for reading) was achieved in these metal documents as follows (cf. figs. 1–4).

C. MANUFACTURE
The list of people to whom privileges were to be given was prepared by the commander of the relevant unit, usually the governor or naval prefect, and submitted to the central imperial administration, which in most cases meant to Rome. The constitution was drawn up there, in an *officium*, probably that of the *ab epistulis* [1], that is, the office responsible for imperial correspondence. It included all relevant details and the names of those privileged, where appropriate arranged by unit. The resultant text was sent to the emperor for approval. It then went to an *officina* specializing in the manufacture of these documents, which often (and later always) began producing them before the constitution itself was published [3.73–76]; [26]. This can be deduced from certain details on the diploma's exterior: dates of publication and other movable elements left blank or entered in a different hand, discrepancies in enumerations of consulships in the weeks around year end, and the renewal of the emperor's *tribunicia potestas* ('tribunician power') on December 10. The text was prewritten in ink, as some surviving residues show (RGZM 33) [14]. The date of the constitution indicates the day on which it was published on the large bronze *tabula*. None of these large *tabulae*, of which there must have been tens of thousands, have been found. As yet, all that survive are small excerpts, cut to size for use in military diplomas in AD 224/25, 243 and 248 (RMD V 465; CIL XVI 147; 153).

The custom of having the emperor approve the constitution when the manufacture of the diploma was only beginning sometimes had unforeseen consequences if the emperor died abruptly. In such a case, the military diplomas would often be made, and the constitution published in the reign of his successor, with the later date but, of course, still in the name of the deceased emperor. Such cases are known from the period of transition from the reign of Trajan to that of Hadrian, when more than a year passed after Trajan's death until publication [9], and also in the period following the murder of Commodus on December 31, AD 192. Two constitutions approved by Commodus shortly before his death were only implemented during the turbulent year of AD 193 – the first on March 16, in the reign of Pertinax, who also implemented other *dona* ('gifts' or 'rewards') of Commodus (SHA Pert. 6,6), and the second on August 11 in the reign of Septimius Severus, as the dates on the military diplomas reveal [29]; [30.147ff.].

D. RECIPIENTS, PRIVILEGES
The Privileges bestowed by the emperor via the military diploma were generally associated with the *honesta missio*, honourable discharge on completion of the term of military service. Until the reign of Hadrian, they were sometimes – in special cases – granted before this, *ante stipendia emerita* ('before the pay was earned') for notable feats of service, as by Trajan in the Second Dacian War of AD 105/06 (CIL XVI 160; RMD V 343), and by Hadrian himself in 121 when he honoured soldiers' entire families (RMD V 357; VII 704–706). These privileges affected the recipient's personal legal status. They consisted in the award of Roman citizenship, *civitas*, and *conubium*, the right to marry

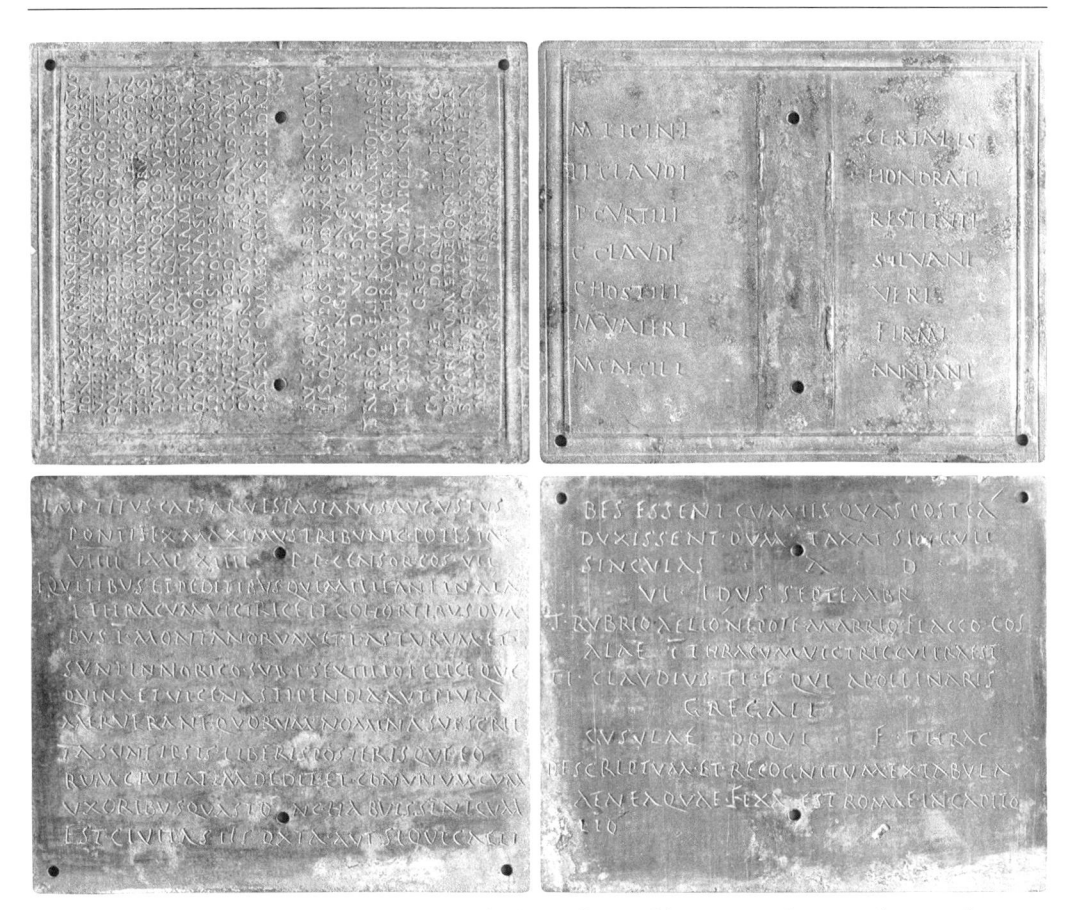

Figs. 1–4: Diploma of Titus from September 8, AD 79 for the auxiliaries of the province of Noricum (two-part document on metal tablets) [14]. The military diplomas comprised two rectangular tablets, *tabella* I (left) and *tabella* II (right). The constitution text with certification was written horizontally and continuously across the insides of *tabellae* I and II (below), beginning on *tabella* I top left and ending on *tabella* II bottom right. The tablets with the text inside were then folded together and joined and locked with metal threads running through several stamped holes on both tablets (two in the middle, one at top and bottom of the right edge, abandoned in the final phase). On the exterior of *tabella* I (top left), the entire constitution with certification was engraved in upright format for reading. On the exterior of *tabella* II (top right), seven seals of seven witnesses were arranged downwards in horizontal format, giving their names in the genitive case to the left and right (i.e. 'seal of...'). These seals, which were made of organic materials, were protected by an elongated metal capsule that was soldered on and that rarely survives. Both exteriors were furnished with frames, which at first were lavishly decorated. The entire design is most unusual for an official document. Behind it is an innovative and successful idea: every individual soldier should receive his own personal miniature copy of the great framed *tabula aenea/aerea* at Rome, as a way of forging a lasting emotional connection between the privileged veterans, usually including their families, and the emperor. Furthermore, this elaborate and unmistakable design was nearly impossible to counterfeit.

a foreign woman (*peregrina*). Recipients of both privileges were very often members of units that largely consisted of *peregrini*, that is, provincials from somewhere other than Rome – in practice, many belonged to one of the *auxilia*, including the provincial fleets. The second, somewhat smaller category of recipients of *civitas* and *conubium* close to the emperor were soldiers serving in the two higher-ranking Praetorian → fleets at Misenum and Ravenna, and in the unit of imperial mounted guards founded by Trajan, the *equites singulares Augusti* ('imperial mounted guards'), who would already have received the *ius latii* ('Latin rights') on admission to these units. Previously, in the crisis-ridden year of AD 68, Galba granted *civitas* and *conubium* to legionary veterans who were not Roman citizens, and Vespasian later did the same in 70 and 71, including to legionaries unfit for service, and to soldiers of the two Praetorian fleets (CIL XVI 7–11 mit RMD V App. II; RMD III 136; V 323). The granting of *civitas* also extended to existing children of a concubinate formed during military service and their offspring in turn. *Conubium* applied to the soldier's current partner or – if the soldier had no partner at the time – to one and only one future wife. The formula for the *auxiliarii* ('auxiliaries') at this period was expressed in a single sentence, for example: *Imp(erator) Caesar P. Aelius Hadrianus Aug(ustus)* [full appellation] *equitibus et peditibus, qui militaverunt in alis* [number] *et cohortibus* [number], *quae appellantur* [names of units] *et sunt in* [name of province] *sub* [name of governor], *quinque et viginti* [or more] *stipendiis emeritis, dimissis honesta missione, quorum nomina subscripta sunt, ipsis, liberis posterisque eorum civitatem dedit et conubium cum uxoribus, quas tunc habuisssent, cum est civitas iis data, aut si qui caelibes essent cum iis, quas postea duxissent, dumtaxat singulis singulas* ('Imperator Caesar Hadrianus Augustus (full appellation) granted to the cavalrymen and infantrymen having served in ala [number] and cohort [number] named [names of units] and stationed in the province of [name of province] under [name of governor] and having served 25 years [or more] for themselves, their children and descendants, citizenship and the right of matrimony with such spouses as they had at the time citizenship was granted or, if they were unmarried at this time, such spouses as they married later, but one each only').

Antoninus Pius, who also intervened in other aspects of military diplomas [5], imposed considerable restrictions on this long-standing and generous practice. Working to consolidate the institution of Roman marriage after the death and consecration of his wife Faustina Augusta in November 140, he greatly limited the granting of citizenship to children born from concubines during military service. The *equites singulares Augusti* and auxiliaries no longer received retroactive citizenship [27.30ff.]; [21]. The formula excluding such children read as follows: [Imperator and the subsequent elements as above] *civitatem Romanam, qui eorum non haberent, dedit et conubium cum uxoribus, quas tunc habuissent, cum est civitas iis data, aut cum iis, quas postea duxissent, dumtaxat singulis* ('Imperator Caesar ... Augustus ... granted Roman citizenship to those that did not yet have it, and the right of matrimony with such spouses as they had at the time citizenship was granted, or with those that they took later, but one each only'). Children fathered by all ranks of *auxiliarii* and conceived before the father's enlistment in the army were exempt from this exclusion, but their status had to be verified before the governor [15]; [6]. This benefit was added to the text of the constitution in a special sentence that began as follows: *Praeterea praestitit, ut* [etc.] ('He also provided that ...'). The prior practice was retained for natural children of soldiers in the two imperial fleets – *filii* ('sons') of *mulieres* ('women'), as the phrase goes in such cases, continued to be recognized as *liberi* ('children') born of *uxores* ('wives') [22.146ff.]. Here too, however, a formal declaration was required. All subsequent emperors retained these regulations.

For soldiers of the citizen units, the only privilege that could possibly be given was *conubium*. It was granted on completion of military service, bestowed using the formula *nomina militum, ... qui pie et fortiter militia functi sunt ...* ('the names of soldiers ... who have served loyally and valiantly'). The only recipients of military diplomas of this type were soldiers of the ten *cohortes praetoriae* ('praetorian guards') and the four *cohortes urbanae* ('urban guards') of the city of Rome and the *cohors urbana* ('urban guard') of Lugdunum. These types were not available to legionaries. Such diplomas were very rare throughout the first two centuries. Beginning in the reign of Septimius Severus, who dismissed the old Praetorian Guard in AD 193 and then reestablished it – at twice its former strength – with soldiers from his own army (mostly from the Balkans), military diplomas were given in abundance, especially to the Praetorians. During the last phase of the document's history, these were the only diplomas to be issued [7].

E. WITNESSES

During the first phase, seven *ad hoc* witnesses would add their seals, including soldiers. Vespasian then transferred the accreditation process to a group of professional lawyers at Rome between AD 75 and 78 [17.467ff.], and a selection of seven of these would perform the notarial act. The group was reduced to a seven-man committee in February 138, no doubt at the behest of Antoninus, the new emperor and adoptive son of Hadrian [27.30f.]; [7.41ff.]. When a member of the committee retired, he was replaced by a successor according to a principle of hierarchy. These colleges can be traced through the mid-3rd century almost without interruption (updated in the appendices to RMD). In the case of the Praetorians and the *urbaniciani* (troops garrisoned in the city), seven comrades signed, a different seven for each diploma.

F. DEVELOPMENTS AND DISRUPTIONS

Until the reign of Domitian, military diplomas were up to 20 × 16 cm in size, weighing over 1 kg. They were already becoming smaller, thinner and lighter under Nerva and Trajan. From the reign of Antoninus Pius onwards, their size varied between c. 15 × 12 and c. 12 × 10 cm, and they sometimes weighed less than 200 g. Larger and heavier examples appeared again in their final phase. Towards the end of the 1st century, less care began to be taken with the actual constitution text on the interior than with the showy exterior text. This is noticeable in the use of a looser script, more abbreviations and, from the reign of Trajan onwards, the omission of the witnessing. In the reign of Antoninus Pius, unit numbers were being left off auxiliary diplomas, until a directive from the emperor brought an end to such errors [5]; [7.44ff.]. During the double principate of Marcus Aurelius and Lucius Verus, lasting stylistic improvements appeared in place of customary formulas, such as *praeest* for the established contraction *praest*. Archaizing locatives in names of provinces were even introduced in the spirit of the Second Sophistic, for example *et sunt Thraciae* and *Lyciae Pamphyliae* in place of *et sunt in Thracia* and *in Lycia Pamphylia* – these changes probably originated from suggestions made by Marcus Aurelius, who was an excellent stylist [30.138ff.].

The crisis of the Marcomannic Wars brought a radical change. Between 168 and 177, the use of bronze in the manufacture of military diplomas was suspended entirely. The lists of witness colleges, however, shows that they were still at work – in other words, that documents were still being issued, but presumably on perishable materials, probably *tabulae ceratae* ('wax (covered) tablets') made of wood [3]; [7.46ff.]; [30.141]. After ascending to the throne in AD 180, Commodus apparently decided to keep both forms of military diploma: bronze for the units close to the emperor – the Praetorians, urban cohorts, *equites singulares Augusti* ('imperial mounted guards') and the two Praetorian fleets – and perishable materials for the mass of auxiliaries in the provinces, who now only received bronze military diplomas in exceptional cases [30.145ff.]. Septimius Severus continued this practice. Production for the various units continued uninterrupted under the Severan rulers and under Maximinus Thrax. The last of two known bronze military diplomas made for an *auxiliarius* dates from AD 206 (RMD VII 798) [6]; [11]. Until the reign of Gallienus, other than diplomas for the *equites singulares* and the Italic fleets, the only known military diplomas are those issued to Praetorians, but these were very few in number under this emperor ([8.333ff.]; see the lists in the vols. of RMD). After this, the production of metal documents was abandoned altogether for over thirty years, before finally being abolished after the Second Tetrarchy.

The break between 168 and 177, with its long interruption of the regular practices of artisans, had a marked effect on manufacturing standards [23.526ff.]; [24.248ff.]; [30.142ff.]. This especially affected the interior texts, which had always tended to be neglected. The prescribed division of the texts across *tabellae* I and II was abandoned – some now began on *tabella* II. Above all, the quality of the texts on the closed interiors of the *tabellae* II (which were sometimes covered with smooth, linear marks) deteriorated further, sometimes dramatically, in terms of the legibility of the sometimes cuneiform-like cursive, and often in the correctness of the language.

Sometimes, the interiors were even left blank (e.g. RMD III 199), or contained text from a different constitution (RMD V 471a/b). It was now entirely clear that the outside represented the actual text of the document. These texts were designed very lavishly, with large letters visually highlighting the recipient section. Once again, elements of spoken language crept into the witness attestations: *que* (= *quae*) *est* and *postemplum* (= *post templum*). Increasingly, fragmentary bronze inscriptions of all kinds were used for *tabellae* II, with the written side turned inwards [2]; [18], or simply thin sheets of scrap metal (e.g. RMD V 455) [23.528f.].

G. Significance

For almost every year between AD 61 and AD 254, one or more military diplomas are known, with a gap during the Marcomannic Wars. To date, almost 500 constitutions have been identified, but this amounts not even to one half of one percent of the documents that once existed [3]; [7]. The information they contain has advanced our understanding in many fields, clarifying matters of dispute and closing gaps in knowledge. These advances include details of emperors' titles and official powers, the prosopography of senators as governors and consuls, and of *equites* ('equestrians') as governors and commanders, the composition of auxiliary units in almost all provinces, the changes and relocations of auxiliary units, and recruitment in general and on specific occasions. All this information is precisely dated. Above all, however, the mass of military diplomas provide physical proof of the colossal integrative function that the Roman army performed through its routine bestowal of citizenship and marital rights.

H. Related documents, *honesta missio*

Two other types of documents were manufactured in the form of classical military diplomas in the early 2nd century – only for Praetorians, and both highly exceptional cases: in AD 106, certificates of discharge (RMD IV App. I A) and in AD 119 documents bearing an edict of Hadrian that retroactively granted *civitas Romana* ('Roman citizenship') to Praetorians whose citizenship status was in doubt [10]; [12]. Technically, the Roman army did not issue certificates of discharge (on the *honesta missio* in detail [19]). For soldiers who received military diplomas after honourable discharge, thereby receiving *civitas* and *conubium*, or else the latter alone, failure to receive a certificate of discharge posed no problem, because the military diploma confirmed honourable discharge either directly (through the formula *dimissis honesta missione*) or indirectly (*qui pie et fortiter militia functi sunt*). However, all legionaries had to take upon themselves the responsibility of making their privileges, which were called *commoda*, appear credible. A few bronze tablets dating from the first half of the 3rd century have been found that were intended to verify the privileges granted, and so were made in the form of a certificate or in imitation of one (RMD IV App. I.1–I.3; RGZM 73–75) [19.310ff.]; [28.23ff.]. In one major exception of AD 240, a governor of Germania superior, or perhaps Gordian III himself, approved the manufacture of large diplomas in bronze for veterans of the two legions of that province, probably in recognition of their notable role in the power struggle that followed the death of Maximinus Thrax in Italy [28]. It was only in AD 311 that private copies were replaced by documents issued by commanders of the border units (*duces*) [28.70f.]; [13].

Bibliography

[1] T. Carboni, Emeritae missionis epistulae: sulla prassi amministrativa del congedo, in: Rivista storica italiana, 2019, 411–439   [2] W. Eck, Bronzeinschriften von Ehrendenkmälern in Rom. Zu dem neuen Militärdiplom von der unteren Sava, in: ZPE 133, 2000, 275–282   [3] W. Eck, Der Kaiser als Herr des Heeres. Militärdiplome und kaiserliche Reichsregierung, in: J. Wilkes (ed.), Documenting the Roman Army. Essays in Honour of Margaret Roxan, 2003, 55–87   [4] W. Eck et al., Die Krise des römischen Reiches unter Marc Aurel und ein Militärdiplom aus dem Jahr 177(?), in: Chiron 33, 2003, 365–377   [5] W. Eck, Die Veränderungen in Konstitutionen und Diplomen unter Antoninus Pius, in: M.A. Speidel / H. Lieb (eds.), Militärdiplome. Die Forschungsbeiträge der Berner Gespräche von 2004, 2007, 87–104   [6] W. Eck, Septimius Severus und die Soldaten. Das Problem der Soldatenehe und ein neues Auxiliardiplom, in: B. Onken / D. Rohde (eds.), In omnia historia curiosus. Studien zur Geschichte von der Antike bis zur Neuzeit. Festschrift für Helmut Schneider zum 65. Geburtstag, 2011, 63–77   [7] W. Eck, Bürokratie und Politik in der römischen Kaiserzeit. Administrative Routine und politische Reflexe in Bürgerrechtskonstitutionen der römischen Kaiserzeit, 2012   [8] W. Eck, Diplomata militaria für Prätorianer, vor und nach Septimius Severus. Eine Bestandsaufnahme und ein Erklärungsversuch, in: Athenaeum 100, 2012, 321–336   [9] W. Eck, Konsuln des Jahres 117 in Militärdiplomen Traians mit tribunicia potestas XX, in: ZPE 185, 2013, 235–238   [10] W. Eck et al., Edikt Hadrians für Prätorianer mit unsicherem römischen Bürgerrecht, in: ZPE 189, 2014, 241–253; ZPE 191, 2014, 266–268 und ZPE 206, 2018, 199–201   [11] W. Eck, Das letzte Diplom für einen Auxiliarsoldaten aus dem Jahr 206 n.Chr. – der Text der Innenseite, in: ZPE 208, 2018, 237–244   [12] W. Eck, Soldaten aus den Donauprovinzen in der Prätorianergarde. Zum Erdbeben in Syrien aus dem Jahr 115 und zum Edikt Hadrians aus dem Jahr 119, in: ZPE 206, 2018, 199–201   [13] W. Eck, Eine dritte Kopie der Tafel von Brigetio aus dem Jahr 311 n.Chr., in: Quaderni Lupinesi 9, 2019, 53–57   [14] W. Eck / A. Pangerl, Zur Herstellung der diploma militaria. Tinte auf einem Diplom des Titus für Noricum, in: ZPE 157, 2006, 181–184   [15] W. Eck / P. Weiss, Die Sonderregelungen für Soldatenkinder seit Antoninus Pius. Ein niederpannonisches Militärdiplom vom 11. Aug. 146, in: ZPE 135, 2001, 195–208   [16] W. Eck / H. Wolff (eds.), Heer und Integrationspolitik. Die römischen Militärdiplome als historische Quelle, 1986   [17] R. Haensch, Die Verwendung von Siegeln bei Dokumenten der kaiserlichen Reichsadministration, in: M.-F. Boussac / A. Invernizzi (eds.), Archives et sceaux du monde hellénistique. Archivi e sigilli nel mondo ellenistico, Torino, Villa Gualino, 13–16 Gennaio 1993 (BCH Suppl. 29), 1996, 449–496   [18] M. Mirković, Euphrata et Romano consulibus auf einem neuen Militärdiplom von der unteren Sava, in: ZPE 133, 2000, 286–290   [19] M.A. Speidel, Honesta missio. Zu Entlassungsurkunden und verwandten Texten, in: M.A. Speidel, Heer und Herrschaft im Römischen Reich der Hohen Kaiserzeit, 2009, 317–346   [20] M.A. Speidel / H. Lieb (eds.), Militärdiplome. Die Forschungsbeiträge der Berner Gespräche von 2004, 2007   [21] S. Waebens, Imperial Policy and Changed Composition of the Auxilia. The 'Change in A.D. 140' Revisited, in: Chiron 42, 2012, 1–23   [22] P. Weiss, Zwei Diplomfragmente aus dem pannonischen Raum, in: ZPE 80, 1990, 137–156   [23] P. Weiss, Ausgewählte neue Militärdiplome. Seltene Provinzen (Africa, Mauretania Caesariensis), späte Urkunden für Prätorianer (Caracalla, Philippus), in: Chiron 32, 2002, 491–543   [24] P. Weiss, Neue Fragmente von Flottendiplomen des 2. Jahrhunderts n.Chr. Mit einem Beitrag zum Urkundenwert des Außentexts bei den Militärdiplomen, in: ZPE 150, 2004, 243–252   [25] P. Weiss, Zwei vollständige Konstitutionen für die Truppen in Noricum (8. Sept. 79) und Pannonia inferior (27. Sept. 154), in: ZPE 146, 2004, 139–254   [26] P. Weiss, Von der Konstitution zum Diplom. Schlussfolgerungen aus der 'zweiten Hand', Leerstellen und divergierenden Daten in den Urkunden, in: M.A. Speidel / H. Lieb, Militärdiplome. Die Forschungsbeiträge der Berner Gespräche von 2004, 2007, 187–207   [27] P. Weiss, Die vorbildliche Kaiserehe. Zwei Senatsbeschlüsse beim Tod der älteren und jüngeren Faustina, neue Paradigmen und die Herausbildung des 'antoninischen' Prinzipats, in: Chiron 38, 2008, 1–45   [28] P. Weiss, Eine honesta missio in Sonderformat. Neuartige Urkunden für Veteranen der Legionen in Germania superior unter Gordian III., in: Chiron 45, 2015, 23–75   [29] P. Weiss, Konstitutionen eines toten Kaisers. Militärdiplome von Commodus aus dem Jahr 193 n.Chr., in: S. Panzram et al. (eds.), Menschen und Orte der Antike. Festschrift für Helmut Halfmann zum 65. Geburtstag, 2015, 273–280   [30] P. Weiss, Die Militärdiplome unter Marc Aurel und Commodus. Kontinuitäten und Brüche, in: V. Grieb (ed.), Marc Aurel. Wege zu seiner Herrschaft, 2017, 135–153.

Peter Weiss

Military law

A. Greece
B. Rome

Neither Greece nor the Roman Republic had any codified military law. The establishment of the standing professional army under Augustus created the need for consistent legal norms for soldiers. Consequently, individual judgments already rendered began to be collated into digests in the Severan period. In addition to military criminal law, these dealt with provisions of property law, privileges and prohibitions.

A. GREECE

A.1. Classical period
A.2. Hellenistic period

A.1. CLASSICAL PERIOD

No specific military law is preserved from the Greek *poleis*. From at least the 5th century BC onwards, the citizens of individual city states were obliged to perform military service. In a sense, military service was a privilege reserved for citizens, and the armies of the Greek cities of the Classical period were the community of their citizens under arms (→ Conscription). In Athens, all citizens from the ages of 18 to 59 were eligible for conscription. The armies of the Greek *poleis* were based on the concept of the militia. Soldiers did not receive pay, but they were compensated for lost earnings. The popular assembly determined the deployment and recruitment (full (*pandemei*) or partial levy) of the army [2.141–158, 569–573]. Punishments for military offenses were settled in the courts. Accusations against generals and monarchs in both Athens and Sparta who were called to account after a defeat are well documented [13.4–33]. Desertion (*lipotaxion/lipotaxia*), cowardice (*deilia*), and refusal to serve in the army (*astrateia*) were punished with the loss of civic rights (*atimia*) (→ Cowardice; → Avoidance of military service).

A.2. HELLENISTIC PERIOD

Unlike in the Classical period, military service in many Hellenistic *poleis* was no longer an essential prerequisite for citizenship [4.20–26]. In general, the source material for the armies of the Hellenistic monarchies is better; case studies show that soldiers and their wives and children enjoyed special rights. In the 3rd century BC, members of the military above a certain rank had special tax status as *hellenes* and were exempt from the obol tax [5.71f.]. A royal decree also dating from the 3rd century shows that soldiers in the field received special legal protection for themselves and their families while they were absent from home. For example, it was forbidden to initiate legal proceedings against a soldier who was absent on duty, and trials already ongoing when a soldier was assigned for deployment had to be suspended. Wives and children of soldiers away on campaign also had legal immunity. In the case of proceedings already initiated at the husband's or father's departure, the same regulations applied to families as for the soldiers themselves. However, cases that came due for trial during the soldier's absence were dealt with by a special court [9]. The wife of a soldier also enjoyed noticeably more rights during her husband's absence and following his death. From the 2nd century BC onwards, for instance, the widow of a soldier was able to act as *kleros* (land allotment) administrator on behalf of her sons, and as from the 1st century BC, she could even become their guardian [15.142–194].

B. ROME

B.1. Military criminal law – crimes and punishments
B.2. Place of jurisdiction
B.3. Civil proceedings
B.4. Privileges and prohibitions

According to Republican military principles the soldier was a citizen and the citizen was a soldier. It was the military's right to conscript people into the army, provided that the person possessed citizenship and had enough wealth to finance equipment and weapons. Only with the establishment of the standing army under Augustus (27 BC–AD 14) did a real professional army emerge, and with this came new legal problems that required regulation. Military law began to be codified under the Severans (193–235), and it is preserved in the *Digests*, the *Codex Iustinianus* and the *Codex Theodosianus* [8.1011f.].

B.1. MILITARY CRIMINAL LAW – CRIMES AND PUNISHMENTS

During the Monarchical and Republican periods, the general had absolute authority over the soldiers who served under him. No regulations that were set down in writing under the Republic were applied generally. Creating a documentary record was merely part of the traditional practice of a good general [8.964f., 969]. The Romans had no military criminal law in the modern sense. What would be a crime under such a system was considered a breach of the *disciplina militaris* (→ Discipline, B.), and the soldier faced the disciplinary authority of the officers who were his immediate superiors. Offences were not precisely defined, and neither were the punishments they incurred. Soldiers had no right of provocation. Even in the last days of the Republic, the general held the power of life or death over his soldiers. Punishments imposed were determined according to military expediency [8.967, 973]. Over the course of Republican history, offences came to be associated with particular punishments, but not in any legally binding way. Abandoning the standard or a position, stealing from the camp, bearing false witness and homosexual activities were punished with *fustuarium*, a form of ritual cudgelling that frequently led to death. In the *decimatio*, every tenth man of a convicted unit was selected by lot and flogged to death by his comrades.

In the Imperial period, the supreme commander – now the emperor – was still responsible for maintaining military order and discipline. The legal venue for trying soldiers' military offences was the unit camp. Less serious cases came under the responsibility of the centurions. *Principales* were also passing judgment by the reign of Septimius Severus (AD 193–211), if not before [17.147–152].

Dig. 49,16,2, pr. makes a distinction between crimes exclusive to the military (*delicta propria militum*) and those that could also be committed by civilians – which, in some cases, were punished more harshly when committed by soldiers, such as adultery (*delicta cum ceteris communia*). The degree of punishment, dependent on the circumstances of the case, ranged from *castigatio* (corporal punishment), *pecunaria multa* (fines) and *munerum indictio* (punitive service) to death. For especially serious crimes, such as defection to the enemy, soldiers were tried not as *milites* ('soldiers'), but as *hostes* ('enemies'). This made it possible to impose punishments that were not given to soldiers (e.g. torture, *damnatio ad metalla* or *ad bestias* ('condemnation to the mines', or 'to the beasts'), hanging, and crucifixion). Military punishments tended to reduce the guilty person's status, for example relegation to inferior duties (*militiae mutatio*), degradation (*gradus deiecto*) or dishonourable discharge from the army (*missio ignominiosa*). Crimes that were exclusive to the military involved breaches of the *disciplina militaris*, which depending on context (time of → war or → peace, rank of those involved) could incur the death penalty. These included lack of discipline, insubordination, disregard of orders, fomenting disobedience, insurgency, causing injury to comrades, and resisting corporal punishment. A soldier who sold all his weapons in peacetime was considered a deserter. During wartime, selling a single weapon was enough to invite the death penalty. In cases where a soldier was absent from his unit or position without leave, jurists distinguished between *desertio* ('desertion') and *emansio* (absence beyond one's furlough) (→ Avoidance of military service). Mitigating circumstances were taken into consideration for the latter. Cowardice in the face of the enemy was punished with degradation. Fleeing while on *exploratio* (→ Reconnaissance) in contact with the enemy, leaving one's position in war, and feigning illness out of fear of the enemy were punishable by death. The most serious offence of all, however, was defection to the enemy. Captured *transfugae* ('defectors') were tried not *pro milite* ('as a soldier'), but *pro hoste* ('as an enemy'), and were released from their soldier's oath. Even a mere attempt at defection was punishable by death, but in this case the individual was tried *pro milite* [8.977–1003]; [3.300–311]; [17.150–156].

B.2. PLACE OF JURISDICTION

During the Republican and Imperial periods and through Late Antiquity, soldiers' immediate superiors were responsible for military trials arising from breaches of the *disciplina militaris*. If a general legal norm was broken as well as a military obligation, the soldier was subject to both authorities for the relevant infractions. During the Republican period, the general held the *ius gladii* ('the right of the sword', i.e. the right to impose the death penalty). In the Imperial period, this right passed to the governor as the supreme commander of the units stationed in his province, but he had the power to delegate it to unit commanders. For military offences, private cases involving soldiers, and possibly also cases in which soldiers were passive defendants (scholars differ on this category), the place of jurisdiction was the unit's camp, and the commander held jurisdiction. If a soldier wished to appear as a plaintiff against civilians, he had to avail himself of the ordinary courts; this required his commanding officer's permission to be absent from the unit. The *de facto* immunity of soldiers referenced by Juvenal (Iuv. 16) implies that a special place of jurisdiction was also used in cases involving civilians, but whether this was the case for soldiers, and if so from what date, is open to doubt. Dig. 5,1,7 may indicate a *privilegium fori* (the legal privilage of being tried in a specific court) for soldiers, but in military criminal law, penal authority lay with superior officers, and the place of jurisdiction was always the camp [1.219–224]; [8.947–964, 1007f.]; [17.147]; [10].

The reforms of Diocletian (284–312) and Constantine I (306–337) separated civilian and military authority in the provinces, these having hitherto been held as one by the governor. Under Diocletian, it seems, courts that were strictly military were set up among the military commanders (*duces* ('Commanders'), *comites rei militaris* ('Associates in Military Affairs'), *magistri militum* ('Masters of Soldiers')), but these did not exercise jurisdiction over matters of military discipline. The exact judicial responsibilities are not clear [16.409]. Further complicating the question of jurisdiction for soldiers in cases of civil and criminal law was the classification system that emerged about this time, according to which soldiers were subject to different military judges depending on their commander. The *comitatenses* ('court troops'), who were soldiers of the mobile army, were answerable to the *magistri militum*, the *limitanei* ('border troops') were answerable to the *comites rei militaris* or *duces*, and – beginning with the reign of Valentinian I (364–375) – the *palatini* ('palace troops') were considered a distinct troop category under the *magistri militum praesentales* ('Master of Soldiers in the (Imperial) Presence'). Thus it was that soldiers in a single province might answer to three different judges.

By no means was jurisdiction placed under military control starting in the 4th century AD. Several imperial edicts stated explicitly that all civil legal disputes were to be heard before the civilian governor, even if one party was a soldier (Cod. Theod. 2,1,2; 9). A criminal case with a soldier as plaintiff was also to be negotiated before the civilian court. Only a soldier accused in a criminal case would be brought before a military court. When offenses were improperly brought before the military court, punishments were sometimes severe. The situation changed to some extent in AD 413, when it became permissible for civil suits against soldiers to be heard by the *magister militum* who was responsible (Cod. Iust. 3,13,6). Soldiers' civil suits continued to be negotiated before the civilian court ([16] sees this as less clear-cut). The rule that a soldier as claimant in civil cases or as the accused in criminal cases had to go before the military court, while as plaintiff in both cases he had to go to the civilian court, may have persisted until the reign of Justinian (527–565). Civilians could not be brought before a military court, either in criminal or in civil cases. The unification of civilian and military authority in the hands of the *duceset Augustales* under Justinian probably led to some changes in practice. Egyptian papyri show that, even before this, realities of judicial practice did not always reflect the provisions of the codices [12.377–380].

B.3. CIVIL PROCEEDINGS
Soldiers were only permitted to initiate proceedings in their own interests. They were not allowed to appear as *cognitores* (representatives) in proceedings. This prohibition probably dated back to Augustus, and it was reaffirmed in the reign of Hadrian (117–138) if not before [8.948–953]; [3.260f.]. It is uncertain whether soldiers were allowed to appear as *adsertores in libertatem* (one who asserts that another person is free). During the Principate, it seems that they were at least allowed to do so when the case concerned a close relative. In a dispute before a court concerning one's own freedom, an *adsertor in libertatem* was required, because the person under scrutiny could not be simultanously subject and object of the proceedings [8.953f.].

Soldiers were probably allowed certain rights as *absentes rei publicae causa* ('absent for the sake of the state') in the Republican period (Dig. 4,6,45). After all, while serving in the army they could not leave the standard without incurring danger to themselves, but there was often no one at home to deal with their affairs. One of these rights was the *restitutio in integrum* ('restitution to the original condition'), which required the praetor in certain circumstances to suspend all legal consequences triggered by a certain situation as if that situation had never come about. This applied, for instance, if a soldier missed a deadline in a case and consequently lost the case because of his absence [8.947–953].

B.4. PRIVILEGES AND PROHIBITIONS
Any privileges granted to a soldier during the Republic were between him and his general. Caesar was the first (46–44 BC) to enshrine in statute some of the benefits he bestowed on his men. He was the first to revive the old privilege of the *testamentum in procinctu* ('will on the battlefield'), permitting his soldiers to make a will without meeting the legal requirements (*libera testamenti factio*; Dig. 29,1,1). This privilege applied to all soldiers on active service from the reign of Trajan (AD 98–117) onwards. The will had to be made during military service. The regulation was justified in terms of soldiers' 'artlessness' (*simplicitas*) and 'ignorance' (*imperitia*). Soldiers were privileged in terms of the form of the will, the persons to whom they were allowed to make bequests and the right to make changes to an existing will. The *testamentum militare* ('military will') remained valid even if the strict legal conditions for a Roman will, namely, the prescribed number of witnesses and an official statement, were not met, or if the will was written in Greek. Beyond this, even incomplete wills or wills made verbally before witnesses were recognized. Soldiers were allowed to name heirs in two or more wills, distinguish between military and civilian property, bequeath only some of their assets while leaving the remainder intestate, and appoint heirs for limited periods or on certain conditions. Furthermore, no *querella inofficiosi testamenti* ('complaint because of a will contrary to duty') could be raised against a soldier's will, nor could such a will be challenged so as to invalidite it. This range of privileges appears to have come about unsystematically, beginning in the reign of Hadrian. Unlike civilians, who were only allowed to name heirs who themselves were legally competent to make a will, soldiers faced few legal restrictions on their heirs. One was the requirement that slaves had to be freed before inheriting. Soldiers were permitted to make bequests to peregrines (non–citizen foreigners), Latins, and childless and unmarried persons. Veterans had one year after leaving military service to compose a regular will. Their military will would cease to be valid thereafter [3.210–216].

One important privilege for soldiers was the *peculium castrense* ('camp property'). The Roman *filius familias* (son under the authority of his father) whose father was still alive was subject to the *patria potestas* ('father's authority'). This meant that he held no property and could not make a will. But there was an exception here for Roman citizens in military service. They had full power of disposal over the *peculium castrense*, the property they acquired through or during their army service. The fact that Roman citizen soldiers who were *filii familias* were allowed to make a will at all, despite remaining in the *potestas* of their fathers, is closely related to this. The privilege of the *peculium castrense* was first introduced by Augustus, later to be reaffirmed by Nerva (96-98) and Trajan. Hadrian finally extended the right to apply also to veterans. Soldiers' fathers had no access to the *peculium castrense*, but if the soldier died intestate, the *peculium* went to the father – as likewise if the designated heirs did not accept the inheritance.

Augustus intervened drastically in the traditional rights of the testator to protect soldiers in their absence. For example, they could not be disinherited – even by their own father – while in the field. Moreover, without the privilege of the *peculium castrense*, many soldiers would not have had right of disposal over their own pay. Soldiers' primary sources of income were the *stipendium* ('pay'), paid out several times a year, their share of the war booty, and the monetary gifts known as *donativa*, which became increasingly important over the course of the Imperial period, [11].

In contrast to the above privileges, some legal business was forbidden to soldiers. For example, they could neither buy nor lease land in the provinces where they were stationed (→ Civilians). From at least the reign of Augustus until after that of Septimius Severus (193-211), soldiers were also prohibited from marrying (→ Marriage) [8.919]; [6].

☞ Customs of war; Law of war; State and army

BIBLIOGRAPHY
[1] O. BEHRENDS, Die römische Geschworenenverfassung, 1970 [2] J. BLEICKEN, Die athenische Demokratie, ⁴1995 [3] J.B. CAMPBELL, The Emperor and the Roman Army, 31 BC-AD 235, 1984 [4] A. CHANIOTIS, War in the Hellenistic World. A Social and Cultural History, 2005 [5] W. CLARYSSE / D.J. THOMPSON, Counting the People in Hellenistic Egypt, vol. 2, 2006 [6] W. ECK, Septimius Severus und die Soldaten. Das Problem der Soldatenehe und ein neues Auxiliardiplom, in: B. ONKEN / D. ROHDE (eds.), In omni historia curiosus. Studien zur Geschichte von der Antike bis zur Neuzeit. Festschrift für Helmuth Schneider, 2011, 63-77 [7] J.H. JUNG, Das Eherecht der römischen Soldaten, in: ANRW II.14, 1982, 302-346 [8] J.H. JUNG, Die Rechtsstellung der römischen Soldaten. Ihre Entwicklung von den Anfängen Roms bis auf Diokletian, in: ANRW II.13, 1982, 882-1013 [9] E. KIESSLING, Aposkeuai und die prozessrechtliche Stellung der Ehefrauen im ptolemäischen Ägypten, in: APF 8, 1927, 240-249 [10] C. KREUZSALER, Zwischen Privilegierung und Diskriminierung. Die Sonderstellung der Soldaten im römischen Recht, in: B. PALME (ed.), Die Legionäre des Kaisers. Soldatenleben im römischen Ägypten, 2011, 27-39 [11] B. LEHMANN, Das Eigenvermögen der römischen Soldaten unter väterlicher Gewalt, in: ANRW II.14, 1982, 183-284 [12] B. PALME, Spätrömische Militärgerichtsbarkeit in den Papyri, in: H.-A. RUPPRECHT (ed.), Symposion 2003. Vorträge zur griechischen und hellenistischen Rechtsgeschichte, 2006, 375-408 [13] W.K. PRITCHETT, The Greek State at War, vol. 2, 1974 [14] E. SANDER, Militärrecht, in: RE Suppl. 10, 1965, 394-410 [15] S. SCHEUBLE-REITER, Die Katökenreiter im ptolemäischen Ägypten, 2012 [16] A.J.B. SIRKS, Antwort auf Bernhard Palme, in: H.-A. RUPPRECHT (ed.), Symposion 2003. Vorträge zur griechischen und hellenistischen Rechtsgeschichte, 2006, 409-414 [17] G. WESCH-KLEIN, Soziale Aspekte des römischen Heerwesens in der Kaiserzeit, 1998.

ANNA MARIA KAISER

Military literature

A. Introduction
B. Origins in Greece
C. Taktika
D. Poliorketika
E. Rome
F. Comprehensive Roman treatises

A. INTRODUCTION

War existed long before any attempt was made to analyze it in writing. It should not be imagined that military treatises exactly reflect military practice – the latter comprising military knowledge, largely unwritten, and military instruction, which in societies before the advent of state structures was given verbally or through experience in the field. The appearance of military literature in part depended on a society's transition from oral to written culture. Military writings take the form of histories, personal memoirs, philosophical treatises, novels, encyclopaedias, technical manuals, political pamphlets, war reports and collections of exempla.

B. ORIGINS IN GREECE

B.1. Historiography and military theory
B.2. Early specialist treatises

In western history, military writing began with the Homeric epics. The quest for heroic manly 'excellence' (*arete*) as a guarantee of everlasting renown invited imitation. By the 5th century BC, Homer had become an encyclopaedia of knowledge, not least in the art of war. The inclusion of quotations from Homer in historiographic and military writings was almost obligatory. Ultimately, Homeric epic as military encyclopaedia gave rise to the genre of the Homeric Tactica, in which quotations offered instructions for training, tactics, and generalship. Traces of this genre survive particularly in the Homeric scholia and works by authors of the Second Sophistic (e.g. Polyaenus, Strat. 1 pr. 4–13; Frontinus' lost Homeric *Tactica* [16. 25–27]).

Numerous factors encouraged the proliferation of military treatises from the time of the Persian Wars (490–478 BC) onwards: (1) Changes in Greek warfare were complicating the job of the → general. By 400 BC, his sphere of responsibility extended far beyond the battle itself. (2) Beginning in the 5th century, war was becoming more secular and more rational. It was becoming possible to plan wars and battles, and the talents of individual generals were becoming more important. To some extent, the concept of *tyche* ('chance') was replacing the role of the gods in determining the outcome of war. Thucydides bears witness to this shift. Accordingly, some military treatises emphasize factors of prescience, calculation, and good timing (Greek *kairos* / Latin *occasio*). (3) The choice of generals (*strategoi*) at Athens generated debates on the question of what constituted a 'good general'. (4) The emergence of the hoplite phalanx (c. 700–500 BC), in which those not of noble birth served as warriors, made demonstrating *arete* for the glory of the *polis* a collective matter, alongside the indidivual quest for *arete*. *Arete* was evolving from an innate privilege of the wellborn to a quality that could be learned. (5) The Sophists' new definition of knowledge as a collection of individual aptitudes (*technai*) also made war a *techne* – like rhetoric, medicine and other spheres of life. Some itinerant Sophists also taught tactics, while others, the *hoplomachoi*, taught fighting techniques; they were the first professional military trainers (→ Education) [11]. (6) The transition from oral to written culture inspired the creation of manuals on *technai* and political pamphlets. Both were avenues for writing on military matters.

B.1. HISTORIOGRAPHY AND MILITARY THEORY

Historiography also gave rise to military literature. The *Histories* of Herodotus (c. 484–c. 425 BC) established war as the chief subject of written history. Herodotus blended the era's interest in great deeds with a focus on human action, and applied the Ionian method of investigation (*historia*), which looked for causes (*aitiai*) and origins (*archai*), to war. He formulated a great many key themes and 'theories', even before categories for the study of military matters had emerged. These included geographical and cultural influences, the efficacy of stratagems, the importance of knowing one's enemy, and differences in weaponry.

Thucydides (c. 460–c. 400 BC) undertook the description of warfare in the Peloponnesian War (431–404; → Wars of note, H.) as a manual for generals and statesmen (1,21f.): it was an analytical case study of the clash between a land power and a sea power, which included commentaries on strategic and tactical decisions, the art of war and siege warfare. Themistocles, as the ideal general (Thuc. 1,138), became the standard by which subsequent historians would evaluate the capabilities of generals. That a good general was thought to be shrewd and clever was in harmony with the high regard paid to stratagems of war (Thuc. 5,8f.). Thucydides' unique study of war as a phenomenon remained unsurpassed until Clausewitz' treatise *Vom Kriege* (1832; 'On War'). The unpredictable way in which war unfolded, its many shifts and reversals, and the constant need to adapt to changing circumstances lent new meaning to the concept of good timing (*kairos*). Thucydides also considered factors of national character and psychology. He reduced success to the correct application of human intelligence and financial resources.

Thucydides' military analysis inspired imitators, notably Polybius (c. 200–118 BC). Polybius was writing during the Hellenistic period when the general's role had been firmly established, and he further developed Thucydides' focus on the general's acumen, quick analysis of a situation (*anchinoia*), planning, prescience, and the timing necessary to take advantage of opportunities. Polybius was also interested in national character, institutions (especially of the Roman army, Pol. 6,19–58), available resources and geography. Precise analysis of victories and defeats was required to explain Roman hegemony in the Mediterranean (Pol. 11,19a; 15,15f.). Polybius' interest in the art of war led him into digressions (e.g. Pol. 9,12–21; 11,8; 11,19) – and also into prejudice: his excursus on the superiority of the Roman legion over the Greek phalanx (Pol. 18,28–32) exhibits inaccuracies and rhetorical misdirections. Josephus' long passage on the superiority of the Roman army (Jos. BI 3,70–109) was driven by a similar motive: to deter resistance against Rome.

The first Greek military treatise that was not a work of history was a political pamphlet about naval power [4]: The *Constitution of the Athenians*, wrongly attributed to Xenophon and dated variously (late 440s to mid-420s BC), praised the strategic benefits of naval power for Athens (2,1–16). Thucydides (1,142f.) was reacting to this view. Despite the significance attached to fleets in the works of Pseudo-Xenophon, Thucydides and many other historians, there was no theoretical discussion or specialist treatment of sea power in treatises – although naval matters may have formed part of the lost *Poliorketika* (cf. Aen. Tact. 40,8; Philo of Byzantium, *Poliorketika* C.51–71; D.101–110; Frontinus, Strat. 3; *De rebus bellicis* 17; Veg. Mil. 4,31–46).

B.2. Early specialist treatises

No longer simply one topic among many as in historiography and other genres, war became a subject in its own right with the work of Xenophon (368–355 BC). His *Hellenika*, reporting on the years 411–362, included military commentaries. Xenophon's *Anabasis*, the first surviving war memoir, describes the experience of a mercenary commander. Many of its topics (e.g. crossing rivers and mountain ranges in the face of enemy resistance) were included in subsequent collections of stratagems. His account of Spartan organization, drilling, and field camps in his *Constitution of the Lacedaemonians* (Xen. Lac. 11f.) anticipates similar discussions in later tactical works. The first comprehensive treatment of the art of military command, the *Cyropaedia* – a romanticized tale of the youth and accomplishments of Cyrus the Younger (in which Spartans frequently appear in Persian garb) – explores → education, drilling, organization, nutrition, the setting up of field camps, supply operations, marches, creative aspects of command, and the general's oversight of morale and → discipline. The first independent Greek military treatise, Xenophon's *Hipparchikos*, a technical manual, proposes reforms and specific training for the Athenian cavalry in preparation for the defence of Attica against the Thebans. This work incorporates two of Xenophon's favorite themes: stratagems and good timing.

A contemporary of Xenophon, Aeneas Tacticus, a Peloponnesian with a Sophist education, made an attempt at the first military encyclopaedia (*Strategika*, Pol. 10,44; Aen. Tact. 1,2). All that survives is one lengthy fragment about the defence of a hypothetical city. The work may have consisted of eight parts: preparations, finances, camps (announced), stratagems, inspirational speeches (*akousmata*: military rhetoric?), siege warfare (a lost section on the topic of attack?), tactics (?) and naval matters (?).

Xenophon and Aeneas established models for subsequent military writings. The distinction between *Strategika* (discussions of all aspects of the arts of military command) and *Taktika* (treatises on organization, drilling and battlefield manoeuvres) emerged around 400 BC, but the lack of surviving texts and laxness in recording titles in manuscripts prevent a clear categorization of the material into one genre or the other. The Greeks made no distinction between *Strategika* and collections of stratagems (e.g. Polyaenus' *Strategika*). In addition to Xenophon's 'Socratic' and Aeneas' 'Sophist' perspectives, Aristotle offered a third perspective, which included just war and international relations among military interests. Aristotle's treatise (fragmentary) on 'just negotiations of war' (*Dikaiomata polemon*, written 334–330) is the first known monograph on just war and may have inspired Varro's lost work *De bello et pace* (Gell. NA 1,25,1–11). Demetrius of Phalerum wrote *Strategika* (Diog. Laert. 5,80) for Ptolemy I. Clearchus of Soli composed a work entitled *Taktika* and another on the topic of panic, perhaps in connection with the Peripatetic interest in Homer as a tactician [12]. The collection of data characterized the approach of this school, as examples were always important in military education. One early Peripatetic writer collected exempla to illustrate the acquisition of military materials (Aristot. Oec. 2,2,1–41). Collections of exempla – a Hellenistic phenomenon about which little is known – primarily served rhetorical purposes; but they did contain sections on military subjects (e.g. Val. Max. 7,2–4; 9,6). Frontinus' *Strategemata*, the first known collection that was purely military in subject matter, was followed in the Antonine period by the *Strategemata* of Hermogenes of Smyrna (FGrH 579) and the *Strategika* of Polyaenus, which supposedly guided Lucius Verus in the Parthian War (161–166).

Peripatetic interest waned in the first generation after Aristotle. The title *Strategika* disappeared with the exception of one treatise by the Athenian Melesermus (1st cent. AD or later; *Suda* s.v. M489). Interest in encyclopedic works, however, persisted. Xenophon's *Cyropaedia* and Cineas' epitome of Aeneas Tacticus were read in Rome. Later, the Platonist Onasander summarized Greek thinking on the art of military command in his *Strategikos* (dated to 49–59), and added to it some Roman material.

C. Taktika

As from the 3rd century BC, *Taktika* was the most common title given to military treatises. Aelianus Tacticus (1,2) made a catalogue of authors, but did not include many introductions (*eisagogai*) or specialist works. His list begins with the Aeneas epitome of Cineas, followed by Pyrrhus of Epirus (319/18–272 BC), Pyrrhus' son Alexander, Clearchus of Soli, Pausanias and Evangelus. The other authors probably date from the 2nd or early 1st centuries BC: Polybius, Eupolemus, Iphicrates and the Stoic Poseidonius.

At some point, the content of works with the title *Taktika* diverged into two strands, one practical and the other philosophical. Philosophers (except the Pythagoreans) considered tactics a variant of mathematics (Geminus fr. 2 Aujac). This development may have begun with Clearchus of Soli, who emphasized the importance of geometry for the organization and structure of the army (7,526d). Interest in this subject continued among the Platonists: Onasander also wrote a work entitled *Taktika* (?: *Suda* s. v. O 386). At Frontinus' suggestion, Aelianus Tacticus dedicated his *Taktike theoria* to Trajan. The title distinguishes his Platonic approach from Stoic discussions of the same material – to which Asclepiodotus and Arrian gave the title *Techne taktike*.

All three versions of the essentially identical text describe the organization, drilling and marching formations of an ideal Hellenistic phalanx: 16,384 men (2^{14}, a perfect power of two), taking into consideration the geometrical forms of armies and the arrangement of units, even down to subunits, to ensure a mathematical equivalence of formation strength. The three versions, however, differ in detail. It has been conjectured that Polybius' *Taktika* is the original source for Poseidonius' treatise. The textual and chronological kinship of Arrian's work with the treatise of Aelianus suggests that Arrian is an adaptation of Aelianus, although Arrian replaces many of the mathematical arguments with references to Roman practice and to his own campaign against the Alani (AD 135). He also adds the account of cavalry exercises in Cappadocia in celebration of Hadrian's *vicennalia* (AD 136) and of military reforms. Far from pure antiquarianism, Roman descriptions of the Hellenistic phalanx make reference to legions' deployment in phalanx-like formations [14].

The Stoics admired Xenophon from the earliest days of their school, and they imitated many of his writings. Odysseus became a Stoic hero. The Stoics argued that the true sage (*sophos*), outstanding in all *technai* including the art of military command, made the best general. Stoic interest in ethics and the *ius naturale* ('natural right') engendered debates on just war and military ethics.

Another form of *Taktika* appeared in the pseudo-Democritean school associated with Bolus of Mendes, who researched alchemy and sympathetic magic in the late 2nd century BC. The *Taktika* of Damocritus (FGrH 730) was probably the work wrongly attributed to Democritus of Abdera (5th cent. BC; Diog. Laert. 9,48). Its content – apparently collections of exempla of botanical, biological and magical materials put to military use – recur (directly or indirectly) in the *Kestoi* (Book 7) of the Christian Sophist Iulius Africanus: The success of the Roman Empire would require antidotes against Persian magic. Africanus, who was acquainted with collections of stratagems, hippological treatises and other works of medicine and science, advocated (in spite of its general repudiation) for the use of poison, as recommended in military treatises on siegecraft (e.g. Aen. Tact. frg. 4; Philo of Byzantium, *Poliorketika* B.53; D.91–92).

D. POLIORKETIKA

The *Strategika* of Aeneas Tacticus established the second main category of military writing, the *Poliorketika* ('Things Related to Sieges'), comprising both general works on siegecraft and treatises on the construction of artillery and siege equipment (→ Siege warfare). The surviving Aeneas fragment (32–37) discusses defensive measures to counter a besieging force. The invention of non-torsion catapults in Syracuse by the *mechanici* ('engineers') of Dionysius I in about 399 BC, together with the invention of torsion catapults in the reign of Philip II of Macedon around 350 BC (→ Generals of note, M.), expanded military technology to include a new category. Like the earlier *hoplomachoi* ('fighters in arms'), the *mechanopoioi* ('engineer–designers'), itinerant engineers specializing in siege engines and → artillery, found work with the major military powers. The art of building siege equipment and catapults was still largely limited to the verbal instruction given to apprentices by masters. Supposed treatises by *mechanici* may have been merely annotated diagrams or construction plans. Archimedes refused to record in writing the designs for the machinery he deployed against the Roman siege of Syracuse (Plut. *Marcellus* 14,7–17, esp. 17,3f.).

The only attested writing to come from the engineers of Philip and Alexander is the 'Mechanical Treatise' (*Mechanikon syngramma*, Athenaeus Mechanicus 10,10f.) by a certain Diades. The number of works on siegecraft grew sharply in the 3rd century BC. Pyrrhus wrote a work titled *Poliorketika* (Athenaeus Mechanicus 6,1; 31,6–10), while another work of the same title composed by Daimachus of Plataeaa (Athenaeus Mechanicus 5,12) dates back at least to the reign of Antiochus I (281–261). At Alexandria, probably in the reign of Ptolemy II (283–246), Ctesibius discussed a mechanized scaling ladder in his 'Commentaries' (*Hypomnemata*) (Athenaios Mechanicus 29,9–31,5). His treatise on the 'manufacture of catapults' (*Belopoiika*) describes the first non-torsion and torsion catapults. By contrast, Hero of Alexandria (60s AD) wrote a work for specialists on the 'construction and dimensions of the *cheiroballistra*', a kind of catapult similar to those depicted on the Trajan Column. Biton, an engineer in the service of Attalus II of Pergamum, wrote about highly developed versions of non-torsion artillery in his 'War machines and artillery constructions' (probably 156–155) [6].

Philo of Byzantium (c. 200 BC), a scientist familiar with the artillery workshops of Rhodes and Alexandria, was the author of the most comprehensive account of siegecraft since Aeneas Tacticus, from whose work he borrowed. His compendium of mechanics (*Mechanike Syntaxis*) also includes the *Belopoiika*, updating Ctesibius' work on torsion catapults, as well as one book each on 'Preparations' (*Paraskeuastika*) and siege techniques (*Poliorketika*) for attack (Part D) and defence (Part A–C) – the only surviving treatment of offensive and defensive siege techniques before Vegetius. The 'Preparations' (Part A) are the only classical treatise on the building of fortifications and defensive exterior structures to survive.

A century after Philo, a Rhodian 'school' of *Poliorketika* flourished. Apollonius provides a stemma: having worked on repelling the siege of Rhodes by Mithridates VI Eupator in 88/87 BC, he taught Agesistratus, who in turn taught Athenaeus (a Peripatetic from Seleucia in Cilicia) and Vitruvius (Pollio, Caesar's artillery officer). The last two of these relied on the work of Agesistratus, both enjoying the patronage of Augustus' sister Octavia. Athenaeus' work 'On Machines' (*Peri mechanematon*), dedicated to Octavia's son, M. Claudius Marcellus (*cos.* 25 BC), contains alongside his own inventions a survey of the history of various kinds of siege ramps (*testudines*) and engines [5]. Vitruvius placed chapters on artillery (10,10–12) and siege engines (10,13–16) at the end of his treatise *De architectura* (after 27 BC). He updated Agesistratus, translated Greek technical terms into Latin, and added more recent historical examples.

The last Roman treatise on poliorcetics to bear the title *Poliorcetika*, a text with many interpolations that is attributed to Trajan's architect Apollodorus of Damascus, essentially deals with machines, similar to the work of Athenaeus. The traditional association of this treatise with Trajan's Dacian Wars (101–102, 105–106) is disputed, as is its dedication to Trajan. The list of military writers in John Lydus (*De magistratibus populi Romani* 1,47,1), which does not distinguish between *tactici* and *mechanici*, mentions Apollodorus as well as the otherwise unattested treatise *Peri mechanematon* ('On Machines') by the Emperor Julian.

With the exception of Vegetius' Book 4, the Roman *Poliorcetika* end with Ammianus' excursus on artillery and siege engines (Amm. Marc. 23,4) and the proposals for reform contained in the anonymous work *De rebus bellicis*. As in his other excursus, Ammianus largely recycles known material. The only new contribution is his description of the *onager* (or *scorpio*, a machine for hurling rocks; Amm. Marc. 23,4,4–7), an important weapon of the 4th century. *De rebus bellicis*, the work of a retired bureaucrat (probably 366–370), makes proposals for reducing defence costs and manning levels. His inventions, none of which has been successfully reconstructed despite the surviving illustrations, were essentially altered versions of old equipment presented under new names, e.g. the *quadrirotis* (7): a four-wheeled version of the *carroballista*. There is still debate as to whether this work is a satirical fantasy or a presentation of serious proposals.

Few of the surviving Roman treatises on siegecraft and artillery, however, are of any practical value. Exhortations to pursue a strategy in Aeneas Tacticus, Philo and Biton are exceptions. Even the experienced artilleryman Vitruvius adopted the framework of an academic discussion of architecture and mechanics. With the exception of Hero's *Cheiroballistra*, instructions on mechanical engineering remained verbal, or else appeared in technical manuals that do not survive. Hero's antiquarian edition of Ctesibius' *Belopoiika* may have inspired Frontinus' assertion that progress in siege technology had reached its limit (Frontinus, Strat. 3 pr.). Many works belonging to the genres of theoretical mechanics or technological history [7] only touch fleetingly on warfare and siegecraft. The treatises of Philo and Apollodorus appear in the form of epistolary tracts, a common format for Hellenistic mechanical dissertations.

E. ROME

In Rome, Cato the Elder (234–149) was the first to write a military treatise. His work *De re militari* ('On Military Matters') dealt with the art of military command, organization and military law. We know that Cato urged the deployment of archers (Veg. Mil. 1,15,4). Vegetius' seven orders of battle (Veg. Mil. 3,20) derive ultimately from Cato, probably through Frontinus (e.g. Frontinus, Strat. 4,1,16). Like Cato's treatise *De agricultura* ('On Agriculture'), *De re militari* translated Greek theory into Latin. Vegetius' idea that the Spartans were the first *tactici* ('tacticians') and authors of military treatises (Veg. Mil. 3 pr. 2), also found in the Homeric scholia, likewise goes back to Cato [14. 337–342].

Generals of the Late Republican period, including Lucullus, Pompey and Caesar, read Greek military writings. The polymath and antiquarian M. Terentius Varro also dealt with *bellica disciplina* ('war practices'; Cic. Ac. 1,9), although it is not clear what is meant by this expression. Under Augustus, the antiquarian Lucius Cincius examined legal aspects of war and military law in *De re militari* (Gell. NA 16,4), following Cato's example [2]. Antiquarianism was also characteristic of military treatises of the Julio-Claudian period. The *Libri memorialium* ('Books of Memoirs') by the jurist Masurius Sabinus dealt with military honours (*coronae*) for valour and the rules governing triumphs. The exempla collection of Valerius Maximus (*Facta et dicta memorabilia*) also contained a treatment of *ius triumphi* ('right of triumphal procession'; 2,8), as well as exempla on military discipline (2,7), stratagems (7,2–4) and related military topics such as errors, recklessness, treachery, hatred and cruelty (9,2f.; 9,6; 9,8f.). Concerns for republican legality stand here in ironic contrast to the contemporary reality of imperial control of the army.

Greek military treatises served as models for Roman authors. The treatise on javelin-throwing on horseback (*De iaculatione equestri*: Plin. HN 8,159; 8,162; Plin. Ep. 3,5,3) by Pliny the Elder, which was influenced by his experiences in equestrian service on the Rhine (47–52 and 56–58), was intended as a parallel to Xenophon's *Hipparchikos*. Cornelius Celsus' encyclopaedia *De artibus* dealt with military topics among others. No indication survives of the treatment of military topics in the compilation by Frontinus (Veg. Mil. 1,8,11), unless he should be identified with the Roman *taktikos* Celsus, to whom was attributed a monograph on the victory of Domitius Corbulo over the Parthians in a surprise attack (Lyd. Mag. 3,33,2–34; cf. 1,47,1). Another manual, of uncertain date, *De munitionibus castrorum* ('On Camp Fortification') by Pseudo-Hyginus Gromaticus, claims to offer the most detailed account of a Roman field camp since Polybius (6,27–34). The author declares that he has compiled all other treatises on the subject. However, the details, often accepted by archaeologists, should be treated with caution.

In the Late Republican period, the memoirs and autobiographies of Hellenistic generals and rulers merged with the Roman practice of writing *commentarii*, which were reports of deeds (*res gestae*) presented in an unadorned style. Caesar's *Bellum Gallicum* and *Bellum Civile* developed this genre further – albeit to his own purposes and often distorting the 'facts' (e.g. Caes. B Gall. 1 as a treatise on just war). The influence of Xenophon's *Anabasis* (narrative in the 3rd person singular) is unmistakable. This set a precedent. Trajan wrote a (lost) *Dacica* describing his campaigns in Dacia. Arrian's *Alanica*, dealing with his campaign as governor of Cappadocia fighting the Alani (AD 135), may have belonged to this genre. Arrian had read Caesar's *Gallic War*. The long fragment of this treatise, a hypothetical battle ('array') against the Alani (*Extaxis kat' Alanon*; cf. Thymbrara in Xenophon's *Cyropaedia*), contains the most detailed description of a Roman marching column and battle formation of the 2nd-century Imperial period.

Taruttienus Paternus (Praetorian Prefect 177–c. 182), another of Vegetius' sources, followed Catos' model of combining tactical and legal topics. His work *De re militari* dealt mainly with the duties of officers, the status of the military ranks (e.g. the *immunes*, specialists exempt from other duties) and punishments.

F. COMPREHENSIVE ROMAN TREATISES

Perhaps the greatest loss of all military treatises is Sextus Iulius Frontinus' work 'On the Duties of a Legate' (*De officio legati*), which can be identified with 'On the Office of General' (*Peri strategias*: Lyd. Mag. 1,47,1; 3,3). It is earlier than his *Strategemata* (84–88), and its contents can be deduced from the latter and from Vegetius. Frontinus boasts of having created a 'military science' (*rei militaris scientia*, Greek *episteme*), a higher level of knowledge than a *techne* (Frontinus, Strat. 1 pr. 1). The *Strategemata*, which is structured like the other work, consists of four books: (1) preparations for deployment (modelled on Aeneas Tacticus), (2) battle and subsequent action (*tactica*), (3) attack and defence in sieges (*poliorcetica*), (4) appendix of general topics in the art of military command (*strategikon*). As the *Strategemata* treats stratagems by providing exempla to imitate or by focusing on the invention of new tricks, each book offers a table of contents for quick reference. This was an innovation of Frontinus in the field of military literature, which Aelianus Tacticus later adopted. Even more influential was Frontinus' division of military procedures according to the type of situation. This first known classification system justifies his claim to have developed a *scientia belli*. Vegetius' 'general rules of war' (*regulae bellorum generales*, Veg. Mil. 3,26,1–32) – not the chapter's title – may derive from Frontinus, as may the seven orders of battle (Veg. Mil. 3,20). Frontinus only quotes Pyrrhus and Cato, but dependence on Xenophon, Onasander, the Corpus Caesarianum and many annalists of the Roman Republic may be inferred. Vegetius' references to 'good generals' (*bonus dux* etc.) reveals his use of Frontinus. Earlier collections of exempla form the basis for Book 4 of the *Strategemata*.

About three centuries later, the reform of the Roman infantry led Flavius Vegetius Renatus, the first Christian tactician since Iulius Africanus, to write his *Epitoma rei militari* ('Abridged Treatment of Military Matters'). Quite apart from its importance for its own time, this compendium of ancient military thought became the most-read military treatise until the appearance of Clausewitz' *Vom Kriege* ('On War', posthumous 1832–1834). Vegetius' identity and dates remain controversial. His description of Emperor Gratian as *divus* ('deity'; Veg. Mil. 1,20,3) suggests that his work dates from 383 or later. A high-ranking official (*vir illustris, comes*) at Constantinople and supporter of Theodosius I seems the likeliest profile [15].

The poor quality of the Roman infantry – because of bad → recruitment, training, discipline and especially the use of 'barbarians' – motivated Vegetius more than the catastrophe of Adrianople in AD 378 (to which 3,11,7–9 perhaps refers) (→ Battles of note, B.). The Roman cavalry, based on Goths, Alani and Huns, needed no reform (Veg. Mil. 1,20,2; 3,26,34; 3,26,36). Mounted archers merited only a single mention in Vegetius (Veg. Mil. 2,16,1). Books 1–3 deal with (1) the selection and recruitment of recruits, field camps; (2) the structure of legions, duties of officers, administration, battle order and training; (3) the organization and planning of a campaign (supplies, troops' health, signalling, camps), concerns prior to the battle, and provisions after it – for victory and defeat alike. Book 4 is an appendix on siege techniques and naval issues. The publication of the individual books at different times explains the repetition of some topics from different sources. Military sources mentioned by name are Cato, Celsus, Frontinus, Paternus and the *Constitutiones* of Augustus, Trajan and Hadrian (Veg. Mil. 1,8,10f.; 2,3,6f.). Although he was familiar with Greek *Taktika* (1,8,9; 3 pr. 2), Vegetius patriotically emphasized Roman authors and thus ignored the Greek origins of material in Cato and Frontinus. One exception concerns the genre of the manual, which he does refer to. There are visible borrowings from Onasander through Frontinus. The source or sources for Book 4 cannot be determined if they are not from Frontinus [8].

Writing as an antiquarian as he often does, Vegetius argues for the superiority of a citizen army as compared to mercenaries ('barbarians') and strives for the revival of 'ancient Roman' *virtus* and *disciplina*. His *antiqua legio* ('the ancient legion'), a theoretical construct, does not resemble the army of any era. His skillful blending of contemporary and Republican practices prevents us from identifying actual realities of the 4th century. The training system, for instance, may be from Cato. The details he gives regarding battle orders further illustrate this chronological blending, although the deployment of a phalanx-shaped formation does reflect contemporary practice. Battle should only be sought if a general is confident of his superiority and is able to exploit advantages of terrain or choice of time. A victory without battle is preferable, which leads to the doctrine of stratagems: exhaustion of the enemy through hunger, postponement of confrontation or victory through ruse. Such practices enable a smaller force to defeat a larger one, and they help minimize losses [13].

Flavius Eutropius revised the text at Constantinople in 450. He may have brought all four books together into one, and he changed some chapter titles (e.g. 3,26: *regulae bellorum generales*). An expanded form of these *regulae*/rules and other sections of Vegetius appeared in Greek around 600 ([Maur.] Strat. 8,2). Eutropius may have omitted the name of the emperor addressed in order to confer universal validity on the treatise.

☞ Battle; Camp; Discipline; Education; Eve-of-battle speech; March; Recruitment; Siege warfare; Strategy; Training

BIBLIOGRAPHY
[1] J. ANDERSON, Military Theory and Practice in the Age of Xenophon, 1970 [2] V. GIUFFRÈ, La letteratura 'de re militari', 1974 [3] M. JÄHNS, Geschichte der Kriegswissenschaften vornehmlich in Deutschland, 1889–1891 [4] D. LAPSE / C. SCHUBERT, Seemacht, Seeherrschaft und Seestrategie bei Pseudo-Xenophon, in: Klio 94, 2012, 55–81 [5] O. LENDLE, Texte und Untersuchungen zum technischen Bereich der antiken Poliorketik, 1983 [6] E. MARSDEN, Greek and Roman Artillery. Technical Treatises, 1971 [7] B. MEISSNER, Die technologische Fachliteratur der Antike, 1999 [8] D. SCHENK, Flavius Vegetius. Die Quellen der Epitoma Rei Militaris, 1930 [9] A. SCHILLER, Sententiae Hadriani de re militari, in: W. Becker / L. Schnoss von Carolsfeld (eds.), Sein und Werden im Recht. Festgabe für Ulrich von Lübtow, 1970, 295–306 [10] O. Spaulding, Pen and Sword in Greece and Rome, 1937 [11] E. WHEELER, The Hoplomachoi and Vegetius' Spartan Drillmasters, in: Chiron 13, 1983, 1–20 [12] E. WHEELER, Polla kena tou polemou. The History of a Greek Proverb, in: GRBS 29, 1988, 153–184 [13] E. WHEELER, Stratagem and the Vocabulary of Military Trickery, 1988 [14] E. WHEELER, The Legion as Phalanx in the Late Empire. Part I, in: Y. Le Bohec / C. Wolff (eds.), L'Armée romaine de Diolétian à Valentinien Ier, 2004, 309–358 [15] E. WHEELER, Review of M. Charles, Vegetius in Context, in: BMCR, 2008 (https://bmcr.brynmawr.edu/2008/2008.06.42/) [16] E. WHEELER, Polyaenus. Scriptor Militaris, in: K. Brodersen (ed.), Neue Studien zu Polyän–New Studies in Polyaenus, 2010, 7–54.

EVERETT L. WHEELER

Military service

A. Greek
B. Roman

A. GREEK

A.1. Preparations for war
A.2. In the field
A.3. The process of battle
A.4. After the battle

War service was already a status symbol in the Homeric period and in the era of the Mycenaean warrior lords of the Bronze Age [21]. As a mark of distinction, it was not reserved only for the elites of society. As Greek society developed from the Archaic period through the Classical to the Hellenistic period, ordinary citizens increasingly performed military service on behalf of those of higher status. By doing so, they earned freedom and civic rights, thereby acquiring the external trappings of membership in the upper echelons (Aristot. Ath. pol. 4,1f.). Comedy in Hellenistic literature presented the 'vainglorious soldier' alongside Achilles. Professional soldiers such as Aeneas Tacticus wrote of war and society, complementing the accounts of the upper-class Athenians Thucydides and Xenophon. These diverse treatments of war and military service culminated in the Roman Empire, perhaps best articulated in the works (in Greek) by the Roman senator, soldier and historian Lucius Flavius Arrianus (Arrian). His *Anabasis of Alexander* and *Tactica* are studies of war from both historical and practical perspectives [16]. The experiences of warfare in all its dimensions in the Grecian world – preparations for war, the prosecution of war, and the consequences of war – reveal the nature and general condition of military service.

A.1. PREPARATIONS FOR WAR

A.1.1. Preparation and training
A.1.2. Military equipment

A.1.1. PREPARATION AND TRAINING

Preparations for war took place in familiar and family surroundings. From the Homeric period onwards, warriors were organized into kinship groups. The fighting forces of the *Iliad* are thus shown as units of tribes and clans (Hom. Il. 2,362f.). Military and social organization of this kind continued into later eras, as at Athens, for instance (following the reforms of Cleisthenes), when men served in ten contingents or regiments (*taxeis*) by tribe, each under the command of a *taxiarchos*, with smaller units led by younger officers, the *lochagoi* (Aristot. Ath. pol. 30,2; 31,3; 61,3). In short, men fought alongside their kinsmen, friends and neighbours. This reality inspired deeds of heroism, and it also intensified the shock of death on the battlefield, as in the case of Aeschylus, who in ca. 490 BC witnessed the death of his brother Cynaegeirus at the Battle of Marathon (Hdt. 6,114).

While the roots of Greek soldiery lay in family connections, the rise of the *polis* (ca. mid-7th cent. BC) saw communities begin to regularize and systematize military training. The purported reforms of Lycurgus in → Sparta are the best-known examples, but other polities likewise introduced formal military → training. A recently discovered text from ancient Arcadia, dated to about 500 BC, attests to such training of citizens, which may have been mandatory up to the age of 50 [7. 1–30]. Lycurgus' Spartan system spawned the famous lifestyle of *agoge* (literally 'guidance'), in which military training and service began at the age of seven and continued to the age of 60 (Plut. *Lycurgus* 4. 16,4–18,4). In the funeral oration he attributes to Pericles, Thucydides (2,39,1f.) depicts a far less militant Athens, but this may be rhetorical and ideological exaggeration. During the 4th century, young Athenians received military training in a youth corps, the *ephebeia* (source collection in [3]). Although the source material is unclear, this training was probably in effect already in the 5th century. Around 458/57 BC, the Athenians sent a force of old and young soldiers to fight the Corinthians (Thuc. 1,105,4). The fact that young men – essentially 'recruits' – were required to perform active war service indicates that the military training of young citizens was already well established.

The emergence of formalized military exercises coincides with the rise of the *polis*, but kinship relations and age groupings as already attested in Homer forged ties of no less significance. A contingent of Athenians organized by *phylai* ('clans') usually consisted of a large body of fighters – sometimes hundreds of fighters when the situation was critical, as at the Battle of Chaeronea between Athens and Macedonia in 338 BC. Within the context of the Lycurgan reforms (and subsequent changes), Sparta also established a complex military structure of divisions or companies (*lochoi*), subdivided into smaller units of *pentekostyes* ('fifties') and *enomotiai* ('[men] bound by oath') (Thuc. 5,68,3). In pressing circumstances, fighters from such units could be temporarily assigned to a special task, as when the Spartans set up a garrison on the island of Sphacteria when Athens threatened it (Thuc. 4,8,9).

Such divisions complemented the deployment of 'peer groups'. As noted above, young (aged 18–20) and old (over 55) men at Athens formed a civic militia with responsibilities for security and as an army reserve (Thuc. 1,105,4). Similar classifications were made in Sparta, where citizens were placed in a sequence of 40 age groups from men of 20 years up to 60 (Thuc. 5,64; Xen. Hell. 6,4,17; Xen. Lac. pol. 2,1–4,7). Organizational forms like this offered what scholars now call 'unit cohesion': the power that inspires men to defend their 'brothers' and fight well in front of them. Both Athens and Sparta kept registers or lists of names of those who were accountable to military service (Aristot. Ath. pol. 42,1; Thuc. 6,43; 5,64). The Monument of the Eponymous Heroes in the Athenian Agora functioned as a 'bulletin board' listing the age groups called up for army service [4. 157–159].

Little is known with certainty about how Greek soldiers were trained or how preparations were made for battle. The → phalanx, the basic formation in traditional hoplite combat, certainly required drilling and exercises, because marching in step while keeping ranks is not easy to do while performing complex turning manoeuvres (as anyone who, for example, has taken part in a marching band knows). At Marathon, the Athenians and their allies from Plataeae moved forward steadily and methodically before finally advancing on the larger Persian army at the double (Hdt. 6,112) (→ Battles of note, F.). The Macedonian phalanx of Philip and Alexander, armed with the long pike (*sarissa*), was well able to manoeuvre skilfully in uneven terrain, even in the face of the enemy (Arr. An. 1,6,1–4). Manoeuvres like these would only be possible after much drill practice.

Group dancing may have further assisted this practice. Such a dance is depicted on the Atarbos Relief, a work of art dedicated at Athens around 322 BC. It shows young men engaged in the *pyrrhiche* war dance, a performance that was associated with the Panathenaic Games, but that was also known to other Greeks. The men danced in time with their shields, and spectators and perhaps even jurors joined in [8. 256–267]. The historians Xenophon (Xen. An. 6,1,5–12) and Arrian (Arr. An. 2,24,6) report celebrations after battle where the *pyrrhiche* (along with further contests, as at the end of Homer's *Iliad*) also played a part, albeit in this case as a cathartic ritual for coping with the trauma of war [17. 189–191].

Fighting in battle involved physical exhaustion. Men trained for this through the *hoplitodromos*, a foot race in full armour, and with wrestling matches. The *hoplitodromos* was a prestigious contest held, for instance, at the Panhellenic Games at Olympia and Delphi – which suggests that all Greeks of an age liable for military service performed it. A drinking vessel decorated by the Antiphon Painter (c. 480 BC) shows young men training for the race [14. 8]. Wrestling matches formed part of the contests. They enabled the revolutionaries in the circle of Epameinondas at Thebes to gather and prepare openly for the rebellion by which they expelled the Spartan occupiers from their city in 379/78 BC (Plut. *Pelopidas* 8; → Generals of note, F.).

Men of the Homeric era learned the skills of warfare, as they learned much else, by observing their older relatives. Early in the 4th century BC, teachers of warfare began touring the Greek city states. Xenophon, in his *Memorabilia*, relates a conversation between Socrates and Pericles the Younger, in which are mentioned the collections of *strategemata* that were available to young men for the study of the art of war (Xen. Mem. 3,5,22). One surviving example is the 4th-century BC manual by Aeneas Tacticus on the subject of 'How to withstand a siege' [1]. Manuals such as this and reports of trainers teaching lessons continue to be attested in abundance down to the Roman Imperial period (→ Military literature). They include the *Strategemata* of the war veteran Frontinus (1st cent. AD), actually a guide to conduct in politics and the military, and the treatise by the Macedonian author Polyaenus (c. AD 160), which is more of a rhetorical work. Treatises such as these supply us with valuable information, not only about renowned generals and their victories and defeats, but also about tactics and methods of battle [2].

A.1.2. MILITARY EQUIPMENT

As modern archaeology demonstrates, the manufacture of military equipment is thousands of years older than Greek culture. Since the Homeric period, such products have included helmets, shields, armour, and a plethora of weapons made of bronze or other materials (Hom. Il. 1,17; 2,578; 13,130–135). There are depictions on some ceramic vessels of workshop scenes in which bronzesmiths are busy making helmets [14. 52], with a selection of their finished workpieces hanging on the wall. The manufacturing of and trading in arms were activities as widespread in Greek antiquity as they are in the modern age. Aristophanes, for instance, makes reference to the sufferings of weapons dealers and makers of spears and helmets whose livelihoods disappeared as a result of the Peace of Nicias (421 BC), when the Peloponnesian War was suspended for a time (Aristoph. Pax 1209–1264).

The various pieces of equipment that different men took with them into battle exhibited stark differences in cost and scope. A member of the elite such as the extravagant Athenian aristocrat Alcibiades bore a lavishly worked shield that was decorated with gold and with an armed Eros hurling thunderbolts (Plut. *Alcibiades* 16,2). Less wealthy Athenians like Socrates generally needed 75–100 drachmas – three months' earnings for a specialist laborer – to equip themselves with just a shield, a spear, and – as a helmet – perhaps a head covering made of nothing but felt (*pilos*). During the Peloponnesian War (→ Wars of note, H.), the Athenians recruited about 700 *thetes* (men from the lowest category of the property census) to provide a naval force for the Sicilian Expedition (Thuc. 6,43,3). These men were equipped out of the public purse, although presumably only with the most basic weapons, if any at all (cf. Thuc. 4,32,2).

A.2. IN THE FIELD

A.2.1. Camp life
A.2.2. Discipline

A.2.1. CAMP LIFE

In all periods, soldiers probably spent more time on the march and in field camps than in battle. Like the Roman army after them, the Greeks took steps to defend their camps. The palisade fence in Homer's *Iliad* may be the oldest and best-known example of such defensive workings (Hom. Il. 15,345). Another example is the camp protected by a ditch that was built by the Athenians in their effort to put down a rebellion on Euboea in 349/48 BC (Plut. *Phocion* 12,3). Camp life was seldom easy. There was always work to do, whether obtaining provisions and other essential goods, or securing the location. The classic example of a negative outcome when a camp was put in the wrong place and not secured properly is offered by the Athenian fleet at Aigos potamos in 405 BC. While the sailors and soldiers went off searching for provisions and water with no plan in place, the Spartans seized the poorly located army camp with a lightning surprise attack (Xen. Hell. 2,1,25f.).

Unlike today's soldiers, who are responsible for the condition of their own weapons and equipment and sometimes for preparing their own food, Greek warriors delegated these tasks to companions and servants. From the Homeric period to the Archaic, these were invariably dependents or slaves. The best-known example is Patroclus, a *therapon* ('attendant') of Achilles who served him in various matters and also fought, as his famous death proves (Hom. Il. 11,611–615; 11,786–787; [21.

42–44]). The role of slaves in the Archaic and Classical periods was similar (e.g. at Marathon: Paus. 1,32,3). They sometimes attained a status equal to that of their former masters (e.g. ca. 494 in Argos, cf. Hdt. 6,83; although their exact rank is unclear). Slaves often received a 'diluted' citizenship of lesser value, as happened at Plataeae for the slaves who volunteered to fight for Athens at the naval battle of Arginusae in 406 BC. In Aristophanes' comedy *The Frogs*, the slave Xanthias complains that he did not take part in the battle, and hence must remain a slave (Aristoph. Ran. 33f.; 192; 693–699).

The Spartans and their helots offer by far the best evidence in regard to Greek soldiers and their companions on campaign and in battle. Herodotus reports that at the decisive battle against the Persians at Plataeae, each of the 5,000 Spartans was accompanied by seven helots (Hdt. 9,28,2). This, however, may have been an unusually large number, reflecting the fear that sending off so many Spartan citizens might trigger one of the helot rebellions that posed such a constant terror for Sparta. In the field, the helots supported their Spartan lords in various functions. They prepared food and took care of equipment, but in battle they also took their places in the midst of the fighting. Herodotus tells us that during the inspection of the battlefield after the Battle of Thermopylae, the Persians identified many fallen Spartans as helots who had lost their lives fighting alongside their lords (Hdt. 8,25). During the late 5th century, the Spartans came to accept the growing importance of auxiliaries, and granted them the status of *neodamodeis* ('newly belonging to the people'), which conferred freedom.

As Greek society made the transition from the Classical to the Hellenistic period, military structures also evolved. The famous campaign of the Persian prince Cyrus included numerous support staff, such as mule drivers and servants, who are rarely unmentioned by Xenophon. He only takes note of their presence when they come into direct contact with the warriors they serve (Xen. An. 5,8,5). The numbers of non-combatants were sometimes significant. The army of Alexander the Great was accompanied not only by the usual groups described above, but also by a staff of technical military advisors, scientists and entertainers. Many of them were Greeks; all were there to support the king and his court and the army as a whole, and to keep up morale [19. 122–129].

A.2.2. DISCIPLINE

Even if the necessities of life were provided through the efforts of others, camp life was monotonous and strenuous. Many issues needed to be addressed. For the generals, the most pressing issues were the need to maintain discipline and problem of desertion (*lipotaxia*). Bored by the monotony of camp life and drilling, soldiers sometimes deserted and returned home, as happened in 349/48 BC in the case of the Athenian army commanded by Phocion (Plut. *Phocion* 12,3). Democratically elected generals had little authority to act against such lack of discipline. The inflexible discipline demanded by the Athenian mercenary general Iphicrates, for instance, would be unthinkable. Iphicrates killed a guard whom he found sleeping, later remarking, 'I sent him back where I found him' (Frontinus, Str. 3,12,2f.; cf. also Xen. An. 2,6,9f.; 2,6,14f.; 5,8,8–25 and the discipline of the mercenary force of Cyrus).

The life of a soldier was unlike any other. Such a life could inspire the ideas of a literary genius such as Aeschylus (as is clear in the epitaph that survives in his *vita*, as in his plays *The Persians* and *Seven Against Thebes*) or a thinker such as Socrates. In Potidaea in the early phase of the Peloponnesian War, Plato tells us, Socrates astonished his comrades with his aesthetic reflections amidst much adversity on a campaign dominated by great suffering and losses (cf. Thuc. 2,58) (Plat. Symp. 219e). There is increasing awareness today that the consequences of these experiences of war were of great significance to the philosophy of Socrates and his famous trial and execution [12. 131–153].

A.3. THE PROCESS OF BATTLE

Animal sacrifices and urging on from the generals preceded the meeting of the rival battle lines. A rapid advance accelerating to a run in the final steps seems to have been the preferred mode of attack in many places (which also explains the aforementioned prestige of the *hoplitodromos* at the Panhellenic Games). The Spartans, however, were known for advancing at a moderate pace set by their buglers (Thuc. 5,70; Ath. 14, 627D, 630E). At all events, the clash of weapons, shouting and groaning will have been immense, with the bronze-covered shields of the hoplites only adding to it. The results were as brutal as they were chaotic. A 30 cm spear tip causes terrible wounds. It penetrates shields and inflicts lethal injury. A Spartan officer buried in an Athenian grave died with the blade lodged in his ribcage [4. 133]; [13. 234]. The *kopis*, a heavy, single-edged sword particularly valued by the cavalry was capable of slicing a man's face almost completely in two, as happened to a Theban soldier ('Gamma 16') who fell at Chaeronea [18. 102]. Spears sometimes splintered, sword blades broke, and shields failed. At times like this, stones became deadly weapons, like the lump of rock hefted by the Spartan Arimnestus to kill the Persian general Mardonius at Plataeae (Plut. *Aristides* 19,1).

Corpses piled up in such carnage. At Delium (424 BC), 14% of all Athenian hoplites who had had contact with the enemy died (c. 1,000 of 7,000 men). A further thousand suffered slight or serious injuries and many of those died in the wake of the battle. At Sphacteria (425 BC), 33% of the Spartans fell in battle (148 of 440), with many more doubtless suffering injuries (cf. Thuc. 4,38,1). A 'normal' death rate of 5% has been postulated, but the evidence from Delium and Sphacteria suggests that this is an overly conservative estimate (→ Consequences of war, A.; cf. [9]). It has also been suggested that hoplite battles were over in a matter of minutes (e.g. [10. 221]). This is also doubtful. The Battle of Delium probably started in mid-afternoon and continued until nightfall, thus lasting about three hours (Thuc. 4,90,4; 4,93,1). A hard battle with heavy losses between Mantinea and Tegea in the winter of 423/22 only ended as night fell (Thuc. 4,134), which is evidence of a battle lasting longer than mere minutes (what would be the purpose of starting a battle after sunset?). The battle between the Athenians and Spartans at Sphacteria was not fought in one place, but on the move and on uneven terrain. It began before sunrise and lasted almost the whole day (Thuc. 4,32; 4,36). A similarly drawn-out campaign by the Athenians in Aetolia in 427 BC took a similar toll in dead and wounded (Thuc. 3,93–102; → Timeframe of war).

Brutality on the battlefield would seem to be an obvious occurrence, but it was probably only one side of the reality. In his collection of character sketches, Theophrastus, Aristotle's successor as principal of the Lycaeum, depicts the 'coward': a soldier able to shirk battle because he has supposedly forgotten his sword, and who leads a wounded comrade from the battlefield (Theophr. char. 25,3–6). Although Theophrastus' main intent is to praise the more disciplined and soldierly Macedonians of his own time, he also reveals the laxity of the Greek phalanx and the readiness of some individuals simply to escape the dangers of the fight (→ Cowardice).

A.4. AFTER THE BATTLE
As in the modern era, war reports and details about battles were keenly awaited. Plato tells of the homecoming of Socrates from Potidaea early in the Peloponnesian War, and the plethora of questions his friends had for him (Pl. Chrm. 153b–c). News from distant fronts reached home only belatedly and often came as a shock. For instance, when an anonymous traveller told of the Sicilian catastrophe, thinking it widely known, the consternation among those hearing him was all the greater (Plut. *Nicias* 30). Greek communities were tightly woven, and news of a defeat sometimes triggered violent reactions. For instance, the sole Athenian survivor of a campaign in Aegina was killed by angry widows on his return home. Soon afterwards, a law was passed banning Dorian costume with its long and lethal cloakpins (Hdt. 5,87f.).

In some communities, the dead also came home. While the heroes of Marathon were famously buried where they fell, the practice emerged from the 460s onwards of cremating fallen Athenians on the battlefield, then sending them home in small caskets (Aesch. Ag. 437–444; cf. [17. 174]). The remains were taken to the official public tomb (*demosion sema*) in the Athenian district of Kerameikos, where burial took place with a wake and a dedicatory oration by a leading citizen (Thuc. 2,34–46). Later, the names of the fallen, listed by affiliation, would be taken to their respective *phylai*, just as when organizing for war. Other communities practised similar rituals. For example, there was a similar park set up as a memorial site in Thespiae, also with lists of names and heroic statues in memory of the fallen. Thebes had Delia, a memorial park built from the spoils that came from the victory over the Athenians at Delium [11]; [20. 104]. The Spartans had no such rituals or ceremonies. They buried their dead where they fell, with few pains taken back home for those who died of their wounds. Exceptions may have been made in the case of Spartan kings, for example Leonidas (Paus. 3,14,1), or Agesilaus, whose body was embalmed on the North African coast (in wax; honey was usual) and brought home (Plut. *Agesilaus* 40,3).

The Homeric heroes appear unmoved by the horrors of the battlefield. Later sources evoke those horrors in different ways. It was possible to depict pale, shaking soldiers with chattering teeth in the minutes leading up to battle (Polyaeus, Strat. 9,1,8; Gorg. Hel. 16–18; cf. [18. 158–160]). Another picture presents men going blind from the shock of close combat and from witnessing the deaths of others, as with the Athenian Epizelus at Marathon (Hdt. 6,117) or Anticrates of Cnidus (of whom an inscription survives at Epidaurus [6]). Yet, on closer inspection, Homer too offers Antilochus' tearful account to Achilles of the killing of Patroclus by Hector (Hom. Il. 18,17), and Achilles' ensuing reaction, driven by grief and guilt. Homer describes Achilles as sleepless and refusing to eat, intent only on vengeance (Hom. ll. 19,213f.). Symptoms of psychological trauma like these are a well-known phenomena in modern in modern experiences of war. Scholars today approach such evidence in the Greek sources with greater understanding [15]; [17].

A battle was a terrible experience in the Greek world. The frequency of such experiences has been called into question, perhaps on the assumption that the effects of trauma are somehow dose-dependent (i.e. if one is exposed only rarely, the consequences are less severe). This must be false. In reality, a single experience of battle can cause lifelong trauma [20]. Exemplifying this is the story of Epizelus, who remained behind blind at Marathon and, according to Herodotus (who wrote his *Histories* 50 years later), spent the rest of his life there.

☞ Cowardice; Emotions; Fleet; Slavery

BIBLIOGRAPHY

SOURCES
[1] AINEIAS THE TACTICIAN, How to Survive Under Siege, translation, introduction and commentary by D. Whitehead, 1990 [2] B. CAMPBELL, Greek and Roman Military Writers. Selected Readings, 2004 [3] P. HARDING (ed.), From the End of the Peloponnesian War to the Battle of Ipsus, translated by P. Harding, 1985.

SECONDARY LITERATURE
[4] J. CAMP, The Archaeology of Athens, 2001 [5] J. DUCAT, Perspectives on Spartan Education in the Classical Period, in: S. Hodkinson / A. Powell (eds.), Sparta. New Perspectives, 1999, 43–66 [6] E.J. EDELSTEIN / L. EDELSTEIN, Asclepius. Collection and Interpretation of the Testimonies, 1945 (reprint 1998) [7] J. HEINRICHS, Military Integration in Late Archaic Arkadia. New Evidence from a Bronze Pinax (ca. 500 BC) of the Lykaion, in: W. Heckel et al. (eds.), The Many Faces of War in the Ancient World, 2015, 1–89 [8] J.M. HURWIT, The Athenian Acropolis, 1999 [9] P. KRENTZ, Casualties in Hoplite Battles, in: GRBS 26, 1985, 13–21 [10] P. KRENTZ, The Battle of Marathon, 2010 [11] P. LOW, Remembering War in Fifth-Century Greece. Ideologies, Societies, and Commemoration beyond Democratic Athens, in: World Archaeology 35, 2003, 98–111 [12] S.S. MONOSON, Socrates in Combat. Trauma and Resilence in Plato's Political Theory, in: P. Meineck / D. Konstan (eds.), Combat Trauma and the Ancient Greeks, 2014, 131–162 [13] C.F. SALAZAR, The Treatment of War Wounds in Graeco-Roman Antiquity, 2000 [14] N. SEKUNDA, Greek Hoplite 480–323 BC, 2000 [15] J. SHAY, Achilles in Vietnam, 1994 [16] P.A. STADTER, Arrian of Nicomedia, 1980 [17] L.A. TRITLE, From Melos to My Lai. War and Survival, 2000 [18] L.A. TRITLE, A New History of the Peloponnesian War, 2009 [19] L.A. TRITLE, Alexander and the Greeks. Artists and Soldiers, Friends and Enemies, in: W. Heckel / L.A. Tritle (eds.), Alexander the Great. A New History, 2009, 121–140 [20] L.A. TRITLE, 'Ravished Minds' in the Ancient World, in: P. Meineck / D. Konstan (eds.), Combat Trauma and the Ancient Greeks, 2014, 87–104 [21] H. VAN WEES, Status Warriors, 1992.

LAWRENCE A. TRITLE

B. ROMAN

B.1. From the origins to the Imperial period
B.2. Conditions of military service
B.3. Term of military service
B.4. Legal and financial situation
B.5. Specialist roles
B.6. Exiting service

B.1. FROM THE ORIGINS TO THE IMPERIAL PERIOD

In the earliest phase, the militia system reflected the small city state, which fought wars close to home between the sowing of the seed and the harvest [47]. Recruitment at first was based on the structure of the *comitia curiata*, 'Curiate Assembly' [5]. Because the call-up for active military service depended on the assets of the person concerned (cf. the structure of the *comitia centuriata*, 'Centuriate Assembly' with its five *classes* for the infantry), a heavy burden developed on those groups that only just met the minimum census, whereas the *proletarii* (citizens without property) or *infra classem* ('beneath the class') were not generally called up to serve in a legion. Obligatory military service extended to all *cives Romani* ('Roman citizens') from the ages of 16 to 46 [50]. The fact that many wars were fought far away and often offered little promise of booty created a crisis in the system of war service in the late 2nd century BC [19]. This was especially difficult for smallholders because of the long absences involved [49]. The army reform of Marius (→ Generals of note, K.) addressed issues that had long been affecting the military [47]. Recruitment was now extended to those who did not fulfil the admission criteria (*capite censi*) of the *census* (e.g. Liv. 1,43) [1]. The prospect of booty (*praeda* or *spolia*) was one of the most important motivations for war service [63]. Soldiers owed obedience first and foremost to their commander, to whom they were connected by the *clientela*, the patron–client relationship [50]. Generals like these fought out the civil wars of the later Republic [17]. By the end of these wars, Augustus had an army of 60 legions, which he managed to reduce to 28 [47]. The professional army of the Imperial period was characterized by obligation and continuity [52]. Standing at the pinnacle of the military administration was the emperor. The role of Praetorian Prefect now also developed into a centerpoint of army administration [30]. During the 1st century AD, the annual military budget ran to approximately 500 million sesterces (HS), a sum that probably tripled by the Severan period [9]. Two thirds of the legionaries in Italy were still recruits under the Julio-Claudian dynasty [32], with forced recruitment probably more common than scholars long assumed [11]. Roman conquests went hand in hand with the integration into the army of new allies and subjugated enemies [22]. → Auxiliaries in the Republican period were provided as part of a *foedus*, 'treaty' [27]. In the Imperial period, *ad hoc* allies of the Republic were replaced by regular auxiliary units (*auxilia*) [46]. The annual recruitment requirement for the auxiliary forces was greater than that for the legions [11]. The recruitment of so many people to the *auxilia* weakened the military capabilities of the affected territories to counter possible rebellions [47]. Proper management of citizenship as a privilege that could be earned through military service was one key to Rome's lasting success in dealing with the *auxilia* [19].

B.2. CONDITIONS OF MILITARY SERVICE

Beginning with the Marian army reform, if not before, drilling (*disciplina militaris*) came to primary importance [4]. This was harshly enforced in the professional army founded by Augustus (Suet. Aug. 24,2). The centurions embodied Roman severity, as Tac. Ann. 1,23 reports on their right of punishment. Daily service for a soldier began with morning roll-call [24]. One ubiquitous component of everyday camp life was a strictly regulated guard duty [43]. Alongside the training of recruits (*tirones*), there were regular combat exercises for soldiers, with participation compulsory for as long as they were in army service [37]. Depending on the unit, there was required training for deployment preparation, for example with horses and their care [31]. The use of artillery firing weapons (catapults) also had to be practised [6]. Specialist authors such as Vegetius offer details on the various aspects of training (Veg. Mil. 1,8–28). Jos. BI 3,72–76 calls military drilling 'battle without bloodshed', and he calls battle 'drilling with bloodshed'. Furthermore, there were regular administrative tasks, one important one being the setting up of a *pridianum*, a personnel inventory for the unit concerned [30]. The proper supply of provisions was crucial to maintaining soldiers' satisfaction [18]. Meat, fish and shellfish enriched the otherwise grain-based menu [19]. The food provisions offered on campaign usually differed, relying more heavily on grain, if for no reason other than logistics and perishability. The staple food was 'soldiers' bread' (*panis militaris*) (→ Supply, B.). Of no less importance to soldiers' daily lives were the camp villages (*canabae*) directly adjacent to the base, which offered a broad spectrum of services and industries (from workshops to brothels). Admission to the army, with its associated administrative procedures, and especially with the performance of the *sacramentum* (service oath; Epikt., *Diatribaí* 1,14,15) to the emperor, should be understood as a rite of initiation [21]. A soldier had the right to bear arms [3]. However, members of the military were recognizable even when not in full kit. One way of identifying a soldier permanently was tattooing [25]. The quintessential emblem of a soldier was the *cingulum*, the army belt. This symbol began to grow in importance after AD 200, as society became more and more heavily militarized [49]. Service in the *auxilia* led to the integration of provincials into Roman society and accelerated the Romanization of provinces [29]. Cottage industries specializing in the manufacture of weapons and other equipment settled in the *canabae* [14]. Living in these settlements were the families of soldiers who, despite the ban on marriage, participated in illegitimate relationships [53]. Like civilians, army members joined together in *collegia* ('associations'), although Septimius Severus cracked down on this practice (Dig. 47,22,1) [38]. Another important aspect of military life was involvement in ceremonies (e.g. military parades) [41]. Late Antiquity was characterized by the barbarization of the army [60].

B.3. TERM OF MILITARY SERVICE

The term of military service in the Republican militia army is often given as 16 years with reference to Pol. 6,19,2, but it is also possible, as Plut. C. Gracchus 2,5 implies, that it was ten years [28]. Augustus in 13 BC initially set the term of service at 16 years for legionaries and 12 years for Praetorians (Cass. Dio 54,25), before raising it to 20 years for legionaries and 16 for Praetorians in AD 5 (Cass. Dio 55,23) [40]. Ultimately, the term of service for legionaries was extended to 25–26 years. This was done primarily to reduce costs. The more men who died before achieving their *honesta missio* (honourable discharge), the less had to be paid out in discharge settlements [17]. Soldiers were sometimes forced to serve more than 30 years to win their discharge (Tac. Ann. 1,17) [24]. Up to 10,000 recruits had to be found every year to maintain the legions' fighting strength [21]. Peregrines, slaves and *liberti* (freedmen) were excluded from serving in legions [24].

B.4. LEGAL AND FINANCIAL SITUATION

No relationship between a soldier and a woman during his term of service was valid in law; in other words, there could never be a *iustum matrimonium* ('legal marriage') [36]. Septimius Severus lifted the ban on marriage in AD 197 [29]. Augustus introduced a special status among the *cives Romani* for soldiers who had been subject to the *patria potestas* ('father's authority') in civilian life, whereby – regardless of the wishes of their *pater familias* ('father of the family') – they had, among other things, rights of disposal over their *bona castrensia*, that is, everything they acquired in the course of their service in the way of pay, booty, *donativa* (supplementary payments), and so forth, and the right to carry out legal transactions accordingly (Inst. Iust. 2,12) [10]. Legionaries in field or permanent camps lived in the *contubernium*, that is, a 'tent community' of roughly eight men [21]. This way of life instilled strong cohesion within *contubernia*, and this cohesion played an important role in the legion's fighting strength [19]. The size of accommodations in a permanent camp made the private lives of officers considerably more pleasant than life in the *contubernium*. They had about twenty times as much room as a common soldier [18]. Yet, military service offered men from the lower social classes benefits that included a regular income, ample provisions and a roof over their head [16]. Passing sentence on a soldier fell under military jurisdiction, as did civilian complaints against soldiers [21]. The catalogue of punishments for offences was comprehensive and merciless. The *decimatio* was one of the harshest methods in the army's repertoire of disciplinary measures (e.g. Amm. Marc. 24,3,2; App. Civ. 2,48,195): every tenth man of the unit was taken to be executed by his own comrades [19]. On the other hand, soldiers were exempt from labouring in the mines and from torture (Dig. 49,16,3,1). On each payday, an auxiliary infantryman received 250 HS, a legionary 300 HS and a cavalryman – whether of a legion or an auxiliary unit – 350 HS, until pay was raised in the reign of Domitian [58]. A legionary's annual → pay was 225 *denarii* under Augustus, 300 in the reign of Domitian, 550 under Septimius Severus and 750 starting in the time of Caracalla [1]. A *centurio* ('centurion') who did not belong to the *primi ordines* (the 1st cohort of a legion) received 15 times the pay of a common soldier in the legion, the *praefectus castrorum* ('camp commander') no less than 60 times as much [57]. Soldiers could also expect *donativa*, for instance on the accession of a new emperor or in situations of crisis [29]. Augustus, for instance, bestowed 75 *denarii* to every legionary in his will (Suet. Aug. 101,2). The army of the Imperial period accelerated the process by which the Roman Empire came increasingly to be dominated by monetary factors [9]. A professional soldier had to spend up to 30% of his pay on board [18]. Rampant inflation in the 3rd century made military service drastically less attractive [35]. Soldiers now took on additional work in infrastructure, agriculture, forestry, logistics, communications, policing and justice [52]. Another important area of responsibility was the administrative control of the stationing zone of each region and its hinterland [34]. Army bases of the Imperial period should be seen as catalysts of local and regional economic life in view of the production, distribution and consumption of goods [20]; [18]. Soldiers sometimes obtained building materials, or even made them (e.g. brickworks), and they also organized the procurement of food and animal feed (→ Supply, B.) [13]. In addition to state-regulated forced recruitment campaigns, the crisis of the 3rd century also led to some payments for military service being made in kind [25]. The provision of these goods in kind was a tax payment and classified as *annona militaris* ('military annual income'), the intention being to help lessen the effects of inflation on the purchasing power of the army wage [26]. This flow of goods had to be monitored and coordinated by the army.

B.5. SPECIALIST ROLES
The professionalization of the army went hand in hand with the creation of expert and specialist roles [32]. Centurions of the *primi ordines* in particular tended to receive administrative assignments [30]. Such roles regularly went to men of relatively advanced age [44]. These were, for instance, specialists in the fields of administration and logistics. A legion had some *immunes*, that is, men exempt from the 'everyday service' of the *milites gregarii*, or common soldiers. The number of likewise 'exempt' and higher-ranking *principales* ran to about 500 per legion, and that of the *immunes* to about 600 [19]. The *immunes* were used in a wide range of roles within the unit [47]. These included work as secretaries, *venatores* ('hunters') or *tubicen* ('army musicians') (→ Specialists, B.) [30]. *Immunes*, however, could suffer the punishment (*munerum indictio*) of being returned to the duties of a common soldier [57]. There were also some roles that would fall within the areas of responsibility of specialist forces today. The *frumentarii* (literally, 'purveyors of corn') performed duties in → reconnaissance (B.) and military policing. They were recruited from within the legions, and they had a headquarters at Rome [2]; [15]. Protecting the imperial family was a task entrusted to the army, but the emperor's personal life guards, the *corporis custodes* ('bodyguards'), were not members of regular units [55]. In addition to its other duties, the Praetorian Guard carried out assignments like assassinations [15]. The capital was home to special units of a quite different kind: the *cohortes urbanae* ('urban guard') founded in the reign of Augustus functioned as a municipal police force, and the *cohortes vigilum* ('cohorts of the watchmen') as a fire brigade [51]. In Late Antiquity, there emerged the *agentes in rebus* ('agents in matters'), who performed a range of special functions as a kind of military espionage service [62].

B.6. EXITING SERVICE
In wartime, especially during drawn-out conflicts, most soldiers' deaths may be assumed to have resulted from disease (army epidemics), rather than from battle [19]. During the so-called Antonine Plague, for instance, the army proved to be a major center of infection [8]. A soldier could be discharged honourably, on medical grounds, or dishonourably (Dig. 49,16,13,3). It is assumed for the Imperial period that over 30% of soldiers died by natural causes alone before achieving their *missio honesta* (honourable discharge) [39]. Modern estimates of soldiers' life expectancy put the average age of new recruits at about 20. Some 15% of men were allowed to leave military service prematurely, for example because of wounds, and another 40% died before the end of their term of service [18]. Statistically speaking, it may be assumed that about 250 soldiers per legion achieved the *missio honesta* each year [9]. Only the *missio honesta* and the *missio causaria* (discharge for health reasons following a wound or similar) entitled the soldier to access the privileges of a → veteran [21]. Once an army medic had diagnosed the soldier's permanent unfitness for service, an administrative process

was triggered that involved the relevant governor and ultimately led to the *missio causaria* [61]. One problem the army faced was that of desertion, not least because deserters would embark on criminal lives, for example in bandit gangs [23]. Augustus established legal certainty in regard to the privileges of *veterani* [7]. The regulations set for military service in 13 BC already needed revision in AD 5, especially in regard to terms of service, which were now extended [54]. Also in AD 5, the level of veterans' benefits was set: 20,000 HS for the Praetorians, 12,000 HS for other army members [59]. Augustus in AD 6 set up the *aerarium militare* (a military fund) and filled it with 170 million HS from his own private fortune (R. Gest. div. Aug. 17) to finance the discharge payments. Later, this army fund was replenished with the earnings from an auction tax of 1% and an inheritance tax of 5% [32]. Only after the death of Augustus did soldiers' dissatisfaction with the revised service conditions lead to a major → mutiny of the legions on the Danube and Rhine [12]. One of the mutineers' key demands was that the contractually regulated discharge of provisions be consistently followed [59]. On discharge from service, many men sold their privately owned weapons and equipment to the army, which came under the responsibility of the unit's quartermaster (*custos armorum*) [14]. Discharge was not carried out individually, but for the entire affected cohort, usually in December or January [56]. Once their (probably) 25-year term of service ended, the auxiliaries of the Imperial period received a document that today is known as a military diploma, a practice that can be traced back to the reign of Claudius (AD 41–54). They also received citizenship. This privilege extended even to auxiliaries' children [51]. On discharge, a soldier passed out of the jurisdiction of the *ius militare* ('military court') [56]. There was a possibility to return to service, or, in the case of especially competent soldiers, to continue in service as *evocati* ('those with extended service') [56]. The grant of land to veterans continued under the Principate. The key difference as compared with the care of veterans in the Republican period was that land was now allocated not in Italy, but mainly in the *provinciae* ('provinces') [4]. Most veterans settled near where they had formerly served [29]. Together with the lifting of the marriage ban, this had the effect of making the profession 'hereditary', with the son of a soldier also becoming a soldier [1]. It is therefore easy to see why settlements near camps and their hinterlands represented an important recruitment base for the army in Central Europe [48]. Under the Republic, establishing veteran colonies was, where possible, prevented by the senate, because the mechanisms of the *clientela* (patron–client relationship) unfortunately meant that such processes caused enormous growth in the power of the statesmen responsible for founding the colonies [4]. In Egypt, veterans are found to be landowners and representatives of the upper classes in villages [48].

☞ Administration; Army; Auxiliaries; Camp; Honours; Legion; Military law; Motivation; Society and army; Training; Veterans

BIBLIOGRAPHY
[1] G. ALFÖLDY, Römische Sozialgeschichte, 2011 [2] F.M. AUSBÜTTEL, Die Verwaltung des römischen Kaiserreiches, 1998 [3] M.C. BISHOP / J.C.N. COULSTON, Roman Military Equipment, 2009 [4] L. BURCKHARDT, Militärgeschichte der Antike, ³2020 [5] G. CAIRO, Origins of the Roman Army, in: Y. Le Bohec (ed.), The Encyclopedia of the Roman Army, vol. 2, 2015, 714–715 [6] B. CECH, Technik in der Antike, 2010 [7] P. COSME, Augustus's Army, in: Y. Le Bohec (ed.), The Encyclopedia of the Roman Army, vol. 1, 2015, 66–67 [8] D.H. CRAWFORD, Deadly Companions. How Microbes Shaped Our History, 2007 [9] H.-J. DREXHAGE ET AL., Die Wirtschaft des römischen Reiches, 2002 [10] M. DUCOS, Bona castrensia, in: Y. Le Bohec (ed.), The Encyclopedia of the Roman Army, vol. 1, 2015, 106–107 [11] W. ECK, Friedenssicherung und Krieg in der römischen Kaiserzeit. Wie ergänzt man das römische Heer?, in: A. Eich (ed.), Die Verwaltung der kaiserzeitlichen Armee, 2010, 87–110 [12] A. EICH, Die römische Kaiserzeit. Die Legionen und das Imperium, 2014 [13] T. FISCHER, Die römische Armee als Wirtschaftsfaktor, in: L. Wamser (ed.), Die Römer zwischen Alpen und Nordmeer, 2000, 49–52 [14] T. FISCHER, Die Armee der Caesaren. Archäologie und Geschichte, 2012 [15] C.J. FUHRMANN, Policing the Roman Empire, 2012 [16] A.K. GOLDSWORTHY, The Roman Army at War, 2009 [17] K. HOPKINS, The Political Economy of the Roman Empire, in: I. Morris / W. Scheidel (ed.), The Dynamics of Ancient Empires, 2009, 178–204 [18] M. JUNKELMANN, Panis militaris, 2006 [19] M. JUNKELMANN, Die Legionen des Augustus, 2015 [20] H. KLOFT, Die Wirtschaft des Imperium Romanum, 2006 [21] R. KNAPP, Römer im Schatten der Geschichte, 2012 [22] T. KOLNBERGER, Das Konzept der Militärzone. Die geographische Reichweite militärischer Systeme, in: G. Mandl / I. Steffelbauer (ed.), Krieg in der antiken Welt, 2007, 115–128 [23] J.-U. KRAUSE, Kriminalgeschichte der Antike, 2004 [24] Y. LE BOHEC, Die römische Armee, 2009 [25] Y. LE BOHEC, Das römische Heer in der späten Kaiserzeit, 2010 [26] A.D. LEE, War in Late Antiquity, 2007 [27] C. LETTA, Allies. Republic, in: Y. Le Bohec (ed.), The Encyclopedia of the Roman Army, vol. 1, 2015, 31–32 [28] E. LO CASCIO, Demography and Army. Republic, in: Y. Le Bohec (vol.), The Encyclopedia of the Roman Army, vol. 1, 2015, 312–313 [29] C. MANN, Militär und Kriegführung in der Antike, 2013 [30] A.R. MENÉNDEZ ARGÜÍN, Administration. Principate, in: Y. Le Bohec (ed.), The Encyclopedia of the Roman Army, vol. 1, 2015, 5–11 [31] H. MÜLLER, Tiere als Kostenfaktor in antiken Kriegen, in: R. Pöppinghege (ed.), Tiere im Krieg, 2009, 15–31 [32] E. NEMETH / F. FODOREAN, Römische Militärgeschichte, 2015 [33] M. NG, Cohorts of Vigiles, in: Y. Le Bohec (ed.), The Encyclopedia of the Roman Army, vol. 1, 2015, 257–258 [34] B. PALME, Militärs in der administrativen Kontrolle der Bevölkerung im römischen Ägypten, in: A. Eich (ed.), Die Verwaltung der

kaiserzeitlichen Armee, 2010, 149–164 [35] B. PALME, Die Armee der römischen Kaiserzeit in ihrer historischen Entwicklung vom 1.–7. Jh. n.Chr., in: B. Palme (ed.), Die Legionäre des Kaisers, 2011, 1–10 [36] B. PFERDEHIRT, Die Rolle des Militärs für den sozialen Aufstieg in der römischen Kaiserzeit, 2002 [37] S.E. PHANG, Roman Military Service, 2008 [38] S.E. PHANG, Colleges, Military, in: Y. Le Bohec (ed.), The Encyclopedia of the Roman Army, vol. 1, 2015, 259–260 [39] S.E. PHANG, Demography and Army. Prinicipate, in: Y. Le Bohec (ed.), The Encyclopedia of the Roman Army, vol. 1, 2015, 313–314 [40] N. POLLARD / J. BERRY, Die Legionen Roms, 2012 [41] G. POMA, Ceremonies, Military. Republic, in: Y. Le Bohec (ed.), The Encyclopedia of the Roman Army, vol. 1, 2015, 191 [42] B. RANKOV, Military Forces, in: P. Sabin et al. (eds.), The Cambridge History of Greek and Roman Warfare, vol. 2, 2007, 30–75 [43] B. RANKOV, Camp Security. Principate, in: Y. Le Bohec (ed.), The Encyclopedia of the Roman Army, vol. 1, 2015, 141–142 [44] M. REUTER, Wie alt man wurde. Die Angaben auf Grabsteinen, in: H.-J. Schalles / S. Willer (eds.), Marcus Caelius. Tod in der Varusschlacht, 2009, 44–48 [45] P. ROUSSEL, Barbarization, in: Y. Le Bohec (ed.), The Encyclopedia of the Roman Army, vol. 1, 2015, 78–81 [46] D.B. SADDINGTON, Allies. Principate, in: Y. Le Bohec (ed.), The Encyclopedia of the Roman Army, vol. 1, 2015, 32–33 [47] P. SÄNGER, Augustus – Herr über 28 Legionen. Das militärische Erbe der Republik und die kaiserzeitliche Armee, in: G. Mandl / I. Steffelbauer (eds.), Krieg in der antiken Welt, 2007, 64–84 [48] P. SÄNGER, Römische Veteranen in Ägypten (1.–3. Jh. n.Chr.). Ihre Siedlungsräume und sozio-ökonomische Situation, in: P. Herz et al. (eds.), Zwischen Region und Reich, 2010, 121–133 [49] H. SIDEBOTTOM, Der Krieg in der antiken Welt, 2008 [50] M. SOMMER, Römische Geschichte, vol. 1, 2013 [51] P. SOUTHERN, The Roman Army, 2007 [52] M.A. SPEIDEL, Augustus' militärische Neuordnung und ihr Beitrag zum Erfolg des Imperium Romanum. Zu Heer und Reichskonzept, in: M.A. Speidel, Heer und Herrschaft im Römischen Reich der Hohen Kaiserzeit, 2009, 19–51 [53] M.A. SPEIDEL, Das römische Heer als Kulturträger. Lebensweisen und Wertvorstellungen der Legionssoldaten an den Nordgrenzen des Römischen Reiches im ersten Jahrhundert n.Chr., in: M.A. Speidel, Heer und Herrschaft im Römischen Reich der Hohen Kaiserzeit, 2009, 515–544 [54] M.A. SPEIDEL, Geld und Macht. Die Neuordnung des staatlichen Finanzwesens unter Augustus, in: M.A. Speidel, Heer und Herrschaft im Römischen Reich der Hohen Kaiserzeit, 2009, 53–84 [55] M.A. SPEIDEL, Germanische Verbände im römischen Heer, in: M.A. Speidel, Heer und Herrschaft im Römischen Reich der Hohen Kaiserzeit, 2009, 109–120 [56] M.A. SPEIDEL, Honesta Missio. Zu Entlassungsurkunden und verwandten Texten, in: M.A. Speidel, Heer und Herrschaft im Römischen Reich der Hohen Kaiserzeit, 2009, 317–346 [57] M.A. SPEIDEL, Rang und Sold im römischen Heer und die Bezahlung der 'vigiles', in: M.A. Speidel, Heer und Herrschaft im Römischen Reich der Hohen Kaiserzeit, 2009, 381–394 [58] M.A. SPEIDEL, Roman Army Pay Scales, in: M.A. Speidel, Heer und Herrschaft im Römischen Reich der Hohen Kaiserzeit, 2009, 349–380 [59] M.A. SPEIDEL, Sold und Wirtschaftslage der römischen Soldaten, in: M.A. Speidel, Heer und Herrschaft im Römischen Reich der Hohen Kaiserzeit, 2009, 407–437 [60] M.P. SPEIDEL, Ancient Germanic Warriors. Warrior Styles from Trajan's Column to Icelandic Sagas, 2008 [61] K. STAUNER, 'Rationes ad milites pertinentes'. Organisation und Funktion der Binnenadministration militärischer Einheiten in der frühen und hohen Kaiserzeit, in: A. Eich (ed.), Die Verwaltung der kaiserzeitlichen Armee, 2010, 37–85 [62] I. SYVÄNNE, Agens, agentes in rebus, in: Y. Le Bohec (ed.), The Encyclopedia of the Roman Army, vol. 1, 2015, 20–21 [63] J. THORNE, Booty. Principate, in: Y. Le Bohec (ed.), The Encyclopedia of the Roman Army, vol. 1, 2015, 109–110.

JOSEF LÖFFL

Militia

A. Local militias
B. Growth of self-defence in Late Antiquity

With the exception of the garrison in Rome and the urban cohorts stationed in Carthage and Lugdunum (Lyon), central authorities maintained no police militias in the cities of the Roman world. However, provincial garrisons were often entrusted with the job of maintaining order, all the more so when, between the principates of Tiberius and Marcus Aurelius, the empire faced no serious external threat. In Italy and in all the provinces, soldiers could be deployed for police interventions, particularly to counter → banditry, which was widespread in some regions such as Anatolia [10].

A. LOCAL MILITIAS

The Roman army's staffing levels did not always permit it to take on additional tasks such as policing duties. There are indications that some cities raised local militias for maintaining public order. More evidence for these militias is found in the Greek-speaking provinces, where epigraphic – and in Egypt papyrological – documents mention magistrates commissioned for this purpose. One such magistrate was the irenarch ('justice of the peace'), attested mostly in Asia Minor and Egypt starting in the reign of Trajan. Militias of this kind constituted a municipal public organization created to combat bandits. Within the province of Asia, every city submitted a shortlist of ten men to the proconsul, who selected one to be irenarch [2]. In Egypt, with its less dense cities, irenarchs were assigned to a nome or a toparchy. To help in the fulfilment of his role, the irenarch had at his disposal a unit of *diogmites* ('pursuers'), very lightly armed infantrymen, whom the irenarch may have been required to finance for the duration of his term in office. We also know of *paraphylakes* ('chief guardians'), who are attested from the late 1st century BC onwards and apparently performed a very similar function, with *paraphylakites* under their command. They perhaps differed from the irenarchs in that they took on policing duties in rural areas. There is also evidence of *orophylakes* ('mountain guards'), who did similar work in mountainous regions, 'night commanders' in Syria and Egypt, *strategoi* ('commanders') for the *chora* ('territory') of Carian cities, and also *hipparches* ('cavalry commanders'), *archontes* ('commanders'), *eparchoi* ('rulers') and *peripoloi* ('patrollers'), who formed patrols.

These diverse and multifaceted titles always correspond to public service organizations, which seem to have been especially numerous – and financially burdensome – in Egypt. This focus on Egypt is also a function of the abundance of papyrological evidence, in which are referenced *irenophylakes* ('guardians of the peace') and *archephodoi* ('chiefs of police') responsible for the territory of a village, as well as guard teams – *magdophylakes* ('tower guards') – conducting night watches on towers, and even 'bandit-hunters'.

Besides these police forces, inhabitants of a town or city sometimes took their defence into their own hands, as inscriptions and some Greek romances attest. These local militias were on the front line putting down the Jewish Revolt in Egypt and Cyrenaica in AD 115–117, because many of the legionaries of Trajan's army had gone off to fight the Parthians. They were also deployed against the *boukoloi* ('herdsmen') from 172 onwards [10]. It is difficult in the case of the archers attested at Palmyra to determine whether they were members of an urban militia or a unit of the imperial army. Such problems of interpretation often arise in the east, where the documentary record is less reliable than in the west. Two prefects charged with combating banditry are nevertheless attested, one at Nyon [5] and the other at Bois-l'Abbé. These appear to have been municipal positions created in the late 2nd or early 3rd centuries, as the Gallic provinces suffered a period of crisis [4]. Specific events sometimes show that cities had police forces. In AD 69, the coastal cities of Gallia Narbonensis and the Alpes Maritimae were attacked by the fleet from Misenum and mixed divisions of the garrison of Rome sent by Otho. That same year, the Haedui faced a rebellion led by the Boian Mariccus. In both cases, the cities' *iuventus* ('youth') were called up. This probably refers to the colleges of *iuvenes* ('young men') that were able to take on policing duties. In the Alpes Maritimae, it was the governor of the province who mobilized them, while the city of the Haedui organized the repression of those led by Mariccus. This logically related to the different magnitudes of the threat: in one case, much of the province was affected; in the other, just one city and a few districts. It was probably to this type of paramilitary organization that Vindex was alluding when, in the spring of 68, he declared that he had a potential force of 100,000 men available to deal with a rebellion against Nero in his province [3]. A local militia of this type also intervened in Africa in 238, to support the power grab by the proconsul Gordian at the expense of Maximinus Thrax.

These schools for *iuvenes* were not reserved for some urban elite made up of sons of decurions. They brought together young *honestiores* ('privileged') and *humiliores* ('members of lower classes'), and they may have contributed to the integration of the cities' rural and urban populations by organizing their participation in key aspects of civic life, such as protecting the city. However, the few references to these forces, which were invariably overwhelmed by regular army units, highlight their poor military quality and thus suggest that their original purpose was not to fight [7]. According to the *Histories* of Tacitus (2,12f.), it is possible that in mountain regions such as the Alpes Maritimae, the *iuvenes*, who are sometimes called *Montani* and *Alpini*, also served as mountain guides and porters. This type of association is also attested in inscriptions in Raetia. We also learn through Tacitus that some places had paid garrisons, something in between the citizens' militia and the regular army, which were maintained locally by specific communities such as the Helvetii [3]. The significance of youth associations is also attested in the Greek-speaking provinces through the terms *ephebes* (young men aged 18–20 registered for military service) and *neoi* ('youths'), for example in carved decrees in Cyrenaica regarding the invasion of the Garamantes [10].

B. GROWTH OF SELF-DEFENCE IN LATE ANTIQUITY

As central authority waned in Late Antiquity, paramilitary citizen militias acquired an ever more significant role, and the distinctions between them and the regular army were increasingly effaced. This period saw the involvement of bishops in the organization of city defence, as well as the development of self-defence units on a more or less spontaneous basis and of forces raised more or less legally by major landowners. In theory, only civilian and military representatives of the emperor were allowed an escort of *bucellarii* (elite escort troops, lit. 'biscuit eaters'), but the rule was not always strictly applied. Papyrological documents make such phenomena more visible in Egypt than elsewhere. The papyrus archives of Abinnaeus (mid-4th cent.) show the new division of civil and military responsibilities gradually becoming a reality. Similar phenomena are apparent in the Balkans at the time of the Slavic invasions of 570–580, which had the effect of weakening links between Constantinople and the provinces, even ones that were relatively close to the capital. In 594, supported by their bishop, the citizens of Asemus on the Danube refused to allow their garrison to be incorporated into the imperial army. In AD 580 and 610, despite the withdrawal of most of the imperial forces, the citizens of Thessalonica repelled attacks by the Slavs and Avars. Such civilians who participated in civic defence probably received training to prepare them to withstand sieges. In cities that had circus parties, such as Constantinople and Antioch, they probably helped defend against possible attackers. Evidence is much rarer in the west, but Gregory of Tours mentions the role played by some local militias in the cities of Poitiers and Tours at a time when the Roman Empire had given way to the Merovingians [10].

→ State and army

BIBLIOGRAPHY
[1] E. BIRLEY, Local militias in the Roman Empire, in: Bonner Historia-Augusta-Colloquium 1972/1974, 1976, 65–76 [2] C. BRÉLAZ, La sécurité publique en Asie Mineure sous le Principat, 2005 [3] P. COSME, L'année des quatre empereurs, 2012 [4] M. DONDIN-PAYRE, Magistratures et administration municipale dans les Trois Gaules, in: M. Dondin-Payre / M.-T. Raepsaet-Charlier (eds.), Cités, municipes, colonies. Les processus de municipalisation en Gaule et en Germanie sous le Haut-Empire romain, 1999, 127–230 [5] R. FREI-STOLBA, Recherches sur les institutions de Nyon, Augst et Avenches, in: M. Dondin-Payre / M.-T. Raepsaet-Charlier (eds.), Cités, municipes, colonies. Les processus de municipalisation en Gaule et en Germanie sous le Haut-Empire romain, 1999, 29–95 [6] P. GINESTET, Les organisations de la jeunesse dans l'Occident romain, 1991 [7] F. JACQUES, Humbles et notables. La place des humiliores dans les collèges de jeunes et leur rôle dans la révolte africaine de 238, in: Antiquités africaines 15, 1980, 217–230 [8] T. MOMMSEN, Die römischen Provinzialmilizen, in: Hermes 22, 1887, 547–558 [9] M. WHITBY, Armies and Society in the Later Roman World, in: A.M. Cameron (ed.), CAH 14: Late Antiquity. Empire and Successors, 2001, 469–496 [10] C. WOLFF, Les brigands en Orient sous le Haut-Empire romain, 2003.

PIERRE COSME

Motivation

A. Greek
B. Roman

A. GREEK
Despite the ubiquity of war in the surviving sources, only a few commentators give explicit indications as to why soldiers of classical antiquity took on the rigours of war and accepted the risks of suffering grave injury or losing their lives in battle. The chief explanations given in the texts are the quest for renown and *polis* patriotism, with material motives often indirectly discernible. In general, soldiers were motivated by a combination of different factors.

A.1. Quest for renown and *polis* patriotism
A.2. Material motivations
A.3. Social ties

A.1. QUEST FOR RENOWN AND *POLIS* PATRIOTISM
The Homeric heroes, who played an important part in the military history of the classical world as exemplary warriors (on which in detail [13]), rapidly flared up in murderous rage on seeing their honour threatened. As a child, Patroclus killed another boy when tempers were lost during a game of knucklebones (Hom. Il. 23,85–88). Ajax and Idomeneus almost drew their weapons when arguing over who was leading during a chariot-race, with Achilles just barely able to pacify them (Hom. Il. 23,448–498). It is only through the intervention of Athena that Achilles himself is prevented from instigating a bloodbath among the Greeks in his rage at the taking of Briseis (Hom. Il. 1,188–194). Above and beyond any rational motivation, the impulse to protect one's own honour by all means could lead to conflict. But the Homeric heroes also reflect on what makes valiant combat worthwhile. Although the individual's quest for renown offers the primary motivation, this quest manifests itself in different ways. Achilles prefers a glorious, early death outside the walls of Troy to a long life (Hom. Il. 9,410–416), although there is no clear indication of which group is to hold him in such renown. Sarpedon, on the other hand, when urging Glaucus to fight bravely, is thinking of the community in their Lycian homeland (Hom. Il. 12,310–328). Warlike feats, he argues, are needed in order to legitimize their prominent social status, for lasting honour is only accorded to valiant leaders. Hector states that the supreme objective of battle is the protection of one's homeland (Hom. Il. 12,243), but in the end, he too is motivated by the quest for personal renown.

In the post-Homeric period, the urban community became much more important as the target audience for feats of battle. In the battle paraeneses of Callinus of Ephesus and Tyrtaeus of Sparta (both 7th cent. BC), motivation is related wholly to the *polis*. Powerful songs composed in elegiac couplets urge citizens to abandon lazy indolence and the quest for wealth or sporting excellence, and instead to devote themselves to fighting for the *polis* with all their might. The rewards for the valiant citizen who stands his ground in the hoplite battle are the highest honours in the *polis*, whether he loses his life or not. 'For the loving grief of all the people belongs to the powerful man – if thus he dies. If he survives unscathed, his worth is like that of the demigods' (Callinus 1,18f. G.-P.). On the other hand, if the *polis* was defeated by its enemies and its citizens were forced to flee with their families, this was a man's ultimate shame (Tyrt. Frg. 6/7,3–10 G.-P.). Callinus further intensified the soldier's motivation for battle by arguing that the time of a man's death was predetermined by the gods, and his only choice was whether to die gloriously or ingloriously (Callinus 1,12–15 G.-P.). These battle songs, particularly those of Tyrtaeus, enjoyed wide reception and were often used to urge soldiers to embrace a heroic death for their homeland's sake. In evaluating them, however, it is important to remember that they were written for people whose very existence was under threat: for the people of Ephesus under threat from the Cimmerians in the case of Callinus, and for the Spartan order in the Second Messenian War in the case of Tyrtaeus. Unlike some modern receptors of their work, these poets did not demand that soldiers die in battle, only that they give their utmost for the good of the *polis* (→ Death).

Sparta is especially known for honouring valiant warriors, but other *poleis* also sought to increase soldiers' motivation by recognizing achievements. This pertained primarily to the fallen. During the Classical period, it was customary in many *poleis* to put up monuments bearing the names of citizens killed in battle. At Athens, a public ceremony of mourning was held at the end of a campaigning year in honour of the fallen, who were buried in communal graves (Thuc. 2,34). An oration was given that situated the recent hostilities within a long tradition and endowed them with a mythical aura. This ceremony was not directed at future soldiers alone, but at the entire citizenry, who had suffered privations of war and whose belief that these sacrifices were meaningful needed to be reinforced.

Corresponding to the honour bestowed on valiant soldiers was the public shame ascribed to those who had displayed cowardice in battle. According to Tyrtaeus (Frg. 8,14 G.-P.), such men would be expelled from the *polis*, and the loss of civic rights is attested at Athens (Aesch. Tim. 29). Punishments were imposed by courts at home; there is generally no evidence of officers' imposing disciplinary penalties to maintain fighting morale. One exception to this is Sparta, in whose army the flogging of wayward soldiers was customary. This reflects the more extensive hierarchy among Sparta's forces and their greater number of officers in comparison with other *poleis* (→ Sparta) [11]. Some scholars suggest that there was a fundamental difference in motivation between Spartan and Athenian hoplites: whereas the valour of the former depended on strict obedience and traditional concepts of honour, the Athenians were motivated by their sense of the superiority of their political order, since they fought on the basis of rational thought on behalf of democracy, liberty and equality [2]. Given the disparate nature of the sources, however, this cannot be confirmed. Certainly, the ancient testimonies yield no evidence that Athenian soldiers had a higher motivation.

A.2. MATERIAL MOTIVATIONS

A.2.1. Pay
A.2.2. Booty

A.2.1. PAY
No general rules are observable for the payment of the citizen soldiers who made up the core of the *polis* armies. Practices differed greatly from one place to another and across time (seminal [18. 3–29]). In Classical Athens, galley service in the fleet was regarded as a source of income for poorer citizens (Thuc. 6,24; Ps.-Xen. Ath. pol. 1,13), who manned the oars alongside metics, → mercenaries and sometimes → slaves. Prospects of better → pay feature as a motivation for characters in comedy (Aristoph. Ach. 600). As for the level of pay, indications vary between 2 obols and 1 drachma per day (Thuc. 3,17,4; 8,45,2; Aristoph. Vesp. 1188f.), while for hoplites, a daily wage of 1 drachma with another to subsidize a servant is mentioned (Thuc. 3,17,4). During the final phase of the Peloponnesian War, levels of pay were much discussed, particularly in the Spartan-Persian camp. It was anticipated that increasing pay would markedly improve motivation in the fleet, and if they substantially outbid the opposing side, it was expected that Athenian oarsmen would desert their own navy and defect for the sake of better pay (Xen. Hell. 1,5). The sources do not reveal whether such behaviour was expected only of mercenaries, slaves and metics, or whether Athenian citizens were also imagined as defecting.

While the role of pay as compared to *polis* patriotism is difficult to assess in the case of citizen soldiers, the motivation of mercenaries was primarily financial. The first Greek mercenaries are attested in the service of Near Eastern monarchs in the 8th century BC [14], and their significance began to increase in the late 5th century BC. The increase in mercenary activity owed as much to the devastation caused by the Peloponnesian War and to the intensification of social conflicts as to increased demand from potential new employers such as the younger tyrants and the pretenders to the Persian throne [20]. Most mercenaries came from remote and impoverished regions such as Arcadia, and they were driven by material need, but some among them were aristocrats who had been banished from their *poleis* and saw military service as an opportunity to win renown and influence far from their homelands (→ Mercenaries). Discussing why mercenaries joined the march of the Ten Thousand for Cyrus the Younger, in addition to financial motives Xenophon mentions the desire for adventure and the quest to prove themselves as men (An. 6,4,8).

A treaty between Eumenes I of Pergamum and a contingent of troops (IPerg 13, c. 260 BC; see [8. 282–288]) affords insight into what mercenaries were seeking. Clearly looking to end a rebellion, Eumenes made concessions to the soldiers' demands, and promised to move from payments in kind to monetary payments, to reduce the annual term of service to ten months, to guarantee the mercenaries tax privileges and to give financial support to the orphaned children of the fallen. In return, the mercenaries promised him unconditional loyalty against his internal and external enemies. The document reveals not only the troops' material motivations, but also their desire to be recognized as a group especially close to the king. Considerations of status played an important role.

A.2.2. BOOTY

Although the sources place more emphasis on the quest for renown, prospects of → booty were a powerful motivation for ancient communities to wage war and for men to take part in it. Besides money and other objects of value, cattle and people are often mentioned as spoils of war, and it was possible to regard territory of defeated enemies as booty (in detail [18. 53–100] and [19. 68–541]). The Homeric world was already familiar not only with grand heroic wars, but also with small and unheroic conflicts over herds of cattle (Hom. Il. 18,509–540), which reflects the social realities of the Geometric period. Minor wars of this kind between neighbouring communities squabbling over land or movable booty continued into the Hellenistic period [15]; [5. 129–137]. For Greek monarchs – from Archaic tyrants to Hellenistic kings – wars were not just an opportunity for showing off their glory; they were also a means for obtaining booty in order to pay their troops (e.g. Plut. Pyrrhus 26,2; further examples from the Hellenistic period in [1]). For citizens of a *polis*, too, the prospect of acquiring booty was an inducement to start a war. The economic impact of booty was enormous (see in detail [7]) – Alexander the Great's seizure of the Persian royal treasury, for example, transformed the Greek economy. Soldiers who became wealthy through service in war were eloquent examples that inspired young men to devote themselves to military service, too.

A.3. SOCIAL TIES

A.3.1. Comradeship
A.3.2. Army leaders
A.3.3. Religion and rituals

A.3.1. COMRADESHIP

It is a commonplace of Greek literature that soldiers fight more bravely when they form up according to lineage and stand with their kinsmen in battle (Hom. Il. 2,362–366; Onas. 24). Greek *poleis* did generally arrange their formations according to local origins. There was a practical reason for this: community registers could be consulted for recruitment. Nevertheless, there was also an intention that social influence would drive soldiers to fight with more valour [6. 40–69]. Another principle was recruitment by year, with military units arranged according to age group. Here, too, it was hoped that each individual would be more highly motivated if he was fighting with members of his own group. Unlike the Roman cohorts or modern regiments, the tactical units of the Greek *polis* armies never developed a strong → esprit de corps, because campaigns were too short for this to develop ([6. 70–79] *contra* [10. 117–125]). Only rarely is mention made of the specific accomplishments of a particular *taxis* ('regiment'; Lys. 16,14–16), the exception being elite units such as the Theban 'Sacred Band'. Rather than relying on esprit de corps, trust was placed in the efficacy of pre-existing social ties. Mercenary armies and the forces of Hellenistic rulers were likewise usually arranged according to criteria of common origin. There is a suggestion in the case of some units that homosexual relations among fighters were encouraged as a way of intensifying motivation (e.g. Plut. *Pelopidas* 18), although the historicity of such statements is dubious [16].

A.3.2. ARMY LEADERS

Ancient historiography offers a great many eve-of-battle orations by generals. Commanders would make vividly clear for their men how noble the objectives of battle were, why their cause was just, and why their army was superior to the enemy, so that victory would be theirs. Practical considerations call into question the historical accuracy of such lengthy speeches, given that acoustics would dictate that only a few soldiers would be able to hear them, and the danger of a surprise enemy attack would forbid gathering the entire force for a peroration [9]. In reality, generals' morale-boosting speeches would mostly have been confined to acclamations and a few pithy words of encouragement. Aristotle mentions the use of short quotations from the *Iliad* to spur on troops (Aristot. Rhet. 1395a 10–14).

One major influence on the morale of the troops was the personality of the general, especially in the Hellenistic period. Alexander the Great (→ Generals of note, B.) embodied the ideal of the heroic general urging his troops on through personal example. He would fight at extreme risk to himself at the focal points of battles and sieges, sharing the travails and dangers of campaigns in unknown country. Through symbolic acts, he also conveyed to his soldiers a feeling that they were taking part in an epoch-making event under the command of a general beloved by the gods. This bond with Alexander was a crucial factor that led his troops to follow him for long periods on enterprises that went far beyond what anyone believed was possible at the time [4]. Alexander's example was a formative influence on the Hellenistic kings at war, as they emulated their ideal hero. The often diverse contingents of Hellenistic armies were motivated to fight with valour primarily by charismatic, herioc kings [3].

A.3.3. RELIGION AND RITUALS

Ancient Greece had no concept of waging war in order to propagate a religion. By the same token, soldiers drew no motivation from a notion of fighting a war on behalf of 'their' god, who would take them to victory and reward the fallen in the afterlife. The so-called 'Sacred Wars' had nothing in common with wars of religion, but were fought for influence in the Delphic Amphictyony. It is impossible to ascertain whether the idea that the moment of a person's death was predestined – an idea reflected in many written sources – influenced the motivation of individual soldiers to any significant degree. Certainly, no Greek army exhibits any discernible fatalism.

Religious portents, however, were important to troops' morale. The Homeric epics show celestial phenomena or the flight of birds influencing the moral of particular heroes or entire armies. It was a common theme in Greek literature that favourable portents motivated troops, and that unfavourable ones demoralized them. Throughout the Archaic and Classical periods, it was customary to slaughter an animal before an army set out, and to predict the course of the battle or war by reading its entrails (Thuc. 6,69,2; Xen. Oec. 5,19). Generals, however, always had ways of influencing the portents, even by repeating the sacrifice if necessary [17. 307]. Onasander expected competence in divination from generals, so that they could conduct a positive reading of signs themselves, and he also called for capable seers to be brought along. Soldiers, he argued, would in any case be on the lookout for portents, and it was important for managing the army that an interpretative authority over such omens be upheld. In the end, soldiers would fight more bravely if they believed that the gods were on their side (Onas. 10,25–28). The story is told that Attalus I of Pergamum inscribed a promise of victory into the liver of a sacrifical animal before a battle against the Gauls in order to motivate his troops (Polyaenus, Strat. 4,20). In general, however, extispicy was on the wane in the Hellenistic period, with religious motivation now fed more by faith in the commander's heroic power [17. 301–305].

Another sacrifice was performed immediately before battle commenced. The goal was no longer to ascertain the divine will, but to increase troops' aggression through a symbolic killing [12]. Fanfares not only conveyed signals, but also raised spirits ahead of hostilities. So too did the *paian* sung by the soldiers. There is much talk of alcohol consumption in Greek armies [10. 126–131]; increased wine consumption before the Battle of Leuctra (371 BC) is said to have influenced the Spartans to take the field (Xen. Hell. 6,4,8f.). There is no evidence, however, for the suggestion that alcohol was deliberately served before battles to increase motivation and reduce inhibitions in regard to killing.

BIBLIOGRAPHY

[1] M.M. AUSTIN, Hellenistic Kings, War and the Economy, in: CQ 36, 1986, 450–466 [2] R.K. BALOT, Courage in the Democratic Polis. Ideology and Critique in Classical Athens, 2014 [3] P. BESTON, Hellenistic Military Leadership, in: H. van Wees (ed.), War and Violence in Ancient Greece, 2000, 315–335 [4] E. CARNEY, Macedonians and Mutiny. Discipline and Indiscipline in the Army of Philip and Alexander, in: CPh 91, 1996, 19–44 [5] A. CHANIOTIS, War in the Hellenistic World. A Social and Cultural History, 2005 [6] J. CROWLEY, The Psychology of the Athenian Hoplite. The Culture of Combat in Classical Athens, 2012 [7] Y. GARLAN, Guerre et économie en Grèce ancienne, 1989 [8] G.T. GRIFFITH, The Mercenaries of the Hellenistic World, 1935 [9] M.H. HANSEN, The Battle Exhortation in Ancient Historiography. Fact or Fiction?, in: Historia 42, 1993, 161–180 [10] V.D. HANSON, The Western Way of War. Infantry Battle in Classical Greece, ^{2}2000 [11] S. HORNBLOWER, Sticks, Stones, and Spartans. The Sociology of Spartan Violence, in: H. van Wees (ed.), War and Violence in Ancient Greece, 2000, 57–82 [12] M.H. JAMESON, Sacrifice before Battle, in: V.D. Hanson (ed.), Hoplites. The Classical Greek Battle Experience, 1991, 197–227 [13] J.E. LENDON, Soldiers and Ghosts. A History of Battle in Classical Antiquity, 2005 [14] N. LURAGHI, Traders, Pirates, Warriors. The Proto-History of Greek Mercenary Soldiers in the Eastern Mediterranean, in: Phoenix 60, 2006, 21–47 [15] J. MA, Fighting Poleis of the Hellenistic World, in: H. van Wees (ed.), War and Violence in Ancient Greece, 2000, 337–376 [16] D. OGDEN, Homosexuality and Warfare in Classical Greece, in: A.B. Lloyd (ed.), Battle in Antiquity, 1996, 107–168 [17] R. PARKER, Sacrifice and Battle, in: H. van Wees (ed.), War and Violence in Ancient Greece, 2000, 299–314 [18] W.K. PRITCHETT, The Greek State at War, vol. 1, 1971 [19] W.K. PRITCHETT, The Greek State at War, vol. 5, 1991 [20] M.F. TRUNDLE, Greek Mercenaries from the Late Archaic Period to Alexander, 2004.

CHRISTIAN MANN

B. ROMAN

B.1. Survival of the Republic
B.2. The professionalization of the army
B.3. Imperial period

Dulce et decorum est pro patria mori ('It is sweet and decorous to die for one's country'), intoned Horace (Carm. 3,2,13) [15]. On the funerary altar of Adamclisi (Tropaeum Traiani; Romania), erected at the end of Trajan's Dacian War, the following words introduce the list of fallen Roman soldiers: '[in honour? and] in memory of the [most] valiant [men, who] met their deaths [fighting?] for the republic' ([*in honorem? et*] *memoriam fortis*[*simorum virorum qui pugnantes?*] *pro rep*(*ublica*) *morte occubu*[*erunt*]; CIL III 14214 = ILS 9107 = IScM IV 8; cf. also the tribute on the tomb of Marcus Claudius Fronto in Rome, CIL VI 41142 = ILS 1098: *huic senatus auctore Imperatore M*(*arco*) *Au/relio Antonino Aug*(*usto*) *Armeniaco Medico / Parthico maximo quod post aliquot se/cunda proelia aduersus Germanos / et Iazyges ad postremum pro r*(*e*) *p*(*ublica*) *fortiter / pugnans ceciderit armatam statuam* [*poni*] */ in foro diui Traiani pecunia publica cen*[*suit*]) [14].

The prime motivation for a member of the Roman army was thus held to be his personal undertaking to fight for the Roman Republic. Of course, it is no longer possible to establish how far ordinary soldiers took to heart such pronouncements of public propaganda. Other forms of motivation differed from those in the Monarchical and Republican periods, for although conscription in theory still applied from the reign of Augustus onwards, it was only imposed in the event of a shortage of volunteers. The numerous levies (Latin *dilectus*) attested in the first three centuries AD prove that this was done whenever necessary. Patriotism alongside *virtus* on the battlefield served as key ideals of the early Republic (cf. Sall. Catil. 7,4–6) and fundamental concepts of Roman military → discipline. Admittedly, it is impossible to draw a clear distinction between patriotism and loyalty to the state, but swearing one's readiness to die for the *res publica* was certainly part of the Roman military → oath (*sacramentum*, cf. Veg. Mil. 2,5,5: *iurant autem milites omnia se strenue facturos, quae praeceperit imperator, nunquam deserturos militiam nec mortem recusaturos pro Romana re publica*, 'but the soldiers swore that they would diligently do whatever the emperor ordered, that they would never desert their service, nor would they flinch from dying for the Roman Republic'); cf. also Serv. Aen. 8,1) [14. 142f.].

B.1. SURVIVAL OF THE REPUBLIC

During the Monarchical and Republican periods, the most important motivation was quite simply the survival of Rome in the face of threats from its neighbours – initially the Latin League and the Etruscans (especially Veii) [1. 167–217], later the warlike tribes of the Central Apennines such as the Samnites. The Roman soldier also had dealings with enemies outside Italy that brought the state to the brink of annihilation. In 390 BC, Gaulish warriors under Brennus even overran the city of Rome itself and plundered it, and they were defeated only with great difficulty (according to tradition, the victory was won in 390/89 by the dictator Marcus Furius Camillus (MRR I, 95; 97) (critical assessment of the annalistic sources: [1. 314–322]), and in 275–272 BC, Pyrrhus crossed the Adriatic and attacked Roman interests in the south of the Italian peninsula. By far the greatest danger faced by the Roman Republic and its army on Italian soil, however, came from the campaign of Hannibal. In perilous situations like this, the most important motivation consisted in saving the state and its citizens from extinction. Augmenting this motivation was the upgrade in service conditions with the introduction of the *stipendium*, a day wage of about 120 *denarii* per year, in about 160 BC (Pol. 6,39,12–15). C. Iulius Caesar raised this to an annual sum of 225 *denarii* in 49 BC (Suet. Iul. 26,3; → Pay). It transformed the Roman hoplite army, actually a citizens' militia, into an army of recruits (Liv. 4,59,11–60,8; 8,8,3; Diod. Sic. 14,16,5) [8. 18–32].

Even in the Middle Republican period, the long term of service (six, seven or more years, up to 16 in special cases) was already creating what was effectively a professional army, with experienced soldiers who had fought in Italy, Sicily, Spain and North Africa [7. 1–19]. The persistent wars in the Iberian Peninsula were instrumental in bringing about changes in the structures of the Roman army, both in terms of recruitment of troops and their caliber, including a tendency towards increasing professionalism. Given these new conditions of service, soldiers' motivation readily shifted – away from patriotism and the defence of state and families (Pol. 6,52,4–7) and towards prospects of wealth from participation in successful campaigns. The first of the military to become professionalized were the centurions (officers) in command of what would become the army's key tactical unit, the *centuria*. Two centurions (*centurio prior* and *centurio posterior*) led a maniple, a very mobile formation of 120 soldiers and the smallest tactical unit (Pol. 6,24). Six centuries (*centuriae*) or three maniples made one cohort (*cohors*). The maniple was replaced as the smallest tactical unit by the *centuria* of 80 men, probably at the time of the Second Punic War (218–202 BC), but certainly by the 1st century BC.

Whereas many soldiers were discharged at the end of a campaign to return to their farms, numerous centurions continued serving for many more years, because this had become a likely path to social advancement. Worthy of mention here is the long and illustrious career of Spurius Ligustinus, who began as an ordinary soldier (*miles gregarius*) and proceeded by way of various promotions to reach the highest rank as centurion (*primus pilus*). Ligustinus was an outstanding war hero, serving for 22 years in Macedonia, Spain, Greece and twice more in Spain, and taking part in the triumph of Quintus Fulvius Flaccus in 180 BC (Liv. 42,34,1–11) [8. 53–56]; [2]. His motivations for serving for over two decades included prospects of affluence, promotion within the army, honours (Pol. 6,39,3) and social prestige.

Senior officers – the military tribunes serving alongside the consuls – were young aristocrats, that is, members of senatorial families at the beginning of their civic and military careers. For many of them, taking part in campaigns gained them important military experience that would put them in good stead when the time came for them to lead their own forces, which in turn opened their path to the consulship (Publius Cornelius Scipio Aemilianus, for instance, served as military tribune in the 4th Legion in Africa in 149 BC before becoming consul in 147; cf. Cic. Rep. 6,9,1: *cum in Africam venissem M. Manilio consuli ad quartam legionem tribunus*; MRR 1, 459; 463). There were also some military tribunes of equestrian rank. Besides prospects of riches, they were motivated by the opportunity to secure essential overseas relations for their families or the *publicani* (tax farmers) – all of the same social background.

After the Second Punic War and the first campaigns in the eastern Mediterranean, fierce competition within the nobility over the higher magistracies, especially the consulship, led to numerous military adventures in the new provinces. Army leaders had to rely on experienced soldiers (cf. e.g. Liv. 32,3,2–7; 32,9,1 on the levy for the Macedonian War against Philip V, 199–198), who were motivated by the promise of a suitable share of the spoils of war and other benefits. Soldiers, their officers and junior officers attained a rank just below the elites of Roman society [11. 13]. Ordinary soldiers and senior commanders used each other to attain their respective goals. Soldiers and centurions wanted to leave poverty behind, while the nobles aimed to secure magistracies and senior position. They thus offered *donativa* ('supplementary monetary payments') or land to common soldiers, or simply gave them permission to plunder. For elites and their fellow citizens, common interests were a motivation for joining the army.

B.2. THE PROFESSIONALIZATION OF THE ARMY

The situation changed profoundly following the army reforms instigated by Marius in the year of his first consulship (107 BC) during the war against Jugurtha and the outbreak of the civil wars of the 1st century BC (cf. Sall. Iug. 86,2: *Ipse interea milites scribere, non more maiorum neque ex classibus, sed uti libido cuiusque erat, capite censos plerosque*, 'he now called up soldiers no longer according to the censitary classes as by ancient custom, but taking whoever was willing, even from the mass of the propertyless'; MRR 1, 550; → Generals of note, K.). Levying the *proletarii* ('citizens without property') and the *capite censi* ('those counted by head') proved to be the first step towards recognizing the need for a professional army [8. 61–68]. From then on, the prime motivations were probably payment – for many soldiers were poor (Sall. Iug. 86,3: *inopia bonorum*) –, booty and the prospect of being settled in a veteran colony somewhere in Italy (Sall. Iug. 87,1: *sed consul expletis legionibus cohortibusque auxiliariis in agrum fertilem et praeda onustum proficiscitur, omnia ibi capta militibus donat*). These prospects strengthened the bonds between the common soldiers and the competing members of the elites into a typically Roman relationship based on *fides* between patrons and clients (*patronus – cliens*), which guaranteed that veterans would later receive a plot of land. These bonds were so strong that → veterans often returned to the battlefield to defend the (purported) rights of their patron [7. 20–69].

Until 90 BC, contingents of the Italic *socii* ('allies') fought side by side with the Roman legions, forming the *alae sociorum* ('allied forces'). Their motivation was similar to that of their Roman comrades-in-arms, but with the added inducement of the prospect of Roman citizenship (Cic. Balb. 51; cf. also the *foedus* ('treaty') with Camerinum: soldiers of two cohorts received Roman citizenship *virtutis causa* ('for valour'), Val. Max. 5,2,8; Plut. Marius 28,3; Cic. Balb. 46). The reluctance of the authorities in Rome to grant this triggered the Social War (*bellum sociale*, 90–88), which ended in the award of Roman citizenship to the Italic allies *en masse*.

Other → auxiliaries were recruited from the provinces or directly from theatres of war, such as the African allies in the Second and Third Punic Wars, men from small Numidian kingdoms eager to escape the influence of the Carthaginians, or the Hispanic tribes during the many campaigns on the Iberian Peninsula, who regarded the Roman army as an important support in their own conflicts among themselves. Conditions specific to the Hispanic context included the promise of land and even Roman citizenship (e.g. the well-known example of the cavalry of the *turma Sallvitana*, granted citizenship *en bloc* in 89 BC; cf. ILS 8888 = FIRA I^2 17 = ILLRP 515 [10. 64, 116]).

The *senatus consultum de Asclepiade sociisque* of 78 BC granted various privileges to three Greek *navarches* ('ships' captains') for their twelve years of service (CIL I 203 = I^2 588 = IG XIV 951 = FIRA I^2 35 [16. 56–68]). It is impossible to say whether they had been motivated by the prospect of privileges upon entering service, but they probably always knew that their service for Rome would lead to some kind of benefit. At some point between 42 and 38, Caesar the Younger, *imperator* and *triumvir rei publicae constituendae* (the future Augustus), granted citizenship under the *lex Munatia Aemilia* (42 BC) to Seleucus of Rhosus (son of Theodotus), along with his parents, wife and children. As Imperator Caesar, *divi filius*, in 33 BC, he granted the same privilege to his own veterans, their parents, children and wives (IGLS 718; FIRA I² 56 = CPL 103 [16. 68–97]). The chance of attaining Roman citizenship and other benefits – the most highly prized of which was *immunitas* (exemption from paying duties and performing services to the state) – might thus have been the most important motivation for peregrines (non-citizens) to join the Roman army, alongside the desire for pay and booty.

The motivations of soldiers thus differed during the civil wars of the 1st century BC. Roman citizens found the prospect of being settled in colonies inside or outside Italy attractive. Non-citizens, on the other hand, coveted Roman citizenship and other privileges, especially *immunitas*. Both groups were also interested in opportunities for pay, booty and social advancement. Within a deeply hierarchical society, and particularly in uncertain times, military service was seen as one of the best ways to escape poverty and enhance social prestige.

B.3. IMPERIAL PERIOD

These trends continued, with the most important motivations remaining the same under the Principate, as the army finally became a professional force. The former sailor Lucius Trebius (*Titi filius*), for instance, announced on his gravestone, 'I was born in poverty, thereafter doing service as a naval soldier alongside Augustus for 17 years without reluctance, without offence, and was honourably discharged' (*natus sum summa in pauperie, merui post, classicus miles, ad latus Augusti annos septemque decemque nullo odio, sine offensa, missus quoq(ue) honeste*: CIL V 938 = ILS 2905 = CLE 372 = AE 1972, 194) [12. 525]). As this inscription clearly illustrates, after 27 BC it was the emperor alone, as head of the entire army and holder of the *imperium maius* [6], who guaranteed that soldiers would receive their pay, their decorations, their honourable discharge with land or money (*missio agraria* and *missio nummaria*) and other privileges. For non-citizens serving in the auxiliary units, sailors in the Praetorian or provincial fleets, and the *equites singulares Augusti* ('imperial mounted guards'), those privileges included Roman citizenship or (for the Praetorians) the right of lawful marriage to a non-citizen woman [3]; [4].

Experience gained could prove very useful, not only in the military sphere, but also in the administrative and judicial machinery of the empire. This was particularly true for officers and junior officers, the *principales* (soldiers with specialist duties) and *immunes* or *beneficiarii*, who worked in the various *officia* of the provincial governors or within their own units. Many former officers and soldiers are later attested as senior figures in their communities, applying experience gained in military service to work on behalf of their fellow citizens. The numbers of serving soldiers were quite high, at around 150,000–180,000 legionaries and 220,000 auxiliaries. Because with few exceptions the army relied upon voluntary recruitment, motivation must have been of considerable importance [5]. The prospect of gaining Roman citizenship and entitlement to legal marriage (*ius conubii*) proved attractive to many non-citizens from all corners of the empire. Family tradition also induced many children of legionaries, mainly those born in the *canabae* [*castris*] (settlements outside military camps), to volunteer for the army (→ Camp, B.).

However, the system established by Augustus was seriously called into question in AD 68–69, when 'the secret of the empire was laid bare: the *princeps* could be made elsewhere than in Rome' (Tac. Hist. 1,4,2: *evulgato imperii arcano posse principem alibi quam Romae fieri*). Now, as during the → civil wars, soldiers tended to be motivated more by future advantage and booty rather than loyalty to the reigning emperor. During the Year of the Four Emperors, AD 69, it became abundantly clear that any charismatic governor touting social promises could make a play for the throne, if he could rely on a large provincial army that was motivated by personal ties to him and the promise of future *donativa*. The events that followed the death of Commodus, and the crisis of the 3rd century, show just how fragile and fleeting the relationship between the emperor and his army really was. Even before that, the period of an emperor's accession sometimes brought rebellions (*seditiones*) in the army, as soldiers sought to exploit the transfer of power – one example being the revolt of the legions of Illyricum and Germania in AD 14/15 (Tac. Ann. 1,16–51; 16,1: *cum Pannonicas legiones seditio incessit, nullis novis causis, nisi quod mutates princeps licentiam turbarum et ex civili bello spem praemiorum ostendebat*; 31,1: *isdem ferme diebus isdem causis Germanicae legiones turbatae*).

These realities help explain the motivation of the Roman elites, that is, members of the senatorial and equestrian classes (*ordo senatorius, ordo equester*). As during the Republic, a leadership position in army service was the perfect path for *equites Romani* who were seeking higher offices and entry into the *ordo senatorius*. Illustrating this are well-known cases of equestrian officers who attained the consulship and took power in the most important provinces. One of the most impressive examples is the career of Marcus Valerius Maximianus, member of the equestrian order and son of a senior magistrate of the *colonia Poetovio* in Pannonia superior (Diana Veteranorum, Numidia, AE 1956, 124 = IDRE II 445). During the crisis of the

3rd century, even ordinary soldiers could become emperors, or at least usurpers, beginning with Maximinus Thrax (the 'Soldier-Emperors'). All this was made possible by serving in the army, which facilitated rapid social advancement. After AD 260, senators were excluded from army command. Equestrian officers even took control of the legions, in what was the first step towards the transformation of the Roman army in the late 3rd and early 4th centuries.

Motivations even now were probably not much different from before. Naturally, loyalty to the state and the emperor – combined from the second half of the 4th century onwards with devotion to the Christian faith – was fundamental. Prospects of good pay, the *donativa* that were distributed regularly every five years during an emperor's reign (Procop. Arc. 24,27–29), tax exemptions during and after military service (Brigetio, AD 311: AE 1937, 232; Durostorum: AE 2007, 1224 = 2009, 1204), the chance of a share in spoils of war and family tradition (the children of veterans also joining up) – all these were motivations for military service [9. 51–60, 79–89, 101–105].

The declining numbers of epigraphic sources permit few specific insights. Nor is it possible in this new system, where promotion seems to have been more fluid than before, to trace complete careers. There are a great many examples in the 4th century AD of soldiers who began serving on the borders (*ripenses*, 'riverbank troops'/ *limitanei*, 'border troops') and then graduated to the mobile army of the *comitatenses* ('court troops'). Having fought for their own lives on the frontier, they took on a more political role in the *comitatenses*, where they could expect more wealth and promotion. The role played by soldiers in imperial successions continued to increase in importance, which was also a major cause of increasing instability. The advent of *foederati*, professional army groups of various backgrounds – but always from outside the empire – [13], makes it even more difficult to attempt general statements about the motivation of soldiers in this heterogeneous army of the empire of Late Antiquity.

☞ Discipline; Esprit de corps; Eve-of-battle speech; Honours; State and army; Valour

BIBLIOGRAPHY
[1] A. ALFÖLDI, Das frühe Rom und die Latiner, 1977 [2] L. DE BLOIS, Army and Society in the Late Roman Republic. Professionalism and the Role of the Military Middle Cadre, in: G. Alföldy et al. (eds.), Kaiser, Heer und Gesellschaft in der Römischen Kaiserzeit. Gedenkschrift für Eric Birley (HABES 31), 2000, 11–31 [3] W. ECK, L'empereur romain chef de l'armée. Le témoignage des diplômes militaires, in: Cahiers de Centre Gustave Glotz 13, 2002, 93–112 [4] W. ECK, Der Kaiser als Herr des Heeres. Militärdiplome und kaiserliche Reichsregierung, in: J.J. Wilkes (ed.), Documenting the Roman Army (BICS Supplement 81), 2003, 55–87 [5] W. ECK, Friedenssicherung und Krieg in der römischen Kaiserzeit. Wie ergänzt man das römische Heer?, in: A. Eich (ed.), Die Verwaltung der kaiserzeitlichen römischen Armee, 2009 [6] W. ECK, Das kaiserliche Heereskommando und die Rolle des Heeres in der Administration des Reiches, in: J.-L. Ferrary / J. Scheid, Il princeps romano. Autocrate o magistrato? Fattori giuridici e fattori sociali del potere imperiale da Augusto a Commodo, 2015 [7] E. GABBA, Republican Rome, the Army and the Allies, 1976 [8] L. KEPPIE, The Making of the Roman Army. From Republic to Empire, 1984 [9] A.D. LEE, War in Late Antiquity. A Social History, 2007 [10] V.A. MAXFIELD, The Military Decorations of the Roman Army, 1981 [11] S.E. PHANG, Roman Military Service. Ideologies of Discipline in the Late Republic and Early Principate, 2008 [12] M. REDDÉ, Mare Nostrum. Les infrastructures, le dispositif et l'histoire de la marine militaire sous l'Empire Romain, 1986 [13] R. SCHARF, Foederati. Von der völkerrechtlichen Kategorie zur byzantinischen Truppengattung (Tyche suppl. vol. 4), 2001 [14] M.A. SPEIDEL, Pro patria mori ... La doctrine du patriotisme romain dans l'armée impériale, in: Cahiers Glotz 21, 2010, 139–154 [15] H.P. SYNDIKUS, The Roman Odes, in: G. Davis (ed.), A Companion to Horace, 2010, 194–198 [16] H. WOLFF, Die Entwicklung der Veteranenprivilegien vom Beginn des 1. Jahrhunderts v.Chr. bis auf Konstantin d.Gr., in: W. Eck / H. Wolff (eds.), Heer und Integrationspolitik. Die römischen Militärdiplome als historische Quelle, 1986.

FLORIAN MATEI-POPESCU

Music

Music was important in military contexts, and not only for the → transmission of orders and messages. In relation to the Greek military, the genre of work songs, including the *embaterion* and *kastoreion* – is of significance. The latter was named after Castor (cf. Hom. Il. 3,237), the twin of the Dioscuri who was associated with horses, and signified a melody that was sung by the Spartans on their way to → battle, accompanied by an *auletes* (flute-player) (cf. fig. 1). For his part, the king would strike up with the *embaterion*, a military → march (Plut. mus. 26,1140c; Plut. *Lycurgus* 22; Polyaenus, Strat. 1,10). This was sometimes sung, but more usually played by an *auletes* (see Thuc. 5,70; but Ath. 1,21f–22a, which mentions *kineseis embaterius* together with *archaius kitharoidus*).

The meter of the *embaterion* and *kastoreion* was anapaestic (Val. Max. 2,6,2). According to Ath. 14,630f., the Spartans gave the name *enoplia* to their *embateria*, but this should not be confused with the homonymous dance rhythm performed in full armour. The same source reveals that the Spartans sang the songs of Tyrtaeus before battles (→ Sparta). The *Suda* (*Tyrtaíos*, 1205 Adler) does indeed associate the name of Tyrtaeus with war songs (*mele polemisteria*), which may have

Fig. 1: Detail from the upper frieze on the Chigi Vase (Olpe, overall height: 26cm; c. 675–625 BC). This polychrome vase-painting is the oldest depiction of a hoplite phalanx. An *auletes* is seen in the background of the ongoing battle.

included *embateria*. However, the surviving anapaests (Dion Chrys. 2,59 (= PMG 856; cf. 857)) are probably not attributable to him. Tyrtaeus was also known for his battle paraeneses (*hypothekai*, Suda l.c.). These elegies urging war were more likely performed at symposia (perhaps on campaign, cf. Philochorus FGrH 328 F 216) than in combat.

The category of Greek work songs also includes the *paian*. In contexts of warfare, it was sung before the fight (Eur. Tro. 122–128; Bacchylides, *Dithyrambi* 25,1–3; Aesch. Sept. 262–271; Thuc. 6,32,1f.; 7,75,7; Xen. An. 3,2,9; 4,3,19; 4,8,16) and upon its (victorious) conclusion (Hom. Il. 22,391–394; Xen. Hell. 7,2,15; 7,2,23; 7,4,36; Timotheus, *Persae* PMG 791,196–201; *Vita Sophoclis* 3 = TrGF 4 p. 31 Radt), or else used as a battlecry (Aesch. Pers. 386–395 (cf. PMG 858); Eur. Phoen. 1102f.; Thuc. 1,50,5; 4,43,2f.; 7,44,6; Xen. Hell. 2,4,17 etc.). More generally, → mercenaries sang while keeping watch ([8. 11] on Archilochus). Also, an *auletes* provided musical background aboard triremes. He was a member of the crew, and his playing on the *aulos* supported the rhythm of the oarsmen (e.g. IG II^2 1951, 100f.).

There were military musicians (*aeneatores*) in the Roman army. They included *bucinatores*, *cornicines* and *tubicines* (in general see Veg. Mil. 2,22), names deriving from the brass instruments *bucina*, *cornu* and *tuba* (the last of these akin to a signalling trumpet). They were called upon to perform in the camp, on march and during battle, for the communication of orders (→ Specialists). Yet, music in the Roman army was not limited to the signalling function alone. It is clear that men marched to musical signals and knew extended marching melodies (cf. fig. 2) [6]. In AD 69, when Vitellius marched troops into Rome after his victory over Otho, the *classicum*, the best-known of the signals (Veg. Mil. 2,22), was blown (Suet. Vit. 11; Suet. Tib. 37 may also be interpreted in this way). Ammianus Marcellinus (16,12,7) mentions a departure of infantry units accompanied by trumpets, which seems to echo Veg. Mil. 2,22 (*tubicen ad bellum vocat milites et rursum receptui canit*, 'the trumpet calls the soldiers to war and again sounds the retreat').

When Ammianus describes the movements of the army with the words *velut repedantes sub modulis*, 'as if retreating in rhythm' (19,6,9) and *velut pedis anapaesti praecinentibus modulis*, 'as if to the rhythm of the anapaestic foot' (24,6,10), he may mean that men marched to the rhythm of the music. Cass. Dio 56,22,3 (*hoi salpiktai … trochaion ti symbboesantes*) may allude to a march at the double, Lib. Or. 1,144 (*echo te organon symmige*) to a march melody. Trumpeters, *salpiktai*, who marched in → triumphal processions (App. Lib. 66; Plut. *Aemilius Paullus* 33) and military funerals (App. Civ. 1,105f.) while playing, may indicate a backdrop of military music (cf. probably also Sen. Apocol. 12). The aspect of song arises in the *barritus*, originally a Germanic battle song or battlecry (Tac. Germ. 3, where the word is *barditus*; Amm. Marc. 16,12,43; 26,7,17), which was adopted by the Roman army in Late Antiquity (Amm. Marc. 31,7,11; cf. 21,13,15; Veg. Mil. 3,18), and which was sung in the face of the enemy.

☞ March; Parades; Transmission of orders; Triumph

BIBLIOGRAPHY

[1] E.L. BOWIE, Miles Ludens?, in: O. MURRAY (ed.), Sympotica, 1990, 221–229 [2] O. FIEBIGER, Cornicines, in: RE 4/1, 1900, 1602–1603 [3] D.E. GERBER, Tyrtaeus, in: D.E. GERBER (ed.), A Companion to the Greek Lyric Poets, 1997, 102–107 [4] M. IHM, Barditus, in: RE 3/1,

Fig. 2: Detail from the spiral relief on the Trajan Column (Rome, AD 112/13; marble). This marble column, with its spiral frieze approximately 200 m long, was dedicated to the emperor Trajan in AD 113 to commemorate victory in the Dacian Wars, and it still stands today in its original position in the Trajan Forum in Rome. The section shown here shows a sacrificial procession forming part of a *lustratio exercitus*, accompanied by three *cornicines* and (above) three *tubicines*.

1897, 10–11 [5] L. KÄPPEL, Paian. Studien zur Geschichte einer Gattung, 1992 [6] A. MÜLLER, Zur Verwendung der Musik im römischen Heere, in: Philologus 73, 1916, 154–156 [7] M.P. SPEIDEL, Eagle-Bearer and Trumpeter, in: BJ 176, 1976, 123–163 [8] M.L. WEST, Studies in Greek Elegy and Iambus, 1974.

PATRICK SÄNGER

Mutiny

A. Greek
B. Roman

A. GREEK

A.1. The *polis* ideal of citizen hoplites
A.2. Mercenaries and revolts

Mutiny today is understood as a situation in which a group, such as a ship's crew or an army unit, refuses to obey its commander and attempts to seize control from him. In the Ancient Greek world, mutiny in this modern sense was a rarity. In fact, there is no Ancient Greek term that corresponds to the present-day sense of the word. Where Greek authors describe a rebellion, they use the same vocabulary as for civil unrest: *stasis*, that is, a dispute between factions or a civil conflict. Arrian calls the mutinies of the army of Alexander the Great at the Hyphasis and Opis (326 and 324 BC; → Wars of note A.) 'disorder', 'upheaval' (*tarache*) and 'despondency' (*athymia*) (Arr. An. 5,25,2; 7,8,3; 7,11,4).

The first mutiny in Greek literature occurs in Homer's *Iliad*, when Achilles refuses to obey the orders of the Achaean commander Agamemnon. He withdraws his Myrmidons from the war, with ruinous consequences for the Greek army as a whole. Responding to the deputation sent to persuade him to return to the fight, Achilles even calls for a general uprising against Agamemnon: 'As for you others, I advise you thus: set sail for home, for your goal of taking the rearing fortress is a hopeless one. For mighty, far-thundering Zeus holds his hand implacably over it, and its people are filled with new courage. So you be on your way, and convey my message to the leaders of the Achaeans – this being the role of the elders –, that they may devise another scheme, and a better one than this; one that will save their ships and the horde of the Achaeans beside their hollow ships, now that this plan of their invention is no longer viable because of my unrelenting rage' (Hom. Il. 9,417–426). Since Agamemnon has injured Achilles' honour, his behaviour is within the rules of the heroic code, which places a higher priority on the warrior's renown than on any other concern.

Probably the first attested mutiny in Greek military history took place in connection with the foundation of the Delian League (478 BC). After repelling the invasion of Xerxes, the non-Spartan Greek allies resented their harsh and repressive treatment at the hands of Pausanias, commander of the league, and refused to obey him. Pausanias was then ordered back to Sparta: 'His recall came at the very moment when the hatred he had provoked moved the allies (except for the soldiers from the Peloponnese) to desert him and join the Athenian side' (Thuc. 1,95,4). The Athenian hegemony within the Delian League that resulted from the rejection of Pausanias would lead to the rise of the Athenian empire and, ultimately, to the

Peloponnesian War (431–404 BC). These events marked a watershed in Greek dealings with Persia, but they also marked a pivotal moment in the history of the Greek *poleis*.

A.1. The *polis* ideal of citizen hoplites

The above example notwithstanding, mutinies seem to have been rare, or even non-existent, in the era of autonomous Greek city-states. After all, military service in the hoplite phalanx was the most prestigious expression of one's status as a citizen and a citizen's greatest privilege. It was also the fundamental means by which one defended one's own farmland and family against external attack. The relative paucity of structures of command in the hoplite army, along with the egalitarian nature of hoplite tactics, all but ruled out the danger of revolt. The → militias of the city-states could rely on the loyalty of their farming citizen-soldiers, a loyalty that was grounded in the values of the *polis*. 'This is excellence (*arete*) and renown, this is the greatest prize in the world and the best for a youth to win; this pride common to all, the city and her people, when a man stands unflinching in the front rank, relentless, banishing all thought of ignominious flight, lays on the line with patient courage all that life has promised him, and with rousing words stands shoulder to shoulder with his comrade' (Tyrt. 9D,13–19). Furthermore, the very same men who fought in the phalanx would have voted for the war at the assembly.

The importance attached to the wellbeing of the fighting force is further illustrated by the fact that *polis* armies tended to form ranks in the phalanx according to *phyle* ('clan'). Men fought alongside their own brothers, cousins and friends. Hippocrates, the Athenian commander at Delium (424 BC), used his eve-of-battle speech to express his strong identification with the fight for the *polis* and respect for their ancestors. 'Advance to face [the Boeotians] as citizens of a land of which you are all proud, it being the first in Hellas, and as the sons of fathers who defeated them under Myronides at Oenophyta, and thereby took possession of Boeotia' (Thuc. 4,95). The culture of direct personal connections within the *polis* further intensified natural affinities among friends and kinsmen.

In the more professional Spartan armies, with their more developed command structures and hierarchies, obedience was regarded as the foundation of liberty and as a legal principle (Thuc. 1,84,3): 'We are wise, for our education is based on too little learning to despise the laws, and on too strict self-control not to obey them' (→ Sparta). The Spartan poet Tyrtaeus refers to the close connection between freedom within the *polis* and service in the hoplite phalanx: 'If he [the hoplite] falls in the front rank, he loses his life in battle, to the glory of his people, his city and his father. ... The noble repute and name of the hero will never fade away; he lives on, eternal and undying, beneath the earth' (Tyrt. 9D,23–32). The hoplite ideal fundamentally altered the concept of *arete*, which dated back to Homer, for whom the individual honour (*time*) and renown (*kleos*) of a warrior like Hector or Achilles counted for more than the safety of the army or even the survival of the polity.

A.2. Mercenaries and revolts

From the later phases of the Peloponnesian War (→ Wars of note H.) through the 4th century BC and into the Hellenistic period, the increasing use of mercenaries changed the character of Greek armies. In Xenophon's *Anabasis*, for example, the Greek → mercenaries recruited by Cyrus for the fight against his brother, King Artaxerxes II of Persia, refuse to follow him further until he promises them higher pay. The soldiers later threaten outright mutiny when they discover that Cyrus' true intention is to overthrow the Great King.

The widespread hiring of mercenaries testifies to the dissolution of the traditional bond between fighting to defend the *polis* and the exercise of civic privileges. The revolts faced by Alexander the Great in the east reveal the inherent instability of mercenary units and professional forces. For four months in the mid-3rd century BC, for example, mercenaries mutinied against King Eumenes I of Pergamum until they won improved conditions of service at two fortresses in his kingdom, Philetaerea and Attaleia. Such demands – by the king and his soldiers alike – would have been unthinkable in the culture of *polis* militias during the 6th and 5th centuries. The mercenaries wanted guarantees regarding term of service, pay and the treatment of veterans and orphans. Both sides demanded pledges of loyalty and protection against conspiracies.

Even so, mutiny remained an uncommon problem in the Greek world until its integration into the Roman Empire in the 2nd and 1st centuries BC.

Bibliography

[1] P.A. Cartledge, The Birth of the Hoplite, in: P.A. Cartledge, Spartan Reflections, 2001, 153–166 (first published as La nascita degli opliti e l'organizzazione militare, in: S. Settis (ed.) I Greci, vol. 2/1, 1996, 681–714) [2] P.A. Cartledge, Alexander the Great, 2004 [3] P. Ducrey, Warfare in Ancient Greece, 1986 [4] V.D. Hanson, The Other Greeks. The Family Farm and the Agrarian Roots of Western Civilization, 1999 [5] V.D. Hanson, The Western Way of War, 2000 [6] S. Hornblower, Warfare in Ancient Literature. The Paradox of War, in: P. Sabin et al. (eds.), The Cambridge History of Greek and Roman Warfare, vol. 1, 2007, 22–53 [7] S. Hornblower, Sticks, Stones and Spartans. The Sociology of Spartan Violence, in: H. van Wees (ed.), In War and Violence in Ancient Greece, 2009, 57–82 [8] D. Kagan / G. Viggiano (eds.), Men of Bronze. Hoplite Warfare in Ancient Greece, 2013

[9] J. Kromayer / G. Veith, Heerwesen und Kriegführung der Griechen und Römer, 1928 [10] C. Mann, Militär und Kriegführung in der Antike, 2013 [11] W. Rüstow / H. Köchly, Geschichte des Griechischen Kriegswesens von der Ältesten Zeit bis auf Pyrrhos, 1852 [12] H. van Wees, Greek Warfare. Myths and Realities, 2004.

GREGORY F. VIGGIANO

B. Roman

B.1. De-escalation
B.2. Punishment

One of the fiercest conflicts in the history of the Roman army broke out on the announcement of the death of the first *princeps*, Augustus (d. August 19, AD 14; Tac. Ann. 1,16–30: mutiny in Pannonia; 1,31–52: mutiny in Germania). On that occasion, it was Germanicus, adoptive son of Augustus' successor Tiberius, who – with some difficulty – brought the mutinying legions on the Rhine to their senses. To begin with, two legions on the Lower Rhine revolted. Two more were dragged into the uprising, so that about 20,000 men were involved. Exacerbating the situation, the three legions stationed on the Danube had revolted only a short time before, the mutiny brought to an end by Drusus, Tiberius' biological son. The grievances aired by the soldiers seem more than understandable: excessive terms of service (more than 30 years), inadequate pay, hard labour, exploitation and harassment by the centurions. Germanicus, like Drusus, tried various ways to resolve the mutiny. He gave speeches in which he sought to inspire the soldiers' pride and sense of honour, pointing to the greatness of Rome, reminding them of their duty and promising improvements that were later confirmed in Rome. Ultimately, though, Germanicus ended the revolt by severe repression: all leaders of the mutiny were executed – a procedure in line with the *mos maiorum* ('ancestral custom'). He also offered followers the option of redeeming their wrongdoing by delivering up the ringleaders for death.

The events in Pannonia and Germania amply demonstrate how quickly the Roman army could mutate from an instrument of protection for the fledgling Principate into a threat to it. Further illustrating this point are the events following the assassination of Domitian (d. September 18, AD 96), for discontent was rampant in the *exercitus Romanus* ('Roman army') following the accession of Nerva. Unlike his predecessor Domitian, the new emperor, who lacked military experience and made no effort to court the military, was not well-liked (Suet. Dom. 23; Cass. Dio 68,1f.; Philostr. soph. 1,2). If he was not aware of it before, this situation was drawn to Nerva's attention when the Praetorian Guard in Rome arrested him (Plin. Pan. 5,7; Cass. Dio 68,3,2f.; 68,5,4). He promptly adopted Trajan, thereby naming as his successor a man who was popular with the military, which defused the crisis (Plin. Pan. 5,8; 6,1; 6,4; 7,3; 9,2; [4]). Discontent or open mutiny could also arise from frustration at ongoing wars, hostile weather, concern about situations at home and lack of faith in commanders (Tac. Ann. 13,35,5; Hdn. 6,7,2–5; 8,5,8f.).

B.1. De-escalation

It was a goal among leaders that conflict situations should not be allowed to arise in the first place, or, if they did, they should be resolved while they were still controllable. The military writer of Late Antiquity Vegetius gives a very thorough description of tried and tested methods for countering discontent and unrest in the camp (Mil. 3,4). He considered inactivity and a lack of drilling to be the root of the problem. Prevention thus consisted in relentless activity, such that soldiers were unable to think of anything but their duties and assignments, regular manoeuvres and parades, no granting of leave, daily training with weapons to the point of exhaustion, training in running and swimming, heavy physical labour, such as chopping wood, digging ditches, laying paths in difficult terrain and squaring timber for construction. Such measures, however, were also capable of having the opposite effect.

If trouble was brewing in a unit, Vegetius advised the commander to enact measures suitable for prevention: identify the ringleaders and remove them from the camp by giving them an honourable assignment or temporarily appointing them to maintenance duties or a defensive deployment. If the situation was critical, the senior commander should act in accordance with the *mos maiorum* and intervene harshly – as Vegetius put it: impose fear on everyone and punishment on a few. First, however, efforts were made to achieve de-escalation. Frontinus (Strat. 1,9) lists a series of instances where a general successfully defused a situation and restored order. His examples show that a commander was best advised to act with circumspection and wisdom in finding a suitable way to end a mutiny. One effective strategy was to remind soldiers of their honour. C. Iulius Caesar, a charismatic army leader, was said to have ended a mutiny by scornfully addressing his men as *quirites* – 'Civilians!' – rather than as soldiers (Tac. Ann. 1,42; Suet. Caes. 70). On another occasion, he was supposedly compelled to accede to the demand of certain soldiers to be discharged, but he did so with such a thunderous expression of threat that the released soldiers instantly and ruefully returned to the colours (Frontinus, Strat. 1,9,4). Claudius' planned conquest of Britain in

AD 43 was jeopardized when soldiers arriving at the Channel refused to undertake a campaign across the boundaries of the known world. On hearing of the mutiny, Claudius sent his freedman and confidant Narcissus to the legions to urge them to see reason. This made it abundantly clear to the mutineers that, in Claudius' eyes, they were not loyal soldiers who would deserve to be addressed by a freeborn man or even a high ranking officer. The soldiers got the message, and the campaign was successfully prosecuted (Cass. Dio 60,19,1–4).

Of course, not every mutiny ended so mildly. While governor of the province of Britannia (c. AD 185), the future Emperor Pertinax was forced to put down unrest that brought him within a hair's breadth of being killed by mutinous legionaries – an incident he avenged with the utmost ruthlessness. Pertinax then asked to be relieved of his post (SHA Pert. 3,10; PIR² H 73). It is impossible to say whether this was because his drastic response angered the army, because it weighed upon him, or whether he simply thought it better to give the troops a fresh start under a commander without such a history.

B.2. Punishment

The *Digests* contain a number of passages dealing with the punishment of mutineers. Ringleaders guilty of insurrection (*seditio*) could expect death or, in less serious cases, degradation (Dig. 49,16,3,19f.). The pseudo-Pauline *Sententiae* declare that a *miles turbator pacis* ('soldier who disturbs the peace') is punishable with death (5,38,2). Soldiers finding common cause against general discipline, that is, initiating a conspiracy or mutiny, faced dishonourable discharge from the *exercitus Romanus*, the consequence of which, moreover, was *infamia* ('disgrace'; Dig. 49,16,3,21; cf. Suet. Aug. 24,2 and Frontinus, Strat. 4,5,2).

One special form of disobedience was support given to a usurper by an entire unit or part of a unit. In general, the penalty for this was the wholesale or partial dissolution of the unit concerned. Vespasian recreated the Batavian cohorts from scratch following the defeat of the Batavian Revolt [1. 47f.], and Septimius Severus took the lives of all the Praetorians who had participated in the assassination of Pertinax. The remainder were dishonourably discharged and banished from Rome (Hdn. 2,13,2–12; Cass. Dio 75,1,1). He punished the urban cohorts of Lugdunum for their loyalty to Clodius Albinus by dissolving them. Elagabalus either temporarily disbanded the *legio III Gallica* that had supported its legate's usurpation (Cass. Dio 80,7,1), or else he allowed it to survive with the loss of its unit name and under difficult conditions. Severus Alexander restored the legion's former rights.

Given the total strength of the army, we hear relatively little of mutinies in the *exercitus Romanus* during the Roman Imperial period. The reasons for this are many, including the reliability of centurions and senior officers who were careful to ensure calm and good order. Superiors were also expected to pay attention to their soldiers' concerns and grievances (Dig. 49,16,12,2). The overall good conditions under which soldiers performed their duties contributed much to general contentment. Most notably, these included regular payments and bonuses, discharge following a reasonable term of service, decent permanent camps, good medical care (→ Medical corps), assorted comforts such as bath complexes, opportunities for promotion, and privileges for → veterans that eased their return to civilian life.

☞ **Discipline; Military law; State and army**

Bibliography

[1] G. Alföldy, Die Hilfstruppen der römischen Provinz Germania inferior (Epigraphische Studien 6), 1968 [2] J.B. Campbell, The Emperor and the Roman Army, 31 BC–AD 235, 1984 [3] S.E. Phang, Roman Military Service. Ideologies of Discipline in the Late Republic and Early Principate, 2008 [4] M.A. Speidel, Bellicosissimus princeps, in: A. Nünnerich-Asmus (ed.), Traian. Ein Kaiser der Superlative am Beginn einer Umbruchzeit?, 2002, 23–40 (reprinted in: M.A. Speidel, Heer und Herrschaft im Römischen Reich der Hohen Kaiserzeit, 2009, 121–166) [5] G. Stern, Mutiny, Military, in: S. Bagnall et al. (eds.), The Encyclopedia of Ancient History, vol. 8, 2013, 4646–4647 [6] G. Wesch-Klein, Soziale Aspekte des römischen Heerwesens in der Kaiserzeit (HABES 28), 1998, esp. 169–178.

GABRIELE WESCH-KLEIN

Oath

The oath (*horkos, ius iurandum, sacramentum*) played a key role in public and private life during Antiquity, and especially in the military sphere, whether at war or peace. By calling on gods or higher powers as witnesses, a person or group could guarantee the truthfulness of something said about the past or present (assertory oath), or the uprightness of intentions (promissory oath). The verbal promise was usually confirmed with rituals, and any breach of an oath could incur punishments or sanctions [3].

Traces of verbal oaths among warriors or hostile camps are already found in Homer's *Iliad* (Hom. II. 3,264–301). As a crucial element in diplomatic agreements, alliances and peace treaties, an oath bound members of the Delian League and the Peloponnesian League alike (Hdt. 9,106,4; Xen. Hell. 5,3,26) [5]; [1]; [8]. With varying modalities (Thuc. 5,47,8–10), it was intended to guarantee the 'good faith' (*pistis*) of the parties, who in some instances renewed their oaths on a regular basis and interpreted them with a measure of flexibility (Thuc. 1,99; 5,30). The oath also played a part in the relationship between soldiers and their commanders (Aesch. Sept. 43–53). In the form of a vow made before battle (Xen. An. 3,2,12), it imposed responsibilities on every individual combatant. By making an oath, every citizen declared his membership in the polity and his readiness to defend it. This strengthened the cohesion of the phalanx and any other battle formation. Sometimes, a written declaration augmented a verbal oath. An inscription from the second half of the 4th century BC records the oath that Athenian *ephebes* (young men between 18 and 20 years of age) had to take: submission to the *polis*, solidarity with comrades, obedience to rationally acting commanders, and a promise not to desert the colors [6. 296–316]. The same inscription also preserves an apocryphal version of the oath supposedly taken by the Athenians at Plataeae (479 BC) [7]. The importance of the oath in kingdoms and city-states and among soldiers (including mercenaries) remained unabated in the Hellenistic period (IK 28,1,2f.).

Loyalty (*fides*) was of the highest importance in Rome, where treaties (*foedus*) were also associated with oaths (Liv. 1,24). Foreigners were often regarded as less trustworthy and more prone to perjury (*Punica fides*), although they did have regard for the value of an oath (Caes. B Gall. 7,66,7), and Rome itself did not always act in an exemplary way. Soldiers were expected to respond to their call-up to the military, but for a time it was left to them to swear oaths among themselves. This changed in 216 BC, when they were systematically required to utter the *sacramentum militare* before the tribunes (Liv. 22,38,2–5) [2. 19–32]. Making the oath transformed *quirites*, plain 'civilian' citizens, into *milites*, citizens under arms (Tac. Ann. 1,42,3). The most prestigious oath was the military one (Dion. Hal. Ant. Rom. 11,43,2), which reinforced the bond between the commander and his troops. Even it, however, was to some extent undermined in the fratricidal wars towards the end of the Republican period. The force of this oath revived under Augustus, who introduced a mandatory *sacramentum* for soldiers, affirming their loyalty to him personally and to his authority. It was sworn at the time of enlistment and at the accession of a new emperor, and it was renewed in January every year, and perhaps on the *dies imperii* (annual holiday marking the emperor's accession) and on paydays. This took place in a ceremony that displayed the religious dimension of the act, thus strengthening the soldiers' *esprit de corps* and encouraging participation in the ruler cult (on the *genius* of the *sacramentum* itself: AE 1924, 135). In reality, mutinies, usurpations and civil wars did on occasion tarnish the oath's lustre (Tac. Hist. 1,12,1). The exact wording of the oath in the Imperial period is not recorded, but since Republican times, it contained a pledge to obey and not to desert (Pol. 6,21,1–3; Dion. Hal. Ant. Rom. 10,18,2; Liv. 22,38,4). In a paraphrase dating from the late 4th century, Vegetius (Veg. Mil. 2,5; see also Serv. Aen. 8,614) also mentions readiness to die for the *res publica*. That this requirement for self-sacrifice for the state continued into the Imperial period need not be doubted, as it was in previous scholarship [9]. Even if Christian soldiers of the 3rd and early 4th centuries found their faith irreconcilable with the demands of the oath and endured persecution as a result (*Passio S. Marcelli* 1f.), Vegetius suggests that in his day, the oath was sworn before Father, Son and Holy Spirit as well as the *maiestas imperatoris* ('emperor's majesty').

☞ Discipline; Military law

BIBLIOGRAPHY

[1] S. BOLMARCICH, Oaths in Greek International Relations, in: A.H. Sommerstein / J. Fletcher (eds.), Horkos. The Oath in Greek Society, 2007, 26–38, 223–227 [2] J.B. CAMPBELL, The Emperor and the Roman Army, 1984 [3] F. GRAF, Eid, in: ThesCRA 3, 2005, 237–246 [4] S.E. PHANG, Roman Military Service. Ideologies of Discipline in the Late Republic and Early Principate, 2008, 117–120 [5] P.J. RHODES, Oaths in Political Life, in: A.H. Sommerstein / J. Fletcher (eds.), Horkos. The Oath in Greek Society, 2007, 11–25,, 220–223 [6] L. ROBERT, Études philologiques et épigraphiques, 1938 [7] P. SIEWERT, Der Eid von Plataiai, 1972 [8] A.H. SOMMERSTEIN / A.J. Bayliss (ed.), Oath and State in Ancient Greece, 2012, 147–306 [9] M.A. SPEIDEL, Pro patria mori... La doctrine du patriotisme romain dans l'armée impériale, in: Cahiers du Centre Gustave Glotz 21, 2010, 139–154.

PATRICE FAURE

Officers

A. Greek
B. Roman

A. Greek

A.1. Athens
A.2. Sparta
A.3. Other *poleis*
A.4. Hellenistic armies

Below the level of the generals (i.e. the chief commanders), Greek armies had various branches of arms and tactical units, each headed by its own officers. The militia armies of the Archaic and Early Classical periods had no such officers below the general. Only later, and especially in the Hellenistic mercenary armies, did a fixed structure and hierarchy develop, and with it a distinct officer corps, although this differed greatly by era and army.

Personal wealth was always an important consideration for a military career in the militia armies, so that officer positions not only expressed a social hierarchy, they also reinforced it. Higher → pay for officers was also an issue of status [4. 75–97]; [5. 35f.].

A.1. Athens

Almost all officers were elected annually by the *ekklesia* ('assembly'), because their work required a certain level of professional qualification (Xen. Ath. pol. 1,3; Aristot. Ath. pol. 61,1). As from 501/500 BC, ten *strategoi* ('commanders') operated as supreme commanders of the army and navy [9], and they could be re-elected (Aristot. Ath. pol. 22,2; cf. 62,3). Their competencies were strictly military, but they also gained political influence through the military successes of Athens and the Delian League. Originally, they were assigned to specific, situation-dependent missions, but by the mid-4th century BC, a distribution of responsibilities into individual areas had developed (Aristot. Ath. pol. 61,1; on their competencies, cf. 61,2).

Under the *strategoi*, there were ten *taxiarchoi* ('regiment commanders') for the infantry (Thuc. 4,4,1; 8,92,4; Dem. Or. 4,26; Poll. 8,94), each in command of a *taxis* ('regiment'). They in turn appointed the *lochagoi* ('company captians'; Aristot. Ath. pol. 61,3) and kept the draft lists for the *phylai* ('divisions'; Aristoph. Pax 1179–1181).

For the cavalry, there were two *hipparchoi* ('cavalry commanders'), who each commanded the horsemen of five *phylai*. The cavalry of one *phyle* was commanded by a *phylarchos* ('division commanders'; Aristot. Ath. pol. 61,5), and for each *phyle*, ten *dekadarchoi* commanded one *dekades* ('unit of ten men'; Xen. hipp. 1,8). *Hipparchoi* and *phylarchoi* were responsible with the *katalogeis* for the squad lists (Aristot. Ath. pol. 49,2; cf. [14. 676–688]), for mustering, → education and → training (Xen. Hipp. 1,12; 1,17; 1,21; 1,25; 2,1; 2,7; 3,13), for care of the horses and → equipment (Xen. Hipp. 1,22; 1,25), and for the disbursement of pay (SEG 21, 525, ll. 18–21).

Nothing is known of the conditions or careers of officers, except the fixed minimum for personal assets. For cavalry officers, membership in the *hippeis* ('equestrian') censitary class was certainly one condition (SEG 21, 525, ll. 12–15). There is no evidence of a fixed career path as in the Roman army, and given that this was a citizen militia, none would be expected. The Athenians were advised by Hagnon (5th cent. BC) to mix younger and older officers, as some smaller *poleis* did, and to elect former *taxiarchoi* and *phylarchoi* as *strategoi taxiarchoi phylarchoi* (Theophr. De eligendis magistratibus, MS Vat. gr. 2306, B, ll. 10–170 and 172–183). It is not clear to what extent Athens heeded this advice, but it seems at least possible that they did to some degree (cf. Xen. Mem. 3,4,1; Aristoph. Av. 799; Syll.³ 1074; IG II² 2854; [8. 1087]).

A.2. Sparta

The Spartan army was notable for its abundance of officer ranks (cf. Thuc. 5,66,4; Xen. Lac. pol. 11,6; cf. [9]) – five beneath the king in Xenophon's day [1. 67–83]. Six *polemarchoi* ('warleaders') elected for one year each commanded a *mora* (a military unit), 24 *lochagoi* ('company captains') commanded a *lochos*, 48 *pentekonteres* or *pentekosteres* commanded a *pentekostys* (unit of 50 men) and 96 *enomotarchoi* commanded an *enomotarchia* (unit bound by oath) (Thuc. 5,66,3f.; Xen. Lac. pol. 11,4). *Protostatai* (lit. 'those who stand before') commanded the first rank in battle (Xen. Lac. pol. 11,5) (→ Sparta).

Xen. Lac. pol. 13,11 also mentions *hellanodikai* ('battle judges'), *tamiai* ('treasurers'), *laphyropolai* ('sellers of spoils') and commanders of the army train (Xen. Lac. pol. 13,4). On the king's *syskenoi* ('tent companions'), cf. Xen. Lac. pol. 13,1,7.

The Spartan fleet was under the command of a *nauarchos* ('fleet commander'), whose authority was independent of the king. This gave him a great deal of power (Aristot. pol. 2,1271a,37–40). This was one of very few opportunities for Spartiates to attain political influence alongside the kings. Although technically the *nauarchia* was a one-year appointment during the Ionian War, and it could only be held once, the ban on repeated appointments could be circumvented by operating as a deputy (*epistoleus*) to the *nauarchos*, whose supreme command would then only be nominal

(Xen. Hell. 2,1,7; cf. [18]). Beginning in the mid-5th century, counsellors (*symbouloi*) were sometimes appointed to work alongside unsuccessful *nauarchoi*, for purposes of supervision and strategic guidance (e.g. Thuc. 2,85,1; 3,69,1; 8,39,2).

The only other position to offer comparable scope for influence was that of the *harmostai* ('governors') (Xen. Lac. pol. 14,2), who had a reputation for being corruptible. They headed garrisons outside Sparta, mostly after the Peloponnesian War, and their ruthless pursuit of mostly personal interests was a major factor in the development of anti-Spartan resentments (e.g. Xen. Hell. 1,1,32).

A.3. OTHER *POLEIS*
Many of the officer ranks recorded in Athens and Sparta were also found in other *poleis*. The Boeotians (Xen. Hell. 5,2,30) and Sicilians (Plut. *Dion* 28,3) had *lochagoi*. *Taxiarchoi* are attested as commanders of mercenary contingents of assorted weapon specialities (Xen. Hell. 6,2,18; Xen. An. 4,1,28; 4,3,22). There are records of *polemarchoi* at Thebes in the early 4th century BC (Xen. Hell. 5,2,25), and in the four tetrads of Thessaly in the mid-4th century BC (IG II² 116, l. 23; IG II² 175, l. 6). *Strategoi* were appointed at Syracuse in the late 5th century BC (Thuc. 6,72,4; Diod. Sic. 13,91–95) and in the Arcadian League in the 360s (Diod. Sic. 15,62,2; Xen. Hell. 7,3,1). The Thebans deployed *harmostai* in their garrisons (Xen. Hell. 7,3,4: 366 BC at Sicyum; Xen. Hell. 7,1,43: 366 BC in Achaean *poleis*).

A.4. HELLENISTIC ARMIES
In the Macedonian army, officers were originally appointed in accordance with regional → recruitment, as part of the regional and municipal organizational structures, and they were invariably members of the Macedonian aristocracy (EKM Beroia 4). By the reign of Alexander the Great (→ Generals of note, B.), if not before, however, senior officer ranks were excluded from this rule, and chosen by the king (Curt. 5,2,2–5; Arr. Anab. 3,16,11). Over time, Alexander appointed more and more of his *syntrophoi* (i.e. those raised with him) and friends as officers, and they in turn came to wield great influence over the king, so that they were able to promote their own favourites to officer positions [10. 3, 57].

The most important infantry ranks were, in descending order of seniority, *strategoi*, *speirarchai* ('cohort commanders'), *tetrarchai* and *lochagoi*. The cavalry ranks were the *ilarchai* and *tetrarchai* (?). There were also five officers *ektos taxeos* ('outside the order'), including the ensign-bearers (*semeiophoros*), trumpeters (*salpigktes*) and heralds (*stratokeryx*) (Asclepiodotus 2,9), as well as other supernumerary officers (SEG 40, 524; cf. [6. 443–460]). However, this hierarchy was already undergoing many amendments during Alexander's campaign [3. 201–212].

The relationship between monarch and (senior) officers in the Hellenistic armies depended primarily on personal relations, that is, on trust and reciprocity, as was the case with Alexander's army (cf. SEG 37, 1020). Those officers were accordingly able to gain great influence over their king (Plut. Mor. 177c; cf. [15. 355–368]). Similarly, garrison officers were able to operate as mediators between the monarch and his subjects, in whom they could instill a positive view of monarchical rule through charitable acts. This was all the more true given that many such men returned to their homelands after they were discharged from the army [5. 35, 88–91]. Over time, some military positions became effectively hereditary [5. 39–41]; [17. 330–335]. However, the relationship between monarch and officer was not so personal that a change of government or king was career-ending for the officer (e.g. IC III,IV 14 and IThSy 318, cf. [16. 41–43]. But changed geopolitical conditions enabled loyal newcomers to forge careers leading to high officer rank (e.g. IFay II 107 and 108; cf. [17. 304]).

On the hierarchies of officer ranks in the Hellenistic armies cf. [2. 85–93] (Seleucids); [7. 155–159]; [13]; [19]; [17. 163–170] (Ptolemies).
☞ General; Mercenaries; Rank

BIBLIOGRAPHY
[1] J.K. ANDERSON, Military Theory and Practice in the Age of Xenophon, 1970 [2] B. BAR-KOCHVA, The Seleucid Army. Organization and Tactics in the Great Campaigns, 1976 [3] H. BERVE, Das Alexanderreich auf prosopographischer Grundlage, vol. 1, 1926 [4] T. BOULAY, Arès dans la cité. Les poleis et la guerre dans l'Asie Mineure hellénistique, 2014 [5] A. CHANIOTIS, War in the Hellenistic World, 2005 [6] M.B. CHATZOPULOS, Macedonian Institutions under the Kings, vol. 1, 1996 [7] C. FISCHER-BOVET, Army and Society in Ptolemaic Egypt, 2014 [8] F. GSCHNITZER, Phylarchos (4), in: RE Suppl. 11, 1968, 1086–1090 [9] N.G.L. HAMMOND, Strategia and Hegemonia in Fifth-Century Athens, in: CQ 19, 1969, 111–144 [10] W. HECKEL, The Marshals of Alexander's Empire, 1992 [11] J.F. LAZENBY, The Spartan Army, 2012 (reprinted from 1985) [12] L. MOOREN, La hiérarchie de cour ptolémaïque. Contribution à l'étude des institutions et des classes dirigeantes à l'époque hellénistique, 1977 [13] W. PEREMANS et al., Prosopographia ptolemaica, vol. 2, 1952 [14] P.J. RHODES, A Commentary on the Aristotelian Athenaion Politeia, 1993 (reprint 2006) [15] I. SAVALLI-LESTRADE, Les philoi royaux dans l'Asie hellénistique, 1998 [16] S. SCHEUBLE-REITER, Loyalitätsbekundungen ptolemäischer Phrurarchen im Spiegel epigraphischer Quellen, in: A. Çoskun et al. (eds.), Identität und Zugehörigkeit im Osten der griechisch-römischen Welt. Aspekte ihrer Repräsentation in Städten, Provinzen und Reichen, 2009, 35–53 [17] S. SCHEUBLE-REITER, Die Katökenreiter im ptolemäischen Ägypten, 2012 [18] R. SEALEY, Die

spartanische Nauarchie, in: Klio 58, 1976, 335–358 [19] E. Van't Dack, La littérature tactique de l'Antiquité et les sources documentaires, in: E. Van't Dack, Ptolemaica selecta. Études sur l'armée et l'administration lagides, 1988, 47–64.

SANDRA SCHEUBLE-REITER

B. Roman

B.1. Definition and evolution to the end of the Republic
B.2. Principate
B.3. The 3rd century and Late Antiquity

B.1. Definition and evolution to the end of the Republic

The modern term 'officer', for which neither Latin nor Ancient Greek has an exact equivalent, denotes the holder of a senior military authority or command. Modern armies distinguish between various types of officers (e.g. 'generals', 'staff officers', 'subalterns', 'junior officers', 'commissioned' and 'non-commissioned' officers), but none of the present-day categories can be exactly applied to the Roman army, where officer rank combined multiple dimensions of meaning: military (status, function and experience in the army), political (relationship to the central power) and social and cultural (origins and status in society).

War was fought according to aristocratic practices at first, but the increasing shift to a censitary army from the 6th century BC onwards brought wider → recruitment and systematization of the command structure. Magistracies with *imperium* (giving the right to command the army) and the military tribunate (six *tribuni* of variable experience per → legion: Pol. 6,19–21 on their ranks, functions, and appointment by the consuls or the people) were reserved for the the equestrian censitary class. The selection of officers from the elite of society for time-limited commands was closely bound up with the political principles of the Republic [8]. On a lower level, the centurions made up the junior command level in the legion. As intermediaries to the senior commanders, the *centuriones* (60 per legion, each heading a century; the *decuriones* in an analogous position leading the cavalry *turmae*: Pol. 6,24f.) served at close proximity to the deployment zone and to the soldiers of the subordinate units – the role of the latter increasingly important (maniples in the 4th century BC and cohorts in the 2nd). Members of the lowest censitary classes, they were chosen from among the most courageous and experienced individuals each campaign, with no guarantee that their appointment would be systematically ongoing (Liv. 42,32–34 on these issues and the figure of Spurius Ligustinus 171 BC). The internal hierarchy within the centurionate, where a distinction was increasingly apparent between the *primi ordines* and the *primus pilus* (centurion of the first century of the first cohort), stimulated competition (Caes. B Gall. 5,44). The *praefecti* who headed the confederate contingents (*socii*) were recruited from among Rome's neighbouring subjugated Italic tribes, sometimes belonged to those tribes, and were sometimes Romans themselves. *Duoviri navales* ('two-men dealing with naval matters') are attested in the navy.

Beginning in the 2nd century BC, the growing geographical range and duration of military campaigns, together with the increase in the number of legions, led the senate to delegate far-reaching military powers of decision-making to *legati* of senatorial rank. Such legates are found working alongside the *imperatores* of the 1st century BC, such as Pompey and Caesar, who appointed them personally. Caesar had a particularly close relationship with his officers. He entrusted command of the *auxilia* to external (e.g. Gallic) commanders, who received Roman citizenship as their reward, and like Sulla before him, he put centurions in the senate. During the Civil Wars of the years 40–30 BC, the *imperatores* courted the support of officers, who became guarantors of soldierly *disciplina* and *fides*.

B.2. Principate

The establishment of the Principate [6] led to a compromise between Augustus, supreme commander of the new professional army, and the senatorial and equestrian elites who formed the command under his authority (which limited their autonomy – Tac. Ann. 11,20,1 –, without eliminating it completely). In provinces that only had one legion, the *legati Augusti pro praetore* ('legate of the emperor, acting on behalf of the praetor') took on both its command and the provincial governorship. The *legati legionum*, meanwhile, commanded legions in provinces with more than one legion. They were assisted by six *tribuni militum*, one of senatorial rank (called *laticlavius*, for the broad purple stripe he wore), the other five of equestrian rank (*angusticlavi*, with a narrower stripe). The terminology reflects the importance of the markings (CSIR-Öst. 1/3, 319) and privileges (in pay, accommodation, marital rights, residences for relatives, etc.) that distinguished officers among themselves and from the members of their units (cf. fig. 1). Claudius reorganized (Suet. Claud. 25,1) command of the *auxilia*, which was occasionally transferred to officers of the same ethnicity as the units themselves (e.g. Arminius, who rebelled despite being a Roman *eques*). This marked the advent of the equestrian career path, which gradually became formalized with three *militiae equestres* (*praefectus cohortis, tribunus legionis, praefectus alae*; from the reign of Hadrian even *praefectus alae miliariae* in the 4th *militia*) [3]. All these senior officers,

Fig. 1: The so-called 'Praetorian relief' (marble, 163 × 134 × 28 cm; found in Rome). This relief must have belonged to the arch that Claudius had built around 51/52 at the passage of the Via Lata under the Aqua Virgo – to celebrate the conquest of Britain from 43 and the capture of the Britannic leader Caratacus in 51. The scene was to take place in front of an imposing backdrop showing a triumphal procession: note the contrast between the soldiers depicted in bas-relief in the background and those in high relief in the foreground. The latter must be officers, as they stand out due to their position in the scene, but also due to their clothing (anatomically shaped breastplates, one of which – that of the third figure from the left – with a *gorgoneion*; *cingulum* around the breastplate; *calcei* on the feet; carrying a sword). They do not necessarily have to be Praetorians, and the question of which troop they belong to remains controversial.

from among the social elites, exercised command in the context of careers that encompassed military and civilian positions alternately (CIL VIII 9990; XI 3364). From this stems the debate among historians regarding the 'amateur' status of senior Roman officers – a phenomenon that requires nuanced consideration [2].

Above all, the senior officers could rely on the experience of centurions serving in the legions and the auxiliary troops, Praetorian, urban and *vigiles* ('watchmen') cohorts (and that of the decurions in the cavalry). As professional soldiers, centurions now mainly came from the lower orders, although some were *equites* (CIL VII 217; 11301; CIL III 1480). Much better paid than ordinary soldiers, equipped with a prestigious rank (with the *vitis*, the vine as its emblem), and sometimes posted from one unit to another (in Rome or the provinces for missions within or outside the camp), the centurions embodied the figure of the professional officer [1];

[4]. Becoming *primipilus* ('chief centurion') might crown a long career (AE 1985, 735), but some *primipili* went even farther, as *praefectus castrorum* ('camp commander', by rank the 3rd officer of a legion), tribune of the *vigiles* ('watchmen'), *urbaniciani* ('troops garrisoned in the city') or Praetorian cohorts, or even a second term as *primipilus*. At the end of their first or second such term, a very few, now *equites* ('equestrians'), received procuracies (CIL II 484; XI 395). During the 2nd and 3rd centuries, some even became Praetorian prefects or senators (CIL VI 41141; Cass. Dio 79,14,1–4). The most brilliant careers were furthered by periods of unrest or civil war, in which tribunes and centurions (especially Praetorians) often carried out political assassinations (Cass. Dio 77,3,2–4).

The professional soldier's career required ability, education (at least in reading, writing and arithmetic), successful outcomes, and recommendations (the ultimate boon was to serve close to the seat of power, especially in the imperial guard). Such a career was a means of social advancement that stimulated competition, which could also be found among the senatorial and equestrian elites, who likewise wanted to advance their career opportunities. Great generals (such as Agrippa, Corbulo (→ Generals of note, D.) and Agricola) distinguished themselves through their qualities as *viri militares* ('military men'), and some emperors achieved great experience as senior officers (Tiberius, Vespasian, Titus, Trajan, Hadrian, Pertinax: CIL III 550). Gradually, recruitment of senior and subaltern officers expanded to all provinces of the empire. A strict hierarchy and radical social distinction were preserved between these two groups, but they were in constant contact with each other and all played important parts in everyday army life (→ discipline, → training, → administration, religious ceremony, administration of justice etc.: Dig. 49,16,12). In the navy, equestrian prefects commanded the main fleets at Misenum and Ravenna as well as the other fleets. Trierarchs (of the same rank as centurions) commanded ships and *navarches* commanded squadrons (RMD IV 205).

Over time, the command structure was adapted, for example in the 2nd century AD with the introduction of the ranks of *dux* ('commander') and *praepositus* ('officer in charge') for officers heading detachments and expeditionary corps (CIL VI 1408). Some centurions and senior officers (e.g. M. Valerius Maximianus: AE 1956, 124) distinguished themselves in combat. For this they won *dona militaria* ('military decorations'; corresponding to their rank: IGLS VI 2796), renown and, in some cases, promotion. On the other hand, there was still the risk of → mutiny (Tac. Ann. 1,23,3–5 and 1,32,1; relations among soldiers could vary depending on the persons and situations involved) and the often heightened risk of dying in combat (as already at Cannae in 216 BC (→ Battles of note, C.) and in AD 9 in the Teutoburg Forest (→ Battles of note, J.)).

B.3. THE 3RD CENTURY AND LATE ANTIQUITY

Serious losses increased with the military difficulties of the 3rd century. The situation now favoured the rise of more experienced career officers. Rising to outrank the *primipilus*, and often of Illyrian background, these career officers frequently served in the army that accompanied the emperor (the *comitatus*, in which the tribunes and centurions held the title of *protector Augusti*: CIL XI 1836). In the 260s – whether *de facto* or *de iure*, for the existence of an 'Edict of Gallienus' is disputed – this trend led to the disappearance of the senatorial ranks from the legions (*legati* and *tribuni laticlavii*) in favour of equestrian *praefecti* (already found previously in Egypt and the three *legiones Parthicae*). Some career officers, such as Maximinus Thrax, Probus and Aurelian even reached the imperial throne through acts of violence and usurpation. These 'soldier-emperors' or 'Illyrian emperors' may have protected the empire, but the classical authors, who belonged to the supplanted class of elites, criticized them harshly [5. 583–632].

Coming from the same military world, Diocletian and the Tetrarchs, then later Constantine (who returned military responsibilities to the reformed senatorial class), conducted a thorough reorganization of the army and its command structures. The old terminology (*tribuni, praefecti, praepositi, centuriones*) was retained, albeit in altered form, in which certain units were developed further (legions) and others vanished (Praetorian cohorts), while still others were newly created (*comitatenses*, 'court troops', *limitanei*, 'border troops', *scholae palatinae*, 'palace guards' and *foederati*, 'allied troops', the last of these with commanders from their own people) [7]. The separation of the military from the administrative career path also helped create a civilian bureaucracy of *officiales*, who took over the old military terminology (e.g. the *primipilarii*: AE 2005, 1328–1330). Some new ranks were already appearing in the 3rd century, for example *ordinarius, centenarius, ducenarius, primicerius*, as attested in the 4th-century *scholae*.

The death rate of officers in combat was high, for example at Adrianople in AD 378 (→ Battles of note, B.). The *Notitia Dignitatum* gives a list of officer positions that were in existence at the turn of the 4th/5th centuries, but nothing more can be said about them in the absence of other sources (despite the work of the former officer Ammianus Marcellinus, the treatise by Vegetius and the papyrus collection of Flavius Abinnaeus, P. Abinn.). The percentage of officers of 'barbarian' background (Alamanni, Franks, Goths etc.), some of whom rose to very high ranks (e.g. Stilicho; → Generals of note, P.), increased through the 4th and 5th centuries until the fall of the Western Empire. These were men who were well integrated into the military and social structures of Rome. In their own way, they illustrate the rich history of the Roman command structures, which were informed by long tradition and many adaptations over the course of the centuries.

☞ Administration; Army, C. Roman; Auxiliaries; Guards; Legion; Rank

BIBLIOGRAPHY

[1] D.J. BREEZE / B. DOBSON, Roman Officers and Frontiers, 1992 [2] P. COSME, Qui commandait l'armée romaine?, in: S. Demougin et al. (eds.), H.-G. Pflaum, un historien du XXᵉ siècle, 2006, 137–156 [3] H. DEVIJVER, The Equestrian Officers of the Roman Imperial Army, 2 vols., 1989–1992 [4] P. FAURE, L'aigle et le cep. Les centurions légionnaires dans l'Empire des Sévères, 2013 [5] K.-P. JOHNE et al. (eds.), Die Zeit der Soldatenkaiser. Krise und Transformation des Römischen Reiches im 3. Jahrhundert n.Chr. (235–284), 2008 [6] L. KEPPIE, The Making of the Roman Army. From Republic to Empire, 1984 [7] Y. LE BOHEC / C. WOLFF (eds.), L'armée romaine de Dioclétien à Valentinien Iᵉʳ. Actes du Congrès de Lyon (12–14 septembre 2002), 2004 [8] J. SUOLAHTI, The Junior Officers of the Roman Army in the Republican Period. A Study on Social Structure, 1955.

PATRICE FAURE

Parades

A. Introduction
B. Types of parades in Greco-Roman Antiquity
C. Functions of parades

A. Introduction

The term 'parade' is a modern umbrella term that covers – in relation to Greco-Roman antiquity – various forms of processions, concentrations of troops and military performances, typically with some reference to war or the army. The military elements were either the participants themselves (generals, soldiers armed or unarmed) or particular objects (weapons, of the participants or seized from the enemy, other objects with connotations of war). It is suggested here that another fundamental criterion for the use of the term is that the procession possessed a performative dimension – as Bömer proposed, that 'the pomp of a true *pompa* was present along with the participation of those around' [3. 1891]. Unlike today, when the military aspect of parades is typically prominent, Greco-Roman Antiquity had not only movements and processions such as the Roman triumph or the *decursiones* (see below) that were primarily military in nature, but also other kinds of processions that were mainly religious and did not centre on military elements, but contained them alongside other elements. Still, this inclusion of the military was a function of the central role of warfare in the social, cultural and religious constitution of ancient communities [16]; [17]; seminal for Greece already [23. 9–30]. It is therefore natural that parades were often community rituals, too.

Parades in Greco-Roman Antiquity cannot be strictly defined according to practical utility or symbolic function. Rather, they often incorporated multiple dimensions, including display of the community's military strength (inwardly and outwardly; see below, C.). A basic distinction can be drawn between the regular, recurring processions that were generally performed according to a festival calendar (e.g. the Panathenaea at Athens, the *pompa circensis* at Rome), and sporadic events marking particular occasions (the victory procession of Antiochus IV Epiphanes at Antioch, the triumph ritual at Rome). Different again from these are parades that were only organized once (e.g. the transfer of the remains of important persons). A further distinction can be made on the basis of the form of the parade route, between circular processions (e.g. *lustrationes*) and those that functioned as escorts, in which certain objects, often sacrificial, were taken from one place to another, usually ending at a temple or altar [6]; [22].

The various forms of parades, which were given many different names, from *pompa* (Latin)/*pompe* (Greek), *decursio* and *eishodos* to *apopompos* or *pyrriche*, can only be categorized in an approximate way. They underwent many changes from the time of their origin in the Homeric period through Late Antiquity, and no systematic study has yet been made of them all. Sources for reconstructing ancient parades are descriptions of processions in literary texts and epigraphic documents, which give sporadic information about the makeup of processions and those participating in them, chiefly in the Greek world. Pictorial testimonies of various kinds (friezes, reliefs, vase paintings, coin images) can supplement these, but it is often difficult to reconstruct from them the reality of the specific parade [6. 34f.].

The Greek world had the various *pompai*, *pyrrichai* and other processions (e.g. victory processions and transfers of prominent deceased figures). Besides the triumph (*pompa triumphalis*), Rome had the funeral procession (*pompa funebris*) and the circus procession (*pompa circensis*), processions of moving out and returning home (*profectio*, *adventus*), the *lustratio* and the *census*, which like the *ludus Troiae* and the *transvectio equitum* were also rituals. The *decursiones* were performed in general army exercises, marches connected with the detachment of troops, weapons inspections (e.g. Jos. BI 5,9,1; Arr. Peripl. p. eux. 6,2; 10,3) and, more generally, in parades associated with imperial *adlocutiones* ('addresses') to the army. The various forms of parades in the Greek and Roman worlds respectively had only a few phenomena in common or directly comparable. Although literary sources sometimes suggest processes of reciprocal reception (e.g. Dion. Hal. Ant. Rom. 7,71,3; 7,72,6 for the reception of Greek sword dances in the *pompa circensis*), some scholars call this into question (see below, B.1. and B.2. on the *pompa* of Antiochus IV at Antioch).

It is possible to make a systematic distinction among the various parades according to the varying prevalence of military elements and the quality of allusions. The chronological dimension is only considered here in specific cases.

B. Types of parades in Greco-Roman Antiquity

B.1. Parades of a purely military character
B.2. Parades with military elements
B.3. Parades with a symbolic military presence

B.1. Parades of a purely military character

The Roman → triumph was the Roman victory ritual, celebrated, as ancient sources attest, from the foundation of Rome until Late Antiquity and beyond. Classical authors provide ample accounts of it. In the triumph, the military dimension was unambiguously dominant, by virtue of the occasion and the participants (e.g. general as *triumphator* on the triumphal quadriga, → booty, prisoners of war, and soldiers crowned with laurels).

Another example of a purely military parade was the *decursio* (also: *decursus, exercitus, exercitatio militaris*), the systematic and publicly visible drilling of of soldiers. Attested in ancient sources for the Republican period from the Second Punic War onwards, the *decursio* was intended to improve the Roman army's → discipline and efficiency (first Scipio 210 BC in Spain: Pol. 10,20; Liv. 26,51,3–7; → Generals of note O.). It involved the military → education of recruits (Liv. 23,35,6; 24,48,11; Veg. Mil. 1,3), the → training of infantry and cavalry (Liv. 40,47,8; 44,9,5; Tac. Ann. 2,55; 3,33) and, in general, the improvement of the fighting power of the participating divisions of the army (Liv. 29,22,2; 40,47,8; Jos. BI 3,72–75; Veg. Mil. 2,22). Already during the Republic, a symbolic dimension was sometimes evident alongside the pragmatic functions, particularly in regard to reinforcing units' cohesion and self-understanding (cf. e.g. Liv. 44,9,5–9). But in the Imperial period, the public and performative aspect of the event became dominant, for instance when the emperor attended military parades in the presence of the urban populace, especially at Rome, and even joined in exercises with the soldiers (Plin. Paneg. 13,1–3; Suet. Nero 10) or took part in the *decursio* (Suet. Nero 7; [19. 460f.]). The term *decursio* is also attested, from the Republic until the High Imperial period, as referring to the funeral rites for Roman generals and emperors (Liv. 25,17,5 on the Second Punic War; cf. the *decursiones* at the cremations of Antoninus Pius and Septimius Severus).

As a special form of the *lustratio* ('purification'), the *lustratio exercitus* ('purification of the army') gave attention to the *pax deorum* ('peace of the gods') alongside the military dimension. In this ritual, the army was purified by encircling it with the sacrificial animals of the *suovetaurilia* (offering of boar, ram and bull; Cass. Dio 47,38,4; cf. in general Liv. 23,35,5). There are illustrations of this ritual on the Trajan Column (Scenes 8, 52f., 102f.; cf. [6. testimony no. 122]) and on the Arch of Constantine in Rome (attica on the southern side). The *transvectio equitum* ('review of the cavalry') was an annual parade at Rome, attested from the 4th century BC onwards, involving the youth of the Roman equestrian class, and it may have been associated with the equestrian *census* and aptitude testing of horses (Liv. 9,46,15; Vir. Ill. 32,2). From the time of Augustus onwards, this ritual acquired more significance, as the title of its leader, the *princeps iuventutis* ('first among the young'), became an honorific title for the heirs of the Roman imperial house (coins of Augustus 2/1 BC: BMCRE 1, pl. 14,7).

It may be assumed that military manoeuvres in preparation for campaigns also took place in Greece, but less is known about how they were conducted. Xenophon's description of cavalry parades led by the cavalry commander in Athens during the great *polis* festivals (Hipp. 3,2–4) is largely prescriptive and thus hypothetical, and its relationship with reality is difficult to estimate. Livy reports that the Macedonian army held *decursiones* (Liv. 40,6,5; 40,9,10).

A widely documented form of military parade that was well established in Greece, and that some Roman authors also report taking place in the Roman world (cf. e.g. Plin. HN 7,204; Amm. Marc. 16,5,10), was the sword dance, or *pyrrhiche*, in which military exercise, performance and contest often merged together (cf. Xen. An. 6,1; [5]; [4]). Evidence for these is particularly strong in Sparta (for boys aged 4 and up: Ath. 14,29,19–22; Lucian. Salt. 10), but is also found in Athens and other cities, especially in inscriptions (Megara: IG VII 190; Rhodes: SEG 39, 759). Men and women alike performed such dances solo, in pairs or in choruses. Dancers were usually naked with hoplite weaponry (helmet, shield and lance), and they danced to the accompaniment of the flute. *Pyrrhichai* were frequently integrated into processions (e.g. at the Panathenaic Games in Athens: Lys. 21,1; Isaios 5,36; IG II 3,2311; generally [15]; [8]) and other social practices (symposium: Xen. An. 6,1). Recently, their function as an initiation ritual has been highlighted [4].

There was no direct equivalent in the Greek world to the triumph as a victory parade held on a special occasion and focusing on the general and his accomplishments. While Polybius certainly saw the victory celebration held by Antiochus IV Epiphanes at Antioch in 166 BC as a deliberate echo of the victory games of L. Aemilius Paullus at Amphipolis (Macedonia) (Pol. 30,25), recent research has tended to emphasize the independence of the Hellenistic tradition [14]. It was more common in Greece to hold periodic, usually annual festivals to commemorate particular victories (cf. the procession with armed participants in honour of Artemis Agroterai in Athens, which was associated with the annual festival remembering the Battle of Marathon (→ Battles of note, F.): Plut. Mor. 862a; IG II² 1006; 1008; 1011; 1028–1030; 1040).

B.2. PARADES WITH MILITARY ELEMENTS
In many processions of the Greco-Roman world, soldiers, usually in military formation, comprised one element among many. The most obvious examples in Greece are the religious processions held from the Classical period onwards in many

poleis, often on a regular basis. Here, the armed participants in processions were usually the *ephebes* (young men aged 18–20 registered for military service), often accompanied by their teachers or *choregoi* (e.g. the processions at the Theseia in Athens, attested in inscriptions: IG II² 1006; 1008f.; 1028–1030; 1032; 1043). Epigraphic records show that Eretria held a procession to Amarynthus in honour of Artemis, and that it involved musical contests, choruses and sacrifices, as well as the participation of 3,000 hoplites and 600 cavalry (Str. 10,1,10; cf. IG XII 9,189; 236f.). Another interesting example is the Pythaïs procession from Athens to Delphi, which was escorted by mounted soldiers [10].

There is good evidence for the grand *pompai* ('sacrificial processions') of the Hellenistic kings [1. 114–150]. Ptolemy II Philadelphus and Arsinoë held a procession at Alexandria in honour of *Pantes theoi* ('all the gods'), in about 275/74 BC. Besides the abundant religious personnel, some 80,000 soldiers (infantry and cavalry) are said to have taken part (Callixenus of Rhodes, FGrH 627 F 2 = Ath. 5,196a–203b; [24]; [21]). The festival was probably repeated every five years. In 166 BC, Antiochus IV Epiphanes held a parade in honour of Apollo at Antioch, marking his victory over Egypt, with the participation of infantry, cavalry and war chariots. Many *ephebes*, sacrificial animals and statues of deities were also involved, and contests followed (Pol. 30,25). This appears to have been the continuation of a practice dating back to Alexander III of Macedon, whereby groups of soldiers under arms were integrated into existing religious processions (procession in honour of Artemis at Ephesus: Arr. An. 1,18,2; cf. the Apollo procession on Zakynthos under Dion: Plut. *Dion* 23,3f.). A similar example is attested for Athens as early as 403 BC, when the citizens of Pireaus entered the city accompanied by hoplites to sacrifice to Athena on the Acropolis following the overthrow of the Thirty Tyrants (Xen. Hell. 2,4,39).

Soldiers frequently participated in one-off processions, as when the remains of a deceased hero or ruler were transferred from one place to another (return of the urn of Philopoemen by the Achaeans: Plut. *Philopoemen* 21; Syll.³ 624).

In Rome, the ruler's departure (*profectio*) and homecoming (*adventus*) ceremonies acquired a military dimension in the Imperial period, as military formations along with citizens and senators began to accompany the emperor (Nero: Cass. Dio 63,20,4; Vitellius: Suet. Vit. 11; Trajan: Plin. Paneg. 23,3; Julian: Amm. Marc. 21,10,1; cf. on Trajan's departure e.g. RIC Traianus II,297) or, in the case of an *adventus*, went out to greet him (reception of Caligula by the Praetorians: Suet. Cal. 4; [12. 284–303]).

There is occasional evidence for soldiers' participation in other rituals central to civic life, such as the *lustratio* ('purification') of the Capitol under Emperor Vespasian in AD 70 (Tac. Hist. 4,53,1–3). The army probably also took part in the quinquennial *lustrum* ('purificatory sacrifice'), as the *census* relief in the Ara Domitii Ahenobarbi (early 1st cent. BC) suggests [6. 56].

Finally, soldiers are recorded as taking part in emperors' regnal jubilees, for example the *decennalia* of Gallienus in AD 262 (SHA Gall. 7,4–8,7).

B.3. PARADES WITH A SYMBOLIC MILITARY PRESENCE

Finally, in many different processions of the Greek and Roman worlds, the military was present in a symbolic way, with participants from the military showing to the public objects related in some way to warfare and military service.

In Greece, weapons with symbolic significance or mythological overtones were often brought along on religious processions, for example at the Hyacinthia in Sparta (Aristot. frg. 532R) or on the procession for Athena at Argos (Callimachus, *Hymn to Athena* v. 35; Aen. Tact. 17,2). Such weapons were sometimes used in the contests that accompanied the festival, before being consecrated to the deity thereafter (e.g. in honour of Athena at Elis, where the victor brought the weapons to the temple in a procession: Ath. 13,90,10–16). Otherwise, they were carried in the *pompa*, to be used in the contests afterwards (Syll.³ 419: Delphi).

Many pictorial records of processions in the Roman world show figures wearing tunics and carrying long shields, but any relation between these images and actual parades is unclear. The previously mentioned sword dances (*pyrrhichai*) could be said to have had a symbolic dimension, as could the armed dancers (*ludiones* or *lydiones*) in the *pompa circensis* ('Circus Parade') at Rome (Dion. Hal. Ant. Rom. 7,72,5–10). The *ludus* (or *lusus*) *Troiae* ('Game of Troy') is also open to such an interpretation – a wargame for boys and youths on horseback, which Virgil (Aen. 5,548–603) associated with the foundation legend of Rome. The first solid evidence for the festival may date from the Sullan period (Plut. Cato minor 3), otherwise certainly from the time of C. Iulius Caesar (e.g. Suet. Iul. 39). Similarly, the *salii*, priests of Mars at Rome whose weapon dance marked the ritual opening and closing of the campaigning season, were not personal representatives of the Roman army. Rather, as 'religious specialists' [18. 177], they sought to obtain the favour of the war god for the campaigns of the coming year (Liv. 1,20,4; Varro, Ling. 5,85; Hor. Carm. 4,1,28).

Other references to symbolic military presence in parades relate to the wearing of military clothing by key participants in the various processions. In Rome, from the Republican period onwards, the clothing most often in view was the regalia of the general as *triumphator*, which invoked the image of the victorious general. For example, the magistrate hosting the *pompa circensis*, which was not a military parade *per se*, invoked the image of the *triumphator* when he claiming the right to ride on the triumphal quadriga (Juv. 10,39–49). In the Republican period, the same was true of the *pompa funebris* ('funeral procession'), which was primarily a civilian procession, but one in which the military merits of ancestors were given expression by the wearing of appropriate regalia (Pol. 6,53). Beginning in the late 2nd century AD, the funeral procession for deceased emperors occasionally acquired an even clearer military stamp. At the funeral for Pertinax in AD 193, for example, not only were famous Romans arranged among (and in place of) ancestors of the late emperor (as at the funeral of Augustus), but images of defeated enemies, children's choirs, colleges and groups of soldiers were also displayed (Cass. Dio 75,4,2–6).

C. Functions of parades

The functions of parades in Greco-Roman Antiquity were many and varied. Besides straightforward, practical consideratinos such as increasing the efficiency of the units of soldiers that participated in the exercises (somewhat comparable to modern military manoeuvres), political, social and religious functions also played a major part.

For instance, the structured processions in which soldiers or weapons representing acts of war were paraded before the assembled community served to strengthen the identity and cohesion of those involved and the audience. The prominent role of the *ephebes* (young men registered for military service) in parades in the Greek world also contributed to defining roles and creating self-image among different age groups within the community. Parades marking victories commemorated (and, where held regularly, immortalized) collective achievements. In Greece at least, they also offered an opportunity to remember those members of the community who had fallen in battle.

Besides calling to mind the drama of real military campaigns, the various forms of weapons games, dances and contests provided an opportunity for competition (whether real or symbolic) within the home community or against others. Communities of Greek and Roman citizens alike used such parades, which always included a religious component, to secure the goodwill of their gods.

The Hellenistic kings and Roman emperors used parades of soldiers not only to present a powerful image of themselves and lend legitimacy to their position of authority, but also to demonstrate the physical resources at their disposal in defence of that authority. It is thus far from a coincidence that during both the Hellenistic period and the Roman Imperial period, more and more soldiers were appearing in religious and communal processions (on the Hellenistic period: [22. 8]).

☞ **Honours; Training; Triumph**

Bibliography

[1] A. Bell, Spectacular Power in the Greek and Roman City, 2004 [2] B. Bergmann / C. Kondoleon (eds.), The Art of Ancient Spectacle, 1999 [3] F. Bömer, Pompa, in: RE 21, 1952, 1878–1993 [4] P. Ceccarelli, La pirrica nell'antichità greco-romana. Studi sulla danza armata, 1998 [5] M.-H. Delavaud-Roux, Les danses armées en Grèce antique, 1993 [6] F. Fless, Römische Prozessionen, in: Thesaurus Cultus et Rituum Antiquorum, vol. 1, 2004, 34–58 [7] P. Johanek / A. Lampen (eds.), Adventus. Studien zum herrscherlichen Einzug in die Stadt, 2009 [8] A. Kavoulaki, Processional Performance and the Democratic Polis, in: S. Goldhill / R. Osborne (eds.), Performance Culture and Athenian Democracy, 1999, 293–320 [9] J. Köhler, Pompai. Untersuchungen zur hellenistischen Festkultur, 1996 [10] S. Kühn, Die Pythaïs-Prozession. Neue Untersuchungen zu der Prozession von Athen nach Delphi, 2018 [11] J.A. Latham, Performance, Memory, and Processions in Ancient Rome, 2016 [12] J. Lehnen, Adventus Principis. Untersuchungen zu Sinngehalt und Zeremoniell der Kaiserankunft in den Städten des Imperium Romanum, 1997 [13] L. Maurizio, The Panathenaic Procession. Athens Participatory Democracy on Display?, in: D. Boedeker / K.A. Raaflaub (eds.), Democracy, Empire, and the Arts in Fifth-Century Athens, 1998, 297–317, 415–421 [14] P.F. Mittag, Antiochos IV. Epiphanes. Eine politische Biographie, 2006 [15] J. Neils, Pride, Pomp, and Circumstance. The Iconography of Procession, in: J. Neils (ed.), Worshipping Athena. Panathenaia and Parthenon, 1996, 177–197 [16] K.A. Raaflaub / N. Rosenstein (eds.), War and Society in the Ancient and Medieval Worlds, 1999 [17] J. Rich / G. Shipley (eds.), War and Society in the Greek World, 1993 [18] J. Rüpke, Die Religion der Römer. Eine Einführung, 2001 [19] M.A. Speidel, Albata decursio – ein kaiserliches Siegesmanöver. Zu einer neuen Inschrift aus Ankara, in: M.A. Speidel, Heer und Herrschaft im römischen Reich der Hohen Kaiserzeit, 2009, 451–462 [20] R. Strootman, The Hellenistic Royal Courts. Court Culture, Ceremonial and Ideology in Greece, Egypt and the Near East, 336–30 BCE, 2007 (Diss. Utrecht) [21] D.J. Thompson, Philadelphus' Procession. Dynastic Power in a Mediterranean Context, in: L. Mooren (ed.), Politics, Administration and Society in the Hellenistic and Roman World, 2000, 365–388 [22] M. True et al., Greek Processions, in: Thesaurus Cultus et Rituum Antiquorum, vol. 1, 2004, 1–20 [23] J.-P. Vernant, Introduction, in: J.-P. Vernant (ed.), Problèmes de la guerre en Grèce ancienne, 1968, 9–30 [24] F. Walbank, Two Hellenistic Processions. A Matter of Self-Definition, in: Scripta Classica Israelica 15, 1996, 119–130.

TANJA ITGENSHORST

Pay

A. Greek
B. Roman

A. GREEK

A.1. Before the *misthos*
A.2. Introduction of payment
A.3. Public finances
A.4. Influence on warfare
A.5. Peloponnesian War
A.6. After the Athenian Empire
A.7. Philip, Alexander and the Hellenistic kingdoms

A.1. BEFORE THE *MISTHOS*

Before the Persian Wars, Greek soldiers did not receive pay (*misthos*, 'pay'). They rarely went into the field, and when they did, in most cases it was only to secure disputed border territories [3. 7–15]. Wars were generally started by wealthy leaders, without authorization by a *polis*. These leaders acquired their troops simply by promising them a share of any booty and land that could be gained from the war (e.g. Plut. *Solon* 9,2f.). Hoplite volunteers at this period usually numbered only a few hundred men. They had to supply their own armour, weapons and provisions, and most of them also belonged to the wealthier classes of society. The wars they fought lasted only a few days or weeks, and were usually decided in a single battle. During the Archaic period, war was thus a private enterprise financed by the participants themselves.

A.2. INTRODUCTION OF PAYMENT

Two major changes took place in Classical Greece [5. 170f.]. Both are most evident at Athens. This *polis*, which became a superpower in the 5th century, was responsible for the shift to payment-based warfare. The first innovation was that war became a public matter. At Athens, this happened as a result of the democratic reforms introduced by Cleisthenes after 508 BC, which transferred sole responsibility for waging war to the *demos* ('people'), and provided them with a new public army for doing it (e.g. Hdt. 5,77f.). The second new development involved war at sea. The Athenians knew that the Ionian Revolt (499–494) had failed because of the superiority of the Persian navy. They also knew that the Persian triremes had given them trouble at Marathon in 490 (→ Battles of note, F.). Accordingly, seven years later, the Athenian *demos* decided to launch a massive shipbuilding programme in preparation for the Persians' anticipated return [5. 67f.]. Trireme crews needed to be paid: because these warships had no room for the storage of food, seafarers had to buy provisions every day from local markets (cf. e.g. Dem. Or. 50,22; 50,53–55).

A.3. PUBLIC FINANCES

Financing these payments proved a huge challenge for the Athenian state. A seaman received one drachma per day (e.g. Thuc. 3,17). With 200 sailors aboard a trireme, keeping such a vessel at sea for a month cost 6,000 drachmas (i.e. one talent; e.g. Thuc. 6,8). Athens therefore had to spend hundreds of talents to send out even just a small percentage of its 200 new triremes. During the Second Persian War (480/79; → Wars of note, J.), the Athenians resorted to emergency measures to pay these wages (e.g. Plut. *Themistocles* 10). A new source of finance had to be found, if the naval forces of the *polis* were to be maintained in the long term [5. 172f.]. This was achieved in 478, when the Ionian Greeks invited the Athenians to take charge of the ongoing war against Persia (Thuc. 1,94–97). The → alliance now founded by Athens is known today as the Delian League. Its members adopted the Persians' methods for financing naval war: each of them guaranteed to pay an agreed annual tribute (*phoros*). The Athenians quickly realized that their military power (*dynamis*) depended on these payments, so they tightened their control over the *poleis* who paid them [5. 126–129]. As a result, the League transformed into the Athenian Empire.

A.4. INFLUENCE ON WARFARE

According to the traditional view, Athens waited another 40 years to pay its hoplites [6. 11–13]. During that period, it prepared the political ground for the introduction of public service for pay (*misthophoria*) [4. 7f.]. Pericles in the 450s argued for paying jurors. Pay (*misthos*) for council members and magistrates followed in the 440s. Most Athenians were poor. What they lacked was leisure (*schole*), for they had to work hard for their living (e.g. Lys. 24,16). In order to take an active part in democracy, they needed compensation for lost income (cf. e.g. Aristot. Pol. 1293a1–10). The first mention of *misthos* for hoplites dates from 433 BC (Thuc. 3,17,4). The argument is made that hoplites only began to receive pay after payment in political life had established the principle that public service warranted compensation.

Logistical considerations, however, disprove this traditional view. From the outset, the campaigns of the Delian League were conducted at sea and on land (e.g. Thuc. 1,96–114). They involved hundreds or thousands of supposedly unpropertied hoplites, and they lasted months, or in the case of sieges, perhaps even several years. Because transport triremes had no cargo space, it was impossible for hoplites to bring their own stores with them. Being poor, they were also unable to pay for their own meals over long periods. Therefore, the Athenian hoplites must have been paid. Classical Greece – and this is an important point – had military pay even before it introduced the *misthos* for political activity.

Paying all combatants led to more frequent and much larger wars. The wage of one drachma per day equalled that of a trained labourer [2. 97–120]. Each combatant typically had to spend only two of the six obols (that made up one drachma) on food [2. 35]. So unpropertied hoplites and seafarers were paid rather handsomely – which helps to explain the steep increase in rates of participation in the armed forces. Only five percent of Athenians opted to become hoplites in the Archaic period [3. 13]. By 432, this percentage had risen to 30 percent [5. 36–38]. The rest of the *demos* regularly signed up for navy service. Athens was now able to send thousands of hoplites and naval personnel off to war. When the popular assembly voted in favour of a war of this magnitude, the men voting knew that their personal participation in that war was a real possibility. But they also knew that they would be well paid for it. This had the effect of encouraging assembly members to approve wars more often, and sometimes wars that would last for months or years. Thus, military pay tended to make the Athenian *demos* more inclined towards war (e.g. Thuc. 6,24,3f.).

A.5. PELOPONNESIAN WAR
By 450 BC, Athens had become a threat to the other superpowers of the Grecian world. → Sparta, however, was finding it difficult to oppose Athens effectively. The Spartans were the dominant power on land, because as full-time hoplites they fought far better than all others [5. 174]. Sparta was also able to draw on many thousands of hoplites from the members of the Peloponnesian League, and they did not need to pay them. But during the Peloponnesian War (431–404 BC; → Wars of note, H.), whenever the Spartans and their huge coalition army entered Attica, the Athenians simply withdrew behind their walls and waited out the siege for weeks until the Spartans and their allies were forced to withdraw because of a shortage of supplies [6. 38f.]. Sparta accordingly recognized that it could only defeat Athens by becoming a naval power itself (e.g. Thuc. 8,2–5). To do so, however, Sparta would need to find a way to bear the enormous costs of a navy. It found such a way in 412 BC, when Persia decided to provide the required financing. In exchange for the right to reimpose *phoros* ('tribute') on the Greek cities of Asia Minor, the Persians helped Sparta pay for a large fleet (e.g. Thuc. 8,18; 8,37; 8,58). In 405 BC, that → fleet destroyed the last Athenian warships. Sparta was now able to crush the Athenian Empire.

A.6. AFTER THE ATHENIAN EMPIRE
Athens tried to restore its tribute-based empire during the Corinthian War (395–387 BC). Persia put an end to this by again financing a large Spartan fleet. The Athenian *demos* now had to seek other ways of paying its hoplites and seafarers. A reform of 378 BC therefore put in place a system for wealthy citizens to pay temporary taxes on their assets to fund wars [5. 176]. In 373, the Athenians persuaded members of the Athenian League to make annual contribution payments (*syntaxeis*) (e.g. Dem. Or. 18,234). Meanwhile, they also created a dedicated military fund (*stratiotika*), into which any surplus in the public finances would be paid. Despite these financial reforms, however, Athenian generals (*strategoi*) were still regularly sent into battle without sufficient funds. The *demos* authorized them to make up the difference with booty, plunder or extortion [5. 177f.].

Because collecting these funds took time, commanders were often able to provide their hoplites and seafarers only enough money to cover their food, leaving the rest of their pay outstanding. This shift was reflected in terminology. During the 5th century, the usual terms for 'pay' were *misthos* and *trophe* ('sustenance'). Both were used for the one drachma per day earned by a combatant [6. 3–6]. By the 360s BC, *siteresion* ('provision money') referred to a combatant's daily two obols (e.g. Dem. Or. 4,28), and *misthos* to the balance payable later [2. 52f.].

A.7. PHILIP, ALEXANDER AND THE HELLENISTIC KINGDOMS
These sources of finance enabled Athens to prosecute its wars with great success. It was able to keep Sparta in check, and it rapidly ascended to become a regional superpower [5. 17–19]. It was not, however, successful enough to stop the rise of King Philip II. By 338, Philip had defeated the other leading Greek *poleis*, thereby making Macedonia the new hegemonic power. His military success depended largely on his ability to secure rich sources of public revenue [5. 178f.]. As a result, Philip II was able to pay for an unrivalled training program for the Macedonian army (e.g. Dem. Or. 9,47–52) and to enlist vast numbers of → mercenaries.

Philip's son, Alexander, was less concerned about public revenues when he conquered Persia. The booty he won enabled him to pay his army with ease. However, the Hellenistic kingdoms that emerged in the wake of his death had to manage their public finances carefully. Because of their much larger tax bases, they were able to finance mercenary armies many times larger than the armies of Athens and Sparta in the Classical period (e.g. Pol. 5,65; 5,78–87). The war for primacy in the Greek world now went far beyond the confines of the *poleis*.

☞ Military service; State and army

BIBLIOGRAPHY
[1] F. BURRER et al., Kriegskosten und Kriegsfinanzierung in der Antike, 2008 [2] W.T. LOOMIS, Wages, Welfare Costs and Inflation in Classical Athens, 1998 [3] D.M. PRITCHARD, The Symbiosis between Democracy and War. The Case of Ancient Athens, in: D.M. Pritchard (ed.), War, Democracy, and Culture in Classical Athens, 2010, 1–62 [4] D.M. PRITCHARD, Public Spending and Democracy in Classical Athens, 2015 [5] D.M. PRITCHARD, Athenian Democracy at War, 2019 [6] W.K. PRITCHETT, The Greek State at War, vol. 1, 1974.

DAVID M. PRITCHARD

B. ROMAN

B.1. Monarchical and Republican periods
B.2. Imperial period and Late Antiquity

B.1. MONARCHICAL AND REPUBLICAN PERIODS

In the early days of Rome, citizens liable for military service were required to provide their own equipment according to their assignment to a property class. However, they received no pay. Their most important source of income during army service was booty, of which, following a victory, they were entitled to expect a share to be assigned by the general. According to Roman tradition, army soldiers were first paid in 406 BC during the Siege of Veii (Diod. Sic. 14,16,5; Liv. 4,59,11–4,61,8). How this payment was made is unclear, for Rome was not yet minting coins at this period. According to Polybius, an ordinary soldier received pay of two obols (= three asses) per day in the 2nd century BC, a centurion (i.e. commander of a *centuria*) received double that, and a cavalryman was paid one drachma (= 1 *denarius*?) (Pol. 6,39,12 with [2. 22f., 146f.]). However, it is unlikely that pay was actually disbursed daily. It was probably reckoned in the first instance as compensation for soldiers' loss of income arising from their military service. Although confederates (*socii*) received no pay from Rome, they were granted the same free grain rations as Roman soldiers.

According to Suetonius, C. Iulius Caesar (perhaps in 49 BC) permanently doubled legionaries' pay (*in perpetuum*: Suet. Iul. 26,3). This change was differed fundamentally from the occasional individual rewards and promotions that were regularly granted, including by Caesar (e.g. Caes. B Civ. 3,53).

B.2. IMPERIAL PERIOD AND LATE ANTIQUITY

Augustus created an entirely new pay system over the course of his reign. He had a service contract drawn up for all troop types and all ranks in 13 BC (apparently in connection with preparations for the Germanic Wars), and he presented this to the senate. Innovations mainly concerned the minimum term of service, discharge payments, and pay (Cass. Dio 54,25,5f.; Suet. Aug. 49,2). Pay was issued to soldiers in three instalments (*stipendia*), on January 1, May 1 and September 1. A weapons inspection also seems to have taken place (Jos. BI 5,9,1; Arr. Peripl. p. eux. 6,2; 10,3), and the military → oath was ceremonially renewed on January 1 (*sacramentum*: Tac. His. 1,55; Epict. 1,14,15).

A soldier's pay depended on the basic rate for his troop type and his rank (*gradus*), which assigned him to one of three pay categories: those earning the basic amount, those earning one and a half times the basic rate (*sesquiplicarii*), and those receiving double (*duplicarii*). A sole inscription from the mid-1st century attests to a triple payment (*triplicarius*) for an *evocatus* ('individual with extended service') of an *ala* ('auxiliary force') (AE 1976, 495). It is very doubtful, however, whether this was a regular category or an extraordinary payment, and whether any such payment was still being made later. Cavalrymen received a somewhat higher basic amount (*equestria stipendia*: CIL XII 2602 = ILS 2118).

Neither in 13 BC nor as part of adjustments made in AD 5, however, does Augustus seem to have made any changes to the basic rates of pay in the legions (Cass. Dio 55,23,1; RGDA 17; cf. tab. 1). Basic annual pay was 225 *denarii* (= 900 *sestertii*), and it was paid out in *stipendia* of 75 *denarii* (= 300 *sestertii*). At this period, pay was calculated on the basis of whole *denarii* (not *aurei*; [8. 57]; otherwise: [1. 114]). Domitian was the first, in AD 84 following his victory over the Chatti, to raise basic pay in the → legions: by one third, to 300 *denarii* (= 1,200 *sestertii*) per year (Suet. Dom. 7,3). Later pay rises are attested for the reigns of Septimius Severus (AD 197, by 100% (?) to 2,400 *sestertii*: SHA Sept. Sev. 12,2f.; Hdn. 3,8,5), Caracalla (AD 212, by 50% to 3,600 *sestertii*: Hdn. 4,4,7) and Maximinus Thrax (AD 235, by 100% to 7,200 *sestertii*: Hdn. 6,8,8) [7. 350, 419–427]. There is no record of later pay increases. Doubtless, basic pay rates for other troop types of the imperial army would have been raised at the same time, and by the same percentages.

Tab. 1: Annual basic pay in the Roman army in *denarii* (from: [7. 427]). Underscored figures are taken from surviving source data.

	Augustus (13 BC)	Domitian (83/84)	Severus (197)	Caracalla (212)	Maximinus (235)
cohortes praetoriae					
miles	750	1,000	2,000	3,000	6,000
centurio	3,750 (?)	5,000 (?)	10,000 (?)	15,000 (?)	30,000 (?)
cohortes urbanae					
miles	375	500	1,000	1,500	3,000
centurio	3,750 (?)	5,000 (?)	10,000 (?)	15,000 (?)	30,000 (?)
cohortes vigilum					
miles	187.5	250	500	750	1,500
centurio	(less than the *centuriones* of the Praetorians and *urbaniciani*?)				
Legions					
miles	225	300	600	900	1,800
eques	262.5	350	700	1,050	2,100
centurio	3,375	4,500	9,000	13,500	27,000
prim. ord.	6,750	9,000	18,000	27,000	54,000
prim. pil.	13,500	18,000	36,000	54,000	108,000
cohortes civium Romanorum					
miles	225	300	600	900	1,800
centurio	3,375 (?)	4,500 (?)	9,000 (?)	13,500 (?)	27,000 (?)
Auxiliaries					
mil. coh.	187.5	250	500	750	1,500
eq. coh.	225	300	600	900	1,800
eq. alae	262.5	350	700	1,050	2,100
cent. coh.	937.5	1,250	2,500	3,750	7,500
dec. coh.	1,125	1,500	3,000	4,500	9,000
dec. alae	1,312.5	1,750	3,500	5,250	10,500

Basic pay in the Praetorian, urban and citizens' cohorts can be deduced from the amounts that Augustus bequeathed to soldiers of these units in AD 14 (Tac. Ann. 1,8; cf. Suet. Aug. 101; Cass. Dio 56,32,2), since it appears that these sums equalled one individual instalment of pay (*stipendium*). Accordingly, annual payments would have been 3,000, 1,500 and 900 *sestertii* respectively [7. 420]. Before AD 84, annual basic pay in the Roman urban *cohortes vigilum* was probably 750 *sestertii* [7. 389–394]. There are no clues to annual basic pay rates in the → fleets at Misenum or Ravenna (perhaps 750 *sestertii* before AD 84?) or for soldiers of the mounted imperial life guard (*equites singulares Augusti*) (perhaps 2,800 *sestertii* in the 2nd century) [7. 377].

The literary sources offer no indication of the annual basic pay disbursed to the regular → auxiliaries of the Principate from the reign of Augustus onwards. However, pay amounts are preserved in the (generally epigraphic) records of individual soldiers' careers, and in a very few documentary sources (on papyrus and wooden tablets) [7]; [8]. Understanding the sums recorded is difficult and not without difference of opinion (cf. [1]; [5]; [8]), as they are seldom given as full figures, and the documents concerned usually omit relevant information, such as payment dates, troop types, and ranks of payees. Nevertheless, pay can be reconstructed for this troop type under specific methodological conditions [7]; [8]. Scholars specializing in this area now largely agree that the basic pay of infantry soldiers in the auxiliary units was at a ratio of 5:6 to basic pay in the legions. Admittedly, minor deductions or bonuses not specified in the documents must be assumed in order to explain some sums in the documentary record, but a basic wage of 750 *sestertii* per year has been established for infantry soldiers in an auxiliary cohort, and 1,050 *sestertii* per year for a cavalry soldier in an *ala*, prior to Domitian's pay rise [7. 349–371].

The same method also makes it possible to reconstruct the pay of centurions in the legions, established as coming (before AD 84) to 13,500 *sestertii* per year for an ordinary centurion, 27,000 *sestertii* for a centurion of the first cohort, and 54,000 *sestertii* for the *primipili* (Chief Centurion). Centurions in the auxiliary cohorts accordingly received 3,750 *sestertii* per year, and decurions in the *alae* received 5,250 *sestertii* [7. 371–378]. However, soldiers did not have all this money at their disposal, since deductions were made for various purposes. In the 1st century AD, for instance, money was reserved for foodstuffs, shoes and clothing, weapons, the *epulum* ('banquet'), etc, and taken together, this might comprise the greater part of a soldier's pay (Tac. Ann. 1,17; [7. 359f.]). The deductions were reduced in the 2nd century, before finally being replaced by Roman state contributions to soldiers' expenses [7. 365f.]. By the beginning of the 4th century, the regular imperial monetary gifts (*donativa*) and allowances (*annona*) had already far outstripped the *stipendia* [3. 114–117]. Ultimately, over the course of the 4th century, the *stipendia* became so insignificant that they ceased to be paid, while the *donativa* and *annona* were raised.

Recruits of all troop types received a payment of 300 *sestertii* on enlistment, and → veterans who received honourable discharge were paid a substantial sum (*praemia militiae*) that was calculated according to rank and period of service (Suet. Aug. 49,2): 12,000 *sestertii* for ordinary legionaries and 20,000 *sestertii* for Praetorians (Cass. Dio 55,23,1). Caracalla raised these sums to 20,000 and 25,000 *sestertii* respectively (Cass. Dio 77,24,1). During the Imperial period, soldiers could also expect occasional bonuses, gifts of money from commanders or the emperor, and booty in addition to their regular income. Although some soldiers regarded basic pay in the legions as low in AD 14 (Tac. Ann. 1,17; 1,35), the regularity of such pay, together with additional payments, prospects of promotion, the guaranteed → supply of requirements and pay increases contributed greatly to making service in the Roman Imperial army an attractive proposition [7. 428–437].

☞ Military service, B. Roman; Rank; State and army, B. Roman Republic; State and army, C. Imperial period

BIBLIOGRAPHY
[1] R. ALSTON, Roman Military Pay from Caesar to Diocletian, in: JRS 84, 1994, 113–123   [2] M. CRAWFORD, Coinage and Money under the Roman Republic. Italy and the Mediterranean Economy, 1985   [3] R. DUNCAN-JONES, Structure and Scale in the Roman Economy, 1990   [4] J. HALDON, Warfare, State and Society in the Byzantine World, 1999   [5] P. LE ROUX, Duplicarius, duplarius, sequiplicarius. Un réexamen, in: C. Wolff (ed.), Le métier de soldat dans le monde romain, 2012, 523–532   [6] M.A. SPEIDEL, Roman Army Pay Scales, in: JRS 82, 1992, 87–106   [7] M.A. SPEIDEL, Heer und Herrschaft im Römischen Reich der Hohen Kaiserzeit, 2009, 349–437   [8] M.A. SPEIDEL, Roman Army Pay Scales Revisited. Responses and Answers, in: M. Reddé (ed.), De l'or pour les braves! Soldes, armées et circulation monétaire dans le monde romain, 2014, 53–62   [9] W. TREADGOLD, Byzantium and Its Army, 1995, 284–1081.

MICHAEL A. SPEIDEL

Peace

A. Peace as an ideal
B. Regulations for the preservation of peace
C. International arbitration
D. Agreements to establish peace

A. PEACE AS AN IDEAL

Peace and war are conditions of human reality upon which people have reflected since time immemorial [23]. The description of Achilles' shield in the *Iliad* (18,490–540) juxtaposes the city at peace with the city at war, and evokes the joys of peace far from the battlefield as a past ideal or future hope [26]. Peace – including peace within a city – repeatedly appears as the goal of human effort [33]. Hesiod names Eirene (peace) alongside Dike (justice) and Eunomia (good lawfulness) as the daughters of Themis (Theog. 901–906), and it is Eirene who rules over the just city (Op. 228; cf. Pl. Leg. 628c). Even war was merely a means of restoring peace (Aristot. Eth. Nic. 1177b4), although Augustine added the detail of peace with victory (Civ. 19,12): in the Roman tradition, he understood *pacare* ('to make peaceful') as the process of establishing an order under the hegemony of Rome. Aristophanes brought Eirene to the stage as a power conferring blessings in his comedy *Peace* (421), and Cephisodotus created her statue in the first half of the 4th century BC [16]. Peace as the ultimate state of salvation, as promised by the prophet Isaiah (11) and in the Revelation of John (21), is also found in *Eclogue 4* by Virgil.

B. REGULATIONS FOR THE PRESERVATION OF PEACE

Not until the Briand-Kellogg Pact of 1928 would a state's right to wage a war of aggression (*ius* AD *bellum*) be prohibited in international law, and the adoption of this principle into Article 2 Clause 4 of the United Nations Charter established an organizational framework for it. No such peace regulation existed in Antiquity. Warfare was any state's right, although many felt the need to assert a 'just cause' for war, or, in Roman parlance, to wage a *bellum iustum* [7]. Meanwhile, the principle upheld chiefly by Rome, whereby a 'natural enmity' pertained between states and required a treaty of friendship to suspend it, is rejected today. In the Greek world, the Delphic Amphictyony of the 7th century (StV II, Nr. 104) can at most be said to have restricted the modalities of war among its members. The Hellenic League of 481 (StV II, no. 130) established a temporary general peace to counter the Persians (→ Wars of note J.) [10]. Beginning in 386, several attempts were made to bring about a lasting, general peace through a *koine eirene* ('common peace'). The guiding principle, upheld by all, was the autonomy of the *poleis*, but this peace could only be guaranteed by the strongest power at the time – Sparta in 386, and later Philip II of Macedon (Corinthian League, 338 BC) – which could then make use of the situation for its own purposes. Accordingly, the *koine eirene* never won universal acceptance [13]; [31]; [22].

The peace established by Rome as it expanded its rule, initially in Italy through to 264 BC, then throughout the Mediterranean by the Augustan period, was more successful. Imposed as a practical fact, it would endure at least until the crisis of the 3rd century, and much longer than that across much of the empire. However, the function of the Imperium Romanum as a guarantor of peace for all its inhabitants only gradually became associated with the evolving concept of empire. Cicero was still thinking mainly of the (urban) Romans themselves when he demanded that the goal of external wars should be 'that without affronts [i.e. in security], life may be lived in peace' (*ut sine iniuria in pace vivatur*, Off. I 11,35). To his brother Quintus, however, he justified the taxes raised in the province of Asia with the argument that Rome was guaranteeing its external and internal peace (*pax sempiterna atque otium*, AD Q. fr. 1,1,34). Augustus too proclaimed the peace he had established, the *pax Augusta*, primarily in relation to the period of → civil war, which he had brought to an end. A decree of the senate on July 4, 13 BC ordered the construction of the monumental Ara Pacis Augustae in the Field of Mars to commemorate it, and the structure was duly dedicated on January 30, 9 BC. Yet the actual occasion – Augustus' victorious return from the provinces in Hispania and Gaul (R. Gest. div. Aug. 12) – involved the entire empire, as did the closure on three occasions of the gates of the Temple of Janus *cum esset parta victoriis pax* ('when peace was with victory won') (R. Gest. div. Aug. 13) [9]. The peoples of the empire likewise thanked their emperor for his gift of peace, for example the provincial assembly of Asia Minor in 9 BC (OGIS 458). Luke the Evangelist (2,14) equated the imperial peace with the peace on Earth promised by the birth of Christ. Vespasian's Templum Pacis, on the other hand, although it celebrated the victory over the Jews in AD 71, cannot be isolated from the ending of the civil wars in AD 69. During the Imperial period, the term *pax Romana* was used to denote the peace guaranteed by the Roman Empire and requiring protection, mainly against external barbarian attack, with force of arms (first Sen. Dial. 1,4,14). In this sense, its most striking praise came from Aelius Aristides in his *Roman Oration* (69–71; 103f.) of AD 143. Tacitus has the Caledonian prince Calgacus voice criticism of the *pax Romana* thus: *ubi solitudinem faciunt, pacem appellant* ('Where they create their solitude, they call it peace') (Agr. 30,4; [30]).

C. INTERNATIONAL ARBITRATION

In the evolution of international arbitration proceedings, the Greeks made a distinct contribution. L. Piccirilli has collected instances of arbitration up to 338 BC [3], A. Magnetto those dated between 337 and 196 [17], and S.L. Ager those from 337 to 90 BC [5]. What is clear, however, is that negotiating the resolutions of disputes between major powers often did not succeed, even when treaties were agreed upon and signed, as between Athens and Sparta in the 5th century [3. 21; 25; 27]. The various offers made to Athens by Philip II of Macedon between 346 and 341 [3. 56; 58; 59] were also spurned. The Hellenistic monarchs never submitted themselves to such proceedings: Philip V of Macedon rejected a Roman demand in 200 BC [5. 59]. Rome, meanwhile, repudiated offers of mediation from Pyrrhus in 280 [5. 27] and from Ptolemy II in 252 [5. 35], but imposed just such proceedings on Greek states, for example in the Peace of Apamea of 188 BC [5. 97], occasionally also acting as arbitrator itself [18]; [14].

D. AGREEMENTS TO ESTABLISH PEACE

D.1. Truce
D.2. Capitulation/*deditio*
D.3. Peace treaty

Peace in Antiquity was established in various ways, temporarily or permanently: through a formal truce, by the capitulation of a belligerent party, or through a peace treaty. P. Kehne offers an overview of '1,000 selected international treaties of Greco-Roman Antiquity' [15]; [14], while treaties between 700 and 200 BC are examined in detail in *Staatsverträge des Altertums* (StV) [1]; [2]; [4].

D.1. Truce

Spondai ('truces') to the Greeks were any mutually agreed protection against force of arms – for a short term, for instance, to retrieve the bodies of the fallen. Agreements of longer duration were also made, for example the five-year truce agreed between the Athenians and Peloponnesians in 451/50 BC (StV II, no. 143). Truces with detailed conditions were concluded, for example, between Athen and Sparta in the region of Pylos in 425 (StV II, no. 176), and in 423 (StV II, no. 185). Both were intended to facilitate peace negotiations, but they did not lead directly to the Peace of 421 (Peace of Nicias: StV II, no. 188). That peace, too, was no more than a *sponde* limited to 50 years (like the 'Thirty Years' Peace' agreed by the Athenians and Peloponnesians in 446/45: StV II, no. 156) [6]. The truces with Persian satraps during the campaign of Spartan king Agesilaus in Asia Minor between 397 and 395 were likewise intended to enable further peace negotiations (StV II, no. 219f.; 222). The sacred laying down of arms (*ekecheiria*) that enabled Panhellenic religious festivals (especially the Olympic Games) to take place was a special case.

The Romans attached farther-reaching conditions to their truces (*indutiae*). Several early (prior to 293 BC) references to cessations of hostilities for periods of between one and forty years, mainly with Etruscan cities, are of doubtful historicity (StV III, Nr. 435; 439; 461f.) [21]. The tradition, at least, reflects the Roman principle that for the duration of a truce, responsibility for the maintenance and pay of Roman forces was imposed on the adversary. Likewise, Scipio, in the autumn of 203 and late autumn of 202, during the final phase of the Second Punic War (→ Wars of note K.) in Africa, issued demands at peace negotiations in Rome for the maintenance and payment of the Roman army. On the second occasion, this was probably also intended as compensation for the Roman grain fleet that the Carthaginians had hijacked during the first truce (StV III, no. 548). Three truces preceded the peace agreement between Philip V of Macedon and Rome in 197. The boundary between truces and temporary peace treaties sometimes blurred during Late Antiquity [34].

D.2. Capitulation/*Deditio*

Surrenders by individual soldiers or units will not be addressed here. The capitulation by treaty of a Greek community – which unlike in early modern Europe was always dictated unilaterally by the victor [29] – might mean its annihilation or dissolution as an independent polity. In the cases of Plataeae in 427 (StV II, no. 171), Melos in 415 (Thuc. 5,116) and very nearly Mytilene in 427 (StV II, no. 170; Thuc. 3,50), this could even mean the execution of all the men and the sale of the women and children into slavery. Often, however, the populace was permitted to leave on surrender of its property, as Sparta required of the Messenians in 460/59 (StV II, no. 138), as Athens required of the inhabitants of Potidaea in 429 (StV II, no. 168), as the Spartan general Lysander required of the Samians in 404 (StV II, no. 212), and as Philip II of Macedon required of the people of Methone in 354 (StV II, no. 314). If a *polis* was allowed to survive, the costs of the war and other conditions might be exacted, as when the Athenians stripped the island of Thasos of its mainland territorial possessions and ships in 463 and had its city walls torn down (StV II, no. 135). Samos had to accept similar conditions in 439, and its oligarchic regime was forced to give way to a democracy (StV II, no. 159). The Spartan general Brasidas displayed generosity in 424, limiting himself to making Acanthus (StV II, no. 181) and Amphipolis (StV II, no. 182) into Spartan confederates. Following its defeat in the Peloponnesian War in 404, Athens lost its Long Walls, its fleet and its external possessions. It became a member of the Peloponnesian League (StV II, no. 211). Similarly, Alexander of Pherae had to accept territorial losses and join the Boeotians in 363 (StV II, no. 288), and in 362 the island of Ceos was forced to rejoin the Athenian League (StV II, no. 289). In 322 after the Lamian War, according to terms set by Antipater, Athens was compelled to adopt an oligarchic constitution and pay reparations, and it also lost Samos. The former confederacy was renewed (StV III, no. 415).

The Roman form of capitulation, the *deditio* (*in fidem*), was likewise always dictated unilaterally by the victor. Based on its form (Liv. 1,38,1f.), therefore, it is not generally described as a treaty. Instead, it is understood as the yielding party's legal self-annihilation [11]; [8]; [12]. It could certainly lead to the dissolution of the polity, one prominent instance being when Capua, which had defected to Hannibal, was forced to surrender to Rome in 212 (Liv. 26,16,6–11; 34,1–12). Still, the fact that a *deditio* was no longer permissible if the battering-ram (*aries*) had already touched the wall (Caes. B Gall. 2,32,1) shows that it was clearly distinct from a simple conquest. It spared the participants further costs of war. There are numerous examples of a victor giving assurances before a surrender that give every appearance of being a capitulation treaty [20]; [32], for example Panormus in 254 (StV III, no. 484). Elsewhere, the *deditio* was often followed by the restitution of the community. An inscription dating to 104 BC from Spain, which attests to the *deditio* of the people of Seano[corum] to the governor of the province of Hispania ulterior, L. Caesius, provides evidence of this procedure [19]. The act of outright surrender (*se suaque*) and its acceptance were followed by provisional instructions, such as the surrender of weapons and the return of captured spoils.

Thereafter, the capitulating polity was immediately released to freedom in its former state and with its former constitution, subject to approval by the senate and people of Rome. This approval was sought by having the community, now recognized once more as a subject of international law and capable of action, send emissaries to Rome. On principle, communities were only allowed restitution if they had accepted *deditio* peacefully. The Mamertines of Messana probably received a treaty of confederacy (*foedus*) in 263, following their *deditio* in 264 (StV III, no. 478), while the Latins and Campanians who surrendered in 338 were granted a range of legal benefits, from entry into full or partial (*civitas sine suffragio*) Roman citizenship to continued independence. While Velitrae lost its walls and council, Antium gained a citizen colony (StV III, no. 347). The exclusive primacy of Rome increasingly made empty many international legal forms that had been operative since the late 2nd century BC. Caesar in Gaul, for instance, made the *deditio* a precondition for any kind of international relationship with Rome [27]. The *deditio* was still being used with Germanic tribes in the 4th century AD, although it had lost its real legal force [25].

D.3. PEACE TREATY

Peace treaties in the Greek world were initially truces (*spondai*; see above, D.1.) of many years' duration. Such truces were concluded on several occasions with Argos: by Sparta in 451/50, for 30 years (StV II, no. 144), in 420 for 50 years (although the peace broke down; StV II, no. 192), and in 418 for 50 years (StV II, no. 194); and by Athens in 420 for 100 years (StV II, no. 193). The last two of these were also alliances (*symmachiai*), which kept the peace much like treaties of amity. Formal treaties establishing peace (*eirene*) only began to be made in the 4th century, at first often as *koine eirene* (see above, B). Peace treaties between tyrants of Syracuse and Carthage date back to Gelon in 480 BC (StV II, no. 131). These and the capitulations of rebellious League confederates of Athens are the only agreements to make mention of war reparations [28].

As far as Rome was concerned, any form of treaty could in principle establish peace (*pax*) [35]. Livy preserves the older wording used in the ceremonial form of *foedus* ('treaty') involving the fetial priests (1,24,4–9), who were no longer involved after 201 BC. Whether a peace treaty was valid that was concluded solely through the promise (*sponsio*) of the generals was an issue of some controversy in Rome in light of the *pax Caudina* of 321 (StV III, no. 416). In 137 BC, the peace with Numantia was annulled and the general who concluded it, Mancinus, was surrendered to the enemy. Normally, a peace had to be approved at Rome by the senate and people. Thus, the preliminary peace established in 241 by the generals Lutatius Catulus and Hamilcar Barcas was rejected by the popular assembly at Rome, and replaced with a peace treaty that imposed harsher terms on Carthage (StV III, no. 493). From this point on, peace treaties were always dictated by Rome as victor. Exceptions arising out of peculiar circumstances were the 205 BC peace with Philip V after the First Macedonian War (StV III, no. 543) and the Peace of Dardanus that was concluded between Sulla and Mithridates VI of Pontus in 85 BC.

The structure of peace treaties was highly regular. They began with a friendship clause that restored the condition of peace. Allies were included here. Next came specific provisions, including the return of prisoners, defectors, absconded slaves, warships and elephants, and the reimbursement of costs of war. In the conflicts with Carthage and Rome's subsequent expansion into the Greek east, these costs gradually grew excessively high. Hostages were taken until payment was made, which was took a very long time. Territorial provisions were of great importance, and included the surrender of land, sometimes to Rome's allies, and occasionally naval exclusion zones or prohibitions on warfare. A delegation of ten senatorial legates could impose individual provisions. Formally, however, peace treaties were concluded between equal partners. The *maiestas* clause found at the beginning of the treaty signed with the Aetolians in 189 BC, *imperium maiestatemque populi Romani gens Aetolorum conservato sine dolo malo* ('The Aetolians shall acknowledge without malicious intent the authority and majesty of the Roman people'; Liv. 38,11,2), is probably not an indication of a specific type of *foedus iniquum* ('treaty of unequals').

Rome's dominance in the Mediterranean region now left no partners for regular peace treaties. The only equal counterpart left was the Parthian Empire. Beginning with Augustus, authority to conclude a treaty was reserved for the emperor (*lex de imp. Vesp.* l. 1). Nevertheless, peace treaties continued to be signed: in AD 102, Trajan even had the treaty with the Dacian prince Decebalus confirmed by the senate (Cass. Dio 68,9,7). Rome gradually found itself in the position of having to make payments, whether as subsidies for military support, such as those agreed with Germanic tribes by Marcus Aurelius and Commodus in 175 and 180 [24], or as reparations, such as those paid by Macrinus to the Parthian Great King Artabanus IV in AD 218. Bilateral sworn *foedera* revived in the 4th and 5th centuries, with the preliminary peace that was made in the field now confirmed by the *magistri militum* ('Masters of Soldiers') concerned.

☞ **Alliances; Costs of war; Diplomacy; Enemies; Hostages; Victory; War**

Bibliography

Sources
[1] H. Bengtson / R. Werner (eds.), Die Staatsverträge des Altertums, vol. 2: Die Verträge der griechisch-römischen Welt von 700 bis 338, ²1975 [2] R.M. Errington (ed.), Die Staatsverträge des Altertums, vol. 4: Die Verträge der griechisch-römischen Welt von ca. 200 v.Chr. bis zum Beginn der Kaiserzeit, 2020 [3] L. Piccirilli, Gli arbitrati interstatali greci, vol. 1, 1973 [4] H.H. Schmitt (ed.), Die Staatsverträge des Altertums, vol. 3: Die Verträge der griechisch-römischen Welt 338 bis 200 v. Chr., 1969.

Secondary literature
[5] S.L. Ager, Interstate Arbitrations in the Greek World, 337–90 B.C., 1996 [6] E. Baltrusch, Symmachie und Spondai. Untersuchungen zum griechischen Völkerrecht der archaischen und klassischen Zeit (8.–5. Jahrhundert v.Chr.), 1994 [7] S. Clavadetscher-Thürlemann, Polemos dikaios und bellum iustum, 1985 [8] W. Dahlheim, Struktur und Entwicklung des römischen Völkerrechts im dritten und zweiten Jahrhundert v.Chr., 1968, 5–67 [9] W. Dahlheim, Augustus, 2010, 250–254 [10] A. Graeber, Friedensvorstellung und Friedensbegriff bei den Griechen bis zum Peloponnesischen Krieg, in: ZRG 109, 1992, 116–162 [11] A. Heuss, Die völkerrechtlichen Grundlagen der römischen Aussenpolitik in republikanischer Zeit, 1933, 60–77 [12] K.-J. Hölkeskamp, Fides – deditio in fidem – dextra data et accepta. Recht, Religion und Ritual, in: Senatus populusque Romanus. Die politische Kultur der Republik, 2004, 105–135 [13] M. Jehne, Koine Eirene, 1994 [14] V. Kasceev, Schiedsgericht und Vermittlung in den Beziehungen zwischen den hellenistischen Staaten und Rom, in: Historia 46, 1997, 419–433 [15] P. Kehne, 1000 Selected International Treaties of Graeco-Roman Antiquity, in: BNP Index Lists and Tables, 2010, 350–451 [16] P. Kranz, Krieg und Frieden als Themen antiker Bildkunst, in: G. Binder / B. Effe (eds.), Krieg und Frieden im Altertum, 1989, 68–84 [17] A. Magnetto, Gli arbitrati interstatali greci, vol. 2, 1997 [18] A.J. Marshall, The Survival and Development of International Jurisdiction in the Greek World under Roman Rule, in: ANRW II.13, 1980, 626–661 [19] D. Nörr, Aspekte des römischen Völkerrechts. Die Bronzetafel von Alcántara, 1989 [20] D. Nörr, Die Fides im römischen Völkerrecht, 1991 [21] S.P. Oakley, A Commentary on Livy, Books VI–X, Bd. 3: Book IX, 2005, 538–541 [22] K.A. Raaflaub, Greek Concepts and Theories of Peace, in: K.A. Raaflaub (ed.), Peace in the Ancient World. Concepts and Theories, 2016, 122–157 [23] K.A. Raaflaub (ed.), Peace in the Ancient World. Concepts and Theories, 2016 [24] F. von Saldern, Studien zur Politik des Commodus, 2003, 33–40 [25] R. Schulz, Die Entwicklung des römischen Völkerrechts im vierten und fünften Jahrhundert n.Chr., 1993, 133–152 [26] O. Taplin, The Shield of Achilles within the 'Iliad', in: J. Latacz (ed.), Homer. Die Dichtung und ihre Deutung, 1991, 227–253 [27] D. Timpe, Rechtsformen der römischen Außenpolitik bei Caesar, in: Chiron 2, 1972, 277–295 [28] J. von Ungern-Sternberg, Kriegsentschädigungen im griechisch-römischen Bereich als eine vertraglich geregelte Form des Beutemachens?, in: Griechische Studien, 2009, 205–224 [29] J. von Ungern-Sternberg, Europäische Kapitulationsurkunden. Genese und Rechtsinhalt, in: K. Brüggemann et al. (eds.), Die baltischen Kapitulationen von 1710, 2014, 17–42 [30] K.-W. Welwei, 'Si vis pacem, para bellum'. Eine Maxime römischer Politik?, in: G. Binder / B. Effe (eds.), Krieg und Frieden im Altertum, 1989, 85–109 [31] J. Wilker, War and Peace at the Beginning of the Fourth Century. The Emergence of the Koine Eirene, in: J. Wilker (ed.), Maintaining Peace and Interstate Stability in Archaic and Classical Greece, 2012, 92–117 [32] A. Zack, Forschungen über die rechtlichen Grundlagen der römischen Außenbeziehungen, Teil 8: Die juristische Form und der rechtliche Zweck der intergesellschaftlichen deditio und die Bedeutung der fides im Zusammenhang mit der deditio, in: Göttinger Forum für Altertumswissenschaft 19, 2016, 89–163 [33] G. Zampaglione, The Idea of Peace in Antiquity, 1973 [34] K.-H. Ziegler, Kriegsverträge im antiken römischen Recht, in: ZRG 102, 1985, 40–90 [35] K.-H. Ziegler, Friedensverträge im römischen Altertum, in: Archiv des Völkerrechts 27, 1989, 45–62.

Jürgen von Ungern-Sternberg

Phalanx

A. Definition
B. Equipment and qualifications
C. Formation and method of fighting
D. Evolution
E. Political consequences
F. Impact, limits
G. Later history

A. Definition
In the epics, the Greek *phalanx* (plural *phalanges*) denotes massed ranks of soldiers in battle (Hom. Il. 6,6; 19,158; see 5,96; 11,90; Hes. Theog. 935f.). From Xenophon (An. 1,8,17; 6,5,27) onwards, the word generally refers to the massed battle formation of hoplites bearing standard weapons who fought in the wars of the Greek *poleis*. This formation was subsequently adopted by the Romans. Later, it applied to the infantry (armed with long lances) of the Macedonian kings beginning with Philip II ('Macedonian phalanx'), and there came to be a non-specific sense whereby phalanx was used for any massed formation of infantry, as for instance in describing the Celts (Gauls) and Germani (Caes. B Gall. 1,24,5; 1,52,4; Liv. 10,29,6; Plut. Marius 20,6). Detailed discussions of the matters presented here are found in [8]; [10]; [11]; [35]; [29]; [13]; [2]; [20].

B. Equipment and qualifications
The word 'hoplite' (*hoplites*) derives from *hopla*/*hoplon*, which had a general meaning of 'weapon' and a specific sense in reference to the typical hoplite shield. The hoplite's equipment (*panoplia*) was protective: a bronze helmet with slit apertures only for eyes, nose and mouth; a bronze breastplate ('bell' breastplate) and bronze greaves;

perhaps also arm guards and cuisses; and semicircular metal pieces to protect the lower abdomen. Attack weapons were the spear, approximately 2 m long with an iron tip and spike (so that if it broke, either half could be used as a weapon), the iron sword, and perhaps a lighter javelin. The large, round wooden shield (diameter approx. 1 m), covered with leather or bronze plate and with its edges reinforced with bronze, was markedly concave. It was borne on the left arm using a grip (*porpax*) and handle (*antilabe*). Its shape allowed the soldier to rest it on his shoulder, freeing his arm, and it could be used as a defensive or offensive weapon [30. 25–101]; [17] (→ Equipment, A.).

In early Greek history (7th/6th centuries), fighting in the *polis* army was a privilege reserved for citizens. Wars were short and, with the exception of raiding campaigns by noble warrior bands, mostly limited to feuds with neighbouring *poleis* [21. 51–53]. Participants were expected to provide their own equipment and supplies. The panoply (the warrior's equipment) was expensive [7. 351–353] – around 30 drachmas (ML 14), or the value of 30 sheep. This limited hoplite warfare to the landowning middle and upper classes.

Smaller *poleis* had fully equipped hoplites only in the front ranks. Farther back, rather than helmets and breastplates, fighters wore a felt and leather cap and a canvas or leather jerkin (see also [35. 55–57]). Where necessary (but as a matter of course in the case of Sparta), slaves were used as reinforcements (Hdt. 9,10,1; 9,28,2) [12. 31–39], and they occupied the rear ranks.

C. FORMATION AND METHOD OF FIGHTING

The phalanx comprised a wide block of hoplites, about eight ranks deep, divided into ranks and divisions (*stichos*, *lochos* etc.), but not into separate units. The width was dictated by the number of fighters and the width of the enemy phalanx, which it was necessary to match to avoid being outflanked. The phalanx specialized in frontal assault, and achieved its best results on relatively flat and unobstructed ground.

The 'pure' phalanx included neither light infantry fighting with bows, slings or javelins, nor cavalry. Members of the social elite rode to the battlefield, but dismounted to join the phalanx for battle. Except in peripheral regions (Macedonia, Thessaly), where mounted combat was preferred, organized cavalry units did not begin to appear until the 5th century BC [31]. In skirmishes before the battle proper, specialists (often → mercenaries: light infantry from Thrace, archers from Crete) sought to disrupt the order of the enemy formation [35. cap. 5]; [13. 119–124]. *Poleis* only began to acquire their own units of light infantry towards the end of the 5th century.

Hoplite combat was not characterized by tactical finesse. The general led his army to the battlefield, set up the formation and exhorted the soldiers to fight bravely. He then took up his position in the front rank. It was only in the major battles of the 5th and 4th centuries, where contingents of allied *poleis* fought alongside each other, that it became possible, for instance, for one wing's victory to be used to rescue another wing from defeat through skillful maneuvering.

How compact the formation was is a matter of debate. The round shield worn on the left arm protected the right side of the man standing to the left. Soldiers sought this protection, and as a result, the formation tended to drift right (Thuc. 5,71,1). The epics' metaphors already emphasize tightness and compactness of formation [22. 247–250]. Still, the hoplites needed space to fight and evade enemy thrusts. Some distance between individual fighters was therefore required. There are also references to jostling and thrusting (*othismos*), with men 'fighting, killling and dying shield to shield' (Xen. Hell. 4,3,19; see Thuc. 4,96,2). This is already a motif in epic poetry (Hom. Il. 4,446–451; 13,131–133, which Pol. 18,29,5f. saw as the hoplite phalanx), but it can only have applied to the front ranks.

Sacrifices and consultation with soothsayers were followed by the sounding of the signal. Giving the battlecry (paean), the armies advanced, either at a steady march (the Spartans to the rhythm of the double flute), or else finishing at a run in order to avoid enemy projectiles, raise fighting spirit and win dynamic advantage (Caes. B Civ. 3,92; → Music).

The initial collision was followed by close combat with spears and swords. Warriors moved in from behind to replace the fallen. Homer depicts in its full horror the brutality of this type of fighting on a slippery, stinking battlefield [33] strewn with corpses, dying people and weapons [27]. The key to effectiveness was to preserve the formation. Generally, the battle was over as soon as one side achieved a breakthrough. Before the advent of reserves and units capable of independent manoeuvres, the losing side had little or no chance of restoring equilibrium to the battle, unless they could gain a territorial advantage or if delayed contingents arrived. They would therefore flee, often throwing away their heavy shields (Archil. 5 West). The victors would use spoils to build a monument on the battlefield (*tropaion*, 'trophy'), while the losers would request a truce to collect their dead, thereby acknowledging their defeat.

In early times, what mattered was → victory, not the destruction of the enemy, so pursuit was no more than cursory. Battle was fought for control of disputed land, but also for → honour among neighbouring rivals. Polybius mentions a negotiated battle (1,87,9). Wars between hoplites contained ritual elements (→ peace, for example, was often agreed for 30 years, until a new generation could grow up), but talk of 'ritual warfare' [4] goes too far. Other constraints arose from traditional norms, adherence to which was in the best interests of the social classes involved [18. 53–71]; [15. 25–34]. Because of these constraints, death rates were relatively low. When social constraints fell away in the 5th century and losing sides were more vigorously pursued, including by cavalry, the losses on the part of the losing side were sometimes extremely high [14]. This was particularly true of Greek victories over non-Greeks, because of differences in armament and methods of fighting. For Marathon (490; → Battles of note, F.), Herodotus (6,117,1) gives a figure of 6,400 Persian dead (exaggerated), and 192 Athenian (genuine). Those among the wounded who could be moved were cared for and taken away. Others were presumably delivered from their sufferings by friend or foe. There is good evidence for psychological trauma akin to what is now known as post-traumatic stress disorder (PTSD) [32]; [29. 202–211].

One description of a battle illustrates how matters proceeded, although by this time the battle involved hybrid armies (415 BC). 'First, the stone-throwers, slingers and archers from both sides began their skirmish ahead of the battle lines... The soothsayers then presented the usual sacrifices, and the trumpeters signalled the attack. They accordingly marched ahead ... When the time came for fighting at close quarters, the battle long remained in the balance ... At last, the Argives pushed back the Syracusan left, then the Athenians repelled those ranked against them. The remainder of the Syracusan lines were thus broken and took flight. The Athenians did not pursue them far [for fear of the superior enemy cavalry], but soon pulled back and set up a *tropaion* ... They collected their dead, laid them on a funeral pyre and spent the night there. Next day, they returned their dead [about 260 of them] to the Syracusans under armistice, collected the remains of their own dead [some 50 in number] and set sail with the captured weapons' (Thuc. 6,69–71).

D. EVOLUTION
The epic *aoidoi* ('bards') concentrated their attention on the heroic acts of leaders, whose ideal qualities consisted of being the best in battle and speech (Hom. Il. 6,208; 9,440–443). Yet the *Iliad* (c. 700 BC) also offers solid testimony of mass combat in compact formations (15,277; 16,212–217). Victory depended on the efforts of all fighters, even the lowliest (13,223; 13,237). Everyone had a share in the spoils (9,318–319). An exchange of arms, intended to provide the best fighters with the best weapons, makes clear that the 'best' were not always members of the elite (14,370–384). The principle of the phalanx is already clearly formulated here: fight strictly in formation, to the detriment of individual acts of heroism. 'Fewer of them by far were falling, for they were taking constant pains in the throng of battle to save each other from the sheer slaughter' (17,356–365). Hoplite weapons are found in graves dating from the late 8th century. It therefore seems justified to see the Homeric phalanxes as a precursor to the hoplite phalanx ([22]; contra: [35. 153–157]).

Development through the 7th century aimed at maximizing the force of the phalanx by concentrating on pure frontal combat [8]. Early vase paintings and episodes in the *Iliad* show archers with heavy infantry. Van Wees [34] infers from this that the phalanx was long hybrid in composition, and that 'pure' hoplite combat was only achieved at a very late date, if at all [15]. Such images may also be explained in terms of Near Eastern influences or, as in early Italy, with reference to mixed warrior bands [26. 355f. (English: 17f.)]. Despite minor variations in armament, the 'pure phalanx' is well documented in vase paintings prior to 600 BC. At the same time, various indications attest to the military and social dominance of the hoplite [25. 360f. (English: 97)].

Hoplite combat spread rapidly throughout Greece, perhaps from Sparta [3. 153–166]. External influences on specific weapon forms are probable. A massed formation of heavily armed infantry appears on the Sumerian 'Stele of the Vultures' [19. 247], but to my knowledge there is no evidence of a tradition associated with it. On the whole, the hoplite phalanx seems to have been a Greek invention that emerged through an interactive process with the *polis*, its institutions and its sense of community [25].

The introduction of large-scale naval warfare and the incorporation of cavalry and light infantry led to the emergence of hybrid (5th cent.) and ultimately integrated armies (late 4th cent.). The future belonged to these, although Greek hoplites would continue to be indispensable.

E. POLITICAL CONSEQUENCES
The phalanx, in which landowning classes fought for their *polis*, their territory and their own interests, helped create and maintain an egalitarian political order [28], as is reflected in communal legislation and the regulation of decision-making processes (as in Sparta's 'Great Rhetra'). In → Sparta, this regulation took on extreme forms because of the need to maintain control over non-citizen contingents (helots and *perioikoi*), who were by far more numerous [3. 21–38]; [37. 52–93]. The lower classes not qualified for hoplite service remained excluded from active citizenship (oligarchy).

Persian forces operated on land and at sea, which forced Athens, the primary target of Persian aggression (480/79), to become a naval power. In consequence of Athens' → fleet -based authority in the Delian League, the engagement of the lower classes in the navy became permanent, leading by the mid-5th century to the full-fledged emergence of democracy in an interactive process with Athenian imperial authority [36. 1–139]; [23]; [24]. The hoplites, still important in warfare, thereby lost their primacy [20]. Two short-lived oligarchic coups (411, 404) limited active citizenship to an arbitrary number of 5,000 and 3,000 hoplites respectively (Thuc. 8,65,3; Xen. Hell. 2,3,18).

F. IMPACT, LIMITS

The success of the hoplite phalanx depended on its armament, cohesion and discipline. The 'bronze men' quickly became popular as mercenaries in the Near East and Egypt [1]. Xenophon's *Anabasis* describes the attempt by Cyrus the Younger to seize the Persian throne with 10,000 Greek mercenaries (401 BC). Hoplites fought on both sides in Alexander's battles in Persia (→ Wars of note, A.; → Mercenaries).

Even so, the efficacy of the phalanx was limited. To match the width of the enemy formation, smaller armies were forced to thin out their own ranks. It was difficult to maintain the cohesion of the phalanx on terrain that was uneven or complicated by obstacles. Skilfully deployed, light infantry or cavalry could cause a phalanx difficulties (Thuc. 3,97f.; Xen. Hell. 4,4f.). As a monolithic block, the phalanx was unable to react to attacks on the flank or from the rear. Psychological factors (Xen. Hell. 4,3,17) and superstitions (Thuc. 6,70,1) influenced morale, which was especially important for the phalanx. Other weapons types and strategies, such as the use of territorial advantage, were neglected.

There were discussions of the advantages and disadvantages of phalanx combat, as there were regarding naval warfare (Thuc. 1,142f.). Herodotus, for instance, has the Persian Mardonius criticize the 'clumsy' manner of Greek warfare: 'When they declare war on each other, they look for the fairest and flattest terrain. There, they march up and fight their battle,' with the result that both sides suffer grave losses. Instead, he argues, 'each party should ascertain where the other is at the greatest disadvantage, and challenge him there' (Hdt. 7,9b,1f.).

G. LATER HISTORY

At the Battle of Leuctra (371), the Theban Epaminondas (→ Generals of note, F.) defeated the Spartans with an 'oblique phalanx', deploying his best troops on a left wing that was reinforced to 50 ranks, thereby overcoming the Spartan elite on their right wing. Their allies on the left wing took flight when they saw the Spartiates facing defeat (Xen. Hell. 6,4,12–14) [6. 166–170]; [9. 44–51].

Philip II of Macedon (→ Generals of note, M.) created a revolutionary 'integrated army', with which the brilliant tactician and strategist Alexander the Great succeeded in conquering the Persian Empire [6. 175–215]. In the 'Macedonian phalanx', soldiers were equipped with smaller round shields (*pelta*) worn round the neck, since they needed both hands to wield their long, heavy spears (*sarissa*; c. 6 m, 5.5–6.5 kg) [16]. The spears of several ranks projected out ahead of the front rank in a 'thicket' of spears, preventing opponents from reaching those wielding them, while the ranks behind held their *sarissai* to deflect showers of enemy arrows. This phalanx was almost invincible in frontal combat, but it lacked mobility and required suitable terrain, and it was vulnerable to outflanking, which made protection of the flanks by mobile troops vital. When Ptolemy IV defeated Antiochus III at the Battle of Raphia near Gaza (217), in which tens of thousands of phalangites fought on both sides, large contingents of cavalry, → elephants and all manner of light infantry took part, but the battle was decided between the phalanxes (Pol. 5,79–86). In integrated armies of this kind during the Hellenistic period, the Macedonian phalanx played a crucial role.

Warfare in early Italy was dominated by the private campaigns of noble warrior bands that included horsemen, archers and hoplites. The Greek phalanx reached Rome by way of the Etruscans, and the Romans used it mainly in conflicts with other cities (e.g. Veii). However, the rigid phalanx was not successful in conflicts with mountain tribes such as the Samnites. The Romans enlarged their army by introducing different tiers with regard to soldiers' armament requirements (and the qualifying census) (Liv. 1,43), and they increased their mobility by dividing the legions into independently mobile units (initially maniples, then cohorts), whose rear ranks could move up to replace units that were exhausted in battle (on the history of the Roman army, see [5. cap. 1–10]). Caesar's war reports illustrate the ability of the cohort army to react with flexibility to unforeseen developments (Caes. B Gall. 1,25; Caes. B Civ. 3,89,4; 93,3–5). Ultimately, the cohort army proved its superiority even over the integrated armies of the Hellenistic monarchies with their massed phalanxes.

☞ Battle; Cavalry, A. Greek; Infantry

BIBLIOGRAPHY

[1] I. BETTALLI, I mercenari nel mondo greco, vol. 1, 1995 [2] B. CAMPBELL / L. TRITLE (eds.), The Oxford Handbook of Warfare in the Classical World, 2013 [3] P. CARTLEDGE, Spartan Reflections, 2001 [4] W.R. CONNOR, Early Greek Land Warfare as Symbolic

Expression, in: P&P 119, 1988, 3–29 [5] P. ERDKAMP (ed.), A Companion to the Roman Army, 2007 [6] A. FERRILL, The Origins of War, 1997 [7] J.P. FRANZ, Krieger, Bauern, Bürger, 2002 [8] V.D. HANSON, Hoplite Technology in Phalanx Battle, in: V.D. HANSON (ed.), Hoplites, 1991, 63–84 [9] V.D. HANSON, The Soul of Battle, 1999 [10] V.D. HANSON, The Wars of the Ancient Greeks and Their Invention of Western Military Culture, 1999 [11] V.D. HANSON, The Western Way of War. Infantry Battle in Classical Greece, ²2000 [12] P. HUNT, Slaves, Warfare, and Ideology in the Greek Historians, 1998 [13] P. HUNT, Military Forces, in: P. Sabin et al. (eds.), The Cambridge History of Greek and Roman Warfare, vol. 1, 2007, 108–146 [14] P. KRENTZ, Casualties in Hoplite Battles, in: GRBS 26, 1985, 13–20 [15] P. KRENTZ, Fighting by the Rules. The Invention of the Hoplite Agōn, in: Hesperia 71, 2002, 23–39 [16] M.M. MARKLE III, The Macedonian Sarissa, Spear and Related Armor, in: AJA 81, 1977, 323–339 [17] C. MATTHEW, A Storm of Spears. Understanding the Greek Hoplite at War, 2012 [18] J. OBER, The Athenian Revolution, 1996 [19] J.N. POSTGATE, Early Mesopotamia, 1992 [20] D.M. PRITCHARD, Athenian Democracy at War, 2018 [21] K.A. RAAFLAUB, Soldiers, Citizens and the Evolution of the Early Greek Polis, in: L. Mitchell / P.J. Rhodes (eds.), The Development of the Polis in Archaic Greece, 1997, 49–59 [22] K.A. RAAFLAUB, Homerische Krieger, Protohopliten und die Polis. Schritte zur Lösung alter Probleme, in: B. Meißner et al. (eds.), Krieg, Gesellschaft, Institutionen, 2005, 229–266 [23] K.A. RAAFLAUB et al., Origins of Democracy in Ancient Greece, 2007 [24] K.A. RAAFLAUB, The Breakthrough of Dēmokratia in Mid-Fifth-Century Athens, in: K.A. Raaflaub et al., Origins of Democracy in Ancient Greece, 2007, 105–154 [25] K.A. RAAFLAUB, Proto-Phalanx und Polis. Der frühgriechische Massenkampf im interkulturellen Zusammenhang des östlichen Mittelmeerraumes, in: T. Brüggemann et al. (eds.), Studia Hellenistica et Historiographica. Festschrift für Andreas Mehl, 2010, 357–372 (English: Early Greek Infantry Fighting in a Mediterranean Context, in: D. Kagan / G.F. Viggiano (eds.), Men of Bronze. Hoplite Warfare in Ancient Greece, 2013, 95–111) [26] K.A. RAAFLAUB, Auf dem Streitwagen des Sängers. Die Suche nach einer historischen 'epischen Gesellschaft', in: C. Ulf et al. (eds.), Lag Troia in Kilikien? Der aktuelle Streit um Homers Ilias, 2011, 341–374 (English: Riding on Homer's Chariot. The Search for a Historical 'Epic Society', in: Antichthon 45, 2011, 1–34) [27] K.A. RAAFLAUB, Homer and the Agony of Hoplite Battle, in: AHB 27, 2013, 1–22 [28] K.A. RAAFLAUB / R. WALLACE, 'People's Power' and Egalitarian Trends in Archaic Greece, in: K.A. Raaflaub et al., Origins of Democracy in Ancient Greece, 2007, 22–48 [29] L. RAWLINGS, The Ancient Greeks at War, 2007 [30] A. SCHWARTZ, Reinstating the Hoplite. Arms, Armour and Phalanx Fighting in Archaic and Classical Greece, 2009 [31] I.G. SPENCE, The Cavalry of Classical Greece, 1993 [32] L.A. TRITLE, From Melos to My Lai. A Study in Violence, Culture and Social Survival, 2000 [33] L.A. TRITLE, Inside the Hoplite Agony, in: AHB 23, 2009, 50–69 [34] H. VAN WEES, The Development of the Hoplite Phalanx. Iconography and Reality in the Seventh Century, in: H. van Wees (ed.), War and Violence in Ancient Greece, 2000, 125–166 [35] H. VAN WEES, Greek Warfare. Myths and Reality, 2004 [36] K.-W. WELWEI, Das klassische Athen, 1999 [37] K.-W. WELWEI, Sparta, 2004.

KURT A. RAAFLAUB

Plunder

☞ Booty; Scorched earth

Policing

There was no police force in the modern sense in the ancient world [3. 4–6]; [6]. In general, the regular armies of a Greek *polis* or a Hellenistic kingdom, and the soldiers of the early and later Roman army, were deployed to maintain public order and guarantee the safety and property of citizens. No information on this subject survives from the Archaic or Classical periods in Greece. This suggests that the hoplites of every *polis*, working with the municipal authorities, took responsibility for law and order and the defence of the territory against → bandits.

During the Hellenistic period, it seems that the royal armies had little to do with what might be called police actions, with the exception of the army of the Ptolemies, which had inherited specialized policing units from the Pharaonic tradition (*phylakitai*). Each individual *polis* was responsible for fighting all kinds of bandits, and for protecting its own territory. To this end, military units were stationed in the *phrouria* (fortresses) within the territory, especially along its frontiers. Many epigraphic witnesses attest that police in many places kept watch at city walls and gates and patrolled dangerous roads at night (e.g. Tomis: IScM II.2, 2nd cent. AD). In the heartlands of the Hellenistic monarchies, royal units despatched to cities had the job of maintaining public order. In the Seleucid Empire, colonists were settled in certain regions to guarantee public safety and forestall any attempt at rebellion or secession and also to combat banditry of all kinds (Palaemagnesia in Lydia: OGIS 229) [8. 135–138].

In the early Roman Empire, the army was charged with combating enemies of public order. However, this policy does not seem to have been standardized across the whole empire. There is evidence of diverse practices and strategies in the provinces, arising in many cases from adaptation to local exigencies and circumstances. In Rome and Italy, the *cohortes praetoriae* ('Praetorian Guard') and *cohortes urbanae* ('Urban Guard') could be said in light of their specific responsibilities to resemble police forces rather than army units.

In regions along the *limes* ('boundaries') and within the imperial domains, there is evidence of soldiers being temporarily assigned as *centuriones regionarii* ('Regional Centurions') from their legions. Such *regionarii* are attested in the provinces along the lower Danube (Montana and Samum) [4], but also, for instance, in

Britain (Vindolanda: Tab. Vindol. 250; 255; 653. Bath / Aquae Sulis: RIB 152), Asia Minor (Antioch in Pisidia: IGRR III 301) and Egypt [1. 81–96]; [2. 67–86]. Pliny the Younger wrote to Trajan requesting permission to ask the governor of Moesia inferior to send a *centurio regionarius* to Pliny's own province, Pontus et Bithynia (Plin. Ep. 10,77f.). Besides the *regionarii*, the *beneficiarii consularis* ('Consular Adjutants') and *stationarii* ('those stationed at a post') serving in the *stationes* ('posts'; e.g. Osterburken and Sirmium) – at crossroads and provincial boundaries, in mining and quarrying districts and even inside imperial domains – performed policing assignments (Tert. Apol. 2,8) alongside various administrative duties. This was a widespread phenomenon throughout the entire empire, as attested in numerous inscriptions [5. 133–210, 220–243]; [7. 85–129].

Side by side with men of the Roman army, special officers whose positions dated back to old Hellenistic traditions took command in the provinces of Asia Minor, Macedonia and Thrace. These were the *irenarchi/irenarches* ('Justices of the Peace'; Dig. 50,4,18,7, armed municipal departments of *diogmitai*). The *paraphylakes* ('Chief Guardians') safeguarded public order and citizens' safety within the urban area. Not all of these, however, were regular and permanent citizen militias. The *lex Ursonensis* (CIII) also permitted Roman colonies to maintain civic defence forces. In colonies in Macedonia (Philippi) and Galatia (Antioch in Pisidia, Comama and Iconium), the *irenarchi/irenarches* are attested as components of the local authorities [3. 90–157, 193–196, 206–213].

The thorough reforms to the Roman army that began in the reign of Diocletian, as well as a lack of epigraphic evidence, make it impossible to establish anything definite for Late Antiquity about police actions as distinct from ordinary military actions to counter external or internal threats, definitions having become increasingly blurred.

☞ **Militia; State and army**

BIBLIOGRAPHY
[1] R. ALSTON, Soldier and Society in Roman Egypt. A Social History, 1995 [2] R.S. BAGNALL, Army and Police in Roman Upper Egypt, in: JARCE 14, 1977, 67–86 [3] C. BRÉLAZ, La sécurité publique en Asie Mineure sous le Principat (Ier–IIIème s. ap. J.-C.). Institutions municipales et institutions impériales dans l'Orient romain, 2005 [4] G. CUPCEA, On Police and Administrative Duties of the Roman Military: regionarii, in: Acta Musei Napocensis 53/I, 2016, 151–176 [5] J. NÉLIS-CLEMENT, Les beneficiarii. Militaires et administrateurs au service de l'Empire (Ier s. a. C.–VIe s. p. C.), 2000 [6] W. NIPPEL, Police, in: BNP 11, 2007, 463–464 [7] J. OTT, Die Beneficiarier. Untersuchungen zu ihrer Stellung innerhalb der Rangordnung des römischen Heeres und zu ihrer Funktion, 1995 [8] M. SARTRE, Anatolie hellénistique. L'Anatolie hellénistique de l'Egée au Caucase (334–31 av. J.-C.), 1995.

FLORIAN MATEI-POPESCU

Prisoners

A. Definition
B. Greek and Hellenistic worlds
C. Rome

A. DEFINITION

Captivity is the most frequent consequence of war alongside → death and wounding. Warfare was total, directed at the entire enemy 'people', including non-combatants: women, children and the elderly (→ Civilians; → Marriage), and sometimes even animals (Pol. 10,15,4f.; Liv. 42,63,10; Tac. Ann. 1,51; 14,37; [15]; [14]). The Greek term *aichmalotos* ('taken by the spear'), first regularly used as a term for prisoners of war in the Hellenistic period, then in the Roman Imperial period, expresses the concept particularly well [4]. Other attested terms are *andrapodon/captivus* and *captivi/mancipia*. Dig. 1,5,4,3 offers the following etymology: 'they – namely, slaves – are called *mancipia* because they were captured by the hand (*manu capere*) of the enemy'; *servus*, 'slave', comes from *servare* ('to keep protected') (Dig. 1,5,4,2). In law, slavery and captivity were thus understood as the human aspect of warfare (but cf. Tac. Ann. 2,21: 'no prisoners', and Tac. Ann. 12,17; Amm. Marc. 16,11,9; 24,4,25). Captivity applied to individuals, settler communities and political or ethnic units, and it went hand in hand with murder, plunder, rape, abduction, deportation and enslavement. The taking of prisoners is regarded as the most important exogenous source for the insitution of slavery. Classified as → booty, prisoners of war represented an economic commodity. At all periods of Antiquity, their sale to traders in the field or at markets, their contributions in the form of labour to agriculture, mining and the trades, their specialist knowledge, and the possibility of their gaining freedom through a 'ransom' paid by a third party – all of these made prisoners of war a lucrative category of spoils (*laphyron/leia/praeda/manubiae*) [12]; [14].

B. GREEK AND HELLENISTIC WORLDS

Prisoners of war in the Greek and Hellenistic worlds were the property of the victor. There was criticism of the enslavement of Greeks by Greeks (e.g. Aristot. Pol. 1255a 21–31, Pl. Rep. 469b–c), but throughout the wars of the *poleis*, especially the brutal Peloponnesian War (431–404 BC), captivity (killing, enslavement), forced labour, deportation and banishment were regarded as fully acceptable in dealing with defeated foes. Thucydides in particular offers several accounts of massacres in conquered *poleis*, with men executed and women and children sold into slavery (3,50; 3,68; esp. Melos/'Melian Dialogue': 5,84–116; slave markets with prisoners of war: 5,3,4; also Xen. Hell. 1,6,13–15). We know of 'Athenian slave labourers' in the quarries of Syracuse, who were prisoners of war from the Sicilian Expedition defeated in 413 BC (Thuc. 7,86,1; 7,87). Of course, there is also evidence for the freeing of prisoners by treaty (Thuc. 5,18,7; 5,35,4), as part of exchanges, or for the price of a ransom (*lytron*: first in Hom. Il. 24,686; prices determined by custom, treaty and/or status and military significance: Xen. Hell. 4,8,21; 6,2,36). Sale into slavery was more frequent than redemption, which took place in the context of treaties or at the initiative of individuals (Dem. Or. 53,6–10). Those involved generally had to produce the payment themselves. Treaties and undertakings between *poleis* offered some hope of redemption in cases of collective captivity. Anyone who won freedom with a loan and failed to pay it off faced debt servitude (Dem. Or. 53,11). Conversely, ransoms and exchanges were sometimes dispensed with (Thuc. 2,103,1; Polyaenus, Strat. 4,11,1), although diplomatic solutions were rare (Pol. 5,10,4). In the Hellenistic mercenary armies (3rd–1st centuries BC), prisoners from the enemy side were sometimes enlisted in the victorious army (Diod. Sic. 18,29,5). It was also possible, for instance in Hellenistic Egypt, that they might be settled (as *klerouchoi*: P. Petr. III 104) or else used as forced labourers (in mines: Diod. Sic. 3,12,2). They might be freed for a ransom (Diod. Sic. 20,84,6; Plut. *Philopoemen* 4,3), or they could be released as a political move by the ruler, who thereby gained popularity and renown (Diod. Sic. 19,85,3; Plut. *Demetrius* 17,1). Defeat, destruction, deportation – many prisoners of war shared the same fate from the Classical through the Hellenistic periods (Xen. Hell. 2,3,6; Pol. 2,58; 23,10,4–6). Mass enslavement and plunder in the territory of the enemy were customary under the → law of war (Pol. 5,11; but criticism of the plunder of Greek *poleis* e.g. here: Pol. 15,22,2), where such actions filled the war chest or secured → supplies for troops (Pol. 16,24,9). Still, the exchange of prisoners and their release, in exchange for ransom or not, were frequent components of peace agreements in the Hellenistic period (StV III, Register II Cc9, p. 418; [1]; [4]).

C. ROME

C.1. External enemies
C.2. Romans

War and captivity were 'everyday' matters in Rome. Enslavement was an instrument of warfare. All the way from Rome's expansion in Italy, beginning in the 4th century BC, and the epoch-making conflicts of the Punic Wars (→ Wars of note, K.) against Carthage, and the campaigns in the Hellenistic world (3rd/2nd cents. BC), to the Imperial period (in the Jewish War (→ Wars of note, E.) under Vespasian and Titus, and later Trajan (Dacian Wars; → Wars of note, C.) and Marcus Aurelius (Marcomannic Wars, 1st/2nd cents AD), a great many combatants and civilians on both sides became prisoners of war. All legal systems of Antiquity reduced prisoners of war to the status of slaves. Accordingly, regulatory treaties between polities, truces and peace agreements contained clauses concerning the fate of prisoners, deserters and defectors. This continued on all fronts during the 3rd century AD and through Late Antiquity, as attested by historical and legal sources and, less frequently, inscriptions (AE 1895, 58; SEG 49, 1989, 1379; 'Augsburg Victory Altar' = AE 1993, 1231b, which reports on the freeing of thousands of Italic prisoners of war from Iuthungian captivity: *excussis multis milibus Italorum captivorum*; [2]; [8]; [6]; [9]; [11]).

C.1. EXTERNAL ENEMIES

Capturing and enslaving enemy soldiers and civilians, for instance when a city was taken, were common practices. From the 3rd century onwards (Punic Wars, e.g. Liv. 32,26,6), prisoners of war began to come to Italy in large numbers – as resources for labour in the private sphere, in the trades and especially in agricultural production, they only added to the social inequality ('large estates'/'small-scale farmers') that came in the wake of Rome's expansion and the increasing demands on citizens (militia army), and that culminated in the collapse of the Republic. Between the 3rd and 1st centuries BC, mass enslavements (Liv. 41,28,8; 45,34,5) brought tens of thousands of prisoners of war to markets, for instance on Delos, the main trading centre for slaves in the Mediterranean [12]; [13]. Old and unusable prisoners might be killed, while the young were put to forced labour, as when Jews were abducted to work on the Corinth Canal in Greece in AD 67 (Jos. BI 3,539). There were still large numbers of prisoners of war in the Imperial period (e.g. Dacian Wars: 50,000). Given Rome's merciless practice of war, which did not spare women, children or the elderly (Pol. 10,15,4f.; Liv. 42,63,10), it is unsurprising that mass killings and suicides are reported, as in the notorious example of Masada (960 people, AD 74: Jos. BI 7,389–401; suicide of the besieged as an escape: see e.g. Xen. An. 4,7,1–14 for the 4th century BC). Cassius Dio (78,14,2, but see also Tac. Germ. 8) observes the hopeless condition of women prisoners of war: in AD 213, Germanic women in Roman captivity preferred to take their own and their children's lives rather than be sold [15]. On campaign, for instance after the plundering of a city, the general had the power to order the proceeds of the sale of booty, which included prisoners of war, to be distributed among the soldiers (Cic. Att. 5,20,5; Pol. 10,16f.; Liv. 45,34; see also Tac. Hist. 3,19,2). To this end, the army train included professional slave dealers [13]. Some prisoners of war, such as the craftsmen of Cartagena in 209 BC, were made 'public slaves' (*servi publici*: Pol. 10,17,6f.) by virtue of their skills. Occasionally, prisoners of war were not sold, but assigned to soldiers by the general (Caes. B Gall. 7,89,5). It was natural that official rituals, such as the triumphal processions, for which one condition was a tally of at least 5,000 enemy dead (Val. Max. 2,8,1; 'balance sheets' of dead and captured in *commentarii*, e.g. Plut. *Caesar* 15,5; high 'sale prices' of prisoners of war: Caes. B Gall. 2,33,7) and which involved the parading and killing of prisoners (enemy generals: Plut. *Marius* 12; Cass. Dio 40,41), and such as spectacles and executions in the circus or amphitheatre (e.g. prisoners of war as gladiators – e.g. Spartacus: App. Civ. 1,116), as well as official imagery (e.g. the column reliefs of Trajan and Marcus Aurelius in Rome), architecture (Trajan Forum/Arch of Constantine), and other genres of art (e.g. coins) made a point to put 'foreign' prisoners of war on display, emphasizing their defeat, deportation and maltreatment, temporarily and 'for all eternity' [5].

C.2. ROMANS

C.2.1. Attitudes to captivity and defeat
C.2.2. Right of return and peace treaties
C.2.3. Prisoners of war, deportation and technology transfer
C.2.4. Redemption and its consequences

C.2.1. ATTITUDES TO CAPTIVITY AND DEFEAT

Conversely, Roman soldiers and civilians could fall into enemy hands as a result of military conflict (cf. the famous *Vae victis* episode of 387 BC: Liv. 5,48,8f. or Verg. Aen. 2,354: the only certainties for the captured were an absence of certainty and 'humiliation rituals' such as being put under the yoke: *sub iugum mittere*). Legally, they became *servi hostium*, 'slaves to the enemy' (Gai. Inst. 1,129; Dig. 49,15,24). Such was not the case, however, in civil war. In Cremona in AD 69, the soldiers of Vespasian 'enslaved' the captured inhabitants after pillaging and plundering the city. When no buyers proved willing to purchase their 'fellow citizens', the victims were simply murdered (Tac. Hist. 3,34,2). *Captivitas* and the loss of liberty (*capitis deminutio maxima*; Dig. 49,15,5 pr.) signified the loss of all legal rights and relationships arising from Roman citizenship. This meant, for example, that marriages were annulled, property was forfeited, and the capacity to make a will or inherit was abolished. The prisoner was deprived of all legal standing. The legal status of a prisoner of war was equivalent to that of a dead person (Dig. 49,15,18), although their legal affairs were merely suspended, not permanently abolished. Livy (Liv. 22,59,1) was not alone in painting a bleak picture of the 'value' attached to those taken captive. No state had less respect for prisoners of war than Rome. Many examples illustrate the contempt in which Rome held Roman soldiers who were taken prisoner rather than – as their oath and the Roman military ethos demanded – winning victory or dying for the republic in the attempt (oath: Veg. Mil. 2,5,2; 'victory or death' ethos: Cic. Off. 3, 114; Pol. 6,58,2–9; preference for death in battle: Amm. Marc. 16,12,22). During the Punic Wars after the catastrophic Battle of Cannae (216 BC), the senate refused to buy the freedom of those taken captive (Liv. 22,59–61,4) – even though it was customary for peace treaties to provide for the handing over of prisoners of war (Pol. 1,62,8f.). Prisoners of war were tortured and tormented, killed or sacrificed (Flor. Epic. 30,24, e.g. in the wake of the Varian Disaster / *clades Variana*: Tac. Ann. 1,61,3f.). *Strategemata* sometimes recommend parading prisoners before the troops in a degrading way (naked, emaciated) to boost moral (Frontinus, Str. 1,11,17f.; Maur. Strat. 7,1,5), or else killing them and displaying the corpses as a deterrent (Frontinus, Str. 2,9,4). Officers opted for suicide to avoid being taken prisoner, for this was considered morally superior to captivity (Vell. Pat. 2,120f.; Cass. Dio 68,12,1–5). Ordinary soldiers, too, chose this means of avoiding the brutality of captivity (Jos. BI 6,186–187; Cass. Dio 40,52,2). Captivity implies → cowardice – thus, soldiers who survived the Varian Disaster and were released or bought out of captivity were treated as 'dishonorable' discharges (*missio ignominiosa*; after being bought free by relatives or private individuals, they had to continue their lives outside Italy: Cass. Dio 56,22,4), while those who escaped captivity went back into the army (Tac. Ann. 1,61,4) [2]; [9]. A freed or escaped prisoner of war (e.g. Cass. Dio 72,20,1) who came back across the 'threshold of the empire' (*limen*: Inst. Iust. 1,12,5) was permitted under the *ius postliminii/postliminium* (Dig. 49,15,4f.; 49,15,13; 49,15,19 [9]; [10]) – if he had been a soldier, it was first to be established whether he had deserted (*desertio, emansio*: punishments included slavery, Frontinus, Str. 4,1,20; or death: Jos. BI 3,103; Amm. Marc. 21,12,20) or defected to the enemy (*transfuga*: traitors: Dig. 49,15,5; 49,16,7; treaty clauses preventing the acceptance of *transfugae*: Cass. Dio 68,10,3) or whether he had been taken prisoner honorably (without surrendering, weapon in hand) – to regain his liberty and Roman citizenship. Beginning at least with the reign of Hadrian onwards, returnees were subjected to a test (*probatio*) before having their old rights restored, apparently because they were under suspicion of collaboration with the enemy. The test included an investigation of whether the returnee had remained with the enemy despite an opportunity of escape (Dig. 49,16,3,12; 49,16,5,5f.). Interestingly, rank, length of service, leadership experience, and leadership among comrades played a part in these deliberations. The *bonus miles*, the 'good soldier', did not lie, and thus did not come under suspicion with regard to his captivity. Where desertion or defection were established, the death penalty was the consequence, at least in wartime (Dig. 49,16,5,1). Defectors (*transfugae*) were treated as enemies and could expect torture and ignominious execution (Dig. 49,16,7). If it was found that a soldier or civilian could be classified as a 'defector', the *postliminium* was rendered ineffective (Dig. 49,15,19,4), and the 'renegade' (Dig. 4,5,5,1) was punished with death.

C.2.2. RIGHT OF RETURN AND PEACE TREATIES

The *postliminium*, the 'right to return home', generally treated the returned Roman citizen as if he had always been in possession of his rights (Gai. Inst. 1,129; Dig. 49,15,24), although this did not automatically extend to a marriage that had been in effect prior to his captivity. The returnee had no claim to retroactive pay, extraordinary payments or *donativa* (Dig. 49,16,5,6). Because prisoners of war were often in captivity for long periods (resold in enemy territory: Tac. ann. 2,24,4; Cass. Dio 72,16,2; freed after 40 years: Tac. Ann. 12,27,3; 100-year-old 'veteran': Amm. Marc. 24,1,10), neither discharge payments nor veteran privileges were denied after their return and *probatio*, if their regular term of service had ended while they were held prisoner (Dig. 49,16,3,12; 49,16,5,7). However, if the prisoner died in captivity, his rights were regarded as extinguished from the time of capture, and all the consequences in property and inheritance law that followed upon death came into effect as if the man had died in freedom. Peace treaties that contain a return clause sometimes attest to substantial numbers of Roman prisoners of war, for example 13,000 with the Quadi and Marcomanni, 100,000 with the Iazyges (Cass. Dio 71,11,2–4; 71,16,2; 72,3,1f. – Marcomannic Wars of Marcus Aurelius and Commodus [3]; [2]; [8]; [9]).

C.2.3. PRISONERS OF WAR, DEPORTATION AND TECHNOLOGY TRANSFER

Roman soldiers and artisans (and other 'specialists') captured in war, some of whom were deliberately 'chosen' and carried off, played their part in evening out a 'cultural gradient', particularly in the fields of military technology, construction, artisanal crafts and trades, and agriculture (Tac. Hist. 5,23,3; Faustus of Byzantium 5,4). The sources regularly mention truce agreements in which the return of such groups is stipulated – on all the 'major fronts' on which Rome fought, in its confrontations with the Germanic tribes, the Dacians and its great adversaries in the east, the Parthians and Sassanids, for whom the mass deportation and resettlement of Roman prisoners of war in certain cities was a frequent phenomenon, particularly in the reigns of Sapor I and Chosroes I in the 3rd and 6th centuries respectively (Plut. *Crassus* 31,7; Zon. 12,23; Amm. Marc. 19,6,2; 20,6,1; 7; Rome buying prisoners' freedom: Zos. 3,32,4; Amm. Marc. 25,7,9–11: Procop. Pers. 2,5,29f.). Sassanid public reliefs offer the only pictorial representations of Roman prisoners of war. The capture of Emperor Valerian (AD 260) was especially exploited in word and image for propaganda purposes here, and also in Sapor I's *Res gestae*. The latter account describes the emperor and others taken prisoner by Sapor in person (cf. *mancipia / manu capere* in Roman law: Dig. 1,5,4,3). Roman sources mention this event as a Roman digrace (Zos. 1,36,2). The emperor died in captivity and was not ransomed [11]; [7].

C.2.4. REDEMPTION AND ITS CONSEQUENCES

In the case of redemption (*redemptio ab hostibus*), the effect of the *postliminium* for the *captivus redemptus* was postponed until he had paid back or worked off the purchase price to the buyer (Cod. Iust. 8,50,17 pr.). Until then, the redeemed individual was the property of the *redemptor*. From the 2nd century onwards, so many Romans were in captivity that state treaties and family interventions no longer sufficed for their return and ransom. The work was increasingly taken on by traders, who then enjoyed the aforementioned 'retention rights' over the redeemed. In Late Antiquity, the church often became involved in buying the freedom of prisoners. From about AD 300 onwards, this came to be seen as a Christian duty, and liturgical equipment and apparel could even be sold to finance it (Cod. Iust. 1,2,21,2). Bishops often intervened personally (Procop. Pers. 2,5,29f. – 12,000 prisoners freed by the Bishop of Sergioupolis, 6th century AD; [10]; [14]).

☞ Civilians; Consequences of war; Marriage

BIBLIOGRAPHY
[1] A. BIELMAN, Retour à la liberté. Libération et sauvetage des prisonniers en Grèce ancienne. Recueil d'inscriptions honorant des sauveteurs et analyse critique, 1994   [2] K.R. BRADLEY, On Captives under the Principate, in: Phoenix 58, 2004, 298–318   [3] L. D'AMATI, Civis ab hostibus captus. Profili del regime classico, 2004   [4] P. DUCREY, Kriegsgefangene im antiken Griechenland, in: R. Overmans (ed.), In der Hand des Feindes. Kriegsgefangenschaft von der Antike bis zum Zweiten Weltkrieg, 1999, 63–81   [5] H. VON HESBERG, Die Wiedergabe von Kriegsgefangenen und Sklaven in der römischen Bildkunst, in: H. Heinen (ed.), Antike Sklaverei. Rückblick und Ausblick. Neue Beiträge zur Forschungsgeschichte und zur Erschließung der archäologischen Zeugnisse, 2010, 179–191   [6] J. KOLENDO, Les Romains prisonniers de guerre des Barbares au Ier et au IIe siècles, in: Index 15, 1987, 227–234   [7] N. LENSKI, Captivity and Romano-Barbarian Interchange, in: R.W. Mathisen / D. Shanzer (eds.), Romans, Barbarians, and the Transformation of the Roman World. Cultural Interaction and the Creation of Identity in Late Antiquity, 2011, 185–198   [8] L. DE LIBERO, Surrender in Ancient Rome, in: H. Afflerbach /

H. Strachan (eds.), How Fighting Ends. A History of Surrender, 2012, 29–38 [9] J. RÜPKE, Kriegsgefangene in der römischen Antike. Eine Problemskizze, in: R. Overmans (ed.), In der Hand des Feindes. Kriegsgefangenschaft von der Antike bis zum Zweiten Weltkrieg, 1999, 83–98 [10] M.V. SANNA, Nuove ricerche in tema di postliminium e redemptio ab hostibus (Biblioteca di studi e ricerche di diritto romano e storia del diritto 5), 2001 [11] O. STOLL, 'Nulla erunt bella, nulla captivitas'? Aspekte der Kriegsgefangenschaft und Gefangene als Mediatoren römischer Technologie im Sasanidenreich, in: S. Günther et al. (eds.), Pragmata. Beiträge zur Wirtschaftsgeschichte der Antike im Gedenken an Harald Winkel, 2007, 117–149 [12] H. VOLKMANN, Die Massenversklavungen der Einwohner eroberter Städte in der hellenistisch-römischen Zeit (Forschungen zur antiken Sklaverei 22), ²1990 [13] K.-W. WELWEI, Sub corona vendere. Quellenkritische Studien zu Kriegsgefangenschaft und Sklaverei in Rom bis zum Ende des Hannibalkrieges (Forschungen zur antiken Sklaverei 34), 2000 [14] K.-W. WELWEI, Kriegsgefangenschaft, in: H. Heinen (ed.), Handwörterbuch der Antiken Sklaverei 2, 2017, 1691–1697 [15] K.-H. ZIEGLER, Vae victis. Sieger und Besiegte im Lichte des Römischen Rechts, in: O. Kraus (ed.), 'Vae victis!' Über den Umgang mit Besiegten, 1998, 45–66.

OLIVER STOLL

Production system

A. Imperial period
B. Procurement of raw materials

Production of goods needed by the military in the Roman Republic was organized mainly through private enterprise. A clear example is offered by Liv. 28,45,14–21 on preparations for the African campaign of Scipio Africanus (→ Generals of note, O.). The system seems primarily to have been based on work contracts (*locatio conductio operum*) in which private contractors produced weapons and goods to state specifications (in general [1]). There was always scope, however, to turn to other means of production. After taking Carthago Nova, for instance, Scipio made 2,000 craftsmen into slaves of the Roman people (Liv. 26,47,2), with the promise of prompt manumission if they worked well for the republic. Nothing is known of the specialities of these craftsmen or exactly what work they did.

A. IMPERIAL PERIOD
Little is known of the production system under the Principate, suggesting that methods of the Republican period probably persisted [17]. In frontier regions that lacked the developed economic structures necessary to supply large armies, the services of the indigenous population were apparently utilized by force (cf. in general [11]).

This seems to have caused particular problems in regard to the supply of troops along the Rhine. In all probability, the Gallic communities involved were required to supply the army not only with provisions, but also with equipment, which imposed a severe burden and ultimately provoked what became known as the Revolt of Sacrovir [9]. The Gallic communities were probably required within a few years not only to make good the material losses from the Varian Disaster, but also to take on the heavy burdens (replacement of lost equipment, work related to shipbuilding, etc.) arising from the campaigns of Germanicus in AD 14–16.

Although the legions had plenty of qualified craftsmen available [21]; [23]; [26], the production of large series of weapons was mostly contracted out. During the High Imperial period, a system came into being in most regions whereby craftsmen were obliged to produce weapons and other goods for the military. In one such case, raw materials (iron and other substances) and probably charcoal were provided by the state. Cass. Dio 69,12,2 suggests the existence of such a system in Judaea ahead of the Bar Kochba Revolt. Jewish smiths secretly took possession of swords rejected by Roman quality control.

By contrast, there are indications in Britain of a central production site for weapons at Bath (ILS 2429 = RIB 156), assigned to the *legio XX Valeria victrix*. In other regions, private craftsmen seem to have been dominant, as suggested by the inscription CIL XIII 2828 = ILS 7047, which mentions manufacturers of armour (*loricarii*) from the territory of the Haedui who were in a working relationship with a *centurio* (*frumentarius*?) that is not defined in detail. There is also evidence of a private sword dealer (*negotiator gladiarius*) who may have supplied the *legio XXII Primigenia* at Mogontiacum (Mainz) with weapons (CIL XIII 6677 = ILS 2472).

Nothing is known of the composition of the workforce in these workshops. The man working at the *fabrica* in Bath may have been a soldier, while the papyrus ChLA X 409 (Egyptian *fabrica* attached to the *legio II Traiana*) reveals a mixed workforce of soldiers and persons (*pagani*) who were probably civilians [11].

In the Transpadana (Mediolanum), the inscription CIL XIII 6763 = ILS 1188 AD. along with Hdn. 7,12,1 (AD 238) attest to the existence of private weapons manufacturers who were probably not tied to the state by permanent contracts. Tacitus (Hist. 2,82,1) suggests something similar for the year AD 69 in the east of the empire. Both of these cases, however, represent unusual situations during a civil war, and it is not known whether these craftsmen were working to produce weapons at other times, too.

During Late Antiquity, there were state-organized weapons production centres in selected regions, probably assigned to units within the comitatensian army (Not. Dign. Or. 11,19–39; Not. Dign. Occ. 9,16–39), and each making specific types of weapon (armour, shields, bows, etc.) (cf. in general [6]; [14]; [18]). This new organization seems to date from the reign of Diocletian [6]; [14]. The craftsmen working at these centres were probably only obliged to meet certain production quotas within a specific period (cf. in this sense Cod. Theod. X 22,1, March 11, 374). In regard to free movement of labour, they were subject to state monitoring (tattooing of craftsmen). In return for their work, however, these craftsmen – like soldiers and civilians in public administration – received regular deliveries of foodstuffs (*annonae*) from the state. They were also entitled to produce from the private market after fulfilling their public supply obligations. Not even by the 6th century were all craftsmen who produced weapons subsumed under state workshops, as shown by Nov. 85 (June 25, 539) to Basilides, the *magister officiorum* (on the role of the *magister officiorum* cf. [4]). Of special interest is the detailed information regarding weapons that private individuals were seemingly still able to obtain without difficulty. This text also highlights the obligation to deliver weapons to the state arsenals.

B. PROCUREMENT OF RAW MATERIALS

Virtually all raw materials (wood, metal, leather, etc.) that were needed for producing military goods were of types that were not exclusively military, but were also widely used in civilian life. They only became 'military goods' when put to military use. It follows that the Roman military was in principle able to obtain almost all the goods and raw materials it needed on the free market. This could be done by direct requisition from producers or traders, or else through a compulsory purchase (*coemptio*) by the state. In the latter case, the Roman state was the only legitimate purchaser, and was accordingly able to influence the price.

The system for obtaining raw materials for the production of military goods in the Imperial period seems to have been a flexible one, heavily dependent on the economic conditions in the particular region where the military was stationed or deployed. In most regions, soldiers could gather certain basic materials such as wood directly from forests, where these were publicly owned. For instance, fatigue details of the Mainz legion felled timber in the Odenwald, for use in shipbuilding at Mainz [9].

Metals could be obtained either by fatigue details that operated warehouses and smelting operations, or from civilian metal producers who were required to supply a portion of their production to the state [24]. There is evidence in Britain for the army organizing mining operations. In the Balkans, major mining regions such as Bosnia-Herzegovina were utilized and placed under the direct administration of the Roman state [12]; [19]. The same was probably true of the *ferrum Noricum* from Styria.

In Late Antiquity, iron supplies were organized as a special form of tax on property (*ferraria praestatio*) (Basil. epist. 110; cf. also [3] and [14. 519]), that is, those liable to pay taxes had to deliver certain quantities of iron to state locations. A similar system seems to have been introduced for receiving bronze, which was generally obtained by melting down bronze statues and other bronze items, although this was explicitly prohibited by the government (Cod. Theod. XI 21,2,1, April 7, 371).

The flexible operation of this system is exemplified in the case of leather. From the early Imperial period, for instance, we know of the Germanic tribe of the Frisii, from whom Drusus during the conquest demanded tanned leather hides (*coria*) as tribute (*tributum*) (Tac. Ann. 4,72,1; cf. [13]), with the army being named specifically as the recipient. A *centurio* ('centurion') oversaw the delivery of these supplies. Nothing is said of the purposes to which these leather hides were put.

Later evidence from Vindolanda (II 343; cf. also [7. esp. 111–113]), on the other hand, shows the army supplying itself through the local market with raw materials (100 pounds of sinews), which craftsmen could then process in the camp.

The general tendency seems to have been for labour-intensive or particularly noxious components of the production process (e.g. the tanning of leather) to be contracted out to the civilian sphere, and for only the final phase of production to be performed by the military itself or under military supervision.

☞ Administration; Civilians; Equipment; Infrastructure; Legion; Supply

BIBLIOGRAPHY

[1] H. AIGNER, Zur Wichtigkeit der Waffenbeschaffung in der späten römischen Republik, in: GB 5, 1976, 1–24 [2] A.K. BOWMAN / A.D. THOMAS (ed.), The Vindolanda Writing-Tablets. Tabulae vindolandenses, vol. 2, 1994 [3] J. BURIAN, Canon metallicus, in: R. Stiehl / H.E. Stier (eds.), Beiträge zur alten Geschichte und deren Nachleben. Festschrift für Franz Altheim 2, 1970, 91–95 [4] M. CLAUSS, Der magister officiorum in der Spätantike (4.–6. Jahrhundert). Das Amt und sein Einfluß auf die kaiserliche Politik, 1981 [5] P. CONNOLLY, The Roman Saddle, in: M. Dawson (ed.), Roman Military Equipment. The Accoutrements of War. Proceedings of the Third Roman Military Equipment Research Seminar, 1987, 7–27 [6] A. DEMANDT et al. (eds.), Diokletian und die Tetrarchie. Aspekte einer Zeitenwende, 2004 [7] C. VAN DRIEL-MURRAY, The Leather Trades in Roman Yorkshire and beyond, in: P. Wilson / J. Price (eds.),

Aspects of Industry in Roman Yorkshire and the North, 2002, 109–123 [8] M. FORLIN PATRUCCO, Aspetti fiscalismo tardo-imperiale in Cappadocia. La testimonianza di Basilio di Cesarea, in: Athenaeum 51, 1973, 294–309 [9] P. HERZ, Zeugnisse römischen Schiffbaus in Mainz. Die Severer und die expeditio Britannica, in: JbRGZM 32, 1985, 422–435 [10] P. HERZ, Der Aufstand des Iulius Sacrovir (21 n.Chr.). Gedanken zur römischen Politik in Gallien und ihren Lasten, in: Laverna 3, 1992, 42–93 [11] P. HERZ, Die Versorgung des römischen Heeres mit Waffen und Ausrüstung, in: A. Eich (ed.), Die Verwaltung der kaiserzeitlichen römischen Armee. Studien für Hartmut Wolff, 2010, 111–132 [12] A.M. HIRT, Imperial Mines and Quarries in the Roman World. Organizational Aspects 27 BC– AD 235, 2010 [13] K.-P. JOHNE, Die Römer an der Elbe. Das Stromgebiet der Elbe im geographischen Weltbild und im politischen Bewusstsein der griechisch-römischen Antike, 2006 [14] A.H.M. Jones, The Later Roman Empire, 284–602. A Social, Economic and Administrative Survey, 1964 [15] J. KARAJANOPOULOS, Das Finanzwesen des frühbyzantinischen Staates, 1958 [16] Y. LE BOHEC, Das römische Heer in der späten Kaiserzeit, 2010 [17] R. MACMULLEN, Inscriptions on Armour and the Supply of Arms in the Roman Empire, in: AJA 64, 1960, 23–40 [18] M. NICASIE, Twilight of Empire. The Roman Army from the Reign of Diocletian until the Battle of Adrianople, 1998 [19] H.U. NUBER, Zwei bronzene Besitzermarken aus Frankfurt-Heddernheim. Zur Kennzeichnung von Ausrüstungsstücken des römischen Heeres, in: Chiron 2, 1972, 483–509 [20] J. OLDENSTEIN, Die Ausrüstung römischer Auxiliarsoldaten. Studien zu Beschlägen und Zierat an der Ausrüstung der römischen Auxiliareinheiten des obergermanisch-raetischen Limesgebietes aus dem zweiten und dritten Jahrhundert n.Chr., in: BRGK 57, 1976, 49–284 [21] F. PERGAMIN (ed.), La legislazione di Valentiniano e Valente (264–375) (Materiali per una palingenesia della costituzioni tardo-imperiali 2/4), 1993 [22] H. VON PETRIKOVITS, Militärische Fabricae der Römer, in: Actes du IXe congrès international d'études sur les frontiers romains, Mamaia 6.–13.9.1972, 1974, 399–407 (reprinted in: Beiträge zur römischen Geschichte und Archäologie, 1976, 612–619) [23] H. VON PETRIKOVITS, Römisches Militärhandwerk. Archäologische Forschungen der letzten Jahre, in: AAWW 111/1, 1974, 1–21 (reprinted in: Beiträge zur römischen Geschichte und Archäologie, 1976, 598–611) [24] M. POLFER, Production et travail du fer en Gaule du Nord et en Rhénanie à l'époque romaine. Le rôle des établissements ruraux, in: M. Polfer (ed.), Artisanat et production artisanales en milieu rural dans les provinces du nord-ouest de l'Empire romain. Actes du colloque organisé à Erpeldange (Luxemburg) les 4 et 5 mars 1999, 1999, 45–76 [25] P. RICHARDOT, La fin de l'armée romaine (284–476), 1998 [26] E. SANDER, Der Praefectus fabrum und die Legionsfabriken, in: BJb 162, 1962, 139–161 [27] D. SIM, Roman Chain-Mail. Experiments to Reproduce the Technique of Manufacture, in: Britannia 28, 1997, 359–371 [28] S.A. SIMON, Les Guerres daciques de Domitien et de Trajan. Architecture militaires, topographie, images et histoire, 2005 [29] A. ŠKREGO, The Economy of Roman Dalmatia, in: D. Davidson et al. (eds.), Dalmatia. Research in the Roman Province 1970–2001. Papers in Honour of J.J. Wilkes, 2006, 149–173 [30] P. STOFFEL, Über die Staatspost, die Ochsengespanne und die requirierten Ochsengespanne. Eine Darstellung des römischen Postwesens auf Grund der Gesetze des Codex Theodosianus und des Codex Iustinianus, 1993 [31] B. TREUKKER, Politische und sozialgeschichtliche Studien zu den Basilius-Briefen, 1961

[32] H. UBL, Was trug der römische Soldat unter dem Panzer?, in: Bayerische Vorgeschichtsblätter 71, 2006, 261–276.

PETER HERZ

Rank

A. Greek
B. Roman
C. Late Antiquity

A. GREEK

A.1. Hellenistic period
A.2. Antigonids
A.3. Ptolemies
A.4. Seleucids

A.1. HELLENISTIC PERIOD

Supreme command in all the Hellenistic armies lay with the king himself, and he appointed his closest confidants to senior ranks (on ranks and hierarchies in the Greek armies of earlier periods see e.g. [8]). Very little information is preserved regarding the occupants of lower ranks. For the Ptolemaic army, it is only rarely possible to trace careers, such as the ascent of cavalry officers to the position of *strategos* of a nome, or family traditions, whether in certain regions (see below) or fulfilling specific functions ([14. 130f.]: genealogies of Jewish officers). Despite the importance of personal relationships and family connections, it seems that, unlike in Rome, energetic newcomers were able to advance their careers to high officer rank. The promoting of ordinary soldiers to officer rank is attested in Ptolemaic Egypt (cf. e.g. *Prosopographia Ptolemaica* II 2185, 2747; VI 16975).

The most important ranks and functions of the tactical units along with their hierarchies as described by the classical tacticians (→ Military literature) seem largely to have been common to all the Hellenistic armies. However, these armies had no system of fixed command structures and tactical units, so their organization was characterized by a certain flexibility. At the same time, variations are apparent from the outset, and these were further accentuated by numerous reforms in army organization, above all by the introduction of additional levels of command. We know almost nothing of the junior officer ranks.

A.2. ANTIGONIDS

Our information about officer ranks in the Antigonid army is deficient. The senior commander in the Macedonian cavalry was a *hipparches* (Pol. 18,22,2). There were also other *hipparchoi* lower in the hierarchy (SEG 49, 722, l. 7). Infantry officers were *hegemones*. The basics of the phalanx command structure recorded by classical tacticians are confirmed by the battle arrangements at Amphipolis (ISE II 114) and a letter from Philip V to Archippus (ISE II 110). In descending order of rank, the officers were *strategos*, *chiliarches*, *tetrarches* and *lochagos*. As in the Ptolemaic army, the respective levels of hierarchy also had other officers *exo taxeon* ('outside the companies'), that is, with special, sometimes administrative functions. On the level of the the *speira* ('cohort'), there were five such officers (*semeiophoros*, 'standard-bearer'; *ouragos*, 'tail-leader'; *salpigtes*, 'trumpeter'; *hyperetes*, 'adjutant'; and *stratokeryx*, 'herald'), and on the level of the *strategia*, there were the *grammateus*, 'secretary'; *archyperetes*, 'chief adjutant'; and *cheiristes*, 'administrator' (→ Administration A.). Presumably, every *tetrarchia* of 64 men would have four officers, every *speira* would have 21 officers, and every *strategia* would have more than 336 officers [7. 76–79]; [6. 454].

Naturally, the commanders of the royal guards (*hypaspistai*, later *argyraspides* and *basilike ile*) and the *peltastai* ('light armed footsoldiers') came from the immediate entourage of the king. Senior officer posts (*chiliarchai* and *speirarchai*) were filled at a public meeting on merit and without regard for territorial responsibilities, by the king himself or by judges appointed by him (Arr. Anab. 3,16,11; Curt. 5,2,2–5), while the remainder (e.g. *lochagoi* and *tetrarchai*) were appointed on the level of cities or units in accordance with their regional recruitment bases [6. 444–459]; [7. 38–40].

A.3. PTOLEMIES

The Ptolemaic military hierarchy is still controversial, because many terms, such as *strategos*, *hegemon* and *hipparches* occur on more than one level. Often, it is only possible to achieve clarity when they are combined with other titles or functions or titles of courtly rank, or are found within a wider context [9].

At the top of the hierarchy undoubtedly were the so-called eponymous officers; each soldier was assigned to one of them (i.e. 'one of the men of ~'). These officers were members of the highest aristocracy of Alexandria. It has recently been suggested that their function was not – as is generally assumed – exclusively eponymous, but that they served as supreme commanders (under the *strategos*) [4. 158f.].

Below them in Egypt were the *strategoi* of one or more nomes, to whom the troops in those nomes were answerable. Their rank depended on the size and status of their territories. Despite the evolution of their office into an instrument of civilian administration, they seem to have retained some military functions until the 1st century BC [4. 157f.]. Following the great revolt in Upper Egypt (206–186 BC), the *strategoi* were put under the command of an *epistrategos* (→ Army, B.).

The occasional titles preserved in papyri and the ranks attested by the classical tacticians allow the listing of the following officer ranks for the cavalry – in descending order and by number of soldiers under their command: *hipparches* (of the *epitagma*), *telarches*, *ephipparches*, *hipparches* (of a *hipparchia*), *epilarches*, *ilarches*, *epilochagos*, *lochagos* and *dekanikos*. Officer ranks for the infantry were the *chiliarchos*, *pentakosiarchos*, *syntagmatarches* and *taxiarches*, and after the restructuring of the infantry (→ Army, B.), the *chiliarchos*, *hegemon* (of a *syntagma/semeion*), *hekatontarches*, *pentekontarches* and *ouragos* [13. 50f.]. Standard-bearers (*semeiophoroi*) and heralds (*kerykes*) are also attested. High-ranking *laarchai* (in courtly ranks 'one of the first friends') headed the units made up mainly, but not exclusively, of Egyptian *machimoi*.

Garrison commandants were *phrourarchoi*, but *phrourarchos* was a military rank rather than a function, so not all garrison commandants were permitted to use the title. Their status within the military hierarchy depended on the garrison they commanded. For example, the *phrourarchoi* of Philae and Syene in Upper Egypt in the 2nd century BC held the second-highest courtly title, 'one of the first friends', while other *phrourarchoi* at the same period did not.

In the Ptolemies' external land possessions, the governor had command of the forces and held the title of *strategos*. These governors outranked the Egyptian nome *strategoi*: the *strategoi* of Cyprus, for instance, bore the highest court title, 'kinsman [of the king]' (*syngenes*). These governors belonged to the king's closest circle, and some families provided several *strategoi* in a region (e.g. that of Aetus in Cilicia in the 3rd century BC [12]). Serving under them were the fortress commandants (*phrourarchoi*), whom the king also appointed.

We also know of assorted *hegemones* and *hipparchai exo taxeon* (*hipparchai* 'outside the companies'), who did not necessarily outrank cavalry or infantry officers. Their titles alone permit no inferences, but some of them did belong to the highest authorities in Alexandria.

A.4. SELEUCIDS
Because of the shortage of documentary sources, we only have detailed information about senior officer ranks, and the hierarchy of the military terms is unclear. For lower ranks, we know only the titles. Nothing is known of the identities, backgrounds or careers of these officers.

The supreme commander (*strategos*) was the king, who would sometimes leave the actual command in battle to a deputy or provincial governor. Every unit had its own commanders, who were generally referred to simply as *hegemon* (for the infantry) or *hipparchos* (for the cavalry). In his function as a leader of a company of men, an officer (including the king) would also be called *strategos*. The commander of the elephant unit was addressed as *elephantarches* (App. Syr. 32; 2 Macc 14,12), and the naval commander was addressed as *nauarchos* (Pol. 5,43,1; IEry 28). The ethnic contingents were led by their own commanders, some of whom took their titles from the people group itself (e.g. the Mysians were commanded by a *mysarchos*). Commanders of the individual contingents seem to have answered directly to the king or supreme commander.

The highest commands were mainly held by Greeks and senior Macedonians, although some defecting Ptolemaic mercenary commanders joined them following the Fourth Syrian War (219–217 BC). Many officers seem to have come from the small circle of Macedonian nobility at court (see e.g. Pol. 5,82,8; 5,82,13), but it was also possible in principle to advance on merit. No established career paths or principles are evident, either because of a lack of documentation or simply because none existed (thus [2. 64–67]; [5. XI]; but see [1. 85–93]). Elevation to higher positions, at any rate, was not through incremental promotion, but by royal appointment. At a certain level, being in the immediate presence of the king was necessary in order to achieve further promotion. In the case of appointments to governor positions, however, military experience does seem to have been an important consideration [3].

☞ **Administration, B. Hellenistic period; Army, B. Hellenistic period; Officers, A. Greek**

BIBLIOGRAPHY
[1] B. BAR-KOKHVA, The Seleucid Army. Organization and Tactics in the Great Campaigns, 1976 [2] E. BIKERMAN, Institutions des Séleucides, 1938 [3] L. CAPDETREY, Le pouvoir séleucide. Territoire, administration, finances d'un royaume hellénistique (312–129 avant J.-C.), 2007 [4] C. FISCHER-BOVET, Army and Society in Ptolemaic Egypt, 2014 [5] J.D. GRAINGER, A Seleukid Prosopography and Gazetteer, 1997 [6] M.B. HATZOPOULOS, Macedonian Institutions under the Kings, vol. 1: A Historical and Epigraphic Study, 1996 [7] M.B. HATZOPOULOS, L'organisation de l'armée macédonienne sous les Antigonides. Problèmes anciens et documents nouveaux, 2001 [8] P. HUNT, Military Forces, in: P. Sabin et al. (eds.), The Cambridge History of Greek and Roman Warfare, 2007, 108–146 [9] L. MOOREN, La hiérarchie de cour ptolémaïque. Contribution à l'étude des institutions et des classes dirigeantes à l'époque hellénistique, 1977 [10] S. SCHEUBLE-REITER, Die Katökenreiter im ptolemäischen Ägypten, 2012 [11] N.V. SEKUNDA, The Antigonid Army, 2013 [12] J.D. SOSIN, P.Duk.inv. 677. Aetos, from Arsinoite Strategos to Eponymous Priest, in: ZPE 116, 1997, 141–146 [13] E. VAN'T DACK, La littérature tactique de l'antiquité et les sources documentaires, in: E. Van't Dack (ed.), Ptolemaica selecta. Études sur l'armée et l'administration lagides, 1988, 47–64 [14] E. VAN'T DACK, Les armées en cause, in: E. Van't Dack et al., The Judean-Syrian-Egyptian Conflict of 103–101 B.C. A Multilingual Dossier Concerning a 'War of Sceptres', 1989, 127–136.

SANDRA SCHEUBLE-REITER

B. Roman

B.1. Origins
B.2. Republic
B.3. Imperial period

Like all armies in all eras, the Roman army was organized to serve the interests of state, and it reflected the society of its day. However, it displayed one peculiarity. Until the early 3rd century AD, the army was led entirely by the aristocracy.

B.1. Origins

As is well known, Roman origins are obscure and interwoven with myth and legend, which conceals realities and requires decipherment. All that is known for certain is that the king commanded the army personally, although he had nobles represent him for certain misisons, especially when he agreed to have a battle decided by proxy through a duel of heroes. Accounts from the *Iliad* give a good idea of the situation in such cases. After a revolution that replaced the monarchy with what was essentially an aristocratic regime (traditionally dated to 509 BC), power went to two consuls, who functioned as political leaders in Rome and supreme commanders of the army. Tribunes who functioned as senior → officers and centurions who functioned as subaltern officers also emerged at a very early date.

B.2. Republic

The latter part of the Early Republican period (509–201) and the Middle (201–133) and Late Republican periods (133–31 BC) were characterized by increasing warfare [1]; [2]; [4]; [5]; [6]. This increase was driven by the expansion of Roman conquests and attacks from outside (e.g. Hannibal (→ Generals of note, G.)). The Roman state found itself having to mobilize three or four armies at once. The first difficulty was to find sufficient men to command these armies at the same time. At first, the forces were under the command of the two consuls – alone, according to tradition –, with the later addition of praetors, then extraordinary magistrates, proconsuls and propraetors. In especially grave circumstances, overall military command was handed to a dictator. Without doubt the most famous of these was Fabius 'the Delayer' (*Cunctator*), so called for the strategy he employed against Hannibal. This was a highly illustrious title ('dictator'), and remained so until its abuse by Sulla and especially Caesar (→ Generals of note, C.). The dictator appointed a legate, called the 'master of horse' (*magister equitum*), whose authority was not limited to the cavalry: he supported his superior at all times, everywhere and in all functions. All such commanders developed the habit of entrusting legates (*legati*) with various assignments. Caesar usually put a legate in charge of each legion during the Gallic Wars (→ Wars of note, D.). Among the lower ranks of junior officers and centurions, a hierarchy developed from the moment the legion was divided into three ranks. The equivalent of the centurion in the cavalry was the decurion.

This command structure had three characteristics that later became still more pronounced. At first, every officer had a council of war (*consilium*), which he was required to consult before every major decision, but obviously not during the battle itself. He was required to hear the council, but not necessarily to follow its recommendations. Curio, for example, consulted his war council in Africa before engaging with the enemy. Secondly, the Romans had a large leadership cadre. Every soldier in battle was subject to the attention of one or more superiors. Finally, and *pace* the textbooks of the 20th century, these officers were of great value. There may have been no military academies like Saint-Cyr or West Point, but the training given to young nobles (with lots of sports and history lessons) did prepare them for war.

The navy was long seen as a weakness of the Roman military, and it is true that there was no standing → fleet in the Republican period. However, the *coloniae maritimae* and some allies, especially those from the ports of Southern Italy (*socii navales*), provided ships and crews whenever needed. Special magistracies were created to command them, the *quaestores classici* ('naval quaestors'), and the *duoviri navales* ('admirals').

More attention has been paid to land forces. They were divided into legions and units of the *socii* ('confederates'), the latter provided by the Latins and other peoples living in Italy.

The legions were commanded by tribunes and centurions. During the final phase of the Republic, some ranks appeared that we might call junior officers, although the term is not entirely fitting: perhaps they would better be called → specialists. In Latin they were known as *principales*. They were exempt from heavy labour. This group included the standard-bearers, who were responsible for the eagle and the *signum* (the *signum* belonged to a maniple, a group of two centuries – it is uncertain whether the cohort that superseded it had one or not). There were certainly other functions, too.

Legions were supported by units of the *socii*, totalling 70,000 cavalry and 700,000 infantry. The latter, comprising both heavy and light infantry, were divided into cohorts of 500 men, each under the command of a cohort prefect (*praefectus cohortis*). The cohorts were grouped into wings of 4,000–5,000 men, each answering to a confederate prefect (*praefectus sociorum*). The vocabulary does little to explain the actual conditions, since mounted troops were divided into wings of 300 [6] or 900 men (Pol. 6,20; 6,26; 6,30), each commanded by a *praefectus sociorum* and 30 decurions under his command.

B.3. IMPERIAL PERIOD

The situation became more complex in the early Imperial period. Control over soldiers during battle was increased, and army organization in general was refined [3]. Under Augustus, the military was finally professionalized and became a standing army – two trends that had largely been underway in the latter phase of the Republic. Augustus also set up permanent garrisons.

Supreme command was in the hands of the emperor, who might lead the troops himself (e.g. Trajan) or delegate the task to a family member (Drusus and Tiberius under Augustus) or a competent general (Vespasian for Nero). In Rome and in the field, he was assisted by the Praetorian Prefect(s). These commanders of the imperial guard soon became trusted advisors, although occasionally prone to excess (Sejanus with his plot against Tiberius). The Praetorian Prefect was a member of the *princeps*' council (*consilium principis*), even leading it in the absence of the emperor.

The key forces present in the city of Rome were the nine Praetorian cohorts, the three urban cohorts and the seven cohorts of the *vigiles*, 'watchmen' (numbers and strengths vary over the centuries, but were always of approximately this order). Each of these corps was commanded by a prefect, and the Praetorian Prefect outranks the two others, the urban prefect and the prefect of *vigiles*. Each unit, a cohort of about 500 men, was led by a tribune and six centurions. As in the legions, there are records of *principales*, to be discussed below.

Starting with the reign of Augustus, the real strike forces of the Roman army were stationed along the → borders. They comprised 25–30 legions, supported by auxiliary units.

The frontier provinces had armies of one or more legions with auxiliary units, or else armies of auxiliary units alone. Three cases were distinguished: provinces with several legions, those with one legion, and those with no legions. In all cases, the governor exercised civil and military authority in the name of the emperor. Alongside his body of soldiers, he also had at his disposal a limited administrative apparatus (no more than a few dozen imperial slaves and freedmen). With their help, he administered justice and supervised tax collection, the maintenance of temples and roads, and similar projects. If he commanded more than one legion (Britannia, Germania, Moesia, Syria etc.), he would be a member of the senate with the title 'legate of the emperor in place of a praetor' and would already have held the consulship once (*legatus Augusti pro praetore, consularis*). In most cases, he was called simply 'consular'. He had under his command people who had the same title as his own and who came from the same background, but who held a lower rank: former praetors who were called *legati Augusti propraetore* or simply *legati legionis*. If he had only one legion (Numidia, Dacia etc.), the governor was simply a *legatus Augusti propraetore* and was counted among the former praetors. In provinces with no legion but only auxiliary units (Mauretania etc.), the governor would be an equestrian and called *procurator Augusti*.

Each → legion (cf. also → Army) was headed by one legate and seven senior officers. The first was the *tribunus laticlavius* ('broad-striped tribune'), who would be a son of a senator. After him came *equites* (members of the equestrian order): the camp prefect (*praefectus castrorum*) took care of the buildings and upheld discipline; the five *tribuni angusticlavii* ('narrow-striped tribunes') each commanded two cohorts. The duties of the *tribunus sexmestris* ('six-month tribune') are unclear, but he may have commanded the cavalry. Next came the subordinate officers, the centurions, who were mostly from the urban nobility, although there were exceptions. First among them, the *primus pilus* ('chief centurion') or *primipilus*, was consulted in discussions and his opinion was highly regarded. The others followed a career path that is very difficult for historians to reconstruct: as they advanced, they changed position both within the cohort and from one cohort to another – towards the most prestigious first cohort. There were supposed to be only 59 of them, the same number as of centurions, but larger numbers are found because some were consigned to isolated posts.

The positions that proliferated the most in this period were the *principales* or *immunes*, that is, those who were exempt from hard labour. Many of these were given more pay: some received one and a half times basic pay (*sesquiplicarii*), others received double pay (*duplicarii* or *duplarii*), and one instance is known of triple basic pay (*triplicarius*). Their total numbers are estimated at about 500 in a legion of 5,000, and they took on many jobs, in four categories:

(1) Military assignments in the strict sense: (1a) Weapons. Although the infantry had the key role in battle, the legion also needed its horsemen, 120 in number. It also had artillerymen, all called 'men of the *ballistae*' (*ballistarii*). (1b) Orders were conveyed through military music (*tubicines*, *cornicines* and *bucinatores*) and movements of the standard (*aquilifer* and *signiferi*). (1c) Various watchmen were responsible for security. (1d) A great many quartermasters and *principales* supervised → training.

(2) Services: (2a) Several soldiers dealt with supplies, mainly receiving provisions and storing them in the camp warehouses. (2b) Engineers and the workshop. The geometer (*librator*) and

surveyor (*mensor*) helped with building the camp. The workshop (*fabrica*) enabled weapons to be repaired. (2c) → Medical corps. Each legion had a field hospital (*valetudinarium*) with physicians (*medici*), archivists (*librarii*) and *capsarii* (who managed a chest containing medications and recipes). (2d) Priests served in every unit.

(3) Administrative duties (→ Military service; → Military literature): Every camp commandant, regardless of the importance of his garrison, was informed at all times of the personnel, supplies and materials at his disposal. The Roman military was obsessed with archiving, which it entrusted to *librarii*, *act(u)arii* and *notarii*, to mention only the best-known titles.

(4) Judiciary and policing: Every camp had a policing post (*statio*); military police work was the job of *statores*. Where misdeeds required judges, these were chosen from the ranks of the officers.

The commanders of the auxiliary units (→ Auxiliaries) were directly answerable to the legionary legate if stationed in a province with a legion. Otherwise, they answered directly to the equestrian procurator. Units of 500 men were commanded by prefects, units of 1,000 men were commanded by tribunes. Under them were decurions in the cavalry and centurions in the infantry. A group of *principales* is attested for every corps.

Beginning in the reign of Augustus, the navy became a permanent institution. It was divided into two major fleets (at Misenum and Ravenna), which were commanded by high-ranking prefects and provincial squadrons. The *praepositus reliquationis* ('officer in charge of the reserve') was in charge of the reserves or the depot. A fleet was commanded by a navarch, and each vessel – regardless of size – was commanded by a subaltern officer with the rank of centurion. *Principales* are attested.

Officers' status remained unaltered throughout the Principate (1st-2nd cents.). As discussed above, their numbers even grew, and soldiers were accordingly well supported in battle. However, the notorious 'Crisis of the 3rd Century' brought changes. The senatorial officers vanished, doubtless because their families feared losses and because the state was neither disposed to lose its aristocracy nor eager to pay their high salaries.

☞ Administration, C. Roman; Officers, B. Roman

BIBLIOGRAPHY

[1] G. BRIZZI, Studi militari romani, 1983 [2] G. CASCARINO, L'esercito romano. Armamento e organizzazione, vol. 1: Dalle origini alla fine della Repubblica, 2007 [3] A. VON DOMASZEWSKI, Die Rangordnung des römischen Heeres, Introduction, Corrections and Additions by B. Dobson, ²1967 [4] P. FRACCARO, Opuscula, vol. 2, 1957 [5] P. FRACCARO, Opuscula, vol. 4, 1975 [6] J. HARMAND, L'armée et le soldat à Rome de 107 à 50 avant notre ère, 1967 [7] L. KEPPIE, The Making of the Roman Army, from Republic to Empire, ²1998 [8] Y. LE BOHEC (ed.), La hiérarchie (Rangordnung) de l'armée romaine sous le Haut-Empire, 1995 [9] Y. LE BOHEC, L'armée romaine sous le Bas-Empire, 2006 [10] G.R. WATSON, The Roman Soldier, 1969 (reprint 1985) [11] G. WEBSTER, The Roman Imperial Army of the First and Second Centuries AD, ⁴1998

YANN LE BOHEC

C. LATE ANTIQUITY

C.1. Sources
C.2. General developments
C.3. The 'old-style' rank system
C.4. The 'new-style' rank system
C.5. Function descriptors
C.6. Careers

Despite intensive recent efforts by scholars, the ranks of the later Roman army have not been explained to the same degree as for the early Imperial period. The sources are abundant, but less than revealing, leaving many details unclear and controversial. In the case of some terms, it is even difficult to determine if they refer to a rank, a function (post) or a pay grade. To establish duties and competencies, we must often rely on uncertain derivations from etymology. Beginning from the division into a *militia armata* ('military public service') and a *militia inermis* ('civil public service'), which took effect across the whole empire around AD 308, military ranks were also reflected in the civilian *officiales* ('offices').

C.1. SOURCES

Our knowledge of ranks for Late Antiquity is drawn from literary, patristic and juristic sources and from epigraphic and papyrological evidence. Military textbooks supply abundant information, but it is sometimes problematic, because antiquarian erudition, wishful thinking and recommendations intermingle with statements about actual conditions (→ Military literature). Vegetius, in his *Epitoma rei militaris*, which was probably written in the reign of Valentinian II (375–392), is vague in terms of temporal horizons when he discusses the (Severan?) *antiqua ordinatio legionis* ('old order of the legion') as both the starting point and model for his analysis of the situation in his own day. John Lydus, *De magistratibus* (mid-6th cent.), gives a detailed description of the civil *officium* ('chancellery') of the Praetorian Prefect of his time, but his comprehensive list (1,46) of military ranks and posts refers to the legion of the time before the Tetrarchy. Maurice's *Strategikon* (c. 600) is intended as a structuring manual for the cavalry in particular [25]. In order to describe the organizational model in general terms and in isolation from the various categories of troops, it makes use of an artificial terminology rather than the rank and regiment titles that were in use at the time [23. 397f.]. Even well-informed historians such as Ammianus Marcellinus (last quarter 4th cent.) and Procopius of Caesarea (mid-6th cent.) avoid specialist military jargon in favour of anachronistic, archaizing expressions. Inscriptons on solders' gravestones from the 3rd, 4th and early 5th centuries deliver more precise information.

For the later centuries, the Constitutions of Anastasius (491–518), which are preserved in epigraphic form, are of tremendous importance, especially the edict (c. 491–502) against corruption in giving promotions found at Perge [20]: Appended to the *sermo* of the emperor (A 1–71) and the corresponding *edictum* of the *magister militum* ('Master of Soldiers'; B 1–71) is a *gnosis* (*notitia*) on the pay schedule (C 1–29), which supplies the most reliable information on the ranks in a legion of Late Antiquity. There are also many rank titles and descriptions of functions from the Late Antique army contained in imperial constitutions (Cod. Theod., Cod. Iust.) and papyri, particularly contract documents, where soldiers give their full titles, and documents from the military chancelleries (e.g. ChLA XLIII 1248 [399]). Because sources of this kind presuppose knowledge of the terminology, they give no explanations, but they do attest to the essential continuity of the rank system established around AD 300 until at least the early 7th century.

C.2. General developments

One peculiarity of the Late Roman army was that two rank systems coexisted side by side. Regiments that had been established prior to the Tetrarchy according to the traditional scheme of *legiones* ('legions'), *alae* ('auxiliaries') and *cohortes* ('cohorts') retained the 'old style' rank system. Units that were recruited for the mobile field army from the mid-3rd century onwards followed a 'new-style' rank system that was used for the infantry (*auxilia*) and cavalry regiments (*equites, vexillationes, cunei*) alike. Constantine seems to have standardized what were originally regionally diverse systems when he was sole emperor (from 324). The rank system was always tied to the type of regiment, even after units were divided into the three major categories of the mobile field army (*comitatenses*, first in Cod. Theod. 7,20,4, AD 325), the border army (*limitanei*, by AD 363, Cod. Theod. 12,1,56) and the guard (*palatini*, a category in its own right first in Cod. Theod. 8,1,10, AD 365). There was, however, a clear gradation in rank and status between the *palatini*, *comitatenses* and *limitanei*, which impacted the prestige and pay of their soldiers.

The most senior ranks – *tribunus* and *primicerius* – and the highest-ranking functions (posts) – *vicarius* and *campidoctor* (see below) – occurred in both the 'old-style' and 'new-style' rank systems. Departing from traditional appellations, *tribunus* in the late 4th century became the universal title for commanders of any regiments of cavalry and infantry. From the mid-5th century onwards, the honorific title of the tribunes, *comes*, was more and more frequently conflated with the rank title itself (*comes vel tribunus, komes etoi tribunos*), and eventually replaced it from the 6th century onwards. After the tribunes, the second most senior rank was the *primicerius*, in both the infantry and cavalry [23. 400f.]. Men rose from the ranks to become *primicerius* after many years of service and multiple promotions. Generally, the *primicerius* was an experienced soldier who attained this prestigious rank, which placed its holder in charge of regimental administration, just before his *missio* ('discharge from service'). On ranks in the Late Roman army, see in general [5]; [6. 107–151]; [12. vol. 2, 633–649]; [10. vol. 1, 75–81]; [27]; [16]; [23]; [28. 219–236].

C.3. The 'old-style' rank system

C.3.1. Legions
C.3.2. Alae
C.3.3. Cohortes

Units that had been founded before about AD 290–300 retained their traditional structure, regardless of whether they were classified as belonging to the guards, field army or border army. For instance, a legion always preserved its 'old-style' rank system, no matter whether it was assigned to the *comitatenses* or *limitanei*.

C.3.1. Legions

Our knowledge of the ranks in a Late-Antique legion is on firm footing thanks to the *gnosis* with the pay schedule in the inscription of Anastasius at Perge (c. 491–502) (C 1–29; [20]). The description of the *antiqua ordinatio legionis* given in Veg. Mil. 2,7f., which largely agrees with this, supplements it. The papyrus dossier of the soldier Fl. Patermuthis of Syene shows that the ranks of the legions remained essentially unchanged until around AD 600 [14]. However, many legions of Late Antiquity developed out of detachments and off-shoots from existing legions, so that they were considerably smaller than legions of the Principate. The legions established under the Tetrarchy still followed the old model with ten cohorts [3]; [2], and the Perge inscription confirms that this remained the case: all standard-bearers were ten in number, and the highest ranks (*ordinarii, Augustales, Flaviales*) were always multiples of ten. The inscription also testifies to a highly sophisticated rank system that (ideally) divided almost 1,100 individuals of various gradations into two dozen ranks.

During the 4th century, a *legio limitanea* was commanded by a *praefectus*, and a *legio palatina* or *comitatensis* was commanded by a *tribunus* (on the terminology see → Army, D.). The title *tribunus* later became established everywhere. In second place after the *tribunus numeri*, according to the Perge inscription, is the *tribunus minor*. This agrees with Veg. Mil. 2,7,1, where the *tribunus maior* is the highest rank for the legion, nominated *per epistulam sacram imperatoris iudicio* ('by letter from the emperor on the basis of a decision by the emperor'). He was followed by the *tribunus minor*, who achieved this post *ex labore* ('by diligent service'). This was probably the *primicerius*, risen through the ranks, mentioned elsewhere as the highest rank after the *tribunus*. The term *tribunus minor* refers to his function as deputy (*vicarius*) to the *tribunus maior* (see below).

The tactical subsidiary units of the legion remained the centuries. Some *centuriones* began to be called *ordinarii* or *ordinati* in the early 3rd century, but exactly what this meant is controversial [11]. The traditional hierarchy of the *centuriones* (which was divided into 59 steps under the Principate) is no longer mentioned after the Tetrarchy (AE 1981, 777), but there were still *centuriones* in the legions (e.g. P. Lond. V 1722 [530]; 1734 [526–575], P. Münch. I 8 [540]). The Constitution of Anastasius on the Perge inscription and Veg. Mil. 2,7 list *ordinarii*, *Augustales* and *Flaviales* in descending order after the two *tribuni*. The *gnosis* in the inscription lists 20 men as *ordinarii*, the highest-ranking centurions. The *Augustales* are divided into three pay categories, the highest of which also numbers 20 men, with the others at 30 and 70 respectively. The *Flaviales* also had two pay groups of 60 and 140 men respectively. In the case of the *Augustales*, the presumption on the basis of Veg. Mil. 2,7,3 (*Augustales ... ordinariis iuncti sunt*, 'the *Augustales* are joined with the *ordinarii*') and P. Münch. I 8 ([540] *ordinarios augystalios*) is that they belonged to the *ordinarii* (*centuriones*), and the same with the *Flaviales* (*Flaviales item, tamquam secundi Augustales*: 'also the *Flaviales*, as it were *Augustales* of second rank') [13]. But given their large numbers (200 *Flaviales*, 120 *Augustales*), it seems implausible to classify them all as *ordinarii* in the centurion ranking. Arcadius was said to have introduced the *Augustales* (Lydus, Mag. 3,10).

After these ranks, the *gnosis* in the inscription lists *optiones*, who were surprisingly few in number at just ten. After them, Veg. Mil. 2,7,3f. gives the various standard-bearers: *aquilifer*, *imaginarii*, *signiferi* (*quos nunc draconarios vocant*): 'the bearers of the legionary eagle, the bearers of the imperial images and the standard-bearers (who are now called bearers of the dragon standard')

(→ Specialists B.). The Perge inscription does not mention an *aquilifer* (perhaps an anachronism on Vegetius' part), but lists ten *signiferi*, ten *vexillarii* ('flag-bearers') and ten *imaginiferi* (= *imaginarii*). The imperial *sermo* (A 52–53) and the edict of the *magister militum* (B 55–56) mention that the *draconarii* (an umbrella term for the assorted standard-bearers) were under the authority of a *magister draconum* [29], who exercised this function (*chreia*) for two years before returning to his former position (B 58–60).

The next group listed in the inscription and Veg. Mil. 2,7,8 is the signal-blowers (*tubicines*, *cornicines*, *bucinatores*) and the weapons trainers *armaturae duplares* (who received double *annona* ('rations/pay') and *armaturae semissales* (who received one-and-a-half times *annona*; Veg. Mil. calls them *simplares*, 'recipients of single pay'). As tactical ranks, they were – according to A 55–56 and B 56–58 – under the *campidoctor*. This title (like the *magister draconum*) described a function (not a rank) and does not appear in the rank system (see below). Other ranks (or positions) mentioned in the inscription and by Vegetius are *librarii* ('bookkeeper'), *beneficiarii* ('seconded (to administrative duties)'), *mensores* ('quartermasters'). The *metatores* ('surveyors'), *tesserarii* and *campigeni* (subaltern ranks, both anachronistic?) appear only in Vegetius. Besides the aforementioned ranks, the inscription also includes, together with the *optiones*, the *veredarii* ('couriers') in two pay categories, a *praeco* ('herald'), and *torquati semissales* and *bracchiati semissales* (wearers of torques and arm clasps, as emblems of valour), who received one-and-a-half times regular pay. Veg. Mil. 2,7,10 also mentions the ranks *torquati duplares* and *simplares* (torque-wearers receiving double and single pay), which were awarded for bravery. However, given that the inscription lists 136 *torquati* and 156 *bracchiati*, this etymology seems questionable. Veg. Mil. 2,7,1 and 2,7,11 refers anachronistically to this entire body of individuals as *principales*, and in accordance with the newer terminology (*ut proprio verbo utar*, 'that I may use the correct term'), as *principia*.

Beneath these ranks were the *munifices* (regular soldiers), for whom the number given in the inscription is lost. Then came *clerici* and *deputati*. There seem to have been army chaplains in the staff of the army from the time of Constantine onwards [24]. Separated from the hierarchy of ranks, the *clerici* were in a category of their own, which is also highlighted in CPR XXIV 15 (5th cent.). *Deputati* were generally soldiers sent out with raw materials to supply the army. Maur. Strat. 2,9, however, describes them as orderlies charged with bringing back the wounded from the battlefield. In Late Antiquity, too, the smallest administrative and tactical unit remained the *contubernium*, the 'tent fraternity'. Maur. Strat. 12.B,9,20–29 still attests to the traditional eight-man *contubernium* in the late 6th century.

C.3.2. ALAE

Papyrological evidence is especially illuminating in regard to the rank system in the *alae*. As before, the commander held the title of *praefectus*, with *praepositus* also being used (synonymously) by the mid-4th century. This is apparent in the dossier of Fl. Abinnaeus, who is usually addressed as *eparchos* (= *praefectus*: P. Abinn. 3,2; 44,1; 45,1 etc.), but sometimes as *praipositos* (P. Abinn. 13,20; 25,1; 26,33 etc.). A *centurio* sometimes functioned as an interim commander (P. Oxy. XLI 2953 [ca. 300], L 3580 [4th cent.]; [35]). The squad list ChLA XVIII 660 (326/329) shows the *princeps* (= *decurio princeps* of the first *turma*) in second place after the commander, just as in the High Imperial period, followed by ten more *decuriones*. Then came the *summus* (= *summus curator*) and *actuarius*, who were responsible for cash management and catering, and whose designations were perhaps function descriptors rather than ranks. The eleven *turmae* in ChLA XVIII 660 may indicate a reduction in hypothetical strength compared with the Principate (16 *turmae*). A change is evident in ranks beneath the *summus* and *actuarius* from the time of the Tetrarchy onwards (P. Panop. Beatty 2,28f. [300] SB XVIII 13852,28 [309]; ChLA XVIII 660): in place of the *sesquiplicarius* and *duplicarius*, the *catafractarius* appears as the rank above the simple *eques*. The documents of the cavalryman Fl. Sarapion (ChLA XLIII 1248 [399], see [26]) exhibit the same sequence of ranks: *munifex* (= *eques*), *catafractarius*, *decurio*. In accordance with the old principle that better weapons correlated with higher pay (already referenced in the *adlocutio* of Hadrian in AD 128: ILS 2487), the *catafractarius* probably received one-and-a-half times or double regular pay [34]. The troop lists of the *Notitia Dignitatum* show the *alae* still making up a significant part of the cavalry in the early 5th century. New *alae* were established in the reign of Arcadius (Not. Dign. Or. XXVIII 21: *ala Arcadiana nuper constituta* – '... recently constituted'). Later, the non-specific regiment descriptor *numerus/arithmos* became established, which prevents identification of the *alae*.

C.3.3. COHORTES

The *Notitia Dignitatum* lists 118 *cohortes*, all classified as *limitanei*. Documentary evidence, however, shows the cohorts already disappearing in the early 4th century, so that information about their internal structure is scanty. Papyri come to our aid again for understanding the development: of the 19 cohorts that Not. dign. Or. XXVIII and XXXI place in Egypt, none is mentioned by name in papyri of the late 4th and early 5th centuries, but there are indirect indications. Not. dign. Or. XXVIII 46 states that the *cohors IV Numidarum* was based in Narmouthis (Faiyum). P. Sakaon 9,4 (314/15) mentions a *praepositosen Narmouthei*, and P. Sakaon 62,2 (328) mentions a soldier and *praepositos [e]n kastrois Nar[mouthe]o[s]*. Although both texts mention only the garrison site, the troops stationed there were probably the *cohors IV* listed in the *Notitia*. A second example is provided by the *cohors I Felix Theodosiana*, which Not. Dign. Or. XXXI 64 has stationed *apud Elephantinem*. A dozen documents from the Patermouthis dossier mention between 578 (P. Münch. I 2) and 613 (P. Lond. V 1737) soldiers of an *arithmos Elephantines*, probably identifiable with the *cohors I Felix* in the *Notitia*. Here as elsewhere, the non-specific term *arithmos/numerus* has displaced the traditional name *cohors*, but the presence of *ordinarii* (P. Münch. I 2,18–20) proves that behind the term *arithmos Elephantines* there was a cohort that preserved its 'old-style' rank system into the 7th century. It was commanded by a *praepositus* (= *praefectus*), and later by a *tribunus*; and it was divided into centuries under *centuriones* (*ordinarii*).

C.4. THE 'NEW-STYLE' RANK SYSTEM

The newly established regiments of the field army (*scholae palatinae*, *vexillationes*, *auxilia* and *cunei*) followed a new rank system that first emerged under the Tetrarchy, but that only reached its final form and empire-wide reach in the 320s. Some of its ranks are already attested in the mid-3rd century [32], but Constantine standardized the changes, with new types of units (e.g. *equites*) created before ca. 260–290 adapted to the new rank system.

Jerome describes this 'new-style' rank system in his treatise *Contra Iohannem Hierosolymitanum episcopum* 19 (PL XXIII, c. 386/87), giving the ranks in descending order of seniority: *numquid ex tribuno statim fit tiro? non, sed ante primicerius, deinde senator, ducenarius, centenarius, biarchus, circitor, eques, dein tiro* ('Do we proceed directly from tribune to new recruit? No: before that, we have *primicerius*, then *senator, ducenarius, centenarius, biarchus, circitor, eques* and only then new recruit'). Jerome cites the career of a cavalryman, but the new system also applied to infantry units, as demonstrated, for example, by the purchase contract BGU I 316 = M. Chr. II 271 (359) between the *senator* of an auxiliary *numerus* and the *biarchus* of a *vexillatio*. The same hierarchy is found in the ranking of the naval infantry (ILS 2787 [306–363]) and the *agentes in rebus* ('commissioners of state': Cod. Just. 12,20,3 [457–470]): *ducenarius, centenarius, biarchus, circitor, eques*. The *officiales* in civil offices also followed this system (Cod. Just. 1,27,2,19–36 [534]), which is widely attested through the late 6th century at least. The functions of most of these ranks can only be guessed at [6. 107–138].

The *circitor* first appears around AD 233 in army records from Dura-Europus (RMR 47 = ChLA VII 337 and RMR 49 = ChLA VII 343). Epigraphic evidence also begins soon after the middle of the 3rd century [30]. Veg. Mil. 3,8,18 offers the plausible explanation that the term *circitor* was an abbreviation of *circumitor*, and that this was originally a function descriptor: diligent soldiers were selected to inspect the guards in a 'circuit'. Only later, he suggests, did *circitor* become a rank (*gradus*). Conversely, the definition of *circitor* as a soldier's weapons assistant, given in Lydus, Mag. 1,46, cannot be correct, because *circitores* were senior to the *equites*. In AD 326, Constantine agreed to allow sons of cavalry veterans who provided their own horses to be enlisted with the immediate rank of *circitor* (Cod. Theod. 7,22,2,1).

The rank name *biarchus* derives from *exarchus*, a title of eastern origin that is first attested around AD 250 (CIL III 4832 = ILS 2528) in a unit of guards (*ala celerum*) [31. 70f.]. It was possible for this rank to be awarded twice to the same soldier, who then became *bis exarchus* ('twice *exarchus*'; CIL III 14214,24 [early 4th cent.]), giving rise to the abbreviated form *biarchus*. *Exarchus* disappears in the early 4th century (last attested P. Oxy. XLIII 3143 [305], M. Chr. 196 [309] or P. Aberd. 21 [276–325]), whereas *biarchus* was in regular use from the reign of Constantine onwards (first attested: P. Col. VII 188 = SB XII 11042; duplicate: SB XX 14379 [320]; AE 1995, 1338 [324]; P. Oxy. LX 4084 [339]).

The titles *centenarius* and *ducenarius* also emerged around the mid-3rd century. They were derived from the older rank and pay classes of equestrian officials and were bestowed upon selected centurions in the new elite regiments of the field army [32. note 13]. Reflecting the status of their regiments, they outranked centurions of the legions and cohorts. The new titles were probably intended to signify an alignment with the old equestrian *militiae*. The same thinking probably also led to the naming of the next-highest rank as *senator*, attested from the early 4th century onwards. The few epigraphic testaments [10. vol. 1, 75–77, 280]; [32] and the sole attestation in papyrology (BGU I 316) date from the 4th century. The *senator* is not mentioned again.

Within each regiment, individuals of equal rank were brought together in *scholae* (much like the *officiales* in civil offices: Veg. Mil. 2,21). The *Augustales*, for instance, formed a *schola* (P. Ross. Georg. III 10 [ca. 400]), as did the *Flaviales*, the *centenarii* and the *ducenarii*. The internal organization of the *scholae* was based on seniority, and it strengthened the internal hierarchies. Formalized in the 3rd century, the *scholae* lasted until at least the late 6th century (Maur. Strat. 1,8,18). The highest ranks below the tribunes were considered *priores/protoi*, and they could also act as a formal body. The *priores* included the *primicerius* and the *ordinarii* (P. Münch. I 2 [578]: *ordinarioi kai hoi loipoi priores*, '*ordinarii* and the other *priores*', i.e. at least the *ducenarii*). Meritorious soldiers and protegés advanced to the rank of *protector* [4]. From the reign of Diocletian onwards, the *protectores* were a special corps at court, under the command of the *magister militum praesentalis*. Later, they served as a pool of qualified military staff who could be used for administrative, organizational and logistical duties, and who might attain commands (P. Abinn. 1) or even more senior posts (ILS 2788).

C.5. Function descriptors

The ranks of *centenarius*, *ducenarius*, *senator* and *primicerius* qualified their holders for a number of tactical and administrative functions in the regiments, although there was no rigid correlation between rank and function: some functions could be fulfilled by men of various ranks. Such flexibility was essential, becuase units were sometimes split up, and often permanently: *vexillationes* of the cavalry were split into two *cunei* [18], and *auxilia* were split into *banda* (AE 1995, 1427 [531], see [36]). Maur. Strat. 12.B,8,16–20 even mentions the AD *hoc* split of an *arithmos* into two *tagmata* in the field, each receiving its own standard. The original unit remained under the command of the *tribunus*, the new one under a *vicarius* or *campidoctor*. Unlike in the numerical system of 'the olden days' (*hoi archaioi*), regiments by AD 600 varied in size and were reformed as needed (Maur. Strat. 1,4,8f.; 1,4,23–25; 1,4,32–35).

Between the 4th and early 7th centuries, a *vicarius* is often attested as commanding a unit or subunit. *Vicarius* was not a rank in the rank system, but a temporary title for someone substituting short-term for the regular commander (*tribunus*). Veg. Mil. 3,4,3; 3,6,23 and other literary and juristic sources mention *tribuni vel vicarii* ('tribunes or vicars') as commanders. The phrase *apo bikarion* (*ex vicariis*, 'former vicar') in papyri of the 6th century shows that the higher position was used as an honorific title after the substitution ended: P. Lond. V 1724, 83 (578–582) *str(atiotes) leg[(eonos)] S[y]e[n]e[s] kai apo bikar(ion)*, 'soldier of the legion of Syene and former vicar'. It was usually the *primicerius*, the highest-ranking officer after the tribune, who substituted for his commanding officer as *vicarius* (AE 1933, 185). Maurice only uses *vicarius* in reference to infantry regiments (Strat. 12.B,8,20), and instead he uses *ilarches* for cavalry (1,3,17f.). Older military writers use this term as an equivalent for *decurio*. When cavalry regiments were split up, the *ilarches* commanded the second unit.

The *domesticus* was the tribune's adjutant and/or chief of staff for a unit (in the *militia inermis* he was the personal assistant to the official and/or head of a chancellery). It was likely that the *primicerius*, being the highest-ranking qualified individual, would be appointed to the post of *domesticus*, but it was in the tribune's power to call up men from lower ranks (*senator, ducenarius, centenarius*).

The *campidoctor* is attested from the late 2nd century onwards (ILS 2416), particularly in the Praetorian Guard. This may simply have been a new title for the highest-ranking weapons trainers and cavalry captains (*exercitatores, doctores armorum*), who were responsible for training, tactical manoeuvres and the parade ground (*campus*). Generally, *centuriones* and *evocati* were appointed to this position. As from the 4th century, the *campidoctor* is found in infantry regiments of both old and new types. His status appears to have risen between the 4th and 6th centuries. According to Maur. Strat. 12.B,8,20, when large infantry regiments were split up, the *campidoctor* sometimes – like the *vicarius* – commanded one part with its own standard. As the third-most senior officer after the tribune and *vicarius*, he had similar duties of tactical leadership in the field. References in Ammianus Marcellinus (15,3,10 etc.) and Veg. Mil. (3,6,23; 3,8,11 etc.) suggest that it was mainly senior *centuriones* (*ordinarii*) who took this post (cf. also *apo kampiduktoron ordenariou* (MAMA I 86, no. 168 [late 4th cent.]: *ordinarius* in the rank of a *campidoctor*). The phrase *ex campidoctoribus*, which also appears in P. Lond. I 113.5(a) (498), reveals that, as with the *vicarius*, the post was temporary and regarded as a mark of distinction [33. 168f.]. This elevated status is also reflected in the role played by two *campidoctores* in the praesental armies during the emperors' enthronement ceremonies at Constantinople in the 5th and 6th centuries: they laid a torque on the head of the new ruler as a crown (Constantinus Porphyrogennetos, *De ceremoniis* 1,91–93).

C.6. CAREERS

Length of service and mechanisms of advancement can only be described in rough outline for soldiers in Late Antiquity. Despite being mentioned several times in the sources, a regular progress *secundam matriculam* ('in the order of matriculation', i.e. by seniority) was not always observed. According to the Edict of Anastasius from Perge (A 13f.), promotions were decided on the basis of *digna* (*axia*), *labores* (*ponoi*), *stipendia* (*stratias chronoi*): 'Dignity/valor, proving oneself by hard service, seniority'. The same edict shows that corruption and protection also played their part.

In the 4th century, Fl. Marcus, after serving for 23 years in a *vexillatio*, attained the rank of *protector*, and then served for a further five years in the *schola protectorum* (ILS 2783). The career of Fl. Memorius was even more impressive: he served with the *Ioviani* for 28 years, then for six years as *protector domesticus*, before being appointed *praefectus* of the *Lanciarii Seniores* for three years, and finally achieving the rank of *dux* (ILS 2788). Abinnaeus (1st half of 4th cent.) completed a more modest, but successful and perhaps typical career. He served for 33 years in the *vexillatio Parthusagittariorum*, rising to the rank of *ducenarius*. The *dux* then selected him to conduct Blemmyan 'defectors' (*refugae*) to the imperial court at Constantinople. While performing this duty in the summer of 336, he received the privilege of the *adoratio purpurae* ('adoration of the imperial purple', i.e. an audience with the emperor), thus advancing to *protector*, and finally, after three more years, he became *praefectus* of the *ala V Praelectorum* (P. Abinn. 1, on which [1]; [28. 459–478]). Fl. Callinicus Iovinianus in AD 502 was still an ordinary soldier with the *Leontoclibanarii*, but he was promoted to *biarchus* in 509, and in 523 he finally became *centenarius*. Even if he had already been a *centenarius* for a few years in 523, it would still have taken him about ten years to advance beyond *biarchus* [21]. A generation after him, Fl. Menodorus of the same unit advanced through the ranks: in 546 he was *primicerius*, having still been a *centenarius* fifteen years before, in 531. In the intervening years, he must have held the ranks of *ducenarius* and *senator* [22]. Accordingly, he was promoted approximately every five years, so that his career progressed more quickly than that of Callinicus Iovinianus.

Organization and rank as described in the *Strategikon* are often understood as the turning-point from the Late Roman to the Byzantine Army, but this may instead be attributed to the artificial terminology used by Maurice [23. 397]; [25]. The rank titles of Late Antiquity are still sporadically attested in the late 7th century. The rank systems of 'old' and 'new' styles lasted until the Arab expansion, and only disappeared in the reorganization of the Byzantine military in the mid-7th century [7. 138, 288f., 293f.]; [8]; [9. 107–110]. Middle Byzantine sources reveal that certain ranks, such as *senator*, *ducenarius* (as *dukin(i)ator*) and *centenarius* (as *kentarchos*) were still in use in the 9th century. In continuation of a development that can be traced back to the 5th century, the title *comes* ultimately replaced *tribunus* as the name for the army commander (Leo, *Taktika* 4,6; 4,12).

☞ Administration, C. Roman; Officers, B. Roman

BIBLIOGRAPHY
[1] T.D. BARNES, The Career of Abinnaeus, in: Phoenix 39, 1985, 368–374 (reprinted in: T.D. Barnes, From Eusebius to Augustine. Selected Papers 1982–1993, 1994, XV) [2] D.N. CHRISTODOULOU, Galerius, Gamzigrad, and the Fifth Macedonian Legion, in: JRA 15, 2002, 275–281 [3] K. DIETZ, Cohortes, ripae, pedaturae, in: K. Dietz et al. (eds.), Klassisches Altertum, Spätantike und frühes Christentum, 1993, 279–329 [4] M. EMION, Des soldats de l'armée romaine tardive. Les protectores (IIIe–VIe siècles

ap. J.-C.), 2 vols., 2017   [5] R. Grosse, Die Rangordnung der römischen Armee des 4.–6. Jahrhunderts, in: Klio 15, 1918, 122–161   [6] R. Grosse, Römische Militärgeschichte von Gallienus bis zum Beginn der byzantinischen Themenverfassung, 1920   [7] J.F. Haldon, Byzantine Praetorians. An Administrative, Institutional and Social Survey of the Opsikion and Tagmata, c. 580–900, 1984   [8] J.F. Haldon, Administrative Continuities and Structural Transformation in East Roman Military Organisation ca. 580–640, in: M. Kazanski / F. Vallet (eds.), L'armée romaine et les barbares du IIIe au VIIe siècles, 1993, 45–53   [9] J.F. Haldon, Warfare, State and Society in the Byzantine World, 1999   [10] D. Hoffmann, Das spätrömische Bewegungsheer und die Notitia Dignitatum, 2 vols. (Epigraphische Studien 7/1–2), 1969–1970   [11] S. Janniard, Centuriones ordinarii et ducenarii dans l'armée romaine tardive (IIIe–VIe s. apr. J.-C.), in: A.S. Lewin / P. Pellegrini (eds.), The Late Roman Army in the Near East from Diocletian to the Arab Conquest (BAR International Series 1717), 2007, 383–394   [12] A.H.M. Jones, The Later Roman Empire 284–602. A Social, Economic and Administrative Survey, 3 vols., 1964   [13] J.G. Keenan, An Instance of the Military Grade Flavialis, in: BASP 10, 1973, 43–46   [14] J.G. Keenan, Evidence for the Byzantine Army in the Syene Papyri, in: BASP 27, 1990, 139–150   [15] Y. Le Bohec (ed.), La hiérarchie (Rangordnung) de l'armée romaine sous le Haut-Empire (Actes du congrès de Lyon, 15–18 septembre 1994), 1995   [16] Y. Le Bohec, L'armée romaine sous le Bas-Empire, 2006   [17] Y. Le Bohec / C. Wolff (eds.), L'armée romaine de Dioclétien à Valentinian Ier (Actes du congrès de Lyon, 12–14 septembre 2002), 2004   [18] A.S. Lewin, The Egyptian cunei, in: Tyche 18, 2003, 73–76   [19] A.S. Lewin / P. Pellegrini (eds.), The Late Roman Army in the Near East from Diocletian to the Arab Conquest (BAR International Series 1717), 2007   [20] F. Onur, The Anastasian Military Decree from Perge in Pamphylia. Revised 2nd edition, in: Gephyra 14, 2017, 133–212   [21] B. Palme, Flavius Callinicus Iuvinianus, in: F.A.J. Hoogendijk / B.P. Muhs (eds.), Sixty-Five Papyrological Texts Presented to Klaas A. Worp (Papyrologica Lugduno-Batava 32), 2008, 231–242   [22] B. Palme, Flavius Menodorus, Offizier der Leontoclibanarii, in: R. Eberhard et al. (eds.), '... vor dem Papyrus sind alle gleich!' Papyrologische Beiträge zu Ehren von Bärbel Kramer (Archiv für Papyrusforschung, Beiheft 27), 2009, 154–162 (no. 13)   [23] P. Rance, Campidoctores Vicarii vel Tribuni. The Senior Regimental Officers in the Late Roman Army and the Rise of the Campidoctor, in: A.S. Lewin / P. Pellegrini (eds.), The Late Roman Army in the Near East from Diocletian to the Arab Conquest (BAR International Series 1717), 2007, 395–409   [24] P. Rance, An Unnoticed Regimental Diaconus in the Correspondence of Theodoret of Cyrrhus, in: Historia 63, 2014, 117–128   [25] P. Rance, Maurice's Strategicon and 'the Ancients'. The Late Antique Reception of Aelian and Arrian, in: P. Rance / N.V. Sekunda (eds.), Greek Taktika. Ancient Military Writing and Its Heritage, 2017, 217–255   [26] J.R. Rea, A Cavalryman's Career, A.D. 384 (?)–401, in: ZPE 56, 1984, 79–88   [27] P. Richardot, Hiérarchie militaire et organisation légionnaire chez Végèce, in: Y. Le Bohec (ed.), La hiérarchie (Rangordnung) de l'armée romaine sous le Haut-Empire (Actes du congrès de Lyon, 15–18 septembre 1994), 1995, 405–428   [28] M. Rocco, L'esercito romano tardoantico. Persistenze e cesure dai Severi a Teodosio I, 2012   [29] M.P. Speidel, The Master of the Dragon Standards and the Golden Torc. An Inscription from Prusias and Prudentius' Peristephanon, in: Transactions of the American Philological Association 115, 1985, 283–287   [30] M.P. Speidel, Der Circitor und der Untergang des Numerus Cattharensium beim Fall des obergermanischen Limes, in: Saalburg-Jahrbuch 46, 1991, 148   [31] M.P. Speidel, Riding for Caesar, 1994   [32] M.P. Speidel, The Origin of the Late Roman Army Ranks, in: Tyche 20, 2005, 205–207   [33] E.L. Wheeler, The Legion as Phalanx in the Late Empire, Part 2, in: Revue des études militaires anciennes 1, 2004, 147–175   [34] C. Zuckerman, Le camp de Ψῶβθις/Sosteos et les catafractarii, in: ZPE 100, 1994, 199–202   [35] C. Zuckerman, Deux centurions commandants d'ailes en Égypte vers 300, in: Y. Le Bohec (ed.), La hiérarchie (Rangordnung) de l'armée romaine sous le Haut-Empire (Actes du congrès de Lyon, 15–18 septembre 1994), 1995, 385–387   [36] C. Zuckerman, Constantiniani – Constantiniaci from Pylai. A Rejoinder, in: Tyche 13, 1998, 255–258.

BERNHARD PALME

Rear

A. Introductory remarks
B. Infrastructure work

A. Introductory remarks

The term 'rear' denotes the territory behind the zone of conflict or deployment (i.e. not the 'front'), in which combat troops were able to march into position and where deployment and supplies had to be organized. 'Rear' also describes the organizational structures that were set up here. Setting up and maintaining a militarily usable infrastructure within the rear zone was particularly important.

From the Late Republican period onwards, the Romans had the indisputable advantage of exercising essential control over all coasts of the Mediterranean, and thus being able to accomplish much of their supply effort and the transportation of their troops by ship (Tac. Ann. 1,9: *mari Oceano aut amnibus longinquis saeptum imperium: legiones, provincias, classes, cuncta inter se conexa*, 'an empire with the the sea, ocean and distant rivers as boundaries; the legions, provinces, divisions – all things are connected'). This advantage would only be lost in the 5th century, when the Vandals succeeded in establishing their kingdom in North Africa [4]; [3]; [19].

Besides the preparation of stores and depots, work on military infrastructure also included the building and development of sea and river ports and the construction and maintenance of roads and other structures necessary for troop movements and supply. Also subsumed under the category of the 'rear' were the mostly unpaid contributions required of the civilian population for the supply of troops.

B. Infrastructure work

B.1. Construction

B.1. CONSTRUCTION

The Romans usually made use of existing harbours for their maritime transport, expanding them to meet their needs. Examples include the ports of Ancona (CIL IX 5894 = ILS 298; cf. [17]) and Seleucia Pieria (cf. [42] and Theod. hist. mon. 13,15). Although the port of Caesarea Maritima in Palaestina was built on the initiative of the client king Herod, it was certainly used by Roman troops from the outset [16. 70–105].

Road construction for military reasons included not only the building of the actual roadway, but also the installation of bridges and buildings needed for ongoing operations (cf. e.g. the great Danube bridge of Trajan (CIL III 8267 = ILS 5863); cf. [40. 491–496] for infrastructure measures at the Iron Gates and [40. 647f. with fig. 267] on the Danube bridge at Drobeta).

The category of buildings also included change stations (*mutationes*) and overnight accommodations (*mansiones*) for the state mail (*cursus publicus*) and requisite warehouses (*horrea*), which also became important as collection and preparation points for the *annona militaris* ('military annual income') in Late Antiquity (cf. [19]; [29]; [28]).

Infrastructure also involved resettlement measures driven by state privileges, as in the case of Pizus in the province of Thracia (modern Bulgaria) [31]. Such measures were intended to stimulate serviceable markets along the most important marching routes, where units could supplement their supplies on the free market as they marched through (cf. Syll.³ 880 = IGRR 1,766 = IGBR 3,2 no. 1690).

Large construction projects and projects close to the borders of the empire appear to have been carried out by military engineering detachments. In interior provinces, the subsequent maintenance of the most important roads seems to have been achieved by calling on the services of the civilian population, too [26]. The inscription CIL IX 6075 = ILS 5875 is one piece of evidence indicative of such a financing model. It documents the financial obligations imposed on owners of land adjacent to the *via Appia* for repairs during the reign of Trajan. In principle, such services are comparable to the annual five days of *pro bono* work that most Egyptians were required to perform maintaining dykes and canals [5].

Constructing and maintaining buildings for the *cursus publicus* or for the storage of military goods were obligations regularly imposed on communities along roads, in Late Antiquity at least. Relevant legal texts provide evidence for this (cf. Dig. 50,4,18).

The scope and spatial extent of the rear stage area were heavily dependent on what would be required for the future theatre of war and on the particular local conditions, that is, the economic viability of the immediate hinterland.

In the case of the frontier province along the Rhine and Danube, the civilian provinces immediately adjacent must be seen as the natural area for the rear (cf. e.g. [6]; [8]). This is apparent even in the title of the *procurator Belgicae et duarum Germaniarum*, whose responsibility it was, from the early Imperial period on, to supply the troops in Germania. As for the province of Mauretania Tingitana (modern Morocco), it appears that the littoral Iberian provinces of Lusitania (Portugal) and Baetica (Andalusia) functioned as the rear, with transport by sea being easier and quicker than other options, such as land transport from the neighbouring provinces of Numidia and Africa proconsularis (modern Tunisia). It was probably for this reason that still in Late Antiquity, Mauretania Tingitana belonged administratively to the *dioecesis Hispaniarum* (Not. Dign. Occ. 21,14; cf. [43]).

The province of Raetia, on the other hand, was organizationally part of the *dioecesis Italia annonaria* in Late Antiquity, and was probably supplied mostly from Northern Italy, even though this required transport by land via the Alpine passes (Not. Dign. Occ. 35,32f.).

The situation was more complex in the case of the provinces of the southern Balkans, where the hinterland seems regularly to have stretched out into the coastal regions of Asia Minor. While this area seems to have been used only on an AD *hoc* basis at first (cf. the jurisdiction of Timesitheus during the Balkan Wars in the reign of Maximinus Thrax (235–238 according to CIL XIII 1807 = ILS 1330) [14]), a more permanent organizational structure apparently existed there in Late Antiquity and later (cf. e.g. [29]; [28]).

We know of civilian officials (*primipilares*) from Asia Minor responsible in the 4th century for the transfer of military supplies to the Danube provinces and expected to perform this task in the form of a *munus* ('obligation') [9]. In AD 537, in the reign of Justinian I (527–565), the permanent office of a *quaestor exercitus* ('Quaestor of the Army') was created to bring the frontier provinces of Scythia and Moesia II (modern Bulgaria) along the lower Danube and the interior provinces of Insulae (islands of the Aegean), Caria (modern Turkey around Halicarnassus/Bodrum) and Cyprus under a unified command (introduced by Iust. Nov. 41, also mentioned in Nov. 163,2 (575); cf. [12]).

In the case of the Syrian military provinces along the Euphrates and Tigris, the Anatolian rear regularly appears to have extended from Cilicia (region around Tarsus and Adana) into the neighbouring coastal provinces of Pamphylia and Lycia. It is unclear to what extent the Romans in the east of the empire were able to make use of organizational structures built by their predecessors in these lands [7]; [11]; [12].

Egypt had a double function in this system. Its capacities were used not only for supplying its own garrison, but frequently also to → supply troops in Syria and expeditionary forces from Syria (cf. [2]).

In terms of its organizational capabilities, the Roman Empire was clearly superior to all its potential enemies. Only in conflicts with the Parthian and Sassanid Empires did adversaries have comparable organizational structures.

☞ Infrastructure; Vehicles

Bibliography

Sources
[1] The Chronicle of Pseudo-Josua the Stylite, translation and introduction with notes by F.R. Trombley and J.W. Watt, 2000.

Secondary literature
[2] C.E.P. Adams, Land Transport in Roman Egypt. A Study of Economics and Administration in a Roman Province, 2007 [3] P. Arnaud, Maritime Infrastructure. Between Public and Private Initiative, in: A. Kolb (ed.), Infrastruktur und Herrschaftsorganisation im Imperium Romanum. Herrschaftsstrukturen und Herrschaftspraxis III. Akten der Tagung in Zürich 19.–20.2.2012, 2014, 161–179 [4] P. Arnaud, The Interplay between Practioners and Decision-Makers for the Selection, Organization, Utilization and Maintenance of Ports in the Roman Empire, in: J. Preiser-Kapeller / F. Daim (eds.), Harbours and Maritime Networks as Complex Adaptive Systems. International Workshop 'Harbours and Maritime Networks as Complex Adaptive Systems' at the Römisch-Germanisches Zentralmuseum in Mainz, 17.–18.10.2013 within the Framework of the Special Research Programme (DFG-SPP 1630) 'Harbours from the Roman Period to the Middle Ages' (Römisch-Germanisches Zentralmuseum. RGZM-Tagungen 23), 2015, 61–81 [5] D. Bonneau, Le régime administratif de l'eau dans l'Égypte grecque, romaine et byzantine (Probleme der Ägyptologie 8), 1993 [6] C. Cavallo et al., Food Supply to the Roman Army in the Rhine Delta during the First Century A.D., in: S. Stallibrass / R. Thomas (eds.), Feeding the Roman Army. The Archaeology of Production and Supply in NW Europe, 2008, 69–81 [7] M.-L. Chaumont, Chaumont, Études d'histoire parthe V. La route royale des Parthes de Zeugma à Séleucie du Tigre d'après l'itinéraire d'Isidore de Charax, in: Syria 61, 1984, 63–107 [8] M. Derreumaux / S. Lepetz, Food Supply at Two Successive Military Settlements in Arras (France). An Archaeobotanical and Archaeozoological Approach, in: S. Stallibrass / R. Thomas (eds.), Feeding the Roman Army. The Archaeology of Production and Supply in NW Europe, 2008, 52–68 [9] B. Dobson, Die Primipilares. Entwicklung und Bedeutung, Laufbahnen und Persönlichkeiten eines römischen Offiziersranges, 1978 [10] D.F. Graf, The Persian Royal Road System in Syria-Palestine, in: Transeuphratène 6, 1983, 149–168 [11] D.F. Graf, The Persian Royal Road System, in: H. Sancisi-Weerdenburg et al. (eds.), Continuity and Change. Proceedings of the Last Achaemenid History Workshop, April 6–8, 1990, Ann Arbor, Michigan (Achaemenid History VIII), 1995, 167–189 [12] J.F. Haldon, Economy and Administration. How Did the Empire Work?, in: M. Maas (ed.), The Cambridge Companion to the Age of Justinian, 2005, 28–59 [13] P. Herz, Zur Karriere des Lucius Septimius Flavianus Flavillianus aus Oinoanda, in: B. Takmer et al. (eds.), Vir doctus anatolicus. Studies in the Memory of Sencer Sahin, 2016, 464–470 [14] P. Herz, Gedanken zur Karriere des Timesitheus, in: Philia 3, 2017, 69–78 [15] F. Himmler, Untersuchungen zur schiffsgestützten Grenzsicherung auf der spätantiken Donau (3.–6. Jh. n.Chr.) (BAR International Series 2197), 2011 [16] K.G. Holum et al. (eds.), King Herod's Dream. Caesarea on the Sea, 1988 [17] M. Horster, Bauinschriften römischer Kaiser. Untersuchungen zu Inschriftenpraxis und Bautätigkeit in Städten des westlichen Imperium Romanum in der Zeit des Prinzipats, 2001 [18] C. Johnstone, Commodities or Logistics? The Role of Equids in Roman Supply Networks, in: S. Stallibras / R. Thomas (eds.), Feeding the Roman Army. The Archaeology of Production and Supply in NW Europe, 2008, 128–145 [19] A. Kolb (ed.), Infrastruktur und Herrschaftsorganisation im Imperium Romanum. Herrschaftsstrukturen und Herrschaftspraxis III. Akten der Tagung in Zürich 19.–20.2.2012, 2014 [20] M. Lenoir, À propos de C. Iulius Pacatianus, gouverneur de Maurétanie Tingitane, in: L'Africa Romana, vol. 7, 1990, 897–892 [21] N. Lenski, Failure of Empire. Valens and the Roman State in the Fourth Century A.D., 2002 [22] A. Luther, Die syrische Chronik des Josua Stylites, 1997 [23] N.P. Milner, Athletics, Army Recruitment and Heroisation. L. Sep. Fl. Flavillianus of Oinoanda, in: AS 61, 151–167 [24] A. Mócsy, Das Lustrum Primipili und die Annona Militaris, in: Germania 44, 1966, 312–326 (again in: Pannonien und das römische Heer. Ausgewählte Aufsätze (MAVORS 7), 1992, 106–120 (with supplement)) [25] J. Preiser-Kapeller / F. Daim (eds.), Harbours and Maritime Networks as Complex Adaptive Systems. International Workshop 'Harbours and Maritime Networks as Complex Adaptive Systems' at the Römisch-Germanisches Zentralmuseum in Mainz, 17.–18.10.2013 within the Framework of the Special Research Programme (DFG-SPP 1630) 'Harbours from the Roman Period to the Middle Ages' (Römisch-Germanisches Zentralmuseum. RGZM-Tagungen 23), 2015 [26] M. Rathmann, Untersuchungen zu den Reichsstraßen in den westlichen Provinzen des Imperium Romanum (Beihefte der Bonner Jahrbücher 55), 2003 [27] J. Remesal Rodriguez, Die procuratores Augusti und die Versorgung des römischen Heeres, in: H. Vetters / M. Kandler (eds.), Akten des 14. Internationalen Limeskongresses 1986 in Carnuntum, pt. 1, 1990, 55–65 [28] E. Rizos, Centres of the Late Roman Military Supply Network in the Balkans. A Survey of Horrea, in: JRGZ 60, 2013, 659–696 [29] E. Rizos, Remarks on the Logistics and Infrastructure of the Annona Militaris in Eastern Mediterranean and Aegean Areas, in: Antiquité Tardive 23, 2015, 287–302 [30] S. Rocca, Herod's Judaea. A Mediterranean State in the Classical World (Texts and Studies in Ancient Judaism 122), 2008 [31] K. Ruffing, Städtische Wirtschaftspolitik im hellenistisch-römischen Kleinasien? Zur Funktion der Emporia, in: H.-U. Wiemer (ed.), Staatlichkeit und

politisches Handeln in der römischen Kaiserzeit (Millennium-Studien 10), 2006, 123–149 [32] M.A. SPEIDEL, Heer und Straßen, Militares viae, in: R. Frei-Stolba (ed.), Siedlung und Verkehr im römischen Reich. Römerstrassen zwischen Herrschaftssicherung und Landschaftsprägung. Akten des Kolloquiums zu Ehren von Prof. H.E.Herzig vom 28. und 29. Juni 2001 in Bern, 2004, 331–344 (again in: Heer und Herrschaft im römischen Reich der hohen Kaiserzeit (MAVORS 16), 2009, 501–513) [33] M.A. SPEIDEL, Rekruten für ferne Provinzen. Der Papyrus ChLA X 422 und die kaiserliche Rekrutierungszentrale, in: ZPE 163, 2007, 281–295 (again in: Heer und Herrschaft im römischen Reich der hohen Kaiserzeit (MAVORS 16), 2009, 213–234) [34] M.A. SPEIDEL, The Development of the Roman Forces in Eastern Anatolia. New Evidence for the History of the exercitus Cappadocicus, in: A.A. Lewin / P. Pellegrini (eds.), The Late Roman Army in the Near East from Diocletian to the Arab Conquest. Proceedings of a Colloquium Held at Potenza, Acceranza and Matera, Italy (May 2005) (BAR International Series 1717), 2007, 73–90 (again in: Heer und Herrschaft im römischen Reich der hohen Kaiserzeit (MAVORS 16), 2009, 595–631) [35] M.A. SPEIDEL, Dressed for the Occasion. Clothes and Context in the Roman Army, in: Heer und Herrschaft im römischen Reich der hohen Kaiserzeit (MAVORS 16), 2009, 235–248 [36] M.A. SPEIDEL, Les longues marches des armées romaines. Réflets épigraphiques de la circulation des militaires dans la province d'Asie au IIIe siècle apr. J.-C., in: Cahiers du Centre Gustave Glotz 20, 2009, 188–210 [37] M.A. SPEIDEL, 'Auf kürzestem Weg und gut verpflegt an die Front'. Zur Versorgung pannonischer Expeditionstruppen während der severischen Partherkriege, in: E. Eich (ed.), Die Verwaltung der kaiserzeitlichen römischen Armee. Studien für Hartmut Wolff, Stuttgart (Historia Einzelschrift 211), 2010, 133–147 (previously in: Heer und Herrschaft im römischen Reich der hohen Kaiserzeit (MAVORS 16), 2009, 255–271) [38] M.A. SPEIDEL, Herrschaft durch Vorsorge und Beweglichkeit. Zu den Infrastrukturanlagen des kaiserzeitlichen römischen Heeres im Reichsinneren, in: A. Kolb (ed.), Infrastruktur und Herrschaftsorganisation im Imperium Romanum. Herrschaftsstrukturen und Herrschaftspraxis III. Akten der Tagung in Zürich 19.–20.2.2013, 2014, 80–99 [39] M.P. SPEIDEL, The Army at Aquileia, the Moesiaci Legion and the Shield Emblems of the Notitia Dignitatum, in: SJb 45, 1990, 68–72 (again in: Roman Army Studies, vol. 2, 1992, 414–418) [40] A.S. STEFAN, Les guerres daciques de Domitien et de Trajan. Architecture militaire, topographie, images et histoire, 2005 [41] K. STROBEL, Untersuchungen zu den Dakerkriegen Trajans. Studien zur Geschichte des mittleren und unteren Donauraumes in der Hohen Kaiserzeit, 1984 [42] D. VAN BERCHEM, Le port de Séleucie de Piérie et l'infrastructure logistique des guerres parthiques, in: BJb 185, 1985, 47–87 [43] N. VILLAVERDE Verga, Tingitana en la antigüedad tardia (siglos III–VII). Autoctonía y romanidad en el extremo occidente mediterráneo, 2001.

PETER HERZ

Reconnaissance

A. Greek
B. Roman

A. GREEK

A.1. Information provision
A.2. Information transfer

It was of fundamental importance for a general's strategic and tactical planning that he should have precise information about the topographical, economic and political conditions of the region to be entered, the exact position, military strength, plans and weaknesses of the enemy, and the geography of the battlefield (see e.g. Hdt. 3,134f.; Xen. Hipp. 4,7; Aen. Tact. 16,19f.). Collecting and providing such information is known as reconnaissance. In the Greek army, as in almost all premodern armies, reconnaissance was not institutionalized, that is, it was neither professionalized nor was it carried out by a specially designated unit.

A.1. INFORMATION PROVISION

A.1.1. Introduction
A.1.2. Defectors and captives
A.1.3. Scouts and reconnaissance units
A.1.4. Spies

A.1.1. INTRODUCTION

A first step in gaining information might be to consult historical works, such as those of Herodotus, Thucydides, Xenophon, Ctesias or Polybius [2. 328]; [10. 37f.]. Information from locals (Curt. 5,3,5f.; 8,11,3f.), merchants (Xen. Hell. 3,4,1), travellers and foreigners (Plut. *Nicias* 30) was also useful. Alcibiades (c. 450–404/03 BC), for example, had merchant vessels confiscated so that his enemies would not learn of his approach (Plut. *Alcibiades* 28,2; Xen. Hell. 1,1,15). Such information, however, was often inexact or packed with rumours [7. 92f.]; [10. 22–25]. Therefore, accounts given by banished individuals were usually more valuable, being more precise and reliable (Plut. *Aratus* 5). The banished Hippias and Demaratus delivered significant information to the Persian kings Darius I and Xerxes I on their Greek campaigns (see e.g. Thuc. 6,59,4; Hdt. 7,101–104). *Proxenoi* (citizens of one city who represented another) also sometimes proved credible informants (Thuc. 3,2; Xen. Hell. 6,1; Aeschin. Leg. 172; cf. [3]). The young Alexander the Great (356–323 BC) supposedly questioned Persian emissaries at the court of his father Philip II of Macedon as to the lengths and conditions of their roads, the military talents of their king Artaxerxes III, and the bravery and ability of the Persians (Plut. *Alexander* 5,1).

A.1.2. DEFECTORS AND CAPTIVES

Defectors were a particularly important source of information (Hdt. 3,4; Thuc. 4,68,6; Xen. Hipp. 4,7). Alexander the Great in particular was said to have made regular use of information from such people (e.g. Curt. 4,13,36; 5,13,2f., see [2. 333f.]). With regard to further strategic or tactical information, however, ordinary soldiers were only in a position to supply information that was circulating in the camp, or even rumours. Accordingly, traitors or banished individuals who had formerly held high offices in their *polis* or army were of greater use because of their insider knowledge and authority (Hdt. 8,128; 9,45; Plut. *Aristides* 13; Plut. *Alcibiades* 30,2; 31,2; Arr. Anab. 3,19,4f.; Curt. 3,13,2f.; 5,13,9–12).

Another potentially fruitful source of information was captive locals or enemy scouts, soldiers, etc. (Hdt. 7,195). The successful return of the Ten Thousand from Mesopotamia via the mountains of Armenia, for instance, would not have been possible without continuous consultations with locals who were incidentally or purposefully taken captive (Xen. An. 3,5,14; 4,1,22; 4,4,16–18). Alexander the Great also frequently took enemy soldiers or locals prisoner to question them (e.g. Curt. 3,13,4).

With defectors and even with prisoners, however, there was inevitably the risk that they might be spying for the other side and deliberately passing on false information (e.g Polyaeus, Strat. 1,46; Thuc. 6,64–66; Arr. An. 3,7,4; cf. [7. 190–225]; [10. 14–16]). Various approaches were taken to counter this risk: threat of execution (Xen. An. 3,2,20), taking family members hostage (Xen. An. 4,6,1; Curt. 8,11,3f.), exceptionally large rewards, honours bestowed for correct information (Diod. Sic. 17,68,4–6; 17,83,8; 17,85,4–6; Curt. 5,7,12), and use of other informants (Xen. An. 4,1,21–25) or scouts (Thuc. 1,91,1–3) to confirm reports.

A.1.3. SCOUTS AND RECONNAISSANCE UNITS

In addition to this more passive form of information gathering, generals also conducted active reconnaissance by sending out scouts. Scouts of all kinds were known as *kataskopoi* (or *proskopoi*, *skopoi* or *proodoi*) in Greek [4. 129–132]. According to Aeneas Tacticus (6,1), scouts should have military experience in order to judge a situation correctly (see also Xen. An. 4,4,15).

If an army was on the move, scouts would be sent out primarily in difficult and unclear terrain to determine the route, detect ambushes and locate the enemy (Xen. Hipp. 4,4–6; Onas. 6,7). Either single individuals or small groups would be used, since they would be able to occupy elevated observation positions unnoticed (e.g. Hom. Il. 2,790–794; Thuc. 8,100,2; Xen. Cyr. 6,3,2).

However, the advance guard (*prodromoi*) was also used for reconnaisance where contact with the enemy was expected, especially from the 4th century BC on (Hdt. 4,121; 9,14). These soldiers generally carried only light weapons, so that they could be used either in skirmishing or in regular combat [8. 457]. In Athens in the 4th century BC, mounted *prodromoi* served as scouts, seemingly replacing the *hippotoxotai*, mounted archers, who also functioned as a kind of advance guard and skirmish group (Aristot. Ath. pol. 49,1; Xen. Mem. 3,3,1). In terms of rank and social status, these horsemen stood higher than other riders (Photius s.v. *prodromoi*; *adoxoi*) [1. 222f.]. Four *ilai prodromoi* (also known as *sarissophoroi*, 'pike-bearers' because of their weaponry) were used for reconnaissance in the army of Alexander the Great (Arr. An. 1,14,1; 1,14,6; Pol. 12,20,7; Arr. An. 1,12,7; 1,13,1; 3,7,7). They were also regular members of the cavalry, taking part in battle ahead of the right wing of the main army (Arr. An. 2,9,2).

Among those used by the Spartans as scouts were Sciritae, inhabitants of the northern frontier regions of Laconia (Xen. Lac. pol. 12,3). According to Xenophon (Lac. pol. 13,6), these Sciritae and 'outriders' (*proereunomenoi hippeis*) went ahead of the Spartans on the march. They, too, were regular members of the Spartan army (Diod. Sic. 15,32,1).

According to Xenophon, other scouts disguised as robber bands were sent out ahead of the advance guard proper, either to take prisoner anyone who might report their presence, or, if an informant escaped, to provoke an attack typical of bandits (Xen. Cyr. 2,4,23; Xen. Hipp. 4,5).

A.1.4. SPIES

Generals also used spies, not so much to investigate topography and routing, but rather to obtain information about the enemy's capabilities and tactical plans [6]. In disguise and under false identities, these spies sometimes infiltrated the enemy camp or a besieged city (see e.g. already Hom. Od. 4,244–250; Hom. Il. 10,204–459). Emissaries sometimes operated as spies (Hdt. 3,17). To avert secret deals among spies and to identify false information, the *strategos* ('commander') Pompiscus (4th cent. BC?) selected one Arcadian and three men unknown to each other, and prevented communication between them (Polyaenus, Strat. 5,33,6). To detect spies in his mercenary army, the Athenian *strategos*Chares (4th cent. BC) had every soldier tell his comrades exactly who he was and to which unit he belonged (Polyaenus, Strat. 3,13,1; cf. 5,28,2; on precautions against espionage, see also Xen. Hipp. 4,8; Aen. Tact. 10,11–15; Polyaens, Strat. 5,33,1 [6. 6–10]). The military scientist Aeneas Tacticus (first half of 4th cent. BC) is a particularly prolific and important source on the military use of spies (in city sieges).

A.2. Information transfer

Where scouts were unable or forbidden to convey information in person, several possibilities were open to them. They could send communications verbally or in writing through messengers (Polyaenus, Strat. 5,26; Xen. An. 1,2,21), although letters could easily be captured or opened by the messenger (Thuc. 1,132,5). During a city siege, it was possible to fire the missive over the city walls using a bow (Hdt. 8,128; Aen. Tact. 31,25–27). Fire signals are also attested [6. 14f.], as are flags (Pol. 2,66,10; Plut. *Philopoemen* 6,3) and the use of shields to flash reflections (Hdt. 6,115; Xen. Hell. 2,1,27; Plut. *Lysander* 11,2). The Spartans had their own particular method for transmitting secret information: the *skytale*. A leather strap was wound around a staff. A message was then written on the leather across the winding, and the unwound strap was sent. Only someone with a staff of the same dimensions would be able to decipher the text (Plut. *Lysander* 19,5; Gell. NA 17,9,6–15). Aen. Tact. 18,20f.; 31 offers our most thorough review of the sometimes outlandish methods used to transmit secret messages.

☞ Avoidance of military service; Battle; Cavalry; Hostages; Infantry; Prisoners; Strategy

Bibliography
[1] G.R. Bugh, The Horsemen of Athens, 1988 [2] D. Engels, Alexanders' Intelligence System, in: CQ 30, 1980, 327–340 [3] A. Gerolymatos, Espionage and Treason. A Study of the Proxenia in Political and Military Intelligence Gathering in Ancient Greece, 1986 [4] W.K. Pritchett, The Greek State at War, vol. 1, 1971, 127–133 [5] W.K. Pritchett, The Greek State at War, vol. 2, 1974, 188–189 [6] J.A. Richmond, Spies in Ancient Greece, in: G&R 45, 1998, 1–18 [7] F.S. Russell, Information Gathering in Classical Greece, 1999 [8] F.S. Russell, Finding the Enemy. Military Intelligence, in: B. Campbell / L.A. Tritle (eds.), The Oxford Handbook of Warfare in the Classical World, 2013, 474–492 [9] I.G. Spence, The Cavalry of Classical Greece, 1993 [10] C.G. Starr, Political Intelligence in Classical Greece, 1974.

Sandra Scheuble-Reiter

B. Roman

B.1. Roman Republic
B.2. Principate
B.3. Roman Empire in Late Antiquity

As in any state, Rome's military strength in part depended on its ability to obtain reliable information on its present and potential enemies. Starting from relatively meagre beginnings, Rome's abilities in this area, especially at the strategic level, gradually improved as the Roman Empire grew and the threats and opportunities that it faced changed over time.

B.1. Roman Republic

B.1.1. Strategic reconnaissance
B.1.2. Tactical reconnaissance

B.1.1. Strategic reconnaissance

The political and military structures of the Roman Republic – magistracies elected annually, rudimentary archives and no standing army – were poorly suited to the gathering and processing of strategic intelligence. Armies themselves, however, did generally (although not always) possess sufficient competence in tactical reconnaissance as they marched and on the battlefield.

Strategic reconnaissance in the first place involves estimating the intentions of the enemy and its ability to wage war. One factor that greatly hindered this in Republican Rome was a lack of geographical information, both in general and in detail. Rome only began to acquire such information during its wars of conquest (e.g. Caesar in Gaul). Some geographical and military information could be learned in advance from confederates or client states, for example Saguntum in Spain before the Second Punic War (218–201 BC; Pol. 3,15,1f.) – but such sources were seldom impartial and could therefore be unreliable.

In a number of cases, the senate tried to fill the gaps in its knowledge by sending out a few men in a reconnaissance team, but this was only possible with the approval of states that Rome was able to intimidate (e.g. Carthage before the Third Punic War, 149–146 BC), and the limitations of such ventures are obvious. Nevertheless, there is no evidence to suggest that the Romans were conducting strategic espionage on a permanent basis.

Information more likely to be reliable came from Rome's own colonies outside Italy, its provincial governors who had some contact with immediate neighbours, and Romans engaged in long-distance trade. There are some indications that such sources passed strategic information to the senate – both to individual senators and to the body as a whole. However, where we are able to follow this in detail – in Caesar's *Commentarii* and the private letters of Cicero –, it is clear that the picture they were able to obtain and pass on to the senate was often highly deficient.

In Gaul, Caesar was operating in uncharted territory about which little was known. When advancing, he therefore had to obtain the most basic information himself, either through diplomatic contacts or from tribes already conquered. Prior to his first expedition to Britain, he separately sent one Roman officer and one Gallic chief to the island to investigate the situation there. However, both returned empty-handed, and Caesar's own questioning of men who traded across the English Channel also proved fruitless. He finally decided to undertake a 'blind' invasion. The military gains from the expedition proved meagre (Caes. B Gall. 4,20–36), but it was a political triumph, celebrated in Rome with twenty days of thanksgiving festivities (Cass. Dio 39,33). This shows how Caesar was able to exploit his dispatches and *commentarii* to shape the senate's and people's view of his achievements.

Cicero likewise tried to obtain intelligence during his only governorship, which took place in Cilicia (51 BC), when he had serious concerns about a possible Parthian invasion. Yet, his letters from this period show that he often relied on rumours (Cic. Att. 5,16) and reports from unreliable client princes (Cic. Fam. 5,3,1; Cic. Att. 5,18,1; 5,20,2), while treating with scepticism information from his own cavalry and the governor of the neighbouring province of Syria (Cic. Fam. 3,8,10; 15,2; 15,4). As a result, he seriously underestimated the actual threat, and his reports to the Roman senate were misleading, sporadic and often arrived too late (Cic. Fam. 15,3,2; cf. 15,9,3). The fact that they took 74 days to reach Rome (Cic. Fam. 15,1,2; 15,2,3; Cic. Att. 5,19,1; 5,21,2) illustrates another great shortcoming of Roman reconnaissance: information that reached the capital from the frontiers of the empire was almost always out of date.

It was nearly impossible to operate a centralized intelligence system in Rome that would have enabled incoming information to be sorted, evaluated and communicated back to commanders so as to guide further intelligence-gathering. In practice, this meant that Roman commanders such as Caesar and Cicero had to be given free rein to deal with local situations as they saw best. This sometimes brought unintended or undesirable consequences.

B.1.2. TACTICAL RECONNAISSANCE

Tactical reconnaissance is the process of ascertaining the position, strength and intentions of an immediate enemy as it approaches or on the battlefield. While marching, Caesar and other Roman generals usually deployed a protective shield by sending much of the cavalry on ahead of the main marching column. In addition, some selected horsemen (usually local allies) would conduct reconnaissance even farther ahead of the troops as *exploratores* (explorers), checking or identifying routes and selecting the location for the overnight camp (e.g. Caes. B Gall. 2,17,1; 7,44,1–3). When close to an enemy camp or settlement, *speculatores* (scouts) might conduct further covert operations, often at night or in disguise (Bell. Afr. 35,2–5). Close to the enemy, some commanders even deemed it necessary to see the situation for themselves, despite the great dangers involved. It was during just such a personal inspection that the two consuls for the year 208 BC, Marcus Claudius Marcellus and Titus Quinctius Crispinus, fell into a deadly ambush set by Hannibal's Numidian cavalry (Pol. 10,32; Liv. 27,26f.; Plut. *Marcellus* 29).

Another source of information was prisoners, whether soldiers or civilians, who could be interrogated. Cato the Elder was said to have attacked an enemy position for the very purpose of capturing a prisoner to interrogate when he was in Spain in 195 BC (Frontinus, Strat. 1,2,5). Deserters and refugees also sometimes volunteered information. For instance, it was through such informants that Caecilius Metellus learned of a failed plot against Jugurtha (109 BC, cf. Sall. Iug. 73,1). Information of this kind was priceless: military intelligence is most useful when confirmed by multiple sources.

Roman generals seem very rarely to have dispensed with military reconnaissance altogether. When they did so, the results were sometimes catastrophic, as Gaius Flaminius discovered to his loss in 217 BC, when he decided to march *inexplorato* ('unreconnoitred': Liv. 22,4,4) past Lake Trasimene. He lost his entire army and his life.

B.2. PRINCIPATE

B.2.1. Strategic reconnaissance
B.2.2. Tactical reconnaissance

B.2.1. STRATEGIC RECONNAISSANCE

The Principate witnessed a considerable improvement in Roman military reconnaissance. Emperors had direct control over the standing army, which was commanded by generals they had appointed. That army was distributed across the frontier provinces and housed in permanent camps along fortified border roads (*limites*), protected by great rivers or defensive structures like palisades, embankments and ditches. They were thus far better placed, strategically and geographically, to obtain information. Moreover, the development of the bureaucracy essential to the everyday operation of permanent professional units provided the means for recording and analyzing information on the ground. It was now easier for the emperor in Rome than it had been for the Republican senate to obtain an overview of military threats and opportunities. Still, there remained great limitations on the emperor's knowledge and his ability to act upon it. Reconnaissance cycles remained largely in the hands of provincial governors.

The main sources of reconnaissance information that was available to the emperors were embassies to Rome, rulers of client states and provincial governors. As in the Republic, the value of such information was admittedly limited by the general tendency of the sources to pursue their own interests, but governors at least were officials who were appointed personally by the emperor. Furthermore, all incoming information could be evaluated with the support of the reliable imperial conciliar committee (*consilium*), and this could be done in the light of written information (maps in itinerary form, geographical treatises, and memoirs written since the Late Republican period). However, the distance between the emperor and the frontier and the slowness of communications – information and dispatches frequently took a month or more to reach their destination – generally did not permit him to react personally to a situation as it developed, or to take direct control. It was thus chiefly the *legati Augusti* responsible for the military provinces on the frontiers who received and processed military reconnaissance, rather than Rome itself.

Frontier governors were expected to acquaint themselves with their province and their army as soon as they took up their posts, by making inspection tours and meeting local client rulers (cf. Arrian's *Periplus Ponti Euxini*). They were also able to consult their large staff (*officia*) of experienced subordinate officers temporarily assigned from the legions in the province. Since each legion provided around 100 such men, the size of the governor's staff was directly proportional to the strength of the particular provincial army. The staff officers (*officiales*) included the *beneficiarii consularis*, each of whom was stationed for six months to *stationes* ('stations') far from the provincial capital, so they were familiar at first hand with the frontier regions. Meanwhile, the *officiales* stationed at provincial headquarters were acquainted with the bigger picture, as they processed all the governor's correspondence. Given that governors changed every three years or so, these men represented an invaluable element of continuity.

The entire correspondence was systematically stored, with thematically related letters and documents stuck together, numbered and sorted into appropriate boxes or pigeonholes. This made it possible to retrieve, analyse and comment on information as needed. There are, for instance, numerous indications that files of individual soldiers (cf. P. Oxy. 7.1022 = RMR 87) and even individual army horses (P. Dur. 130 = RMR 116) in a province were stored in camps and headquarters, and that they were updated when men were transferred or promoted, or retired or died. This degree of bureaucracy only became possible as frontiers became fixed.

It was not customary during the Principate, however, for governors to conduct active reconnaissance beyond the frontier, although – like the emperor – they were privy to some information received from client kings or obtained through bribes given to potential enemies (e.g. Cass. Dio 67,6,5; 68,6,1). There is little or no evidence of foreign espionage (as it would be called now) under the Principate. There was no general practice of operating advance posts beyond river frontiers, but there are occasional examples on the eastern frontier and in Africa from the late 2nd century AD onwards. At about the same period, in Germania (e.g. CIL XIII 6814; 7750; 7751) and elsewhere, units of specialist explorers (*exploratores*) emerge; but many of these may have been created *ad hoc* for specific campaigns, and later when they were assigned to forts as permanent units, they may not have retained their specialist reconnaissance function. There is some evidence to suggest that signalling systems were set up (→ Transmission of orders), but this was normal practice along a border or in a hinterland, for example at Hadrian's Wall [7]. Except in active wartime, Roman reconnaissance, while highly effective, appears to have been mostly passive and reactive.

B.2.2. TACTICAL RECONNAISSANCE

Unlike strategic reconnaissance, which under the Principate evolved as a side effect of broader structural changes in the army, little changed regarding the acquisition of tactical information compared to the days of the Republic. As before, marching armies sent an advance guard of cavalry on ahead as a scouting force (Jos. BI. 3,6,2; Arrian, *Acies contra Alanos* 1). Explorers were selected and assembled into units for specific campaigns (e.g. Ti. Claudius Maximus and his men during the Second Dacian War, AD 105–106: AE 1969/70, 583; cf. Trajan Column, scene cxlv). Some commanders still risked their lives conducting reconnaissance in person – one example being the future emperor Titus, who almost lost his life on a scouting mission during the Siege of Jerusalem (Jos. BI 5,2,1f.). Prisoners of war and deserters were still interrogated (e.g. Tac. Ann. 4,73).

The most striking change in this period was that some emperors from the 2nd century onwards, such as Marcus Aurelius, Lucius Verus and Septimius Severus spent a great deal of time at the frontiers of the empire. They thus took direct control of all military operations in the field, including the gathering and processing of tactical and strategic intelligence. This made decision-making easier and facilitated better coordination between provinces than had been possible during much of the early Principate.

B.3. ROMAN EMPIRE IN LATE ANTIQUITY

During the period of the Late Roman Empire when two legitimate emperors were regularly in place at once and both were increasingly involved at one or other of the empire's borders, whichever of the two faced a problem in his zone of control was responsible, along with his conciliar committee (*consistorium*), for reconnaissance at the highest level. The historian Ammianus Marcellinus (30,3,1–3) reports that in AD 374 the Western Emperor Valentinian received word near Basle that the Quadi had invaded Illyricum. He sent the secretary of the *consistorium*, Paternianus, to investigate the situation. When Paternianus confirmed the gravity of the problem, the *consistorium* had to dissuade Valentinian from military intervention.

Intelligence was gathered by the commanders (*duces*) at the frontier, and from the late 4th century onwards by the commanders of the field army (*magistri*) who were deployed everywhere across the empire. Ammianus Marcellinus (18,6,17–7,6), who served on the staff of one such *magister peditum* ('master of foot soldiers') by the name of Ursicinus, tells of the scouting expedition he personally conducted across the Euphrates in 359 at his superior's command. (There are many references to actual acts of espionage in the Roman Empire of Late Antiquity, particularly on the eastern front bordering Persia (cf. Procop. Pers. 1,21,11f.)). The findings of this expedition were supplemented by information obtained from embassies (Amm. Marc. 18,6,17–19) and merchants (cf. Cod. Iust. 4,63,4). We know that irregular troops were scouting out the situation beyond the border at the northern perimeters of the empire, for example the *areani*, who in the 4th century 'ventured across long distances' in the Scottish Lowlands (Amm. Marc. 28,3,8), and that patrol boats were used for this purpose on the lower Danube in 412 (Cod. Theod. 7,17,1).

Where possible, local commanders reacted directly to information learned through reconnaissance, but they also cooperated with other commanders and high-ranking officials in the region. Such cooperation is attested, for instance, between the *dux Mesopotamiae* Cassianus and the *praefectus praetorio per Orientiem* Strategius Musonianus, when in AD 355 they both independently learned from their own spies (*speculatores*) that the Persian king Sapor II was facing problems with hostile tribes elsewhere in his empire. They consequently worked together to persuade the nearest Persian commander, Tamsapor, to persuade his king to accept a peace with Rome. Strategius informed Emperor Constantius of this plan, but it ultimately came to nothing (Amm. Marc. 16,9,2–4; 16,10,21; 17,5,15). The proliferation of frontier and field army commanders in response to growing threats to the empire in the 4th century thus led to overlapping spheres of activity and cooperation on reconnaissance missions.

The Romans' ability to conduct good reconnaissance did, however, vary from frontier to frontier. Obtaining intelligence was a great deal easier in the east, where Rome faced the Persian Empire, with its major urban centres and large army, whose movements were slow and impossible to conceal [3]. Along the Rhine and Danube frontier, by contrast, reconnaissance was more difficult because the enemy forces were relatively small groups of bandits and plunderers that could appear and disappear suddenly. Even so, the empire of Late Antiquity established fortified advance posts in front of all its frontiers, which were intended to stop enemy incursions into imperial territory and provide an early warning system.

On the tactical level, the *Notitia Dignitatum* notes the continued use of explorer units (*exploratores*), such as had operated along Rome's borders since the 2nd century AD. But as in other cases, it is not clear whether such units retained their specialist function beyond their initial mission, or whether they had merely served originally as reconnaissance units on a campaign. There is no doubt, however, that Roman armies still deployed explorers and the shield protection of cavalry while marching (e.g. Amm. Marc. 31,9,2; 31,12,2f.). It is also certain that some commanders still insisted on scouting the situation with their own eyes. During his campaign against the Persians in AD 363, for instance, Emperor Julian rode ahead to the Tigris to conduct reconnaissance and fell victim to an ambush (Amm. Marc 25,3,2ff.), just as the consuls Marcellus and Crispinus had done over half a millennium before him.

☞ **Avoidance of military service; Battle; Cavalry; Hostages; Infantry; Prisoners; Strategy**

BIBLIOGRAPHY
[1] N.J.E. AUSTIN / N.B. RANKOV, Exploratio. Military and Political Intelligence in the Roman World from the Second Punic War to the Battle of Adrianople, 1995 [2] R. HAENSCH, Das Statthalterarchiv, in: Zeitschrift der Savigny-Stiftung für Rechtsgeschichte 190, Romanistische Abteilung, 1992, 209–317 [3] A.D. LEE, Information and Frontiers. Roman Foreign Relations in Late Antiquity, 1993 [4] W. RIEPL, Das Nachrichtenwesen des Altertums mit besonderer Rücksicht auf die Römer, 1913 [5] R.M. SHELDON, Intelligence Activities in Ancient Rome. Trust in the Gods, but Verify, 2005 [6] D.J. WOOLISCROFT, Das Signalsystem an der Hadriansmauer und seine Auswirkungen auf dessen Aufbau, in: V.A. MAXFIELD / M.J. DOBSON (eds.), Roman Frontier Studies 1989. Proceedings of the XVth International Congress of Roman Frontier Studies, 1991, 142–147 [7] D.J. WOOLLISCROFT, Roman Military Signalling, 2001.

BORIS RANKOV

Recruitment

A. The Greek world
B. The Roman world

A. The Greek world

A.1. Archaic and Classical periods
A.2. The Hellenistic period

A.1. Archaic and Classical periods

Thanks to literary sources, inscriptions (military catalogues, regulations, edicts, treaties, epitaphs) and the abundant papyrus material, we are in a position to achieve an overall picture of both long-term and temporary military commitments. Although the citizen militia is still acknowledged as the norm, historians are now more willing to entertain the diversity of military recruitment – including mercenaries, → auxiliaries and allies – in all periods.

Conditions at Athens are the best known, and they illustrate the model citizen army and citizen soldier: mainly hoplites with accompanying cavalry and an increasingly significant → fleet (trireme oarsmen). Recruitment was based on a census, which combined civil affiliation (*demos*, *phyle*) and age categories. These demands explain the great importance attached to the military training of *ephebes* (young men aged 18–20 registered for military service) in the gymnasium, which continued into the Hellenistic period, as well as the fact that cities kept updated lists of those fit for → military service. Because service in the military was mandatory to an advanced age and could be called upon year after year, cities were occasionally forced to expand their thinking and offer pay. Yet, the model of the citizen soldier was not even the only one. In Classical Syracuse, for instance, particularly during its confrontation with Athens, there was a prominent role for the *epilektoi* ('chosen'), a military group located between the regular forces and mercenaries. In the Boeotian Laegue, the armed forces of the cities were supplemented through mobilization. Sparta had a flexible system that combined the elite of *homoioi* ('peers') with *perioikoi* ('dwellers around [Sparta]') and allies (*xenoi*, *symmachoi*). In exceptional cases, voluntary service by → slaves or the unfree (*penestai* in Thessaly, helots in Sparta), in exchange for the promise of freedom, was preferred. Because of the structural peculiarities of the Lacedaemonian army, demographic decline (oliganthropy) and slowing recruitment went hand in hand in Sparta.

The phenomenon of mercenary service (*misthophoroi*; → Mercenaries) had existed since time immemorial and was used by a variety of regimes [4]. Sufficient examples are provided by the Greeks and Carians in Egypt under the New Kingdom and in Persia: the ten thousand Greek mercenaries in the service of Cyrus the Younger (Xen. An.), and the reputation of the Arcadians, Cretans and (to non-Greeks) Thracians. Although beginning as no more than marginal support for the citizen militias, mercenary service increasingly evolved into an alternative to them. Mercenaries did not necessarily come from disadvantaged regions, and in most cases their service was rooted in reputation and tradition. Insofar as the involvement of mercenaries continued to be seen in Hellenistic societies as a counterpart to civic military service, mercenary activity reflected the growing professionalization of warfare.

A decree of the late 3rd or early 2nd century BC, preserved in two incomplete versions (SEG 49, 722; 855), offers information about recruitment in Macedonia. This Antigonid *diagramma* ('edict') clearly shows the censitary aspect of recruitment, based on a basic unit, the 'hearth' (*pyrokausis*), and on a military district defined by the administrative sphere of an *epistates* (senior administrator of each citizen unit), who was responsible for registration and mobilization. The censitary classes for this purpose were defined within each *politeuma*. This enabled cities to perform partial and general mobilizations (cf. Liv. 33,3; 19,3), which continued to form the basis for recruitment and deployment [26].

A.2. The Hellenistic period

The Hellenistic period brought diversification in the composition and professionalization of armies. The Hellenistic kings relied on recruits from military settlements, the purposes of which were not confined to controlling the territory and retaining the soldiers. They also encouraged soldiers' sons to take up arms. Monarchs relied on diverse and cosmopolitan armed forces, and they standardized recruitment in order to ensure a regular reserve for controlling their whole territory. The Ptolemaic kingdom, for instance, arranged the settlement of *klerouchoi* ('holders of land allotments') in the Egyptian *chora* ('territory'). This created a category of soldiers affiliated with an *ethnos* or pseudo-*ethnos*, followed by the category *tes epigones* ('descendants'). These sons of soldiers in turn served as soldiers or reservists. Among the Egyptian *klerouchoi*, the most important groups by ethnicity or designation were Macedonians (one quarter), Thracians (at least one fifth), Cyrenians, Jews, Thessalians, Cretans, Anatolians and Syrians – essentially reflecting the Ptolemaic sphere of influence [3]. The army also opened up to Egyptian recruitment (*machimoi*), especially after the Battle of Raphia (217 BC). In much the same way, soldiers of various population groups (Macedonians, Mysians and other Anatolians, Jews, Thracians, Persians etc.) were settled in the *katoikiai* ('military settlements') of the Seleucids in Asia Minor (and of other kings), whereupon these communities were able to attain the status of *polis* [9].

Beyond the standing and professionalized royal armies, which had considerable resources at their disposal, because of the increasing contribution of epigraphy and shifts of perspective in contemporary historiography, a reevaluation is underway of citizen armies in the Hellenistic period and the role of the *ephebeia* as a civic institution on the Athenian model as it preserved its military character [6]; [11]. Through the agency of their supreme commander (*hegemon*) or a mercenary recruiter (*xenologos*), mercenaries were integrated into royal and civic armies. Sources often mention problems with recruitment and payment, for example the agreements made between Eumenes I of Pergamum and his soldiers concerning remuneration (OGIS 266), or the difficulties of an Ionian city trying to pay its mercenaries (IEry. 24).

B. The Roman world

B.1. Republic
B.2. Imperial period
B.3. Late Roman army

B.1. Republic

According to tradition, it was Servius Tullius who organized the Roman army by census, assigning 193 centuries to the five property classes that formed the basis for recruitment under the Republic until the reforms of Marius and the enlistment of the *capite censi*, 'those counted by head' (107 BC). The *dilectus*, the consuls' call-up of mobilized citizens, involved the creation of archived lists on the basis of which the military tribunes conducted recruitment in the name of the consuls to form *legiones* ('legions') of equal strength. However, Rome also resorted to recruiting among its allies (*socii*) in Italy and *auxilia externa* ('outer auxiliaries'), which retained their specializations (Hispania, Africa and Gaul).

B.2. Imperial period

B.2.1. General basis
B.2.2. Development of individual units

B.2.1. General basis

The creation of a standing army by Augustus entailed standardization of the legions and auxiliary units (*alae* and cohorts). Under the Empire, only the emperor was entitled in the name of the *imperium* to order a levy of troops, whether by calling up volunteers or through conscription. In Italy, recruitment was the responsibility of special commissioners of senatorial rank (*missi ad dilec-*

tum iuniorum) appointed by the emperor, especially for the urban and Praetorian cohorts, while in the provinces the governor managed recruitment as directed by the emperor. In the senatorial provinces, the *dilectus* was the responsibility of the proconsul, or occasionally it was done by a special appointee of senatorial rank (*legatus as dilectum*) who was supported by subordinates of equestrian rank (*dilectatores*). In smaller, especially procuratorial provinces, the governor might himself assume the function of *dilectator*, while the largest provinces were divided into districts assigned to *dilectatores*. Assisted by imperial officials, they would conduct a preliminary inquiry (*inquisitio*), consulting the censitary register, to evaluate the potential for mobilized recruits. The emergence of the term *dilectarius* to denote legionary recruits is noteworthy (→ Military diplomas of the 3rd century AD; cf. fig. 1).

The documentation of recruitment is at its best for the Imperial period. Valuable sources include soldier lists (including the *origo*, the recruit's place of origin), epitaphs, papyri (RMR; [1]) and especially the remarkable collection of military diplomas (CIL XVI; RMD I–V; RGZM)

Fig. 1: Imperial rescript of Gordianus III, dated December 13, AD 240 (transcript on bronze). The missive grants a *honesta missio* ('honourable discharge') to *Marcus Aure*[*lius* ---]*alus Disae* [*f*(*ilius*)?] *T*(*h*)*rax*. This soldier of the *legio VIII Augusta* (Germania superior) was recruited to one of the legionary *vexillationes* participating in Caracalla's eastern expedition on February 28, AD 214 (following the *probatio* late in 213). The document attests to a massive enlisting of troops (*dilectus*, hence the term *dilectarius*) in the Balkans [38].

with chronological and geographical details of the recruited population groups, and sometimes even records of decisions in individual cases [19]; [31].

In principle, legal status determined assignment to the various army corps. Other criteria included *origo* by ethnicity/province, age and physical stature, along with any letters of recommendation (*litterae commendaticiae*). Slaves were forbidden to perform military service. If they applied as volunteers, they were punished with death, and if they took someone's place, the fault lay with whoever they were replacing (Plin. Ep. 10,30). Recruitment took place in two stages: (1) muster (*probatio*), with verification of physical suitability and legal status; (2) assignation (*signatio, in numeros referre*), with recruits entered into the registers of the first unit to which they were assigned. After daily training that lasted at least four months, the *tiro probatus* ('acceptable recruit') became a *miles* ('soldier'). To receive this basic training, the *tiro* ('recruit') was assigned to a unit by the authority that had performed the muster. Egyptian and Syrian papyri include letters giving the names of *tirones probati* and their basic data (age, distinguishing marks). For instance, a letter of February 103 from the Prefect of Egypt to the prefect of the *coh. III Ituraeorum* includes the assignment of six new recruits to be enlisted in the latter's cohort (P. Oxy. 7,1022; ChLA III 215; RMR 87; CPL 111).

Historians of the modern era have often been led astray by the persistent literary stereotype of the warlike character of the Thracians (Hdt. 5,6; Thuc. 7,29,4; Amm. Marc. 26,7,5; *Expositio totius mundi et gentium* 50; Cod. Iust., *Nov.* 26 pr. 1) and the Balkan tribes (Veg. Mil. 1,28: *bellicosi*). The Thracians and Illyro-Pannonians remained the most important pool of recruits in the 3rd century and later, partly as a result of existing traditions, but partly also because of the many changes of circumstance that affected the Danube provinces in particular, and because recruits from this region made up most of the elite corps that accompanied the emperor, such as the Praetorian cohorts, the Imperial Guard (*equites singulares Augusti*), the *legio II Parthica*, and later the *protectores* and *domestici*. Besides stereotypes of ethnic *origo*, the question of social background drew on other prejudices, such as the supposedly greater hardiness of rural recruits (Veg. Mil. 1,7). In any case, it may be assumed that the majority of soldiers came from humble backgrounds.

Only Roman citizens were allowed to serve in the legions and Praetorian cohorts, but special cases did occur. For instance, a long register of soldiers from Viminacium, preserved only in part (CIL III 14507 = IMS II 53 = AE 2004, 1223), lists about 280 soldiers of the *legio VII Claudia* who were recruited during the major crisis of the Marcomannic Wars in AD 169, and who were discharged in 195. Two thirds of them came from the same province (Moesia superior), and the remainder came from neighbouring provinces. Their names, which are mostly imperial gentilics, indicate that they were mostly *peregrini* (foreigners), who were granted Roman citizenship on enlistment [34]. It is said that Marcus Aurelius even recruited bandits (*latrones*) from Dalmatia and Dardania (SHA Aur. 21,2,7). With regard to this practice, one inscription from Philippopolis in Thrace contains the extraordinary expression *ord(inatos) lestologesas*, 'official bandits' (IGBulg III.1 1126).

B.2.2. DEVELOPMENT OF INDIVIDUAL UNITS

The general contexts of recruitment are explained by the conditions of the specific campaigns, the need for recruits, the development of provinces and the stereotypes concerning the warlike aptitudes of certain population groups. Compared to conscription, voluntary service (there were *cohortes voluntariorum* and *cohortes civium Romanorum*) is elusive and less visible [7]. There were considerable differences between provinces regarding their degree of Romanization and their geostrategic importance. Some provided mainly legionaries, others auxiliaries, yet others marines. For the 2nd century, the number of new recruits is estimated at 9,000–14,000 men for the 30 legions and 10,000–18,000 men for the auxiliary forces.

Under the Julio-Claudian Dynasty, the portion of citizens from Italy and the most heavily Romanized provinces (Gallia Narbonensis, Hispania, Africa) in the legions is striking. Beginning with the reign of Vespasian, the proportion from the first group declined in comparison with the second group and citizens from the Greek east. During the 2nd century, local recruitment became the norm for most legions. In addition, there was the recruitment of soldiers' sons 'born in the camp' (*castris*), before citizens from the Danube and Balkan provinces (Thracians and Pannonians) began to be recruited on a large scale in the 3rd century [21].

The *auxilia* retained an ethnic component in the Julio-Claudian era, with a greater proportion from the provinces of the Alps, Danube and Balkans. As from the reign of Hadrian, local recruitment began to prevail, and the number of Roman citizens began to increase [29]. In general, there has been less sustained and probing interest in the study of recruitment to the auxiliary units than to the legions, partly because of the (apparent) shortage of sources and greater difficulty in interpreting them. There has likewise been a measure of disregard for auxiliary soldiers, who were seen as mere foreigners, although recent studies have been reevaluating the role of provincials [27]. It has proved useful in regard to auxiliaries to ask questions about matters other than their originally ethnic-based recruitment – even if the term 'ethnic soldiers' as a novelty of the Imperial period is valid in the case of the Batavians and other population groups [15]. The data taken as a whole allow us to trace the evolution of recruitment in terms of population groups across centuries and to identify the possible continuities using various recruitment models in order better to understand the regular mix of provincial populations in the Roman army [13]. Many *peregrini* recruits in the auxiliary forces who were already married when enlisted took their families with them to the province where they served. Military service proved the most suitable way for *peregrini* to achieve social advancement, as beneficiaries of a system established by the imperial administration. Besides the potential for upward mobility within the empire and the considerable financial rewards, they would enjoy high status as soldiers and veterans: the *honesta missio* ('honourable discharge') granted them and their children (until AD 140) *civitas Romana* ('Roman citizenship') as well as *conubium* (the right to marry) with their partner.

In the Praetorian fleets, whose soldiers were originally *peregrini* (Egypt, Asia Minor, Dalmatia and Pannonia, Thracia, Sardinia and Corsica), the granting of Roman citizenship at the time of recruitment became automatic in the late 1st century. This explains why it was possible for them to transfer seemlessly to the legions. This was the situation at the time of the war against Bar Kochba (→ Wars of note, B.): marines of the *classis Misenensis* ('Fleet of Misenum') were transferred to the legions following heavy losses in Judaea, leading to a massive recruitment program for marines (especially in the Balkans) between 133 and 135, as documented in the military diplomas awarded in AD 160 [18].

In addition, the military diplomas have made it possible to detect a 25-year cycle of large-scale recruitment among the *Daci* (probably from Moesia inferior) on the basis of discharge dates (127, 153, 178) [12]. The reality must have been exceedingly complex: forced recruitment, at least at first, following the wars and uprisings; then the call-up of ethnic units (Thracians, *Brittones*, Dacians, etc.); and finally, in a critical period, local recruitment and family traditions.

Such a recruitment operation would involve the call-up of hundreds or thousands of recruits in one province, to be sent elsewhere to fill vacancies in assorted units. This was a system coordinated from Rome, its implementation guaranteed by the provincial authorities, as is shown by a papyrus from the reign of Hadrian (ChLA X 422): [*milites di*]*gesti per co(n)sules et nationes et* [*patrias*] (cf. fig. 2) [35], and the AD 68 reference to a group of 500 recruits from Pannonia on the way to Germa-

Fig. 2: Latin papyrus from the reign of Hadrian (ChLA X 422). The text conveys an impression of the annual recruitments of soldiers of different origins, and of how these recruits were distributed to every province: [*milites di*]*gesti per co(nsules) et nationes et* [*patrias*] ('Soldiers sent by the consuls to different tribes and lands'). This was a large-scale recruitment system coordinated from Rome, its implementation guaranteed by the provincial authorities [35].

nia (Tac. Hist. 2,14: *quingenti Pannonii nondum sub signis*). We know of 1,000 *iuniores Bessi* (recruits from Thracia) early in the 3rd century, whom Sextus Iulius Iulianus took to Mauretania Tingitana (CIL VIII 9381; ILS 2763) for integration into the *auxilia* there [37]. Even at this late date, multiple forms of recruitment were running in parallel: local (provincial), regional (from a group of provinces), and general recruitment or on a large scale – all centrally coordinated. A papyrus informs us of the entry of a group of *tirones Asiani* into the *coh. I. Lusitanorum* in Egypt in AD 117 (PSI IX 1063; RMR 74). We learn of an immense recruitment operation in a precisely defined region of southern Asia Minor (province of Lycia-Pamphylia) from four copies of the same constitution (dated March 7, AD 160) for the troops of Syria-Palaestina, attesting to recruits from Aspendus (RGZM 41), Telmessus (RMD III 173), Sagalassus (AE 2011, 1810) and Suedra (AE 2005, 1730) in four different auxiliary units.

B.3. LATE ROMAN ARMY

For the Roman army of Late Antiquity, the legislation of Diocletian in the Tetrarchy introduced a system for enlisting recruits that was linked to a tax revenue. The 'system of patrimonial supply of recruits' created more binding recruitment procedures by assigning the responsibility for recruitment to a new contribution unit (*capitulum* as a body of *collatores*), with payment in kind in the form of actual recruits (*corpora*), and recruitment through monetary payment (i.e. a payment in lieu of service, *aurum tironicum*). The series of laws passed by Diocletian and Constantine (Cod. Theod. 7,22,1–3; 7,23,1) aimed to make 'soldier' status hereditary by introducing a legal requirement for sons of soldiers to enlist. In his constitution of 375, Valens made it the duty of a recruit to provide *ex agro ac domo propria* ('from his own land or house'; Cod. Theod. 7,13,7), in order to put a stop to abuses of the system (use of proxies, *vicarii*). This confirms the continuance of the system of tax-based recruiting [8]. Alongside the creation of new units, which were occasionally recruited from defeated tribes, allies played a prominent role. In the Early Byzantine period, the army was made up of professional soldiers who were paid from tax revenues. The papyri of late Egypt attest to the importance of local recruits in the overall pattern of forces [28].

☞ Army; Auxiliaries; Education; Legion; Mercenaries

BIBLIOGRAPHY

SOURCES

[1] S. DARIS, Documenti per la storia dell'esercito romano in Egitto, 1964.

SECONDARY LITERATURE

[2] R. ALSTON, Soldier and Society in Roman Egypt. A Social History, 1995   [3] R.S. BAGNALL, The Origins of Ptolemaic Cleruchs, in: BASP 21, 1984, 7–20   [4] M. BETTALLI, I mercenari nel mondo greco, vol. 1: Dalle origini alla fine del V sec. a.C., 1995   [5] L. DE BLOIS / E. LO CASCIO (eds.), The Impact of the Roman Army (200 BC–AD 476). Economic, Social, Political, Religious and Cultural Aspects, 2007   [6] T. BOULAY, Arès dans la cité. Les poleis et la guerre dans l'Asie Mineure hellénistique, 2015   [7] P.A. BRUNT, Conscriptions and Volunteering in the Roman Imperial Army, in: SCI 1, 1974, 90–115   [8] J.-M. CARRIÉ, Le système de recrutement des armées romaines de Dioclétien aux Valentiniens, in: Y. LE BOHEC / C. WOLFF (eds.), L'armée romaine de Dioclétien à Valentinien Ier. Actes du congrès de Lyon (12–14 septembre 2002), 2004, 373–387   [9] G.M. COHEN, Katoikia, Katoikoi and Macedonians in Asia Minor, in: AncSoc 22, 1991, 41–50   [10] J.-C. COUVENHES et al. (eds.), Pratiques et identités culturelles des armées hellénistiques du monde méditerranéen. Hellenistic Warfare, vol. 3, 2011   [11] J.-C. COUVENHES / H. FERNOUX (eds.), Les cités grecques et la guerre en Asie Mineure à l'époque hellénistique. Actes de la journée d'études de Lyon, 10 octobre 2003, 2004   [12] D. DANA / F. MATEI-POPESCU, Soldats d'origine dace dans les diplômes militaires, in: Chiron 39, 2009, 209–256   [13] D. DANA / B. ROSSIGNOL, Entrer dans l'armée romaine. Bassins de recrutement des unités auxiliaires (Ier–IIe s. après J.-C.), in: HiMA 6, 2017, 3–11   [14] R.W. DAVIES, Joining the Roman Army, in: BJ 169, 1969, 208–232   [15] C. VAN DRIEL-MURRAY, Ethnic Soldiers. The Experience of the Lower Rhine Tribes, in: T. GRÜNEWALD / S. SEIBEL (eds.), Kontinuität und Diskontinuität. Germania inferior am Beginn und am Ende der römischen Herrschaft. Beiträge des deutsch-niederländischen Kolloquiums in der Katholieke Universiteit Nijmegen (27. bis 30.06.2001), 2003, 200–217   [16] C. VAN DRIEL-MURRAY, Ethnic Recruitment and Military Mobility, in: Á. MORILLO et al. (eds.), Limes XX. XX Congreso internacional de estudios sobre la frontera romana. XXth International Congress of Roman Frontier Studies, vol. 1, 2009, 813–822   [17] W. ECK, Friedenssicherung und Krieg in der römischen Kaiserzeit. Wie ergänzt man das römische Heer?, in: A. EICH (ed.), Die Verwaltung der kaiserzeitlichen römischen Armee. Studien für Hartmut Wolff, 2010, 87–110   [18] W. ECK / A. PANGERL, Die Konstitution für die classis Misenesis aus dem Jahr 160 und der Krieg gegen Bar Kochba unter Hadrian, in: ZPE 155, 2006, 239–255   [19] W. ECK / H. WOLFF (eds.), Heer und Integrationspolitik. Die römischen Militärdiplome als historische Quelle, 1986   [20] C. FISCHER-BOVET, Army and Society in Ptolemaic Egypt, 2014   [21] G. FORNI, Il reclutamento delle legioni da Augusto a Diocleziano, 1953   [22] G. FORNI, Esercito e marina di Roma antica. Raccolta di contributi, 1992   [23] E. GABBA, Esercito e società nella repubblica romana, 1973   [24] S. GALLET / Y. LE BOHEC, Le recrutement des auxiliaires d'après les diplômes militaires et les autres inscriptions, in: H. LIEB / M.A. SPEIDEL (eds.), Militärdiplome. Die Forschungsbeiträge der Berner Gespräche von 2004 (Mavors 15), 2007, 267–292   [25] G. GIGLI, Forme di reclutamento militare durante il basso impero, in: RAL 8/2, 1947, 268–289   [26] M.B. HATZOPOULOS, L'organisation de l'armée macédonienne sous les Antigonides. Problèmes anciens et documents nouveaux, 2001   [27] I. HAYNES, Blood of the Provinces. The Roman Auxilia and the Making of Provincial Society from Augustus to the Severans, 2013   [28] A.M. KAYSER, Rekrutierungspraxis im spätantiken Ägypten, in: C. WOLFF (ed.), Le métier de soldat dans le monde romain. Actes du cinquième congrès de Lyon (23–25 septembre 2010), 2012, 99–120   [29] K. KRAFT, Zur Rekrutierung der Alen und Kohorten an Rhein und Donau, 1951   [30] M. LAUNEY, Recherches sur les armées hellénistiques, 2 vols., 1949–1950 (reprinted in 1987)   [31] H. LIEB / M.A. SPEIDEL (eds.), Militärdiplome. Die Forschungsbeiträge der Berner Gespräche von 2004 (Mavors 15), 2007   [32] F. LIEBENAM, Dilectus, in: RE 5/1, 1903, 591–639   [33] J.C. MANN, Legionary Recruitment and Veteran Settlement during the Principate, 1983   [34] M. MIRKOVIĆ, The Roster of the VII Claudia Legion, in: ZPE 146, 2004, 211–220   [35] M.A. SPEIDEL, Rekruten für ferne Provinzen. Der Papyrus ChLA X 422 und die kaiserliche Rekrutierungszentrale, in: ZPE 163, 2007, 281–295 (reprinted in: M.A. Speidel, Heer und Herrschaft im Römischen Reich der Hohen Kaiserzeit, 2009, 213–234)   [36] M.P. SPEIDEL, The Rise of Ethnic Units in the Roman Imperial Army, in: ANRW II.3, 1975, 202–231 (reprinted in: M.P. Speidel, Roman Army Studies, vol. 1, 1984, 117–148)   [37] M.P. SPEIDEL, A Thousand Thracian Recruits for Mauretania Tingitana, in: AntAfr 11, 1977, 167–173 (reprinted in: M.P. Speidel, Roman Army Studies, vol. 1, 1984, 341–347)   [38] P. WEISS, Eine honesta missio in Sonderformat. Neuartige Bronzeurkunden für Veteranen der Legionen in Germania superior unter Gordian III., in: Chiron 45, 2015, 23–75   [39] L. WHITBY, Recruitment in Roman Armies from Justinian to Heraclius (ca. 565–615), in: A. CAMERON (ed.), The Byzantine and Early Islamic Near East, vol. 3: States, Resources and Armies, 1995, 61–124.

DAN DANA

Refusal of military service

☞ Avoidance of military service

Religion

A. Greek
B. Roman Republic
C. Roman Imperial period
D. Late Antiquity

A. Greek

A.1. Connectedness
A.2. Consultation of oracles
A.3. Religious specialists
A.4. Divine aid
A.5. Before battle
A.6. Divine intervention
A.7. After battle

A.1. Connectedness

In Ancient Greece, every aspect of war had, in today's terms, a 'religious' aspect. The Greeks had no equivalent to the word 'religion', and seemingly no sense that religious acts, rituals and undertakings belonged to a distinct sphere of human experience [12]. To them, the gods participated in every moment of war, from the initial decision to launch hostilities to the truce or → peace agreement that ended the conflict. The many rites associated with war probably evolved over time, and there seem to have been differences in practice and emphasis between cities and ethnicities (especially between Dorians and Ionians). Still, evidence suggests a high degree of continuity in this sphere throughout the Classical and Hellenistic periods (490–30 BC).

Wars were not started solely for religious reasons [16. 130f.], but given the interweaving of religion and politics [21], the pretexts for attacking another city generally had a religious dimension. For instance, an enemy might stand accused of breaking a treaty or peace agreement (all treaties were ratified by an oath before the gods), or of having committed a particular offence, such as building on sacred land (as the Athenians accused Megara of doing around 432 BC; cf. Thuc. 1,139,2) or desecrating a sanctuary (cf. the First and Second Sacred Wars over control of Delphi). Philip II (→ Generals of note, M.) and Alexander the Great (→ Generals of note, B.) both declared their intention to punish the Persians for burning down Greek temples (Diod. Sic. 16,89; Arr. Anab. 3,18,12).

A.2. Consultation of oracles

No official decision to start a war was made without consulting the gods through one or more methods of divination. Despite the claim by the Eleans that it was not customary to consult the oracles at Panhellenic sanctuaries concerning wars among Greeks (Xen. Hell. 3,2,22), many cities did precisely this – either before the final decision to wage war or ahead of an important battle [8. 49–54]; [13. 87f.]; [16. 124f.]. In 432 BC, for instance, the popular assembly in Sparta voted to declare that the Athenians had broken the 30-year peace. It went on to consult Apollo at Delphi, as to whether it was advisable to start a war (Thuc. 1,118) [3. 4f.]. The Athenians turned to three oracles before invading Sicily in 415 BC: Zeus Ammon at the Libyan oasis of Siwa, the Dodona Zeus at Epirus, and Apollo at Delphi (Plut. *Nicander* 13f.; Plut. Mor. 403B; Paus. 8,11,12) [3. 9f.]. Before the Battle of Leuctra (371 BC), the Spartans consulted the oracle of Zeus at Dodona 'regarding victory' (Cic. Div. 1,74 and 2,54–57, a quotation from Callisthenes from Olynthus, FGrH 124, F 22a). In 336 BC, Philip II asked Delphi whether he would defeat a king of the Persians (Arses) (Diod. Sic. 16,91,2). Alexander the Great intended to ask a similar question, but found the Delphic oracle closed when he visited (Plut. *Alexander* 14, 6f.; Diod. Sic. 17,93,4).

A.3. Religious specialists

Independent religious specialists – seers (*manteis*) and oracle singers (*chresmologoi*, sometimes translated as 'oracle gatherers') – played an important role before and during campaigns, and charged fees for their services [1]; [2. 153–187]. Oracle singers, who did not generally take part in campaigns, owned collections of supposedly very ancient oracles, which they recited and interpreted in reference to contemporary conditions or problems. Their services were especially in demand immediately before a war (Hdt. 7,6; 7,142f.). According to Thucydides (Thuc. 2,8,2; 2,21,3), oracle singers in cities all over Greece made numerous prophecies at the outbreak of the Peloponnesian War (431–404 BC). Their influence was such that the Athenians reacted to the destruction of their expeditionary force in 413 BC with anger at the seers and oracle singers who had given them hope that they would conquer Sicily (Thuc. 8,1).

Seers, who were experts in the art of divination, always accompanied generals on campaigns. The aim of their work was to ascertain the will and intentions of the gods with regard to human actions. They did this by interpreting divine signs, which were either requested and obtained – such as features in the entrails of sacrificial animals – or occurred unsolicited as natural phenomena. Seers attached themselves as personal advisors to prominent generals and statesmen. It was even believed that they had the power to 'win' battles (Hdt. 9,33,2; 9,35) [2. 94–96].

During a campaign, seers looked for omens or portents and performed divinatory sacrifices at every stage of the war: before the army set out from home or from camp, prior to crossing frontier lines, and ahead of battle. Two forms of sacrificial divination were of particular significance before battles: the sacrifice in the field camp (*hiera*) and the sacrifice on the battle line (*sphagia*). The *hiera* included studying the viscera of the sacrificial animal (usually a sheep), especially the liver, while the *sphagia* involved cutting the throat of the animal (goat or ram) and observing its movements and blood flow [9]; [14]. When a seer declared the omens favourable, this did not mean that success or victory was guaranteed. The sacrifice was only intended to establish whether matters should proceed towards an encounter with the enemy [9. 205]. The gods revealed their will, but did not guarantee victory. Even if a commander followed the advice of his seer, it was still considered entirely possible for him to lose the battle if he committed a strategic or tactical error.

A.4. DIVINE AID
Unfavourable omens or ominous portents (especially earthquakes) could put a stop to a campaign (Thuc. 3,89,1; 6,95,1; 8,6,5) or halt military operations. An eclipse of the Moon in 413 BC, for example, prevented the Athenians from setting out from Syracuse (Thuc. 7,50,4). Since a seer would be able to sacrifice up to three times daily, it was rare for negative omens to prevent an imminent battle. Before the Battle of Plataeae (479), the seers on both sides announced that the omens were good for mounting a defence, but unfavourable for launching an attack (Hdt. 9,36f.).

Festivals sometimes delayed hostilities, especially among the Spartans. Their three most important festivals were the Hyakinthia (late spring/early summer, 3 days' duration), the Gymnopaidia (high summer, 3–5 days) and the Karneia (late summer, 9 days). Whether by chance or planning, the timing of these festivals limited the duration and spatial extent of Spartan military operations at the peak of the war season. Religious festivals served to regulate Spartan military morale, while also forging the social context that justified the acceptance and upholding of this ethos [5. 428–430].

Success in war depended on obtaining and keeping the goodwill and support of the gods. Good omens alone did not suffice, for both opposing armies usually received them before the fight began. Frequent sacrifices, vows in the event of victory and the avoidance of impious acts were all important ways of securing divine aid (cf. fig. 1). The best-known example is that of the Athenians before the Battle of Marathon (→ Battles of note, F.), who promised to offer Artemis one sacrificial goat for every Persian they killed (Xen. An. 3,2,12). Xenophon, whose religious views seem to have been standard [4]; [15], repeatedly emphazises the necessity of constantly seeking divine advice and support (Xen. Hipp. 9,8f.; Xen. Cyr. 1,6,46; Xen. Oec. 5,19f.). He also stresses the importance of making every effort to win the gods as allies (e.g. break no oaths, plunder no temples, never use violence against supplicants). This was crucial, for the gods were able at will to make the great small and to protect the weak (Xen. An. 3,2,10).

Fig. 1: Frieze from a red-figured *stamnos* (c. 450–400 BC, attributed to the Cleophon Painter). The scene shows a warrior about to go to war, offering a libation to the gods. The person facing him is probably his wife. At the far left stands his father (probably a seer), and another woman to the right.

A.5. BEFORE BATTLE

Once the *hiera* and *sphagia* proved favourable, a catchphrase was spread along the battle lines for the troops already formed up, for example 'Zeus the Saviour and Victory' (Xen. An. 1,8,16; 6,5,25). Then, when the opposing armies clashed, the soldiers would sing a paean to Apollo (Str. 9,3,12; less plausibly to Ares, despite [11. 118f.]). This was immediately followed by a battle-cry to Enyalios (byname of Ares as god of war; cf. Xen. An. 1,8,18; 4,3,19; 5,2,14; Xen. Cyr. 7,1,26; Arr. Anab. 1,14,7). Evidence for the singing of a paean before battle is especially strong in the case of the Dorian *poleis* [17. 105–108], but there are indications that the Athenians did the same (Thuc. 6,32; Xen. Hell. 2,4,17).

A.6. DIVINE INTERVENTION

In the Homeric epics, the gods join the fight in person and sometimes even make themselves visible to the dying. Gods and especially heroes are still present in the historians' battle reports, although less frequently [19. 11–46]. There are many examples of epiphanies from the Persian Wars: it was said that several heroes, includiung Theseus, joined battle at Marathon in 490 BC [19. 23f.]. In 480 BC, during the Persian attack on the temple at Delphi, divine powers intervened in spectacular fashion (Hdt. 8,37): sacred weapons appeared before the temple, followed by thunder, lightning and falling rocks. A divine battle-cry was then heard, and two local heroes appeared. After the Battle of Plataeae, it was discovered that not a single Persian had fallen in the sacred precinct of Demeter, even though battle had raged immediately beside it (Hdt. 9,65). In 424 BC, the Spartan Brasidas attributed his capture of a fortress on Chalcidice to the intervention of the goddess Athena, whose temple was nearby (Thuc. 4,116). Furthermore, it was believed that the gods intervened invisibly on behalf of their favourites. Actions of gross impiety, on the other hand, could lead to catastrophic defeat. According to Xenophon, it was the Spartans' capture of the Acropolis of Thebes in 382 – contrary to their sworn oath – that ultimately led to the destruction of their army at the Battle of Leuctra (371), and thereafter to the collapse of their hegemony in Greece (Xen. Hell. 5,4,1; 6,4,2f.) [6. 318–322].

A.7. AFTER BATTLE

When a land battle ended, it was expected that both sides would allow the bodies of their fallen enemies to be buried during a truce. Some *poleis* (e.g. Sparta) buried their dead immediately on the battlefield. Others (e.g. Athens) took them home for public funerals. The return of the dead was negotiated by heralds, who were under the protection of the god Hermes and thus inviolable. The side claiming victory now sang another paean to Apollo (Xen. Hell. 4,3,21; 7,2,15) and built a tropaeum at the place where the enemy had turned to take flight (Thuc. 2,92; 7,54). This took the form of a wooden pillar with a full set of enemy armament hung from it [8. 64–70]; [18. 246–275] (cf. fig. 2). After a victory at sea, the tropaeum was put up as close to the battle site as possible (Thuc. 8,42,4). These acts were essentially religious in nature, so it was sacrilege to refuse the burial of the fallen or to desecrate a victory monument. Sacrifices were made to accompany both the building of the tropaeum and the thanksgiving after news the victory reached home (Isoc. Or. 7,10; Xen. Hell. 1,6,36f.) [8. 69].

It was customary after a victory for both cities and individuals to present votive gifts to the gods at temples and sanctuaries. Cities generally gave one tenth of the spoils (including weapons and armour), which may also have served an economic purpose [10. 176–202]. During the 5th and 4th centuries BC, the Athenians used spoils of war to build at least twelve six-foot 'Golden *Nikaí*' on the Acropolis – bronze statues of the goddess of victory, each coated in 120 pounds of gold. These

Fig. 2: Silver tetradrachma of Agathocles, tyrant of Syracuse (310/08–306/05 BC; 17.18 g; diameter: ca. 24.4 mm). Garlanded head of Kore-Persephone, looking right. On the reverse, Nike, standing turned to the right, brandishes a trophy. Persephone and her mother Demeter were goddesses of particular importance to Agathocles: he saw them as protectresses of Sicily. When he invaded Africa in 310 BC, he burned his ships, fulfilling a vow to the two goddesses, and announced to his troops that the goddesses had, through omens obtained from the sacrifice (*hiera*), foretold victory in the entire war (Diod. Sic. 20,7; Iust. 22,6). The image of the goddess of victory brandishing the trophy was intended to embolden the troops, who included a considerable number of mercenaries. Despite initial military successes against Carthage, however, the campaign would ultimately fail.

were later melted down to pay the costs of the Peloponnesian War and later conflicts [7. 60 with 335 note 144].

In addition to votive gifts to sanctuaries in one's own territory, it was common to build monuments and dedicate objects elsewhere, especially at the Panhellenic sanctuaries of Delphi and Olympia, where they would serve both as thankofferings to the gods and as propaganda aimed at other Greeks. Following his victory over the Athenians at Aigos Potamos, the Spartan *strategos* ('commander') Lysander dedicated an immense gathering of monuments at Delphi. It comprised 37 bronze statues of deities and admirals – including one of himself being crowned by Poseidon (Paus. 10,9,7) [20. 105–107]. After the Battle of the Granicus in 334 BC, Alexander sent 300 complete sets of Persian armour to Athens as votive gifts for Athena, bearing the pointed inscription, 'Alexander, son of Philip, and the Greeks (except the Spartans), from the barbarians who live in Asia [Minor]' (Arr. Anab. 1,16,7; Plut. *Alexander* 16,17f.). Greek *poleis* could boast at others' expense even while honouring the gods.

☞ State and army, A. Greek

BIBLIOGRAPHY
[1] J. DILLERY, Chresmologues and Manteis. Independent Diviners and the Problem of Authority, in: S.I. JOHNSTON / P.T. STRUCK (eds.), Mantikê. Studies in Ancient Divination, 2005, 167–231 [2] M.A. FLOWER, The Seer in Ancient Greece, 2008 [3] M.A. FLOWER, Athenian Religion and the Peloponnesian War, in: O. PALAGIA (ed.), The Timeless and Temporal. The Political Implications of Athenian Art, 2009, 1–23 [4] M.A. FLOWER, Piety in Xenophon's Theory of Leadership, in: R.F. BUXTON (ed.), Aspects of Leadership in Xenophon (Histos Supplementary 5), 2016, 85–119 [5] M.A. FLOWER, Spartan Religion, in: A. POWELL (ed.), The Blackwell Companion to Ancient Sparta, 2017, 425–451 [6] M.A. FLOWER, Xenophon as a Historian, in: M.A. FLOWER (ed.), The Cambridge Companion to Xenophon, 2017, 301–322 [7] J.M. HURWIT, The Athenian Acropolis. History, Mythology, and Archaeology from the Neolithic Era to the Present, 1998 [8] A. JACQUEMIN, Guerre et religion dans le monde grec (490–322 av. J.-C.), 2000 [9] M.H. JAMESON, Sacrifice before Battle, in: V.D. HANSON (ed.), Hoplites. The Classical Greek Battle Experience, 1991, 197–228 [10] T.S.F. JIM, Sharing with the Gods. Aparchai and 'Dekata' in Ancient Greece, 2014 [11] R. LONIS, Guerre et religion en Grèce à l'époque classique, 1979 [12] B. NONGBRI, Before Religion. A History of a Modern Concept, 2013 [13] R. PARKER, Greek States and Greek Oracles, in: R. BUXTON (ed.), Oxford Readings in Greek Religion, 2000, 76–108 [14] R. PARKER, Sacrifice and Battle, in: H. VAN WEES (ed.), War and Violence in Ancient Greece, 2000, 299–314 [15] R. PARKER, One Man's Piety. The Religious Dimension of the Anabasis, in: R. LANE FOX (ed.), The Long March. Xenophon and the Ten Thousand, 2004, 131–153 [16] R. PARKER, War and Religion in Ancient Greece, in: K. ULANOWSKI (ed.), The Religious Aspects of War in the Ancient Near East, Greece, and Rome, 2016, 123–132 [17] W.K. PRITCHETT, The Greek State at War, vol. 1, 1971 [18] W.K. PRITCHETT, The Greek State at War, vol. 2, 1974 [19] W.K. PRITCHETT, The Greek State at War, vol. 3, 1979 [20] M. SCOTT, Delphi and Olympia, 2010 [21] K. TRAMPEDACH, Politische Mantik. Die Kommunikation über Götterzeichen und Orakel im klassischen Griechenland, 2015.

MICHAEL A. FLOWER

B. ROMAN REPUBLIC

B.1. Going to war
B.2. Evocatio
B.3. Trophy, triumph, ovatio

Reliable information is available from about the 3rd century BC onwards and will be used here to reconstruct religious rituals in the context of military life and activity.

B.1. GOING TO WAR

B.1.1. Declaring and preparing for war
B.1.2. In the field

In order to lead an army into battle, a consul or praetor not only needed to be elected and confirmed in office by auspices, he also needed to observe the *feriae Latinae* ('Latin Festival' on Monte Cavo) and perform the requisite sacrifices at Lavinium.

B.1.1. DECLARING AND PREPARING FOR WAR
As soon as it was decided to embark on military action, whether through the sending of the *fetiales* (an official body of priests) to deliver an ultimatum or through the senate's decision to wage war, and the consuls, praetors or dictator were instructed to conduct the war, the legionaries lined up on the Capitol and followed the legates and tribunes in swearing their → oath (*sacramentum*) [16. 76–91]. According to Livy (22,38,1–6), the *sacramentum*, which was a special form of *iusiurandum* ('vow'), was voluntary and taken within one's unit in Rome's early history, but in 216 BC it became obligatory and the military tribunes were put in charge of having soldiers recite it. This procedure did not change during the latter centuries of the Republican period. The oath listed a number of actions that the soldier was required to do or forbidden to do, on pain of punishment by the gods. The gods, invoked as witnesses and bondsmen for the oath, would be insulted if the oath were broken and could be expected to take revenge for the affront. The *sacramentum* was indispensable because, according to Cato the Elder (Cic. Off. 1,37), it authorized the soldier to kill an enemy. Its validity was limited to the duration of the campaign. The Latins and *socii* ('allies') independently

assembled and swore in their own troops, who then made their way to a specific place at a specified time in accordance with an edict from a consul (Pol. 6,21,4).

The prelude to hostilities came with proclamations by two *fetiales*: the *pater patratus* accompanied by the *verbenarius*, who brought herbs picked on the Capitol. From the 3rd century BC onwards, increasing distances prevented the *fetiales* from conveying the senate's decisions in person, so a legal fiction was adopted. From that point on, the *pater patratus*, who remained in Rome, declared war by hurling a lance into a plot of land near the Temple of Bellona that had been purchased by a prisoner of war, and was thus technically speaking 'enemy' territory (Serv. Aen. 9,52; Serv. Auct.).

As soon as the army was assembled in Rome, the commander – consul, praetor or dictator – took the auspices for the march out and went to the Capitol to make a vow to Jupiter, Juno and Minerva that he would win victory and return uninjured. He then went to the Forum and the *sacrarium* (place for holy things) of Mars in the Regia (seat of the *pontifices* ('priests') and *flamines* (lit. 'those who burn', a type of priest) on the south side of the Forum Romanum), to shake the *ancilia* (the shields of the *salii*, who were a body of twelve priests) and the lance representing Mars, while speaking the formula *Mars vigila* ('Mars, awake!'; Serv. Aen. 8,3; 7,603). Finally, he marched the army out. Clearly, these rituals could only be performed when it was possible to march the army out in an orderly manner. Various rituals at the start of the military campaigning season addressed war horses and weapons. On March 19, which was the *quinquatrus* of Minerva, the *salii* processed through the streets of Rome, performing their war dances armed in the old style (*ancilia movere*, 'moving the shields'). The races of the Equirria were celebrated close to the Altar of Mars on February 27 and March 14.

B.1.2. IN THE FIELD

Before marching out, a *lustratio* ('purification') of the army was held in the Field of Mars. A gathering of units and divisions formed into a unified army and called upon Mars to protect it. In times when confederates from outside Rome joined the legionary army, a *lustratio* of the entire army was presumably held at the place where the various parts of the army met. The same was true of a fleet (Liv. 36,42,2).

As the deployment continued, the commander would regularly hold auspices, especially before a military operation and before crossing rivers. During the period of the Punic Wars, a form of auspices became customary during military campaigns in which, rather than studying the flight of birds, the priests would observe the behaviour of hens in cages [18]. Gradually, a sacrifice also became established, with *haruspices* ('diviners') in the commander's entourage conducting prophecies from it, while *pullarii* ('hen-keepers') were responsible for the hen auspices. Because failure or other difficulties often called the status of the commander into question, and because it was becoming more and more difficult for such a commander to return to Rome to obtain new auspices concerning his legitimacy in office, a new practice took hold. It now became usual to dedicate as a *templum* ('temple') a piece of land in the region where operations were ongoing, which was thus seen as 'Roman'. This fiction of religious law enabled the holder of an *imperium* (command authority) to take legitimizing auspices on campaign as if he were in Rome, and thus assure himself of renewed legitimacy in his right to command. Daily auspices and prophetic sacrifices were performed to inquire into details of the operation. They took place in the *templum* built in the camp (Liv. 41,18,8) or the surrounding land.

In general, commanders made specific vows before battles, making an assortment of promises that might range from a bowl of sweet wine (*pocillum mulsi*), a drink that symbolized the authority of Jupiter (on the legend [19. 99ff.]), to a large-scale sacrifice or the dedication of a temple or public games. The deities receiving these vows would not only be Jupiter, Juno and Minerva, Mars and Apollo, but also others connected in some way with the ongoing war: Bellona victrix, Fors Fortuna, Fortuna equestris, Venus victrix, and, later Apollo and Diana (Octavian), Isis and Serapis (Vespasian). Soldiers also appear to have made vows, but the sources of the Republican period reveal little or nothing about them. As in the case of most military rituals under the Republic, the sources only give information about religious rites connected with warfare.

One particularly spectacular military ritual was the *devotio*. This involved the consul, his head cloaked and standing on a spear laid beneath his feet, dedicating himself and the enemies he was about to face in battle to the *Dii Manes* (the collected deities of the dead) and the goddess Tellus, so that they would grant victory to the Roman people. He then plunged into the enemy battle line to drag his adversaries down to death with him. This ritual was performed three times by members of the *gens Decii* (340, 295 and 279 BC).

B.2. EVOCATIO

One unusual ritual consisted of an invitation to the enemy's gods to come to the aid of the Romans in exchange for a promise to build them a temple and establish a regular cult (Plin. HN 28,18). The first known examples concern Castor, cardinal deity of Tusculum, at the Battle of Lake Regillus

(Liv. 2,20,12), who received a temple in the Forum, and Juno regina of Veii, whose statue was taken to Rome after the victory and for whom a temple was built on the Aventine (Liv. 5,21,3–7). The *evocatio* of Juno of Carthage by Scipio Africanus became famous (Serv. Aen. 2,244, 351), as did the prayer of evocation supposedly offered by Scipio Aemilianus in the Third Punic War (149–146 BC) (Macrob. Sat. 3,9,7f.). Following the recitation of the prayer, a prophetic sacrifice was performed to establish the deity's assent to the *evocatio* (invitation to Rome, where the deity would receive a public cult; Macrob. Sat. 3,9,9).

The sole piece of direct documentary evidence, an inscription on the capture of Isaura Vetus in 75 BC, does not recount the same procedure. The stone describes the fulfilment of a vow to *Sive deus sive dea cuius in tutela oppidum vetus Isauricum fuerat* ('the god or goddess in whose protection the old town of Isauricum stood') after the capture of the town and the sale of its surviving inhabitants. The ritual does not correspond to the accounts in the literary sources, being directed, as in 146 BC, merely to *Sive deus sive dea* ('the god or goddess'; see [3]). The inscription simply mentions the fulfilment of the vow made before the capture of the city, and it may represent only that part of the ritual that was performed in this location. Nothing rules out the possibility that this deity may also have been taken to Rome and given a cult there.

B.3. TROPHY, TRIUMPH, OVATIO

After a victory, the commander, wearing his toga in the form of the *cinctus Gabinus* (girded in the manner of the city of Gabii), burned the weapons of the → enemy and dedicated them – in the early period to Vulcan, once to Jupiter Victor (295), and in the 2nd century BC chiefly to the deities of war, including Mars, Minerva and Lua Mater. Sometimes these deities were associated with Vulcan, whose consuming fire destroyed the defeated enemy's weapons. In 121 BC, the Greek practice of setting up trophies was adopted, and some texts also mention thanksgiving offerings, generally offered in the field at the end of a war (Plut. *Marcellus* 22,1–3; perhaps also Liv. 41,18,3). Finally, the campaign might culminate in a → triumph at Rome, at which the *triumphator*, who on this day was dressed like a statue of Jupiter, performed a sacrifice to Jupiter on the Capitol, thus fulfilling the vows spoken before the army marched out. Sacrificial banquets, increasingly splendid as Rome's successes multiplied and grew, concluded the ceremony. The *triumphator* fully completed his obligations when he built any temple or held any games he may have promised during the campaign. In the scaled-down version of the triumph, the *ovatio*, the victorious army leader rode on horseback into the city and laid his wreath on the knees of the statue of Jupiter on the Capitol. As his *ex voto* (offering made in fulfillment of a vow) from the Civil Wars, Augustus in 2 BC had built not only the Forum of Augustus, but also a new Temple of Mars Ultor, which now became the military centrepiece of the state (cf. fig. 3).

Traditionally, the military season ended with the races and sacrifice of the *October equus* ('October Horse') on the Field of Mars on October 15, and the placing of the *ancilia* ('shields') into storage by the *salii*, who processed them (*ancilia condere*) one final time through Rome on October 19, the festival day of the Armilustrium.

☞ **Legion; State and Army**

Fig. 3: Louis Noguet, reconstruction of the main façade of the Temple of Mars Ultor (watercolour, ink, gold highlights, 1868/69). Immediately after his victory over Brutus and Cassius at Philippi (Macedonia, 42 BC), Octavian began planning the construction of this temple to Mars the Avenger as a votive gift. The standards of the defeated legions were to be dedicated there to the war god. However, the purchase of the land took an inordinate time, and the temple was not dedicated until August 1, 2 BC. The temple itself contained images not only of Mars Ultor, but also of the deified Caesar (Divus Iulius). Augustus instructed that the senate should henceforth meet in this temple to discuss matters of war and peace, and proconsuls and legates taking command in provinces were to set off from it. The temple, moreover, served as the place of arrival for *triumphatores*, who presented their spoils there. Boys were able to put on the *toga virilis* at the temple. The columned halls were decorated with statues of the great men of Rome and eulogies to them. Standing in one *exedra* were Aeneas with the kings of Alba Longa and members of the *gens Iulia*, and in the other *exedra* stood Romulus.

Bibliography

[1] E. BIRLEY, The Religion of the Roman Army, 1885–1977, in: ANRW II.16, 1978, 1506–1541 [2] A. VON DOMASZEWSKI, Die Religion des römischen Heeres, in: A. VON DOMASZEWSKI, Aufsätze zur römischen Heeresgeschichte, 1972, 81–209 [3] G. FERRI, Una testimonianza epigrafica dell'evocatio? Su un'iscrizione di Isaura Vetus, in: S. ANTOLINI et al. (eds.), Giornata di studi per di Lidio Gasperini, 2010, 183–194 [4] R.O. FINK et al., The Feriale Duranum, in: Yale Classical Studies 7, 1940, 1–222 [5] I.P. HAYNES, The Romanization of Religion in the Auxilia of the Roman Imperial Army from Augustus to Septimius Severus, in: Britannia 24, 1993, 141–157 [6] J. HELGELAND, Roman Army Religion, in: ANRW II.16, 1978, 1470–1505 [7] J. HELGELAND, Christians and the Roman Army, in: ANRW II.23, 1979, 724–834 [8] A.H.M. JONES, The Social Background of the Struggle between Paganism and Christianity, in: A. MOMIGLIANO (ed.), Conflict between Paganism and Christianity in the Fourth Century, 1963, 17–26 [9] G. KREMER, Götterdarstellungen, Kult- und Weihdenkmäler aus Carnuntum (CSIR, Österreich, Suppl. 1: Carnuntum), 2012 [10] P. LE ROUX, Soldats et cultes indigènes dans les provinces occidentales au Haut-Empire, in: P. LE ROUX, Scripta varia, vol. 1: La toge et les armes. Rome entre Méditerranée et Océan, 2011, 239–252 [11] J. NÉLIS-CLÉMENT, Le monde des dieux chez les beneficiarii, in: Der römische Weihebezirk von Osterburken. 2. Kolloquium 1990 und paläobotanische Untersuchungen, 1994, 251–260 [12] J. NÉLIS-CLÉMENT, Les beneficiarii. Militaires et administrateurs au service de l'Empire (1er s. a.C.–VIe s. p.C.), 2000 [13] A.D. NOCK, The Roman Army and the Roman Religious Year (1952), in: A.D. NOCK, Essays on Religion and the Ancient World, 1972, 736–790 [14] G. PICARD, Les trophées romains. Contribution à l'histoire de la religion et de l'art triomphal de Rome (Bibliothèque des Écoles françaises d'Athènes et de Rome 187), 1957 [15] M. REDDÉ, Réflexions critiques sur les chapelles militaires (aedes principiorum), in: JRA 17, 2004, 443–462 [16] J. RÜPKE, Domi militiae. Die religiöse Konstruktion des Krieges in Rom, 1990 [17] J. SCHEID, Commentarii fratrum arvalium qui supersunt. Les copies épigraphiques des protocoles annuels de la confrérie arvale (21 av.–304 ap. J.-C.) (Roma antica 4), 1998 [18] J. SCHEID, Le rite des auspices à Rome. Quelle évolution? Réflexions sur la transformation de la divination publique des Romains entre le IIIe et le Ier siècle avant notre ère, in: S. GEORGOUDI et al. (eds.), La raison des signes. Présages, rites, destin dans les sociétés de la Méditerranée ancienne, 2012, 109–128 [19] R. SCHILLING, La religion romaine de Vénus depuis les origines jusqu'au temps d'Auguste (Bibliothèque des Écoles Françaises d'Athènes et de Rome 178), ²1982 [20] C. SCHMIDT HEIDENREICH, Les lieux de culte des génies de centuries dans les camps militaires du Haut-Empire romain, in: XII Congressus internationalis epigraphiae graecae et latinae, 2007, 1325–1330 [21] J.F. SHEAN, Soldiering for God. Christianity and the Roman Army, 2010 [22] O. STOLL, The Religions of the Armies, in: P. ERDKAMP (ed.), A Companion to the Roman Army, 2007, 451–476.

JOHN SCHEID

C. Roman Imperial period

C.1. Collective cult sites of the army corps
C.2. Cults practised in the Roman army: the official calendar of the Roman army
C.3. Private cults

Rituals related to war did not change significantly during the Imperial period, but the source material is much better, especially regarding military life itself. As a result, we know far more details about the obligations and ceremonies that developed as military service and army camps became permanent phenomena.

The emperor's departure was always accompanied by vows for marching out, as the commentaries of the Arval Brethren attest (cf. e.g. [17. 178–180]), but we lack information about the marching out of the *legati Augusti pro praetore* ('legates of the emperor, acting on behalf of the praetor') and the legionary legates, and about the rituals they performed. There is, however, evidence for the rituals they performed in the provinces before returning home. In 18 BC, Augustus restricted the triumph to members of the imperial family. From then on, triumphal processions in the true sense became rarities, but the emperor's return to Rome in the form of a triumphal procession became more frequent. Following a victory and before returning to Rome, the emperor would make votive offerings at the site of the victory, and troops would acclaim the emperor as *imperator* (e.g. Jos. BI 6,6,1).

Legionaries, meanwhile, no longer left Rome for the theatre of war in a ceremonial way; at least, as far as we know, their departure was no longer ritualized. Recruitment and the performance of the *sacramentum* ('oath') took place in the camps, which were now permanent, at least in times of peace. Until at least AD 69 (Tac. Hist. 1,55), the *sacramentum* was sworn on January 1, but after this it seems to have been merged into the annual *vota pro salute principis* ('vows for the health of the *princeps*) on January 3 [4. 65f.]. The oath was renewed annually, and soldiers formally ended it on completion of their term of service (Dig. 49,18,2). As soon as auxiliary troops began to receive pay from Rome, they also probably began swearing oaths within the units and camps to which they were posted.

It is reported that the future Augustus revived the college of the *fetiales* (an official body of priests), rebuilding the Temple of Jupiter Feretrius that served as its headquarters. In fact, he himself performed the ritual declaring war on Egypt by hurling a spear into the aforentioned 'enemy' territory near the Temple of Bellona (see above, B.). It nevertheless seems worth asking whether the two Roman emissaries who performed a sacrifice at the conclusion of an agreement with the Lycians in 46 BC might have been *fetiales* (AE 2005, 1487, Z. 74f.). If they were, the college must have survived into the 1st century BC, unless it was Caesar who revived it.

C.1. COLLECTIVE CULT SITES OF THE ARMY CORPS

C.1.1. Rome
C.1.2. Cult sites in the provincial castra

There were cult sites in barracks and military camps throughout Rome and the provinces.

C.1.1. ROME

For the most part, the locations and arrangements of collective cult sites are unknown. Some information can be gleaned from literary sources and inscriptions. When Nero was appointed emperor, he went to the Praetorian camp and apparently he took the auspices (Suet. Nero 8). This ritual had to be performed in a *templum*, which no doubt would have been set up on the *tribunal*, which must have resembled the *auguratorium* of the legionary camp (see below). From Herodian (5,8,5f.), we know that there was a camp temple, presumably the Temple of Mars, the *aedituus* ('temple superintendent') of which is mentioned in an inscription (CIL VI 2256). We also know from their *castra* ('camps') about countless dedications and votive tablets offered by groups of Praetorians. It must be assumed that there were small sanctuaries scattered around the barracks, either standing alone or in the *scholae* ('schools', 'divisions') of the cohorts, associated with the statue of the *genius* of the cohort (cf. CIL VI 213–3) or century (CIL VI 29822). The first barracks of the *equites singulares* ('mounted guards'), northeast of S. Giovanni in Laterano, had a sanctuary with the *genius* of a *turma* ('unit') and a plethora of dedications to Roman deities from soldiers' places of origin. Besides dedications to the *genius* of a *turma*, the second barracks of the *peregrini* ('foreigners') has only yielded one hall, identified as an Augusteum. The *castra peregrinorum* ('camp of the *peregrini*') at S. Stefano rotondo contained a temple of Jupiter redux and a Mithraeum. One apse in the remains of the camp is dedicated to the *genius castrorum* ('the *genius* of the camp'). We know of only one dedication to the *genius* of a century from the *castra urbanorum* ('camp of the city men'), while all that is preserved from the *stationes* ('stations') of the *vigiles* ('watchmen') is one tiny *excubitorium* ('sentry station'), that of the VIIth cohort. It contains an *aedicula* ('small sanctuary') to the *genius* of the cohort. Finally, mention should be made of the Augusteum at the barracks of the *vigiles* in Ostia. It may serve as an example of the Augustea that must have been present at all city barracks.

C.1.2. CULT SITES IN THE PROVINCIAL CASTRA

Collective cult sites were at the heart of the *castra* in the *praetorium*. This was also the location of the room in which the commander took the auspices in the name of the emperor (Ps.-Hyg. mun. cast. 11). The fact that no trace remains of such an *auguratorium* in the *praetoria* or *principia* of the legionary camps undoubtedly shows that the legate took the hen auspices on the *tribunal* or in the courtyard of the *praetorium*, like the consuls and praetors of the Republican period. The prophetic sacrifices were performed on one of the altars of the *praetorium*.

Neither temples nor *aedicula* were built at marching camps during military operations, but they are found at the permanent camps. The *principia* contained the sanctuary of the *signa* ('standards'), which – if there were no specially built *aedicula* of the *domus Augusta* – would contain the *genius imperatoris* along with statues or honorary inscriptions for Jupiter, the *genius signorum* or the *Disciplina* (in Britannia and North Africa). Many dedications were placed at the exit from this *aedicula* (cf. [15]; [22. 521f.]).

It became increasingly common for camps to contain a room similar to the Augusteum at the barracks of the *vigiles* in Ostia, containing alongside the *genius* of the emperor statues of the *divi* ('gods') and *divae* ('goddesses') that formed part of the public cult of the army and the cities of the empire. At Carnuntum, the *principia* included a cult site with statues of Jupiter, a *genius* and Venus, and, on the two short sides of the basilica, one *aedicula* for the *genius* of the *castra* and Jupiter and another for Hercules (on Carnuntum in general cf. [9. 346–403]). At Lambaesis, there were altars to Mars and the *genius* of the *castra*.

Soldiers formed up for the common rituals according to rank. Only officers were allowed into the inner courtyard of the *praetorium*. When colleges were allowed in the army, the *principales* would gather in their respective *schola* and the legionaries would gather outside the *praetorium* on the camp's *via principalis*.

There were small cult sites near the rooms where soldiers' activities took place. These were *aediculae* with an altar in front, around which other altars were raised. In the *principia*, the *tabularia* ('archives') contained dedications to Minerva, Jupiter or Victoria, and of course the *genius* of the *tabularium* itself. The *armamentarium* ('armoury') contained dedications to Mars and Minerva or the *Genius armamentorum*. In soldiers' quarters and in the service premises of the legion or auxiliary unit one regularly finds the *genius* of the particular service or the *genii* of the centuries [20]. The *valetudinarium* ('infirmary') sometimes – as at Novae or Carnuntum – contains a small Asclepieum or at least a designated place with dedications to Aesculapius, Hygieia, Apollo, Sirona, Jupiter or Hercules. Numerous dedications reveal small cult sites at the camp gates. Jupiter, Victoria, Mars, Neptune and Fortuna were the main deities venerated here, with Mithras, Isis and Serapis joining them from the Flavian period onwards and Jupiter Dolichenus later still.

Homage was also paid in the buildings outside the camp, especially on the Campus to the Dii Campestres (e.g. at Gemellae), who were venerated in particular by the cavalry, and to Mars and Victoria. Cult sites consecrated and used by groups of soldiers on their own, that is, as private associations, such as that of the *beneficiarii* at Osterburken (Sanctuary of the *Beneficiarii*), lay outside the camp. The cult there was devoted to Jupiter and Juno, and it also adopted the local goddess Dea Candida Regina in a subordinate position – by no means an exceptional case. A large temple to the Matres Aufaniae, among the most important deities at Cologne, was built in the camp of the *Legio I Minervia* at Bonn. Baths near the camps contain conventional dedications to Fortuna, Aesculapius and Salus, but they show no specific connection to the military.

Soldiers, who were frequently relocated, and the army corps, while conducting operations all over the Mediterranean, were undeniably initiated into cults and the worship of new deities. It is therefore entirely possible that the public cult of the Alexandrian deities was introduced because of the city's support for the Flavian party in 69/70 and because of its popularity in the army of Vespasian. Such currents did not, however, run only in an east-to-west direction, as is generally assumed. Cults also migrated to the east, as the presence of Silvanus near Zeugma in a unit of the *Legio IV Scythica* proves. But transfers of this kind conducted through the army were far from consistent. cMithras, whose cult was widespread among soldiers (albeit less than is sometimes claimed) and even more so among officers, is not attested in Germania superior or Egypt. Conversely, the deities of cities near military facilities became so connected with the army that they began to be portrayed in Roman military garb (Horus, Harpocrates and Anubis in Egypt, Yarḥibol and Malakbel in Syria and – more generally – Jupiter Optimus Maximus Dolichenus). Analysis of the transfer of deities and cults must therefore be made with caution, especially concerning the 'Oriental' cults, since these were often associated with the religious cultures of relocated military units. It was noticed early on that Syrian and Egyptian cults could be found in regions where soldiers were stationed.

C.2. CULTS PRACTISED IN THE ROMAN ARMY: THE OFFICIAL CALENDAR OF THE ROMAN ARMY

Besides the major ceremonies of marching out, returning home and triumph, the Roman army had a specific calendar used by all corps. Special ritual observances could be added to this, as in all cities of the Roman world. An extraordinary papyrus from Dura-Europus provides us with the cultic calendar of the Roman army ([4]; cf. [13]). It dates from between AD 224 and 235, in all probability between 225 and 227, and it originated in the *officium* of the barracks of the XXth cohort of Palmyrenes. It is without doubt the official calendar of the unit, written in Latin, and it largely corresponds to the official festival calendar of the Roman state, comparable with those known from the *Commentarii* of the Arval Brethren or the festival calendars (*fasti*) of the Julio-Claudian period. It follows that it is not specifically military, even though it was established by the emperor and the supreme command of the Roman army and contains some rituals particular to military life. The fact that it comes from a camp of an auxiliary cohort proves that the old distinction between legionaries and auxiliaries had by this time ceased to apply. The entire Roman army was subject to the common religious calendar.

C.3. PRIVATE CULTS

C.3.1. Collective cults
C.3.2. Individual cults
C.3.3. Celebrants

Apart from these public religious services performed outside temples and other official cult sites at the camp, which involved the entire unit, soldiers of all ranks also performed joint and individual religious acts.

C.3.1. COLLECTIVE CULTS

As in civilian life, the individual's religious activity consisted – besides occasional participation in official festivals – in certain ceremonies and votive acts.

Every unit, for instance, might have a *natalis* ('birthday'), actually the birthday of its *aquila* ('legionary eagle') or *signa* ('standard'; Plin. HN 13,23; CIL II 2552–2555; 6183; III 7591). Tacitus calls the eagle and the standard *legionum numina* ('gods of the legions'; Ann. 2,17), and Tertullian claims that the standards outranked the gods, even Jupiter (Apol. 16,8; Ad nat. 12,15), although he exaggerates. The → standards were, however, treated with the utmost respect, with cult activities performed in their honour (ILS 9127). This would not, however, suffice to make them gods as such, let alone gods greater than the greatest gods. Along with other deities particularly associated with a legion, an auxiliary unit, and their constituent elements, the *genius* of such a unit, service or subordinate group expressed the deified abilities of the collective and contributed to the representation of its identity. The unit or its subsidiary elements, the legate, officers or ordinary soldiers made many dedications to the various gods and goddesses for the wellbeing of the emperor.

Votive acts were of great importance. Collective vows for the wellbeing (*salus*) of the ruler, the army and groups of soldiers were made everywhere in the Roman Empire. Vows to the unit were also frequent, especially during a campaign. Finally, series of inscriptions reveal to us the fulfilment of vows at the moment of the *honesta missio* ('honourable discharge'), as well as promotions in the units of Rome such as the provincial army.

C.3.2. INDIVIDUAL CULTS

Besides private dedications and those related to camp life, most of the known individual religious acts were those performed when making the formal commitment to join up, receiving promotion or reaching the end of the term of service. Several documents record the vows made by soldiers on joining up or leaving their home, which were fulfilled at the moment of their return. Votive texts in camps attest to individuals' fulfilment of vows made on promotion or on discharge from service (Osterburken). Individual vows or dedications increasingly invoke Roman deities (including the *genius loci* and deities imported to Rome), but occasionally address local deities. Auxiliaries and legionaries alike performed such devotions. Alongside these rituals associated with a soldier's military career, there are further testimonies found at cult sites in the provinces and where a soldier has left traces while marching through.

C.3.3. CELEBRANTS

The major ritual acts that concerned the entire unit and the Roman people – such as those on the festival calendar from Dura-Europus – were primarily performed by the legate or commanding officer of the camp. The legionary legate was assisted in his duties by *apparitores* ('public servants'), who ranged from the *pullarii* ('hen-keepers') and *haruspices* ('diviners') responsible for divination to attendants at sacrifices. Besides the tribunes, one of the most religiously active of the officers of the *principia* was the *primipilus* ('chief centurion'). More generally, centurions and decurions performed collective rituals for the community in the various barracks and posts.

☞ Legion; State and Army

BIBLIOGRAPHY
[1] E. BIRLEY, The Religion of the Roman Army, 1885–1977, in: ANRW II.16, 1978, 1506–1541 [2] A. VON DOMASZEWSKI, Die Religion des römischen Heeres, in: A. VON DOMASZEWSKI, Aufsätze zur römischen Heeresgeschichte, 1972, 81–209 [3] G. FERRI, Una testimonianza epigrafica dell'evocatio? Su un'iscrizione di Isaura Vetus, in: S. ANTOLINI et al. (eds.), Giornata di studi per di Lidio Gasperini, 2010, 183–194 [4] R.O. FINK et al., The Feriale Duranum, in: Yale Classical Studies 7, 1940, 1–222 [5] I.P. HAYNES, The Romanization of Religion in the Auxilia of the Roman Imperial Army from Augustus to Septimius Severus, in: Britannia 24, 1993, 141–157 [6] J. HELGELAND, Roman Army Religion, in: ANRW II.16, 1978, 1470–1505 [7] J. HELGELAND, Christians and the Roman Army, in: ANRW II.23, 1979, 724–834 [8] A.H.M. JONES, The Social Background of the Struggle between Paganism and Christianity, in: A. MOMIGLIANO (ed.), Conflict between Paganism and Christianity in the Fourth Century, 1963, 17–26 [9] G. KREMER, Götterdarstellungen, Kult- und Weihdenkmäler aus Carnuntum (CSIR, Österreich, Suppl. 1: Carnuntum), 2012 [10] P. LE ROUX, Soldats et cultes indigènes dans les provinces occidentales au Haut-Empire, in: P. LE ROUX, Scripta varia, vol. 1: La toge et les armes. Rome entre Méditerranée et Océan, 2011, 239–252 [11] J. NÉLIS-CLÉMENT, Le monde des dieux chez les beneficiarii, in: Der römische Weihebezirk von Osterburken. 2. Kolloquium 1990 und paläobotanische Untersuchungen, 1994, 251–260 [12] J. NÉLIS-CLÉMENT, Les beneficiarii. Militaires et administrateurs au service de l'Empire (1er s. a.C.–VIe s. p.C.), 2000 [13] A.D. NOCK, The Roman Army and the Roman Religious Year (1952), in: A.D. NOCK, Essays on Religion and the Ancient World, 1972, 736–790 [14] G. PICARD, Les trophées romains. Contribution à l'histoire de la religion et de l'art triomphal de Rome (Bibliothèque des Écoles françaises d'Athènes et de Rome 187), 1957 [15] M. REDDÉ, Réflexions critiques sur les chapelles militaires (aedes principiorum), in: JRA 17, 2004, 443–462 [16] J. RÜPKE, Domi militiae. Die religiöse Konstruktion des Krieges in Rom, 1990 [17] J. SCHEID, Commentarii fratrum arvalium qui supersunt. Les copies épigraphiques des protocoles annuels de la confrérie arvale (21 av.–304 ap. J.-C.) (Roma antica 4), 1998 [18] J. SCHEID, Le rite des auspices à Rome. Quelle évolution? Réflexions sur la transformation de la divination publique des Romains entre le IIIe et le Ier siècle avant notre ère, in: S. GEORGOUDI et al. (eds.), La raison des signes. Présages, rites, destin dans les sociétés de la Méditerranée ancienne, 2012, 109–128 [19] R. SCHILLING, La religion romaine de Vénus depuis ses origines jusqu'au temps d'Auguste (Bibliothèque des Écoles Françaises d'Athènes et de Rome 178), ²1982 [20] C. SCHMIDT HEIDENREICH, Les lieux de culte des génies de centuries dans les camps militaires du Haut-Empire romain, in: XII Congressus internationalis epigraphiae graecae et latinae, 2007, 1325–1330 [21] J.F. SHEAN, Soldiering for God. Christianity and the Roman Army, 2010 [22] M.A. SPEIDEL, Heer und Herrschaft im Römischen Reich der Hohen Kaiserzeit, 2009 [23] O. STOLL, The Religions of the Armies, in: P. ERDKAMP (ed.), A Companion to the Roman Army, 2007, 451–476.

JOHN SCHEID

D. LATE ANTIQUITY

Although earlier traditions continued into the 4th century, the Roman army was also recruiting Christian soldiers by the mid-3rd century. Radical changes on the level of supreme command occurred after the Battle of the Milvian Bridge (→ Battles of note G.). Like all his predecessors, Constantine chose a patron deity. As one would expect, this led him to sanction that deity's cult as a form of religious expression. Less customary, however, was his refusal to celebrate his victorious entry into Rome with the obligatory visit to the Capitol, the laurel ritual and, doubtless, the usual offering to Jupiter. This break with tradition, which was lamented by conservatives, heralded a series of measures that over the course of the 4th century would destroy not only the army's religious practices, but the entirety of traditional religion. Within the army itself, the number of Christians had been increasing since the reign of Marcus Aurelius. Proof of this is found in various traditions, such as a report about the *Legio XII fulminata* under Marcus Aurelius [7. 766–773], a hypothetical tradition concerning the Theban Legion [7. 774–777]; [22. 667–677] and a report of soldiers who died Christian martyrs in the late 3rd century (e.g. [7. 774–783]). Further evidence can be seen in the sarcophagus of the Praetorian centurion Aelius Martinus, which bears a depiction of Jonah with a gourd leaf and must be regarded as Christian (AE 1939, 171; for other inscriptions, cf. [21. 183–185]).

It is impossible to estimate the number of Christians in the Roman army, but Tertullian's assertion (Apol. 37,4) that there were a great many Christians in the camps must be an exaggeration for his day. There was no Christian problem in the army prior to the great persecution. Any Christians among the soldiery remained silent during the traditional ritual ceremonies. Christians sometimes encountered difficulties when they rose to higher ranks that required active participation in the units' communal cult, but we have virtually no information about such situations. Even after Constantine's victory at the Milvian Bridge, the religious context for soldiers did not dramatically change. The two religious traditions simply coexisted, while gradual changes were taking place [7]; [21. 177–215]. For example, it would not be until the *Codex Iustinianus* that the wording for Constantine's acclamation by his soldiers, *Auguste Constantine, dei te nobis servent* ('Augustus Constantinus, may the gods preserve you for us!'), was changed to *Deus te nobis servet* ('... may God preserve you for us!') ([8]; Cod. Theod. 7,20,2 = Cod. Iust. 12,46,1). The standards retained their significance, as did the homage paid to the emperor as supreme commander of the army.

When the public cult was prohibited after the interlude of the reign of Julian, religious practices changed, and the old temples, aediculae and altars were destroyed or turned into churches. However, there are not many examples to set alongside Dura-Europus, where a church was set up in camp during the Severan period – further proof of religious tolerance. It was always the emperor who accepted the *sacramentum*, but the oath was now made to the Holy Trinity (*iurant autem per Deum et Christum et sanctum Spiritum*) and the emperor's *maiestas* (Veg. Mil. 2,5,3–5). The army accepted Germanic recruits who practised their own, non-Christian rituals until AD 416. After that, pagans were formally excluded from the army (Cod. Theod. 16,10,21).

☞ Legion; State and army

BIBLIOGRAPHY
[1] E. BIRLEY, The Religion of the Roman Army, 1885–1977, in: ANRW II.16, 1978, 1506–1541 [2] A. VON DOMASZEWSKI, Die Religion des römischen Heeres, in: A. VON DOMASZEWSKI, Aufsätze zur römischen Heeresgeschichte, 1972, 81–209 [3] G. FERRI, Una testimonianza epigrafica dell'evocatio? Su un'iscrizione di Isaura Vetus, in: S. ANTOLINI et al. (eds.), Giornata di studi per di Lidio Gasperini, 2010, 183–194 [4] R.O. FINK et al., The Feriale Duranum, in: Yale Classical Studies 7, 1940, 1–222 [5] I.P. HAYNES, The Romanization of Religion in the Auxilia of the Roman Imperial Army from Augustus to Septimius Severus, in: Britannia 24, 1993, 141–157 [6] J. HELGELAND, Roman Army Religion, in: ANRW II.16, 1978, 1470–1505 [7] J. HELGELAND, Christians and the Roman Army, in: ANRW II.23, 1979, 724–834 [8] A.H.M. JONES, The Social Background of the Struggle between Paganism and Christianity, in: A. MOMIGLIANO (ed.), Conflict between Paganism and Christianity in the Fourth Century, 1963, 17–26 [9] G. KREMER, Götterdarstellungen, Kult- und Weihdenkmäler aus Carnuntum (CSIR, Österreich, Suppl. 1: Carnuntum), 2012 [10] P. LE ROUX, Soldats et cultes indigènes dans les provinces occidentales au Haut-Empire, in: P. LE ROUX, Scripta varia, vol. 1: La toge et les armes. Rome entre Méditerranée et Océan, 2011, 239–252 [11] J. NÉLIS-CLÉMENT, Le monde des dieux chez les beneficiarii, in: Der römische Weihebezirk von Osterburken. 2. Kolloquium 1990 und paläobotanische Untersuchungen, 1994, 251–260 [12] J. NÉLIS-CLÉMENT, Les beneficiarii. Militaires et administrateurs au service de l'Empire (1er s. a.C.–VIe s. p.C.), 2000 [13] A.D. NOCK, The Roman Army and the Roman Religious Year (1952), in: A.D. NOCK, Essays on Religion and the Ancient World, 1972, 736–790 [14] G. PICARD, Les trophées romains. Contribution à l'histoire de la religion et de l'art triomphal de Rome (Bibliothèque des Écoles françaises d'Athènes et de Rome 187), 1957 [15] M. REDDÉ, Réflexions critiques sur les chapelles militaires (aedes principiorum), in: JRA 17, 2004, 443–462 [16] J. RÜPKE, Domi militiae. Die religiöse Konstruktion des Krieges in Rom, 1990 [17] J. SCHEID, Commentarii fratrum arvalium qui supersunt. Les copies épigraphiques des protocoles annuels de la confrérie arvale (21 av.–304 ap. J.-C.) (Roma antica 4), 1998 [18] J. SCHEID, Le rite des auspices à Rome. Quelle évolution? Réflexions sur la transformation de la divination publique des Romains entre le IIIe et le Ier siècle avant notre ère, in: S. GEORGOUDI et al. (eds.), La raison des signes. Présages, rites, destin dans les sociétés de la Méditerranée ancienne, 2012, 109–128 [19] R. SCHILLING, La religion romaine de Vénus depuis les origines jusqu'au temps d'Auguste (Bibliothèque des Écoles Françaises

d'Athènes et de Rome 178), ²1982 [20] C. SCHMIDT HEIDENREICH, Les lieux de culte des génies de centuries dans les camps militaires du Haut-Empire romain, in: XII Congressus internationalis epigraphiae graecae et latinae, 2007, 1325–1330 [21] J.F. SHEAN, Soldiering for God. Christianity and the Roman Army, 2010 [22] M.A. SPEIDEL, Heer und Herrschaft im Römischen Reich der Hohen Kaiserzeit, 2009 [23] O. STOLL, The Religions of the Armies, in: P. ERDKAMP (ed.), A Companion to the Roman Army, 2007, 451–476.

JOHN SCHEID

Representations of war

A. Pictorial
B. Coins

A. PICTORIAL

A.1. Archaic Greece
A.2. Classical Greece
A.3. Hellenistic world
A.4. Etruria and Roman Republic
A.5. Roman Imperial period

Monuments to war announce achievements and victories in public spaces, transcending the constraints of space and time to which the original event was subject, and keeping it present in memory. They are informed by the political intentions of those commissioning them, are indeed 'monumental' in form, and present their 'message' to a 'public' audience. *Representations* of war include not only public monuments, but also works in genres of 'private' pictorial art. Within a variety of spaces and situations in the lived world, they express a broad spectrum of societal ideas, cultural attitudes and psychological experiences. Monuments and representations reproduce the realities of war not as factual depictions, but within a 'conceptual realism', that is, as they were perceived, selected, intended and to some extent modified in the light of societal models and political ideologies.

A.1. ARCHAIC GREECE

War is a dominant theme of vase-painting in Greek Geometric and Archaic art (8th–6th cents. BC) [1]. With the advent of figural subjects in visual art at Athens around 750 BC, funerary vessels began to feature multi-figure scenes of warriors in single combat. These warriors were usually depicted on foot, although sometimes they were alighting from a war chariot, and generally no central figure was highlighted and no distinction was made between warring parties. There are also scenes of fighting aboard and around ships – again, the fighters are collective and anonymous. The combat is shown to be fierce, sometimes with piles of corpses on the ground and bodies floating in water. In general, focus is not on the victorious dead, but on war as a dangerous endeavor by which warrior elites prove their mettle. In depictions of high-status funeral processions of the same period, the peers of the deceased take part wearing warrior garb and riding in chariots. The figure of the warrior often consists primarily of the symbols of the shield, helmet and spear.

Beginning in the middle of the 7th century, vessels from Corinth (notably the Chigi olpe) start to show dense ranks of warriors facing off in full hoplite gear, with round shields, cuirasses and spears [22]; [16]; [18]. This style of portrayal corresponds in general to the emergence of new forms of combat in the closed formation known as the → phalanx. The scenes are less concerned with precision in rendering the fighting techniques than with expressing warrior solidarity in the newly formed citizen armies of the *polis*. Alongside these scenes, portrayals of single combat remain dominant at this period as representations of personal courage in battle. Even within dense scenes of mass fighting, individual warriors are seen facing each other without being subsumed into large bodies of men. The two modes of depiction do not represent alternative styles of combat – nor do they betray an antithesis between reality and a 'Homeric' ideal. Rather, they reflect two complementary aspects of warfare: the collective cohesion of the army unit and the individual test in head-to-head combat.

The black-figured Attic vessels of the 6th century BC show three fundamental aspects of war: the warrior's preparations and departure from his family in the face of the threat of → death; fighting on the battlefield as proof of manly courage; and the retrieval of a fallen comrade to illustrate glorious death and religious concern for the body [21]; [9]; [18]. There are, however, no illustrations of → victory or → triumph. Rather than emphasizing victory as the desired outcome, interest is focused on the individual, the battle and the fate of the warrior. For a long time, illustrious hoplites remain the almost exclusive subject matter, shown either in full armour or athletically unclothed (with no indication of heroization). Sometimes, forms representing high status are included in the illustration as defining motifs, even though they were of secondary or marginal significance in warfare of the period, for example cavalry, the four-horse chariot, or the ceremonial 'Boeotian' shield. Contrasted with this are depictions of those killed in battle – portrayed with increasing drama – to illustrate downfall and misery [23]. Only towards the end of the 6th century do other groups of warriors enter the frame: Scythian archers, Thracian *peltastai* ('light armed footsoldiers'), Greek light infantry – all providing a social context for the normative figures of the hoplites.

Wars did not build foundations for lasting power in the unstable world of the Greek city-states. Therefore, visual art focuses more on heroic combat and fate than on final victory. In reality, too, little emphasis was placed on rituals of victory. The only permanent monuments to military victories are very limited in scope. Polities and individuals dedicated their own weapons, or weapons taken as booty, at sanctuaries, sometimes suspending them on tall posts with carved inscriptions that indicated who offered the dedication and mentioned specific victories (Olympia), but even these were removed after a time [4]; [11]. It was probably in the 6th century BC that the practice began of setting up a 'commemoration of the [enemy's] turn [to flight]' (*tropaion*) – visible from far and wide, but likewise temporary – at the place on the battlefield where the enemy took flight. It took the form of a pillar draped with armour [26]; [19]. As permanent memorial acts after victories, temples, treasuries and votive gifts could be donated to sanctuaries (Megarian Treasury at Olympia), and statues could be built for the war dead (Croesus *kouros* of Anavyssos), although these did not make explicit reference to war and victory. True victory monuments were an innovation of the 5th century BC.

A.2. CLASSICAL GREECE

From about 500 BC onwards, conflicts and wars among the city-states and between the Greeks collectively and the Persians and other external adversaries came to be seen in a new light, as a struggle for a defined political identity. This was expressed in public monuments that presented victories as matters of political interest. Many of these were votive donations at sanctuaries, which, however, now took on an explicitly political character.

Immediately after the 'democratic' reforms of Cleisthenes, the Athenian *polis* built a monument on its Acropolis to a victory against Chalcis and the Boeotians (506 BC), which was seen as proof of the strength of the new form of government. The monument was a four-horse chariot, with the iron shackles of the many → prisoners of war hanging beside it, all in memory of this foundational victory on behalf of the new political identity (Hdt. 5,77). After the wars against the Persians (490, 480–479 BC) (→ Wars of note J.), the allied *poleis* jointly dedicated monumental votive thanksgivings at the leading Greek sanctuaries, expressive of a new Panhellenic identity, but in the process triggering fierce disputes over participation and distinction in the victories [12]. Certain *poleis* put up separate monuments at Delphi and in their own cities to highlight their own particular accomplishments. Athens went further, immortalizing its fame as victor at Marathon (→ Battles of note F.) with retrospective monuments through which it sought to portray itself as the singular leading force in Greece: the first permanent *tropaion* on the battlefield, a group of statues portraying the general Miltiades and the mythical heroes of Athens at Delphi (Paus. 1,28,2), and a colossal statue of Athena as *promachos*, 'forefighter' on the Acropolis. A cycle of patriotic paintings was installed in the 'Painted Porch' (*Stoa Poikile*) in the Agora (c. 460 BC), beginnig with the mythical victories of Athenian heroes over the Amazons and Troy and leading to the Battle of Marathon against the Persians (Paus. 1,15,1–3). This, the first Greek history painting, depicted the battle in a novel spatial and chronological sequence of action scenes that highlighted the military protagonists on both sides and incorporated the presence of gods and heroes helping the Athenians. Not only was emphasis given to the great victory under the command of Miltiades, but also to the readiness of the fighters to die for the *polis*. In view of the great political significance of the subject matter, the painting sparked intense controversy over the acceptance of this particular version.

Over the ensuing decades, Athens and Sparta, together with their respective allies, fought an intense war of commemoration [15]: the *poleis* put up monuments that boldly advanced their own claims at the great Panhellenic sanctuaries of Delphi and Olympia and in participating cities, brazenly associating themselves with monuments built by their allies and reacting polemically against those put up by their enemies. A focal point in this conflict was the Nike of Paeonius at Olympia, which showed the goddess of victory hovering above an eagle (425 BC; cf. fig. 1). Athens' Messenian and Naupactian allies intended this statue to outdo the Spartan victory shield dedicated at the Temple of Zeus. It was later outdone by the Spartan general Lysander, who had two Nikai on eagles built in Sparta (405 BC).

At Athens, the Temple of Athena Nike represents a high point of political sculpture. The friezes gird the building with battle scenes from the wars with the Persians and enemies within Greece. The pediments form a bridge to the mythical battles of the gods against the giants and of the Athenians against the Amazons, while on the balustrade running round the sanctuary a swarm of *nikai* celebrates an allegorical victory festival, with the construction of *tropaia* and the sacrifice of bulls, to commemorate the victories of Athens in its great past [14]. Public portrait statues of illustrious citizens, some put up privately in sanctuaries, others from the 4th century onwards put up by the *polis* in the Agora, often used the prestigious 'Corinthian' helmet of the *strategos* ('commander') to highlight accomplishments in war.

valour and portents of death [28]; [23]. Depictions of battles with Persians often follow the same plan, but evoke through bodies and equipment the contrast between Greek *arete* ('valour') and Oriental luxury, effeminacy and unscrupulousness [27]; [23].

A.3. HELLENISTIC WORLD

Alexander the Great and the Hellenistic kings based their authority in large measure on the charisma demonstrated through military victories. Accordingly, they developed new forms of monuments and images of war to express the uniqueness of their victorious power. At the farthest point of his campaign, by the River Hyphasis, Alexander had twelve monumental altars constructed to mark his claim to world dominion (Diod. Sic. 17,95,1). The gigantic pyre for Hephaestion was decorated with a comprehensive pictorial scheme of allegorical and symbolic victory motifs, which were destroyed in spectacular fashion when the pyre was lit (Diod. Sic. 17,114f.). On the vehicle carrying Alexander's dead body, the sarcophagus was placed among symbols and images of him as a victorious general, eliciting a powerful emotional response on its journey from Babylon to Egypt (Diod. Sic. 18,26).

After Alexander's death, the Diadochi and other rulers sought to strengthen their own claims to power with monuments that attested to their close relationship with him. It must have been such a ruler who was responsible for a famous battle painting of which an excellent copy is preserved in the Alexander Mosaic at Pompeii [14]; [8]. In a novel coherence of space and time, this work depicts Alexander's (→ Generals of note B.) victory over Darius (the exact battle is disputed). The conflict is portrayed as a contest between the rulers with their armies in the background, with vivid realism and dramatic tension that reflect the 'tragic' historiography of the early Hellenistic period. In the same spirt, the relief sarcophagus of the local king Abdalonymus of Sidon reinforces his position by depicting the victory of Alexander (Issus) that put him on the throne.

A new center of focus arose throughout the Hellenistic world in the 3rd century BC as a result of invasions of Greece and Asia Minor by Celtic groups. With the Persians defeated and integrated into Hellenistic culture, the Celts as embodiments of savage natural power became stylized as the new 'arch enemy' of the Greek world. In ideological analogy with the Persian Wars of the Classical period, all the major powers of the Grecian world sought to define themselves as victors over the Celts in wars and monuments [20]. The Aetolian League, which had saved Delphi from the Celts, built a new kind of statue in the sanctuary there, depicting Aetolia sitting on a pile of Celtic armour. The Antigonids, Seleucids and even Ptole-

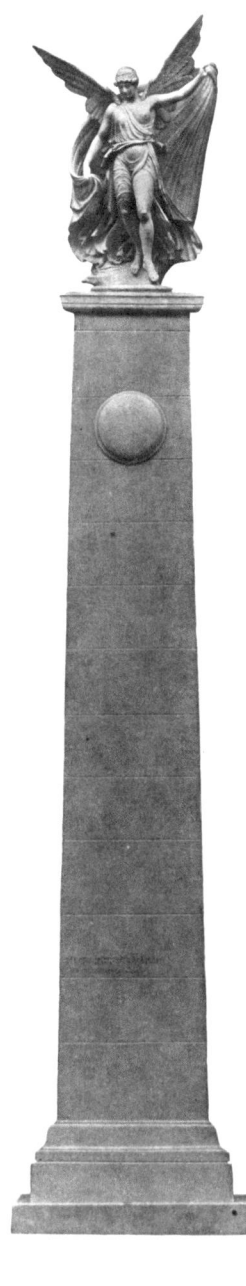

Fig. 1: Greek victory monument: *Nike, Goddess of Victory, atop a pillar* (Olympia, Sanctuary of Zeus, 425 BC; reconstruction). Built by order of Messenians and Naupactians, allies of Athens, after their joint victory over Sparta at the Battle of Sphacteria during the Peloponnesian War. This construction forms part of a symbolic 'war' of monuments, fought out by the rival parties at the great Panhellenic sanctuaries over a period of decades. Each party demonstrated its own strength by creating a network of monuments, while also trying to surpass the monuments put up by its enemies. Monuments can represent identity, and in this function they were used as symbolic weapons to take possession of these living spaces and to humiliate one's rival.

One establishment unique to Athens as a democracy was the *demosion sema* ('public cemetery'), with communal graves of all those who died in battle each year. The reliefs above the lists of the fallen show anonymous battle scenes and emphasize the fighting courage of the fallen and their spirit of self-sacrifice. This undoubtedly helped the living process the mass death of so many citizens. Private tombs with depictions of warriors were built either to honor men who excelled in war but did not die in battle, or to serve as cenotaphs built by families to show glorious battle scenes [24]; [3].

Attic red-figured vases illustrate combat between Greek warriors in motifs of individual

mies built monuments to celebrate victories – of varying degrees of significance – over the new enemy. Among the numerous efforts to bolster royal authority through monuments to victories over the Celts, the strongest was that of the Attalids of Pergamum, who used these monuments to raise themselves to the level of the other Hellenistic monarchies. Roman copies are preserved of figures depicting defeated Celts from a monument of Attalus I (c. 220 BC). The figures include a prince, who dramatically kills his wife and himself while fleeing, and a mortally wounded trumpeter. The victories were celebrated in the halls of the Sanctuary of Athena at Pergamum with the earliest monumental example of a frieze containing fragments of the weaponry of the victors and their enemies. Later, a multi-figure group of statues on the Athenian Acropolis, probably commissioned by Attalus II, placed the Pergamene victories over the Celts on par with the great mythical victories of the gods over the giants and the Athenians over the Amazons, and with the Greek victory over the Persians. The struggle and downfall of the enemy is portrayed with great pathos, while the victorious rulers appear in separate statues. The pillar monument of Aemilius Paullus at Delphi stands in the same tradition, with its battle frieze at the upper end and the equestrian statue of the general on top.

Although cities were constantly involved in wars with one another, monuments were usually only created to recognize rulers and their victories over foreign enemies. One rare exception is the *Winged Victory (Nike) of Samothrace*. Charging forward like the figurehead on the bow of a ship, she evidently commemorates a Rhodian naval victory of the early 2nd century BC. Themes of war are infrequently seen in the private sphere on funerary reliefs of the 3rd century BC [5]; [24].

In general, Hellenistic art depicted war with dramatic exaggeration. As in the Classical period, the focus is on the decisive *peripeteia* ('turning point') of victory and defeat, in which the victor's charisma and the adversary's pathetic downfall emerge through stark contrasts.

A.4. ETRURIA AND ROMAN REPUBLIC
The Etruscans' representations of war and victory were essentially confined to the sphere of tombs, with public monuments largely missing [13]; [24]. Compared with Greece, there is a stronger emphasis on the rituals of victory. Relief sarcophagi of the 5th–3rd centuries BC show processions of people returning from war and other public displays involving military aspects. Unique to date is the *Tomba François* in Vulci, with its frescos portraying not only topics from Greek myth, but also a scene from the Archaic history of the city in which Vulcian representatives led by the brothers Vibenna fought a coalition of neighbouring cities, including Rome. During the 3rd century, leading families in Etruscan cities began to have themselves depicted on sarcophagi and urns fighting Celtic invaders, who were characterized here in particular as desecrators and plunderers of sanctuaries.

In Rome, meanwhile, a new practice of public commemoration was developing, stimulated by the city's expansion into a territorial state [13]; [16]. The senate began to honour outstanding *triumphatores* with public statues, while generals themselves illustrated their campaigns in their → triumphal processions with portable paintings and models. They went on to exhibit pictorial works and collections of booty in the city as monuments, and they dedicated temples to deities who embodied the ideological principles of their victories, for example Victoria, Fides, Honos, Virtus and Pietas ('victory', 'trustworthiness', 'honour', 'valour' and 'sense of duty [to gods and men]'). As a result, Rome developed a monumental and religious topography of commemoration that proclaimed its imperial might. Besides the monuments in public places, illustrious families such as the Fabii and Scipiones increasingly used their tombs to display their military accomplishments. Alongside victorious battles, they highlighted rituals marking the signing of treaties and triumphs as concrete manifestations of types such a *fides* and *virtus*.

During the last century of the Republic, powerful generals turned this practice into a 'war of monuments' as they vied for political dominance [17]. Marius (→ Generals of note K.) built *tropaea* (victory memorials) over Jugurtha and the Germani to enhance his claim to universal victory. Sulla replied with a monument of King Bocchus of Mauretania showing Jugurtha being handed over to himself. Caesar (→ Generals of note C.) had a statue erected of himself astride the globe with an inscription celebrating him as 'demigod'. They used monuments to provoke others, they destroyed opponents' monuments, and they restored those of their own protagonists. Generals set up spectacular monuments across the empire to document that they had extended Roman rule to the 'limits of the world'. Sulla did this at Chaeronea to mark his victory over Mithridates, Pompey did so in the Pyrenees after pacifying Spain, and Caesar set up such momuments at Zela in Asia Minor after defeating Pharnaces II.

A.5. ROMAN IMPERIAL PERIOD

A.5.1. Rome
A.5.2. The empire

A.5.1. ROME
Augustus devised a way of representing war and victory in monuments that remained dominant throughout the Imperial period [30]. Following his victory at Actium (→ Battles of note A.), he

and the senate staged an act of mutual recognition. He put up a statue of Victoria on a globe in the *curia* of the senate, thereby symbolically handing the global dominion he had won to the people of Rome. In return, the senate and people gave the *princeps* a golden shield honouring him for his *virtus* (especially in war), *clementia, iustitia* and *pietas*, and in the process they bound him to these principles for the future. Augustus also made it a rule that all public monuments in his honour, especially for his successes in war, should be initiated not by himself, but by other authorities – in Rome, in particular, by the senate and people. He did this to demonstrate the consensus on which his rule was built.

Beginning in the Augustan period, a repertoire of scenes showing the *princeps* involved in political actions of war and in religious ritual appeared in relief decorations on major political monuments, especially arches and columns. The focus was on topics of ritual representation that expressed the ruler's ideological principles. An early example is a pair of silver beakers from Boscoreale dating from the late Augustan period with reliefs clearly modelled on large monuments of state [2]: Augustus receiving the surrender of a Gallic prince and depicting himself in an allegorical scene of world dominion; Tiberius performing the sacrifice for the march out to war and returning in his triumphal procession. A wide range of such scenes is preserved in a series of relief plaques based on a triumphal arch of Marcus Aurelius [2]: *profectio* (*virtus*), *lustratio* (*pietas*, religious *providentia*), *adlocutio* (*fides, concordia*), surrender of enemies (*clementia, iustitia* or *severitas*), installation of a client king (political *providentia*), *adventus* (*virtus, felicitas*), triumph (*virtus*), thank-offering (*pietas*), distribution of *donativa* (*liberalitas*). A pictorial language was being developed that combined the factual illustration of ritual reality with the inclusion of significant deities and ideological personifications. The overall effect was a relatively constant concept of the victorious emperor. Thus it was possible for the reliefs of Marcus Aurelius, together with reliefs from monuments of Trajan and Hadrian, to be reused on the Arch of Constantine with their heads replaced with Constantine's own. The reign of Constantine also saw the appearance of relief friezes showing the emperor's campaign against Maxentius – the first time a war against Roman citizens had been celebrated in this way [2].

A new narrative structure was developed in the pictorial reports on the commemorative column monuments of Trajan for the Dacian Wars and of Marcus Aurelius for the wars in Germania [6]; [7]. In spherical relief bands running up the column shaft, the campaigns are illustrated 'continuously' in chronological and geographical sequence in characteristic landscape formations with fortresses and settlements. Numerous individual events create a highly detailed pictorial chronicle, but there are also elements of pictorial strategies that incorporate many ritual scenes and serve an ideological purpose. The Trajan Column shows the three offensive campaigns as a systematic sequence of stereotypical scenes: *profectio*, council of war, sacrifices, *adlocutio*, construction of camps and fortresses, march out and battle, defeat of enemies, and consequences for the local popula-

Fig. 2: Roman war scene: relief on the Column of Marcus Aurelius in Rome (Field of Mars, Rome, AD 180–192). Romans taking a settlement of the Germanic Marcomanni. The scene is meant to illustrate the harsh punishment meted out for the uprising of the 'barbarians' against the Roman Empire. The Roman soldiers, in heavy armour, proceed unopposed against helpless men, women and children. The unprotected wooden buildings suggest primitive defencelessness. A battered adversary illustrates hopeless inferiority. A captive enemy is executed before the eyes of the emperor, who is devoid of any humanity. Total Roman victory is presented as just retribution for the enemy' attack on the Roman way of life, as given by the gods.

tion. The Marcus Aurelius Column, on the other hand, portrays the campaigns in a more emotional way, as quick successions of enemy uprisings and cruel punishments (cf. fig. 2). On the Arch of Septimius Severus in Rome, the continuous portrayal of events of war in staggered landscape is transposed into large, rectangular relief plaques.

From the time of the new defensive wars under Marcus Aurelius, senior military figures presented themselves on sarcophagi in sequences of ritual scenes closely patterned on the monuments to the emperors: battle (*virtus*) with surrender (*clementia*), sacrifices at the march-out (*pietas*) and a handshake with the wife (*concordia*). Sarcophagi also begin to display large-scale battle scenes against 'barbarians'. At first, these are anonymous conflicts that only implicitly reference the deceased, but from the late 2nd century onwards, compositions appear showing the general on horseback in the centre, with the Romans below dramatically destroying their enemies [2].

A.5.2. THE EMPIRE

Distinct regional forms of monuments developed in the provinces [2]. In Gallia Narbonensis, Roman victories over local populations are celebrated on triumphal arches of the early Principate (e.g. Orange) in battle scenes and portrayals of defeated enemies. A unique monument to Antoninus Pius at Ephesus – its overall design is unclear – has a monumental frieze that depicts (among other things) a turbulent battle against assorted foreign peoples in which the emperor is presented as a 'Greek' hero on a triumphal two-horse chariot. A *tetrapylon* with a variety of battle scenes on its pillars was built to honour Septimius Severus in his home city of Leptis Magna. On the attic, monumental friezes glorify the emperor's family at major state sacrifices and triumphal processions, in both Rome and Leptis, which is thereby placed on par with the capital. Galerius had a *tetrapylon* with abundant relief decoration built at the entrance to his palace over the *via Egnatia* in Thessalonica. Here, the emperors of the Tetrarchy are celebrated chiefly as victors over the Near East. The form of the monumental honorific column with scenes of war on a spherical relief band was revisited for the last time at Constantinople by Theodosius I and Arcadius: a testament to the strong ideological continuity characteristic of the representation of the Roman emperors in contrast with the Greek city-states and Hellenistic realms.

BIBLIOGRAPHY

[1] G. AHLBERG, Fighting on Land and Sea in Greek Geometric Art, 1971 [2] B. ANDREAE, Römische Kunst, vol. 3: Von Augustus bis Constantin, 2012 [3] N.T. ARRINGTON, Ashes, Images, and Memories. The Presence of the War Dead in Fifth-Century Athens, 2015 [4] H. BAITINGER, Waffenweihungen in griechischen Heiligtümern, 2011 [5] A. CHANIOTIS, War in the Hellenistic World, 2005 [6] F. COARELLI, La colonna Traiana, 1999 [7] F. COARELLI, La colonna di Marco Aurelio, 2008 [8] A. COHEN, The Alexander Mosaic. Stories of Victory and Defeat, 1997 [9] C. ELLINGHAUS, Aristokratische Leitbilder – demokratische Leitbilder, 1997 [10] S. FAUST, Schlachtenbilder der römischen Kaiserzeit, 2012 [11] H. FRIELINGHAUS, Die Helme von Olympia, 2011 [12] W. GAUER, Weihgeschenke aus den Perserkriegen, 1968 [13] P.J. HOLLIDAY, The Origins of Historical Commemoration in the Visual Arts, 2002 [14] T. HÖLSCHER, Griechische Historienbilder des 5. und 4. Jahrhunderts v.Chr., 1973 [15] T. HÖLSCHER, Die Nike der Messenier und Naupaktier in Olympia, in: JdI 89, 1974, 70–111 [16] T. HÖLSCHER, Images of War in Greece and Rome, in: JRS 93, 2003, 1–17 [17] T. HÖLSCHER, Provokation und Transgression als politischer Habitus in der späten römischen Republik, in: MDAI(R) 111, 2004, 83–104 [18] T. HÖLSCHER, Krieg und Kunst im antiken Griechenland und Rom, 2019 [19] L. KINNEY, The Greek and Roman Trophy, 2018 [20] E. KISTLER, Funktionalisierte Keltenbilder, 2009 [21] F. LISSARRAGUE, L'autre guerrier, 1990 [22] H.L. LORIMER, The Hoplite Phalanx, in: BSA 42, 1947, 76–138 [23] S. MUTH, Gewalt im Bild, 2008 [24] F. PIRSON, Ansichten des Krieges, 2014 [25] E. POLITO, Fulgentibus armis, 1998 [26] B. RABE, Tropaia, 2008 [27] W. RAECK, Zum Barbarenbild in der Kunst Athens im 6. und 5. Jahrhundert v.Chr., 1981 [28] T. SCHÄFER, Andres agathoi, 1997 [29] A.B. SPIESS, Der Kriegerabschied auf attischen Vasen der archaischen Zeit, 1992 [30] P. ZANKER, Augustus und die Macht der Bilder, ^{4}2003.

TONIO HÖLSCHER

B. COINS

B.1. Archaic, Classical and Hellenistic periods
B.2. Roman Republic
B.3. Roman Imperial period
B.4. Contexts and quantifications

War and victory were emphasized through the manner in which ancient polities and their rulers were represented on coins. This is true not only because these were prominent themes within the relevant canon of values, but also because soldiers were one of the largest recipient groups for newly minted coins, and it was possible to address them directly through the disbursement of pay. Gods of war and victory were referenced in image and word, as were rulers in their military role, army units and soldiers, equipment and weapons, fallen or captured enemies, consequences of war and monuments commemorating victories. Depictions might refer to specific occasions or else make statements of timeless validity. The types of portrayal range from highly detailed representations to significant abbreviations (not least because of the small area of the coin circle) to encrypted images, which which can only be clearly understood through contextual and iconographic analysis. It

Fig. 3: Quintuple shekel (c. 327 BC; 40.08 g; diameter: c. 34 mm). These coins, which on the reverse side perhaps reproduce the painting of Alexander with the attributes of Zeus painted by Apelles for Ephesus (Plin. HN 35,92), may be the gift from Taxiles to the Macedonian king, which he prized highly (Curt. 8,12,15f.; [8]; [9]: also discussed are other nominals of this series with depictions of war).

can be assumed that everything depicted on coins represents an official perspective (→ Sources D.).

B.1. ARCHAIC, CLASSICAL AND HELLENISTIC PERIODS

Greek coin images were mainly designed to show that the coin belonged to a specific *polis*. These *parasema* (city emblems) generally remained unchanged for centuries. They were often illustrations of myths, gods and heroes associated with the *polis*, or references to its landscape or, as a 'speaking coin type', to the name of the city. The first martial images appeared on Persian gold and silver coins, showing the Great King in the *Knielaufschema* ('kneeling-running motif') form, firing arrows or with bow and spear. In the Grecian world, warriors standing, kneeling or on horseback and shown with lances, spears, swords, clubs, slings, helmets, armour and shield are almost always references to myths. Helmets, greaves, shields, axes, bows, galleys and ships' hulls appeared as coin images in their own right [2. esp. part 3: War; part 5: Naval and Marine]. Portrayals of Nike increase in number beginning in the Hellenistic period. Shown with stylis and victor's laurels, Nike circulated widely on the gold *stateres* of Alexander the Great. Elsewhere, she appears, for instance, on a ship's hull from the reign of Demetrius Poliorketes (→ Generals of note, E.) in reference to his naval victory of 306 BC (examples in [10. 72–76]). In a class of its own is the multi-figure composition on a quintuple shekel which – very much in the spirit of the Alexander Mosaic at Pompeii – shows Alexander the Great (→ Generals of note, B.) on horseback, attacking Porus, who is already fleeing on his war elephant (cf. fig. 3).

B.2. ROMAN REPUBLIC

As the Roman Empire expanded throughout the Mediterranean, Roman currency outstripped all competitors. As a result, there was no need, as in the world of the Greek *poleis*, to use coins to achieve external recognition. Instead, they were used increasingly for internal communication. This paved the way for a new range of images. Mint masters responsible for coin production began in the last third of the 2nd century BC to use silver coins for family representations as well as to comment on current developments. War *exempla* and military successes had a prominent role to play. As early as the beginning of the 3rd century BC, the depiction of an → elephant and pig on *aes signatum* ('stamped bronze') referenced a contemporary experience from the war with Pyrrhus (RRC 9/1; Ael. NA 1,38). There is a direct association between portrayals of the *prora* ('prow') on bronze coins of the Republican period and the development of the Roman navy.

Variations and additions were made to existing coin motifs, for example to include a recent victory, but new multi-figure portrayals also appeared. A recurring theme among Italic rebels was that of mlitary commanders swearing an oath in an 'oath scene' (RRC 29; 234/1). Prisoners and personifications of foreign peoples whose ethnicity was indicated by hair, hair accessories, clothing and weapons were depicted under *tropaea* ('trophies'). More complex scenes show combat between riders on horseback or after dismounting (RRC 264/1; 327/1; cf. also 454/1), the defence of a fallen comrade on foot or on horseback (319/1; cf. fig. 4; 429/1), an attack on a fortification (514/1f.), or a scene such as the *exemplum* of Sergius Silus, who, after losing his right arm, stormed ahead on horseback while holding his sword and the severed head of an enemy in his left hand (286/1; Plin. HN 7,104f.; cf. fig. 5) (generally [4]; [6. 15–26]; [18]).

B.3. ROMAN IMPERIAL PERIOD

Portrayals of the military and victory in the Roman Imperial period made reference exclusively to the emperor and the ruling dynasty. Busts in armour and a general's cloak, headgear such as laurels or a helmet, and a text enumerating acclamations as *imperator* and victory titles set the tone on the obverse [3]. Annotated action scenes on the

Fig. 4: *Denarius* of mint master Q. Minucius Thermus (Rome, 103 BC; RRC 319/1; 4.02 g; diameter: 19 mm). The obverse shows the head of Mars looking left. The reverse has a Roman soldier to the left protecting his comrade, who has collapsed to the ground, against an attacking barbarian warrior with horned helmet.

Fig. 5: *Denarius* of mint master M. Sergius Silus (Rome, 116/115 BC; RRC 286/1; 3.92 g; diameter c. 20 mm). The obverse shows the head of helmeted Roma looking right. On the reverse is the mint master's ancestor of the same name fighting with his left hand only, as he was wounded in battle 23 times fighting the Celts and Carthaginians and is said to have escaped twice from captivity in Carthage.

Fig. 6: *Sestertius* of Hadrian (Rome, c. AD 130–133; RIC 915; 26.66 g; diameter: c. 33 mm). The obverse shows the bust of Hadrian wearing a laurel crown, armour and general's cloak, looking right. On the reverse, Hadrian is on horseback greeting his Dacian army (*EXERC[ITVS] DACICVS*), represented by three standard-bearers. The coin forms part of a large series showing Hadrian in front of various parts of his army, which are introduced by name (*EXERCITVS BRITANNICVS, CAPPADOCICVS, GERMANICVS, HISPANICVS* etc.).

reverse showed the ruler in various military roles, at the *ADLOCVTIO* (cf. fig. 6), *PROFECTIO, EXPEDITIO, TRAIECTVS, ADVENTVS* or at his acclamation as *IMPERATOR*.

The emperor was portrayed as victorious on land and sea, crowned by Victoria or placed alongside Jupiter as victor. Until the 3rd century, a depiction of the emperor on horseback leaping a fallen enemy always appeared in combination with his personal participation in a campaign. The outcome of the war was illustrated with defeated enemies, kings subjugated or taken captive, hostages received, or the installation of kings. *Tropaea*, arch monuments, emperors in triumphal chariots, and the Temple of Janus were all symbols of victory and the peace that came with it, while the legends *RECEPTA, DEVICTA* and *CAPTA* described the different outcomes of war more specifically ([5. vol. 2, 122–124, 142–261]; [7]; [1. 83–116]; [15. 213–378]; cf. [14]; [16]; [17]).

Types of the *DECVRSIO* show the emperor interacting with his army. Empresses of the late 2nd and early 3rd centuries were celebrated on coins as *MATER CASTRORVM*. The *DISCIPLINA* and regular *FIDES* or *CONCORDIA MILITVM/ EXERCITVM* appealed to soldiers. Specific unit types also appeared, such as cohorts, fleets, Praetorians or sections of the army (*EXERCITVS BRITANNICVS, DACICVS, GERMANICVS* etc.). Legends sometimes explicitly named individual legions (most famously the 'legion coins' of Mark Antony (RRC 544/1–39); for the Imperial period: [5. vol. 2, 192–194]; [14. 2–19]). A lead medallion from Late Antiquity shows in great detail the resettlement of defeated barbarians across the Rhine [14. 52f.]. Constantine II was shown fighting as *DEBELLATOR GENTIVM BARBARORVM* (cf. fig. 7).

B.4. CONTEXTS AND QUANTIFICATIONS

The relative completeness of the material in terms of types permits comparative quantitative analysis, and also allows for inferences concerning what is missing. More light can be shed by associating coins with the contexts of their issuing, so that, for example, a Victoria with no explanatory text can be related to a specific event. The number of different types of coins issued for a particular occasion is independent of the amount of money produced and the outcome of the communicative intentions. One promising method for quantifying the 'communicative weight' of coin types is to evalute their appearance in coin finds [12]; [13]. Indications are growing that the circulation of particular coin images in the Roman Imperial period was not

Fig. 7: Bronze medaillon from the reign of Constantine II (Rome, AD 337/340; RIC 347; 31.68 g; diameter: 38.7 mm). Constantine II is shown with diadem and armour on the obverse. The reverse depicts the emperor on horseback with his lance, stabbing an infantryman – armed with sword and shield – who is sinking to the ground. One fallen enemy already lies beneath the horse. The legend calls Constantine 'subduer of the barbarian peoples': *DEBELLATORI GENT{T}(IVM) BARBAR{R}(ORVM)*.

a matter of chance, but that particular regions or recipient groups – such as soldiers in particular – were intentionally supplied with specially chosen coin images [11].

☞ Honours; State and army

BIBLIOGRAPHY

[1] M.R. ALFÖLDI, Bild und Bildersprache der römischen Kaiser, 1999   [2] L. ANSON, Numismata Graeca, Greek Coin Types, 6 pts., 1910–1916   [3] P. BASTIEN, Le buste monétaire des empereurs romains, 3 vols., 1992–1994   [4] G.G. BELLONI, Figure di stranieri e di Barbari nelle monete della repubblica romana, in: M. SORDI (ed.), Conoscenze etniche e rapporti di convivenze nell'antichità, 1979, 201–228   [5] M. BERNHART, Handbuch zur Münzkunde der römischen Kaiserzeit, 2 vols., 1926   [6] S. BÖHM, Die Münzen der Römischen Republik und ihre Bildquellen, 1997   [7] K. CHRIST, Antike Siegesprägungen, in: Gymnasium 64, 1957, 504–533   [8] W. HOLLSTEIN, Taxiles' Prägung für Alexander den Grossen, in: SNR 68, 1989, 5–17   [9] F.L. HOLT, Alexander the Great and the Mystery of the Elephant Medallions, 2003   [10] C. HOWGEGO, Geld in der antiken Welt, 2000   [11] F. KEMMERS, Buying Loyalty, in: M. REDDÉ, De l'or pour les braves, 2014, 229–241   [12] E. MANDERS, Coining Images of Power, 2012   [13] C.F. NORENA, Imperial Ideals in the West, 2011   [14] B. OVERBECK, Rom und die Germanen, 1985   [15] F. SCHMIDT-DICK, Typenatlas der römischen Reichsprägung von Augustus bis Aemilianus, vol. 2: Geographische und männliche Darstellungen, 2011   [16] M. VITALE, Das Imperium in Wort und Bild. Römische Darstellungsformen beherrschter Gebiete in Inschriftenmonumenten, Münzprägungen und Literatur, 2017   [17] R. WOLTERS, Tam diu Germania vincitur, 1989   [18] B. WOYTEK, Der Fremde im Münzbild, in: A. PÜLZ / E. TRINKL (eds.), Das Eigene und das Fremde, 2015, 105–122 (with plates 19–22).

REINHARD WOLTERS

Rewards

☞ Honours

Rules of engagement

☞ Customs of war; Law of war

Scorched earth

A. Persians and Greeks
B. Romans
C. Military manuals

There are numerous examples from the ancient world of the use of the scorched earth tactic, which entails the destruction of the resources of an area of (usually home) territory to deny its use to the enemy [1]. However, since for understandable reasons the tactic was rather unpopular with the affected population and landowners, tradition usually attributes it to that enemy or to 'barbarians' in general.

A. Persians and Greeks

Herodotus reports that the Scythians were already using this tactic to resist the invasion by Darius I in 514 BC, and that it caused the Persian army grave difficulties (Hdt. 4,120). The troops of Artaxerxes II burned feed stocks and all materials ahead of the Battle of Cunaxa in 401 BC (Xen. An. 1,6,2; on Xenophon's remarks regarding the importance of the provision of feed for the flow of supplies [3]). The tactic was also used against Greek mercenaries after the battle. Some villages went up in flames, but the *strategoi* ('commanders') succeeded in obtaining provisions in the communities that were spared – before setting fire to those themselves as they marched out (Xen. An. 3,5,13). The Drilai, a tribe living near Trebizond, employed such tactics against the Ten Thousand (Xen. An. 5,2,3) [5].

The Greeks made use of the scorched earth tactic, too. For example, at the beginning of the Peloponnesian War, Pericles had the Athenian cattle herds moved to Euboea and other islands, and the rural districts evacuated, with all tools removed down to the wooden components of farms (Thuc. 2,14,1) [4]. In 370 BC, Theban forces were compelled to withdraw from Lacedaemon, because all supplies there had been burned or destroyed (Xen. Hell. 6,5,50).

There is a record dating from 334 BC of the mercenary leader Memnon of Rhodes suggesting to the satraps of Asia Minor that they might lay waste to their own arable land to halt the Macedonian advance. The satraps, however, rejected this as dishonourable conduct (Diod. Sic. 17,18,2; Curt. 3,4,3–5; Arr. Anab. 2,1).

B. Romans

Following the Roman defeat at Lake Trasimene in 217 BC, the (pro-)dictator Q. Fabius Maximus gave the order to tear down houses and destroy harvests in order to disrupt Hannibal's advance on Rome (Liv. 22,11,4f.) [2]. During Caesar's war against the Gallic coalition led by Vercingetorix, the Gauls systematically burned down villages and farmsteads ahead of the Battle of Avaricum in 52 BC. By doing so, as the author of the *Bellum Gallicum* points out, they were putting the interests of the many ahead of those of the one (Caes. B Gall. 7,14,2; 7,14,5). Entire *oppida* ('towns') were burned down if they were difficult to defend (Caes. B Gall. 7,14,9; 7,64,3). Both sides in the Roman-Parthian wars of the 4th century likewise left scorched earth behind them. Seeking to stall the Parthian advance in northern Mesopotamia, the Romans withdrew farmers and livestock breeders and evacuated the citadel of Carrhae (Amm. Marc. 18,7,3). Libanius mentions deliberate destruction during Julian's Parthian campaign (Lib. Or. 1,132). In AD 363, following the failed Siege of Ctesiphon, the forces of Sapor II set fire to the meadows, fields and harvests in the area east of the city. The ensuing famine weakened the Roman fighting force (Amm. Marc. 25,2,1f.) [6].

The Goths also seem to have adopted the tactic of destroying resources to harm the enemy during their wars with the Romans in the reign of Justinian. In a letter to the *spectabilis* (a high officer) Valerianus (c. 535/36), the *praefectus praetorio* ('Praetorian Prefect') Cassiodorus describes how the Gothic troops, 'though appointed to defend the Republic, devastated the fields of Lucania and the Brutti, and in their unbridled rapacity severely injured the prosperity of those regions' (Cassiod. Var. 12,5,3). Although Cassiodorus is mainly concerned with conveying landowners' claims for compensation, this may be a further example of the tactic of scorched earth.

C. Military manuals

Classical military treatises begin to discuss this subject in the 4th century BC (→ Military literature). Aeneas Tacticus recommends responding to an invasion by hostile troops by destroying all material that the enemy might use to build walls, tents and other fortifications, and by eliminating stores and harvests and poisoning drinking water (Aen. Tact. 8,3f.; the topic is also examined in the *paraskeuastike* (war planning and armament); Aen. Tact. 21,1). Onasander considers it essential to burn and destroy enemy fields, for 'a loss of materials and shortage of harvests shortens a war, while a surplus lengthens it'. Accordingly, everything that is not needed for supplying one's own troops should be destroyed (Onas. 6,11f.).

☞ **Strategy; Supply**

Bibliography
[1] W. Clausen, The Scorched Earth Policy, Ancient and Modern, in: CJ 40, 1945, 298–299 [2] T. Cornell, Hannibal's Legacy. The Effects of the Hannibalic War (BICS Suppl. 67), 1996, 97–117 [3] M. Gabrielli, Transports et logistique militaire dans l"Anabase', in: Pallas 43, 1995, 109–122 [4] V.D. Hanson, Warfare and Agriculture in Classical Greece, ²1998 [5] J.F. Lazenby,

Logistics in Classical Greek Warfare, in: War in History 1, 1994, 3–18 [6] R. SEAGER, Perceptions of Eastern Frontier Policy in Ammianus, Libanius, and Julian (337–363), in: CQ 47/1, 1997, 253–268.

GIUSTO TRAINA

Seasonality of war

☞ Timeframe of war

Siege warfare

A. Siege, encirclement, blockade, storming
B. Greek poliorcetics
C. Roman siege warfare

A. SIEGE, ENCIRCLEMENT, BLOCKADE, STORMING

The word 'siege' is here understood in the general sense of 'all operations and works undertaken by a hostile army to bring a city or fortress under its control' (translated from [2. 1187]). In a stricter sense, the term 'poliorcetics', derived from the Greek, denotes laying siege to cities. A fortress can be conquered in two ways: passively, by encirclement, that is, surrounding it so as to cut it off from all supplies and support; or: actively and violently by storming it, which includes killing the enemies and inflicting material destruction. Encirclement and blockade are synonymous. The besieged location is taken by causing a famine, but without inflicting material damage. Encirclement and storming can, however, be employed in concert.

B. GREEK POLIORCETICS

B.1. Siege warfare in the Classical period
B.2. The invention of the catapult, and Hellenistic poliorcetics

B.1. SIEGE WARFARE IN THE CLASSICAL PERIOD

The word *poliorkia* is first attested towards the end of the 5th century BC. Thucydides uses it in the sense of 'encirclement'. The Plataeans' *poliorkia* began once the attackers had decided to refrain from a direct attack (Thuc. 2,77). The term did not necessarily imply a surrounding siege, but more generally an effort to cut off the city's freedom of action. *Poliorkia* did, however, include the act of storming the city once that form of assault became more widespread.

The mighty Cyclopean walls at Mycenaean acropolis sites from the mid-14th to late 13th centuries already attest to the implementation of sieges. That this was a frequent occurrence is demonstrated by the proliferation of city walls in the Archaic period. Encirclement was still the usual tactic at this period. Sieges might last for years, and an enemy had to practice patience. Prior to the Persian Wars (490–479), the aim of war was not to capture the city itself, but to occupy its lands. A typical strategy involved launching attacks ever more deeply into the enemy's territory or conducting forays and subjecting them to attrition, so as to force the enemy to accept negotiations or submit to a pitched battle.

In terms of defense, Pericles shifted the priority to the defence of the urban area rather than the entire territory. Experience showed that the city had to be defended if the *polis* was to preserve its independence. The siege of the Athenian Acropolis by the Persians served as an example. Thick walls had to be built to withstand enemy attacks. On the eve of the Peloponnesian War, a significant event took place related to the trust Athens placed in its fleet after the Battle of Salamis. Instead of moving out from the city to join battle, the Athenians fled into the city to defend it. In a sense, the stone bulwark was meant to replace the human bulwark of the phalanx. From this point on, the art of fortification became increasingly effective, with a corresponding effect on siege warfare. However, the strategy of taking refuge inside city walls was soon abandoned, because it allowed the enemy free rein to ravage the territory outside and obtain food supplies. Moreover, the excess population in the city as a result of this strategy led to hygiene problems and the spread of the 'plague' epidemic. From then on, the focus was on fortifying borders (Xen. Mem. 3,5,25–27) and seeking a better balance between defending the city and defending the territory (Aen. Tact. 16,19). The new strategy aimed to defend the territory while keeping the city as a last defensive bastion, or as a base for advances into the surrounding territory.

Encirclement was a common and often decisive strategy during the Peloponnesian War (431–404), as it was frequently accompanied by a linear structure (a palisade or wall of dry stone or unfired bricks) that blocked movement or surrounded the city's outer limits and was sometimes equipped with towers. Those surrounded hindered the enemy's advance by installing inclined obstacles (palisades or ditches). Only rarely were cities stormed. For such an attack to succeed, one needed not only favourable circumstances (weak city walls and few guards), but also special equipment, such as a battering-ram or a 'turtle-ram' (*chelone*) (Thuc. 2,76,4) – in use by the Siege of Plataea in 429 BC at the latest – or a flamethrower (Thuc. 4,100,1–4; 4,115,2f.), which was better able than flaming arrows to target weak spots in the walls and thereby cause devastating fires. In order to break through the upper part of city walls, such machines had to be brought up inclined attack ramps (Thuc. 2,75,2f.), which were built of earth and reinforced with various materials. The use of saps (covered trenches) for opening breaches in city walls, and the digging of mines (tunnels leading underneath the walls into the besieged town) are also attested for this period (Plataeae). These would only succeed if the attackers were able to exploit the element of surprise. Mobile protective devices allowed the machines to be brought closer to the fortress wall while shielding soldiers from the fire of those under siege.

B.2. The invention of the catapult, and Hellenistic poliorcetics

Spectacular advances were soon made in Sicily under Dionysius I (405–367) as he fought his war with Carthage. Dionysius introduced the mobile siege tower to the Grecian world (Siege of Motya, Diod. Sic. 14,51,1–7). It had been known to the Babylonians before reaching the Carthaginians via the Phoenicians. The apparatus has an upper deck at or above the level of the walkway around the enemy walls. Likewise, according to Diodorus Siculus (14,42), it was in the workshops of Dionysius that the catapult was invented. In all versions of this early period, this device was used exclusively to shoot arrows (Diod. Sic. 14,43,3; 50,4; cf. fig. 1). These tripod-mounted machines unleashed a destructive power never before seen in the history of warfare, for no defensive weapon (helmet, armour or shield) could protect a soldier against fire from a catapult.

Greek siegecraft developed particularly under the influence of the Macedonian engineers of Philip II (→ Generals of note M.) and Alexander the Great (→ Generals of note B.), Polyidus and Diades, who constructed more practical and effective battering rams as well as gigantic towers 40–55 m in height, which were called *helepoleis* ('takers of cities'; cf. fig. 2). This pursuit of immensity reached its zenith with Demetrius Poliorketes (→ Generals of note E.), who in 305 BC deployed turtle-rams with ridge beams 50 metres long (Diod. Sic. 20,95,1) and a *helepolis* weighing about 75 tons (Vitr. De arch. 10,16,4) against the walls of Rhodes. The construction of artillery weapons was not left behind in this arms race. Alexander the Great often used *oxybelai* ('sharp missiles'), and the catapult appeared at the Siege of Tyre (332) to launch stones or rock chunks (Diod. Sic. 17,42,7). Both types of machines were deployed on many occasions during the Hellenistic period, mostly in combination. The centrality of siege machinery shows that storming the besieged location was now the main priority. Such a victory demonstrated the commander's military value and enhanced his reputation, and could even break the morale of his opponents in advance.

C. Roman siege warfare

C.1. Early and Middle Republic
C.2. Late Republic and Imperial period

C.1. Early and Middle Republic

Until the time of the Punic Wars, the period when the Romans conquered Italy and defeated countless fortified places, their siege warfare was far inferior to that of the Greeks. They may not even have used battering rams. They had only runged ladders and light protective equipment (the *vineae*) consisting of a wooden frame with a wall made of wicker, which was intended to provide enough protection to allow fighters to approach fortified walls. The ladders, which were probably made on site to better adapt to the height of the walls, often seem to have been the only effective aid to capturing a location. Yet these rudimentary

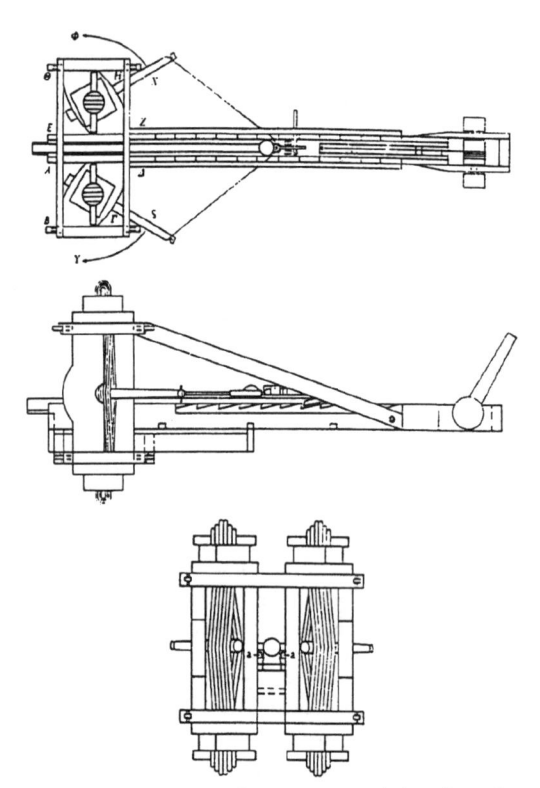

Fig. 1: Reconstruction of a stone catapult based on the manual by Hero of Alexandria (drawing, from [7. vol. 2, 56, fig. 20]). Stone catapults were larger than arrow catapults, but both functioned according to the same principle: they were driven by torsion and detorsion (winding tight and sudden release) in two cords of strong but elastic fibres fixed to two metal rods anchored to a frame (centre and bottom). An arm was inserted into each of these cords. To achieve torsion and thus tension in the fibres, both arms were connected to a rope that was drawn back with the help of a rail running along the barrel of the weapon, then locked with a bolt (top). Knocking out the bolt with a heavy blow sent the arms, and thus the projectile, hurtling forward towards the target.

Fig. 2: Reconstruction of a *helepolis*, a turtle-ram and a battering ram (etching; after *Les dix livres d'Architecture de Vitruve*, trans. C. Perrault, 2nd edition 1684, 345). This reconstruction is based on a passage in Vitruvius discussing the machines designed by Diades (10,3–7). The illustration shows that wheeled *helepoleis* could sometimes be very tall so as to rise over the the besieged walls, and that they consisted of multiple storeys (between 10 and 20 at this period) with apertures on all sides. Men posted at these apertures on every storey could use assorted weapons and pieces of siege machinery, especially catapults and siege hooks to collapse the battlements of the wall. The turtle-ramshown at the left was a battering ram with a wooden structure on wheels covering its central section to protect the men who were attacking the walls. The ram inside was fitted on a mount with rollers that enabled the shaft to be pushed forward. Crowning the construction was a turret for those who operated the catapult. The ram in the foreground likewise rested on rollers, but it was mounted on a mobile frame that gave it more precision and enabled it to break through walls rather than merely shock them. The etching shows only the interior, but this ram, too, must have had a wooden cover. All these pieces of siege equipment were covered with animal skins to make them less vulnerable to fire.

technologies were fully consistent with Roman strategy and tactics.

In fact, the Romans owed their almost perfect success to such strategies and tactics. During the 5th and 4th centuries BC, a siege would end in an orderly battle that decided the fate of the town. After the victory was won, the Romans would either climb the now-vacated city walls, or they would enter the town close behind those who were fleeing into it, if the gates were not shut in time. These were the most common scenarios when Roman soldiers armed with hand-held weapons assaulted a city to capture it. It was not possible to use machinery to capture such places, which were elevated, steeply inclined and often fortified. Those under siege sometimes chose to shut themselves inside their city. In such cases, rather than surround the city and launch a protracted war that would bring supply problems, the Romans chose another option: the tactical assault, which replaced the practice of violently assaulting a city after battle when the assualt proved impossible. The tactics most often adopted were diversion and encirclement. The former, which dated back at least to the capture of Veii (396 BC), involved tricking the besieged populace into thinking that their attackers were focusing on one specific point along the walls so that they would gather as many defenders there as possible – meanwhile, another detachment of besiegers would climb the walls at a different location, which had been left defenseless. The second tactic was meant to sow panic and disperse the city's defences. It involved attacking the city walls from all directions using a ring of soldiers (*corona*), who, equipped with ladders or pushing against the gates in turtle formation, would all move against the city at once (Sieges of Satricum, 386 and 347, and of Cominium 293).

This way of conducting siege warfare – without siege engines – certainly had its heroes, such as Camillus and the consul Valerius Corvus, but it was clear on the eve of the Punic War (264–241) that Roman practice in this area was deeply inadequate. It was probably in the wake of Rome's war against Tarentum (275 BC) – which incidentally boasted a number of famous engineers who had no doubt read Greek treatises on poliorcetics – that the Romans began to acquaint themselves with siege technology. The path from theory to practice, however, was often difficult, as they found themselves confronting heavily fortified walls and other masterpieces of Greek military architecture (Agrigentum, Syracuse). With the help of the turtle-rams provided by Hieron II, Tyrant of Syracuse, the Romans made titanic efforts to break the defensive walls of Lilybaeum, but the resolve of its Carthaginian defenders forced them to abandon their attempt to storm the city and led them instead to set up a blockade. The Romans also introduced new earthwork techniques in this period: digging under city walls to destroy them, and enclosing the city to lay siege to it – practices which the Greeks had long since mastered effectively. From this time on, the Romans began to understand that deploying heavy and cumbersome equipment left them open to counterattack from the outside, and that an attack using machinery needed to be combined with the use of linear protective measures (making walls or connecting links between guardposts). This combination of frontal assault and linear installation became a speciality of the Romans. Caesar also used it (Caes. B Gall. 2,30,2; 7,11,1; 7,36).

C.2. LATE REPUBLIC AND IMPERIAL PERIOD

During the Second Punic War (218–201), Rome became involved in genuine siege warfare in all theatres of the war: in Iberia, Italy, Sicily and Africa. Obviously, most sieges took place in Italy. The Romans were trying to reconquer all the cities Hannibal had subjugated. After taking Syracuse (212), which had allied with the Carthaginians after the death of Hieron II, and then Tarentum and Carthage itself in 209, the Romans took possession of the arsenals of those cities, and therefore, it must be presumed, the very latest equipment. Their machines had certainly improved somewhat by that point, but there had been no radical changes. The first Roman use of the *sambuca* came only at the Siege of Syracuse commanded by M. Claudius Marcellus. This siege engine, said to have been invented by the Tarentine engineer Heraclides, was a large ladder installed horizontally across two quinqueremes lashed together. On approaching a defensive wall, it could be raised by means of a rope winch, enabling the attackers to reach the besieged wall via the sambuca's upper platform (Pol. 8,4,2–11). As for Roman torsion engines (*tormenta*), they had considerable but not extraordinary striking capability. At the Siege of Utica, *oxybelai* fired projectiles about 150 cm long, and catapults launched stones weighing 26 kg – hardly comparable to the '120 very large *catapultae*' (for firing arrows) and '23 larger *ballistae*' (for throwing bolts or stones) from the Carthage arsenal (Liv. 26,47,5f.). The practice of violently assaulting a city with weapons in hand remained prevalent in Italy, although faced with the impregnable walls of Sicily, the Romans had to resort to diversion, cunning and sometimes treachery.

During the Macedonian and Syrian Wars (215–167), the Romans found themselves up against Hellenistic siege technology and experienced opponents. They were wise enough in this situation to rely on their Greek allies, with whom they apparently worked in tandem. The Romans specialized in destroying and capturing walls, as is shown by the predominant use of the battering ram, which was always associated with the tactic of coordinated assaults, and was less commonly associated with undermining (famously at the Siege of Ambracia, Pol. 21,28,1–4), while they entrusted the → artillery to their allies. None of this, however, prevented them from continuing to do what they did best: storm enemy positions to take them by force. In difficult situations, the tactic of coordinated assults was combined with the tactic of inflicting relentless attacks day and night so that the enemy would soon become exhausted, as at Heraclea in Phthiotis in 191 BC (Liv. 36,23,6–10). Contrary to expectations, perhaps, artillery was no silver bullet in these siege wars.

There was, in fact, no set role for artillery in the Roman army before Caesar. They used *tormenta* when the need arose, being content to confiscate them, borrow them, or have engineers build them when the need arose. It seems that Caesar was the first to equip his army with catapults as standard equipment. He used them after landing in Britain, on the battlefield to protect his army's flanks, in the defence of forts, and in sieges, of course. For example, *tormenta* proved highly useful in repelling the Gauls at the Siege of Gergovia (Caes. Gall. 7,41,3). Their considerable firepower compensated for the army's numerical disadvantage. It was probably Augustus who assigned a certain number of artillery engines to every legion. Under the principate, the Roman army had neither an artillery corps nor a supreme artillery commander. Every legion had its own artillery. Every legionary had to be capable of operating these machines.

At the beginning of the imperial period, the firepower of catapults and *ballistae* (the name often given by the Romans to machines for hurling stones) was increased at the urging of Vitruvius. It was very likely in the reign of Trajan, at the time of the Dacian Wars (cf. reliefs on the Trajan Column) that a new engine first appeared, the *carroballista*, a catapult mounted on a car (*carrus*). This gave the Romans the most powerful *oxybeles* ever built. It remained in use until at least the 4th century AD.

☞ **Fortification; Military literature**

BIBLIOGRAPHY

SOURCES
[1] VITRUVE, De l'Architecture. Livre X, commentary by P. Fleury, translated and edited by L. Callebat, 2002 (¹1986)

SECONDARY LITERATURE
[2] Siège, in: La grande Encyclopédie. Inventaire raisonné des sciences, des lettres et des arts, par une société de savants et de gens de lettres, vol. 29, 1901, 1182–1188 [3] D. BAATZ, Bauten und Katapulte des römischen Heeres, 1994 [4] Y. GARLAN, Recherches de Poliorcétique grecque, 1974 [5] O. LENDLE, Schildkröten. Antike Kriegsmaschinen in poliorketischen Texten, 1975 [6] O. LENDLE, Texte und Untersuchungen zum technischen Bereich der antiken Poliorketik, 1983 [7] E.W. MARSDEN, Greek and Roman Artillery, 2 vols., 1969–1971 [8] J. NAPOLI, Effets et méfaits des machines à torsion dans l'Antiquité romaine, in: J. BEL (ed.), Actes et Machines de Guerre (Les Cahiers du Littoral 1/13), 2012, 321–349 [9] J. NAPOLI, Évolution de la poliorcétique romaine sous la République jusqu'au milieu du IIe siècle avant J.-C., 2013

JOËLLE NAPOLI

Slavery

A. Introduction
B. Classical Greece
C. Hellenistic period
D. Rome

A. INTRODUCTION

Slaves were always categorically forbidden to perform military service in Greco-Roman Antiquity. Military service was always the exclusive prerogative of free men, because the social order and the organization of the military were tightly interwoven. Anyone who contributed to the military potential of his home country was also entitled to a political say. Moreover, slave owners were afraid that slaves, once armed, might rise against them. As a rule, then, slaves – who were often regarded as cowardly – and members of other unfree or dependent population groups were not generally deployed as combatants in regular fighting forces. Nor were they typically used as oarsmen in the fleets. However, exceptions to this general rule were often made, particularly in crisis situations.

The Greek *poleis* in particular were frequently compelled by their often meagre recruitment base to resort to exceptional measures. On the other hand, the practice of using slaves in the baggage train to perform auxiliary service was common throughout antiquity. For labour in this function, the use of unfree people was even more common than that of free people.

B. CLASSICAL GREECE

B.1. Land forces
B.2. Fleet
B.3. Ancillary military duties

B.1. LAND FORCES
The use of slaves in land forces was essentially an emergency measure in Classical Greece. It was a last resort for times of extraordinary danger. One example was in the face of the Persian threat in the early 5th century, when the Athenians are said to have deployed unfree combatants for the first time at the Battle of Marathon (490 BC; Paus. 1,32,3; 7,15,7), manumitting them prior to the battle. This, however, did not set a precedent, although Xenophon recommends recruiting slaves for the fleet and land forces in his treatise on public revenues (Vect. 4,42). The Athenians would not again make such a decision until after the Battle of Chaeronea (338 BC) (Lycurg. Leocr. 41; Ps.-Plut. Mor. 849a; Dion. Chrys. 15,21), and even then, changed political conditions meant that the plan was not put into practice.

There are sporadic records of slaves being used in combat by other polities of Classical Greece. Likewise in these cases, arming the unfree was done mostly in connection with immediate, severe threats or sieges imposed on particular cities, for example Plataeae in 431 BC, when slaves hurled rocks and bricks down on the invaders from the roofs (Thuc. 2,4,2), or Thebes as it was besieged by Alexander the Great in 335 BC, when all slaves fit for combat were freed and armed (Diod. Sic. 17,11,2).

As is often the case, Sparta (→ Sparta) was an exception in how it dealt with the unfree. The claim that freed helots were already reinforcing the Spartan army – and gaining citizenship – during the Second Messenian War (7th cent. BC; Paus. 4,16,6; Just. Epit. 3,5,4–7), cannot be true. However, during the emergency of the Peloponnesian War (431–404 BC) battle groups of helots and *neodamodes* ('new citizens', i.e. freed helots who, however, did not earn full citizenship) were formed. In 424 BC, a force of 1,000 mercenaries and 700 helots was sent to Thrace under the command of Brasidas (Thuc. 4,80,5). The unit proved its worth, and its surviving members were manumitted. It was later stationed at Lepreum as a border force. Some 600 helots and *neodamodes* led by Eccritus were sent to support the Syracusans on Sicily in 413 BC (Thuc. 7,19,3; 7,58,3). Despite the constant danger the helots posed to the Spartiates, the latter evidently did not see their recruitment as a major cause for concern. Thucydides reports that their fear of the people whom they were oppressing led the Spartans to murder 2,000 helots who were eager to take part in military campaigns (4,80,3f.), but the veracity of this report must be doubted. *Neodamodes* were deployed in many, mostly foreign theatres of war between 420 and 370 BC, and they became a trusted instrument of Spartan power politics. This practice ended with the Spartan defeat at the Battle of Leuctra in 371 BC. The following year, when Epaminondas (→ Generals of note, F.) advanced into Laconia, over 6,000 helots are said to have volunteered for military service (Xen. Hell. 6,5,28f.). These high numbers again sparked fears that the unfree might rise up, and indeed numerous helots do seem to have defected to the enemy (Plut. *Agesilaus* 32,7). Many helots, however, were steadfast in battle and earned the reward of freedom (Diod. Sic. 15,65,6). It appears significant that when helots were used in combat, the armed unfree were always Laconian, who seem to have borne their fate with more resignation than their Messenian fellow sufferers.

B.2. Fleet

Using slaves as oarsmen in the Greek → fleets was likewise an emergency measure rather than a regular practice during the Classical period. Athens resorted to the unfree when, in times of exceptional demand – such as during the Persian or Peloponnesian Wars (→ Wars of note, J.; → Wars of note, H.) –, the number of thetes and metics did not suffice to man the great Athenian fleet. Slaves served in many squadrons during the last decade of the Peloponnesian War in particular. There is good evidence for their use, for example, aboard the vessels participating in the Battle of the Arginusae (406 BC; Xen. Hell. 1,6,24; Hellanicus, FGrH 4 Frg. 171; cf. also the allusions in Aristoph. Ran. 33; 191ff.; 692ff.). The lists of crew members given in inscriptions (IG II/III² 1951) on the Acropolis record many unfree *therapontes* ('squires'), who were emancipated after their deployment – which was an unusual outcome for the unfree who were enlisted in the fleets. Slaves were put to use as oarsmen after the reconstruction of the Athenian fleet in the 4th century BC, but the recorded cases again show that these were not regular, systematic recruitments, but emergency measures – undertaken, for instance, during the Lamian War (323–322 BC; IG II/III² 554).

The fleets of other Greek *poleis* also used slaves as oarsmen. The Syracusan Tyrant, Dionysius I, for instance, recruited slaves who were manumitted in advance for his fleet in 397 BC (Diod. Sic. 14,58,1).

Helots served alongside free *periokoi* ('dwellers around [Sparta]') in the Spartan fleet (e.g. Xen. Hell. 7,1,12).

It must, of course, be noted that it would never have been possible to put slaves to use in the fleet at short notice, for the work of an oarsman required some training and experience.

B.3. Ancillary military duties

Rare as it was for slaves to be used as combatants in regular land forces or as oarsmen on warships in Classical Greece, it was entirely normal for them to be put to work in the army train. Free classes also worked here, but most of those working as stable hands, weapons handlers, porters, animal handlers, builders, scribes and orderlies in the 5th and 4th centuries BC were unfree. Their numbers exactly reflected the strength of the hoplite complement. The use of these men, who were called *therapontes* ('squires'), *hypaspistai* ('shieldbearers'), *opeones* ('escorts'), *akolouthoi* ('attendants'), *hoplophoroi* ('weapon porters'), *skeuophoroi* (equipment porters), *hippokomoi* ('grooms') and *paides* ('servants'), appears – occasional complaints notwithstanding (e.g. Xen. An. 4,2,20) – to have been thoroughly successful, and some of these unfree weapons handlers even became close confidants of their masters.

The Spartan army made use of helots and slaves from the *periokoi* for ancillary military services, as weapons handlers and retinue servants (Thuc. 4,8,9; Xen. Hell. 4,5,14). Herodotus, for instance, reports that at the Battle of Plataeae (479 BC), every Spartiate was accompanied by seven helots (Hdt. 9,29), although he probably exaggerates.

Regulations concerning retinue servants are preserved from Macedonia, where Philip II stipulated as part of his army reform that every cavalryman should have only one stable attendant and every *dekas* (unit of men) should have a porter (Frontin. Str. 4,1,6).

C. Hellenistic period

C.1. Land forces
C.2. Fleet
C.3. Ancillary military services

Examples are recorded of the use of slaves as defensive reinforcements in the Hellenistic world. Smaller polities in particular were forced to do this because of their insufficient recruitment base. This practice can also be seen as a consequence of the increasing prevalence of slavery.

C.1. Land forces

The use of slaves as combatants in land forces was not customary in the period just after the Wars of the Diadochi. It was only when the Hellenistic potentates had to defend themselves against the Romans that the practice resumed. In 143 BC, for instance, a certain pseudo-Philip raised a slave army of 16,000 against the Romans, although he was ultimately defeated (Eutr. 4,15). In its final stand against Rome, the Achaean League under Diaeus mobilized 12,000 slaves, but Mummius vanquished them (Pol. 38,15,3f.; Paus. 7,15,7). Fifteen thousand *therapontes* ('squires') fought in the army of Mithridates VI of Pontus at the Battle of Chaeronea (Plut. *Sulla* 18,5f.).

It became more common in the Hellenistic period than it had been in the Classical period for slaves to be recruited as an emergency measure in defense of besieged cities. When Zopyrion laid siege to Olbia in 331 BC (?), the attack was repelled when the slaves were manumitted, foreigners were granted citizenship, and a general cancellation of debts was implemented to strengthen the defense (Macrob. Sat. 1,11,33). At Megalopolis, when Polyperchon stood outside the city gates in 318 BC, 15,000 citizens were mobilized alongside foreigners and slaves (Diod. Sic. 18,70). All slaves who were fit to fight were enlisted for combat and ancillary duties during Demetrius Poliorketes' siege of Rhodes in 305/04 BC. As reward for their service, they were promised not only freedom, but also citizenship, and they consequently played a prominent part in the successful defence of the city (Diod. Sic. 20,84,2f.). When Philip V besieged Chios in 201 BC, it is said that the slaves volunteered to fight for its defence.

C.2. FLEET

On the whole, slaves played only a minor role in the fleets of the Diadochi and the successor kingdoms. In practice, the demand for unfree oarsmen varied widely among the various Hellenistic states. Unlike the smaller realms, the great kingdoms had no need for unfree oarsmen, having large reservoirs of free candidates. Moreover, slave oarsmen were not usually emancipated, whereas the manumission of slaves fighting in land armies was expected – although they were not ordinarily granted citizenship (the aforementioned action by the Rhodians was an exception).

C.3. ANCILLARY MILITARY SERVICES

In the Hellenistic period as before, it was common for unfree men to work as retinue servants, weapons handlers, artisans and orderlies. Freemen were occasionally recruited (e.g. young relatives or hired servants), but most ancillary military personnel were slaves. However, differences in practice can be seen between the various Hellenistic states. The Ptolemaic army, for instance, had no need of slaves for ancillary services, since it had an ample pool of free indigenous people available for such work.

D. ROME

Throughout Rome's history, it was strictly forbidden for slaves to enter the Roman army (Serv. Aen. 9,544). In AD 380, a constitution of the emperors Gratian, Valentinian II and Theodosius I emphatically confirmed this prohibition (Cod. Theod. VII 13,8). A constitution of the emperors Arcadius and Honorius again confirmed it in AD 396 (Cod. Theod. VII 18,9). Mechanisms for enforcing this prohibition, however, regularly malfunctioned (Plin. Ep. 10,29). Escaped slaves often attempted, despite the severe penalties involved (Dig. 49,16,11: *ab omni militia servi prohibentur: alioquin capite puniuntur*; 'all military service is prohibited for slaves; otherwise they will be punished with death'), to pass themselves off as free men and thus vanish out of sight into the army. Even freedmen (*liberti*) were excluded from armed service until 217 BC, and foreigners (*peregrini*) enlisted in the army had to be free.

D.1. LAND FORCES

Slaves were officially recruited into Roman land forces only in situations of extreme emergency. The first such instance came after the Roman defeat at the Battle of Cannae in 216 BC (Liv. 22,57,11f.; → Battles of note, C.). The shortage of soldiers led to the recruitment of 8,000 slaves, who volunteered for armed service and were thus categorized as *volones*. Their masters received a purchase price set by the senate and paid from the public purse as compensation. When these slaves proved their worth at the Battle of Beneventum (214 BC) (Liv. 24,14–16), they were manumitted (Flor. Epit. 1,22,23 states that they were freed on recruitment).

In AD 6, Augustus recruited 3,500 freed slaves to form the paramilitary fire brigade (*vigiles*) of the city of Rome (Cass. Dio 55,26,4f.). Other recruitments from the unfree population are recorded for the year AD 6/7, when in response to the Pannonian-Dalmatian uprising a security force of slaves was sent to the Illyrian border, and then again after the Roman defeat in the Teutoburg Forest in AD 9/10 (→ Battles of note, J.), when a force of unfree soldiers recruited in Italy was sent to the Rhine frontier on guard and protection duties (Suet. Aug. 25,2).

In the 2nd century AD, Marcus Aurelius (→ Generals of note, L.) is said to have recruited slaves while preparing for his war against the Germani and Marcomanni after the death of Lucius Verus (SHA Ant. Phil. 21,6), but this information is not necessarily credible.

Unfree soldiers were deployed as combatants against Radagais in AD 406. However, as in earlier cases, they were granted their freedom when they were first recruited (Cod. Theod. VII 13,16). Still, as throughout Roman history, unfree combatants remained a rarity in the armies of Late Antiquity.

Early in the 5th century, the *coloni* were also prohibited from performing military service. These had originally been free tenant farmers, but starting in the late 3rd century AD, they became ever more dependent, entering into living conditions that were akin to slavery.

D.2. FLEET

In the Roman navy, too, recruiting slaves was an exceptional measure reserved for times of extraordinary crisis. As with land forces, it was during the Second Punic War (218–201 BC) that high demand for crews first led to the recruitment in 214 and 210 BC of numerous unfree oarsmen (Liv. 24,11; 26,35).

Slaves were only recruited again for galley service in the wars of the late Republic, such as under the triumvirs ahead of the Battle of Philippi in 42 BC (Cass. Dio 47,17,4), then again in 37 BC by Octavian, after he suffered massive losses (Suet. Aug. 16,1; Cass. Dio 49,1,5). It was the civil war raging at that time that led to these extraordinary measures. A similar context lay behind the mass use of *fugitivi* aboard the warships of Sextus Pompeius (R. Gest. div. Aug. 25; App. Civ. 5,131; Cass. Dio 49,12,4; Oros. hist. 6,18,33).

During the Imperial period, those deployed as seamen in the Roman navy were mainly non-citizens (*peregrini, liberti*), and they were granted Latin rights at the end of their term of service (the *constitutio Antoniniana* of AD 212 also made these free men Roman citizens).

D.3. RETINUE SERVICE

As in the Greek world, the most significant use of unfree people among the Romans was in the army train. These retinue servants were generally called *calones*, but they were also described as *agasones, muliones* or – less frequently – *caculae, armigeri* or *lixae*. These men performed valuable ancillary services. Their tasks included transporting baggage, provisioning mounts and pack and draught animals, taking part in foraging (*pabulatio*), gathering wood, and building infrastructure. Sometimes, however, they were lightly armed, and thereby acquired some military experience.

Good evidence exists for the use of unfree retinue servants during the Second Punic War. Although there are reported instances in the 3rd century BC (Pol. 1,67,7; 1,69,4) and by the early 2nd century BC of such unfree people escaping (Liv. 38,11,4; 38,38,7), their work was nonetheless productive, and they were present at virtually all battlefields of the Middle and Late Republican periods. They were present with the forces of Manlius Vulso (Liv. 38,41,3), the army of Aemilius Paullus (Plut. *Aemilius* 22,2), outside Numantia (Plut. *Tiberius Gracchus* 5), in the war against Jugurtha (Sall. Iug. 45,2 – where it is reported that Metellus forbade his men from bringing their own servants into camp; 66,1), and in the confrontation with the Cimbri and Teutones (Plut. *Marius* 19,1–3). It is not usually possible to ascertain their numbers. The assertion that 80,000 Roman soldiers and *socii* ('confederates'), along with 40,000 *lixae* (non-combatants of unknown function within the Roman army), fell at the Battle of Arausio is undoubtedly an exaggeration. Normally, a total of 400–600 retinue servants may be assumed per legion. According to Vegetius, these servants were organized into units of 200 under the command of a selected retinue servant (Veg. Mil. 3,6). The entire army train was answerable to the camp prefect (*praefectus castrorum*; Veg. Mil. 2,10). The unfree retinue servants were frequently accompanied by considerable numbers of slaves, who came into the possession of soldiers as booty over the course of extended campaigns. The army leadership dipped into this reservoir of private slaves as conditions required.

BIBLIOGRAPHY
[1] B. BERTOSA, The Social Status and Ethnic Origin of the Rowers of Spartan Triremes, in: War and Society 23, 2005, 1–20   [2] H. CHANTRAINE, Kaiserliche Sklaven im römischen Flottendienst, in: Chiron 1, 1971, 253–265   [3] V. GABRIELSEN, Financing the Athenian Fleet. Public Taxation and Social Relations, 1994   [4] A.J. GRAHAM, Thucydides 7.13.2 and the Crews of Athenian Triremes, in: Transactions of the American Philological Association 122, 1992, 257–270   [5] A.J. GRAHAM, Thucydides 7.13.2 and the Crews of Athenian Triremes. An Addendum, in: Transactions of the American Philological Association 128, 1998, 89–114   [6] P. HUNT, The Helots at the Battle of Plataea, in: Historia 46, 1997, 129–144   [7] P. HUNT, Slaves, Warfare, and Ideology in the Greek Historians, 1998   [8] P. HUNT, The Slaves and Generals of Arginusae, in: AJPh 122, 2001, 359–380   [9] P. HUNT, Arming Slaves and Helots in Classical Greece, in: C.L. BROWN / P.D. MORGAN (eds.), Arming Slaves. From Classical Times to the Modern Age, 2006, 14–39   [10] S. JAMES, The Roman Galley Slave. Ben-Hur and the Birth of a Factoid, in: Public Archaeology 2, 2001, 35–49   [11] Y. LE BOHEC, Die römische Armee, 1993   [12] N. ROULAND, Les esclaves romains en temps de guerre, 1977   [13] K.-W. WELWEI, Unfreie im antiken Kriegsdienst, vol. 1: Athen und Sparta (Forschungen zur antiken Sklaverei 5), 1974   [14] K.-W. WELWEI, Unfreie im antiken Kriegsdienst, vol. 2: Die kleineren und mittleren griechischen Staaten und die hellenistischen Reiche (Forschungen zur antiken Sklaverei 8), 1977   [15] K.-W. WELWEI, Unfreie im antiken Kriegsdienst, vol. 3: Rom (Forschungen zur antiken Sklaverei 21), 1988.

JOSEF FISCHER

Society and army

A. Greek
B. Roman

A. GREEK

A.1. Cavalry and the upper class
A.2. Foot soldiers
A.3. Unfree combatants

Little is known of the relations between the military and society in the early phases of Greek history, other than what we find in the Homeric epics, but opinion is divided over the reliability of the picture painted there. In general, Homer portrays only the wealthiest as participating in single combat, for which they dismount from their war chariots. Only as the Greek city-states begin their rise does the relationship between society and army begin to become clearer.

A.1. CAVALRY AND THE UPPER CLASS

Prior to the the 8th century BC and the invention of the horse collar, which enabled the use of horses' pulling power for agricultural purposes, only the very wealthiest members of society could afford to keep horses. As a result, the most affluent strata of society were generally called upon directly or indirectly to provide horses for the cavalry.

We do now know how the mounted forces of early history were maintained. In aristocratic Thessaly, for example, a fragment of Aristotle's *Constitution of the Thessalians* (Aristot. fr. 498) tells us that a certain Aleuas (probably Aleuas 'the Red' in the second half of the 6th century) divided the estates under his control into units called *kleroi* (land allotments). Every *kleros* was expected to provide 40 cavalrymen and 80 hoplites for the confederate army. Researchers suggest that there was a total of 150 *kleroi*, which would imply a total of 6,000 horse and 12,000 hoplites in the confederate army. Another polity in early possession of a cavalry was the Boeotian League, the constitution of which (preserved in the *Hellenika Oxyrhynchia* 16[9],3f.) probably dates back to the time of the league's foundation in 447 BC. Boeotia was divided into eleven military districts, each of which provided 1,000 hoplites and 100 cavalry. Here, too, we have no knowledge of how riders' expenses were defrayed.

Sparta only founded its first cavalry regiment – of 400 horsemen – in 424 BC (Thuc. 4,55,2), and did so by requisitioning the horses of its richest citizens. This system remained in place until the Battle of Leuctra in 371 BC (Xen. Hell. 6,4,11). Such a procedure would have been impossible in oligarchic Corinth. The Corinthians maintained their cavalry horses using revenues gathered from taxing the publicly administered assets of widows and orphans (Cic. Rep. 2,20). The Spartans adopted an array of methods of recruitment among their allies to provide for their cavalry. In 396 BC, King Agesilaus recruited the richest men in the cities of Asia Minor, who were able to maintain cavalry horses, but exempted them from serving in the military themselves if they were able to supply a substitute (Xen. Ag. 1,23f.). By about the mid-4th century BC, even rather insignificant Greek city-states had cavalry units.

It was only as the institution of public finances emerged that it became possible to compensate horse owners for expenses such as the loss of their animals in battle, depreciation or feed costs. In about 443 BC, Athens expanded its cavalry to 1,000 men, with an additional 200 mounted archers. The 'settlement' (*katastasis*) paid to every cavalryman ensured the replacement of a lost horse, and a daily feed allowance (*sitos*) of one drachma was also introduced. Athens was able to afford this thanks to its regular influx of tribute from its empire. Other Greek *poleis* had to resort to other methods.

Two texts (*Paroem.* I,257; II,464) show that a war horse was a royal gift during the reign of Philip II of Macedon. It is unclear who was responsible for providing feed. It seems that later, members of the Macedonian *hetairoi* ('companions', i.e. the noble class) cavalry of Alexander the Great were expected to provide their own horses and stable hands, paying for these from the rights of land usage that they received from the king. This arrangement may have been set up prior to the commencement of the Asia campaign. Plutarch tells us that Alexander would not set foot aboard his ship before he had been apprised of the financial circumstances of his 'companions', and allotted to them variously an estate, a village or the revenue from a particular hamlet or harbour (Plut. *Alexander* 15). Under Alexander (→ Generals of note, B.), squadrons bore geographical names, and in the case of more than half of the units known to us, those names were of subjugated Greek cities. The 'companions' probably received crown land in the territory of the city concerned, seized at the time of that city's conquest.

A.2. FOOT SOLDIERS

Financing hoplite forces was easier. Practices varied, but in general every physically fit male citizen of a *polis* was required to perform military service. Information is most plentiful in the case of Athens. At the ages of 18 and 19, the *epheboi* (young men registered for military service) underwent a program of physical and military → training. The date at which this *ephebeia* system was officially established is disputed. It only emerged in its fully developed form at Athens in 335 BC, when the training program was reformed; from this point on, every *ephebos* received a hoplite shield and spear from the state (Aristot. Ath. pol. 42,4). Young men completed their training in their 20th year, becoming members of the regiment of their *phyle* ('clan', of which there were ten in Athens), and they were now required to perform military service away from home. This obligation remained until their 50th year. Athenian citizens aged 18, 19 and between 50 and 60 were subject to call-up to defend their home city. During a mobilization involving 'the entire people' (*pandemei*), all age groups served. When fewer men were needed, the call-up could be limited to citizen-soldiers either up to a certain age group, or according to regiment (or a combination of both). Recruitment of the citizenry remained the most important procedure for setting up confederate armies (*koina*) even in the Hellenistic period.

Of all the Hellenistic monarchies, only Macedonia had a population large enough to recruit an infantry. Other kingdoms had to establish an infantry first. Egypt created a reserve of troops available for mobilization by settling soldiers on allotted parcels of land (*kleroi*), the size of which depended on their form of service. This system, the *klerouchia*, was founded by Ptolemy I Soter, who after the Battle of Gaza (312 BC) settled 8,000 prisoners of war there, and who may have done the same earlier with part of the defeated army of Perdiccas (321 BC) [1]. The system in the Seleucid Empire has yet to be researched; there are only hints. Cyrrhus is the name of one city in Macedonia and another in northern Syria. Polybius reports that 6,000 inhabitants of Cyrrhus rebelled in 221 when a Seleucid army gathered at Apamea (Pol. 5,50,8). These were probably descendants of Macedonians who had been settled in the Syrian city. The kingdom of the Attalids apparently operated a system of military settlements (*katoikiai*) in which traders, mostly Mysian in origin (as well as Macedonians after the collapse of their state in the wake of the Battle of Pydna in 168 BC), could be enlisted to fight in place of their landlessness.

In some polities, those too poor to equip themselves as hoplites were excluded from public office. There is no evidence, however, that they were also denied citizenship. On the contrary, some polities made efforts to secure the services of this group in roles other than as hoplites. At Athens before 335 BC, the *peripoloi* ('patrols') seem to have been *epheboi* who were too poor to equip themselves as hoplites [5]. They served in wartime as lightly armed javelin throwers.

A.3. UNFREE COMBATANTS

Hoplites' personal servants, who were mostly slaves, were sometimes called upon to fight as lightly armed troops (*psiloi*). This is the background to Herodotus' remark (Hdt. 9,29,2) that for every hoplite there was one *psilos* fighting. These men were the hoplites' porters (*skeuophoroi*). We do not understand exactly what Thucydides means when he writes that the Athenian army at Delium in 424 was accompanied by a great many *psiloi* (Thuc. 4,94,1) who 'were not properly equipped, most of them unarmed, for there had been a general taxation of all foreigners then living at Athens'. Such troops were usually of little value, although in 457, the Athenian general Myronides was able to destroy some of the Macedonian hoplite force with the help of his *psiloi* (Thuc. 1,106,2).

The Greeks were reluctant to recruit their unfree dependents; they did so only in times of extraordinary threat. In 479 BC at Plataeae, 35,000 helots fought as *psiloi* side by side with 5,000 Spartiates – seven for each of them (Hdt. 9,28f.). Two *lochoi* ('companies') of manumitted helots, the *Brasideioi* ('Brasidas' men') and *neodamodeis* ('newly belonging to the people'), took part in the first Battle of Mantinea (418), together with five *lochoi* of Spartans (Thuc. 5,67,1). We later learn of *neodamodeis* as different units that have already been granted their freedom (e.g. Xen. Hell. 3,1,4), and we likewise learn of helot hoplites. These were recruited not among the Messenian helots, but among the Laconians, upon whose loyalty the Spartans were more willing to rely (Plut. *Lycurgus* 28,5).

Another class of unfree combatants were the Thessalian *penestai* ('poor men', 'labourers'). Demosthenes mentions that in 424, Menon of Pharsalus supported the Athenians with a cavalry unit of 200 or 300 of his own *penestai* (Dem. Or. 13,23; 23,199).

Under extraordinary circumstances, even slaves could be enlisted for battle. A fragment (29) of the Attic orator Hypereides contains his proposal – never implemented – that, given the crisis following the Athenian defeat at Chaeronea (338 BC), 150,000 of the slaves working in mining and agriculture should be granted citizenship and armed. The testimony of Thucydides (7,13,2) and epigraphical evidence [3] show that slaves regularly comprised a considerable portion of the oarsmen aboard Athenian triremes, and that some of their masters were their comrades.

☞ Administration; State and army

BIBLIOGRAPHY

[1] R.S. BAGNALL, The Origins of the Ptolemaic Cleruchs, in: Bulletin of the American Society of Papyrologists 21, 1984, 7–20 [2] G.R. BUGH, The Horsemen of Athens, 1988 [3] A.J. GRAHAM, Thucydides 7.13.2 and the Crews of Athenian Triremes. An Addendum, in: Transactions of the American Philological Association 128, 1998, 89–114 [4] P. HUNT, Slaves, Warfare and Ideology in the

Greek Historians, 1998 [5] N.V. SEKUNDA, IG ii² 1250. A Decree Concerning the Lampadephoroi of the Tribe Aiantis, in: Zeitschrift für Papyrologie und Epigrafik 83, 1990, 149–182 (plate IV.) [6] K.-W. WELWEI, Unfreie im antiken Kriegsdienst I–III, 1974–1988.

NICHOLAS SEKUNDA

B. ROMAN

B.1. Initial considerations
B.2. Forms of interaction with civilians

B.1. INITIAL CONSIDERATIONS

The first important point to bear in mind is that study of the Roman army invariably concerns a particular segment of its history. During the Roman Republic, until about the first quarter of the 1st century BC, the Roman army was a true citizen militia, meaning that it essentially comprised the body of adult male Roman citizens. Only with the rise of exceptionally powerful individuals who used the armed forces to further their own political aims did the army begin to separate from society at large. It was then that Augustus, the first to impose personal rule on the empire, formally established a professional army. From this point on, it becomes salient to examine the relations between the army and the communities surrounding it [23]; [25]; [26]. The focus here will be upon this, Imperial army.

Second, it is important to recognize that conditions for the units of the Imperial army differed from region to region, resulting in differing relations between army and society. In Britain or Northern Europe, many units were stationed in relatively wild environs, meaning that the soldiers and their entourage often were effectively synonymous with (Roman) society in the locality. In the Greek-speaking east, on the other hand, military units were often located within urban centres. This naturally gave rise to quite different developments. Egypt in some respects offered its own unique conditions. Certainly, the papyri preserved in Egypt enable us to examine various aspects of the relationship between soldiers and civilians in more detail than elsewhere, even if the surviving evidence tends to be limited to Middle Egypt. In North Africa and Spain, different conditions again prevailed. Finally, attention must be paid to the capital, Rome, where the Praetorian Guard, the *cohortes urbanae* ('urban guard'), the *equites singulares* ('mounted guards') and the *vigiles* ('watchmen') were active. Here, in the 'city' (*urbs*), as Rome was usually called, the situation was again quite different. As in Rome, the soldiers stationed in the provinces belonged to different troop types. A basic distinction must be made between legionaries (Roman citizens; → Legion) and → auxiliaries (units of non-citizens). All this can only be sketched in outline here (see e.g. [14]; [27]; [3]; [21]; [22]; [6]; [25]; [11]; [5]; on specific issues cf. [7]; for an excellent overview of the problems facing any attempt to ascertain the impact of the army on a particular region, see [4], a discussion of [3]).

B.2. FORMS OF INTERACTION WITH CIVILIANS

The best way to understand the relationship between army and society in the Roman world may be to study it from several slightly different perspectives (principles: [17]). First, individual soldiers interacted with individual → civilians in numerous situations and with a variety of outcomes. Second, army units were stationed permanently at many locations around the Roman Empire, and many specific relationships developed at these garrison sites. Third, the army – as a group of soldiers or a collection of groups arranged into hierarchies – moved with some frequency through regions inhabited by civilians, which often brought unwelcome consequences. Fourth, it is probably useful to consider the army itself as a 'society', a parallel community or a society of its own embedded in the wider Roman world and comprising a great many men (and women) from all relevant social strata [1] (cf. also [2] on the army as an environment conducive to social advancement). Recruitment, the ethnic diversity of army units, colonization, and the settlement of veterans all played significant roles in this respect (in general on soldiers' social life [28]; [24]).

Roman soldiers were often perceived as extremely aggressive, and their interactions with members of civilian society often led to violence. Juvenal, for instance, in his 16th *Satire*, asked, 'Who [...] can list the happy advantages of military life?' (*Quis numerare queat felicis praemia [...] militiae?* Iuv. 16,1f.). In Juvenal's opinion, these advantages primarily consist in the soldier's licence to abuse any civilian he meets in the most brutal way and with effective impunity. A similar picture emerges in other texts such as Apuleius' *Metamorphoses*, although here, the civilian – a gardener – wins a temporary victory over the soldier (Apul. Met. 9,39–42). Other literary sources, however, contradict Juvenal's and Apuleius' accounts of the relationship between civilians and soldiers. Dion of Prusa, for instance, can imagine that the relationship between a good emperor and his soldiers resembles that of a herdsman and his dogs, or a ship's captain and his crew (Dion Chrys. 1,28f.). In the first case, the soldier or dog helps to protect civilians or the herd; in the second case, the soldier or sailor works with the emperor or captain to keep the empire's civilian population or the ship's passengers safe (ibid.). To sum up, the literary tradition does not offer a unanimous verdict on relations between soldiers and civilians.

Documentary sources must therefore be examined for further evidence. Yet, the picture that emerges here also seems contradictory [25]. On the one hand, a great many petitions are preserved in which private individuals seek the help of members of the army to resolve a dispute or enforce a civilian's rights, and there are abundant indications that soldiers to a large extent fulfilled the functions of the modern police [19]. Associated with these two areas of military activity, some ancient inscriptions show civilians praising the honesty or fairness of soldiers [20]; [9. 123–146, 201–238] (although some have cast doubt on the authenticity of the feelings expressed in these inscriptions [14. 283]; [22. 88]). At all events, it seems permissible to infer that some soldiers, at some times and in certain circumstances, provided a welcome source of security and stability for the local populace.

On the other hand, other testimonies highlight abusive and often violent plundering carried out by soldiers (especially by those marching through) [13]. There is even concrete evidence – to take just one example – of money extorted by soldiers being dutifully entered in the personal account books of a man in Roman Egypt [8. 248f.].

In summary, the picture is mixed. Regardless of whether they were temporarily assigned for specific duties or merely marching through, the presence of individual soldiers among the civilian population seems sometimes to have brought positive effects and sometimes decidedly negative ones. In the complete absence of usable statistical evidence, we cannot say with any certainty which of these tendencies was more common [25]. Scholarly estimations certainly cannot be accused of excessive optimism – they tend to echo Juvenal's allegations.

Much the same can be said regarding army units stationed in urbanized areas or passing through them – on the way to battle, for instance, or accompanying the emperor on his travels (→ Guards). The dominant view (although not based on reliably quantifiable data) is that such deployments and encounters were not well received by most of the local population, and that Roman soldiers who overstepped the bounds of their already considerable privileges were only rarely and with great difficulty held accountable for their wrongs [8. 243–263]; [22. 85–110].

As for the army as a distinct society in itself, an important 1984 article imaginatively describes how Roman soldiers of assorted ethnicities found cohesion in their units through emotional ties, helping them to weather the terrors of the battlefield [18]. Another important contribution from the late 20th century postulates that such men developed a sense of community through the concept of → honour – both their own, personal honour and the communal honour of their unit [15. 237–266]. Another question that has caused some consternation concerns whether the Roman provincial armies should be seen as 'total institutions', that is, as independent social groups isolated from the surrounding civilian population, or as embedded in the local social order. There are no simple answers to these questions. We are still in the process of gleaning insights into exactly what made the Roman army a coherent entity and community, and how that community functioned within the contexts of the society around it [10] (relevant observations also in [16]; [12]).

☞ State and army; Administration

BIBLIOGRAPHY
[1] G. ALFÖLDY, Das Heer in der Sozialstruktur des römischen Kaiserreiches, in: G. ALFÖLDY et al. (eds.), Kaiser, Heer und Gesellschaft in der römischen Kaiserzeit. Gedenkschrift für Eric Birley, 2000, 33–57 [2] G. ALFÖLDY, Kaiser, Heer und soziale Mobilität im Römischen Reich, in: A. CHANIOTIS / P. DUCREY (eds.), Army and Power in the Ancient World, 2002, 123–150 [3] R. ALSTON, Soldier and Society in Roman Egypt. A Social History, 1995 [4] R. BAGNALL, A Kinder, Gentler Roman Army?, in: JRA 10, 1997, 504–512 [5] S. BINGHAM, The Praetorian Guard. A History of Rome's Elite Special Forces, 2013 [6] A.R. BIRLEY, Garrison Life at Vindolanda. A Band of Brothers, 2002 [7] L. DE BLOIS / E. LO CASCIO (eds.), The Impact of the Roman Army (200 BC–AD 476). Economic, Social, Political, Religious and Cultural Aspects, 2007 [8] B. CAMPBELL, The Emperor and the Roman Army, 31 BC–AD 235, 1984 [9] C.J. FUHRMANN, Policing the Roman Empire. Soldiers, Administration, and Public Order, 2012 [10] A. GOLDSWORTHY / I. HAYNES (eds.), The Roman Army as a Community, 1999 [11] R. HAENSCH, The Roman Army in Egypt, in: C. RIGGS (ed.), The Oxford Handbook of Roman Egypt, 2012, 68–82 [12] I. HAYNES, Blood of the Provinces. The Roman Auxilia and the Making of Provincial Society from Augustus to the Severans, 2013 [13] P. HERRMANN, Hilferufe aus römischen Provinzen. Ein Aspekt der Krise des römischen Reiches im 3. Jhdt. n.Chr., 1990 [14] B. ISAAC, The Limits of Empire. The Roman Army in the East, 1992 (2nd, revised edition) [15] J.E. LENDON, Empire of Honour. The Art of Government in the Roman World, 1997 [16] J.E. LENDON, The Roman Army Now, in: CJ 99, 2004, 443–446 [17] R. MACMULLEN, Soldier and Civilian in the Later Roman Empire, 1963 [18] R. MACMULLEN, The Legion as a Society, in: Historia 33, 1984, 440–456 [19] B. PALME, Zivile Aufgaben der Armee im kaiserzeitlichen Ägypten, in: A. KOLB (ed.), Herrschaftsstrukturen und Herrschaftspraxis, 2006, 299–328 [20] M. PEACHIN, Petition to a Centurion from the NYU Papyrus Collection and the Question of Informal Adjudication Performed by Centurions, in: A.J.B. SIRKS / K. WORP (eds.), Papyri in Memory of P.J. Sijpesteijn, 2007, 79–97 [21] N. POLLARD, The Roman Army as 'Total Institution' in the Near East? Dura-Europos as a Case Study, in: D.L. KENNEDY (ed.), The Roman Army in the East, 1996, 211–227 [22] N. POLLARD, Soldiers, Cities, and Civilians in Roman Syria, 2000 [23] D. POTTER, The Roman Army, in: M. PEACHIN (ed.), The

Oxford Handbook of Social Relations in the Roman World, 2011, 516–534 [24] M.A. SPEIDEL, Das römische Heer als Kulturträger, in: M.A. SPEIDEL, Heer und Herrschaft im Römischen Reich der Hohen Kaiserzeit, 2009, 515–544 [25] M.A. SPEIDEL, Soldaten und Zivilisten im römischen Reich. Zu modernen Rekonstruktionen antiker Verhältnisse, in: M.A. SPEIDEL, Heer und Herrschaft im Römischen Reich der Hohen Kaiserzeit, 2009, 473–500 [26] M.A. SPEIDEL, Actium, Allies, and the Augustan Auxilia. Reconsidering the Transformation of Military Structures and Foreign Relations in the Reign of Augustus, in: C. WOLFF / P. FAURE (eds.), Les auxiliaires de l'armée romaine. Des alliés aux fédérés, 2016, 79–95 [27] M.P. SPEIDEL, Riding for Caesar. The Roman Emperors' Horse Guards, 1994 [28] G. WESCH-KLEIN, Soziale Aspekte des römischen Heerwesens in der Kaiserzeit, 1998.

MICHAEL PEACHIN

Sources

A. Literary sources
B. Greek inscriptions
C. Latin inscriptions
D. Coins
E. Papyri

A. LITERARY SOURCES

A.1. Defining terms
A.2. Significance
A.3. Survey of the most important literary sources (excluding legal sources).
A.4. Legal sources
A.5. Problems of literary sources

A.1. DEFINING TERMS

War and its consequences played a crucial role in the lives of people in Greco-Roman Antiquity. Almost all literary sources [2. 46–90]; [5. 9–15, 252f., 470–473] therefore make some reference to it, albeit to differing degrees. In listing these, it will clearly be necessary to confine ourselves to the most important, and to individual examples from the various genres whose subject is not normally war. The definition of literary sources in this article includes legal sources.

Specialist literature on the subject includes works by Hero of Alexandria, Philo of Byzantium, Biton of Pergamum, Apollodorus of Damascus and Vitruvius' *De architectura* (catapults, artillery; 1st cent. BC). Not properly included in the category of specialist literature are authors such as Frontinus (late 1st cent. AD), whose *Strategemata* ('Stratagems of War') is based on extracts from literary works, and Valerius Maximus (first half of 1st cent. AD), whose *Facta et dicta memorabilia* belongs to the genre of exemplary literature and contains sections, for example, on *strategamata* (7,4), Marius' novel recruitment practices (2,3,1), war etiquette (2,7) and *virtus* (3,1). His presentation relies on excerpts from literary works, for example Livy, Pompeius Trogus and Cicero.

The anonymous *De rebus bellicis* (AD 350–400) discusses machines of war, investigates general problems connected with warfare in Late Antiquity, and makes proposals for reform.

A.2. SIGNIFICANCE

Literary sources are of particular significance. Where they are narrative in nature, they make it possible to see the processes and historical contexts of the military apparatus and the political and societal issues connected with it. For instance, they yield information about the courses of battles, levies (*dilectus*), the applications and consequences of legal provisions, and → mutinies and the reasons behind them. Naturally, this does not mean that no mention is made in them of matters such as military installations and laws, or that these are not sometimes described in detail. Pol. 6,19–42, for example, reports on Roman army organization, and especially the building of camps.

Lists reveal nothing about processes. They give information on military units and command structures, but in terms of what they reveal they are closer to epigraphic sources or papyri. Nor do legal sources portray processes. They show legal regulations, such as those regarding recruitment, or the penalties for breaches of → discipline.

A.3. SURVEY OF THE MOST IMPORTANT LITERARY SOURCES (EXCLUDING LEGAL SOURCES).

A.3.1. Historiography
A.3.2. Orations
A.3.3. Philosophy
A.3.4. Epic and other poetry
A.3.5. Lists
A.3.6. Biography
A.3.7. Other sources

A.3.1. HISTORIOGRAPHY

The most important sources are the great works of historiography that offer detailed descriptions of military processes and their political background, as well as related genres, such as the commentaries of Caesar on the Gallic Wars and the Civil Wars, and the other surviving writings attributed to him (*Corpus Caesarianum*) [2]. It must always be remembered that only a tiny fraction of historical works have been preserved, even in fragments. Of the historiographic works originally written in Greek, for example, the fraction is around one fortieth [15]. The unfinished collection of *Fragments of the Greek Historians* (FGrH) alone contains the names of 856 historians. There are many long periods of history that lack any detailed chronological account – the first half of the 4th century AD is one example. The Greek historians Herodotus (c. 485–425 BC, the 'Father of History'), Thucydides (c. 460–400), Xenophon (c. 430–355, author of the *Anabasis* and *Hellenika*) and Polybius (c. 200–120) all left comprehensive accounts of this kind. So too did the Latin authors Sallust (86–34, author of the *Bellum Iugurthinum*, the *Coniuratio Catilinae* and the *Historiae*, of which only fragments survive), Livy (59 BC–AD 17), Tacitus (c. AD 55–116/20, author of the *Annales*, the *Historiae* and the *Agricola*) and Ammianus Marcellinus (c. 330–390). Writing in Greek about Roman history, Cassius Dio (c. 150–235) left a narrative history of the Imperial period, and Procopius (c. 500–560) did so for Late Antiquity. Flavius Josephus (37–c. 95) wrote in Greek about Jewish history, especially for the years AD 66–70, providing detailed accounts of the conquest of Jerusalem by the future emperor Titus, and the later capture of Masada.

Most of these histories also discuss matters of military technology (e.g. Jos. BI 3,214–217, Amm. Marc. 23,4, Procop. Goth. 1,21,14). However, such descriptions are less technical than the descriptions given by true military writers, and their relevance for reconstructing apparatuses such as catapults and siege engines is disputed.

A.3.2. ORATIONS

The analysis or description of historical and military events in orations began soon after the emergence of historiography and rhetoric in the Classical period.

The Athenian Isocrates, for instance, described the confrontation between the Greeks and Persians in his *Panegyricus* (380 BC; 86–98). He also mentions these conflicts in his *Panathenaicus* (342–339 BC), placing particular emphasis on the role of Athens at the Battle of Salamis (96–98; → Battles of note I.).

This tradition persisted throughout Antiquity. The *Roman Oration* of Aelius Aristides, delivered in Greek (probably around AD 143), deals thoroughly with issues of the army, military service and strategy (72–89). It discusses whether the empire should expand further, or whether it should remain within its current boundaries.

The Latin panegyrists of the 4th century AD discussed and celebrated military successes. For instance, Paneg. 9(12) gives a detailed description of the war between Maxentius and Constantine, including a very thorough description of the Battle of the Milvian Bridge (Paneg. 9(12),16,2ff.).

A.3.3. PHILOSOPHY

Discussions of military history also found their way into the philosophical literature of the Classical period. Examples include Pl. Menex. 239a ff. on the Persian Wars as part of a discussion of the masses and virtue; Pl. Rep. 2,14 (373d–374e) on the necessity of war and an army; and Pl. Rep. 5,14–16 (466e–471c) on ways and means of waging war.

A.3.4. EPIC AND OTHER POETRY

For the period before the emergence of true historiography in the 5th century BC, epic poetry in the form of Homer's *Iliad* remains an important source for most matters of warfare. Thuc. 1,4–15 already drew on Homer in his survey of the history of war in Greece. Later epic too – insofar as it constitutes a historical narrative – offers a source on military processes. In fact, the genre persisted throughout Antiquity, although it dwindled in importance compared to historiography. Lucan's (AD 39–65) *Bellum civile*, for instance, gives an account of the civil war between Caesar and Pompey (→ General, C.; → Generals of note, N.).

Early Greek lyric poetry is of similar significance [2. 48–52]; [10. 33–44]. The elegiac poetry of Tyrtaeus, for example, who was active in Sparta during the second half of the 7th century BC, reflects the historic shift towards → phalanx combat. The fate of the *polis* now lay in the hands of the mass of its wealthy citizens, not in the hands of individual noble warriors.

A.3.5. LISTS

The *Notitia dignitatum* (c. AD 400), a list-like survey of the administrative structure of the late Roman state, includes lists of the military units extant at the time, along with the command structures.

A.3.6. BIOGRAPHY

Plutarch (c. AD 45–125) offers thorough accounts of battles. For example, he is an important source on the Battle of Salamis of 480 BC (Plut. *Themistocles* 12,1–15,2). An account of comparable detail is offered by Cornelius Nepos (c. 100–28 BC) on the Battle of Marathon (Nep. Milt. 5; → Battles of note, F.).

A.3.7. OTHER SOURCES

Examining the historical record concerning battles gives an idea of the many different kinds of sources that can contribute to our knowledge of military history. Three battles may serve as examples here: Marathon (490 BC); Actium (31 BC), and the Frigidus (AD 394) [3]; [6]; [16]. The basis for our knowledge of the Battle of Marathon comes from the account by Herodotus (6,109ff.), with important additional information from: Nep. Milt. 5; the *Suda* article (Byzantine encyclopaedia, c. AD 970) *Choris hippeis* (X 444, IV, p. 818, 12–16 Adler); Aristot. Rh. 1411a 10 (on the Miltiades decree); Schol. Dem. 19,303; Plut. Mor. 628e; Paus. 1,32,3 (on slaves fighting for the Greeks at Marathon).

On the Battle of Actium (→ Battles of note, A.), sources include Plut. *Antonius* 64–68; Cass. Dio 50,16–31 (the eve-of-battle speeches of Antony and Octavian); 50,31–51,1 on the battle itself.

On the Battle of the Frigidus, we find the main pagan sources: Zos. 4,58; Joh. Antiochensis fr. 187 Müller = 280 Roberto; the main Christian sources: Rufin. 11,33; Oros. 7,35,13–19; Philostorgius 11,2; Socr. 5,25; Sozom Hist. eccl. 7,24,3–7; Theod. Hist. eccl. 5,24,13–17; allusions or partial descriptions: Claud. Carm. 1,103–112; 7,89–105; 8,80–93; Ambr., *Explanatio XII psalmorum* 36,25; Epist. 62,4; Obit. Theod. 7; 23; Aug. Civ. 5,26; Chron. min. 1,650,30.

A.4. Legal sources

No codifications [14] or substantial legal texts containing laws pertaining to soldiers survive as independent literary sources from the Greek *poleis*, the Hellenistic kingdoms or the Roman Republic. Most relevant legal provisions from these periods that do survive are found in epigraphic and papyrological sources or in brief quotations in literary texts ([9. 233f.: Attic orators]; Gell. NA 6,10: *aes militare*) or histories (cf. e.g. Liv. 1,43: the law concerning centuries; Thuc. 5,34,1; 5,60,6; 5,72,1; Pol. 6,37f.). Little survives in later legal sources (e.g. Gai. Inst. 4,27: *aes militare*). The situation is quite different in regard to the Roman Imperial period and Late Antiquity, although sporadic references (e.g. Amm. Marc. 20,4,11; Cass. Dio 60,24,3) also play an important part here.

Leaving aside individual provisions contained in sources such as the *Institutions* of Gaius (c. AD 161) (e.g. Gai. Inst. 1,57: marital law concerning soldiers; 1,129: marital law concerning soldiers; 2,109: soldiers' wills), the legal collections of Late Antiquity offer abundant material. These are the *Codex Theodosianus* (AD 438, esp. Book VII: *De re militari*) and its supplementary *Novellae* and the *Corpus iuris civilis* in its three constituent parts (between AD 529 and 534), which collate old law – especially the *Codex Iustinianus* (imperial law) and the *Digesta* (jurists' law), less so the *Institutiones* (textbook with legal force). On the *Digesta*, example passages are 48,4,3f.; 49,16,3,1: list of military penalties. The *Novellae constitutiones* of Justinian also contain legal provisions concerning soldiers (cf. e.g. 130,9 Scholl), but are disregarded here.

The variety of problems that needed to be regulated [11]; [12]; [13] indicates that soldiers enjoyed a special status in the Roman state and its society.

A.5. Problems of literary sources

A.5.1. Historicity and authenticity
A.5.2. Legal sources

A range of problems surround the use of literary sources. Scholars usually deal with these as they relate to individual authors, rarely attempting a cross-sectional approach. Some such problems are discussed below.

A.5.1. Historicity and authenticity

It is generally safe to assume that events described by reliable historians, such as Thucydides or Polybius, really took place. Battles, for instance, were not invented. However, authors attach no importance to the completeness of their descriptions. The locations of battlefield sites, for instance, often cannot be precisely identified (e.g. Cannae; → Battles of note, C.). In the main, historians describe the details that they think are important or that seem important for reasons of rhetorical intent – a problem that was already recognized in Antiquity (Cic. De or. 2,51ff.; Pol. 5,21; 16,14–20). They tend to avoid technical terms. It is certainly possible for them to invent places or people – a technique that can be seen in historiography from the 4th century BC onwards and that the Roman annalists continued [1].

One particular problem lies in the speeches inserted into these histories. It is not certain in every case that such speeches were really given, and no claim to their authenticity is generally made. The speech supposedly made by Maecenas before Augustus in 29 BC, for instance (Cass. Dio 52,14–41), is obviously invented. Forming part of a discussion of strategic issues, it presents perspectives of the Severan period (AD 193–235). Maecenas is speaking out against the eastward expansion of the empire (Cass. Dio 52,18,5). He also recommends the establishment of a professional army (Cass. Dio 52,27–28,3).

Particularly in non-historiographic sources, technical information on matters such as fighting methods and armament frequently reflect situations in other periods – a problem that already occurs in Homer's *Iliad*, where a number of different historical periods of warfare are discernible [10. 30].

A.5.2. Legal sources

Assorted problems apply to legal sources. The scope of a particular provision's applicability is often not immediately apparent. When legal provisions are quoted in literary sources, it is not always easy to ascertain whether they are complete and neither abridged nor altered. It is also difficult to determine how far particular regulations were implemented in reality [9. 243–245].

The differences between the sources for Greek and Roman legal history and the absence of any true → military law among the Greeks are of considerable consequence to scholars [9. 232]. As yet, for instance, no coherent account or encyclopaedia article exists on the law as it applied to soldiers throughout Greek history.

Bibliography

[1] B. BLECKMANN, Von Theopomp zur Historia Augusta. Zu einer Technik historiographischer Fälschung, in: F. PASCHOUD / G. BONAMENTE (eds.), Historiae Augustae Colloquium Genevense, 1999, 43–57 [2] B. CAMPBELL / L.A. TRITLE (eds.), The Oxford Handbook of Warfare in the Classical World, 2013 [3] N.A. DOENGES, The Campaign and Battle of Marathon, in: Historia 47, 1998, 1–17 [4] D. FLACH, Römische Geschichtsschreibung, ⁴2013 [5] J. KROMAYER / G. VEITH, Heerwesen und Kriegführung der Griechen und Römer, 1928 [6] D. LASPE, Actium. Die Anatomie einer Schlacht, in: Gymnasium 114, 2007, 509–522 [7] O. LENDLE, Einführung in die griechische Geschichtsschreibung. Von Hekataios bis Zosimos, 1992 [8] K. MEISTER, Die Griechische Geschichtsschreibung. Von den Anfängen bis zum Ende des Hellenismus, 1990 [9] W.K. PRITCHETT, The Greek State at War, vol. 2, 1974 [10] W.K. PRITCHETT, The Greek State at War, vol. 4, 1985 [11] E. SANDER, Das Recht des römischen Soldaten, in: RhM 101, 1958, 152–191 und 193–234 [12] E. SANDER, Das römische Militärstrafrecht, in: RhM 103, 1960, 289–319 [13] E. SANDER, Militärrecht, in: RE Suppl. 10, 1965, 394–410 [14] G. SCHIEMANN, Law, codification of, in: BNP 7, 2005, 320–322 [15] H. STRASBURGER, Umblick im Trümmerfeld der griechischen Geschichtsschreibung, in: Historiographia antiqua. Commentationes Lovanieses in honorem W. Peremans septuagenarii editae, 1977, 3–52 [16] ZOSIME, Histoire nouvelle. Text established and translated by F. Paschoud, vol. 2, pt. 2, bk. 4, 1979, 474–500 (Description of the Battle of Frigidus by the editor).

JOACHIM SZIDAT

B. Greek inscriptions

B.1. Treaties of alliance
B.2. Hegemonial treaties of alliance
B.3. Organizing and financing military campaigns
B.4. Treaties of capitulation and peace treaties
B.5. Monuments to the fallen
B.6. Victory dedications and monuments

Inscriptions carved in stone or cast in bronze tablets offer abundant and varied information on ancient military history, and represent an indispensable source in this field.

B.1. Treaties of alliance

Many treaties that formed the basis for 'amity and → alliance' (*philia/xenia kai symmachia*) between two *poleis* are documented in bronze and stone inscriptions. The oldest documented *symmachia* treaty is that preserved on a bronze tablet dating from about 500 BC that was found at Olympia, recording a hundred-year pact concluded between Elis and Heraea, with the obligation 'to support each other in all things in word and deed, and especially in war' (Syll.³ 9). The prohibition against damaging the bronze tablet shows the legal weight of its publication [2. 10f.]. Treaties preserved in inscriptions permit us to distinguish between those with friend-enemy clauses, which were generally directed against a particular enemy and required both parties to pursue a joint foreign policy (e.g. IG I³ 76), and those requiring support in the event of a hostile action in the ally's territory (e.g. IG I³ 53, SEG 60, 69; ICret. 1, xxx (Tylisus), no. 1, 307) [2. 15–91]. In addition to the friend-enemy clause, the treaty of 423/22 BC between Athens and Perdiccas contains the latter's agreement to supply wood for oars to Athens alone (IG I³ 89). Many such treaties are attested in inscriptions relating to the *poleis* on Crete in the Hellenistic period, with provisions addressing support in case of a war of aggression, recognition of boundaries, sacrifices to be offered, the provision of maintenance to combatants, and the division of spoils, and also prohibitions against concluding other treaties without the consent of the other party and against unilaterally declaring war or concluding peace or a truce [6. 87–93].

B.2. Hegemonial treaties of alliance

The treaty between the Serdaeans and the 'Sybarites and their allies' (SEG 22, 336; 31, 357; *hoi Sybaritai kai hoi symmachoi*, 6th cent. BC) is the first known example of a hegemonial treaty of alliance. The legal basis of the Spartan alliance system (the Peloponnesian League) derived from the treaties concluded between Sparta and its allies, one of which – with the Aetolian Erxadieis – is preserved in an (albeit fragmentary) inscription. The treaty (*synthekai*) includes the friend-enemy clause, a hegemonic clause (i.e. the obligation to follow Sparta to war), the prohibition against a unilateral peace and on receiving refugees (i.e. escaped helots) and a protection clause applying to the territories of both parties (SEG 26, 461; 51, 449) [2. 19–30] (Sparta). The Delian League was founded on a symmachy directed against the Persians. Treaties of the second half of the 5th century, preserved in inscriptions, show Athens imposing unequal provisions on allies that had defected and then been forced back into the symmachy, binding them to Athens in foreign and domestic policy. The oaths to be sworn, requiring fulfilment in word and deed, were included in the treaty texts as published in the inscriptions (IG I³ 14; 37; 48) [2. 52–64]. Whoever complied received Athens' assurance that it would expel no citizen of the allied city 'nor destroy the city' (IG I³ 40, SEG 60, 81). The declaration, preserved in inscription form, by which the 'Athenians and allies of the Athenians' issued an invitation to join the Second Athenian League, guarantees the ally's freedom and autonomy, the undisputed integrity of its territories, and exemptions from hosting garrisons in its cities and paying tribute. The declaration also promises defensive support (IG II² 43) [7]. Hegemonial treaties from Hellenistic Crete sometimes require troops to be provided to the other party and warn against betraying the *hegemon* [6. 87–100; Edition und Übersetzung der Verträge: 179–451].

B.3. Organizing and financing military campaigns

In connection with the transfer of the league treasury from Delos to Athens in 454 BC, tallies of the *aparchai* (taxes; literally 'first-fruits') received from allies were published on stone in Athens, and these enable us to calculate the rates of tribute in the Delian League (IG I³ 259–290; SEG 59, 60; ATL) [19]. Tribute received was used primarily to finance the building and maintenance of the → fleet stationed at Piraeus [11]. When Athens forced Samos, which had defected, back into the league, it demanded reparations for the costs it had incurred for the war in 441–439 BC, which the treasurers of Athens had given to the *strategoi* ('commanders') in charge of the campaigns (IG I³ 363; SEG 48, 64) [11. 57]. In much the same way, the treasurers gave money to cover the deployment of two contingents of ships to the *strategoi* dispatched to Corcyra in 433/32 BC. The inscription documenting this, which notes the names of the treasurers and the *strategoi*, certified the payment and receipt of these monies (IG I³ 364). The Callias Decree (IG I³ 52) not only records the rulings that tribute be levied, but also indicates a sum of money for boathouses and walls. In 407/06, Athens decided to honour the Macedonian king Archelaus for supplying it with timber for shipbuilding and long logs for oars (IG I³ 117). Inscriptions of this kind enable us to reconstruct the foundations of authority and the political workings within Athens [13]. There is lively debate among scholars regarding the often uncertain dating of inscriptions [17]; [14]. IG II2 505 (302/01 BC) testifies to annual war taxes for the construction of wharves and to a storehouse for ships' equipment (*skeuothekai*). Exact architectural details are extant for the construction of the *skeuotheke* of Philo at Piraeus (IG II² 1668) [9. 149, 247]; [11].

Inscriptions also reveal something about the types of ships that were used in the war fleets (IG I³ 18, l. 15f.; IG II² 1627, ll. 17–21: triaconters and penteconters). Particularly significant are the naval inventories set up at Piraeus (*tabulae curatorum navalium*). The officials responsible for these, the *epimeletai* (special curators) of the *neoria* (dock yard), had lists published in stone of all warships and their equipment, and passed these on to their successors. The lists, which are arranged according to harbours and ships of the first, second and third classes, reveal the following: the names of warships, the *trierarchoi* ('commanders of triremes') and chairmen of the *symmoriai* (taxation groups), wooden equipment (oar blades, rudders, ships' ladders, oar poles, mast supports, mainmasts, yardarms, foremasts) and 'hanging equipment' (sails, ropes, belts, ship covers, anchors). They also sometimes name the ships' architects and indicate unpaid contributions awaited from *trierarchoi* who were required to pay for repairs or for the replacement of equipment (IG II² 1604–1632 of 378/77–323/22 BC) [8]; [10]; [11. 62f.]; [14. 16f.]; [18]. For some years, the lists convey the total size of the fleet, its increase due to vessels confiscated, and the approximate costs of building a ship's hull and equipping it in various ways. [11] estimates the total value of the war fleet stationed at Piraeus (at least 400 triremes) in 427/26 at around 2.9 million drachmas, and in 325/24 (417 ships) at around 3.9 million drachmas. Inscriptions sometimes also record pay and maintenance issued to hoplites and marines [5. with tables 81–84]; [20]. They also yield information concerning loans and subscriptions for the financing of wars (e.g. IG II² 791) [16].

B.4. Treaties of capitulation and peace treaties

A victor in war could impose a treaty of capitulation on the defeated party (IG I³ 38; cf. Thuc. 1,108). Renegade allies of Athens were required to swear an oath promising loyalty to Athens in the future (Samos: IG I³ 48; 439/38 BC). The treaties of alliance that were concluded after wars ended (see above, B.2.1.) often rendered separate peace treaties superfluous. If agreed, they addressed territorial issues, the release of prisoners and the provision of hostages [6. 61 with epigraphic sources]. More frequent than these are *spondai* ('truces') – treaties suspending war and pledging not to use force of arms so as to allow the retrieval of the fallen, retreat, or consultation and negotiation. These are not peace treaties in the strict sense [2. 92–188].

B.5. Monuments to the fallen

Beginning in the early 5th century, there is evidence for monuments to the fallen that were furnished with inscriptions specifying the *poleis* to which the dead belonged and the war in which they fell, either in the form of short couplets, as for the Corinthians who fell at Salamis and were buried on that island (IG I³ 1143, 480 BC; Plut. Mor. 870e), or in the form of longer epigrams, such as the one composed by Simonides to the Megarian 'heroes' who fell 'in the Persian War', which is preserved on an inscription made in the Roman period (IG VII 53; SEG 61, 327). The fragments of lists of Athenians who fell at Marathon, which were discovered a few years ago (SEG 56, 430–432), were part of a *polyandreion* (communal grave) that was set up at the battle site. There are parts of several stelae bearing the names of the fallen from the ten Attic *phylai* ('clans'), each headed with its own epigram (cf. Paus. 1,32,3). The list of the fallen of the Attic *phyle* Erechtheis, perhaps dating from the 420s (IG I³ 1147, SEG 52, 60; [14. 13]; on the *phyle* Aigeis see SEG 34, 35) lists in three columns the names of the dead who fell 'in the war in Cyprus, Egypt, Phoenicia, Halieis, Aegina and Megara in the course of the same year' (cf. Thuc. 1,104f.). The list of the dead IG I³ 1162 also classifies the names of fallen Athenians according to theatre of war (Chersones, Byzantium and other wars on the Hellespont) and by *phyle*. *Strategoi* and seers are highlighted in the lists. Cavalrymen are also noted as such (SEG 48, 83) [14. 14–16], as are archers (*toxotai*) and sometimes foreigners and slaves [1]; [3], [4]; [12]. A naval battle off Egypt between the Persians and Greeks was commemorated on a block set up at the Heraeum of Samos that may have listed fallen Samians by name (ML 34; LSAG 342, no. 21). Sometimes, the fallen were not buried in their native soil, as in the case of the Argives who fell 'at Tanagra by Lacedaemonian hands' and were buried at Athens (IG I³ 1149).

B.6. VICTORY DEDICATIONS AND MONUMENTS

Victors in battle dedicated one tenth of their spoils to a deity (e.g. ML 36, 57). Tripods and Nike statues were often dedicated to the gods, as were weapons (especially shields and helmets) and ships' bows. Other dedications included bronze quadrigas and even columned halls or victory columns such as the famous Serpent Column commemorating the united Hellenes against the Persians (Syll.³ 31). Inscriptions associated with such dedications often mention, alongside the names of the victor, the vanquished and the deity, the artist and the value of the dedication. Retrospective votive inscriptions celebrated the memory of historic battles, such as the victories at Marathon (→ Battles of note, F.), Salamis (→ Battles of note, I.) and Plataeae, and the heroic fight of the fallen to prevent the subjugation of all Hellas (e.g. Syll.³ 23, IG I³ 503/4). Votive dedications were set up in the home city or in sanctuaries of transregional significance, especially at Delphi and Olympia. Besides victorious cities, individuals also made votive dedications (IG I³ 784) or commemorated a victory on a gravestone (IG I³ 823) (→ Victory).

Also relevant to military history are inscriptions that record decisions regarding the building of walls (*teichopoia*) and the defence of cities, sporting and military training in the gymnasium and during the period of the *ephebeia* (ICret. 1, ix (Drerus), no. 1, 84–88) [16]; military reports published as inscriptions (e.g. OGIS 54); and honorary resolutions for the dispatch of soldiers and military equipment, for the fortification of harbours or walls (e.g. IG II² 834; BCH 63, 1939, 133ff.), for the payment of ransoms for prisoners of war (e.g. Chiron 5, 1975, 59ff.), or for the liberation of victims of piracy (Syll.³ 521; 535f.).

☞ Descriptions of war, A. Monuments with Greek inscriptions: Greek and Hellenistic periods

BIBLIOGRAPHY

[1] N.T. ARRINGTON, Inscribing Defeat. The Commemorative Dynamics of the Athenian Casualty Lists, in: Classical Antiquity 30, 2011, 179–212   [2] E. BALTRUSCH, Symmachie und Spondai. Untersuchungen zum griechischen Völkerrecht der archaischen und klassischen Zeit (8.–5. Jahrhundert v.Chr.), 1994   [3] D.W. BRADEEN, Athenian Casualty Lists, in: Hesperia 33, 1964, 16–62   [4] D.W. BRADEEN, The Athenian Casualty Lists, in: CQ 19, 1969, 145–159   [5] F. BURRER, Sold und Verpflegungsgeld in klassischer und hellenistischer Zeit, in: F. BURRER / H. MÜLLER (eds.), Kriegskosten und Kriegsfinanzierung in der Antike, 2008, 74–90   [6] A. CHANIOTIS, Die Verträge zwischen kretischen Poleis in der hellenistischen Zeit, 1996   [7] M. DREHER, Hegemon und Symmachoi. Untersuchungen zum Zweiten Athenischen Seebund, 1995   [8] V. GABRIELSEN, Contributions of Ship's Equipment in the Athenian Naval Records, in: ZPE 98, 1993, 175–183   [9] V. GABRIELSEN, Financing the Athenian Fleet. Public Taxation and Social Relations, 1994   [10] V. GABRIELSEN, The Naval Records from the Athenian Agora, in: CeM 50, 1999, 25–60   [11] V. GABRIELSEN, Die Kosten der athenischen Flotte in klassischer Zeit, in: F. BURRER / H. MÜLLER (eds.), Kriegskosten und Kriegsfinanzierung in der Antike, 2008, 46–73   [12] P. LOW, Remembering War in Fifth-Century Greece. Ideologies, Societies, and Commemoration beyond Democratic Athens, in: World Archaeology 35, 2003, 98–111   [13] J. MA et al. (eds.), Interpreting the Athenian Empire, 2009   [14] A.P. MATTHAIOU, The Athenian Empire on Stone Revisited, 2010   [15] H.B. MATTINGLY, The Athenian Empire Restored. Epigraphic and Historical Studies, 1996   [16] L. MIGEOTTE, Kriegs- und Verteidigungsfinanzierung in den hellenistischen Städten, in: F. BURRER / H. MÜLLER (eds.), Kriegskosten und Kriegsfinanzierung in der Antike, 2008, 151–160   [17] N. PAPAZARKADAS, Epigraphy and the Athenian Empire. Re-shuffling the Chronological Cards, in: J. MA et al. (eds.), Interpreting the Athenian Empire, 2009, 67–88   [18] J.L. SHEAR, Fragments of Naval Inventories from the Athenian Agora, in: Hesperia 64, 1995, 179–224 (pl. 42–44)   [19] R.S. STROUD, The Athenian Empire on Stone. David M. Lewis Memorial Lecture, 2006   [20] H. VAN WEES, 'Diejenigen, die segeln, sollen Sold erhalten'. Seekriegsführung und -finanzierung im archaischen Eretria, in: F. BURRER / H. MÜLLER (eds.), Kriegskosten und Kriegsfinanzierung in der Antike, 2008, 128–150.

WINFRIED SCHMITZ

C. LATIN INSCRIPTIONS

C.1. General overview
C.2. Scope and geographical spread of military inscriptions
C.3. Content

C.1. GENERAL OVERVIEW

Individual inscriptions with content in some way related to the Roman military first appear as early as the mid-3rd century BC (*Elogium C. Duilii*, consul 260 BC, following the naval victory over Carthage at Mylae; ILLRP 319). At first, however, these are primarily restricted to inscriptions of senior magistrates who were victorious in battle (cf. ILLRP 100: ... *de praidad Fortune*; 122; 124). Only slowly do other aspects of military life begin to appear in epigraphic monuments, a tendency that increased from the time of Augustus onwards, reaching its widest range of representation in about the mid-1st century AD and maintaining that level well into the 4th. By the 5th and 6th centuries, references to military matters again become rare in inscriptions. The majority of inscriptions referring to the military are written in Latin, but many were composed in Greek in the east of the empire, mainly by veterans after leaving active service.

Not all aspects of military life appear in inscriptions. This format almost exclusively reflects situations in which the author wanted a longer preservation for his 'message' in a public space. Most inscriptions on perishable materials are lost, although this also applies to many inscriptions on metal. It is primarily the following types of inscriptions, mostly on stone, that provide us with information about the military (representative selection: ILS 1986–2914; 9052–9227; also IGR I, III, IV; [19]):

- Triumphal and victory monuments (see → Descriptions of war B.);
- Inscriptions below honorific statues, for members of the military or put up by them; particularly numerous for emperors and senior commanders of senatorial or equestrian rank;
- Architectural inscriptions for or by the military; also inscriptions made by the producers of building materials such as bricks, water pipes or stones;
- Inscriptions on votive monuments built by military units or individual army members;
- Funerary inscriptions for members of the army during active service and for veterans and their families;
- Ownership inscriptions on objects from military units, especially *centuriae*, or on pieces of equipment belonging to individual army members, generally on bronze plaques.

→ Military diplomas belong to the legal sphere and in fact have a private character.

C.2. SCOPE AND GEOGRAPHICAL SPREAD OF MILITARY INSCRIPTIONS

We cannot know precisely how many inscriptions in total contained information about the military, because there is no corpus of military inscriptions. The Epigraphik-Datenbank Clauss-Slaby (EDCS) contains about 20,000 entries under the heading *legio* ('legion'), at least that number for *cohors* ('cohort') and *ala* ('auxiliaries'), and over 3,000 for the navy. Also listed are inscriptions about *vexillationes* ('temporary detachments'), *veterani* ('veterans'), *missicii* ('discharged') and *evocati* ('extended service') with no further specification of unit. For Latin inscriptions, texts referring to the military probably make up considerably more than 10% of the total 500,000 or more inscriptions. Figures for Greek inscriptions cannot be ascertained. The high proportion of military texts in the epigraphic record is explained on the one hand by relatively high levels of literacy in the military, and on the other by the military's sound financial position.

As for geography, inscriptions with military connections are found everywhere in the empire, with greater concentrations in provinces and locations where army units were stationed, namely, Britain, Germania, Pannonia, Moesia, Dacia, Syria, Arabia and Numidia. Some locations offer especially abundant information thanks to the quantity of monuments (sometimes resulting from unusual preservation conditions): at Rome for the *equites singulares Augusti* ('imperial mounted guards'), because their burial grounds, complete with inscriptions, were systematically levelled in AD 312 [20]; in Lambaesis for the *legio III Augusta*[12]; in Bostra for the *legio III Cyrenaica* (IGLS XIII 1); for the *beneficiarii consularis* in the sanctuaries of Osterburken and Sirmium [17]; [15]; in Gholaia for the life of one *vexillatio* of the *III Augusta* [14]; at Vindolanda for several auxiliary units ([1]: about 800 ink tablets have so far been discovered); and for the army as a stabilizing factor along the overland route in the eastern desert of Egypt [2]. Misenum has a concentration of inscriptions concerning the fleet that was there (CIL X). In terms of content, the *diplomata militaria* ('military diplomas') are of particular significance, because as serial sources – most of which are precisely datable – they allow developments to be traced over long periods of time.

C.3. CONTENT

In almost all cases, the content of these inscriptions is 'personalized', that is, a person is mentioned who has a link to the army, or else an individual unit is referenced. This is particularly but not exclusively true of the votive and funerary inscriptions. Collating these texts and their chronological and topographical orders permits general inferences to be made. In this way, analyses have established which legions and/or auxiliary units were present in which province or at which location at a particular time – for example, the sequence of legions at Mainz, where nine legions were successively stationed in the 1st century AD [16]. Inscriptions often show which people or units took part in particular campaigns, such as Trajan's Dacian War (CIL XI 5992; XVI 160; AE 1951, 52; 1972, 573; 2005, 838; 2008, 1736; ILS 308; 1350; 1352; 2081; 2309; 2647; ILTun 720; → Wars of note, C.) or the suppression of the Bar Kochba Revolt (IGR III 174f.; → Wars of note, B.). IGR IV 284 and 285 prove that King Eumenes II of Pergamum took part as a *socius* ('confederate') in Roman military actions against Nabis of Sparta in 195 and 192 BC.

It is thanks almost exclusively to inscriptions that we are able to reconstruct the evolution of the internal structure of the army, its ranks and military distinctions over several centuries [5]. The same is true of the origins of many soldiers and of senatorial and equestrian → officers (see e.g. PME; [4]). Some inscriptions mention a soldier's *origo* directly, while in other cases the name makes the matter clear (e.g. soldiers from Thrace with typical names: [3]). The settlements of → veterans after discharge in most cases can only be traced through inscriptions – with the numerous military diplomas revealing that many veterans, at least from the auxiliary units, returned to their homelands [6. 84]. Information on mortality during service, and hence the need for increased → recruitment, can likewise only be derived from epigraphic documents [18. cap. 3]. Many texts mention active soldiers' *uxores* ('wives') and children, despite the general ban on marriage [19. 330–332]. It is clear that the development towards quasi-marital relationships only began to acquire statistical significance in the late 1st century AD, especially in connection with the tendency towards stationing soldiers in permanent camps on an almost continuous basis. It is also clear that veterans took part only to a small extent in the lives of the communities where they settled, because they were not required to do more, due to their privileges. Finally, inscriptions clarify the importance of the worship of the gods among soldiers, along with the influence of the deities of the region in which they were stationed alongside the imperial pantheon (e.g. for Egypt see [11]). Statistical conclusions can be drawn with reasonable certainty concerning longer-term developments in these areas based on military inscriptions because most of these inscriptions can be dated with at least reasonable precision, especially at locations where chronological sequences are apparent in long series of similar inscriptions. Where this is not the case, even military inscriptions are often only approximately datable.

Inscriptions are also illuminating with regard to the Roman army's participation in the development of infrastructure in the provinces. It is often assumed that the army's participation was very high, but the inscriptions contradict this. Individual army units, with their high levels of literacy, were little involved in the general development of → infrastructure [10], with the exception of installations that were essential to the army itself [7]. Much more common, although rarely attested directly, was the temporary assignment of individual soldiers to building work in the civilian sphere – one example being the *mensor* ('surveyor') Nonius Datus of Lambaesis, who was sent tocSaldae in Mauretania Caesariensis (ILS 5795).

Documents in which the emperor communicated directly with army units rarely survive. Because their intent was immediate, they were not typically put on durable materials. One exception is Hadrian's criticism of manouevres at Lambaesis (CIL VIII 18042 = ILS 9133 = [13]), and another is the same emperor's decree by which he rectified the lack of citizenship for members of the Praetorian Guard ([8]; cf. [9]).

☞ Descriptions of war, B. Monuments with Latin inscriptions

Bibliography

Sources
[1] A.K. Bowman et al., The Vindolanda Writing-Tablets, vols. 2 and 4, 1994–2010.

Secondary literature
[2] H. Cuvigny, Praesidia du désert de Bérenice, vol. 1: La route de Myos Hormos. L'armée romaine dans le désert oriental d'Egypte, 2003 [3] D. Dana, Onomasticon Thracicum, 2014 [4] H. Devijver, The Equestrian Officers of the Roman Imperial Army, vol. 2 (MAVORS 9), 1992, 109–128 [5] A. von Domaszewski, Die Rangordnung des römischen Heeres, edited by B. Dobson, ²1967 [6] W. Eck, Der Kaiser als Herr des Heeres. Militärdiplome und die kaiserliche Reichsregierung, in: J.J. Wilkes (ed.), Documenting the Roman Army, 2003, 55–88 [7] W. Eck, Das Heer und die Infrastruktur von Städten in der römischen Kaiserzeit, in: C. Ohlig (ed.), Cura Aquarum in Israel II, 2014, 207–214 [8] W. Eck et al., Edikt Hadrians für Prätorianer mit unsicherem römischen Bürgerrecht, in: ZPE 189, 2014, 241–253; ZPE 191, 2014, 266–268 und ZPE 206, 2018, 199–201 [9] W. Eck, Soldaten aus den Donauprovinzen in der Prätorianergarde. Zum Erdbeben in Syrien aus dem Jahr 115 und zum Edikt Hadrians aus dem Jahr 119, in: ZPE 206, 2018, 199–201 [10] M. Horster, Bauinschriften römischer Kaiser, 2001, 168–187 [11] D. Kossmann, Untersuchungen zur Religion der römischen Armee in Ägypten, (http://kups.ub.uni-koeln.de/5896/) [12] Y. Le Bohec, La troisième légion Auguste, 1989 [13] Y. Le Bohec, Les discours d'Hadrien à l'armée d'Afrique, 2003 [14] R. Marichal, Les ostraca de Bu Njem, 1992 [15] M. Mirković, Beneficiarii consularis in Sirmium, in: Chiron 24, 1994, 345–404 [16] B. Rossignol, Quis fratrem mihi reddit? Notes sur la famille des légionnaires de Mayence, in: Cahiers du Centre Gustave Glotz 24, 2013, 286–289 [17] E. Schallmayer et al., Der römische Weihebezirk von Osterburken, pt. 1: Corpus der griechischen und lateinischen Beneficiarier-Inschriften des römischen Reiches, 1990 [18] W. Scheidel, Measuring Sex, Age and Death in the Roman Empire. Explorations in Ancient Demography, 1996 [19] M.A. Speidel, The Roman Army, in: C. Bruun / J. Edmundson (eds.), The Oxford Handbook of Roman Epigraphy, 2014, 319–344 [20] M.P. Speidel, Die Denkmäler der Kaiserreiter, 1994.

Werner Eck

D. Coins

D.1. Value as sources
D.2. Significance to military history

D.1. Value as sources

State authorities embraced the idea of manufacturing metal pieces that were standardized in weight and substance for monetary use, and marked to this effect, soon after the technology first emerged in the mid-7th century BC. On the one hand, coins enabled them to issue an appropriately strong financial guarantee, and on the other, they could use the coins themselves for their own payment purposes and the images on the cions for representational purposes. The interplay between image and wording on coins, the diversity of their motifs, their mass production, their immediate material survival, the usually good datability of coins, and their inherent completeness as objects make them extremely valuable as sources [9]; [11]; [15].

D.2. Significance to military history

D.2.1. Coin images
D.2.2. Finances
D.2.3. Coin finds
D.2.4. Miscellaneous phenomena

In all eras of Antiquity, payments to the army represented the state's largest expenditure. Coins are therefore important as a source for military history.

D.2.1. Coin images

The images and legends on coins, which always represent an official perspective, yield information about political systems and conditions, rulers, events and ideas. Throughout Antiquity, it was of fundamental importance for official powers to represent themselves as victorious in war (→ Representations of war B.). The possibility of tracing the progress of wars by evaluating coins within the contexts of their minting has not yet been fully explored ([18]; [21]; cf. also [23]).

D.2.2. Finances

Intermittent minting rhythms and changing quantities were to a large degree dictated by the type of military deployment and the events and → consequences of war. Crucial influences on the monetization of the ancient world were the dominance of Athenian coins during the period of the Delian League, the minting of the immense Persian treasure by Alexander the Great (→ Wars of note, A.), and the rise of Roman silver minting after Rome's expansion into Iberia and the east in the 2nd century BC ([7]; [5]; [2]; on quantifications: [4]). Micro-studies demonstrate how precisely numismatic material can reveal financial, organizational, economic and political strategies and aspects of society, particularly during times of war ([3]; [22]; cf. [1]).

Some emergency measures that can be directly attributed to war include the extraordinary minting of gold coins during the Peloponnesian War (431–404 BC) at Athens and Syracuse, the issue of overvalued replacement coins [19. 136–146], and the debasement of coin materials (Athenian silver during the Peloponnesian War; Greek cities of Southern Italy during the Pyrrhic War, 280–275 BC; Carthaginian gold and silver in the 3rd century BC; Roman *quadrigati* during the Second Punic War, 218–201 BC, etc.). The dramatic debasement of Roman silver coins during the 3rd century AD was mostly caused by → pay increases, which caused government spending to explode [6]; [20].

D.2.3. Coin finds

Only for a fraction of the coins that survive today are the locations where they were found known. Knowing where coins were found can enable scholars to trace the occupancy dates and intensities of military sites and patterns of deployment [13]; [16]; [8]. Major increases in the number of coins concentrated in specific areas may indicate patterns of unrest [10]. Coins found in barbarian territories suggest subsidies and → mercenary activity, offerings and deposits to ritual and cult, even in military contexts. Within the discipline of numismatics, the analysis of find locations has long since become a subdiscipline with its own comprehensive questions and spectrum of methods [12]; [14]; [17].

D.2.4. Miscellaneous phenomena

Graffiti and countermarks with names of military units placed on coins, emergency and substitute military money, and imitation coins originating from mercenaries (e.g. among the Celts) are only some of the other indications of the close connection between the military and coins.

Bibliography

[1] F. Burrer / H. Müller (eds.), Kriegskosten und Kriegsfinanzierung in der Antike, 2008 [2] M.H. Crawford, Coinage and Money under the Roman Republic, 1985 [3] F. De Callataÿ, L'histoire des guerres mithridatiques vue par les monnaies, 1997 [4] F. De Callataÿ (ed.), Quantifying Monetary Supplies in Greco-Roman Times, 2011 [5] F. De Callataÿ, Royal Hellenistic Coinages. From Alexander to Mithradates, in: W.E. Metcalf (ed.), The Oxford Handbook of Greek and Roman Coinage, 2012, 175–190 [6] R. Duncan-Jones, Money and Government in the Roman Empire, 1994 [7] T.J. Figueira, The Power of Money, 1998 [8] M.P. García-Bellido, Las legiones hispánicas en Germania, 2004 [9] R. Göbl, Antike Numismatik, 2 vols.,

1978 [10] J. VAN HEESCH, Coin Hoards and Invasions? The Evidence of Sites, in: L. BRICAULT et al. (eds.), Rome et les Provinces. Monnayage et histoires. Mélanges offerts à Michel Amandry, 2017, 400–413 [11] C. HOWGEGO, Geld in der antiken Welt, 2000 [12] H.-M. VON KAENEL / F. KEMMERS (eds.), Coins in Context, vol. 1, 2009 [13] F. KEMMERS, Coins for a Legion, 2006 [14] C.E. KING / D.G. WIGG (eds.), Coin Finds and Coin Use in the Roman World, 1996 [15] W.E. METCALF (ed.), The Oxford Handbook of Greek and Roman Coinage, 2012 [16] M. PETER, Untersuchungen zu den Fundmünzen aus Augst und Kaiseraugst, 2001 [17] R. REECE, Roman Coins and Archaeology, 2003 [18] W. SCHEIDEL, Der Germaneneinfall in Oberitalien unter Marcus Aurelius und die Emissionen der kaiserlichen Reichsprägung, in: Chiron 20, 1990, 1–18 [19] R. SEAFORD, Money and the Early Greek Mind, 2004 [20] R. WOLTERS, Nummi Signati, 1999 [21] R. WOLTERS, Wiedergewonnene Geschichte, in: H. PÖPPELMANN (ed.), Roms vergessener Feldzug, 2013, 116–123 [22] B. WOYTEK, Arma et Nummi, 2003 [23] R. ZIEGLER, Kaiser, Heer und städtisches Geld, 1993.

REINHARD WOLTERS

E. PAPYRI

E.1. Introduction
E.2. Civilian duties of the army
E.3. Documents from soldiers' private lives
E.4. Late Antiquity
E.5. Soldiers' dossiers
E.6. Structural changes

E.1. INTRODUCTION

Documentary papyri offer all kinds of information about the internal affairs of the Roman army of Antiquity and Late Antiquity and about the living conditions of soldiers and → veterans within the local society and economy of Egypt. Texts related to army administration are mostly written in Latin until the early 6th century AD. Documents pertaining to internal army administration in the High Imperial period come primarily from an archive find at Dura-Europus, but also from Egyptian papyri [19]. Lists of personnel (RMR 1–5), service allocations (RMR 10–19), losses (RMR 34) and promotions (P. Mich. III 164) reveal the daily activities of units over a period of time (cf. fig. 1). Accounts, reports and *pridiana* (personnel inventories) illustrate routine service (RMR 64). The *Feriale Duranum* (RMR 117) of 223–227 gives unique insights into a unit's official festival calendar. Individual texts give detailed information about recruitment processes (BGU II 423, 2nd cent.), assignment to specific corps (P. Mich. VIII 491, 2nd cent.) and discharge (*missio*; PSI IX 1026, AD 150). Along with inscriptions, papyri document the increasing use of local recruitment. By the 1st century AD, men from Egypt were already the second-largest group after recruits from Asia Minor (ILS 2483), while a list of discharged legionaries from the Severan period (CIL III 6580) shows that three quarters of them came from Egypt, and that two thirds of those were *castrenses* (soldiers' children born in the *canabae*). Greek Egyptians took Latin names when they joined the army (P. Oxy. XXII 2349, AD 70; BGU II 423, 2nd cent.; P. Oxy. XLI 2978, 3rd cent.). Equestrian officer positions were often taken by prominent Alexandrians (M. Chr. 116; PSI VIII 962; P. IFAO III 11, all 2nd cent.). Official correspondence, invoices and control stamps on *ostraka* show the army patrol services along the trade routes from the Nile Valley to the ports of the Red Sea and guard units at the quarries (O. Claud., O. Krok., O. Did.; [3]). O. Krok. 87 contains a report of an attack by barbarian bandits on a small guard post (*praesidium*) in the eastern desert and a circular communication from the commander warning neighbouring posts.

E.2. CIVILIAN DUTIES OF THE ARMY

A second group consists of documents showing the army's role in administrative processes, tax collection, the census, and in work to improve the infrastructure (construction and irrigation) in the Egyptian *chora* ('territory') [14]. Dozens of papyri reveal *centuriones*, *beneficiarii* and *stationarii* in their functions as policing and security bodies to whom local populations appealed in complaints and petitions. Illustrating how the army was supplied are receipts for foodstuffs and animal feed, raw materials and clothing (RMR 76, AD 179). Hundreds of relevant texts permit the reconstruction of army supplies from the 3rd century to the end of Roman rule [12].

E.3. DOCUMENTS FROM SOLDIERS' PRIVATE LIVES

The third and largest group of illuminating texts consists of soldiers' private papers, with letters to families and friends particularly prominent (BGU II 632; P. Mich. VIII 490; 491) – some having been sent home from Italy (BGU II 423; P. Mich. VIII 491, both 2nd cent.) or the Danube frontier [1]. Legal documents such as testaments (BGU I 326, AD 194), loans (ChLA XLV 1340, AD 27) and slave purchases (ChLA III 200, draughted in Syria, AD 166) illustrate economic activities and interactions between army members and local society (→ Society and army B.). Many texts shed light on the social lives of soldiers [2. 117–142]; [11] and veterans [17], showing their strong financial positions (thanks to pay) and social prestige but also occasional points of friction and legal disputes. Some papyrus dossiers reveal soldier families like the family of Claudius Tiberianus and his son Claudius Terentianus (P. Mich. VIII, early 2nd cent.; [21]). Such families served in the army for several generations, building networks and in some villages

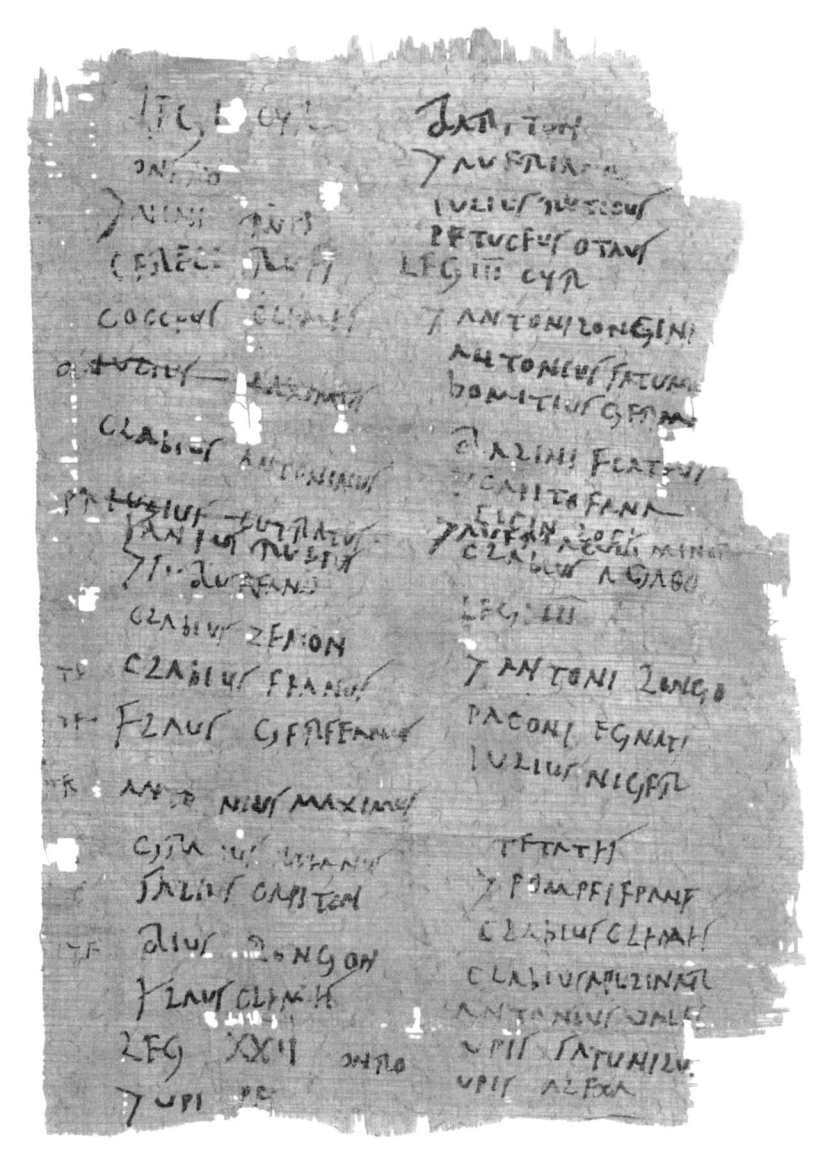

Fig. 1: List of soldiers of the *legio III Cyrenaica* and *legio XXII Deiotariana* (P. Vindob. L 2, edited as ChLA XLIII 1242; SB XXII 15638; origin: Aegyptus, AD 98–120). The list identifies soldiers of the two legions stationed in Egypt in the 1st and early 2nd centuries AD. Given that the *legio III Cyrenaica* was moved to the province of Arabia around AD 120, the list must have been made before this time. In front of the legionaries' names are various entries typical of Roman military documents: > for (*centuria*), tr for *tr*(*anslatus*) – 'moved' –, te for *te*(*tatus*) – 'deceased'. Since eight of the 28 soldiers listed are given as deceased, the document may date from the time of the great Jewish Revolt in Egypt (AD 115–177) and thus attest to heavy losses in the Roman army at this time.

(e.g. Caranis) establishing prominent circles of soldiers in the midst of the indigenous population. Rare insights into soldiers' religious lives are also available. Besides appeals to gods (usually Sarapis) in private letters (P. Turner 18, 89–96; BGU II 423, 2nd cent.), the most widespread type is the *proskynemata* (religious graffiti) at cult sites (over 50, for instance, at the Temple of Mandulis at Kalabsha) and on roads in Egypt and Nubia, which express devotion chiefly to Egyptian deities [20].

E.4. LATE ANTIQUITY
The weight of papyrological evidence shifts from villages more into towns and cities in Late Antiquity, and the 5th century exhibits a still unexplained decline in the number of texts compared to the 4th and 6th centuries. Even more than in earlier periods, findings are concentrated in a few large archives, which influence our knowledge of social and economic developments (emergence of large-scale land ownership, peasant dependency) and religious turmoil (Christianity, monasticism). In the military sphere, papyri illustrate the organizational changes of the late 3rd and early 4th centuries. The new unit types (*equites*, *vexillationes*, *cunei*, etc.) joined the existing traditional army formations (*legiones*, *alae*, *cohortes*), and supreme command now lay with a *comes* (*rei militaris*) *Aegypti*, to whom a *dux Thebaidos* answered. The rank titles and functions of the army of Late Antiquity appear in hundreds of papyri (→ Rank C.). The number of troop types seems to have increased

considerably, but unit strengths (except those of the legions) probably did not exceed 300–400, so that the total occupying force remained at about the same level. For the period around AD 400, the *Notitia dignitatum orientis* lists a total in excess of 70 garrisons in towns and cities and as outposts on desert margins. The papyri confirm these details without exception, and thus provide welcome proof of the accuracy of the *Notitia* [6]. The diffusion of forces into smaller units of *limitanei* ('border troops') across the entire country reflected new thinking about defence. We hear only sporadically of *comitatenses* ('court troops'), which may sometimes have been stationed at Alexandria (BGU I 316, AD 359; P. Paramone 15, 592/93) or may have been passing through (*comitatus* of Diocletian: P. Panop. Beatty 1 and 2, AD 298 and 300). Papyri reveal that the Egyptian campaign of Diocletian and the campaigns against the Blemmyes in the reign of Justinian all led to new military dispositions [15].

Some documents of internal military administration are in Latin, such as the personnel list (*matricula*?) of a unit in P. Mich. X 592 (AD 311–321), and some are in Greek, such as the *brevis* ('short summary') of a cavalry unit in P. Mich. X 593 (AD 312) that gives precise assignments of duties. Individual documents offer snapshots of military administration, but in such a way that shows them to have originally been part of everyday routines [19]: SB XXIV 16282 (late 4th cent.) concerns recruitment and the army → oath, and P. Lond. V 1655 (AD 364), P. Oxy. VIII 1103 (AD 360) and LXIII 4373 (AD 364) deal with landowners' responsibility for provision of recruits, conscription, and compensation for recruits. Almost two centuries later, the Latin letter from a *comes Thebaidos* to the tribunes at Hermoupolis addresses the criteria and procedures for recruitment (P. Ryl. IV 609, early 6th cent.). ChLA XLIII 1248 contains the official transcript of three Latin files on the career of a cavalryman around AD 395–401. The document may have originated in an army chancellery and have been prepared in connection with a *missio* ('discharge') as confirmation of service performed. The only two surviving sheets from the official journal of a *mansio* ('stopping place') near Oxyrhynchus show us the considerable number of travelling soldiers and officers (P. Oxy. LX 4087, 4th cent.; P. Oxy. LX 4088, AD 347–350), while the sole original *evectio* (permit for use of the *cursus publicus*) is intended for staff officers (*protectores*) travelling to the imperial court to pay homage to the imperial purple (ChLA XLV 1320, 399). The billeting of soldiers (*hospitalitas*), which was a perennial problem in other parts of the empire, appears as a problem in Egypt only as attested in P. Oxy. L 3581 (5th cent.).

E.5. SOLDIERS' DOSSIERS

Soldiers of all ranks are attested in great numbers in the papyri of Late Antiquity, but as in the High Imperial period, most of this evidence comes from soldiers' private lives (letters, legal documents, payment receipts). They offer valuable insights into soldiers' socioeconomic position, for example the detailed testament of the *centurio* Valerius Aion (P. Col. VII 188, AD 320). Private dossiers dominate: over 80 writings by Flavius Abinnaeus (c. 340–351) illustrate his career across 45 years of service, including his command of an *ala* ('auxiliary unit') at Dionysias (Fayum), his agenda and his unit's sphere of activities (P. Abinn.). The archive of Flavius Taurinus, his son Flavius Johannes and grandson Flavius Taurinus (II) documents the economic rise of a military family through three generations (BGU XII, CPR XXIV 4–7, 5th cent.). Taurinus and later his son Johannes rose to become *primicerius* ('chief official') of the *Mauri scutarii*, a cavalry unit that is attested at Hermoupolis in dozens of texts between about AD 340 and 540, which makes it the best documented formation of the Roman army of Late Antiquity [8]. The dossier of Flavius Patermuthis, a soldier in the *arithmos Elephantines*, dates from AD 575–613. The texts within it mention by name over a hundred soldiers and veterans of various units stationed at the First Cataract, and in the process they reveal the rank titles of the Late Antique legion as well as the business activities that soldiers were pursing as sidelines. The overlap between military service and secondary private business may have been typical of the situation in the *limitanei* around AD 600 [7]. Private documents belonging to army members also survive from Nessana (P. Ness., 6th cent.) and Petra (P. Petra I–V, AD 537–593), and are important because they originate outside Egypt (Palaestina III and Arabia).

E.6. STRUCTURAL CHANGES

The papyri bring to light a number of long-term developments, such as processes of → recruitment [18], the emergence of soldier families and the establishment of preferential settlement areas for army members in the Faiyum. For Late Antiquity, they reveal the clear separation of functions between a *militia armata* and a *militia officialis* [15], the altered structures of the army and its ranks, especially in the *limitanei*, the scattering of units across the whole country, and the changed dispositions of the Justinianic period [10]; [16]; [22]; [13]. However, papyrological evidence offers almost no information about historical or military events. The special value of this category of evidence consists in its revealing details about institutions and administrative processes, and its rendering visible the nuances of soldiers' connections with the society and economy of the provinces. Given the unified organization of the Roman army, it may be assumed that this real-life view not only represents realities in Egypt, but also reflects general conditions in the Roman army [9]; [4]; [5].

☞ **Administration, C. Roman**

BIBLIOGRAPHY
[1] G. ADAMSON, Letter from a Soldier in Pannonia, in: The Bulletin of the American Society of Papyrologists, 49, 2012, 79–94 [2] R. ALSTON, Soldier and Society in Roman Egypt. A Social History, 1995 [3] H. CUVIGNY (ed.), La route de Myos Hormos. L'armée romaine dans le désert oriental d'Égypte, 2 vols., 2003 [4] H. DEVIJVER, L'Égypte et l'histoire de l'armée romaine, in: L. CRISCUOLO / G. GERACI (eds.), Egitto e storia antica dell'ellenismo all'età arabo, 1989, 37–54 [5] R. HAENSCH, The Roman Army in Egypt, in: C. RIGGS (ed.), The Oxford Handbook of Roman Egypt, 2012, 68–82 [6] A. KAISER, Egyptian Units and the Reliability of the Notitia Dignitatum, pars Oriens, in: Historia 64, 2015, 243–261 [7] J.G. KEENAN, Evidence for the Byzantine Army in the Syene Papyri, in: BASP 27, 1990, 139–150 [8] J.G. KEENAN, Soldiers and Civilian in Byzantine Hermopolis, in: Proceedings of the 20th International Congress of Papyrologists, Copenhagen 1993, 1994, 444–451 [9] J. LESQUIER, L'armée romaine d'Égypte d'Auguste à Dioclétien, 1918 [10] J. MASPERO, Organisation militaire de l'Égypte byzantine, 1912 [11] F. MITTHOF, Soldaten und Veteranen in der Gesellschaft des römischen Ägypten (1.–2. Jahrhundert n.Chr.), in: G. ALFÖLDY et al. (eds.), Kaiser, Heer und Gesellschaft. Gedenkschrift für Eric Birley, 2000, 377–405 [12] F. MITTHOF, Annona militaris. Die Heeresversorgung im spätantiken Ägypten. vol. 1: Darstellung; vol. 2: Katalog, 2001 [13] B. PALME, Die römische Armee von Diokletian bis Valentinian I. Die papyrologische Evidenz, in: Y. LE BOHEC / C. WOLFF (eds.), L'armée Romaine de Dioclétien à Valentinien Ier. Actes du Congrès de Lyon 12–14 septembre 2002, 2004, 101–115 [14] B. PALME, Zivile Aufgaben der Armee im kaiserzeitlichen Ägypten, in: A. KOLB (ed.), Herrschaftsstruktur und Herrschaftspraxis, 2006, 299–328 [15] B. PALME, Imperial Presence. Government and Army, in: R.S. BAGNALL (ed.), Egypt in the Byzantine World, 300–700, 2007, 244–270 (ch. 12) [16] R. RÉMONDON, Soldats de Byzance d'après un papyrus trouvé à Edfou, in: Recherches de Papyrologie 1, 1961, 41–94 [17] P. SÄNGER, Veteranen unter den Severern und frühen Soldatenkaisern. Die Dokumentensammlungen der Veteranen Aelius Sarapammon und Aelius Syrion, 2011 [18] M.A. SPEIDEL, Rekruten für fremde Provinzen. Der Papyrus ChLA X 422 und die kaiserliche Rekrutierungszentrale, in: M.A. SPEIDEL (ed.), Heer und Herrschaft im römischen Reich der Hohen Kaiserzeit, 2009, 213–234 [19] K. STAUNER, Das offizielle Schriftwesen des römischen Heeres von Augustus bis Gallienus, 2004 [20] O. STOLL, Integration und doppelte Identität. Römisches Militär und die Kulte der Soldaten und Veteranen in Ägypten von Augustus bis Diokletian, in: R. GUNDLACH / C. VOGEL (eds.), Militärgeschichte des pharaonischen Ägypten, 2009, 419–458 [21] S. STRASSI, L'archivio di Claudius Tiberianus da Karanis, 2008 [22] C. ZUCKERMAN, Comtes et ducs en Égypte autour de l'an 400 et la date de la Notitia Dignitatum Orientis, in: AnTard 6, 1998, 137–147.

BERNHARD PALME

Sparta

A. Introduction
B. Military character
C. Military potential
D. Army system and reforms
E. Tactics and logistics
F. Oliganthropy

A. INTRODUCTION

Sparta has been remembered as the most striking example of a warlike society and military state in Classical Antiquity. This is due partly to how it portrayed itself, and partly to external perspectives. The city of Sparta expanded throughout the region of Lacedaemon (Laconia) on the southeastern Peloponnese and pursued a long rivalry with Athens. The traditional scholarly account of Sparta depicted a society that was festive and materially prosperous at first (cf. Alcmaeon: ceremonial choral songs), but in the 7th century BC changed into an inward-looking society that was isolated from the outside world, lacked culture, and drilled its citizens into blind obedience through strict military discipline (cf. Tyrtaeus: battle paraeneses). This view has been challenged in recent decades, with Sparta increasingly characterized as a 'normal' Greek *polis* that did not differ fundamentally from other Greek city-states [12]; [17]; [18]; but such revisionist positions have met with opposition [14]; [33. 180–224].

B. MILITARY CHARACTER

Public education (*agoge*), which young males had to undergo from the ages of 7 to 20 or 30 (Xen. Lac. pol. 2–4; later Plut. *Lycurgus* 16–22), gives some indication of the military nature of Spartan society. Yet, while emphasis was certainly placed on obedience, fortitude and endurance, civic virtues were also a priority, and there is no indication of military training before the age of 20 ([12. 36, 44]; cf. [17. 136]). Apart from the communal accommodation of young males and the practice of adults dining in communities (*syssitia/syskenoi*), the city design of Sparta differed little from that of other Greek *poleis*, featuring the usual public facilities (*acropolis*, *agora*, *gymnasium*, etc.), and otherwise dominated by private houses – hardly a city of tents or barracks, or a permanent field camp (Pl. Leg. 666e; Isoc. Or. 6,81; Plut. *Lycurgus* 24) [37]. The popular assembly could vote on any issue brought before it, decide on matters of war and peace, and elect the general to command a campaign. Over time, generals ceased to be drawn exclusively from the ranks of the kings. It was decided in 506 BC that only one of the two kings should be allowed to go to war, although according to Herodotus (5,75; 6,56), the kings had the power to wage war against any enemy they chose.

Still, all Spartan citizens (Spartiates) remained liable for military service from the ages of 19 to 59, and the ephors (a council of overseers in Sparta) could call up whatever range of ages they chose (Xen. Lac. pol. 11,2). Because Spartiates were relieved of daily labour by the services of unfree helots, they were available to the community and were probably equipped with personal weapons by the state (Xen. Hell. 3,3,7), unlike in other *poleis* [7. 27]; [5. 44]. During the Classical period, their shields bore a uniform lambda, but individual shield insignia accompanied it (Theop. FGrH 115 F 402 = Phot. s.v. la{m}bda; Plut. Mor. 234c–d). Citizens in the army stood out with their purple cloaks (*phoinikis*; Xen. Lac. pol. 11,3; Aristot. frg. 542R; [38. 79]), long hair (Hdt. 1,82,8; Xen. Lac. pol. 11,3) and shaved moustaches (Aristot. frg. 539R). Everlasting renown in the community awaited whoever died bravely in battle (Tyrt. frg. 9G–P), while cowards (*tresantes*) were officially ostracized (Hdt. 7,229–232; 9,71; Plut. *Agesilaus* 30,2f.). Women were expected to place their sons at the disposal of the state, but performed no military duties themselves [11].

C. MILITARY POTENTIAL

One early and important stimulus to military preparedness among the Spartans was that Sparta absorbed the neighbouring territory of Messenia as early as the late 8th century BC, and therefore they needed to be armed and ready to keep in check the subjugated population, who were relegated to the status of helots [5. 15f.]. This seems to be the origin of the tactics of the hoplite phalanx that spread throughout Greece [7]; [6]. Besides citizens, the free *perioikoi* ('dwellers around [Sparta]') of Laconia were also enlisted. Helots were called up for auxiliary duties (as weapons porters, light infantry), but not for service in the → phalanx, as was assumed on the basis of Herodotus' account (9,28f.) of the Battle of Plataeae (479 BC) [19. 31–39]. From the mid-6th century BC onwards, Sparta operated an alliance system on the Peloponnese (Peloponnesian League), in which many *poleis* placed themselves under Spartan military control and, on deployments, under the command of Spartan officers (Thuc. 2,75,3: *xenagoi*), which made the city appear stronger to the outside world.

D. ARMY SYSTEM AND REFORMS

D.1. *Phylai* and *lochoi*
D.2. *Perioikoi*
D.3. *Lochoi* and *morai*
D.4. Innovations

Establishing the structure of the Spartan army poses problems, because the ancient authors give conflicting information that resists reconciliation. As a result, it has often been supposed that various army reforms took place, although fundamental continuities have also been postulated [24. 68f.].

D.1. PHYLAI AND LOCHOI

The earliest piece of evidence concerning the Spartan army comes from Tyrtaeus (frg. 10aG–P, v. 16), who mentions a division of the hoplites into the three Dorian *phylai*, 'tribes' (Pamphylians, Hylleis, Dymanes) and the lightly armed *gymnetes* (frg. 8G–P, vv. 35–38). Herodotus (1,65) then mentions *lochoi* ('divisions'), probably numbering five (Aristot. frg. 541R: Edolos/Aidolios, Sinis, Arimas/ Sarimas, Ploas, Messoages/Mesoates) – and as the smallest units the *syssites* (Plut. Lycurgus 12: c. 15 men), *triakades* (companies of thirty; [27]) and *enomotiai* (bands of sworn soldiers), which later numbered around 32–38 men (Thuc. 5,68,3; Xen. Hell. 6,4,12). An early reform ([5. 430]: first half of 7th cent. BC) that replaced the old 'tribal' system thus seems to have taken place. The citizenry, however, never entirely gave up the original system, as shown by the 27 *phratrai* attested later (Ath. 141f.). It is debated whether the *lochoi* really reflect a new, regional division by 'villages' (*obai*) of Sparta (Pitana, Mesoa, Cynosura, Limnae), with Amyclae to the south reckoned as the fifth *oba* (IG V 1,26). The sole early reference to such a local division comes from Herodotus (9,53,2f.), who mentions a *lochos Pitanates*, the existence of which, however, Thucydides dismisses (1,20,3). Efforts have been made in recent times to identify this division (attributed to the kings) with the 300 *hippeis* (elite corps/life guard made up of those aged between 20 and 29; cf. Xen. Lac. pol. 4,3) or with one of their three Hundreds (Hdt. 6,56) [21]; [26]. The Three Hundred won fame under Leonidas at the Battle of Thermopylae (480 BC), such that their 'sacrificial deaths' were thereafter celebrated as an example to others (Hdt. 7,224; 7,228; Cic. Tusc. 1,101f.).

D.2. PERIOIKOI

The first indication that *periokoi* ('dwellers around [Sparta]') were fighting within the *lochoi* dates from 425 BC and the conflicts near Sphacteria during the Peloponnesian War (→ Wars of note H.) (Thuc. 4,8; 4,38; in proportion 3:2 to citizens). There may therefore have been another army reform during the 5th century BC that saw the *periokoi* incorporated into the Spartiate battle lines [20. 300]; [4. 710f.]; [23. 37]; [5. 42]. More recently, however, there has again been support for the contrary position that the *periokoi* always fought in separate units (*lochoi*) ([24]; [16]; cf. [2. 63f.]). Xenophon (Hell. 4,5,11; 6,1,1; 6,4,15; 7,4,20; 7,4,27), Aristotle (frg. 540R) and Isocrates (12,180) suggest the combined force. The 600 or so *periokoi* of the Sciritae, from the northern frontier territory of Sciritis, made up their own company (*lochos*) that formed the left wing of the army and was also assigned the roles of vanguard and camp guard (Thuc. 5,67f.; Xen. Lac. pol. 12,3; 13,6).

D.3. *LOCHOI* AND *MORAI*

Discussing the Battle of Mantineia (418 BC), Thucydides (5,68) goes on to enumerate seven *lochoi* (each consisting of four *pentekostyes*, each of these consisting of four *enomotiai*), each 512 men strong (and eight men deep in formation). Yet another army reform might therefore be postulated. However, in Xenophon (Lac. pol. 11,4), the *lochoi* appear to be subdivisions, while the largest groups now comprise six *morai* (each consisting of four *lochoi*, each of these consisting of two *pentekostyes*, and each of these are two *enomotiai*), each 576 men strong (Hell. 6,4,12; cf. Aristot. frg. 540R). Yet, all the Amyclaeans were not assigned to the same *mora*, and neither were fathers, brothers and sons (Hell. 4,5,10f.); this shows that the *morai* were not (or were no longer) defined by locality. The discrepancy between Thucydides and Xenophon has been variously explained, for instance in terms of Thucydides mistakenly using the word *lochos* instead of *mora* ([39. 378]; [5. 41]; cf. [2. 58]: deliberately) and adding a *lochos* of Brasideans (700 helots recruited, then manumitted by Brasidas in 424 BC; Thuc. 4,80,5; 5,34,1) and also adding neodamodes as new citizens [2. 63]; [4. 710]; [5. 429] – or, the discrepancy has been explained in terms of army reform ([20. 303]: on the diminution of the *enomotiai* because of a shortage of citizens; [23. 35]: on the proliferation of commands; [34. 15] and [32. 118]: on the consolidation of the permanent occupying force outside Decelea). A final adjustment may have been made after the Battle of Leuctra (371 bc), or after the secession of the Messenians, because the sources now speak of twelve *lochoi*, meaning that each *mora* now contained only two *lochoi* instead of four (Xen. Hell. 7,4,20; 7,5,10).

D.4. INNOVATIONS

During the Peloponnesian War (outbreak 424 BC), foot soldiers were for the first time joined by riders (Thuc. 4,55,2 mentions 400), who were probably also divided into six *morai* (of approx. 100 men each) (Xen. Hell. 4,2,16; 4,5,12), and a few warships, of which allies provided greater numbers (Thuc. 8,3,2; [20. 318–322]; [10. 196]; [31. 308–310]), and which, with Persian support, ultimately decided the war. Increasingly, too, freed helots (as neodamodes) (Xen. Hell. 3,4,2: in their own contingent of 2,000 men) and impoverished citizens of limited rights (*hypomeiones*; Xen. Hell. 3,3,6) were incorporated into the battle lines, and contingents of mercenaries were brought in, financed principally from → booty [20. 297–299]; [29]; [38. 46–53, 99–107]. Attempts were made in the Hellenistic period to repopulate the citizen army once more, and to adapt it to the new Macedonian weaponry (including cavalry). Finally, a new, independent coinage was introduced [38. 86, 138, 143].

E. TACTICS AND LOGISTICS

For its equipment and supplies, the army relied on its baggage train and on specialist technical personnel (Xen. Lac. pol. 11,2: artisans; 13,7: soothsayers, physicians, flute-players; 13,11: *hellanodikai*/judges for courts martial, *tamiai*/paymasters, *laphyropolai*/booty sellers; cf. Xen. Hell. 3,4,22). These traveled with the king who served as commander. Accompanying these were two ephors (members of the council of overseers) as supervisors (Xen. Lac. pol. 13,5) or a number of *symbouloi* ('advisors') [4. 708]; [5. 212f.], forming a 'tent companionship' with the *polemarchoi* ('warleaders') as commanders of the *morai* (military units) (Xen. Lac. pol. 13,1; Xen. Hell. 6,4,14; [28. 265f.]). The king performed the prescribed sacrifices to the gods that were the precondition for initiating military action (Hdt. 6,56; Xen. Lac. pol. 13; Xen. Hell. 3,4,23; 4,2,20).

The Spartan army was renowned for its military techniques (Xen. Lac. pol. 13,5) and tactics, although the diverse composition of the force limited the opportunities for training. In the field, the thoroughly organized chain of command (from the king through the *polemarchoi, lochagoi* and *pentekonteres* to the *enomotarchoi*; Thuc. 5,66,3f.) permitted the rapid transmission of orders, enabling the army to form up and manoeuvre (countermarch, left and right turns; Xen. Lac. pol. 11,5–10; 13,6; 13,9) quickly, thereby gaining tactical advantage ([25]: archers).

F. OLIGANTHROPY

Despite its striking successes, the Spartan army also endured painful defeats. Furthermore, like the city's entire citizenry, the Spartan army suffered from declining numbers (*oliganthropia*; Aristot. Pol. 1270a), which the introduction of people from outside was intended to offset. Some 5,000 Spartiates and 5,000 *periokoi* ('dwellers around [Sparta]') fought at Plataeae (479 BC)(Hdt. 9,10f.), but by the Battle of Mantinea (418 BC), the tally of hoplites stood around 3,584 (Thuc. 5,68), suggesting that the entire Spartan army was probably only about 6,000 men, a comparatively small number [23. 36]; [28. 239–241]. At Nemea (394 BC), about 2,000 Spartiates were counted among the 6,000 Lacedaemonians (Xen. Hell. 4,2,16; but [24. 138]), and at Leuctra (371 BC), there were only 700 – alongside about five times as many *periokoi* (Xen. Hell. 6,4,15). Four hundred of those 700 fell, putting an end to the Spartan ascendancy and spelling the loss of Messenia. Finally, by the 3rd century BC, there were said to be only 700 citizens left (Plut. *Agis* 5), and the citizen army needed to be replenished to exceed 4,000 men (Plut. *Agis* 8; Plut. *Cleomenes* 11). Cleomenes III therefore enlisted 2,000 manumitted helots into the army (Plut. *Cleomenes* 23; cf. 28: also *kryptoi*). Despite the presence of many → mercenaries, the resulting force was unable to avert a heavy defeat at the hands of the overwhelmingly superior Macedonians at Sellasia (222 BC). Nabis made a further attempt to replenish the army by freeing helots, but, in the end, Sparta proved no match for the Romans as they pacified Greece in 195 BC [38. 145-148].

☞ Society and army; State and army

BIBLIOGRAPHY
[1] J.K. ANDERSON, Military Theory and Practice in the Age of Xenophon, 1970 [2] J. BELOCH, Griechische Aufgebote II., in: Klio 6, 1906, 58-78 [3] G. BUSOLT, Spartas Heer und Leuktra, in: Hermes 40, 1905, 387-449 [4] G. BUSOLT / H. SWOBODA, Griechische Staatskunde, vol. 2 (HbAW 4,1,1), 1926, 703-718: Heer und Flotte [5] P. CARTLEDGE, Agesilaos and the Crisis of Sparta, 1987 [6] P. CARTLEDGE, The Birth of the Hoplite. Sparta's Contribution to Early Greek Military Organization, in: P. CARTLEDGE, Spartan Reflections, 2001, 153-166 [7] P.A. CARTLEDGE, Hoplites and Heroes. Sparta's Contribution to the Technique of Ancient Warfare, in: JHS 97, 1977, 11-27 (German in: K. Christ (ed.), Sparta, 1986, 387-425 with Addendum 470) [8] P. CONNOLLY, Greece and Rome at War, 1981 (reprinted 1988) [9] U. COZZOLI, Proprietà fondiaria ed esercito nello stato spartano dell'età classica (Studi pubblicati dall'istituto italiano per la storia antica 29), 1979 [10] M. DREHER, Die Seemacht Sparta, in: E. BALTRUSCH et al. (eds.), Seemacht, Seeherrschaft und die Antike, 2016, 189-204 [11] J. DUCAT, La femme de Sparte et la guerre, in: Pallas 51, 1999, 159-171 [12] J. DUCAT, La société spartiate et la guerre, in: F. PROST (ed.), Armées et sociétés de la Grèce classique. Aspects sociaux et politiques de la guerre aux Ve et IVe s. av. J.-C., 1999, 35-50 [13] T.J. FIGUEIRA, The Spartan Hippeis, in: S. HODKINSON / A. POWELL (eds.), Sparta and War, 2006, 57-84 [14] M.H. HANSEN, Was Sparta a Normal or an Exceptional Polis?, in: S. HODKINSON (ed.), Sparta. Comparative Approaches, 2009, 385-416 [15] M.H. HANSEN / S. HODKINSON, Spartan Exceptionalism? Continuing the Debate, in: S. HODKINSON (ed.), Sparta. Comparative Approaches, 2009, 473-498 [16] C. HAWKINS, Spartans and Perioikoi. The Organization and Ideology of the Lakedaimonian Army in the Fourth Century B.C.E., in: GRBS 51, 2011, 401-434 [17] S. HODKINSON, Was Classical Sparta a Military Society?, in: S. HODKINSON / A. POWELL (eds.), Sparta and War, 2006, 111-162 [18] S. HODKINSON, Was Sparta an Exceptional Polis?, in: S. HODKINSON (ed.), Sparta. Comparative Approaches, 2009, 417-472 [19] P. HUNT, Slaves, Warfare, and Ideology in the Greek Historians, 1998 [20] U. KAHRSTEDT, Griechisches Staatsrecht, vol. 1: Sparta und seine Symmachie, 1922 [21] D.H. KELLY, Thucydides and Herodotus on the Pitanate Lochos, in: GRBS 22, 1981, 31-38 [22] J. KROMAYER, Studien über Wehrkraft und Wehrverfassung der griechischen Staaten, vornehmlich im 4. Jahrhundert v.Chr., pt. 2: Die Wehrkraft Lakoniens und seine Wehrverfassung vom 5. bis zum 3. Jahrhundert, in: Klio 3, 1903, 173-212 [23] J. KROMAYER / G. VEITH, Heerwesen und Kriegführung der Griechen und Römer (HbAW 4,3,2), 1928, 28-44: Sparta und der Peloponnesische Bund [24] J.F. LAZENBY, The Spartan Army, 1985 [25] L. LECLERCQ, L'emploi des archers dans l'armée lacédémonienne. Une évolution des valeurs liée au pragmatisme militaire, in: A. GONZALES / M.T. SCHETTINO (eds.), L'idéalisation de l'autre. Faire un modèle d'un anti-modèle, 2014, 53-77 [26] M. LUPI, Amompharetos, the Lochos of Pitane and the Spartan System of Villages, in: S. HODKINSON / A. POWELL (eds.), Sparta and War, 2006, 185-218 [27] M. LUPI, The Spartan τριηκάδες (Hdt. 1.65.5), in: Hermes 143, 2015, 379-383 [28] H. MICHELL, Sparta. τὸ κρυπτὸν τῆς πολιτείας τῶν Λακεδαιμονίων, 1964, 233-280: Spartan Military and Naval Organisation [29] E. MILLENDER, The Politics of Spartan Mercenary Service, in: S. HODKINSON / A. POWELL (eds.), Sparta and War, 2006, 235-266 [30] E. MILLENDER, The Greek Battlefield. Classical Sparta and the Spectacle of Hoplite Warfare, in: W. RIESS / G.G. FAGAN (eds.), The Topography of Violence in the Greco-Roman World, 2016, 162-194 [31] E. MILLENDER, The Spartans 'at Sea', in: G. CUNIBERTI et al. (eds.), Great Is the Power of the Sea. The Power of the Sea and Sea Power in the Greek World of the Archaic and Classical Period (Historika 5), 2016, 299-312 [32] S.M. RUSCH, Sparta at War. Strategy, Tactics, and Campaigns, 550-362 BC, 2011 [33] W. SCHMITZ, Die griechische Gesellschaft. Eine Sozialgeschichte der archaischen und klassischen Zeit, 2014 [34] N.V. SEKUNDA, The Spartans, 1998 (= Elite Series 66: The Spartan Army, 1998) [35] H. SINGOR, The Spartan Army at Mantinea and Its Organisation in the Fifth Century BC, in: W. JONGMAN / M. KLEIJWEGT (eds.), After the Past. Essays in Ancient History in Honour of H.W. Pleket, 2002, 235-284 [36] J.G. TEXIER, Un aspect de l'évolution de Sparte à l'époque hellénistique. La modification de l'armée lacédémonienne et ses implications, in: AFLD 6, 1976, 69-86 [37] L. THOMMEN, Der spartanische Kosmos und sein 'Feldlager' der Homoioi. Begriffs- und forschungsgeschichtliche Überlegungen zum Sparta-Mythos, in: R. ROLLINGER / C. ULF (eds.), Griechische Archaik. Interne Entwicklungen. Externe Impulse, 2004, 127-141 [38] L. THOMMEN, Die Wirtschaft Spartas, 2014 [39] A. TOYNBEE, Some Problems of Greek History, 1969, 365-404: Changes in the Strength and in the Organization of the Lacedaemonian Army after the Establishment of the 'Lycurgan' Regime at Sparta [40] S. VALZANIA, L'esercito spartano nel periodo dell'egemonia. Dimensioni e compiti strategici, in: QS 43, 1996, 19-72 [41] S. VALZANIA, Brodo nero. Sparta pacifica, il suo esercito, le sue guerre, 1999 [42] H. VAN WEES, Greek Warfare. Myths and Realities, 2004 [43] H. VAN WEES, 'The Oath of the Sworn Bands'. The Acharnae Stela, the Oath of Plataea and Archaic Spartan Warfare, in: A. LUTHER et al. (eds.), Das frühe Sparta, 2006, 125-164 [44] K.-W. WELWEI, Unfreie im antiken Kriegsdienst, vol. 1: Athen und Sparta (Forschungen zur antiken Sklaverei 5), 1974

LUKAS THOMMEN

Specialists

A. Greek
B. Roman

A. Greek

A.1. Communications specialists and musicians
A.2. Interpreters (*hermeneus*)
A.3. Attendants (*thetikon* or *stratos skeuophorikos*)
A.4. Medical services (*iatrikon*)
A.5. Seers (*manteis*)
A.6. Technical department: engineers (*mēchanopoioi, organopoioi*) and artisans (*cheirotechnai*)
A.7. Administrative and clerical staff

The evolution of warfare led to the emergence and use of specialist units responsible for particular military functions other than combat in the Greek armies of the Classical and Hellenistic periods. Ancient military treatises call these 'non-combatant units' (*amachon*). The Spartans pioneered the use of these kinds of specialists in the early 5th century BC. Other armies followed their example, especially in the Hellenistic period. The presence of specialists is an indicator of the professional level of the army concerned.

The following specialized non-combatant units were found in Greek armies:

A.1. Communications specialists and musicians

Commands were communicated in three ways: by voice (*phone*), by visible signals (*horatois semeiois*) and by trumpet (*salpinx*) (Arr. Tact. 27,1). The trumpet signal was the usual method (Xen. Hell. 5,1,9; Xen. An. 4,3,29–34), because the noise of battle often drowned out heralds' voices and clouds of dust hid standard-bearers' signals. A *syntagma/speira* ('cohort') of the Macedonian phalanx usually had one herald (*keryx, stratokeryx*), one standard-bearer (*semeiophoros*) and one trumpeter (*salpinktes*) (Ascl. 2,9; 6,3; Arr. Tact. 10,4), charged with communicating commands. Soldiers often marched to the accompaniment of flute players (*auletes*), who dictated the tempo of the soldiers' paces (Thuc. 5,70; Xen. Lac. pol. 13,7; → Music).

A.2. Interpreters (*hermeneus*)

Interpreters had an important job in an army, conducting negotiations with enemies who spoke other languages, holding conversations with the indigenous civilian populace, prisoners and defectors in order to obtain information or supplies, and conveying orders to non-native soldiers [15. 142–144]. For this reason, generals were usually accompanied by professional interpreters who knew specialist military terminology. Some rose into the elite of the army and gained military positions (Arr. An. 4,3,7).

A.3. Attendants (*thetikon* or *stratos skeuophorikos*)

Ever since the Archaic period, Greek hoplites were accompanied by servants (*skeuophoroi, hypaspistai, akolouthoi, therapontes* or *hyperetai*), who were usually → slaves (or *heilotes* in the case of Spartan hoplites). These attendants carried the army's equipment and supplies, and provided services to soldiers. Until the 5th century BC, campaigns were usually short, so these servants were adequately able to deal with soldiers' supplies. As warfare intensified from the 5th century BC onwards, baggage animals and carts were increasingly used, and these had to be organized by a leader as they followed the army (*archon*Sparta: Xen. Lac. pol. 13,4; *hegemon* in Hellenistic armies: Arr. Tact. 30,1). Baggage attendants generally carried tools and materials for building war machines or bridges, and only incidentally foodstuffs (mainly grain), because traders often came with the army train and offered goods for private sale, or else soldiers provided for their needs through plunder. These servants became too numerous and dangerous for the army's rations, so Philip II reduced their numbers to one servant per cavalryman or ten infantrymen (Frontin. Str. 4,1,6). The military treatises (Ascl. 2,9; 6,3; Arr. Tact. 10,4) report that the Hellenistic armies had one *hyperetes* ('servant') per *syntagma/speira* (the smallest independent unit of the army in the Macedonian system, approximately 256 soldiers), whose job was to bring what soldiers needed from the baggage train.

A.4. Medical services (*iatrikon*)

Homer mentions physicians (*iatroi*) caring for injured or sick soldiers. The first evidence for the recruitment of physicians to Greek armies dates from the 5th century BC (sources in [14]). The gradual professionalization of warfare made the deployment of physicians in the field indispensable.

A.5. Seers (*manteis*)

The Greeks attached great importance to seers, who used the observation of sacrifices or portents to interpret the will and sympathies of the gods, and in this way sought to foretell the outcomes of battles. Seers' prophecies could fundamentally affect the prosecution of a battle or even encourage planning for one. Generals were sometimes wont to manipulate prophecies to boost the fighting moral of their troops. Therefore, seers always accompanied an army.

A.6. TECHNICAL DEPARTMENT: ENGINEERS (*MĒCHANOPOIOI, ORGANOPOIOI*) AND ARTISANS (*CHEIROTECHNAI*)

The development of siegecraft demanded specialist engineers who could build and operate the needed siege and → artillery engines. Artillery pieces were also to a lesser extent used on the battlefield [10. 164–168]. Other engineers (*technitai, architektones*) travelled with an army to build bridges for river crossings or support the Hellenistic monarchs in constructing new military settlements. Besides engineers, it was also important for an army to have access to many artisans with different specialities, such as smiths, carpenters, tanners and stonemasons, whose services were needed for the construction and maintenance of machinery, bridges, weapons and fortifications. Xenophon (Lac. pol. 11,2) reports that the Spartans were among the first to employ craftsmen for their military campaigns.

A.7. ADMINISTRATIVE AND CLERICAL STAFF

Secretaries (*grammateis* or *oikonomoi*, and their assistants, *episkopoi* or *cheiristai*) were responsible for the bureaucracy of army and garrison administration, for example the cataloguing of recruits or maintaining records regarding supplies [5. 33, 79–81]. The armies of the Hellenistic kings also had staffs of scribes that included not only secretaries, but also historians, other scholars, and philosophers. Alexander the Great had a special corps of pace counters (*bematistai*), whose job was to measure distances and map the army's route in unknown lands (→ Maps). Their findings were of importance to ancient geography (e.g. Str. 11,8,9).

☞ Military service

BIBLIOGRAPHY
[1] J.K. ANDERSON, Military Theory and Practice in the Age of Xenophon, 1970   [2] D.W. ENGELS, Alexander the Great and the Logistics of the Macedonian Army, 1978   [3] P.R. FRANKE, Dolmetschen in hellenistischer Zeit, in: C.W. MÜLLER et al. (eds.), Zum Umgang mit fremden Sprachen in der griechisch-römischen Antike (Palingenesia 36), 1992, 85–96   [4] Y. GARLAN, Recherches de poliorcétique grecque, 1974   [5] M.B. HATZOPOULOS, L'organisation de l'armée macédonienne sous les Antigonides (Meletémata 30), 2001   [6] P. HUNT, Military Forces, in: P. SABIN et al. (eds.), The Cambridge History of Greek and Roman Warfare, vol. 1: Greece, the Hellenistic World and the Rise of Rome, 2007, 108–146   [7] P. KRENTZ, The Salpinx in Greek Warfare, in: V.D. HANSON (ed.), Hoplites. The Classical Greek Battle Experience, 1991, 110–120   [8] P. KRENTZ, War, in: P. SABIN et al. (eds.), The Cambridge History of Greek and Roman Warfare, vol. 1: Greece, the Hellenistic World and the Rise of Rome, 2007, 147–185   [9] J. KROMAYER / G. VEITH, Heerwesen und Kriegsführung der Griechen und Römer, 1928   [10] E.W. MARSDEN, Greek and Roman Artillery. Historical Development, 1969   [11] W.K. PRITCHETT, Provisioning, in: W.K. PRITCHETT, The Greek State at War, vol. 1, 1974, 30–52   [12] W.K. PRITCHETT, Sacrifice before Battle, in: W.K. PRITCHETT, The Greek State at War, vol. 1, 1974, 109–115   [13] C.F. SALAZAR, The Treatment of War Wounds in Graeco-Roman Antiquity, 2000   [14] E. SEMAMA, La médecine de guerre en Grèce ancienne, 2017   [15] C. WIOTTE-FRANZ, Hermeneus und Interpres. Zum Dolmetscherwesen in der Antike, 1997.

CHARALAMPOS I. CHRYSAFIS

B. ROMAN

B.1. Republic
B.2. Imperial period
B.3. Late Antiquity

The Roman army had soldiers with special expertise and abilities in all periods of its history. Admittedly, as is well known, the sources on the army of early Roman history are extremely sporadic. In fact, they are so unreliable that nothing can safely be said about the internal structure of the army in this phase. It nonetheless seems safe to assume that even at this early time, the warriors of Rome were already fighting with assorted weapons on foot and on horseback. This, along with the introduction of new weapon types and new tactics over the centuries, and the social and (in the case of the confederates and auxiliaries) ethnic associations with specific classes of weapons, meant that specialization in the mastery and use of weapons was already a feature of the Republican → army (→ Rank; → Cavalry; Weapons; → Infantry; → Auxiliaries; → Cavalry; → Camels). The shift to a standing army in the final years of the Republic and the switch to a professional army under Augustus were especially important for excelerating and solidifying this development. From this time onwards, Roman soldiers were to an increasing extent specialists in particular classes of weapons [11. 439–449].

B.1. REPUBLIC

Non-combatants with specialist skills served in the Roman army, at least from the latter part of the Monarchical period. They were registered in two special centuries as buglers (*cornicines*), trumpeters (*tubicines*) and unarmed artisans (*fabri*) (Liv. 1,43,3; 1,43,7; Dion. Hal. Ant. Rom. 4,17; 7,59; Cic. rep. 2,39). The *fabri* appear to have specialized in woodwork and metalwork (*fabri tignarii* and *fabri aerarii*). Nothing more can be ascertained from the sources, however, about the precise nature of their work, although Livy mentions that it involved siege engines. At an unknown date, the *fabri* came under the command of a *praefectus fabrum* [1]; [6. 1920]; [12]. It is no longer clear beyond doubt how long this organizational form endured, but by the Late Republican period, the *fabri* were certainly counted among the legion's regular combatants and were no longer separated into their own divisions (Caes. B Gall. 5,11,3).

Unarmed non-combatants took on many other duties for the army and for individual soldiers and officers during the Republican period. At first, however, many of them were not considered members of the army proper, but worked as slaves or private contractors on their own account. They included specialists in divination and field medicine (→ Medical corps). → Supplies were also to some extent in private hands. Before the army became professional, ordinary soldiers with relevant knowledge and expertise from their civilian experience were commissioned to provide many services. Because of this practice, which was typical of the army in the Republican period, it was initially unnecessary to train numerous individuals within the army's own → ranks to be specialists.

B.2. IMPERIAL PERIOD

B.2.1. Immunes
B.2.2. Administration
B.2.3. Artisans
B.2.4. Weapons, armaments and supplies
B.2.5. Medical services, cult and communication

The shift to a professional army in which men served twenty or more years without interruption led (especially in the legions) to the creation of increasing numbers of positions for soldiers with special technical, administrative or medical skills. People with suitable aptitudes were found through targeted recruitment, but suitable soldiers were also given training during their military service (Veg. Mil. 1,7; 2,19; AE 1942/43, 93; CIL VIII 18086).

B.2.1. IMMUNES
Specialists in these positions were termed *immunes* ('immune') [2. 3]. The privilege (*beneficium*: Paul. Fest. Gloss. lat. p. 30 L; cf. Veg. Mil. 2,7) of their *immunitas* ('immunity') related to exemption from the heaviest labour that formed part of the service of ordinary soldiers (*munifices*) (Dig. 50,6,7; Veg. Mil. 2,7; 2,19). *Immunitas* on its own, however, conferred neither higher rank nor better pay [8. 687]; [11. 382–386, 439–449]. A long (but incomplete) list of such *immunes* specialists dating from the second half of the 2nd century AD is found in a passage preserved in the *Digesta* and originating in a work by the Praetorian prefect and jurist P. Taruttienus Paternus (Dig. 50,6,7). Many other of these positions are recorded in epigraphic and papyrological sources [8. 687f.]; [11. 440f.]; [13. 31–41] (cf. fig. 1). Some *immunes* achieved promotion into the category of soldiers called *principales*, where they received one and a half times or double regular pay. Other than reading, writing and arithmetic, however, specialist knowledge played no part in this promotion [11. 439–449]. Positions for highly specialized individuals among the *principales* were mainly in the fields of bookkeeping, administration, accounting and to some extent medical services.

B.2.2. ADMINISTRATION
The sources show that the *immunes* fulfilled numerous different functions using their specialized knowledge. One large and particularly important group consisted of *immunes* who were able to read and write and master basic arithmetic. Because of these skills, according to Paternus, they took on administrative duties, mostly as secretaries and bookkeepers in the various offices of their units (e.g. *horreorum librarii, librarii depositorum, librarii caducorum*), and they also worked as teachers (*librarii quoque qui docere possint*) and assistants (e.g. *adiutores corniculariorum*): cf. Dig. 50,6,7; Veg. Mil. 2,7; AE 1983, 42; AE 2004, 1069; CIL III 885; 7684; 7688; 8120; CIL XIII 6133; ILS 2393; 2398; 2422a; 2423; 2427; 9076.

B.2.3. ARTISANS
According to Paternus, *immunes* with technical skills were put to work as specialist artisans (*artifices, fabri, optiones fabricae*). They worked as specialists in the *fabricae* (ChLA X 409), working with glass, bronze, lead, iron or stone (*specularii, aerarii, plumbarii, ferrarii, lapidarii*). During the Imperial period, soldier-*fabri* were assembled into groups for team tasks (CIL XIII 12214,29). *Fabri* also worked as carpenters aboard ships of the Imperial navy (CIL X 3418–3427). Some artisanal labour for the army was concentrated in *fabricae legionis* during the Imperial period, with soldiers (*milites*) and *immunes* of the legion working alongside auxiliaries (*cohortales*) and civilians (*pagani*), and with *fabri* (or *fabricienses*: RIB 156 = ILS 2429; AE 1982, 916) apparently also supervising other artisans as project foremen (P. Berlin 6765 = ChLA X 409; Tab. Vindol. 155, 160, 862; cf. Tab. Vindol. III App. 155). Still other *immunes* were temporarily assigned to do construction work, for example as roof shinglers (*scandularii*), ditch diggers (*ii qui fossam faciunt*), surveyors (*mensores*), levellers (*libratores*) and water inspectors (*aquilices*) (see fig. 1).

B.2.4. WEAPONS, ARMAMENTS AND SUPPLIES
Paternus mentions another group of *immunes* who were involved with the manufacture and repair of weapons and other armaments. They included makers of projectile weapons, bows, arrows, swords, catapults and chariots (*ballistarii, arcuarii, sagittarii, gladiatores = gladiarii, architecti, carpentarii*), trumpets and bugles (*tubarii, cornuarii*). The *immunes* also included lime burners (*qui*

valetudinarii) (Dig. 50,6,7; cf. also Tab. Vindol. 155; 156; ILS 2117; 2437; 2438); others worked as vets (*veterinarii*; cf. also *pequarii*: ILS 2431). Regarding the cult, Paternus mentions slaughterers of sacrificial animals (*victimarii*). Other specialists in religious cults and rites may have served among the *immunes*, particularly from the Severan period onwards ([3]; [9. 97]; anders: [14]). In communications, the herald (*praeco*) and trumpeters (*bucinator*) were *immunes*.

B.3. LATE ANTIQUITY

The dwindling of documentary evidence after AD 300 leaves little information available about the specialists in the Roman Army of Late Antiquity. Many of the armaments that would previously have been made in legions' own facilities were later manufactured in state *fabricae* [4]; [5. vol. 1, 670f.]. However, units' administrative and medical services continued to operate in the army of Late Antiquitiy (→ Rank C.) [7. 91]; [10].

☞ Legion; Military Service

BIBLIOGRAPHY

[1] B. DOBSON, The praefectus fabrum in the Early Principate, in: B. DOBSON / D.J. BREEZE, Roman Officers and Frontiers, 1993, 218–241 [2] A. VON DOMASZEWSKI, Die Rangordnung des römischen Heeres, 2nd, revised edition. Introduction, Corrections and Additions by B. Dobson, 1967 [3] R. HAENSCH, Pagane Priester des römischen Heeres im 3. Jahrhundert nach Christus, in: L. DE BLOIS et al. (eds.), The Impact of Imperial Rome on Religions, Ritual and Religious Life in the Roman Empire, 2006, 208–218 [4] S. JAMES, The fabricae. State Arms Factories of the Later Roman Empire, in: J. COULSTON (ed.), Proceedings of the Fourth Roman Military Equipment Conference, 1988, 257–331 [5] A.H.M. JONES, The Later Roman Empire, 284–602. A Social, Economic and Administrative Survey, 3 vols. and map vol., 1964 [6] E. KORNEMANN, Fabri, in: RE 6/2, 1909, 1918–1925 [7] Y. LE BOHEC, L'armée romaine sous le Bas-Empire, 2006 [8] J. NÉLIS-CLÉMENT, Non-Commissioned Officers, NCOs. Principate, in: Y. LE BOHEC (ed.), The Encyclopedia of the Roman Army, 2015, 687–691 [9] B. PALME, Corpus Papyrorum Raineri Archeducis Austriae, vol. 24: Griechische Texte, subvol. 17: Dokumente zu Verwaltung und Militär aus dem spätantiken Ägypten, 2002 [10] P. RANCE, Health, Wounds and Medicine in the Late Roman Army, in: L. BRICE (ed.), New Approaches to Greco-Roman Warfare, 2019, 173–185 [11] M.A. SPEIDEL, Heer und Herrschaft im Römischen Reich der Hohen Kaiserzeit, 2009 [12] K.E. WELCH, The Office of praefectus fabrum in the Late Republic, in: Chiron 25, 1995, 131–145 [13] G. WESCH-KLEIN, Soziale Aspekte des römischen Heerwesens in der Kaiserzeit, 1998 [14] E.L. WHEELER, Pullarii, Marsi, Haruspices, and Sacerdotes in the Roman Imperial Army, in: V.E. HIRSCHMANN et al. (eds.), A Roman Miscellany. Essays in Honour of Anthony R. Birley on His Seventieth Birthday, 2008, 185–201.

MICHAEL A. SPEIDEL

Fig. 1: Gravestone of the *structor* M. Iulius Maximus, soldier of the legio XI at Vindonissa (AD 70–101). Maximus, a specialist artisan, was one of the *immunes* of his legion, and was answerable to the *praefectus castrorum*, 'camp commander' (Veg. Mil. 2,11; Dig. 50,6,7). The relief beneath the inscription shows his most important pieces of work equipment: square and compasses (*CIL XIII* 5209).

calcum cocunt), woodcutters (*qui silvam infindunt*), woodchoppers (*qui carbonem caedunt*) and charcoal burners (*qui carbonem torrent*), hunters (*venatores*), butchers (*lani*) and grooms (*stratores*). Ships' carpeneters (*naupegi*) and steersmen (*gubernatores*) were also among the *immunes* aboard legions' vessels.

B.2.5. MEDICAL SERVICES, CULT AND COMMUNICATION

Immunes worked in field hospitals as medics (*medici*), orderlies (*capsarii*), nurses (*qui aegris praesto sunt*) and hospital administrators (*optio*

Standard

A. Introduction
B. Greek and Hellenistic world, 'enemies of Rome'
C. Roman world

A. INTRODUCTION

Tactical commands were communicated by voice and signal instruments, but their visual transmission required the use of standards, *signa* (Veg. Mil. 3,5,3–8; *signifer* – standard-bearers in general: Veg. Mil. 2,7,5). Soldiers were required to follow the *signa* (*aquilae, dracones, vexillae*: Veg. Mil. 3,5,8) and were not allowed to lose sight of them (*signa sequi*: Liv. 10,5,1; Veg. Mil. 2,22,5f.; 3,5,1; 3,5,10; movements on the battlefield were described in terms relating to the *signa*: *signa tollere* – 'raising' of the standards = march out; *signa ferre* = 'carrying' of the standards = march; *signa vertere* = turn, etc.; [5. 5f.]). There was a clear connection between the visual standards and the signal instruments, for the various soundings of the instruments indicated actions and movements: engage, halt, pursue – the standards followed the instruments (Veg. Mil. 2,22,1–4), and the soldiers followed the standards (→ Music). Josephus admired the exact movements of the battle lines, with the soldiers' gazes directed towards the standards (Jos. BI 3,102–108). Precise guidance depended on this sophisticated system of standards and signal instruments. The appearance of standards can be reconstructed from portrayals on public monuments (e.g. Trajan Column; cf. fig. 1) and funerary reliefs (cf. fig. 2a/b), the latter also providing information about those carrying them (inscriptions).

The best known type of standard was the *aquila*, the legionary eagle – symbol and 'emblem of the entire legion' (Veg. Mil. 2,6,2). The legion also had a *vexillum* ('flag') with the name of the unit (and the *centuriae*?: Veg. Mil. 2,13), and auxiliary units had regimental flags. Cavalry units of the legion carried *vexilla*, as did 'detachments' from the regiment (*vexillatio/-nes*) and army groups (Plut. *Crassus* 19,4–8; ILS 2343; *vexillum* of the general: Cass. Dio 40,18,3; Caes. B Gall. 2,20,1; Tac. Ann. 1,39,4). This was a standard pole with a cloth flag attached to a crossbeam, the colourful cloth being embroidered (with names, numbers, 'crests'). Standards (*signum/signa*) of subordinate units were used for tactical control. They consisted of a wooden shaft with metal and other decorative objects (tassels, ribbons) and a plaque to display the name of the unit or division (on a small *vexillum* or a metal plate on a horizontal wooden block). During the Republican period, the apex of the standard was a spear tip, but in the Imperial period, depictions of hands (right hand – for swearing the oath?) also served this function. It is not clear whether this latter type was the 'manipular standard'. There were differing numbers of *phalerae* ('medallions') on the shaft, and these were probably *dona*/distinctions won by the unit or its commander, like *coronae*, garlands/crowns (e.g. 'Wall Crowns'). The number and order of these 'decorations' contributed to the standards' individuality. The *imago*, the emperor's bust on the standard shaft, is a phenomenon of the professional army founded by Augus-

Fig. 1: Detail from the relief band of the Trajan Column (Scenes IV–V; Rome, AD 112/13; plaster cast, 1861). This depiction of Roman troops crossing the Danube during the Dacian Wars in the reign of Trajan (→ Wars of note C.) shows the two legionary units carrying different types of standards ('manipular standard', one *vexillum*, legionary eagle).

Fig. 2a/b: Funerary stele of Gnaeus Musius from Veleia, *aquilifer* of the *legio XIIII Gemina* (relief; found in Mainz). The inscription of the gravestone, which dates from the time of Tiberius (CIL XIII 6901), mentions the rank (*aquilifer*) and the legion. The full-body image of the *aedicula* stele shows a soldier in full gear standing with the legion's eagle standard. The shaft, curved handle, capital with the crowning eagle on a thunderbolt are clearly recognisable. The eagle's wings are spread upwards and entwined with a laurel wreath; an acorn can be seen in the bird's beak.

tus. The first attestation of the *draco* comes in the 2nd century AD: a 'dragon's head' was fixed to a shaft and a long, colourful tube of cloth was sewn on to it. The *dracones* replaced the standards of the *alae* ('auxiliary troops'). Standards were more than 'tactical media' – they were also reference points for tradition, symbols of identity closely bound up with soldiers' histories and destinies, and objects of an almost sacred character.

B. Greek and Hellenistic world, 'enemies of Rome'

Standards were widespread in Egypt and the Ancient Near East, but there is no evidence for them in the Classical Greek world or in the armies of Alexander the Great. Evidence for them in Hellenistic armies is slight (Liv. 33,10,8; 37,59,3). Signals were given through coloured standards (Pol. 2,66,10f.) and through military musicians (1 Macc 9,12). Roman influence may be possible in these cases (Pol. 18,28; 31,33). Many enemies of Rome had standards: the Celts, for example, carried boar standards (Caes. B Gall. 7,88; Tac. Hist. 4,62,2). Although there are indications that Germanic armies had standards (Plut. *Marius* 23; 27: Cimbri) that were religious in nature (Tac. Germ. 7; Amm. Marc. 31,5,8), there is nothing to indicate a tactical function. Even so, the terrified reactions of barbarians at seeing the glint of Roman standards – a commonplace of Roman literature (e.g. Amm. Marc. 18,2,17; 27,2,6) – cannot be explained in terms of religious awe. Tacitus (Tac. Ann. 1,61,4) mentions the mocking of the standards that were captured during the defeat of the Varian legions (Tac. Hist. 4,18,2; cf. Amm. Marc. 27,1,6).

C. Roman world

C.1. Roman Republic
C.2. Imperial period
C.3. Late Antiquity
C.4. Standards and regimental identity
C.5. Standards and army religion
C.6. Standards and omens

C.1. Roman Republic

Romulus was said to have given animal symbols (eagle, wolf, horse, boar, minotaur) to the first → legion as standards (Plin. HN 10,16), and bundles of hay as manipular standards (Ov. Fast. 3,115; 3,117f.). The army reforms initiated by Marius (→ Generals of note K.; late 2nd cent. BC: Plin HN 10,16) made the 'eagle' the chief standard of the legions: a shaft crowned by an eagle made of precious metal above a bolt of lightning. In the manipular era (4th cent. BC), each of the 30 maniples (= 2 *centuriae*) had a *signum*, 'standard' (Ov. Fast. 3,115). Pol. 6,24,6 mentions two standard-bearers per maniple, which suggests that the *centuriae* had their own. Later, when the 'cohort legion' took over (late 2nd/early 1st cents. BC; but see Liv. 25,39,1), each of the ten cohorts had a *signum* (or dual function of the first manipular standard in a cohort?). Opinions differ here. The *turmae* ('units') of the legionary cavalry had *vexilla* ('flags'). During times of peace, the standards and eagles were kept in the *aerarium populi Romani*, 'treasury of the Roman people' (Liv. 3,69,8; 4,22f.).

C.2. IMPERIAL PERIOD

The eagle (*aquila*) continued to serve as the standard for the legion and the focal point of regimental identity. It went ahead of the marching legion (Liv. 34,46,11; Tac. Hist. 2,89; Jos. BI 3,115–126; Cass. Dio 40,18), and in battle it was held at the front with the first cohort (Tac. Hist. 2,43; Veg. Mil. 2,6,2–4), whose senior *centurio*, the *primipilus*, took responsibility for it, defending and protecting it (Veg. Mil. 2,6,2; 2,8,1). The eagle was the symbol of the *primipilus* (Plin. HN 10,5; Artem. 2,20). *Primipili* would die to save their legion from losing the eagle, which would mean the end of the regiment (Tac. Hist. 3,22,4; but see Vell. Pat. 2,97; Suet. Vesp. 4; sacrificial death of *aquiliferi*: Caes. B Gall. 5,37,5; Flor. Epit. 2,30,29–31). The loss of a standard was a disgrace (Caes. B Gall. 2,25,1; Liv. 10,4,4; Frontin. Str. 2,8,8; Caes. B Gall. 4,25; dissolution of units/symbolic destruction of the *signa*: SHA Sept. Sev. 7,1; Amm. Marc. 25,1,8; honourable capitulation: departure with one's own standards – Tac. Hist. 3,63,1); recovery of a lost standard was always celebrated (Augustus/*signa recepta*: R. Gest. Div. Aug. 29: safekeeping in Temple of Mars Ultor; Cass. Dio 57,18; 60,8 and Tab. Siar. Frg. I 28,29). In extreme circumstances, the standards were gathered in one place and defended: *signa conferre in unum locum* (Caes. B Gall. 2,25,1). 'Leaving behind the standards' (e.g. *a signis discedere*: Caes. B Gall. 5,16,1), was tantamount to abandoning them and synonymous with desertion and breach of the army oath (*sacramentum militiae*). The eagle-bearer, the *aquilifer*, a *principalis* (junior officer), was positioned in the first cohort in the century of the *primipilus* (Veg. Mil. 2,6,2; CIL III 6178; 6180). The *imaginifer*, bearer of a separate standard bearing the *protome* (*imago*) of the emperor (Veg. Mil. 2,7,3), was one of the *principales*. According to Veg. Mil. 2,6,2, he was put with the first legionary cohort (but see CIL III 195). All types of units had 'bearers of the imperial image' (Veg. Mil. 2,7, e.g. *alae*: CIL VIII 9291 or *cohortes*: CIL XIII 7705), even those in Rome (e.g. CIL VI 218, *cohortes urbanae*), except the Praetorians. Smaller portrait medallions bearing the imperial image on *signa* were a decoration granted to all unit types before the Flavian period. After this, they were reserved for Praetorian standards, on which – since they were richly adorned with highly valuable decorations – *phalerae* ('medallions') with the emperor's image replaced the *imago*. Crests were also important to regimental identity, such as the standard animals (of which a legion might have several), which, like the eagles, were carried as heraldic animal standards (e.g. ram of the *legio I Minervia* in Scene 48 on the Trajan Column, Rome) or used as *protomai* on the shafts of standards. The unit's name banner completed their 'heraldic value' (e.g. CIL VII 495; RIB 2426.1). As for the tactical and administrative subdivisions of the legions, namely, the *centuriae* (60 or 59 after the 'reform of the 1st cohort' in the 1st century AD), we may assume that they had a *signum* carried by a *signifer* (but see Veg. Mil. 2,13: centuries with *vexilla*?). Since the division of legions into cohorts (10 in number) and maniples (29/30) continued in the Imperial period, their standards must be assumed to have continued to exist. Each of the *signa* of the six *centuriae* of a cohort and the highest-ranking centurion standard of one of the three maniples of a cohort may have had a 'double function' (or was there a special *vexillum* for the legionary cohort [16. 14f.], or was there a *vexillum* with a number or letter on the corresponding *signum*, as in the reverse image on RRC 365,1; 384,1; RIC 98?). We do not know how they may have differed from other standards (in height, colours, crowning features). There were probably about 67–68 standards in a legion of the Imperial period, and accordingly the same number of *signiferi* of *principalis* rank (*aquilifer, signifer, imaginifer, vexillarius*) along with possible understudies and 'standard-bearers in training' (*discens signiferum*: AE 1992, 1867a; CIL VIII 18086; *discens aquiliferum*: ILS 2344; *aquiliferi/imaginiferi*: SHA Aurelian. 31,7; CIL III 3256). Standard-bearers had special equipment (e.g. bearskins over helmets: Veg. Mil. 2,16,2), and they were 'selected' soldiers who were also entrusted with keeping the books and accounts of regiments and men (Pol. 6,24,6; Veg. Mil. 2,20,7; PSI 1063; weight of the standards: Hdn. 4,7,7) and with undertaking sensitive negotiations (*aquilifer* as 'spokesman' of the *legio IIII* at Cologne, AD 69: Tac. Hist. 1,56,2; positions of trust – *curator veteranorum*: ILS 2338, 2339; CIL VIII 217: *signifer ex suffragio*, i.e. at the request of the men). The 'standard systems' of the *auxilia* were based on those of the legions. The main standards of the *alae* and cohorts were a *vexillum* (e.g. fresco of Dura-Europus: *cohors XX Palmyrenorum* [12. 367–378]), and *imaginiferi* are also attested, with occasional indications of crest standards, that is, animal images. The *turmae* of the *alae* and the cohorts with cavalry elements, their *centuriae* and those of the infantry regiments carried *signa* with medallions (*phalerae*). The units in the city of Rome (Praetorians, urban cohorts, *vigiles*) also had *vexilla* for their regiment and *signa* for the centuries. At permanent camps, the standards were kept in the *sacellum* (also *aedes signorum*), an architecturally prominent room within the *principia* ('staff building'), and guards of the standards looked after them there.

C.3. LATE ANTIQUITY

Signa disappeared from the legions in the 3rd and 4th centuries AD, replaced by *vexilla* for the centuries and *dracones* for the cohorts (ILS 2805), although there were still eagles in the 4th century (Amm. Marc. 15,8,4; 16,12,12; 20,5,1). During the 3rd and 4th centuries, the emperors had a uniquely ornate *draco*, with purple tubing and a gilded pole set with precious stones (Amm. Marc. 16,10,7; 16,12,39). The *draco* was carried by the *draconarius*. A new type of imperial standard of the 4th century was the *labarum*, a *vexillum* with Christogram and other decorative elements that was carried and guarded by 50 men selected from the life guard for their strength, courage and piety (Euseb. VC 2,8,1f.). Constantine introduced an emperor standard with the image of the emperor and his sons (Euseb. VC 1,31,1f.). We may assume that the status accorded to the standards in 'Christian Late Antiquity' (e.g. Agath. 3,24,7) was a legacy of Pagan Antiquity, not least in the focus on the person of the emperor, expressed for instance in the oath to the standards, in which the Holy Trinity was invoked as witness (Veg. Mil. 2,5,3–5). Christianity now appropriated the terminology: the Cross became the *vexillum crucis* or *vexillum veritatis*, and Jesus himself, as general and emperor, became the *signifer*, who carried the Cross forward as a symbol of victory [7. 705–710].

C.4. STANDARDS AND REGIMENTAL IDENTITY

The anniversary of the award of the eagle or the traditional date of the bestowal of the *signa* to other unit types were important in the life of the regiments ([2. 28–44]; auxiliaries, e.g. *cohors I Gallica*: ILS 9130, 9131). The name plate on the pole of the *signum* (silver plaquette of the *cohors VII Raetorum*, Niederbieber; CIL XIII 7765; Praetorian *signa*: *cohors III Praetoria* – funerary relief of M. Pompeius Asper in Rome; ILS 2662; Veg. Mil. 2,13) guaranteed the 'individuality' of a unit's standard. There is evidence for regimental names or numbers on the flags of *vexilla*, which could serve as standards for an entire unit, even a legion ([3] on the *leg. II Augusta*). Individuality was also guaranteed by the decorations for a unit's military achievements fitted to the pole. Unsurprisingly, concepts of *honos* and *virtus legionis* ('honour' and 'valour') are particularly prominent in the context of the 'cult of the standards' (*victoria legionis*: CIL III 11082; *virtus legionis*: CIL III 7591; *pietas legionis*: CIL XIII 6752; *honos legionis*: CIL XIII 6749). Renown was based on success or accomplishments in battle (Tac. Hist. 2,11,1; 2,32,2; 2,66,1); traditions were long upheld and instrumentalized in the interests of 'fighting spirit' (Tac. Hist. 3,24,1–3). Venerable regiments had 'renown affixed to their standards', while new ones had to earn theirs (Tac. Hist. 2,43,1; 5,16,3). The 'guardian spirits' of entire regiments were closely associated with the standards: the *genius legionis* with the eagle (AE 1935, 98; CIL XIII 6690), and for the *auxilia* the *genius cohortis* with the *signa* (RIB 1262; 1263). Crest animals were very important to regimental identity, as their use on the 'legionary coins' of the 3rd century (reigns/usurpations of Gallienus, Victorinus and Carausius), which combine the animal symbol with the name of the legion, clearly shows (e.g. RIC V2 468 nos. 57–59 – *legio II Augusta*/ Capricorn) [12. 551–564].

C.5. STANDARDS AND ARMY RELIGION

Standards played a unique role in the everyday and ritual lives of units. The *rosaliae signorum* made a 'festival of the rose-bedecked standards' part of the religious calendar followed by all regiments (P. Dura 54). The standards were a perennial presence at all rituals: the oath of service was sworn before them, sacrifices were made in their presence, and they were → paraded (care/ anointing of the standards: Plin. HN 13,4). These were symbols of the collective identity of every Roman regiment [2. 28–44]; [12. 257–294]. The notion that the 'religion of the camps amounted to the worship of the *signa*', which were preferred to all the gods, is an exaggeration on the part of Christian and Jewish authors (Tert. Apol. 16,8; Min. Fel. 29,6f.) who were offended by the idolatry and image worship [12. 281–293] that took place in front of images of emperors and gods as part of the religion of the army (such images were sometimes attached to the *signa* themselves as *imagines/protomai*, often made of precious metals). The ruler cult stood alongside veneration of the pantheon as the essence of army religion and an important factor reinforcing ties of loyalty between the emperor and the army. The *imago*, the 'portable image' of the emperor on standards, and perhaps also the emperor statues in the *principia* of permanent camps, also played an important role in ceremonies of the army calendar, effectively functioning as substitutes for the physical presence of the emperor (Artem. 4,31; Tac. Ann. 15,29; cf. also in mutinies: Tac. Hist. 1,55,2f.; 3,12,1f.). The annual loyalty oath and oath to the standards, as acts of loyalty, were sworn before them (and the *signa*), in other words, in the symbolic presence of the emperor and on the *dies imperii* (annual holiday marking the emperor's accession). The standards were likewise present at the end of a soldier's career, for the ceremonial cancellation of the oath of service (*honesta missio/sacramentum solvere:* PSI 9,1026; Dig. 49,18,2). The birthday of the standards, the date of their presentation by the emperor (Tac. ann. 1,42,3), was celebrated, as evidenced in dedications *ob diem natalem aquilae* ('on the occasion of the birthday of the eagle': ILS 2293; AE 1967, 229, 230), *honori aquilae legionis* ('for the honour of the eagle of the legion': CIL XIII 6679; 6690; [2. 38–42]), *ob natalem aprunculorum* ('on the occasion of the birthday of the boar') and *ob natalem signorum* ('on the occasion of the birthday of the *signa*') for auxiliary units (ILS 9127, 9129, 9130). Auxiliaries had individual *signa*, such as the 'boar standards' (CIL XIII 8094: standard decorated with the skull of a bull). The *primipilus* is often associated with the 'veneration' of the legionary eagle and the standard (AE 1935, 98; CIL XIII 6679). This is confirmed by Vegetius (Veg. Mil. 2,6,2; 2,8,1), who mentions the *primipilus'* 'sacred duties': to watch over the legionary eagle and emperor images (AE 1991, 1572: *aquilifer* in the century of the *primuspilus*; CIL III 6178 Col. I l. 20: *imaginifer* of the first cohort). Consecrations by the *primipili* were an expression of the unit's esprit de corps.

C.6. STANDARDS AND OMENS

Standards had a handle at the centre of the pole. The spike at the base of the pole was rammed into the earth when the regiment made camp on campaign. Standards offered omens concerning the outcome of a military operation (Liv. 4,47). If, on departure, they 'would not come out of the ground', this was a bad omen (Cannae: Liv. 22,3,12; Crassus: Val. Max. 1,6,11; Varus: Cass. Dio 56,24,4). It was also portentous when standards could not be decorated (Suet. Claud. 13; Plut. *Sulla* 7), when they caught fire ('burning standards' – Tac. Ann. 12,64), when bees or spiders congregated around them (Cass. Dio 41,14,1; Val. Max. 1,6,12), and when the wind tore the *vexillum* away (Cass. Dio 40,18). It was a good omen, on the other hand, when eagles flew ahead of the army and standards, or 'hovered around' the standards on the march out (Tac. Ann. 2,17,2; Suet. Vit. 9).

☞ Legion; Military Service

BIBLIOGRAPHY

[1] C.-G. ALEXANDRESCU, Blasmusiker und Standartenträger im Römischen Heer. Untersuchungen zur Benennung, Funktion und Ikonographie, 2010 [2] H. ANKERSDORFER, Studien zur Religion des römischen Heeres von Augustus bis Diokletian, 1973 (Diss. Konstanz) [3] D.J. BREEZE, The Flag of Legion II Augusta on the Bridgeness Distance Slab, in: D.J. BREEZE / B. DOBSON, Roman Officers and Frontiers (MAVORS 10), 1993, 78–87 [4] J.C.N. COULSTON, The 'Draco' Standard, in: Journal of Roman Military Equipment Studies 2, 1991, 101–114 [5] A. VON DOMASZEWSKI, Die Fahnen im römischen Heere, in: Abhandlungen des Archäologisch-Epigraphischen Seminars der Universität Wien, Heft 5, 1885, 1–80 (again in: A. von Domaszewski, Aufsätze zur römischen Heeresgeschichte, 1972, 1–80) [6] H. REICHERT, Feldzeichen, in: RGA 8, 1994, 307–326 [7] W. SESTON, Feldzeichen, in: RAC 7, 1969, 689–711 [8] M.P. SPEIDEL, Eagle-Bearer and Trumpeters. The Eagle-Standard and Trumpets of the Roman Legion, Illustrated by Three Tombstones Recently Found at Byzantion, in: BJ 176, 1976, 123–163 (again in: M.P. Speidel, Roman Army Studies, vol. 1, 1984, 3–43) [9] J. STÄCKER, Princeps und miles. Studien zum Bindungs- und Nahverhältnis von Kaiser und Soldat im 1. und 2. Jahrhundert n.Chr., 2003 [10] O. STOLL, Der Adler im 'Käfig'. Zu einer Aquilifer-Grabstele aus Apamea in Syrien, in: Archäologisches Korrespondenzblatt 21, 1991, 535–538 (again in: O. Stoll, Römisches Heer und Gesellschaft. Gesammelte Beiträge 1991–1999, 2001, 13–46) [11] O. STOLL, Excubatio ad signa. Fahnenwache, militärische Symbolik und Kulturgeschichte, 1995 [12] O. STOLL, Zwischen Integration und Abgrenzung. Die Religion des Römischen Heeres im Nahen Osten. Studien zum Verhältnis zwischen Armee und Zivilbevölkerung im römischen Syrien und den Nachbarprovinzen, 2001 [13] O. STOLL, The Religions of the Armies, in: P. ERDKAMP (ed.), A Companion to the Roman Army, 2007, 451–476 [14] K.M. TÖPFER, Signa militaria. Die römischen Feldzeichen in der Republik und im Prinzipat, 2011 [15] H. UBL, Waffen und Uniform des römischen Heeres der Prinzipatsepoche nach den Grabreliefs Noricums und Pannoniens, 1969 (Diss. Wien) (reprinted and edited by P. Scherrer, Austria Antiqua 3, 2013) [16] W. ZWIKKER, Bemerkungen zu den römischen Heeresfahnen in der älteren Kaiserzeit, in: BRGK 27, 1937, 7–22.

OLIVER STOLL

State and army

A. Greek
B. Roman Republic
C. Imperial period

A. GREEK

A.1. Military service
A.2. Training
A.3. Waging war and supreme command
A.4. Costs and finances
A.5. Rituals
A.6. Separation of the civil and military spheres
A.7. Hellenistic period

Established polities with central institutions and cults, reasonably well defined territories and an overall sense of cohesion only emerged gradually in Archaic Greece. One of the most important tasks facing an emerging *polis* was managing internal conflicts and guarding against attacks from outside (e.g. Hom. Il. 18,509–540 (*polis* in war on the Shield of Achilles); Od. 2,6ff., esp. 30 (assembly at Ithaca); Hes. Op. 38f. (judges as incipient state authorities)). To a large extent, the early Greek state was a defensive community, and its structures were not yet highly developed. Warfare was in the hands of those who could afford to arm themselves, and the wealthiest and most assertive became the leaders. Battles were fought for land, → booty and renown, and most of these local wars were short-lived. The growth of *poleis* and the occurrence of more intense conflicts such as the war waged by Sparta on Messenia led to the emergence of → phalanx tactics ([16. 222–230]; [20]; rather differently [21]; [22]) and an increasing institutionalization of war. Compulsory military service for free farmers who were able to arm themselves as hoplites and thus fight in the phalanx probably developed at an early date. As a result, this social group developed more political rights than poorer farmers and the landless. The traditional elite whose status was based on wealth and lineage (*basileis*) took command in war. In Sparta, this generally meant the kings, whereas in Athens it meant the leaders of the *naukraria* (organization of warships) who were appointed by the nobility, or the *archon polemarchos* ('war leader'). The state's monopoly on the use of force took hold slowly. Individual nobles were still recruiting volunteers for private military campaigns in the later Archaic period – examples include the Spartiate Dorieus (Hdt. 5,44–48) and the Athenians Miltiades the Elder and Younger (Hdt. 6,34–41). Little is known, however, of the actual institutions dealing with war and the military.

During the Classical period, the dimensions, frequency and intensity of warfare changed in the aftermath of the Persian Wars, and communities resorted more often to military means. The character of warfare became heavily dependent on the political order and the societal structure of the *polis* concerned. Several issues were crucial to their waging of war, and these will be discussed below.

A.1. Military service

In most *poleis*, military service was in principle compulsory for all citizens, but its actual performance depended on the social status of the individual [21]; [22]; [5]. Only the very wealthy could afford to keep a horse, so only they were mobilized to the cavalry. Athens supported its cavalrymen with a subsidy for maintaining a horse, although this was subject to strict oversight (Aristot. Ath. pol. 49,1f.; in general [2]). Wealthy citizens also served in the phalanx, and the lowest class – at Athens the *thetes* – served either as light infantrymen or oarsmen. Private ownership of weapons was customary for citizens (e.g. Alc. 140V; Thuc. 8,69; Aen. Tact. 4,3; 10,7; 11,8; 17,2; cf. Aristot. pol. 1268a17ff.; 1289b31), but after the Battle of Chaeronea (338 BC), if not before, the Athenian state issued shields and spears (*aspis kai dory*) to the *ephebes*, young men aged 18–20 registered for military service (Aristot. Ath. pol. 42,4; weapons were also distributed in the city imagined in Aen. Tact.: 16,3, cf. 3,5). Oligarchies were able to limit the ownership of weapons to the dominant group ([21. 62]; [6]; Aristot. pol. 1297b2ff. envisages linking weapon ownership with participation in politics).

In any case, warfare and defence remained a key obligation upon citizens throughout the Classical period. The structuring of the hoplite armies (e.g. at Athens by *phylai*, 'clans', and in the Boeotian League by *poleis*) reflected the civil structures of the citizenry and emphasized their close association with the military. → Mercenaries grew in number during the 4th century, but they remained a subsidiary phenomenon until the Hellenistic period. Beginning with the phase of Athenian expansion and the proliferation of wars in Greece, it was no longer just specific groups who were directly involved in hostilities, but almost all citizens were involved, whether as cavalrymen, hoplites, light infantrymen or oarsmen. More so than during the Archaic period, warfare was now every man's concern.

A.2. Training

Physical → training and practice with weapons, however, long remained the responsibility of the individual. Except in Sparta, where the *agoge* (military training) and *krypteia* ('secret service') to be completed by every Spartiate were intended to develop fitness, polities left it up to the individual citizen to train himself. Only towards the end of the Classical period was the *ephebeia*, in which young citizens received military training, systematized by the Athenian *polis* (Aristot. Ath. pol. 42,1–5), with most 18- to 20-year-old men probably participating in it [3. 26ff.]. Only with an abundance of caution can it be suggested that similar developments took place in other *poleis*, but it is known, at least, that towards the end of the Classical period, elite units of the best-trained soldiers were being educated and schooled in several communities, which entrusted to them the most perilous tasks in battle [15. Bd. 2, 208–231].

A.3. Waging war and supreme command

In democratic Athens, the body that decided on the declaration and financing of war was the popular assembly. It formulated the commission for the generals in command and decided on the use of resources. In accordance with this key role, information about the military situation had to be presented as every general meeting (Aristot. Ath.

pol. 43,4; cf. Aristoph. Ach. 19–27). From about 500 BC on, ten *strategoi* ('commanders') were responsible for warfare. It has not been explained beyond doubt exactly how they were elected [4]; [15. vol. 2, 34–58]. The abandonment of selection by lot, which was the customary method for most other official appointments in democracies, in favour of an election was intended to ensure that the office of *strategos* was taken by men with reasonably suitable qualities (Ps.-Xen. Ath. pol. 1,3). In → Sparta, the kings remained the supreme commanders by tradition. However, the increasing geographical dispersal of theatres of war required the appointment of other leading Spartiates as generals (*nauarches* or *harmostes*), chosen by the popular assembly. In oligarchies, the supreme body – a council or some citizens' committee – made the decision on war or peace.

Military leaders enjoyed considerable tactical freedom in the field, but they were subject to close monitoring by the home authorities. Such authority was generally exercised in Sparta by the *ephores* ('overseers'), at Athens by the *boule* ('council'), *ekklesia* ('assembly') and the courts, and in Boeotia by the federal council (Hell. Oxyrh. 19,3f.). It was therefore quite unusual for generals to embark on schemes of their own devising [15. vol. 2, 34–58; cf. 59–116]; [4]; [7]. In Athens, an unsuccessful general ran the risk of prosecution at the people's court [15. vol. 2, 4–33]; [8]. The trials of Epaminondas (→ Generals of note F.) for extending his command without authority (Nep. Epam. 7f.; App. Syr. 41,212–218; Plut. *Pelopidas* 24f.; Ael. VH 13,42) reveal possible tensions between operational and political leadership.

It was a considerable disturbance to the political order and the military constitution when a tyranny became established in a *polis*. Tyrants sought to keep citizens as powerless as possible unless they had the citizens' support, and they often resorted to external forces [1. vol. 1]; [10].

A.4. Costs and finances

Even if citizen-soldiers provided their own equipment and had to bring their own provisions at least for the first phase of a campaign, warfare still presented a *polis* with an economic burden. Only after a certain length of time did the state intervene to underwrite → pay, provisions and other supplies (according to Aen. Tact. 13,1–4, mercenaries were ultimately employed and maintained by the *polis*). To be sure, the state or its generals bore the responsibility for army logistics, and this sometimes became a considerable problem for the public purse. If a campaign was successful, some of the expense would be offset by spoils, or by the tribute that Athens required its confederates to pay in the 5th century.

There was need for sophisticated planning, organization and financing, especially when it came to developing the → fleet. Establishing maritime power required ships, harbours, wharves, rigging, oars and other equipment, as well as enough specialist personnel. Athens provided the infrastructure and hulls at public expense (cf. for Chios Aen. Tact. 11,3), but relied on private wealth for equipping them. Private sponsors, called trierarchs, were expected to provide for a ship's readiness for battle through a competitive process. A special institutional structure for developing and expanding the fleet emerged in Athens, which consumed resources but also provided employment (on the → costs of war for Athens [14. 91–113]). This, however, led to an increase in public functions and institutional complexity, and hence an expansion of the state [19. 96ff.]. This tendency was amplified by the establishment of the Athenian maritime empire, which gave rise to numerous administrative, fiscal and military systems, and thereby increased the profile of the *polis* and its political instruments [17]; [18].

A.5. Rituals

War involved shared rituals that were meant to secure the protection, consent or aid of the gods or generally to bring a conflict to a desired end (survey: [9]). Many communities had rituals or sacrifices for the march out or the beginning of a battle, to be performed by authorities or generals as representatives of the *polis* [15. vol. 1, 109–115]; [13]. A dignified and identity-shaping end to a year of war at Athens was achieved through public burials of the fallen, with each burial accompanied by a eulogy (*epitaphios*) given by a leading politician. These speeches exaggerated the achievements of the deceased and linked them with the accomplishments of part generations [11]; [12], thereby suggesting the continuity of the *polis* and demonstrating the meaning of conflict and death. Burials on the battlefield or near the theatre of war were also frequent [15. vol. 4, 94–259, esp. 249ff.]. Dedicating weapons or other spoils to deities were a way of giving thanks for the gods' help in war and guaranteeing their future goodwill [15. vol. 3, 240–276].

A.6. Separation of the civil and military spheres

The close interconnection between the citizens, the political order, military service and warfare prevented Greek polities of the Classical period from developing a distinct military sphere or military caste. Until the Hellenistic period, military service remained a key duty for citizens of a *polis*, who were fulfilling military and political roles simultaneously. During this period, however, warfare began to fragment. On the one hand, smaller and medium-sized *poleis* with their militaries – even if dependent on a major power – continued to exist and wage war among themselves. On the other, the powerful monarchies that emerged from the empire of Alexander created new forms and dimensions of warfare. In the former case, many continuities are evident in the military system. In the latter, profound changes took place in the relationship between the state and the army.

A.7. Hellenistic period

In the personalized monarchy of Macedonia, the king, being the symbol of the community, was also supreme commander of its armed forces. He determined the political direction and established the aims of war – but in order to achieve these aims, he relied on his own charisma and the vacillating will of the nobility and the people to follow him. During the second half of the 4th century BC, the intensive military activity of Philip II and Alexander the Great effectively transformed the Macedonian peasant army into a professional, standing army.

This process continued throughout the Hellenistic period. The rulers of the great kingdoms relied on professional armies tasked with securing the survival of the dynasty in the face of external and internal threats. Because (with the partial exception of Egypt) the Hellenistic kingdoms consisted of conquered conglomerates of highly diverse territories, it was impossible to cultivate a political base rooted in citizenship and tradition. Instead, the state was embodied in the person of the monarch along with his bureaucracy, his officer corps and his armies. The organization of military order and the responsibility for waging war lay in their hands. For the most part, the armies of the Seleucids and Ptolemies consisted of professional soldiers who were initially recruited from the remnants of the Macedonian and Greek forces that went to the eastern Mediterranean with Alexander and the Diadochi, and who were later recruited from other groups. The control of the army and the loyalty of its members were the essential and indispensable support for royal power. At the same time, the subjects of these monarchies went from being participants – as they had been in the *poleis* – to merely being ruled.

Bibliography

[1] H. Berve, Die Tyrannis bei den Griechen, 2 vols., 1967 [2] G.R. Bugh, The Horsemen of Athens, 1988 [3] L. Burckhardt, Bürger und Soldaten, 1996 [4] P. Ducrey, Armée et pouvoir dans la Grèce antique, d'Agamemnon à Alexandre, in: A. Chaniotis / P. Ducrey, Army and Power in the Ancient World, 2002, 51–60 [5] V. Gabrielsen, The Impact of Armed Forces on Gorvernment and Politics in Archaic and Classical Greek Poleis, in: A. Chaniotis / P. Ducrey (eds.), Army and Power in the Ancient World, 2002, 83–98 [6] S.-G. Gröschel, Waffenbesitz und Waffeneinsatz bei den Griechen, 1989 [7] D. Hamel, Athenian Generals. Military Authority in the Classical Period, 1998 [8] M.H. Hansen, Eisangelia. The Sovereignty of the People's Court in Athens in the Fourth Century B.C. and the Impeachment of Generals and Politicians, 1975 [9] A. Jacquemin, Guerre et religion dans le monde grec (490–322 av. J.-C.), 2000 [10] L. de Libero, Die archaische Tyrannis, 1996 [11] N. Loraux, L'invention d'Athènes, 1981 (^{2}1993) [12] P. Low, Commemorating of the War Dead in Classical Athens. Remembering Defeat and Victory, in: D.M. Pritchard (ed.), War, Democracy and Culture in Classical Athens, 2010, 341–358 [13] R. Parker, Sacrifice and Battle, in: H. van Wees (ed.), War and Violence in Ancient Greece, 2000, 299–314 [14] D.M. Pritchard, Public Spending and Democracy in Classical Athens, 2015 [15] W.K. Pritchett, The Greek State at War, 5 vols., 1971–1991 [16] K. Raaflaub, Homer und die Geschichte des 8. Jahrhunderts v.Chr., in: J. Latacz (ed.), Zweihundert Jahre Homer-Forschung (Colloquium Rauricum 2), 1991, 205–256 [17] K. Raaflaub, Learning from the Enemy. Athenian and Persian 'Instruments of Empire', in: J. Ma et al. (eds.), Interpreting the Athenian Empire, 2009, 89–124 [18] W. Schuller, Die Herrschaft der Athener im ersten Attischen Seebund, 1974 [19] R. Schulz, Feldherren, Krieger und Strategen, 2012 [20] A. Schwarz, Reinstating the Hoplite. Arms, Armour, and Phalanx Fighting in Archaic and Classical Greece, 2009 [21] H. van Wees, Tyrants, Oligarchs and Citizen Militias, in: A. Chaniotis / P. Ducrey (eds.), Army and Power in the Ancient World, 2002, 61–82 [22] H. van Wees, Greek Warfare. Myths and Realities, 2004.

Leonhard Burckhardt

B. Roman Republic

B.1. The problem
B.2. Warfare and statehood
B.3. Citizens and army
B.4. Relationship between the military and civilian spheres

B.1. The problem

'Every political constitution is originally a constitution of war, of the army.' The Prussian historian Otto Hintze (1861–1940) suggested that this generalization should be a 'verified law of the comparative history of peoples'. He outlined an evolutionary model that had long been accepted in the study of ancient history, based on the expansion of Rome [10. 7f.]. The citizen militia organized according to land ownership reflected the nature of the city-state. The conquests in Italy were accompanied by a 'systematic military colonization', while the war against Hannibal saw 'the old principle of general mobilization put into full, actual practice'. Expansion beyond Italy led to the replacement of the citizen militia by a standing army, and generals with lengthy commands had to sent far away into distant provinces. The close relationship between these commanders and their troops undermined the republican constitution. Ultimately, 'in Rome the standing army created the monarch, whereas elsewhere the monarch created the standing army'.

B.2. Warfare and statehood

This model has been modified by classical historians (see in general [17]). In general, the process of state formation in the Roman Empire as the objectification, centralization and institutionalization of public action mainly grew out of warfare (overview: [9]). In the early phase of the Republic (5th century BC), groups devoted to individuals such the 'Companions of Mars' of Valesios Poplios, and also contingents put together by clans for campaigns of plunder (Fabii: Liv. 2,48–50), were still an important factor [13. 15f.]. It is uncertain, however, whether such operations took place alongside an already developed public military organization (as [16] argues) or whether public military efforts only took shape after they overcame the unstable decentralized enterprises. Whatever the case may be, the specific conferral of *imperium* ('command authority') on a commander, the allocation of a geographical zone of responsibility (*provincia*) by the senate, and the practice of having the fetial priests officially demand compensation from an enemy (*rerum repetitio*) prior to the launch of hostilities can all be seen as factors that brought war under state control [8. 33–45]; [12]. So, too, can the reduction in the number of regular holders of *imperium* to three (two consuls, one praetor) in 367 BC, in place of what had at first been an unspecified number of 'leaders' (*praitores*), and later colleges of differing sizes (*tribuni militum consulari potestate*, 444–367 BC). Also part of the same process were the introduction (at about the same date) of army pay (*stipendium*) and (around 400 BC) a tax (*tributum*) imposed on citizens, along with the monetization that set in around the time of the Pyrrhic War (280–275), with regular issues of silver coins by the *res publica*.

The configuration of human resources by the *res publica* was geared towards military needs and Roman expansion. Citizens were classified according to their capacities in war based on the *census*. In the beginning, the popular and military assemblies were virtually identical. During military service, a citizen was removed from the private legal sphere, including the *patria potestas* ('father's authority'), and was subject to the *disciplina militaris* alone. The complex structure of the Roman political system in Italy, which gave the *hegemon* ('leader') a military power far superior to all opponents, was also a product of the warfare of the 5th–3rd centuries. The disposition of the *provincia* as a district of rule that brings the empire with it followed the logic of military conquest, pacification and further expansion. The overwhelming majority of the incomes and expenditures of the *res publica* arose in the military sphere. Wars such as the Second Punic War brought considerable financial burdens, but the successful expansion in Italy greatly alleviated social conflicts between landowners and landless citizens (foundation of colonies on conquered land). After 167 BC, thanks to the huge accumulation of booty from the war with Perseus (Third Macedonian War, 171–168 BC) and regular inflows from the provinces, citizens no longer had to pay any *tributum* (Plin. HN 33,56).

The protracted wars (with many defeats) against the Latins, Samnites and King Pyrrhus between 340 and 272, saw the formation of the nobility as a political elite (summary [14]). These were men who after their military service (ten campaigns: Pol. 6,19) took public office and strove to attain the consulship. Having done so, they would wage war more or less constantly or else seek other ways to expand Rome's domains. It is true that the senate, that experienced body of former officials, was increasingly deciding important questions related to military activity (appointment to a *provincia*; granting of funds; orders for levies; accompaniment in the field by senators on staff; extension of command through prorogation; see Pol. 6,15; [11. vol. 3.2, 1071–1110]). Still, commanders tended – under the pressure of aristocratic competition for → honour and prestige, and given that their regular terms of office were just one year – to take full advantage of their opportunities for making decisions on the spot, and sometimes they took considerable risks (on the First Punic War see e.g. [2]).

B.3. Citizens and army

The Roman army of the Republican period was based on military service by all citizens aged 17–46. The exceedingly complex levy process ([3. 152f.]; seminal [5. 391–415]) sought to reconcile demands of quality and fairness. The mass of citizen soldiers came from the countryside, as recruitment from the city of Rome more or less dried up after the 2nd century BC [6. 140f., 171–174]. This posed a potential political problem, since the world of of the legionaries was no longer identical to that of the citizens who voted at the popular assemblies (structured according to *tribus*) on the motions put before them. C. Marius was the first holder of *imperium* to recruit propertyless citizens as legionaries on a large scale (Sall. Iug. 86,2). This, however, did not make the army 'professional' – levies of conscripts continued into the Imperial period. Marius' (→ Generals of note K.) professionalization of warfare [15. 227–244] did, however, mean that reactivated → veterans (*evocati*) came to be known as the best soldiers, and many of them became alienated from republican modalities of obedience and civilian life [7]. It was not inevitable that soldiers' expectations of a comfortable life after leaving service – and hence their loyalties – would become increasingly focused on their commanders; rather, this was a development that was greatly advanced by the ignorance of Senate politics (see below, B.4.).

B.4. Relationship between the military and civilian spheres

The relationship between the military and civilian spheres was defined by separations and interconnections. Within the sphere of the *militiae*, namely, wherever and as soon as war was waged, the commander had by virtue of his *imperium* a nearly unlimited authority of decision-making with the aim of enforcing Rome's will with maximum force. By contrast, the sphere of the *domi* ('at home'), which always included the city of Rome, but in times of peace also included the citizens' lands outside it, was strictly demilitarized. The *imperium* of the consuls and praetors probably did not apply here, and there was no military presence in Roman towns and cities, where no weapons were generally carried. The popular assembly (*comitia centuriata*), which was structured in imitation of military units (*centuriae*) and which elected holders of the *imperium* and decided questions of war and peace, met in the Field of Mars outside the *pomerium* (see [1]). When a general wished to present his victorious army in a → triumph at Rome, he needed a formal permit of exception to allow him to exercise his *imperium* in the city for this one day and occasion. In light of this, the capture of Rome by Roman troops, as Sulla was the first to dare to do in 88 BC, was a shocking blow to the established order. Thus, while the political centre was for a long time largely untouched by the influence of the military sphere, the separation did not apply in reverse. For one thing, the senate had a considerable say in the waging of war (see above, B.2.), and from about 150 BC on, it came increasingly under the influence of domestic political conflicts. The senate lost its monopoly over the civilian control of military action in the *res publica* when individual aristocrats laid claim to what had hitherto been the rather irrelevant right of the popular assembly to make decisions on all matters. By this means, they bestowed important command positions (sometimes for several years), bypassing the senate and sometimes in spite of its resistance (P. Cornelius Scipio Aemilianus in 147 and 134; Marius in 107; Cn. Pompeius in 67; C. Iulius Caesar in 59).

The partial distance between the city of Rome and military activity contributed, from the 2nd century BC onwards, to the 'military dequalification' of the nobility [4. 152–154, 266–270]. Since most aristocrats were no longer competing with their political rivals by seeking distinction on the battlefield, military expertise was becoming limited to a small number of actors who, in the 1st century, were conducting their campaigns essentially beyond the control of the senate, and were thus able to bind the loyalty of their troops to themselves personally (see above, B.3.). By doing so, they gained access to power that ultimately upended the 'rules of the game' of a political world that was tied to the civilian sphere (→ civil wars of 88, 83/82, 49–45, 43/42 and 31/30).

☞ Society and army; Army; Military law

Bibliography
[1] M. Andreussi, Pomerium, in: LTUR 4, 1999, 96–105 [2] B. Bleckmann, Die römische Nobilität im Ersten Punischen Krieg. Untersuchungen zur aristokratischen Konkurrenz in der römischen Republik, 2002 [3] J. Bleicken, Die Verfassung der römischen Republik, ^{7}1995 [4] W. Blösel, Die römische Republik. Forum und Expansion, 2015 [5] P. Brunt, Italian Manpower 225 B.C.–14 A.D., 1971 [6] P. Brunt, Die Beziehungen zwischen dem Heer und dem Land im Zeitalter der römischen Revolution, in: H. Schneider (ed.), Zur Sozial- und Wirtschaftsgeschichte der späten römischen Republik, 1976, 124–174 [7] W. Dahlheim, Die Armee eines Weltreiches. Der römische Soldat und sein Verhältnis zu Staat und Gesellschaft, in: Klio 74, 1992, 197–220 [8] F. Drogula, Commanders and Command in the Roman Republic and Early Empire, 2015 [9] P. Erdkamp, War and State Formation in the Roman Republic, in: P. Erdkamp (ed.), A Companion to the Roman Army, 2007, 96–113 [10] O. Hintze, Staatsverfassung und Heeresverfassung, 1906 [11] T. Mommsen, Römisches Staatsrecht, 3 vols., ^{3}1887–1888 [12] L. Rawlings, Condottieri and Clansmen, in: K. Hopwood (ed.), Organised Crime in Antiquity, 1999, 97–127 [13] J. Rich, Warfare and the Army in Early Rome, in: P. Erdkamp (ed.), A Companion to the Roman Army, 2007, 7–23 [14] N. Rosenstein, Military Command, Political Power, and the Republican Elite, in: P. Erdkamp (ed.), A Companion to the Roman Army, 2007, 132–147 [15] R. Schulz, Feldherren, Krieger und Strategen. Krieg in der Antike von Achill bis Attila, 2012 [16] D. Timpe, Das Kriegsmonopol des römischen Staates, in: W. Eder (ed.), Staat und Staatlichkeit in der frühen römischen Republik, 1990, 368–387 [17] U. Walter, Politische Ordnung in der römischen Republik, 2017

Uwe Walter

C. Imperial period

C.1. Costs and benefits of the armies
C.2. Army strength, soldiers and citizens
C.3. Emperor, army and authority

C.1. Costs and benefits of the armies

The armies of Rome were an extremely important component of the Roman Empire. Its rulers generally began their communications to the senate with the words, 'The army and I are in good health' (Cass. Dio 69,14,3). Tacitus similarly emphasized the importance of Rome's various armies in a well-known passage in which he declared that it was possible 'to be made emperor elsewhere than in Rome' (Tac. Hist. 1,4). The status of Rome's legions and auxiliaries is also evident from the high percentage of expenditure on military matters – an estimated three quarters of all imperial revenues [9]. To cover these costs, the senate imposed structural taxes. If the funds for particular campaigns were not sufficient, special taxes could be collected, with most of the burden falling on provincials. Marcus Aurelius was said to have financed a war by putting up imperial furniture for public auction (SHA Aur. 17,4). The decline in tax revenues in the later empire caused problems. A law of AD 444 explicitly stated that the current tax base was not adequate to maintain an army of sufficient size (Novellae Valentiniani 3,10) [14].

The armies, however, were not only a cost. They also generated capital, because they functioned as a well organized reservoir of labour. They took responsibility for major infrastructure projects, contributed to production in quarries, and supported civilian construction [16]; [24]. The impact of the military on everyday life was enormous. Late in the 2nd century, armies were stationed permanently in nineteen provinces. In frontier regions, these units brought peace and stability. Soldiers were available to help with major construction projects and local administration. At the same time, many sources indicate that soldiers also made demands on residents of the empire, often with threats of violence [23].

Soldiers were not the only source of violence. Reports of banditry occur with great regularity throughout the history of the Roman Empire [13]. Robber bands sometimes joined up to form gangs of several hundred men with such good organization that they were able to foment disorder throughout the empire – in the case of the notorious bandit Bulla Felix in the reign of Septimius Severus, even in the immediate hinterland of Rome itself (Cass. Dio 77,10). Roman law permitted the use of a weapon in self-defence (*telum*; Cod. Iust. 3,27,1), although elsewhere it stated that 'absolutely no one is granted the right to use a weapon' (Cod. Iust 11,47(46),1). This legal restriction was probably lifted in AD 440. The law concerned listed a broad spectrum of weapon types. The sale of weapons to 'barbarians' (i.e. non-Romans), however, was strictly forbidden (Cod. Iust. 4,41,2). Bearing arms within the city of Rome (and later Constantinople) was subject to the strictest conditions. The Roman state was concerned to maintain a kind of monopoly on the use of force for its military, but without disarming its subjects entirely [5].

C.2. ARMY STRENGTH, SOLDIERS AND CITIZENS

The number of Roman soldiers fluctuated greatly over time. The total number of men in the → legions, the → auxiliaries and the Praetorian Guard was about 250,000 in the reign of Augustus, about 380,000 under Hadrian and about 450,000 by the early 3rd century, shrinking again to roughly 300,000 later that century [8]. The strength of the army seems to have remained more or less constant through the 4th and 5th centuries, although Late Antique sources, such as Agathias, Zosimus and the *Notitia Dignitatum*, suggest a total of about 600,000 soldiers (Jones [18] proposes a higher number, Elton [12] a smaller). These are significant tallies. However, it must be remembered that only a fraction of the 50–80 million inhabitants of the Roman Empire served in the military. This created a dynamic quite different from the earlier phases of Roman history, when citizen soldiers formed the nucleus of the state [1]; [23. 474–477].

'Soldier' and 'citizen' had ceased to be synonymous long before Augustus. A distinction between legionaries and auxiliaries was maintained for soldiers throughout the Imperial period. Legionaries had to be Roman citizens, while auxiliaries only earned citizenship after serving long years in the Roman military. The legionaries had a certain status, and often a close bond with their legion, the prestige of which was measured by its success in the field [20]. Members of the auxiliary units received bronze diplomas when discharged, as proof of their new legal status as Roman citizens. The first known diplomas of this kind date from the reign of Claudius. Unsurprisingly, all trace of them disappears after 212, when the *Constitutio Antoniniana* conferred Roman citizenship on all free inhabitants of the empire. Still, these diplomas are an important source of information (→ Military diploma) [11]. Auxiliary units often possessed a certain ethnic identity, sometimes even drawing strength from this if their people were regarded as warlike and ready to fight [22].

At all events, the huge number of citizenship awards meant that, alongside the armies' roles in construction projects and administration, soldiers were actively contributing to the spread of Roman values and the Latin language. Legionaries and auxiliaries alike were relatively well paid (→ Pay), although pay scales differed markedly [25]. Conscription was expanded in the empire's late phase. Furthermore, recruits from outside the empire began playing an ever more important role, especially once Germanic and Sarmatian ethnic groups were granted permission to settle on Roman territory in return for their military support (*foederati*, → Alliances). Some units subsequently adopted foreign names and customs. By the late 4th century, about 25% of officers appear to have had 'barbarian' names [12].

C.3. Emperor, army and authority

Given the enormous number of soldiers, maintaining troop → discipline was an important aspect of Roman authority. The supreme commander was the emperor, whose relationship with his armed forces was politically vital throughout the history of the Roman Empire [6]; [2]. Many Roman emperors were experienced generals. Rulers without military experience, however, also had to portray themselves as skilled soldiers and show themselves capable of defending the *pax Romana*. In the 3rd century, as the Roman Empire came under sustained pressure, military competence became the sole criterion for ascending the imperial throne – particularly in the case of the 'soldier-emperors' in the second half of that century [17]. Ever since the Late Republican period, the pivotal role of the legions in taking and consolidating power had been a fixture of Roman politics. Establishing a standing army with a clearly defined code of military conduct (*disciplina Augusti*) further reinforced the bond between soldiers and their commanders. Those bonds were cemented with the soldiers' oath to the emperor, regular *donativa* (monetary gifts) and various rituals.

Discontented soldiers, however, were readily incited to → mutiny against certain emperors, especially if they had served under a competent general for a long period of time. The revolt of Vindex and Galba against Nero in AD 68, for instance, marked the end of the Julio-Claudian Dynasty. Similarly Nerva, confronted with Trajan's control over the legions that were stationed near the Apennine Peninsula, found himself in AD 97 compelled to adopt him and install him as his heir [10]. The more pressure the empire faced, the greater the army's significance for political power. During the 4th and 5th centuries, however, it was no longer essential for emperors to demonstrate their personal qualities as generals, not least because a separation had taken place between the civilian and military spheres, which also had the effect of raising the standards for professional commanders. Nevertheless, it was primarily his history of military successes that led Julian to be proclaimed *augustus* in AD 360. At all periods, Roman emperors either had to be victorious generals or else they had to give the appearance of being so. The portrait of Victoria widely seen on coins and monuments in Italy and the provinces attests to the unwavering importance of this aspect of authority [19].

The emperor was the official supreme commander, and thus the recipient of all honorific titles and grants of triumphs. In practical reality, the legions and auxiliary units were led by a variety of commanders. Intense discussion still surrounds the question of just how professional these officers were, especially prior to the separation of administrative and military powers introduced in the late 3rd century. Military commands formed part of the *cursus honorum* ('course of honours', i.e. the sequential order of public offices), which implies that new officers might have brought with them a primarily civilian education. For actual campaigns, however, it seems that commanders with more military experience were selected [3]; [7]. Occasionally, officers who had risen from the ranks were commissioned, but one could only guarantee to find long-term military expertise in the lower ranks, up to that of *centurio*. It seems plausible that junior officers such as these, with their greater military experience, were the ones who largely determined what soldiers did on a daily basis. This practice was further formalized from the 3rd century onwards. Systematic warfare and the importance of military logistics (e.g. the drastic requisitioning of food, goods and services) meant that the imperial government required new aptitudes and expertise. Military personnel had these to offer, which opened their path to more senior positions. As a result, a range of military duties were taken away from civilian senators and given to the *equites* (members of the equestrian order) in the army, who had relevant practical experience and came to represent a new, military middle structure, anticipating the split between civilian and military commands among the senior leadership of the next generation [4]; [15].

The growing influence of soldiers in various spheres of state activity – from the choice of emperor to authority over much Roman territory – has led some to detect a 'systematic militarization of government' [21. 448]. From this perspective, the later Roman Empire could be characterized more as a Dominate than a Principate, with a military bureaucracy having pushed out the old elites. The 3rd and 4th centuries have been called a period of 'appalling turmoil', in which the theory of an elected emperor governing his diverse subjects with goodwill was replaced by a governmental practice in which ambitious generals with no real ties to the state seized control [21]; [26]. From this perspective, the final replacement of Roman rule in the Western Empire of the 5th century by generals such as Odoacer and Theoderic was a result of this militarization of the Roman state. However, this is an exaggeration. From the outset, the Roman armies had been an essential component of the state, and throughout the Imperial period they remained highly present, both in their actions and in how they were presented. Over time, change did occur in the extent to which soldiers' central position in state affairs was openly visible. The composition of the armies also shifted. These changes reflected developments in Roman society. The army and the state were closely intertwined.

☞ Empire, B. Roman

BIBLIOGRAPHY

[1] G. ALFÖLDY, Das Heer in der Sozialstruktur des Römischen Kaiserreiches, in: G. ALFÖLDY et al. (eds.), Kaiser, Heer und Gesellschaft in der Römischen Kaiserzeit. Gedenkschrift für Eric Birley, 2000, 33–58 [2] A.R. BIRLEY, Making Emperors. Imperial Instrument or Independent Force?, in: P. ERDKAMP (ed.), A Companion to the Roman Army, 2007, 379–394 [3] E. BIRLEY, Senators in the Emperors' Service, in: Proceedings of the British Academy 39, 1953, 197–214 [4] L. DE BLOIS, Roman Jurists and the Crisis of the Third Century AD in the Roman Empire, in: L. DE BLOIS (ed.), Administration, Prosopography and Appointment Policies in the Roman Empire, 2001, 136–153 [5] P.A. BRUNT, Did Imperial Rome Disarm Her Subjects?, in: Phoenix 29, 1975, 260–270 [6] J.B. CAMPBELL, The Emperor and the Roman Army, 31 BC–AD 235, 1984 [7] J.B. CAMPBELL, Teach Yourself how to Be a General, in: JRS 77, 1987, 13–29 [8] J.B. CAMPBELL, The Army, in: CAH 12, ²2005, 110–130 [9] R. DUNCAN-JONES, Money and Government in the Roman Empire, 1994 [10] W. ECK, An Emperor Is Made. Senatorial Politics and Trajan's Adoption by Nerva in 97, in: G. CLARK / T. RAJAK (eds.), Philosophy and Power in the Graeco-Roman World, 2002, 211–227 [11] W. ECK / H. WOLFF (eds.), Heer und Integrationspolitik. Die römischen Militärdiplome als historische Quelle, 1986 [12] H. ELTON, Warfare in Roman Europe, AD 350–425, 1996 [13] T. GRÜNEWALD, Bandits in the Roman Empire. Myth and Reality, 2004 [14] P. HEATHER, The Fall of the Roman Empire. A New History of Rome and the Barbarians, 2005 [15] O.J. HEKSTER, Rome and Its Empire, AD 193–284, 2008 [16] P. HERZ, Finances and Costs of the Roman Army, in: P. ERDKAMP (ed.), A Companion to the Roman Army, 2007, 306–322 [17] K.-P. JOHNE, Das Kaisertum und die Herrscherwechsel, in: K.-P. JOHNE (ed.), Die Zeit der Soldatenkaiser. Krise und Transformation des Römischen Reiches im 3. Jahrhundert n.Chr. (235–284), vol. 1, 2008, 583–632 [18] A.H.M. JONES, The Later Roman Empire, 284–602. A Social, Economic and Administrative Survey, 3 vols., 1964 [19] R. KOUSSER, Conquest and Desire. Roman Victoria in Public and Provincial Sculpture, in: S. DILLON / K.E. WELCH (eds.), Representations of War in Ancient Rome, 2006, 218–243 [20] Y. LE BOHEC / C. WOLFF (eds.), Les légions de Rome sous le Haut-Empire. Actes du Congrès de Lyon (17–19 septembre 1998), 2 vols., 2000 [21] M.I. ROSTOVTZEFF, The Social and Economic History of the Roman Empire, 2 vols., ²1957 [22] N. ROYMANS, Ethnic Identity and Imperial Power. The Batavians in the Early Roman Empire, 2004 [23] M.A. SPEIDEL, Soldaten und Zivilisten im römischen Reich. Zu modernen Konstruktionen antiker Verhältnisse, in: M.A. SPEIDEL, Heer und Herrschaft im Römischen Reich der Hohen Kaiserzeit, 2009, 473–500 [24] M.A. SPEIDEL, Herrschaft durch Vorsorge und Beweglichkeit. Zu den Infrastrukturanlagen des kaiserzeitlichen römischen Heeres im Reichsinneren, in: A. KOLB (ed.), Infrastruktur und Herrschaftsorganisation im Imperium Romanum, 2014, 80–99 [25] M.A. SPEIDEL, Roman Army Pay Scales Revisited. Responses and Answers, in: M. REDDÉ (ed.), De l'or pour les braves! Soldes, armées et circulation monétaire dans le monde romain, 2014, 53–62 [26] F.W. WALBANK, The Awful Revolution. The Decline of the Roman Empire in the West, 1969.

OLIVIER HEKSTER

Strategy

A. General remarks
B. War/campaign
C. Grand strategy

A. GENERAL REMARKS

A.1. Elements of strategy
A.2. Setting strategies
A.3. Intelligence

Etymologically the word 'strategy' is based on the Greek root *strat-*, from which derive the terms for a military campaign, an army, and the duties of a general (*strategos*). The French *stratégie* was coined by Joly de Maizeroy (*Théorie de la guerre*, 1777) – inspired by the *Strategikon* of Pseudo-Maurice (539–602) – which he employed essentially as a synonym for the French expression used at that time, *projet de campagne*. The modern sense of 'strategy' (nearly synonymous with 'plan') is represented in Greek as *boule*, *epibole*, *prothesis* and *prolepsis*, and in Latin as *consilium* or *ratio belli* [9. 217]. Strategies on land or water may be offensive or defensive (Syrianus Magister, de re strategica 4,15–17 Dennis; cf. Onas. pr. 8; Frontin. Str. 1 pr. 4). Strategy is a skill (*techne/ars*), not a science, for luck and the unforeseen (or, to Clausewitz: *Friktion*) can thwart even the best plans. Often not openly referred to as such, strategy emerges from behaviour. This 'strategy' is not found in a document, but in the actions of states and their generals when implementing plans or dealing with unexpected situations [7. xi].

Strategy is a form of state polity. Clausewitz' understanding of war as the continuance of politics by other means is a Greek concept (Pl. Prot. 322b–c; Aristot. Eth. Nic. 1094a26–b11). Strategy seeks to enforce a state's military objectives. First, however, it is necessary to establish the manner of warfare (Frontin. Str. 1,3; App. Ib. 376). Complexity and expense need to be proportionate to the aims. All those waging war seek to win, but → victory is a means, not an end in itself, because military success can lead to unexpected political, economic and social consequences and even cause further wars. In reality, neither victory in a major battle nor taking captive the enemy leader necessarily breaks the opponent's spirit. The key to power and to the enemy's will of resistance, Clausewitz' 'centre of gravity' (*Schwerpunkt*), may lie elsewhere (cf. e.g. Thuc. 3,13,5f.; 6,91,7). Wars rarely go as planned, either militarily or with regard to interstate politics. Poor or failing strategies do not necessarily indicate lack of strategic concepts or practices.

A.1. ELEMENTS OF STRATEGY
Strategic factors include geography (e.g. the proximity of the belligerents, topography of the theatre of operations, routes of access and retreat, supply options), types of belligerent (states, alliances, non-state actors; land power/sea power; national character; personalities of leaders), symmetry/asymmetry of forces (level of cultural/technological development, strength), resources (human potential, finances, raw materials), allies (number, reliability, resources, positions relative to enemy), war aims (e.g. remedying wrongs, defending or conquering territories, demonstrating military superiority, access to raw materials, suppressing a revolt, prevention, genocide motivated by cultural, racial or religious factors) and, not least, unforeseen circumstances.

Also influencing strategy are psychological and cultural factors, which are not always well considered either rationally or in terms of preparation and detailed information-gathering. Fear and a perception of threat (whether real or imagined) can generate enmities. States may cultivate an image of their power as a strategy to deter potential rivals or intimidate smaller states. In practice, appearance can surpass reality (Thuc. 6,11,4). Punitive expeditions into the territory of bandits (a common Roman practice) aimed to create psychological deterrence for the future. Similarly, the Roman custom of massacring every living thing in a stormed city (Pol. 10,15,4f.) and of rejecting negotiations and capitulations the moment the battering ram touched the wall (Caes. B Gall. 2,32,1; cf. Sall. Iug. 91,7) was intended to discourage opposition in other places. Such 'rules', which were not set in stone, exerted psychological pressure (→ Terror). The ancient law of war left the fate of any conquered city (including its property and its inhabitants) to the whim of the victor, which was subject to the influence of political and strategic considerations. Julius Caesar's (→ Generals of note C.) policy of *clementia* ('clemency') during the civil war with Pompey (49–45 BC; → Generals of note N.) also contained an element of strategy.

Culture dictates how war is seen and waged, and how its goals are determined. War amounts to normative rather than unchecked violence. Intercultural conflicts can differ from extracultural conflicts in terms of their 'rules' and levels of violence. The often misunderstood words of the Persian Mardonius (Hdt. 7,9b,1f.) compared limited Greek warfare with the unlimited war aims of a non-Greek imperial power. In a similar way, the struggle for dominance and renown among the successors of Alexander, although it was hardly without bloodshed, pursued only limited aims (Plut. *Demetrius* 5,3; 6,2; Just. Epit. 15,1,7–9). The Romans distinguished between wars over control of the empire and wars for survival in the struggle against 'barbarians' (Cic. Off. 1,38: a Stoic idea?). The *limes* ('boundaries') of the Roman Empire could be regarded as a kind of moral frontier that defined behaviour inside and outside Roman territory [1].

Strategy takes place on various levels of military activity. In ascending order of its extent in space and time, it concerns the battle, the campaign, the war and the grand strategy (see below, C.). The boundaries between adjacent categories here are fluid: tactics may blur into battle strategy. Strategy for a campaign may be identical to that for a war if operations are limited to a single theatre or battle. The same principle applies on other levels. Surprise and subterfuge may either be strategic or tactical. The Greek verb *phygomachein* could mean to refuse to form a flank in battle or to feign tactical withdrawal, but it could also denote the process of exhausting an enemy over time either by staying close without engaging (Fabius Maximus against Hannibal) or by luring an enemy invader deeper into home territory (e.g. the Scythians against Darius I). Campaign, war and grand strategy may also extend beyond purely military considerations and into the sphere of diplomacy, for example in the occupation of strategic locations, the acquisition of allies or the creation of diversions (Liv. 35,18,8).

Sometimes a dichotomy is suggested [2] between a 'strategy of defeat' and a 'strategy of exhaustion' with regard to campaign and war strategies, although neither is exclusively offensive or defensive. In the first case, the most common type of traditional strategy, the goal of a campaign may be a decisive battle. Yet, even a battle won does not necessarily mean the end of the war. The victor must know how to make military and/or political use of a victory with the aim of achieving the state's military objectives. Hannibal and Pompey were criticized for not having capitalized on their victories (→ Battle). A 'strategy of exhaustion' seeks by the avoidance of battles or by repeated skirmishing to exhaust the enemy psychologically and/or materially, thereby achieving the enemy's abandonment of immediate operations or the entire war.

A.2. SETTING STRATEGIES
The state determines all forms of strategy, except in a battle, where the general sets the positions and orders for his troops. In monarchies, the

ruler (king, emperor) decides the strategy, sometimes with the support of advisors (cf. Onas. 3). In non-monarchical states, annual magistrates and legislative or consultative committees decide strategy, especially for a war and its grand strategy. Usually, the state's general instructions for a campaign could be adapted to unforseen circumstances. In the 5th century BC, Athenian strategy was publicly debated in the popular assembly, but more detailed private consultations were reserved for the *boule* ('Council') and the committee of ten *strategoi* ('commanders'). Campaign strategies were sometimes very specific. An edict on the Sicilian Expedition (415 BC) preserved in fragments may have ordered the *strategoi* to keep to their orders and ignore opportunities for raids in pursuit of booty elsewhere on their route (IG I^3 93 fr. g.). In Rome in the Middle Republican period, the senate, many of whose members had previously held military commands as consuls or praetors, discussed strategies of war, grand strategy and even campaign strategies. The consuls for the year 216 BC, Terentius Varro and Aemilius Paullus, were instructed to seek a decisive battle with Hannibal (Pol. 3,107,6f.; 3,108,1f.). During the Third Macedonian War (171–168 BC), before Aemilius Paullus took command in 168 BC, the senate tried to regulate the details of the campaigns against Perseus (Liv. 44,22,8). Wars far away in the provinces and extended military commands weakened the senate's control over strategies in the era of unlimited imperialism. This was a factor in the fall of the Republic. Beginning under Augustus, the governors of the imperial provinces served as *legati Augusti* ('legates of the emperor'), with specific *mandata* ('mandates') for their military commands.

A.3. INTELLIGENCE

Despite a degree of public debate regarding strategies, there was an appreciation of the value of secrecy in respect of details. Frontinus devoted the first two chapters of his *Strategemata* (1,1f.) to disguising one's plans while discovering the plans of the enemy. Tacticians stressed the importance of keeping campaign plans secure (Onas. 10,22–24), and of conducting intelligence work during a military operation (Veg. Mil. 3,6,8–10). However, reconnaissance in the field, which had not been a regular part of Greek campaigns before the 4th century BC, was not consistently practiced even later. It remained at the discretion of the general – or at his lack of discretion. The same applied to Roman military → reconnaissance. Obtaining information for wars and campaigns depended on spies, traitors, merchants, the local populace and reports from provincial governors. Such information-gathering sometimes relied on chance, and some states and rulers paid more attention to it than others.

It would be anachronistic, however, to dismiss the ancients' reconnaissance simply because they lacked a central intelligence authority.

Not all reconnaissance is accurate, and even good intelligence needs to be put into practice. Before the catastrophe in the Teutoburg Forest (AD 9; → Battles of note, J.), P. Quinctilius Varus ignored warnings concerning Arminius (Cass. Dio 56,19,2f.; Vell. Pat. 2,118,4). The available sources are not complete. Historians sometimes knew of secret diplomacy but did not report it (e.g. Pol. 29,5,1–3). Cassius Dio (53,19,2–6) lamented the difficulty of obtaining information about Rome's external relations from the reign of Augustus onwards. Surprise – and not necessarily due to a failure of intelligence – was easier to achieve in a battle than at the level of an invasion, because concentrating a state's forces took time, which allowed word to spread. Responding to an unexpected invasion was challenging even if advance warning was given. The Syracusans, for instance, knew that the Athenians were on their way in 415 BC. At the end of the reign of Antoninus Pius in AD 161, a Parthian attack on Syria surprised the Romans even though it had been foreseen.

B. WAR/CAMPAIGN

A brief survey such as this can highlight only a few aspects of ancient strategies, not least because, besides purely military practices, they also included → diplomacy, → alliances and foreign relations. In a war formally declared between two *poleis*, traditional Greek land strategy (up to 500 BC) expected an outcome decided by a single encounter between hoplite forces, a direct collision on an open field without manoeuvres. If either side refused battle, it could be provoked by invasion or the destruction of crops. The aims of war were limited to rectifying wrongs. There was no thought of conquering the opposing city, especially since Greek siegecraft (mainly involving blockades) was not yet developed. To destroy a Greek city was considered 'barbaric'. Limited capacity for supplying an army ruled out campaigns that ranged far over time and space. Given the Greek 'rules' in force at this period, there was no need for strategy. Greek strategic thinking was born with the Persian attack (480–479 BC), when an invasion by a foreign power forced the Greeks to establish a coalition of *poleis* to defend their homeland on land and at sea against a non-Greek assailant that was intent on conquest.

Strategy developed as war aims widened, military action became more geographically widespread, warring parties diversified (alliances, empires, coalitions – although wars between individual city-states certainly continued to occur), resources necessary to warfare increased (raw materials, financial requirements, strength of forces), officers and soldiers became professionalized (use of mercenaries), and technological demands grew. The conflicts between the Spartan Peloponnesian League and the Athenian maritime empire (431–404 BC) – to this day the cardinal example of war between a land power and a sea power – exemplified the changes in Greek warfare and heralded further changes to come. At first, neither belligerent acknowledged the strength of the other. Poor strategic decisions, failed plans, disunity in command, unreliable allies, political unrest at home and chance occurrences all extended the hostilities. Inspired in part by Themistocles' concepts of sea power, Pericles threw out the traditional practices of Greek warfare [8]. His strategy formed the basis for what Delbrück described as the 'strategy of exhaustion'. Trusting in Athens' superior sea power and greater wealth, he abandoned the defence of Attica, refused a decisive battle with Sparta, and relied for supplies on naval operations and raids along the coast of the Peloponnese. He hoped to exhaust the Spartans' resources and will to fight. The repeated ravaging of Attica by Sparta in the 4th century led Athens to develop an interest in defending its territory by building long walls and frontier fortifications (the latter were not a new idea) and by threatening invaders with cavalry and light infantry – topics of Xenophon's *Hipparchikos* and Aeneas Tacticus' → military literature.

→ Supplying an invading army was often fraught with difficulty. Invaders took for granted that they would be able to feed themselves in enemy territory through plunder or access to local markets. It was sometimes possible to establish full-fledged supply lines of storehouses. Rivers offered quicker and more reliable transport options than wagon trains, which were plagued by raids and ambushes (cf. Tac. Ann. 2,5,3). However, refusing to engage in battle, combined with strategic retreat and a scorched-earth policy, hindered the enemy's ability to supply itself. There is abundant evidence that this approach reduced the attackers' supply of food and forced them to fan out, which made it possible to ambush the dispersed groups (Hdt. 4,120f.; Arr. An. 1,12,8f.; 2,43; 3,28,8; Pol. 18,3,3; Caes. B Gall. 7,14; Sextus Iulius Africanus, *Kestoi* 1,2,13–16; Amm. Marc. 18,7,3; Syrianus Magister, *de re strategica* 33,35–39). Starving the enemy was a principle of strategic doctrine (Caes. B Gall. 7,17,1f.; Frontin. Str. 4,7,1; Veg. Mil. 3,3,1; 26,4).

The Romans attempted the strategy of starvation against the Goths (Amm. Marc. 31,7,2; 31,7,6; 31,8,1; 31,11,5; Eun. fr. 44,1 Blockley; Zos. 4,23,6) and Isaurians (Amm. Marc. 14,2,13; 27,9,6). Even without the scorched-earth aspect, it was possible to use time rather than space to exhaust an invader – as the Scythians did with Darius I. The Parthians and early Sassanids often permitted invaders to reach the environs of Ctesiphon – knowing that trying to storm the city while supplying the army would exhaust the Romans. During Julian's retreat from Ctesiphon, Sapor II implemented scorched earth to increase the Romans' supply difficulties (Amm. Marc. 24,7,4–8; 25,2,1f.; 25,7,4). The Germanic tribes used their terrain tactically by withdrawing into forests and marshes to escape Roman pursuers [5]. Domitian reacted by trying to alter the shape of the border (Frontin. Str. 1,3,10). From an attacker's perspective, a scorched-earth practice (which also included plunder) was part of a process for thinning defensive resources. Motives varied: to force battle (App. Ib. 380; Sall. Iug. 54,5f.), to break the enemy's will in a war of conquest (Tac. Agr. 30,4f.; Sextus Iulius Africanus, *Kestoi* 2,2f.), and to punish the enemy for past raids.

By 400 BC at the latest, the Greeks were drawing a distinction between tactics (army organization, fighting techniques, manoeuvres on the battlefield) and strategy (overall command, supervisory authority on the battlefield and beyond, → General; → Military literature). Neither the Greeks nor the Romans distinguished among the various levels of strategy (*strategika*), so their theories do not explicitly work with modern categories, although their existence is attested. Theory, whether descriptive or prescriptive, often lagged behind practice. War existed long before attempts were made to set down its principles in theory. Still, the lack of treatises on strategy (in the modern sense) by tacticians obscures their actual ideas and practices. The Athenians exaggerated their victory at Marathon (→ Generals of note, F.), presenting it as the defeat of Persian hordes. Persian strategy was thus reduced to numerical advantage (cf. Hdt. 1,161,1). The doctrine of stratagems, as summarized by Frontinus, Polyaenus and Vegetius (→ Military literature), emphasized deception, betrayal and surprise in both strategy and tactics. Pseudo-Xenophon preached the advantages of sea power (Ps.-Xen. Ath. pol. 2,1–6) [7]; [11. 526–528]. Catalogues of strategic options, including the use of alliances, appeared in rhetorical training manuals (Aristot. Rhet. 1359a–1360a; Anaximen. Rhet. Alex. 1424b–1425b; cf. Xen. Mem. 3,5f.; Cic. Leg. 3,41). Thucydides (e.g. 2,13,2) reduced the field of strategy to intelligence and money. Polybius highlighted the need for intelligence, numbers and resources. A Roman view (Liv. 9,17,3) emphasized the number and valour of soldiers, the talent of the general – and good luck.

Along with collections of stratagems that encouraged imitation of examples from the past, history itself offered paradigms of strategy. In 49 BC, Pompey found in Themistocles and Pericles two opposing alternatives: relinquish the city to fight elsewhere, or stay and defend it (Cic. Att.

7,11,3; 10,8,4; cf. Plut. *Pompeius* 63,1). Agathocles' march into North Africa (309–307 BC) was the model for the Roman campaigns against Carthage, led by Regulus (256–255 BC) and Scipio Africanus (204–202). The liberation of Messene by Epaminondas (369 BC) broke Spartan power and its rule over much of the Peloponnese. Hannibal's invasion of Italy similarly aimed to destroy Rome's alliance with the Italic confederates (*socii*).

All these examples illustrate the principle that 'the best defence is a good offense', in other words, that one can neutralize an attack at home by taking the war to the attacker's territory or opening a second front on the enemy's flank or rear. In the 190s, when war loomed in the east between Rome and the Seleucids, Hannibal urged Antiochus III to provide him with funds for an attack on Italy. On the eve of his third war with Rome (70s BC), Mithridates VI of Pontus negotiated with Sertorius in Spain, and he later considered sending the Bastarnae down the Danube as his allies to attack Italy from the north. Later, rumour spread of Decebalus' attempt during the First Dacian War (101–102) to induce the Parthian Pacorus II to attack the Roman Empire from the east (Plin. Ep. 10,74; → Wars of note, C.). The principle of responding to an enemy invasion by invading the enemy's territory was well enough known in Late Antiquity to receive its own Greek technical term: *antiperistasis* (Syrianus Magister, *de re strategica* 6,14–24). A variant of this principle, according to which the enemy is pressured on several fronts simultaneously, can be seen in the Roman preference for multiple attack columns performing a 'pincer movement'. Trajan used this manoeuvre against the Dacians in 101/02 and 105/06. Coordinated offensives against the Germani from the Rhine and Danube are known to have taken place in the 1st and 4th centuries, and Julian planned for simultaneous columns to move along the Rivers Euphrat and Tigris during his attack on the Sassanids (363).

The concept of a base of operations, so important to the military theorists of the Napoleonic period, Jomini and Clausewitz, while never mentioned by the classical tacticians, was not unknown to ancient practice. Alexander the Great (→ Generals of note B.) in 334–332 BC protected his contact with the Greek mainland against Persian threat from the sea by occupying the coast from the Hellespont to Egypt, thus cutting off the Persian fleet from its bases. In much the same way, Caesar in his first two years in Gallia Transalpina (58–57) concentrated on securing the Rhine from the Alps to the North Sea in order to cut off the Gauls from the Germans and Celts in the east. Strabo emphasized the geographical importance of a base of operations (*homereion*), both for campaigns and in the sense of 'grand strategy' [10. 528f.].

C. Grand strategy

C.1. Greek superpowers
C.2. Rome

During the Cold War, 'grand strategy', a concept originating in the two world wars, acquired the meaning of a superpower's planning, in reference not only to the scale, stationing and use of conventional and nuclear forces, but also to the deployment of all resources (economic means, human resources, scientific innovation), to complement diplomatic initiatives. Grand strategy presupposes a long-term and geographically wide perspective. The grand strategies of ancient states served as the foundations for their actions – how they positioned and built their cities and frontier fortifications, how they organized their available forces, how they divided up the administration of regions, and how they worked to improve communication routes and diplomacy. Establishing to what extent state imperialism was rooted in grand strategy (and not in greed, personal ambition, the quest for renown, 'divine' directives etc.) is not straightforward. Motivations for aggression must not disregard planning and long-term aims (→ Empire), but the grand strategy of a state, never an unchanging blueprint, can evolve in light of circumstances and regime changes.

C.1. Greek superpowers

Sparta's network of offensive and defensive alliances (c. 550–366 BC), generally known as the Peloponnesian League, embodied grand strategy in its long-term function: to consolidate Spartan power on the Greek mainland and exploit the human potential of its allies. In terms of infrastructure, sustained strategic planning is evident in Themistocles' belief in the superiority of sea power and his decision to turn Athens into an island by building city walls and fortifying its main port of Piraeus, a project that Pericles developed further with the building of the Long Walls linking Piraeus with Athens (Thuc. 1,93; 1,143). From the 4th century BC until the Byzantine period, political theorists debated the correct site for a city, its defensive needs, its vulnerability to attack, the resources it required, and its proximity to the sea – all these being considerations of grand strategy. After Sparta's defeat at Leuctra (371 BC), Epaminondas (→ Generals of note, F.) launched a fortification program to cut off Spartan access to Boeotia and confine Sparta to Laconia. Geostrategic considerations were also a factor. Xenophon mentions the Persian Empire's helplessness in the face of surprise attacks (Xen. An. 1,5,9). The wide spread of the empire's troops and its poor communication routes worked against its immense size and human potential. When Philip V of Macedon surveyed geographical perspectives from the summit of Mount Haemus, he considered the feasibility of a new war with Rome (Liv. 40,21). The Greeks' weaknesses were well known to outsiders. The Persian king Artaxerxes II (404–356 BC) always sided with the losers in intra-Greek conflicts in order to hold Greek power as a whole in check in relation to Persia (Polyaenus, Strat. 7,16,2). The ancients were familiar with the concept of 'balance of power'.

C.2. ROME

The Romans' 'grand strategy' is a matter of fierce debate (e.g. [5]; [7]; [9]; [11]). For the Imperial period in particular, arguments focus on the nature of the Roman frontier, geographical knowledge (the use of maps), and central control of the army and planning. Denials of such strategy ignore the precedent of Greek strategic theory and practice as well as tangible evidence from the Roman Republic. If there had really been no maps, in any case, this would hardly have prevented the development of campaign strategy or a grand strategy (Str. 1,1,16; → Maps) [3]; [9. 220f., 236–239].

Roads and the monitoring of population are two constants of Roman grand strategy (→ Infrastructure). From the 4th century BC on, roads linked the capital with the → colonies and with confederates across Italy in order to facilitate troop movements. Rome placed colonies and *socii* ('confederates') strategically, at the rear or flank of potential enemies. By the late 2nd century BC, Italy was linked to the Spanish provinces by roads through Gallia transalpina. The *via Egnatia*, which ran from the Adriatic to Byzantium, anticipated the later road system in Asia Minor, which enabled the rapid transfer of troops from the Danube to the Euphrates. Ever since the beginnings of the Republic, the Roman census had registered numbers of available troops. Moreover, the *breviarium totius imperii* attested for the reign of Augustus, which listed all armed forces and where they were stationed, along with the fleets, client kingdoms and assorted incomes, makes clear that there was a controlling central administration. Files were even kept on individual soldiers as part of supervised and monitored recruitment processes. The *Notitia dignitatum* (c. AD 400) shows that such listings of units and locations continued into the empire of Late Antiquity. The Roman concept of expandable citizenship also had a strategic purpose. The use of *auxilia* ('auxiliary troops') comprising non-citizens doubled the size of the armed forces and offered people a path to citizenship. The fact that auxiliary units recruited in newly created provinces were generally posted to serve elsewhere was another sign of grand strategy at work.

Augustus regulated the frontiers of Rome by completing the conquest of Iberia, annexing the Alpine regions, expanding the empire up to the Danube, and other similar actions – even if the subjugation of Germania ended with the disaster in the Teutoburg Forest (→ Empire; → Battles of note, J.). A plan to make the Black Sea an inland Roman body of water failed because of the secession of the Bosporan kingdom from Pontus (8 BC). Client kingdoms continued to offer a relatively cost-effective frontier buffer zone (cf. Liv. 33,12,10f.) against 'barbarians' or enemies (e.g. the Parthians), given that there were no annexation or administrative costs involved. Pompey's reorganization of the east (63 BC) saw the province of Syria flanked by client kingdoms in the north (buffering the Caucasus) and south (buffering Egypt). Still, client kings were sometimes difficult to manage (e.g. Decebalus in Dacia), and they ceased to be useful when circumstances changed. Some of them received subsidies, as did some barbarian tribes, whose good conduct was thereby guaranteed. The practice of buying peace with subsidies became still more important in the empire of Late Antiquity. Another way of keeping barbarian tribes in check was to engage in war with other barbarians (Tac. Ann. 12,48,2; Tac. Agr. 12,2; 32,1; Tac. Germ. 33,2; Iul. or. 1,12a–b; Claud., *Panegyricus dictus Honorio Augusto sextum consuli* 218–222; Oros. 7,43,14f.).

There is no space here to discuss the role of grand strategy in designing frontier defences (→ Borders), but the fluidity of tactical and strategic concepts should be noted (e.g. *phygomachein*). The deployment of heavy infantry as a defensive bulwark (*probole*) and as a tactical base formed part of the strategy (→ Battle). Septimius Severus justified his annexation of Mesopotamia as a *probole* for the province of Syria (Cass. Dio 75,3,2), and Herodian used the verb *proaspizein* ('to protect', 'to cover', related to the Greek *aspis*, 'shield') to describe fortresses that secured the Roman Empire against the Sassanids. This use of words may have been Hellenistic in origin: Herod the Great settled the Parthian fugitive Zamaris and his retinue at Batanasa to serve as a *problema* ('obstacle') against the Trachonites and bandits (Jos. Ant. Iud. 17,15–26).

☞ Battle; Borders; Empire; Maps; Military literature; Reconnaissance; Terror

BIBLIOGRAPHY

[1] A. ALFÖLDI, The Moral Barrier on Rhine and Danube, in: The Congress of Roman Frontier Studies, 1949, 1–16 (ed. E. Birley (Durham, 1952)) [2] H. DELBRÜCK, Die Strategie des Perikles erläutert durch die Strategie Friedrichs des Großen, 1890 [3] G. GREATREX, Roman Frontiers and Foreign Policy, in: R. ALSTON / S.N.C. LIEU (eds.), Aspects of the Roman East. Papers in Honour of Professor Fergus Millar, 2007, 103–173 [4] H. GUNDEL, Die Bedeutung des Geländes in der Kriegskunst der Germanan, in: Neue Jahrbücher für Antike und deutsche Bildung 3, 1940,

188–190 [5] B. Isaac, The Limits of Empire. The Roman Army in the East, 1990 [6] D. Laspe / C. Schubert, Seemacht, Seeherrschaft und Seestrategie bei Pseudo-Xenophon, in: Klio 94, 2012, 55–81 [7] E. Luttwak, The Grand Strategy of the Roman Empire, 2016 [8] C. Schubert / D. Laspe, Perikles' defensiver Kriegsplan. Eine thukydideische Erfindung?, in: Historia 58, 2009, 373–394 [9] E. Wheeler, Methodological Limits and the Mirage of Roman Strategy, in: Journal of Military History 57, 1993, 7–41, 215–240 [10] E. Wheeler, Strategie, in: H. Sonnabend (ed.), Mensch und Landschaft in der Antike. Lexikon der Historischen Geographie, 1999, 524–533 [11] C. Whittaker, Frontiers of the Roman Empire. A Social and Economic Study, 1994.

EVERETT L. WHEELER

Supply

A. Greek
B. Roman

A. Greek

A.1. The arming of citizen soldiers
A.2. Food supplies
A.3. The role of the *strategos* with garrison soldiers

A.1. The arming of citizen soldiers

Supplying the army was a constant and primary concern for military leadership. Ancient city-states put a college of magistrates in charge of it. In monarchies, it was dealt with by the king and his army leaders. Supply included equipment (and clothing) and provisions. For armies in the field and troops stationed at fortified sites, supply was a key element of logistics. To manage this, it was necessary to implement mechanisms that were generally at work in ancient economies: markets, government control and regulation.

Historians have all too often treated the topic of arming citizens from the perspective of citizens' ownership of their weapons. The idea thus prevails that citizens armed themselves at their own expense in the Classical period. This capacity to pay for one's own armaments is generally accepted whether one adheres to Aristotle (Ath. pol. 4,2; 3 1279b 4f.), that it was a criterion of citizenship, or whether, with Xenophon (Hell. 5,2,21–23), one sees it as a form of taxation imposed on the first three classes established by Solon. Yet, the fact that during the Classical period citizens had a shield hung up at home (Aristoph. Ach. 279) or owned a lance or a spear (Xen. Hell. 5,1,22) in no way meant that the state surrendered all control over weapons [5]. Plato (Mx. 248e–249b) mentions a law requiring the *polis* to equip the son of a fallen citizen with full armour (*panoplia*), if the fallen citizen's estate had been held in trust by the community, and the son now came into possession of his father's estate. A Thasian law of the mid-4th century said much the same [10].

There is direct evidence for the arming of citizen soldiers by the *polis* beginning in the 4th century BC in Athens. Weapons were either taken from the city's own stores (for distribution) or acquired at markets. There was a city arsenal on the Acropolis: an inventory of the Treasurer of Athena dated 369/68 BC lists 318 cases of arrows in the *opisthodomos* ('rear room') and eight and a half cases in the Hecatompedon (IG II^2 1424a (add.), ll. 121f.). The *chalkotheke* ('bronze storehouse') was also used as a weapons depot. A weapons list probably dating from 343/42 was found in Panactum, where there was a fortress for the defence of Attica. After the reforms of 335 at the latest, the *ephebes* (young men aged 18–20 registered for miltary service) were given a shield and a lance when they had completed their first year of service (Aristot. Ath. pol. 42,4). A passage in Isocrates (7,82) written in 354 BC, however, seems to indicate that Athenian citizens received money to buy weapons. This is confirmed by remarks of Xenophon (Hipp. 1,22f.; shortly after 362 BC) concerning the equipping of cavalrymen. The phylarchs, he says, 'are also given authority under the legislation – with no expenditure of their own – to compel their people to arm themselves out of their received pay (*misthos*)'. It is therefore quite possible that the Athenian infantry and cavalry were given money to arm themselves, with the state relying on the private market for the production, import and sale of weapons. Aeneas Tacticus (30,1) explains that the *polis* under siege had to 'take account of the weapons brought in for sale and placed in the *agora*'.

In the Hellenistic period, it was not uncommon for military magistrates, following a euergetic logic, to help with the purchase of weapons and clothing for their troops. In a decree dated 220/19 BC, which was issued by the Athenians in the garrisons of Eleusis, Panactum and Phyle, honour is paid to the hipparch Theophrastus 'not only for his care of the horses (*hippotrophia*), but also for having ensured that the horsemen were equipped with the best possible weapons by allowing a voluntary contribution (*epidosis*) of 10 *mnai* to be given to officers (*lochagoi*)' (IG II^2 1303, ll. 13–17). More evidence comes from the decree of 211/10 for the *strategos* ('commander') of Eleusis, Demaenetus, whose soldiers praise him for having provided money (*argyrion*) for their clothing (*estheta*) (IG II^2 1304, ll. 34f.; cf. fig. 1). The justification for the honorary decree for the Athenian taxiarchs of 271/70 is also relevant: 'They each took care of their own tribe in such a way that the equipment should be in the best possible condition to go to

Fig. 1: Demaenetus Decree from Eleusis (211/10 BC; IG II21304, ll. 32 ff.). Declaration by the Athenians at the fortresses of Eleusis, Panactum and Phyle and in the open countryside in honour of the *strategos* Demaenetus: [line 19] ἐπεμελήθη δὲ καὶ τῆς τῶν ὀ[ψωνίων δ]ιαδόσεως, σῖτον τε παρατι-θέμενος ἐξ ἑτοίμου ὅ[πως ἔχ]ωσιν ὡς λυσιτελέστατ[ο]ν, καὶ ἐν πᾶσι τοῖς ἔτεσι[ν αὐ]τοῖς προδιδοὺς ἀργύριον εἰς ἐσθῆτα ('and he ensured that pay was disbursed and that grain was obtained at fair prices, and he gave them every year money for clothing'). This honorary inscription from Eleusis also contains formulaic texts honouring with crown and statue the *strategos* Demaenetus for his achievements on behalf of the Athenian *polis* and the soldiers of the garrisons. Alongside many other accomplishments, the recipient is praised for the ample and affordable provisions, pay and kit with which he furnished the men under his command. While tributes like this were not unusual, especially in the Hellenistic period, they were not to be taken for granted, any more than the smooth supply of troops was to be taken for granted. Effectiveness in this difficult task was one of the many reasons given for why the soldiers honored their commander.

the fortresses and checkpoints and take part in inspections (*exetasmos*)' [1. no. 1, ll. 13–15 (= ISE I, no. 18, ll. 13–15)]. At this period, however, the contribution of military magistrates was merely a supplement to equipment provided by the *polis*. The *polis* appears to have used a token system [12], with vouchers probably conferring the right to be equipped with weapons [5].

A.2. Food supplies

Food supplies were essential for the proper functioning of an army in the field or in a garrison. In this respect, the material needs of a citizen soldier and a mercenary were similar. An army carried up to three days' supply of provisions on military expeditions. For any longer than that, the weight of the food would hinder the foot soldiers' progress. Thucydides indicates that everyone was responsible for his own provisions on short expeditions. For a longer campaign in remote areas, the city of Athens (which could afford it) required its men to bring their own rations only for the first three days, and the city paid all subsequent expenses for food. The term *trophe* ('food', 'nourishment') was used for monetary payments to Athenian and Peloponnesian soldiers and sailors, implying that this was not a 'payment' as such but a 'compensation for foodstuffs' [15]. Historians have long had to grapple with the abundance of words found in texts and inscriptions (*itometria, opsonion, misthos, sitos, trophe, siteresion, sitonion, metrema, prodoma, doma, sitarchia*, etc.) variously describing one or the other of two conditions: (1) the provision of supplies in their natural form or in the equivalent amount of money; (2) the payment of a wage to → mercenaries or citizen soldiers. Some scholars [9. 276] have suggested the idea of 'composite pay', while others [13] emphasize the specific conditions in view: it is advisable to consider the specific details of each case rather than seeking to oversystematize the evidence [4].

A state sometimes made logistical preparations to supply an army for more than the first three days. To meet all requirements, however, carts and beasts of burden were needed. The sources refer to these – if they are mentioned at all – with the term *aposkeue*, the army train or 'baggage' [11]. If, looking at the campaign of Alexander, we multiply the weight of grain needed for humans, war horses and draught animals by the known troop strength, we reach staggering figures [8] – figures that should be viewed with caution, because they seem disproportionately large and hard to reconcile with reality. It is more likely that an army in the field would quickly find itself having to live off plunder, theft or requisitions. The Archaic poet Archilochus wrote, 'Here the spear gives me bread,/ and the wine of Ismarus is given me/ here by my spear, and I drink,/ leaning here on my spear' (Elegies Fr. 7). Xenophon explains, 'It is often safer in war to seek food with weapons rather than with agricultural tools in one's hands' (Oec. 5,13). Crossing Susiana in 317 BC, Eumenes of Cardia had to supply his troops entirely with local products: 'He had rice, sesame and dates distributed among the men, for the land had such crops in abundance' (Diod. Sic. 19,13,6).

When food could be supplied neither from the army's own logistics nor from whatever the land could provide, it was possible to make use of markets as intermediaries. For this, special payments of ration money were made for the purchase of provisions, especially grain, or sometimes regular pay was simply increased. During the march of the Ten Thousand, the soldiers had a provisions market at their disposal: an *agora* with market traders (Xen. An. 1,2,18) in the barbarian camp of Cyrus' army (Xen. An. 1,3,14), known as the 'Lydian *agora*' (Xen. An. 1,5,6). Wheat and barley were available there, but the prices sometimes terribly high [6]. Merchants and traders often followed armies on marches. This travelling market also accepted the army's booty: discussing the Siege of Syracuse by the army of Hamilcar in 309 BC, Diodorus Siculus (20,29,6) mentions the presence of 'many people of different backgrounds outside the formation, who only wanted to make booty but offered nothing of military use – and yet, they were the cause of much rowdiness and pointless confusion. Such people often give rise to fateful dangers.'

Military leadership did not shy away from regulating the market, one instance being the stratagem devised by Timotheus at the Siege of Olynthus around 360 BC (Aristot. Oec. 2,2,23a). Having run out of money, the Athenian *strategos* had an emergency copper coin minted to allow his soldiers to buy food at the market, even though bronze coins were normally used for purchases in the *agora*. Other kinds of regulatory intervention also occurred: again at Olynthus, Timotheus came up with another ruse (Aristot. Oec. 2,2,23.d): 'And when there was a shortage of food in the camp because of the new arrivals, he forbade the grinding of grain or its sale in quantities less than a medimnos, and of liquid foodstuffs less than a metrete. The taxiarchs and *lochagoi* then bought up larger quantities and distributed the food to their men – but those newly arrived brought what they needed with them. Yet, whenever they departed, they sold what they had left over. Thus it was that the soldiers finally had food in abundance' (cf. also [2]).

A.3. THE ROLE OF THE *STRATEGOS* WITH GARRISON SOLDIERS

In the fortresses of Attica, the regulatory intervention of the *strategos* – who also held power of command over part of the urban territory of Athens – was crucial to the grain supply [14]. In effect, the military commander operated as a regulator guaranteeing fair grain prices. He had a number of measures available to him. A decree from Rhamnous dated 244 BC (as yet unpublished) states that the *strategos* Archander, 'when grain was scarce, ensured that the city supplied the quantity of wheat stipulated for the garrison of the fortress and the citizens living in Rhamnous'. Given that two population groups – soldiers and citizens – were involved, we may suppose that distribution took place in the form of sale, the soldiers using their pay to participate. When the money ran out, the city offered another solution. The decree issued by the Athenians at Eleusis under the archontate of Menecles (267/66 BC) mentions the furnishing of grain to the garrison of Athenians in honour of Dion, the treasurer responsible for grain (IG II^2 1272), as well as the giving of an *ekklesiastikon* to every soldier to buy that grain (ll. 12f.). As far as we known, this is the only instance of such an authorization in the context of a garrison. Perhaps this was a financial ploy that enabled the city to deprive the soldiers of their rations at a future date. By using such tokens, it was possible to avoid the use of cash, which at the outbreak of the Chremonidean War was first and foremost needed to pay mercenaries [3]. In the previously mentioned 211/10 decree of the Athenians at Eleusis, Panactum and Phyle, pay is treated separately from the grain supply. The *strategos* 'looked after the disbursement of pay (*misthos*) and also put aside grain so that the Athenian garrison soldiers would have convenient access to it, and over the course of the year he gave out money for clothing and thereby ensured that those serving under his command were dressed well' (IG II² 1304, ll. 31–35). Storing up grain enabled the *strategos* to reduce the grain prices in the *agora* where the Athenian garrison soldiers were supplied, if the prices in the *agora* became too high.

Soldiers were very sensitive to the prices they paid for their provisions, and they showed gratitude whenever their superiors were able to reduce those prices. Eumenes I, reaching an agreement with rebellious soldiers at Philetaerea and Attaleia, was forced to make the concession that 'for grain, a price of four drachmas per medimnos should be payable, for wine four drachmas per metretes' (OGIS 266 = StV III, no. 481, ll. 3f.). By this clause, the soldiers probably made an agreement with Eumenes on what the monarch was allowed to charge for grain and wine. In Egypt, where the Ptolemaic administration consistently carried this thinking to its logical conclusion, sale at low prices was probably called *agora*: what mattered for soldiers, in addition to their → pay (*opsonion*) and wheat rations (*metremata*), was their right to buy at fair prices. This was guaranteed by verification documents called *symbola* [13].

☞ Administration; Equipment; Pay

BIBLIOGRAPHY

SOURCES
[1] Nouveaux choix d'inscriptions grecques, edited by L'Institut Fernand Courby, 1971 [2] ARISTOTELES, Le second livre de l'économique, edited with introduction and commentary by B.A. Van Groningen, 1933.

SECONDARY LITERATURE
[3] J.-C. COUVENHES, Les garnisons de l'Attique, du milieu IVᵉ siècle au Iᵉʳ siècle av. J.-C. L'apport des inscriptions, 2000 [4] J.-C. COUVENHES, La place de l'armée dans l'économie hellénistique. Quelques considérations sur la condition matérielle et financière du soldat et son usage dans les marchés, in: R. DESCAT (ed.), Approches de l'économie hellénistique (Entretiens d'archéologie et d'histoire 7), 2006, 397–436 [5] J.-C. COUVENHES, La fourniture d'armes aux citoyens athéniens du IVᵉ au IIIᵉ s. av. J.-C., in: P. SAUZEAU / T. VAN COMPERNOLLE (eds.), Les armes dans l'Antiquité. De la technique à l'imaginaire, 2007, 521–540 [6] R. DESCAT, Marché et tribut. L'approvisionnement des Dix-Mille, in: P. BRIANT (ed.), Dans les pas des Dix-Mille. Peuples et pays du Proche-Orient vus par un Grec (Pallas 43), 1995, 99–108 [7] P. DUCREY, L'armée, facteur de profits, in: A. CHASTAGNOL (ed.), Armées et fiscalité dans le monde antique (Colloque CNRS), 1977, 421–434 [8] D.W. ENGELS, Alexander the Great and the Logistics of the Macedonian Army, 1978 [9] G.F. GRIFFITH, The Mercenaries of the Hellenistic World, 1935 [10] P. HAMON / J. FOURNIER, Les orphelins de guerre de Thasos. Un nouveau fragment de la stèle des Braves (ca 360–350 av. J.-C.), in: BCH 131/1, 2007, 309–381 [11] M. HOLLEAUX, Ceux qui sont dans le bagage, 1926, 355–366 (again in: Études d'épigraphie et d'histoire grecque 3, 1968, 15–26) [12] J.H. KROLL, Some Athenian Armor Tokens, in: Hesperia 46, 1977, 141–146 [13] M. LAUNEY, Recherches sur les armées hellénistiques, 2 vols., 1949–1950 (new edition 1987) [14] G. OLIVER, War, Food, and Politics in Early Hellenistic Athens, 2007 [15] E. WILL, Notes sur ΜΙΣΘΟΣ, in: J. BINGEN (ed.), Le monde grec. Pensée, littérature, histoire, documents. Hommages à Claire Préaux, 1978, 426–438 (again in: E. Will, Historica graeco-hellenistica. Choix d'écrits 1953–1993, 1998, 569–584).

JEAN-CHRISTOPHE COUVENHES

B. ROMAN

B.1. Beginnings in the Republic
B.2. Organization in the Imperial period
B.3. State interference in private business
B.4. The organization of campaigns
B.5. Services of civilian society
B.6. Transportation structure
B.7. Organizational measures

In considering the supply of an army, we must first distinguish between (1) supply with perishable consumables (foodstuffs, etc.) and (2) supply with more durable, longer-term goods (weapons, equipment, etc.).

Furthermore, the organization of supplies involved both supplying permanent locations and supplying troops on detachment, on the march or on deployment.

B.1. BEGINNINGS IN THE REPUBLIC
As soon as the Roman Republic moved away from its original method of waging war – conducting short summer campaigns – supplying its troops became a problem. It was solved, at first, by pillaging enemy fields, which was considered an exigency of war, or by the compulsory requisitioning of grain from allies or from defeated opponents [13].

There was some recourse to private enterprise, for instance during the Second Punic War (218–201 BC), when Rome supplied its army in Iberia [3]. During the Second Macedonian War (200–197 BC), a special levy was imposed on grain harvests in Sicily and Sardinia, while Carthage was required to send additional grain supplies. L. Hortensius extorted grain from the Thracian city of Abdera during the Third Macedonian War (171–168 BC). As a rule, the Republican armies were supplied through quasi-taxes in kind imposed within the regions where they were stationed (surveys [16]; [15]).

B.2. ORGANIZATION IN THE IMPERIAL PERIOD
During the Imperial period, the supply of troops in permanent garrisons was generally guaranteed by receipts from non-personal taxes (e.g. the

decuma on grain) within the surrounding region or neighbouring provinces. Some siphoning off from tax farmers in public or imperial domains is also conceivable. AE 1956, 123 seems to indicate a connection of this kind (honorific inscription for the *procurator* of the *quattuor publica Africae* by an imperial *libertus*, who functioned as *tabularius legionis III Augustae*) [8]. Comparable links are also implied for other units.

If these resources were insufficient, they could be augmented at any time through the *coemptio* of whatever goods were needed. In the *coemptio*, the *res publica* acted as prime buyer of the required goods, usually paying below the applicable market price. The cash required for supplying troops was obtained through regular deductions from soldiers' pay. A pay settlement of AD 81 (P. Gen. Lat. 1 r = RMR 68) shows that from the gross pay of 247.25 drachmas received by an ordinary soldier, there were regular deductions of 10 drachmas' hay allowance, 80 drachmas for provisions and 12 drachmas for shoes. Further deductions were made as necessary, for example for soldiers' clothing. This money also enabled payments to be made for olive oil and wine units delivered by civilian traders.

When troops were to move across long distances, another instrument of public authority took effect: the obligation on populations to provide board, lodging and necessary means of transport (carts, pack animals – along with the relevant operational personnel) to anyone travelling on Roman state business.

Most of the transport requirements for such movements – equipment and animals – were provided by private individuals in the form of a *munus* ('duty'). The jurist Arcadius Charisius later classified such services as encumbrances on the person (Dig. 50,4,18,21, also 18,3f.) and on the estate (Dig. 50,4,18,21). Other services to be provided by imperial subjects without charge included the task of accompanying transportations essential to the military as far as the border or a specific handover point. Only active soldiers and → veterans were exempt from these services (Dig. 50,4,18,29). See also (for example) P. Oxy. XLIII 3111 (May 15, AD 257): two local dignitaries responsible for supplying the army with wine hired a ship to transport wine to the soldiers of the *legio II Traiana* [1].

The inscription AE 1976, 653 formulates the scope of the services demanded in the reign of Tiberius [39]. We cannot know, however, how widely the obligation to supply these services, which was stipulated and may have been nominal, was enforced in reality.

The extraordinary burdens borne by the civilian population in some regions where the military made unreasonable demands are documented in a number of inscriptions [21].

B.3. State interference in private business

As a way of ensuring the provision of means of transport, there is evidence in the Imperial period to suggest that the state took control of the stock of riding horses (cf. BGU XVII 2699 with a sworn declaration on the ownership of mares from AD 209) and draught and pack animals (Ulp. Opiniones 1 (Dig. 50,13,2) may also indicate state control of the equine population). The Roman state perhaps also exercised control over the inventory of transport ships (cf. P. Grenf. I 49 with the registration of a river boat with a capacity of 250 artabas). In organizational terms, this was probably based on local organizations of riverboat operators (the regional associations of boatmen on the Rhône and Saône are especially well known) [5]. State-operated transport ships are first attested in the year AD 298 in P. Panop. Beatty 1,167ff. (ships belonging to the *fiscus*).

For transporting military goods by sea, the Roman state, which had no transport capacities of its own, drew on private fleets of seagoing vessels. Organization was eased by the presence in many regions (Africa, Sardinia, Iberia, Egypt) of existing associations of ship owners (*navicularii*) whose vessels were available for use [6]; [10]. These associations were already bound to the state by long-term contractual commitments to supply grain to Rome (*annona*), which rewarded their commitments with privileges (citizenship, etc.) and exemptions from public obligations (*immunitates*). The system was managed by the *praefectus annonae* ('prefect of provisions') at Rome and the *procuratores* ('procurators') in the provinces [45]; [44].

B.4. The organization of campaigns

During the Imperial period, high-ranking *equites* (members of the equestrian order) were usually appointed to organize the supply of troops during major campaigns: Ti. Claudius Candidus (inscriptions from Tarraco no. 130 = CIL II²/14, 975: second Germanic campaign of Marcus Aurelius), and M. Rossius Vitulus (Pflaum no. 224: march to Rome under Septimius Severus). C. Valerius Marianus of Tridentum (CIL X 5036 = ILS 5016) accompanied transports to supply the *legio III Italica*. We are particularly well informed about the *expeditio orientalis* of Severus Alexander. Besides C. Iulius Alexander, who functioned as commander of the rear for the two fleets at Misenum and Ravenna (NdS 1909,210 = ILS 9221), we know of two officials working for him. P. Sallustius Sempronius Victor (CIG 2509 a), as *procurator* of Bithynia and Pontus, organized supplies from this region to Syria. C. Furius Sabinius Aquila Timesitheus (CIL XIII 1807 = ILS 1330) as *procurator* ensured supplies from the province of Syria Palaestina [31]. In this work, they were supported by civilian officials

[4. nos. 19–21], who were required to accompany transports from Cilicia to Syria (Dig. 50,4,18,3f.).

B.5. SERVICES OF CIVILIAN SOCIETY

Grain appears to have been delivered unmilled to soldiers in the Imperial period, and they would need to grind it before consuming it. By Late Antiquity at the latest, the supplies were changed to bread, which had to be produced by the civilian population (P. Panop. Beatty 1,77ff. (four bakers for one fort); 1,332ff. (public bakery); Pseudo-Josua Stylites 54; 77; Iul. epist. ad Athen. 286 B). Meat was not originally part of the basic provisions to the military, but it was provided to soldiers at least from the reign of Diocletian onwards (P. Panop. Beatty 1,276ff. etc.). It was obtained from communities as a service in kind (P. Cair. Isid. 52 (20.10.312)).

Money was retained from soldiers' pay at irregular intervals to cover the costs of clothing (P. Gen. Lat. 1 r I = RMR 68). The papyrus known as Hunt's Pridianum (RMR 63) dating from AD 105 shows soldiers on detachment from Gaul who were required to obtain clothing for a unit in Stobi (Macedonia), while another testimony (BGU VII 1564 = Sel. Pap. II no. 395) records the supply of blankets from Egypt to the army in Cappadocia (eastern Anatolia). The basic clothing supply was financed with a specific duty called the *vestis militaris*, which was imposed on taxpayers in Late Antiquity (Cod. Theod. 7,6,1 (18,4,365), 12,6,4 (18,6,365)). Goods were transported to soldiers using the *cursus publicus*. Besides actual delivery of goods, payment in lieu was also possible, having been introduced in AD 377 for most of the *dioecesis Oriens* (Cod. Theod. 7,6,5 = Cod. Iust. 12,39,4 (9,3,377)). Later evidence (Cod. Theod. 7,6,4 = Cod. Iust. 12,39,3 (17,1,396), Cod. Theod. 7,6,5 = Cod. Iust. 12,39,4 (9,3,423)) shows that most of this money would be paid out to soldiers so that they could supply themselves on the free market. Such payments had previously been used to remunerate those who produced the goods (cf. P. Cair. Isid. 54 with a delivery of 22 tunics and eight cloaks).

B.6. TRANSPORTATION STRUCTURE

The proper functioning of supplies depended heavily on transportation infrastructures and the keeping of stores. Although the Roman Empire had a well developed system of roads, waterways seem to have been used wherever possible for transporting bulk goods (grain) for the military. The Roman victory in the Second Punic War came about thanks in large part to control of the seas and the most important ports in Campania. Controlling river routes was another important element of Roman strategy. During the Augustan conquest phase in Germania, supply lines were established along the Lippe (Haltern and elsewhere) and Main (Marktbreit), complete with large, fortified camps and depots. The absence of such structures would later force Germanicus to confine himself to short summer campaigns before withdrawing to bases on the Rhine.

During the First Marcomannic War (166/67–175) in the reign of Marcus Aurelius, troops in Pannonia had to be temporarily supplied by ship from Germania and eastern Gaul by way of the Danube when the usual supply route to Aquileia was broken (AE 1956, 124; cf. fig. 2). In the reign of Julian,

Fig. 2: Detail from the relief band of the Trajan Column (Rome, AD 112/13; plaster cast, 1861). Roman soldiers unload bales of supplies near a fortified facility on the Danube.

Fig. 3: *Horreum* at the Roman fort of Vercovicium on Hadrian's Wall (built AD 122; Housesteads Roman Fort near Hexham, Northumberland, England). The remains of the grain storage facility, which was built of massive stone masonry, show that the installation was raised up – on a wooden floor that has now disappeared – to provide better aeration. This protected the grain from dampness at floor level.

the troops on the Rhine were supplied with grain from Britain (Amm. Marc. 18,2,3f.). Valens took supplies for his planned Gothic campaign by way of the Black Sea, where they were reloaded on to river boats at the Danube Delta to be taken to the camps (Zos. 4,10,4; [35]). It was only during wars with the Parthians or Sassanids that the Romans were largely dependent on transport by land from the Mediterranean, although even here attempts were made to use the Euphrates as a transport route (Cass. Dio 75,9,3: campaign of AD 197; Zos. 3,13,3: campaign of AD 363; cf. [9]).

When troops were moved around within the empire, the → infrastructure offered by the established system of the *cursus publicus* was used. The *mansiones* ('stopping places') seem to have been used not just as accommodations, but also as places to gather and distribute provisions. The basic structure can be inferred from the *Tabula Peutingeriana*.

Establishing depots (*horrea*) was just as important. Every permanent Roman camp needed sufficient stores of grain and fodder, which as far as possible were obtained from the areas surrounding of the camp (cf. fig. 3). When major campaigns were planned, attempts were made to set up large depots near the anticipated front – the example at South Shields (for the Britannic campaign of Septimius Severus) could be supplied by sea [11]. Relatively little is known about the depot system within the empire. The system implicit in P. Panop. Beatty 1,131ff., involving public depots in each toparchy of a nome, seems to have been typical of the Egyptian province only. It is possible that in the Anatolian region, the *castellum* ('fort') of Aulutrene performed this kind of task (with AE 1988, 1030 = AE 1993, 1512: *milites conductores*, cf. the *colle(c)tiones* from Freis no. 136).

B.7. Organizational measures

Responsibility for supplying the legions with provisions and materials apparently rested with the first centurion of the *triarii* of the first cohort (the *primipilus*). In addition to his own officials, he could call on the services of soldiers on detachment, who were sometimes sent great distances from their places of deployment (Aquileia) [41]. In legionary *vexillationes* ('detachments') of the Diocletianic period, the responsibility appears to have been held by the *centurio supernumerarius* (P. Panop. Beatty 2,183, 264, 269, 289), while the *summus curator* did the job for the auxiliary units [25].

During the Imperial period, much was done within the military's own organizational sphere, but in Late Antiquity, there was a tendency towards organizational models in which supplies were entrusted to civilians, with the required goods only passing into the hands of the military at the very end of the supply chain. Thus, the *praefecti praetorio* ('praetorian prefects'), *vicarii* ('deputies') and provincial governors now held responsibility for supplies, which were organized as part of the taxation system of Late Antiquity. This shift is most clearly seen in the replacement of the *primipilus* ('chief centurion') and his duties with the institution of the *primipilares*, which undertook the work as a civilian *munus* ('duty') [7]. Even transport was now in civilian hands, as evidenced by the placing of the *praepositi bastagae* ('officer in charge of goods') under the command of the *comes sacrarum largitionum* ('official in charge of sacred contributions') (cf. Not. Dign. Occ. 11,77–85).

☞ **Administration; Equipment; Infrastructure; Pay**

Bibliography

[1] C. Adams, Land Transport in Roman Eygpt. A Study of Economics and Administration in a Roman Province, 2007 [2] R. Alston, Soldier and Society in Roman Egypt, 1995 [3] E. Badian, Zöllner und Sünder. Unternehmer im Dienst der römischen Republik, 1997 [4] G.E. Bean / T.B. Mitford, Journeys in Rough Cilica in 1964–1968 (Österreichische Akademie der Wissenschaften. Philosophisch-Historische Klasse, Denkschriften 102), 1970 [5] W. Boppert, Caudicarii am Rhein? Überlegungen zur militärischen Versorgung durch die Binnenschiffahrt im 3. Jahrhundert am Rhein, in: Archäologisches Korrespondenzblatt 24, 1994, 407–424 [6] W. Brokaert, Navicularii et negotiantes. A Prosopographical Study of Roman Merchants and Shippers, 2013 [7] J.-M. Carrié, Primipilaires et taxe du 'primipilon' à la lumière de documentation papyrologique, in: Actes du XVe Congrès international de papyrologie IV (Papyrologica Bruxellensia 19), 1979, 156–176 [8] M. Christol, Ti. Claudius Proculus Cornelianus, procurateur de la région du Théveste, in: L'Africa Romana 7, 1990, 893–905 [9] E. Dabrowa, Naval Operations during Persian Expedition of Emperor Julian (363 AD), in: A.S. Lewin / P. Pellegrini (eds.), The Late Roman Army in the Near East from Diocletian to the Arab Conquest. Proceedings of a Colloquium Held at Potenza, Acceranza et Matera, 2007, 237–242 [10] L. De Salvo, Economia privata e pubblici servizi nell'impero romano. I corpora naviculariorum, 1992 [11] J.N. Dore / J.P. Gilliam, The Roman Fort at South Shields, 1979 [12] C. Drecoll, Die Liturgien im römischen Kaiserreich des 3. und 4. Jh. n.Chr., 1997 [13] A.M. Eckstein, Unicum subsidium populi romani. Hieron II and Rome, 263–215 BC, in: Chiron 10, 1980, 175–190 [14] H. Elton, Military Supply and the South Coast of Anatolia in the Third Century AD, in: S. Mitchell / C. Kaisari (eds.), Patterns in the Economy of Roman Asia Minor, 2005, 289–304 [15] P. Erdkamp, Hunger and the Sword. Warfare and Food Supply in Roman Republican Wars (264–30 BC), 1998 [16] P. Erdkamp (ed.), The Roman Army and the Economy, 2002 [17] P. Erdkamp (ed.), A Companion to the Roman Army, 2007 [18] E. Faure, Italia annonaria. Notes sur la fiscalité du Bas-Empire et son application dans les différents régions de l'Italie, in: RIDA 11, 1964, 149–231 [19] L. Gracco Ruggini, Stato e associazioni professionali dell'età imperiale romana, in: Akten des VI. Internationalen Kongresses für griechische und lateinische Epigraphik, 1972–1973, 271–311 [20] H. Halfmann, Itinera principum. Geschichte und Typologie der Kaiserreisen im Römischen Reich, 1986 [21] P. Herrmann, Hilferufe aus römischen Provinzen. Ein Aspekt der Krise des römischen Reiches im 3. Jhdt. n.Chr., 1990 [22] P. Herz, Studien zur römischen Wirtschaftsgesetzgebung. Die Lebensmittelversorgung, 1988 [23] P. Herz, Organisation und Finanzierung der spätantiken annona, in: A. Giovannini (ed.), Nourir la plèbe. Actes du Colloque tenu à Genève les 28 et 29. IX. 1989 en hommage à Denis van Berchem, 1991, 161–188 [24] P. Herz, Kampf den Piraten? Zur Deutung zweier kaiserzeitlichen Inschriften, in: ZPE 107, 1995, 195–200 [25] P. Herz, Der centurio supernumerarius und die annona militaris, in: Laverna 10, 1999, 165–184 [26] P. Herz, Die Logistik der kaiserzeitlichen Armee. Strukturelle Überlegungen, in: P. Erdkamp (ed.), The Roman Army and the Economy, 2002, 19–46 [27] P. Herz, Der römische Staat und die Wirtschaft. Staatliche Eingriffe in das Wirtschaftsleben (Kontrolle von Ressourcen), in: M. Polfer (ed.), Artisanat et économie romaine. Italie et les provinces occidentales de l'Empire. Actes du 3e colloque international d'Erpeldange (14–16 octobre 2004), 2005, 17–30 [28] P. Herz, Finances and Costs of the Army, in: P. Erdkamp (ed.), A Companion to the Roman Army, 2007, 306–322 [29] P. Herz, Die Versorgung des römischen Heeres mit Waffen und Ausrüstung, in: A. Eich (ed.), Die Verwaltung der kaiserzeitlichen römischen Armee. Studien für Hartmut Wolff, 2010, 111–132 [30] P. Herz, Wirtschaft und Militär in der römischen Provinz Raetia, in: P. Herz et al. (eds.), Handel, Kultur und Militär. Die Wirtschaft des Alpen-Donau-Adria-Raumes, 2011, 79–107 [31] P. Herz, Gedanken zur Karriere des Timesitheus, in: Philia 3, 2017, 69–78 [32] N. Hodgson, The British Expedition of Septimius Severus, in: Britannia 45, 2014, 31–51 [33] J.E. Jones, The Maritime and Riverine Landscape of the West of Roman Britain. Water Transport on the Atlantic Coasts and Rivers of Britain, 2009 [34] T.K. Kissel, Untersuchungen zur Logistik des römischen Heeres in den Provinzen des griechischen Ostens (27 v.Chr.–235 n.Chr.), 1995 [35] N. Lenski, Failure of Empire. Valens and the Roman State in the Fourth Century A.D., 2002 [36] J. Mathews, The Journey of Theophanes. Travel, Business and Daily Live in the Roman East, 2006 [37] K. Miller, Itineraria romana. Römische Reisewege an der Hand der Tabula Peutingeriana dargestellt, 1916 (reprint 1988) [38] P. van Minnen / J.D. Sosin, Imperial Pork. Preparation for a Visit of Severus Alexander and Iulia Mamaea in Egypt, in: AncSoc 27, 1996, 171–181 [39] S. Mitchell, Requisitioned Transport in the Roman Empire. A New Inscription from Pisidia, in: JRS 66, 1976, 106–131 [40] F. Mitthof, Annona militaris. Die Heeresversorgung im spätantiken Ägypten. Ein Beitrag zur Verwaltungs- und Heeresgeschichte im römischen Reiches im 3. bis 6. Jh. n.Chr., 2 vols., 2001 [41] A. Mocsy, Das Lustrum Primipili und die Annona Militaris, in: Germania 44, 1966, 312–326 [42] M. Nicasie, Twilight of Empire. The Roman Army from the Reign of Diocletian until the Battle of Adrianople, 1998 [43] B. Palme, Die Legionäre des Kaisers. Soldatenleben im römischen Ägypten, 2011 [44] J. Remesal Rodríguez, Die procuratores Augusti und die Versorgung des römischen Heeres, in: H. Vetters / M. Kandler (eds.), Akten des 14. Internationalen Limeskongresses 1986 in Carnuntum, vol. 1, 1990, 55–65 [45] J. Remesal Rodríguez, Heeresversorgung und die wirtschaftlichen Beziehungen zwischen der Baetica und Germanien, 1997 [46] G. Rickman, The Corn Supply of Ancient Rome, 1980 [47] J.P. Roth, The Logistics of the Roman Army at War (264 BC–AD 235), 1999 [48] J. Scheuerbrand, Gerste, Heu und frische Pferde. Die Reitereinheiten als Verwaltungsproblem, in: M. Kemkes / J. Scheuerbrand (eds.), Zwischen Patrouille und Parade. Die Reiterei am Limes, 1997, 19–21 [49] J.A. Sheridan (ed.), Columbia papyri IX. The Vestis Militaris Codex, 1998 [50] M.A. Speidel, Auf kürzestem Weg und gut verpflegt an die Front. Zur Versorgung pannonischer Expeditionstruppen während der severischen Partherkriege, in: A. Eich (ed.), Die Verwaltung der kaiserzeitlichen römischen Armee. Studien für Hartmut Wolff, 2010, 133–147 (reprinted in: M.A. Speidel, Heer und Herrschaft im Römischen Reich der Hohen Kaiserzeit, 2009, 255–272) [51] M.P. Speidel, Summus

curator. Zu Inschriften aus dem österreichischen Oberpannonien und Noricum, in: Römisches Österreich 1, 1973, 53–56 [52] K. STAUNER, Parapomé des Kaisers und seines Heeres im nordwestlichen Kleinasien, in: Gephyra 4, 2007, 1–35 [53] C. VACANTI, Guerra per la Sicilia e guerra della Sicilia. Il ruolo delle città siciliane nel primo conflitto romano-punico, 2012.

PETER HERZ

Symbols

A. Greek
B. Roman

A. GREEK

Symbols (*sema, semeion*) were primarily used in warfare as *episema* or *episemon*, that is, symbols painted – or, if made of metal, riveted – on shields. According to Herodotus (1,171), the Carians were the first people to put symbols on their shields (cf. Str. 14,2,27). There may have been several motivations for the practice, but the fundamental one was the need to distinguish friend from foe in battle. The spread and use of helmet types such as the Corinthian helmet, which hid most of the warrior's face behind the nose protector and side flaps, made it increasingly difficult to identify individuals without some special identifying mark. Symbols on shields were usually of considerable size, so that they might be easily visible. As shown by the iconographic variety of shield symbols on vase-paintings, at first the choice was left to the individual. The meanings of the symbols were not uniform, but must be interpreted on a case by case basis. Some were apotropaic, warding off the dangers of battle or instilling terror in the enemy (e.g. Gorgoneion), while others were decorative or representative (usually depicting animals, such as lions, boars, roosters or horses), or they emphasized the lineage or personal qualities of the warrior (e.g. Plut. Mor. 234,41). The detailed descriptions of the shield symbols of ancient heroes in epic and classical drama are of little help for interpreting the actual reality, because these representations are *topoi* that express the hero's valour, strength and character (e.g. Hom. Il. 18,516ff.; Aesch. Sept. passim).

Polis symbols came into use in the 5th century BC, to identify the origins or civic identities of fighters in a unit or an army. Examples of such symbols include the initial letters of the city name, such as Λ for the Lacedaemonians, M for the Messenians (Phot. *Lexicon* s.v. Λάμβδα) and Σ for the Sicyonians (Xen. Hell. 4,4,10), or the city's emblem (*parasema*), which was often representative of its primary deity, such as the Theban club (Xen. Hell. 7,5,20) or the Mantinean trident (Bacchylides, *Epinician Odes* fr. 1). This development had much to do with the 'democratization' of the *poleis* and the evolution of civic identities [2. 66–69]. Warriors were primarily fighting for their cities, which sometimes even now paid for their equipment, which they no longer had to buy for themselves.

According to coin images and wall-paintings in Macedonian tombs, the Hellenistic kings whose stores provided weapons for their soldiers used a plethora of symbols as *episemata* for their Macedonian shields: cult symbols (e.g. lightning bolt or eagle for Zeus; head of Artemis Tauropolos), dynastic symbols (e.g. club, *kerykeion* or star for the Macedons; anchor for the Seleucids; heroes' heads or monograms as symbols of individual kings, such as Pan for Antigonus II Gonatas and Perseus for King Perseus), or military symbols with a variety of decorative elements or colours (e.g. *Leukaspides, Chalkaspides*) [3]. Different symbols may also have been used to tell apart the various units of an army during battle.

Symbols were also used for warships (figureheads or other symbols; Hdt. 8,92), for the general's tent (Xen. Cyr. 8,5,13), and to identify different units within an army. Commands were also conveyed to soldiers by means of symbols.

Occasionally, civic emblems were used to mark prisoners [1]. Tattooing was intended to humiliate the prisoner, since it was generally only slaves who were branded in this way. A few cases are known from the 5th century BC (secession of Samos, 441/40 BC: Plut. *Pericles* 26; Ael. VH 2.9; Sicily, 411 BC: Plut. *Nicias* 29). Tattooing of prisoners was a practice probably adopted from the Persians, since it is first mentioned in connection with Theban prisoners at the Battle of Thermopylae (Hdt. 7,233).

☞ Specialists

BIBLIOGRAPHY
[1] C.P. JONES, Stigma. Tattooing and Branding in Graeco-Roman Antiquity, in: JRS 77, 1987, 139–155 [2] S. KILLEN, Parasema. Offizielle Symbole griechischer Poleis und Bundesstaaten (Archäologische Forschungen 36), 2017 [3] K. LIAMPI, Der makedonische Schild, 1998 [4] H. PHILIP, Archaische Silhouettenbleche und Schildzeichen in Olympia, 2004 [5] A.M. SNODGRASS, Arms and Armour of the Greeks, 1999.

CHARALAMPOS I. CHRYSAFIS

B. ROMAN

B.1. Signs and objects
B.2. Rituals
B.3. Militaria in public pictorial language

The word 'symbol' is used in different ways, especially among scholars [3]. Here, it will be understood to refer to a socially recognized vehicle of meaning that carries specific connotations and that references something that is not present, or a concept that clearly goes beyond what is present. Based on this definition, many symbols can be identified in the life of the Roman military, including signs and objects as well as ritualized actions. Furthermore, depictions of militaria could acquire specific symbolic meaning within Roman imagery.

B.1. Signs and objects

B.1.1. Ruler images
B.1.2. Depictions of deities
B.1.3. Apotropaic function
B.1.4. Standards
B.1.5. Emblems
B.1.6. Shield symbols
B.1.7. Staurogram and Christogram
B.1.8. The cingulum militare

B.1.1. Ruler images

There is evidence for images of the emperor and his relatives from the Augustan period onwards, both in the pictorial repertoire of militaria and on → standards. As permanent → camps developed, portraits and statues also appeared. We do not know whether images of generals were already being used like this in the Late Republican period. The sources (Cass. Dio 42,15,5) mention only the fitting of name banners to pieces of → equipment.

Images were intended to make the emperor – the supreme commander – at least a visible, if not an actual presence. They also evoked a binding relationship of loyalty between troops and their emperor, and other members of the imperial family were included so as to secure the future of the dynasty. On several occasions, the sources refer to the removal or destruction of such images by soldiers as symbolic of a breach of loyalty.

Standing out from the body of emperor images in the military context are the *imagines* carried as → standards in their own right. This type of standard was probably introduced already in the Augustan period, and certainly during the reign of Tiberius, by virtually all unit types. Though the sources are virtually silent regarding their use, similar phenomena in the civilian sphere and the circumstances of their introduction suggest that they were meant as symbolic representations of the absent emperor on official occasions. This was necessary, for instance, at the swearing of the → oath, the disbursement of → pay, the bestowal of → honours, and at key religious rituals. In light of the structures of obligation in Roman society, all these events could either establish or strengthen a relationship of patronage, which made the presence of the one who held overall command (*imperium*) indispensable [7]; [8. 15f., 84–86]; [11. 153–291]; [12. 106–132]; [14. 26f., 45–50].

B.1.2. Depictions of deities

Images of deities always had a symbolic meaning, for they referred not just to the divine figure in question, but also to its power, cult and mythical context. Like Roman culture as a whole, the Roman military was full of divine images, which appeared as decorations on militaria such as honours, equipment, weapons and standards, as well as on stone monuments and as statuettes in camps [12. 99–105].

Images referred to different spheres of life and ideas according to the purview of the particular deity. Minerva and Mars, for instance, referred to aspects of the military sphere, Dionysus and Venus to concepts of general fortune and happiness, Victoria to victory and Jupiter to the Roman state. The choice of a particular decoration, particularly for personal items, would usually be based on individual religious preferences and the desire for divine assistance [4. 29–32]; [8. 11–20]; [14. 62f.].

B.1.3. Apotropaic function

Various signs and symbols were believed to repel evil in Antiquity, and some of these were used to decorate personal items of equipment. The head of the Gorgon Medusa was an especially popular choice, appearing often on equipment and honours, but almost never on attack weapons. Depictions of deities and divine attributes, such as eagles or thunderbolts, were also thought to repel evil thanks to the divine assistance they brought [4. 29–32]; [8. 11–13, 62].

B.1.4. Standards

The various → standards had symbolic connotations that differed according to their specific functions. The legionary eagle, for instance, was on the one hand the most important standard for every legion and the symbol of its very existence, but on the other it was also closely associated with the most important god of the Roman state, Jupiter, and was regarded as the symbol *par excellence* of the Roman army. Losing a legionary eagle was therefore a very serious matter. Other emblems carried as standards were symbols of identification specific to the unit concerned, not unlike modern crests. The *imagines* symbolized the soldiers' loyalty to the reigning emperor, so they were usually replaced when a new emperor succeeded to the throne. By contrast, the standards of subsidiary units, which were used for the everyday business of signalling and the → transmission of orders, were primarily practical in function – although because of their use in orientation on the battlefield, they also developed into critical points of reference for the collective identity of the soldiers. They likewise symbolized the close bond of loyalty between soldiers and general.

The loss of a standard was a great disgrace, not just for the soldiers, but for all Roman citizens. Recovering lost standards was accordingly an achievement of great prestige. The standards had a sacred aura, the importance of which only grew over the course of the Imperial period. For instance, dedications made directly to the standards themselves begin to be reported in the late 2nd and 3rd centuries AD [11. 153–221]; [13. 257–294]; [14. 186–198, 203].

B.1.5. EMBLEMS

There is evidence that a number of Roman units used specific emblematic symbols that, in representing the identity of the group concerned, acquired a significance akin to a coat of arms. For the legions, two such emblems are usually attested, including one zodiac sign, which suggests a connection with the anniversary of the → legion or its founder. Animals, deities and objects are also found as emblems. Emblems are attested for a few → auxiliary units – a boar, for instance, for some Gallic cohorts. The scorpion associated with the Praetorians may be derived from the zodiac sign of the emperor Tiberius, who gave the unit its camp on the Quirinal. Emblems were carried as separate standards alongside the others, and they were also used for decorative purposes on items such as bricks, architecture, altars, inscriptions, equipment and tombstones. They are also found on coins (→ Representations of war B.; → Sources D.) [13. 380–417, 504–571]; [14. 20–25, 63f.].

B.1.6. SHIELD SYMBOLS

Various literary sources (Tac. Hist. 3,23; Cass. Dio 64,14,2; Veg. Mil. 2,18,1f.) and the *Notitia Dignitatum* of Late Antiquity suggest that Roman units used specific shield markings for purposes of recognition. However, most pictorial sources, especially in official public art, exhibit only a small repertoire of standardized shield symbols, perhaps because monuments were not supposed to draw attention to any specific unit. Thunderbolts appear frequently on shields, probably – as with the legionary eagle – to symbolize the support of the supreme state god, Jupiter. Constantine's purpose was similar when before the Battle of the Milvian Bridge in AD 312, he had the symbol of the Christian god put on his soldiers' shields (Lactant. De mort. pers. 44,5; → Battles of note G.). Units' emblems were sometimes used as shield symbols. A few fragments of original shields, for instance from Dura-Europus, have highly detailed figural images, which may indicate their use in parades [6. 115–124]; [8. 12–17, 106, 131–135]; [13. 24f.]; [15. 80–99].

B.1.7. STAUROGRAM AND CHRISTOGRAM

It was probably some time after the Battle of the Milvian Bridge (AD 312) that the *labarum* was introduced as the new imperial standard. This was a *vexillum* ('flag') with a purple cloth and a monogram of Christ (Staurogram, the monogram of a cross), initially placed on the top, then later on the cloth. This standard, which was intended to symbolize the sacred background of the empire, subsequently became one of the most important symbols of the power of the Christian emperors. Standards that were formally similar to this seem to have been introduced later into the army. The Christogram is also found on shields and helmets, but the few known instances probably belong to the emperor's immediate retinue or his → guards, which calls into question how widespread this phenomenon actually was [8. 131–135].

B.1.8. THE CINGULUM MILITARE

It seems that the *cingulum militare*, the soldier's belt, was seen as the quintessential symbol of soldiery, both by the soldiers themselves and by the civilian populace (Serv. Aen. 8,724). In keeping with this function as a mark of social distinction, it was often ostentiously displayed on soldiers' gravestones, even in combination with otherwise civilian apparel [5].

B.2. RITUALS

B.2.1. Sacramentum
B.2.2. Lustratio
B.2.3. Adlocutio
B.2.4. Triumph

B.2.1. SACRAMENTUM

The *sacramentum*, the → oath of loyalty, ritually established and renewed the relationship of loyalty between the → general or emperor and the soldiers. Unity and mutual trust were thus celebrated in ritual. During the Imperial period, there was an important role here for the *imago* as the symbolic representative of the absent emperor. A violation of the *sacramentum*, depending on the severity of the violation, resulted in various → disciplinary measures, and given the religious context, it was also regarded as an offense against the gods [9. 293–308].

B.2.2. LUSTRATIO

In addition to the sacrificial feasts laid down in the festival calendar, → religious ceremonies also included occasional rituals, one of which – a key component of any campaign – was the *lustratio exercitus* ('purification of the army'). This was originally performed on the Field of Mars in Rome before the army marched out, and later also outside the city. The ritual involved a procession around the assembled army, followed by an appearance at the altar of the war god Mars to perform the sacrifice of the *suovetaurilia* (a boar, a ram and a bull). Until recently, most scholars understood the *lustratio* as primarily a purification ceremony, but a recent interpretation suggests, among other things, an apotropaic function, based on the timing of the ritual [1]; [9. 144-146].

B.2.3. ADLOCUTIO
In the *adlocutio*, the general's personal address to the soldiers (→ Eve-of-battle speech), the bond of loyalty that was affirmed in the *sacramentum* was demonstrated to all, so that this address became a symbol of the unshakable relationship of loyalty between the general and his men. *Adlocutiones* were thus a key element of every Roman depiction of war and an integral part of imperial tours of inspection and troop visits [1]; [11. 126-145]; [13. 237f.].

B.2.4. TRIUMPH
The triumphal procession through Rome was a ritual of special relevance, with many layers of social and political meaning (→ Triumph). Among other things, the procession before the eyes of the populace and the political elite made clear the close relationship between the general and his troops in emphatic style. The triumph was the only occasion on which the general and the troops were able to celebrate their successes together in the capital and to parade their collective glory before the people [2]; [11. 405-445].

B.3. MILITARIA IN PUBLIC PICTORIAL LANGUAGE
Roman iconography was informed by the extensive use of signs and symbols, including some militaria. Standards, for instance, were used on coins as symbols of military authority (*imperium*) and as symbols of the army as a whole [14. 199-226]. In the aftermath of the murder of Caesar, depictions of daggers were briefly used as code for liberation [8. 46-48]. The *parma equestris*, the round shield used by the cavalry, developed into a status symbol of the social class of the *equites* (knights) during the Republican period. Under Augustus, it became a symbol of the planned transfer of power to his biological grandsons, since they were given the title *princeps iuventutis* ('first among the [equestrian] youth') to express this designation.

In addition, supposedly everyday pieces of equipment had deeper meaning in the narrative images of official 'statecraft', as there was no intention to portray particular units and their equipment in a correct, antiquarian and thus documentary way. The selection and placement of militaria were based on prevailing pictorial conventions with a view to narrative strategies [1]. → Standards, for instance, were usually shown in the immediate vicinity of the emperor, contrary to reality, in order to identify him as the commander. Specific pieces of equipment such as the *scutum* (long shield) and greaves were easily recognizable references to legionaries, but it would be wrong to conclude from this that all legionaries and only legionaries wore them. This phenomenon can be seen clearly in the representation of helmet shapes, which were often antiquated and did not correspond to the Roman militaria found at that time. Rather, older pictorial and motif traditions were used. [16]. Depictions of 'statecraft' and the equipment shown in these depictions should therefore be understood to a large extent as constructed visual worlds.

☞ Transmission of orders; Society and army

BIBLIOGRAPHY
[1] L. BAUMER et al., Narrative Systematik und politisches Konzept in den Reliefs der Trajanssäule, in: JDAI 106, 1991, 261-295 [2] M. BEARD, The Roman Triumph, 2007 [3] R. ECKARD, Symboltheorien, 2006 [4] J. GARBSCH, Römische Paraderüstungen, 1978 [5] S. HOSS, Der Gürtel als 'Standeszeichen' der römischen Soldaten, in: Mannheimer Geschichtsblätter 19, 2010, 96-110 [6] J. JUNKELMANN, Reiter wie Statuen aus Erz, 1996 [7] M. KEMKES, Zu Ehren des Kaisers, in: S. MÜLLER (ed.), Gebrochener Glanz, 2014, 109-119 [8] E. KÜNZL, Unter den goldenen Adlern, 2008 [9] J. RÜPKE, Domi militiae. Die religiöse Konstruktion des Krieges in Rom, 1990 [10] M.P. SPEIDEL, Emperor Hadrian's Speeches to the African Army, 2006 [11] J. STÄCKER, Princeps und miles. Studien zum Bindungs- und Nahverhältnis von Kaiser und Soldat im 1. und 2. Jahrhundert n.Chr., 2003 [12] O. STOLL, Die Skulpturenausstattung römischer Militäranlagen an Rhein und Donau, vol. 1, 1992 [13] O. STOLL, Zwischen Integration und Abgrenzung. Die Religion des römischen Heeres im Nahen Osten, 2001 [14] K.M. TÖPFER, Signa militaria. Die römischen Feldzeichen in der Republik und im Prinzipat, 2011 [15] H. TRAVIS / J. TRAVIS, Roman Shields, 2014 [16] G. WAURICK, Die militärische Rüstung in der römischen Kunst, in: C. VAN DRIEL-MURRAY (ed.), Roman Military Equipment. The Sources of Evidence, 1989, 45-60.

KAI MICHAEL TÖPFER

Tactics

☞ Strategy

Terror

A. Concept
B. Greek
C. Roman

A. Concept

Terror is the systematic use of fear and dread as a weapon, to achieve compliance in people by using or threatening violence. It must first be noted that no such abstract definition existed in the vocabularies or conceptual worlds of classical ancient societies. The nuanced semantic fields revolving around fear (Latin *terror, pavor, metus*; Greek *phobos, demos*), for instance, all concern the resulting emotions, not the abstract intention [45], which manifests itself practically as physical violence (e.g. torture, massacres, rape).

Ancient texts' attitudes to such actions always depend on perspectives, status and morality, with differences sometimes emerging in language (e.g. Latin *vis – violentia, crudelitas*; Greek *bia – hybris*; [8]; [34]; [16]). Terror is thus characterized by an asymmetry of perspective. Implemented by one's own side, it appears as legitimate force, and the terminology is almost entirely functional, for example as a means of defining the other [1]; [15]. Examining terror in the ancient world is therefore a task of historical interpretation [52], which recent scholarship has sought to approach through a plethora of methodological angles, ranging from archaeology [41] to political science [28], to social psychology [7] and the historical study of emotions [5].

The following article will confine itself to manifestations of terror in military contexts, that is, armed confrontations between communities. Attention must be paid to the status of perpetrators and victims, their respective relationships, situational differences, and degrees of technologization and systematization. The evaluation of military terror must also be considered. We must remember, however, that the basic level of experience of war and violence was much higher in the ancient world than it is today [13].

B. Greek

The *Iliad* contains a great many scenes of terror (e.g. Hom. Il. 21,17–135), in which the meticulously described fear of the vanquished and the destructive violence of the hero contribute to the epic's exploration of the human and divine limits of heroic violence, in relation to factors such as honour, *hikesia* ('supplication') and divine punishment (Hom. Il. 24,33–54; [3]; [23]). The *Iliad* does not so much shed light on the realities of terror in the Archaic period as it reflects its diffuse functions.

The better source material for the Classical period permits a clearer view, although the emergence of a literary type for the ideal war, together with scholarly debates about whether hoplite warfare followed a contest/rules-based approach or pursued 'total war', make a final assessment difficult [49]; [12]. While Herodotus (7,9B,1) and later Polybius (13,3,2–5) reject on principle the use of psychological warfare in battle, this should be taken merely as a loose convention for opponents who were peers [30]; [26]. When opposing forces were not equal, it was legitimate to use surprise attacks, deception and similar stratagems, which could have a psychological effect (Xen. Hell. 5,2,41f.). It was customary throughout this period for a victorious force brutally to afflict a fleeing enemy (Tyrt. F23a20–22 West; Thuc. 4,96,7f.; 7,84f.; Xen. Hell. 4,4,12, 7,4,31; Diod. Sic. 12,10,1). Such massacres, as well as the pillaging of territories, the ruining of fields and orchards, and the enslaving of rural populations were considered legitimate acts of terror against a defeated opponent in the late 5th and 4th centuries BC (Xen. hell. 4,6,4–6; 6,2,6; 6,5,22; [9]).

Terror acquired a particular intensity in → civil wars (*staseis*), because violence in such cases was considered an unnatural injury to the community represented by the *polis* (Hdt. 8,3,1). Excesses of violence in civil wars were therefore recounted in detail. Thucydides' paradigmatic description of such conflicts on Corcyra contains assassinations, random acts of pillaging, disregard for *hikesia* and blood ties, mass suicides, mass executions, and reports of fellow citizens being walled up alive (Thuc. 3,70–72). The passage serves to condemn the disintegration of values and the undermining of manly character that come with war (Thuc. 3,82–84). Depictions of the cruelties of war that make similar points are also found pertaining to non-Greeks (Hdt. 3,147; 8,32,2; Thuc. 7,29,4f.).

Military terror against dependent persons, such as women, children, the elderly and the sick was understood primarily as a failure on the part of male defenders. It was therefore legitimate, but it also evoked pity [44]. This was especially true when cities were conquered, occasions on which Homeric heroes would kill the men and sell the other victims into slavery (Hom. Il. 6,447–465; Hom. Od. 9,39–61). The Classical period continued in the same vein: Xenophon considered it a universal and undisputed custom for defeated persons and their property to be placed at the disposal of the victor (Xen. Cyr. 7,5,73; Thuc. 3,68). The execution of the conquered, and thus at least the partial elimination of the opposing political body, was a real option (Thuc. 5,116; Xen. Hell. 7,1,28), and taking captives was a legitimate means of exerting political and economic pressure (Thuc. 7,86,1; 7,87; [11]). It may thus be concluded that eradicating a defeated enemy was considered valid in view of the comprehensive rights of the victor, economic and political calculations, and concepts of revenge and reciprocity, with the practice of *hikesia* and the concept of justice setting at least theoretical limits (Thuc. 3,37–48; 3,66; [29]; [51]).

Overall, however, terror was not an instrument of warfare that was used systematically in Ancient Greece, but rather it was normalized in various ways. The beginnings of deliberate use can perhaps be seen in imperialistic endeavors such as the Delian League (Thuc. 3,40,7; 3,42,5; 5,116,2–4; Diod. Sic. 12,76,3; [17]). A good general was said to limit the suffering caused by war, while the tyrant exploited such suffering (Xen. Cyr. 7,2,5–14; 7,3,1; Diod. Sic. 20,71,1–4), and in such accounts the literary treatment of suffering was detached from the actual experiences of those who suffered. In particular, rape and gang rape, which were seen as harm done to the men who were responsible for the women, were normalized, although the actual extent of these actions remains unclear due to the vagueness of language (Xen. Hell. 3,2,27; [10]; [14]). Only on an individual level (Eur. Hec. 240–290; Aristoph. Pax 263–267) and in a rudimentary way by philosophers (Aristot. Pol. 1,1255a; Pl. Leg. 1,625e–626d; [33]) were such experiences ever reflected upon, but there was no impact on military practice.

Beginning with Alexander's campaign, the increasing technologization of warfare and the incorporation of war into monarchical ethics altered the picture somewhat, because it now became possible for the immense destructive potential [21] to be constrained by appeals to the monarchical values of magnanimity and goodwill (Plut. *Demetrius* 21,1f.; 22,4; Diod. Sic. 20,83,1–84,1; 20,99f.; [4. 57–114]). Although the use of → elephants as an instrument of terror was not a lasting success [42], a critical awareness gradually developed throughout the Hellenistic period that kingdoms could use terror – especially the destruction of cities – to consolidate their power (Diod. Sic. 32,2; 32,4; [46]). Alexander the Great (→ Generals of note, B.) became an influential point of comparison [25].

C. ROMAN

Despite basic similarities with previous tradition, the discourse around terror intensified in the Roman period. Polybius was already aware of the Romans' greater range of violent tactics and greater willingness to use them (1,37,7–10; [19]). Livy's narrative of early Roman history, with acts of terror such as the Rape of the Sabine Women portrayed as legitimate (1,9–13), exemplified how violence became a core element of Roman identity. Roman culture exhibited greater clarity and openness about portraying their own acts of military violence [38]; [48] Exemplary figures such as M. Porcius Cato (Liv. 39,40,3–41,4; [27]), for instance, established a sometimes brutal ideal of generalship, according to which deliberate acts of extreme terror were considered legitimate [35].

In the field, battlecries were the first means of intimidating the enemy (Caes. B Civ. 3,92). Salvos of projectiles, the use of artillery (Veg. Mil. 2,25), and a rushing attack accompanied by hurled javelins could have a psychological effect and break up enemy lines (Pseudo-Caesar, *De bello Hispaniensi* 31; Tac. Hist. 3,23; Plut. *Sulla* 18,6; [18]). The pursuit of enemies was carried out with great brutality, ideally with support from cavalry and projectiles (Caes. B Gall. 2,27f.; 4,26; 4,35; Tac. Ann. 2,17f.; Liv. 6,9,11; 44,42).

Sieges in particular illustrate the systematic and self-conscious use of terror. The asymmetrical power dynamic involved in most sieges (Caes. B Gall. 2,12; Jos. BI 3,262; 5,512–524), the proximity of the conflict to the defenders' families, and the tactical need to end the siege quickly gave a sense of legitimacy to the use of terror, despite occasional references to pity (Caes. B Gall. 7,78–81; 8,27–34; Liv. 1,29,1–6; Jos. BI 5,7,567–6,1,8). The mutilation and execution of captive soldiers, commanders and fleeing residents with the explicit purpose of wearing down and subjugating the survivors can be seen on many occasions (Caes. B Gall. 6,34,8; 8,38; 8,44). Josephus' account of the Jewish War includes examples of this type of warfare, with Roman soldiers crucifying hundreds of Jews to demoralize the besieged enemy (Jos. BI 5,446–455; [36]; [37]). The use of encircling embankments and siege engines made it possible to threaten inhabitants even behind city walls, reflecting the technological superiority of Roman warfare (Jos. BI 3,257; 5,502–507).

Theoretically, the plunder of captured cities was under the control of the general, and he could prohibit his men from taking plunder as a sign of his leniency and fairness (Liv. 38,23,2; Onas. 34; Caes. B Gall. 2,33; Caes. B Civ. 3,97; Tac. Hist. 3,33). The normal scenario, however, was chaotic looting that served as a reward for the soldiers, accompanied by acts of cruelty that were only occasionally mentioned by the sources (Liv. 24,39,4–8; Plut. *Sullva* 14,3f.). The killing and mutilating of those defeated, especially men fit for military service, were common, as was rape. This was followed by the actual plundering, and in some cases the total destruction of the city (Pol. 10,15,4–8; Liv. 29,17,15f.; Tac. hist. 3,33,1–3; App. Pun. 19,129; [53]; [31]). Surviving captives were sometimes pardoned or sold into slavery, but they might equally be executed if circumstances required (Tac. Ann. 4,25; 12,17). The terrors experienced by victims in the course of conquests and plundering were explicitly thought of as a weapon, especially on expeditions with a punitive purpose. This was justified as a necessary demonstration of Roman authority. It was thus intended both to restore peace and to deter revolts and raids. Success, of course, was not guaranteed (Cic. Off. 1,35; Cic. Fam. 15,4,10; Liv. 24,39,8f.; [32]; [19]).

Behind this, all the way through to Late Antiquity, lay a harsh, Roman-centric concept of justice that saw excessive violence as a legitimate means of securing world dominion (Cic. Off. 2,27; Verg. Aen. 6,851–853; Them. Or. 10,138d), and that was also applied in dealings with criminals and bandits (Dig. 48,19,28,15; [20]; [43]; [40]). Although Roman literature always found room for a critical, anti-imperialistic perspective (Sall. Hist. 4,67; Tac. Agr. 30–32; Aug. Civ. 4,3–4; [6]), this seems to have had no corresponding manifestation in practice. The use of terror was celebrated (Jos. BI 7,5,5), and the Roman Empire remained fundamentally aggressive [24].

Accordingly, realities of military terror did not change noticeably in Late Antiquity (Amm. Marc. 19,1,7–10; 19,2,3–15; 19,5,5f.; 21,13,15; Procop. Goth. 5,23,9–12), although the discourse surrounding terror was increasingly subjected to Christian logic. Early Christianity rejected military service primarily on the grounds of idolatry (Tert. Idol. 19), but this opposition evaporated by the time of the Council of Arles, if not before [22]. Moreover, the terrors suffered became stylized as trials of Christian faith (Jer. Ep. 127,12f.), while the spread of Christianity was supposedly reflected in the purported decline in excessive military violence (Origen, Contra Celsum 8,69f.; [47]). Orosius, for instance, claims that violence decreases as Christianization increases (Hist. 7,37,14). Terror as a theme in military contexts, for example in connection with the executions and acts of mutilation ordered by Roman generals after combat in Spain (Oros. Hist. 4,21,10; 5,2,3; 5,4,12), are thus subordinated to new motifs, although the tendency to regard terror as a means of othering remains undiminished (Lactant. De mort. pers. 27,2–6; Procop. Vand. 3,2,11f.; [2]).

BIBLIOGRAPHY

[1] V. ANDÒ / N. CUSUMANO (eds.), Come bestie? Forme e paradossi della violenza tra mondo antico e disagio contemporaneo, 2010 [2] T.S. BURNS, Rome and the Barbarians, 100 B.C.–A.D. 400, 2003 [3] D.L. CAIRNS, Poine and Apoina in the Iliad, in: M. LINDER / S. TAUSEND (eds.), Böser Krieg. Exzessive Gewalt in der antiken Kriegsführung und Strategien zu deren Vermeidung, 2011, 35–50 [4] A. CHANIOTIS, War in the Hellenistic World, 2005 [5] A. CHANIOTIS, Violence in the Dark. Emotional Impact, Representation, Response, in: M. CHAMPION / L. O'SULLIVAN (eds.), Cultural Perceptions of Violence in the Hellenistic World, 2017, 100–115 [6] D. CLOUD, Roman Poetry and Anti-Militarism, in: J. RICH / G. SHIPLEY (eds.), War and Society in the Roman World, 1993, 113–138 [7] J.P. CROWLEY, The Psychology of the Athenian Hoplite. The Culture of Combat in Classical Athens, 2012 [8] F. D'AGOSTINO, Bia. Violenza e giustizia nella filosofia e nella letteratura della Grecia antica, 1983 [9] J.C. DAYTON, The Athletes of War. An Evaluation of the Agonistic Elements in Greek Warfare, 2005 [10] G. DOBLHOFER, Vergewaltigung in der Antike, 1994 [11] P. DUCREY, Le traitement des prisonniers de guerre dans la Grèce antique. Des origines à la conquête romaine, 1968 [12] B. ECK, La mort rouge. Homicide, guerre et souillure en Grèce ancienne, 2012 [13] G.G. FAGAN, Violence in Roman Social Relations, in: M. PEACHIN (ed.), The Oxford Handbook of Social Relations in the Roman World, 2011, 467–497 [14] K.L. GACA, Martial Rape, Pulsating Fear, and the Sexual Maltreatment of Girls (paides), Virgins (parthenoi), and Women (gynaikes) in Antiquity, in: S.L. JAMES / S. DILLON (eds.), Women in the Classical World, vol. 3: Women in Public Life, 2017, 103–149 [15] M.R. GALE / J.H.D. SCOURFIELD (eds.), Texts and Violence in the Roman World, 2018 [16] B. GIBSON, Tacitus and the Language of Violence, in: M.R. GALE / J.H.D. SCOURFIELD (eds.), Texts and Violence in the Roman World, 2018, 269–285 [17] L. GIL, Terror e imperialismo. El caso de Mitilene, in: Cuadernos de Filología Clásica. Estudios griegos e indoeuropeos 17, 2007, 163–181 [18] C.M. GILLIVER, Battle, in: P. SABIN et al. (eds.), The Cambridge History of Greek and Roman Warfare, vol. 2, 2007, 76–121 [19] A.K. GOLDSWORTHY, War, in: P. SABIN et al. (eds.), The Cambridge History of Greek and Roman Warfare, vol. 2, 2007, 76–121 [20] T. GRÜNEWALD, Räuber, Rebellen, Rivalen, Rächer. Studien zu latrones im Römischen Reich, 1999 [21] W. HECKEL / J.L. MCLEOD, Alexander the Great and the Fate of the Enemy. Quantifying, Qualifying, and Categorizing Atrocities, in: W. HECKEL et al. (eds.), The Many Faces of War in the Ancient World, 2015, 233–267 [22] J. HELGELAND, Christians and the Roman Army A.D. 173–337, in: Church History 43/2, 1974, 149–163 [23] U. HERRMANN, Anthropos Deinos. Zur Rolle der Gewalt in der griechischen Archaik im Spiegel der epischen und lyrischen Dichtung, 2014 [24] B. ISAAC, Limits of Empire. The Roman Army in the East, 1992 [25] C. JOUANNO, Un épisode embarrassant de l'histoire d'Alexandre. La prise de Thèbes, in: Ktèma 18, 1993, 245–258 [26] D. KAGAN / G.F. VIGGIANO (eds.), Men of Bronze. Hoplite Warfare in Ancient Greece, 2013 [27] B. KIERNAN, The First Genocide. Carthage 146 BC, in: Diogenes 51/3, 2004, 27–39 [28] B. KIERNAN, Blood and Soil. A World of Genocide and Extermination from Sparta to Darfur, 2007 [29] D. KONSTAN, Anger, Hatred, and Genocide in Ancient Greece, in: Common Knowledge 13, 2007, 170–187 [30] P. KRENTZ, Fighting by the Rules. The Invention of the Hoplite Agôn, in: Hesperia 71, 2002, 23–39 [31] F. MARCO SIMÓN, Intimidación y terror en la época de las guerras celtibéricas, in: G. URSO (ed.), 'Terror et pavor'. Violenza, intimidazione, clandestinità nel mondo antico, 2006, 197–213 [32] S.P. MATTERN, Rome and the Enemy. Imperial Strategy in the Principate, 1999 [33] S.S. MONSON, Socrates in Combat. Trauma and Resilience in Plato's Political Theory, in: P. MEINECK / D. KONSTAN (eds.), Combat Trauma and the Ancient Greeks, 2014, 131–162 [34] D.D. PHILIPS,

Xenophon and the Muleteer. Hubris, Retaliation, and the Purposes of Shame, in: W. RIESS / G.G. FAGAN (eds.), The Topography of Violence in the Greco-Roman World, 2016, 19–59 [35] A. POWELL, Julius Caesar and the Presentation of Massacre, in: K. WELCH / A. POWELL (eds.), Julius Caesar as Artful Reporter. The War Commentaries as Political Instruments, 1998, 111–137 [36] J.J. PRICE, Jerusalem under Siege. The Collapse of the Jewish State 66–70 C.E., 1992 [37] C.A. REEDER, Pity the Women and Children. Punishment by Siege in Josephus's 'Jewish War', in: JSJ 44/2, 2013, 174–194 [38] N. RICHER, La violence dans les mondes grec et romain. Introduction, in: J.-M. BERTRAND (ed.), La violence dans les mondes grec et romain, 2015, 7–35 [39] W. RIESS / G.G. FAGAN, The Topography of Violence in the Greco-Roman World, 2016 [40] O.F. ROBINSON, Penal Practice and Penal Policy in Ancient Rome, 2007 [41] N. ROYMANS / M. FERNÁNDEZ-GÖTZ, Caesar in Gaul. New Perspectives on the Archaeology of Mass Violence, in: T. BRINDLE et al. (eds.), TRAC 2014. Proceedings of the Twenty-Fourth Annual Theoretical Roman Archaeology Conference, 2015, 70–80 [42] P. SCHNEIDER, Les éléphants de guerre dans l'Antiquité, IVe–Ier siècles avant J.-C., 2015 [43] P. DE SOUZA, Piracy in the Graeco-Roman World, 1999 [44] P. DE SOUZA, Civilians under Siege in the Ancient Greek World, in: A. DOWDALL / J. HORNE (eds.), Civilians under Siege from Sarajevo to Troy, 2018, 207–232 [45] J.-F. THOMAS, De 'terror' à 'vereri'. Enquête lexicale sur des formes de peur et de crainte en latin, in: RPh 86/2, 2012, 143–168 [46] J. THORNTON, Terrore, terrorismo e imperialismo. Violenza e intimidazione nell'età della conquista romana, in: G. URSO (ed.), 'Terror et pavor'. Violenza, intimidazione, clandestinità nel mondo antico, 2006, 157–196 [47] A. TRATTNER, 'Böser Krieg' aus christlicher Sicht. Darstellungen exzessiver Gewalt im Geschichtswerk des P. Orosius, in: M. LINDER / S. TAUSEND (eds.), 'Böser Krieg'. Exzessive Gewalt in der antiken Kriegsführung und Strategien zu deren Vermeidung, 2011, 207–226 [48] F. TUTRONE, Confini in discesa. Rappresentazioni della violenza e della bestialità nella cultura romana, in: V. ANDÒ / N. CUSUMANO (eds.), Come bestie? Forme e paradossi della violenza tra mondo antico e disagio contemporaneo, 2010, 209–234 [49] H. VAN WEES, Greek Warfare. Myths and Realities, 2004 [50] H. VAN WEES, Defeat and Destruction. The Ethics of Ancient Greek Warfare, in: M. LINDER / S. TAUSEND (eds.), 'Böser Krieg'. Exzessive Gewalt in der antiken Kriegsführung und Strategien zu deren Vermeidung, 2011, 69–110 [51] H. VAN WEES, Genocide in Archaic and Classical Greece, in: V. CASTON / S.-M. WEINECK (eds.), Our Ancient Wars. Rethinking War through the Classics, 2016, 19–37 [52] M. ZIMMERMANN (ed.), Extreme Formen von Gewalt in Bild und Text des Altertums, 2009 [53] A. ZIOLKOWSKI, Urbs disrepta, or How the Romans Sacked Cities, in: J. RICH / G. SHIPLEY (eds.), War and Society in the Roman World, 1993, 69–91.

HENRY HEITMANN-GORDON

Timeframe of war

Thucydides considered the Peloponnesian War (→ Wars of note, H.) more important than the Persian War (→ Wars of note, J.), partly because the latter was decided in two battles at sea and on land, while the former 'lasted very long, and during it sufferings spread across Greece unlike at any other time' (Thuc. 1,23,1; cf. 5,26). The duration of a war in Antiquity depended on the strategic and tactical aims of the conflict, the available resources and logistics, the type of weaponry and military technology used, the status of the fighters themselves (militiamen, mercenaries, professional soldiers), the size and political organization of the belligerents, and the prevailing geographical and ecological conditions. Quantitative attempts at analysis taking historical conditions into account have not proved especially useful [1]. Still, trends may be observed. War in early city-state or ethnic systems (Archaic Greece, early Rome, Celtic Gaul) were generally short and were fought seasonally. Because they needed to work in the fields, citizen militias were only available for a few weeks. Fighting longer wars required troops who were free from the agricultural subsistence economy, as memebrs of a warrior caste (→ Sparta), → mercenaries (Hellenistic states, Carthage) or professional soldiers (Roman Empire). Above all, wars lasting several years required resources that could only be afforded by large entities, such as the Delian League, the Hellenistic kingdoms, the Roman social system, or the Roman Empire of the Principate. Celtic and Germanic warrior groups could only conduct raids and wars on a seasonal basis. Only when they were transformed into large, mobile conglomerates were they able to transition to permanent military activity.

The importance of central decision-making and mobilization of resources is already apparent in the Ancient Near East, for instance in the Siege of Tyre by Nebuchadnezzar, which allegedly lasted for 13 years [4. 7046]. Republican Rome's principle of only ending a war when it had won led – despite the ruling aristocracy's obsession with 'decisive' battles – to wars that were sometimes very long (First Punic War 264–241; Second Punic War 218–201 BC) and wars that kept flaring up again (First to Third Samnite Wars, 343–341, 326–304, 298–290 BC). Under the altered strategic conditions of the Principate, however, it became possible to halt resource-draining offensive wars (Germanic campaign of Germanicus, AD 16; Persian War of Emperor Julian, AD 363). Within certain political and strategic regions of conflict, new wars simply kept breaking out (e.g. six 'Syrian Wars' fought between the Ptolemies and Seleucids, 274–168 BC).

As in modern times, an unexpectedly long war – where the prospects were uncertain – placed belligerent societies under considerable stress. In the case of the Peloponnesian War, the fighting became more brutal the longer the war dragged on [5. 122]. The timeframe of a war could not always be defined as clearly as with the wars between Rome and Carthage, which were neatly bookended by initial hostilities and peace treaties or final destruction. Combating pirates or pacifying provinces often involved phases of inactivity, with sporadic operations and occasional major campaigns. In imperial systems in particular, wars might simmer for some time, with varying degrees of intensity, as 'background noise' at the peripheries.

Environmental factors played a major role in the annual rhythm of the timeframe of war. The Greeks called the season unfit for agriculture, seafaring and war *cheimon* ('winter'), the active season *theros* ('summer') (cf. Thuc. 2,1: Report 'by summers and winters'). Rome held the festivals of its war god in March. Mediterranean naval warfare was more strictly governed by weather and visibility conditions than operations on land. The period from late May to mid-September was regarded as safe (Veg. Mil. 4,39), but in practice vessels put to sea between March and the end of October. The factors discussed above, however, sometimes overrode these considerations for naval enterprises, too (Thuc. 2,69; 3,88; Diod. Sic. 20,74; [3. 201–203]). From the last third of the 5th century BC onwards, far-reaching operations, combinations of different weapon types, the increasing use of mercenaries, and the increasing frequency of siege warfare (see e.g. Pl. Symp. 220a–b) extended the seasonal timeframe of war. Alexander and the Diadochi fought whenever necessary, even in winter [2. 388f.]. The citizens' sons of the Roman army under the Republic were available for longer, and were also often compensated for their time with booty. Overseas campaigns were sometimes continued through winter (e.g. App. Pun. 18,120; Liv. 35,7,7). A semi-professional army could deploy continuously for several years, as did the army of Caesar, and could operate even in the most hostile winter conditions (Caes. B Gall. 7,8,1–3). Campaigns in Africa (47/46 BC) and Iberia (46/45 BC) were usually fought in that season. The permanent, logistically well organized army of the Imperial period used the winter for → training (Tac. Ann. 13,35). Winter campaigns were recommended for actions against mobile enemies such as the Slavs (Ps.-Maurice, *Strategikon* 11,4,19). Seasonal limitations on warfare were minimized by keeping a permanent presence in the operational area (Spartan base at Decelea founded 413 BC; Roman winter camps (*hiberna*)). During the time of the Delian League, the Athenians were capable of exerting power and fighting at any time, thanks to their garrisons, naval bases and supply stations [5. 113].

BIBLIOGRAPHY

[1] W. ECKHARDT, Civilizations, Empires and Wars. A Quantitative History of War, 1992 [2] J.P. ROTH, War (The Hellenistic World and the Roman Republic), in: P. SABIN et al. (eds.), The Cambridge History of Greek and Roman Warfare, vol. 1, 2007, 368–398 [3] E. DE SAINT-DENIS, Mare clausum, in: REL 25, 1947, 196–247 [4] I. SCHRAKAMP, Warfare, Ancient Near East, in: R.S. BAGNALL et al. (eds.), The Encyclopedia of Ancient History, vol. 12, 2013, 7046–7048 [5] R. SCHULZ, Feldherren, Kriege und Strategen. Krieg in der Antike von Achill bis Attila, 2012.

UWE WALTER

Training

A. Classical and Hellenistic Greece
B. Roman Republic and Principate
C. Late Antiquity

A. CLASSICAL AND HELLENISTIC GREECE

Close attention was paid to the training of soldiers throughout Antiquity. It was not, however, well documented in the Archaic and Classical periods, since only a few military treatises have been preserved, the main ones being by Xenophon, who was well known to have been an experienced soldier. Information increases for the Hellenistic period, thanks to authors such as Polybius. Epigraphic material contributes to our knowledge of military training under the Hellenistic monarchies and the Roman Republic.

Xenophon's treatise on hunting provides some information. Hunting was an activity well suited for the training and sharpening of citizen-soldiers' fighting skills (Xen. Cyn. 12,1–4). Xenophon emphasizes the need for good physical condition, which was to be obtained through daily training (Xen. Mem. 3,12,1–4). Training could also improve the fighting capabilities of cavalrymen, as all cavalry commanders were expected to remember. The focus of training should be riding in different types of terrain and mastering the use of weapons, for example throwing spears or fighting with a spear while on horseback (Xen. Hipp. 1,5f.; Xen. Equ. 8,1f.; 12,12f.). Training was the optimal way to find out which horses were best suited for use in the army, since a cavalryman was of no use if he could not control his horse on the battlefield (Xen. Hipp. 1,13–15). At Athens, cavalry exercises and parades were held in public in the Lycaeum (Xen. Hipp. 3,6–8), the Hippodrome and the Academy (Xen. Hipp. 3,10–14). The cavalry's success in battle depended entirely on continuous practice and training (Xen. Hipp. 8,2).

The commander was responsible for ensuring the training of his unit. In 395 BC, when the Spartan king Agesilaus gathered his troops at Ephesus, he announced prizes for the most skilful cavalry units, the most accomplished infantry units and the most proficient archers. Every Spartan gymnasium was filled with exercising soldiers, cavalrymen on horseback and shooters (Xen. Ag. 1,25). Such intense training proved its worth in the same year when Agesilaus won a glorious victory over Tissaphernes near Sardeis (Xen. Ag. 1,30–34; Plut. *Agesilaus* 10). Xenophon also emphasizes and praises the psychological training of these soldiers, who were better trained and more battle-ready in support of Agesilaus' victory (Xen. Ag. 2,7f.).

The first volume of Arrian's *Tactica* offers a valuable account of the standard training of Macedonian and Hellenistic armies (1–32). This work, which examines the Greek military tradition, was the last in a long series of treatises, of which only a few fragments of works by Asclepiodotus (a disciple of Posidonius, who made use of his treatise, which is mentioned by Aelianus and Arrian, but is lost) and Aelianus (who wrote in the reign of Trajan) survive. The most important Hellenistic treatise on tactics seems to have been that of Posidonius. Aelianus and Arrian rely on a common source and probably also drew on a tradition originating with Posidonius (→ Military literature) [19]. As part of the same tradition, Polyaenus (Str. 4,2,10) mentions that the Macedonian king Philip II trained his army by marching it in full kit. It is probable that all Hellenistic rulers and senior commanders were heavily invested in the military training of their soldiers. Although most of their men were professional soldiers who were expected to demonstrate excellent training, they still had to keep up their battle-readiness with regular exercises. For an infantry army, the best way to preserve fitness was through marching and running in full kit. Fighting skills were also honed by training in close combat. As for the cavalry, riders and horses would train to develop the needed bond between man and animal, and to teach the horse to respond correctly to commands in battle.

B. ROMAN REPUBLIC AND PRINCIPATE
During the Roman Republic, the proconsul was responsible for training his men. Direct information comes from Polybius (10,20,1–5) and Livy (26,51,4), who report the special instructions for training the infantry that P. Cornelius Scipio Africanus gave to his military tribunes during the Roman Siege of Carthago Nova (Spain) in 209 BC (→ Generals of note, O.). He also took over the training of combat manoeuvres for the fleet. Infantry training consisted of running, cleaning and preparing weapons, and combat drills [21. 219]. After a rest day, the running resumed. As Livy points out, the proconsul took part in all exercises side by side with his soldiers. → Discipline was also restored by means of marching and training, for example by the other Scipio (P. Cornelius Scipio Aemilianus) at Numantia in 134/33 (Frontin. Str. 4,1,1).

At the beginning of the Roman Empire, training was part of everyday life for all soldiers and was associated with *disciplina* (Tac. Ann. 3,42,1: *militia disciplinaque nostra*), which became one of the key concepts of imperial propaganda (*disciplina Augusti*) [17. 26–35]. Deficiencies in training would mean the spread of disobedience and misconduct among the men, and the loss of consistent standards [2. 105–119]. Most information on training comes to us from Tacitus (Tac. ann. 13,35), Flavius Josephus (Jos. BI 3,71–76; 3,85–88; 3,102–107) and Vegetius, complemented by other sources such as Arrian's *Tactica* (on the cavalry: 36f., 40; 43f.; most thorough treatment in [12]; [3. 42–153]; [7. 41–43]; [6. 93–124], cf. [14. 38–72]) and the speeches given by Hadrian at Lambaesis on the exercise grounds of the *legio III Augusta* in July 128 (CIL VIII 2532 = ILS 2487 = [1. no. 328]) [8. 545]; [18]. Arrian reveals that he himself wrote not only a treatise on cavalry training (*hippika gymnasia*), but also one on infantry training dedicated to Hadrian (Arr. Tact. 32,3). This, however, has not survived.

Vegetius opens his military treatise with the words *nulla enim alia re videmus populum Romanum orbem subegisse terrarum nisi armorum exercitio, disciplina castrorum usuque militia* ('We consider that the Roman people has conquered the globe by means of nothing other than training in arms, discipline and military experience'; Veg. Mil. 1,1,2). Training consisted of exercises involving tree felling, carrying loads, leaping ditches, sea and river swimming, marching at pace and running in full kit (*silvam caedere, portare onera, transsilire fossas, natare in mari sive fluminibus, gradu pleno ambulare vel currere etiam armatos cum sarcinis suis frequentissime convenit*, Veg. Mil. 2,23,12). Recruits and new soldiers (*iuniores quidem et novi milites*) were expected to exercise twice daily (mornings and afternoons) in order to attain the training level of older and more experienced fighters (*veteres autem et eruditi*), who had to train only once a day (Veg. Mil. 2,23,1f.).

The exercise grounds (Latin *campus*, Veg. Mil. 2,23,11) were under the supervision of a sergeant (*campidoctor*) and the *doctor cohortis* ('drill instructor') and his adjutant (*optio campi*) who were subordinate to the sergeant. Cavalry training was supervised by an *exercitator equitum* ('trainer of the cavalry soldiers') and a *magister campi* ('master of camp'). They all made votive gifts to Mars campester (CIL II 4083 = ILS 2416, Tarraco, Hispania citerior: *campidoctor* of the *equites singulares*, 'mounted guards' of the governor) [15. 266], to horse deities such as the Celtic goddess Epona, or to the Dii Campestres in general (CIL III 7904 = ILS 2417 = IDR III/2, 205: *exercitator equitum singularium*, 'trainer of the mounted guard', Ulpia Traiana Sarmizegetusa, Dacia: dedication to Epona and the Campestres; Dii Campestres: CIL VIII 2635 = ILS 3157, with Mars Augustus, CIL VIII 10760, Lambaesis, Numidia; CIL XIII 6449 = ILS 2604, Benningen am Neckar; CIL XIII 6470,

Bockingen; AE 2003, 1274, Obernburg am Main, Germania superior).

Training had to be conducted continuously, regardless of weather or season (Veg. Mil. 2,23,10f.; 3,2). Centurions of the legions and senior officers of the guard units at Rome were sent out to serve in different legions, helping to maintain uniform standards across the entire army. Where possible, soldiers trained in the open air, and where this was not possible, they used specially designed buildings such as the *basilica equestris exercitatoria* (CIL VII 965 = ILS 2619 = RIB I 978, Castra exploratorum, Netherby, Britannia, AD 222: *coh(ors) I Ael(ia) / Hispanorum m(illiaria) eq(uitata) devota numina / maiestatique eius baselicam* (sic!) */equestrem exercitatoriam / iam pridem a solo coeptam / aedificavit consummavitque*; cf. also CIL III 6025 = ILS 2615, Syene, Egypt: a *basilica* built by the *cohors I Flavia Cilicum equitata* in AD 140). *Basilicae* were dedicated buildings within fortresses and forts in the northwestern provinces of the Roman Empire, where the harsh winters did not permit outdoor training all year round (Veg. Mil. 2,23,10: *Missibilia quoque vel plumbatas iugi perpetuoque exercitio dirigere cogebantur usque adeo, ut tempore hiemis de tegulis vel scindulis, quae si deessent, certe de cannis, ulva vel culmo et porticus tegerentur ad equites et quaedam velut basilicae ad pedites, in quibus tempestate vel ventis aëre turbato sub tecto armis erudiebatur exercitus*; 'They were also so concerned to keep up training with throwing and slinging projectiles that they roofed over training areas for the horsemen in winter with bricks and shingles and, where these were absent, at least with reeds, rushes or straw, and made makeshift halls for foot soldiers so that the army could conduct weapons training indoors when storms and gales were blowing outside'). On *basilicae* in the Roman military context see [13]. The *basilicae* in the east, for example at Syene, were probably built to permit regular training in the extreme summer heat of these regions.

Amphitheatres near military fortifications and forts were used for cavalry and infantry training; *ludi castrenses* ('camp games') and *hippika gymnasia* ('horse exercises'), or even circular fencing (installations called *gyrus* could be built for the same purpose: Tab. Vindonissa 43). The exercises were probably very similar to those of gladiators [2]. Provincial governors and commanders of legions and auxiliary units, as well as the officers within a unit, were responsible for the training of all soldiers, as can be seen in literary sources and the speeches of Hadrian at Lambaesis in AD 128.

There was a frequently cited Roman opinion that the units stationed in the east suffered weaker discipline and training than those on the northwestern frontiers (Tac. Ann. 13,35; Suet. Vesp. 4,6; Fronto, *Principia historiae* 12f.; Fronto, *Epistulae ad Verum imperatorem* 2,1,22f.; SHA Avid. 5). Of course, this was merely a commonplace that contrasted the purportedly luxurious lifestyle of Roman soldiers in the east, who were in close proximity to magnificent cities and who supposedly viewed weapons and fortifications as novel and curious sights, with the more austere and harsh lifestyles of soldiers in the western provinces (Tac. Ann. 13,35,1: *satis constitit fuisse in eo exercitu veteranos, qui non stationem, non vigilias inissent, vallum fossamque quasi nova et mira viserent, sine galeis, sine loricis, nitidi et quaestuosi, militia per oppida expleta*; 'It is well enough known that there were veterans serving in this army who had never yet seen an army station or guard post, to whom ramparts and ditches were unheard-of wonders, and who, because they performed their military service in cities, ran around spruced up, helmetless and unarmoured, eager for gain' – referring to the army in Syria in AD 57) [23]. This commonplace may have originated with Sallust, who in reference to the army of Sulla returning from the east accused the general of ruining the youth of the Roman Republic. Sallust established the literary tradition of the 'deviant east', which first corrupted the Roman army and then Rome's youth (Sall. Catil. 11,5f.: *Huc accedebat quod L. Sulla exercitum, quem in Asia ductaverat, quo sibi fidum facere, contra more maiorum luxuriose nimisque liberaliter habuerat. Loca amoena, voluptaria facile in otio ferocis militum animos molliverant. Ibi primum insuevit exercitus populi Romani amare, potare, signa, tabulas pictas, vasa caelata mirari, ea privatim et publice rapere, delubra spoliare, sacra profanaque omnia polluere*; 'Here it was that Lucius Sulla, seeking to curry favour with the forces he commanded in Asia, allowed them – contrary to the customs of our forefathers – immoderate and excessive freedoms. The agreeable amenities easily available in their rest periods rendered the rough spirits of these soldiers effeminate. It was here that the army of the Roman people first learned to love and to carouse, to wonder at statues, paintings and exquisite vessels, to rob private and public property, to plunder sanctuaries and befoul everything sacred and profane'; cf. Sall. Catil. 12,2). However, epigraphic and archaeological evidence clearly contradict this commonplace. There is nothing to suggest that army discipline and training were not maintained identically across the whole empire. Tacitus, however, indicates – probably with some justification – that Corbulo found the forces for his upcoming campaign to be inadequately trained, and that he had to act quickly to restore his army to its former state of fitness (→ Generals of note, D.). Like the early Republican proconsuls, Corbulo is shown here as an example to his soldiers – always the first to start training and always encouraging the others [3. 44–48]; [17. 32f.]. Although there is no direct evidence for this, it seems likely that this kind of intensive training was the norm before a major military undertaking – as in the case of Trajan, who went to the provinces to inspect his armies before launching the Dacian War (ILS 1019: [dum] / exercitus suos circumit) [17. 121–165].

The sources offer no information about the training of sailors in the Praetorian and provincial fleets. Nevertheless, it is conceivable that, in addition to small mock-war exercises using a few ships, the constant routine patrols were used to achieve the necessary training. Such exercises probably resembled the *naumachiae* ('naval battles') performed in flooded amphitheatres.

As mentioned above, one of the most reliable sources on military training in the Roman Principate is the series of speeches delivered by Hadrian on the training grounds of the *legio III Augusta* in the summer of AD 128. The cavalry exercises referred to here resemble very closely the descriptions in Arrian's *Tactica*, even though these amounted to no more than training for sport and were called *ludi castrenses* or *armatura* (Veg. Mil. 2,23,3: *armaturam, quae festis diebus exhibetur in circo*) [3]; [19]; [22]. Following his inspection of the training exercises (*exercitationes militares*; *exercitationibus inspectis*), Hadrian spoke to the legionaries and the legion's cavalrymen. He then criticized the infantrymen of one cohort (*cohors II Hamiorum*) and turned to address the horsemen of the *ala I Pannoniorum* and the *cohors VI Commagenorum equitata* (*cohortales equites*). His comments were extensive: he expressed praise or criticism, offered advice and emphasized that the exercises had to be as close as possible to real battles ([*verae di*]*micationis imaginem accepit*).

C. LATE ANTIQUITY

By the reign of Gallienus at the latest, frontier units were no longer at full strength, for many of their soldiers had been assigned to Northern Italy and elsewhere in the empire (e.g. Sirmium, Poetovio), where they formed large field armies. Perhaps training was not needed, because the wars against foreign invaders were unrelenting. This well-trained army of Gallienus defeated the Goths at Naissus in 269 and became the nucleus for the *comitatenses* ('court troops') units of the later empire. The remaining frontier troops formed the basis for the later *limitanei* ('border troops') units (brief updated survey: [20]). Both, however, followed the same training system, for both were under central imperial commmand and many *limitanei* joined the *comitatenses*. One example is Valerius Thiumpo during the reign of Diocletian. Thiumpo had served in the *legio XI Claudia* at Durostorum in Moesia II, and was reassigned for five years to the *sacer* ('imperial retinue') as *lanciarius* ('lancer') and *protector*, then ordered back to the imperial frontier at the lower Danube as commander (*praefectus*) of the *legio II Herculia* at Troesmis in the province of Scythia (CIL III 6194 = ILS 2781 = IIFDR 236: *D(is) M(anibus) / Val(erius) Thiumpo qui / militavit in leg(ione) / XI Cl(audia) lectus in sacro / comit(atu) lanciarius / deinde protexit / annis V missus / pr(a)ef(ectus) leg(ionis) II Hercul(iae) / [e]git annis II semise et / decessit, vixit annis / XXXXV m(ensibus) III d(iebus) / XI. Aurel(ius) / [- - -]*. Cf. also AE 1922, 72 = 1976, 631 = 1995, 1338 = 1997, 1317 = IIFDR 206 from Ulmetum, Scythia: a soldier who served as *biarc(h)us in sacro palatio* and fell at the Battle of Chrysopolis/Calchedon between Constantine and Licinius in AD 324). No specialist training was required, which clearly shows that there was no real difference between the *limitanei* and *comitatenses*. Indeed, the experience that Valerius Thiumpo gained in the field enabled him to attain the highest possible command in a Roman legion of his day.

There are many reports from the later Roman Empire of failures to perform the rigorous training programme that was expected, which inevitably led to lack of discipline and many military failures and defeats. Ancient historians, however, tended to exaggerate this sort of thing, one example being Zosimus describing the inadequate training of Roman soldiers on the eve of the Battle of Adrianople against the Goths (AD 378) (4,23,4). The situation was exacerbated by the growing tendency to house entire units in civilian settlements and towns that were wholly unsuited to daily exercise and training [16. 170–172]. Authors of the 2nd century, such as Tacitus (Ann. 13,35) and Cornelius Fronto (*Epistulae ad Verum imperatorem* 2,1), were already telling stories of Roman units' lack of discipline and training when stationed in cities in the east of the empire – which was a trope of traditional Roman historiography [17. 33, 524f.]; [11. 269f.]. Yet, as noted above, this was simply perpetuating former eras' propaganda about the lack of discipline and training in units stationed in the east.

Emperors, especially in the Eastern Empire, tried on many occasions to reorganize the army and revive training. Even Heraclius was still trying to do so in AD 621/22, during his protracted Persian campaign, when he moved virtually all the units still in Europe to Asia Minor [9. 35–40]. This shows the importance that central Roman authorities attached to soldiers' training and discipline, until the introduction of the new Byzantine system of the *themata*. The *themata* made the individual units, which were housed in their different garrisons, ever more isolated and autonomous. Soldiers were increasingly busying themselves with livestock farming and tilling the land. A central professional army was, however, still maintained at the capital, along with some professional units out in the *themata* [9. 66f.].

☞ **Discipline; Education; Military service; Motivation**

Bibliography

Sources
[1] E.M. Smallwood, Documents Illustrating the Principates of Nerva, Trajan, and Hadrian, 1966.

Secondary literature
[2] Y. Le Bohec, The Imperial Roman Army, 1994 [3] R.W. Davies, Peace-time Routine in the Roman Army, 1967 (Theses, Durham University: http://etheses.dur.ac.uk/8075/) [4] R.W. Davies, Roman Military Training Grounds, in: E. Birley et al. (eds.), Roman Frontier Studies 1969. Eighth International Congress of Limesforschung, 1974, 20–26 [5] R.W. Davies, Fronto, Hadrian and the Roman Army, in: R.W. Davies, Service in the Roman Army, edited by D. Breeze and V.A. Maxfield, 1989, 71–92 [6] R.W. Davies, Service in the Roman Army, 1989 [7] R.W. Davies, The Daily Life of the Roman Soldier under the Principate, in: R.W. Davies, Service in the Roman Army, edited by D. Breeze and V.A. Maxfield, 1989, 33–70 [8] M. Le Glay, Les discours d'Hadrien à Lambèse, in: J. Fitz (ed.), Limes. Akten des XI. Internationalen Limeskongresses (Székesfehérvár, 30.8.–6.9.1976), 1977, 545–558 [9] J.F. Haldon, Recruitment and Conscription in the Byzantine Army c. 550–990. A Study on the Origins of the Stratiotike Ktemata, 1979 [10] B. Hobley, The 'Lunt' Roman Fort, England. Summary of the Excavations 1967–1972, in: D.M. Pippidi (ed.), Actes du IXe Congrès international d'études sur les frontières romaines, Mamaïa, 6–13 septembre 1972, 1974 [11] B. Isaac, The Limits of Empire. The Roman Army in the East, 1990 (updated edition) [12] F. Kiechle, Die 'Taktik' des Flavius Arrianus, in: BRGK 45, 1964, 87–129 [13] C.C. Petolescu, Un edificiu militar roman. Basilica [A Roman Military Building. Basilica], in: Arhivele Olteniei 10, 1995, 29–36 [14] S.E. Phang, Roman Military Service. Ideologies of the Discipline in the Late Republic and Early Principate, 2008 [15] P. Le Roux, L'armée romaine sous les Sévères, in: ZPE 94, 1992, 261–268 [16] P. Southern / K.R. Dixon, The Late Roman Army, 1996 [17] M.A. Speidel, Heer und Herrschaft im Römischen Reich der Hohen Kaiserzeit, 2009 [18] M.P. Speidel, Emperor Hadrian's Speeches to the African Army. A New Text, 2006 [19] P.A. Stadter, The Ars Tactica of Arrian. Tradition and Originality, in: ClP 73, 1978, 117–128 [20] R. Tomlin, A.H.M. Jones and the Army of the Fourth Century, in: D.M. Gwynn (ed.), A.H.M. Jones and Later Roman Empire, 2008, 143–165 [21] F.W. Walbank, A Historical Commentary on Polybius, vol. 2: Commentary on Books VII–XVIII, 1967 [22] E.L. Wheeler, The Occasion of Arrian's Tactica, in: GRBS 19, 1978, 351–365 [23] E.L. Wheeler, The Laxity of Syrian Legions (1st to 3rd c. A.D.), in: D.L. Kennedy (ed.), The Roman Army in the East, 1996, 229–276.

Florian Matei-Popescu

Transmission of orders

A. Greece
B. Rome

A. Greece

A.1. Archaic warfare and hoplite combat
A.2. The Spartan and Macedonian phalanxes

A.1. Archaic warfare and hoplite combat

Warfare in the Archaic Greek world was not well organized. Instead, it relied on individual courage, particularly among members of the elites who could afford the necessary weaponry, equipment and horses. This meant that specific orders rarely needed to be given, and it was often impossible to communicate them once battle had been joined.

Even the better organized hoplite combat that emerged around the end of the 8th century BC required only limited management and command structures. It was therefore well suited to citizen armies in which → discipline was achieved only with difficulty, if at all. A general would sometimes give a passionate speech to his men shortly before battle, but this was more to instil courage than to convey orders. Sacrifices were made and trumpets gave the signal to advance (Thuc. 6,69,1f.). The Spartans sang war songs or the Paean (a hymn to Apollo) and marched into battle in time with flute accompaniment (Thuc. 5,70; Plut. *Lycurgus* 22,2f.). They performed sacrificial rituals shortly before the two sides engaged (Xen. Hell. 4,2,20). The battle lasted until one side collapsed and fled, with no central commands needed. The hoplite commanders usually themselves fought in the front rank, and from there they were hardly in a position to issue orders, even if they wanted to.

In the 5th century, heavily armed troops were separated from those lightly armed. This and other tactical developments that continued into the first half of the 4th century created the need for a sophisticated system of command and control. Out of this came a hierarchical structure of ranks. A reorganization of the → phalanx gave rise to smaller subordinate units, each with its own commander, whose job, however, was limited to using verbal commands to get his phalanx unit into position on the battlefield (cf. Xen. An. 1,8,11f.) and have it advance on the enemy. The men literally followed their direct superior wherever he took them (cf. Xen. Cyr. 2,2,6–9), arranging themselves into battle lines three to eight ranks deep.

A.2. The Spartan and Macedonian phalanxes

The Spartan phalanx soon became especially hierarchical. Thucydides (5,66) in the late 5th century BC describes the developed command chain that was established there: 'When the king is leading them all, all commands come from him. He tells the *polemarchoi* (regiment leaders) what he requires. They tell the *lochagoi* (company leaders), who tell the *pentekonteres* (line commanders), who tell the *enomotarchoi* (section leaders). The *enomotia* (sections of 40 men) then learn it from them ... because almost the entire Spartan army (except for a small part) consists of commanders of commanders' (→ Sparta). Xenophon tells how these structures enabled the army to manoeuvre before the start of battle: 'On a command, the regiments (*morai*) form into sections (*enomotiai*), in groups of two, three or six... In the Spartan formation, the men in the front rank (*protostatai*) are commanders ... Some of the men are entrusted with command, while others are commanded to obey. Changes in the formation are ordered by verbal command from the section commander (*enomotarches*), who functions as herald... When they march in formation, one section follows the next. If an enemy phalanx appears before them in this situation, the command goes to the section leader to form the battle line towards the shield side (i.e. leftwards), and so it continues throughout the entire marching column, until the phalanx is facing the enemy. If the enemy approaches from the rear in the same situation, each rank turns around abruptly so that the best men are always facing the enemy' (Xen. Lac. pol. 11,5–8).

Thucydides and Xenophon, however, describe all this in a tone that suggests that the Spartans were extraordinary in their degree of organization and discipline. Most *poleis* had fewer subordinate units and commanders. Xenophon's account suggests that their armies often became confused during manoeuvres that the Spartans could perform with ease. As in earlier periods, though, there were no real manoeuvres to perform once the battle was underway, and they could usually go without giving any orders at all. Such armies had no practical need of flags or standards, although the troops of some states did bear insignia on their shields. The Spartans, for instance, used the letter lambda to help distinguish friend from foe.

Nevertheless, the development of new tactics intensified the trend towards ever more elaborate command structures in the second quarter of the 4th century, for example for the Thebans at Leuctra in 371 and Mantinea in 361. Further driving the process were advances in the equipment and training of light → infantry, for instance as developed by Iphicrates in Athens in the early 4th century. Battle signals on land seem to have first been made by raising a → standard or flag (*semeion*: Polyaenus, Str. 3,9,27; cf. Nep. Iph. 11,2,2) in Iphicrates' day, if not before. Trumpets and visual signals had been employed for this purpose since at least the 5th century at sea (Aesch. Pers. 395; Thuc. 1,49; Polyaenus, Str. 1,48,2), where it was much more difficult to coordinate units.

The Macedonian phalanx of Philip II and his son Alexander the Great, which built on the achievements of Iphicrates, confronted its enemy with a thicket of spears at least 4.6–5.3 m long. This phalanx was divided into *lochoi* of 512 men apiece, arranged in sixteen ranks. A *dekadarchos* stood in the front rank of each of these divisions, with a more junior officer in the eighth, ninth and sixteenth ranks. This made it possible to split the *lochos* into two halves and establish a tight formation only eight men deep. This structure once more suggests that commands were given in a decentralized way by voice alone, and that troops literally followed their leaders in the front rank, who in turn followed their company commanders, and so on.

B. Rome

B.1. Verbal commands
B.2. Signals, standards and messengers

B.1. Verbal commands

Unsurprisingly, the Romans used the same basic methods to convey commands as their Greek and Hellenistic predecessors: verbal commands supported by acoustic and optical signals. As the Roman army developed and became more professional during the Middle and Late Republic, however, these methods were supplemented, firstly by the use of written orders and watchwords, and secondly by the use of standards for the individual units on the battlefield, all of this to enhance the army's flexibility and manoeuvrability. Literary and epigraphic sources supply far more details about these methods for the Roman era than for earlier periods in history. Their use is reflected in the command structure of the basic unit of the Roman legions, the century (*centuria*). Besides the commanding centurion (*centurio*) and his deputy (*optio*) – who was probably placed at the century's rear on the battlefield and was armed with a long, gnarled club to drive the men forwards and prevent them from fleeing – every maniple (group of two centuries) had a standard bearer (*signifer*) and a junior officer who passed on the watchword (*tesserarius*, see below).

In the camp, the watchword for the night was conveyed verbally by the legion's commander to its tribunes, who in turn passed it to the centurions. They then gave it to their men, either directly or via the *tesserarius* (Pol. 6,34,5f.; Jos. BI 3,87; Veg.

Mil. 2,7). Polybius (6,34,8f.) describes the duties of this subordinate officer in the mid-2nd century BC: 'A man was chosen by lot to be exempted from watch duties and to go to the tribune's tent every evening at sunset to receive the watchword [*synthema*] in the form of a written tablet [Latin *tessera*], and then to go again. Returning to his maniple, he would pass the wooden piece with the watchword to the commander of the next maniple before witnesses. This man then passed it to the commander of the next maniple, and everyone then did this in sequence until the watchword came back to the first maniples camping closest to the tribunes. These men had to bring the tablet back to the tribunes before darkness fell.'

B.2. SIGNALS, STANDARDS AND MESSENGERS

In camp and on the battlefield, the Romans deployed not only trumpets for acoustic signals, but a whole range of musical instruments with different tonal registers in order to communicate a wide range of commands (→ Music). Under the Principate, and perhaps even before, signals were given by the *cornu* (a spiral-shaped horn played by a *cornicen*), the *tuba* (a straight brass instrument played by the *tubicen*) – these two often together (Tac. Ann. 1,28,3; 1,68,3; Veg. Mil. 2,22) – and the shorter *bucina* (played by a *bucinator*; Frontin. Str. 1,5,17). It appears that all these instruments remained in use through Late Antiquity and into the Byzantine period (cf. Veg. Mil. 3,5,6f.), although in the late 6th century AD, Emperor Maurice ordered (Ps.-Mauricius, Strat. 2,17) that, to avoid confusion, only one instrument (the trumpet, *boukinon*) should sound on the battlefield, and, if necessary, its signal should be passed on by other trumpets in the various divisions.

According to Flavius Josephus, the *salpinx* (*tuba*) announced the time for sleeping and the change of watch (Pol. 14,3,6; but cf. the *boucina* in Pol. 6,36,5 and Frontin. Str. 1,5,17), gave the signal for waking up, and announced the commands to take down the tents, prepare to march, and finally to march. The herald would then ask the men three times if they were ready, to which they replied three times with 'Ready!' and then they marched out. Other commands known to have been conveyed by musical instruments include the signal to gather in the camp (Liv. 5,47,7; 7,36,9 etc.) or on the battlefield, and the order to engage the enemy (Pol. 8,30,7; Caes. B Civ. 3,90,3; Luc. 6,129f. etc.) or withdraw (Pol. 15,14,3; Caes. B Gall. 7,47,1; Liv. 37,29).

→ Standards (*semeia*) doubtless gave a visual signal to join battle in the Greek and Hellenistic armies (see above), but it is not known whether individual units were equipped with standards prior to the reforms under Roman influence in the 2nd century BC, or whether they were used for conveying commands. Certainly, the earliest illustration of a standard being used by a 'Macedonian' army dates from the 2nd century. It appears on a bronze relief from Pergamum [2. 250]. The Roman armies of the Republican period, on the other hand, carried standards (*signa*) in all kinds of animal forms – eagles for the legions; wolves, minotaurs, horses and goats for their individual ranks – and in the form of a human hand (*manus*) for the individual maniples (see above) within these ranks. The Roman general C. Marius is said to have abolished the animal standards as part of his army reform, excepting only the eagle (*aquila*), which accordingly became the symbol of the Roman legions (Plin. HN 10,16).

The *aquilifer* carried the eagle atop a pole. After the centurion (*centurio*), he was the highest ranking officer in a legion and placed at the far right wing next to the highest ranking centurion, the *primipilus*. Each legion comprised ten cohorts, each of which in turn was made up of six centuries and thus three *signiferi*, each carrying a *signum* (a hand fitted at the top of a pole above a number of medallions perhaps indicating the number of the cohort). Under the Principate, the auxiliary infantry units and maniples each had their own *signa*. The cavalry divisions (*turmae*) had cloth flags (*vexilla*) hanging horizontally from a crossbar, carried by a *vexillarius*. An as yet undated example of a red *vexillum* with an image of Victoria astride the globe has been found intact in Egypt. The standard poles were usually fitted with metal spikes so they could be rammed into the ground. Handles halfway up the shaft helped raise them. Movements of the units and their maniples or centuries were steered initially by blasts of the horn (*cornu*) to attract attention, then by the raising of the standards (Frontin. Str. 2,8,1–9; Veg. Mil. 2,22).

These types of standard continued to be used in Late Antiquity and the Byzantine period. Only the *signa* of the maniples gradually disappeared. *Vexilla* were then introduced for the auxiliary cohorts, and dragon standards (*dracones*) for the cavalry and some high-ranking officers (cf. Ps.-Mauricius, Str. 2,14; 7,16). These standards, adopted from the Dacians – enemies of Rome – in the 2nd century, had a serpent head and a fabric tail that fluttered and hissed in the breeze. An example made from a copper alloy and dating from the late 3rd century has been found at the Roman *castellum* ('fort') of Niederbieber (Rhineland-Palatinate, Germany).

Beacons could be used to convey commands and information over great distances. Polybius (10,43–47) describes an elaborate system to this effect, although its practical value in sending specific messages seems doubtful. Nonetheless, Caesar (Caes. B Gall. 2,33,3; Caes. B Civ. 3,65,2) and Appian (Ib. 90) confirm that simple smoke and fire signals were used to communicate between camps and *castella* (cf. also Liv. 21,27,7; Onas. 6,8; Veg. mil. 3,5), and it has been suggested that such signals were also used along permanent Roman frontier installations such as Hadrian's Wall [4]; [10].

In all likelihood, however, the most efficient way of conveying detailed orders over long distances was to send a messenger by cart or on horseback. For hundreds of years, the imperial *frumentarii* (literally, 'purveyors of corn', a kind of intelligence agency) delivered messages between Rome and the governors of border provinces.

☞ Legion; Military service

Bibliography
[1] A. Abuin, Standards and Insignia of Byzantium, in: Byzantion 71, 2001, 5–59 [2] A. Conze, Altertümer von Pergamon, vol. 1, Text 2: Stadt und Landschaft, 1913 [3] G.T. Dennis, Byzantine Battle Flags, in: ByzF 8, 1982, 51–60 [4] G.H. Donaldson, Signalling Communications and the Roman Imperial Army, in: Britannia 19, 1988, 349–356 [5] Y. Le Bohec, L'armée Romaine sous le Haut-Empire, 1989 [6] N. Maliaras, Die Musikinstrumente im byzantinischen Heer vom 6. bis zum 12. Jahrhundert, in: JÖB 51, 2001, 73–104 [7] N. Sekunda, Military Forces. A. Land Forces, in: P. Sabin et al. (eds.), The Cambridge History of Greek and Roman Warfare, vol. 1: Greece, the Hellenistic World and the Rise of Rome, 2001, 325–357 [8] M.P. Speidel, Eagle-Bearer and Trumpeter, in: BJ 176, 1976, 123–163 [9] H. van Wees, Greek Warfare. Myths and Realities, 2004 [10] D.J. Woolliscroft, Roman Military Signalling, 2001.

BORIS RANKOV

Triumph

A. Introduction
B. Early history and Republic
C. Imperial period
D. Monumentalization of the triumph in the Republican and Imperial periods

A. Introduction

The Roman triumph was a victory ritual that classical historians (e.g. Dionysius of Halicarnassus, Livy, Plutarch; cf. InscrIt 13,1, 534) tell us had been performed since the foundation of Rome, and whose existence continued to be attested through Late Antiquity and beyond (→ Parades). At the heart of the ritual was a procession (*pompa triumphalis*) that took the victorious general, his soldiers and the spoils and prisoners of war from the Field of Mars outside the municipal boundary (*pomerium*) into Rome and up to the Temple of Jupiter on the Capitol. The triumph generally marked the conclusion of a victorious campaign. Its functions were religious, political, social and cultural, though they underwent changes through the long history of the tradition. The literary sources of the Principate sometimes describe a development from the religious ritual of the Monarchical period to a secularized victory celebration emphasizing self-glorification in their own time (e.g. Dion. Hal. Ant. Rom. 2,34,1–4; Plut. *Romulus* 16,5–8). Today, historians argue that the triumph fulfilled multiple functions in parallel, as attested by its persistence, vitality and dynamism over nearly a millennium of ancient history.

Scholars long discussed the origins and early history of the triumph from a perspective of religious science. Besides the Etruscan elements, which suggest a history dating back to the 6th century BC, there have also been attempts to identify connections with rituals of greater antiquity from Asia Minor [26]. It was in this context that the role of the *triumphator* as (Etruscan) king and/or the embodiment of Jupiter was discussed [3]. During the Republican period, the legal status of the *triumphator* (as magistrate and bearer of military authority with *imperium*) was of considerable importance. Over the past two decades, scholarly interest has shifted increasingly to issues of cultural history. The study of victory and triumphal monuments, especially in the context of the city of Rome, has brought the spatial dimension of the triumph into the focus of attention. With each individual triumph being celebrated in a setting dominated by the memory of previous triumphs, a complex and semantically charged 'landscape of memory' emerged [7]; [8]. The route of the triumph has again been hotly debated in this context [24]; [16]; [20]. Meanwhile, greater interest has arisen in the performative dimension of the triumph, leading to research into the interaction among the actors and groups of actors participating in it [7]; [15]; [20]. Attention here has increasingly focused on political communication in the Republican and Imperial periods, between the senate, magistrates (or emperor) and people [1]; [7]; [6]. Recently, especially for the Republican period, scholars have examined more closely the role of defeats in the Roman people's self-image, which was typically characterized by → victories and triumphs [4]. Fresh analysis has also been given to triumphs held after civil wars [11].

B. Early history and Republic

B.1. Forms of triumph
B.2. Qualifying for a triumph
B.3. Sociological perspective and functions

B.1. Forms of triumph

The 'Capitoline Triumph List' (*Fasti Triumphales Capitolini*, after its place of safekeeping on the Capitol in Rome; cf. InscrIt 13,3), dating from the

Augustan period, details almost 300 triumphs for the Monarchical and Republican periods overall, not all of which are accepted as historical fact ([9] with the catalogue of triumphs 340–19 BC; [21. 244–252]: survey of triumphs 753–19 BC). Several different forms are distinguished. Besides the full triumph (*triumphus*), there were also the (rarely celebrated) triumph on the Alban Mount (*triumphus in monte Albano*), which was probably held at the general's own expense, and the *ovatio*, the lesser victory celebration [21]. The naval triumph (*triumphus navalis*; the term is used in the Augustan triumph catalogue and elsewhere) was granted after a victory at sea, but whether its form differed from a regular triumph is unknown.

In the full triumph, the procession ideally included the booty displayed on chariots, the prisoners of war, the victorious soldiers, and finally the general in triumphal regalia riding in a triumphal car usually drawn by four horses (*currus* or *quadriga*). The procession passed from the Field of Mars into the city through the Triumphal Gate (*porta triumphalis*), crossing Rome by way of several interim stations (Velabrum, Forum Boarium, Circus Maximus, Velia, Forum Romanum, Clivus Capitolinus), and ended outside the Temple of Jupiter Optimus Maximus on the Capitoline Hill, where the *triumphator* placed a laurel wreath in the lap of the statue of the god and made a sacrifice, followed by a banquet for Roman citizens. Scholars continue to dispute the location of the Triumphal Gate and the detailed reconstruction of the triumphal route through the city of Rome (most recently [24]; [16]; [20]). The *ovatio* probably took the same route as the triumph, though the general did not ride in the triumphal car, but generally walked into the city (Dion. Hal. Ant. Rom. 5,47,2f.; Plut. *Marcellus* 22,1ff.). No details are known of the design or route of the triumph on the Alban Mount, except that it ended at the Sanctuary of Jupiter there (cf. on Q. Minucius Rufus in 197 BC Liv. 33,23,8f.).

B.2. Qualifying for a triumph

During the Republican period, the victory celebration was in the gift of the senate. Key sources include the debates in the senate preceding the granting of a triumph – reported by Livy among others – and Val. Max. 2,8. Scholars still debate the qualifying criteria. *Pace* Valerius Maximus, there was no established, comprehensive 'triumphal law'. Besides the status of the general (as holder of *imperium* and *auspicium*) and his military accomplishments, the course of the debate in the senate itself played an important part (cf. e.g. on the triumph of Cn. Manlius Vulso in 187 BC: Liv. 38,44,9–50,3; in general [9]; [19]; [13. 178–253]). If the senate was reluctant to award a full triumph, it might allow the general an *ovatio* (as e.g. for M. Claudius Marcellus in 211 BC: Liv. 26,21,1–5). If he was denied a triumph, the general could choose on his own initiative (and probably at his own expense) to hold a triumph on the Alban Mount outside Rome (as Q. Minucius Rufus for instance did in 197 BC: Liv. 33,22f.; cf. in general [22]). As from 27 BC, the granting of triumphs was firmly under the aegis of the *princeps*. The last triumph celebrated by a general who was not a member of the imperial house (L. Cornelius Balbus) took place in 19 BC. This victory celebration is also the last entry in the Augustan triumph catalogue.

B.3. Sociological perspective and functions

For the day of the triumph, the *triumphator* was elevated above all his peers. Probably for this reason, the serving consuls (if the *triumphator* was not one of them) did not attend the concluding banquet (*cena*) (Val. Max. 2,8,6). Ancient sources sometimes report that the general was made to resemble the statue of Jupiter on the Capitol (especially with the sceptre and face painted red: Liv. 10,7,10; Plin. HN 33,111f.; [23. 224]). However, this special status was unquestionably temporary. Attempts by some Republican generals to wear the triumphal regalia after the day of the victory celebration were typically thwarted by opposition from the senate (C. Marius in 104 BC: Liv. Per. 67; Plut. *Marius* 12,5; otherwise with L. Aemilius Paullus after 167 BC and Cn. Pompeius Magnus (Pompey) after AD 61). This changed with the dictatorship of Caesar.

During the Republican period, this prominent exposure of one man ran counter to the idea of the essentially collective and collegial rule of the senatorial aristocracy. This explains why, throughout the history of the Republic, fierce debates in the senate apparently preceded decisions concerning triumphs [1]. From the senate's perspective in view of its collective authority, triumphs served the purpose of giving strategic focus to conflicts and dampening rivalries within this body, although it was not always possible to eliminate conflicts. This also explains why the granting of triumphs did not simply follow set criteria, but always had to be negotiated anew [13. 252f.]. On the whole, the senate succeeded in maintaining control over the bestowal of triumphs until late in the Republican period.

From a religious studies perspective, the sacrifice to Jupiter on the Capitol that concluded the triumph ended the campaign, which had begun with the vow to the same god at the initial march out (*profectio*) [23]. At the same time, by crossing the city boundary (*pomerium*), the soldiers were brought from the sphere outside the city (*militiae*, 'the field') to the pacified space of the city of Rome (*domi*, 'at home'). After the triumph, the army received rewards in the form of *donativa*, scaled by military rank (e.g. Liv. 37,59,6; 41,7,3; 45,43,7). It is no longer assumed today that crossing the city boundary had a purifying effect on the army, which had been tainted by the brutality of war [26. 152f.]; [23. 229].

There was also an economic dimension to the triumph, since the procession brought to the city spoils of war (→ Booty), especially minted and unminted precious metals, that were probably transferred directly into the public treasury (*aerarium*) [15].

The triumph was also a communication event, in that it presented evidence of the campaign's military successes to the urban Roman public. The booty – enemy weapons and prisoners of war – exhibited in the procession, for instance, served as material proof of victory. Because prisoners of war were put on show in the procession in their own distinctive costumes, they served to illustrate how the rule of Rome was extending across an ever growing empire encompassing many different cultures [15]. There was a special role here for the defeated rulers who were sometimes exhibited, such as King Perseus of Macedonia (at the triumph of L. Aemilius Paullus in 167 BC) or Vercingetorix (at the triumph of C. Iulius Caesar (→ General, C.) over Gaul in 46 BC). At Octavian's triumph over Egypt in 29 BC, a portrait was displayed of Queen Cleopatra, who had taken her own life the year before (Cass. Dio 51,21). The soldiers functioned before the Roman public in the triumphal procession as eye witnesses to their general's military achievements. Sources sometimes make reference to the relationship between the soldiers and the *triumphator*. At the triumph of L. Aemilius Paullus, the army is said to have sung patriotic songs and songs in praise of the *triumphator*, mixed with laughter (Plut. *Aemilius Paullus* 34). Reports of the triumph of Caesar in 46 BC preserve the soldiers' satirical verses referring to the general's personal qualities (Suet. Caes. 49f.; Plin. HN 19,144). This is open to various interpretations: as an expression of latent tensions, a Saturnalian inversion of ritual, or evidence of close comradeship.

C. IMPERIAL PERIOD

C.1. Forms and conditions of the triumph
C.2. Functions of the triumph

C.1. FORMS AND CONDITIONS OF THE TRIUMPH

The ritual of the triumph was modified in various ways in the Imperial period. The triumph on the Alban Mount no longer took place. Besides the full triumph and the *ovatio* ('ovation'), which was still celebrated, Augustus' reign saw the creation of 'triumphal honours' (*ornamenta triumphalia*), by means of which victorious generals who were not members of the ruling dynasty could also be publicly celebrated.

As from the reign of Augustus and the completion of the triumphal catalogue after AD 19 (date of the last triumph entered in it), triumphs were only celebrated by the emperor or a potential successor (sometimes together: Vespasian and Titus in AD 71). The only decisive factor in the design of the event was the ruler's will. Some emperors did not hold triumphs (e.g. Nerva, Hadrian, Antoninus Pius, Septimius Severus), while others celebrated several, sometimes despite questionable military achievements (Domitian, Trajan). Overall, the frequency of triumphs was less than in the Republican period, and the link between military victory and triumph that was recognizable through into the Late Republican period was not now always apparent. There is consequently signiciant scholarly discussion of the ritual character of the victory celebration for the whole Imperial period [6].

The triumph continued to exist in Late Antiquity, but scholars today disagree as to the definition and nature of the ritual. For instance, the theory of the steady 'Christianization' of the triumph beginning in the 4th century [14] is now disputed [18]. The pagan triumph actually survived the end of Antiquity, as seen for instance in the triumph of Byzantine Emperor Constantine V after a victory over the Bulgars in 763 (Theophanes Confessor, *Chronographia* a. m. 6254 (p. 433 de Boor); Niceph. brev. 76).

C.2. FUNCTIONS OF THE TRIUMPH

As a symbol of victory, the triumph was a key facet of imperial self-image. Beginning with Augustus, pictorial representations (statues, coins, triumphal arches) tended to play a larger role than the ceremony itself [10]. Triumphs were increasingly celebrated in cities other than Rome (e.g. Trier, Constantinople). The elements of the ceremony of arrival (*adventus*) and the ruler jubilees (*decennalia*, *vicennalia*) were sometimes mixed [6]. There are reports from the reigns of Caligula and Nero of public processions taking on elements of a triumph, but the conditions and course (and sometimes destination) of these processions was so radically altered that it is extremely doubtful that they should be considered triumphs (Caligula's crossing of the Bay of Baiae in the late 30s: Suet. Cal. 19; Cass. Dio 59,17; Nero's reception of the Armenian king Tiridates at Rome in AD 66: Suet. Nero 13; Cass. Dio 63,2–7; Nero's return from Greece to Rome: Suet. Nero 25; Cass. Dio 63,20). Vespasian, having won the civil war and the Jewish War (→ Wars of note, E.), returned to the traditional model of the triumph as the victorious general entering the city of Rome. Despite some modifications, the triumph remained closely tied

D. Monumentalization of the triumph in the Republican and Imperial periods

While many literary sources beginning in the 2nd century BC attest to the perennial presence of the victory festival in the everyday life of the city of Rome, the triumph also became, from the Augustan period at least, a topic in Roman fiction [10].

While the victory celebration was fleeting, individual triumphs left many material and immaterial traces behind, and from at least the Middle Republic, these were used by victorious generals to emphasize the 'symbolic capital' (P. Bourdieu) of the triumph in front of their senatorial peers and the Roman people, or to keep it in their remembrance permanently. Fleeting elements included exhibiting paintings of battles in the procession (first permanent exhibition of a painting at the senate building in Rome 263 BC by M.' Valerius Messalla: Plin. HN 35,22), holding victory games (L. Caecilius Metellus 250 BC: Plin. HN 8,17), and portraying past *triumphatores* ('those celebrating a triumph') among the ancestors in aristocratic funeral processions (*pompa funebris*; cf. Pol. 6,53,7f.). Some generals took bynames after their triumphs alluding to their victories (P. Cornelius Scipio Africanus (→ Generals of note, O.), Q. Caecilius Metellus Numidicus, P. Servilius Vatia Isauricus; other bynames are inventions of the antiquarian tradition, e.g. Q. Fabius Maximus Allobrogicus) (→ Victory titles). Beginning in the Republican period, coins began to display victory symbols (victory goddess Victoria, monuments of spoils: Greek *tropaia*) to allude to victories and triumphs, and the emperor appeared in the guise of *triumphator* on coins of the Imperial period [6].

Among permanent monuments recalling victories and triumphs, perhaps the most important were dedications of booty. The first occasion of this at Rome was in 338 BC, when following a victory over the Antiates the ram bows (*rostra*) of captured ships were fitted to the orators' daises in the Forum Romanum. Booty was increasingly dedicated outside Italy from the 220s onwards, for example by M. Claudius Marcellus at Delphi in 222 BC.

Temple dedications were important, resulting from the vows (*vota*) made by the general before the war and the support of the deity granted during the war. Generals often made direct or indirect reference to their military accomplishments in these dedications (e.g. dedication of the Temple of Hercules at Rome after 145 BC by L. Mummius: CIL I² 626). There is occasional evidence in the Republican period of victorious generals endowing arch monuments, but not always with a clear link to military successes (e.g. by P. Cornelius Scipio Africanus in 190 BC; Q. Fabius Maximus Allobrogicus in 120 BC). References to military success became more explicit on arches from the reign of Augustus (e.g. Cass. Dio 53,26,5; 56,17,1f.). Scholars disagree over whether, at least in some phases of the Republican period, all *triumphatores* were honoured with a statue in Rome. There is also disagreement over whether this took place by senatorial decree or on the initiative of the family concerned. The attested removal of statues in 158 BC suggests that the latter occurred (Plin. HN 34,30f.; [25. 152–159]). Beginning with Augustus, however, the decision was directly or indirectly in the hands of the emperor. After his inauguration, all recipients of the *ornamenta triumphalia* ('triumphal honors') were honoured with a statue in the Forum Augusti (Cass. Dio 55,10,3; [5]). The emperors sometimes aligned entire areas of the forum with the theme of a triumph (Trajan Forum).

Over the centuries, all these monuments in Rome gave rise to a 'triumphal space', which continued to play a part in the celebration of triumphs by emperors, as this space formed the backdrop for staging the emperor's victorious nature [6]. Triumphal monuments of earlier emperors began to be reused and redesigned in the 4th century, to commemorate new victories (Arch of Constantine in Rome: reuse of the friezes of the emperors Trajan and Marcus Aurelius; [27. 212–220]).

☞ **Booty; Parades; Victory; Victory titles**

Bibliography

[1] J.-L. Bastien, Le triomphe romain et son utilisation politique à Rome aux trois derniers siècles de la République, 2007 [2] M. Beard, The Roman Triumph, 2007 [3] L. Bonfante-Warren, Roman Triumphs and Etruscan Kings. The Changing Face of the Triumph, in: JRS 60, 1970, 49–66 [4] J.H. Clark, Triumph in Defeat. Military Loss and the Roman Republic, 2014 [5] W. Eck, Kaiserliche Imperatorenakklamation und ornamenta triumphalia, in: ZPE 124, 1999, 223–227 [6] F. Goldbeck / J. Wienand (eds.), Der römische Triumph in Prinzipat und Spätantike, 2016 [7] K.-J. Hölkeskamp, Pomp und Prozessionen. Rituale und Zeremonien in der politischen Kultur der römischen Republik, in: Jahrbuch des Historischen Kollegs, 2006–2007, 35–72 [8] T. Hölscher, The Transformation of Victory into Power. From Event to Structure, in: S. Dillon / K. Welch (eds.), Representations of War in Ancient Rome, 2006, 27–48 [9] T. Itgenshorst, Tota illa pompa. Der Triumph in der römischen Republik, 2005 [10] H. Krasser et al. (eds.), Triplici invectus triumpho. Der römische Triumph in augusteischer Zeit, 2008 [11] C.H. Lange, Triumphs in the Age of Civil War. The Late Republic and the Adaptability of Triumphal Tradition, 2016 [12] C.H. Lange / F.J. Vervaet (eds.), The Roman Republican Triumph. Beyond the Spectacle, 2014 [13] C. Lundgreen, Regelkonflikte in der römischen Republik. Geltung und

Gewichtung von Normen in politischen Entscheidungsprozessen, 2011 [14] M. MCCORMICK, Eternal Victory. Triumphal Rulership in Late Antiquity, Byzantium, and the Early Medieval West, ²1990 [15] I. ÖSTENBERG, Staging the World. Spoils, Captives, and Representations in the Roman Triumphal Procession, 2009 [16] I. ÖSTENBERG, Circum metas fertur. An Alternative Reading of the Triumphal Route, in: Historia 59, 2010, 303–320 [17] A. PETRUCCI, Il trionfo nella storia costituzionale romana dagli inizi della repubblica ad Augusto, 1996 [18] R. PFEILSCHIFTER, Der römische Triumph und das Christentum. Überlegungen zur Eigenart eines öffentlichen Rituals, in: F. GOLDBECK / J. WIENAND (eds.), Der römische Triumph in Prinzipat und Spätantike, 2016, 455–486 [19] M.R.P. PITTENGER, Contested Triumphs. Politics, Pageantry, and Performance in Livy's Republican Rome, 2008 [20] M.L. POPKIN, The Architecture of the Roman Triumph. Monuments, Memory, and Identity, 2016 [21] J. RICH, The Triumph in the Roman Republic. Frequency, Fluctuation and Policy, in: C.H. LANGE / F.J. VERVAET (eds.), The Roman Republican Triumph. Beyond the Spectacle, 2014, 197–252 [22] V. ROSENBERGER, Verwehrte Ehre. Zur Wertigkeit des triumphus in monte Albano, in: Klio 91, 2009, 29–39 [23] J. RÜPKE, Domi militiae. Die religiöse Konstruktion des Krieges in Rom, 1990 [24] S.T. SCHIPPOREIT, Wege des Triumphes. Zum Verlauf der Triumphzüge im spätrepublikanischen und augusteischen Rom, in: H. KRASSER et al. (eds.), Triplici invectus triumpho. Der römische Triumph in augusteischer Zeit, 2008, 95–136 [25] M. SEHLMEYER, Stadtrömische Ehrenstatuen der republikanischen Zeit. Historizität und Kontext von Symbolen nobilitären Standesbewusstseins, 1999 [26] H.S. VERSNEL, Triumphus. An Inquiry into the Origin, Development, and Meaning of the Roman Triumph, 1970 [27] J. WIENAND, Der Kaiser als Sieger. Metamorphosen triumphaler Herrschaft unter Constantin I., 2012.

TANJA ITGENSHORST

Valour

A. Greek
B. Roman

A. Greek

A.1. Concept
A.2. Valour as disposition
A.3. Valorous action
A.4. Valour as an aspect of the doctrine of virtue
A.5. Valour in women
A.6. Personification of valour

A.1. Concept

In the course of the gender debate in classical studies, the conception of valour has attracted increasing attention, for example in the anthology [6]. The word most commonly used for the concept in Classical Greece invites such attention. Whereas Homeric epic uses a variety of words such as *alke* ('strength', 'prowess'), *menos* ('drive'), *thymos* ('surging spirit', 'courage'), often in combination with the adjective *agenor* ('manly') or *tharsos* ('courage'), to denote valour (LfgrE s. vv.), the usual word for valour in Classical Greece, alongside terms such as *tharsos* or *tolma* ('boldness'), was *andr(e)ia* (which occurs in Homer as *enoree* or *agenoree*). Derived via the adjective *andreios* from *aner*, it strictly speaking means 'manhood'. This gendering of the concept is already apparent in Homer to the extent that he has battle paraeneses begin with the exhortation 'Be men!' (*aneres este*) [2. 33]. The context is thus that of a typically masculine activity, namely, warfare and fighting, and to Homer valour is the defining virtue of the hero.

A.2. Valour as disposition

Plato discusses the nature of valour in detail [4]; [5]. In the *Republic*, he assigns it as one of the cardinal virtues (along with wisdom, prudence and justice) to the guards who are responsible for the preservation (*soteria*) of ethical ideas (Rep. 429a–430c). However, whether valour is a virtue like the other three is called into question in the *Protagoras* (349dff.). Valour appears in an expanded catalogue of virtues in the *Rhetoric* (I 9, 1366b) of Aristotle, where valour and justice are deemed the most highly esteemed, the former being useful only in war and the latter also in peace. Above all, though, valour is a disposition of the soul. Plato in the *Republic* describes the *physis* (i.e. the natural capacity) required of the guards, and draws an analogy with guard dogs, which – besides keen perceptions and speed – also need strength and 'valour' (Rep. 375a). Plato assigns valour to the *thymos* or *thymoeides*, that is, that part of the soul that lies between the rational (*logistikon*) and the desirous (*epithymetikon*). However, whereas in the Homeric battle paraeneses, attention is paid exclusively to the combatants' fighting capacity (cf. the formulaic expression *mnesasthe de thouridos alkes*: 'remember our ferocious strength'), the valour of the guards – while rooted in the *thymoeides* – must be combined with a friendly demeanour towards their own people (Pl. Rep. 375c–376c).

In addition to natural capacities, other factors came into play. For instance, there was the idea that innate valour could be strengthened through appropriate exercise (Xen. Mem. 3,9). While Hippocrates (Aër. 16) attributes the → cowardice or valour of a particular people to *physis* insofar as the changing seasons 'toughen up' a people, so to speak, and thereby foster valour, whereas steady temperatures cultivate cowardice, there is within this comparison between Asian and European peoples also a crucial political dimension. Anyone fighting not for himself, but for the benefit a ruler, cannot be valorous, even if he is so by nature.

A.3. Valorous action

Athenian and Spartan self-portrayals in which valour figures prominently should be understood in this context. In the eulogy to the fallen by Pericles recounted by Thucydides (2,35–46), valour is an important Athenian trait that is closely associated with a frame of mind and attitude that prizes freedom, as opposed to a valour that is enforced through hard training. In a similar way, Isocrates in his *Panathenaikos* (12,197f.) sees the valour of the ancestors not as a quality in isolation, such as barbarian enemies might share, but as one that could only manifest itself in conjunction with a noble lineage and upbringing [1. 160–163]. The allusion to Sparta is one of many sources indicating that Sparta operated a state-regulated education program geared towards the → education of warriors and inculcating valour (e.g. also Plut. *Lycurgus* 28). If we are to believe Tyrtaeus and his elegies exhorting valour in battle (frg. 10; 11; 12 W.), behaviour that was expected of a soldier included advancing with determination, where possible with the vanguard, with the aim of entering close combat, and persevering in battle formation, so that the phalanx would not be breached (similarly Callinus frg. 1 W.). Valour here was not just about attacking, but even more so, it was about standing one's ground. In Plato's *Laches*, too, the title character answers Socrates' question as to what valour is without much deliberation: it is, he says, the willingness to repel the enemy steadfastly in the battle line, and not to take flight (Lach. 190e). While under certain circumstances, particularly for the cavalry, flight can be an opportunity to display valour, just as other dangers and crises, and even dealing with desires, can be occasions for proving one's courage (191a–c), prudent persistence is a crucial component of valour (*meta phroneseos karteria*, 192c). In contrast to the Homeric model that focuses on heroic single combat, of interest here is a hoplite ethic: behaviour that secures the preservation of the phalanx. Still, valour brings no less honour to the hoplite than it does to the Homeric hero. Callinus and Tyrtaeus (see above) contrast the honour of the man fallen in battle with the disgrace that awaits the coward. The undercurrent here is the idea of the community – whether the unit or the *polis* – that these fighting citizens are defending. This context gives rise to the notion of sacrificial courage. In Tyrtaeus, the city honours the fallen fighter because he died in valorous combat for the city's sake. By the same token, a brave fallen soldier brings renown to his *polis* and family. The valour of fighting citizens is thus an important component in the identity of the city-state.

A.4. VALOUR AS AN ASPECT OF THE DOCTRINE OF VIRTUE

Aristotle's definition of valour attaches great weight to the idea of honour both in military and non-military spheres (on traditional elements in Aristotle's concept of valour: [8. 187–209]). In the *Rhetoric* (1366 b 11–13), he argues that valour is the virtue that enables a man to perform noble deeds in dangerous situations in accordance with the law and in its service. The idea of nobility emerges even more strongly in the *Nicomachean Ethics* (1115 a 4–1115 b 5), where as part of his doctrine of the *mesotes* ('middle', 'mean'), Aristotle assigns valour to the midpoint between fear and (reckless) audacity (*phobos* and *tharre*, likewise Pl. Lach.). Aristotle makes a distinction between fearlessness and valour, for valour only exists when there is fear of an evil. Yet, not every evil is to be feared. The most fearful of all is death. Valour manifests itself in fear of death – but not in every situation, only those involving the noblest form of death: death in battle. It manifests itself in situations in which one can defend oneself and it is honourable to die. Thus, given that nobility is the defining characteristic, no other conceivable motivation for dealing with fear can be seen as valour, although other motivations are often claimed as such. Valour is also a regular feature in the Stoic doctrine of virtue (e.g. SVF I 200; 201; III 256).

A.5. VALOUR IN WOMEN

Aristotle declares that Socrates ascribed valour to women, but as with all virtues, Aristotle considers the valour of women to be of lesser value than that of men (Pol. 1260a20–24; see also 1277b20–22). Plato in principle considers that women are fit for military service (Rep. 456a), and the Stoic C. Musonius Rufus (Diatr. 4) makes plain that women must act like men and avoid the appearance of cowardice in order to preserve their chastity; as the example of the Amazons shows, women in no way lack valour in combat. Still, it was only exceptional women who excelled in valour, one example being the Queen of Halicarnassus, Artemisia, of whom Herodotus (7,99) reports that she 'waged war with will and valour [*andreies*], under no compulsion', and she commanded troops. Here, as so often, the valour of a woman is contrasted with the faintheartedness of men [3. 86], a great embarrassment to the latter (cf. e.g. Dem. Or. 60,29). In Aristophanes' *Lysistrata*, for instance, the men's failure is contrasted with female descendants 'of manliest [*andreiotaton*] grandmothers and nettlesting mothers' (549). This becomes clearer still in Greek tragedy, where Alcestis, for example, is praised for her bravery in sacrificing herself for her husband Admetus, while a sharp contrast is drawn with Admetus' father, who is not prepared to do so (Eur. Alc. 471ff.; 741f.). Female valour is often 'extreme', in which case it is classed not as *andreia* but as *tolma* (which is common in tragedy), for example that of Euripides' Medea (Med. 1051; 1326). Sophocles' Electra, on the other hand (El. 983), uses *andreia* of her own actions where she sees herself and her sister in roles of masculine action [9. 197–236]; [2. 40f.]. In the context of a woman's sacrificial death, however (the theme of several of the tragedies of Euripides [7]), the women concerned generally remain firmly in their traditional, passive roles, even if their valour is praised or constitutes a motivation for them. A typical word for this kind of 'valour', which is more of a sacrificial courage, is *eupsychia*.

A.6. PERSONIFICATION OF VALOUR

Personifications (cf. *Kebetos Thebaiu Pinax* 20.3.) and pictorial representations of valour seem to have been rare. One relief of Andreia is preserved from the 1st or 2nd century AD. Mosaics are preserved depicting Evandria from the 4th or 5th centuries (LIMC, s. vv.).

BIBLIOGRAPHY

[1] R.K. BALOT, Courage in the Democratic Polis, 2014 [2] K. BASSI, The Semantics of Manliness in Ancient Greece, in: R.M. ROSEN / I. SLUITER (eds.), Andreia, 2003, 25–58 [3] S.E. HARRELL, Marvelous Andreia, in: R.M. ROSEN / I. SLUITER, Andreia, 2003, 77–94 [4] A. HOBBS, Plato and the Hero, 2000 [5] A.L. RABIEH, Plato and the Virtue of Courage, 2006 [6] R.M. ROSEN / I. SLUITER (eds.), Andreia, 2003 [7] J. SCHMITT, Freiwilliger Opfertod bei Euripides, 1921 [8] É. SMOES, Le courage chez les grecs, d'Homère à Aristote, 1995 [9] J. WISSMANN, Motivation und Schmähung. Feigheit in der Ilias und in der griechischen Tragödie, 1997.

JESSICA WISSMANN

B. Roman

B.1. Fear
B.2. Courage

Everyone who goes into battle feels fear. Overcoming or at least mitigating this feeling requires mustering all of one's valour. Latin has three words that express 'valour': *fortitudo*, *animus* and *virtus*, which are not entirely synonymous. (1) Closest to the meaning of 'valour' is *fortitudo*, which the Greek glossaries translate as *andreia*, *arete*, *ischys* and *rome* – the last of which enables the wordplay *Roma-rōme*, the city of strength and valour. The meaning of the first Greek word is 'strength' and 'steadfastness', physical and moral – and it is from this second sense that the meaning arises of a 'valour' that is political, civic (very frequent in Cicero), and finally purely military. The noun *fortitudo*, however, is rarer than the corresponding adjective, *fortis* ('valorous', 'brave'), which is well attested from Terence (Eun. 814) to Vegetius (Mil. 1,6) and also occurs in epigraphic sources (CIL VIII 22765). A legion, the *II Traiana*, received the byname *fortis*, and soldiers are described as *fortissimi*. Several other words belong to the same semantic field: *fortesco, -ere* ('to become brave'), *forticulus* ('somewhat brave'), *fortificatio* ('reinforcement'), *fortifico, -are* ('to fortify'), and finally *fortiter* ('bravely'). (2) *Animus*, *anemos* in Greek, denotes the invisible part of a person, the spirit as distinct from the body. Similar in meaning to *voluntas*, the word also describes the will or 'heart' in the sense of valour. Caesar (B Gall. 7,70,3) and Cicero (Phil. 5,4) use it synonymously with *fortitudo* and speak of the *animus* of soldiers. The same meaning is found in Livy (2,47,3f.; 9,40,4f.; 44,3,8), who generally uses this noun in the plural. The contrast between *animus* and *anima* ('spirit' and 'soul') arose in the Middle Ages. The psychologist Carl Gustav Jung took this up, and the writer Paul Claudel later revisited it in a well-known dialogue. (3) *Virtus* today is often translated as 'valour', but this is not always accurate. *Virtus*, *arete* in Greek, is what characterizes a man (*vir*), and while what best defines him is no doubt manliness, it is also and especially public service. For his sacrifices of devotion Augustus received from the senate a golden shield, the *clipeus virtutis*, on which were engraved his other related qualities – clemency, justice and piety. In fact, *virtus* was primarily a civil virtue, and therefore belonged to the sphere of philosophy in general and morality in particular. It also acquired a military significance, and thus encompassed valour to the point where it ultimately came (if only rarely) to be used as a synonym for *fortitudo* (Cic. Tusc. 2,18). Finally, it was regarded as a deity and capitalized. As such, it was often associated with Honos ('honour'), and temples were dedicated to the divine pair, first in 222 BC, then in 133 BC.

B.1. Fear

Interestingly, texts rarely mention *fortitudo* in battle, because it was taken for granted. Writers thus describe valorous acts without calling them valorous. After the civil war of AD 68–69, for example, Cerialis came to Rigodulum (now Riol, near Trier), where rebels had occupied and fortified a hilltop. The Romans, infantry ahead of cavalry, advanced in rank and file under heavy fire, and drove the enemy off (Tac. Hist. 4,71,6–9). There was no need for Tacitus to write the word 'valour': the concept was present in the reader's mind without being explicitly mentioned in the text. Other similar descriptions abound.

Valour is an attitude that is identified *ex negativo*. A valorous soldier is not one who feels no fear (there are such soldiers, but they are rare, and without doubt cases for the psychiatrist), but one who feels it and overcomes it [2. 223–233]. Colonel Charles Ardant du Picq, who died in battle in the Franco-Prussian War in 1870, took an interest in soldiers' emotional states in combat, and came to the conclusion that feeling fear was normal. This French officer in turn inspired John Keegan, who in an important work published in 1976, *The Face of Battle*, developed his predecessor's perspective further. Keegan's aim was to begin at the time of Caesar, but his memory of Latin literature was deficient and his descriptions fragmentary. Nevertheless, it is worth studying some of the passages in which he describes the circumstances that increase fear. Soldiers proved more susceptible to fear when tired (men who are not well rested should not be sent into battle), when the weather was hostile (too cold, too hot, rain, snow etc.), when logistics were lacking (hunger and thirst have a weakening effect), and when the soldier becomes isolated on the battlefield.

Other factors escaped John Keegan's attention. First, the Romans pushed piety to the point of superstition and feared bad omens (→ Religion). For example, if a general fell, they considered this an omen of disaster. To overcome such a situation required all the talents of a Caesar. On landing in Africa, Caesar fell face to the ground. His men fell silent. He reassured them by explaining that he was taking possession of African soil (Cass. Dio 42,58). The appearance of soldiers also had an influence, as was well understood in Classical Antiquity. The plumes affixed to helmets were designed to make men look bigger than they were. Archaeologists who find helmets forget these additions because they often do not survive. Yet they were not merely decorative, but also functional. Finally, as is well known, the element of surprise is important, especially in ambushes. The Romans sometimes used ambushes, but they were not their preferred form of battle because they ran counter to *fides* ('trustworthiness') and *honos* ('honour').

The state provided generals with a range of methods for increasing valour. Some were purely military, others psychological. In the first category, → training was effective [2. 162–169]. Designed as basic and advanced → education, it consisted of three elements. Sport improved physical condition and thereby raised morale. Weapons training gave the combatant a sense of security. Manoeuvres gave him confidence in the commands he received. As many texts attest, people in Classical Antiquity had a clear understanding of the importance of such training, not primarily based on personal experience and practice, but based on reflection. Cicero likened a man without training to a woman (Tusc. 2,16,37), and he did not intend this as a compliment. Flavius Josephus attributed the Romans' success to their training practices (BI 3,5,7,102). Vegetius reminded his readers that 'in war, mistakes cannot be put right' (Mil. 1,13).

B.2. COURAGE

Having become a real soldier, the young Roman went off to war. He must have had the moral conviction that the gods protected the arms of Rome, and the gods themselves had demands arising from law, the *ius fetiale*. Numerous steps were prescribed that the Roman state had to perform. In theory at least, war had to be defensive. It was therefore essential that an emissary had demanded reparations and been unsuccessful, and war had to be declared against the enemy in an orderly fashion. Several rituals followed: the hurling of the spear by a fetial priest; the dance of the Salii; the opening of the gates of the Temple of Janus; and the interpretation of omens.

Once deployed, the young man was motivated to exhibit valour by means of various factors, some psychological. One of these, however, had nothing to do with valour: fear was countered by means of another, more immediate fear. The soldiers of the third rank, the *triarii*, pushed anyone who shrank from the fight forward again, and would even kill them. Deserters, when caught, were punished with death. They were whipped until they lost consciousness, then revived with water. Finally, they were beheaded with an axe. This procedure was conducted in the presence of the other soldiers.

Other elements came into play that partly explain the success of the Roman army. A sense of esprit de corps bound the soldier to his commander and his fellow soldiers. This sense was evoked by the oath (*sacramentum, ius iurandum*), and it was expressed in the standards of the legion and maniple, the eagle and the *signa*. But what most powerfully drove the soldiers to face danger head on was the lure of spoils. An unwritten, purely oral 'law of nations', the *ius gentium*, legitimized this practice, even causing disappointment among soldiers when they found themselves having to go to war against a less than wealthy people. In this respect, the entire first book of the *City of God* may be cited, remembering that Augustine cannot be suspected of any laxness in matters of morality.

Did the fear disappear when the campaign was over? Psychiatrists have known for some time that people exposed to danger suffer long-term effects known as post-traumatic stress disorder (PTSD). As far as we can see, the Romans suffered fewer adverse effects in the face of death than people today. Killing a barbarian was not a traumatic event. Still, at least one reference to psychological disturbance comparable to PTSD is found in Lucretius: 'Then the minds of men that perform great feats with great passion, often will do and dare the same in sleep' (*porro hominum mentes, magnis quae motibus edunt magna, itidem saepe in somnis faciuntque geruntque*) (4,1011f.).

☛ Battle; Esprit de corps

BIBLIOGRAPHY

[1] W. EISENHUT, Virtus romana, 1973 [2] Y. LE BOHEC, La guerre romaine, 2014 [3] D. WARDLE, Virtus, in: BNP 15, 2010, 459–460 [4] G.R. WATSON, The Roman Soldier, 1969 (reprint 1985) [5] G. WEBSTER, The Roman Imperial Army of the First and Second Centuries AD, [4]1998.

YANN LE BOHEC

Vehicles

All armies of the ancient world had vehicles, although they were only usable in regions with navigable roads or tracks. Chariots were used in battle and → hunting, but for the most part they disappeared with the advent of phalanx tactics. However, it was always important to rely on carts, lightweight or heavyweight (two or four wheels), to transport people and materials, such as equipment, weapons, baggage, provisions, building materials or booty. Such vehicles were drawn by mules, donkeys, horses or oxen. Carts were mainly used to carry heavy goods or large quantities of goods, both in the baggage train of an army on expedition, and for the supply of troops at permanent stations. Aeneas Tacticus (16,14f.) reports that the Cyrenians used carts as transport vehicles, as instruments of defence, to deliver soldiers to their place of deployment, and to set up as barricades in emergency circumstances. Xenophon (Cyr. 6,1,27; 6,2,8) describes the Cyrenians as still using chariots in the old manner.

As for the armies of the Greek *poleis*, an organized supply train with carts was generally rare, although common for the Spartans [8. 104–108], and also in the Persian and Hellenistic expeditionary armies (Thuc. 5,72,3; Xen. Cyr. 6,2,34) [5. 132–137]. In the Macedonian army under Philip II and Alexander the Great, the rule was that no transport vehicles should be used, for reasons of speed and mobility. Although this rule was sometimes bent (as by Alexander in Iran), the Macedonians mostly used carts only for siege equipment and transporting the sick and injured. They also did without heavy ox carts [1. 11–17]. Such armies therefore attached greater importance to pack animals (mules, donkeys, → camels) and sometimes porters (e.g. *skeuophoroi* in Athens). Some Roman generals also forbade the use of carts and excessive baggage (App. Ib. 14,85; Sall. Iug. 45), and they required soldiers to carry as much of their own equipment and supplies as they could – hence their nickname *muli Mariani* (Marius' mules) (Frontin. Str. 4,1,7; Plut. *Marius* 13). Caesar, too, seems to have used only pack animals [4. 82f.], although it was otherwise normal in the Roman army for carts to carry equipment (including raw materials), heavy artillery, provisions and the wounded [7. 208–212]. How many carts were used depended on several factors, in particular the size of the army, the terrain to be crossed, and the organization of supplies. As a result, no general description can be attempted. Even the classical authors themselves rarely give specific numbers, and how reliable such numbers are cannot be known. Hundreds of transport vehicles accompanied Xenophon's march (Xen. An. 3,2,27), and thousands of mules traveled with Alexander the Great (Curt. 3,13,16). In 87 BC, Sulla supposedly deployed 10,000 teams of (two) mules to transport siege engines at Athens (Plut. *Sulla* 12). Mark Antony was said to have taken 300 carts on his Parthian campaign for the same purpose (Plut. *Antonius* 38). Information from Vegetius indicates that a legion needed 59 two-wheeled and 10 four-wheeled carts (with 158 draught animals) for siege equipment alone. A legion would thus need no fewer than 1,000 animals for its transportation needs [2. 288–290].

Various types of carts (general term *hamaxai/vehicula*) can be distinguished, like the omnipresent Greek *hamaxa* (usually with two wheels) and the heavier, four-wheeled *tetrakukloi*. The usual types of Roman vehicles were also used in the army, although the terminology in the sources is not always precise. The *plaustrum* was a (normally) two-wheeled oxcart for heavy transport; there were also Livy's *iuncta vehicula* (42,65,2) and the *angaria* of the *cursus publicus* (Cod. Theod. 8,5,11). The *carpentum* was lighter, two-wheeled like the *birota* (Cod. Theod. 8,5,8), and drawn by mules (or horses) (Liv. 35,5,13). Four-wheeled carts included the *carrus* (according to Ed. Diocl. 15,38–40 it sometimes had two wheels) and *raeda*. That these were used in the *cursus publicus*, which members of the military also used [3], and in the army itself, is confirmed by the reliefs on the Trajan and Marcus Aurelius Columns and on a few funerary monuments to soldiers (cf. fig. 1). Estimates of transportation speeds and carrying capacities rely on only a few ancient testimonies (Cato Agr. 22,3; AE 1976, 653 (Sagalassus AD 14–20); OGIS 2,29 (Palmyra AD 137); Ed. Diocl. 17; Cod. Theod. 8,5 passim) and on comparisons with conditions in the 19th and early 20th centuries [2. 294]; [7. 211f.]; [6. 585–590]. According to this evidence, a two-wheeled, mule-drawn cart could carry 270–500 kg for a distance of 30 km per day, and a four-wheeled cart could carry 450–650 kg. An oxcart with two wheels could transport 360–500 kg up to 20 km per day; one with four wheels could transport 430–650 kg. Larger loads or longer distances could be achieved by adding more draught animals.

☞ **Infrastructure; Rear; Supply**

Fig. 1: Gravestone from Viminacium (near Kostolac, Serbia, CIL III 1650). The relief shows the *speculator* Lucius Blassius Nigellio (seated behind the driver) in a four-wheeled cart. His servant is holding the *beneficiarius* spear, the symbol of the *principales* of the Roman army.

BIBLIOGRAPHY
[1] D. ENGELS, Alexander the Great and the Logistics of the Macedonian Army, 1980   [2] A. GOLDSWORTHY, The Roman Army at War, 100 BC–AD 200, 1996   [3] A. KOLB, Army and Transport, in: P. ERDKAMP (ed.), The Roman Army and the Economy, 2002, 161–166   [4] A. LABISCH, Frumentum Commeatusque. Die Nahrungsmittelversorgung der Heere Caesars, 1975   [5] J. LEE, A Greek Army on the March. Soldiers and Survival in Xenophon's Anabasis, 2007   [6] G. RAEPSAT, Land Transport, pt. 2: Riding, Harness and Vehicles, in: J.P. OLESON (ed.), The Oxford Handbook of Engineering and Technology in the Classical World, 2008, 580–605   [7] J.P. ROTH, The Logistics of the Roman Army at War (264 BC–AD 235), 1999   [8] H. VAN WEES, Greek Warfare. Myths and Realities, 2004.

ANNE KOLB

Veterans

A. Republic and early Principate
B. Imperial Period and Late Antiquity

A. REPUBLIC AND EARLY PRINCIPATE

A.1. Introduction
A.2. Republic
A.3. Reign of Augustus (Principate)

A.1. INTRODUCTION
The army of the Roman Republic was a citizens' militia raised annually by a levy (Latin *dilectus*; → Recruitment). As in other polities of the ancient world, only those meeting a particular property qualification were required to perform military service, because only men with a personal interest and share in the republic could be expected to defend it. The first indication of the duration of → military service comes from an emended passage in Polybius (c. AD 160; Pol. 6,19,1f.). This has been understood to mean that a man had to serve up to six years of uninterrupted military service. After this, he held the status of an *evocatus* (an individual with extended service), and as such he could be called up for as many as 16 more years [8. 35f.]. The defence of Rome, and later the desire to expand the empire, must have been motivating factors, but there was also a financial inducement. Modern-day armies disapprove of plunder, but the Roman army deliberately planned to despoil the vanquished of all their property, and when a campaign came to an end, a veteran could expect to receive his share of the booty. Occasionally, he might also enjoy the prospect of joining a settlement that was set up in the territory won from the enemy (on the return to civilian life of soldiers discharged from Greek and Roman armies, see [10. 183–185]; [17. 472–476]).

A.2. REPUBLIC

A.2.1. Emergence of the veterans issue and attempts at regulation up to the Gracchi
A.2.2. Reforms of Marius
A.2.3. Soldiers and veterans in the Civil Wars

Enough is known of the earliest wars of the Roman Republic to suggest a pattern in their campaigns against their immediate neighbours. Ploughing in the Mediterranean region can begin in September, and the harvest lasts from June to August. Accordingly, it would be possible to fight short wars in spring and summer, which would allow soldiers to return to their farms for the harvest and prepare for the next season's sowing [14. 27–31]. This invites three observations: the word 'veteran' is derived from the Latin *vetus* ('old'). Given that recruitment began at the age of about 17, men were called veterans when they had completed only one or two campaigns, or when they had completed the entire required term of service. Second, the Romans typically attacked opponents who were not much richer than themselves, so the → booty may often have been meagre (although plentiful enough for people who themselves had little). Third, and most importantly: the society of the Roman Republic was stable. The demands of civilian and military life did not conflict.

A.2.1. EMERGENCE OF THE VETERANS ISSUE AND ATTEMPTS AT REGULATION UP TO THE GRACCHI
It has been widely assumed that conditions changed probably around the time of the war with Hannibal, and certainly during the wars of the 2nd century BC, when soldiers served for years without interruption, only to return to farms that were overburdened with debt or financially ruined [4. 11, 39]. Meanwhile, the argument goes, the nobility, having enriched themselves in these same wars, were starting to create large-scale estates and use slaves to work them, often at the cost of ordinary farmers (App. Civ. 1,7). As a result, many of these farmers sank below the property threshold for military service. This threshold was twice reduced as the numbers of qualified men declined [4. 1–10]. Finally, legislation was found necessary, and around the middle of the 2nd century C. Laelius introduced a bill to effect changes (the details of which are unclear), but withdrew it in the face of opposition.

In 133 BC, the tribune Ti. Sempronius Gracchus issued an agrarian law. Not all land from conquest was distributed. Individuals were allowed to take up to 500 *iugera* (125 hectares) of this public land (*ager publicus*). However, this provision was often circumvented, and numerous illegal requisitions of this land took place. Gracchus' law restored the upper limit and took the rest for distribution to the poor. As is well known, he was then murdered, but the commission for implementing his law continued to work until 111 BC. For some time, one member of this commission was his brother C. Sempronius Gracchus, who also reinstated Tiberius' law (App. Civ. 1,9; 1,18; 1,27; Plut. C. Sempronius Gracchus 5; Plut. Ti. Sempronius Gracchus 8).

A.2.2. REFORMS OF MARIUS

The effects of these measures were limited: in 107 BC, the consul Marius, needing to replenish the army for his war against Jugurtha, was forced to abandon the property qualifications and accept anyone (Sall. Iug. 86) (→ Generals of note, K.). Marius was acting out of necessity rather than ideology. His decision was the natural consequence of the steady erosion of conscript numbers, which had become evident in the preceding years. However, his decision would have far-reaching consequences: it meant the birth of the professional army. Armies of men who owned no land and who owed loyalty as clients not to the state, but to their generals, would fight for those same generals in → civil wars. They showed no political interests, but as veterans they expected material compensation from their leaders [4. 1–52].

Recent scholarship has modified this picture. It is now believed that year-long campaigns began a century earlier than previously assumed. The introduction of army → pay (*stipendium*) for the Siege of Veii in 406 BC (Liv. 4,59,11) indicated the shape of things to come. A number of factors ensured that this change did not have immediate negative consequences. If someone was called up, other family members, including women, could work the land, while the veteran could benefit from booty and occasionally from a distribution of land. The supposed reduction in the property threshold is problematic [13. 309–316], and the growth of estates may have only become significant around the time of Sulla. Casualties in the field had been high since the war against Hannibal, but the population was rising and, along with this, poverty was becoming more frequent. Too many people were competing for too little land. The literary tradition claiming a decline in population can be explained by the lack of accurate information available to contemporaries of Ti. Sempronius Gracchus. Without suitable and sophisticated methods of measurement, their assumption that the population was falling was simply wrong [14].

Many of the recent approaches are useful, but more attention might be paid to the Roman and Latin colonies, and to land allocations made to individuals up to 181 BC, in which veterans were certainly involved [15. 13–111]; [4. 39]. One might also find acceptable the suggestion that farmers showed such perseverance that they were able to survive on very little, which made their ruin a slow process that lasted until the mid-2nd century. It is unlikely that the Romans misunderstood the nature of the crisis afflicting them. And it is difficult to believe that the declining figures evident in the census resulted simply from omissions, rather than population decline. Tiberius Sempronius Gracchus himself, travelling through Etruria, saw the slave estates with his own eyes and knew about a slave war that was raging on Sicily (Plut. Ti. Sempronius Gracchus 8; App. Civ. 1,9) [7. 16–23].

Accepting that there was a crisis in the recruitment base, however, does not necessarily mean accepting the usual explanations for Marius' actions in 107 BC. The numbers of those enlisted without the requisite property qualifications were small. Nor did Marius abolish the *dilectus*. Landowners still served in the army, and men without these qualifications were only admitted in times of emergency, as during the Social War. The armies of the Late Republic therefore consisted of both landowners and landless, but without statistics, it is impossible to say in what proportions. Both had the same → esprit de corps and were generally indistinguishable. Based on these findings, one can better assess the role of veterans in the last century of the Republic.

A.2.3. SOLDIERS AND VETERANS IN THE CIVIL WARS

Legionaries still wanted to fight the enemies of Rome and they still wanted to profit from it, but the two ideals were both now corrupted. In terms of patriotism or politics, it can be recognized that, during the two phases of internal conflict – the first Civil War (88–82), then the second and the era of the Triumvirates (49–31) –, soldiers' enemies were now fellow Romans, not foreigners. Authority was no longer in just one pair hands. Still, soldiers were not at first clients, and they were certainly politically aware. They had to be convinced of the justice of the cause for which they fought. Sulla, therefore, had to convince his men that they should right the wrongs done to him as consul in 88 BC, as Cinna would do the following year. A generation later, Caesar too referred to injustices done to him when he attacked his opponents, who under the leadership of Pompey declared themselves the legitimate authority in the state (→ Generals of note, C.; → Generals of note, N.). After Caesar's death, Mark Antony and Octavian urged their men to avenge his murder, while Brutus and Cassius proclaimed themselves to be the restorers of the Republic. Later, Octavian styled himself as the defender of Rome against Cleopatra and Mark Antony.

But a change occurred between these two periods and generations. The troops had found their voice. In the earlier phase, they appeared content to react to a program laid out before them. In the later, with political authority weakened, they often took control of setting the political agenda themselves. For example, when Octavian and Mark Antony seemed to be moving too slowly in confronting Caesar's killers, their troops urged them to act. Those same troops then won Octavian a consulship, and later arranged for him to marry into the house of Mark Antony [7. 37–55].

Similar developments took place in the world of economics. In the earlier phase, most booty was coming from foreign enemies, although Sulla's opponents in Rome also suffered losses. During the second phase, → booty was chiefly extorted from provincial populations. Even Caesar on two occasions had to deal with rebels (49 and 47 BC) who were demanding *donativa* (monetary gifts) (App. Civ. 2,47; 2,92–94). It became normal between 44 and 31 to enrich one's soldiers with money at the expense of Italy and the provinces – an approach the triumvirs and their Republican opponents also allowed. This continued until after Philippi (42 BC). However, the acute phase was between 44 and 36 BC, when there were no wars against foreigners [7. 47–53].

A veteran wanted booty, but he also wanted land. It is possible to trace the history of veteran settlements in the Late Republican period. Marius acquired land for his veterans with the help of the tribune Saturninus in 103 BC and again in 100. On the first occasion, the senate approved, but the fall of Saturninus meant that the second settlement was not carried out (Vir. Ill. 73; Liv. Per. 69) [4. 199 n. 167]. The next settlement of veterans, by Sulla, was on a vast scale. He obtained for his veterans land in Italy in order to punish his enemies and remedy the harm done in the war (81 BC) [6]. By contrast, the first attempts by Pompey to obtain land for his veterans followed the traditional pattern. Following the elimination of Q. Sertorius, the senate granted his veterans land, but it was not in a position to meet its own obligation (Cass. Dio 38,5,1f.) [7. 60]. Two attempts to procure land for Pompey's men, who were veterans of the war with Mithridates, failed in 63 and 60 BC. To achieve his aims, Pompey made common cause with Caesar, who as consul for 59 BC forcibly passed a law according to which war plunder was used to buy land in Italy to provide settlements for the urban *plebs* and veterans [7. 60f.].

During the second phase of civil war, soldiers became just as proactive economically as they did politically. Caesar began allocating land to his veterans in 47 BC, a process that continued until his death [8. 49–52]. He had planned the program himself. It was first triggered by the rebellion of 47 BC, when soldiers demanded not only the *donativum*, but also their own discharge, since they had completed their terms of service (App. Civ. 2,92). Unlike Sulla, Caesar proceeded to acquire land by buying it, not confiscating it (App. Civ. 2,94). But faced with the impending discharge of the veterans, the triumvirs returned to Sulla's methods. At Bononia in 43 BC, they agreed to confiscate the estates of 18 Italic cities, chosen on the basis of wealth, not political affiliation. Caesar the Younger (Octavian) then had to implement this policy in 41 BC. Efforts to alleviate the suffering of those who were dispossessed provoked rebellion and encroachment on unassigned land (App. Civ. 4,3; 5,13; 5,16) [7. 58–69]. Following his victory over Lepidus and Sextus Pompeius, Caesar the Younger in 36 BC declared the civil war to be at an end, and he requested a campaign against the Illyrians. This request was granted, but only after the rebellious veterans' demands for land and discharge had been met (App. Civ. 5,128f.) [7. 88f.].

Caesar the Younger's victory at Actium (31 BC) put an end to the civil war, and with it the Roman Republic. The ex-Octavian Caesar the Younger became Augustus, and he began to create the imperial state. Among his concerns were the imperial army and providing for its veterans.

A.3. REIGN OF AUGUSTUS (PRINCIPATE)

A.3.1. New conditions
A.3.2. Other innovations by Augustus

A.3.1. NEW CONDITIONS
Augustus created a professional army that replaced the citizen militias of the Republic. It was not, however, an entirely new creation. This accomplishment shows how Augustus reacted not only to his own experience, but also to the events of the preceding century. As a bridge between republic and empire and acting much as he did in other areas of state, he was pragmatic in his efforts to end the chaos (which was partly of his own making) and to prepare the army for the new world. Four perspectives on his actions are possible: leadership, conditions of service, compensation and provision for veterans' life after service.

The era of fragile authority, when various men vied for legitimate authority, was over. There was only one ruler now. The *imperium* (military authority) was in the hands of Augustus alone, with virtually all the armies of the empire under his command. Soldiers swore an oath of loyalty to him and his legates, and they fought under his patronage [3. 25, 32]. Augustus set the conditions of their service. The *stipendium* (soldiers' → pay) had always been subject to interruptions. Soldiers had been paid throughout the Republic. By Augustus' day, they were earning 225 *denarii* per year, although still with interruptions [20. 89–91]. To earn this, a soldier after 13 BC had to serve for

16 years, a member of the Praetorian Guard for twelve. These terms were increased to 20 and 16 years respectively in AD 5 (Cass. Dio 54,25,6; 55,23,1). A veteran also had to serve more years *sub vexillo* ('under the standard'), under a special officer, the *curator veteranorum* [18. 325f., 409f.]. At the end of their service, Praetorians as *evocati Augusti* could rise at least to the rank of legionary centurions [20. 11f., 18]. The 16-year term in the reign of Augustus largely corresponded to the Republican practice, but unlike under the Republic, soldiers were now explicitly forbidden to marry, which may have improved mobility [9. 147f.]. This was no obstacle to unofficial relationships, which were then made legitimate when the soldier left the army. Cassius Dio (54,25,6) lays out the reasons behind Augustus' military reforms: demands for early discharge led to rebellions. That the term of service was now precisely prescribed was intended to eliminate this cause for complaint. Dio also indicates that veteran's demands for land became a chronic problem. Now they were to receive money instead – a change that was especially popular with citizens who feared for the land they owned.

A.3.2. OTHER INNOVATIONS BY AUGUSTUS

Now to Augustus' innovations concerning veterans after their discharge. He offers two important pieces of information himself. According to his own testimony, he purchased land for settlements in Italy and the provinces (R. Gest. div. Aug. 16) and established → colonies in many parts of the empire, 28 colonies in Italy alone (R. Gest. div. Aug. 28). The specifics can be made clearer: after Actium, Augustus donated land to men who had served on his campaign, and money to the followers of Mark Antony. He came up with the land in Italy by expelling those who had taken Antony's side. To them, instead, he offered land in the provinces or money in compensation (Cass. Dio 51,4) [8. 73–80]. The next settlement phase lasted until 14 BC, and is often associated with Augustus' actions in the provinces. His visit to Sicily in 21 BC, for instance, led to the foundation of colonies including at Syracuse. There also seem to have been new foundations in Italy; but only a few, vague details remain. However, there is no evidence of further settlements from 14 BC until the foundation of Emona in AD 14, the last year of Augustus' reign [8. 83–86, 208]. This may be associated with the special payments made to veterans in lieu of land in 13 BC (s.o.), which may indicate a shortage of suitable land. We do not know the size of these payments, but an amendment to the edict in AD 5 stipulates that they are to be raised to 3,000 *denarii* for a legionary and 5,000 for a Praetorian (Cass. Dio 55,23,1). Meanwhile, the funding of such special payments was guaranteed by the setting up of an *aerarium militare* ('military treasury'). Augustus filled this treasury with donations from his own fortune, but the regular funds came from an auction duty and inheritance taxes [3. 172].

In his will, Augustus, who gave few *donativa* in his lifetime, left bequests to his troops (Suet. Aug. 101) [3. 166]. Shortly after his death, rebellions broke out in the armies of Pannonia and Germania inferior. There were many injustices. Service was hard, and men were kept in active service long after reaching their age of discharge. The obligation to serve in the reserve (*sub vexillo*) also caused resentment. Citing the better conditions offered to Praetorians, soldiers demanded → pay increases, a maximum service term of 16 years and a cash lump sum payable on discharge, as soldiers were assigned land in marshes and mountainous terrain unfit for cultivation. The rebels were promised a service term of 16 years, with an obligation of a maximum of four more years in case of an enemy attack. Augustus' legacies were to be doubled (Tac. Ann. 1,16–49).

A few observations are worth making here. For one thing, Augustus' regulations were not working. Some scholars blame him personally for this [8. 209]. The funds provided would not have sufficed for such generous discharge payments [3. 172f.]. Although there is no evidence of settlements after 14 BC (see above), the complaints about poor land suggest that land was assigned when money was tight. Augustus can hardly be held responsible for this, for it strains credibility to suggest that the man who expended so much effort on solving such problems in the time of the triumvirate would now let them happen again. What was happening was that soldiers were again making their feelings known in the wake of his death. Politically speaking, they were calling into question the authority of Tiberius, as some wanted to see Germanicus on the throne. Economically speaking, there were two well-known demands: timely discharge from military service and a special payment. This crisis eventually passed, and in the following year Tiberius restored the obligatory 20-year term of service (Tac. Ann. 1,78).

Hadrian put an end to the settlement of veterans in colonies [20. 137, 148], but the system established by Augustus would endure for over 200 years. For all that time, financing the army remained one of the emperor's chief concerns [3. 161–176].

☞ **Administration; Civil war; State and army**

BIBLIOGRAPHY

[1] Y. LE BOHEC, L'armée Romaine sous le Haut-Empire, 1989 [2] H. BOTERMANN, Die Soldaten und die römische Politik in der Zeit von Caesars Tod bis zur Begründung des Zweiten Triumvirats, 1968 [3] J.B. CAMPBELL, The Emperor and the Roman Army 31 BC–AD 235, 1984 [4] E. GABBA, Republican Rome. The Army and

the Allies, 1976 (trans. by P.J. Cuff) [5] J. HARMAND, L'armée et le soldat à Rome de 107 à 50 avant notre ère, 1967 [6] A. KEAVENEY, Sulla and Italy, in: Critica Storica 19.4, 1982, 499–544 [7] A. KEAVENEY, The Army in the Roman Revolution, 2007 [8] L. KEPPIE, Colonisation and Veteran Settlement in Italy 47–14 BC, 1983 [9] L. KEPPIE, Colonisation and Veteran Settlement in Italy in the First Century A.D., in: Papers of the British School at Rome 52, 1984, 77–114 [10] P. KRENTZ, War, in: P. SABIN et al. (eds.), The Cambridge History of Greek and Roman Warfare, 2007, 147–185 [11] M.D. PARKER, The Roman Legions, 1958 [12] S.E. PHANG, The Marriage of Roman Soldiers (13 BC–AD 235). Law and Family in the Imperial Army, 2001 [13] J.W. RICH, The Supposed Roman Manpower Shortage of the Later Second Century B.C., in: Historia 32, 1983, 287–331 [14] N. ROSENSTEIN, Rome at War. Farms, Families and Death in the Middle Republic, 2004 [15] E.T. SALMON, Roman Colonisation under the Republic, 1970 [16] H.C. SCHNEIDER, Das Problem der Veteranenversorgung in der späten römischen Republik, 1977 [17] J. SERRATI, Warfare and the State, in: The Cambridge History of Greek and Roman Warfare, 2007, 461–497 [18] M.A. SPEIDEL, Heer und Herrschaft im Römischen Reich der Hohen Kaiserzeit, 2009 [19] A. THEIN, Sulla's Veteran Settlement Policy, in: F. DAUBNER (ed.), Militärsiedlungen und Territorialherrschaft in der Antike, 2010, 79–99 [20] G.R. WATSON, The Roman Soldier, 1969 [21] G. WEBSTER, The Roman Imperial Army, 1969.

ARTHUR KEAVENEY

B. IMPERIAL PERIOD AND LATE ANTIQUITY
By establishing a standing professional army, Augustus regulated soldiers' service duration and solved the problem of provisions to veterans that had made them a political football and flashpoint of the Late Republican period. Their military potential, however, meant that veterans remained a group of some political relevance in the later empire and Late Antiquity. The founding of colonies through the *deductio* ('transplanting') of entire bodies of veterans posed another, albeit passive problem of political security. The relevance of such colonies, however, diminished with the advent of thedefensive strategy of stationing troops of the imperial army all around the empire. The entire policy of colonial foundations, which had declined in number between the reigns of Augustus and Trajan, was wholly abolished in the reign of Hadrian. Even so, the meeting documented in Cod. Theod. 7,20,2 between Constantine I and a group of veterans probably in Gaul may indicate that veterans still had a measure of influence until Late Antiquity, and that they found it relatively easy to obtain a hearing from the emperor.

In socioeconomic terms, imperial veterans at the outset of their civilian lives could draw on the money they had saved up during their military service, and in the case of legionaries, they could draw on benefit from a land grant (*missio agraria*) or the payment of a discharge bonus (*missio nummaria*), the latter form of settlement being more usual after 13 BC. For veterans from the Danubian provinces, a picture has emerged of a sophisticated and economically active population that was engaged in agriculture and devoted to the production and sale of goods [3. 160f.]; [6. 123–132]. In Egypt, sources related to the settlements of Caranis [1. 139–142] and Philadelphia [11. 12–15] in the Arsinoites (Middle Egypt) show that veterans in the Imperial period comprised a homogeneous population group. As former soldiers, most of whom came from families of artisans or small-scale farmers [8. 389], they were, in all likelihood, already economically comfortable before their army service [10. 26].

The tendency has been noted in the case of the Rhine and Danube provinces for veterans to enter municipal councils (*ordo decurionum*), but those involved amounted to no more than 5.8 percent of the group [9]. Similar results emerge for the four African provinces (Mauretania, Numidia, Africa proconsularis and Cyrenaica), where only 33 of the 421 veterans, that is, around 8 percent, are identifiable as municipal dignitaries [5. 626–629]. There is no evidence as yet of any veterans becoming members of the *ordo decurionum* in Britain [13. 197]. The situation is similar in Egypt, where the kind of social advancement that, after discharge from the military, would be crowned by entry into the *ordo decurionum* has yet to be conclusively proven in the career of a single soldier, or among the descendants of a single (former) military family [10. 27f.]. In light of this, it seems reasonable to locate the socioeconomic status of veterans of the Imperial period mainly in the environs of a 'middle class' [12. 287]; [4. 125], whose wealth did not usually suffice for promotion into the provincial elite [10. 33f.]; cf. [7. 530].

Even in Late Antiquity, veterans were still guaranteed a settlement in money or a land grant to help them on their way in civilian life. However, there is no information regarding their actual socioeconomic status in this period. The *Abinnaeus Archive* of the mid-4th century AD offers some insight into the living conditions of the veterans residing near the auxiliary fortress built at the village of Dionysias in the Arsinoites during the reign of Diocletian. It has been argued that they belonged to a 'minor rural middle class', with members settled in a village and only owning land in this single village [2. 119]. The socioeconomic position of veterans living at Caranis and Philadelphia in the Imperial period was similar.

BIBLIOGRAPHY
[1] R. ALSTON, Soldier and Society in Roman Egypt. A Social History, 1995 [2] J. BANAJI, Agrarian Change

in Late Antiquity. Gold, Labour, and Aristocratic Dominance, 2002 [3] A. CHAUSA SÁEZ, Veteranos en el África romana, 1997 [4] R. HAENSCH, Der Exercitus Aegyptiacus – Ein provinzialer Heeresverband wie andere auch?, in: K. LEMBKE et al. (eds.), Tradition and Transformation. Egypt under Roman Rule, 2010, 111–132 [5] F. JACQUES, Le privilège de liberté. Politique impériale et autonomie municipale dans les cités de l'Occident romain (161–244), 1984 [6] K. KRÓLCZYK, Veteranen in den Donauprovinzen des römischen Reiches (1.–3. Jh. n.Chr.), 2009 [7] Y. LE BOHEC, La troisième légion Auguste, 1989 [8] F: MITTHOF, Soldaten und Veteranen in der Gesellschaft des römischen Ägypten (1.–2. Jh. n.Chr.), in: G. ALFÖLDY et al. (eds.), Kaiser, Heer und Gesellschaft in der Römischen Kaiserzeit. Gedenkschrift für Eric Birley, 2000, 377–405 [9] L. MROZEWICZ, Die Veteranen in den Munizipräten an Rhein und Donau zur Hohen Kaiserzeit (I.–III. Jh.), in: EOS 77, 1989, 65–80 [10] P. SÄNGER, Veteranen unter den Severern und frühen Soldatenkaisern. Die Dokumentensammlungen der Veteranen Aelius Sarapammon und Aelius Syrion, 2011 [11] P. SCHUBERT, Philadelphie. Un village égyptien en mutation entre le IIe et le IIIe siècle ap. J.-C., 2007 [12] O. STOLL, Legionäre, Frauen, Militärfamilien. Untersuchungen zur Bevölkerungsstruktur und Bevölkerungsentwicklung in den Grenzprovinzen des Imperium Romanum, in: JRGZ 53, 2006, 217–344 [13] G. WESCH-KLEIN, Soziale Aspekte des römischen Heerwesens in der Kaiserzeit, 1998.

PATRICK SÄNGER

Victory

A. Concept
B. Greek
C. Roman Republic and Imperial period
D. Late Antiquity

A. CONCEPT

Victory is a broad and conceptually vague term that essentially refers to the outcome successfully achieved by an individual or party in some kind of competition with another individual or party (Greek *nike*, Latin *victoria*). In a military context, victory in the strict sense (as distinct from its opposite, defeat) means the successful conclusion of a violent conflict between polities (or, in the case of a → civil war, parties within a single polity). Victory in Greco-Roman Antiquity was often personified and viewed as a deity (esp. Nike, Victoria, with similar connotations, but also e.g. Athena, Apollo, Sol Invictus), and venerated accordingly in ritual. Given the special significance of victory for ancient communities (as seen clearly in the Romans), these cults could serve to justify political legitimacy. It would therefore be invalid to make a sharp theoretical distinction between politics and religion on this topic.

Military victory as a historical reality is of particular interest for the study of culture, given its frequent use to represent processes of societal reorganization or reaffirmation. Victory achieved through military means becomes the starting point and point of reference for relationships of newly negotiated (or to be negotiated) power, which are dominated by victorious party. It serves as a justification for supremacy and subjugation, while providing symbolic capital for a recalibration of the status, rank and prestige of the participants. In monarchical systems in particular, victory is both a pivotal point in the constitution of power and a discursive instrument of authority (in Max Weber's sense), which also explains frequent efforts to turn a momentary victory into a permanent state by means of appropriatevstrategies of political communication (victory festivals and thanksgivings, burial of the fallen and funerary cult, dedications of spoils and monumentalizations, ceremonial and victory titles, etc.).

The shifts in the spheres of trade, economy and (public) finance that generally came with the end of a military conflict (e.g. through the taking of spoils, enslavements, reparation payments, tribute) usually amplified these effects. However, compensatory mechanisms within society took effect – albeit more effectively in aristocracies and democracies than in monarchies – to stabilize established structures and hierarchies against potential turmoil arising from sudden reallocations of renown and prestige within a victorious polity. The particular historical significance of a military victory thus depended on a sometimes complex web of related structural changes and definitions of meaning resulting from changes in power relations, altered scope for action and design, and a newly adjusted repertoire of narratives and symbols – even if it is not always possible to identify beyond doubt a clear victory or victor (e.g. in a 'Pyrrhic' victory or in conflicts with an unclear outcome).

Ancient historiography first developed a detailed understanding of the political, social, religious and ceremonial dimensions of this complex of phenomena (e.g. [29]; [28]; [17]; [89]; [64]; [8]; [42]; [73]; [87]), but since the 1980s, the discipline of cultural studies has been reevaluating victory and victoriousness in the Archaic, Classical and Hellenistic periods [30]; [96]; [86]; [33], in Republican and Imperial Rome [26]; [9]; [6]; [7]; [46]; [47]; [65]; [49]; [34]; [67]; [40]; [48]; [20]; [32] and in Late Antiquity [56]; [63]; [41]; [62]; [92]; [32]; [57], with questions of political semantics to the fore along with issues of societal normativity and the role of victory and victoriousness in memorialization and the construction of history. There is now increasing interest in the importance of peace as a concept of power [20], the implications of military defeats [78]; [19]; [68], and the problem of victories in civil wars, analysis of which is particularly apt for the study of sociocultural processes of disintegration and reintegration [75]; [96]; [47]; [91]; [92]; [34]; [93]; [18]; [36]; [40]; [48]; [14]; [37].

B. Greek

B.1. Archaic and Classical periods
B.2. Hellenistic period

B.1. Archaic and Classical periods
During the Archaic period, military successes were decorated with ritual elements, as already illustrated in Homeric epic: the plunder of the enemy dead, the singing of the paean, private dedications of booty in sanctuaries, thank-offerings (e.g. Hom. Il. 10,570f.) and lavish warrior funerals with contests in honour of the fallen (Patroclus: Hom. Il. 23, Hector: Hom. Il. 24, Achilles: Hom. Od. 24). There is no evidence, however, to suggest organized public victory festivals. Tropaea (monuments of victory) were built, at first in sanctuaries (Olympia: [4]), but the later ubiquitous building of temporary tropaea on the battlefield only seems to have emerged as a Greek way of staging a victory in the context of the Persian Wars (→ Wars of note, J.) ([84]; [86]; in general on tropaea see also [77]). The victors built the usually human-shaped tropaeum at the place where the battle began or where it took its decisive turn (*trope*), using plundered weapons and pieces of armour (occasionally, the sources indicate rival tropaea: Thuc. 1,105,6; 4,72,4; Xen. Hell. 5,4,65f.; 7,5,26), while the defeated party was required to make public acknowledgment of its defeat by pleading for a truce and releasing the bodies of the fallen.

In aristocratic societies, the focus in staging military accomplishments was on individual *arete* ('valour'), which was assessed without regard to the outcome of the conflict as a whole. As the civic communities later grew in political importance, the *polis* gradually became the primary point of reference for commemorating victory, for example through municipal dedications and foundations using the spoils (e.g. the dedication of one tenth of the booty at Olympia by a victorious *polis*, or the establishment of treasuries: [2. 125]; [3. 84]), and increasingly through public festivals, rituals and monuments referencing victories [76. 154–229]. Victory offered to a *polis* a range of opportunities for strengthening civic identity and the image of prestige, but the outcome of a conflict seems to have remained of little significance to the evaluation of individual accomplishments in battle (probably a relic of former times, when a prince's *arete* was expected to outshine the efforts of the collective), both in public and private commemorations (the latter especially apparent in private dedications and gifts accompanying private burials). Burying the fallen seems to have been primarily the responsibility of the *polis* at an early date, as illustrated by the Archaic *polyandria* (communal graves) of Paros [97]. At first, oustanding individuals might still be honoured with their own public grave or cenotaph, but spaces for representing personal or family-related military feats were increasingly restricted in democratic polities (this is clearly apparent in burial practices at Athens for the time between the reforms of Cleisthenes and the Peloponnesian War (→ Wars of note, H.), when the sumptuary laws relating to burials mentioned in Cic. Leg. 2,64f. were in force).

During the Classical period, public commemoration of military conflicts was increasingly dominated by focus on the civic and military community, and some *poleis* even sought to market their successes on a transregional scale symbolically in Panhellenic sanctuaries (especially Olympia, Delphi, Isthmia, Dodona). Where public victory festivals took place, however (e.g. in Syracuse after successfully repelling the Athenians: Thuc. 7,73), they do not seem to have followed any typical pattern. Athens, in particular, thanks to its revenues from the Delian League, was able to emphasize its military dominance and resulting victories by making foundations (e.g. the Athenian Treasury at Delphi: [15]; [31]), holding public festivals (especially the Great Dionysia: [81]), conducting impressive funerals for the fallen [53]; [83]; [95], and pursuing monumental building programs (e.g. the Temple of Nike: [60]; [39]; [44]). The achievements of the citizen collective were celebrated regardless of the success of the particular enterprise. This is seen in funerary epigrams and the trial of the generals after Arginusae: even if a battle was won, it was more important that the fallen should be retrieved and buried [11. 509–571]. While genres such as Atthidography (local historiography) and eulogies to the fallen emphasized the success of the citizen collective in Athens, different developments can be traced in independent *poleis* and symmachies (especially 'old' and 'new' tyrannies), and some of these attached greater importance to the individual. Epinicia (victory odes) to individuals, for instance, attest to the importance of individual feats (often likewise in the sphere of the contests).

B.2. Hellenistic period
Military success in the service of mobilizing, integrating and legitimizing authority was personalized in Alexander the Great (→ Generals of note, B.), as the strategic, tactical and military achievment of the leading figure. The developing tendency to emphasize individual accomplishments, which increased through the 4th century, culmi-

nated with him. Soli (where Alexander sacrificed to Asclepius, held a military parade, and organized a torch relay and gymnastic and musical contests: Arr. Anab. 2,5,8; see [23. 271]) exemplifies the new concept of victoriousness that Alexander likewise fostered elsewhere. The problem of his succession solidified the new paradigm: after Alexander, the claim to rule could only be justified by the personal performance of the Diadochi, and for the construction of merit based on the charisma of an individual, a reputation for victory was crucial [30]. If the *poleis* were to accept Hellenistic kingship, it was vital that the kings should attain victories, since monarchy could best be reconciled to the autonomy of the city-states through the ruler cult, which externalized the kings as quasi-divine beings and required succes in order to carry out their euergetism [55].

Because of the constant need to prove themselves in war, the charismatic authority of the Hellenistic kings was inherently unstable. Efforts to promote the king's warlike prowess were accordingly legion (e.g. in monumental art, as in the battle pictures from the era of Alexander and the Diadochi, the 'Alexander Sarcophagus', the 'Dying Gaul', the frieze of the Pergamum Altar; see [43]; [16. 189–213]). However, no standard victory ritual akin to the later Roman triumph developed under the Hellenistic monarchies. What processions did take place (e.g. the 'Great Procession' of Ptolemy II Philadelphos in Alexandria or the procession of Antiochus IV in Daphne in 166 BC) were not, formally speaking, victory celebrations [25]; rather, they recalled the municipal *pompai* of the Classical period, with their roots in the religious festival calendar, transforming these into impressive manifestations of the king's renown and benevolence. As the sphere of Roman influence expanded, victoriousness ultimately lost its importance in the later Hellenistic monarchies (key milestones being the 'Day of Eleusis' in 168 BC, the 'Ephesian Vespers', and the reorganization of the east by Pompey). What remained were rulers who, in charismatic terms, could be understood as 'castrated kings' [33].

C. Roman Republic and Imperial period

C.1. Republic
C.2. Imperial period

C.1. Republic

More than any other ritual in Rome, the triumphal procession symbolized military victory. Although it absorbed elements of the Hellenistic → parades (especially during the Late Republican period), the Roman → triumph assumed its own status with distinct social functions in the political culture of Republican society dominated by aristocratic 'checks and balances', especially in the course of successful imperial expansion (contra [82]). The annalistic tradition traced the triumph back to Romulus (InscrIt 13,1 p. 534; see [27]), but the origins of the ritual in the early history of Rome are largely obscure. What evidence is available from the 6th and 5th centuries reveals the early prominence of warrior *condottieri* ('[military] leaders') and their clans [17. 130–132]; [12. 52f.]; [1]; [79]; [88], whose status within society may have given rise to the personalized aspects of the triumphal procession (distribution of booty, central position of the *triumphator* in the procession, and personal dedication on the Capitol). Key elements of the ritual's early evolution remain unclear (e.g. the significance of painting the face of the *triumphator* red – cf. [80] contra [87]; in general on the problem of the sources: [7]).

From its Archaic beginnings as a public celebration of the return of a successful warlord (or 'company leader') with his soldiers and booty, the triumph ultimately preserved its sacred dimension as a ritual that ended war, closely associated with the cult of Jupiter. However, especially in the Middle and Late Republican periods, it became increasingly regulated and developed into a ritual complex that brought together the very broadest spectrum of civic society, all the while keeping clear focus on the figure of the victorious general (now the magistrate furnished with *imperium*). Still, by the senate claiming the right to award a triumph, the Roman aristocracy kept in its hands this important mechanism of societal control and correction, even if there was never any such thing as an explicit *ius triumphandi* ('right of triumphal procession'). The republican practice of approving or refusing triumphs is more accurately described as a result of processes of negotiation within the aristocracy. Although legal arguments no doubt carried much weight in these processes, a variety of other formal and informal means of persuasion were also employed (see e.g. [6]; [71. 33–53]; [54]; [49]; [48]).

Within the context of these influences, the triumph proper (in addition to the *triumphus navalis*, 'naval triumphal procession', the *triumphus in monte Albano*, 'triumphal procession on the Alban Mountain', and the *ovatio*, 'ovation') became the most important means by which ambitious magistrates put their military victories on display in the capital, which was particularly important because most of these victories were won far away. The specific design of each victory procession in Rome differed according to the circumstances and political significance of the victory concerned. The procession, comprising the *triumphator*, his soldiers and the senators typically included not only prestigious items of plunder and selected prisoners, but also portrayals of the battles, wonders of nature and striking cultural products from faraway lands [65]. The efforts of victorious generals to perpetuate the memory of their contributions to successful outcomes brought about a proliferation of triumphal monuments in Rome, especially along the course of the *via triumphalis* ('Triumphal Road') and in the Forum Romanum [66]; [74].

As rivalries within the aristocracy intensified in the 1st century BC, the tendency to highlight individual accomplishments increased. Processions, for instance, became ever more lavish, and festivities were extended to last several days. Certain acts were designed to make symbolic points, as when Pompey wore the cloak of Alexander rather than the usual purple toga (App. Mithr. 117; on which [85]). The increasing scale of military successes escalated triumphal competition, as these processions acquired correspondingly great symbolic and economic significance. Only recently have scholars paid close attention to the strategies of ambitious commanders as they sought to express their successes in the Roman civil wars through triumphs (see esp. [48]; [40]).

C.2. IMPERIAL PERIOD

The transformation from an aristocratic *res publica* to a monarchy led to a profound shift in the form and function of the triumph. The military victories of Marius, Pompey, Caesar (→ Generals of note, K., → Generals of note, N., → Generals of note, C.) and finally Octavian brought these men harvests of prestige that could no longer be reconciled through traditional mechanisms to the political system of the aristocratic republic. Under the conditions of an empire, the triumph could no longer be permitted to function as a medium of intra-aristocratic rivalry. In practice, it was now only the ruler himself or his presumptive heir who was permitted to hold a triumph (although members of the aristocracy who achieved military success were at first honoured with *ornamenta triumphalia*, 'triumphal honours' until this form of distinction became obsolete in the 2nd century). As it became monopolized by the *princeps*, the now rare triumph acquired great significance as a ceremonial means of highlighting the emperor's military role. As such, it became a key facet in the emperors' strategy for representing himself symbolically, effecting political integration, and preserving his authority.

According to [80], the *princeps* could turn any public appearance into a triumph. The accuracy of this observation is shown by the triumphs of Caligula, Claudius and Nero (sources and discussion in [94. 12f.]). It was only with the Flavian triumph of AD 71 that the empire developed the paradigm for a monarchical triumph aimed at building consensual authority, which was able to create a normative bonding effect for the institution as a whole, apart from the variable profiles of the individual emperors. With the increasing importance of the military, the gradual shift from a monarchy of the capital to a residential empire, and the formation of standing army units along the empire's frontiers, the triumphal representation of power became one of the most important fields of communication between the sovereign and his subjects across the empire, and it developed more and more into an institution amplifying the emperor's victorious nature. Indicative of this reality are, for instance, the provincial victory monuments from the reigns of Trajan, Hadrian and the Severans. Imperial coins and medallions were increasingly used to represent promises of military success to the units stationed near the borders.

D. LATE ANTIQUITY

D.1. Triumphal authority and Christianity
D.2. Empire of the military residence
D.3. Imperial palace in the capital

D.1. TRIUMPHAL AUTHORITY AND CHRISTIANITY

Military success continued to be one of the most important building blocks of monarchical legitimacy in Late Antiquity. The economic (→ booty, tribute, → slaves) and symbolic (→ peace, virtue, divine support) potential of good fortune in war tended to outweigh any Christian criticisms against military facets of the representation of rulers [70], who continued to base their prestige on military success long after actual command in the field had passed to the *magistri militum* ('Masters of Soldiers'). Throughout Late Antiquity, Roman emperors continued to be portrayed in imperial pictorial programmes (especially on monumental reliefs and coins) as eternal victors, and they celebrated victories with spectacular processions that were still regularly called 'triumphs' (*thriambos/triumphus*) – regardless of whether they marked victories over external or internal enemies (Pan. Lat. 12(9), 23, 3; 2(12), 37, 1–4, Prisc. *De laude Anastasii Imperatoris* 174–177; see [63. 35–79]). Festivities of this kind were usually accompanied by banqueting, imperial orations and gifts (*donativa, largitiones*) and panegyric speeches. Traditional games and contests were also held (seminal [56]; also [92]). The virtuous character of the emperor was reflected in material culture, for example in statues, coins, medallions and inscriptions, and sometimes also in large-scale monuments, such as triumphal arches, relief columns, obelisks and church foundations.

After Constantine broke the traditional link between the triumph and pagan religion, the victory celebrations of Late Antiquity at first became neutral or ambivalent in terms of religion. Although Christian elements increasingly appeared as part of the staging and reception of the triumph [51], the triumphal ritual proper only became thoroughly Christianized in the Middle Byzantine period – unlike, for example, the *adventus* ritual of Late Antiquity, which was typically staged in the manner of a triumph [56]; [70]. The contemporary debate over the depaganization of triumphal representation can be seen clearly in the controversy over the altar of Victoria. This controversy ended in the second half of the 4th century when the Altar of Victoria was removed once and for all from the Roman Curia (Symmachus, Relat. 3; Ambr. Epist. 17f.; see [73]; [45]). The enduring significance of victory for rulers in Late Antiquity, however, meant that Victoria kept her key position in triumphal iconography, albeit now regarded as a personification of the concept rather than as a goddess [52].

D.2. EMPIRE OF THE MILITARY RESIDENCE
Despite the high degree of continuity, it cannot be ignored that the significance of military victories and the emperor's victorious nature changed in Late Antiquity – and that the triumphal representation of authority likewise underwent profound changes. For example, the importance of the *caput imperii* ('head of the empire', i.e. Rome) in the staging of victory changed radically. In the decentralized empire of the late 3rd and 4th centuries, victory celebrations over foreign enemies were typically held in imperial residences (e.g. Trier, Sirmium and Antioch), while the city of Rome became the primary stage for triumphal entries (*adventus*) after victories in civil wars. On the one hand, presence in the 'Eternal City' as a victorious general enabled the emperor to highlight his proximity to the senate and his claim to supremacy over the whole empire (e.g. Constantine in 312, 315 and 326, Constantius II in 357, Theodosius I in 389 and Honorius in 403/04 and 416). On the other hand, presence in the frontier regions enabled him to demonstrate his proximity to the soldiers and to the leading figures of the *apparatus imperii* (the extended imperial system of government).

Alongside these developments, and becoming apparent at least by the late 3rd century AD, there was a tendency to replace the *propagatio imperii* ('enlargement of the empire') with less elaborate demonstrations of military excellence, for example with infrastructure programs that had military applications (e.g. the building of bridges and fortifications), usually intended for no more than limited pillage and plunder expeditions into enemy settlement areas. The traditional quest for renown through a great victory over external enemies could come at a very high cost. This is exemplified by the death of Emperor Julian during his Persian campaign in AD 363 (→ Generals of note, H.). Risks of this kind were subsequently lessened by shifting the emperor's active presence on the frontiers more into the sphere of → diplomacy [57], but the death of Valens at the Battle of Adrianople in AD 378 (→ Battle, B.) shows that an emperor's active engagement in battle against 'barbarians' was now potentially a problem even deep inside the empire's own territories [50].

D.3. IMPERIAL PALACE IN THE CAPITAL
In this context, the emperor's withdrawal into the palace, and the transfer of military leadership duties to the *magistri militum*, appear as entirely consistent developments (imperial palace: [90]; *magister militum*: [72]). The victory ideology continued to focus on the figure of the ruler, but this was only possible when innovative means were found to honour successful generals (e.g. Eutropius, Stilicho, Belisarius), while still assigning the highest honour to the emperor (e.g. the *proskynesis* ('prostration') of Belisarius before Justinian: Procop. Pers. 4,9,1–16; see [13]).

As from the reign of Theodosius I, Constantinople, as the new capital with a strengthening imperial palace, became the most important stage for Roman victory celebrations [21]; [58]; [61]; [22]; [10]; [59]; [5]; [69]. Although the emperors generally stopped taking the battlefield in person after the late 4th century, it was still extremely important for them to be honoured through triumphal representation (obelisks, Forum of Theodosius with relief column and triumphal arch, relief column of Arcadius, Golden Gate, Marcian Column, equestrian statue of Justinian). The staging of victories, however, was changing. Over the course of the 5th and 6th centuries, increasing tendencies towards Christianization transformed official celebrations into triumphal processions of thanksgiving in honour of God [24]. Such processions might still on occasion be led by the emperor (in a carriage, on horseback or on foot), but they usually led *to* the emperor, enthroned in the Hippodrome awaiting the masses [13. 69–71]. Biblical and eschatological concepts were more and more woven into the idea of triumphal authority, as evidenced by the *adventus* of Heraclius into Jerusalem in AD 630 with the restitution of the True Cross [35]. In the post-Roman west, victory celebrations were largely performed in the guise of thanksgivings in honour of God, albeit generally with less pomp and pageantry [38].

☞ Battle; Booty; Consequences of war; Honour; Parades; State and army; Strategy; Triumph

BIBLIOGRAPHY
[1] J. ARMSTRONG, Claiming Victory. The Early Roman Triumph, in: A. SPALINGER / J. ARMSTRONG (eds.), Rituals of Triumph in the Mediterranean World, 2013,

7–21 [2] H. BAITINGER, Waffen und Bewaffnung aus der Perserbeute in Olympia, in: AA, 1999, 125–139 [3] H. BAITINGER, Die Angriffswaffen aus Olympia (Olympische Forschungen 29), 2001 [4] J.M. BARRINGER, Zeus at Olympia, in: R.N. BREMMER / A. ERSKINE (eds.), The Gods of Ancient Greece. Identities and Transformations, 2010, 155–177 [5] S. BASSETT, The Urban Image of Late Antique Constantinople, 2004 [6] J.-L. BASTIEN, Le triomphe romain et son utilisation politique à Rome aux trois derniers siècles de la République, 2007 [7] M. BEARD, The Roman Triumph, 2007 [8] A.R. BELLINGER / M.A. BERLINCOURT, Victory as a Coin Type, 1962 [9] S. BENOIST, Rome, le prince et la cité. Pouvoir impérial et cérémonies publiques (Ier siècle av.–début du IVe siècle apr. J.-C.), 2005 [10] A. BERGER, Streets and Public Spaces in Constantinople, in: Dumbarton Oaks Papers 54, 2000, 161–172 [11] B. BLECKMANN, Athens Weg in die Niederlage. Die letzten Jahre des Peloponnesischen Kriegs, 1998 [12] L. BONFANTE WARREN, Roman Triumphs and Etruscan Kings. The Changing Face of the Triumph, in: JRS 60, 1970, 49–66 [13] H. BÖRM, Justinians Triumph und Belisars Erniedrigung. Überlegungen zum Verhältnis zwischen Kaiser und Militär im späten Römischen Reich, in: Chiron 43, 2013, 63–91 [14] H. BÖRM, Mordende Mitbürger. Stasis und Bürgerkrieg in griechischen Poleis des Hellenismus, 2017 (Habil. Konstanz) [15] H. BÜSING, Das Athener Schatzhaus in Delphi. Neue Untersuchungen zur Architektur und Bemalung, 1994 [16] A. CHANIOTIS, War in the Hellenistic World, 2005 [17] G. CHARLES-PICARD, Les trophées romains. Contribution à l'histoire de la religion et de l'art triomphal de Rome, 1957 [18] B. CHRUBASIK, Kings and Usurpers in the Seleukid Empire. The Men who Would Be King, 2016 [19] J. CLARK, Triumph in Defeat. Military Loss and the Roman Republic, 2014 [20] H. CORNWELL, Pax and the Politics of Peace. Republic to Principate, 2017 [21] G. DAGRON, Constantinople imaginaire. Études sur le recueil des Patria, 1984 [22] S. DIEFENBACH, Frömmigkeit und Kaiserakzeptanz im frühen Byzanz, in: Saeculum 47, 1996, 35–66 [23] J. DILLERY, Xenophon, Military Review and Hellenistic Pompai, in: C.J. TULPIN (ed.), Xenophon and His World, 2004, 259–276 [24] P. DUFRAIGNE, Adventus Augusti, Adventus Christi. Recherche sur l'exploitation idéologique et littéraire d'un cérémonial dans l'antiquité tardive, 1994 [25] A. ERSKINE, Hellenistic Parades and Roman Triumphs, in: A. SPALINGER / J. ARMSTRONG (eds.), Rituals of Triumph in the Mediterranean World, 2013, 37–55 [26] J.R. FEARS, The Theology of Victory at Rome. Approaches and Problems, in: ANRW II.17.2, 1981, 736–826 [27] D.C. FEENEY, Caesar's Calendar. Ancient Time and the Beginnings of History, 2007 [28] J. GAGÉ, La théologie de la victoire impériale, in: RH 58, 1933, 1–43 [29] J. GAGÉ, Σταυρὸς νικοποιός. La victoire imperiale dans l'empire chrétien, in: RHPhR 13, 1933, 370–400 [30] H.-J. GEHRKE, Der siegreiche König. Überlegungen zur Hellenistischen Monarchie, in: AKG 64, 1982, 247–277 [31] M.B. GENSHEIMER, Metaphors for Marathon in the Sculptural Program of the Athenian Treasury at Delphi, in: Hesperia 86, 2017, 1–42 [32] F. GOLDBECK / J. WIENAND (eds.), Der römische Triumph in Prinzipat und Spätantike, 2017 [33] U. GOTTER, The Castrated King, or: The Everyday Monstrosity of Late Hellenistic Kingship, in: N. LURAGHI (ed.), The Splendors and Miseries of Ruling Alone. Encounters with Monarchy from Archaic Greece to the Hellenistic Mediterranean, 2013, 207–230 [34] B. GRAY, Stasis and Stability. Exile, the Polis, and Political Thought, c. 404–146 BC, 2015 [35] L. GREISIGER, Messias – Endkaiser – Antichrist. Politische Apokalyptik unter Juden und Christen des Nahen Ostens am Vorabend der arabischen Eroberung, 2014 [36] M. HAAKE, 'Trophäen, die nicht vom äußeren Feinde gewonnen wurden, Triumphe, die der Ruhm mit Blut befleckt davon trug …'. Der Sieg im imperialen Bürgerkrieg im 'langen dritten Jahrhundert' als ambivalentes Ereignis, in: H. BÖRM et al. (eds.), Civil War in Ancient Greece and Rome. Contexts of Disintegration and Reintegration, 2016, 237–301 [37] M. HAAKE, Zwischen Severus Alexanders Triumph über die Sāsāniden im Jahre 233 und den Triumphfeierlichkeiten Diocletians und Maximians im Jahre 303. Zum römischen Triumph im dritten Jahrhundert n.Chr., in: F. GOLDBECK / J. WIENAND (eds.), Der römische Triumph in Prinzipat und Spätantike, 2017, 357–395 [38] G. HALSALL, The Decline and Fall of the Ancient Triumph, in: F. GOLDBECK / J. WIENAND (eds.), Der römische Triumph in Prinzipat und Spätantike, 2017, 555–568 [39] E.B. HARRISON, The Glories of the Athenians. Observations on the Program of the Frieze of the Temple of Athena Nike, in: D. BUITRON-OLIVER (ed.), The Interpretation of Architectural Sculpture in Greece and Rome, 1997, 109–125 [40] W. HAVENER, Imperator Augustus. Die diskursive Konstituierung der militärischen 'persona' des ersten römischen 'princeps', 2016 [41] F. HEIM, La théologie de la victoire de Constantin à Théodose, 1992 [42] T. HÖLSCHER, Victoria Romana. Archäologische Untersuchungen zur Geschichte und Wesensart der römischen Siegesgöttin von den Anfängen bis zum Ende des 3. Jhs. n.Chr., 1967 [43] T. HÖLSCHER, Griechische Historienbilder des 5. und 4. Jahrhunderts v.Chr., 1973 [44] T. HÖLSCHER, Ritual und Bildsprache. Zur Deutung der Reliefs an der Brüstung um das Heiligtum der Athena Nike in Athen, in: MDAI(A) 112, 1997, 143–166 [45] R. KLEIN, Der Streit um den Victoriaaltar. Die dritte Relatio des Symmachus und die Briefe 17, 18 und 57 des Mailänder Bischofs Ambrosius, 1972 [46] H. KRASSER et al. (eds.), Triplici invectus triumpho. Der römische Triumph in augusteischer Zeit, 2008 [47] C.H. LANGE, Res Publica Constituta. Actium, Apollo and the Accomplishment of the Triumviral Assignment, 2009 [48] C.H. LANGE, Triumphs in the Age of Civil War. The Late Republic and the Adaptability of Triumphal Tradition, 2016 [49] C.H. LANGE / F.J. VERVAET (eds.), The Roman Republican Triumph. Beyond the Spectacle, 2014 [50] N.E. LENSKI, Failure of Empire. Valens and the Roman State in the Fourth Century A.D., 2002 [51] P. LIVERANI, Roma tardoantica come spazio della rappresentazione trionfale, in: F. GOLDBECK / J. WIENAND (eds.), Der römische Triumph in Prinzipat und Spätantike, 2017, 487–510 [52] F. LÓPEZ SÁNCHEZ, Victoria Augusti. La representación del poder del emperador en los reversos monetales romanos de bronce del siglo IV d.C., 2004 [53] N. LORAUX, L'invention d'Athènes. Histoire de l'oraison funèbre dans la 'cité classique', 1981 [54] C. LUNDGREEN, Regelkonflikte in der römischen Republik. Geltung und Gewichtung von Normen in politischen Entscheidungsprozessen, 2011 [55] J. MA, Antiochos III and the Cities of Western Asia Minor, 1999 [56] S.G. MACCORMACK, Art and Ceremony in Late Antiquity, 1981 [57] F.K. MAIER, Palastrevolution. Der Weg zum hauptstädtischen Kaisertum im Römischen Reich des vierten Jahrhunderts,

2019 [58] C. Mango, Le développement urbain de Constantinople, IVᵉ–VIIᵉ siècles, 1985 [59] C. Mango, The Triumphal Way of Constantinople and the Golden Gate, in: Dumbarton Oaks Papers 54, 2000, 173–188 [60] I.S. Mark, The Sanctuary of Athena Nike in Athens. Architectural Stages and Chronology, 1993 [61] J. Martin, Zum Selbstverständnis, zur Repräsentation und Macht des Kaisers in der Spätantike, in: Saeculum 35, 1985, 115–131 [62] J. Martin, Das Kaisertum in der Spätantike, in: F. Paschoud / J. Szidat (eds.), Usurpationen in der Spätantike. Akten des Kolloquiums 'Staatsstreich und Staatlichkeit', 6.–10. März 1996, 1997, 47–61 [63] M. McCormick, Eternal Victory. Triumphal Rulership in Late Antiquity, Byzantium, and the Early Medieval West, 1986 [64] J.H. Oliver, Demokratia, the Gods, and the Free World, 1960 [65] I. Östenberg, Staging the World. Spoils, Captives, and Representations in the Roman Triumphal Procession, 2009 [66] I. Östenberg, Circum metas fertur. An Alternative Reading of the Triumphal Route, in: Historia 59, 2010, 303–320 [67] I. Östenberg et al. (eds.), The Moving City. Processions, Passages and Promenades in Ancient Rome, 2015 [68] I. Östenberg, Defeated by the Forest, the Pass, the Wind. Nature as an Enemy of Rome, in: J.H. Clark / B. Turner (eds.), Brill's Companion to Military Defeat in Ancient Mediterranean Society, 2018, 240–261 [69] R. Pfeilschifter, Der Kaiser und Konstantinopel. Kommunikation und Konfliktaustrag in einer spätantiken Metropole, 2013 [70] R. Pfeilschifter, Der römische Triumph und das Christentum. Überlegungen zur Eigenart eines öffentlichen Rituals, in: F. Goldbeck / J. Wienand (eds.), Der römische Triumph in Prinzipat und Spätantike, 2017, 455–485 [71] M.R.P. Pittenger, Contested Triumphs. Politics, Pageantry, and Performance in Livy's Republican Rome, 2008 [72] A. Poguntke, Das römische Heermeisteramt im 5. Jahrhundert. Überlegungen zum Verhältnis zwischen Kaiser und Heermeister in Ost und West, in: C. Föller / F. Schulz (eds.), Osten und Westen 400–600 n.Chr. Kommunikation, Kooperation und Konflikt, 2016, 239–262 [73] H.A. Pohlsander, Victory. The Story of a Statue, in: Historia 18, 1969, 588–597 [74] M.L. Popkin, The Architecture of the Roman Triumph. Monuments, Memory, and Identity, 2016 [75] J.J. Price, Thucydides and Internal War, 2001 [76] W.K. Pritchett, The Greek State at War, pt. 3, 1979 [77] B. Rabe, Tropaia. τροπή und σκῦλα – Entstehung, Funktion und Bedeutung des griechischen Tropaions, 2008 [78] J. Rich, Roman Attitudes to Defeat in Battle under the Republic, in: F. Marco Simón et al. (ed.), Vae victis! Perdedores en el mundo antiguo, 2012, 83–111 [79] J.W. Rich, Warlords and the Roman Republic, in: T. Ñaco del Hoyo / F. López Sánchez (eds.), War, Warlords and Interstate Relations in the Ancient Mediterranean, 2017, 266–294 [80] J. Rüpke, Domi militiae. Die religiöse Konstruktion des Krieges in Rom, 1990 [81] B. Smarczyk, Untersuchungen zur Religionspolitik und politischen Propaganda Athens im Delisch-Attischen Seebund, 1990 [82] A. Spalinger / J. Armstrong (eds.), Rituals of Triumph in the Mediterranean World, 2013 [83] C. Stöhr, Tod für die Patris. Das Gefallenengedenken in den griechischen Poleis klassischer und hellenistischer Zeit, 2016 (Diss. Heidelberg) [84] J. Stroszeck, Greek Trophy Monuments, in: S. Des Bouvrie (ed.), Myth and Symbol, pt. 2: Symbolic Phenomena in Ancient Greek Culture. Papers from the Second and Third International Symposia on Symbolism at the Norwegian Institute at Athens, September 21–24, 2000 and September 19–22, 2002, 2004, 303–331 [85] K. Trampedach, Zwischen Alexander und Augustus. Pompeius' Neuordnung des Ostens, in: H.-J. Gehrke (ed.), Rom und der Osten im 1. Jahrhundert v.Chr. Akkulturation oder Kampf der Kulturen?, 2009, 393–416 [86] M. Trundle, Commemorating Victory in Classical Greece. Why Greek Tropaia?, in: A. Spalinger / J. Armstrong (eds.), Rituals of Triumph in the Mediterranean World, 2013, 123–138 [87] H.S. Versnel, Triumphus. An Inquiry into the Origin, Development and Meaning of the Roman Triumph, 1970 [88] J. Walter, Monarchen im frühen Rom. Traditionen – Konzepte – Wirklichkeiten, in: S. Rebenich (ed.), Monarchische Herrschaft im Altertum, 2017, 119–139 [89] S. Weinstock, Victor and Invictus, in: The Harvard Theological Review 50, 1957, 211–247 [90] M. Whitby, From Frontier to Palace. The Personal Role of the Emperor in Diplomacy, in: J. Shepard / S. Franklin (eds.), Byzantine Diplomacy, 1992, 295–303 [91] J. Wienand, Der blutbefleckte Kaiser. Constantin und die martialische Inszenierung eines prekären Sieges, in: M. Fahlenbock et al. (eds.), Inszenierung des Sieges – Sieg der Inszenierung. Interdisziplinäre Perspektiven, 2011, 237–254 [92] J. Wienand, Der Kaiser als Sieger. Metamorphosen triumphaler Herrschaft unter Constantin I., 2012 [93] J. Wienand (ed.), Contested Monarchy. Integrating the Roman Empire in the Fourth Century AD, 2015 [94] J. Wienand et al., Der römische Triumph in Prinzipat und Spätantike. Probleme – Paradigmen – Perspektiven, in: F. Goldbeck / J. Wienand (eds.), Der römische Triumph in Prinzipat und Spätantike, 2017, 1–26 [95] J. Wienand, Die Politisierung des Todes. Gefallenenbestattung und Epitaphios logos im demokratischen Athen, 2018 (Habil. Düsseldorf) [96] A. Wolpert, Remembering Defeat. Civil War and Civic Memory in Ancient Athens, 2002 [97] P. Zaphiropoulou, I due polyandria dell'antica necropoli di Paros, in: Annali di archeologia e storia antica 6, 1999, 13–24.

JOHANNES WIENAND

Victory titles

A. The Greek Macedonian kingdoms
B. Roma victrix
C. Developments in the Imperial period

To the political powers and societies of the ancient world, victory (*nike*, *victoria*) was the ultimate goal of all armed conflicts. As such it had enormous military, political, religious and ideological significance. Personified in allegories and as deities, victory was prominent in Greek and Roman toponymy and anthroponymy, and from the 4th century BC to the 6th century AD it inspired the formation of victory titles and bynames, especially for active kings, princes, generals and emperors. This thousand-year practice gave rise to a diverse tradition of titles in terms of their meaning, conferring and reception, and also with regard to the selection and aims of their recipients.

A. The Greek Macedonian kingdoms

A.1. Requirement of victory
A.2. Multiple functions
A.3. Participants and awards

The victorious power of the rulers of the ancient Near East, such as the Pharaohs of Egypt or the Assyrian or Persian kings, underwent a notable degree of glorification. In Greece, by contrast, it was primarily the gods who were associated with → victory, whether through victory surnames (Zeus Nikator, Heracles Aniketos, Athena Nike etc.) or the worship of Nike ('Victory') as a goddess in her own right. During the Classical period, military leaders were generally under the authority of civic institutions, and the glory of victory was in theory shared by the whole collective (Thuc. 1,132,2f.). Beginning in the 4th century BC, the rise of the Macedonian and Hellenistic kingdoms allowed monarchs to adopt the use of victory titles.

A.1. Requirement of victory

Although he later received the byname 'the Great' (*Megas*), Alexander III (336–323 BC) was first known by the victory title *Aniketos* ('unconquerable'), recalling Achilles and Heracles, ancestors of the Macedonoian royal house. The ground had been laid for the use of this formal title, which is attested in connection with divine honorifics from 324/23 onwards (Hyp., *Contra Demosthenem* 7,32), in the earlier establishment of the motif of the king's invincibility (Diod. Sic. 17,16,2; 17,93,4). As embodied in the exceptional figure of Alexander, and driven by the Macedonian military tradition and myths of power and conquest (e.g. Odysseus and Theseus), the ability of the ruler to win victory by taking an active part in battles (Pol. 5,85,8) became the pivotal point of Hellenistic monarchical ideology [1. 457–459]; [14]. The title *basileus* ('king') tended to be awarded after a genuine victory (Diod. Sic. 20,53; App. Syr. 54,275–277). That gave legitimacy to the exercise of power over the 'land won by the spear' (*doriktetos chora*), or the world saved from barbarian threat (Pol. 18,41,7). Some kings now adopted victory titles emphasizing their military virtues and victorious qualities to cement their political and ideological image.

A.2. Multiple functions

The general proliferation of royal epithets in the Hellenistic period (one ruler could hold several such titles) also included the use of victory titles, which in this context comprised just one specific, albeit significant aspect [11. 333–352]; [12. 183–186]; [8. 276–279]. These titles, limited in number, did not celebrate particular victories over an enemy or a people, but were of a general character: *Nikator* ('victor'), *Kallinikos* ('glorious victor'), *Nikephoros* ('who carries off victory'), *Aniketos* ('undefeated' and especially 'unconquerable').

Of all the Hellenistic royal houses, the Seleucids were the first to use victory titles, and they used them the most. Seleucus I Nikator (305–281), founder of the Seleucid Empire, was probably the only one of the Diadochi to use a victory title during his lifetime. This seems to have been guided by his desire to call to mind Alexander Aniketos, while also distinguishing himself from Ptolemy I Soter ('Saviour') and his victory ideology. The title Nikator was also given to Zeus, the family's patron deity, while Nike was one of the kingdom's guardian deities. After surviving to be the last of the Diadochi (and according to Just. Epit. 17,2,2 to become *victor victorum*, 'victor of victors'), Seleucus in death rested in a tomb called Nikatoreion ('belonging to the victor') at Seleucia Pieria (App. Syr. 63,336). Of his successors, only Demetrius II (145–139 and 129–125) – who was embroiled in internal conflicts and anxious to associate himself with the founder of the dynasty – and Seleucus VI (c. 96–94) took the title Nikator, which is also attested in Parthia in the 1st century BC. The other Seleucids preferred other victory titles, with Kallinikos – the surname of Heracles – chosen by Seleucus II (246–226), Antiochus VII (138–129), Antiochus VIII (125–96), Demetrius III (97–87) and Antiochus XII (c. 87–83), whereas Nikephoros – the surname of Zeus – was taken by Antiochus IV (175–164) and others. These two titles were also used in Commagene and Cappadocia, but above all in the Greco-Bactrian and Greco-Indian kingdoms, where rulers were particularly receptive to the victory ideology, whether in titles (Nikephoros or Aniketos with their Sanskrit translations *Jayadhara, Aparajita*) or in coin images of Nike. Motivations for such decisions might be political (reference to ideals of Alexander and Seleucus), military (importance of victory to the warrior aristocracy) or religious (possible association with Mithra, the unconquerable Sun). One exception was Aśoka (269–232), king of the Maurya Dynasty, who after a warlike phase turned to Buddhism, rejected victory and praised peace.

The use of victory titles in the other Hellenistic kingdoms pales in comparison with the Seleucids and South Asia. The Ptolemies sometimes adopted names connected with war (e.g. Nikephoros (OGIS 89) for Ptolemy IV after the Battle of Rhaphia in 217 BC), but never permanently or officially. The title Soter could take on the meaning 'victorious' in reference to a king who successfully defended his country, but the multivalence of the term was never constrained to this. The concept of victory in connection with title 'ultimate saviour' manifested itself most clearly in opposition to a barbarian threat. In Pergamum, for instance, Attalus I (241–197) and Eumenes II (197–159), both victors over the Galatians, each took the title Soter. The restoration of peace and prosperity after victory by a savior and liberator, sometimes with the use of the title Eirenopoios ('Bringer of Peace'), was celebrated in official discourse and through various honours bestowed by the cities. Finally, the victor's ideology was expressed in more isolated or diffuse usage, whether in actual titles (Demetrius Poliorketes used 'Besieger, Conqeror of Cities' as his unofficial title), in the names of military units (Liv. 43,19,11 on the *nikatores*, soldiers of Perseus), or as traces in anthroponymy (Berenice, 'She who Brings Victory') or toponymy (Nikopolis, 'City of Victory').

A.3. Participants and awards

In few cases is it known for certain by whom, how and why victory titles were bestowed on those bearing them, whether this was an official procedure, and whether it took place during the subject's lifetime or posthumously. The literary, epigraphic, numismatic and papyrological sources are sometimes lacking or contradictory, aside from the possibility of discrepancies between official and unofficial texts. The honours and epithets bestowed by cities, along with later literary reconstructions, complicate the situation even further. The sources might, for example, state that a victory title was bestowed long after a ruler's death, when in fact he was already using it during his lifetime. In some cases, there is a concrete connection between the adoption of a victory title and an actual military victory (e.g. Antiochus IV Nikephoros after an Egyptian campaign in 170–169), but not in other cases (e.g. Ptolemy X and Ptolemy XII). At least initially, the acclamation of the soldiers may have triggered the award of a victory title (Lucian. Zeux. 11), which later might acquire an official character (or might not). A victory title was sometimes awarded by the will of the king himself, or on the initiative of his enourage or court. The later recognition of Alexander as 'the Great' (Megas) may have originated from his court or from ongoing developments within Hellenistic political thought. The Greek Hellenistic sources in general call him simply Basileus ('king'), and some intellectuals criticized the vanity of his conquests as well as the presumption of kings in taking certain titles. It is, therefore, mostly Latin sources that call him Magnus ('the Great') (Plaut. Most. 775f.). Although Latin sources, too, were sometimes critical, they were unable to prevent the figure of the conqueror from inspiring Roman generals and emperors.

B. Roma victrix

B.1. The Republican *imperatores*
B.2. Appropriation by the emperors

Victoria [5], the personification of victory and a goddess, was worshipped from an early date at Rome, where several deities, including Hercules, Jupiter, Mars and Venus received the surname *Victor* or *Victrix*. From the Middle Republican period onwards, and even more so under the Principate, powerful individuals also took victory bynames. These were considered important for political recognition, which was largely based on military reputation.

B.1. The Republican *imperatores*

Rome's military expansion brought some magistrates and promagistrates of the Republic the status of *imperatores*, that is, military commanders honoured by the senate with a triumph [2]. Beginning in the 4th century BC, some of them also acquired *cognomina* that referenced their place of victory, for example the consul L. Aemilius Mamercinus Privernas in 329 BC. The first to receive a victory byname based on the name of a defeated people (*nomen victae ab se gentis*: Liv. 30,45,7), however, was P. Cornelius Scipio Africanus (→ Generals of note, O.), *imperator* starting in 209 BC (Pol. 10,40,2–5; Liv. 27,19,4), after he defeated Carthage in 202 BC. The title Imperator first appears on an official inscription in honour of L. Aemilius Paullus (ILS 8884), victor over King Perseus in 168 BC, for which he was honoured with the victory byname Macedonicus. During the 2nd century BC, many *imperatores* who were honoured with a triumph took a victory byname that was not officially granted by the senate, but had the support of their soldiers, their followers or the people, and which brought them great advantage (Liv. 30,45,6). P. Cornelius Scipio Aemilianus, who captured Carthage in 146 BC and Numantia in 133 BC, was honoured as Africanus and Numantinus. Inspired by Hellenistic examples, these practices had their origins in political ambitions fueled by military successes, and also in the antagonistic spirit of the Roman aristocracy. The bestowing of titles based on geographical or tribal names differed from the practice of Greek and Hellenistic rulers who adopted more general victory titles.

As bynames grew more and more commonplace, they were devalued and lost relevance among the great *imperatores* of the 1st century and the civil wars. Sometimes endowed with extraordinary command authority, these men took the rewards of their legates' military successes as their own. Rather than content themselves with weaker victory titles, they developed a discourse that was in part inspired by Hellenistic victory ideology.

After his victories over the followers of Marius in 82 BC, Pompey accepted from his soldiers the byname Magnus ('The Great'), which Sulla later recognized (Plut. *Pompeius* 13,7–11) and was reactivated for the eastern campaign that won him a triumph in 61 BC. Victory was now increasingly associated with the *virtus* ('valour') and charismatic personality of the *imperator*, who was sustained by his *felicitas* ('good fortune') or his patron deity, for example Venus Victrix ('Victorious') for Pompey or Venus Genitrix ('Begetter') for Caesar. At the Battle of Pharsalus, the appellation of the former was 'unconquerable Hercules' and that of the latter was 'victorious Venus' (App. Civ. 2,76). Meanwhile, the political importance of the goddess Victoria was affirmed, as she was associated with both generals. She was celebrated explicitly in the *ludi Victoriae* ('Victory Games') of Sulla (82 BC) and Caesar (46 BC) [3]. Caesar the Younger, the former Octavian, who had emerged victorious from the civil wars, in turn made victory one of the pillars of his new imperial ideology when he dedicated an altar to Victoria (*ara Victoriae*) in 29 BC.

B.2. APPROPRIATION BY THE EMPERORS

Augustus (reigned as *princeps* 27 BC–AD 14) held to the principle of an indissoluble bond between → victory and his *virtus* as charismatic *imperator*, promoting the *victoria Augusti* ('Victory of Augustus') as the prerequisite for the *pax Augusta* ('peace of Augustus'). Titles honouring victories were also given to legions, such as the *VI Victrix*. But where this ideology really made its presence felt was in the new system of imperial titles, which were promoted on a massive scale through inscriptions and coins. Like their earlier Greek equivalents, Latin victory titles continued to evolve in response to the demands of power through the end of Antiquity. The ex-Octavian made Imperator his imperial praenomen. Tiberius (14–37), Caligula (37–41) and Claudius (41–54) did not follow this example, but Nero (54–68) revived it towards the end of his reign and established it for the future. The title Imperator was followed by an adverb of quantity to indicate the number of acclamations received from troops after important victories (Cass. Dio 52,41,4). Octavian received the title in 43 BC; then, beginning with Claudius, ascending the throne was counted as the first acclamation. The three most important privileges of victory were soon claimed by the emperor and the imperial family. Outside this group, these honours went only to a few aristocrats in the early years of the principate. The last to receive a triumph was L. Cornelius Balbus in 19 BC; the last to be named *imperator* was Q. Iunius Blaesus in AD 23 (Tac. Ann. 3,74,4); and the last to take a victory title was P. Gabinius Secundus Chaucius (victor over the Chauci in AD 41; Suet. Claud. 24,7).

C. DEVELOPMENTS IN THE IMPERIAL PERIOD

C.1. The *cognomina devictarum gentium*
C.2. Late Antiquity

C.1. THE *COGNOMINA DEVICTARUM GENTIUM*

Augustus took no victory titles derived from tribal names. However, this tradition did revive during his reign, with Nero Claudius Drusus (called 'The Elder'), brother of Tiberius. The senate granted Drusus the posthumous *cognomen* of Germanicus ('victor over the Germani') in 9 BC for his victories on the Rhine. This honour was also passed on to his descendants (Germanicus, Caligula, Claudius and Nero), although being an inherited title, it was a subordinate one and – except in the case of his son Germanicus – not one that reflected an actual victory over the Germanic tribes. Claudius in AD 43 took the title Britannicus for the conquest of Britain, but he transferred this title to his young son. Beginning in his reign, various Victorias associated with particular tribes were venerated besides the *victoria Augusti*, for example the *Victoria Britannica*. A change came with Domitian, who in 83 took the title Germanicus. This was a genuine victory title, and it was adopted as such into his official title. Thereafter, many emperors opted to use *cognomina devictarum gentium* ('bynames after defeated peoples') and *cognomina ex virtute* ('bynames from valour') [7].

These victory titles were granted after victories over external enemies by the *princeps* or his generals acting on his behalf by virtue of a transfer of *imperium* (Cass. Dio 60,8,7) [6. 35–38]; [9. 39–41, 84–87]. Although these were more specific than acclamations, they still passed through the filter of imperial ideology, which excluded victory titles arising from putting down internal rebellions or civil wars. Some victories, meanwhile, were not as clear-cut as certain titles implied. This sometimes gave rise to mockery and wordplay (SHA Carac. 10,6). Victory titles were officially approved by the senate (or confirmed by it following a prior military acclamation), but only after receipt of an imperial victory report and with at least some pressure from the sovereign (Hdn. 3,9,12), who could also refuse (Cass. Dio 79,27,3).

Domitian (81–96) and Trajan (98–117, also *Germanicus*, *Dacicus* and *Parthicus*) made abundant ideological use of their victory titles on coins and inscriptions. Other emperors, by contrast, used none at all – for instance, Hadrian (117–138) and Antoninus Pius (138–161). The attitudes of Marcus Aurelius (161–180) and Lucius Verus (161–169) exemplify the range of ways this issue could be handled within a single shared reign. Verus used three victory titles, two of which were new

(*Armeniacus, Medicus*), the third being the first instance of a compound with *maximus* (*Parthicus maximus*, 'greatest conqueror of the Parthians'). After Verus' death in AD 169, his adoptive brother Marcus Aurelius, a philosopher with no particular fondness for victory bynames, dropped them, and instead made rather limited use of the titles *Germanicus* and *Sarmaticus*, which he shared with *caesar* Commodus. Having succeeded as *augustus*, Commodus (180–192) also called himself *Germanicus maximus* and *Britannicus*, before assuming the title *Invictus Romanus Hercules* towards the end of his reign in reference to the invincible Hercules.

Balancing tradition and innovation, the Severans made extensive ideological use of victory titles. As emperor at the start of a civil war, Septimius Severus (193–211) emphasized his victories over foreign enemies: *Arabicus, Adiabenicus* (195) and *Parthicus maximus* (198, together with Caracalla). He was also *Britannicus maximus* (210, with both his sons). Imitating Alexander, Caracalla (211–217) also called himself *Magnus* ('the Great') and conqueror of the Germani. His reign saw the start of the systematic use of the adjective *maximus*, and the use of *Invictus* spread to such an extent that practically all emperors of the 3rd century adopted it. Acclamations of emperors, now mentioned less frequently, were less and less related to victories: finally, in the reign of Diocletian (284–305), titles began to be renewed on an annual basis. Moreover, victory bynames diversified – *Carpicus, Persicus, Gothicus* in the 3rd century, and even *Alamannicus* and *Francicus* in the 4th – and the Tetrarchs and Constantine sometimes used two or three of them. More and more, however, they were replaced by more general victory titles in attempts to compensate for the fragility of power in the 3rd century and suggest its resurgence.

C.2. LATE ANTIQUITY

Beginning with the Tetrarchy and continuing until the mid-5th century, the use of pompous introductory formulae took hold, in praise of victories over barbarians and usurpers, for example: *liberator orbis Romani fortissimus ac piissimus invictissimusque dominus noster* (AE 1939, 58: Diocletian, 'most fearless, pious and invincible liberator of the Roman world, our Lord'), and *victoriosissimus Augustus omnium barbararum gentium debellator* (IK 12,313a: Julian, 'most victorious Augustus, conqueror of all the barbarian peoples') [13. 45–47, 53–61]. *Imperator* was preserved as a *praenomen*, but from the Tetrachy onwards, it took second place to the formula *dominus noster*. *Invictus*, much used in the 3rd century, persisted at least until 450, particularly in the superlative *invictissimus*. The preferred alternative became *victor* and cognates, particularly after 324 and Constantine's victory over Licinius (Euseb. VC 2,19,2). This was a move away from a title associated with the solar cult (Mithras, Sol) in favour of a more neutral one that soon acquired a Christian connotation (Euseb. *Triakontaeterikos* 3,3; 7,13) [4]. It was sometimes used as the *praenomen* in place of Imperator. Constantine (who celebrated his triumph in 326) and his successors often combined it with *triumphator* and various suffixes (*semper et ubique, toto orbe, omnium gentium, victoriosissimus*; victor 'ever and everywhere', 'in the whole world', 'over all peoples', 'most victorious'). The imperial acclamations and *cognomina devictarum gentium*, still present in the classical titles of the inscription on the Gratian Bridge of AD 369 (ILS 771), subsequently vanished. A more sober title system prevailed, preserving above all the victory titles such as *victor ac triumphator* (or *triumphalis*), which barbarian rulers sometimes imitated (CIL X 6850, for Theoderic) [10]. After 533, Justinian adopted titles, including *cognomina devictarum gentium* (CIL III 13673), that more or less reflected actual facts and were in some cases new (e.g. Alanicus, Anticus, Vandalicus). This can be explained in connection with his project of the military reconquest and reestablishment of the empire. After a few final innovations, such as Gepidicus and Herullicus (from the Gepids and Heruli) in the reign of Maurice (582–602), the *cognomina devictarum gentium* disappeared once and for all in 629 when Heraclius adopted his new system of titles.

BIBLIOGRAPHY

[1] M.M. AUSTIN, Hellenistic Kings, War, and the Economy, in: CQ 36/2, 1986, 450–466 [2] R. COMBÈS, Imperator. Recherches sur l'emploi et la signification du titre d'imperator dans la Rome républicaine, 1966 [3] J.R. FEARS, The Theology of Victory at Rome. Approaches and Problems, in: ANRW II.17.2, 1981, 736–826 [4] F. HEIM, La théologie de la Victoire. De Constantin à Théodose, 1992 [5] T. HÖLSCHER, Victoria Romana. Archäologische Untersuchungen zur Geschichte und Wesensart der römischen Siegesgöttin von den Anfängen bis zum Ende des 3. Jhs. n.Chr., 1967 [6] D. KIENAST et al., Römische Kaisertabelle. Grundzüge einer römischen Kaiserchronologie, [6]2017 [7] P. KNEISSL, Die Siegestitulatur der römischen Kaiser. Untersuchungen zu den Siegerbeinamen des ersten und zweiten Jahrhunderts, 1969 [8] P. LÉVÊQUE, La guerre à l'époque hellénistique, in: J.-P. VERNANT (ed.), Problèmes de la guerre en Grèce ancienne, 1968, 261–287 [9] A. MAGIONCALDA, Lo sviluppo della titolatura imperiale da Augusto a Giustiniano attraverso le testimonianze epigrafiche, 1991 [10] M. MCCORMICK, Eternal Victory. Triumphal Rulership in Late Antiquity, Byzantium, and the Early Medieval West, 1986 [11] F. MUCCIOLI, Gli epiteti ufficiali dei re ellenistici, 2013 [12] C. PRÉAUX, Le monde hellénistique. La Grèce et l'Orient de la mort d'Alexandre à la conquête romaine de la Grèce (323–146 av. J.-C.), vol. 1, 1978 [13] G. RÖSCH, ΟΝΟΜΑ ΒΑΣΙΛΕΙΑΣ. Studien zum offiziellen Gebrauch der Kaisertitel in spätantiker und frühbyzantinischer Zeit, 1978 [14] B. VIRGILIO, Lancia, diadema e porpora. Il re e la regalità ellenistica, [2]2003 (new expanded edition with a documentary appendix).

PATRICE FAURE

War

A. Greek
B. Roman

A. Greek

A.1. Beginning: Mycenae and the Homeric world
A.2. Advent of the hoplite phalanx
A.3. Upholding Homeric warrior values in the Hellenistic period
A.4. Defensive territorial war
A.5. Athenian maritime imperialism
A.6. Peloponnesian War
A.7. Evolution of warfare in the 4th century BC
A.8. Hellenistic warfare

Achieving a satisfactory definition of war is difficult. It is best understood as an organized use of force by politically independent communities. Even here, however, boundaries blur with other forms of organized violence, such as piracy or banditry. The Greeks were aware of this, because they developed customs of war based on public declarations of war and other religious and judicial practices. They also initiated reflection on tactics and strategy, the notion of just war, the rules of war, the limits of its destructive effects, and the evils it inflicts on human societies. They made the *polemos akeryktos*, 'war without [declaration by] a herald', into an object lesson – a form of war that was always possible, but never desirable. A war of destruction was also admitted as a possibility, but as a convulsive event. Day by day, war tended to affect only the lives of combatants, because the surrender of prisoners was initially limited to hostages, and later involved mostly slaves. The 'sacred wars' (*hieros polemos*) fought over the Panhellenic sanctuary of Delphi between about 600 and 338 BC cannot be regarded as wars of religion.

The way in which classical scholars approach war in the Greek world has developed considerably over time, and a great many approaches are now available. Traditional military history, which has focused on strategy, tactics, armies and the battlefield, should continuously be examined from new angles. War must be studied as a political, legal, institutional, economic, religious, social and cultural phenomenon in equal measure.

A.1. Beginning: Mycenae and the Homeric world

The Greeks of the Mycenaean world populated the Balkans around the mid-17th century BC and spread to Crete and finally around the Aegean from the mid-15th to the early 14th century, benefiting from the extinction of the Minoan culture. Mycenae was particularly notable for its defensive walls, already known as 'Cyclopean' in Antiquity because only Cyclops were believed capable of having built them. The same kind of effort at creating a bulwark to protect a palace, its granaries, storehouses, administration, and presumably its king's subjects is also seen at Tiryns, Athens and Gla. Linear B inventory tablets show the control exercised by the palace as a storehouse for materials and perhaps war chariots. Goods found at graves include offensive (swords, daggers) and defensive weapons (Dendra panoply, helmets topped with wild boar tusks), which archaeologists interpret as symbols of power and social hierarchy. A fresco at Akrotiri (excavation site on Santorini) shows that the Mycenaeans engaged in pillaging: war was a means of acquiring riches (Aristot. pol. 1,1225b). Rooted in the right of the strongest, it was a privilege of the mighty, but also a means for legitimizing political violence in the eyes of the weak.

Following the 'Dark Ages' (11th–9th centuries BC), Homer's *Iliad* and *Odyssey* emerge as the link between the Mycenaean world and Greece of the Archaic, Classical and Hellenistic periods. These two verse epics, composed by an *aiodos* ('singer'), the first around 740 BC, the second around 700, represent the advent of writing in a culture of oral traditions perhaps dating back to the Mycenaean period. The work of Moses Finlay has shown that the world of Odysseus was part historical, part literary. For instance, the helmet of Meriones described in the *Iliad* (10,260–271) resembles the one found at Dendra. But the Trojan War did not take place – at least, not in the way described by Homer. In the *Iliad*, which recounts the consequences of the wrath of Achilles, the heroes' war is based on a sequence of confrontations in single combat. The poet describes the combatants' arrival on the battlefield in their war chariots, their genealogies, their weapons, and the insults they exchange. They are then seized by a destructive rage – the influence of Lyssa, daughter of Mania, goddess of madness – and the 'Red Death' strikes them down one after another, either directly by the sword, or from a distance by spear or arrow. The Homeric epics reflect the social realities of a war of plunder. Raiding expeditions made possible the capture of slaves and cattle. Homer expressed the military values of the entire Greek world, laying the foundations for the education of young men (*paideia*) for the next thousand years. War displayed the valour (*arete*) and excellence (*aristeia*) of the combatants. It was an encounter with death and it dealt blows of fate. Achilles holds funeral games to honour the memory of Patroclus, who attains an enviable heroic status. Priam, striving to achieve the release of the desecrated corpse of Hector, weeps in the presence of Achilles, who in turn remembers Patroclus (→ Death).

A.2. Advent of the hoplite phalanx

Writing reemerged at the dawn of the Archaic period. Meanwhile, the model of the city-state was developing, new architectural forms were being explored at sanctuaries, and the Greeks were establishing colonies across the Aegean, and then throughout the Mediterranean. A new way of fighting also emerged in this period. Scholars no longer speak of a 'hoplite revolution', but instead they describe a slower development that came to fruition in the 7th century. The Spartan wars of conquest in Messenia are a symptom of this change (→ Sparta). Found in Etruria and dated to around 640 BC, the Chigi Vase (*olpe*) attests to the spread of a coherent form of hoplite combat at around this time. A rank of hoplites, holding their shields tightly against their bodies with the help of a handle (*antilabe*) and an arm strap (*porpax*), advanced on the enemy to the accompaniment of music played by an *auletes* ('flautist'). Each hoplite, equipped with a helmet, a breastplate, greaves and a lance, carried a shield distinguished by its own symbol (*episemon*), indicating that this collective battle was the work of a social class that was able to afford its own equipment. The hoplite was expected to demonstrate *sophrosyne* ('self-mastery') in battle. During this period, the poet Tyrtaeus offers insight into the new ideology of the Spartan hoplite: group cohesion was necessary, but one should also aspire to the 'beautiful death' that had been available to the Homeric heroes. From now on, the aristocratic values of warfare were expressed within the hoplite unit, which was called upon to fight 'shield to shield and helmet to helmet'.

A.3. Upholding Homeric warrior values in the Hellenistic period

By the time Alexander the Great was conquering the Achaemenid Empire between 334 and 323 BC, the hoplite phalanx had evolved into the Macedonian phalanx, but the values remained the same: Alexander (→ Generals of note, B.) was acting the part of a Homeric king, with the gods of Olympus by his side. Crossing the Hellespont, he was the first to leap ashore – like Protesilaus – and declare Asia to be *doryktetos* ('conquered with the spear'). He went to Troy, now the city of Ilium, and – as the new Achilles – dedicated its conquest to the goddess Athena. Outside Tyre, he saw Hercules in a dream, and he took this as a sign that he should capture the city, which was the seat of the cult of the god Melqart, whom the Greeks identified with Heracles. The oracular prophecy of Amun, which he received at Siwa in the Libyan Desert, reinforced in his mind the idea of becoming 'Lord of the World' and son of Zeus. When his empire broke up, the coins minted in 306–304 BC by his 'successors', the Diadochi, who had become kings themselves, show that war legitimized their authority. Following his naval victory over the Ptolemaic fleet off Salamis on Cyprus in 306, Demetrius Poliorketes (→ Generals of note, E.) issued a tetradrachma with a winged Victory (*Nike*) to the right with a trumpet at her lips on the prow of a warship. A helmeted, armed Athena on a war chariot drawn by four elephants appeared on the reverse of a silver tetradrachma minted at Seleucia on the Tigris to commemorate a victory of Seleucus I. In 291 or 290, the Athenians celebrated Demetrius Poliorketes with a hymn called *Ithyphallikos* for its Dionysian character. The citizens lamented that the other gods had no ears to hear them, 'but you we see alive, and not only in wood or stone. Above all, highly honoured one, we beseech you, bring us peace: you have the power to do it' (Duris of Samos, FGrH 76 F 13). The divine cults through which civic communities honoured the Hellenistic monarchs were a sign of subjugation to a military power that was capable of bringing peace or destruction. Between the second half of the 3rd century and the first half of the 2nd, the rulers of Pergamum immortalized their victories over the barbarian Galatians in statues that they presented in a series of large and small offerings at Pergamum itself, on Delos, at Delphi and on the Acropolis in Athens. In the late 2nd and early 1st centuries BC, Mithridates VI Eupator was still portraying himself as the new Alexander throughout his campaign of conquest against the Romans in Asia Minor.

A.4. Defensive territorial war

The first war attested in historical sources has often been interpreted as a ritual one: the conflict between Chalcis and Eretria, two cities on Euboea, over the Lelantine Plain. On the Peloponnese, Sparta and Argos fought similarly over the Thyreatis. These frontier conflicts, about which we ultimately know very little, must be seen in the context of the sacralization of the urban community's territory (*chora*). The territory of the ancestors, the *patria*, had to be defended when it was attacked. A code that was tacitly accepted by both sides limited battle to an advance followed by a phase of close combat, which is largely unknown to us, ending in the flight (*trope*) of one of the two phalanxes. → Religion worked as a significant regulatory element. Sacrifices and libations (drink offerings) were made before the battle, with the favour of one or several deities sought. After the battle, the victor put up a sign of victory (*tropaion*) made from the weapons of the enemy, who had left the battlefield but returned later to reclaim their fallen and acknowledge defeat. Literary sources of the Archaic and Classical periods allow us to reconstruct an idealized version of this combat among equals, which was relatively brief (lasting around 20 minutes), thus limiting the loss of lives, and which always followed the principle of a decisive engagement. V.D. Hanson has identified this as a Western model of war [13], although it was probably only one among many forms of warfare practised among the Greeks, who also used guerrilla tactics and engaged in raiding. Still, the hoplite model spread around the Mediterranean world. Greek → mercenaries skilled in this style of fighting, known as 'brazen men' (Hdt. 2,152), are attested in the armies of Nebuchadnezzar II of Babylon and the last Egyptian pharaohs. During the First Persian War, the Battle of Marathon provided confirmation of the Greeks' technical superiority. Herodotus indicates that on this day, the attack of the Athenians and Plataeans was continuous. The commemoration of the 192 fallen Athenian soldiers (the *Marathonomachoi*) shows that the representation of this battle, both on the battlefield (*soros*) and in Athens itself, was central to religious and political life at the time. Vase paintings portray the superiority of the Greek hoplites over the foreign, brightly coloured Persian barbarians.

A.5. ATHENIAN MARITIME IMPERIALISM
By the law of Themistocles (483 BC), the city-state of Athens resolved to divert all revenues from the mines in the Laurium into building a war fleet. Initially deployed against Athens' rival Aegina, the → fleet proved its worth at the Battle of Artemisium and the Battle of Salamis (→ Battles of note, I.; both 480 BC). Athens equipped itself with triremes – ships with three stacked banks of oarsmen – such as the fleets of Samos and Corinth already possessed a century before. In addition to pentekonters, ships with 50 oarsmen attested in Greek navies from the 7th century onwards, the Athenians had about 200 vessels with rams fitted to their prows (*embolon*) to pierce the hulls of enemy ships. These vessels were also equipped with sails to facilitate longer coastal voyages. Spartan isolationism after the Battle of Plataeae and the Battle of Mycale (both 479 BC), the political ascent of the lowliest citizens (*thetes*) through their role as oarsmen, and the Athenians' determination to liberate the Greek cities of Asia Minor all led to the foundation of the Delian League (478–404). While infantrymen of the Athenian middle class were responsible for their own weapons and equipment (*panoplia*), the construction of triremes was taken on by the municipality, and the obligation to equip them was given to wealthy citizens, who were required to perform a costly public service, the trierarchy, which was subject to constant increase until the last third of the 4th century. Money (*prosodoi*) had to be provided to generate revenues (*poroi*) for the maintenance of war chests, including the *stratiotika* ('military fund'). The maritime imperialism of Athens in the 5th century, which revived in a somewhat altered form in the 4th century (Second Athenian League, 377–337), was a military system that assured citizens of → pay for military service (*misthos, misthophora*) as well as booty, and guaranteed the security of the seas that was necessary for supplies and commerce.

A.6. PELOPONNESIAN WAR
The Peloponnesian War (→ Wars of note H.; 431–404 BC) was a break with the past that cannot only be explained as a product of the radically different source material. This was a major conflict, and although Thucydides tells the story as its historian, it is also documented elsewhere. In this confrontation lasting 27 years, the Delian League (founded 478) and the Peloponnesian League fought each other. Above all, the Peloponnesian War called into question certain traditional assumptions to which the Greeks had grown accustomed. By relying on Athen's maritime empire via the port of Piraeus, whose fortifications were linked to the city by two Long Walls built between 461 and 456, Pericles successfully transformed the city-state into an island for a time, leaving the city's surrounding territory exposed to the assaults of the Peloponnesian forces under the Spartan King Archidamus II. It has been shown that these assaults caused less damage to crops than the sources suggest, and that not all arable land was surrendered, because the Athenian cavalry (which should not be considered synonymous with the censitary class of the *hippeis*) undertook forays to repel some incursions. In 424, Sparta also equipped itself with a cavalry (Thuc. 4,55,2). It remains true, however, that Athens refused to participate in a decisive battle. At Amphipolis, Brasidas demonstrated leadership that was abounding with 'insight and valour' (*xunesis kai arete*), making himself the model general for generations to come.

Lightly armed troops were becoming ever more important. The *peltastai* ('light armed footsoldiers'), equipped with a small, crescent-shaped shield and two javelins, had already been used in the Persian army of the early 5th century, and they now emerged in the form of Thracian contingents, before the Greek armies availed themselves of their unique technical skills. The lightly armed *psiloi* ('light infantry') do not seem to have played a prominent part in the Battle of Plataeae in 479, but at Sphacteria in 425, the *peltastes* certainly did. They trapped the Spartan hoplites on terrain that did not suit them. Javelin throwers, archers, slingers and cavalry all proved to be crucial elements in battles of the 4th century, as they combined even more closely with the phalanx. Many *poleis* also established elite units (→ Elite troops), such as the *logades* ('selected'), *epilektoi* ('chosen'), *aristoi* ('noblemen'), *hieros lochos* ('sacred band'), the Three Hundred, the Five Hundred, and the Thousand, although some of these specialist corps may be reminiscences of the Archaic period.

After the failure of the Peace of Nicias (421), the massacre of the Melians (416), the failure of the Sicilian Expedition (415–413), the foundation of a Lacedaemonian garrison at Decelea in Attica (412), and the building of a Spartan fleet funded with gold from the Great King of Persia (treaties of 412–411), the Peloponnesian War became a global 'total war' that mobilized all available resources of the states involved. Expressed widely in the 4th century by the Greeks and given a theoretical foundation by Isocrates, the desire for a general → peace (*koine eirene*) was fed by the inability to find a common *hegemon* ('leader'). In 404 BC, Athens was forced to cede its hegemony to Sparta.

Over the course of the Peloponnesian War, the → mercenary trade regained social significance. Xenophon's *Anabasis*, which recounts the return of the expedition of the Ten Thousand recruited by the usurper Cyrus the Younger, who had died an unlucky death at the Battle of Cunaxa (401 BC), presents a sociology of professional soldiery for the years 401–399 and bears witness to the deployment of Spartans overseas. In his advice on defending city walls under siege (*Poliorketika*), Aeneas Tacticus describes the fragility of urban communities, especially on the Peloponnese, which – torn apart by → civil war (*stasis*) – drove some of their citizens to become mercenaries. Mercenaries sometimes turned on their employers, leaving to the attackers a place they were hired to defend. Beginning in the 4th century, poor regions and regions where not everyone had access to land (e.g. Crete) became suppliers of soldiers, who – as the circulation of coins reveals – were attracted by money and later returned to their homelands.

A.7. EVOLUTION OF WARFARE IN THE 4TH CENTURY BC

The 4th century witnessed the further development of the phalanx. The use of professional soldiers and light infantry may have been among the reasons behind this. The art of manoeuvre was perfected, which enabled first Sparta and then Thebes to exercise hegemony over the Greek world. This required continuous training, either in the form of a long and rigorous program of exercises (*agoge* in → Sparta) or, for citizens of the other *poleis*, in the gymnasium. From the 5th century onwards, the Thebans adopted a remarkably deep phalanx formation, as at Delium (424), where it consisted of 25 rows. The slanted battle formation of Thebes established by Epaminondas (→ Generals of note, F.) and Pelopidas at Leuctra in 371 won esteem. It involved shifting the main thrust to the left wing, where 50 rows of Theban hoplites faced the stronger flank of the Lacedaemonians. The 'Sacred Band', an elite force of 150 pairs of citizen-soldiers commanded by Pelopidas, established a wedge formation called *embolon* (something inserted, 'wedge') in the sources. The Spartans, meanwhile, limited themselves to *enomotiai* (units of men bound by oath) three men wide and twelve rows deep (Xen. Hell. 6,4,12). In order to counter the mobility of lighter forces, greater maneuverability was achieved through lighter armament. A leap forward in quality came in Macedonia thanks to a reform by Philip II (after 359; → Generals of note, M.), who had been held → hostage at Thebes in his youth. Abandoning heavy defensive armament and equipping his infantrymen with a spear 6–7 m long that was reinforced at both ends and held in both hands, he greatly improved the mobility of the Macedonian phalanx. The equipment was also less costly and better suited to a royal army composed of a large number of Macedonian subjects. Writing two centuries later, Polybius (18,30) described the impact of such a force, which had a depth of 16 rows, with the first five lowering their spears while the rear rows pointed their spears in the air to protect the entire force against the rain of arrows. Philip also reformed the cavalry and developed poliorcetics, the art of capturing city walls, in which Syracuse had developed an interest in the late 5th century (→ Siegecraft). These military innovations enabled Philip to defeat an alliance of Greek *poleis* at the Battle of Chaeronea (338) and to impose on them a general peace along with Macedonian hegemony (Corinthian League of 337).

Chaeronea, however, did not spell the end of the Greek city-state; nor did the spirit of the *polis* disappear altogether in the 4th century. It had certainly become easier to recruit mercenaries, but the declining enthusiasm for military service that ones hears in the Athenian orators was probably chiefly rhetorical. What was taking place was a separation of the political spheres: the public sphere of the *polis*, which was now managed by professional politicians (*politeuomenoi*), and the military sphere, which was embodied by *strategoi* ('commanders'), who had evolved into veritable *condottieri* ('[military] leaders'). On campaign, *strategoi* had to take financial hardships into account and sometimes live off the land. But the *polis* still exercised institutional control over its military officials, and some *strategoi* took the floor before the popular assembly. Meanwhile, the renewal of the Athenian *ephebeia* (group of young men aged 18–20 being trained for military service) in 335, as described by Aristotle, attests to the will to reinvigorate the corps of citizen soldiers that had been defeated at Chaeronea.

A.8. Hellenistic warfare

Between 334 and 323, the Macedonian phalanx of *pezetairoi* ('companions on foot') enabled Alexander to win large pitched field battles (Granicus, Issus, Gaugamela) and to put to flight the Achaemenid army of Darius III before pacifying the Upper Satrapies of his empire. It did not immediately render obsolete the traditional hoplite phalanx, which continued to be deployed. Several Greek *poleis* and confederacies, however, adopted the Macedonian style of combat in the 3rd century, notably Sparta under Cleomenes III (235–222). This form of warfare, which almost all Macedonian kings of the Hellenistic period employed, could only achieve its full effect when cavalry and elite infantry units worked together, as Alexander (→ Generals of note, B.) himself had demonstrated with his companions (*hetairoi*), including the royal squadron (*agema*) and the *hypaspistai*, semi-heavy infantry, including members of the royal guard (*basilikoi hypaspistai*).

New units emerged in the armies of the Seleucids and Antigonids: the 'silver shields' (*argyraspides*), the 'bronze shields' (*chalkaspides*) and the 'white shields' (*leukaspides*), making it sometimes difficult to distinguish *pezetairoi* from *hypaspistai*. The cavalry grew in importance during the 3rd century, and horsemen specializing in needle-prick tactics emerged (*tarentinoi*) along with heavily armed cavalry (*kataphraktoi*) following the Persian model. For a time, Alexander and later the Diadochi used Asian → elephants, a weapon of terror that sometimes proved counterproductive. This Macedonian style of warfare was appropriated by monarchies that sought to demonstrate their affiliation with the Hellenistic world, such as the Hasmonaean Kingdom and the Kingdom of Pontus under Mithridates VI Eupator. However, the Macedonian phalanx met its match at the turn of the 2nd century BC in the form of the Roman manipular legion, which was more mobile and effective on any terrain (Pol. 18,31f.). Despite the defeats that Rome inflicted on Antiochus III at Cynoscephalae (197) and on Philip V at Pydna (168), the Macedonian model persisted, probably thanks to the reforms it underwent in the mid-2nd century. Along with the literary and archaeological documentation of the 2nd century, the *Tactica* of Asclepiodotus, dating from the 1st century but describing an older reality, describes the emergence of a more mobile Macedonian phalanx influenced by manipular tactics.

Naval fleets played a crucial role in achieving mastery of the seas, whether in confrontation with a hostile hegemon or with pirates. Rhodes and later Ptolemaic Egypt attained this status in the late 4th century, although Aetolian 'piracy' and an Antigonid navy also developed. The gigantism of the fleets expressed itself in the number of vessels. 'Quadriremes', 'quinqueremes', 'septiremes', 'undeciremes' and the like were ships that, in reality, had no more than three rows of oars (one above the other) like the trireme, but had more oarsmen per oar. Thus the capacities of ships were increasing. Meanwhile, the Greeks were perfecting siegecraft (or poliorcetics) by means of a whole range of ever more complex engines and techniques, for example the catapult, *oxybeles* ('sharp missile' launcher), *helepolis* ('siege tower'), battering ram and sap – but they were also developing the art of defence, as attested by 'crenellated' city walls, turrets of various shapes, and the publication of learned treatises, some of which are preserved, such as that of Philo of Byzantium.

The royal armies differed markedly from the citizen armies thanks to the abundant funds available to them. This enabled them to employ mercenaries, and prosopographic anlaysis gives us some idea of their geographical origins. Literary texts and epigraphic records give a clearer view of the material conditions of mercenary service and the relationships with the local civilian population, which were sometimes plagued by conflict in times of peace. Mercenaries were often temporarily assigned to garrisons (*phrouria*) that controlled conquered cities. Royal armies also included subjects who were recruited through various means: the 'hearth' (*pyrokausis*) of the army (of the Antigonids), the *klerouchia* (of the Ptolemies, which was open to the indigenous *machimoi*), and the *katoikia* (of the Seleucids and Attalids, although whether it was strictly military in character is disputed). Allies also provided a portion of the kings' armed forces, and the *symmachia* ('alliance') formed the legal basis for recruiting Cretan soldiers. The Greek *poleis* and confederacies (*koina*) continued to maintain armed forces, and they provided contingents to the kings as part of their alliances. All the Greek city-states maintained citizen militias to ensure the security of their territory. Border disputes occasionally flared up, and these were settled by arbitration practices that developed. Citizen units trained (→ Education) in the gymnasium continued to take part in major wars: in 73 BC, Cyzicus provided 1,000 soldiers and ten ships to the Romans who were fighting Mithridates (Plut. *Lucullus* 9,1).

☞ Society and army; State and army

BIBLIOGRAPHY
[1] T. BOULAY, Arès dans la cité. Les poleis et la guerre dans l'Asie Mineure hellénistique, 2014 [2] P. BRUN, Hégémonies et sociétés dans le monde grec. Inscriptions grecques de l'époque classique, 2017 [3] L. BURCKHARDT, Bürger und Soldaten. Aspekte der politischen und militärischen Rolle athenischer Bürger im Kriegswesen des 4. Jahrhunderts v.Chr., 1996 [4] B. CAMPBELL / L. TRITLE (eds.), The Oxford Handbook of Warfare in the Classical World, 2013 [5] A. CHANIOTIS, War in the Hellenistic World. A

Social and Cultural History, 2005 [6] J.-C. COUVENHES (ed.), La symmachia comme pratique du droit international dans le monde grec. D'Homère à l'époque hellénistique (Dialogues d'Histoire Ancienne), 2016 [7] J.-C. COUVENHES / H.-L. FERNOUX (eds.), Les cités grecques et la guerre en Asie Mineure à l'époque hellénistique, 2004 [8] P. DUCREY, Guerres et guerriers dans la Grèce antique, 1985 (reprint 1999) [9] P. DUCREY, Polemica. Études sur la guerre et les armées dans la Grèce ancienne, 2019 [10] P. ELLINGER, La légende nationale phocidienne. Artemis, les situations extrêmes et les récits de guerre d'anéantissement (BCH Suppl. 27), 1993 [11] C. FISCHER-BOVET, Army and Society in Ptolemaic Egypt, 2008 [12] Y. GARLAN, Recherches de poliorcétique grecque, 1974 [13] V.D. HANSON, The Western Way of War, 1989 [14] V. ILARI, Guerra e diritto nel mondo antico, pt. 1: Guerra e diritto nel mondo greco-ellenistico fino al III secolo, 1980 [15] M. LAUNEY, Recherches sur les armées hellénistiques, 2 vols., 1949–1950 (reprint 1997, with bibliographical Addenda) [16] J.F. LAZENBY, The Spartan Army, 1985 [17] J.E. LENDON, Soldiers & Ghosts. A History of Battle in Classical Antiquity, 2005 [18] W.K. PRITCHETT, The Greek State at War, 5 vols., 1971–1991 [19] P. SABIN et al. (eds.), The Cambridge History of Greek and Roman Warfare, vol. 1: Greece, the Hellenistic World and the Rise of Rome, 2007 [20] N. SEKUNDA, Hellenistic Infantry Reform in the 160's BC, ²2006 [21] H. VAN WEES, Greek Warfare. Myths and Realities, 2004.

JEAN-CHRISTOPHE COUVENHES

B. ROMAN

B.1. Beginnings
B.2. Categories of war
B.3. Values
B.4. War and prestige
B.5. Transition from Republic to Principate
B.6. Legal factors, religious concepts and rituals
B.7. War aims and endings

B.1. BEGINNINGS

To the Roman mind, war (*bellum*) [61. s. v. *bellum*] was not merely a form of armed confrontation, but also a judicial process [68]. There was probably no state monopoly on the use of force in early Roman history until the late 5th century [4]. Instead, warfare took place chiefly on the level of the *gentes*, 'clans' (cf. e.g. Liv. 2,48–50), sometimes acting as armed clans in the *bellum familiare* ('private war') [8]. *Gentes* as a whole went to war organized according to the system of the *curiae* [2]. When dealing with barbarians, Rome fought brutally with no recognition of limits (→ Borders) [3]. The distinction between Rome and the 'uncivilized' world was significant with regard to the legitimacy of this form of warfare [51]. Where an opponent was deemed to be an equal, diplomatic solutions were considered, as the policies of Augustus towards the Parthian Empire in the early Principate illustrate (cf. R. Gest. div. Aug. 32f.) [68]. The designation of *imperium* ('command authority') as the legal basis for his actions and the *provincia* ('province') as the geographical location of his mission served as the main lines of control for a magistrate, who enjoyed a high degree of autonomy in the pursuit of war aims [53]. A conferred authority classified as *imperium* generally included military command [35]. The military authority of a magistrate ended at the *pomerium* (the boundary around the city of Rome) [42]. This boundary, defined in religious law, divided all that was concerned with war (*militiae*) from the civilian sector (*domi*) [8]. It was only during a triumphal procession that an army was permitted to cross the *pomerium* under arms [27]. Because Romans understood war fundamentally within a religious context, the persona of the individual general was at first given secondary status behind the idea of victory guaranteed by the gods [56]. In early times, the annual season for Rome' wars began in March and ended in October [52]. The processions of the Salian priests had a part to play here [48]. Other important dates related to war in the Roman calendar included the Ides of October and the *armilustrium* (a festival in honor of Mars) [55].

B.2. CATEGORIES OF WAR

The Roman categories of war included *bellum*, regular warfare, and *latrocinium*, irregular warfare against → bandits [41]. Another category not present in the Roman definition was petty warfare, the dimensions of which fall between *bellum* and *latrocinium*. Rome made a distinction between bandits (*latrones*) and enemies or adversaries in war (*hostes*) [68]. Rome's wars can also be classified into four basic types: wars of conquest, wars to put down rebellions in the empire (including → civil wars), punitive expeditions, and wars against invaders [20]. The three slave wars of the 2nd and 1st centuries BC were special cases in the history of Roman domestic unrest [32]. In studying warfare, a clear distinction must be maintained between the → law of war (*ius belli*) and the definition of a just war (*bellum iustum*): there was no automatic link between these two categories in Antiquity [22]. The fetial rituals give a good idea of the Roman perspective on the *bellum iustum*. War guilt was assigned entirely to the adversary, with Rome taking up arms purely in self-defence [28]. From the Roman point of view, a *bellum iustum* was by its nature automatically a defensive war [18]. A *bellum iustum* presupposed just grounds for war (cf. Cic. Off. 1,36; cf. Cic. Rep. 3,35 [IV A]), which could include an attack on an ally of Rome's (cf. Cic. Off. 2,26), the defection of a confederate, or an attack on an emissary [1]. Caesar as a matter of course justified the Gallic Wars as defensive (e.g. Caes. B Gall. 1,7) [14]. Even at the outbreak of the Civil War, it was important to Caesar that it should not be classified as a *bellum civile* [49]. There was a high degree of continuity in this conception of warfare as defensive [10].

B.3. VALUES

Consideration of whether a war was just focused entirely on the Roman perspective and internal legitimization as a *bellum iustum*. No account was taken of the adversary's perceptions [42]. It is clear from the arguments of Cicero that Republican Rome did not wage war only on the basis of (aggressive) self-defence (cf. Cic. Off. 1,38; cf. Cic. Phil. 8,12). The importance attached to acquiring *dignitas* ('esteem') and *honos* ('honour') should not be underestimated [24]. Polybius had expert knowledge of the Roman military mindset in Italy in the 2nd century BC [45]. He considered the Romans to be aggressive by nature, and he was well aware that invented pretexts and concrete motives went hand in hand when Romans waged war [5]. The tradition of the just war in Christianity is traced back to Augustine [16], who was particularly influenced by Cicero [29]. To Augustine, war was always governed by divine providence [17]. To a certain extent, he considered the use of force and even killing (e.g. Aug., *Contra Faustum Manichaeum* 22,74) as justified in order to repel evil and restore peace (cf. e.g. Aug. Civ. 19,7; 19,13). But individual self-preservation did not, in his opinion, justify killing [19]. His doctrines bridged the gap between pacifist Christianity and the exigency of war to secure peace [62]. Augustine understood peace in the Roman Empire as analogous to the domestic peace guaranteed by the *pater familias* ('father of the family'; cf. Civ. 19,12): Anyone who violates this internal order can legitimately be brought to reason through war [33].

B.4. WAR AND PRESTIGE

The internal structure of the Roman nobility was dominated by competition for prestige in which renown won in war was superior to all else. Roman aggression had its roots in this constant state of rivalry within the republican elite [57]. Fundamental elements of Roman elite values as applicable to warfare, such as the concept of *virtus* (cf. e.g. Plin. HN 7,139–141), survived into Late Antiquity (→ Valour) [40]. Personal participation in combat – as demonstrated, for example, by showing one's battle scars – became an important factor in this rivalry [69]. Participating in a duel or in single combat enjoyed especially high status dating back to the earliest days of Roman history [40]. This form of confrontation was associated the tradition of dedicating the *spolia opima* ('rich spoils') – a tradition traced back to Romulus himself [13]. It involved bringing the armaments of the slain enemy leader to the Temple of Jupiter Feretrius (cf. Liv. 4,20) [28]. Another central element of this competition was the triumph. To prevent generals from claiming a triumphal procession based on minor raids, a quality standard was defined in the 2nd century BC, which was measured by the number of enemy fighters killed and had a minimum threshold of 5,000 (cf. Val. Max. 2,8,1) [8]. The last triumph with accompanying sacrificial acts took place in the reign of Diocletian in AD 303 [36]. This system did not categorically exclude magistrates who had failed in war; it offered opportunities for reintegration [12]. However, defeat in war was deeply shameful for the soldiers returning home (cf. e.g. App. Samn. 4,20f.).

B.5. TRANSITION FROM REPUBLIC TO PRINCIPATE

War was essentially the norm for the Roman Republic [47]. However, military action was not inevitable. The killing of Roman citizens abroad, for instance, by no means necessarily led to a declaration of war [21]. Rome's confederacy system gave it access to the military resources of Italy (cf. e.g. Plut. *Pyrrhus* 21) [4]. Ultimately, war reduced Rome's ability to incorporate conquered territories effectively into its state [9]. The regulations failed to keep pace with the demands of warfare on an ever increasing scale. Particularly difficult in this regard was the principle of collegiality, according to which supreme command changed on a daily basis and the consuls' single-year term placed limits on their authority, although the emergence of the promagistracy offered some relief [25]. The propraetors of Sulla's new order were strictly forbidden to strike out from their provinces to wage war on their own initiative without the permission of the senate [11]. In its final phase, however, the Roman Republic was not able to reintegrate the mighty warlords it helped create, and this led to the civil wars of the 1st century BC [44]. Cicero emphasized the equality of political and military action [47], and he considered all means to be fair and reasonable that were necessary to preserve the *res publica* [60]. During the Late Republican period, wars offering the prospect of enormous spoils were fought by a small circle of generals, some of whom were closely associated with one another, which meant that true military expertise now tended to be passed on from 'master' to 'pupil' [7]. The *pax Augusta* of the Principate must be understood as peace under arms, the essential concept of which is expressed in R. Gest. div. Aug. 26–33 and Verg. Aen. 6,850–853 [31]. During the 3rd century, the empire entered a serious crisis of legitimacy, for it was no longer possible to guarantee the defence of the provinces [66]. The bond between the emperor and the army was now even more important [56]. The legitimacy of the rule of the soldier-emperors was primarily linked to military accomplishments [46]. Suitable leadership qualities in war sufficed for a general to join the ranks of the many soldier-emperors [26]. It was normal for emperors to take part in campaigns in person in the 3rd and 4th centuries [39]. Under Constantine, the program of values for a military leader from the era of soldier-emperors was revised in a Christian direction [64]. Vegetius (Veg. mil. 2,5), for instance, draws attention to the Christian interpretation of the soldiers' *sacramentum* ('oath').

B.6. LEGAL FACTORS, RELIGIOUS CONCEPTS AND RITUALS

Beginning and ending a war were acts of border crossing that were associated with specific rituals [55]. At the heart of these rituals was the need to make the legitimacy of the path to war unassailable [59]. Given such protective mechanisms, there was no possibility of war breaking out by diplomatic accident. The route to just war required a demand for redress that offered the adversary an opportunity to correct the situation; if this opportunity was not taken, it stipulated a declaration of war with due attention to the relevant guidelines. Moreover, the motivation for the war had to be a just cause, and the aim of the war had to amount to restoring a → peace free from injustice (cf. Cic. Off. 1,35) [4]. The legal procedures leading to the declaration of war were not dependent on a vote of the popular assembly [67]. The origins of the fetial law (*ius fetiale*; cf. Cic. Off. 1,36) are disputed and the sources are not helpful in clarifying them. One theory suggests that the process was ultimately a measure for restricting the ability of the *gentes* to wage war on their own initiative [42]. The *pater patratus*, a member of the priestly *fetiales*, took on the task of the *rerum repetitio* (demand for reparations) or *clarigatio* (call for redress), which involved his proclaiming Rome's demands [1]. This was done at the frontier, at the first encounter with a citizen of the adversary, on the way through the adversary's city gates, and in the adversary's forum (cf. Liv. 1,32,8) [23]. After the adversary had been issued with a deadline of about one month (cf. Liv. 1,32,9), senators were asked if they would assent to a potential war (cf. Liv. 1,32,11f.) [68]. If they agreed, the *indictio belli* ('declaration of war') was performed, as part of which the *pater patratus* hurled a spear into enemy territory at the border (cf. Liv. 1,32,13f.) [23]. In the Roman mind, the quality of a space could be transferred. For instance, it was possible to declare an area near the Temple of Bellona enemy territory in order to perform there the rituals of the declaration of war [23]. It must not be thought, however, that every war of the Republican period was associated with a formal declaration of hostilities and the ritual processes that went with it [24]. Caesar the Younger (Octavian) defined his war with Mark Antony as a foreign war against Egypt, and he declared it by means of the fetial rituals [28], but the performance of those rituals under the Principate was essentially an anachronism [22]. Another important component of the path to war was the obtaining of *auspicia* ('auspices') by the *haruspex* ('diviner'), in order to ensure that the gods were favourably disposed towards the enterprise [48]. Also performed before a march to war was the *lustratio* ('purification'), the ritual purification of the army [42]. Entry into the *exercitus Romanus* ('Roman army') was considered a crossing of a boundary analogous to the declaration of war (→ Borders). Entering the professional army of the Imperial period marked the transition from the legal status of *civis Romanus* ('Roman citizen') to that of *miles* ('soldier') [34].

B.7. WAR AIMS AND ENDINGS

The causes of Roman expansion were complex. Possible motivations range from defensive imperialism to economic inducements to Roman elite values [58]. In theory, the aim of a *bellum iustum* was always the attainment of a just → peace [59]. In practical fact, however, one of the key aims was plunder (→ Booty). The property of the defeated party went to the victor [38]. The *deditio* ('surrender') of the enemy was absolute as far as the Romans were concerned, and nothing was guaranteed to the loser. It was a total surrender with no protections [6. 249]. A truce (*indutiae*) was seen merely as a temporary cessation of hostilities, and unlike the *deditio*, it could not bring about the end of a war with Rome [68]. All booty was at the disposal of the general [55]. Prisoners (*captivi* or *capti*) were taken in the Republican period, for instance when a city was conquered, with women and children generally sold into slavery and the men killed [65]. During the Imperial period, however, Rome's defeated enemies were integrated into the military as auxiliaries where necessary [50]. The Roman Empire went on the defensive in the 3rd century, and it was forced to wage unprofitable wars to repel external enemies [15]. Even when fighting defensively, Rome in Late Antiquity was confronted with enemies in the west who were fighting primarily for booty, while in the east the battles were to establish and consolidate centres of power [37]. Accordingly, most wars of Late Antiquity were campaigns of plunder and punitive expeditions [63]. The Roman defeat at Adrianople in AD 378 represents a crucial turning point of Roman warfare in Europe, as it was associated with a permanent diminution (cf. e.g. Amm. Marc. 31,13,18f.) of Rome's military power [30].

☞ Society and army

BIBLIOGRAPHY
[1] S. ALBERT, Bellum Iustum. Die Theorie des 'gerechten Krieges' und ihre praktische Bedeutung für die auswärtigen Auseinandersetzungen Roms in republikanischer Zeit, 1980 [2] G. ALFÖLDY, Römische Sozialgeschichte, ⁴2011 [3] E. BADIAN, Römischer Imperialismus, 1980 [4] E. BALTRUSCH, Außenpolitik, Bünde und Reichsbildung in der Antike, 2008 [5] D.W. BARONOWSKI, Polybius and Roman Imperialism, 2011 [6] C.A. BARTON, The Price of Peace in Ancient Rome, in: K.A. RAAFLAUB (ed.), War and Peace in the Ancient World, 2007, 245–255 [7] W. BLÖSEL, Die Demilitarisierung der römischen Nobilität von Sulla bis Caesar, in: W. Blösel / K.-J. Hölkeskamp (eds.), Von der 'militia equestris' zur 'militia urbana'. Prominenzrollen und Karrierefelder im antiken Rom, 2011, 55–80 [8] L. BURCKHARDT, Militärgeschichte der Antike, ³2020 [9] K. CHRIST, Die Römer. Eine Einführung in ihre Geschichte und Zivilisation, 1994 [10] K. CHRIST, Krise und Untergang der römischen Republik, ⁴2000 [11] K. CHRIST, Sulla. Eine römische Karriere, 2002 [12] T. COREY BRENNAN, Power and Process under the Republican 'Constitution', in: H.I. FLOWER (ed.), The Cambridge Companion to the Roman Republic, 2006, 31–60 [13] R. COWAN, For the Glory of Rome. A History of Warriors and Warfare, 2007 [14] W. DAHLHEIM, Julius Caesar. Die Ehre des Kriegers und die Not des Staates, ²2006 [15] A. EICH, Die römische Kaiserzeit. Die Legionen und das Imperium, 2014 [16] L. FREEDMAN, Defining War, in: J. LINDLEY-FRENCH / Y. BOYER (eds.), The Oxford Handbook of War, 2014, 17–29 [17] T. FUHRER, Krieg und (Un-)Gerechtigkeit. Augustin zu Ursache und Sinn von Kriegen, in: M. FORMISANO / H. BÖHME (eds.), War in Words. Transformations of War from Antiquity to Clausewitz, 2011, 23–36 [18] T. GANSCHOW, Krieg in der Antike, 2007 [19] P. VAN GEEST, Ethik, in: V.H. DRECOLL (ed.), Augustin Handbuch, 2007, 526–539 [20] A. GOLDSWORTHY, War, in: P. SABIN et al. (eds.), The Cambridge History of Greek and Roman Warfare, vol. 2: Rome from the Late Republic to the Late Empire, 2007, 76–121 [21] H. GRASSL, Römische Händlersiedlungen in der späten Republik, in: H. HEFTNER / K. TOMASCHITZ (eds.), Ad fontes! Festschrift für Gerhard Dobesch zum fünfundsechzigsten Geburtstag am 15. September 2004 dargebracht von Kollegen, Schülern und Freunden, 2004, 295–301 [22] N. GROTKAMP, Völkerrecht im Prinzipat. Möglichkeit und Verbreitung, 2009 [23] C. HÄNGER, Die Welt im Kopf. Raumbilder und Strategie im Römischen Kaiserreich (Hypomnemata 136), 2001 [24] W.V. HARRIS, War and Imperialism in Republican Rome 327–70 BC, ²1985 [25] H. HEFTNER, Von den Gracchen bis Sulla. Die römische Republik am Scheideweg 133–78 v.Chr., 2006 [26] O. HEKSTER, Rome and Its Empire AD 193–284, 2008 [27] P. HERZ, Religions. Principate, in: Y. LE BOHEC (ed.), The Encyclopedia of the Roman Army, vol. 3, 2015, 822–828 [28] A. HEUSS, Römische Geschichte, ⁷2000 [29] W. HÜBNER, Klassische lateinische Literatur und Rhetorik, in: V.H. DRECOLL (ed.), Augustin Handbuch, 2007, 49–60 [30] S. JAMES, Rom und das Schwert. Wie Krieger und Waffen die römische Geschichte prägten, 2013 [31] M. JUNKELMANN, Die Legionen des Augustus, ¹⁵2015 [32] A. KEAVENEY, Servile Wars, in: Y. LE BOHEC (ed.), The Encyclopedia of the Roman Army, vol. 3, 2015, 869 [33] A. KELLER, Die politischen Voraussetzungen der Entstehung der 'bellum iustum'-Tradition bei Cicero und Augustinus, in: I.-J. WERKNER / A. LIEDHEGENER (eds.), Gerechter Krieg – gerechter Frieden. Religionen und friedensethische Legitimationen in aktuellen militärischen Konflikten, 2009, 23–41 [34] S. KERNEIS, ius militare, Military Law, in: Y. LE BOHEC (ed.), The Encyclopedia of the Roman Army, vol. 2, 2015, 555–556 [35] W. KUNKEL, Magistratische Gewalt und Senatsherrschaft, in: ANRW I.2, 1972, 3–22 [36] E. KÜNZL, Der römische Triumph. Siegesfeiern im antiken Rom, 1988 [37] Y. LE BOHEC, Das römische Heer in der Späten Kaiserzeit, 2010 [38] Y. LE BOHEC, Economic Warfare. Late Empire, in: Y. LE BOHEC (ed.), The Encyclopedia of the Roman Army, vol. 2, 2015, 354 [39] A.D. LEE, War in Late Antiquity. A Social History, 2007 [40] J.E. LENDON, Soldiers & Ghosts. A History of Battle in Classical Antiquity, 2005 [41] L. LORETO, Small War. Republic, in: Y. LE BOHEC (ed.), The Encyclopedia of the Roman Army, vol. 3, 2015, 902–904 [42] C. MANN, Militär und Kriegführung in der Antike, 2013 [43] D.J. MATTINGLY, Imperialism, Power and Identity. Experiencing the Roman Empire, 2011 [44] C. MEIER, Res publica amissa. Eine Studie zu Verfassung und Geschichte der späten römischen Republik, ³1997 [45] F. MILLAR, The Roman Republic in Political Thought, 2002 [46] R. PFEILSCHIFTER, Die Spätantike. Der eine Gott und die vielen Herrscher, 2014 [47] F. PINA POLO, Rom, das bin ich. Marcus Tullius Cicero. Ein Leben, 2010 [48] G. POMA, Religions. Republic, in: Y. LE BOHEC (ed.), The Encyclopedia of the Roman Army, vol. 3, 2015, 820–822 [49] K.A. RAAFLAUB, Dignitatis contentio. Studien zur Motivation und politischen Taktik im Bürgerkrieg zwischen Caesar und Pompeius (Vestigia 20), 1974 [50] B. RANKOV, Prisoner. Principate, in: Y. LE BOHEC (ed.), The Encyclopedia of the Roman Army, vol. 3, 2015, 781–782 [51] D. ROHMANN, Bilder der Gewalt. Kriegsdarstellungen in der Literatur der frühen Kaiserzeit, in: M. LINDER / S. TAUSEND (eds.), 'Böser Krieg'. Exzessive Gewalt in der antiken Kriegsführung und Strategien zu deren Vermeidung, 2011, 153–165 [52] N. ROSENSTEIN, War and Peace, Fear and Reconciliation at Rome, in: K.A. RAAFLAUB (ed.), War and Peace in the Ancient World, 2007, 226–244 [53] J.P. ROTH, War, in: P. SABIN et al. (eds.), The Cambridge History of Greek and Roman Warfare, vol. 1: Greece, the Hellenistic World and the Rise of Rome, 2007, 368–398 [54] J.P. ROTH, Roman Warfare, 2009 [55] J. RÜPKE, Domi militiae. Die religiöse Konstruktion des Krieges in Rom, 1990 [56] R. SCHULZ, Feldherren, Krieger und Strategen. Krieg in der Antike von Achill bis Attila, 2012 [57] H. SIDEBOTTOM, Der Krieg in der antiken Welt, 2008 [58] M. SOMMER, Römische Geschichte, vol. 1: Rom und die antike Welt bis zum Ende der Republik, 2013 [59] C. STADLER, Krieg, 2009 [60] W. STROH, Cicero. Redner, Staatsmann, Philosoph, 2008 [61] A. WALDE, Lateinisches etymologisches Wörterbuch, vol. 1: A–L, 1965 [62] M. WALZER, Erklärte Kriege – Kriegserklärungen, 2003 [63] C. WHATELY, Booty. Late Empire, in: Y. LE BOHEC (ed.), The Encyclopedia of the Roman Army, vol. 1, 2015, 110–111 [64] J. WIENAND, Der Kaiser als Sieger. Metamorphosen triumphaler Herrschaft unter Constantin I. (Klio Beihefte 19), 2012 [65] C. WOLFF, Prisoner. Republic, in: Y. LE BOHEC (ed.), The Encyclopedia of the Roman Army, vol. 3, 2015, 780 [66] G. WOOLF, Rom. Die Biographie eines Weltreichs, 2015 [67] A. ZACK, Studien zum 'Römischen Völkerrecht'. Kriegserklärung, Kriegsbeschluss, Beeidung und Ratifikation zwischenstaatlicher Verträge, internationale Freundschaft und Feindschaft während der römischen Republik bis

zum Beginn des Prinzipats, ²2007 [68] K.-H. ZIEG-
LER, Das Völkerrecht der römischen Republik, in: ANRW
I.2, 1972, 68–114 [69] M. ZIMMERMANN, Gewalt. Die
dunkle Seite der Antike, 2013.

JOSEF LÖFFL

Wars of note

A. Campaign of Alexander
B. Bar Kochba Revolt
C. Trajan's Dacian Wars
D. Gallic Wars
E. Jewish War
F. Mithridatic Wars
G. Aurelian's Palmyrene War
H. Peloponnesian War
I. Julian's Persian War
J. Persian Wars
K. Punic Wars

A. CAMPAIGN OF ALEXANDER

A.1. Motives for the attack on the Persians
A.2. From the Granicus to Issus
A.3. From Egypt to Persepolis
A.4. To India and back

The Campaign of Alexander lasted from 334 to 323 BC and culminated in the military conquest of the Persian Empire by the Macedonian army under Alexander III ('the Great'). It led to the collapse of Persian rule over Western Asia and the spread of Macedonian dominance and Greek culture in these regions (surveys e.g. [9]; [6]; [4]; [3]; [8]).

A.1. MOTIVES FOR THE ATTACK ON THE PERSIANS

Alexander's father and predecessor Philip II (→ Generals of note, M.; murdered 336 BC) had already planned a campaign against Persia, and in 336 he sent an advance guard into western Asia Minor, commanded by Parmenion and Attalus. According to Polybius (3,6), one motive for the attack was the weakness of Persia as evident from the campaigns of the Ten Thousand (401/00 BC) and the Spartan king Agesilaus, which, given Macedonian military prowess, persuaded Philip that the prospects of victory were good. The pretext was revenge for the burning of the temple on the Athenian Acropolis, along with other injustices the Greeks were said to have suffered at Persian hands in the wars 150 years before. The publicist Isocrates tirelessly championed a war with Persia for the purpose of gaining new territory for Greek colonies. It seems more likely, however, that Philip's main priority was simply to acquire booty and expand his power in western Asia Minor. Any attack was conditional upon the Macedonians' achieving military control over their neighbours, especially the Greeks, who were united under Macedonian hegemony in the Corinthian League in 337 BC.

By the time he crossed the Hellespont in 334 BC, Alexander had at his disposal a well-trained army and an experienced officer corps [5]. He had about 32,000 infantry, made up of around 12,000 Macedonian foot soldiers, 7,000 allies, 5,000 → mercenaries and 7,000 Thracians and Illyrians. There was also a → cavalry of 1,800 Macedonian and 1,800 Thessalian horsemen, along with 600 from elsewhere in Greece and 900 from Thrace, and some lightly armed soldiers (Diod. Sic. 17,17,3–5; cf. Just. Epit. 11,6; Plut. *Alexander* 15; Arr. Anab. 1,11,3). His naval capacities, like his war chest, were modest. 12,000 men were left behind in Macedonia under the command of Antipater to ward off neighbours. The strength of the Macedonians lay in their flexible cavalry, the cavalry of *hetairoi* ('companions', the noble class), which was capable of launching massive assaults in its own right, the hoplite phalanx armed with *sarisai* (long spears measuring 4–6 m), and the *pezetairoi* ('companions on foot'), who generated enormous momentum in the forward march (cf. e.g. Arr. Anab. 1,15,5). Throughout his campaign, Alexander repeatedly replenished his Macedonian recruits, later also recruiting Iranians (e.g. Arr. Anab. 3,16,10; 7,6,1; Diod. Sic. 17,49,1; 17,108,1–3; Curt. 4,6,30; 8,5,1).

A.2. FROM THE GRANICUS TO ISSUS

After symbolically laying claim to the land by hurling a spear into enemy territory and making sacrifices (e.g. to the Trojan Athena), Alexander confronted an army commanded by several Persian satraps in his first land battle near the Granicus River (334 BC). The satraps had decided to fight a pitched battle against Alexander. In doing this, they were disregarding the advice of Memnon, a Greek vassal of the Great King and general in Troas, who thought they should starve the Macedonian army out of its scant resources through a scorched-earth tactic and launch a naval assault on Greece (Arr. Anab. 1,12,9f.; Diod. Sic. 17,18,2). Taking up a position on the riverbank seemed to offer a serviceable defence, but the numerically inferior Persian force was unable to withstand the cavalry attack led in person by Alexander (Arr. Anab. 1,14,4–16,7; Diod. Sic. 17,19–21; Plut. *Alexander* 16; Just. Epit. 11,6). The Persian horsemen were put to flight, and the Greek mercenaries who were working for the Great King were ruthlessly killed or enslaved as traitors. Alexander then set off for Lydia and Ionia, where he assumed the role of liberator from Persian rule. He met resistance only in Miletus, which was inadequately supported by the superior Persian fleet (Arr. Anab. 1,18,3–19,6; Diod. Sic. 17,22; Plut. *Alexander* 17), and at Halicarnassus, where Memnon led the defence. The Macedonians also met little opposition in Caria and Phrygia. Alexander's push into the Anatolian interior ran the risk of losing what he had won but not yet secured, because the Persian fleet was active in the Aegean, while Alexander had disbanded his fleet after the conquest of Miletus (Arr. Anab. 1,20,1; Diod. Sic. 17,22,5). However, the cutting (or untying) of the Gordian Knot showed that his ambition was not limited to Asia Minor, was also aimed at the realm of the Great King Darius III (Arr. Anab. 1,24,3–2,4,6; Plut. *Alexander* 18; Curt. 3,1,12–18; Just. Epit. 11,7). He reached Cilicia in the summer of 333. Once there, he received word that Memnon, whom Darius had entrusted with supreme command in the west, had died that spring after launching a promising naval offensive in the Aegean. Darius, meanwhile, had mobilized much of his imperial force, advanced on Syria, and crossed the Amanus Mountains north of the Levant coast. Having already marched into the coastal plain of Alexandretta, however, Alexander was at Darius' rear. The ensuing Battle of Issus (Nov. 333; Pol. 12,17–23; Arr. Anab. 2,8–11; Diod. Sic. 17,33f.; Plut. *Alexander* 20; Curt. 3,8–11; Just. Epit. 11,9; FGrH 148 F 44) thus took place with the fronts reversed. Alexander was running an enormous risk, since he had no territory into which to retreat and the Persians still had control of the seas. The relatively narrow terrain, however, did not allow the larger Persian army to deploy. Alexander led the cavalry on the Macedonian right, the *sarisa* phalanx faced the Greek mercenaries in the centre, and Parmenion had command along the coast to the left. Once again, it was an attack by Alexander that launched the battle as he moved against the Persian centre where Darius was located. The Persian cavalry could not hold the line. Darius turned to flee, and the Persian army, which up to this point had resisted valiantly, disintegrated. Losses were high. Darius escaped, but his camp with his family and substantial resources fell into Alexander's hands. Supplies for the Macedonian troops were thus secured for the time being. Alexander rejected a peace offer from the Great King that would have granted him the territories west of the Euphrates (or the Halys) and marriage to Darius' daughter (Arr. Anab. 2,14f.; 2,25; cf. Curt. 4,5,1–9; Just. Epit. 11,12).

A.3. FROM EGYPT TO PERSEPOLIS
After Issus, Alexander secured the Levant coast in order to neutralize the Persian fleet. The only resistance came at Tyre, which was besieged at great cost for seven months (Arr. Anab. 2,17–24; Diod. Sic. 17,40,2–46; Plut. *Alexander* 24f.; Curt. 4,2,1–4,19; Just. Epit. 11,10; FGrH 151 F 1,7), and Gaza. Wealthy Egypt came into Macedonian hands without a fight. This left Alexander without enemies to the rear, and with ample resources for his advance into the heart of the Persian Empire. At the Battle of Gaugamela (October 1, 331; Arr. Anab. 3,11,8–12,5; Diod. Sic. 17,57–61; Plut. *Alexander* 32f.; Curt. 4,13,26–35; Just. Epit. 11,13f.), the much larger Persian army found the broad plain conducive to its style of fighting, but even the use of scythed chariots and the construction of obstacles did not bring victory. Alexander commanded the right wing of the Macedonian army, Parmenion the left. Mazaeus put the latter under severe pressure, but Alexander was able to evade the obstacles and attack Darius directly. With clouds and great distance obscuring his view of the battle, Darius again turned to flee, which triggered the collapse of his army. While Darius escaped to Ecbatana, Alexander occupied Babylon, Susa and Persepolis. Persepolis was partly burned to the ground to accomplish the promised revenge (Arr. Anab. 3,18,10–12; Diod. Sic. 17,70–72; Plut. *Alexander* 37f.; Curt. 5,6,1–7,11; Just. Epit. 11,14). Although Alexander discharged his Greek contingents shortly afterwards (Arr. Anab. 3,19,5f.; Diod. Sic. 17,74,3; Plut. *Alexander* 42; Curt. 6,2,17), there was no doubt that his campaign must continue, for Darius was still free and most of the Persian Empire was still unconquered (cf. Map 1).

A.4. TO INDIA AND BACK
Shortly afterwards, Darius was killed by his own people. Alexander had Darius' successor, Bessus, executed. To assert his claim as King of Asia, Alexander conquered Bactria and Sogdiana in gruelling campaigns (329–327). He had to divide his force several times to break the resistance, some of which turned to guerrilla warfare. During this period, Alexander faced several conspiracies, and his plans to introduce Persian ceremonies at court met with resentment (death of Cleitus (Arr. Anab. 4,8f.; Plut. *Alexander* 50–52; Curt. 8,1,19–2,12; Just. Epit. 12,6f.), Callisthenes Affair). Advancing into the Indus Valley, the battle-hardened Macedonian troops proved more than a match for the armies of local princes (despite their use of → elephants), thanks to the forcefulness of the phalanx and the flexibility of the cavalry. When Alexander made known his intent to lead them over the Hyphasis into the Ganges region, the Macedonian soldiers mutinied, citing the duration of the campaign, the uncertain prospects, and the strain caused by harsh weather (monsoon) and relentless fighting (Arr. Anab. 5,25–28; Diod. Sic. 17,93,2–94,5; Plut. *Alexander* 62; Curt. 9,2,12–3,19; Just. Epit. 12,8). Alexander had to give way.

The homeward journey, difficult and overshadowed by conflicts, took them from the Indus Valley to the Indian Ocean, where Alexander divided his force into a navy (led by Nearchus) and a land army. The following poorly prepared march

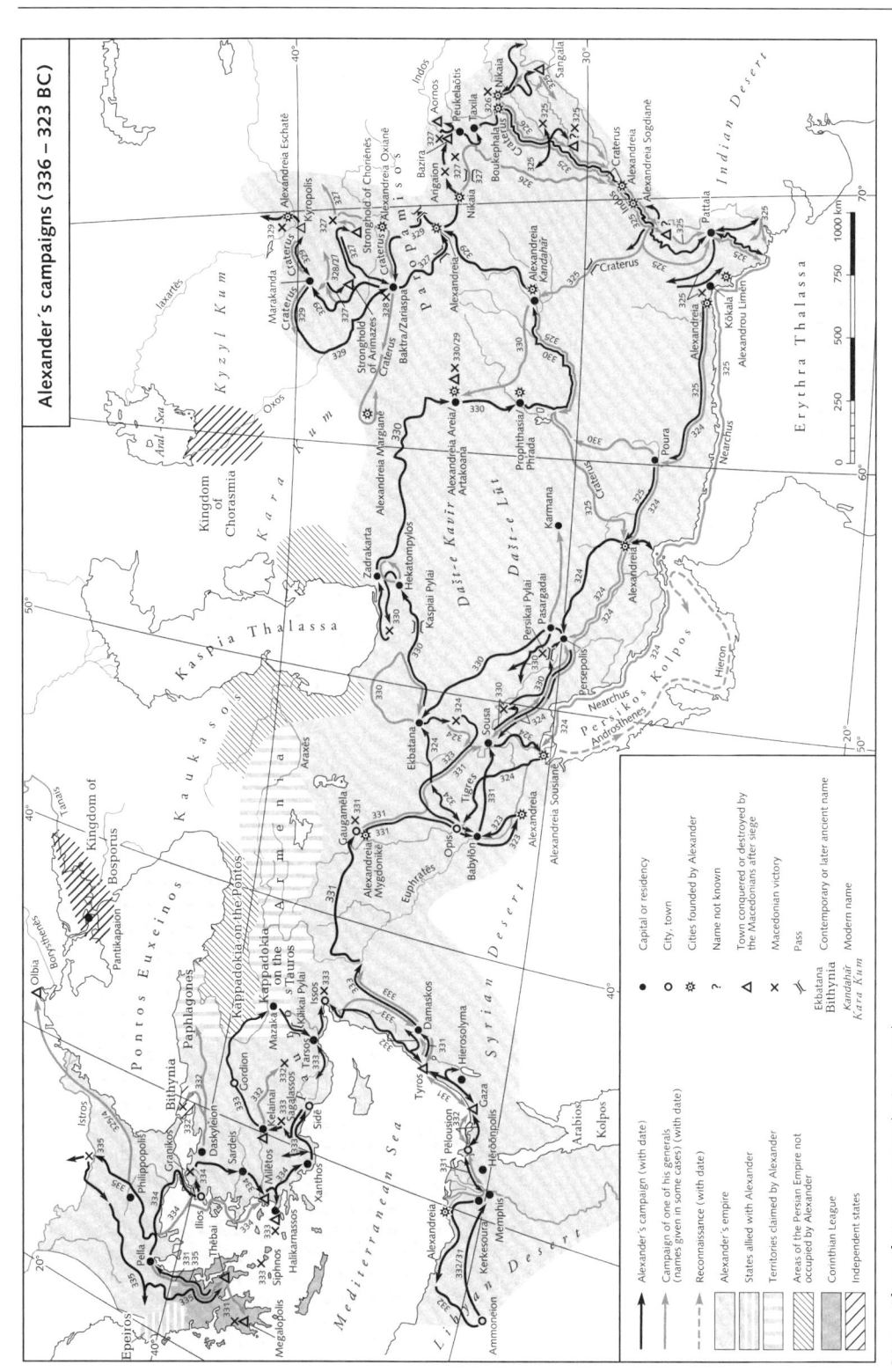

Map 1: Alexander's campaigns (336–323 BC)

through the Gedrosian Desert claimed many Macedonian lives (Arr. Anab. 6,22,1–27,1; Diod. Sic. 17,105,3–106,1; Plut. *Alexander* 66; Curt. 9,10,9–18). Arriving at Opis in Mesopotamia, Alexander sent the older and wounded soldiers home, but he was then faced with another → mutiny, which arose from his adoption of Persian customs and his decision to integrate Iranians into the army. This time, Alexander punished the leaders harshly (Arr. Anab. 7,8–11; Diod. Sic. 17,108,3; 17,109,3; Plut. *Alexander* 71; Curt. 10,2,8–4,3; Just. Epit. 12,11). Alexander's death in June 323 brought the campaign to an end. Its importance lay not just in the political shifts that took place in Western Asia, but also in the opening up of vast regions that were previously little known to Europeans, in the stimulus it gave to the economy, science and scholarship, and in the general transformation that occurred in the Greek and Macedonian world and worldview.

☞ Generals of note, B. Alexander; Mutiny

BIBLIOGRAPHY
[1] D. ENGELS, Alexander the Great and the Logistics of the Macedonian Army, 1978 [2] J.F.C. FULLER, The Generalship of Alexander the Great, 1958 [3] H.-J. GEHRKE, Alexander der Große, ⁶2013 [4] W. HECKEL, The Conquests of Alexander the Great, ²2012 [5] W. HECKEL, Alexander's Marshals, ²2016 [6] R. LANE FOX, Alexander the Great, 2004 [7] J. ROISMAN (ed.), Brill's Companion to Alexander the Great, 2003 [8] H.-U. WIEMER, Alexander d. Gr., ²2015 [9] G. WIRTH, Alexander d. Gr., ⁹1995.

LEONHARD BURCKHARDT

B. BAR KOCHBA REVOLT
The great revolt of AD 66–70 and 73/74 inflicted heavy losses on the Jewish population. However, Jewish life recovered over the ensuing decades, even in the immediate environs of the destroyed Jerusalem. It remains unclear to this day how serious an impact the diaspora uprising of AD 115–117 in Mesopotamia, Cyprus, Egypt and Cyrene had in Judaea. An imperial *legatus* (M. Titius Lustricus Bruttianus) *pro pr(aetore)* ... *exercit(uum) Iudaici et Arabici* ('legate for the praetor of the army of the Jews and Arabs') is attested, probably from early in the reign of Hadrian. This extraordinary merger of the armies of two provinces suggests that major hostilities had occurred in the region ([15] and Epigraphik-Datenbank Clauss-Slaby, EDCS-67400753: inscription beneath a biga: highly problematic [1]). It is still not possible, however, to make any more detailed observations.

The confrontation with Rome that would prove far more catastrophic for the Jews as a people than those before it began unexpectedly in the spring of 132, during the governorship of Tineius Rufus. The causes are disputed. The likeliest trigger appears to have been Hadrian's announcement, during his visit to the province in the summer of 130, that the *colonia Aelia Capitolina* would be founded to replace Jerusalem (AE 2004, 1424 = SEG 55, 1416) (on the possible causes [13]; [3]; [12]). Such a colony would have destroyed all Jewish hopes for the reconstruction of Jerusalem as a Jewish city. The leader of the rebels was Simon bar Kosiba (PIR² S 746), today generally known as Bar Kochba. He was called the Messiah by Rabbi Akiva, and he took as his title *ha Nasi*, Prince (of Israel; see also [20]). Many of his letters were discovered at Naḥal Ḥever and Wadi Murabba'at [21]. They show that non-Jews, probably mostly Nabataeans, also took part in the rebellion (cf. Cass. Dio 69,13,1). The number of rebels is unknown. At first, their key strength was surprise; later, they fought a guerrilla campaign, especially from subterranean 'hiding places' [23]. Roman forces suffered enormous losses, forcing Hadrian to transfer large contingents of soldiers from the fleet at Misenum to the *legio X Fretensis* and other army units in Judaea (PSI 1026 = CIL XVI Suppl. App. 13; [11]). The auxiliary troops also lost many men during these protracted hostilities [6. 29–40]. The territory controlled by the rebels stretched from the Jordan and Dead Sea as far as the last of the Judaean Mountains in the west, at least as far as Hebron in the south and around Jericho in the north. Galilee was not part of the zone under direct control, as evidenced by coin finds and hiding places [22], but it must be remembered that there was a wider area in which engagements may have occurred; in other words, forays to Galilee are possible [14]. The rebels did not take Jerusalem, that is, the *colonia* under construction or the legionary camp. The legend on the Bar Kochba coins, 'For the Freedom of Jerusalem', expressed the aim, not the *status quo* [16]. The Roman army received colossal reinforcements in the form of legionary detachments and auxiliary units transferred from many provinces ([4]; see also CIIP I 2,717). Sex. Iulius Severus succeeded Tineius Rufus as governor, after being transferred to Judaea from Britannia. The legate of Syria, Poblicius Marcellus, and of Arabia, Haterius Nepos, also fought the rebellion, which directly affected Arabia at least. It seems rather unlikely that Hadrian returned to the province in person in the autumn of 132 in response to the seriousness of the military revolt [7]. This assumption is based on the term *expeditio*, found in some inscriptions, but too much significance is perhaps attached to one word here. Severus fought the rebels chiefly by destroying infrastructure and overrunning the hiding places, including at Naḥal Ḥever, where still today remains of small Roman outposts are preserved above the caves (Cass. Dio 69,13,3). The fighting must have continued into the spring of 136, for it was only then that Hadrian accepted the second acclamation as *imperator* (CIL XIV 2088;

before May 31, 136: [17. No. 88] and P. Heid. VII 396; cf. [10]; [6]). The emperor also had the senate award the *ornamenta triumphalia* ('triumphal honours') to the governors of Judaea, Syria and Arabia (CIL III 2830; AE 1904, 9; IGR III 176; CIL XI 5212). Imperial coins make no reference either to the war or to the victory. Only in Judaea did the senate or one of the legions have an arch commemorating the victory built at Tel Shalem south of Scythopolis ([9] *contra* [2], see the arguments in [5]). The consequences of the war were the devastation of the Judaean heartlands, a boost to the diaspora, and a shift in the centre of gravity of Judaism towards Galilee.

☞ Wars of note, E. Jewish War

BIBLIOGRAPHY
[1] M. BEN ZEEV, New Insights into Roman Policy in Judea on the Eve of the Bar Kokhba Revolt, in: JSJ 49, 2018, 84–107   [2] G.W. BOWERSOCK, The Tel Shalem Arch and P. Naḥal Ḥever/Seiyal 8, in: P. SCHÄFER (ed.), The Bar Kokhba War Reconsidered, 2003, 171–180   [3] R. DEINES, How Long? God's Revealed Schedule for Salvation and the Outbreak of the Bar Kokhba Revolt, in: A. LANGE et al. (eds.), Judaism in Crisis. Crisis as a Catalyst in Jewish Cultural History, 2011, 201–234   [4] W. ECK, The Bar Kochba Revolt. The Roman Point of View, in: JRS 89, 1999, 78–86   [5] W. ECK, Hadrian, the Bar Kokhba Revolt, and the Epigraphic Transmission, in: P. SCHÄFER (ed.), The Bar Kokhba War Reconsidered, 2003, 153–170   [6] W. ECK, Rom herausfordern. Bar Kochba im Kampf gegen das Imperium Romanum, 2007   [7] W. ECK, Der Bar Kochba-Aufstand der Jahre 132–136 und seine Folgen für die Provinz Judaea/Syria Palaestina, in: G. URSO (ed.), Iudaea socia – Iudaea capta, 2012, 249–265   [8] W. ECK, Bar Kokhba, in: The Oxford Classical Dictionary, digital edition, 2015 (https://doi.org/10.1093/acrefore/9780199381135.013.1056)   [9] W. ECK / G. FOERSTER, Ein Triumphbogen für Hadrian im Tal von Beth Shean bei Tel Shalem, in: JRA 12, 1999, 294–313   [10] W. ECK / N. MUGNAI, A New Military Diploma for the Troops of Moesia inferior (19 January 136), in: ZPE 198, 2016, 218–222   [11] W. ECK / A. PANGERL, Die Konstitution für die classis Misenensis aus dem Jahr 160 und der Krieg gegen Bar Kochba unter Hadrian, in: ZPE 155, 2006, 239–252   [12] W. HORBURY, Jewish War under Trajan and Hadrian, 2014   [13] B. ISAAC / A. OPPENHEIMER, The Revolt of Bar Kokhba. Ideology and Modern Scholarship, in: A. OPPENHEIMER, Between Rome and Babylon, edited by N. Oppenheimer, 2005, 197–224   [14] U. LEIBNER / G. BIJOVSKY, Two Hoards from Khirbet Wadi Hamam and the Scope of the Bar Kokhba Revolt, in: Israel Numismatic Research 8, 2013, 109–134   [15] J.-M. MIGNON et al., Un nouveau cursus sénatorial ..., in: Cahiers du Centre Gustave Glotz 24, 2013, 294   [16] L. MILDENBERG, The Coinage of the Bar Kokhba War, 1984   [17] J.H. OLIVER, Greek Constitutions of Early Roman Emperors from Inscriptions and Papyri, 1989   [18] G. STEMBERGER, Verfolgung der jüdischen Religion unter Hadrian. Zwischen Wirklichkeit und Martyrologis, in: Scripta Classica Israelica 33, 2014, 255–268   [19] C. WEIKERT, Von Jerusalem zu Aelia Capitolina. Die römische Politik gegenüber den Juden von Vespasian bis Hadrian, 2016   [20] T. WITULSKI, Der Titel Nāśî' bei Ezechiel, in den qumranischen Schriften und bei Bar Kokhba. Ein Beitrag zur ideologischen Einordnung des Bar Kokhba-Aufstandes, in: Liber Annuus 60, 2010, 189–234   [21] Y. YADIN et al. (eds.), The Documents from the Bar Kokhba Period in the Cave of Letters, 2002   [22] B. ZISSU / H. ESHEL, The Geographical Distribution of Coins of the Bar Kokhba War, in: Israel Numismatic Research 14, 2002, 157–167   [23] B. ZISSU / A. KLONER, The Archaeology of the Second Jewish Revolt against Rome, in: Bolletino di Archeologia Online, 2008, 40–52.

WERNER ECK

C. TRAJAN'S DACIAN WARS

As far as the Romans were concerned, the confrontation between Rome and the Dacian kingdom, immediate neighbours since the 1st century, was motivated by military and political rather than economic considerations, although the considerable resources of Dacia went some way to compensating for the enormous expense of the wars. The conflict began in AD 85 when the Dacians attacked the Roman province of Moesia (Iord. Get. 76), forcing Domitian to intervene personally (Iord. Get. 77). Two dramatic events during this war are worthy of special attention: first, a Roman army commanded by Praetorian prefect Cornelius Fuscus was annihilated in inner Dacia in 76 (Iord. Get. 78); and later, the Romans commanded by Tettius Iulianus won a decisive battle at Tapae (Cass. Dio 67,10,1–3). The battle site is located in the northeastern Banat, closer to Voislova-Zăvoi than to the Iron Gates of Transylvania. However, since Domitian was tied down by other events to the middle reaches of the Danube, he was unable to press home the advantage, and found himself compelled to conclude a peace with the Dacian king Decebalus on terms favouring the latter (Cass. Dio 67,7,3f.).

War broke out again in the reign of Trajan, for whom this was one among several opportunities to bolster the legitimacy of his rule. A road was built along the right bank of the Danube at the Iron Gates in preparation (CIL III 8267; AE 1973, 475). The emperor left Rome on March 25, 101 (CIL VI 2074). The Roman attack was divided into several columns, pushing mainly through the Banat and Oltenia. The Romans again broke Dacian resistance at Tapae (Cass. Dio 68,8,1f.). As a diversion, the Dacians combined with the Rhoxolani to attack Moesia inferior through Dobruja. The Romans' subsequent major victory at Adamclisi was commemorated at the site with an extravagant monument (the Tropaeum Traiani; CIL III 12467; 14214).

Trajan won important victories in the Orăştie Mountains, the heartlands of Dacian power (Cass. Dio 68,8,3; 68,9,3). He took the fortress of Costeşti and advanced as far as the settlement of Costeşti, just a few kilometres from the royal seat of Sarmizegetusa Regia (Grădiştea Muncelului). All that was needed was a final effort to capture the royal seat and avert a future war. Instead, Trajan preferred to conclude a peace with Decebalus in 102 (Cass. Dio 68,9,4-6). The most plausible explanation is that the emperor was not yet ready to assume the costs of establishing a new province. For now, it seemed more useful to weaken the Dacian kingdom. The Dacians were required to tear down their fortifications and accept a Roman garrison (Cass. Dio 68,9,7). A far-reaching recruitment was carried out, the Banat and Oltenia remained under Roman occupation, and a bridge was built over the Danube designed by Apollodorus of Damascus.

The Romans, however, had not taken sufficient account of the theocratic, even fundamentalist nature of the Dacian political system. Such a system often disregarded the *ius gentium*, the elementary law that applied between different peoples. Decebalus thus adhered to none of the conditions of the peace. He attacked the Roman garrisons and took the commanding officer Pompeius Longinus prisoner (Cass. Dio 68,12,1). This supplied Trajan with arguments for a *bellum iustum* ('just war'). This time, Trajan had only one option: to incorporate Dacia into the empire as a province. He set off again from Rome on June 4, 105 (Vidman, F. Ost. 46). Once again, the emperor took personal command of the military operations (Cass. Dio 68,10,4). The most spectacular event of the campaign, illustrated on both the Trajan Column and an inscription preserved from Macedonia (AE 1969-1970, 583), was the suicide of King Decebalus as he was pursued by Roman soldiers. The honouring of soldiers of the *cohors I Brittonum* (CIL XVI 160 = IDR I, D 1) on August 11, 106 suggests that the war was essentially over by this date. The head of the Dacian king was put on show on the *scalae Gemoniae* ('Gemonian stairs') in Rome that same year (Vidman, F. Ost. 46f.). The victory over the Dacians was celebrated at Rome in grand style (Cass. Dio 68,15,1). The senate and people commissioned a column for the Trajan Forum with a relief illustrating the most important events of the Dacian Wars. Dacia became a Roman province.

The Dacians' failure is chiefly attributable to their much smaller army (Rome deployed about one third of its entire armed force in this conflict), the limited extent of their settlement area, and the heavy concentration of political authority in the hands of Decebalus.

BIBLIOGRAPHY
[1] C. CICHORIUS, Die Reliefs der Trajanssäule, 1896-1900 [2] C. DAICOVICIU, La Transylvanie dans l'antiquité, 1945 [3] F.B. FLORESCU, Monumentul de la Adamklissi, 1965 [4] C.C. PETOLESCU, Dacia. Un mileniu de istorie, 2010 [5] I. PISO, War die Eroberung Dakiens eine Notwendigkeit?, in: F. MITTHOF / G. SCHÖRNER (eds.), Columna Traiani – Traianssäule. Siegesmonument und Kriegsbericht in Bildern, 2017, 333-342 [6] K. STROBEL, Untersuchungen zu den Dakerkriegen Trajans, 1984 [7] K. STROBEL, Kaiser Traian. Eine Epoche der Weltgeschichte, 2010.

IOAN PISO

D. GALLIC WARS

The 'Gallic Wars' were a series of military campaigns against various Celtic tribes conducted between 58 and 51/50 BC by Caesar as proconsul of Illyria, Gallia cisalpina and Gallia transalpina (cf. Map 2). Over less than a decade, according to Plutarch, Caesar conquered 800 cities, subjugated 300 tribes, confronted 3 million enemy soldiers in battle, and had 2 million of them killed or taken captive (Plut. *Caesar* 15,5). How these operations proceeded [3] is known to us chiefly through the report Caesar himself left in his books, and from a supplementary eighth book by an anonymous author believed by some to have been Caesar's legate, Hirtius [2].

Our perspectives on the phases and significance of these campaigns rely above all on this one key source, other testimonies either being less detailed (Vell. Pat. 2,39; 46; 47; Suet. Iul. 25; Flor. Epit. 1,45; Plut. *Caesar* 18-27) or closely dependent on Caesar's version (Cass. Dio 38,31-50; 39,1-5; 39,40-53; 40,1-11; 40,31-44). It is accepted today that it is not possible to separate the facts in this case from the telling of them [5]; [4].

Book 1 of *De bello gallico* deals with the year 58 BC (campaign against the Helvetii and Ariovistus); Book 2 with 57 BC (campaigns against the confederation of the Belgae and expedition against the tribes in Aremorica); Book 3 with 56 BC (campaigns against the Veneti, Aquitani, Menapii and Morini); Book 4 with 55 BC (campaigns against the Usipetes and Tencteri; crossing of the Rhine; first expedition to Britain); Book 5 with 54 BC (campaigns against the Treveri; second expedition to Britain); Book 6 with 53 BC (campaigns against the Senones, Treveri and Eburones; second expedition across the Rhine); Book 7 with 52 BC (campaign against a large coalition of rebellious peoples commanded by the Arvernian Vercingetorix); Book 8 with 51-50 BC (Siege of Uxellodunum; subjugation of Aquitania). These texts, which were probably edited later to standardize them (the first seven books during the winter of 52-51, the eighth late in 44), deliberately give an impression of coherence. This led modern historians to conclude that the conquest was systematic and planned on a grand scale. A different interpretation is preferred today, namely, that Caesar took advantage of a favourable opportunity to justify military operations in Gaul, so that, by confronting the most feared barbarians

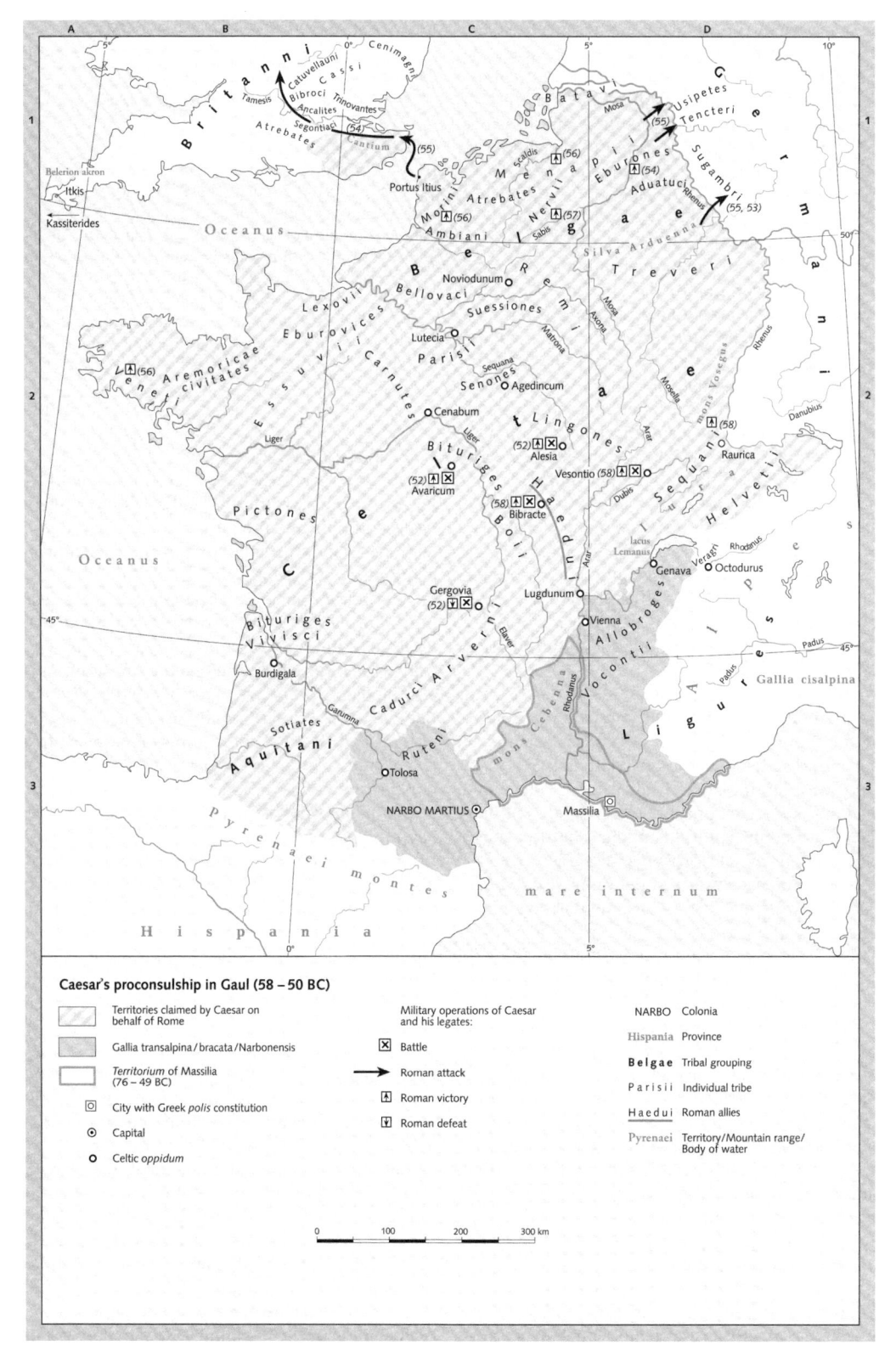

Map 2: Caesar's proconsulship in Gaul (58–50 BC)

in the west in the name of Rome and breaking their resistance through spectacular victories, he might win military renown to match that gained the decade before by Pompey (→ Generals of note, N.) in the east [1]. Regarding the decisions he made in 58 BC (putting a stop to the Helvetian migrations through his province and refusing to tolerate the *superbia* ('insolence') of Ariovistus, supposedly an ally of Rome) and his expedition against the Belgae in 57 BC, Caesar was seeking to fulfil the obligations incumbent upon a proconsul to defend the communities under Rome's protection against any potential threat, and to enforce without mercy the *maiestas* ('greatness') of the Roman people. In all this, he was in line with the expectations of the time, and if his aggressive offensive strategy of hitting hard before annihilating all pockets of resistance was unusual at all, it was only unusual insofar as it was implemented with unprecedented swiftness and audacity [6].

Caesar had a substantial but ultimately limited force at his disposal (6–8 or even 10 legions). Facing politically disunited opponents, however, he was also able to rely on Gallic and Germanic allies, who provided him with equipment, → auxiliaries, and especially a large → cavalry. The Gallic Wars must not be seen simply as a confrontation between Romans and Gauls.

In order to assert Roman authority, Caesar counted on the impression left by a limited number of dramatic military successes. This goal is all the more understandable given that the Roman army was fighting against adversaries whose tactical and strategic concepts were largely familiar. Caesar's account mentions pitched battles, sieges (most famously of Alesia 52 BC, Caes. B Gall. 7,68–89), and even marine operations (e.g. Caes. B Gall. 3,14–16), but contrary to some portrayals, less conventional methods such as guerrilla warfare played little role. It is suggestive that, at the end of his second year of campaigning, after his demonstration of force against the Helvetii, Suebi and Belgae – all of whom are presented as major opponents – Caesar was able to claim unchallenged that all Gaul had been pacified (Caes. B Gall. 2,35,1). Later campaigns are often portrayed as minor expeditions of a punitive nature against rebellious peoples (except in 52 BC), or, conversely, as prestige enterprises conducted with the public in Gaul and Rome in view. It is also relevant that Suetonius felt that he could summarize the entirety of the Gallic campaigns in one brief passage (Suet. Iul. 25,1) that refers only to two notable actions: the crossing of the Rhine in 55 BC and the two landings on the British coast in 55 and 54 (Suet. Iul. 25,2) – operations that most ancient authors considered inconsequential and of negligible military importance (Lucan. 2,570–572; Tac. Agr. 13,2; Plut. *Caesar* 23,4; Cass. Dio 39,53), but which were important in Rome (Catull. 11,9–12; Diod. Sic. 5,21; Quint. Inst. 2,13,2) and could be exploited politically by the proconsul (Flor. Epit. 2,13).

☞ **Generals of note, C. Caesar**

BIBLIOGRAPHY
[1] C. GOUDINEAU, César et la Gaule, 1990 [2] L. GRILLO / C. KREBS (eds.), The Cambridge Companion to the Writings of Julius Caesar, 2017 [3] T.R. HOLMES, Caesar's Conquest of Gaul, 1911 [4] J. OSGOOD, The Pen and the Sword. Writing and Conquest in Caesar's Gaul, in: Classical Antiquity 28/2, 2009, 328–358 [5] A.M. RIGGSBY, Caesar in Gaul and Rome. War in Words, 2006 [6] N. ROSENSTEIN, General and Imperialist, in: M. GRIFFIN (ed.), A Companion to Julius Caesar, 2009, 85–99 [7] M. SCHAUER, Der Gallische Krieg, 2016.

FRANÇOIS CADIOU

E. JEWISH WAR

No military event of the Greco-Roman world is known in such wealth of detail as the war fought between Rome and the Jews (and among different factions of Jews in Palaestina, a not insignificant component of the hostilities as a whole) between AD 66 and 70 or 73/74. The main source is Josephus' *Bellum Iudaicum* in seven books, along with Book 20 of the same author's *Antiquitates Iudaicae* (up to the outbreak of the revolt). Attention must also be paid to short sections of Tacitus' *Histories*, Book 65 of Cassius Dio and Suetonius' *Vitae Vespasiani* and *Titi*, but their importance pales next to Josephus. These latter sources show the Roman perspective, while – apart from Josephus – the Jewish perspective is reflected only on coins. The key problem of interpretation is the credibility of Josephus, who, as a pardoned participant, wrote his work in Rome. On the one hand, he had to keep in mind the Flavian Dynasty and the Roman elites, but on the other hand, he was party to the conflict on the Jewish side. Separating his history from his interpretation is often beyond the powers of analysis.

Very different reasons are offered for why part of the Jewish population revolted. They range from alleged social tensions between large landowners and impoverished farmers (with influence from messianic ideas and the provocation of Roman prefects), to the view that the Jewish community was fundamentally incompatible with Roman rule. Most recently, it has been argued [7] that the crucial period was the last years before the revolt under the prefect Gessius Florus, as the new policies of Nero led to an increase in plundering the countryside and, in Caesarea, to an explosion of tensions between the Jewish populace and the pagan majority, including the auxiliary troops of the prefect. Meanwhile – it is suggested – the indecisive policies of the Syrian governor Cestius Gallus gave Jewish and Idumaean agitators at

Jerusalem the pretext for denouncing Jewish leaders who hoped for a compromise with Rome. In AD 66, when the sacrifices for the emperor were cancelled at Jerusalem and the Roman garrison in the city was massacred, Cestius Gallus brought his army to the city. When he was denied entry and his army suffered heavy losses while it withdrew, there was no avoiding war. Nero ordered Vespasian as legate to put down the rebellion, and by the time of Nero's death in the summer of 68, he had already subjugated most of Judaea. The Roman → civil war largely interrupted hostilities until the Flavians prevailed late in AD 69. At Jerusalem, where hundreds of thousands of Jews had taken refuge, extremist groups took power, including the zealots under Eleazar ben Simon. Much of the city's supplies went up in flames during internal fighting. Vespasian's son Titus advanced on Jerusalem early in AD 70, laying siege to the city for five months starting in spring with four legions and auxiliary troops from the client kingdoms, including King Agrippa II. Ultimately, the Romans' surrounding forces choked off all supplies to the city. The months of famine greatly reduced the population, as did desertion. Even so, the defenders long withstood the Romans' continuous attacks, and even managed to construct new defensive lines. According to Josephus, the Temple went up in flames on 10 Av (= August 30), AD 70 (the later rabbinical tradition says 9 Av). Josephus claims that Titus wanted to save the Temple, but this must be seen as an attempt to divert blame from the Flavian Dynasty. The Temple was a symbol of Jewish independence, which necessitated its destruction. The remainder of the city was captured early in September, and where it was not already burnt to the ground, it was destroyed. At least some of the Temple treasure and the sacred artefacts were saved, and put on show in the Templum Pacis after the triumphal procession in Rome.

The Herodian fortresses still occupied by rebels were captured by 73 or 74, with the last being Masada, taken by governor L. Flavius Silva Nonius Bassus. The Jewish population suffered catastrophic losses, but with the exception of Jerusalem, few settlements were actually destroyed. Across most of what was now the separate province of Judaea, Jewish life was able to proceed without profound change.

☞ Wars of note, B. Bar Kochba Revolt

BIBLIOGRAPHY
[1] E. BALTRUSCH, Die Juden und das Römische Reich. Geschichte einer konfliktreichen Beziehung, 2002 [2] A.M. BERLIN / J.A. OVERMAN (eds.), The First Jewish Revolt. Archaeology, History, and Ideology, 2002 [3] P. BILDE, The Causes of the Jewish War According to Josephus, in: JSJ 10, 1979, 179–202 [4] W. ECK, Die römischen Repräsentanten in Judaea. Provokateure oder Vertreter der römischen Macht?, in: M. POPOVIĆ (ed.), The Jewish Revolt against Rome. Interdisciplinary Perspectives, 2011, 45–68 [5] A. GIAMBRONE (ed.), Rethinking the Jewish War (66–74 CE). Archeology, Society, Traditions, 2021 [6] M. HENGEL, Die Zeloten, 1976 [7] S. MASON, A History of the Jewish War, AD 66–74, 2016 [8] M. POPOVIĆ (ed.), The Jewish Revolt against Rome. Interdisciplinary Perspectives, 2011 [9] J. PRICE, Jerusalem under Siege. The Collapse of the Jewish State, 66–70 CE, 1992.

WERNER ECK

F. MITHRIDATIC WARS

The three wars that Rome fought against King Mithridates (also Mithradates) VI Eupator of Pontus (121–64 BC) took place in 89–84, 83 and 73–64 BC. The third ended with the king's death and the reorganization of the East, producing the Roman provinces of Pontus and Bithynia, Cilicia, and Syria (main sources: Memnon, FGH 434, 31–58; App. Mithr.; Plut. *Sulla*; Plut. *Lucullus*; Plut. *Pompeius*; Cass. Dio 36f.; literature: [9]; [7]; [6]; [4]).

Under Mithridates VI, the kingdom of Pontus emerged as a power in Anatolia and the Black Sea that the Romans were not disposed to tolerate [7]. Mithridates was reticent at first in his conflict with Bithynia and Cappadocia, but when Roman emissaries incited the Bithynian king Nicomedes IV to plunder Pontic cities, he hit back. Early in 89 BC, he won the Battle of the Amnias Valley. He then switched from pursuing his enemies to an attack on the province of Asia. The Roman regime was anathema to the cities of Asia Minor, and they betrayed Rome almost without exception and defected to Mithridates. The massacre of Romans and Italics that became known as the 'Ephesian Vespers' followed in 88 BC (App. Mithr. 22f.).

The king's naval operations against Rhodes and Patara failed. In spite of these reverses, however, his generals crossed to Greece, where the Athenians defected from Rome [3]. Mithridates was now at the zenith of his power. He installed sons to reign over Pontus, Cappadocia and Lesser Armenia, Colchis and the Crimea. His satraps controlled the rest of Anatolia while he himself resided at Pergamum.

When Sulla arrived in Greece with five legions in 87 BC, the tide turned. Taking Athens and winning victories in Boeotia, Sulla put Mithridates on the defensive. Having been proscribed at Rome by the regime of Cinna and relieved of his command, Sulla was keen to bring the war to a quick conclusion. In the summer of 85, he reached an agreement with the king, who was forced to pay reparations and withdraw to his ancestral kingdom.

The Second Mithridatic War is the name given to a campaign to Cappadocia and Pontus by the proconsul Murena (83 BC). While Mithridates was still regarded as a threat by Rome, the Armenian Tigranes II was expanding into the vacuum that was the remains of the Seleucid Empire. Early in the 70s BC, an alliance between the kings of Pontus and Armenia created a power bloc to eclipse the other Hellenistic monarchies.

Mithridates launched the Third Mithridatic War in 73 BC to fight Rome for the inheritance of the late Nicomedes IV [1. 227–230]. The king, heavily armed, maintained relations with pirates in Asia Minor and the Roman dissident Sertorius in Hispania. However, his offensive in Bithynia failed on land and at sea. Lucullus spent the years between 74 and 70 operating along the coasts and forcing his way into the heartland of the kingdom. Mithridates fled to Tigranes, who held him in custody. An audacious march through eastern Anatolia took Lucullus to Tigranocerta, where he defeated the Armenian army. The kings escaped. Rome stripped Lucullus of his command. Mithridates was able to retake the Pontic heartland early in 67. The following year, Pompey (→ Generals of note, N.) took supreme command under the provisions of the *lex Manilia*. He won a devastating victory in the Lycus Valley. Mithridates escaped in a daring flight north, and recaptured the renegade Crimea. For now, Pompey turned on Armenia and accepted Tigranes' capitulation outside Artaxata. From there, he moved upriver along the Araxes Valley before descending into the Cyrus Valley (in modern-day Georgia), where he broke the resistance of the Iberians and finally moved through the Phasis Valley to reach the coast of Colchis [2].

In the spring of 64 BC, legates, client kings and municipal delegations met at Amisus, where Pompey began his administrative reorganization. The general decided not to cross to the Cimmerian Bosporus, but instead ordered a naval blockade. He marched through Cappadocia and Commagene towards Syria and Palaestina. There, he received word of Mithridates' death (Plut. *Pompeius* 41,3–5). Given the circumstances, there were many defections and acts of treason. Mithridates' own son Pharnaces had finally forced him to take his own life. His body was buried at Sinope, but his grave has yet to be discovered [6].

Mithridates defied the greatest power of the ancient Mediterranean for 26 years. Six generals of consular rank marched out against him, and he survived a chain of catastrophic defeats as well as 20 months of internment in Armenia. Seemingly defeated at last and in his late sixties, he still had the tenacity to save himself with a march of several hundred kilometres through difficult terrain to establish a new front.

Only after the Mithridatic Wars was Rome's strategic presence along the coasts of Asia Minor and Syria established, forming the basis for Roman rule across the Near East as far as the Euphrates.

☞ **Generals of note, N. Pompey**

BIBLIOGRAPHY
[1] E. BADIAN, Zöllner und Sünder, translated by W. Will and S. Cox, 1997 [2] M. DREHER, Pompeius und die kaukasischen Völker. Kolcher, Iberer, Albaner, in: Historia 45, 1996, 188–207 [3] C. HABICHT, Athen. Die Geschichte der Stadt in hellenistischer Zeit, 1995, 297–313 [4] J.M. HØJTE (ed.), Mithridates VI and the Pontic Kingdom, 2009 [5] J.M. HØJTE, The Death and Burial of Mithridates VI, in: J.M. HØJTE (ed.), Mithridates VI and the Pontic Kingdom, 2009, 121–130 [6] M. KALLET-MARX, Hegemony to Empire. The Development of the Roman Imperium in the East from 148 to 62 B.C., 1995 [7] B.C. MCGING, The Foreign Policy of Mithridates VI Eupator, King of Pontus, 1986 [8] B.C. MCGING, Mithridates VI Eupator. Victim or Agressor?, in: J.M. HØJTE (ed.), Mithridates VI and the Pontic Kingdom, 2009, 203–216 [9] T. REINACH, Mithradates Eupator, König von Pontos, translated by A. Goetz, 1895.

CHRISTIAN MAREK

G. AURELIAN'S PALMYRENE WAR

From AD 253 to 268, the Syrian oasis city of Palmyra under its king, Odaenathus, functioned as an ally of Rome, successfully fighting the Persian king Sapor I. After Odaenathus' death, however, his son Vaballathus and widow Zenobia plotted a more independent course. Palmyrene armies conquered Egypt and expanded their sphere of control to the Syrian provinces, Mesopotamia, Arabia and eastern Asia Minor. Rome's former ally now became a threat, as Palmyra was developing from a city-state under Roman control and a hub of the caravan trade into an independent kingdom between Roman and Persian territory. Zenobia established a vibrant court that attracted such figures as the Greek philosopher Longinus, and even Christian dignitaries such as Paul of Samosata, Bishop of Antioch. It is clear that Zenobia's ambitions went beyond functioning as a mere client of Rome with a royal title.

After fighting brutal wars in Italy and the Balkans, Aurelian finally found time for a campaign against the growing power of the Palmyrene monarchy. The Greek historian Zosimus of Constantinople [3] wrote an unusually detailed account of it during the reign of the Eastern Roman Emperor Anastasius I (491–518) (Zos. 1,50–58), which was undoubtedly based on exhaustive sources. Aurelian took with him a battle-hardened army made up of detachments (*vexillationes*) from the Danube region, his Dalmatian and North African cavalry, and the Praetorian Guard (Zos. 1,52,3f.). For his part, Zabdas, the Palmyrene commander, had excellent heavy cavalry units, along with Syrians and stragglers from the former Roman army of the east. After their defeat in the first battle, Zenobia reportedly boasted that she had lost not a single Palmyrene soldier, for all the fallen in her army had been Romans (Anonymus Continuator Dionis FHG IV,197, frg. 10,5).

Aurelian sped across Asia Minor at a forced march, and after a protracted siege took the pro-Palmyrene city of Tyana. He exercised leniency by preventing his soldiers from plunding the city, which enhanced his reputation in the Roman east. He easily overcame the passes of the Taurus Mountains, then won a first battle near Antioch. Continuing south, he chose a surprising route along the east bank of the Orontes. This enticed the heavy Palmyrene cavalry to undertake an exhausting ride east, after they had earlier secured access to the wealthy city of Antioch farther west. They were duly defeated at Immae by Aurelian's lighter and more mobile Dalmatian and African troops, who were still fresh.

The Palmyrenes withdrew their remaining forces to the city of Emesa, at an important crossroads in a valley between ridges of mountains – an ideal place to set up a central provision camp. They recruited local troops and called up remaining reserves, thereby replenishing their ranks. Aiming to halt Aurelian's advance, they had left a division on a hill near Daphne to keep watch on the main road south from Antioch. The emperor's forces rapidly overran this unit. Because Aurelian intended to win back wealthy provinces and secure his rear ahead of the southward march to Emesa, he sent units into Roman Mesopotamia and Arabia. He also recruited more men in those provinces and in Syria and Palaestina, obviously finding enough supporters there who were ready to serve him.

The decisive battle between Aurelian and the Palmyrene general Zabdas came at Emesa in June or July 272. Zabdas had reason to be confident. Although his army was of mixed quality, it was very large, whereas Aurelian had sent some of his best men off to various provinces in the east. Nevertheless, the Palmyrenes lost. Although the mounted Roman units were defeated by the numerically superior enemy cavalry and suffered major losses, Zabdas' motley band of footsoldiers was crushed by the Imperial infantry. The victory of Zabdas' cavalry could not offset this massacre. The remnants of the Palmyrene army withdrew to Palmyra itself, which – as archaeology attests – was only weakly fortified, and so capitulated quickly. Zenobia fled east, but was captured by the Euphrates. The Palmyrene populace was treated mercifully, but Aurelian's spoils were colossal. The emperor set off westwards, heading for the Balkans, but turned around on hearing of an uprising at Palmyra. He returned to the east at a forced march and took Palmyra for a second time in AD 273. This time, the city faced harsher treatment. Although it was not razed to the ground, it was reduced to an ordinary border town along Rome's fortified eastern frontier.

☞ Borders

BIBLIOGRAPHY
[1] L. DE BLOIS, Image and Reality of Roman Imperial Power in the Third Century AD, 2019   [2] U. HARTMANN, Das palmyrenische Teilreich, 2001 (esp. 231–402)   [3] M. MEIER, Zosimus, in: BNP 15, 2010, 971–973.

LUKAS DE BLOIS

H. PELOPONNESIAN WAR

H.1. Prior history and causes
H.2. Archidamian War
H.3. War on Sicily and Decelean-Ionian War
H.4. Historical significance

H.1. PRIOR HISTORY AND CAUSES
Since Diodorus Siculus (12,37,2 etc.), who was probably drawing on historiographers of the 4th century BC, the term Peloponnesian War has been used to describe the conflicts, which were already seen as a coherent body of events by Thucydides, that took place between Athens and Sparta and their respective allies during the period 431–404 and involved much of the Greek world. A first war between the two major powers (which will not be discussed here) is known to scholars as the 'First Peloponnesian War' and was fought between 458 and 451 (truce) and then 446 (peace), after hostilities had broken out around 460 between Sparta's allies, including Corinth and Aegina, and Athens over control of the Saronic Gulf, which caused → Sparta to intervene. The trigger for the Peloponnesian War that broke out in 431 was again conflict between Athens and its neighbours in the late 430s. There were tensions with Corinth, for instance, when it fought with Corcyra over control of the city of Epidamnus and primacy in the Ionian Sea, and Athens supported Corcyra as part of a defensive alliance. Athens also declared a trade embargo that excluded Megara from all ports in the Delian League (formally because of supposed border violations, but perhaps more because it was operating as a supply port for Corinth: [20. 200–227]; cf. [32. 610–614]). Corinth, for its part, supported a rebellion by the League city of Potidaea. Finally, in 432, the Corinthians, Megarans and other allies persuaded Sparta to declare its peace with Athens broken. Athens refused to relinquish Potidaea and Aegina and cancel the trade embargo against Megara, as Sparta demanded in exchange for peace. War therefore broke out in 431. In Thucydides' view, war had become inevitable because 'the growth in power of the Athenians filled the Spartans with

fear and drove them to war' (Thuc. 1,23,5; 1,118,2 etc.). But this view is much disputed among scholars, just as great controversy surrounds the question guilt and the reasons for the war in general. It may be that in the tense situation of 432/31, the fear of losing authority on both sides simply drove them to war – Sparta fearing the consequences if it did not enforce the demands of its allies, and Athens fearing if it yielded to these demands (overview of debate in [23] and [24]; recently important [2. 20–39]; [22. 86–105] and [32]; [9]; cf. for contemporary views only Aristoph. Ach. 496ff. and Pax 604ff.).

H.2. Archidamian War

The course of the first phase of the Peloponnesian War (cf. Map 3), the 'Archidamian' (first use Lys. in Harpocrat. A 247 Keaney s.v.), 'Ten-Year' (Thuc. 5,25,1) or 'Attic' (Thuc. 5,28,2) War of 431–421, was determined by a military stalemate. Sparta and its allies were superior on land and so tried to bring about a decisive pitched battle. King Archidamus II (who gave the war its name) invaded Attica in 431, 430 and 428, then Cleomenes invaded in 427, and they devastated the land [6. 35–64] – in this phase mainly symbolically. The Athenians, however, avoided fighting a decisive battle by withdrawing their rural population behind the city walls of Athens. Instead, they made use of their naval superiority by sending the → fleet to attack and plunder Laconia and its allies. Following the Spartan withdrawal, Megara had to endure annual Athenian invasions that sought to control Megaris and thereby block Sparta's land route to central Greece. This hardly reflects a defensive strategy, as was attributed to Pericles in Thuc. 2,65,7. Like Sparta, Athens was more intent on wearing down its enemy through symbolic humiliations such as plundering and injuring the enemy's allies, until the enemy gave way and accepted the victor's demands (on the debate over aims and tactics [6. 65–88]; [27]; [22. esp. 375–381]; [7]). The lack of a decisive battle led to a considerable expansion of the war in order to put indirect pressure on the other side. One important theatre was the northwest, especially the Gulf of Corinth, the Ionian Islands and Acarnania, where protracted proxy wars raged. Another theatre was Boeotia, where Sparta destroyed Plataeae in 427 after a two-year siege, and Athenian offensives failed in 426 and 424 (with heavy losses at the Battle of Delium). As for the Delian League, Athens put down rebellions by Potidaea in 429 and Mytilene in 427. The war gained new momentum in 425, when the Athenians fortified the promontory at Pylos in Messenia, and Sparta feared a helot uprising. The attacks on Attica now ceased, but in 424 a commando operation by the Spartan general Brasidas took Athenian possessions on the Chalcidice and especially Amphipolis. An Athenian counterattack under Cleon failed in 422, whereupon advocates of peace prevailed on both sides and the Peace of Nicias was agreed in 421.

H.3. War on Sicily and Decelean-Ionian War

The Peace of Nicias hurt Sparta's reputation with its disappointed allies, who then joined forces against Sparta in the Mantinea-Elis-Argos axis and allied with Athens. Sparta put an end to this insubordination at the Battle of Mantinea in 418 – according to Thuc. 5,74,1, this was the largest land battle of the war to date and one of the few decisive ones. There was still no direct confrontation with Athens, however, in spite of the latter's aggressions (416 overthrow of the pro-Spartan party in Argos, attack on Melos). At Athens, a plea from the city of Segesta on Sicily in 415 to help against Syracuse and Selinus offered an opportunity to implement apparently long-standing plans to attack Syracuse, with the ultimate aim of preventing the cities of Sicily with their powerful navies from allying with Sparta (Thuc. 6,1,1 and 6,6,1 overstate irrational motivations such as megalomania; cf. [12. 159–191] and [2. 75–91]). Despite the benefit of reinforcements, however, the belated Siege of Syracuse did not go well due to tactical errors, and the enterprise went on the defensive in 414 when Sparta intervened to support Syracuse. The starving Athenian army was forced to capitulate while withdrawing in 413, with supposedly 40,000 citizens, confederates and mercenaries killed or dying in captivity. The impending defeat emboldened Sparta to resume the war back in Greece, with the first invasion of Attica since 427 taking place in the spring of 413, leading to the permanent occupation of the town of Decelea, which forced the Athenians behind their city walls for years and gave Sparta, the Thebans and others free rein for plunder. Sparta opened another front in the Aegean in 412, supporting the defection of important Athenian allies in Ionia, including Chios and Miletus, and receiving from Persia vast subsidies for the maintenance of a fleet. The conflicts of the following years, which were concentrated in Ionia and the Hellespont (hence 'Decelean-Ionian War'), were indecisive. After initial Spartan successes, Athens won a devastating victory at the naval battle of Cyzicus in 410. Sparta won victories in 407 at Notium near Ephesus and in 406, but Athens prevailed again in 406 at the Battle of the Arginusae. The dynamic of this phase of the war, which on the Athenian side was dominated by Alcibiades as admiral from 410 to 407 and on the Spartan by Lysander from 407 onwards, was significantly affected by the availability of money to finance the fleets (see below). Sparta as the favoured partner of the Persians

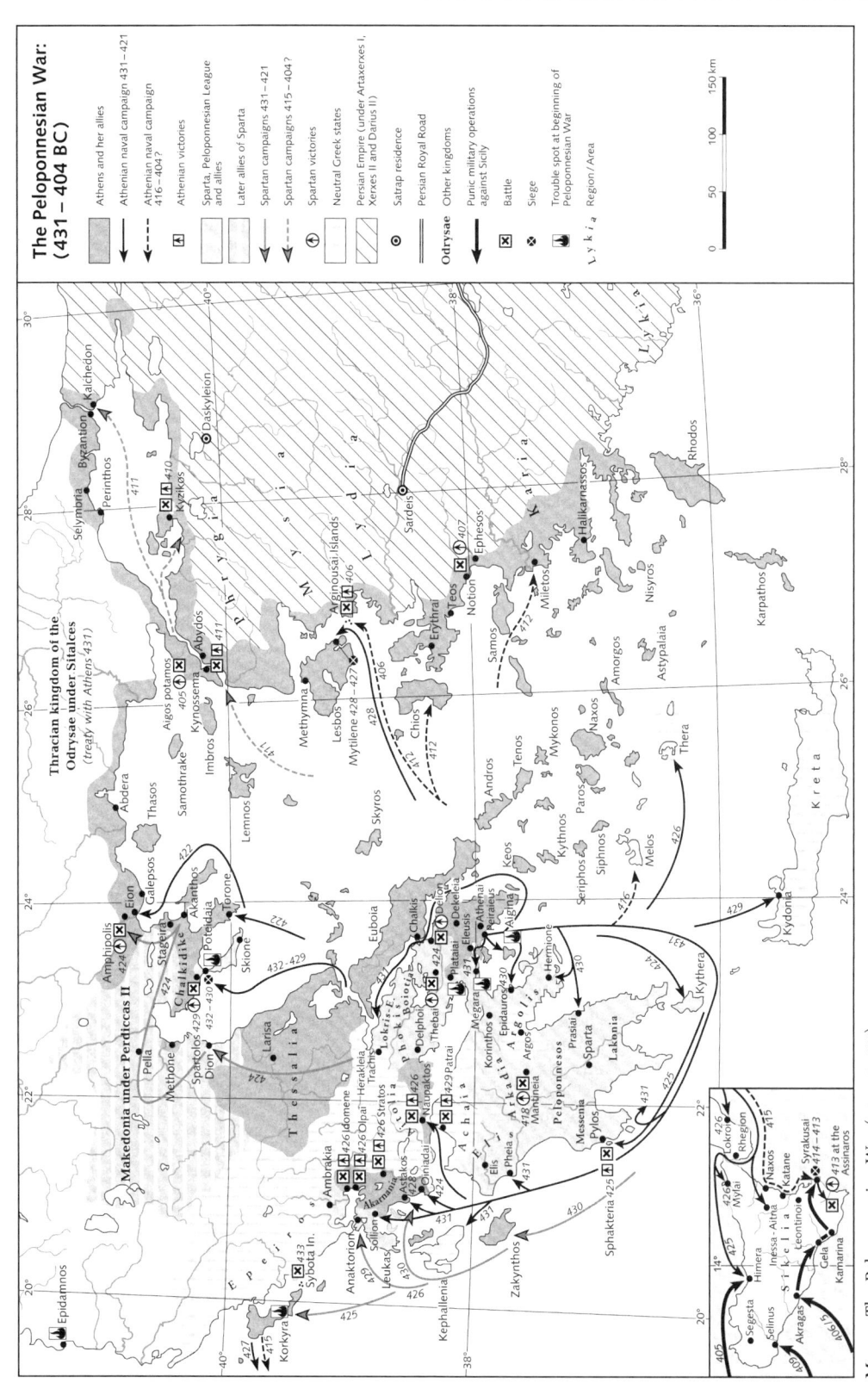

Map 3: The Peloponnesian War (431–404 BC)

was in a better long-term position in this respect. Even so, victory came only in 405, when Lysander used a ruse to destroy the Athenian fleet in a surprise attack, as most of this fleet had been pulled up on land at Aigos Potamos on the Hellespont. Exhausted, Athens was unable to build a new fleet, and the city was forced to surrender in 404 after months of siege.

H.4. HISTORICAL SIGNIFICANCE

The outcome of the war was of historical importance insofar as it gave Sparta hegemony in the Greek world for about 30 years. Moreover, the collapse of Athens gave Persia control over the west coast of Asia Minor once more, restoring its position as a major Aegean power.

The Peloponnesian War was viewed even by contemporaries as a turning point, not just historically but also in the history of warfare. According to a widespread opinion, the Peloponnesian War put an end to the practice of deciding wars in large, ritualized hoplite battles, as Herodotus, writing at the time of the war, describes (Hdt. 9,3). Emerging instead were (seaborne) raids, long sieges (examples of both being Plataeae, Pylos, Decelea and Syracuse; on which [28]), surprise and deception manoeuvres, and the increased use of light and heavy infantry and cavalry (e.g. at the Battle of Delium: [6. 89–161]); but cf. also e.g. [31. 115–197] and [21. 78–90], according to which the ritualized hoplite battle had always been more an ideology than a reality). One characteristic of the Peloponnesian War was that the citizen armies were considerably augmented with mercenaries (but cf. the debate in [31. 41f.]), slaves (e.g. Xen. Hell. 1,6,24) or, in the case of Sparta, helots (first used as regular fighters 424: Thuc. 5,34,1) or *neodamodes*, 'new citizens' (Thuc. 7,58,3; cf. on both [29. 23–27]). Much of this anticipates the 4th century. What decided the war, however, was naval warfare. This made war more dependent than ever on access to money. Even in the Archidamian War, Athens had to contend with financial shortages despite its high reserves (Thuc. 2,13,3–5) and regular revenues. An *eisphora* ('tax') was exacted from wealthy Athenians in 428/27 to finance the sometimes months-long naval deployments, and it seems that special duties were imposed on allies (both Thuc. 3,19,1). The collection of tribute was professionalized (IG I^3 34 = HGIÜ I, 75; IG I^3 68 = HGIÜ I, 111), and tributes may have been raised (IG I^3 71 = HGIÜ I, 113, 'Cleon's Assessment'; on all this see [26. 171–221]; [15]). Monetary constraints were an even stronger influence on the course of the Ionian War. Sparta's fleet, consisting of its own ships (Thuc. 8,3) and especially contingents from its allies, were heavily dependent on Persian financial support (Thuc. 8,5,5; 8,29 etc.; overviews on the Spartan fleet in the Peloponnesian War [17]; [3]), and Athens, too, faced increasing difficulties, as attested in 413 by the temporary replacement of tribute from the Delian League with harbour tolls that promised higher revenues (Thuc. 7,28,4). Other measures attesting to Athen's financial need include the use of the 'iron reserve' of 1,000 talents in 412 (Thuc. 8,15,1), the melting down of temple treasures (see e.g. Philochorus, FGrH 328 Frg. 141), special requisitions from allies, and Athenian generals' raids for booty (on all these [26. 249–292]; [16. esp. 183–284]).

Contemporaries already found the practice of warfare to be highly brutal during the Archidamian War. This is examined, for instance, in Thuc. 1,23,2; 3,28–50 (Mytilene) and in Euripides' *Hecuba* and *Trojan Women*. Excessive violence, mass executions and mass enslavements were the order of the day (e.g. besides the above, Thuc. 3,68; 5,18,8; 5,32,1; 5,116,4f.; 7,29,2–4; Xen. Hell. 2,1,31f.). This tendency was exacerbated by numerous internal conflicts (*staseis*), which were fueled by the polarization of the Greek world between Sparta and Athens and likewise fought in extremely brutal ways (classic account Thuc. 3,70–83 on Corcyra; cf. Euripides, *Orestes* and *Phoenician Women*; cf. [4. esp. 254–261]). Contemporaries lamented the loss of loyalty and faith, and of ethical principles in general (classic accounts Thuc. 3,52–68 on Plataeae in 427, 3,82,3–83 on the *stasis* in Corcyra, 4,74 on Megara in 424, and 4,80 on the mass killing of helots; cf. also Sophocles, *Philoctetes*). All this was in some cases probably the result of the harsh warfare of goading attacks, pillaging raids and proxy wars during the Archidamian and Decelean Wars, and, on a psychological level, of the bitterness that grew on all sides through the long duration of the conflict. In other cases, violence and deceit were used deliberately as deterrents and demonstrations of power (on all this [6. 97–109]; [30]).

☞ Sparta

BIBLIOGRAPHY

[1] B. BLECKMANN, Athens Weg in die Niederlage. Die letzten Jahre des Peloponnesischen Kriegs, 1998   [2] G. CAWKWELL, Thucydides and the Peloponnesian War, 1997   [3] C. FALKNER, A Note on Sparta and Gytheum in the Fifth Century, in: Historia 43, no. 4, 1994, 495–501   [4] H.-J. GEHRKE, Stasis. Untersuchungen zu den inneren Kriegen in den griechischen Staaten des 5. und 4. Jh. v.Chr., 1985   [5] D. HAMEL, The Battle of Arginusae. Victory at Sea and Its Tragic Aftermath in the Final Years of the Peloponnesian War, 2015   [6] V.D. HANSON, A War like No Other. How the Athenians and Spartans Fought the Peloponnesian War, 2005   [7] P. HUNT, Thucydides on the First Ten Years of the War (Archidamian War), in: R.K. BALOT et al. (eds.), The Oxford Handbook of Thucydides, 2017, 125–144   [8] J.O. HYLAND, Persian Interventions. The Achaemenid Empire, Athens, and Sparta, 450–386 BCE, 2018   [9] S.N. JAFFE, Thucydides on the Outbreak of War. Character and Contest, 2017   [10] D. KAGAN, The Outbreak of the Peloponnesian War, 1969

[11] D. KAGAN, The Archidamian War, 1974 [12] D. KAGAN, The Peace of Nicias and the Sicilian Expedition, 1981 [13] D. KAGAN, The Fall of the Athenian Empire, 1987 [14] D. KAGAN, The Peloponnesian War, 2004 (summary from [10]-[13]) [15] L. KALLET-MARX, Money, Expense, and Naval Power in Thucydides' History 1–5.24, 1993 [16] L. KALLET-MARX, Money and the Corrosion of Power in Thucydides. The Sicilian Expedition and Its Aftermath, 2001 [17] T. KELLY, Peloponnesian Naval Strength and Sparta's Plans for Waging War against Athens in 431 B.C, in: R.H. SACK (ed.), Studies in Honor of Tom B. Jones, 1979, 245–256 [18] P. KRENTZ, The Strategic Culture of Periclean Athens, in: C.D. HAMILTON / P. KRENTZ (eds.), Polis and Polemos. Essays on Politics, War, and History in Ancient Greece in Honor of Donald Kagan, 1997, 55–72 [19] J.F. LAZENBY, The Peloponnesian War. A Military Study, 2004 [20] R.P. LEGON, Megara. The Political History of a Greek City-State to 336 B.C., 1981 [21] J.E. LENDON, Soldiers & Ghosts. A History of Battle in Classical Antiquity, 2005 [22] J.E. LENDON, Song of Wrath. The Peloponnesian War Begins, 2010 [23] E.A. MEYER, The Outbreak of the Peloponnesian War after Twenty-Five Years, in: C.D. HAMILTON / P. KRENTZ (eds.), Polis and Polemos. Essays on Politics, War, and History in Ancient Greece in Honor of Donald Kagan, 1997, 23–54 [24] E.W. ROBINSON, Thucydides on the Causes and Outbreak of the Peloponnesian War, in: R.K. BALOT et al. (eds.), The Oxford Handbook of Thucydides, 2017, 115–124 [25] J.B. SALMON, Wealthy Corinth. A History of the City to 338 B.C., 1984 [26] L.J. SAMONS II, Empire of the Owl. Athenian Imperial Finance, 2000 [27] C. SCHUBERT / D. LASPE, Perikles' defensiver Kriegsplan. Eine thukydideische Erfindung?, in: Historia 58, no. 4, 2009, 373–394 [28] M. SEAMAN, The Peloponnesian War and Its Sieges, in: B. CAMPBELL / L.A. TRITLE (eds.), The Oxford Handbook of Warfare in the Classical World, 2013, 642–655 [29] R.J.A. TALBERT, The Role of Helots in the Class Struggle at Sparta, in: Historia 38, no. 1, 1989, 22–40 [30] L.A. TRITLE, A New History of the Peloponnesian War, 2010 [31] H. VAN WEES, Greek Warfare. Myths and Realities, 2004 [32] M. ZAHRNT, Das Megarische Psephisma und der Ausbruch des Peloponnesischen Krieges, in: HZ 291, 2010, 593–624.

SEBASTIAN SCHMIDT-HOFNER

I. JULIAN'S PERSIAN WAR

In AD 363, the emperor Julian (361–363) launched a major offensive against the Sassanid Empire under Sapor II (309–379). This, the largest campaign ventured by the late Roman Empire on its eastern frontier, became Julian's last campaign, ending in his death. The most detailed account is contained in the *Res Gestae* of Ammianus Marcellinus, who suplemented his personal recollections of the events with other eye-witness accounts that are now lost. Later authors, notably Zosimus, relied indirectly on similar source material. Persian perspectives must be derived from this Roman-centric tradition.

Julian's intentions defy easy explanation. He rejected Sapor's offer to negotiate, yet there was no obvious need for an expedition. His extensive preparations suggest ambitions far beyond a simple punitive action against the Persians or minor adjustment to the border. Julian's stratagy of a rapid advance along the Euphrates with the goal of capturing the Sassanid capital of Ctesiphon calls to mind the successful invasions by Trajan (115), Septimius Severus (197) and Carus (283), whose aim had been to break the military power of their neighbour empire. The Roman army included a Persian prince and defector, Sapor's brother Hormizd (Hormisdas), whom Julian may have hoped to install as a compliant ruler. The motive of wanting to achieve personal renown is certainly evident in the emulation of Alexander and Trajan, but the historical reality is difficult to extract from the literary representation. Such military adventurism may have been driven by the practical need for Julian, a western usurper, to gain prestige and legitimacy in the east by winning a triumph there, and to reestablish the institutional cohesion of an army that was still suffering internal tensions caused by the most recent power struggles within the empire.

On arrival at Antioch in the summer of 362, Julian embarked on large-scale preparations. These included building a navy on the upper reaches of the Euphrates to accompany the army and provide logistical support. On March 5, 363, he marched to Hierapolis, where the army assembled to cross the Euphrates. He divided his army at Carrhae, sending Procopius and Sebastianus east with a large contingent (between 16,000 and 30,000 men according to various accounts), to coordinate defensive operations with his ally Arsaces II of Armenia, and if possible, to continue down the Tigris to reunite with the main army in lower Mesopotamia. Julian meanwhile led the main army southeastwards, after a diversionary move in the direction of the Tigris, and reached the Euphrates at Callinicum. Reunited with the fleet farther south, its 65,000 men crossed the river near Circesium on April 6 (Julian. Ep. 58; Lib. Or. 18,213–215; Amm. Marc. 23,2f.; 23,5; Zos. 3,12f.; Ioh. Mal. 13,19–21). Continuing its march along the east bank, this army met with only occasional resistence, but left scorched earth behind. With exceptions such as Pirisabora, few fortresses offered opposition, and local Persian troops contented themselves with ambushes when a favorable opportunity arose. The whereabouts of Sapor's army remained unknown (Lib. or. 18,216–231; Amm. Marc. 24,1–3,9; Zos. 3,14–19,2). Julian pulled away from the Euphrates in early May, marching slowly through canals and flooded fields towards the Tigris. Resistance now intensified, especially at Maiozamalcha, and the heat became burdensome. Julian had a disused canal cleared in order to bring his fleet to the Tigris (Lib. or. 18,232–247; Amm. Marc. 24,3,10–6,3; Zos. 3,19,3–24,2).

The army crossed the Tigris on May 29 in an amphibious night attack and defeated a Persian force outside Ctesiphon (Lib. Or. 18,248–255; Amm. Marc. 24,6,4–14; Zos. 3,25). Because Julian was unable to capture the heavily fortified city, however, his campaign stalled. Early in June, he decided to burn his fleet and march east into enemy territory, but why he did this remains unclear. After two weeks, the Persian scorched-earth strategy forced the Romans to turn northwest and withdraw north along the Tigris Valley in hopes of reaching Roman territory and reuniting with Procopius' Roman-Armenian force, which – for reasons unknown – had not moved south (Lib. Or. 18,261–263; Amm. Marc. 24,6,17–8,5; Zos. 3,26; Ioh. Mal. 13,22). The Persian army now began to attack the rear and flanks of Julian's column, and it destroyed supplies along the route of the march (Lib. Or. 18,264–268; Amm. Marc. 24,8,5–25,3,2; Zos. 3,27–29). In one of these skirmishes near Samarra on June 26, Julian was fatally wounded (Lib. Or. 18,268–276; Amm. Marc. 25,3; Sozom. Hist. Eccl. 6,1f.; Zos. 3,28,4–29,2; Ioh. Mal. 13,23–25).

After long deliberations, senior officers chose Jovian (363–364) as Julian's successor. After several days of forced marches under difficult conditions, Jovian decided to accept Sapor's humiliating conditions in order to save the army from its plight. According to this agreement, Jovian ceded five provinces and 18 fortresses, including the key strongholds of Nisibis and Singara, and he consented to Sapor's subsequent occupation of Armenia (Amm. Marc. 25,5–9; Zos. 3,30–34). The campaign shows that the Roman army still had a high level of operational competence, but it also reveals the limits of its strategic, logistical and reconnaissance abilities in difficult environments far from supply bases when dealing with an elusive enemy. While the losses of soldiers and materials seem not to have had any long-term consequences, the reshaping of the eastern frontier shaped the character of the Roman-Sassanid rivalry for more than two centuries.

BIBLIOGRAPHY
[1] J. DEN BOEFT et al., Philological and Historical Commentary on Ammianus Marcellinus XXIII, 1998 [2] J. DEN BOEFT et al., Philological and Historical Commentary on Ammianus Marcellinus XXIV, 2002 [3] J. DEN BOEFT et al., Philological and Historical Commentary on Ammianus Marcellinus XXV, 2005 [4] M.H. DODGEON / S.N.C. LIEU (eds.), The Roman Eastern Frontier and the Persian Wars, AD 226–363, 1991 [5] C.W. FONARA, Julian's Persian Expedition in Ammianus and Zosimus, in: JHS 111, 1991, 1–15 [6] T. GNOLI, Le guerre di Giuliano imperatore, 2015 [7] W.E. KAEGI, Constantine's and Julian's Strategies of Strategic Surprise against the Persians, in: Athenaeum 59, 1981, 209–213 [8] J. MATTHEWS, The Roman Empire of Ammianus, 1989.

PHILIP RANCE

J. PERSIAN WARS

J.1. Darius' attack
J.2. The campaign of Xerxes

According to Herodotus and implicitly Thucydides (1,97), the Persian Wars were the conflicts fought between the Greeks and Persians in the Aegean from the Ionian Revolt (499–494 BC) to the defeat of the Persian fleet at Mycale (479 BC). Our knowledge of the wars comes almost entirely from Greek sources, yielding a one-sided view of events even among scholars. Recent efforts [1]; [2] have not achieved much change in this respect. The *poleis* of western Asia Minor, under Persian suzerainty since the subjugation of Lydia by Cyrus the Great and the conflicts that followed, were confederates in the Ionian League, a primarily religious affiliation. Led by Miletus, they rose up with the aim of throwing off the tyrant installed by the Great King Darius I, and with him Persian rule (according to [3]; see also [2]). Their only support from the Greek mainland came from Eretria and Athens (Hdt. 5,97f.), although Darius had regarded the latter as a tributary since its plea for help to him in 507 (Hdt. 5,73). After an initially successful advance on Sardes, seat of the satrap Artaphernes, the Ionian forces were defeated at Ephesus in 498 BC, whereupon the Athenians withdrew. Although Cyprus and the Carians joined the revolt, it ultimately failed because of Persian military superiority and Ionian disunity. The rebel *poleis* were recaptured one by one over the years that followed. The fate of Miletus was sealed with its defeat in the naval battle of Lade (494; Hdt. 6,11–17).

J.1. DARIUS' ATTACK
Darius soon demanded that the mainland Greeks recognize Persian supremacy. Some *poleis*, mainly of the islands and northern Greece, did so. But most – including Sparta and Athens – did not. Darius sent an expeditionary force to put the insubordinate Athenians in their place, but the campaign failed on the plain of Marathon (→ Battles of note, F.; 490). The Persians did, however, occupy and plunder much of the Aegean, including Samos, Naxos, Delos and Euboea. During a ten-year suspension of hostilities, Athens took the advice of Themistocles and built a fleet of triremes, but it is not clear whether its intended purpose was to counter Athens' rival Aegina or to defend against an impending Persian invasion (Hdt. 7,144; Thuc. 1,14; Plut. *Themistocles* 4).

J.2. THE CAMPAIGN OF XERXES
The design of the campaign launched ten years later by Xerxes, Darius' successor, shows that his purpose was to subjugate the whole of Greece (e.g. Aesch. Pers. 231–234; 475f.). The Greek resistance

organized itself in the Hellenic League led by Sparta (481; Hdt. 7,132; 7,145; 7,148; Theop. FGrH 115 Frg. 153; Plut. *Themistocles* 20; Tod I² 19), with members outside the Peloponnese including Athens, Aegina, the Phocians and several small *poleis*. The Great King advanced with enormous forces by land and sea (although Hdt. 7,60–99 exaggerates fulsomely). Northern Greece and Macedonia rapidly fell to him, and the Thessalians defected when the Greeks abandoned their attempt to protect them. A Greek advance guard of around 7,000 hoplites commanded by the Spartan King Leonidas took up positions at Thermopylae, a narrow pass in Phocis. Most of the Hellenic force withdrew after the Persian elite units slipped past them. The remaining 300 Spartiates and 700 Thespians were wiped out after stubborn resistance. Their futile struggle gave birth to the legend of the heroic Spartan state ([5]; already Hdt. 7,207–233, legendary in many respects; cf. Simon. Frg. 5; 92 Diehl) (→ Sparta). Although a storm did some damage to the Persian fleet and a naval battle ended in a standoff, the Greek fleet withdrew from Artemisium on the northern tip of Euboea into the Straits of Salamis on hearing word of the defeat.

The Persians then occupied central Greece and the evacuated city of Athens without encountering meaningful resistance. The temples on the → Acropolis were destroyed. The defeat at the hands of the Hellenic League fleet in the naval battle of Salamis (→ Battles of note, I.) induced Xerxes to withdraw with his ships, but a powerful land army under Mardonius wintered in Thessaly. It moved against Boeotia in the spring of 479, and again occupied Athens. The Spartans and the Peloponnesian League mobilized, fortifying the Isthmus of Corinth and marching a united pan-Hellenic army under the Spartan Pausanias to Plataeae. After several days' inaction, supply problems provoked the battle. In the end, the outcome of the battle was decided by the close-combat superiority of the Greeks, especially the Spartans, which rendered the Persians' ranged weapons ineffective. Herodotus (9,28f.) suggests that the strength of the Greeks was around 100,000 men, including 5,000 Spartiates, 5,000 *perioikoi* ('dwellers around [Sparta]') and 35,000 lightly armed helots – although this last figure is probably too high. The Persians were purportedly far superior in numbers, but this cannot be true. In the same year, a Greek army defeated the Persians on land and at sea at Mycale (near Miletus) (Thuc. 1,89), after some Ionians had already defected.

In addition to sheer luck and Persian errors in leadership, the decisive factor in the success of the Greeks was the military effectiveness of the hoplite phalanx. Furthermore, it can be assumed that the western periphery of the empire was not a top priority for the Great King. The two battles had considerable military and political consequences: in the Aegean, the offensive posture was now on the side of the Greeks, or more specifically the Delian League founded by Athens to succeed the Hellenic League (Thuc. 1,96; Aristot. Ath. pol. 23,5; Plut. *Aristides* 25). The dynamic of Persian expansion was broken in the region, creating the conditions for Athens' rise to dominance. Moreover, there was an increasing sense in Greece of being in conflict with barbarians. Preserving the freedom of the Greeks against barbarian forces was considered the most important and celebrated outcome of the Persian Wars [6].

BIBLIOGRAPHY
[1] P. BRIANT, Histoire de l'empire Perse de Cyrus à Alexandre, 1996, 158–173, 531–585 [2] G. CAWKWELL, The Greek Wars. The Failure of Persia, 2005 [3] J. FISCHER, Die Perserkriege, 2013 [4] A. KEAVENEY, The Persian Invasions of Greece, 2011 [5] M. MEIER, Die Thermopylen – 'Wanderer, kommst du nach Spa(rta)', in: E. STEIN-HÖLKESKAMP / K.-J. HÖLKESKAMP (eds.), Die griechische Welt. Erinnerungsorte der Antike, 2010, 98–113 [6] K. RAAFLAUB, Die Entdeckung der Freiheit, 1985 [7] P. TOZZI, La rivolta ionica, 1978 [8] H.T. WALLINGA, Xerxes' Greek Adventure. The Naval Perspective, 2005 [9] W. WILL, Die Perserkriege, 2010.

LEONHARD BURCKHARDT

K. PUNIC WARS
None of the many armed conflicts of the Roman Republic comes close to epitomizing Rome's rise to global dominance as emphatically as the three engagements known to the Romans as the Punic Wars (264–146 BC). After centuries of coexistence regulated by treaties, the extension of Roman interests from Southern Italy to Sicily provoked the first military confrontation (264–241; cf. Map 4), which after twenty years of conflict ended for a time with the cessation of all Carthaginian claims on Sicily. Shortly afterwards, Rome exploited its opponent's relative weakness to annex Sardinia. Regardless of the immediate causes, the two later wars ultimately followed the logic of Roman power politics: to prevent a resurgence of its defeated enemy on the Iberian Peninsula, Rome provoked the Second Punic War (218–201; cf. Map 5), which reduced Carthage to a North African client state of Rome. Half a century later, in 150 when the Carthaginians reacted to repeated attacks by Rome's ally King Massinissa of Numidia by launching military action, the senate voted for the destruction of the Carthaginian state (Third Punic War 149–146).

The question of whether or not Rome was legitimately entitled to accept the request for assistance from the mercenary colony of Messana (Messina) in 264 BC depends entirely on the authenticity of a treaty which, according to the historian Philinus, defined a boundary separating Roman and

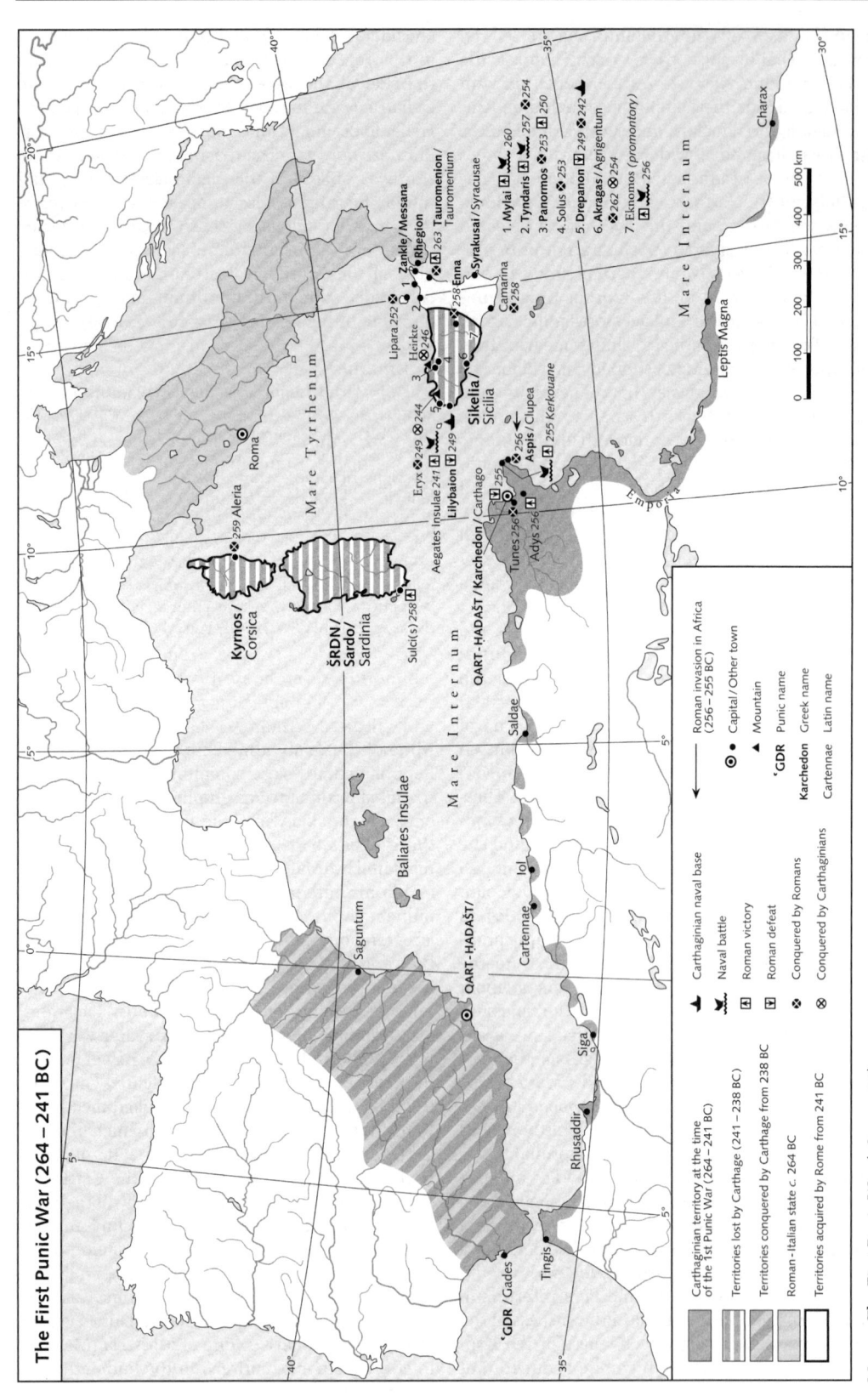

Map 4: The First Punic War (264–241 BC)

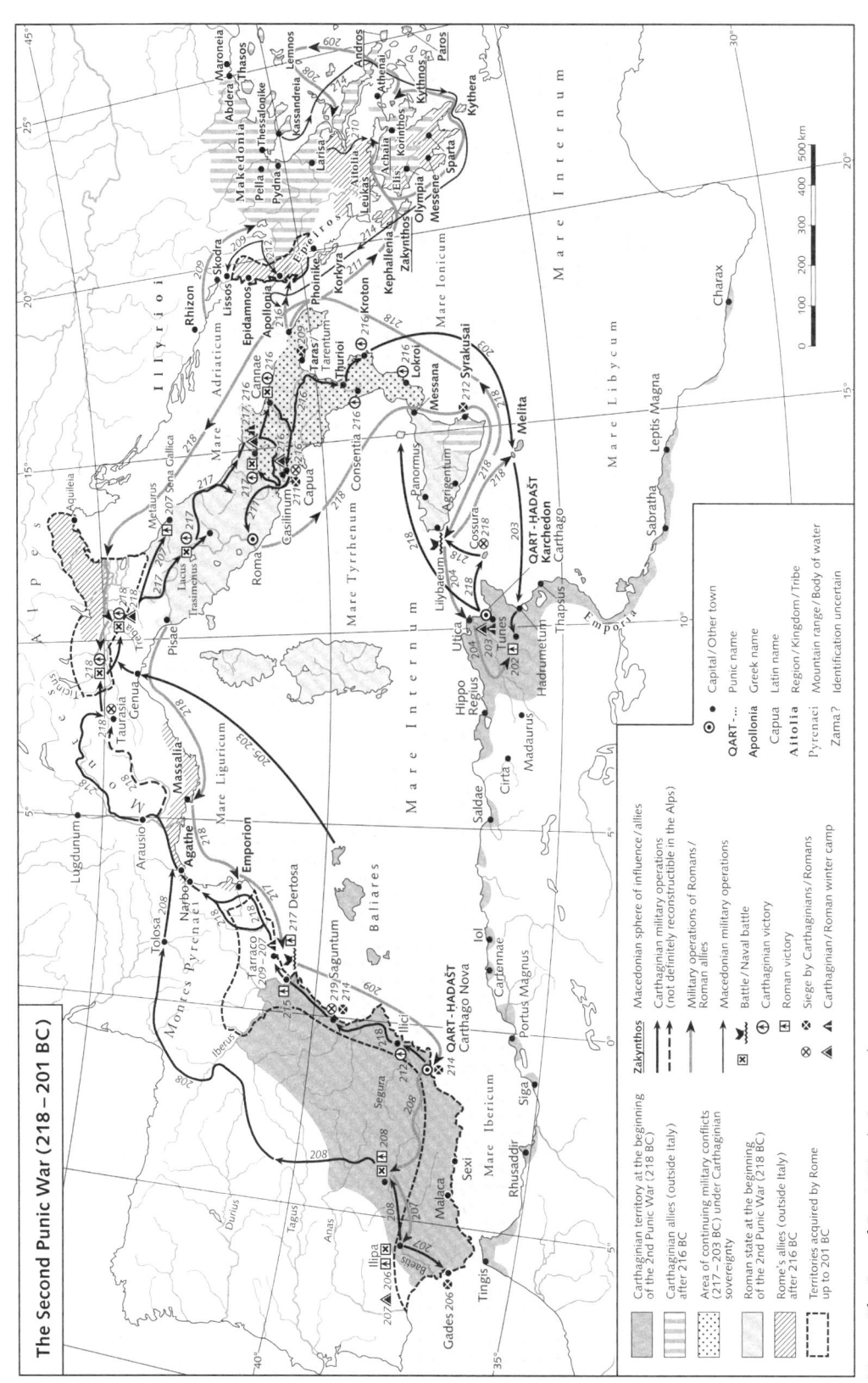

Map 5: The Second Punic War (218–201 BC)

Carthaginian spheres of interest between Southern Italy and Sicily. Pol. 3,26 disputes the existence of such an agreement, pointing out that it was not to be found in the archive of the aediles in Rome. At all events, it must have been clear to the Romans that intervening on Sicily as the protector of Messana against Carthage would mean war with the Phoenician maritime power. Rome forced Carthage's ally Syracuse to capitulate in just the second year of the war (263 BC). However, following a failed invasion of Africa (256/55) and repeated heavy losses at sea, victory came only when a fleet built with private funds was deployed at the Battle of the Aegates (241).

Seeking to offset its loss of Sicily and Sardinia, Carthage in 237 began a phase of intensive expansion in southern and eastern Iberia, bringing it back into the sights of the Roman political world. Once again, it was a plea for help from a city in the Carthaginian sphere of influence (Saguntum, on this occasion) that triggered the Second Punic War by providing the Romans with legal grounds for intervention. Here again, Polybius found no evidence in the archives of the *aerarium* of the treaty of 226/25 that purportedly defined the Iber (Ebro) as the boundary of Carthaginian interests (2,13,7). Hannibal forestalled a planned Roman invasion of Africa by advancing into Italy, but his victories there in the first years of the war (218–216) failed to damage the Roman alliance system. Roman successes in the Iberian and Sicilian theatres forced the Carthaginians back into North Africa, where Hannibal finally faced defeat at Zama at the hands of the Roman general P. Cornelius Scipio (202).

Neither amity nor alliance (App. Lib. 237) could free the Carthaginians from their role as adversary. They appealed in vain to Rome to halt the ongoing annexations of Massinissa, before taking up arms themselves in 151, thereby breaching the treaty of 201 BC. This may have provided a legal basis for the disproportionate decision to annihilate Carthage, but it can no more explain it than can Roman suspicions regarding what archaeology has shown to be the city's economic resurgence. During a period in which dominance in the Mediterranean world was fragile and constantly under threat, Carthage offered the Roman senate an opportunity to set a highly visible example, without having to take into account a Greek public, as they had to do regarding the more moderate punishment of Corinth in the same year (146).

It is clear that the initiative in all three Punic Wars came from Rome. One can attribute the cause of each war to 'security reasons', if one is prepared to adopt the participants' understanding of 'security': the need to safely assert one's own hegemonic claims within an ever-expanding horizon of interests. This way of thinking no doubt informed the senate's debates considerably. Here as elsewhere, the Romans were no strangers to the concept of preventative action to counter threats they considered plausible [8]. What distinguished the Punic Wars from the plethora of Roman wars of expansion was their duration and intensity, which made them at times an incalculable risk to Rome itself, and elevated them to the status of key narratives in the panorama of Roman history. This became a story of hereditary enmity and rivalry projected back into the mythical past (Verg. Aen. 4,622–629), with the proverbial perfidy of the enemy (Cato, Orig. 4 fr. 84) contrasted with the shining *exemplum* of Roman *fides* in the legend of Regulus (Cic. Off. 3,99–101).

☞ **Generals of note, G. Hannibal; Generals of note, O. Scipio Africanus**

BIBLIOGRAPHY
[1] K. BRINGMANN, Punic Wars, in: BNP 12, 2008, 205–213 [2] A. GOLDSWORTHY, The Punic Wars, 2000 [3] D. HOYOS (ed.), A Companion to the Punic Wars, 2011 [4] D. HOYOS, Mastering the West. Rome and Carthage at War, 2015 [5] W. HUSS, Geschichte der Karthager, 1985 [6] G. MANZ, Roms Aufstieg zur Weltmacht. Das Zeitalter der Punischen Kriege, 2017 [7] S. MODROW, Vom punischen zum römischen Karthago. Konfliktreflexionen und die Konstruktion römischer Identität, 2017 [8] T. MUST, Präventivkriege und Sicherheitspolitik. Bestimmende Motive römischer Außenpolitik zwischen 171 und 133 v.Chr., 2018 [9] A. ZACK, Forschungen über die rechtlichen Grundlagen der römischen Außenbeziehungen während der Republik bis zum Beginn des Prinzipats X: Gesamtschau und die wesentlichen Zusammenhänge in den 'Forschungen I–IX', in: GFA 20, 2017, 113–126 [10] K. ZIMMERMANN, Rom und Karthago, ³2013.

KLAUS ZIMMERMANN

Weapons

☞ **Armament**

Index

Note on the indices

There are three indices to the article texts, covering people, geographical names and technical terms. Index entries do not mark every occurrence in an article text, but are given only once (generally the first occurrence) for each context. It is therefore advisable always to investigate the environs of an index location in the texts to find more information on the name, place or term searched for. Separate references are given where a search term occurs more than once in separate contexts within a single article.

The index term is followed by the page number(s) and title of the article. Differing transcription and scholarly conventions (not all of which can be covered here) mean that it is advisable also to look up other variants of entries that come from ancient sources or scripts not based on the Latin alphabet (e.g. Greek or Arabic). The same applies to complex and multipart names.

Entries marked * have their own lemma in *Brill's New Pauly* – some in the Antiquity volumes (1–15), others in the Classical Tradition volumes (I–V), some in both (please also include in research the addenda at the ends of volumes 15 and V). Where the keyword given here differs from the lemma title (which is invariably stylistically related) in *Brill's New Pauly*, the *Pauly* form is also shown. Numerals in square brackets refer to the number of a homonym in *Brill's New Pauly* (e.g. Theodora [2]*; Alexandria [1]*), in order to facilitate identification and the location of the correct article in the main encyclopaedia.

A. Index of Persons

The index of persons references the personal names given in the compendium. The main name form is always given, along with any surname and/or forename(s). Searches should include all name elements in case of complex and multipart names. Mythological figures can be found in the subject index.

A. Index of persons

Abdalonymus*   Representations of war 381
Abgar [1]* II   Battles of note 57
Abinnaeus, Flavius   Language 246, Militia 300, Officers 319, Rank 353, Sources 412
Acilius [I 10]* Glabrio, Marcus   Diplomacy 132
Aelianus [1]* Tacticus   Military literature 286, 289
Aelius Aristides (Aristides [3]*, P. Aelius)   Peace 329, Sources 402
Aelius [II 11]* Gallus, Lucius   Fleet 178
Aelius [II 19]* Seianus (Sejanus), Lucius   Guards 211, 212, Honours 222, Rank 347
Aelius Martinus   Religion 378
Aemilius [I 12]* Lepidus, Marcus   Consequences of war 109, Veterans 474
Aemilius [I 24]* Mamercinus Privernas, Lucius   Victory titles 485
Aemilius [I 31]* Paullus, Lucius   Battle 48, Battles of note 55, Booty 69, Heroism 216, Representations of war 382, Slavery 396, Strategy 435
Aemilius [I 32]* Paullus, Lucius   Booty 68, Consequences of war 107, Parades 321, Triumph 463, 464, Victory titles 485
Aemilius [I 35]* Regillus, Lucius   Consequences of war 111
Aemilius [I 37]* Scaurus   Infrastructure 232

Aeneas [2]* Tacticus   Military literature 286, 287, 289, Military service 290, 292, Reconnaissance 358, Strategy 436, War 491
Aeschylus [1]*   Battles of note 63, Descriptions of war 127, Enemies 159, Military service 291, 293
Aetius [2]*, Flavius   Generals of note 190, Honours 225
Aetus [1]*   Rank 345
Agathocles [2]*   Strategy 437
Agelaus [7]*   Enemies 159
Agesilaus [2]* II   Alliances 12, Borders 70, Camels 79, Equipment 163, 164, Military service 294, Peace 330, Society and army 397, Training 455, Wars of note 497
Agesistratus   Military literature 288
Agis [2]* II   Discipline 136
Agrippa [1]*, Marcus Vipsanius   Battles of note 53, Empire 153, Enemies 162, Fleet 178, Honours 221, Infrastructure 231, Officers 318
Akiva ben Yosef (Aqiba*)   Wars of note 500
Alaric (Alaricus [2]*)   Enemies 162, Generals of note 190, 208
Alcaeus [4]*   Mercenaries 271
Alcibiades [3]*   Descriptions of war 126, 127, Military service 292, Reconnaissance 357, Wars of note 508
Aleuas   Society and army 397
Alexander [II 2]* I of Macedon   Army 24
Alexander [II 4]* the Great, Alexander III of Macedon   Alliances 13, Army 24, 25, Battle 47, Borders 71, Camels 79, Camp 80, Cavalry 86, 87, Civil war 92, Costs of war 113, Descriptions of war 128, Elephants 143, Elite troops 145, Emotions 149, Empire 150, 151, Enemies 159, 160, Equipment 164, 165, Esprit de corps 168, Fleet 175, 176, Garrison 184, General 188, 189, Generals of note 191, 192, 198, 204, 205, Guards 210, Heroism 215, 217, Honour 218, Hunting 226, Infrastructure 232, Innovation 239,

241, Language 245, Law of war 248, March 261, 263, Mercenaries 273, Military literature 287, Military service 291, 293, Motivation 303, Mutiny 310, State and army 428, Officers 316, Parades 322, Pay 325, Phalanx 335, Reconnaissance 357, 358, Religion 368, 371, Representations of war 381, 385, Siege warfare 390, Slavery 393, Society and army 397, Sources 409, Specialists 418, Standard 422, State and army 428, Strategy 437, Supply 441, Terror 452, Timeframe of war 455, Transmission of orders 460, Vehicles 471, Victory 478, Victory titles 484, 485, 487, War 489, 492, Wars of note 497, 511

Alexander [II 8]*, Son of Polyperchon Camp 80
Alexander [II 10]* of Epirus Military literature 286
Alexander [II 15]* of Pherae Peace 330
Alexander V Generals of note 195
Alyattes* II Dogs 139
Ambiorix* Honour 219
Ambrose (Ambrosius*) Enemies 157
Ameinocles Fleet 172
Ammianus Marcellinus* Battles of note 54, Descriptions of war 128, Generals of note 198, Guards 213, Military literature 288, Officers 319, Reconnaissance 362, Sources 402, Wars of note 511
Amyntas [3]* III Generals of note 203
Anastasius [1]* I Army 34, Hunting 227, Rank 349, 353, Wars of note 506
Andriscus* Pseudophilippus Slavery 395
Anicius Faustus, Quintus Discipline 137
Anticrates Military service 294
Antigonous, army physician Medical corps 270
Antigonus [1]* I Monophthalmos Generals of note 195, Infrastructure 232, Innovation 242
Antigonus [2]* II Gonatas Generals of note 195, Symbols 447
Antigonus [3]* III Doson Alliances 13, Battle 48, Customs of war 118, Emotions 149
Antimenides Mercenaries 271
Antiochus [2]* I Soter Military literature 287
Antiochus [5]* III Megas Army 26, Battle 48, Battles of note 58, Consequences of war 105, Diplomacy 132, Elephants 144, Empire 153, Enemies 161, Fleet 177, General 189, Generals of note 197, 207, Innovation 242, March 262, Phalanx 335, Strategy 437, War 492
Antiochus [6]* IV Epiphanes Army 26, Hostages 226, Parades 320, 321, 322, Victory 479, Victory titles 484, 485
Antiochus [7]* V Eupator General 189
Antiochus [9]* VII Euergetes Sidetes Victory titles 484
Antiochus [10]* VIII Epiphanes Philometor Victory titles 484
Antiochus [13]* XII Dionysus Epiphanes Philopator Callinicus/Kallinikos Victory titles 484
Antipater [1]* Generals of note 195, Peace 330, Wars of note 497
Antiphon Painter* Military service 292
Antistius [II 12]* Vetus, Lucius Infrastructure 232

Antistius Turpio Heroism 216
Antoninus [1]* Pius Borders 74, 75, Generals of note 202, Honours 223, Innovation 240, Marriage 265, Military diploma 278, Triumph 464, Parades 321, Representations of war 384, Strategy 435, Victory titles 486
Antonius [I 9]*, Marcus/Mark Antony Battles of note 53, 57, Civil war 94, 95, Consequences of war 107, 109, Discipline 138, Empire 153, Enemies 160, Fleet 177, 178, Guards 210, Honour 218, 219, Innovation 237, 242, Medical corps 268, Representations of war 386, Sources 403, Vehicles 471, Veterans 473, 475, War 495
Antonius [II 15]* Saturninus, Lucius Military diploma 276
Apollodorus, Son of Pancrates Bandits 44
Apollodorus [14]* of Damascus Military literature 288, Sources 401, Wars of note 502
Apollonius, Siege warfare specialist Military literature 287
Appuleius (Ap(p)uleius [I 11]*) Saturninus, Lucius Generals of note 202, Veterans 474
Arbogast (Arbogastes*) Army 32
Arcadius* Generals of note 208, 209, Rank 350, 351, Representations of war 384
Archander, Strategos Supply 441
Archelaus [1]* of Macedon Infrastructure 232, Sources 405
Archelaus [7]* Sisines Philopatris of Cappadocia Empire 154
Archestratus, Macedonian officer Consequences of war 106
Archidamus [1]* II of Sparta Emotions 147, Eve-of-battle speech 169, Innovation 241, War 490, Wars of note 508
Archilochus* Honour 218
Archimedes [1]* Honour 219, Innovation 241, Military literature 287
Archippus, Macedonian official Rank 344
Ardabur [2]* Aspar, Flavius Army 32, General 187
Arimnestus, Spartan soldier Military service 293
Ariovistus* Alliances 14, Wars of note 502
Aristides [1]* Fleet 173, Generals of note 199
Aristocles, Spartan officer Discipline 136
Aristodemus [2]* Heroism 215
Aristophanes [3]* Descriptions of war 126, 128, Heroism 217, Peace 328
Aristotle (Aristoteles [6]*) Armament 17, Discipline 135, Emotions 146, Enemies 159, Military literature 286, Motivation 303, Valour 468
Arminius* Avoidance of military service 42, Battles of note 64, Consequences of war 110, Enemies 162, Officers 317, Strategy 435
Arrian of Nicomedia (Arrianus [2]*, Lucius Flavius) March 262, Military literature 286, 289, Military service 290
Arrius [II 5]* Menander Avoidance of military service 41
Arsaces [4]* II of Armenia Wars of note 511

INDEX OF PERSONS

Arsinoe [II 3]* II   Parades 322
Artabanus [8]* IV   Camels 79, Peace 331
Artaphernes [2]*   Battles of note 59
Artaphernes [3]*   Wars of note 512
Artavastes [2]* II   Battles of note 56
Artaxerxes [2]* II   Army 23, Costs of war 113, Mercenaries 272, Mutiny 311, Scorched earth 388, Strategy 438
Artaxerxes [3]* III   Reconnaissance 358
Artaxerxes [4]* IV (Arses)   Religion 368
Artemisia [1]*   Valour 468
Asclepiodotus [2]*   Military literature 286, War 492
Asinius [I 4]* Pollio, Gaius   Battles of note 61
Aśoka*   Victory titles 484
Athenaeus [5]*   Military literature 288
Atilius [I 21]* Regulus, Marcus   Enemies 160, Honour 219, Innovation 242, Strategy 437
Attalus, Macedonian general   Wars of note 497
Attalus [4]* I   Motivation 304, Representations of war 382, Victory titles 485
Attalus [5]* II Philadelphos   Military literature 287
Attalus [6]* III Philometor Euergetes   Empire 153
Attila*   Generals of note 190
Augustine of Hippo (Augustinus Aurelius*)   Descriptions of war 130, Diplomacy 133, Enemies 157, Valour 470, War 494
Augustus* (Octavian, Gaius Octavius, Julius Caesar the Younger)   Administration 7, Alliances 14, Army 28, Auxiliaries 37, 38, 39, Battle 50, Battles of note 53, Booty 65, 67, Borders 73, 74, 75, 76, Camp 81, Cavalry 88, Civilians 96, 98, Civil war 94, 95, Conscription 102, Consequences of war 107, 109, 110, Costs of war 115, Death 119, Descriptions of war 124, Diplomacy 132, 133, Discipline 137, 138, Elite troops 145, Empire 153, 155, Enemies 160, 161, Esprit de corps 168, Fleet 178, Fortification 181, Garrison 185, General 188, 189, Guards 210, 211, Honour 219, Honours 221, 222, Infrastructure 231, 233, Innovation 237, 239, 243, Law of war 250, Legion 254, 255, 257, Marriage 264, Medical corps 267, Mercenaries 274, Military law 280, 281, 283, 284, Military literature 288, 290, Military service 295, 296, 297, 298, Motivation 305, 306, 307, Mutiny 312, Oath 314, Officers 317, Parades 321, 323, Pay 326, 327, Peace 329, 331, Rank 347, 348, Recruitment 364, Religion 372, 373, 374, Representations of war 382, 383, Siege warfare 392, Slavery 395, 396, Society and army 399, Sources 403, 407, Specialists 418, Standard 421, 423, State and army 431, Strategy 435, 438, Symbols 450, Triumph 464, 465, Valour 469, Veterans 473, 474, 475, 476, Victory 480, Victory titles 486, War 493, 495
Aurelian (Aurelianus [3]*, Lucius Domitius)   Army 29, 31, Borders 77, Cavalry 89, Empire 154, Fortification 182, General 189, Innovation 240, Officers 319, Wars of note 506, Wars of note 506
Aurelius [10]* Cleander, Marcus   Guards 212
Aurelius [18]* Scaurus, Marcus   Honour 219
Aurunculeius [3]* Cotta, Lucius   Honour 219

Avidius [1]* Cassius, Gaius   Consequences of war 111, General 189
Axius, Medicus ocularius   Medical corps 270

Bardylis [1]*   Generals of note 203
Bar Kochba* (Simon ben Koseba)   Consequences of war 110, Wars of note 500
Basilides   Production system 342
Bauto*, Flavius   Army 32
Belisarius*   General 189, Guards 213, Honours 225, Victory 481, Victory 481, Wars of note 498
Biton*   Artillery 35, Military literature 287, Sources 401, Sources 401
Bocchus [1]*   Generals of note 201, Representations of war 382
Bolus of Mendes   Military literature 287
Bonifatius [1]*   Generals of note 190
Boudicca*   Garrison 185, Alliances 12, Fleet 174, General 186, March 260, War 490, Peace 330, Religion 370, Slavery 393, Sparta 415, War 490, Wars of note 508
Brennus [1]*   Motivation 305
Britannicus* (Tiberius Claudius Caesar Germanicus)   Enemies 161
Bulla Felix*   Bandits 44, State and army 431

Caecilius [I 10]* Metellus, Lucius   Honour 219, Triumph 465
Caecilius [I 30]* Metellus Numidicus, Quintus   Discipline 137, Generals of note 192, 201, Reconnaissance 360, Slavery 396, Triumph 465
Caecilius [I 32]* Metellus Pius Scipio, Quintus   Elephants 144
Caecina [II 1]* Alienus, Aulus   Booty 68, Consequences of war 108
Caelius, Marcus   Death 119
Caesar* (Gaius Iulius Caesar)   Artillery 36, Auxiliaries 37, Battles of note 57, 61, Booty 68, 69, Chariot 91, Civil war 94, Consequences of war 107, 109, 110, 111, Descriptions of war 129, Diplomacy 133, Discipline 138, Education 141, Elephants 144, Emotions 149, Empire 153, 155, Enemies 160, 162, Fleet 178, General 188, 189, Generals of note 192, 198, 206, Guards 210, Infrastructure 234, Innovation 237, 242, Language 245, March 261, 263, Medical corps 267, Mercenaries 274, Military law 283, Military literature 288, 289, Motivation 305, Mutiny 312, Officers 317, Parades 322, Pay 326, Peace 331, Rank 346, Reconnaissance 359, Religion 375, Representations of war 382, Scorched earth 388, Siege warfare 392, Sources 401, 402, State and army 430, Strategy 434, 437, Symbols 450, Timeframe of war 455, Triumph 463, 464, Valour 469, Vehicles 471, Veterans 473, 474, Victory 480, Victory titles 486, War 493, Wars of note 502
Caesennius [3]* Paetus, Gnaeus   Generals of note 194
Caesius, Lucius   Peace 330
Calamis*   Military diploma 276
Calgacus*   Enemies 162, Peace 329

INDEX OF PERSONS

Caligula* (Gaius Iulius Caesar Augustus Germanicus)
  Civil war 95, Guards 212, Legion 257, Parades 322,
  Triumph 464, Victory titles 486
Callias [5]*   Infantry 229
Callicratidas [1]*   Booty 66, Honour 218
Callimachus [1]*   Battles of note 59
Callinicus Iovinianus, Flavius   Rank 353
Callinus [1]* of Ephesus   Descriptions of war 126,
  Motivation 301, Valour 468
Callisthenes [1]*   Wars of note 498
Calpurnius Macer [II 11]* Caulius Rufus, Publius
  Consequences of war 110, Policing 337
Cambyses [2]* II   Fleet 172
Canidius* Crassus, Publius   Battles of note 53
Caracalla* (Marcus Aurelius Antoninus Caesar)
  Army 29, Auxiliaries 41, Cavalry 89, Consequences
  of war 109, Costs of war 115, Descriptions of
  war 125, Elephants 144, Honours 224, Legion 254,
  Marriage 266, Military service 297, Pay 326, 328,
  Victory titles 487
Caratacus*   Officers 318
Carausius*   Fleet 179, Standard 424
Carus [3]*   Wars of note 511
Cassander*   Camp 80, Consequences of war 104,
  Generals of note 195
Cassianus   Reconnaissance 362
Cassiodorus*   Scorched earth 388
Cassius [I 10]* Longinus, Gaius   Auxiliaries 37, Battles
  of note 56, Veterans 473
Cassius [III 1]* Dio   Sources 402, Wars of note 504
Catilina* (Lucius Sergius Catilina)   Education 141
Cato [1]* the Elder (Marcus Porcius Cato)   Booty 67,
  69, Consequences of war 108, 109, Enemies 162,
  Generals of note 207, March 264, Military
  literature 288, 289, Reconnaissance 360, Religion 371,
  Terror 452
Cato the Younger (Marcus Porcius [I 7]* Cato)
  Enemies 160, Honour 220
Celsus [7]* (Aulus Cornelius Celsus)   Medical
  corps 270, Military literature 288, 289
Censorinus   Battles of note 57
Cephalus, Athenian armourer   Innovation 240
Cephisodotus [4]*   Peace 328
Cerialis, Flavius   Hunting 227
Cersebleptes*   Generals of note 204
Cestius Gallus, Gaius   Wars of note 504
Chandragupta (Sandracottus*)   Army 26
Chares [1]*   Reconnaissance 358
Charias   Innovation 241
Charisius [1]*, Aurelius Arcadius   Supply 443
Chosroes [2]* I   Diplomacy 133, Prisoners 340
Cicero* (Marcus Tullius Cicero)   Descriptions of
  war 129, Enemies 157, 160, Reconnaissance 359,
  Sources 401, War 494
Cimon [2]*   Battles of note 59, Diplomacy 132,
  Fleet 173, Generals of note 199
Cincius [1]*, Lucius   Booty 68, Military literature 288
Cineas [1]*   Military literature 286

Claudius Drusus [II 1]*, the Younger, Nero
  Mutiny 312
Claudius [I 2]* Caecus, Appius   Army 28, Cavalry 88
Claudius [I 11]* Marcellus, Marcus   Booty 67,
  Heroism 216, Honour 219, Reconnaissance 360, 362,
  Siege warfare 392, Triumph , 463
Claudius [II 17]* Candidus, Tiberius   Supply 443
Claudius [II 24]* Drusus, the Elder, Nero   Death 120,
  Fleet 178, Infrastructure 232, Production system 342,
  Rank 347, Victory titles 486
Claudius [II 31]* Fronto, Marcus   Motivation 305
Claudius [II 42]* Marcellus, Marcus   Military
  literature 288
Claudius [III 1]* (Tiberius Claudius Nero Germanicus)
  Administration 7, Auxiliaries 38, Borders 74,
  Consequences of war 111, Descriptions of war 124,
  Empire 154, Fleet 178, Generals of note 194,
  Guards 212, Honours 222, 223, Marriage 264, Military
  diploma 275, Military service 298, Mutiny 312,
  Victory 480, Victory titles 486, Officers 317, 318, State
  and army 431, Victory 480, Victory titles 486
Claudius Maximus, Tiberius   Honours 224,
  Reconnaissance 361
Claudius Ulpianus, Tiberius   Hunting 226
Clausewitz, Carl von   Military literature 285,
  Strategy 433, 437
Clearchus [2]*   Army 23
Clearchus [6]* of Soli   Military literature 286
Cleisthenes [2]*   Borders 69, Civil war 92, Military
  service 291, Pay 324, Representations of war 380
Cleitus [6]*   Wars of note 498
Cleitus [7]*   Fleet 176
Cleombrotus [2]* I   Education 141, Generals of
  note 196
Cleomenes [3]* I   Alliances 12
Cleomenes [4]*   Wars of note 508
Cleomenes [6]* III   Armament 17, Consequences of
  war 103, 105, Education 140, Eve-of-battle speech 169,
  Sparta 416, War 492
Cleon [1]*   Descriptions of war 127, Emotions 149,
  General 186, Infantry 229, Wars of note 508
Cleonymus [1]*   Cowardice 116
Cleopatra [II 12]* VII   Battles of note 53, Borders 73,
  Civil war 95, Enemies 160, Fleet 178, Guards 210,
  Honour 219, Law of war 250, Triumph 464,
  Veterans 473
Cleophon [1]*   Descriptions of war 127
Clodius [II 1]* Albinus, Decimus   Civil war 95,
  Mutiny 313
Clodius [II 7]* Macer, Lucius   Legion 257
Cloelia [1]*   Hostages 225
Commodus* (Lucius Aurelius Commodus)
  Bandits 44, Borders 75, Civil war 95, Enemies 161,
  Honours 223, Military diploma 276, 279,
  Motivation 307, Victory titles 487, Peace 331,
  Prisoners 340
Conon [1]*   Fleet 175
Constans [1]* (Flavius Iulius Constans)   Army 32

Constantine (Constantinus [1]*) I   Army 29, 30, 31, 32, Auxiliaries 41, Battles of note 60, Borders 77, Cavalry 90, Diplomacy 133, Education 142, Elite troops 146, Enemies 157, 162, Fleet 179, General 189, Generals of note 200, Guards 212, Infantry 230, Innovation 238, Military law 282, Sources 402, Symbols 449, Victory 480, Officers 319, Rank 349, 350, 351, 352, Recruitment 367, Religion 378, Representations of war 383, Sources 402, Veterans 476, Victory 481, Victory titles 487, War 495

Constantine (Constantinus [2]*) II   Army 32, Representations of war 386

Constantine (Constantinus [3]*, Flavius Claudius) III   Generals of note 209

Constantine/Konstantinos (Constantinus [7]*) V   Triumph 464

Constantius [1]* I (Flavius Valerius Constantius)   Generals of note 200

Constantius [2]* II   Army 32, Generals of note 198, Reconnaissance 362, Victory 481

Constantius [6]* III   Generals of note 191

Coponius   Battles of note 57

Cornelius [I 7]* Balbus, Lucius   Triumph 463, Victory titles 486

Cornelius [I 18]* Cinna, Lucius   Generals of note 202, Veterans 473, Wars of note 505

Cornelius [I 20]* Cossus, Aulus   Booty 67

Cornelius [I 70]* Scipio Aemilianus Africanus (Numantinus), Publius   General 188, Generals of note 192, 201, Heroism 216, Hunting 226, Motivation 306, Religion 373, State and army 430

Cornelius [I 71]* Scipio Africanus, Publius   Battle 50, Booty 66, 68, 69, Consequences of war 110, 111, Discipline 137, Emotions 147, Enemies 161, General 188, Generals of note 192, 197, 206, Guards 210, Language 245, Parades 321, Peace 330, Production system 341, Religion 373, Strategy 437, Triumph 465, Victory titles 485, Wars of note 516

Cornelius [I 72]* Scipio Asiaticus, Lucius   Battles of note 58, Enemies 161, Generals of note 207

Cornelius [I 83]* Scipio Nasica Corculum, Publius   Enemies 162

Cornelius [I 90]* Sulla Felix, Lucius   Civil war 93, 94, Consequences of war 107, 108, 109, 111, General 189, Generals of note 192, 201, 205, Guards 210, Heroism 216, March 262, Officers 317, Parades 322, Peace 331, Rank 346, Representations of war 382, State and army 430, Vehicles 471, Veterans 473, 474, Victory titles 486, Wars of note 505

Cornelius [II 12]* Dolabella, Publius   Descriptions of war 124

Cornelius [II 16]* Fuscus   Wars of note 501

Cornelius [II 26]* Lentulus, Cossus   Descriptions of war 124

Cornelius Scipio, Publius (son of Scipio Africanus?)   Honour 219

Cornelius Sisenna*, Lucius   Descriptions of war 128

Crastinus   Heroism 216, Camels 79, Descriptions of war 127, Enemies 156, Mercenaries 271, Representations of war 380

Ctesias*   Reconnaissance 357
Ctesibius [1]*   Military literature 287
Curtius [II 8]* Rufus, Quintus   Descriptions of war 128
Cynaegeirus*   Military service 291
Cypselus [2]*   General 189
Cyrus [2]* II, the Great   Camels 79, Consequences of war 104, Empire 151, Enemies 156, 159, Infrastructure 232, Army 23, Empire 151, Equipment 164, Mercenaries 272, Military literature 286, Military service 293, Motivation 302, Mutiny 311, Wars of note 512, Phalanx 335, Recruitment 363, Supply 441, War 491

Daimachus [1]* of Plataeae   Military literature 287
Damocritus   Military literature 287
Darius [1]* I   Battles of note 59, Enemies 159, Infrastructure 232, Reconnaissance 357, Scorched earth 388, Strategy 434, 436, Wars of note 512
Darius [3]* III   Camp 80, Equipment 165, General 188, Generals of note 191, Representations of war 381, War 492, Wars of note 498
Datis   Battles of note 59
Datus, Nonius   Sources 408, Enemies 162, Honours 224, Peace 331, Strategy 437, Wars of note 501
Decidius [1]* Saxa, Lucius   Honour 219
Decius [I 2]* Mus, Publius   Heroism 216
Decius [II 1]* (Gaius Messius Quintus Traianus Decius)   Consequences of war 107, Discipline 137, Guards 212
Deiotarus*   Empire 154
Demaenetus, Strategos of Epirus   Supply 439
Demaratus   Reconnaissance 357
Demetrius [2]* I Poliorketes   Alliances 13, Battle 48, Consequences of war 106, Equipment 165, Fleet 176, Generals of note 195, Honour 218, Innovation 238, 241, 243, Representations of war 385, Siege warfare 390, Slavery 395, Victory titles 485, War 489
Demetrius [4]* of Phalerum   Consequences of war 104, Military literature 286
Demetrius [8]* II Theos Nikator Philadelphos   Victory titles 484
Demetrius [9]* III Eukairos   Victory titles 484
Demetrius I (Syria)   Hostages 225
Democritus [1]* of Abdera   Military literature 287
Demosthenes [1]*   Army 24, Infantry 229, Innovation 238
Demosthenes [2]*   Administration 3, Emotions 148, Enemies 158
Diades   Innovation 241, Military literature 287, Siege warfare 390
Diaeus*   Slavery 395
Didius [II 6]* Severus Iulianus, Marcus   Guards 212, Honours 223
Diocletian (Diocletianus*, Gaius Aurelius Valerius Diocletianus)   Administration 8, Army 29, 30, Auxiliaries 41, Borders 77, Camels 79, Civil war 95, Consequences of war 109, Education 142, Generals of note 200, Guards 212, Honours 223, Infantry 230,

INDEX OF PERSONS

Infrastructure 234, Innovation 238, Legion 255, Military law 282, Officers 319, Policing 337, Production system 342, Rank 352, Recruitment 366, Sources 412, Supply 444, Victory titles 487, War 494
Diodorus [18]* Siculus   Wars of note 507
Diodotus [1]*   Emotions 147
Dion, Treasurer at Eleusis   Supply 441
Dion [I 1]*   Enemies 158, Parades 322
Dionysius [1]* I   Equipment 164, Fleet 175, Fortification 180, General 189, Innovation 241, 243, Mercenaries 272, Military literature 287, Siege warfare 390, Slavery 394
Dionysius [18]* of Halicarnassus   Infantry 229
Dioscurides   Administration 4
Domitian (Domitianus [1]*, Titus Flavius Domitianus)   Borders 74, Camp 85, Empire 154, Guards 211, Honours 223, Infrastructure 234, Innovation 240, Legion 257, Military diploma 276, 278, Military service 297, Mutiny 312, Pay 326, 328, Strategy 436, Triumph 464, Victory titles 486, Wars of note 501
Domitius [I 3]* Ahenobarbus, Gnaeus   Dogs 139
Domitius [I 8]* Ahenobarbus, Lucius   Battles of note 61
Domitius [II 11]* Corbulo, Gnaeus   Consequences of war 110, General 189, Hostages 225, Infrastructure 232, March 262, Military literature 289, Officers 318
Dorieus   State and army 426
Dryton*   Administration 4
Duilius [1]*, Gaius   Descriptions of war 123, Sources 406

Eccritus   Slavery 393
Echetlus, Echetlaeus*   Battles of note 59
Elagabalus [2]*, Marcus Aurelius Antoninus   Mutiny 313
Eleazar [11]* ben Simon   Wars of note 505
Ennius [1]*, Quintus   Descriptions of war 128, 129, Enemies 161
Epaminondas*   Alliances 12, Army 24, Battle 48, Consequences of war 104, Education 141, Generals of note 196, Honour 218, Innovation 238, Military service 292, Phalanx 335, Slavery 394, State and army 427, Strategy 437, War 491
Ephialtes [2]*   Fleet 174
Epizelus   Military service 294
Eratosthenes [2]* of Cyrene   Maps 259
Eubulus [1]*   Fleet 175
Eugenius [1]*, Flavius   Generals of note 208
Eumenes [1]* of Cardia   Heroism 215, Supply 441
Eumenes [2]* I   Descriptions of war 121, Mercenaries 273, Motivation 303, Mutiny 311, Recruitment 364, Supply 442
Eumenes [3] II Soter   Battles of note 58, Generals of note 197, Sources 407, Victory titles 485
Eunapius   Generals of note 198
Eupolemus   Military literature 286
Euripides [1]*   Valour 468
Euromus*   Alliances 13

Eusebius [7]*   Enemies 157
Eutropius, Flavius   Military literature 290
Evagoras [2]*   Costs of war 113
Evangelus, Author of a Tactica   Military literature 286

Fabius [I 24]* Maximus Allobrogicus, Quintus   Consequences of war 111, Triumph 465
Fabius [I 28]* Maximus Rullianus, Quintus   Consequences of war 108
Fabius [I 30]* Maximus Verrucosus Cunctator, Quintus   Battles of note 55, General 188, Generals of note 192, 207, Honour 219, Rank 346, Scorched earth 388, Strategy 434
Fabius [I 35]* Pictor, Quintus   Generals of note 197
Fabius [II 21]* Valens   Consequences of war 108
Fausta* (Flavia Maxima Fausta)   Battles of note 60
Faustina [2]* the Elder (Annia Galeria Faustina)   Honours 223, Military diploma 278
Faustina [3]* the Younger (Annia Galeria Faustina)   Honours 223
Felix [6]*, Flavius Constantius   Generals of note 190
Flaminius [1]*, Gaius   Battle 49, Booty 68, Reconnaissance 360
Flavius [II 44]* Silva Nonius Bassus, Lucius   Wars of note 505
Flavius Johannes   Sources 412
Flavius Marcus   Rank 353
Flavius Taurinus, Primicerius (grandfather of the scriniarius of the same name)   Sources 412
Flavius Taurinus, Scriniarius (grandson of the primicerius of the same name)   Sources 412
Flavius Virilis   Marriage 266
Fritigern   Battles of note 54
Frontinus*, Sextus Iulius   Military literature 286, 288, 289, Military service 292, Mutiny 312, Sources 401
Fulvius [I 8]* Flaccus, Marcus   Consequences of war 111
Fulvius [I 9]* Flaccus, Marcus   Booty 68
Fulvius [I 12]* Flaccus, Quintus   Motivation 305
Fulvius [I 15]* Nobilior, Marcus   Honours 221
Furius [I 13]* Camillus, Marcus   Heroism 215, Motivation 305, Siege warfare 392
Furius [II 5]* Sabinius Aquila Timesitheus   Gaius, Rear 355, Supply, 443
Furius Octavius Secundus, Decimus   Honours 224

Gabinius [II 3]* Secundus Chaucius, Publius   Victory titles 486
Gainas*   Army 32
Gaius, Aurelius   Cavalry 90
Gaius [2]*   Marriage 265, Sources 403
Gaius Caesar (Iulius [32]* Caesar, C.)   Battles of note 57, Consequences of war 110, Honours 222
Galba [2]* (Servius Sulpicius Galba)   Cavalry 88, Civil war 95, Discipline 138, Guards 211, Honours 223, Legion 257, Military diploma 277, State and army 432, State and army 432
Galerius [5]* (Gaius Galerius Valerius Maximianus)   Representations of war 384

INDEX OF PERSONS

Gallienus* (Publius Licinius Egnatius Gallienus) Army 29, 30, 31, Cavalry 89, Innovation 238, Military diploma 279, Officers 319, Parades 322

Gaudentius [4]* Generals of note 190

Geiseric (Geisericus, Geiseric*) Consequences of war 108

Gelon [1]* General 187, 189, Mercenaries 271, Peace 331

Germanicus [2]* (Nero Claudius Drusus/Nero Iulius Caesar) Avoidance of military service 42, Battle 51, 52, Battles of note 57, 64, Consequences of war 107, Death 120, Descriptions of war 124, Enemies 161, General 189, March 262, Medical corps 268, Mutiny 312, Production system 341, Supply 444, Timeframe of war 454, Veterans 475, Victory titles 486

Gessius Florus* Wars of note 504

Gildo* Enemies 161, Generals of note 208

Gordian I (Gordianus [1]*, Marcus Antonius Gordianus Sepronianus Romanus Africanus) Militia 300

Gordian III (Gordianus [3]*, Marcus Antonius Gordianus) Auxiliaries 40, Medical corps 268, Military diploma 280

Gorgias [2]* Descriptions of war 127

Gratian (Gratianus [2]*, Flavius Gratianus) Battles of note 54, Victory titles 487

Gregorius [I 3]* of Nazianzus (Gregory of Nazianzus) Enemies 157

Gregory of Tours (Gregorius [II 4]*) Militia 301

Gylippus* Fleet 175, Administration 7, 8, Auxiliaries 39, Avoidance of military service 43, Borders 74, 75, Camp 82, Cavalry 89, Colonies 101, Consequences of war 109, Descriptions of war 125, Discipline 137, Empire 154, Honours 222, 223, Innovation 240, Marriage 267, Military diploma 276, 279, Military law 283, Military literature 287, 290, Triumph 464, Victory 480, Officers 317, 318, Prisoners 339, Rank 351, Recruitment 365, Representations of war 383, Sources 408, State and army 431, Veterans 475, 476, Victory 480, Victory titles 486, Wars of note 500

Hamilcar [2]* Supply 441

Hamilcar [3]* Barcas Generals of note 197, Peace 331, Battle 50, 52, Battles of note 55, Booty 68, Consequences of war 107, 108, Death 119, Elephants 143, Empire 152, Enemies 161, Eve-of-battle speech 169, Fleet 176, General 188, Generals of note 197, 206, 207, Innovation 239, Language 245, Motivation 305

Hasdrubal [3]* Generals of note 197

Haterius [6]* Nepos, Titus Wars of note , 500

Hecateius [3]* of Miletus Maps 259

Hephaestion [1]* Emotions 149, Representations of war 381

Heraclianus* Consequences of war 108

Heraclides [11]* of Tarentum Siege warfare 392

Heraclius [7]* General 189, Victory 481, Victory titles 487

Herianoupis Administration 4

Hermogenes of Smyrna Military literature 286

Herod Agrippa II (Marcus Iulius [II 5]* Agrippa) Wars of note 505

Herodes [14]*, Strategos Garrison 184

Herod I (Herodes [1]*), the Great Diplomacy 133, Guards 210, Rear 355, Strategy 438

Herodotus [1]* Battles of note 59, Descriptions of war 126, 127, 128, Enemies 159, Eve-of-battle speech 170, Garrison 184, Heroism 214, Military literature 285, Reconnaissance 357, Sources 402, Wars of note 512

Hero* of Alexandria Artillery 35, Military literature 287

Hesiod (Hesiodus*) Descriptions of war 126

Hieron [2]* II Empire 152, Siege warfare 392

Hieronymus [3]* Generals of note 197

Hintze, Otto State and army 428

Hippias [1]* Alliances 12, Battles of note 59, Reconnaissance 357

Hippocrates [3]* Mutiny 311

Hipponoidas Discipline 136

Hirtius*, Aulus Consequences of war 108, Wars of note 502

Homer (Homerus [1]*) Alliances 10, Army 23, Cavalry 86, Cowardice 116, Descriptions of war 125, 127, 128, Discipline 134, Emotions 147, Enemies 156, 158, 161, Eve-of-battle speech 170, Heroism 215, Innovation 240, Military literature 284, Phalanx 333, Sources 402, 403, Valour 467

Honorius [3]* (Flavius Honorius) Slavery 395, Victory 481, Enemies 162, Generals of note 208, Slavery 395

Horatius [4]* Cocles Heroism 215

Hormisdas [3]* (Hormizd) II Wars of note 511

Hortensius [1]*, Lucius Supply 442

Hostilius [8]* Mancinus, Gaius Honour 219, Peace 331

Hyginus (Gromaticus) (Pseudo-) Camels 79, Military literature 289

Hyperbolus* Descriptions of war 127

Hypereides* Society and army 398

Iason [2]* Mercenaries 272

Ignatius Battles of note 57

Iohannes [7]* Primicerius Generals of note 190

Iphicrates, Author of a Tactica Military literature 286

Iphicrates* Army 24, General 186, Infantry 229, Innovation 238, Mercenaries 272, Military service 293, Transmission of orders 460

Isidorus [2]* of Charax Consequences of war 110

Isocrates* Descriptions of war 127, Emotions 147, Enemies 159, Sources 402, War 491, Wars of note 497

Iugurtha* Army 28, Consequences of war 107, 110, Generals of note 201, Honour 219, Legion 253, Motivation 306, Reconnaissance 360, Representations of war 382, Slavery 396, Veterans 473

Iulius Dexter, Gaius Administration 8

Iulius [II 3]* Agricola, Gnaeus Borders 74, Chariot 91, General 189, Officers 318

Iulius [II 8]* Alexander, Gaius   Supply 443
Iulius [II 43]* Civilis, Gaius   Auxiliaries 38, Enemies 160
Iulius [II 133]* Severus, Sextus   Wars of note 500
Iulius [II 150]* Vindex, Gaius   Militia 300
Iulius Iulianus, Sextus   Recruitment 366
Iunius [I 10]* Brutus, Marcus   Auxiliaries 37, Veterans 473
Iunius [II 6]* Blaesus, Quintus   Victory titles 486

Jerome (Hieronymus [8]*, Eusebius Sophronius)   Enemies 157
John Lydus (Lydus [3]*, Iohannes)   Military literature 288
Jomini, Antoine-Henri   Strategy 437
Josephus (Iosephus [4]* Flavius), Titus Flavius   March 262, Military literature 285, Sources 402, Wars of note 504
Jovian (Flavius Iovianus* Augustus)   Generals of note 198, Guards 213, Honour 220, Wars of note 512
Juba [1]*   Civil war 94, Elephants 144
Juba [2]*   Diplomacy 133
Julian (Iulianus [11]*, Flavius Claudius)   Battle 51, Booty 68, Consequences of war 107, 108, Elephants 145, Generals of note 198, Heroism 217, Honour 220, Honours 225, Maps 259, Military literature 288, Wars of note 511, Parades 322, Reconnaissance 362, Religion 378, Scorched earth 388, State and army 432, Strategy 436, Supply 444, Timeframe of war 454, Victory 481, Victory titles 487, Wars of note 511
Justinian I (Iustinianus [1]*, Flavius)   Army 32, 34, Camels 79, Diplomacy 133, Education 143, Honours 225, Military law 283, Rear 355, Scorched earth 388, Sources 403, 412, Victory 481, Victory titles 487
Justin I (Iustinus [1]* I)   Army 32, Guards 213

Kikkuli, Hurrian horse trainer   Chariot 90

Laches, Taxiarch   Discipline 136
Laches [1]*   Valour 467
Laelius [I 2]*, Gaius   Veterans 472
Lamachus*   Descriptions of war 127, Heroism 217
Leo [4]* I   Army 32, Guards 213
Leonidas [1]*   Descriptions of war 128, Heroism 214, Honour 218, Military service 294, Sparta 414, Wars of note 513
Lesbonax [2]* of Mytilene   Eve-of-battle speech 170
Libanius*   Generals of note 198
Licinius [I 11]* Crassus, Marcus   Battles of note 56, 57, Consequences of war 107, Diplomacy 133, Discipline 138, Generals of note 193, Honour 219, 220, Standard 425
Licinius [I 13]* Crassus, Marcus   Booty 67
Licinius [I 14]* Crassus, Publius   Auxiliaries 37
Licinius [I 16]* Crassus, Publius   Battles of note 56
Licinius [I 24]* Lucullus, Lucius   March 262

Licinius [I 26]* Lucullus, Lucius   Battles of note 56, Generals of note 192, 193, Military diploma 276, Military literature 288, Wars of note 506
Licinius [I 32]* Murena, Lucius   Wars of note 505
Licinius [II 4]* (Valerius Licinianus Licinius)   Army 30, Battles of note 60, Fleet 179, Generals of note 200, Victory titles 487
Ligustinus, Spurius   Honours 221, Motivation 305, Officers 317
Litorius*   Generals of note 190, Avoidance of military service 42, Descriptions of war 128, Infantry 229, Sources 402
Lollia Bodicca   Marriage 266
Longinus [1]*, Cassius   Wars of note 506
Lucan (Lucanus [1]*, Marcus Annaeus)   Battles of note 61, Descriptions of war 128
Lucius Caesar (Iulius [33]* Caesar, L.)   Honours 222
Lucius Verus (Verus*, Lucius Aurelius Verus)   Generals of note 202, Honours 223, Military diploma 279, Military literature 286, Reconnaissance 361, Slavery 395, Victory titles 486
Lupus   Death 120
Lusius* Quietus   Cavalry 88
Lutatius [1]* Catulus, Gaius   Peace 331
Lutatius [3]* Catulus, Quintus   Booty 67, 68, Generals of note 202
Lyciscus [2]*   Enemies 159
Lycurgus [1]*   Alliances 10
Lycurgus [4]*   Discipline 135, Equipment 164, Military service 291
Lycurgus [9]*   Honour 218, Booty 69, Consequences of war 104, Customs of war 118, Empire 151, General 186, Peace 330, Religion 371, Representations of war 380, Wars of note 508
Lysias [1]*   Consequences of war 106
Lysicles   Honour 218
Lysimachus [2]*   Generals of note 195, Guards 210

Machanidas*   Heroism 215
Macrinus* (Marcus Opellius Severus Macrinus)   Battle 45, Consequences of war 108, Guards 212, Peace 331
Magnentius* (Flavius Magnus Magnentius)   Enemies 161
Magnus Maximus (Maximus [7]*)   Generals of note 208
Maizeroy, Joly de   Strategy 433
Manlius, Aulus   March 262
Manlius [I 20]* Torquatus, Titus   Discipline 137, Heroism 216, 217
Manlius [I 24]* Vulso, Gnaeus   Booty 69, Honours 221, Slavery 396, Triumph 463
Manlius [I 26]* Vulso, Lucius   Booty 68
Marcianus [5]*   Generals of note 191
Marcus [2]* Aurelius   Auxiliaries 40, Bandits 44, Borders 73, 76, Camels 79, Conscription 102, Consequences of war 108, Generals of note 202,

Honour 220, Honours 223, 224, Law of war 249, 250, Legion 257, Medical corps 268, Military diploma 279, Militia 299, Peace 331, Prisoners 338, 339, 340, Reconnaissance 361, Recruitment 365, Religion 378, Representations of war 383, 384, Slavery 395, State and army 431, Supply 443, 444, Triumph 465, Victory titles 486

Mardonius [1]*   Battles of note 59, 63, Military service 293, Phalanx 335, Strategy 434, Wars of note 513

Mariccus*   Militia 300

Marius [I 1]*, Gaius   Army 28, Civil war 94, Conscription 102, General 186, 188, Generals of note 192, 201, Guards 210, Honour 219, Infrastructure 232, Innovation 236, Legion 253, March 262, Military service 295, Motivation 306, Recruitment 364, Representations of war 382, Sources 401, Standard 422, State and army 429, Transmission of orders 461, Triumph 463, Veterans 473, Victory titles 486

Marius [II 4]* Celsus, Aulus   Descriptions of war 125

Massinissa*   Wars of note 513

Maurice (Mauricius* Flavius Tiberius)   Army 32, Transmission of orders 461, Victory titles 487

Maxentius* (Marcus Valerius Maxentius)   Army 30, 31, Battles of note 60, Descriptions of war 124, Generals of note 200, Representations of war 383

Maximilian(us) of Tebessa   Avoidance of military service 42

Maximinus [2]* Thrax   Costs of war 115, Heroism 217, Military diploma 279, 280, Militia 300, Motivation 308, Officers 319, Pay 326, Rear 355

Mazaeus*   Wars of note 498

Megabacchus   Battles of note 57

Mehmed II   Enemies 161

Melesermus   Military literature 286

Memnon [3]*   Scorched earth 388, Wars of note 497

Memorius, Flavius   Rank 353

Menander [13]* Protector   Diplomacy 133

Menecles   Supply 441

Menodorus, Flavius   Rank 353

Menon [1]* of Pharsalus   Society and army 398

Merobaudes [1]*   Army 32

Michael Kritoboulos   Enemies 161

Miltiades [1]* the Elder   Borders 70, State and army 426

Miltiades [2]* the Younger   Battles of note 59, Generals of note 199, Representations of war 380, Sources 402, State and army 426

Minucius [I 12]* Rufus, Marcus   Descriptions of war 123

Minucius [I 13]* Rufus, Quintus   Triumph 463

Minucius [I 16]* Thermus, Marcus   Generals of note 193

Mithridates [6]* VI Eupator   Camels 79, Civil war 94, Empire 153, Fleet 177, Generals of note 193, 202, 205, Military literature 288, Peace 331, Representations of war 382, Slavery 395, Strategy 437, Veterans 474, War 489, 492, Wars of note 505

Modestinus Herennius*   Discipline 138

Molon*   General 189

Mummius [I 3]*, Lucius   Descriptions of war 123, Enemies 160, Slavery 395, Triumph 465

Muwattalli II   Army 22

Myronides [2]*   Mutiny 311, Society and army 398

Nabis*   Sources 408, Sparta 416

Naevius [I 1]*, Gnaeus   Descriptions of war 128, Enemies 161

Narcissus [1]*   Mutiny 313

Narses [4]*   Honours 225

Nearchus [2]*   Wars of note 498

Nebuchadnezzar [2]* II   Enemies 156, Timeframe of war 454, War 490

Necho [2]* II   Fleet 172, Infrastructure 232

Neoptolemus [5]*   Heroism 215

Nepos [2]*, Cornelius   Sources 402

Nero* (Nero Claudius Caesar Drusus Germanicus)   Auxiliaries 39, Battles of note 61, Civil war 95, Consequences of war 108, Enemies 157, Fleet 178, General 189, Generals of note 194, Honours 223, Infrastructure 233, Legion 257, Militia 300, Parades 322, Rank 347, Religion 375, State and army 432, Triumph 464, Victory 480, Victory titles 486, Wars of note 504

Nerva [2]* (Marcus Cocceius Nerva)   Military diploma 278, Military law 284, Mutiny 312, State and army 432

Nicanor [4]*   Camp 80

Nicias [1]*   Battle 51, Descriptions of war 127, Fleet 175, March 260, Peace 330

Nicomedes [4]* IV Philopator   Wars of note 505

Numa* Pompilius   Descriptions of war 129

Numonius [2]* Vala, Gaius   Honour 220

Octavia [2]*   Military literature 288

Odaenathus [2]*   Wars of note 506

Odoacer*   Enemies 162

Olympias [1]*   Generals of note 191, 204

Onasander [2]*   Military literature 286, 289, Motivation 304

Onomarchus*   Battle 48

Orodes [2]*   Battles of note 56

Otho* (Marcus Salvius Otho)   Civil war 95, Medical corps 269, Militia 300

Pachrates   Administration 4

Pacorus [3]*   Strategy 437

Pancrates [4]*   Administration 4

Pantites   Honour 218

Papirius [I 15]* Cursor, Lucius   Booty 65

Parmenion [1]*   Wars of note 497, 498

Patermuthis, Flavius   Rank 349, 351, Sources 412

Paternianus   Reconnaissance 362

Pates   Administration 4

Paulus [1]* of Samosata   Wars of note 506

Pausanias [1]*   Camels 79, Descriptions of war 123, Discipline 136, Mutiny 310, Wars of note 513

Pausanias [2]*   Customs of war 118, Wars of note 513
Pausanias [8]*   Military literature 286
Peisistratus [4]*   Civil war 92, General 189, Guards 209, Mercenaries 271
Pelopidas*   Army 24, Generals of note 196, Innovation 238, War 491
Perdiccas [2]* II   Fleet 174, Sources 404
Perdiccas [3]* III   Generals of note 203
Perdiccas [4]*   Society and army 398
Periander, Athenian lawmaker   Administration 3
Periander*   Infrastructure 232
Pericles [1]*   Army 23, Descriptions of war 127, Discipline 136, Empire 150, Fleet 174, Fortification 180, Innovation 238, Military service 291, 292, Scorched earth 388, Valour 467, Pay 324, Strategy 436, 437, War 490, Wars of note 508
Perseus [2]*   Army 25, Battle 48, Booty 67, Diplomacy 132, Equipment 165, Fleet 177, Infrastructure 233, Mercenaries 273, Strategy 435, Symbols 447, Triumph 464, Victory titles 485
Pertinax* (Publius Helvius Pertinax)   Guards 212, Honours 223, Military diploma 276, Mutiny 313, Officers 318, Parades 323
Petreius [1]*, Marcus   Education 141
Petronius, Marcus   Heroism 216
Phanocritus, Honoree   Descriptions of war 122
Pharnabazus [2]*   Fleet 175
Pharnaces [2]* II   Representations of war 382, Wars of note 506
Phila [2]*   Generals of note 195
Philetaerus [2]*   Equipment 164
Philip II (Philippus [2]* II)   Alliances 13, Army 24, 25, Battle 47, 48, Borders 71, Cavalry 86, 87, Consequences of war 103, 106, Customs of war 118, Dogs 139, Elite troops 145, Emotions 148, Empire 151, Enemies 158, 159, Equipment 164, Esprit de corps 168, General 187, Generals of note 191, 203, Guards 210, Heroism 215, Infantry 229, Innovation 236, 239, 241, 243, Law of war 248, March 263, Military literature 287, Military service 291, Pay 325, Peace 329, 330, Phalanx 332, 335, Reconnaissance 357, Religion 368, Siege warfare 390, Slavery 394, Society and army 397, Specialists 417, Transmission of orders 460, Vehicles 471, War 491, Wars of note 497
Philippus [2]* Arabs   Guards 212
Philip V (Philippus [7]* V)   Administration 4, Alliances 13, Army 25, Battle 48, Consequences of war 105, Customs of war 117, Empire 153, Enemies 159, Fleet 177, Garrison 184, Generals of note 197, 207, Innovation 238, Motivation 306, Peace 329, 330, 331, Rank 344, Slavery 395, Strategy 437, War 492
Philocrates [2]*   Generals of note 204
Philo [I 6]* of Eleusis   Infrastructure 231, Sources 405
Philo [I 7]* of Byzantium   Artillery 35, Consequences of war 105, Fortification 180, Military literature 287, Sources 401, War 492

Philopoemen*   Education 140, Heroism 215, Parades 322
Phocion*   Military service 293
Phylarchus [4]*   Emotions 149
Pindar (Pindarus [2]*)   Battles of note 63
Plato [1]*   Descriptions of war 127, Enemies 158, Military service 293, 294, Valour 467
Plautianus (C. Fulvius [II 10]* Plautianus)   Guards 212
Plautus*, Titus Maccius   Descriptions of war 129, Heroism 217, Mercenaries 274
Pliny the Elder (C. Plinius [1]* Secundus)   Military literature 288
Pliny the Younger (C. Plinius [2]* Caecilius Secundus)   Policing 337
Plutarch (Plutarchus [2]*)   Sources 402
Poblicius [II 2]* Marcellus, Gaius   Descriptions of war 125, Wars of note , 500
Polyaenus [4]*   Military literature 286, Military service 292, Strategy 436, Strategy 436
Polybius [2]*   Descriptions of war 127, Emotions 149, Military literature 285, 286, Sources 403, Reconnaissance 357, Sources 402, 403, War 494
Polycrates [1]*   Fleet 172, Infrastructure 231, Innovation 239, Mercenaries 271
Polyidus [2]*   Innovation 241, Siege warfare 390
Polyperchon [1]*   Camp 80, Slavery 395
Pompeius Asper, Marcus   Standard 424
Pompeius [I 3]* Magnus, Gnaeus   Auxiliaries 37, Battles of note 61, Borders 73, Civil war 94, 95, Consequences of war 107, 108, 110, Descriptions of war 124, Diplomacy 133, Education 141, Emotions 149, Empire 153, 155, Enemies 160, 161, Fleet 177, 178, 179, General 188, Generals of note 192, 193, 205, Heroism 217, Honour 220, Honours 221, Innovation 236, Military literature 288, Officers 317, Representations of war 382, Sources 402, State and army 430, Strategy 434, 436, 438, Triumph 463, Veterans 473, 474, Victory 480, Victory titles 486, Wars of note 504, 506
Pompeius [I 5]* Magnus, Sextus   Consequences of war 108, Fleet 178, Slavery 396, Veterans 474
Pompeius [I 8]* Strabo, Gnaeus   Generals of note 205
Pompeius [II 10]* Longinus, Gnaeus   Wars of note 502
Pompeius [III 3]* Trogus, Gnaeus   Sources , 401
Pompeius Niger, Quintus   Heroism 216
Pompiscus   Reconnaissance 358
Pomponius [I 7]* Matho, Marcus   Dogs 139
Pomponius [III 3]*, Sextus   Enemies 159
Popillius [I 2]* Laenas, Gaius   Empire 153
Porsenna*, Lars   Guards 209, Heroism 215, Hostages 225
Porus [3]* the Bad   Elephants 143, Enemies 159, Generals of note 191, Representations of war 385
Poseidonius [3]*   Military literature 286
Postumius Albinus, Aulus   Honour 219
Postumius [I 9]* Albinus, Spurius   Honour 219

Postumius [I 17]* Tubertus, Aulus   Discipline 137
Probus [1]* (Marcus Aurelius Probus)   Army 29, Officers 319
Procopius [1]*   Wars of note 511, 512
Procopius [3]*   Generals of note 191, Sources 402
Prusias [1]* I   Generals of note 197, 207
Psammetichus [1]* I   Mercenaries 271
Pseudo-Hero   Artillery 35
Pseudo-Maurice   Strategy 433
Pseudo-Xenophon   Military literature 285
Ptolemy (Claudius Ptolemaeus [65]*)   Maps 259
Ptolemy (Ptolemaeus [1]*) I Soter   Generals of note 195, Guards 210, Innovation 236, Military literature 286, Society and army 398, Victory titles 484
Ptolemy (Ptolemaeus [2]*) II Philadelphos   Army 26, Military literature 287, Parades 322, Peace 329, Victory 479
Ptolemy (Ptolemaeus [7]*) IV Philopator   Costs of war 113, Diplomacy 132, Phalanx 335, Victory titles 484
Ptolemy (Ptolemaeus [8]*) V Epiphanes   Equipment 164
Ptolemy (Ptolemaeus [9]*) VI Philometor   Garrison 184
Ptolemy (Ptolemaeus [16]*) X Alexander I   Victory titles 485
Ptolemy (Ptolemaeus [18]*) XII Neos Dionysos   Diplomacy 133, Victory titles 485
Ptolemy (Ptolemaeus [20]*) XIII Theos Philopator   Battles of note 61
Pyrrhus [3]*   Armament 17, Avoidance of military service 42, Camp 81, Elephants 143, Enemies 160, 161, Generals of note 195, Heroism 215, Innovation 239, 242, Military literature 286, 287, 289, Motivation 305, Peace 329, Representations of war 385, Sources 409, State and army 429

Quinctius [I 12]* Crispinus, Titus   Reconnaissance 360, 362
Quinctius [I 14]* Flamininus, Titus   Battle 48, Booty 67, Garrison 184

Radagaisus*   Generals of note 209, Slavery 395
Ramesses [2]* II   Army 22
Ramesses [3]* III   Army 22
Rossius Vitulus, Marcus   Supply 443

Sabinus [II 5]*, Mas(s)urius   Military literature 288
Sacrovir (Iulius [III 26]* Sacrovir)   Production system 341
Sallust (C. Sallustius [II 3]* Crispus)   Descriptions of war 128, 129, Sources 402
Sallustius Sempronius Victor, Publius   Supply 443
Sapor [1]* I   Borders 77, Consequences of war 107, Prisoners 340, Wars of note 506
Sapor [2]* II   Reconnaissance 362, Scorched earth 388, Strategy 436, Wars of note 511, 512
Sarapion, Flavius   Rank 351

Scribonius [I 4]* Curio, Gaius   Rank 346
Sebastianus [1]*   Battles of note 54, Wars of note 511
Secundinus   March 263
Sedatius* Severianus, Marcus   Generals of note 202
Seleucus [2]* I Nikator   Army 26, Borders 71, Civil war 92, Generals of note 195, Honour 218, Innovation 242, Victory titles 484, War 489
Seleucus [4]* II Kallinikos   Victory titles 484
Seleucus [8]* VI Epiphanes Nikator   Victory titles 484
Seleucus of Rhosus, Honoree   Motivation 306
Sempronius [I 11]* Gracchus, Gaius   Civil war 93, Conscription 102, Costs of war 114, Veterans 473
Sempronius [I 14]* Gracchus, Tiberius   Booty 68, Death 119
Sempronius [I 15]* Gracchus, Tiberius   Consequences of war 111
Sempronius [I 16]* Gracchus, Tiberius   Civil war 93, Empire 153, Veterans 472
Senecio, Aurelius   Descriptions of war 125
Septimius [II 7]* Severus (Lucius Septimius Severus Pertinax)   Army 30, 31, Borders 76, Cavalry 88, Civilians 96, 98, Civil war 95, Colonies 101, Descriptions of war 124, Discipline 137, Education 142, Empire 154, Guards 212, Legion 257, Marriage 265, Military diploma 276, 278, 279, Military law 282, 284, Military service 296, Mutiny 313, Triumph 464, Victory titles 487, Parades 321, Pay 326, Reconnaissance 361, Representations of war 384, State and army 431, Strategy 438, Triumph 464, Wars of note 511
Serena*   Generals of note 208
Sergius Mena, Gaius   Death 120
Sergius Silus [I 10]* (the Elder), Marcus   Representations of war 385
Sertorius*, Quintus   Enemies 160, Strategy 437, Veterans 474, Wars of note 506
Servilius [I 25]* Pulex Geminus, Marcus   Booty 67, Heroism 216
Servilius [I 27]* Vatia Isauricus, Publius   Enemies 161, Generals of note 193, Triumph 465
Servius Tullius [I 4]*   Army 27, Battle 48, Cavalry 88, Infantry 229, Legion 252, Recruitment 364
Severus [2]* Alexander (Marcus Aurelius Severus Alexander)   Cavalry 89, Mutiny 313, Supply 443
Sextus [2]* Iulius Africanus   Military literature 287, 289
Siccius* Dentatus, Lucius   Honours 221
Silaces, Parthian commander   Battles of note 56
Simon, Athenian delinquent   Discipline 136
Simonides [2]*   Battles of note 63, Sources 405
Simplicinus* Genialis, Marcus   Descriptions of war 125
Sisygambis*   Camp 80
Socrates [2]*   Emotions 148, Honour 218, Military service 292, 293, 294, Valour 467, 468
Solon [1]* of Athens   Civil war 92, Cowardice 116, Discipline 135, Supply 439
Sophagesenus   Elephants 144
Sophocles [1]*   Descriptions of war 127

Spartacus* Enemies 160, Generals of note 193, Prisoners 339
Stertinius [1]*, Lucius Consequences of war 111
Stesichorus [1]* Descriptions of war 127
Stilicho*, Flavius Administration 9, Army 32, Enemies 161, 162, General 187, Generals of note 191, 208, Officers 319, Victory 481
Strategius Musonianus*, Flavius Reconnaissance 362
Suetonius [2]* Tranquillus, Gaius Wars of note 504
Sulpicius Felix, Marcus Civilians 98
Sulpicius [I 13]* Galba Maximus, Publius Booty 66
Sulpicius [I 19]* Rufus, Publius Generals of note 202
Surena Battles of note 56, 57
Symmachus [4]* Eusebius, Quintus Aurelius Enemies 161
Syphax Generals of note 207
Syrianus Magister Eve-of-battle speech 170

Tacfarinas* Descriptions of war 125, Enemies 162
Tacitus* (Publius Cornelius Tacitus) Battles of note 64, Civil war 95, Descriptions of war 128, General 189, March 262, Production system 341, Sources 402, Wars of note 504
Tamsapor* Reconnaissance 362
Tarquinius [11]* Priscus (the Elder), Lucius Booty 67, Cavalry 88
Tarquinius [12]* Superbus, Lucius Guards 209
Taruttienus Paternus*, Publius Military literature 289, Specialists 419, 420
Taxiles* Elephants 143
Terentianus, Claudius Language 245, Sources 410
Terentius [I 14]* Varro, Gaius Battles of note 55, Strategy 435
Tertinia Amabilis Marriage 266
Tertinius Gessius, Marcus Marriage 266
Tettius [2]* Iulianus, Lucius Wars of note 501
Themistocles* Battles of note 62, Descriptions of war 121, Enemies 159, Fleet 173, Fortification 180, Generals of note 199, Innovation 238, Military literature 285, Strategy 436, 437, War 490, Wars of note 512
Theoderic the Great (Theodericus (Theoderic) [3]*) State and army 432, Victory titles 487
Theodosius [2]* I Army 30, Battles of note 55, Enemies 157, Esprit de corps 169, General 189, Generals of note 208, Military literature 289, Slavery 395, Representations of war 384, Slavery 395, Victory 481
Theodosius [3]* II Fortification 182
Theophrastus, Honoured hipparch Supply 439
Theophrastus* Military service 294
Thrasycrates Enemies 159
Thucydides [2]* Descriptions of war 126, 127, 128, Eve-of-battle speech 170, Fleet 174, Garrison 184, Military literature 285, Military service 290, Reconnaissance 357, Sources 402, Wars of note 507, 512

Thutmosis [3]* III Army 22
Tiberianus, Claudius Language 245, Sources 410
Tiberius [1]* (Tiberius Claudius Nero) Auxiliaries 38, Battles of note 63, 64, Borders 74, Camp 85, Consequences of war 107, Diplomacy 133, Empire 154, Fleet 178, General 189, Guards 211, Honour 220, Honours 222, Medical corps 268, Militia 299, Mutiny 312, Officers 318, Rank 347, Representations of war 383, Symbols 449, Veterans 475, Victory titles 486
Tiberius [2]* II Army 32
Tiglath-Pileser [2]* III Enemies 157
Tigranes [2]* II Consequences of war 108, Wars of note 505
Timarchus [4]* General 189
Timotheus [4]* Supply 441
Tineius [3]* Rufus, Quintus Wars of note 500
Tiridates [5]* I March 262, Triumph 464
Tissaphernes* Booty 69
Titius Lustricus Bruttianus, Marcus Wars of note 500
Titurius* Sabinus, Quintus Honour 219
Titus [3]* (Titus Vespasianus) Consequences of war 111, Costs of war 115, Descriptions of war 124, Enemies 161, Officers 318, Prisoners 338, Reconnaissance 361, Sources 402, Triumph 464, Wars of note 505
Totila Enemies 162
Trajan (Traianus [1]*, Marcus Ulpius Traianus) Booty 68, Borders 73, Camels 79, Cavalry 88, Conscription 102, Consequences of war 109, Descriptions of war 124, Discipline 137, Empire 154, Enemies 161, General 189, Generals of note 198, 202, Guards 211, Honours 223, 224, Infrastructure 232, 234, Innovation 239, Legion 257, 258, Medical corps 268, Military diploma 276, 278, Military law 283, Military literature 286, 288, 289, 290, Militia 299, 300, Mutiny 312, Triumph 464, Officers 318, Parades 322, Peace 331, Policing 337, Prisoners 338, 339, Rank 347, Rear 355, Representations of war 383, Siege warfare 393, State and army 432, Strategy 437, Triumph 465, Veterans 476, Victory titles 486, Wars of note 501, 511
Trebius, Lucius Motivation 307
Tyrtaeus* Descriptions of war 126, Motivation 301, Sources 402, Valour 468

Ulpius Telesphorus, Marcus Medical corps 269
Ummidius Durmius Quadratus, Marcus Generals of note 194
Ursicinus* Reconnaissance 362

Vaballathus* Wars of note 506
Valao, Chief of the Naristi Honours 224
Valens [2]* (Flavius Valens) Army 29, 32, Battles of note 54, Consequences of war 107, Diplomacy 133, Generals of note 208, Recruitment 367, Supply 445, Victory 481

Valentinian I (Valentinianus [1]*, Flavius) Army 29, 32, Innovation 243, Military law 282, Reconnaissance 362

Valentinian II (Valentinianus [3]*, Flavius) Rank 348, Slavery 395

Valentinian III (Valentinianus [4]*, Placidus) Generals of note 190, 191, Honours 225

Valerianus, spectabilis Scorched earth 388

Valerian (Valerianus [2]*, Publius Licinius) Borders 77, Consequences of war 107, Diplomacy 133, Guards 212, Honour 220, Prisoners 340

Valerius Aion, Centurion Sources 412

Valerius [I 11]* Corvus, Marcus Siege warfare 392

Valerius [I 33]* Maximus Messalla, Manius Triumph 465

Valerius [II 11]* Maximianus, Marcus Bandits 44, Honours 224, Motivation 307, Officers 318

Valerius [III 5]* Maximus Military literature 288, Sources 401

Valerius Marianus, Gaius Consequences of war 108, Supply , 443

Valesios Poplios (Valerius [I 7]*; P. Valerius [I 44]* Publicola) State and army 429

Vargunteius [2]* Battles of note 57

Varro [2]* Reatinus (Marcus Terentius Varro) Honours 221, Law of war 249, Military literature 286, 288

Varus (Quinctilius [II 7]* Varus, Publius) Army 28, Battles of note 63, 64, Cavalry 88, Descriptions of war 124, Honour 220, Legion 255, 257, Prisoners 339, Standard 422, 425, Strategy 435

Vedennius Moderatus, Gaius Artillery 35

Vegetius* (Flavius Vegetius Renatus) Medical corps 268, Military literature 287, 288, 289, Mutiny 312, Officers 319, Strategy 436, Vehicles 471

Vercingetorix* Scorched earth 388, Triumph 464, Wars of note 502

Vespasian (Vespasianus*) Auxiliaries 39, Borders 75, Civil war 95, Consequences of war 111, Descriptions of war 124, 125, Discipline 137, Education 142, Enemies 160, 161, General 186, Honours 223, Infrastructure 232, Legion 257, March 262, Military diploma 277, 278, Mutiny 313, Officers 318, Parades 322, Peace 329, Prisoners 338, 339, Rank 347, Recruitment 365, Religion 372, 376, Triumph 464, Wars of note 505

Vettius Valens, Marcus March 263

Vibenna*, Aulus Representations of war 382, Caelius, Representations of war 382

Vibius [I 2]* Pansa Caetronianus, Gaius Consequences of war 108

Victorinus [2]* Standard 424

Villius [6]* Tappulus, Publius Battle 48

Virgil (Vergilius [4]* Maro, Publius) Descriptions of war 128, 129, Emotions 147, Peace 328

Viriatus* (Viriathus) Enemies 162

Viridomarus Heroism 216

Vitellius [II 2]* (Aulus Vitellius) Civil war 95, Consequences of war 108, Honour 220, Medical corps 269, Parades 322

Vitricius Avoidance of military service 42

Vitruvius [2]* Artillery 35, Military literature 288, Siege warfare 393, Sources 401

Vologaeses [1]* Hostages 225

Xenophon [2]* Descriptions of war 127, 128, Enemies 159, Infrastructure 232, Mercenaries 272, Military literature 286, 287, 288, 289, Military service 290, Phalanx 335, Reconnaissance 357, Sources 402, Strategy 436, Vehicles 471, War 491

Xerxes [1]* I Alliances 11, Battles of note 62, Camels 79, Customs of war 117, Descriptions of war 126, Enemies 159, Fleet 173, Heroism 214, Infrastructure 232, Law of war 248, Mutiny 310, Reconnaissance 357, Wars of note 512, 513

Zabdas Wars of note 506

Zamaris Strategy 438

Zenobia [2]* Wars of note 506

Zeuxis [2]* Alliances 13

Zopyrion [1]* Slavery 395

Zosimus [5]* State and army 431, Wars of note 506, 511

B. Geographical Index

The geographical index lists place names, regions and bodies of water as well as buildings (the latter under the respective place name).

Abdera [1]*   Fleet 173, Supply 442
Abritus*   Consequences of war 107
Acanthus [1]*   Peace 330
Acarnania (Acarnanians, Acarnania*)   Alliances 13, Battle 47
Achaea (Achaeans, Achaea [1]*)   Alliances 13, Borders 71, Consequences of war 106, Descriptions of war 123, Garrison 185, Infantry 229, Officers 316, Wars of note 508
Achaemenid Empire (Achaemenids [2]*)   Costs of war 113, Enemies 159, War 489
Acrocorinth   Acropolis 1, Garrison 184, Civil war 94, Consequences of war 109, Descriptions of war 124, Fleet 178, 179, Guards 210, Honour 219, Innovation 237, 242, Legion 254, Representations of war 382, Sources 402, Veterans 474, 475
Adamklissi (Adamclisi*)   Battle 52, Enemies 161, Wars of note 501
  – Tropaeum Traiani   Battle 53, Death 120, Motivation 304, Wars of note 501
Adana*   Rear 356
Adrianople/Hadrianople (Hadrianopolis [3]*)   Army 30, Battle 46, Battles of note 54, 55, Consequences of war 107, Diplomacy 133, Enemies 162, Generals of note 200, Military literature 289, Officers 319   Victory 481   War 495
Adriatic Sea   Army 29, Empire 153, Motivation 305, Strategy 438
Aegadian Islands (Insulae Aegates*)   Wars of note 516
Aegaleos* (mountain range)   Borders 71
Aegean Sea   Acropolis 1, Army 26, Battles of note 59, Borders 77, Empire 150, 151, Esprit de corps 168, Fleet 171, 173, 175, 176, 178, Innovation 241, Rear 355, War 488, 489, Wars of note 498, 508, 510, 512, 513
Aegina*   Fleet 173, 174, Infrastructure 231, Military service 294, Sources 406, War 490, Wars of note 507, 512
Aegosthena*   Acropolis 1, Borders 71
Aelia Capitolina   Colonies 100
Aetolia (Aetolians, Aetolia*)   Alliances 11, 13, 14, Auxiliaries 37, Battle 47, Customs of war 117, Diplomacy 132, Military service 294
Africa*   Administration 8, Army 30, Battles of note 60, Borders 74, 76, Cavalry 88, 89, Civil war 94, Descriptions of war 124, Elephants 143, Empire 152, 153, Enemies 162, Garrison 185, Generals of note 190, 197, 200, 201, 205, 207, 208, Honour 220, Legion 253, 257, Militia 300, Motivation 306, Peace 330, Rank 346, Reconnaissance 361, Recruitment 364, 365, Siege warfare 392, Supply 443, Timeframe of war 455, Valour 469, Wars of note 516
Africa* proconsularis   Discipline 137, Veterans 476, Rear 355

Agrieliki (mountain)   Camp 80
Agrigentum/Agragantum (Acragas*)   Elephants 143, Siege warfare 392
Aigos Potamos (Potamoi)*   Religion 371   Wars of note 510, Fleet 175, Military service 292
Ai Khanum*   Acropolis 1
Akrotiri   War 488
Alabanda*
  – Chora   Consequences of war 105
Alalia (Aleria, Alalia*)   Fleet 173
Alba Iulia   Armament 21
Alban Hills (Mons Albanus*)   Triumph 463, 464
Albano Laziale   Hunting 226
Alesia*   Fortification 180, Wars of note 504
Alexandretta   Wars of note 498
Alexandria [1]*   Artillery 35, Borders 76, Fleet 178, Generals of note 206, Infrastructure 231, 232, Military literature 287, Parades 322   Rank 344, 345, Religion 376, Sources 412, Victory 479
Alpes Maritimae*   Militia 300
Alps (Alpes (Alps)*)   Borders 73, Elephants 143, Empire 154, Enemies 161, Generals of note 197, 200, 208, Strategy 437
Alta Italia (Northern Italy)   Rear 355, Empire 153
Althiburus*   Descriptions of war 125
Amanus* (mountain range)   Wars of note 498
Amarynthus*   Parades 322
Ambracia*   Siege warfare 392
Ambracian Gulf   Battles of note 53
Amida*   Elephants 145, Wars of note 506, Alliances 14
Amnias* (river)   Wars of note 505
Amorgos*   Fleet 176
Ampelus [2]*   Acropolis 1
Amphipolis*   Administration 4, Army 25, Generals of note 204, Parades 321, Peace 330, Rank 344, Wars of note 508
Ampurias (Emporiae*)   Artillery 36
Amyclae [1]*   Sparta 414
Anatolia   Legion 255, Militia 299, Wars of note 505
Anatolian Greece   Fleet 174
Anavyssos
  – Croesus kouros   Representations of war 380
Ancona*   Rear 355
Andros*   Fleet 176
Antioch [1]*   Borders 77, Consequences of war 108, Infrastructure 232, Militia 301, Parades 320, 321, 322, Victory 481, Wars of note 507, 511
Antioch [5]*   Policing 337
Antium*   Peace 331
Antonine Wall/Vallum Antonini   Borders 75
Aous* (river)   Battle 48
Apamea [2]*   Battles of note 59, Empire 153, Hostages 226
Apamea [3]*   Society and army 398, Administration 5, Auxiliaries 41, Elephants 144, General 187, Peace 329
Apennine Mountains   Empire 152, Motivation 305
Aquae Granni (Aquae Gran(n)i [III 3]*)   Medical corps 270
Aquae Iasae [III 8]*   Medical corps 270
Aquae [III 6]*/Baden-Baden   Medical corps 270

GEOGRAPHICAL INDEX

Aquae Mattiacorum (Aquae Mattiacae [III 4]*) Medical corps 270
Aquae Sextiae [III 5]* Generals of note 202
Aquae Sulis [III 7]*/Bath Medical corps 270, Policing 337, Production system 341
Aquileia [1]* Descriptions of war 125, Generals of note 191, Infrastructure 231, Supply 444
Aquincum* Death 120, Medical corps 270
Aquitania* Generals of note 190, Wars of note 502
Arabia* Camels 79, Empire 154, Fleet 171, 175, Innovation 239, Sources 407, Wars of note 506
Arabian Desert Language 246
Arausio*/Orange Generals of note 201, Representations of war 384, Slavery 396
Araxes [1]* (river) Wars of note 506
Arcadia (Arcadians, Arcadia*) Borders 70, Consequences of war 105, Military service 291, Motivation 302
Aremorica* Wars of note 502
Argentoratum Generals of note 198
Arginusae* Honour 218, Military service 293, Slavery 394, Wars of note 508
Argos [II]* Alliances 11, 12, Army 23, Borders 69, 70, 71, Customs of war 118, Innovation 236, Law of war 247, Military service 293, Parades 322, Peace 331, War 489, Wars of note 508
 – Chora   Consequences of war 105
Arles (Arelate*) Infrastructure 232, Terror 453
Armenia* Battles of note 56, Consequences of war 108, Generals of note 194, 197, 202, 208, Reconnaissance 358, Wars of note 506, 512
Armenia minor/Lesser Armenia March 263
Armorica Generals of note 190
Arras Fortification 182
Artaxata* March 262, Wars of note 506
Artemisium [1]* Battles of note 62, Descriptions of war 128, War 490, Wars of note 513
Asculum* Battle 45, Elephants 143
Asemus Militia 300
Asia [2]* Battles of note 57, Empire 153, Fleet 177, Garrison 185, Generals of note 191, 193, Hunting 226, Militia 299, Peace 329, Wars of note 498, 505
Asia Minor* Army 26, Bandits 44, Battles of note 53, 59, 63, Civilians 97, Consequences of war 104, 105, 111, Dogs 139, Education 141, Empire 151, 153, Enemies 162, Fleet 171, 173, Generals of note 195, 204, Innovation 241, Legion 255, Militia 299, Pay 325, Peace 329, Policing 337, Rear 355, Recruitment 364, 366, Representations of war 381, 382, Scorched earth 388, Society and army 397, Sources 410, Strategy 438, Supply 445, Triumph 462, War 489, 490, Wars of note 498, 505, 506, 510
Aspendus* Recruitment 366
Assyrian Empire (Assyria*) Infrastructure 232
Astypalaea* Alliances 14
Athens [1]* Administration 2, 3, Alliances 10, 11, 12, Army 23, Bandits 44, Battle 52, Battles of note 59, 62, Borders 70, 77, Cavalry 86, Civilians 96, Civil war 91, 92, Colonies 100, Consequences of war 103, 104, 105, 106, Costs of war 112, 113, Cowardice 116, Customs of war 117, 118, Descriptions of war 122, 127, Diplomacy 131, Discipline 135, 136, Education 140, Emotions 147, Empire 150, 151, Enemies 158, Equipment 165, Fleet 173, 175, 176, Fortification 180, Garrison 184, General 186, Generals of note 195, 199, 204, Guards 209, Infantry 229, Infrastructure 231, Innovation 236, 238, 240, 243, Law of war 248, Mercenaries 272, Military law 281, Military literature 285, Military service 291, 293, Motivation 302, Mutiny 310, State and army 426, War 488
 – **Acropolis**   Acropolis 1, Parades 322, Religion 370, Representations of war 380, 382, Siege warfare 389, Slavery 394, Supply 439, War 489, Wars of note 497, 513
 – **Acropolis, Statue of Athena**   Representations of war 380
 – **Agora**   Battles of note 60, Military service 291, Representations of war 380, Oath 314, Parades 320, 321, 322, Pay 324, 325, Peace 329, 330, 331, Phalanx 335, Reconnaissance 358, Recruitment 363, Religion 370, Representations of war 379, 380, Siege warfare 389, Slavery 393, 394, Society and army 397, 398, Sources 402, 404, 405, 406, 409, Sparta 413, State and army 426, 427, Strategy 435, 436, 437, Supply 439, 440, Transmission of orders 460, Valour 467, Vehicles 471, Victory 478, War 488, 490, Wars of note 505, 507, 508, 510, 512, 513
 – **Chora**   Consequences of war 105
 – **Demosion sema**   Representations of war 381
 – **Olympaeum**   Consequences of war 111
 – **Stoa poikile/'Painted Porch'**   Representations of war 380
 – **Temple of Athena Nike**   Representations of war 380
 – **Temple of Nike**   Victory 478
Athos* Descriptions of war 127, Infrastructure 232
Atlantic Ocean Fleet 178
Attaleia [2]* Mutiny 311, Supply 442
Attica* Battles of note 59, Borders 69, 70, 71, Camp 80, Consequences of war 105, 106, Fleet 175, Fortification 180, Infrastructure 232, Military literature 286, Pay 325, Strategy 436, Supply 439, Wars of note 508
Aufidus* (river) Battles of note 55
Augsburg (Augusta Vindelicum*) Borders 76, Descriptions of war 125
Augst (Augusta Raurica*) Fortification 181
Aulutrene Supply 445
Autun (Augustodunum*) Fortification 181
 – **City wall**   Fortification 181
Avaricum* Scorched earth 388
Avernus (lake) Infrastructure 231

Babylon* Battles of note 63, Elephants 144, Empire 151, Mercenaries 271, Representations of war 381
Bactria* Generals of note 191, Wars of note 498
Bad Gögging Medical corps 270

Baecula* Battle 50, Generals of note 206
Baetica Rear 355
Baiae* Triumph 464
Balearic Islands (Baliares*) Auxiliaries 37, Infantry 229, Mercenaries 274
Balkans Army 25, 31, Battles of note 55, Empire 154, Esprit de corps 168, Generals of note 209, Military diploma 275, 278, Militia 300, Production system 342, Rear 355, Recruitment 366, War 488, Wars of note 506
Banat Wars of note 501
Banna/Birdoswald Camp 84, Hunting 227
Barbaricum Sources 409
Basle (Basilia*) Reconnaissance 362
Batanasa Strategy 438
Bedriacum Medical corps 269
Belgica* Generals of note 190
Belgrade Borders 77
Belich Battles of note 56
Beneventum* Death 119, Elephants 143, Slavery 395
Berenice [8]* Bandits 44
Berkasovo Armament 20
Beroea [1]* Administration 4, Education 141
Berytus* Colonies 100
Bithynia et Pontus* Policing 337, Wars of note 505
Bithynia* (see also Bithynia et Pontus) Empire 153, Fleet 177, Supply 443, Wars of note 505
Black Sea (Pontos Euxeinos*) Borders 76, 77, Consequences of war 106, Fleet 171, 177, 178, Generals of note 204, Infrastructure 231, Strategy 438, Supply 445, Wars of note 505
Boeotia (Boeotia, Boeotians*) Alliances 11, 13, Borders 69, 71, Cavalry 86, Consequences of war 106, Costs of war 112, Customs of war 118, Generals of note 196, Mutiny 311, Society and army 397, State and army 427, Strategy 437, Wars of note 505, 508, 513
Bois-l'Abbé Militia 300
Bonn (Bonna*) Borders 77
– Sanctuary of the Matronae Aufaniae Religion 376
Bononia*/Bologna Veterans 474
Boscoreale* Representations of war 383
Bosnia-Herzegovina Production system 342
Bosporan Kingdom Strategy 438
Bosporus [1]* Consequences of war 106, Fleet 179, Wars of note 506
Bostra* Sources 407
Boulogne Fleet 178
Bowness-on-Solway Borders 74
Brigetio* Motivation 308
Britannia* Administration 8, Auxiliaries 41, Battles of note 60, Borders 74, 76, Camp 82, Chariot 91, Civil war 95, Consequences of war 110, Costs of war 115, Descriptions of war 124, Dogs 139, Empire 154, Fleet 178, Fortification 181, 182, Garrison 185, Generals of note 200, 202, 208, Honours 223, Infrastructure 231, Innovation 239, 240, Legion 255, Marriage 266, Medical corps 268, 270, Mutiny 312, Officers 318, Policing 337, Production system 341, 342, Rank 347, Reconnaissance 359, Religion 375, Siege warfare 392, Society and army 399, Supply 445, Veterans 476, Victory titles 486, Wars of note 500, 502, 504
Brundisium*/Brindisi Civil war 94, Generals of note 206
Budapest Borders 77
Burgundy, Kingdom of Generals of note 190
Byzantium* (see also Constantinople) Consequences of war 106, Diplomacy 132, Enemies 162, Fortification 179, Language 245, Strategy 438

Caerleon Medical corps 270
Caesarea [3]* Maritima Rear 355 Wars of note 504
Callinicum Wars of note 511
Camerinum* Motivation 306
Camirus* Borders 69
Campania* Enemies 159, Supply 444
Camulodunum* Colonies 100
Canaan Enemies 157
Cannae* Battle 46, 52, Battles of note 54, Booty 68, Conscription 102, Consequences of war 108, 109, Generals of note 197, 206, Innovation 239, Legion 253, Officers 319, Prisoners 339, Slavery 395, Sources 403, Standard 425
Cappadocia* Auxiliaries 41, Borders 76, Cavalry 89, Empire 154, Generals of note 202, March 263, Military literature 287, 289, Supply 444, Victory titles 484, Wars of note 505
Capua* Booty 67, Elephants 143, Generals of note 197, Peace 330
Caranis* Language 245, Sources 411, Veterans 476
Caria (Cares, Caria*) Militia 300, Rear 355, Wars of note 498
Carnuntum* Religion 375
Carpow Medical corps 270
Carrhae Battles of note 56, 57, Camels 79, Consequences of war 107, 110, Generals of note 193, Honour 219, Scorched earth 388, Wars of note 511
Carthage* Alliances 13, Booty 67, Consequences of war 103, Descriptions of war 123, Empire 152, 153, 155, Enemies 158, 160, 161, Fleet 172, 173, 175, 176, 178, 179, Generals of note 190, 197, 207, Honour 219, Infrastructure 231, Innovation 241, 242, Mercenaries 274, Militia 299, Peace 331, Prisoners 338, Reconnaissance 359, Religion 373, Siege warfare 392, Sources 406, Strategy 437, Supply 442, Timeframe of war 454, 455, Victory titles 485, Wars of note 513
Carthago Nova*/Cartagena Booty 66, 68, 69, Generals of note 206, Prisoners 339, Production system 341
Carystus [1]* Generals of note 199
Castabala* Dogs 139
Catalaunian Fields (Campi Catalauni*) Generals of note 190
Caucasus* Strategy 438
Caudine Forks March 260
Cecropis* Education 140
Central Asia Borders 71, Empire 151

Central Europe Chariot 91, Military service 298
Central Greece Battles of note 62, Consequences of war 106, Fleet 173, Generals of note 204, Wars of note 508, 513
Central Italy Consequences of war 110, Fortification 181, Guards 209
Ceos [1]* Peace 330
Chaeronea* Alliances 12, 13, Army 24, Battle 46, Cavalry 86, 87, Enemies 158, Generals of note 191, 204, Heroism 215, 216, Honour 218, Military service 291, 293
Chalcidice* Generals of note 204, Religion 370, Representations of war 382, Slavery 393, 395, Society and army 398, State and army 426, War 491, Wars of note 508
Chalcis [1]* Alliances 11, Army 23, Consequences of war 104, Garrison 184, Representations of war 380, War 489
Chersonesus [1]* Borders 70, Generals of note 199, Sources 406
Chios* Alliances 12, Slavery 395, State and army 427, Wars of note 508
Chrysopolis/Calchedon* Generals of note 200
Cibalae* Generals of note 200
Cilicia*/Cilices, Cilicia* Fleet 177, Generals of note 195, Rank 345, Rear 355, Reconnaissance 360, Supply 444, Wars of note 498, 505
Cimmerian Bosporus (Bosporus [2]*, Kerch Strait) Borders 71, Consequences of war 106
Circesium Wars of note 511
Cirta* March 262
Cithaeron* (mountain range) Borders 70
Classe Death 119
Classis Infrastructure 231
Clastidium* Honour 219
Clazomenae* Borders 71
Clyde Borders 75
Cnidus* Fleet 175, Infrastructure 231, Military service 294
Colchis* March 263, Wars of note 505, Wars of note 505, 506
Colonia Agrippinensis*/Cologne Borders 77, Colonies 100, Generals of note 200, Hunting 226, Religion 376
 – **City wall** Fortification 181
Colophon* Dogs 139
Comama Policing 337
Cominium* Siege warfare 392
Commagene* Auxiliaries 38, Empire 154, Victory titles 484, Wars of note 506
Constantinople* (see also Byzantium) Battles of note 54, Enemies 162, Fleet 179, General 189, Generals of note 200, 208, 209, Guards 213, Hostages 225, Militia 300, Triumph 464, Victory 481, Rank 353, State and army 431, Triumph 464, Victory 481
 – **Column of Arcadius** Representations of war 384, Victory 481
 – **Column of Justinian** Victory , 481
 – **Column of Marcian** Victory 481
 – **Column of Theodosius** Representations of war 384
 – **Forum of Theodosius** Victory 481
 – **Hippodrome** Victory 481
 – **Theodosian Walls** Fortification 182
Coolus Armament 19
Corbridge Armament 21
Corcyra* Alliances 12, Civil war 91, Cowardice 116, Fleet 173, 174, Sources 405, Terror 451, Wars of note 507, 510
Corinth (Corinthus/Corinth*) Battles of note 62, Borders 69, Civil war 91, Colonies 100, Descriptions of war 123, Discipline 136, Empire 153, Enemies 160, Fleet 172, 173, 174, Innovation 238, 241, Mercenaries 272, Prisoners 338, Representations of war 379, Society and army 397, War 490, Wars of note 507, 516
Corinth, Gulf of* Fleet 173, Infrastructure 232, Wars of note 508
Coronea* Booty 69, Discipline 136
Corsica* Recruitment 366, Empire 152
Cos* Fleet 176
Costești Wars of note 501
Cremona* Artillery 36, Booty 66, Colonies 100, Prisoners 339
Crenides Generals of note 204
Crete*/Creta Alliances 12, Armament 16, Army 25, Auxiliaries 37, Borders 70, Empire 153, Fleet 171, 177, Infantry 229, Mercenaries 272, 274, Phalanx 333, Sources 404, War 488, 491
Crimea Borders 76, Wars of note 505, 506
Crisa* Borders 70
Ctesiphon* Consequences of war 107, Elephants 145, Generals of note 198, Scorched earth 388, Strategy 436, Wars of note 511, 512
Cumae/Cyme [2]* Fleet 173, Infrastructure 231
Cunaxa* Army 23, Chariot 91, Scorched earth 388, War 491
Cures* Sabini Descriptions of war 123
Cydna/Pydnae Fortification 181
Cyme [3]* Equipment 164
Cynoscephalae* (mountain range) Army 25, Elephants 143, Innovation 238, 239, 242, War 492
Cynosura [2]* (headland) Camp 80
Cynosura [3]* Sparta 414
Cynuria [1]* Army 23, Borders 70
Cyprus* Empire 155, Equipment 165, Fleet 171, 172, 173, Generals of note 195, 199, Wars of note 500, Rank 345, Rear 355, Wars of note 512
Cyrenae (Creta et Cyrenae*) Empire 153
Cyrenaica* Consequences of war 104, Militia 300, Veterans 476
Cyrene* Colonies 100, Fleet 177, Wars of note 500
Cyrrhus [1]* Society and army 398
Cyrrhus [2]* Society and army 398
Cyrus [5]* Valley Wars of note 506
Cythera* Army 23
Cyzicus* Diplomacy 132, War 492, Wars of note 508

Dacia (Daci, Dacia*) Army 31, Borders 74, 75, 77, Empire 154, Enemies 162, Fortification 181, Innovation 239, Rank 347, Sources 407, Strategy 438, Wars of note 501

Dalmatia (Dalmatae, Dalmatia*) Auxiliaries 37, Enemies 162, Garrison 185, Generals of note 190, Recruitment 365, 366

Damascus* Empire 151

Danube (Ister, Istrus [1]*) Army 31, Bandits 44, Borders 74, 75, 76, Camels 79, Camp 82, Education 142, Elite troops 145, Empire 154, 155, Enemies 162, Fleet 178, Generals of note 198, 200, 202, Guards 212, Hunting 226, Infrastructure 231, 234, Innovation 238, 240, Legion 255, Military service 298, Militia 300, Mutiny 312, Rear 355, Reconnaissance 362, Sources 410, Strategy 437, Supply 444, Veterans 476, Wars of note 501

Daphne [4]* Victory 479 Wars of note 507

Dardania Recruitment 365

Dardanus [4]* Peace 331

Dead Sea Wars of note 500

Decelea* Camp 80, Education 140, Garrison 184, Wars of note 510, Sparta 415, Timeframe of war 455, War 491, Wars of note 508, 510

Decumatian Fields/Decumates Agri Empire 154

Delium [1]* Customs of war 118, Law of war 248, Military service 293, 294, Mutiny 311, Society and army 398, War 491, Wars of note 508

Delos* Administration 3, Alliances 12, Consequences of war 110, Empire 150, Fleet 173, 177, Infrastructure 231, Prisoners 338, Sources 405, War 489, Wars of note 512

Delphi* Borders 70, Descriptions of war 123, Enemies 158, Law of war 247, Mercenaries 272, Military service 292, Motivation 304, Parades 322, Religion 368, 371, Representations of war 380, 381, Sources 406, Triumph 465, War 488, 489
 – Monument of Aemilius Paullus Representations of war 382
 – Sanctuary of Apollo Descriptions of war 123
 – Serpent Column Descriptions of war 123, Sources 406
 – Siphnian Treasury Booty 66
 – Statue of the Deified Aetolia Representations of war 381
 – Temple of Athena Religion 370

Dema* (wall) Borders 70

Dendra War 488

Deurne Armament 20

Diana Veteranorum* Motivation 307

Dioecesis Oriens Supply 444

Diolkos* Infrastructure 232

Dionysias Sources 412, Veterans 476

Djerdap/Đerdap Infrastructure 232

Dobruja Wars of note 501

Dodona (Dodona, Dodone*) Victory 478

Dover Fleet 178

Drerus* Education 141

Drobeta* Rear 355

Dunapentele/Dunaújváros Armament 20

Dura-Europus* Acropolis 1, Camels 79, Descriptions of war 125, Generals of note 202, Language 246, Rank 352, Religion 376, 377, 378, Sources 410, Standard 423, Symbols 449

Durostorum* Generals of note 190, Motivation 308

Dyrrhachium* Battles of note 61

Dystus Acropolis 1

East Africa Borders 76

Eastern Anatolia Wars of note 506

Eastern Gaul Generals of note 198

Eastern Mediterranean Sea Army 26, State and army 428

Eastern Roman Empire Army 32, 33, 34, Borders 77, Consequences of war 107, Education 143, Generals of note 208

Eboracum* Generals of note 200

Ebro Wars of note 516

Ecbatana* Wars of note 498

Echzell Medical corps 269

Edessa [2]* Consequences of war 107

Egypt*, Aegyptus Administration 8, Alliances 12, Army 22, 26, 29, Bandits 44, Battles of note 53, 61, Borders 76, Camels 79, Chariot 90, Civilians 97, 98, Civil war 94, 95, Consequences of war 108, 111, Costs of war 112, 115, Descriptions of war 127, Diplomacy 133, Elephants 144, Empire 150, 151, 153, Enemies 156, 161, Equipment 165, Fleet 171, 172, 174, 175, 177, 179, Garrison 184, Hunting 226, Infrastructure 232, Innovation 236, 242, Language 245, Marriage 266, Mercenaries 273, Military service 298, Militia 299, 300, Sources 406, War 492, Wars of note 498, 500, Officers 319, Parades 322, Phalanx 335, Policing 337, Prisoners 338, Rank 344, 351, Rear 356, Recruitment 363, 365, 366, Religion 374, 376, Representations of war 381, Society and army 399, 400, Sources 407, 410, Standard 422, State and army 428, Strategy 437, 438, Supply 442, 443, Transmission of orders 461, Triumph 464, Veterans 476, Victory titles 485, War 495, Wars of note 498, 500, 506

Eining Borders 74, 76

Eion [1]* Generals of note 199

El-Agueneb Hunting 227

Elatea [1]* Consequences of war 103

Elbe Battles of note 63, Consequences of war 107

Eleusis [1]* Battles of note 62, Borders 70, Education 140, Supply 441 Victory 479

Eleutherai* Borders 71

Elis [1]* Borders 70, Customs of war 117

Elis [2]* Alliances 11, 12, Parades 322 Sources 404, Wars of note 508

Elpeus Battle 48

Emesa* Cavalry 89, Wars of note 507

Emona* Veterans 475

Emporion (Chios) Acropolis 1

Enipeus [2]* (river) Battles of note 61

Eordaicus (river)   Battle 48
Ephesus*   Acropolis 1, Civil war 93, Consequences of war 106, Fleet 176, Motivation 302, Parades 322, Wars of note 512
– Great Antonine Altar   Representations of war 384
Ephyra [3]*   Artillery 36
Epidamnus   Wars of note 507
Epidaurus*   Alliances 14, Borders 69, Customs of war 117, Military service 294
Epirus*   Booty 67, 68, Generals of note 204, Religion 368
Eretria [1]*   Acropolis 1, Alliances 11, Army 23, Battles of note 59, Borders 71, Consequences of war 104, Fleet 173
– Acropolis   Acropolis 1, Parades 322, War 489, Wars of note 512
Erythrae [2]*   Garrison 184
Ethiopia   Innovation 242
Etruria (Etrusci, Etruria*)   Chariot 91, Representations of war 382, Veterans 473, War 489
Euboea [1]*   Alliances 11, Consequences of war 104, Fleet 173, Generals of note 199, Scorched earth 388, Wars of note 512
– Temple of Artemis Amarynthia   Enemies 158
Euphrates [2]*   Battles of note 56, 57, Borders 76, Empire 154, Generals of note 198, Infrastructure 231, 232, Rear 355, Reconnaissance 362, Supply 445, Wars of note 498, 506, 511
Europa   Borders 74, Cavalry 89, Empire 153, Peace 330, War 495
Eurymedon [5]* (river)   Fleet 173, Generals of note 199

Failaka   Army 26
Faiyum*   Hunting 227, Sources 412
Farasan Islands   Borders 76, Fleet 178
Firth of Forth   Borders 75
Florence (Florentia*)   Generals of note 209
Fontillet   Armament 18
Fossa [1]* Augusta   Infrastructure 231
Fossa Corbulonis   Infrastructure 232
Fossa Mariana   Infrastructure 232
Fréjus   Fortification 181
Frigidus* (river)   Generals of note 208, Sources 402
Frisia   Medical corps 268

Gabiene   Elephants 143
Galatia*   Empire 154, Legion 257
Galilee (Galilaea*)   Wars of note 500
Gallia cisalpina*   Empire 153, Generals of note 193, Wars of note 502
Gallia*, Gaul (see also Gallia cisalpina, Gallia Narbonensis, Gallia transalpina)   Army 29, Auxiliaries 37, Battles of note 54, 60, Cavalry 88, Consequences of war 107, 110, Dogs 139, Education 141, Elephants 144, Empire 153, 155, Fleet 179, Garrison 185, Generals of note 190, 193, 198, 200, 208, 209, Guards 210, Infrastructure 231, Innovation 242, Language 245, Mercenaries 274, Peace 331, Production system 341, Reconnaissance 359, Recruitment 364, Strategy 438, Supply 444, Timeframe of war 454, Triumph 464, Veterans 476, Wars of note 502
Gallia Narbonensis (Narbonensis*)   Empire 153, Fortification 181, Militia 300, Recruitment 365, Representations of war 384
Gallia transalpina   Empire 153, Generals of note 193, Innovation 237, Strategy 437, Wars of note 502
Ganges* (river)   Wars of note 498
Gaugamela*   Chariot 91, Elephants 143, General 188, Generals of note 191, Innovation 239, War 492, Wars of note 498
Gaza*   Battle 48, Elephants 143, Generals of note 191, 195, Innovation 238, 241, Society and army 398
Gedrosian Desert (Gedrosia, Gadrosia*)   Wars of note 500
Gela*   General 189
Gemellae*   Religion 376
Gergovia*   Heroism 216, Siege warfare 392
Germania (Germani, Germania*; see also Germania inferior, Germania superior)   Battles of note 63, Borders 73, 74, 75, 76, 77, Camp 85, Consequences of war 107, 110, Descriptions of war 124, Education 142, Empire 154, Garrison 185, Infrastructure 232, Motivation 307, Mutiny 312, Sources 407, Timeframe of war 454, Rank 347, Reconnaissance 361, Recruitment 366, Strategy 438, Supply 444
Germania inferior   Generals of note 194, Honours 224
Germania superior   Auxiliaries 40, Borders 74, Generals of note 202, Infrastructure 234, Innovation 240, Military diploma 280, Veterans 475, Religion 376
Gesoriacum*   Descriptions of war 124
Gholaia   Sources 407
Gla   War 488
Glanum*   Booty 66
Gordium*   Generals of note 191, Wars of note 498
Granicus* (river)   Generals of note 191, Heroism 215, March 261, Mercenaries 272, War 492, Religion 371, Wars of note 497
Great Britain   Camp 85
Greece/Hellas [1]*   Alliances 11, Armament 17, Army 22, 24, Battles of note 58, 59, 62, Booty 67, Camels 79, Cavalry 87, Chariot 91, Civilians 96, Consequences of war 111, Costs of war 112, Customs of war 117, Descriptions of war 121, Diplomacy 130, 132, Education 140, Elephants 143, Elite troops 145, Emotions 146, Empire 150, 151, 153, Enemies 159, Equipment 163, Esprit de corps 168, Fleet 171, Generals of note 191, 195, 196, 206, 208, Infrastructure 232, Law of war 248, Mercenaries 272, Motivation 304, 305, Mutiny 311, Parades 321, 322, 323, Pay 324, 325, Peace 331, Phalanx 334, Prisoners 338, Religion 368, 370, Representations of war 381, Slavery 393, 394, Sources 406, Sparta 414, State and army 425, 426, Terror 452, Timeframe of war 454, Triumph 464, Valour 467, Victory titles 484, Wars of note 497, 505, 512

Hadrian's Wall Borders 74, 77, Civilians 96, Innovation 240, Reconnaissance 361, Transmission of orders 462
Haemus* (mountain range) Generals of note 204, Strategy 438
Hagenau Armament 19
Haliartus* Customs of war 118
Halicarnassus*/Bodrum Rear 355, Wars of note 497
Halieis* Sources 406
Haltern Death 119, Medical corps 270, Supply 444, Supply 444
Halys* (river) Wars of note 498
Hasmonean Kingdom Empire 153
Hebron* Wars of note 500
Hebrus* (river) Generals of note 204
Helena (vicus) Generals of note 190
Hellespont (Hellespontus*) Consequences of war 106, Generals of note 199, 200, Heroism 215, Infrastructure 232, Sources 406, Strategy 437, War 489, Wars of note 497, 508
Heraclea [1]* Trachinia Bandits 44, Siege warfare 392
Heraclea [9]* Minoa Acropolis 1, Elephants 143
Heraea* Alliances 11, Sources 404
Hermoupolis (Hermupolis (magna)*) Sources 412
Hesselbach Auxiliaries 40
Hierapolis (Bambyce*) Wars of note 511
Hindu Kush Elephants 144
Hispania* (see also Spain, Hispania citerior, Hispania ulterior) Borders 73, 76, Recruitment 364, 365
Hispania Baetica (Hispania Baetica, Hispania Ulterior*) Garrison 185
Hispania citerior (Hispania Tarraconensis, Hispania Citerior*) Empire 153, 155
Hispania ulterior (Hispania Baetica, Hispania Ulterior*) Empire 153, Generals of note 193, 201, Peace 330
Hittite Empire (Ḫattusa*) Chariot 90
Hromówka Armament 18
Hydaspes* (river) Elephants 143, Generals of note 191
Hyettus* Bandits 44
Hyphasis* (river) Generals of note 192, Mutiny 310, Representations of war 381, Wars of note 498

Ialysus* Borders 69
Iaxartes* (river) Battle 48
Iberia, Iberian Peninsula Civil war 94, Empire 152, 155, Generals of note 197, 202, 206, Honours 221, Legion 255, Motivation 306, Wars of note 513
Ichara* Army 26
Iconium* Policing 337
Idistaviso* Battle 51, March 262
Ilipa* Battle 50, Generals of note 206
Illerup Armament 18
Illyricum*, Illyria (see also Illyricum inferius) Alliances 14, Battle 48, Empire 153, Fleet 176, Generals of note 193, 198, 203, 204, 209, Motivation 307, Reconnaissance 362, Slavery 395
Illyricum inferius Empire 154
Immae Wars of note 507

India* Army 26, Borders 71, 76, Elephants 144, Empire 151, Equipment 164, Fleet 175, Garrison 184, Generals of note 191, Hunting 226, Innovation 241
Indian Ocean* Wars of note 498
Indus Valley Generals of note 191, Wars of note 498
Intercisa [1]* Armament 20
Ionia* Borders 70, Enemies 159, Fleet 173, Wars of note 497, 508
Ionian Islands Wars of note 508
Ionian Sea Wars of note 507
Ipsus* Elephants 143, Generals of note 195, Innovation 242
Iran* Diplomacy 133, Vehicles 471
Iron Gates Infrastructure 232, Rear 355
Isaura Vetus Religion 373
Israel Enemies 156, Wars of note 500
Issus* Battle 46, Camp 80, Generals of note 191, War 492, Representations of war 381, Wars of note 498
Isthmia Victory 478
Isthmus* (of Corinth) Battles of note 62, Borders 70, Enemies 158, Infrastructure 232
Istria Consequences of war 110, Fleet 179
Italia*, Italy Administration 6, Alliances 13, 14, Army 28, Auxiliaries 37, Avoidance of military service 42, Battle 48, Battles of note 53, 55, 60, Borders 73, 76, Cavalry 88, Chariot 91, Civil war 93, 94, 95, Consequences of war 104, 107, 110, 111, Costs of war 114, Death 119, Descriptions of war 129, Diplomacy 133, Discipline 137, Empire 152, Enemies 156, 159, 161, Fleet 178, 179, Generals of note 190, 193, 197, 200, 205, 207, 208, Guards 211, Honour 220, Hostages 225, Infrastructure 231, 232, Innovation 236, 241, 242, Language 245, Law of war 249, Military service 295, 298, Militia 299, Motivation 305, Peace 329, Phalanx 334, 335, Policing 336, Prisoners 338, Rank 346, Recruitment 364, 365, Siege warfare 390, Slavery 395, Sources 410, State and army 428, 429, 432, Strategy 437, 438, Veterans 474, 475, War 494, Wars of note 513, 516
Italia Meridionale (Southern Italy) Consequences of war 108
Italica* Descriptions of war 123, State and army 426
Iudaea, Judaea Auxiliaries 38, Descriptions of war 125, Empire 154, Garrison 185, Production system 341, Recruitment 366, Wars of note 500, 505

Jericho* Wars of note 500
Jerusalem* Booty 66, Borders 76, Consequences of war 110, 111, Costs of war 115, Descriptions of war 124, Enemies 156, Honours 222, Reconnaissance 361, Sources 402, Victory 481, Wars of note 500, 505
 – **Temple** Wars of note 505
Jordan (Iordanes [2]*; river) Wars of note 500
Judah (Judah and Israel*) Enemies 156
Julian Alps Battles of note 60

Kalabsha   Sources 411
Kalkriese*   Armament 20, 21, Battles of note 64
Karasu (river)   Infrastructure 232
Katzenberg   Fortification 183
Kemathen   Armament 18
Kerameikos*   Military service 294
Knossos*   Chariot 91
Koblenz   Borders 77, Fortification 182
Kommos [1]*   Fleet 171
Koroni   Camp 80
Künzing   Armament 19, Medical corps 268

Lacedaemon (see also Sparta)   Scorched earth 388
Laconica*   Borders 69, Sparta 413,
    Reconnaissance 358, Slavery 394, Sparta 413, 414,
    Strategy 437, Wars of note 508
Lade*   Fleet 173, Wars of note 512
Lambaesis*   Administration 7, 8, Cavalry 89,
    Discipline 137, Hunting 227, Medical corps 269,
    Religion 375, Sources 407, 408
Larisa [3]*, Larissa   Consequences of war 105,
    Generals of note 204
Lasithi/Dicte (mountain range)   Consequences of war 105
Latium   Army 27, Descriptions of war 129,
    Diplomacy 133, Enemies 161, Generals of note 201,
    Law of war 249
Lauriacum*   Armament 18, Borders 76
Laurium*   Consequences of war 105, Fleet 173,
    War 490
Lavinium*   Religion 371
Lechaeum*   Infantry 229, Mercenaries 272
Lelantine Plain (Lelantion pedion*)   Alliances 11,
    Army 23, Consequences of war 104, Innovation 238,
    War 489
Le Mans   Fortification 182
Lemnos*   Administration 3
Lepreum*   Slavery 393
Leptis Magna*   Borders 74, Descriptions of war 124
    – Arch of Septimius Severus   Representations of
      war 384, Representations of war 384
Lesbos*   Alliances 12
    – Messon   Borders 69
Leucas, Leucadia*   Battles of note 53
Leuctra*   Army 24, Battle 46, 47, Cavalry 87,
    Education 141, Generals of note 196, Innovation 238,
    Motivation 304, Phalanx 335, Religion 368, 370,
    Slavery 394, Society and army 397, Sparta 415,
    Strategy 437, Transmission of orders 460, War 491
Levant   Chariot 90, Fleet 171, 172, Innovation 241, Wars
    of note 498
Lilybaeum*   Empire 152, Siege warfare 392
Limes*   Army 29, Borders 76, Fortification 182,
    Innovation 240, Policing 336
    – Danube Limes   Army 34
    – Upper Germanic-Rhaetian   Borders 74, 75
Limnae [2]*   Sparta 414
Lindus*   Borders 69, Costs of war 113
Lippe   Medical corps 270

Lisus, Lissus*   Acropolis 1
Liternum*   Generals of note 207
Loire   Generals of note 190
Long Walls   Descriptions of war 127, Fortification 180,
    Strategy 437
Lower Egypt   Administration 4
Lower Rhine   Enemies 162, Infrastructure 232,
    Mutiny 312
Lucania (Lucani, Lucania*)   Scorched earth 388
Lugdunum*/Lyon   Military diploma 278, Militia 299,
    Mutiny 313
Lusitania (Lusitani, Lusitania*)   Enemies 162,
    Rear 355
Lycia et Pamphylia*   Recruitment 366
Lycia (Lycii, Lycia*; see also Lycia et Pamphylia)
    Empire 154, Motivation 301, Rear 356
Lyctus, Lyttus*   Alliances 13
Lycus [19]* (river)   Wars of note 506
Lydia*   Army 26, Battles of note 58, Wars of note 497,
    512
Lyncus*, Lyncestis   Elephants 143, Generals of
    note 203
Lysimachia [1]*   Alliances 13

Maas   Infrastructure 232
Macaria [3]*   Consequences of war 104
Macedonia (Macedonia, Macedones*)   Alliances 12,
    Army 25, 27, Bandits 44, Battles of note 53,
    Cavalry 86, 87, Customs of war 118, Empire 153, Esprit
    de corps 168, Fleet 177, Garrison 185, Generals of
    note 195, 203, 204, Guards 210, Infrastructure 232,
    Innovation 239, 241, 243, Mercenaries 273, Military
    service 291, Motivation 305, Officers 316, Pay 325,
    Phalanx 333, Policing 337, Recruitment 363,
    Slavery 394, Society and army 398, State and
    army 428, Symbols 447, War 491, Wars of note 497,
    513
Magna Graecia*   Consequences of war 110,
    General 186
Magnesia [2]*   Dogs 139
Magnesia [3]*   Army 26, Battle 48, Battles of note 58,
    Camels 79, Chariot 91, Elephants 143, Generals of
    note 207, Honour 219, Mercenaries 273
Mainz (Mogontiacum*)   Armament 18, 19, Borders 77,
    Camp 85, Descriptions of war 124, Fortification 182,
    Production system 341, 342, Sources 407
    – Drususstein   Death 120
Mainz-Weisenau   Armament 19, Death 119
Maiozamalcha, Maogamalcha   Honours 225, Wars of
    note 511
Malla   Alliances 13
Mannheim   Armament 19
Mantinea*   Alliances 12, Battle 46, Booty 69,
    Borders 71, Customs of war 118, Discipline 136,
    Education 141, Emotions 147, 149, Equipment 164,
    Generals of note 196, Heroism 215, Innovation 238,
    Military service 294, Society and army 398,
    Sparta 415, Transmission of orders 460, Wars of
    note 508

GEOGRAPHICAL INDEX

Marathon* Army 23, Battle 46, 52, Battles of note 59, 63, Camp 80, Customs of war 117, Descriptions of war 123, Dogs 139, Emotions 148, Generals of note 199, March 263, Military service 291, 293, 294, Parades 321, Pay 324, Phalanx 334, Religion 369, 370, Representations of war 380, Slavery 393, Sources 402, 405, 406, Strategy 436, War 490, Wars of note 512
– **Sanctuary of Heracles** Battles of note 59, Camp 80
Marcomannic Kingdom (Marcomanni*) Empire 154
Mardia Generals of note 200
Marktbreit Supply 444
Maronea [1]* Alliances 14
Masada* Prisoners 338, Sources 402, Wars of note 505
Massilia (Massalia*) Borders 73, Fleet 173, 176
Mauretania* Auxiliaries 38, Empire 154, Generals of note 201, Rank 347
Mauretania Caesariensis Empire 154, Veterans 476, Sources 408
Mauretania Tingitana Auxiliaries 39, Borders 74, Civilians 98, Empire 154, Medical corps 269, Veterans 476, Rear 355, Recruitment 366
Mayen Fortification 183
Media* Borders 71, General 189
Mediterranean Sea (Mare Nostrum*) Army 26, Cavalry 87, 88, Civil war 94, Diplomacy 132, 133, Empire 153, Esprit de corps 168, Fleet 171, 177, 178, Generals of note 201, 205, 208, Honours 221, Innovation 243, Military literature 285, Motivation 306, Peace 329, 331, Prisoners 338, Rear 354, Religion 376, Supply 445, Timeframe of war 455, Veterans 472, War 489, 490, Wars of note 516
Megalopolis* Booty 69, Camp 80, Consequences of war 103, Slavery 395
Megara [2]* Battles of note 62, Borders 70, 71, Fleet 174, Parades 321, Religion 368, Sources 406, Wars of note 507, 508, 510
Megaris Borders 71, Wars of note 508
Megiddo* Army 22
Melos [1]* Consequences of war 103, Law of war 248, Peace 330, Wars of note 508
Memphis* Army 31, Elephants 144, Empire 151
Meroë Elephants 144
Mesoa* Sparta 414
Mesopotamia* Battles of note 56, Borders 76, Chariot 90, Empire 154, Generals of note 198, Reconnaissance 358, Strategy 438
Messana, Messene [1]*/Messina Consequences of war 103, 104, Empire 152, Generals of note 196, Peace 331, Strategy 437, Wars of note 513
Messenia (Messana, Messena [2]*) Borders 69, Consequences of war 103, 104, Sparta 414, 415, State and army 426, War 489, Wars of note 508
Methone [3]* Consequences of war 103, Customs of war 118, Generals of note 204, Peace 330
Methymna* Booty 66
Middle East Legion 255

Middle Egypt Army 26, Society and army 399
Milan (Mediolan(i)um*) Cavalry 89, Fleet 179, Generals of note 191, 208, Guards 213
Miletus [2]* Colonies 100, Fleet 173, Wars of note 497, 508, 512
Milvian Bridge Battles of note 60, Generals of note 200, 201, Religion 378, Symbols 449
Misenum* Army 29, Infrastructure 231, Marriage 265, Military diploma 277, Militia 300, Officers 318, Pay 327, Rank 348, Sources 407, Supply 443
Mitanni (Mittani*) Chariot 90, Infrastructure 232
Moesia (Moesi, Moesia*; see also Moesia superior, Moesia inferior, Moesia II) Consequences of war 110, Rank 347, Sources 407, Wars of note 501
Moesia II Rear 355
Moesia inferior Borders 76, Policing 337, Recruitment 366, Wars of note 501
Moesia superior Recruitment 365
Mons Amanus Descriptions of war 124
Mons Graupius* Chariot 91, Infantry 230
Montana* Hunting 226, Policing 336
Monte Cavo (Mons Albanus*) Religion 371
Montefortino Armament 19
Morocco Artillery 37
Mosel (Mosella*) Fortification 182, Infrastructure 232
Motya*/Mozia Innovation 241, Siege warfare 390
Munichia, Munychia Camp 80, Garrison 184, Infrastructure 231
Mycale* (mountain range) Battles of note 63, Fleet 173, War 490, Wars of note 512, 513
Mycene (Mycenae*) Army 22, War 488
Mylae [2]* Descriptions of war 123, Sources 406
Myonnesus* Consequences of war 111
Mysia* Army 26
Mytilene* Alliances 14, Consequences of war 103, Customs of war 118, Generals of note 193, Peace 330, Wars of note 508

Nabataea, Nabataean Kingdom Borders 73, Empire 154
Nacone* Civil war 91
Naḥal Ḥever Wars of note 500
Naissus* Generals of note 200
Naples, Gulf/Bay of Infrastructure 231
Naples (Neapolis [2]*) Fleet 178
Narbonne (Narbo*) Generals of note 190
Narmuthis Rank 351
Naulochus* Fleet 178
Nauportus [1]* Armament 18
Naxos [1]* Wars of note 512
Nea Halos Acropolis 1, Army 22, Battles of note 53, Colonies 100, Empire 150, Phalanx 335
Nemea [2]* Battle 46, Enemies 158, Sparta 415
Nesactium* Booty 66
Nessana Sources 412
Newcastle upon Tyne Borders 74
Newstead Armament 18, 21

Nicomedia* Marriage 266
Nicopolis [3]* Battles of note 54, Descriptions of war 124
Niederbieber Armament 19, Standard 424, Transmission of orders 461
Nijmegen Borders 77, Death 119
Nile* Army 26, Civilians 97, Fleet 171, 174, Infrastructure 232, Sources 410
Nîmes (Nemausus [2]*) Fortification 181
– **City wall** Fortification 181
Nimrud (Kalḫu*) Enemies 157
Nisibis* Battle 45, Elephants 145, Wars of note 512
Noricum* Borders 76, Generals of note 190, 203, 209
North Africa Battles of note 53, Borders 74, Empire 154, Fleet 176, 179, Generals of note 190, 208, Innovation 240, Legion 255, Marriage 266, Medical corps 269, Motivation 305, Rear 354, Religion 375, Strategy 437
North Atlantic Ocean Fleet 171
Northeastern Peloponnese Borders 71
Northern Aegean Fleet 174, 176, Generals of note 199
Northern Europe Society and army 399
Northern Greece Wars of note 512, 513
Northern Italy Battles of note 60, Fortification 181, Generals of note 191, Legion 255
Northern Mesopotamia Generals of note 202, Scorched earth 388
Northern Syria Army 26, Borders 71, 76
North Sea (Mare Germanicum*) Fleet 178, Infrastructure 232, Strategy 437
Notium* Wars of note 508
Novae [1]* Religion 376
Novaesium* Medical corps 270
Nubia* Borders 71, Sources 411
Numantia* Consequences of war 110, Discipline 137, Enemies 160, Generals of note 201, Honour 219, Peace 331, Slavery 396, Victory titles 485
Numidia (Numidae, Numidia*) Administration 7, Auxiliaries 37, Borders 73, Elephants 144, Generals of note 201, Sources 407, Veterans 476, Rank 347, Rear 355, Sources 407
Nursia* Descriptions of war 123
Nuzi* Chariot 90
Nydam Armament 18
Nyon Militia 300

Odenwald Production system 342
Oenoe [4]* Borders 71
Oenophyta* Mutiny 311
Olbia [1]* Slavery 395
Oltenia Wars of note 501
Olympia* Enemies 158, Law of war 247, Military service 292, Victory 478, Religion 371, Representations of war 380, Sources 404, 406
– **Megarian Treasury** Representations of war 380
– **Nike of Paeonius** Representations of war 380
Olynthus* Enemies 158, Generals of note 204, Supply 441

Ophir Fleet 171
Opis [3]* Generals of note 192, Mutiny 310, Wars of note 500
Orăștie (mountain range) Wars of note 501
Orchomenus [1]* Alliances 13, Battle 45, Enemies 158
Orient Army 34, Borders 75, 77, Innovation 240, Language 245, Representations of war 384, Standard 422, Victory titles 484
Orontes [7]* (river) Infrastructure 232, Wars of note 507
Oropus* Borders 70
Orșova Artillery 36
Osroene* Cavalry 89
Osterburken Armament 18, Policing 337, Religion 376, 377, Sources 407
Ostia* Fleet 179
– **Augusteum** Religion 375
– **Claudian Portus** Consequences of war 111
Oxyrhynchus* Sources 412

Palaemagnesia Policing 336
Palaestina*, Palestine Camels 79, Consequences of war 110, March 263, Wars of note 507, Rear 355, Wars of note 506, 507
Pallantia March 262
Palmyra* Camels 79, Cavalry 89, Militia 300, Wars of note 506
Pamisos [1]* (river) Consequences of war 104
Pamphylia* Fleet 173, Rear 356, Generals of note 199
Panactum* Borders 71, Education 140, Supply 439, Supply 439, 441
Pangaeum* (mountain range) Army 24, Fleet 174, Generals of note 204
Panium Elephants 143
Pannonia* Auxiliaries 37, Empire 154, Generals of note 191, Mutiny 312, Sources 407, Recruitment 366, Supply 444, Veterans 475
Pannonia inferior Auxiliaries 40, Bandits 44, Death 120, Garrison 185
Pannonia superior Civil war 95, Garrison 185
Panormus [3]* Elephants 143, Peace 330
Paraetacene* Elephants 143
Parma* Descriptions of war 123, Infrastructure 232
Parnassus* (mountain range) Borders 70
Parnes* (mountain range) Borders 70
Paros* Victory 478
Parthia*, Parthian Empire Diplomacy 133, Empire 154, Innovation 239, Peace 331, Rear 356, Victory titles 484, War 493
Patara* Wars of note 505
Patroklou charax Camp 80
Peloponnese (Peloponnesus*) Alliances 11, Borders 70, Cavalry 86, Consequences of war 106, Equipment 164, Fleet 175, Generals of note 196, 208, Sparta 413, Strategy 436, Wars of note 513
Pelusium* Borders 71

Pergamene Kingdom/Attalid Kingdom Society and army 398
– **Sanctuary of Athena** Representations of war 382
Pergamum* Battles of note 59, Empire 153, Fleet 176, Representations of war 382, Transmission of orders 461, Victory titles 485, War 489, Wars of note 505
Perge* Rank 349, 353
Perinthus* Consequences of war 106, Dogs 139
Persepolis* Empire 151, Wars of note 498
Persian Gulf Army 26, Fleet 175
Persia, Persian Empire (Persis*) Alliances 10, 12, 13, Army 24, Battles of note 63, Borders 76, Consequences of war 108, Diplomacy 131, Discipline 135, Empire 151, Enemies 158, Fleet 173, 174, 175, Garrison 184, General 187, Generals of note 191, 208, Infrastructure 232, Mercenaries 273, Mutiny 311, Pay 324, 325, Phalanx 335, Reconnaissance 362, Representations of war 385, Strategy 437, Wars of note 497, 498, 506, 508, 510
Persis Army 26
Perugia (Perusia*) Civil war 94, Infantry 230
Petra [1]* Education 142, Sources 412
Petra [3]* Innovation 243
Phalerum* Battles of note 62
Pharmacussa Battles of note 62
Pharos
– **Lighthouse** Consequences of war 111, Infrastructure 231
Pharos [2]* Alliances 14
Pharsalus* Battles of note 61, Consequences of war 109, Generals of note 193, 205, Heroism 216, Victory titles 486
Phasis [1]* (river) Wars of note 506
Pherae* Generals of note 204
Philadelphia [4]* Veterans 476
Philae* Rank 345
Philetaerea Mutiny 311, Supply 442
Philippi* Generals of note 204, Guards 210, Policing 337, Slavery 396, Veterans 474
Phocaea* Booty 66, Consequences of war 104, Fleet 173
Phocis* Borders 71
Phoenicia Fleet 171, 172, Sources 406
Phrygia (Phryges, Phrygia*) Army 26, Wars of note 498
Phrygius (river) Battles of note 58
Phthiotis* Siege warfare 392
Phyle [2]* Borders 71, Supply 439, 441
Piazza Armerina* Hunting 227
Picenum (Picentes, Picenum*) Generals of note 205
Piraeus* Battles of note 62, Camp 80, Consequences of war 106, Fleet 173, Fortification 180, Infrastructure 231
– **Arsenal of Philo** Sources 405, Parades 322, Strategy 437, War 490
Pi-Ramesses Chariot 90
Pirisabora Wars of note 511

Pisidia* Elephants 143
Pistoria (Pistoriae*) Education 141
Pitana* Sparta 414
Pityus* Artillery 36
Pizus Rear 355
Placentia*/Piacenza Colonies 100
Plataeae* Alliances 11, 12, Army 23, Battle 47, 52, Battles of note 59, 62, Camels 79, Customs of war 117, 118, Emotions 149, Enemies 158, 159, Equipment 164, Fleet 173, Heroism 215, Military service 291, 293, Siege warfare 390, Oath 314, Peace 330, Religion 369, 370, Slavery 393, 394, Society and army 398, Sources 406, Sparta 414, 415, War 490, Wars of note 508, 513
Poetovio* Motivation 307
Poitiers (Lemonum*) Militia 301
Pollentia [1]* Generals of note 208
Pompeii* Armament 18, Costs of war 114
– **Alexander Mosaic** Representations of war 381
Pontine Marshes Infrastructure 232
Pontus* (see also Bithynia et Pontus) Consequences of war 110, Empire 153, Strategy 438, Supply 443, War 492, Wars of note 505
Po (Padus*) Alliances 14, Empire 153
Portus Iulius Infrastructure 231
Potidaea*/Cassandrea Army 25, Consequences of war 103, Customs of war 118, Fleet 174, Military service 293, 294, Peace 330, Wars of note 507, 508
Priene* Acropolis 1
Propontis* Fleet 179
Provincia Insularum Rear 355
Pselchis Language 246
Psophis* Borders 70
Ptolemaic Kingdom Borders 71, Mercenaries 274
Ptolemais [6]* Thērṓn Hunting 226
Punt* Fleet 171
Pydna* Army 25, Battle 47, Booty 68, Consequences of war 107, 108, Empire 153, Equipment 165, Generals of note 204, Innovation 239, Society and army 398, War 492
Pylos [2]* Army 22, Camp 80, Chariot 91, Wars of note 510, Peace 330, Wars of note 508
Pyrenees Borders 73, Enemies 161, Representations of war 382

Qadesh* Army 22, Enemies 156

Raetia, Rhaetia (Raeti, Raetia*) Borders 74, 75, 76, Descriptions of war 125, Generals of note 190, 202, 203, 208, Militia 300, Rear 355
Ravenna* Army 29, Death 119, Fleet 179, Generals of note 190, 209, Infrastructure 231, Marriage 265, Military diploma 277, Officers 318, Pay 327, Rank 348, Supply 443
Red Sea (Erythra thalatta*) Borders 76, Elephants 144, Fleet 171, 176, 178, Infrastructure 232, Sources 410

Regillus (Lacus Regillus*; lake)   Religion 372
Regina Castra*/Regensburg   Borders 76, Medical corps 270
Rhamnous, Rhamnus*   Acropolis 1, Borders 71, Education 140, Supply 441
Rhaphia*   Army 26, Death 120, Elephants 143, Mercenaries 273, Phalanx 335, Recruitment 363, Victory titles 484
Rhine (Rhenus [2]*; river)   Auxiliaries 38, Battles of note 54, 63, 64, Borders 74, 75, 76, 77, Camp 82, 85, Cavalry 89, Consequences of war 107, Descriptions of war 124, Elite troops 145, Empire 153, 154, 155, Fleet 178, Fortification 181, Generals of note 198, 202, 208, 209, Guards 212, Infrastructure 231, 232, 234, Innovation 238, 240, Legion 255, March 262, Medical corps 270, Military literature 288, Military service 298, Mutiny 312, Production system 341, Rear 355, Reconnaissance 362, Representations of war 386, Slavery 395, Strategy 437, Supply 444, Veterans 476, Victory titles 486, Wars of note 502, 504
Rhizus, Rhizous   March 263
Rhodes (Rhodos*)   Artillery 35, Battles of note 59, Borders 69, Civil war 91, Diplomacy 132, Empire 153, Fleet 173, 176, Generals of note 195, Infrastructure 231, 232, Innovation 241, Military literature 287, Parades 321, Representations of war 382, Siege warfare 390, Slavery 395, War 492, Wars of note 505
Rhône (Rhodanus*; river)   Infrastructure 232, Supply 443
Rigodulum*   Valour 469
Rimini (Ariminum*)   Generals of note 190
Roman Empire (Roma*; see also Eastern Roman Empire, Western Roman Empire)
  Administration 5, Alliances 10, Army 22, 30, Auxiliaries 37, 39, 41, Avoidance of military service 42, Bandits 44, Battle 48, 50, Battles of note 54, 55, 57, 59, 63, 64, Booty 65, 67, 69, Borders 74, 75, 76, 77, Cavalry 88, Civilians 97, Consequences of war 107, Costs of war 114, 115, Descriptions of war 123, 124, 125, 128, 129, Diplomacy 132, 133, Discipline 137, Education 143, Elephants 144, Elite troops 145, Emotions 146, Empire 152, 153, 154, Enemies 159, 160, 161, 162, Fleet 176, 177, Fortification 180, Garrison 185, General 186, 188, Generals of note 197, 198, 201, 202, 207, Heroism 216, Hostages 225, Infrastructure 232, Innovation 236, 237, 239, 242, 243, Law of war 247, 248, 249, 251, Legion 252, 255, Military literature 285, 287, Military service 295, 297, Motivation 305, 306, Oath 314, Officers 317, Peace 328, 329, 331, Policing 336, Prisoners 339, 340, Rear 356, Reconnaissance 359, 360, 362, Recruitment 364, 366, Religion 377, Representations of war 385, Siege warfare 392, Slavery 395, Society and army 399, Specialists 418, State and army 428, 429, 430, 431, 432, Strategy 434, 437, 438, Supply 444, Terror 453, Timeframe of war 454, Valour 470, Veterans 473, Victory 481, Victory titles 485, War 492, 493, 494, 495, Wars of note 500, 501, 504, 505, 506, 513

Rome (Roma*)   Administration 6, 7, Alliances 13, 14, Army 28, 29, Avoidance of military service 42, Battle 52, Battles of note 60, Booty 66, Borders 73, 76, Camp 82, Cavalry 88, Civil war 93, 94, 95, Consequences of war 107, 108, 110, 111, Death 120, Descriptions of war 124, Discipline 137, Empire 152, Enemies 161, 162, General 186, 189, Generals of note 191, 194, 200, 202, 208, Guards 211, 212, Honour 219, 220, Honours 223, 225, Hostages 225, Hunting 226, Infantry 229, Innovation 237, 240, Law of war 250, Medical corps 269, Military diploma 275, 276, 278, Military service 297, Militia 299, 300, Motivation 305, 306, 307, Mutiny 312, 313
 – **Amphitheatrum Flavium/Colosseum**   Descriptions of war 124
 – **Apollo magnus (statue on Capitol)**   Military diploma 276
 – **Aqua Virgo**   Officers 318
 – **Arch of Constantine**   Battles of note 61, Descriptions of war 124, Prisoners 339, Representations of war 383, Triumph 465
 – **Arch of Janus**   Legion 254
 – **Arch of Marcus Aurelius**   Representations of war 383
 – **Arch of Septimius Severus**   Officers 318, Parades 320, 321, 322, Pay 326, Peace 330, 331, Phalanx 335, Policing 336, Rank 346, 347, Religion 372, 373, 374, 377, 378, Representations of war 382, 384, Scorched earth 388, Slavery 395, Society and army 399, Standard 423, 424, State and army 429, 430, 431, Symbols 450, Transmission of orders 462, Triumph 462, 463, 464, 465, Victory 479, 481, Victory titles 485, Wars of note 501, 504
 – **Aurelian Walls**   Fortification 182, Guards 211
 – **Aventine Hill**   Religion 373
 – **Bridge of Gratian (Pons Gratiani)**   Victory titles 487
 – **Caelian Hill**   Guards 211, 212
 – **Capitol, Capitoline Hill**   Consequences of war 111, Honours 222, Military diploma 276, Religion 371, 373, 378, Triumph 462, 463, Victory 479
 – **Casa Romuli**   Military diploma 276
 – **Circus Maximus**   Consequences of war 111, Triumph 463
 – **Clivus Capitolinus**   Triumph 463
 – **Curia Iulia**   Enemies 161, Victory 481
 – **Field of Mars (Campus Martius)**   Honours 221, Religion 372, State and army 430, Symbols 449, Triumph 462, 463
 – **Forum Boarium**   Triumph 463
 – **Forum of Augustus (Forum Augustum)**   Honour 219, Honours 223, Triumph 465

- Forum of Caesar (Forum Caesaris/Iulium) Religion 373
- Forum of Trajan (Forum Traiani) Descriptions of war 124, Prisoners 339, Triumph 465, Wars of note 502
- Forum Romanum Religion 373, Triumph 463, Victory 480
- Forum Romanum, Parthian Arch Descriptions of war 124
- Forum Romanum, Rostra Descriptions of war 123
- Gemonian Stairs (Scalae Gemoniae) Wars of note 502
- Lateran Cavalry 88
- Lateran Basilica Guards 212
- Marcus Aurelius Column Enemies 161, Prisoners 339, Representations of war 384
- Minerva Statue Military diploma 276
- Palatine Hill Guards 211
- Porta Capena Honour 219
- Regia Religion 372
- Severan Walls Fortification 181
- Tabularium Military diploma 276
- Temple of Bellona Religion 372, 374
- Temple of Castor and Pollux Religion 373
- Temple of Fortuna Consequences of war 111
- Temple of Hercules Victor Triumph 465
- Temple of Juno Religion 373
- Temple of Jupiter Feretrius Religion 374
- Temple of Jupiter Optimus Maximus Consequences of war 111, Triumph 462, 463
- Temple of Mars Ultor Descriptions of war 124, Religion 373
- Temple of Mater Matuta Consequences of war 111
- Temple of Peace (Templum Pacis) Consequences of war 111, Descriptions of war 124, Wars of note 505
- Tomb of Germanicus (in the Mausoleum of Augustus) Battle 52
- Tomb of Marcus Claudius Fronto Motivation 305
- Tombstone of Gaius Vedennius Moderatus Artillery 35
- Trajan Column Armament 17, Artillery 36, Booty 68, Descriptions of war 124, Enemies 161, Equipment 165, Fortification 181, Military literature 287, Prisoners 339, Representations of war 383, Siege warfare 393, Standard 421, 423
- Velabrum Triumph 463
- Velia Triumph 463
- Via Lata Officers 318
- Via Triumphalis Victory 480
- Viminal Hill Guards 211
Rough Castle Borders 75

Saalburg* Fortification 181
Sagalassus* Recruitment 366
Sagra* (river) Honour 218
Saguntum* Fleet 176, Generals of note 197, Wars of note 516, Reconnaissance 359
Saint-Bertrand-de-Comminges Fortification 182
Sala [2]* Civilians 98
Salamis [1]* Battles of note 62, Enemies 159, Equipment 165, Fleet 173, Generals of note 195, 199, Heroism 215, Innovation 241, Siege warfare 389, Sources 402, 405, 406, War 489, 490, Wars of note 513
Saldae* Sources 408
Samarra* Wars of note 512
Samos* Consequences of war 103, Costs of war 113, Fleet 172, Garrison 184, Infrastructure 231, Innovation 239, Peace 330, Sources 405, Symbols 447, War 490
- Heraeum Sources 406
Samothrace* Consequences of war 105
- Winged Victory (statue of Nike) Representations of war 382
Samum Policing 336
Saône (Arar*; river) Infrastructure 232, Supply 443
Sapaudia* Generals of note 190
Sardeis*, Sardes, Sardis Camels 79, Diplomacy 131, Empire 151, Wars of note 512
Sardinia* Consequences of war 111, Dogs 139, Empire 152, Fleet 171, Supply 443, Recruitment 366, Supply 442, Wars of note 513
Sarmizegetusa Regia Wars of note 502
Saronic Gulf (Saronikos Kolpos*) Battles of note 62, Infrastructure 232, Wars of note 507
Sassanid Empire Generals of note 198, 200, Rear 356, Wars of note 511
Satricum* Siege warfare 392
Sava (Savus*; river) Empire 154
Scamander* (river) Emotions 147
Schinias Camp 80
Sciritis* Sparta 414
Scotland Empire 154
Scyros* Generals of note 199
Scythia* Bandits 44, Rear 355
Scythopolis (Beisan*) Wars of note 501
Segesta [1]* Wars of note 508
Seleucia [1]* Magna Consequences of war 111, War 489
Seleucia [2]* Pieria Rear 355, Victory titles 484
Seleucia [5]* ad Calychadnum Military literature 288
Seleucid Empire Battles of note 56, Borders 71, Civil war 91, Empire 153, General 189, Hunting 226, Policing 336
Selinus* Wars of note 508
Sellasia* Battle 48, 49, Sparta 416
Sentinum* Chariot 91, Consequences of war 108, Heroism 216
Sicily (Sicilia*) Alliances 14, Civil war 94, Consequences of war 104, Costs of war 112, 114, Customs of war 118, Descriptions of war 126, 127, Empire 150, 152, Enemies 158, Fleet 175, 176, Fortification 181, General 187, 189, Generals of

note 193, 200, 205, 207, Honours 221, Motivation 305, Religion 368, Siege warfare 390, 392, Slavery 394, Supply 442, Symbols 447, Veterans 473, 475, War 491, Wars of note 513
Sicyon*   Officers 316
Sidon*   Fleet 171, Representations of war 381
Sinai*   Borders 71
Singara*   Wars of note 512
Sinope*   Wars of note 506
Sirmium*   Policing 337, Sources 407, Victory 481
Siwa (Ammoneion*)   Religion 368, War 489
Sogdiana*   Battle 48, Generals of note 191, Wars of note 498
Soli [2]*   Victory 479
Solygea   Battle 51
Somalia   Fleet 171
South Asia   Victory titles 484
Southern Anatolia   Fleet 171, 172
Southern Arabia   Borders 76, Fleet 178
Southern Crete   Fleet 171
Southern Gaul   Dogs 139, Legion 255
Southern Greece   Generals of note 204
Southern Italy   Alliances 11, Civil war 91, Consequences of war 107, Elephants 143, Rank 346, Sources 409
South Shields   Supply 445
Spain (see also Hispania, Hispania citerior, Hispania ulterior)   Army 29, Battles of note 60, Booty 69, Consequences of war 108, 110, 111, Education 141, Elephants 144, Enemies 161, Fleet 171, 176, 178, 179, Generals of note 200, 205, 206, 208, Heroism 216, March 264, Motivation 305, Parades 321, Peace 330, Reconnaissance 359, Representations of war 382, Siege warfare 392, Society and army 399, Sources 409, Strategy 437, Society and army 399, Supply 443, 442, Terror 453, Timeframe of war 455, Wars of note 506
Sparta*   Administration 2, 3, Alliances 11, 12, Army 23, Battle 47, Booty 65, Borders 69, 70, 71, Cavalry 87, Costs of war 112, Cowardice 116, Customs of war 117, Discipline 135, Education 140, 141, Empire 150, Enemies 158, Esprit de corps 168, Fleet 173, 175, Fortification 180, Garrison 184, General 186, Generals of note 196, 199, Guards 209, Heroism 215, Honour 218, Law of war 247, 248, March 261, 263, Mercenaries 272, Military law 281, Military literature 286, Military service 291, Motivation 302, Mutiny 310, Parades 321, 322, Pay 325, Peace 329, 330, 331, Phalanx 333, 334, Recruitment 363, Religion 368, 370, Representations of war 380, Slavery 393, 394, Society and army 397, Sources 402, 404, 408, Specialists 417, State and army 426, 427, Strategy 436, 437, Timeframe of war 454, Valour 467, Vehicles 471, War 489, 490, 491, 492, Wars of note 507, 508, 510, 512
Sphacteria*   Fleet 174, Infantry 229, Innovation 238, Military service 291, 294, Sparta 414, War 490
Split (Spalatum*)   Fleet 179
Stanegate   Borders 74
Stenyclarus*   Consequences of war 104

Stobi   Supply 444
Strait of Otranto   Fleet 178
Strasbourg (Argentorate*)   Battle 51
Stratos*   Acropolis 1
Straubing   Armament 18
Stymphalus*   Consequences of war 103
Styria, Steiermark   Production system 342
Suedra   Recruitment 366
Sunium* (cape)   Borders 71
Susa*   Empire 151, Wars of note 498
Susiana*   Supply 441
Sybaris [4]*   Alliances 11, Consequences of war 103
Syene*   Army 34, Camels 79, Garrison 184, Rank 345, 349
Symaethum*   March 263
Syracuse (Syracusae*)   Auxiliaries 37, Borders 70, Cavalry 86, Civil war 91, Empire 152, Enemies 158, Fleet 173, 175, 176, Fortification 180, General 189, Honour 219, Innovation 241, 243, March 260, 263, Military literature 287, Officers 316, Prisoners 338, Recruitment 363, Religion 369, Siege warfare 392, Slavery 394, Sources 409, Strategy 435, Supply 441, Veterans 475, Victory 478, War 491, Wars of note 508, 510, 516
– Euryalus Fortress   Fortification 180
Syria*   Administration 8, Army 29, Auxiliaries 39, Battles of note 54, Borders 71, Camels 79, Consequences of war 108, Descriptions of war 125, Empire 153, 154, Enemies 156, Fleet 177, 178, Garrison 185, Generals of note 194, 202, Militia 300, Rank 347, Rear 355, Reconnaissance 360, Religion 376, Sources 407, 410, Strategy 435, 438, Timeframe of war 454, Wars of note 498, 505, 506
Syria-Palaestina   Auxiliaries 39, Death 120, Recruitment 366, Supply 443

Tacape*   Borders 74
Taenarum [1]* (headland)   Mercenaries 274
Tamugadi   Descriptions of war 125
Tanagra*   Sources 406
Tapae*   Wars of note 501
Tarentum/Taranto (Taras [2]*)   Booty 69, Enemies 161, Generals of note 197, Siege warfare 392
Tarraco*   Supply 443
Tarsus*   Rear 355
Taunus* (mountain range)   Borders 75, Battles of note 59, Wars of note 507
Tegea [1]*   Alliances 11, Military service 294
Telmessus*   Recruitment 366
Tel Shalem   Descriptions of war 125, Wars of note 501
Teutoburg Forest (Saltus Teutoburgiensis*)   Battle 53, Battles of note 63, 64, Consequences of war 107, 110, Death 120, Empire 154, Guards 211, Honour 220, Legion 255, Officers 319, Slavery 395, Strategy 435, 438
Thalamae [2]*
– Fortress   Consequences of war 103
Thapsus [2]*   Elephants 144

GEOGRAPHICAL INDEX

Thasos*   Colonies 100, Consequences of war 104, Fleet 173, Generals of note 199, Infrastructure 231, Peace 330, Supply 439
Thebaid, Thebais   Administration 4, Camels 79
Thebes [1]*   Camels 79, Officers 316, Religion 370, Slavery 393, War 491
Thebes [2]*   Alliances 10, Army 24, Battle 47, Education 141, Elite troops 145, Emotions 149, Equipment 164, Esprit de corps 168, Fleet 175, Generals of note 196, 203, Innovation 236, Military service 292, 294
Thelphusa*   Borders 70
Thera*   Colonies 100
Thermaic Gulf (Thermaios Kolpos*)   Generals of note 204
Thermopylae*   Battle 46, Battles of note 58, Borders 70, Customs of war 117, Elephants 143, Elite troops 145, Heroism 214, Honour 218, Military service 293, Sparta 414, Symbols 447, Wars of note 513
Thermus*
  – Temple of Apollo   Booty 66
Thespia*   Military service 294
Thessalonica*/Thessaloniki   Militia 301
  – Arch of Galerius   Representations of war 384
Thessaly (Thessali, Thessalia*)   Battles of note 63, Camels 79, Cavalry 86, Costs of war 112, Fleet 175, Generals of note 204, 205, Honour 218, Infantry 229, Officers 316, Phalanx 333, Recruitment 363, Society and army 397, Wars of note 513
Thoricus*   Borders 71
Thracia*, Thrace   Auxiliaries 38, 40, Bandits 44, Battles of note 54, Colonies 100, Descriptions of war 127, Empire 154, Generals of note 191, 199, 204, 208, Infantry 229, Infrastructure 233, Mercenaries 272, Phalanx 333, Policing 337, Rear 355, Recruitment 366, Slavery 393, Sources 408
Thyreatic Plain   Army 23
Thyreatis   Borders 70, War 489
Thyrrheum*   Alliances 14
Tiber (Tiberis*; river)   Battles of note 60, Empire 152
Ticino (Ticinus*; river)   Generals of note 206
Ticinum*   Generals of note 209
Tigranocerta*   Wars of note 506
Tigris*   Generals of note 198, Rear 355, Reconnaissance 362, Strategy 437, War 489, Wars of note 511
Timavo (Timavus*; river)   Generals of note 208
Timgad   Discipline 137
Tours   Militia 301
Transpadana*   Production system 341
Trasimene (Lacus Trasumenus*; lake)   Booty 68, Consequences of war 110, Generals of note 197, March 260, Reconnaissance 360, Scorched earth 388
Trastevere   Guards 211
Trebia* (river)   Elephants 143, Generals of note 197
Trebizond, Trapezus*   March 263, Scorched earth 388
Tridentum*/Trent   Consequences of war 108, Supply 443

Trier (Augusta [6]* Treverorum)   Fortification 182, Generals of note 200
  – Porta Nigra   Fortification 181
Triphylia*   Borders 70
Troad*   Wars of note 497
Tropaeum Alpium (Tropaea Augusti*; near Monaco)   Descriptions of war 124, Enemies 161
Troy*   Acropolis 1, Alliances 10, Camp 80, Descriptions of war 126, Discipline 134, Emotions 147, Enemies 161, Law of war 247, Motivation 301
  – Acropolis   Acropolis 1, Representations of war 380, War 489
  – Temple of Athena   Acropolis 1
Turin (Augusta [5]* Taurinorum)   Battles of note 60, Generals of note 200
Tuscany   Generals of note 209
Tusculum*   Religion 372
Tyana*   Wars of note 507
Tyriaeum*   Equipment 164
Tyrrhenian Sea (Mare Tyrrhenum*)   Army 29, Fleet 173, 176, 179
Tyrus*/Tyre   Consequences of war 103, Fleet 171, 172, 175, Generals of note 191, Infrastructure 232, Innovation 241, Siege warfare 390, Timeframe of war 454, War 489, Wars of note 498

Uchi maius*   Descriptions of war 125
Ulcisia Castra   Death 120
Upper Egypt   Administration 4, Army 26
Upper Macedonia   Generals of note 203
Ur*   Chariot 90
Urso*   Conscription 102
Utica*   Siege warfare 392
Uxellodunum [1]*   Wars of note 502

Valence (Valentia [2]*)   Generals of note 190
Vallum Aelium   Borders 74
Veii*   Booty 67, Costs of war 114, Descriptions of war 129, Heroism 215, Pay 326, Phalanx 335, Religion 373, Siege warfare 391, Veterans 473
Velitrae*   Peace 331
Venusio   Elephants 143
Vercellae [1]*   Booty 67, 68, Dogs 139, Generals of note 202
Verona   Battles of note 60, Generals of note 200, 209
Veseris (river)   Battle 49, 50
Vesuvius*   Enemies 159
Vetera*   Descriptions of war 125
Via Appia*   Infrastructure 232
Via Egnatia*   Infrastructure 232, Representations of war 384, Strategy 438
Via Flaminia*   Battles of note 60
Via Sacra*   Consequences of war 111
Vienna (Vindobona*)   Borders 76, 77
Viminacium*   Recruitment 365
Vindolanda*   Civilians 96, Equipment 165, Hunting 227, Policing 337, Production system 342, Sources 407

Vindonissa*   Armament 19, Camp 84, 85
Voislova-Zăvoi   Wars of note 501
Volsinii [1]*   Consequences of war 111
Vroulia   Acropolis 1
Vulci (Volci/Vulci*)   Representations of war 382

Wadi Hammamat
 – **Bir Umm el-Fawakhir**   Hunting 227
Wadi Murabba'at   Wars of note 500
Western Anatolia   Fleet 172
Western Asia   Generals of note 191, Wars of note 497, 500
Western Asia Minor   Mercenaries 272, Wars of note 497, 512
Western Balkans   Generals of note 200

Western Europe   Chariot 91
Western Roman Empire   Army 32, 33, 34, Battles of note 60, Generals of note 208
Wyhl   Armament 18

Xanten*   Death 119, Hunting 226

Zagora*   Acropolis 1
Zakynthos*   Parades 322
Zama (Zama [1]* Regia)   Enemies 161, Generals of note 197, 207, Wars of note 516
Zea   Infrastructure 231
Zela*   Representations of war 382
Zeugma [2]*   Religion 376

C. Subject Index

The subject index covers topics and terms, as well as peoples and mythological figures.

Ab epistulis (Epistulis, ab*)   Military diploma 276
Absentes rei publicae causa   Military law 283
Accensi*   Army 28
Achaean League   Alliances 13, Bandits 44
Actuarius (Actarius*)   Administration 7, Rank 348, 351
Adaeratio*   Army 33
Ad bestias   Military law 282
Adlocutio*   Parades 320, Rank 351
Ad metalla   Military law 282
Administration (Political administration*; see also Officium, officiales)   Army 28, 31, 32, Innovation 238, Maps 259, Military diploma 275, 276, Military service 295, 297, Sources 410, 412, Specialists 419, Officers 318, Rank 348
Adventus*   Parades 320, 322, Triumph 464
Aerarium*   Administration 6, Camp 83, Costs of war 114, Standard 423, Triumph 464
Aerarium* militare   Administration 7, Auxiliaries 39, Consequences of war 109, Innovation 237, Legion 254, Military service 298, Veterans 475
Aesculapius (Asclepius*)   Religion 376
Aetolian League   Alliances 13
Agaso   Slavery 396
Age group   Military service 291, Motivation 303, Society and army 398, Parades 323, Recruitment 363
Agema   Army 25, 26, Elite troops 145, Equipment 165, Guards 210, War 492
Agentes in rebus*   Military service 297, Rank 351
Agger   Camp 82, Fortification 182
Aggression   Empire 150, 154, Wars of note 508
Agmen   March 263
Agmen quadratum   March 262
Agoge*   Administration 2, Education 140, Military service 291, Sparta 413
Agon   Battle 45, Civil war 92, Consequences of war 105, Descriptions of war 122, Emotions 148, Enemies 157, Terror 451, Victory 478
 – athletic   Victory 479
 – musical   Parades 322, Victory 479
Agricultural production   Prisoners 338
Agriculture*   Army 23, 28, Consequences of war 105, Mutiny 311, Society and army 398, Timeframe of war 455, Prisoners 337, 340
Ala [2]*   Cavalry 88, 89, Education 142, Infantry 230, March 261, 262, Rank 349, 351, Sources 407, 412
Alae sociorum   Motivation 306
Alamanni*   Battle 51, Borders 76, Generals of note 198, 200, Officers 319
Alcohol   Motivation 304
Alexander Sarcophagus*   Equipment 165
Alliance (see also Foedus)   Borders 74, 76, Consequences of war 103, Costs of war 113, Descriptions of war 121, Diplomacy 131, 132, 133, Elite troops 145, Fleet 174, 176, Innovation 236, Law of war 248, 249, Oath 314, Peace 331, Strategy 435, Sources 404, 405, Strategy 436
Allied states   Alliances 11, Heroism 215, War 492
Allies (see also Foederati, Socii)   Alliances 12, Battle 47, 50, Battles of note 53, Cavalry 88, Diplomacy 130, Discipline 136, Generals of note 196, 197, 199, Honours 221, Military service 295, Peace 331, Reconnaissance 359, Recruitment 363, Religion 371, Strategy 434, Supply 442, War 493
Alpini
 – Iuvenes   Militia 300
Ambush   March 260, Reconnaissance 358, 362, Valour 469
Amicitia* (Friendship*)   Alliances 13, 14, Diplomacy 132, Law of war 249
Amnesia   Civil war 91, 92
Amnesty (Amnestia*)   Civil war 92
Amphictyony (Amphiktyonia*)   Alliances 11, Peace 329
Amphitheatre (Amphitheatrum*)   Prisoners 339
Anatomy*   Medical corps 270
Ancilia (Ancile*)   Religion 372, 373
Animus   Valour 469
Annona (Cura annonae*)   Honours 224, Pay 328, Rank 350, Supply 443
Annona militaris   Military service 297, Rear 355
Antepilani   Battle 49
Antesignani   Elite troops 146
Antigonids   Administration 4, Army 27, Battle 47, 48, Cavalry 86, 87, Consequences of war 104, Empire 151, Fleet 175, 176, Mercenaries 273, War 492, Recruitment 363, Representations of war 381
Anti-Semitism*   Enemies 157
Anubis*   Religion 376
Apollo*   Religion 372, 376
Apopompos   Parades 320
Apotropaic gods*   Symbols 450
Apparitor (Apparitores*)   Religion 377
Aquilifer   Rank 347, 350, Transmission of orders 461
Arable farming   Borders 74
Ara Pacis Augustae*   Peace 329
Arbitration*   Borders 70, Law of war 248, Peace 329
Arche   Empire 150, 151
Archer (Bow-shooting*)   Army 22, 25, Auxiliaries 37, 38, 39, Battle 47, 48, 50, 51, Battles of note 56, 58, 59, 61, Camels 79, Cavalry 86, 89, Chariot 90, Cowardice 117, Education 142, Elephants 144, Fleet 175, Infantry 230, Innovation 242, March 261, 262, 263, Mercenaries 272, 274, Military literature 288, 289, Militia 300, Phalanx 333, 334, 335, Reconnaissance 358, Representations of war 379, 385, Society and army 397, Sources 406, Sparta 415, War 490
Architecture*   Acropolis 1, Borders 75, 77, Fortification 180, Prisoners 339, War 489
Archon, Archontes*   Specialists 417

Arete (see also Virtus)   Army 23, Battle 45, Descriptions of war 122, Discipline 134, 135, General 187, Military literature 284, Mutiny 311, Representations of war 381, Victory 478, War 488

Arginusae*, Trial of the Generals of   Victory 478

Argyraspídes*   Army 25, 26, Battles of note 58, Elite troops 145, Guards 210, War 492

Aristocracy* (see also Nobility)   Army 22, 23, 32, Booty 67, Cavalry 86, Civil war 94, 95, Education 141, Elite troops 145, Empire 155, Fleet 174, General 186, 187, Generals of note 199, 204, Guards 209, Heroism 216, Motivation 302, 306, Society and army 397, State and army 429, 430, Timeframe of war 454, Victory 477, 479, 480, Victory titles 484, 485, 486, Officers 316, 317, 318, Rank 344, 346, War 489

Armament*   Army 23, Costs of war 114, Military law 281, Religion 370, Sources 403

Armamentaria*   Camp 83, 85, Religion 375

Armatura   Rank 350

Armiger   Slavery 396

Armilla   Honours 221, 224

Armorum custos   Administration 8, Military service 298

Armour*   Armament 19, 20, Army 22, 23, 28, Cavalry 86, Dogs 139, Infantry 229, Innovation 238, 240, Military service 292, War 489, Representations of war 379, 385

Army
– Peacetime army   Honours 222
– Wartime army   Honours 222

Army organization   Army 25

Army service, military service   Avoidance of military service 41, Enemies 157

Army supply (see also Logistics)   Administration 6, 8, 9, Army 28, 32, 34, Booty 65, Chariot 90, Civilians 96, 97, 98, Consequences of war 108, Costs of war 114, 115, Equipment 164, Fleet 177, 178, Honours 222, Infrastructure 230, 231, 232, 233, Innovation 235, 236, Maps 259, Medical corps 268, Mutiny 313, Pay 328, Production system 341,, Scorched earth 388, Siege warfare 391, Specialists 419, 435, State and army 427, Rank 347, Rear 354, 355, Wars of note 513

Arrow (Bow and arrow*)   Armament 18, Infantry 229, Phalanx 333, Specialists 419

Arsenal (see also Armamentaria)   Equipment 164, Fleet 177, Production system 342, Siege warfare 392, Supply 439

Artillery (see also Long-range weapons, Firearms)   Battle 48, 51, Cavalry 89, Costs of war 113, Fortification 182, General 187, March 262, Military literature 287, 288, Rank 347, Terror 452, Vehicles 471

Aspis (see also Clipeus, Hypapistai, Shield)   Army 23, Battle 46, 47, 48, 49, Elite troops 145, March 261, State and army 426, Strategy 438

Assyrians   Empire 150, Enemies 157, Infrastructure 232, Victory titles 484

Asylia (Asylon*)   Diplomacy 131, nemies 159

Athenian League (Second)*   Alliances 11, Descriptions of war 123, Garrison 184, Peace 330

Athenians   Military service 294, Sources 405

Attalids   Representations of war 382, Society and army 398, War 492

Auguratorium   Religion 375

Augustales [2]*   Military law 283, Rank 349, 350, 352

Aurum tironicum   Recruitment 367

Auspicia   Booty 67, Honours 221, 222, Innovation 237, Religion 371, 372, 375, Triumph 463, War 495

Autocrat   Generals of note 193

Autonomy (Autonomia*)   Alliances 11, 14, Army 23, 24, Battles of note 55, Borders 73, Colonies 100, Consequences of war 104, 106, Diplomacy 131, Empire 150, 152, Peace 329, Sources 404

Auxilia*, auxiliarii/Auxiliaries   Administration 7, Alliances 14, Armament 18, Army 28, 29, 32, Artillery 37, Battle 50, 51, Battles of note 56, 57, 64, Borders 75, 76, Camp 82, Cavalry 88, 89, Conscription 102, Consequences of war 110, Education 141, Elite troops 146, Empire 152, 154, Fortification 182, Generals of note 190, 193, 208, Guards 211, 212, Honours 222, 224, Hunting 227, Infantry 230, Innovation 237, 240, Law of war 250, Legion 255, March 262, 263, Marriage 264, 265, 266, Medical corps 267, 269, Mercenaries 274, Military diploma 277, 278, 279, Military service 295, 296, 298, Motivation 306, 307, Officers 317, Pay 327, Rank 347, 348, 351, 352, Recruitment 363, 364, 365, 366, Religion 376, 377, Sources 407, 408, Specialists 418, 419, Standard 425, State and army 431, 432, Strategy 438, Symbols 449, Transmission of orders 461, War 495, Wars of note 500, 504, 505

Auxilia externa   Cavalry 88, Recruitment 364

Auxilia palatina   Generals of note 201

Auxiliary ala   Army 29

Auxiliary camp   Medical corps 268

Auxiliary castellum   Camp 81, 82, 84, 85

Auxiliary cohort   March 262, 263, Religion 376

Auxiliary fortress   Esprit de corps 168

Auxiliary infantry   Military service 297

Awe   Emotions 147, 148, Strategy 434, Terror 451, Valour 468, 469

Axe   Battle 48, Valour 470

Ballista*   Fortification 182

Ballistarius   Rank 347

Balteus   Armament 18

Bandum*   Rank 352

Banishment*   Civil war 91, 92, Conscription 102, Honour 220, Reconnaissance 357

Barbarians*   Alliances 10, 14, Army 29, 30, 33, 34, Auxiliaries 41, Battle 45, 50, 51, Battles of note 53, 57, Booty 66, Borders 71, 77, Descriptions of war 126, 127, 129, Education 140, Elite troops 146, Emotions 147, 148, Enemies 157, 158, 159, 161, Equipment 167, Fleet 174, 179, General 187, 189, Generals of note 198, 208, Honour 220, Innovation 240, 242, Language 245,

SUBJECT INDEX

Military literature 289, Officers 319, Peace 329, Representations of war 384, 386, Scorched earth 388, Standard 422, State and army 431, 432, Strategy 434, 435, 438, Valour 467, 470, Victory 481, Victory titles 484, War 489, 490, Wars of note 502, 513

Bar Kochba Revolt (Jewish Wars [III]*)   Honours 223, Production system 341, Recruitment 366, Sources 407

Barracks   Camp 83, Cavalry 88, Guards 212, Religion 375, 376, 377

Basilica*   Camp 83, Religion 375

Batavians (Batavi*), Batavian Revolt*   Auxiliaries 38, Mutiny 313

Battering ram   Siege warfare 390, 392

Battle paraenesis   Descriptions of war 126, 127, Valour 467

Beasts of burden   Vehicles 471

Bellona*   Law of war 250, Religion 372, 374

Belt*   Military service 296, Symbols 449

Beneficiarii*   Motivation 307, Policing 337, Rank 350, Religion 376, Sources 407, 410

Biarchus   Rank 351, 352, 353

Bishop   Prisoners 340, Militia 300, Wars of note 506

Boar   Legion 257, Parades 321, Symbols 447, 449

Bona castrensia   Military service 296

Booty (War booty*)   Administration 4, 6, Alliances 13, 14, Army 27, Bandits 44, Borders 76, Camels 79, Camp 80, Civilians 96, Civil war 94, 95, Consequences of war 107, 108, 110, 111, Costs of war 112, 113, 114, 115, Descriptions of war 122, 123, 128, 129, Empire 151, 153, 155, Enemies 157, 158, Fleet 176, General 186, Generals of note 192, 201, 204, 206, Honours 221, 222, Law of war 250, Mercenaries 274, Military service 294, 295, Motivation 303, 306, 307, 308, Parades 321, Pay 324, 325, 326, 328, Prisoners 337, 338, Religion 370, Sources 404, Sparta 415, State and army 426, 427, 429, Strategy 435, Supply 441, Timeframe of war 455, Triumph 462, 463, 464, 465, Valour 470, Vehicles 470, Veterans 472, 473, 474, Victory 477, 478, 479, 480, War 494, 495, Wars of note 497, 507

Border dispute   Consequences of war 104, Strategy 438

Borders (see also Limes)   Bandits 44, Civilians 96, Education 140, Empire 154, Fortification 182, Garrison 185, Innovation 237, Law of war 250, Legion 254, Mutiny 313, Policing 336, Rank 347, Reconnaissance 360, 361, 362, Sources 404, Supply 443, Transmission of orders 462, War 493, 495

Border troops (see also Limitanei)   Army 31, Rank 349

Border violation   War 495

Bow (Bow and arrow*)   Artillery 35

Bracchiati   Rank 350

Brass*   Military diploma 275

Breastplate   Cavalry 86, Infantry 229, Officers 318, Phalanx 332

Brevis   Sources 412

Bronze*   Administration 7, Armament 16, 20, Equipment 164, Innovation 240, 243, Military diploma 275, 279, Military service 292, 293, Supply 441

Bronze tablets   Sources 404

Brothel*   Military service 296

Brutality   Military service 294, Prisoners 339, Terror 452

Bucellarii*   Elite troops 146

Bucina, bucinatores*   Rank 347, 350, Specialists 420, Transmission of orders 461

Buddhism   Victory titles 484

Buglers   Military service 293

Building trade*   Consequences of war 111, Prisoners 340, Specialists 417

Bull   Parades 321, Legion 257, Symbols 449

Bureaucracy*   Army 22, Costs of war 115, State and army 432, Reconnaissance 360, 361

Burgus*   Bandits 44

Byzantines   Rank 353

Cacula   Slavery 396

Calceus*   Officers 318

Calo   Slavery 396

Camel*   Army 26, Auxiliaries 39, Battles of note 58, Costs of war 115, Vehicles 471

Camp/Castra [1]*   Administration 6, Army 28, 29, 31, 34, Battle 46, Battles of note 54, 58, 62, Booty 68, Borders 75, Camp 80, 81, 85, Civilians 96, Death 119, Emotions 148, Equipment 167, Esprit de corps 168, Fortification 182, Guards 211, Heroism 216, Infrastructure 230, 234, Innovation 237, 239, Legion 253, 255, Maps 259, Marriage 266, Medical corps 267, 270, Military law 282, Military literature 289, Military service 292, 293, 296, Mutiny 312, 313, Officers 318, Rank 347, Reconnaissance 358, 360, 361, Religion 372, 375, 376, 377, Representations of war 383, Sources 408, Sparta 413, Supply 444, Symbols 448, Transmission of orders 460, 461, Wars of note 500, 507

Camp construction   Camp 84, Sources 401

Camp followers   Army 27, Civilians 96, Costs of war 112, Generals of note 202, March 260, Slavery 393, 394, 395, Specialists 417, Vehicles 470, Officers 315

Campidoctor   Rank 349, 350, 352, 353, Training 456

Campigenus   Rank 350

Campus   Rank 353, Religion 376

Canabae   Military service 296, Motivation 307, Sources 410

Capite censi*   Conscription 102, Military service 295, Recruitment 364

Capitulation   Customs of war 118, Diplomacy 132, Standard 423, Strategy 434, Wars of note 516, Peace 329, 330, 331, Prisoners 339

Capitulation treaty   Sources 405

Capitulum   Recruitment 366

Capricornus   Legion 257

Capsarius   Rank 348, Specialists 420

Capture   Strategy 433, Terror 452

Career path   Officers 316, 318, 319, Pay 327, Rank 351, Sources 412
Carroballista   Battle 48
Carthaginians   Elephants 143, Enemies 156, Generals of note 197, 206, Honour 219, Innovation 243, Sources 409
Cartography*   Borders 73
Castellum [1]*   Auxiliaries 39, Camp 81, 82, 84, Civilians 96, Equipment 167, Innovation 240, Medical corps 268, 270, Sources 410, Supply 445, Transmission of orders 461
Castrametation   Camp 80
Castra peregrinorum   Religion 375
Castra praetoria   Battle 51
Castra urbanorum   Religion 375
Castrenses   Sources 410
Cataphract/Catafractarii (Kataphraktoi*)/Equites catafracti   Army 26, 33, Battle 51, Battles of note 57, 58, Cavalry 89, Innovation 240, Rank 351
Catapult*   Artillery 35, 36, 37, Battle 48, Fleet 175, 176, Innovation 241, 242, 243, Military service 296, Siege warfare 390, 392, Sources 402, Specialists 419, War 492
Catella   Honours 221
Catering   Army 32, Consequences of war 108, General 187, Military service 296, 297, Rank 351, Supply 439, 441, 443, Vehicles 471
Causeway   Infrastructure 232
Cavalry* (see also Horseman, Ala, Equites singulares (Augusti))   Administration 5, Armament 16, 17, 19, Army 23, 24, 29, 31, 32, 33, Auxiliaries 37, 38, 39, Battle 46, 47, 48, 50, 51, Battles of note 55, Camp 84, Cavalry 89, Costs of war 112, 114, Education 140, 142, Elite troops 145, Equipment 164, 165, General 187, Generals of note 204, 207, Guards 210, 211, Hunting 227, Legion 253, March 260, 261, 262, 263, Military literature 286, Officers 318, Phalanx 333, 334, 335, Rank 346, 348, 349, 351, 352, Reconnaissance 362, Recruitment 363, War 490, Society and army 397, Sources 412, Sparta 415, State and army 426, Strategy 436, Supply 439, Terror 452, Transmission of orders 461, Valour 469, War 490, 491, 492, Wars of note 506, 507, 510
Celts*   Armament 17, 18, 20, Battle 49, Consequences of war 107, Enemies 156, Fleet 178, Phalanx 332, Representations of war 381, 382, Sources 409, Timeframe of war 454
Cenotaph (Kenotaphion*)   Representations of war 381
Censitarian army   Officers 317
Census*   Army 27, 28, Guards 210, Infantry 229, Military service 295, Parades 321, 322, Phalanx 335, Recruitment 363, 364, Sources 410, State and army 429, Veterans 473
Centaurs*   Legion 257
Centenarius   Officers 319, Rank 351, 352, 353
Cento   Consequences of war 110
Centuria*, Century   Army 28, 29, Battle 48, 49, 50, Camp 83, 84, Cavalry 88, Discipline 138, Esprit de corps 168, Infantry 230, Legion 252, 253, 255, March 261, Motivation 305, Rank 350, Sources 407, Specialists 418, Standard 423, State and army 430, Transmission of orders 460
Centurio*   Administration 6, 8, 9, Armament 18, Army 28, 29, Auxiliaries 38, Battle 50, Battles of note 57, Booty 67, Camp 84, Consequences of war 108, Death 119, Discipline 137, Education 141, Elite troops 145, Guards 211, 212, Heroism 216, Honours 221, 223, 224, Innovation 237, Legion 252, 254, 255, March 262, 263, Marriage 265, 266, Medical corps 269, Military law 282, Military service 296, 297, Motivation 305, 306, Mutiny 312, 313, Officers 317, 318, 319, Pay 326, 328, Production system 342, Rank 346, 347, 348, 350, 351, 352, 353, Religion 377, 378, Sources 410, 412, Standard 423, State and army 432, Transmission of orders 460, 461
Centurio regionarius   Policing 336, 337
Certamen   Battle 45
Chicken*   Religion 372, 375, Symbols 447
Chigi Vase (Chigi Painter*)   Innovation 238, Representations of war 379, War 489
Children (Child, childhood*)   Military diploma 278, Military law 281, 283, Military service 298, Motivation 308, Sources 408
Chremonidean War*   Camp 80
Christianity*   Avoidance of military service 42, Battles of note 60, 61, Descriptions of war 130, Diplomacy 133, Enemies 156, 157, Generals of note 200, 201, Oath 314, Religion 377, 378, Sources 403, 411, Standard 424, Symbols 449, Terror 453, Triumph 464, Victory 481, Victory titles 487, War 494, 495, Wars of note 506
Christianization   Law of war 250
Church*   Prisoners 340
Cimmerii*   Dogs 139
Cingulum   Officers 318, Military service 296
Circitor, circumitor   Rank 351, 352
Circular wall   Acropolis 1
Citadel   Acropolis 1
Citizen army, Citizen soldier   Army 23, 25, 27, Auxiliaries 37, Consequences of war 104, 105, Emotions 146, Innovation 235, Mercenaries 273, Motivation 302, Mutiny 311, Recruitment 363, 364, Society and army 398, Sparta 415, State and army 427, Supply 439, 440, War 491, 492, Wars of note 510
Citizen, Citizenry   Administration 2, Army 29, Borders 69, Civilians 96, Civil war 94, Colonies 100, Consequences of war 103, Costs of war 113, Descriptions of war 123, Diplomacy 131, 133, Discipline 135, 136, Education 141, Empire 155, Fleet 174, General 186, Guards 209, 211, 212, 213, Honour 218, Infantry 229, Law of war 250, Legion 252, 253, 254, Marriage 264, Military diploma 279, Military law 281, Military service 291, Oath 314, Officers 317, Phalanx 333, Prisoners 338, 339, 340, Recruitment 365, Representations of war 381, Society and army 397, State and army 426,

427, Supply 439, Timeframe of war 455, Wars of note 508

Citizen militia Army 23, 27, Innovation 236, Militia 300, Motivation 305, Officers 315, Society and army 399, State and army 428, Timeframe of war 454, Veterans 472, 474, War 492

Citizenship*/Civitas* Peace 331, Prisoners 339, Recruitment 366, Administration 7, Alliances 14, Army 28, Auxiliaries 38, 39, 40, Battles of note 64, Cavalry 89, Civilians 96, Colonies 101, Descriptions of war 122, Diplomacy 133, Empire 155, Enemies 160, Garrison 185, Honours 222, 224, Language 246, Law of war 251, Legion 253, Marriage 265, Military diploma 275, 276, 278, 279, Military law 281, Military service 290, 293, 295, 298, Motivation 306, Slavery 395, Society and army 398, Sources 408, State and army 431, Strategy 438, Supply 443

City state (see also Polis) Auxiliaries 38, Descriptions of war 121, Empire 152, Mutiny 311, Representations of war 380, Society and army 397, War 489, 491

City (Town, city*) Borders 71, 73, 76, Colonies 101, Consequences of war 105, Customs of war 118, Descriptions of war 129, Guards 211, Heroism 215, Innovation 237, 240, 243, Militia 299, 300, Pay 327, Peace 328, Prisoners 338, 340, Recruitment 363, Religion 368, Society and army 397, Sources 411, War 490, 492

City wall Borders 77, Strategy 437

Civil administration Administration 9

Civilian (Paganus*), civilian population Administration 9, Civil war 94, Consequences of war 103, Death 119, Descriptions of war 123, Honours 222, Medical corps 269, Military law 282, 283, Military service 296, Militia 301, Mutiny 312, Prisoners 338, 340, Production system 341, Rear 355, Reconnaissance 360, Society and army 399, 400, Specialists 419, Supply 445

Civil war/Stasis Administration 7, Auxiliaries 37, 41, Battle 51, Battles of note 53, Civil war 91, 93, Colonies 101, Consequences of war 107, 110, Death 120, Descriptions of war 127, 128, 129, Emotions 149, Empire 153, Enemies 158, 160, 162, Fleet 178, Fortification 181, Generals of note 193, 194, 198, 200, 205, 206, Guards 211, Heroism 216, Honour 220, Hostages 225, Innovation 236, 237, Law of war 249, Motivation 307, Mutiny 310, Oath 314, Officers 318, Peace 329, Prisoners 339, Production system 341, Slavery 396, Strategy 434, Terror 451, Triumph 462, Veterans 473, 474, Victory 477, Victory titles 485, 486, 487, War 491, 493, 494, Wars of note 505, 510

Civis Romanus (see also Citizen) Honours 221, 222, Military service 295, 296

Civium Romanorum Honours 224

Clans Customs of war 117, Descriptions of war 129, General 186, 187, Military service 291, Victory 479, War 493

Clericus/Chaplain Rank 350

Clibanarius Army 33

Client, clientele (Cliens, clientes*) Civil war 93, 94

Clientela Diplomacy 132, Military service 295, 298

Client monarchy Alliances 14, Auxiliaries 38, 39, Borders 73, Diplomacy 133, Empire 154, Enemies 159, Rear 355, Reconnaissance 359, 360, 361, Wars of note 513, Strategy 438, Wars of note 505, 506, 513

Clipeus Battle 48, Valour 469

Close combat Armament 18, Army 22, Valour 467

Clothing Administration 6, Consequences of war 103, Costs of war 114, 115, Enemies 162, Equipment 163, 164, 165, 166, 167, Honours 225, Infrastructure 233, Military service 294, Officers 318, Parades 322, Pay 328, Religion 376, Representations of war 385, Sources 410, Supply 439, 442, 443, 444

Cohesion Military service 291

Cohors prima/First Cohort Camp 84, Legion 253, March 263, Military service 297, Officers 317, Pay 328

Cohort (Cohors*) Army 29, 31, Auxiliaries 37, 40, 41, Battle 50, 51, Battles of note 64, Camp 84, Cavalry 88, Education 142, Generals of note 201, Guards 211, Infantry 230, Innovation 236, Legion 253, March 262, 263, Motivation 305, Officers 317, Phalanx 335, Rank 346, 347, 349, 351, 352, Recruitment 365, Sources 407, Standard 423, Transmission of orders 461

Cohortes civium Romanorum/Citizen Cohort Honours 222, Pay 327, Recruitment 365

Cohortes equitatae Army 33, Camels 79, March 263

Cohortes praetoriae/Praetorian Guard (Praetorians*) Administration 7, Army 29, 30, 31, Artillery 36, Battles of note 60, Cavalry 90, Consequences of war 109, Elite troops 145, Guards 210, 211, 212, Honours 222, 223, 224, Innovation 237, March 262, Military diploma 278, 279, Military service 296, 297, 298, Motivation 307, Mutiny 313, Officers 318, 319, Parades 322, Pay 327, Policing 336, Rank 347, 353, Recruitment 364, Sources 408, Standard 423, 424, State and army 431, Symbols 449, Veterans 475, Wars of note 506

Cohortes urbanae/Urban Cohorts/Urbaniciani Honours 224, Military diploma 278, 279, Military service 297, Officers 318, Policing 336, Rank 347, Society and army 399

Cohortes vigilum/Vigiles* Conscription 102, Consequences of war 110, Military service 297, Officers 318, Pay 327, Rank 347, Religion 375, Slavery 395, Society and army 399

Coinage Enemies 162, Fleet 174

Coins Costs of war 114, Enemies 158, 161, Generals of note 195, 203, Pay 326, Representations of war 384, State and army 429, Supply 441, Symbols 449, Triumph 464, Victory 480, Victory titles 486

Collatores Recruitment 366

Collegium* Military service 296

Coloniae maritimae Fleet 176

Colonization* Society and army 399, War 489

Colony, colonist (Coloniae*) Colonies 99, Consequences of war 105, 109, Esprit de corps 168,

Fleet 174, 176, Fortification 181, Garrison 185, Guards 210, Honours 222, Law of war 250, March 260, Policing 336, 337, Reconnaissance 359, State and army 429, Strategy 438, Veterans 473, 475, 476

Columna bellica Law of war 250

Columna rostrata Descriptions of war 123

Comes, comites* Military law 282, Sources 411, 412, Rank 349, 353

Comitatus, comitatenses* Administration 9, Army 30, 31, 33, 34, Auxiliaries 41, Battle 51, Borders 77, Cavalry 90, Elite troops 145, Generals of note 200, Innovation 238, Military law 282, Motivation 308, Officers 319, Production system 342, Rank 349, Sources 412

Comitia* centuriata Honours 221, Military service 295, State and army 430

Command, art of Military literature 286, 287, 288

Commander (see also General, Imperator, Strategos) Maps 259

Command, high command Borders 76

Commerce* Booty 68, Borders 77, Consequences of war 106, 108, 109, Fleet 175, 178, Infrastructure 231, Language 245, Prisoners 338, Production system 341, 342, Reconnaissance 357, 362, Society and army 398, Supply 441, Victory 477

Communication* Army 34, Military service 297

Compassion Emotions 146, 149

Comradeship Death 120, Elite troops 145, Emotions 146, 149, Eve-of-battle speech 169, Triumph 464

Concordia* (see also Cohesion) Civil war 93, Legion 257, Representations of war 383, 384, 386

Condottieri Mercenaries 272, Victory 479, War 491

Conscientious objection* Military law 282

Conscription Conscription 102, Cowardice 116, Death 120, Military law 281, Military service 295, Motivation 305, State and army 426, 427, 428, 429, 431

Consequences of war (War, consequences of*) Descriptions of war 121, 127, Sources 409

Consilium* Generals of note 206, Strategy 433, Rank 346, 347, Reconnaissance 361

Consilium coercendi intra terminos imperii Empire 155

Conspiracy Mercenaries 274, Mutiny 313, Wars of note 498

Constitutio Antoniniana* Empire 155, Honours 223, State and army 431

Consul(es)* Civil war 94, Legion 252, Motivation 306, Officers 317, Rank 346, Religion 371, 372, 375

Contio* Booty 68

Contributions Alliances 14

Contubernalis, contubernium* Battle 50, 51, Camp 84, Esprit de corps 168, March 263, Military service 296, Rank 350

Contus Battle 51

Conubium*/Ius conubii Marriage 264, 265, Military diploma 275, 276, 278, 279, Motivation 307, Recruitment 366

Corinthian War* Consequences of war 106, Infantry 229, Army 24

Cornu, cornicen (Cornicines*)/Horns Infantry 229, Rank 347, 350, Specialists 418, 419, Transmission of orders 461

Corona Generals of note 193, Honours 221, 223, 224, 225, Military literature 288, Standard 421

Corporis custodes (Germani)/Germani corporis custodes Elite troops 145, Guards 209, 211, 212, March 262, Military service 297

Corruption Army 34

Costs of war State and army 427

Coup d'état Civil war 93, 95

Courier Infrastructure 232, Transmission of orders 462

Court* Administration 4, 5, Empire 151, Guards 211, Infrastructure 233, Military service 293, Rank 353, Sources 412, Victory titles 485

Cowardice Avoidance of military service 42, Battles of note 53, Cavalry 87, Discipline 134, 136, 138, Emotions 147, Heroism 215, Honour 218, Law of war 250, Military law 281, Motivation 302, Prisoners 339, Slavery 393, Sources 404, Sparta 414, Valour 467, 468

Crafts, trade* Booty 68, Civilians 96, Costs of war 115, Medical corps 269, Military service 296, Prisoners 337, 338, 339, 340, Production system 341, 342, Slavery 395, Specialists 418, 419, Veterans 476

Crier/Praeco* Customs of war 117, 118, Diplomacy 130, 131, Language 245, Law of war 248, March 260, Rank 345, 350, Religion 370, Specialists 417, 420

Cuisses Phalanx 333

Cult* Acropolis 1, Consequences of war 110, Heroism 214, Religion 373, 375, 376, 377, 378

Cuneus Administration 8, Auxiliaries 41, Rank 351, 352, Sources 411

Curator Administration 8, Veterans 475

Cursus honorum* State and army 432

Cursus publicus* Civilians 97, Rear 355, Sources 412, Supply 444, 445, Vehicles 471

Custos armorum Military service 298

Cyclopean masonry War 488

Dacian Wars Cavalry 88, Honour 219, Military diploma 276, Prisoners 338, Sources 407

Dagger/Pugio Armament 18

Dance* (see also War dance) Discipline 135, Military service 291, Parades 321, 322, Valour 470

Dea Candida Regina Religion 376

Dead in battle Religion 370

Death* Battle 45, Battles of note 64, Descriptions of war 126, Discipline 137, Heroism 216, Honour 217, 218, Honours 223, Law of war 250, Military law 281, 282, Military service 291, 292, 293, 294, Motivation 305, Mutiny 313, Prisoners 337, 339, 340, Representations of war 379, 381, Sparta 414, State and army 427, Valour 468, 470, War 488

Death penalty* Avoidance of military service 41, 42, 43, Conscription 102, Cowardice 116, Discipline 138, Honour 218, Military law 282, Prisoners 340

Decadarch, decadarchy (Dekadarchia [1]*)
   Cavalry 86, Transmission of orders 460
Decas* Cavalry 86, Equipment 164
Decimatio* Cowardice 116, Discipline 138, Military service 297
Declaration of war Administration 5, Borders 73, Customs of war 117, Diplomacy 131, 132, Law of war 248, 249, War 488, 495
Decorations, military*/Honours Descriptions of war 122, Eve-of-battle speech 169, Heroism 216, Honours 221, Military service 290, Motivation 306, Rank 350, Reconnaissance 358, Symbols 448
Decurio, decuria [4]* Administration 9, Army 29, Cavalry 88, Discipline 137, Guards 212, Marriage 265, Militia 300, Officers 317, 318, Rank 346, 348, 351, 352, Religion 377
Decursio Death 119, 120, Parades 320, 321
Dedication State and army 427
Dedication of spoils Triumph 465, Victory 478
Deditio* Booty 66, Diplomacy 132, Hostages 225, Law of war 251, Peace 330, 331, War 495
Defeat Army 28, Battle 45, 46, 51, 52, Battles of note 54, 55, 58, 61, Customs of war 118, Descriptions of war 122, 124, 126, Eve-of-battle speech 169, Fleet 174, 175, General 188, Generals of note 193, 205, 206, 207, Innovation 236, 239, Military law 281, Military service 292, 294, Phalanx 333, Production system 341, Religion 370, Scorched earth 388, Slavery 394, 395, Sparta 415, 416, Standard 422, State and army 429, Triumph 462, Victory 477, 478, War 489, 494, 495, Wars of note 506, 508, 512, 513
Defence Alliances 10, Armament 19, Army 23, 30, 32, Battle 47, 48, Borders 74, 75, 76, 77, Civil war 95, Consequences of war 105, Descriptions of war 121, Enemies 160, Esprit de corps 168, Fortification 181, 182, Garrison 185, Generals of note 191, 200, Infantry 230, Innovation 235, 241, 242, Law of war 249, March 260, Military service 292, Militia 300, Mutiny 311, 312, Representations of war 385, Siege warfare 389, 391, 392, Sources 404, 406, 412, Strategy 436, 437, Supply 439, Valour 470, Veterans 472, 476, War 491, 492, 494, Wars of note 497, 505, 511
Defence costs Military literature 288
Defensive alliance Wars of note 507
Defensive complex Acropolis 1, War 488
Defensive operations Empire 155, Innovation 239, Religion 369, War 495, Wars of note 508
Defensive war War 493
Defensive weaponry Cavalry 86, War 488
Deities Battle 50, Battles of note 60, Booty 65, Borders 70, Descriptions of war 122, 126, Diplomacy 131, 132, Enemies 156, 158, 161, Eve-of-battle speech 169, General 187, Heroism 214, Law of war 247, 248, 249, Medical corps 268, Military literature 285, Motivation 304, Oath 314, Parades 322, Religion 368, 369, 370, 371, 372, 373, 376, 377, Representations of war 382, 383, 384, Sources 408, 411, Sparta 415, State and army 427, Strategy 437, Symbols 448, 449, Terror 451, Triumph 465, Valour 469, Victory 480, 481, Victory titles 483, War 488, 489, Administration 3, Alliances 10, 11, 12, Consequences of war 104, Customs of war 118, Diplomacy 131, Empire 150, Garrison 184, Generals of note 199, Mutiny 310, Oath 314, Officers 315, Pay 324, Phalanx 335, Sources 404, 405, 409, War 490, Wars of note 507, 513, Administration 2, Civil war 92, Discipline 135, Empire 150, Fleet 174, Garrison 184, Generals of note 199, Pay 324, Peace 330, Phalanx 335, Representations of war 380, 381, State and army 426, Symbols 447, Victory 477
Demography Consequences of war 103, 105, 106, 111
Dendrochronology Borders 75
Deportation* (see also Prisoners of war) Prisoners 337
Deputatus Rank 350
Desertion (Desertor*)/Transfuga*/Defection, Defector Avoidance of military service 42, 43, Battles of note 53, Costs of war 112, Cowardice 116, Generals of note 208, Honour 218, Language 245, Military law 281, 282, Military service 293, 298, Mutiny 310, Oath 314, Prisoners 338, 339, 340, Rank 353, Reconnaissance 358, 360, 361, Specialists 417, Standard 423, Wars of note 505
Devotio* Religion 372
Diadochi (Diadochi and Epigoni*) Enemies 159, General 189, Generals of note 192, 195, Guards 210, Mercenaries 273, Slavery 394, Victory 479
Diana* Religion 372
Dictator* Civil war 94, Rank 346, Religion 371, 372
Dignitas War 494
Dii Campestres Religion 376
Dii Manes Religion 372
Dilectator Recruitment 364
Dionysus* Symbols 448
Diplomacy* (see also Emissary, Embassy) Alliances 11, 13, Costs of war 113, Generals of note 206, 207, 208, Language 245, Law of war 247, Oath 314, Prisoners 338, Reconnaissance 359, Strategy 434, 435, 437, Victory 481, War 495
Discens* Cavalry 90, Education 142
Discharge, certificate of Military diploma 279
Disciplina Augusti State and army 432
Disciplina militaris* Administration 5, 7, 8, 9, Avoidance of military service 42, Battle 46, 52, Cavalry 87, Descriptions of war 129, Education 142, Emotions 148, Fortification 181, General 188, Heroism 216, Law of war 249, Legion 255, Marriage 264, 267, Mercenaries 274, Military law 281, 282, Military literature 286, 288, 290, Military service 296, 297, Motivation 302, 305, Mutiny 313, Officers 317, 318, Parades 321, Phalanx 335, Religion 375, Representations of war 386, Sources 401, Sparta 413, State and army 429, 432, Symbols 449, Transmission of orders 459

Disease* Consequences of war 108, 111, Discipline 138, Medical corps 268, 269, Military law 282, Military service 297

Disgrace Honour 218, 220

Ditch Army 29, Battle 46, Borders 75, 78, Camp 81, Fortification 180, 181, 182, Innovation 240, Military service 292, Mutiny 312, Reconnaissance 360

Doctor armorum Rank 353

Documents* (see also Discharge, certificate of, Military diplomas) Language 246, Marriage 267, Military diploma 279, Pay 327, Rank 349, 351, Sources 405, 412

Dolphin [1]* Legion 257, Army 32, General 187, Rank 352, 353, Recruitment 365

Domi State and army 430, Triumph 463

Dona militaria* (see also Corona, Phalera, Hasta, Torques, Fibula, Catella, Vexillum, Armilla) Descriptions of war 125, Honours 221, 222, 223, 224, Officers 318

Donativum* Consequences of war 109, Costs of war 115, Death 120, General 189, Guards 212, Honours 222, 223, Military law 284, Military service 297, Motivation 306, 307, 308, Pay 328, Prisoners 340, State and army 432, Triumph 464, Veterans 474, 475, Victory 480

Draco, Draconarius Rank 350, Standard 422, 424, Transmission of orders 461

Drill Discipline 136, Mercenaries 273, Military literature 286, Sparta 413

Ducenarius* Officers 319, Rank 351, 352, 353

Duovir* navalis Officers 317, Rank 346

Duplarius Honours 224, Rank 350

Duplicarius Cavalry 88, Pay 326, Rank 347, 351

Dux [1]* Military diploma 280, Military law 282, Officers 318, Rank 353, Sources 411

Dux [2]* Military law 283

Eagle* Legion 253, March 262, 263, Rank 346, 350, Religion 376, Symbols 448, 449, Transmission of orders 461, Valour 470

Economy* Sources 413, State and army 427

Education, military (Recruits, training of*) Administration 2, Cavalry 89, Discipline 135, General 187, Generals of note 193, 207, Hunting 227, Innovation 236, Legion 254, Military literature 286, Military service 291, Officers 315, Sources 406, Valour 467, 470, War 492

Eisodos Parades 320

Eisphora* Costs of war 114, Wars of note 510

Elephant* Administration 5, Army 26, Battles of note 58, Hunting 226, Legion 257, Phalanx 335, Rank 345, Representations of war 385, War 492, Terror 452, War 489, Wars of note 498

Elite hoplites Army 24

Elite units, Elite soldiers Army 25, 26, 28, 30, 34, Auxiliaries 39, Battles of note 54, Cavalry 88, Chariot 91, Civil war 92, Consequences of war 106, Education 141, Empire 151, Equipment 165, Fleet 173, Generals of note 201, 204, Guards 209, 211, Innovation 236, 237, March 262, Military service 290, 292, Motivation 306, Officers 319, Phalanx 334, Rank 352, Recruitment 363, 365, Representations of war 379, Sparta 414, State and army 426, 429, 432, Transmission of orders 459, War 490, 491, 492, Wars of note 513

Emansio Military law 282

Emblem Symbols 449

Emissary, Embassy (see also Diplomacy) Civilians 98, Costs of war 114, Customs of war 117, 118, Descriptions of war 127, Diplomacy 130, 131, 132, 133, Law of war 248, 249, Mutiny 310, Peace 331, Reconnaissance 358, 360, 362, Religion 374, Valour 470, Wars of note 505

Emperor (Kaiser (Caesar, Emperor)*; see also Imperator) Military diploma 275, 276, Military law 282, Military service 295, 297, Motivation 308, Parades 323, Religion 374, Symbols 449

Emporion* Colonies 100

Enemy (Hostis*) Army 22, 23, Auxiliaries 37, Avoidance of military service 43, Bandits 44, Borders 73, 75, Camp 80, Consequences of war 105, 108, 110, Descriptions of war 124, 129, Heroism 214, 215, 216, 217, Infantry 230, Infrastructure 234, Law of war 248, 249, 250, March 260, 262, Military law 282, Motivation 301, 305, Prisoners 338, 339, Rank 346, Religion 370, 371, 372, Representations of war 381, Sources 404, War 489, 493, 495, Wars of note 502

Enemy territory War 495

Enomotarchai Officers 315

Enomotarchos Transmission of orders 460

Enomotia* Sparta 415

Enomotiai Military service 291

Epagoge March 262

Eparch (Eparchos) Rank 351

Ephebes (Ephebia*) Administration 2, Borders 70, 71, Descriptions of war 121, Education 140, 141, Infrastructure 230, Innovation 236, Military service 291, Militia 300, Oath 314, Parades 322, 323, Recruitment 363, 364, Society and army 397, 398, Sources 406, State and army 426, Supply 439, War 491

Epilektoi Elite troops 145, Recruitment 363

Epimachia* Diplomacy 131

Epistates (Epistatai*) Recruitment 363

Epistoleus Officers 315

Epiteichismos Camp 80

Eques, ordo equester (Equites romani*) Administration 9, Army 28, 29, 31, Battles of note 64, Camp 83, Cavalry 88, 90, Civil war 94, Death 119, Enemies 158, General 186, Generals of note 201, 205, Guards 212, Honours 223, 224, Legion 252, 255, March 262, Marriage 264, Military diploma 279, Motivation 306, 307, Officers 317, 318, Parades 321, Rank 347, 349, 351, 352, Recruitment 364, Sources 410, 411, State and army 432, Supply 439, Symbols 450

Equipment Administration 3, 5, Armament 16, Army 23, Auxiliaries 38, Battle 48, Booty 66,

Cavalry 88, Costs of war 112, 115, Descriptions of war 121, General 187, Infantry 229, Infrastructure 234, March 261, 263, Military law 281, Military service 293, Officers 315, Phalanx 332, Production system 341, Sources 405, Specialists 417, Supply 439, 442, Symbols 448, 450, Transmission of orders 460

Equites promoti   Army 31, Cavalry 89

Equites singulares* (Augusti) (see also Life guards, Elite units, Cavalry)   Administration 7, Army 31, Battles of note 61, Cavalry 88, 89, 90, Education 142, Elite troops 145, Guards 211, 212, Legion 255, March 263, Marriage 265, Military diploma 277, 279, Motivation 307, Pay 327, Recruitment 365, Religion 375, Sources 407, Society and army 399, Sources 407

Erudition (Education/Culture*)   Officers 318

Esprit de corps   Guards 213, Motivation 303, Veterans 473

Ethnarchy   Empire 153

Etruscans (Etrusci, Etruria*)   Armament 20, Army 27, Battle 48, Legion 252, Motivation 305, Phalanx 335, Triumph 462

Evectio   Sources 412

Evocati*, evocatio (military)   Honours 224, Military service 298, Pay 326, Rank 353, Sources 407, State and army 429, Veterans 472, 475

Evocatio* (religious)   Guards 211

Exarchate*, Exarchus   Rank 352

Excubitores, excubitorium   Army 32, Guards 213, Religion 375

Exercitatio, exercertator (see also Education, Training)   Parades 321, Rank 353

Expansion (see also Imperialism)   Army 28, Battles of note 57, Borders 73, 74, 75, Civil war 94, Colonies 100, 101, Consequences of war 107, Empire 150, 151, Enemies 158, Garrison 185, Generals of note 204, Infrastructure 232, Innovation 237, 239, Representations of war 382, State and army 428, 429, Victory 479, War 495, Wars of note 513, 516

Expeditio, expediti   March 260, 261, 262, Officers 318

Exploratores*   Armament 20, Battles of note 54, March 260, Reconnaissance 358, 360, 361, 362

Extraordinarii*   Elite troops 145, March 261

Fabrica (Fabrica, fabricenses*; see also Crafts, trade)   Rank 348, Specialists 420

Fallen, eulogy to   Heroism 215

Fallen, memorial to   Sources 405

Fallen troops   Battle 51, 52, Consequences of war 111, Customs of war 118, Death 119, Descriptions of war 122, 123, 129, Discipline 135, Elite troops 145, Generals of note 206, Law of war 248, Military service 294, Motivation 302, 303, 304, Phalanx 334, Religion 370, Representations of war 379, 381, 385, 386, Sparta 414, State and army 427, Valour 467, 468, Victory 477, 478

Family*   Military service 296, Sources 410

Fear   Emotions 146, 147, 148, Terror 451, Valour 469, 470

Federalism   Empire 151

Felt   Armament 20, Military service 292, Phalanx 333

Feriae Latinae*   Religion 371

Feriale Duranum*   Sources 410

Festival calendar   Parades 320, Religion 376, 377, Sources 410, Symbols 449, Victory 479

Festival (Festivals; Feasts*)   Sparta 413, Victory 478, 480

Fetiales*   Diplomacy 132, Law of war 249, 251, Religion 371, 372, 374, 375, State and army 429, Valour 470

Fibula   Honours 221

Fidelis   Honours 224

Field army   Rank 352

Firearms (see also Artillery, Long-range weapons)   Innovation 235

Flaviales   Rank 349, 350, 352

Flight, putting to   Battle 52, Battles of note 59, 61, Cowardice 116, Discipline 136, Emotions 147, Generals of note 190, 193, 209, Reconnaissance 360, Siege warfare 391, Slavery 396, Valour 467, Wars of note 497, 498

Flute, flautist/Aulete   Parades 321, Specialists 417, Transmission of orders 459

Foederati* (see also Socii, Allies)   Alliances 13, 14, Army 30, 32, 34, Battles of note 55, Borders 77, Civil war 95, Diplomacy 133, Education 140, Motivation 308, Officers 319, State and army 431

Foedus* (see also Alliance)   Alliances 13, 15, Diplomacy 133, Empire 152, Law of war 249, 251, Military service 295, Motivation 306, Oath 314

Foot soldiers (see also Infantry)   Administration 2, Alliances 12, Armament 16, Army 22, 23, Avoidance of military service 42, Battle 49, Battles of note 53, 55, 58, 59, Cavalry 87, Costs of war 112, Equipment 165, Generals of note 204, 207, Innovation 235, 236, Legion 252, 255, March 262, Mercenaries 272, Supply 440, War 492, Wars of note 497

Forced labour   Prisoners 337, 338

Forced recruitment   Military service 297

Foreigners   Borders 70, Colonies 101, Guards 213, Law of war 249, Prisoners 339, Recruitment 365, Slavery 395, Society and army 398, Sources 406, Veterans 473, 474

Formula togatorum   Alliances 14, Cavalry 88

Fors Fortuna   Religion 372

Fort   Borders 75, Consequences of war 105

Fortifications*   Bandits 44, Battle 46, 48, Borders 73, 74, 75, 77, Camp 82, Cavalry 89, Garrison 184, Heroism 216, Innovation 240, 241, Pay 325, Policing 336, Siege warfare 389, Specialists 418, Supply 439

Fortified settlement   Generals of note 203

Fortitudo   Valour 469

Fortress   Acropolis 1, Army 29, 31, Borders 71, 75, 77, Camp 80, 82, Consequences of war 105, Costs of war 113, Descriptions of war 122, Fortification 179, Hunting 227, Infrastructure 231, 232, Innovation 243,

Mutiny 311, Religion 370, Representations of war 383, Siege warfare 389, 390, Victory 481, Wars of note 511
Fortuna* Religion 376
Fortuna equestris Religion 372
Franks (Franci*) Generals of note 198, 200, Officers 319
Freedmen*/Liberti Administration 6, Army 29, Conscription 102, 103, Fleet 176, Honours 223, Marriage 265, 266, Military service 296, Prisoners 338, Slavery 395, 396, Sparta 415
Freedom* Army 23, 24, Battles of note 62, Consequences of war 104, Descriptions of war 128, Discipline 136, Enemies 159, Hostages 225, Law of war 248, 250, Military law 283, Military service 290, Motivation 302, Mutiny 311, Prisoners 339, Production system 341, Recruitment 363, Slavery 395, Society and army 398, Valour 467, Wars of note 500, 513
Front Borders 75, 76, Guards 212, Heroism 215, Prisoners 338, Reconnaissance 362
Frontier fortification Strategy 436
Frontier province Rear 355
Frontier state Empire 150
Frontier zone Army 23, 24, 31, Bandits 44, Borders 69, 70, 71, 73, 76, Consequences of war 104, Education 140, Innovation 240, Reconnaissance 358, State and army 431
Frumentarii* Transmission of orders 462, Military service 297
Funditores* Armament 18, Mercenaries 274
Funeral, funeral rites (Burial*) Death 119, Law of war 248, Parades 321
Funerary architecture* Battle 52, Death 119, Descriptions of war 122, Heroism 215, Military service 294, Rank 349, Representations of war 381, 382, State and army 427
Funerary cult Victory 477, Death 120, Education 142, Sources 407
Funerary oration Consequences of war 103
Funus militare Death 119
Fustuarium Military law 281

Gallic Wars Rank 346, War 493
Garrison Acropolis 1, Army 25, 26, 27, 29, 31, Auxiliaries 40, Bandits 44, Battles of note 57, Borders 71, 77, Civil war 95, Consequences of war 104, 105, Costs of war 112, Education 140, Fortification 181, Garrison 185, Generals of note 200, Guards 211, Infrastructure 230, Medical corps 270, Mercenaries 273, Militia 299, 300, Society and army 399, Sources 412, Supply 439, 440, 441, 442, War 492, Wars of note 502
General (see also Imperator, Strategos) Battles of note 62, Consequences of war 110, Descriptions of war 129, Heroism 215, 216, Honours 221, 225, Military literature 285, 290, Pay 326, Peace 331, Rank 349
General's oration Enemies 156, Motivation 303, Symbols 450

General's report Descriptions of war 129
Genius* Religion 375
Genius armamentorum Religion 375
Genius castrorum Religion 375
Genius cohortis Religion 375
Genius imperatoris Religion 375
Genius loci Religion 377
Genius sacramenti Oath 314
Genius signorum Religion 375
Genius tabularii Religion 375
Genius turmae Religion 375
Germanic Wars/Bella Germanica Legion 254
Germani (Germani, Germania*) Armament 20, Cavalry 88, 89, Diplomacy 133, Enemies 156, 162, Fortification 183, Generals of note 201, 202, Honour 220, March 262, Phalanx 332, Production system 342, Rear 355, Religion 378, State and army 431, Timeframe of war 454
Gift of money (see also Donativum) Auxiliaries 38
Gladiarius Consequences of war 109
Gladiator* Prisoners 339
Glandes Armament 18
Gloria Honour 219
Goat* Transmission of orders 461
Gorgo [1]* Symbols 448
Gorgóneion* Officers 318
Goths (Goti*) Borders 77, Officers 319
Governor* (Consularis*) Alliances 12, Cavalry 89, Consequences of war 104, Diplomacy 133, Empire 153, General 189, Guards 211, Infrastructure 233, Marriage 265, 266, Military diploma 276, 279, Military law 282, Militia 300, Motivation 307, Mutiny 313, Peace 330, Rank 345, 347, Reconnaissance 360, 361, Wars of note 500
Graffiti Sources 409
Grave mound Heroism 214
Greaves (see also Cuisses) Armament 19, Infantry 229
Greeks Language 245
Griffin* Legion 257
Guard (see also Elite units, elite soldiers) Army 26, 30, 33, Cavalry 88, Civil war 95, Education 143, Elite troops 145, Hunting 226, Military service 297, Officers 318, Rank 344, 347, 349, Recruitment 365, Symbols 449
Guerrilla, guerrilla war(fare) Army 24, Battle 45, Battles of note 55, Education 140, War 490, Wars of note 498, 500, 504
Gymnasium* Descriptions of war 121, Discipline 135, 136, Education 141, Infrastructure 230, Recruitment 363, Sources 406, War 491, 492

Harbours, docks* Fleet 172, 173, 175, Infrastructure 230, 231, Rear 355, Society and army 397, Sources 406, State and army 427, War 490, Wars of note 510
Harmostai* Garrison 184, Officers 316
Harpocrates* Religion 376
Haruspex (Haruspices*) Religion 372

Hasmonaeans* War 492
Hasta [1]* Battle 48, Honours 221, Legion 252, March 263
Hastatus Army 28, Battle 49, 50, Legion 253, March 261
Hatred Emotions 147, Enemies 156, 157
Hegemon, hegemony (Hegemonia*) Alliances 11, 13, Rank 345, Recruitment 364, Specialists 417
Helepolis* Generals of note 195, March 262, War 492
Hellanodikai* Officers 315
Hellenic League* (see also League of Corinth) Alliances 12, Battles of note 62, Fleet 173, Peace 329
Hellenistic period Battle 45, 46, 47, 49, Fleet 175, 176, 177, General 186, 188, Mercenaries 271, Specialists 417, Victory 479, Victory titles 484
Helmet* Armament 19, Battle 48, Cavalry 86, Infantry 229, Legion 252, Military service 292, Parades 321, Phalanx 332, Symbols 447
Helots* Education 140, Enemies 158, Generals of note 199, Military service 293, Phalanx 334, Recruitment 363, Slavery 393, 394, Society and army 398, Sources 404, Sparta 414, 415, Wars of note 510
Helvetii* Auxiliaries 40, Militia 300, Wars of note 502, 504
Hercules (Heracles [1]*) Battles of note 59, Generals of note 191, Legion 257, 258, Religion 375, 376, Victory titles 485
Hero, heroism Battle 45, Descriptions of war 122, Discipline 134, Elite troops 145, Honour 217, Motivation 305, Rank 346, Sources 405, Symbols 447, Terror 451
Hero's death Motivation 302
Hetairoi* Army 24, Battle 48, Cavalry 86, Descriptions of war 126, Elite troops 145, Generals of note 192, Guards 210, Innovation 236, Society and army 397, War 492, Wars of note 497
High treason Enemies 160
Hipparch Cavalry 86, Officers 315, Rank 345
Hippeis (see also Cavalry, Horseman) Cavalry 86, Officers 315
Hippotoxotai* (see also Cavalry, Horseman) Cavalry 86, 87
Hodopoioi* March 262
Homoioi* Consequences of war 103
Homonoia* Civil war 92
Homo novus/Novus homo General 186, Generals of note 201
Homosexuality* Emotions 149, Military law 281, Motivation 303
Honorific title (see also Civium Romanorum, Fidelis, Pia, Torquata) Honours 224, State and army 432
Honour (Honos*) Army 23, Battle 45, Civilians 98, Cowardice 116, Descriptions of war 124, 126, Discipline 135, Emotions 147, Enemies 158, Generals of note 192, 205, Heroism 214, 215, Innovation 237, Motivation 301, Mutiny 310, 311, 312, Phalanx 334, Representations of war 382, Scorched earth 388, Society and army 400, Sources 407, Standard 424, Terror 451, Valour 468, 469, 470, Victory titles 485, War 494
Hoplite battle Battle 52, Consequences of war 103
Hoplite combat Military service 291
Hoplite equipment Parades 321, Representations of war 379
Hoplite (Hoplitai*) Alliances 12, Armament 15, Army 23, 24, 28, Battle 46, 47, Battles of note 59, 63, Cavalry 87, Consequences of war 105, Discipline 135, Education 140, Equipment 163, General 187, 189, Generals of note 196, Heroism 214, 215, Honour 218, Hunting 226, Infantry 229, Innovation 236, 238, 240, March 260, 261, 263, Mercenaries 271, 272, Military service 293, Motivation 302, Parades 322, Pay 324, 325, Phalanx 332, 333, 334, Policing 336, Recruitment 363, Representations of war 380, Society and army 397, 398, Sources 405, Sparta 414, 415, 416, Specialists 417, State and army 426, Transmission of orders 459, Valour 468, War 489, 490, 491, Wars of note 510, 513
Hoplite ideal Mutiny 311
Hoplite oath Borders 70
Hoplite phalanx (Phalanx*) Army 27, Battle 46, 47, Chariot 91, Descriptions of war 126, Discipline 134, Elite troops 145, Emotions 147, Innovation 243, Military literature 285, Mutiny 311, Sparta 414, Wars of note 513
Hoplitodromos Military service 292, 293
Horse* Cavalry 86, 89, Religion 372, State and army 426, Symbols 447, Transmission of orders 461
Horse nomads Dogs 139
Horus* Religion 376
Hospitalitas* Alliances 14, Sources 412
Hostage Garrison 184, Generals of note 190, 203, Law of war 251, Sources 405, War 488
Hostage-taking Reconnaissance 358
Huns (Hunni*) Battles of note 54, Generals of note 190
Hunting* Booty 65, Borders 70, Dogs 139, Vehicles 470
Hybris* Descriptions of war 122
Hygieia* Religion 376
Hypaspistai Army 25, Battle 47, Elite troops 145, Generals of note 204, Guards 210, Infantry 229, War 492

Ilarch (Ilarches) Rank 352
Imago Symbols 448
Imago, imaginifer, imaginarius (Imaginiferi, Imaginifarii*) Rank 350, Standard 423, Standard 423, 425, Symbols 448
Immunes Hunting 226, Legion 255, Medical corps 269, Military literature 289, Military service 297, Motivation 307, Rank 347, Specialists 419, 420
Immunitas* Diplomacy 130, Military law 281, 282, Motivation 307, Supply 443
Imperator* (see also General, Commander, Emperor, Strategos) Battle 52, Booty 65, 67, 68, Borders 73, Civil war 94, Elite troops 145, General 186, Generals

of note 193, 205, Guards 210, Honours 222, Innovation 237, Officers 317, Religion 374, Representations of war 386, Victory titles 487, Victory titles 485, 486

Imperialism (see also Expansion) Diplomacy 131, Empire 150, 151, 155, Enemies 162, General 187, Strategy 435

Imperiogenesis Alliances 10

Imperium* Administration 6, Army 28, Battle 45, Civil war 94, Honours 222, Innovation 236, 237, Officers 317, Recruitment 364, Religion 372, State and army 429, 430, Symbols 448, 450, Triumph 462, 463, Veterans 474, War 493

Infantry (see also Foot soldiers) Administration 5, Armament 18, 19, Army 22, 23, 24, 25, 26, 27, 28, 29, 32, 33, Auxiliaries 37, 38, Avoidance of military service 42, Battle 46, 47, 48, 51, Battles of note 55, Booty 67, Cavalry 86, 88, 89, Chariot 90, Costs of war 112, Education 142, Elite troops 145, Equipment 164, General 187, Generals of note 204, 208, Infantry 229, 230, Legion 253, March 263, Mercenaries 273, Military literature 289, Militia 299, Parades 322, Phalanx 332, 334, Rank 344, 345, 346, 347, 349, Strategy 438, Supply 439, Valour 469, War 491, Wars of note 507

Infrastructure* Camp 85, Chariot 90, Consequences of war 109, Costs of war 115, Military service 297, Rear 354, Sources 408, 410, State and army 427, 431, Strategy 437

Inheritance (Succession, laws of*) Battle 52, Marriage 264, 267, Military law 283, 284

Inheritance tax (Vicesima hereditatium) Army 29, Consequences of war 109, Innovation 237, Marriage 267, Military service 298, Veterans 475

Initiation* Education 140

Innovation Army 22, Civil war 95, Consequences of war 110, Fleet 172, Generals of note 195, 199

Inquisitio Recruitment 364

Inscriptions* Death 120, Sources 407, 408, 410

Inspection Parades 320, Pay 326

Insurgency Discipline 138, Military law 282, Mutiny 313

International law* Law of war 248, 249, Peace 329, 331, Prisoners 338

Irenarch, eirenarch Policing 337, Militia 299

Iron* Innovation 240, 243

Isis* Religion 372, 376

Itinerare* Maps 259, Reconnaissance 361

Iuniores* Battle 48

Ius fetiale Garrison 185, Valour 470, War 493, 495

Ius gentium Diplomacy 130, Law of war 251, Wars of note 502

Ius gladii Military law 282

Ius militandi in legione Legion 254

Ius militare Military service 298

Ius postliminii Honour 220, Law of war 248, 250

Iustum iter March 263

Iustum matrimonium Military service 296

Iuthungi* Borders 76, Prisoners 338

Iuventus (Iuvenes*) Militia 300

Janus/Ianus* Valour 470

Javelin, javelin thrower (see also Lancea, lancearii) Armament 18, Battle 47, 49, Cavalry 86, 87, Infantry 229, March 263, Military service 292, 293, Phalanx 333, State and army 426, Transmission of orders 460

Jewish War Costs of war 115, Militia 300, Prisoners 338, Terror 452

Jews (Judaism*) Enemies 156, 157, Rank 344, Recruitment 364, Standard 424, Terror 452, Wars of note 500, 504

Juno/Iuno* Religion 372, 376

Jupiter Dolichenus Religion 376

Jupiter/Iuppiter* Legion 258, Religion 372, 374, 375, 376, Symbols 448, 449, Victory titles 485

Jurisdiction Military law 283

Just war/Bellum iustum Descriptions of war 129, Diplomacy 131, 132, 133, Enemies 160, Garrison 185, Law of war 249, Military literature 286, Peace 329, War 493, 495, Wars of note 502

Kamax Cavalry 86

Katáphraktoi*/Klibanophóroi War 492

Katoikia Recruitment 364

Katoikos* Army 25

Kellogg-Briand Pact Peace 328

Killing Prisoners 337

King Costs of war 112, Law of war 249, Legion 252, Officers 316, Parades 322, Policing 336, Rank 345, 346, Recruitment 363, Sources 407

Kit Camp 82, March 260, 261, 262, 263

Kleros* Administration 4, 5, Army 25, Costs of war 112

Klerouchoi* Administration 5, Army 25, 26, Cavalry 87, Consequences of war 104, Esprit de corps 168, Generals of note 199, Mercenaries 273, Prisoners 338, Recruitment 363, Society and army 398, War 492

Koine eirene* (see also Peace, Pax Augusta, Pax Romana) Consequences of war 104, Diplomacy 131, Law of war 248, Peace 329, War 491

Kontos March 263

Kopis Cavalry 86

Krypteia* Education 140, State and army 426

Labarum* Symbols 449

Laeti* Borders 77, Law of war 250

Lance Armament 18, Battle 46, 47, Cavalry 86, 87, Law of war 250, Legion 252, Parades 321, Religion 372, Valour 470

Lancea, lancearii*, lanciarii Army 33, Battle 51, Cavalry 90, Education 142, March 262, 263, Rank 353

Laphyropoles Officers 315

Latin* Consequences of war 110, Language 245, Sources 410

Latini (Latini, Latium*) Military law 283

Latin League Motivation 305

Latin rights/Ius Latii Diplomacy 133, Military diploma 277
Latrones Avoidance of military service 43
Law of war (War, law of*) Law of war 247, Strategy 434, War 493
Lead* Armament 18
League of Corinth (see also Hellenic League) Alliances 11, 13, Generals of note 204
Leagues (States, confederation of*) Descriptions of war 121
Leather* Armament 20, Cavalry 86, Phalanx 333
Legatus Augusti pro praetore Officers 317, Rank 347, Religion 374, Strategy 435
Legatus*, Legate Army 29, Battles of note 57, Consequences of war 110, Diplomacy 132, Education 141, Empire 153, Fleet 177, Generals of note 194, 201, 207, Innovation 237, Legion 255, Marriage 264, Officers 317, 319, Peace 331, Rank 346, 347, Religion 375, 377, Veterans 474, Victory titles 485, Wars of note 500, 505
Legatus legionis/Legionary legate Honours 223, March 262, 263, Officers 317, Rank 347, 348, Religion 374, 377
Legionary camp Camp 82
Legionary, Legion (Legio*) Administration 6, Armament 20, Army 28, 29, 31, 32, Artillery 36, Auxiliaries 37, 41, Battle 46, 47, 49, 50, 51, Battles of note 56, 57, 58, 63, 64, Booty 68, Borders 76, Camp 82, 85, Cavalry 88, 89, Civil war 93, Conscription 102, Consequences of war 109, Costs of war 115, Death 119, Descriptions of war 125, Education 141, 142, Elite troops 145, Emotions 147, Empire 154, Esprit de corps 168, Generals of note 201, 202, 203, Guards 211, 212, Heroism 216, Honour 220, Honours 222, 224, Infantry 230, Infrastructure 233, Innovation 235, 236, 237, 239, 240, 242, Language 245, Legion 257, March 261, 262, 263, Marriage 265, Medical corps 267, 269, Military diploma 280, Military literature 287, Military service 295, 296, Motivation 306, 308, Mutiny 312, 313, Officers 317, 319, Pay 326, Phalanx 335, Policing 336, Production system 341, Rank 346, 347, 348, 349, 350, 352, Recruitment 364, Religion 376, Representations of war 386, Sources 407, Specialists 419, Standard 422, 423, State and army 431, 432, Symbols 448, 449, 450, Transmission of orders 460, 461, Valour 470, Vehicles 471, Veterans 473, 475, Wars of note 504, 505
Levy* (Dilectus) Administration 6, Borders 76, Conscription 102, Consequences of war 107, Law of war 249, Legion 254, Medical corps 268, Military law 281, Motivation 305, Sources 401, Recruitment 364, Veterans 473
Lex Oppia Consequences of war 109
Librarius Rank 348, 350
Librator* Consequences of war 110, Rank 348
Libyan Language 245
Life guards (see also Corporis custodes, Equites singulares (Augusti)) Dogs 139, Generals of note 208, Guards 209, 210, Legion 252, Military service 297, Sparta 414
Lighthouses* Infrastructure 231
Light infantry Cavalry 86, Rank 346
Lightly armed personnel Battles of note 58, Innovation 236, 238, 239, Legion 252, March 262, Mercenaries 273, Phalanx 333, 334, 335, Representations of war 380, Society and army 398, Sparta 414, State and army 426, Transmission of orders 460, Wars of note 510, 513
Limes* (see also Border) Army 30, 32, Borders 73, 74, Fortification 182, Garrison 185, Medical corps 268, Reconnaissance 360, Strategy 434
Limitanei* (see also Border troops) Administration 9, Army 30, 31, 33, 34, Auxiliaries 41, Borders 77, Cavalry 90, Generals of note 200, Innovation 238, Military law 282, Motivation 308, Officers 319, Rank 349, 351, Sources 412
Linen (Linen, flax*) Phalanx 333
Line of battle/Acies/Duplex acies/Triplex acies Battle 49, 50, 51, Legion 253, March 261, 262
Lion* Legion 257, Symbols 447
Liturgy* Civilians 99, Militia 299, War 490
Lixa Slavery 396
Lochagos Military service 291, Transmission of orders 460, Officers 315, 316
Lochos* Battle 47, Military service 291, Officers 315, Phalanx 333, Sparta 414, Sparta 414, 415, Transmission of orders 460
Logistics* Administration 6, 7, 8, Army 28, Battles of note 54, 59, Camp 84, Chariot 90, Civil war 95, Costs of war 115, Descriptions of war 122, Generals of note 197, 198, 207, Military service 296, 297, Rank 352, State and army 427, 432, Supply 439, 441, Timeframe of war 454, 455, Valour 469, Wars of note 512
Lonchophoroi March 263
Long-range combat Armament 18
Long-range weapons (see also Artillery, Firearms) Battle 45, 50, 51, Battles of note 59, Elephants 144
Lorica Armament 21, Fortification 181
Losses (see also Death, Death rate, Dead in battle) Production system 341
Loyalty (Fides*) Diplomacy 132, Enemies 160, General 188, Honour 219, Oath 314, Officers 317, Representations of war 382, Symbols 448, 449, Valour 470
Ludiones/Lydiones Parades 322
Ludus Troiae, Lusus Troiae Parades 320, 322
Lustratio* Parades 320, 321, 322, Religion 372, Symbols 449

Maccabean Revolt Civil war 92
Macedonians (Macedonia, Macedones*) Acropolis 1, Armament 17, Battle 46, 47, Civil war 92, Elite troops 145, Equipment 164, Generals of note 191, 195, 203, Language 245, March 263, Mercenaries 273, Pay 325, Siege warfare 390, Symbols 447, Transmission of orders 461

Macedonian Wars*
 – First Macedonian War   Peace 331
 – Second Macedonian War   Consequences of war 103, Motivation 306
 – Third Macedonian War   Avoidance of military service 42, Costs of war 114, Equipment 165

Machaira   Cavalry 86
Machimoi*   Army 26, Rank 345, Recruitment 363, War 492
Magister draconum   Rank 350
Magister equitum*   Cavalry 90, Generals of note 200, Rank 346
Magister militum*   Administration 8, Army 32, 33, 34, Generals of note 190, 208, Innovation 238, Military law 282, 283, Rank 349, 350, 352, Victory 480, 481
Magister officiorum*   Guards 212, Production system 342
Magister peditum   Battles of note 54, Cavalry 90, Generals of note 200
Magister utriusque militiae   Generals of note 190
Magistrate, Magistracy (Magistratus*)   Army 28, Borders 70, Civil war 94, Empire 152, Generals of note 205, Guards 210, Law of war 251, Officers 317, Parades 323, War 494
Maiestas*   Oath 314, Wars of note 504
Mandator   Language 245, Religion 376
Manicae*   Armament 21
Maniple (Manipulus*)   Army 28, 29, Battle 49, 50, Booty 68, Esprit de corps 168, Generals of note 202, Infantry 229, Innovation 236, 237, 239, 243, Legion 252, March 261, Motivation 305, Officers 317, Phalanx 335, Rank 346, Standard 422, Transmission of orders 460, Valour 470, War 492
Manoeuvre   Battle 50, Battles of note 57, 61, 62, Diplomacy 133, General 187, Generals of note 206, Language 246, Military literature 286, Rank 353, Sparta 415, Strategy 435, 436, Valour 470
Mansio*   Infrastructure 233, Maps 259, Rear 355, Sources 412, Supply 445
Maps (see also Cartography)   Reconnaissance 361
Marathonomakoi   Descriptions of war 123, Heroism 215, War 490
Marauder   Borders 71
Marching camp   Battles of note 64
Marching orders   Transmission of orders 461
Marcomannic Wars   Military diploma 279
Marines   Officers 318, Recruitment 365, 366
Market*   Equipment 164, Pay 324, Prisoners 337, Production system 342, Rear 355, Strategy 436, Supply 439, 441, 443
Marriage*/Matrimony (see also Conubium)   Civilians 96, 98, Law of war 250, Marriage 264, 265, 266, Medical corps 269, Military diploma 278, 279, Military law 282, Military service 296, 298, Motivation 307, Officers 317, Prisoners 339, 340, Sources 408
Mars*   Religion 372, 375, 376, Symbols 448, 449, Victory titles 485

Massacre   Battle 45, Battles of note 54, Booty 66, Civil war 92, Consequences of war 103, Emotions 147, Generals of note 209, Prisoners 337, Strategy 434, Terror 451, Wars of note 505, 507
Mater castrorum   Representations of war 386
Matres Aufaniae   Religion 376
Matricula   Administration 9, Rank 353, Sources 412
Mattiobarbulus   Armament 18
Mechanical construction   Military literature 288
Medical services (military)*   Civilians 96, Specialists 419
Medicine*   Marriage 266, Medical corps 268
Medicus   Civilians 97, Enemies 159, Medical corps 268, 269, Rank 348, Specialists 417, 420
Men of Bronze   Phalanx 335
Mensor*   March 262, Rank 348, 350, Sources 408
Mercenaries*/Mercenarius   Administration 5, Alliances 12, 14, Army 23, 24, 25, 26, 27, Auxiliaries 37, Bandits 44, Battle 47, 50, Borders 71, Civil war 92, Consequences of war 109, Costs of war 112, 114, 115, Descriptions of war 121, Education 140, Elite troops 145, Empire 152, Enemies 159, 162, Equipment 164, 165, Esprit de corps 168, Fleet 175, 176, General 186, 187, 189, Generals of note 190, 204, Guards 209, 210, Infantry 229, Innovation 236, Language 245, Mercenaries 271, 274, Military service 293, Motivation 302, 303, Mutiny 311, Oath 314, Officers 315, 316, Phalanx 333, 335, Prisoners 338, Rank 345, Reconnaissance 358, Recruitment 363, 364, Scorched earth 388, Slavery 393, Sources 409, Sparta 415, 416, State and army 426, 427, Strategy 436, Supply 440, 441, Timeframe of war 454, War 490, 491, 492, Wars of note 497, 508, 510, 513
Mercenary commander   Military literature 286
Mercy   Emotions 149
Metator   March 262, Rank 350
Metropolis [1]*, Mother city   Colonies 100
Miles   Honours 222, 224
Miles gregarius   Military service 297, Motivation 305
Military budget   Military service 295
Military deception (see also Ruse de guerre, Stratagem)   Battle 45, Battles of note 61, General 187, 188, Military literature 286, Strategy 434, 436, Supply 441
Military diplomas*/Diplomata militaria   Auxiliaries 39, Cavalry 89, Marriage 265, Military diploma 275, Military service 298, Recruitment 364, 366, Sources 407, 408, State and army 431
Military law*   Hunting 227, Law of war 249, Military literature 288, Sources 403
Military literature   Generals of note 193
Military punishment   Military law 282
Military service, army service   Auxiliaries 38, Battle 46, Battles of note 55, Civilians 96, 99, Consequences of war 109, General 187, Generals of note 193, 205, Innovation 236, Legion 252, Motivation 307, Mutiny 311, Parades 322,

Recruitment 363, 366, Religion 377, Slavery 393, State and army 429, Veterans 472, 476
Military settlement Army 26, Borders 71, Specialists 418
Military technology and engineering* Innovation 242
Militia armata Rank 348, Sources 412
Militia army Costs of war 114, 115, Fleet 176, Innovation 236, Military service 296, Officers 315
Militiae Rank 352, State and army 430, Triumph 463
Militiae mutatio Military diploma 276, Military law 282, Religion 372, 375, Symbols 448
Militia equestris Officers 317
Militia inermis Rank 348, 352
Militia officialis Sources 412
Militia (see also Citizen militia) Auxiliaries 39, March 263, Mercenaries 273, Mutiny 311, Policing 337, Timeframe of war 454
Mines Consequences of war 105, Fleet 173, 174, Siege warfare 390
Mining* Policing 337, Prisoners 337, Production system 342, Society and army 398
Minoan Fleet 171
Minotaur (Minotaurus*) Transmission of orders 461
Minting* Consequences of war 105, Sparta 415, Symbols 450, Triumph 465
Missicius Sources 407
Missio [1]*/Discharge, dismissal Administration 9, Consequences of war 109, Military law 282, Military service 298, Motivation 307, Rank 349, Sources 410, 412
Missio causaria Medical corps 268, Military service 297
Missio honesta/Honesta missio Civilians 98, Consequences of war 110, Medical corps 268, Military diploma 275, 276, 278, Military service 296, 297, Recruitment 366, Religion 377, Standard 425
Missio ignominiosa Military law 282, Prisoners 339
Misthophoría Pay 324
Misthophoroi Mercenaries 271, 273, Recruitment 363
Misthos* Costs of war 112, Pay 324, 325
Misthotos Mercenaries 271
Mithras*, Mithraeum Consequences of war 110, Religion 375, 376
Mobilization Society and army 398
Monarch Parades 323
Monomachy Battle 45
Montani [2]* Militia 300
Monument Armament 17, Battle 52, Battles of note 59, Consequences of war 111, Generals of note 203, Military service 291, 294, Motivation 302, Representations of war 380, 381, 382, 384, Sources 407, Symbols 449
Mora [1]* Officers 315, Sparta 415
Morale Battle 46, 52, Discipline 135, Language 245, Military literature 286, Motivation 304, Phalanx 335, Prisoners 339, Siege warfare 390, Specialists 417, Valour 470

Morality Discipline 134, 136, Emotions 149, Strategy 434, Terror 451, Valour 470
Mortality rate Battle 52, Phalanx 334, Consequences of war 103
Motivation Eve-of-battle speech 170
Mounted guards (see also Equites singulares (Augusti)) Administration 7, Discipline 137
Mourning* Emotions 149, Military service 294
Muli Mariani Generals of note 202, Vehicles 471
Mulio Slavery 396
Munerum indictio Military law 282, Military service 297
Munifex Rank 350, 351
Munus, Munera* Infrastructure 233
Murus Gallicus* Fortification 181
Music* Innovation 238, Military service 291, War 489
Mutatio Rear 355
Mutiny* Civilians 98, Elite troops 145, Generals of note 192, 198, 204, Mercenaries 274, Military service 298, Mutiny 310, 311, 313, Oath 314, Officers 318, Sources 401, State and army 432, Wars of note 500
Mycenaeans Acropolis 1, Alliances 10, Army 22, Fleet 171, Innovation 240, Military service 290, Siege warfare 389, War 488
Mysarchos Rank 345
Myth* Borders 69, Emotions 150, Empire 151, Rank 346, Representations of war 382, 385
Mythologization Battles of note 63
Mythology Battles of note 60, Death 119, Enemies 161, Heroism 214, Motivation 302, Parades 322, Representations of war 380, 382, Symbols 448, Wars of note 516

Natalis Religion 376
Natio, nationes Education 140, 142, Infantry 230
Nauarchia Officers 315
Nauarchos* Motivation 306, Officers 315, 318, Rank 345, 348
Naukraria (Naukraria, naukraros*) Administration 3
Naupegus Consequences of war 109
Naval array Descriptions of war 122, Sources 405
Naval battle Infantry 229
Naval warfare* Phalanx 335
Navy (Navies*)/Classis Administration 3, 5, 7, Army 25, 26, 27, Battles of note 53, 62, Conscription 102, Costs of war 112, 113, Descriptions of war 122, Fortification 180, Generals of note 195, 198, 205, Honours 224, Hunting 226, Infrastructure 231, Innovation 235, 238, 241, 242, Legion 252, Marriage 265, Medical corps 269, Mercenaries 272, 273, Military diploma 277, 278, 279, Military literature 285, Military service 295, Militia 300, Motivation 302, Officers 315, 318, Pay 325, 327, Peace 331, Phalanx 335, Rank 346, 348, Recruitment 363, 366, Religion 372, Representations of war 385, Sources 405, Slavery 393, 394, 395, 396, Sources 405, 407, Specialists 419, State and army 427, Strategy 436, 437, 438, Timeframe of war 455,

War 490, 492, Wars of note 497, 505, 508, 510, 511, 513, 516
Necropoleis* Death 119, 120
Neptune (Neptunus*) Legion 258, Religion 376
Neutrality Law of war 248
Night watch Language 246
Nike* Victory 477, Victory titles 484
Nobility Army 24, Fleet 173, Generals of note 191, Guards 210, Legion 252, Rank 346, State and army 426, 428
Non-combatants Military service 293, Specialists 417, 418
Notarius Rank 348
Notitia dignitatum* Army 33, Auxiliaries 41, Officers 319, Rank 351, Reconnaissance 362, Sources 402, 412, State and army 431, Strategy 438, Symbols 449
Numerus* Camp 85, Cavalry 89, Education 140, 142, Infantry 230, Rank 351, 352, Sources 412

Oarsmen Society and army 398, State and army 426
Oath* (see also Sacramentum) Administration 6, 7, Alliances 10, 11, 13, Army 28, Booty 67, 68, Civil war 92, Consequences of war 104, Descriptions of war 121, Diplomacy 132, Discipline 137, Education 140, 143, Enemies 159, Esprit de corps 169, Generals of note 197, Honours 223, Law of war 251, Motivation 305, Pay 326, Prisoners 339, Religion 369, 371, 374, 378, Representations of war 385, Sources 404, 412, Standard 423, 424, State and army 432, Symbols 448, 449, Valour 470, Veterans 474
Obedience (see also Disciplina militaris) Discipline 137, Generals of note 194, Sparta 413, State and army 430
Oblique order Education 141, Generals of note 196
Occupation, military Army 25, 26, Borders 74, 76, Sources 404, Wars of note 502, 505
Offensive Army 22, 23, Borders 77, Descriptions of war 121, Empire 154, 155, Innovation 235, 239, Timeframe of war 454, Wars of note 504, 508, 511
Offensive weaponry War 488
Officer, officer corps Administration 4, 6, 9, Army 26, 28, Battle 47, Battles of note 54, 55, Booty 67, 68, Civilians 96, 97, 98, Consequences of war 106, Descriptions of war 129, Discipline 138, Eve-of-battle speech 169, General 186, Generals of note 191, 209, Guards 211, Heroism 216, Honour 219, Honours 222, 223, Hunting 227, Innovation 235, Language 245, Legion 254, March 262, Marriage 264, 266, Medical corps 268, Military law 281, 282, Military service 291, 293, 296, Motivation 302, 306, 307, 308, Mutiny 313, Prisoners 339, Rank 344, 346, 348, 353, Reconnaissance 361, Religion 375, 377, Sources 408, Sources 408, 410, 412, State and army 428, 432, Supply 439, Transmission of orders 460, 461, Wars of note 502, 512
Officium*, officiales Camp 83, Military diploma 276, Motivation 307, Officers 319, Rank 348, 351, 352, Reconnaissance 361, Religion 376

Oikoumene* Empire 155
Oliganthropy Consequences of war 106, Civil war 92, Garrison 184, Peace 330, Phalanx 335, Society and army 397, State and army 426
Omen* Valour 469
Onager Artillery 37
Opsonion Costs of war 112
Optimates* Civil war 94, Generals of note 202, Camp 84, Legion 252, Rank 350, Specialists 419, 420, Transmission of orders 460
Oracle* Religion 368
Orderlies Rank 350
Ordinarius, ordinatus Officers 319, Rank 349, 350, 351, 352
Origo* Recruitment 364, Sources 408
Ornamenta triumphalia Descriptions of war 125, Generals of note 194, Honours 223, Triumph 464, 465, Victory 480, Wars of note 501
Orphans* Motivation 303, Society and army 397
Ostrakon* Sources 410
Ovatio* Enemies 160, Triumph 463, 464, Victory 479

Pacifism Avoidance of military service 42, Descriptions of war 129, Diplomacy 133, Enemies 157
Paean* Phalanx 333, Religion 370, Transmission of orders 459, Victory 478
Palatini* Army 32, 34, Military law 282, Rank 349
Palisades Military service 292
Palta Armament 16
Panic Battle 52, Battles of note 60, Emotions 148
Panis militaris Military service 296
Panoplia Phalanx 332
Panoply Battle 51, Innovation 238, Symbols 448
Papilio Camp 84
Parade Death 119, Equipment 164, Military service 296, Parades 320, 323, Standard 424, Triumph 462, Victory 479
Paragoge March 262
Paraphylax Militia 299, Policing 337
Parma (round shield) Armament 20, Infantry 229, Symbols 450
Parthians* Battles of note 56, Camels 79, Consequences of war 107, 108, 109, 111, Empire 154, Enemies 161, Generals of note 194, 202, Honour 219, 220, Innovation 240, Military literature 289, Militia 300, Prisoners 340, Reconnaissance 360
Pater patratus Law of war 249, 250, Religion 372
Patria Motivation 304
Patria potestas* Military law 284, Military service 296
Patriotism Motivation 305
Patron, Patronage Auxiliaries 39, Enemies 160, Marriage 266
Pax* Augusta (see also Peace) Civil war 93, Diplomacy 133, Peace 329, State and army 432, Victory titles 486
Pay (Wages*) Costs of war 112
Peace, conditions of Administration 6, Generals of note 196
Peace, regulation of Generals of note 194

Peace (see also Pax Augusta, Pax Romana)
Alliances 13, Avoidance of military service 42,
Borders 77, Consequences of war 104, 106,
Descriptions of war 121, 126, 128, Emotions 147,
Enemies 158, 160, Fleet 174, Fortification 181, Generals
of note 196, 199, Innovation 242, Law of war 247,
248, 249, Military law 282, Phalanx 334, Religion 368,
Representations of war 386, Sources 404, Sparta 413,
State and army 427, 430, 431, Terror 453, Victory 477,
480, Victory titles 484, War 491, 492, 494, 495, Wars
of note 501, 507

Peace treaty Alliances 12, Battles of note 59,
Consequences of war 104, Diplomacy 130, 131,
Honour 219, Law of war 251, Oath 314, Peace 329, 331,
Prisoners 338, 339, 340, Religion 368, Sources 405,
Timeframe of war 455

Pectorale Armament 20

Peculium* castrense Law of war 249, Military
law 283, 284

Pedites singulares March 262

Pegasus [1]* Legion 257

Peloponnesian League Alliances 10, 11, 12,
Consequences of war 104, Fleet 174, Generals of
note 196, Oath 314, Pay 325, Peace 330, Sparta 414,
Sources 404, Sparta 414, Strategy 436, 437, War 490,
Wars of note 513

Peloponnesian War Acropolis 1, Alliances 12,
Army 23, 24, Consequences of war 104, 105, Costs
of war 113, Descriptions of war 126, Diplomacy 131,
Emotions 147, 149, Fleet 174, Fortification 180,
Garrison 184, Generals of note 199, Infantry 229,
Innovation 236, 238, 240, Law of war 247, 248,
March 260, Mercenaries 272, Military literature 285,
Military service 292, 294, Motivation 302, Mutiny 311,
Officers 316, Pay 325, Prisoners 337, Religion 368, 371,
Scorched earth 388, Siege warfare 389, Slavery 393,
394, Sources 409, Sparta 414, 415, Timeframe of
war 454, Victory 478, War 490, 491, Wars of note 507

Peltastai* Armament 17, Army 24, 25, 26, Battles of
note 58, Infantry 229, Innovation 238, March 261,
Mercenaries 272, Rank 344, Representations of
war 379, War 490

Pelte Armament 17, Battle 47

Penestai* Recruitment 363

Pentecost's Military service 291, Officers 315,
Sparta 415

Pentekonteres, pentekosteres Officers 315,
Transmission of orders 460

Peregrinus* Army 29, Conscription 102, Empire 155,
Enemies 159, Honours 222, Infantry 230,
Marriage 265, Military diploma 275, 277, Military
law 283, Military service 296, Motivation 307,
Recruitment 365, 366, Religion 375, Slavery 395, 396

Pergamonese Battles of note 58

Perioikoi* Phalanx 334

Peripolos Bandits 44, Education 140

Persians Battles of note 59, 62, Camels 79, Camp 80,
Descriptions of war 121, Empire 150, 151, Enemies 156,
158, 161, Equipment 164, Fleet 175, Generals of
note 198, 200, Hostages 225, Infrastructure 232,
Innovation 240, Language 245, Military
literature 286, Military service 293, Motivation 303,
Phalanx 334, 335, Recruitment 363, 364, Religion 368,
Representations of war 380, 381, 382, Siege
warfare 389, Sources 404, 406, Victory titles 484,
War 492, Wars of note 508, 510, 511

Persian Wars* Acropolis 1, Battles of note 59,
Descriptions of war 128, Enemies 156, Esprit de
corps 168, Fleet 173, Fortification 180, Infantry 229,
Military literature 285, Pay 324, Religion 370,
Slavery 394, Sources 405, State and army 426,
Timeframe of war 454, Victory 478, War 490

Pezetairoi (Pez(h)etairoi*) Army 24, 25, 26, Elite
troops 145, Generals of note 204, Guards 210,
Innovation 239, War 492, Wars of note 497

Phalanx* (see also Hoplite phalanx) Armament 15,
17, Army 23, 24, 25, 26, 27, Battle 46, 47, 49, 51, Battles
of note 58, Camp 80, Cavalry 87, Discipline 134, 135,
Education 140, Elephants 144, Esprit de corps 168,
General 187, 189, Generals of note 191, 196, 204,
Heroism 216, Infantry 229, Innovation 236, 238,
239, March 260, 261, 263, Mercenaries 273, 274,
Military literature 285, 287, Military service 291, 294,
Mutiny 311, Oath 314, Phalanx 332, 335, Rank 344,
Representations of war 379, Sparta 414, State
and army 426, Transmission of orders 459, 460,
Valour 467, Vehicles 470, War 489, 490, 491, 492

Phalera Honours 221, 224

Phoros* Alliances 12

Phrourarchos* Rank 345

Phylarchos [1]* Cavalry 86, Officers 315

Phyle [1]* Cavalry 86, Descriptions of war 122,
Equipment 164, Military service 291, Mutiny 311,
Officers 315, Society and army 398, Sources 405,
Sparta 414, State and army 426

Pictorial art Heroism 214

Piety Valour 469

Pili, pilani Battle 49, Legion 253

Pillage Prisoners 339

Pilum* Armament 18, Battle 49, 50, 51, Legion 252,
253, March 263

Pinna Fortification 181

Piracy*, Pirates Borders 76, Consequences of war 106,
108, Enemies 160, Fleet 177, 179, Generals of note 193,
206, Honours 221, Sources 406, Timeframe of
war 455, War 488, 492, Wars of note 506

Pius, Pia Honours 224

Plaision March 260

Plinthion March 260, 262

Plumbata Armament 18

Plunder Bandits 44, Battles of note 54, Booty 65,
66, 68, 69, Civilians 96, Consequences of war 108,
Costs of war 112, Empire 151, Law of war 250,
March 263, Mercenaries 274, Motivation 306,
Pay 325, Prisoners 337, 338, 339, Reconnaissance 362,
Religion 369, Representations of war 382, Society
and army 400, Specialists 417, State and army 429,
Strategy 436, Supply 441, Terror 452, Veterans 472,
Victory 478, 481, Wars of note 508, 510

Poeni (Phoenicians, Poeni*) Language 245

Polemarchos* Officers 315, Transmission of orders 460

Police* Army 29, Borders 76, Camels 79, Education 140, Garrison 185, Military service 297, Militia 299, Policing 336, Rank 348, Society and army 400, Sources 410

Polis citizens Innovation 238, Representations of war 379

Polis patriotism Motivation 301

Polis* (see also City state) Army 23, 24, Cavalry 86, Costs of war 112, 113, Descriptions of war 122, Empire 151, 153, Esprit de corps 168, Heroism 215, Innovation 241, Law of war 247, Military service 291, Motivation 301, Mutiny 311, Peace 329, Phalanx 332, 333, 334, Prisoners 337, Religion 370, Representations of war 385, Society and army 397, Sources 404, Wars of note 512

Polyandreion Sources 405

Polyreme Fleet 175, 176, 178

Pomerium* Civil war 93, Honours 221, 222, State and army 430, Triumph 462, 463, War 493

Pompa Parades 320, 322, 323, Triumph 462

Popular assembly Fleet 173, 174, Strategy 435

Populares* Civil war 94

Porta decumana Camp 82, 83

Porta praetoria Camp 82

Porta quintana Camp 82

Portents Booty 68, Motivation 304, Religion 369

Posteriores Battle 50, Cavalry 88

Post-traumatic stress disorder Consequences of war 111, Phalanx 334, Valour 470

Praeda* Military service 295

Praefectus [1]* annonae Supply 443

Praefectus [5]* castrorum Officers 318, Rank 347, Military service 297, Slavery 396

Praefectus [8]* fabrum Specialists 418

Praefectus alae Auxiliaries 39

Praefectus classis Military diploma 276

Praefectus cohortis/Cohort prefect Rank 346

Praefectus praetorio*/Praetorian Prefect Army 32, Cavalry 88, Generals of note 200, Guards 211, 212, Honours 224, Military service 295, Officers 318, Rank 347, 348, Scorched earth 388, Specialists 419, Supply 445

Praefectus*, prefect Administration 8, Army 29, Camp 83, Guards 211, Honours 224, Innovation 237, Language 246, March 262, 263, Marriage 266, Officers 317, 318, 319, Rank 346, 347, 348, 350, 351, 353, Wars of note 504

Praefectus sociorum Cavalry 88

Praemia, praemia militiae/Veterans' benefits Honours 222, Military service 298, Pay 328

Praepositus* Officers 318, 319, Rank 348, 351

Praesentales Military law 283

Praesidia, praesidium Bandits 44, Camp 81, Sources 410

Praetentura Camp 82, 83, 84

Praetor* Military law 283, Rank 346, Religion 371, 372, 375, State and army 429

Praetorian camp Camp 82, Religion 375

Praetorian tribune Generals of note 208

Praetorium* Camp 83, Religion 375

Pridianum Military service 296, Sources 410

Priests* (see also Clericus/Chaplain) Conscription 102

Primicerius* Officers 319, Rank 349, 350, 351, 352, 353, Sources 412

Primi ordines March 263, Military service 297, Officers 317

Primus pilus, Primipilus* Battle 50, Camp 84, Guards 211, Honours 221, 224, March 262, Motivation 305, Officers 317, 318, 319, Pay 328, Rank 347, Religion 377, Transmission of orders 461

Princeps* Army 28, Battle 49, 50, Cavalry 88, Guards 211, Legion 253, March 261, Rank 351

Princeps iuventutis* Parades 321, Symbols 450

Principales* Legion 255, Military law 282, Military service 297, Motivation 307, Rank 346, 347, 348, 350, Religion 375, Specialists 419

Principia* Camp 84, 85, Rank 350, Religion 375, 377

Priores/Protoi Battle 50, Cavalry 88, Rank 352

Prisoners of war* Army 34, Avoidance of military service 43, Booty 65, 66, 67, 68, 69, Borders 76, Consequences of war 103, 110, 111, Customs of war 118, Enemies 159, 160, Fleet 176, Generals of note 195, Honour 219, 220, Language 245, Law of war 250, Parades 321, Phalanx 333, Reconnaissance 358, 360, 361, Religion 372, Representations of war 380, 385, Society and army 398, Sources 405, 406, Specialists 417, Symbols 447, Terror 452, Triumph 462, 463, 464, War 488, 495, Wars of note 508

Privilege (Privilegium*)/Commoda Administration 7, 9, Civilians 99, Consequences of war 104, 109, Descriptions of war 122, Diplomacy 133, Guards 212, Legion 252, Marriage 264, 265, Military diploma 275, 276, 280, Military law 281, 283, Military service 295, 297, Mutiny 311, Rear 355, Society and army 400, Sources 408, Supply 443

Probatio*, probatus Conscription 102, Education 142, Recruitment 365

Procession* Parades 320, 321, 322, 323, Triumph 462, 463, 464, 465, Victory 480, 481

Proconsul* Militia 299, Rank 346, Wars of note 502

Procurator, procurator* Augusti Rank 347, Rear 355, Supply 443

Prodromoi [2]* Administration 2, Army 25, Cavalry 87, Reconnaissance 358

Production of goods Military service 297

Profectio Parades 320, 322, Triumph 463

Professional army, professional soldier Auxiliaries 37, Camp 81, Civilians 96, Costs of war 115, Education 140, Elite troops 145, Generals of note 201, Infrastructure 230, Innovation 236, 243, Legion 254, Medical corps 267, Mercenaries 271, 273, Military law 280, 281, Military service 295, 296, 297, Motivation 307, Officers 317, Society and army 399,

Sources 403, Specialists 418, 419, State and army 428, Timeframe of war 454, Veterans 476, War 495
Professionalism   Battle 46, 50, State and army 432, Veterans 473, 474
Professionalization   Army 24, 28, 31, Costs of war 114, Empire 151, Esprit de corps 168, Generals of note 204, Honours 222, Innovation 236, Mercenaries 272, Military diploma 278, Military service 297, Motivation 305, Mutiny 311, Officers 318, Rank 347, Recruitment 363, 364, State and army 429, Specialists 417, Strategy 436, Transmission of orders 460, War 491, Wars of note 510
Profession   Discipline 135, Education 140, Garrison 185
Proletarii*   Innovation 236, Military service 295, Motivation 306
Proletarization   Civil war 93
Promachoi   Elite troops 145, Emotions 147
Promagistracy   War 494
Promotion (see also Career path)   Officers 318
Propaganda*   Enemies 159, Prisoners 340
Propagator imperii   Empire 155
Proscriptions*   Civil war 94, Enemies 160
Proskynemata   Sources 411
Prostitution*, Prostitute   Marriage 266
Protective deity   Religion 378
Protector   Army 32, Elite troops 146, General 187, Rank 352, 353, Recruitment 365, Sources 412
Protector Augusti   Officers 319
Protector domesticus   Education 143, Guards 213
Proteichisma   Fortification 180
Protostates   Officers 315
Provincia*, Province   Administration 5, 6, 7, Army 29, Auxiliaries 38, 40, Borders 73, 76, 77, Camp 82, Cavalry 89, Civilians 96, 98, Civil war 95, Colonies 100, Consequences of war 108, Costs of war 115, Education 141, Empire 152, 155, Fortification 181, 182, Garrison 185, General 189, Generals of note 198, 202, Guards 211, 212, Honours 222, Infantry 230, Infrastructure 231, Innovation 237, 238, Legion 255, March 263, Military service 296, Militia 300, Motivation 306, Officers 317, Recruitment 365, Representations of war 384, Veterans 474, Society and army 399, 400, Sources 407, 408, State and army 429, 431, Strategy 435, Timeframe of war 455, Veterans 474, 475, War 493, 494, Wars of note 500, 501, 502, 504, 505, 506
Provisional peace   peace 331, Peace 331
Proxenia, Proxenos*   Diplomacy 132, Law of war 248, Reconnaissance 357
Ptolemies*, Ptolemaic Dynasty   Administration 4, Army 26, 27, Battle 47, Cavalry 87, Civil war 92, Costs of war 112, Elephants 143, Empire 151, 153, Fleet 171, 175, 176, Generals of note 195, Hunting 226, Innovation 236, 241, 242, Language 246, Mercenaries 273, 274, Officers 316, Policing 336, Rank 344, 345, Recruitment 363, Representations of war 382, Slavery 395, State and army 428, Supply 442, Timeframe of war 454, Victory titles 484, War 492
Publicani*   Motivation 306

Public official   Hostages 225
Pullarius   Religion 372, 377
Punic*   Language 245
Punic Wars*   Consequences of war 107, 109, Enemies 156, 161, Legion 253, 254, Motivation 306, Prisoners 338, 339, Religion 372, Siege warfare 390, Supply 444, Timeframe of war 454
  – **First Punic War**   Army 28, Avoidance of military service 42, Descriptions of war 128, Elephants 143, Fleet 176, Innovation 242, Siege warfare 392
  – **Second Punic War**   Administration 6, Battle 49, 50, Battles of note 55, Cavalry 88, Consequences of war 107, 109, Costs of war 114, Elephants 143, Empire 153, Garrison 185, General 188, Generals of note 206, Mercenaries 274, Motivation 305, 306, Reconnaissance 359, Siege warfare 392, Slavery 396, State and army 429, Supply 442
  – **Third Punic War**   Reconnaissance 359, Religion 373
Punishment   Administration 6
Punishment, Criminal law*   Administration 3, Discipline 136, 138, Eve-of-battle speech 169, Honour 220, Marriage 266, Military law 281, 282, 283, Oath 314, Terror 451

Quaestor*   Administration 6
Quaestor classicus   Rank 346
Quaestor* sacri palatii   Administration 9
Quincunx*   Battle 49

Ram (male sheep)   Parades 321, Symbols 449
Rampart   Borders 70, 75
Rank/Gradus   Pay 326
Rank insignia   Equipment 167
Rank system   Army 31
Ransom (see also Redemption)   Battle 52, Costs of war 114, Enemies 160, Prisoners 337, 338
Rape*   Prisoners 337, Terror 451, 452
Ratio   Administration 9
Reading (see also Erudition)   Officers 318
Rebellion   Battle 50, Empire 153, Enemies 162, Fleet 173, 174, Garrison 185, Generals of note 203, 208, Military diploma 276, Motivation 307, Mutiny 310, Recruitment 366, Slavery 395, Valour 469, Veterans 474, 475
Recommendation/Introduction   Officers 318, Recruitment 365
Reconnaissance   Battles of note 54, Cavalry 87, Maps 259, Wars of note 512
Recruit, recruitment/Tiro [2]*/Muster   Administration 4, 6, 9, Army 28, 32, 33, 34, Auxiliaries 41, Avoidance of military service 42, Cavalry 89, Civilians 97, Civil war 94, Conscription 102, Costs of war 114, Education 140, 141, 142, Generals of note 200, 201, 208, Guards 211, 212, Innovation 235, 237, Language 246, Legion 252, 253, Mercenaries 273, 274, Military diploma 279, Military service 291, 295, 296, 297, 298, Motivation 303, Officers 316, 317, 318, Rank 344, 351, Recruitment 363, 365, 367, Religion 374, Slavery 393, 394, 395, 396,

Society and army 398, 399, Sources 408, 410, 412, Specialists 418, 419, State and army 431, Strategy 438, Veterans 472, 473, War 491, Wars of note 497, 502

Redemption (see also Ransom)   Prisoners 338, 340

Reduction in rank/Gradus deiecto   Discipline 138, Military law 282

Refuge   Borders 71

Regionarii   Policing 336

Religion*   Customs of war 117, Descriptions of war 122, Motivation 304, Officers 318, Parades 320, 322, Religion 368, Sources 411, War 489, 493

Religious war   Enemies 157, Motivation 304

Remembrance   Motivation 305

Renown   Battles of note 57, Descriptions of war 122, 126, 130, Discipline 134, 135, Fleet 174, General 186, 187, 188, Generals of note 205, Honour 217, Motivation 301, 302, Mutiny 311, Representations of war 379, Sparta 414, State and army 426, Strategy 437, Valour 468, Victory 481

Requisition   Civilians 96, 97, Production system 342, Supply 441

Reserve, reservist/Reliquatio   Army 25, 27, Battle 49, 51, 52, Battles of note 55, 58, 61, Borders 76, 77, Costs of war 113, Elephants 144, Guards 211, Innovation 237, March 260, Phalanx 333, Rank 348, Recruitment 363, Society and army 398, Society and army 398, Veterans 475, Wars of note 507, 510

Restitutio* in integrum   Military law 283

Retentura   Camp 82

Revenge*   Battles of note 57, Emotions 149, Enemies 157, 158, Fleet 173, Terror 452, Wars of note 497, 498

Revolt   Empire 150, Administration 9, Army 30, 31, Auxiliaries 41, Borders 77, Cavalry 90, Innovation 238

Ritual*   Army 23, Battle 45, Booty 67, Borders 69, Death 119, Descriptions of war 121, Garrison 185, Heroism 214, 216, Law of war 249, Military service 292, 294, Oath 314, Parades 320, 321, 322, Phalanx 334, Religion 368, 371, 372, 373, 374, 375, Representations of war 380, 382, 383, Sources 409, Standard 424, Symbols 449, Triumph 462, 464, Victory 478, 479, War 489, 495, Wars of note 510

Road building (Roads and bridges, building of*)   Infrastructure 232, 234, Rear 355

Roads   Borders 70, Infrastructure 232, 233, Innovation 240

Robbery*, Robbers/Bandits   Bandits 44, Booty 65, Civilians 98, Customs of war 117, Descriptions of war 129, Dogs 139, Enemies 160, Law of war 249, Military service 298, Militia 299, 300, Policing 336, Reconnaissance 358, 362, Recruitment 365, State and army 431, Sources 410, State and army 431, Strategy 434, 436, Terror 452, 453, War 488, 490, 493

Roman Confederation (Socii, Roman Confederation*)   Timeframe of war 454, War 494, Wars of note 516

Rorarii   Army 28

Rules of engagement   March 260, War 488

Ruse de guerre (see also Military deception, Stratagem)   Battle 45, March 260, Military literature 286, Sources 401

Sacramentum* (see also Oath)/Covenant   Legion 255, Military service 296, Oath 314, Religion 371, 374, 378, Symbols 449, Valour 470

Sacred Band (Hieroi lochos)   Army 24, Heroism 215, Innovation 236, Motivation 303, War 491

Sacred Wars* (Hieroi polemoi)   Motivation 304

Sacrifice*   Diplomacy 131, Military service 293, Motivation 304, Parades 322, Phalanx 334, Prisoners 339, Religion 369, 372, 374, 375, Specialists 420, State and army 427, Symbols 449

Saddle   Cavalry 87

Sagittarius (see also Arrow (Bow and arrow))   Armament 18, Mercenaries 274

Salii [2]*   Religion 372, Valour 470

Salpinx   Transmission of orders 461

Salus*   Religion 376, 377

Sambuca   Siege warfare 392

Samnites, Samnium*   Alliances 13, 14, Army 27, 28, Battle 49, Booty 65, Consequences of war 107, 108, Hostages 225, Innovation 236, Motivation 305, Phalanx 335, State and army 429

Samnite War   Timeframe of war 454

Sanctuaries*   Acropolis 1, Booty 68, Borders 69, Camp 83, Customs of war 118, Descriptions of war 121, 122, 127, Education 140, Law of war 247, Triumph 463, Religion 368, 370, 375, 376, Representations of war 380, 382, Victory 478, War 488, 489

Sarisophoroi   Army 25, 26

Sarissa*, sarisa   Armament 17, Army 24, Battle 46, 47, 48, Cavalry 86, 87, Generals of note 191, 204, Innovation 239, Mercenaries 274, Military service 291, Phalanx 335, Wars of note 497

Sarmatians (Sarmatae*)   Cavalry 89

Sassanids*   Borders 76, Cavalry 89, Elephants 144, Prisoners 340

Scamnum tribunorum   Camp 83

Schlieffen Plan   Generals of note 197

Schola   Administration 7, Camp 83, Generals of note 201, Rank 352, 353, Religion 375

Scholae palatinae*   Army 30, 32, 33, Cavalry 90, Elite troops 146, Guards 212, 213, Officers 319, Rank 351

Scorched earth   Consequences of war 108, Generals of note 198, Strategy 436, Wars of note 497, 512

Scorpion   Symbols 449

Scouts   Reconnaissance 358, 360

Scutarius   Guards 212, Sources 412

Scutum   Armament 20, Battle 48, 49, Legion 252, Symbols 450

Scythed chariot   Battles of note 58, Chariot 90, Wars of note 498

Seafaring   Borders 76

Seditio*   Mutiny 313

Seer   Religion 368, 369

Seleucids*   Administration 5, Army 26, 27, Battles of note 58, Camels 79, Cavalry 87, Civil war 92, Costs of war 112, Elephants 143, Empire 151, 153, General 187, 189, Generals of note 207, Mercenaries 273, Officers 316, Policing 336, Representations of war 381, Society and army 398, Society and army 398, State and army 428, Strategy 437, Timeframe of war 454, Victory titles 484, War 492, Wars of note 506

Senate (Senatus*)   Administration 5, 6, Battles of note 53, 55, Borders 73, Camp 83, Civil war 94, Consequences of war 108, 111, Descriptions of war 129, Diplomacy 132, Enemies 160, 161, 162, Eve-of-battle speech 170, Generals of note 201, 205, Heroism 216, Honours 222, Hostages 225, Innovation 237, Law of war 249, 251, Officers 317, Peace 331, Prisoners 339, Representations of war 382, 383, Slavery 395, Sources 408, State and army 429, 430, Strategy 435, Triumph 462, 463, Victory 479, 481, Victory titles 485, War 495, Wars of note 501, 502, 516

Senator   Army 29, Battle 52, Booty 67, Civil war 94, 95, Generals of note 194, Honours 223, Legion 255, Marriage 264, Military diploma 279, Military service 290, Motivation 307, Officers 317, 318, Rank 347, 351, 352, 353, Recruitment 364

Senatorial class   Army 29, 31, Honours 223, 224, Motivation 306, Officers 319

Seniores   Battle 48

Sentry, sentry duty   Administration 6, Army 34, Borders 75, Civilians 97, 98, Education 140, Sources 410

Serapis*   Religion 372, 376

Servant   Slavery 396

Service/Compulsory service   Army 25, 33, Consequences of war 109, Innovation 237, Legion 254, Mutiny 312, Rank 353

Service law   Law of war 249

Sesquiplicarius   Army 33, Pay 326, Rank 347, 351

Shame   Emotions 148, Honour 217

Shield devices   Equipment 164, Symbols 447

Shield* (see also Aspis, Clipeus, Scutum)   Armament 19, 20, Battle 46, 47, 48, 49, Consequences of war 111, Infantry 229, Legion 252, March 261, Military service 291, 292, 293, Parades 321, Phalanx 333, Religion 372, State and army 426, Symbols 447, 450, Transmission of orders 460

Shipbuilding*   Production system 341

Ship (see also Navy, Fleet)   Emotions 148, Symbols 447

Sicilian Catastrophe   Military service 294

Sicilian Expedition   Military service 292

Siege   Army 22, Battle 45, 50, Battles of note 60, Camp 80, Consequences of war 103, 105, 110, Costs of war 113, Customs of war 118, Descriptions of war 129, Elephants 143, Fortification 180, 181, Generals of note 190, 191, 193, 204, Heroism 215, 216, Infantry 230, Infrastructure 231, 232, Innovation 241, 243, Military literature 285, 286, 287, Motivation 303, Pay 324, Slavery 395, Supply 439, 441, Terror 452, Vehicles 471, War 492, Wars of note 504, 508

Siege convoy   March 262, Acropolis 1, Fleet 175, General 187, Generals of note 205, Innovation 241, Military literature 288, 289, Siege warfare 389, 392, Strategy 435, War 491, 492

Siege engine   Battle 48, Generals of note 195, Military literature 287, 288, Sources 402, Specialists 418, Vehicles 471

Siege tower   Innovation 241

Siege warfare   Battle 48

Signals*, signalling systems   Borders 71, Phalanx 333, Reconnaissance 361, Specialists 417, Standard 421, 422, Transmission of orders 460, 461, 462

Signatio   Recruitment 365

Signifer   Administration 8, Camp 84, Rank 347, 350, Transmission of orders 460, 461

Signum   Battle 50, 52, Rank 346, Religion 375, 376, Standard 424, Transmission of orders 461, Valour 470

Silvanus*   Religion 376

Single combat   Booty 65, Emotions 148, General 187, Heroism 216, Society and army 397, War 488, 494

Sirona*   Religion 376

Siteresion*   Pay 325

Skeuotheke*   Infrastructure 231, Sources 405

Skirmish, skirmishers   Army 22, Battle 45, 47, 48

Skytale*   Reconnaissance 359

Slave revolts   War 493

Slavery*, slaves, enslavement   Administration 6, Avoidance of military service 41, Booty 66, 68, Civilians 96, Conscription 102, Consequences of war 103, 105, 109, 110, 111, Customs of war 118, Descriptions of war 126, Emotions 149, Enemies 160, Equipment 163, Fleet 174, 176, 177, General 186, Generals of note 203, Law of war 247, 249, 250, Military law 283, Military service 292, 296, Motivation 302, Phalanx 333, Prisoners 337, 338, 339, Production system 341, Rank 347, Recruitment 363, 365, Society and army 398, Sources 402, 406, 410, Specialists 417, 419, Terror 451, 453, Veterans 472, 473, Victory 477, 480, War 488, 495

Sling (Slinger*)   Armament 18, Army 25, Auxiliaries 37, 38, Battle 48, 50, Battles of note 58, 61, Infantry 229, 230, March 261, 262, Mercenaries 274, Phalanx 333, 334, Representations of war 385, War 490

Smuggling   Alliances 14

Social advancement   Administration 9, Army 33, Consequences of war 109, Guards 212, Motivation 305, 307, Officers 318, Rank 344, Recruitment 366, Society and army 399, Veterans 476

Social inequality   Prisoners 338

Social Wars*   Alliances 14, Army 28, Borders 73, Consequences of war 107, 108, Diplomacy 133, Empire 152, Generals of note 202, 205, Motivation 306

Societas   Law of war 249

Socii navales (see also Navy, Fleet)   Rank 346

Socii* (see also Foederati, Allies)   Administration 6, Alliances 13, 14, Army 25, 26, 27, Battle 50, Battles of note 58, Diplomacy 133, Empire 152,

Fleet 176, Generals of note 197, 207, Honours 221, Infantry 229, Innovation 236, Legion 253, March 261, Mercenaries 271, 274, Officers 317, Pay 326, Peace 330, Rank 346, Recruitment 364, Slavery 396, Sources 408, Sparta 415, Specialists 418, State and army 427, Strategy 437, 438, Veterans 473, Wars of note 497, 508

Soldiers' pay (Stipendium, see also Pay)   Administration 4, 5, 6, Army 28, Avoidance of military service 43, Battle 49, Cavalry 88, Civilians 97, Consequences of war 107, 108, Costs of war 112, 114, 115, Descriptions of war 121, Fleet 174, General 187, Generals of note 201, Guards 210, Honours 221, 222, 224, Innovation 236, 237, Legion 252, 253, 254, Medical corps 269, Mercenaries 274, Military law 281, 284, Military service 297, Motivation 307, Mutiny 312, 313, Officers 315, 317, 318, Pay 326, Peace 330, Prisoners 340, Rank 347, 349, 350, 351, 352, Recruitment 363, Representations of war 384, Sources 405, 409, State and army 427, 429, 431, Supply 439, 441, 442, 443, Symbols 448, Veterans 473, 474, 475, War 490

Spartans (Spartiatae*)   Military service 293, 294, Religion 369

Spatha   Armament 18, Battle 50

Specialism   Elite troops 145, Mercenaries 272

Specialists   Auxiliaries 39, Civilians 96, Infantry 230, Mercenaries 272, 274, Military service 297, Religion 368, Specialists 417

Speculator, speculator Augusti   Cavalry 88, Guards 211

Speirarches   Officers 316

Spolia*   Booty 67, Military service 295

Spolia opima   Booty 67, Heroism 216, Honours 221, War 494

Spy (Espionage*)   Reconnaissance 358, 359, 361, 362, Strategy 435

Stable   Camp 84

Staff   Legion 255

Staging post   Borders 74

Standard, military (Ensigns*; see also Eagle, Draco, Flag, Banner, Imago, Signum, Vexillum)/Flag/Banner   Battles of note 57, 61, Consequences of war 111, Diplomacy 133, Honour 219, Legion 253, 255, Military law 281, Rank 349, 350, 352, Reconnaissance 359, Religion 375, 376, 378, Standard 424, Specialists 417, Standard 421, 422, 423, 424, Symbols 448, 449, Transmission of orders 460, 461, Valour 470

State slaves   Prisoners 339

Statio*   Bandits 44, Medical corps 270, Policing 337, Rank 348, Religion 375

Stationarius   Policing 337, Sources 410

Stator (Statores*), stator Augusti   Guards 211, Rank 348

Statua triumphalis   Honours 223

Status   Motivation 301, Officers 315

Stele of the Vultures   Phalanx 334

Stichos   Phalanx 333

Stirrups   Cavalry 87, 89

Stone   Military service 293

Storehouse (Horrea*; see also Logistics)   Camp 84, Infrastructure 234, Rear 355, Supply 445

Stores   March 263

Stork*   Legion 257

Stratagem (Strategemata*; see also Military deception, Ruse de guerre)   Prisoners 339, Military literature 290, Military service 292, Sources 401, Strategy 435

Strategikon*   Military literature 286, 289

Strategos* (see also General, Commander, Imperator)   Administration 3, Fleet 173, General 186, 189, Officers 315, 316, Pay 325, Rank 345, Representations of war 380, Scorched earth 388, State and army 427, Supply 439, 441

Strategy   Acropolis 1, Administration 5, Army 26, 30, Battle 45, 46, Battles of note 59, 62, Borders 71, 76, 77, Civil war 95, Colonies 100, Consequences of war 105, Discipline 136, Empire 150, Eve-of-battle speech 169, Fleet 175, 176, 178, Fortification 180, General 187, 188, Generals of note 191, 193, 195, 197, 198, 200, 202, 204, 206, Infrastructure 234, Innovation 235, 236, 239, 240, 241, 243, March 263, Military literature 285, 288, Phalanx 335, Policing 336, Rank 346, Reconnaissance 357, 358, 359, 361, Religion 369, Siege warfare 389, 391, Sources 402, 403, 409, Supply 444, Timeframe of war 454, Victory 477, 478, War 488, Wars of note 504, 512

Stratiotika   Pay 325

Subarmalis   Armament 20

Subsidia   Peace 331, Wars of note 508

Suicide*   Civil war 95, Descriptions of war 126, Discipline 138, Generals of note 194, Prisoners 338, 339, Terror 451, Wars of note 506

Sumerians*   Phalanx 334

Summus curator   Rank 351, Supply 445

Suovetaurilia*   Parades 321, Symbols 449

Supplies   Battles of note 53, Camels 79, Cavalry 86, Costs of war 115, Equipment 164, General 187, Generals of note 195, 200, 201, Infrastructure 233, Military literature 286, Scorched earth 388, Strategy 436, Supply 443, 445, Timeframe of war 455, Vehicles 470, Wars of note 497, 505

Supplies, delivery of (see also Logistics)   Production system 342

Supply crisis   Fleet 177, Veterans 476

Swimming*   Education 142, Mutiny 312

Sword*/Gladius   Armament 18, Battle 48, 49, 50, Cavalry 86, Infantry 229, Legion 252, 253, Military service 293, Officers 318, Specialists 419

Symbol   Administration 8, General 188, Motivation 303, Officers 316, Parades 321, 322, Standard 423, State and army 428, Transmission of orders 461, Triumph 465, Victory 477, 478, 480

Symmachial treaty   Sources 404

Symmachy (Symmachia*)   Administration 3, Alliances 11, 13, Diplomacy 131, Sources 404, Victory 478

Syngenes   Rank 345

Synhedrion*   Alliances 13, Empire 150

SUBJECT INDEX

Syntaxis* Administration 3, 4, 5, Pay 325
Syskenoi Equipment 163, Sparta 413

Tabula aenea, tabula aerea Military diploma 276
Tabula* Administration 6, Consequences of war 111, Maps 259, Military diploma 276
Tabula cerata Military diploma 279
Tabula curatorum navalium Sources 405
Tabularium, tabularii Administration 7, Military diploma 276, Religion 375
Tactics* Army 23, 24, 25, 26, 33, Battle 46, 49, 50, 51, Battles of note 60, Camels 79, Cavalry 87, Consequences of war 108, Descriptions of war 121, 127, 129, Discipline 135, Fleet 172, 174, General 187, 188, Generals of note 191, 193, 197, 198, 199, 205, 206, 207, Honour 219, Innovation 235, 239, March 263, Military literature 285, 286, Military service 292, Motivation 303, 305, Rank 352, Reconnaissance 357, 358, 359, 361, Religion 369, Scorched earth 388, Siege warfare 391, 392, Sparta 414, 415, Specialists 418, Standard 421, 422, 423, State and army 427, Strategy 434, 436, 438, Timeframe of war 454, Transmission of orders 459, Victory 478, War 488, Wars of note 497, 504, 508
Tagma Rank 352
Taktika [1]* Military literature 284, 286, 289, 290, Strategy 436
Tamias* Officers 315
Tattooing Military service 296
Taxiarch (Taxiarchos*) Military service 291, Officers 315, 316
Taxis Officers 315
Tax (Taxes*; see also Inheritance tax (Vicesima hereditatium)) Administration 3, Alliances 14, Army 28, 29, Auxiliaries 38, Avoidance of military service 42, Cavalry 89, Colonies 100, Consequences of war 105, 108, 109, 110, Costs of war 113, Descriptions of war 122, Empire 151, 152, 155, Fleet 176, 177, Generals of note 203, Innovation 237, 238, Marriage 267, Mercenaries 274, Military law 281, Military service 297, 298, Motivation 303, 308, Pay 325, 326, Peace 329, Production system 342, Rank 347, Recruitment 366, 367, Society and army 397, 398, Sources 405, 410, State and army 429, 431, Supply 439, 442, 444, 445, Veterans 475
Technological history Innovation 235
Technology* Innovation 241, 242, 243, Sources 402, Timeframe of war 454, War 490
Technology of war Prisoners 340
Tellus* Religion 372
Temple offerings (see also Votive offerings*) Booty 67, Enemies 158, Representations of war 380, Triumph 465, Victory 478
Temple*, templum Battles of note 59, Borders 70, Civil war 93, Consequences of war 111, Customs of war 117, Descriptions of war 123, 125, Empire 151, Enemies 159, 162, Honour 219, Language 245, Religion 368, 369, 370, 372, 373, 375, 378, Representations of war 380, 382, 386, Standard 423, Triumph 465, Wars of note 497, 505, 510

Terror Generals of note 198, Strategy 434
Tessera, tesserarius* Administration 9, Camp 84, Rank 350, Transmission of orders 460
Testamentum militis Law of war 249, Marriage 267, Military law 283, Sources 403, 410, 412
Testudo* Battle 51
Tetragonal March 260
Tetrarch, Tetrarchy (Tetrarches, Tetrarchia*) Civil war 95, Officers 316
Thalassocracy Army 26, Fleet 173, 174
Theban Legion Religion 378
Thetes* State and army 426
Third Sacred War Borders 71, Generals of note 204, Mercenaries 272
Thorax* Armament 20
Thracians (Thraci, Thracia*) Army 25, Auxiliaries 38, Battles of note 58, Borders 70, Generals of note 203, 204, Language 246, Recruitment 363, 365, 366, Wars of note 497
Thunderbolt Legion 257, Symbols 448, 449
Tigurini* Hostages 225
Time* (Attic law) Discipline 135, Honour 217
Tiro probatus Recruitment 365
Torquata, torquatus Honours 224, Rank 350
Torques [1]* Honours 221, 224
Torsion weapons Generals of note 205, Military literature 287
Torture* Prisoners 340
Trade embargo Wars of note 507
Training Cavalry 87, 89, Costs of war 114, Discipline 135, Education 140, 143, Fleet 172, General 186, 187, Generals of note 193, 206, 207, Hunting 226, Infrastructure 230, Innovation 236, March 263, Medical corps 268, Military literature 285, 286, Military service 291, 296, Officers 315, 318, Parades 321, Pay 325, Rank 347, 353, Recruitment 365, Society and army 397, Timeframe of war 455, Transmission of orders 460, Valour 470, War 491
Traitor Prisoners 339
Translator Civilians 97, Language 245, Camels 79, Chariot 91, Civilians 96, Fleet 177, 178, Garrison 185, Medical corps 269, Pay 325, Rear 355, Slavery 396, Strategy 436, Supply 444, 445, Vehicles 470
Transport, means of Supply 443, Vehicles 471
Transport network Infrastructure 232
Transvectio equitum* Parades 320, 321, Consequences of war 111, Emotions 146, Military service 292, 294, Phalanx 334, Valour 470
Treachery Civil war 91, Discipline 138, Enemies 162, Siege warfare 392, Strategy 435, Wars of note 497
Treasury Rank 351
Treaty Hostages 225
Treaty of alliance Alliances 14, Borders 73, Empire 152, War 492
Triarii (Triarius [1]*) Army 28, Battle 49, 50, Legion 253, March 261, 263, Valour 470
Tribuli* Fortification 181
Tribunicia potestas Military diploma 276

SUBJECT INDEX

Tribunus [4]* militum Administration 6, 8, Army 28, 29, Auxiliaries 39, Camp 83, Cavalry 88, Civil war 94, Consequences of war 108, Death 119, Education 141, Generals of note 193, 200, 201, 202, Guards 211, 212, Heroism 216, Honours 224, Legion 252, 255, March 262, 263, Motivation 306, Oath 314, Officers 317, 318, 319, Rank 346, 347, 348, 349, 350, 351, 352, 353, Recruitment 364, Religion 371, 377, Sources 412, State and army 429, Transmission of orders 460

Tribunus [7]* plebis Civil war 94

Tribute (Tributum; see also Taxes) Administration 3, Alliances 12, Consequences of war 104, 108, Costs of war 114, 115, Empire 150, Innovation 236, Pay 324, Production system 342, Sources 405, Society and army 397, Sources 404, State and army 429, Victory 477, 480, Wars of note 510

Triclinium* Camp 83

Trierarchia* Administration 3, Officers 318, Sources 405, State and army 427

Triphalangía March 261, 262

Trireme* Battles of note 59, 62, Costs of war 113, Fleet 172, 173, 174, 175, Generals of note 199, Innovation 241, Legion 257, Medical corps 269, Pay 324, War 490, 492, Wars of note 512

Triumphal arch/Commemorative arch (Triumphal arches*) Consequences of war 111, Representations of war 383, 384, Victory 480

Triumphator Representations of war 382

Triumph, Triumphal procession* Battle 52, Battles of note 60, Booty 69, Consequences of war 107, 110, 111, Costs of war 114, Descriptions of war 124, 128, 129, Elephants 144, Empire 153, Enemies 160, General 188, Generals of note 193, 198, 201, 205, Heroism 216, Honours 221, 223, Innovation 237, Law of war 250, Parades 320, 321, Prisoners 339, Religion 373, 374, 376, Representations of war 379, 382, 383, 386, Sources 407, State and army 430, 432, Victory 479, 480, 481, Victory titles 485, 486, 487, War 493, 494, Wars of note 511

Trooper (see also Cavalry, Equites singulares (Augusti), Ala) Administration 2, 6, Armament 16, 18, Army 25, 26, 27, 28, 29, 31, Avoidance of military service 42, Battle 49, 50, Battles of note 53, 55, 58, 61, Cavalry 86, 88, Costs of war 115, Discipline 135, Elite troops 145, Fleet 175, Generals of note 191, 196, 200, 204, 208, Guards 209, 211, 212, Infantry 230, Innovation 235, 236, 237, 239, Legion 252, 255, March 261, 262, Military service 293, Motivation 306, Officers 315, Parades 322, Pay 326, Phalanx 333, 335, Rank 344, 345, 346, Reconnaissance 358, 360, 361, Representations of war 379, 385, Slavery 394, Society and army 397, Sources 406, Sparta 415, Specialists 417, State and army 426, Transmission of orders 461, Valour 467, Wars of note 497, 504

Tropaion* Battle 52, Customs of war 118, Enemies 158, 161, Phalanx 333, 334, Religion 370, Representations of war 380, 382, 385, Triumph 465, Victory 478

Trophe Pay 325

Trophy Booty 67, 68

Truce Consequences of war 104, Customs of war 117, Diplomacy 131, Hostages 225, Law of war 247, 248, 251, Peace 329, 331, Phalanx 333, Prisoners 338, 340, Religion 368, 370, Sources 404, Victory 478, War 495

Trumpet, trumpeter (see also Bucina, Cornu, Tuba) Infantry 229, March 262, Phalanx 334, Specialists 417, 420, Transmission of orders 459, 460

Tuba, tubicen* Infantry 229, Military service 297, Specialists 418, 419, Transmission of orders 461

Turf Fortification 181

Turma* Army 28, Cavalry 88, 89, Infantry 230, Legion 253, Motivation 306, Officers 317, Rank 351, Religion 375, Transmission of orders 461

Tyrant, Tyranny (Tyrannis, Tyrannos*) Army 23, Battles of note 59, 61, Civil war 92, Consequences of war 104, Costs of war 112, 113, Equipment 164, Fleet 172, 173, Garrison 184, General 189, Generals of note 191, Guards 209, Innovation 239, Mercenaries 271, State and army 427, Terror 452

Unfree Army 27

Uniform Equipment 164, 165

Usurpation*, Usurpator Battles of note 60, Civil war 92, 95, Enemies 161, General 189, Generals of note 198, Guards 212, Innovation 238, Mutiny 313, Oath 314, Officers 319, Wars of note 511

Valetudinarium (see also Medicus, Medicine, Wounded) Medical corps 269, 270, Rank 348, Religion 376

Vallum* Fortification 181

Valour Battle 45, 46, Descriptions of war 129, General 188, Heroism 214, Hunting 226, Rank 350, 353, Representations of war 382, Strategy 436, Victory titles 486, War 488

Vandals (Vandali*) Generals of note 190, 208

Vanguard Reconnaissance 358, 361

Vehicle Equipment 164

Velites* Battle 50, Infantry 229, Legion 252

Venator (see also Hunting) Military service 297

Venus* Religion 375, Symbols 448, Victory titles 485

Venus victrix Religion 372

Verbenarius Law of war 249, Religion 372

Veredarius Rank 350

Verutum Battle 48

Vestiarius (see also Clothing) Consequences of war 109

Vestis militaris Supply 444

Veterans* Administration 7, 9, Army 29, 33, Civilians 99, Civil war 94, Colonies 100, 101, Conscription 102, Consequences of war 109, Death 120, Esprit de corps 168, 169, General 189, Generals of note 200, 202, Honours 222, Innovation 236, 237, March 261, Marriage 266, Military diploma 280, Military law 283, 284, Military service 297, 298, Motivation 306, 308, Mutiny 313, Rank 352, Society and army 399, Sources 407, 408, 410, 412, State and army 429, Supply 443

SUBJECT INDEX

Veterans, care of   General 189, Generals of note 201, Military service 298
Veterans' privilege   Prisoners 340
Veterinarian (Veterinarius)   Specialists 420
Vexillarius   Rank 350, Transmission of orders 461
Vexillatio*   Army 29, 30, 32, Battle 51, Camp 85, Cavalry 89, Generals of note 201, March 263, Officers 318, Rank 349, 351, 352, 353, Sources 407, 411, Standard 421, Supply 445, Wars of note 500, 506
Vexillum (see also Standard, military)   Honours 221, Standard 423, 424, Symbols 449, Transmission of orders 461
Via decumana   Camp 83
Viae militares   Infrastructure 233
Via praetoria   Camp 82, 83
Via principalis   Camp 82, 83, 84, Religion 375
Via sagularis   Camp 82, 85
Vicarius [1]*   Rank 349, 350, 352, 353, Recruitment 367
Victoria [1]*   Enemies 161, Religion 375, 376, State and army 432, Symbols 448, Triumph 465, Victory 477, Victory titles 483, 485, 486
Victoria Augusta   Victory titles 486
Victor, Victrix   Victory titles 485, 487
Victory celebrations   Triumph 462, 463, 464, 465, Victory 478
Victory insignia   Customs of war 118
Victory monuments, victory dedications   Descriptions of war 124, 128, Enemies 159, 161, Generals of note 195, Heroism 216, Representations of war 380, Victory 480
Victory rituals   Parades 320
Victory, victor   Army 31, Battle 45, 52, Battles of note 56, 60, 61, 62, 63, Booty 66, Consequences of war 104, 107, 110, Descriptions of war 122, 123, 124, 125, Enemies 158, 160, Equipment 164, Eve-of-battle speech 169, General 187, 188, Generals of note 191, 195, 196, 198, 209, Heroism 215, 217, Honour 218, Honours 221, Hostages 225, Innovation 237, 239, Law of war 247, March 264, Military service 292, Parades 323, Pay 326, Peace 330, Phalanx 333, Prisoners 337, Religion 369, 372, Representations of war 379, 380, 382, 384, 386, Sources 406, Strategy 433, 434, 436, Terror 451, Triumph 462, 465, Veterans 474, Victory titles 483, 484, 486, War 489, 495, Wars of note 498, 510
Victuals   Military service 292, Specialists 417
Vir militaris   Officers 318
Virtus imperatoria   Empire 155
Virtus* (see also Areté)   Descriptions of war 129, General 188, Generals of note 194, 197, 206, Honour 219, Honours 221, 224, Military literature 290, Representations of war 382, 384, Motivation 305, 306, Sources 401, Standard 424, Valour 469, Victory titles 486, War 494
Vitis   Officers 318
Volones*   Slavery 395
Volunteers   Conscription 102, Generals of note 201, 207, Legion 253, Military service 293, Motivation 305, 307, Pay 324, Recruitment 363, 364, 365, Slavery 395

Votive offerings* (see also Temple offerings)   Representations of war 380
Vow   Booty 67, Religion 369, 372, 373, 374, 377, Triumph 463, 465

Wagon, chariot*   Specialists 419, Supply 441, 443, Vehicles 471
Wall   Acropolis 1, Army 34, Booty 66, Borders 70, 74, 75, Camp 82, 84, Consequences of war 104, Emotions 148, Fortification 180, 181, 182, Guards 211, Honours 221, Infrastructure 231, Innovation 240, 241, Peace 330, 331, Policing 336, Siege warfare 389, 391, 392, Sources 405, 406, Strategy 436, War 491, 492, Wars of note 502, 508
War chariot*   Army 22, 23, 26, Battles of note 58, Descriptions of war 126, Enemies 156, 157, Parades 322, Society and army 397, Vehicles 470, War 488, 489
War customs   Customs of war 118, War 488
War dance (see also Dance)/Pyrrhiche*   Death 119, Discipline 135, Military service 291, Parades 320, 321, 322
Warlords   Victory 479, War 494
War machine   Specialists 418
War of plunder   Enemies 162, War 488
War of vengeance   Enemies 159
War reparations   Peace 331
War service   Army 26, Descriptions of war 129, Military literature 288, Military service 290, Motivation 303
Warship   War 489
Watch towers (see also Burgus)   Innovation 240
Water   Military service 292
Weapons*   Armament 18, Battle 52, Military service 298, Oath 314, State and army 426, 431, Symbols 448, Valour 470
Weapons dealers   Military service 292
Wheat   Camp 84
Widow*   Military law 281, Society and army 397
Wolf*   Legion 257, Transmission of orders 461
Woman*, Wife/Uxor   Civilians 96, 98, Consequences of war 103, 109, 111, Costs of war 112, Cowardice 117, Customs of war 118, Death 119, Enemies 158, Law of war 250, Military law 281, Military service 296, Motivation 307, Parades 321, Sources 408, Sparta 414, Terror 451, Valour 470, Veterans 473
Wounded (see also Valetudinarium)   Battle 52, Consequences of war 103, Equipment 164, Generals of note 191, Medical corps 268, 270, Military service 294, 297, Phalanx 334, Rank 350, Vehicles 471, Wars of note 500
Wrath   Emotions 146, 147
Writing (see also Erudition)   Officers 318

Xenologos   Recruitment 364
Xenos   Mercenaries 271
Xiphos   Cavalry 86

Yarḥibol   Religion 376